CANADIAN GLOBAL ALMANAC 2001

Macmillan Canada
Toronto

Contents

CANADA
AT A GLANCE	1
MAP	2

THE LAND
LANDFORMS	3
VEGETATION	7
AGRICULTURE	7
CLIMATE	9
PROVINCES AND TERRITORIES	24
CANADIAN CITIES	31
NATIONAL PARKS	37

THE PEOPLE
POPULATION	42
VITAL STATISTICS	58
MIGRATION	64
SOCIAL TRENDS	71
EDUCATION	80
CRIME AND JUSTICE	83

THE NATION
NATIONAL SYMBOLS	87
CANADIAN HISTORY	89
GOVERNMENT OF CANADA	137
POLITICS AND ELECTIONS	178
DEFENCE	190

THE ECONOMY
GLOSSARY OF TERMS	194
ECONOMIC INDICATORS	195
FEDERAL GOVERNMENT SPENDING	200
FOREIGN TRADE	210
BUSINESS	216
LABOUR	228
PERSONAL FINANCE	234
INVESTMENT	244

GLOBAL INFORMATION
WORLD MAPS	M1
GLOBAL SUPERLATIVES	247
GEOGRAPHY	248
POPULATION	252
ECONOMY	255
INTERNATIONAL ORGANIZATIONS	257
HISTORY IN HEADLINES	270
NATIONS OF THE WORLD	317

SCIENCE AND NATURE
ASTRONOMY AND SPACE	557
EARTH SCIENCES	570
PHYSICAL SCIENCES	580
SCIENCE AT WORK	586
ATMOSPHERIC SCIENCE	591
LIFE SCIENCES	607

ARTS AND ENTERTAINMENT
ARTS COUNCILS	615
TELEVISION	616

CANADIAN GLOBAL ALMANAC 2001

POPULAR MUSIC	**621**
MOVIES	**632**
PERFORMING ARTS	**637**
THEATRE	**641**
DANCE	**646**
BOOKS, MAGAZINES, NEWSPAPERS	**647**
GALLERIES AND MUSEUMS	**655**
HALL OF FAME	**660**
SPORTS	
BASEBALL	**695**
BASKETBALL	**711**
FOOTBALL	**717**
HOCKEY	**727**
OLYMPICS	**744**
OTHER SPORTS	**779**
QUICK REFERENCE	**795**
OBITUARIES	**809**
NEWS EVENTS OF 1999–2000	**818**
INDEX	**839**
CALENDARS AND HOLIDAYS	**857**

Comments and Suggestions

Please feel free to send us your comments and any suggestions for subsequent editions. Many readers took the time to drop us notes and letters last year and the correspondence is most welcome, although it is not always possible to respond personally to each writer. Address all correspondence to the Publisher, *The Canadian Global Almanac*, c/o CDG Books Canada Inc., Suite 400, 99 Yorkville Avenue, Toronto, Ontario M5R 3K5.
You can also e-mail us. The address is almanac@cdgbooks.com. We look forward to hearing from you.

Publisher and Editor-in-Chief	**SUSAN GIRVAN**
Contributing Editors	**LIBA BERRY** *(Index)*
	ANDREW BORKOWSKI *(Arts and Entertainment)*
	FRANKLIN CARTER *(Politics)*
	DAN CARLE *(Sports)*
	ART CHAMBERLAIN *(News Events)*
	BARBARA LAW *(Statistics)*
	DAVID PHILLIPS *(Climate)*
	DONNA WILLIAMS *(Hall of Fame, Obituaries)*
Typesetting	**HEIDY LAWRANCE ASSOCIATES**
Researchers	**SONJA RUTHARD**
	ANN McILWRAITH
Cover Design	**GORD ROBERTSON**
Maps	**MAPPING SPECIALISTS**

Copyright © CDG Books Canada Inc., 2000

All rights reserved. The use of any part of this publication reproduced, transmitted in any form or by any means, electronic, mechanical, recording or otherwise, or stored in a retrieval system, without the prior consent of the publisher is an infringement of the copyright law. In the case of photocopying or other reprographic copying of the material, a licence must be obtained from the Canadian Reprography Collective before proceeding.

A portion of the information in this publication is made available through the cooperation of Statistics Canada. Integral and/or adapted reproductions are published with permission of the Minister of Industry, Science and Technology. Readers wishing further information on any of the subjects credited "Statistics Canada" may obtain copies of related publications by contacting Publications Sales, Statistics Canada, Ottawa, Ontario, Canada KIA 0T6, or by calling 1-613-951-7277 or 1-800-267-6677 (toll free in Canada and the United States). Readers may also fax orders by dialing 1-613-951-1584 or fax order line 1-877-287-4369 (toll free in Canada and the United States).

Researchers, editors, contributors and Publisher have used their best efforts in preparing this book. CDG Books Canada, the researchers, editors, and contributors make no representations or warranties with respect to the accuracy or completeness of the contents of this book and specifically disclaim any implied warranties of merchantability or fitness for a particular purpose. There are no warranties that extend beyond the descriptions contained in this paragraph. No warranty may be created or extended by sales representatives or written sales materials. The accuracy and completeness of the information provided herein and the opinions stated herein are not guaranteed or warranted to produce any specific results, and the advice and strategies contained herein may not be suitable for every individual. Neither CDG Books Canada, the researchers, editors, nor the contributors shall be liable for any loss of profit or any other commercial damages including but not limited to special, incidental, consequential or other damages.

Canadian Cataloguing in Publication Data

The National Library of Canada has catalogued this publication as follows:

Main entry under title:

The Canadian global almanac

Annual
1992–
"A book of facts".
Continues: Canadian world almanac and book of facts, ISSN 0833-532X.
ISSN 1187-4570
ISBN 0-7715-7704-4 (2001)

1. Almanacs, Canadian (English).* 2. Almanacs.
AY414.C36   031.02   C92-031173-3

Macmillan Canada, an imprint of CDG Books Canada Inc., Toronto

Printed in Canada

CANADA

Canada At-a-Glance

■ LAND

Area:	9 970 610 sq. km
Length of coastline:	243 791 km (longest in the world)
Length of border with U.S. inc. Alaska:	8 890 km
Longitudinal centre of Canada:	97°W (close to Winnipeg)
Latitudinal centre of Canada:	62°N (close to Yellowknife, Northwest Territories)
Geographic centre of Canada:	Arviat, Nunavut (60°06'30"N, 94°03'30"W)
Greatest distance east to west:	5 514 km (Cape Spear, Newfoundland to the Yukon/Alaska border)
Greatest distance north to south:	4 634 km (Cape Columbia, Ellesmere Island to Middle Island, Lake Erie)
Largest island:	Baffin Island, Nunavut, 507 451 sq. km
Northernmost point:	Cape Columbia, Ellesmere Island, Nunavut, 83°06'N–69°57'W
Southernmost point:	Middle Island, Lake Erie, Ontario, 41°41'N–82°40"W
Easternmost point:	Cape Spear, Newfoundland, 47°31'N–52°37'W
Westernmost point:	Yukon-Alaska boundary, 141°00'W
Northernmost community:	Grise Fiord, Ellesmere Island, Nunavut, 76°25'N–82°54'W
Southernmost community:	Pelee Island South, Ontario, 41°45'N–82°38'W
Easternmost community:	Blackhead, Newfoundland, 47°32'N–52°39'W
Westernmost community:	Beaver Creek, Yukon Territory, 62°23'N–140°52'W
Longest river:	Mackenzie River, Northwest Territories, 4 241 km
Largest lake (entirely) in Canada:	Great Bear Lake, Northwest Territories, 31 328 sq. km
Highest waterfall:	Della Falls, Della Lake, B.C., 440 metres (more than one drop)

■ PEOPLE

Population:	30 482 900 (April 1, 1999 projection)
Population growth rate (1999):	1.09%
Life expectancy at birth (1999):	78.6; men: 75.7; women: 81.4
Age structure of the population:	0-14 years: 20%; 15-64: 68%; 65+: 12%
Official Languages:	English and French

■ NATION

Confederation:	July 1, 1867
Governor General:	Her Excellency, the Right Honourable Adrienne Clarkson
Prime Minister:	The Right Honourable Jean Chrétien
Motto:	A Mari Usque ad Mare (From Sea to Sea)
National Symbols:	the Maple Leaf and the Beaver (both official)
National Game:	lacrosse (summer), hockey (winter)
Anthem:	O Canada (National), God Save the Queen (Royal)
National Capital:	Ottawa, Ontario
Date of the last general election:	June 2, 1997
Largest province:	Quebec, 1 540 680 sq. km
Smallest province:	Prince Edward Island, 5 660 sq. km

■ ECONOMY

GDP (1998):	$688.3 billion; $22,400 per capita
Rate of inflation (Mar. 2000):	3.0%
Rate of unemployment (Feb. 2000):	7.3%
Average family income (1998):	$49,626

Source: *Canadian Heritage; Natural Resources Canada; Statistics Canada*

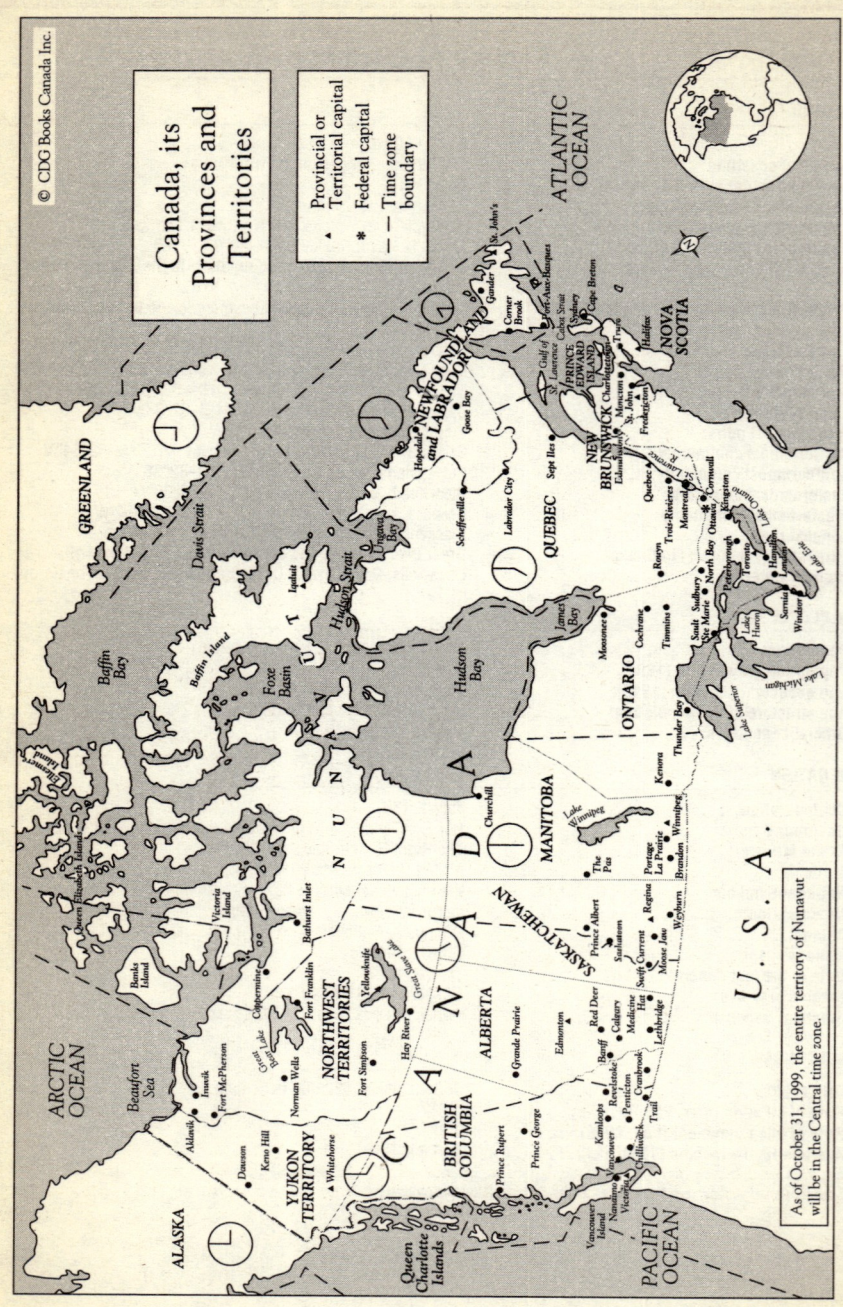

THE LAND

LANDFORMS OF CANADA

Canada is the largest country in the Western Hemisphere and the second largest in the world, with a total area of 9,970,610 sq. km. It stretches north to south from Cape Columbia on Ellesmere Island to Middle Island in Lake Erie, a distance of 4,634 km. The greatest east-west distance is 5,514 km from Cape Spear, Nfld, to the Yukon-Alaska border. Within this vast expanse, Canada contains an extremely wide variety of geographical features: the towering peaks of the Rockies, the flat Prairies, the rugged north and the gently rolling landscape of the east. But within this seemingly wide range of features, five areas with common characteristics are found. These physiographic regions are generally used to describe Canada and form the basis of Canada's geographical landforms and geological regions.

■ The Canadian Shield

Also known as the Precambrian Shield, this area is located in the central part of the continent. Viewed from the air it is a vast, inhospitable land of rocks, lakes and trees. It makes up roughly half of Canada's surface area, sweeping around Hudson Bay like a giant horseshoe, but also is the foundation for the rest of the continent.

The Canadian Shield has not always looked as it does today. Early in the Earth's history this area was the site of towering mountains, deep valleys and mighty rivers. The mountains were thrust up by volcanic activity as long as 3.8 billion years ago, during the Precambrian era. Over time, the forces of erosion—wind, water, freezing temperatures, ice—wore down the rocks that formed the mountain peaks and carried the materials away. Now all that remains are the roots of the once-mighty mountains.

The processes of volcanism present at the time of mountain-building caused minerals to form in the cooling rock of the Precambrian mountains. Deep inside the mountains, minerals such as gold, silver, copper and nickel came together into veins of ore. These ore bodies make the Shield a rich storehouse of mineral wealth.

■ The Appalachian Region

To the east of the Shield, this region was also once the site of massive mountain peaks. The rock that forms these peaks is not as old as the rock of the Shield, and is of a type that is more easily eroded. The Appalachian Region runs in a northeasterly direction from the southern United States to Newfoundland.

The mineral deposits found in the region reflect the complexity of the geology, and include gypsum, barite, salt, copper, zinc, lead, gold and silver. Since the end of the mountain-building period, erosion has worn off the tops of the mountains and filled the valleys with sediments, which gives the area its present-day less rugged appearance.

■ The Interior Plains

West of the Shield, rock which formed at the bottom of ancient lakes and seas gives the Prairies their distinctive flatness.

The Interior Plains occupy the central portion of the continent. Minerals found in the Interior Plains include potash, a substance produced when lakes and shallow seas evaporate, leaving deposits. Potash deposits in Saskatchewan are among the largest in the world. Coal, oil and natural gas were formed from organic materials trapped by the sedimentary layers during Palaeozoic times. An extension of the Interior Plains thrusts up between the Canadian Shield and the Appalachian Region, forming the Great Lakes-St. Lawrence Lowlands landform area. Soils throughout the Interior Plains are fertile, since the sedimentary materials that are found in the Plains break down easily.

Other lowland areas were formed during the Palaeozoic era as a result of the deposit of sediment which created the Interior Plains. The Hudson Bay Lowlands on the southwestern edge of Hudson Bay are relatively thin layers of sedimentary rock on top of the Precambrian Shield. The Arctic Lowlands, between the Shield and the Innuitian Mountains of the high Arctic, are similar in age and characteristics to the material of the Interior Plains.

■ The Western Cordillera

As the Precambrian mountains eroded, the sedimentary layers were deposited over a great distance and formed the Appalachian Region to the east. These deposits also provided the material from which future landforms would be built to the west. These landforms are now known as the Western Cordillera.

When the continent started its westward movement about 200 million years ago, its leading edge was forced against the adjacent oceanic plate and the land moved overtop the ocean. Geologists speculate that the tremendous pressure exerted during this process caused the sedimentary layers of the plate's edge to buckle into a massive dome. Magma, the hot fluid substance below the Earth's crust, flowed into the dome and formed a core which eventually collapsed between 65 and 160 million years ago, breaking the rock layers. This core stretches along the edge of the continental plate and absorbs the pressure of the two plates as they press upon each other.

The Western Cordillera is an area of great complexity; rocks composed of different materials and through different processes are thoroughly mixed. The Coast Ranges which form the leading western edge of the continent are composed of both igneous and metamorphic rock. The interior of the Cordillera is a jumble of plateaus, folded and broken rock layers and recent volcanoes. The sedimentary materials of the Rockies on the eastern edge of the Cordillera were folded and broken during a period of mountain-building in Eocene times, some 40-65 million years ago.

The Cordillera contains minerals associated with all the processes involved in its creation. The igneous rocks of the western part of the Cordillera are a major source of minerals including lead, zinc, silver, copper and gold. The sedimentary deposits of the eastern Cordillera are responsible for the coal and petroleum found there.

■ Innuitian Region

Mountain-building shaped the landforms of the high Arctic during the Devonian period (about 405 million years ago). The most recent activities appear to have occurred about 30 million years ago, which was long after the mountain-building period that thrust up the Rocky Mountains in the Cordillera.

Little detail is known about this region because research is so difficult in the inhospitable climate, but some geologists have suggested mountain-building is the result of the North American plate advancing on the Eurasian plate.

The topography of this region is characterized by low plateau mountains, with ridges as high as 3,000 m. The area is composed mainly of sedimentary rocks but includes some metamorphic and volcanic rocks.

For more information on geological time periods, see the chart in the Science and Nature section.

Highest Point in Each Province and Territory

Province/Territory	Highest Point	Elev. (m)
Newfoundland	Mt. Caubvick[1]	1 652
Prince Edward Island	46° 20'—63° 25' (Queen's County)	142
Nova Scotia	46° 42'—60° 36' (Cape Breton Highlands)	532
New Brunswick	Mt. Carleton	817
Quebec	Mont D'Iberville[2]	1 652
Ontario	Ishpatina Ridge	693
Manitoba	Baldy Mtn.	832
Saskatchewan	Cypress Hills	1 468
Alberta	Mt. Columbia	3 747
British Columbia	Fairweather Mtn.	4 663
Yukon Territory	Mt. Logan[3]	5 959
Northwest Territories	61° 52'—127° 42' (unnamed peak, Mackenzie Mtns.)	2 773
Nunavut	Barbeau Peak (Ellesmere Island)	2 616

Source: *Natural Resources Canada*

(1) On the Nfld/Que. border; also known as Mt. D'Iberville in Quebec; next highest point in Nfld is Cirque Mt. at 1,568 m. (2) On the Nfld/ Que. border; also known as Mt. Caubvick in Newfoundland; next highest point in Que. is Mont Jacques-Cartier at 1,268 m. (3) Name change proposed: Mount Pierre Elliott Trudeau.

Landforms

Largest Lakes in Canada

Lake	Area[1] (sq. km)	Lake	Area[1] (sq. km)
Superior, Ont.[2]	82 100	Nettilling, NT*	5 542
Huron, Ont.[3]	59 600	Winnipegosis, Man.	5 374
Great Bear, NWT	31 328	Nipigon, Ont.	4 848
Great Slave, NWT	28 568	Manitoba, Man.	4 624
Erie, Ont.[4]	25 700	Dubawnt, NT*	3 833
Winnipeg, Man.	24 387	Lake of the Woods, Ont./Man.[6]	4 472
Ontario, Ont.[5]	18 960	Amadjuak, NT*	3 115
Athabasca, Sask.	7 935	Melville, Nfld	3 069
Reindeer, Sask./Man.	6 650	Wollaston, Sask.	2 681
Smallwood Reservoir, Nfld	6 527	Lac Mistassini, Que.	2 335

Source: *Natural Resources Canada* *Nunavut

(1) Total area, including islands except for the Great Lakes, where area does not include islands larger than 0.052 sq. km. (2) Includes 53,400 sq. km in US (3) Includes 23,600 sq. km in US (4) Includes 12,900 sq. km in US (5) Includes 8 960 sq. km in US (6) Includes 1,322 sq. km in US.

The Great Lakes

The Great Lakes form the largest body of fresh water in the world and with their connecting waterways are the largest inland water transportation unit. They enable shipping to reach the Atlantic via the St. Lawrence River; the Gulf of Mexico via the Illinois Waterway, from Lake Michigan to the Mississippi River; a third outlet connects with the Hudson River and thence the Atlantic via the New York State Barge Canal System.

	Superior	Michigan	Huron	Erie	Ontario
Length in km	563	494	332	388	311
Breadth in km	257	190	295	92	85
Deepest soundings in metres	405	281	229	64	244
Volume of water in cubic km	12 100	4 920	3 540	484	1 640
Area[1] (sq. km) in US	53 400	57 800	23 600	12 900	8 960
Area[1] (sq. km) in Canada	28 700	0	36 000	12 800	10 000
Total Area[1] (sq. km) US and Canada	**82 100**	**57 800**	**59 600**	**25 700**	**18 960**
National boundary line in km	430	0	446	404	281

Source: *Natural Resources Canada*   (1) Does not include islands larger than 0.052 sq. km.

Longest Rivers in Canada

River	Length (km)	Flows Into	River	Length (km)	Flows Into
Mackenzie	4 241	Arctic Ocean	North Saskatchewan	1 287	Saskatchewan R.
Yukon	3 185	Bering Sea	Ottawa	1 271	St Lawrence R.
St. Lawrence	3 058	Gulf of St. Lawrence	Athabasca	1 231	Lake Athabasca
Nelson	2 575	Hudson Bay	Liard	1 115	Mackenzie R.
Columbia	2 000	Pacific Ocean	Assiniboine	1 070	Red R.
Saskatchewan	1 939	Lake Winnipeg (via Cedar Lake)	Severn	982	Hudson Bay
Peace	1 923	Lake Athabasca	Albany	982	James Bay
Churchill (Man.)	1 609	Hudson Bay	Back	974	Arctic Ocean
South Saskatchewan	1 392	Saskatchewan R.	Thelon	904	Hudson Bay
Fraser	1 370	Pacific Ocean	La Grande Rivière	893	James Bay

Source: *Natural Resources Canada*

Canadian Heritage Rivers System (CHRS)

On January 18, 1984 a joint program was established to oversee the management and conservation of Canada's rivers. Individual rivers are administered by the government responsible for the land each flows through, be it provincial, territorial or federal lands in national parks, however the CHRS assists by supporting a management plan with funding and policy initiatives. No management plan is put forward until after public consultation is complete and a consensus has been reached. (In the case of rivers that form international boundaries, the consultation is done on both sides of the border. New Brunswick's plan for the St. Croix River was developed in collaboration with the State of Maine and both governments have endorsed it.)

The Heritage Rivers System is overseen by a fourteen member board made up of a representative appointed by each of the provincial and territorial governments, plus a federal appointee from the Department of Indian Affairs and Northern Development and another from Canadian Heritage's Parks Canada. This board meets at least once a year to designate funding and program priorities, and to review and approve new guidelines and policies. 24 rivers have been designated for special management and conservation attention; 11 more have been nominated for CHRS status (Bay du Nord, Newfoundland; Churchill, Saskatchewan; Cowichan, B.C.; Detroit, Ontario; Jacques-Cartier, Quebec; Main, Newfoundland; Missinaibi, Ontario; Rideau, Ontario; St. Mary's, Ontario; Tatshenshini, Yukon; Thames, Ontario.)

For more information about the CHRS and for detailed fact sheets on each river, including information on each river's geography, natural heritage, human heritage and recreation possibilities, visit www.chrs.ca.

Designated Rivers	Location	Length
Alsek River	Kluane National Park Reserve, Yukon	90 km section
Arctic Red River	Arctic Red River (Tsiigèhnjik), Northwest Territories	450 km
Athabasca River	Canadian Rocky Mountains National Parks, Alberta and BC	1 538 km
Bloodvein River	Woodland Caribou Provincial Park/Atikaki Wilderness Park, Ontario/Manitoba	200 km section
Bonnet Plume River	Yukon	350 km
Boundary Waters-Voyageur Waterway	Quetico, Middle Falls and Voyageur Provincial Parks, Ontario	250 km section
Clearwater River	Clearwater River Provincial Wilderness Park, Saskatchewan	187 km section in Sask
Fraser River	British Columbia	1 375 km
French Rivers	French River Provincial Park, Ontario	110 km
Grand River	Ontario	290 km
Hillsborough River	Prince Edward Island	45 km
Humber River	Ontario	100 km
Kazan River	Nunavut	850 km
Kicking Horse	Canadian Rocky Mountains National Parks, Alberta and BC	68 km section
Margaree-Lake Ainslie River System	Nova Scotia	120 km
Mattawa River	Mattawa River Provincial Park, Ontario	43 km section
North Saskatchewan River	Canadian Rocky Mountains National Parks, Alberta and BC	48.5 headwater section
Seal River	Manitoba	260 km section
Shelburne River	Nova Scotia	53 km
South Nahanni River	Nahanni National Park Reserve, Northwest Territories	540 km
St. Croix	New Brunswick	185 km
Thelon River	Nunavut	545 km section
Upper Restigouche	New Brunswick	55 km section
Yukon River	Yukon	Thirty Mile Section 48 km

Source: *Parks Canada*

VEGETATION

Coniferous forests dominated by spruce, fir and pine cover much of the Canadian landscape, sweeping across the continent in a broad band. Through the rest of the country there is a range of forest conditions. To the north, cold temperatures limit growth and the trees become small and fewer in number. At the tree line, trees grow only in sheltered river valleys. The tree line marks the northern extent of forests and the beginning of tundra conditions (moss, lichens and dwarf vegetation with permanent frozen subsoil).

The massive spruce, fir and pine of the forests along the coast of British Columbia are encouraged by a friendly climate. The moisture-laden winds from the Pacific Ocean keep the land well-supplied with rain. Under these conditions tree growth is rapid: the soils are constantly being replenished with minerals by the rains, and plant decay is also rapid in the damp conditions, thereby releasing more minerals for tree growth. With average monthly temperatures seldom going below freezing, the growing season is long. Coniferous trees thrive under such conditions.

The Interior Plains is one region of Canada that is not covered by forests because there is not enough precipitation, or available moisture, to sustain tree growth. In Alberta, Saskatchewan and Manitoba, forests gradually give way from north to south through a transitional area called the park belt, which contains both trees and grassland, before yielding to grasslands. Within these provinces, there are areas where moisture levels are insufficient to support grasslands and even hardy grasses have difficulty growing. During the 1930s, the lack of rainfall in the Interior Plains led to "dust bowl" conditions because vegetation could not grow enough to anchor the soil.

The forests of southeastern Canada are mixed, containing both coniferous and deciduous trees. Adequate rainfall and warm temperatures allow the less hardy species such as oak, maple, hickory and walnut to flourish in southern Ontario and Quebec and the Maritime provinces.

The Arctic tundra is so very dry and cold that the growing season is extremely limited. The vegetation of the tundra consists of mosses, lichen, dwarf bushes and heather. These plants are able to grow because they have adapted to the difficult conditions through characteristics such as small size and slow growth. Some shrubs and lichen grow so slowly that their development must be measured in centimetres per century.

AGRICULTURE

There are four main types of farms in Canada: livestock farms, grain farms producing such crops as wheat and oats, mixed farms producing both grain and livestock, and special crop farms producing vegetables, fruits, tobacco and other products. Both the type and amount of farming within Canada are affected by climate and location.

■ The Atlantic Region

The Atlantic region is an area of diverse agricultural activity. Newfoundland, because of poorly developed soils and a difficult climate, has a limited agricultural industry supplying only local markets. Encouraged by a moist climate and silty, stone-free soils, farming is the leading industry on Prince Edward Island; potatoes are the main crop. The land also supports mixed grains and dairy farms.

Nova Scotia's main agricultural areas surround the Bay of Fundy and Northumberland Strait where they are protected from Atlantic gales; dairy farming and poultry production are common. Nova Scotia's Annapolis Valley is famous for fruit, mainly apples. In New Brunswick, potatoes and livestock are produced in the Saint John River valley, and there is mixed farming in the northwest of the province.

■ The Central Region

In Canada's central region, the fertile soils and moist climate of southern Ontario and Quebec support a thriving agricultural industry. Although these growing conditions allow a variety of crops, the population concentration in this area encourages specialization in products with high transportation costs. Dairy farms are concentrated around Montreal and in southwestern Ontario, supplying milk, butter and cheese to the major centres such as London, Hamilton, Toronto,

Kingston, Montreal and Quebec City. Vegetable crops are also grown near these centres. Farms specializing in poultry and egg production, sheep and hogs are also common.

The Niagara Peninsula, between Lakes Ontario and Erie, is a major fruit-growing centre. The moderating effects of the lakes delay the growth of the fruit trees in the spring until the danger of frost is past. Tender fruit crops—peaches, pears, plums and cherries—as well as grapes thrive in these conditions. Tobacco (and now ginseng) grow well on the glacially-created sand plains of southwestern Ontario.

■ The Prairie Provinces

Manitoba, Saskatchewan and Alberta contain 80 percent of Canada's farmland. Here, a combination of flat, easily-worked land, fertile soils, long sunny summer days and sufficient precipitation encourages the healthy growth of high-quality grains. This area grows most of Canada's wheat, about 90 percent of its barley and rye, and more than 75 percent of its oats.

Manitoba grows canola and flax in addition to wheat and other grains. Mixed farming in the province emphasizes beef cattle. Dairy farms are common around Winnipeg. Saskatchewan grows about 60 percent of Canada's wheat and large quantities of other grains. Mixed farming, poultry, egg and livestock production contribute to the provincial economy. Alberta, also a major grain producer, has more beef cattle ranches than any other province. They are located mainly in the south of the province and in the foothills of the Rocky Mountains where the steep slopes and dry land is unsuited to growing crops.

■ The Pacific Region

In the Pacific region, only 2 percent of British Columbia is agricultural land. But the pockets of farmland are extremely productive. The lower mainland and the southern tip of Vancouver Island comprise the Georgia Strait agricultural region, an area concentrating on dairy farming and poultry raising to supply the province's population centres. Other crops include raspberries, strawberries, peas, tomatoes and flowers.

The Okanagan Valley contains 90 percent of British Columbia's orchards, producing grapes, apples and tender fruit such as peaches, plums, apricots and cherries. Here, local climatic and physiographic characteristics have resulted in conditions suitable for the orchard industry, although irrigation is often necessary and frost damage is a hazard. Beef cattle and sheep are raised in the interior of the province, where growing conditions are not suitable for crops requiring cultivation, but grazing can be carried out.

■ The North

Canada's North generally has soil and climatic conditions unsuited to agriculture. A small number of farms produce some dairy products, beef cattle and vegetables for the local market.

Water Quality and Groundwater

Canada's prevailing images are of rivers, lakes and glaciers that supply abundant, clean water, and attention has focussed on preventing the pollution of those rivers and lakes. More recently, however, concern has shifted to groundwater supplies and the problems keeping that water clean. With good reason: about 25% of us use groundwater for all daily needs.

Groundwater is found in underground spaces between particles of soil and rock or in the cracks and spaces. Most of this water is within 100 m of the surface, with varying levels of saturation. The level below which water saturates all available space is called the water table. Water in the water table is called groundwater. Above the water table is an unsaturated zone; water there is referred to as soil moisture. Pollutants of any kind that leak (or are dumped) into or onto the ground will find their way into the groundwater either by seeping down directly, or in the case of more solid pollutants, being washed into the ground by rainfall. Examples of such a threat are the runoff from the 1990 tire fire at Hagersville, ON and the still undetermined cause of groundwater pollution in Walkerton, ON. For more information, see "The Nature of Water" at www.ec.gc.ca/water.

CLIMATE

Within Canada, climate is primarily affected by surrounding landforms, proximity to large bodies of water and the degree of latitude.

Landforms Air masses are forced to rise over mountains which lie in their path. As this happens, the air cools and its ability to retain moisture is reduced. Condensation then occurs and precipitation falls in the form of snow or rain. For instance, Prince Rupert on the western side (windward) of the Coastal Mountains receives over 2,500 mm of precipitation annually.

On the leeward side of the mountains (the side away from the wind), the air mass descends, warms and is able to once again retain moisture. Moreover, there may be little moisture left in the air mass. Thus precipitation is light and a rain-shadow effect is created. In a rain-shadow area, such as near Kamloops, BC, desert-like conditions exist.

Water Parts of Canada near large bodies of water have more moderate climates due to the differing abilities of land and water to gain or lose heat. Whereas water can act like a heat bank, releasing accumulated heat through the fall and early winter and warming the land nearby, the reverse is also true. In the spring and early summer, the water is cooler than the land and can keep the land temperature lower. [*see also*: Ocean Currents, p.11.]

Wind direction also determines the degree to which this influence is felt. On the Pacific coast the prevailing westerlies blow off the water onto the land and the influence of the Pacific Ocean is keenly felt. On the Atlantic coast, the westerlies blow off the land onto the water so the effect of the Atlantic Ocean is not as pronounced. Victoria's lowest monthly average temperature is 4.6°C in Jan. with an annual range of only 11°C between the warmest and coldest months while Halifax's lowest monthly average is -4.8°C in Feb. with an annual range of 22.7°C.

Latitude Latitude is the distance north or south of the equator and is expressed in degrees. Its effects on climate are twofold. Firstly, the further north the location, the more the curvature of the earth results in the sunlight spreading over a greater surface area. This decreases the solar radiation per unit area of ground so that less warmth from the sun is felt. Secondly, solar radiation has to travel a greater distance through the atmosphere at higher latitudes which again reduces the amount of energy reaching the earth.

Other Factors Because the prevailing wind direction is from west to east, the air masses move eastward across the continent picking up moisture from lakes and rivers and releasing it further along. Therefore, generally, precipitation increases with greater distance eastward from the central continent: the average precipitation in Winnipeg is 504 mm, Toronto 781 mm, Montreal 940 mm and Halifax 1 474 mm.

Also, the Labrador Current affects climate on the Atlantic coast. This cold current within the Atlantic Ocean flows south along the coast of Newfoundland and Labrador and reduces the moderating effect of the ocean on the land. It also causes the thick Newfoundland fog when relatively warm air is cooled from below on contact with the cold waters.

Heating Up

According to Environment Canada's climate change web site (www.climatechange.gc.ca/info) the 20th century has been the warmest in the past six centuries—not just in Canada, but around the world. And the warmest decades on record are the 1980s and the 1990s.

What does this mean for Canadians? For residents of Arviat in Nunavut, it means the Inuktitut language has to come up with a word for "sunburn," something they've never needed before. Is this warming trend bad? Probably; northern plants and animals uniquely adapted to their environment will find it more difficult to survive as growing seasons change, food sources disappear or their usual feeding, nesting or spawning areas become less hospitable. Northern communities will become even more isolated without the firm ice that makes roads and links them during the cold months of the year. And we can all expect more of what Environment Canada calls "severe weather events" such as tornadoes, blizzards and droughts.

Average Weather Data for Selected Airports in Canada

Airport	Temperature °C Winter High	Winter Low	Summer High	Summer Low	Precipitation Annual Snowfall cm	Total Precipitation mm
Vancouver	5.7	0.1	21.7	12.7	55	1 167
Calgary	-3.6	-15.7	23.2	9.5	135	399
Edmonton	-8.7	-19.8	22.5	9.4	127	466
Regina	-11.0	-22.1	26.3	11.9	107	364
Winnipeg	-13.2	-23.6	26.1	13.4	115	504
Toronto	-2.5	-11.1	26.8	14.2	124	781
Ottawa	-6.3	-15.5	26.4	15.1	222	911
Montreal	-5.8	-14.9	26.2	15.4	214	940
Saint John	-2.8	-13.6	22.1	11.6	283	1 433
Halifax	-1.5	-10.3	23.4	13.2	261	1 474
Charlottetown	-3.4	-12.2	23.1	13.6	339	1 201
St. John's	-0.7	-7.9	20.2	10.5	322	1 482
Iqaluit	-21.5	-30.0	11.6	3.7	257	424
Yellowknife	-23.9	-32.2	20.8	12.0	144	267
Whitehorse	-14.4	-23.2	20.3	7.6	145	269

Airport	Wind Average Speed km/hr	Prevailing Direction	Peak Wind km/hr	Sunshine Bright Sunshine hours	Possible Sunshine hours
Vancouver	12	E	129	1 919	4 475
Calgary	16	N	127	2 395	4 483
Edmonton	13	S	146	2 303	4 488
Regina	20	SE	153	2 365	4 483
Winnipeg	18	S	129	2 377	4 482
Toronto	15	W	135	2 038	4 464
Ottawa	14	W	135	2 054	4 469
Montreal	15	W	161	2 015	4 465
Saint John	18	S	146	1 894	4 452
Halifax	18	S	132	1 949	4 488
Charlottetown	19	W	177	1 844	4 467
St. John's	24	W	193	1 527	4 470
Iqaluit	16	NW	141	1 508	4 563
Yellowknife	15	E	113	2 277	4 546
Whitehorse	14	S	106	1 852	4 523

Airport	Annual Number of Days Frost	Wet Weather	Thunderstorms	Freezing Precipitation	Smoke/ Haze	Blowing Snow	Fog
Vancouver	55	164	6	1	120	—	34
Calgary	201	111	25	6	22	9	22
Edmonton	210	122	25	8	16	7	18
Regina	204	109	23	14	3	28	28
Winnipeg	195	119	28	13	20	24	17
Toronto	165	141	28	10	104	9	34
Ottawa	165	159	24	17	80	13	36
Montreal	156	162	26	13	75	12	18
Saint John	173	164	11	12	22	13	102
Halifax	163	170	10	16	17	14	122
Charlottetown	169	177	9	17	20	26	47
St. John's	176	217	4	38	19	27	121
Iqaluit	273	152	<1	5	<1	61	15
Yellowknife	226	118	6	11	6	9	19
Whitehorse	224	122	6	2	1	3	15

Source: *Environment Canada*

Ocean Currents

Oceans or large bodies of water like the Great Lakes affect the climate of the land nearby because they act as heat reservoirs and heat exchangers. Water heats up more slowly than land, and it holds that heat for a longer time. Because of this, the climate in the areas closest to water is more moderate than the climate inland: even though the air over the coastal land is warmer in summer and colder in winter than the air over water at the same latitude, it won't be as hot (or as cold) as the air over land that is far away from the coast.

These water bodies also affect rainfall, wind and clouds: when the water is warmer than the air above it, it generates clouds, rain and wind; when the water is colder than the air above, the opposite happens—there is likely to be fog, less rain, and winds are reduced.

As the ocean currents move heat and cold around the world, Canada is affected by the warm Gulf Stream on the Atlantic coast and the weaker but still warm Alaska Current on the Pacific side; both of these flow northward. Cold currents like the West Greenland Current and the Labrador Current flow south from the Arctic on the east side; the banks of fog off the southeast coast of Newfoundland mark the spot where the Labrador Current meets the Gulf Stream. In general though, because our weather flows from west to east, it is the currents on the Pacific side that have the most effect on Canada's climate.

Inland, the Great Lakes and Hudson Bay are two vast areas of water that affect the climate around them: the Great Lakes act as a huge heat reservoir that moderates the weather in southern Ontario and Quebec, while Hudson Bay is frozen over for six months, and even during the summer months melting ice keeps the surface water temperature close to freezing. Hudson Bay's most common effect is fog in summer and precipitation, cloud and strong winds during the rest of the year.

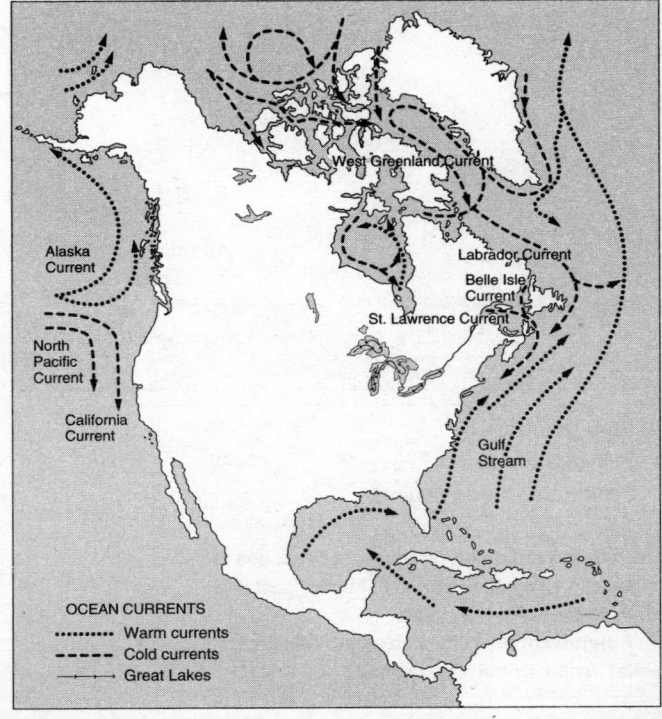

12 *The Land*

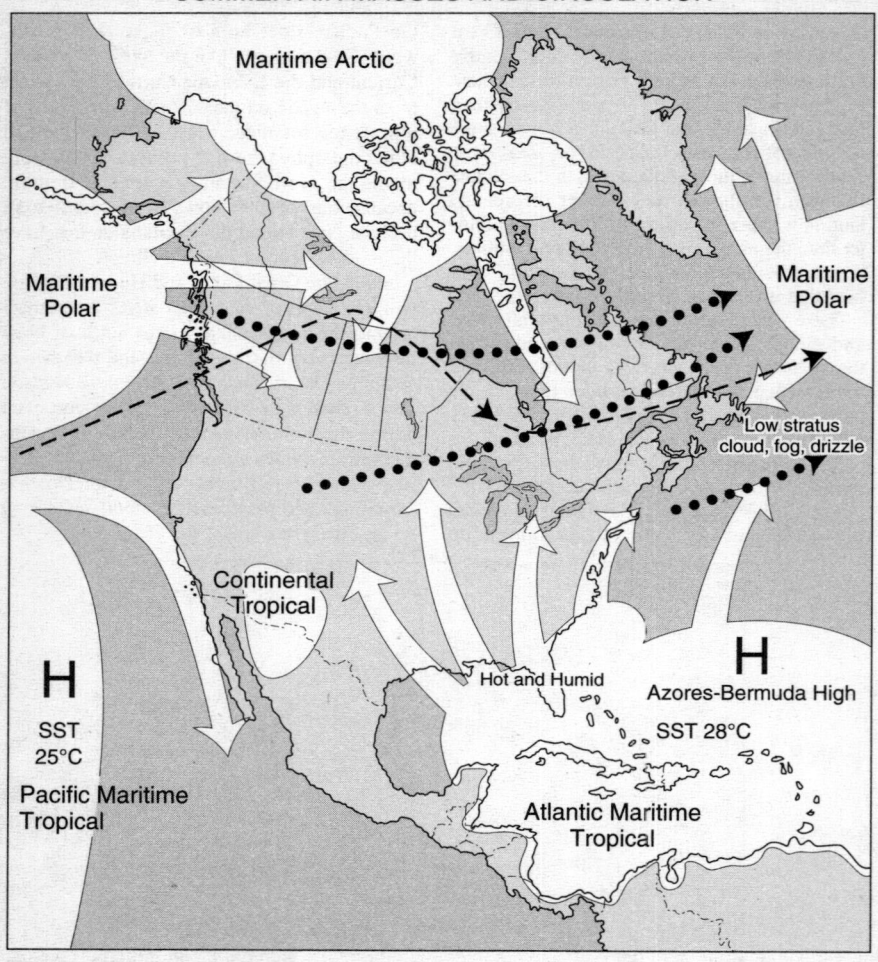

Climate 13

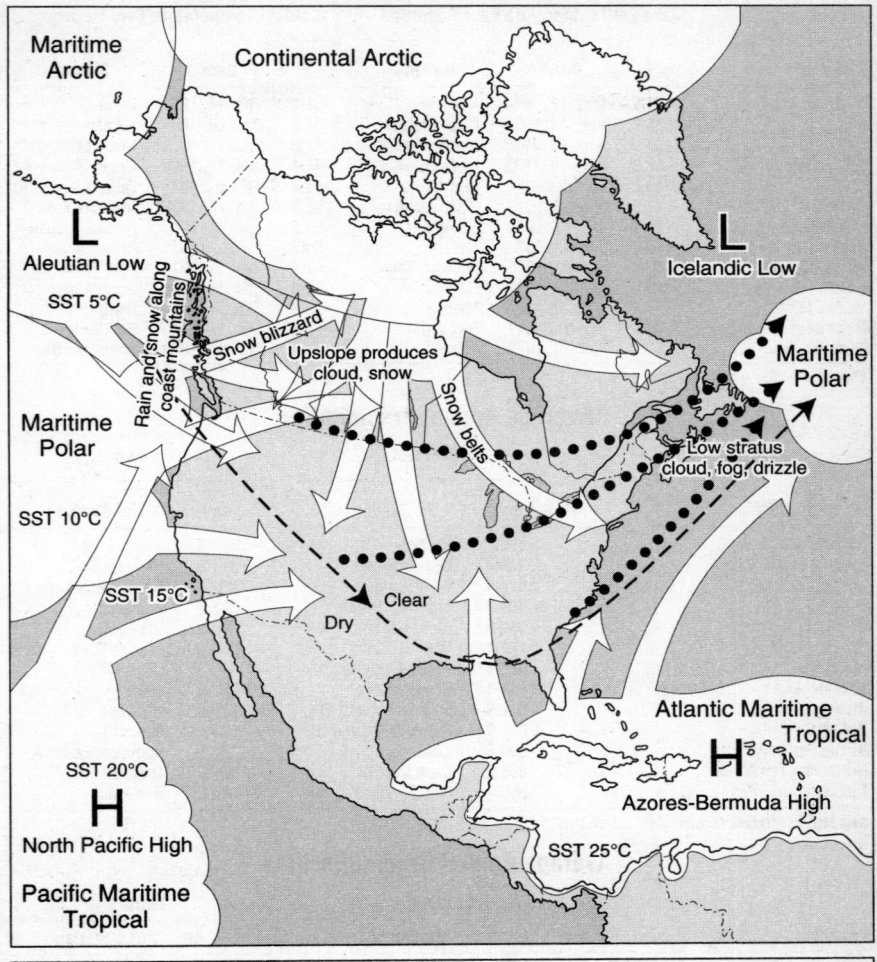

WINTER AIR MASSES AND CIRCULATION

– – – Polar jet stream
••••• Primary storm tracks
SST Sea Surface Temperature

Continental Arctic: very cold, dry, stable
Maritime Arctic: very unstable, clouds, frequent showers or flurries
Maritime Polar: milder, more stable than Arctic air
Pacific Maritime Tropical: stable in lower 1000m
Atlantic Maritime Tropical: warm and humid

Provincial Weather Facts

Province	Warmest Temperature Ever Recorded °C	Date	Station	Coldest Temperature Ever Recorded °C	Date	Station
Newfoundland	41.7	Aug. 11, 1914	Northwest River	-51.1	Feb. 17, 1973	Esker 2
P.E.I.	36.7	Aug. 19, 1935	Charlottetown	-37.2	Jan. 26, 1884	Kilmahumaig
New Brunswick	39.4	Aug. 18, 1935	Nepisiguit Falls	-47.2	Feb. 1, 1955	Sisson Dam
Nova Scotia	38.3	Aug. 19, 1935	Collegeville	-41.1	Jan. 31, 1920	Upper Stewiacke
Quebec	40.0	July 6, 1921	Ville Marie	-54.4	Feb. 5, 1923	Doucet
Ontario	42.2	July 20, 1919	Biscotasing	-58.3	Jan. 23, 1935	Iroquois Falls
Manitoba	44.4	July 11, 1936	St. Albans	-52.8	Jan. 9, 1899	Norway House
Saskatchewan	45.0	July 5, 1937	Midale	-56.7	Feb. 1, 1893	Prince Albert
Alberta	43.3	July 21, 1931	Bassano Dam	-61.1	Jan. 11, 1911	Fort Vermilion
British Columbia	44.4	July 16, 1941	Lillooet	-58.9	Jan. 31, 1947	Smith River
Yukon Territory	36.1	June 14, 1969	Mayo	-63.0	Feb. 3, 1947	Snag
Northwest Territories	39.4	July 18, 1941	Fort Smith	-57.2	Dec. 26, 1917	Fort Smith
Nunavut	33.9	July 22, 1973	Arviat	-57.8	Feb. 13, 1973	Shepherd Bay

Source: *Environment Canada*

Average Annual Precipitation

Province	Greatest mm	Station	Least mm	Station
Newfoundland	1 699.7	Burgeo	739.8	Nain
Prince Edward Island	1 169.4	Charlottetown A	921.0	Montague
New Brunswick	1 444.4	Saint John A	909.6	Upsalquitch Lake
Nova Scotia	1 630.7	Ingonish Beach	973.7	Pugwash
Quebec	1 559.8	Mont Logan	295.9	Cape Hopes Advance
Ontario	1 191.1	West Guilford	569.0	Kenora TCPL
Manitoba	696.1	Peace Gardens	402.3	Churchill A
Saskatchewan	530.1	Brabant Lake	287.9	Nashlyn
Alberta	1 072.0	Waterton Park HQ	270.8	Empress
British Columbia	6 655.0	Henderson Lake	205.6	Ashcroft
Yukon Territory	590.6	Tuchitua	135.9	Komakuk Beach A
Northwest Territories	663.2	Cape Dyer A	137.6	Tuktoyaktuk
Nunavut	355.1	Fort Simpson	61.0	Rea Point

Source: *Environment Canada*

Average Annual Bright Sunshine

Province	Greatest Hrs	Station	Least Hrs	Station
Newfoundland	1 572	Churchill Falls A	1 303	St. Shotts
Prince Edward Island	1 967	Tignish	1 817	East Baltic
New Brunswick	2 010	Chatham A	1 373	Summit Depot
Nova Scotia	1 969	Shearwater A	1 449	Sable Island
Quebec	2 054	Montreal Int'l. A	1 158	Mont Logan
Ontario	2 203	Thunder Bay A	1 635	New Liskeard
Manitoba	2 460	Delta U	1 828	Churchill A
Saskatchewan	2 537	Estevan A	2 073	Cree Lake
Alberta	2 490	Coronation A	1 724	Banff
British Columbia	2 244	Cranbrook A	949	Stewart A
Yukon Territory	1 844	Whitehorse A	1 789	Watson Lake A
Northwest Territories	2 277	Yellowknife A	1 899	Inuvik
Nunavut	2 091	Eureka	1 443	Mould Bay A

Source: *Environment Canada*

Average Annual Snowfall

Province	Greatest cm	Station	Least cm	Station
Newfoundland	322.8	Woody Point	91.6	St. Shotts
Prince Edward Island	330.6	Charlottetown A	173.3	Montague
New Brunswick	448.8	Dawson Settlement	176.2	Southwest Head
Nova Scotia	406.7	Cheticamp	104.1	Baccaro
Quebec	648.4	Mont Logan	161.6	Havre aux Maisons
Ontario	430.0	Searchmount	74.0	Lakeview MOE
Manitoba	332.7	Island Lake	94.9	Lundar
Saskatchewan	348.6	Collins Bay	58.0	Aylesbury
Alberta	642.9	Columbia Icefield	59.9	Empress
British Columbia	1 433.0	Glacier NP Mt. Fidelity	20.4	Carnation Creek
Yukon Territory	365.7	Keno Hill	60.1	Komakuk Beach A
Northwest Territories	234.5	Fort McPherson	65.2	Tuktoyaktuk
Nunavut	602.4	Cape Dyer A	28.6	Rea Point

Source: Environment Canada

Wind

Province	Highest Average Annual Wind Speed km/hr		Station	Highest % of Calms %	Station
Newfoundland	28.0	(W)	Bonavista	17.1	Wabush Lake A
Prince Edward Island	22.4	(SSW)	Summerside A	4.4	Summerside A
New Brunswick	22.4	(W)	Miscou Island (AUT)	11.8	Fredericton A
Nova Scotia	25.7	(W)	Sable Island	16.9	Greenwood A
Quebec	32.0	(NW)	Grindstone Island	20.4	Gaspé A
Ontario	21.0	(SW)	Bruce Ontario Hydro	30.2	White River
Manitoba	22.7	(WNW)	Churchill A	21.0	Norway House A
Saskatchewan	22.9	(W)	Swift Current A	12.8	La Ronge A
Alberta	21.5	(W)	Pincher Creek	39.7	High Level A
British Columbia	33.7	(NW)	Cape St. James	48.5	Quesnel A
Yukon Territory	14.1	(SSE)	Whitehorse A	57.5	Dawson A
Northwest Territories	19.9	(E)	Nicholson Peninsula	18.9	Fort Simpson
Nunavut	35.3	(NW)	Resolution Island	35.1	Eureka

Source: Environment Canada

"Coldest Days" (Wind Chill)

Province	ET/WCF[1]	Location	Date	Temp (°C)	Wind (km/hr)
Newfoundland	-71/2814	Wabush Lake	Jan. 20, 1975	-41	40
Prince Edward Island	-57/2450	Charlottetown	Jan. 18, 1982	-32	37
Nova Scotia	-53/2309	Sydney	Jan. 18, 1982	-25	59
New Brunswick	-61/2547	Charlo	Jan. 18, 1982	-31	54
Quebec	-77/3001	Nitchequon	Jan. 20, 1975	-42	56
Ontario	-70/2753	Thunder Bay	Jan. 10, 1982	-36	54
Manitoba	-76/2938	Churchill	Jan. 18, 1975	-41	56
Saskatchewan	-70/2757	Swift Current	Dec. 15, 1964	-34	89
Alberta	-68/2740	Red Deer	Dec. 15, 1964	-35	61
British Columbia	-69/2749	Old Glory Mtn.	Dec. 15, 1964	-36	58
Yukon Territory	-83/3152	Komakuk Beach	Feb. 12, 1975	-50	40
NWT/Nunavut	-92/3357	Pelly Bay	Jan. 13, 1975	-51	56

Source: Environment Canada

(1) ET is equivalent wind chill temperature in °C. WCF is wind chill factor in watts/square metre

Weather Summaries for 1999–2000

July 1999: In parts of the four Atlantic provinces, drought conditions and intense heat for the third summer in a row wilted crops, endangered the health of livestock and forced open-fire bans in parks and forests.

Calgarians called it "the lousiest summer ever." And not just because July had more snow than February or that every weekend from the first of the summer to Labour day was wet. Overall, the summer was one of the wettest ever and in the top ten in the 20th Century for the cold and cloud. Early in the month, up to 65 cm of snow fell in the high mountains between Lake Louise and Jasper at Saskatchewan Crossing and the RCMP closed the Icefield Parkway.

On July 5, stifling heat and humidity triggered a line of severe thunderstorms across eastern Ontario, the Laurentians and the Eastern Townships of Quebec. The storm packed winds 100 to 120 km/h with gusts to 160 km/h and heavy rains, and felling tall pines and poplars, crushing vehicles, tearing down power lines and shearing off roofs. More than 600,000 households in Montreal and the Eastern Townships were without power (some for a week. Two days later, a tornado touched down and caused considerable damage through the Eastern Townships. At Drummondville, the tornado tore roofs off several houses, leaving 200 people in the need of shelter and 4,000 without power.

August 1999: Summer-like temperatures and rainfalls prevailed across the country in August. Funnel clouds occurred in seven of 10 provinces. One touched down in Pugwash, NS tearing the dining room off a café and carrying it across a parking lot, leaving a dazed cook and her manager behind in the kitchen. In late August, Hurricane Cindy was churning well out in the mid-Atlantic, but a rogue wave drowned two swimming off the coast of Nova Scotia.

For most of summer 1999, Ontarians endured bouts of high heat and humidity. The Ontario Ministry of Environment issued five air quality advisories over a total of nine days. Between May and September, many cities in southern Ontario and Quebec had twice their normal number of hot days with temperatures greater than 30°C. Ottawa had 26 hot days, compared to a normal yearly total of 12.

When it came to the weather, organizers in Winnipeg couldn't have picked a better 17 days to host the Pan-Am Games between July 23 to August 8. Only 21 mm of rain fell in three weeks, with most of it at night although the temperature hit 32.5C° on July 29.

September 1999: Above-average temperatures were observed across most of Canada during September. It was especially warm in Atlantic Canada where several +30°C records were set in Halifax, Sydney and elsewhere. The drought in Atlantic Canada ended in September when heavy rains from tropical storms soaked crops and plants, and replenished wells and groundwater reserves. Unfortunately for PEI potato growers, the deluge swamped fields, delaying harvest a week or more.

While Eastern Canadians nervously readied for Hurricane Floyd, it was his younger brother Harvey that packed the biggest punch. On September 21-23, the moisture from tropical storm Harvey fed a storm passing over Halifax. The intensifying low caused 1-in-100 year rainfalls and strong winds. Several weather stations along the Fundy coast of New Brunswick received over 200 mm. Even more rain, up to 302 mm, fell in northern Nova Scotia, making for the worst flooding in 30 years. On September 23, the remnants of Hurricane Gert sank at least five boats docked in a harbour on Newfoundland's Avalon Peninsula. Winds reached up to 120 km/h over the Grand Banks, and waves peaked at nine m.

On the Friday before Labour Day, dense early-morning fog enveloped sections of Highway 401 near Windsor, contributing to one of the worst road disasters in Canadian history. The horrific accident killed eight people and injured 33 others. In all, the chain-reaction pileup destroyed 82 vehicles, many of them fused together in the intense heat. Just moments before the crash, visibility was reduced to about a metre by a fast-moving blanket of thick fog.

October 1999: After two dry years, the Great Lakes emptied rapidly, but not just because of lower precipitation totals and less runoff from rivers and streams; it was also due to huge evaporation losses. Both water and land surfaces in the basin have been unseasonably warm year-round, resulting in increased evaporation. By the end of October, the levels of all of the Great Lakes were below the 80-year average and, with the exception of Superior and Ontario, were down from their levels of a year ago.

Early in October, Fredericton and district got a dusting of snow, but it melted a few minutes later. In mid-month, several days of strong winds disrupted transport schedules across Newfoundland. Ferry transportation to the island was as much as four to five days behind; container vessels were half a week off; and trucks were held up on both ends of Wreckhouse, likely the windiest stretch of the Trans-Canada Highway. On Halloween, an Alberta storm called a clipper raced through Saskatchewan, bringing several cm of snow to the North Battleford region. Winds reached 70 km/h in Saskatoon and 110 km/h in Regina. They knocked down trees and tore off siding and evastroughs and blew over signs. The wind was so strong that it propelled parked cars.

November 1999: Precipitation was highly variable across Canada throughout November. Below-average precipitation continued across the Prairies and into northern Ontario. For British Columbia and Atlantic Canada, it was another month with above-average precipitation.

On the first day of November, a storm roared across Manitoba at record-breaking speed. For Winnipeg, it was the highest sustained wind speed for November at 87 km/h (previous record was 76 km/h) with gusts to 113 km/h. It was just 2 km/h below the all-time record set in July. The wind knocked trucks on their side, flooded cottages, forced schools to close, and turned stop signs, scaffolding and commercial signs into projectiles. The same storm whipped through southern Ontario knocking out power, uprooting trees and flooding streets. Powerful winds of 90 km/h toppled a 25-metre high mesh curtain just erected at a 9-hole golf course and driving range in Downtown Toronto. On November 17th, freezing rain and fog wreaked havoc on Calgary roads and sidewalks, creating backlogs for ambulances and forcing hospitals to bring in extra staff.

November saw some incredibly warm temperatures in the west. Assiniboia, SK had the highest temperature in the nation 24.7°C on the 7th. For the month, Edmonton was about four degrees warmer than normal.

December 1999: Unseasonably mild temperatures continued into December. Record high Boxing Day temperatures were observed in Alberta. At Calgary the temperature on the 27th reached a phenomenal 19.5°C, breaking the old record set in 1898 by more than 6°C. It had been so warm in parts of Alberta that grass fires broke out and trees sprouted leaves. It was hotter in Alberta than in parts of Mexico.

On December 1, winter's first snowstorm struck Nova Scotia. At the airport, about 35 cm of snow with a consistency of wet cement, gave snow-clearing crews fits and closed the airport for a few hours. On December 11-12, the first snowstorm of the winter in southern Quebec dumped 25 to 40 cm of snow swept by winds of 80 km/h. Many areas along the St. Lawrence from Trois Rivieres eastward faced blizzard-like conditions. Sept-Iles got nearly 40 cm of snow. Slippery roads and black ice conditions caused scores of accidents, leading to 13 fatalities and many injuries. On Christmas Day, hundreds of residents of Churchill, MB sought refuge from a fierce storm that knocked out power in northern Manitoba and northwestern Ontario. Winds peaking at 133 km/h cut most of the power in Churchill on Christmas Day afternoon. 200 residents had to forego turkey and ate baloney sandwiches and slept on bedrolls jammed in a community centre as the town declared a state of emergency.

On the last day of the year, Vancouver got a measurable amount of rain, making it the 193rd wet day this year, breaking a new record by one for number of wet days set in 1981.

January 2000: Although the coldest temperature of the winter occurred at Eureka, Nunavut (-50.2°C) on the 26th, winter was reluctant to take hold of much of Canada until the middle of the month. In London, it was so warm in early January that some sap ran in area maple trees—a full seven weeks early. On January 11, a loud, booming winter thunderstorm could be heard across Nova Scotia. Some houses in Halifax shook and windows rattled. The next day, an equally rare thunderstorm boomed over BC's Lower Mainland bringing a variety of precipitation including rain, hail and snow.

On the 17th, many people in New Brunswick were calling it the Storm of the Century. Saint John was hammered with a massive 58 cm of snow with winds gusting to 70 km/h. Snowbanks of more than a metre completely buried parked cars. On the 21st, another winter blast slammed into parts of Atlantic Canada bringing blinding snow, hurricane-force winds and storm-surge flooding. That blizzard dumped up to 54 cm of snow in some places. But it was water, not white stuff, which caused most of the problems. In Charlottetown, the combination of hurricane-force winds and the highest tides of the season caused harbour water to surge ashore, prompting city work crews to build snow banks to hold back the rising seawater. The next day heavy rain and high seas, backed by gale-force winds from the storm, caused major flooding and extensive property damages on the south coast of Newfoundland. The largest of the waves was between 15 and 18 metres travelling at 90 to 110 km/h. Environment Canada said it was the largest set of waves to strike Newfoundland since the 1929 tsunami in the Burin Peninsula.

February 2000: Above-average temperatures prevailed across most of Canada. In the middle of the month an old-fashioned cold and snow spell forced residents from Calgary to Montreal to hunker indoors. The storm brought more than 20 cm of snow to the Prairies and central Canada resulting in the usual traffic mess. By the 21st, winter had really ended across Canada, making one of the shortest cold seasons on record. The end of February saw record-high temperatures set from the Prairies to the Maritimes. In Ontario, temperatures soared into the double digits. On the 26th residents of London saw the mercury climb to 17.8°C while Windsor temperatures exceeded the unheard of 20°C mark. A "false" spring in Montreal McGill with 11°C temperatures shattered records for the day. Montrealers sunned themselves and enjoyed April in February. At Sherbrooke, the temperature soared to a record-breaking 15°. In Ottawa, it was the warmest February-day ever when temperatures climbed to 12°C warmer in the nation's capital than in other hot spots such as Reno and Jerusalem.

March 2000: While winter weather attempted a comeback in March, warmer than usual temperatures were observed across most of the country. Winnipeg observed its fourth-warmest March on record with a monthly average temperature of -0.1°C. Temperatures in excess of 25°C were observed in southwestern Ontario on the 7th. This was the earliest incidence on record of temperatures exceeding 25°C for the region, beating the old mark by more than three weeks.

Above-average precipitation was observed throughout the Prairie Provinces. Unlike the Prairies, however, below-average precipitation continued into and throughout the month making March 2000 the 11th consecutive month of below-average precipitation in Ontario. In parts of southern and central New Brunswick, a St. Patrick's storm dumped 32 cm of snow. Across Nova Scotia, rain, freezing rain and ice pellets contributed to treacherous driving conditions. In PEI, between 25 and 30 cm of snow forced motorists to abandon vehicles in the middle of highways. A late-season storm commonly known as Sheila's Brush combed central, eastern and southern Newfoundland with a vengeance, dumping a deluge of snow and freezing rain, shutting down highways and causing flooding and wind damage in several towns. St. John's recorded 72 mm of rain.

April 2000: Weather conditions did not vary too far from normal in April, the result of mild to cool weather swings during the month.

Montrealers called it a belated April's Fool's joke, but few were laughing when they awoke to a record April one-day snowfall of 37 cm. As of April 1, Montreal's snow removal contracts with two dozen outside firms had expired.

Windsor received a new record high April rainfall of nearly 100 mm on the 20th. At Toronto Island, winds reached 80 km/h from an easterly direction in a thunderstorm. While temperatures were slightly above normal in the Maritimes, it was not so pleasant at the end of April. In New Brunswick, residents bundled up in winter coats, scarves and gloves and grumbled about the weather. Cold temperatures, rain, freezing rain, snow and overcast skies were the order of the day throughout most of April although April temperatures were close to normal.

On the 27th, northern and central Alberta was hit with a freak windstorm that drove huge chunks of ice onto lakefront property around Lac St. Anne outside Edmonton. Some of the ice sheets were about a half metre thick and 10 square metres in area bunched up and wound up sticking four metres into the air.

May 2000: Cool temperatures and steady precipitation since March helped to extinguish a treacherous spring forest fire season. In March, fire prevention officials from Quebec to Alberta had activated emergency resources five weeks earlier than normal.

Early in May temperatures in southern Ontario soared to 10 degrees warmer than normal. At Toronto the temperatures were above 30°C leading to the earliest smog alert ever.

A sudden spring snowstorm covered parts of Manitoba and Saskatchewan with 20 cm of snow. The bad weather closed the Trans-Canada Highway between Moosomin and Virden, MB. In Alberta the storm dumped up to 45 cm of snow on central and foothill regions.

An intense rainstorm around the middle of May left fields soggy in southern Ontario and prompted flood warnings in the Grand and Saugeen rivers. In Toronto, the storm ripped through the city at 75 km/h leaving downed tree limbs and debris scattered about. The Don Valley Parkway had over 1 metre of water in some parts, forcing its closure. In Niagara-on-the-Lake, property damage from the severe wind, hail and rain exceeded $1 million.

June 2000: Wet, wet, wet best describes the weather across most of southern Canada during the first month of summer. It was especially inclement in the eastern Prairies where cool cloudy weather accompanied the excessively moist conditions. Winnipeg's temperature was 2.5°C cooler than normal; total precipitation was 177.4 mm compared to normal of 83.8 mm making it the sixth wettest June on record and a nasty breeding ground for mosquitoes. Toronto broke records for both the wettest May and June ever: the May-June rainfall totals surpassed records dating back to 1840. In June, it rained on 25 days.

Much of the rain came in huge downbursts. On June 11, an intense rainstorm swamped roads and basements in London and district. Many streets had water right up to doorsteps as swollen sewers struggled to handle the runoff. Some residents were being deluged for the second time this year. In southwest neighbourhoods more than 150 mm of rain fell in six hours. Cool, wet weather hurt farmers in central Canada with many of them not able to complete the seeding that they had started two months ago.

Seasonal Temperature and Precipitation in Canada

*All figures are based on the thirty-year period 1961 to 1990 inclusive.
Airport station unless * designates city office station.*

	January			April		
	Average Temperature (°C)		Total	Average Temperature (°C)		Total
Station	Mid Afternoon	Early Morning	Precipitation (mm)	Mid Afternoon	Early Morning	Precipitation (mm)
Calgary, Alta.	-3.6	-15.7	12.2	10.6	-2.4	25.1
Charlottetown, PEI	-3.4	-12.2	106.3	6.3	-1.8	81.6
Churchill, Man.	-22.9	-30.9	17.3	-5.2	-14.8	22.6
Dawson, Yukon*	-27.1	-34.2	16.5	5.9	-9.7	9.4
Edmonton, Alta.	-8.7	-19.8	22.9	9.9	-2.7	21.8
Fredericton, NB	-4.0	-15.4	93.3	9.4	-1.4	83.4
Iqaluit, NT	-21.7	-30.0	21.8	-9.9	-19.6	28.4
Halifax, NS	-1.5	-10.3	146.9	8.0	-0.9	124.4
Hamilton, Ont.	-2.6	-10.0	61.3	11.3	1.2	74.3
Kitchener, Ont.*	-3.3	-11.4	54.3	11.2	0.4	72.6
London, Ont.	-2.8	-10.7	69.0	11.7	0.7	79.2
Moncton, NB	-3.7	-13.9	119.7	7.7	-2.0	100.9
Montreal, Que.	-5.8	-14.9	63.3	10.7	0.6	74.8
Ottawa, Ont.	-6.3	-15.5	58.0	10.8	0.3	69.0
Quebec, Que.	-7.7	-17.3	90.0	7.9	-1.5	75.5
Regina, Sask.	-11.0	-22.1	14.7	10.5	-2.4	20.4
Saint John, NB	-2.8	-13.6	128.3	7.9	-1.5	109.7
St. John's, Nfld	-0.7	-7.9	147.8	4.8	-2.2	110.4
Saskatoon, Sask.	-12.3	-22.9	15.9	10.0	-2.2	25.7
Sault Ste. Marie, Ont.	-5.5	-15.4	74.4	8.5	-2.0	65.2
Toronto, Ont.	-2.5	-11.1	45.6	11.5	0.6	64.0
Vancouver, BC	5.7	0.1	149.8	12.7	4.9	75.4
Victoria, BC	6.5	0.3	141.1	12.9	3.8	41.9
Whitehorse, Yukon	-14.4	-23.2	16.9	5.7	-5.1	8.3
Windsor, Ont.	-1.3	-8.8	50.3	13.4	2.7	80.3
Winnipeg, Man.	-13.2	-23.6	19.3	9.8	-2.3	35.9
Yellowknife, NWT	-23.9	-32.2	14.9	-0.5	-12.0	10.3

Talkin' About the Weather

What's the difference between a **report**, a **forecast** and an **outlook**?
They all make up what Environment Canada refers to as a public weather bulletin. A description of the current weather conditions at a specific location is a **report**. Information concerning predicted weather conditions for the current day and the next is the **forecast**. An extended forecast—general weather conditions for the coming three days—is the **outlook**.

OK, so what's the difference between a weather **advisory**, a weather **watch** and a weather **warning**?
When Environment Canada issues a weather **advisory** for an actual or expected weather condition (for example, a wind chill advisory), they are telling us that the weather is likely to cause some discomfort or concern, but will not likely be a serious threat. When a weather **watch** is in effect, they are telling us that conditions are favourable for the development of what they call severe weather. The weather event may not happen, but we should pay attention to what's going on around us outside. When a weather **warning** is issued for severe weather (severe thunderstorms, tornadoes, hail etc.) the conditions are either occurring or it's highly probable that they will occur. This means that it's definitely time to take precautions.

Climate

Station	July Average Temperature (°C) Mid Afternoon	July Average Temperature (°C) Early Morning	July Total Precipitation (mm)	October Average Temperature (°C) Mid Afternoon	October Average Temperature (°C) Early Morning	October Total Precipitation (mm)
Calgary, Alta.	23.2	9.5	69.9	12.6	-1.2	15.5
Charlottetown, PEI	23.1	13.6	81.6	12.1	4.0	111.7
Churchill, Man.	16.9	6.8	50.7	1.4	-4.3	46.5
Dawson, Yukon*	22.8	6.5	33.9	-0.5	-10.4	27.9
Edmonton, Alta.	22.5	9.4	101.0	11.3	-2.2	17.7
Fredericton, NB	25.6	12.9	84.5	13.1	1.5	93.1
Iqaluit, NT	11.6	3.7	58.2	-2.1	-7.8	42.4
Halifax, NS	23.4	13.2	96.8	13.0	4.0	128.9
Hamilton, Ont.	26.4	15.1	81.0	13.9	4.7	66.3
Kitchener, Ont.*	26.1	13.6	90.4	13.2	2.9	70.4
London, Ont.	26.4	14.2	76.7	14.2	3.9	76.4
Moncton, NB	24.4	12.5	102.6	12.7	2.1	106.4
Montreal, Que.	26.2	15.4	85.6	13.0	3.6	75.4
Ottawa, Ont.	26.4	15.1	88.1	12.8	3.0	74.8
Quebec, Que.	24.9	13.2	118.5	11.0	2.0	96.0
Regina, Sask.	26.3	11.9	58.9	11.9	-1.7	20.3
Saint John, NB	22.1	11.6	103.7	12.1	2.9	122.5
St. John's, Nfld	20.2	10.5	121.2	10.6	3.4	151.7
Saskatoon, Sask.	25.4	11.7	58.0	11.1	-1.5	16.9
Sault Ste. Marie, Ont.	24.3	11.2	65.6	11.8	2.9	83.2
Toronto, Ont.	26.8	14.2	76.6	14.1	3.6	63.0
Vancouver, BC	21.7	12.7	36.1	13.5	6.4	115.3
Victoria, BC	21.8	10.7	17.6	14.1	5.3	74.4
Whitehorse, Yukon	20.3	7.6	39.3	4.3	-3.1	23.0
Windsor, Ont.	27.7	17.0	85.3	15.8	6.0	57.9
Winnipeg, Man.	26.1	13.4	72.0	11.3	0.1	29.5
Yellowknife, NWT	20.8	12.0	35.2	1.3	-4.2	34.8

Source: *Environment Canada*

Winter Weatherspeak

When the forecast calls for **snow**, it means those hexagonal flakes, falling for a significant time and in quantity. A **snow flurry** or **shower** is intermittent snow falling in a limited quantity. This flurry or shower may often also contain **snow pellets**—these are brittle and break up when they fall on hard ground. (In contrast, **ice pellets** bounce noisily on the ground and don't break up. The lesser-known **snow grains** are tiny, white grains of opaque ice which don't bounce or shatter—or appear in much quantity or ever in showers. **Ice crystals** are tiny sprinkles that hang in the air and sparkle in the light like diamond dust.) A **snow squall** means there will be flurries, accompanied by strong winds and poor visibility. **Drifting snow** will be blown no higher than 2 m off the ground, whereas the wind lifts **blowing snow** 2 m or more. A **blizzard** is a storm that will last three or more hours, with blowing snow, poor visibility and cold.

And then, of course, there's the **wind chill**. The combined effect of wind and cold air temperatures increases the loss of body heat and is something that Canadians should always pay attention to. When Environment Canada discusses the wind chill factor, it means they have factored the effect of the wind into the current or expected temperature. For a wind chill chart and more information on its effect—find out when exposed flesh freezes in 30 seconds!—check the Atmospheric Science section of Science and Nature.

Spring and Fall Frost Dates in Canada

Frost occurs whenever temperatures fall to 0°C or lower. All frost dates and values are based on the available data during the period 1951-1980.

Growing degree-day data are from the period 1961-90. Data reported from airport stations unless * designates city office station.

	1 in 10 Chance Last Spring Frost After Date	1 in 10 Chance First Fall Frost Before Date	Frost-free Period (days)	Growing Degree-Days Above 5°C[1]
Newfoundland				
Corner Brook*	June 10	Sept. 8	139	1 432
St. John's*	June 24	Sept. 19	131	1 262
Prince Edward Island				
Charlottetown	May 27	Oct. 6	151	1 636
Nova Scotia				
Halifax	May 28	Sept. 30	155	1 707
New Brunswick				
Fredericton	June 10	Sept. 13	126	1 760
Moncton	June 10	Sept. 14	124	1 649
Saint John	June 10	Sept. 18	139	1 499
Quebec				
Chicoutimi*	June 4	Sept. 18	135	1 575
Gaspé*	June 12	Sept. 11	123	1 336
Montreal	May 19	Sept. 26	157	2 079
Quebec	May 28	Sept. 14	137	1 688
Schefferville	June 27	Aug. 22	77	604
Ontario				
Kitchener*	May 25	Sept. 17	151	1 992
London	May 25	Sept. 23	147	2 121
Moosonee*	July 6	July 30	70	1 078
Ottawa	May 25	Sept. 21	147	2 045
St. Catharines*	May 18	Oct. 5	173	2 451
Sudbury	June 11	Sept. 11	128	1 680
Thunder Bay	June 13	Aug. 29	104	1 427
Timmins	June 23	Aug. 19	91	1 395
Toronto	May 25	Sept. 18	149	2 090
Windsor	May 10	Oct. 3	177	2 544
Manitoba				
Brandon	June 9	Aug. 31	108	1 652
Churchill	July 7	Aug. 20	76	562
Flin Flon	June 10	Sept. 2	115	1 379
Winnipeg	June 10	Sept. 11	121	1 802
Saskatchewan				
Prince Albert	June 21	Aug. 17	95	1 455
Regina	June 14	Aug. 27	109	1 723
Saskatoon	June 10	Sept. 1	117	1 658
Alberta				
Banff*	June 30	Aug. 6	89	1 124
Calgary	June 10	Aug. 27	112	1 435
Edmonton	June 14	Aug. 13	105	1 352
Fort McMurray	June 30	Aug. 2	84	1 352
Lethbridge	May 31	Sept. 2	124	1 779
Medicine Hat	May 27	Sept. 8	129	1 971
Peace River	June 23	Aug. 13	93	1 276
British Columbia				
Fort Nelson	June 7	Aug. 14	106	1 289
Kamloops	May 18	Sept. 19	149	2 259
Penticton	May 23	Sept. 14	148	2 163
Prince George	July 1	Aug. 11	85	1 238
Prince Rupert	May 25	Sept. 28	156	1 181
Vancouver	Apr. 21	Oct. 13	216	2 018
Victoria	Apr. 30	Oct. 17	201	1 864

Climate

	1 in 10 Chance Last Spring Frost After Date	1 in 10 Chance First Fall Frost Before Date	Frost-free Period (days)	Growing Degree-Days Above 5°C[1]
Yukon				
Dawson*	June 16	Aug. 6	91	1 015
Whitehorse	June 24	Aug. 13	82	871
Northwest Territories				
Yellowknife	June 9	Sept. 3	111	1 039
Nunavut				
Alert*	July 15	July 16	4	30
Iqaluit	July 12	July 26	59	177
Resolute	July 15	July 16	9	29

Source: *Environment Canada*
(1) Growing degree days represent the average total number of heat units (daily mean temp. -5°C) during the growing season

Plant Hardiness Zones in Canada

A plant's hardiness rating is related to its ability to survive in specific climate conditions. Plant hardiness zones were originally based on average minimum winter temperatures in a location, and first developed by the US Department of Agriculture (USDA).

The USDA created 11 zones, each of which have since been split into subzones a and b. Canada's Department of Agriculture and Agri-Food took the concept of hardiness further by including other factors besides minimum temperature in designating Canada's plant hardiness zones. They created a weighted equation that took into account such factors as the average minimum temperature of the coldest month; the average length of the frost-free period; average rainfall between June and November; the average maximum temperature in the hottest month; the amount of snow; and the maximum windspeeds in the last 30 years in any given area.

Canada's zones range from 0a in our coldest regions to 9a in our most temperate locations, and the minimum temperature equivalents are shown below. Canadian gardeners may find themselves in micro-climates that differ from the conditions the zone map indicates, however most should choose perennials based on the zone the garden is in and the hardiness rating of the plant. (A plant can survive in the zone it's rated for or a higher/warmer one.)

To find out what zone you're in, consult a local nursery or visit the map at http://res.agr.ca/CANSIS/SYSTEMS/online_maps.html

Hardiness Zone	Average Minimum Temperature (°C)
0a - 0b	-46 or colder
1a - 1b	-46 to -37
2a - 2b	-37 to -29
3a - 3b	-29 to -23
4a - 4b	-23 to -20
5a - 5b	-20 to -15
6a - 6b	-15 to -12
7a - 7b	-12 to -6
8a - 8b	-6 to -1
9a	-1 to 4 or warmer

Source: *Agriculture and Agri-Food Canada*

What Grows Where? Trees and Shrubs

Trees: White Spruce can survive in Zone 1; Laurel Willow thrives in 1b, White Ash and Hackberry need 2b, European Birch and American Elm hold out for 2 and Black Walnut prefers 3b. Black Locust trees won't survive in much below Zone 4, while English Oak and Norway Maple require the balmier climate of Zone 5. Flowering Dogwood wants 6b and European Beeches prefer 6. In Zones 7 and 8, we find such species as the Dove Tree and Pacific Dogwood, while only those with Zone 9a conditions (yes, residents of Victoria, B.C.) can hope to keep a Southern Magnolia alive.

Shrubs: Those in Zone 1 can raise Mugo Pine and Saskatoon bushes; 2s (including Saskatoon gardeners) can also have Siberian Dogwood. Garland Spirea must be in climate Zone 3 or better, with Japanese Yew demanding Zone 4 and Smokebushes requiring a 5. Japanese Maples grow well in Zone 6, Cherry Laurel in 7, while Sweet Bay Laurel resides best in Victoria or other 9bs in the nation.

PROVINCES AND TERRITORIES

Latitude, Longitude, Elevation of Canadian Cities

City	Lat. N °	Lat. N '	Long. W °	Long. W '	Elev. (m)	City	Lat. N °	Lat. N '	Long. W °	Long. W '	Elev. (m)
Alert, NT*	82	30	62	22	31	Moose Jaw, Sask.	50	23	105	32	544
Brandon, Man.	49	51	99	57	409	Niagara Falls, Ont.	43	06	79	03	180
Brantford, Ont.	43	08	80	15	215	North Bay, Ont.	46	18	79	27	204
Burlington, Ont.	43	19	79	47	87	Ottawa, Ont.	45	26	75	41	56
Calgary, Alta.	51	02	114	03	1 045	Peterborough, Ont.	44	18	78	19	205
Charlottetown, PEI	46	14	63	07	9	Prince Rupert, BC	54	19	130	19	38
Churchill, Man.	58	45	94	10	29	Quebec, Que.	46	48	71	12	50
Dartmouth, NS	44	39	63	34	7	Regina, Sask.	50	27	104	36	577
Dawson, Yukon	64	03	139	26	369	Saint John, NB	45	16	66	03	8
Edmonton, Alta.	53	32	113	29	666	St. John's, Nfld	47	34	52	43	61
Fredericton, NB	45	57	66	38	9	Saskatoon, Sask.	52	07	106	39	484
Guelph, Ont.	43	32	80	14	325	Sault Ste. Marie, Ont.	46	30	84	20	180
Halifax, NS	44	38	63	34	18	Sherbrooke, Que.	45	24	71	53	191
Hamilton, Ont.	43	15	79	52	100	Sudbury, Ont.	46	29	80	59	347
Hull, Que.	45	25	75	42	56	Sydney, NS	46	08	60	11	62
Iqaluit, NT*	63	45	68	31	34	Thunder Bay, Ont.	48	22	89	14	188
Kingston, Ont.	44	13	76	28	80	Toronto, Ont.	43	39	79	23	91
Kitchener, Ont.	43	26	80	29	335	Trois-Rivières, Que.	46	21	72	33	35
LaSalle, Que.	45	25	73	39	34	Vancouver, BC	49	18	123	04	43
Laval, Que.	45	33	73	44	43	Victoria, BC	48	25	123	21	17
Lethbridge, Alta.	49	41	112	49	910	Whitehorse, Yukon	60	43	135	03	703
London, Ont.	42	59	81	14	251	Winnipeg, Man.	49	53	97	08	232
Moncton, NB	46	05	64	46	12	Yellowknife, NWT	62	28	114	22	205
Montreal, Que.	45	30	73	33	27						

Source: *Natural Resources Canada*
*Nunavut

Area[1] of Canadian Provinces and Territories

(sq. km)

	Land	Water	Total	% of Total Area of Canada
Newfoundland and Labrador	373 872	31 340	405 212	4.06
Prince Edward Island	5 660	—	5 660	0.06
Nova Scotia	53 338	1 946	55 284	0.55
New Brunswick	71 450	1 458	72 908	0.73
Quebec	1 365 128	176 928	1 542 056	15.44
Ontario	917 741	158 654	1 076 395	10.78
Manitoba	553 556	94 241	647 797	6.49
Saskatchewan	591 670	59 366	651 036	6.52
Alberta	642 317	19 531	661 848	6.63
British Columbia	925 186	19 549	944 735	9.46
Yukon Territory	474 391	8 052	482 443	4.83
Northwest Territories	1 183 085	163 021	1 346 106	13.48
Nunavut	1 936 113	157 077	2 093 190	20.96
Canada	**9 093 507**	**891 163**	**9 984 670**	**100.00**

Source: *Natural Resources Canada*

(1) Calculated from the National Atlas of Canada 1:1000000 scale hydrology base. (—) = zero

Newfoundland

☐ **CAPITAL:** St. John's, metro pop. (1999) 174 509. **Date entered Confederation:** Mar. 31, 1949.

☐ **POPULATION (1999): 541 000;** Pop. density: 1.5 per sq. km.; **Pop. growth (1996–1999):** -2.0%; **Pop. Urban (1996):** 56.9%; **Official Languages (1996):** 96% English; 3.9% bilingual. **Net interprovincial migration (1999):** -2 794.

☐ **VITAL STATISTICS: Rates** (per 1 000 pop., 1998-99): **Birth:** 9.4; **Death:** 8.2; **Life expectancy at birth** (1996): male: 75; female: 81.

☐ **GEOGRAPHY: Total area** 405 720 sq. km; **Land area** 371 690 sq. km; **Forested land** 142 000 sq. km; **Length of coastline** 19 720 km. **Climate:** ranges from subarctic in Labrador and northern tip of island to humid continental with cool summers and heavy precipitation. **Topography:** Island of Newfoundland: highlands of the Long Range Mtns. (elev. 900 m) along w. coast; barren and rocky central plateau descends to lowlands towards the n. east; coast is deeply indented with bays and fjords. Labrador: mountainous in the n.; rugged coast and interior plateau.

☐ **ECONOMY: Gross Domestic Product** (1998): $11 308 million; **% change GDP** (1997–98): 6.3%; **Per capita GDP** (1998): $20 711. **Employment distrib.** (1999): goods-producing industries (agriculture, primary ind., mfg, construction) 23%; service-producing industries (transpt., trade, finance, service, pub. admin, unclassified) 77%. **Unemployment rate** (1999): 16.9%. **Principal industries:** mining, manufacturing, fishing, logging and forestry, electricity production, tourism.

☐ **EDUCATION (1997–98): No. of schools:** 397 elem. and sec.; 6 post-sec. **Enrolment:** 102 074 elem. and sec.; 21 949 post-sec.

☐ **INTERNATIONAL AIRPORTS:** Gander.

☐ **NATIONAL PARKS:** Gros Morne, Terra Nova.

☐ **PROVINCIAL DATA: Motto:** *Quaerite Prime Regnum Dei:* "Seek Ye First the Kingdom of God." **Flower:** Pitcher plant. **Bird:** Atlantic Puffin (unofficial). **Anthem:** Ode to Newfoundland. **Tartan:** Newfoundland Tartan.

☐ **POLITICS: Premier:** Brian Tobin (Lib.). **Leaders, opposition parties:** Jack Harris (NDP), Ed Byrne (Prog. Cons.). **Date of last general election:** Feb. 9, 1999. **Lt. Governor:** Hon. A.M. House.

Prince Edward Island

☐ **CAPITAL:** Charlottetown, metro pop. (1996) 36 990. **Date entered Confederation:** July 1, 1873.

☐ **POPULATION (1999): 138 000;** Pop. density: 24.4 per sq. km.; **Pop. growth (1996–1999):** 2.5%; **Pop. Urban (1996):** 44.2%; **Official Languages (1996):** 88.9% English; 0.1% French, 11.0% bilingual. **Net interprovincial migration** (1999): 703.

☐ **VITAL STATISTICS: Rates** (per 1 000 pop., 1998-99): **Birth:** 11.3; **Death:** 7.7; **Life expectancy at birth** (1996): male: 74; female: 81.

☐ **GEOGRAPHY: Total area** 5 660 sq. km; **Land area** 5 660 sq. km; **Forested land** 3 000 sq. km; **Length of coastline** 1 107 km. **Climate:** humid continental with temperatures moderated by maritime location. **Topography:** flat through gently rolling hills; sharply indented coastline; many streams but only small rivers and lakes.

☐ **ECONOMY: Gross Domestic Product** (1998): $2 872 million; **% change GDP** (1997–98): 1.4%; **Per capita GDP** (1998): $20 964. **Employment distrib.** (1999): goods-producing industries (agriculture, primary ind., mfg, construction) 27%; service-producing industries (transpt., trade, finance, service, pub. admin, unclassified) 73%. **Unemployment rate** (1999): 14.4%. **Principal industries:** agriculture, tourism, fishing, manufacturing.

☐ **EDUCATION (1997–98): No. of schools:** 71 elem. and sec.; 2 post-sec. **Enrolment:** 24 688 elem. and sec.; 4 629 post-sec.

☐ **INTERNATIONAL AIRPORTS:** none.

☐ **NATIONAL PARKS:** Prince Edward Island (north shore).

☐ **PROVINCIAL DATA: Motto:** *Parva Sub Ingenti:* "The small under the protection of the great." **Flower:** Lady's slipper. **Bird:** Blue Jay. **Tree:** Red Oak.

☐ **POLITICS: Premier:** Pat Binns (Prog. Cons.) **Leaders, opposition parties:** Wayne Carew (Lib.), Dr. H. Dickieson (NDP). **Date of last general election:** April 17, 2000. **Lt. Governor:** Hon. Gilbert R. Clements.

Nova Scotia

☐ **CAPITAL:** Halifax, metro pop. (1999) 352 594. **Date entered Confederation:** July 1, 1867.

☐ **POPULATION (1999): 939 800; Pop. density:** 17.8 per sq. km.; **Pop. growth (1996–1999):** 3.2%; **Pop. Urban** (1996): 54.8%; **Official Languages** (1996): 90.4% English; 0.2% French, 9.3% bilingual. **Net interprovincial migration** (1999): 1 418.

☐ **VITAL STATISTICS: Rates** (per 1 000 pop., 1998-99): **Birth:** 10.3; **Death:** 8.8; **Life expectancy at birth** (1996): male: 75; female: 81.

☐ **GEOGRAPHY: Total area** 55 490 sq. km; **Land area** 52 840 sq. km; **Forested land** 41,000 sq. km; **Length of coastline** 5 934 km. **Climate:** humid continental with some moderating effects due to maritime location. **Topography:** Atlantic Uplands are segmented by river valleys; Cape Breton Is. rises from lowland in the s. to a high plateau; many rivers, lakes and jagged coastline.

☐ **ECONOMY: Gross Domestic Product** (1998): $20 689 million; **% change GDP** (1997–98): 2.4%; **Per capita GDP** (1998): $22 104. **Employment distrib.** (1999): goods-producing industries (agriculture, primary ind., mfg, construction) 22%; service-producing industries (transpt., trade, finance, service, pub. admin, unclassified) 78%. **Unemployment rate** (1999): 9.6%. **Principal industries:** manufacturing, fishing and trapping, mining, agriculture, pulp and paper.

☐ **EDUCATION (1997–98): No. of schools:** 499 elem. and sec.; 18 post-sec. **Enrolment:** 164 715 elem. and sec.; 44 785 post-sec.

☐ **INTERNATIONAL AIRPORTS:** Halifax

☐ **NATIONAL PARKS:** Cape Breton Highlands, Kejimkujik.

☐ **PROVINCIAL DATA: Motto:** *Munit Haec et Altera Vincit:* "One defends and the other conquers." **Flower:** Mayflower. **Bird:** Osprey. **Tree:** Red Spruce. **Gem:** Agate.

☐ **POLITICS: Premier:** Dr. John Hamm (Prog. Cons.). **Leaders, opposition parties:** Wayne Gandet (Lib.), Helen MacDonald (NDP). **Date of last general election:** July 27, 1999. **Lt. Governor:** Hon. Myra A. Freeman.

New Brunswick

☐ **CAPITAL:** Fredericton, metro pop. (1999) 46 507. **Date entered Confederation:** July 1, 1867.

☐ **POPULATION (1999): 755 000**; **Pop. density:** 10.5 per sq. km.; **Pop. growth (1996–1999):** 2.2%; **Pop. Urban** (1996): 48.8%; **Official Languages** (1996): 57.3% English; 10.1% French, 32.6% bilingual. **Net interprovincial migration** (1999): 305.

☐ **VITAL STATISTICS: Rates** (per 1 000 pop., 1998-99): **Birth:** 10.2; **Death:** 8.1; **Life expectancy at birth** (1996): male: 75; female: 81.

☐ **GEOGRAPHY: Total area** 73 440 sq. km; **Land area** 72 090 sq. km; **Forested land** 61,000 sq. km; **Length of coastline** 1 524 km. **Climate:** humid continental climate except along the shores where there is a marked maritime effect. **Topography:** northern upland; rolling central plateau; southern lowland plain with many rivers.

☐ **ECONOMY: Gross Domestic Product** (1998): $17 231 million; **% change GDP** (1997–98): 2.5%; **Per capita GDP** (1998): $22 883. **Employment distrib.** (1999): goods-producing industries (agriculture, primary ind., mfg, construction) 24%; service-producing industries (transpt., trade, finance, service, pub. admin, unclassified) 76%. **Unemployment rate** (1999): 10.2%. **Principal industries:** manufacturing, fishing, mining, forestry, pulp and paper, agriculture.

☐ **EDUCATION (1997–98): No. of schools:** 383 elem. and sec.; 10 post-sec. **Enrolment:** 133 154 elem. and sec.; 27 957 post-sec.

☐ **INTERNATIONAL AIRPORTS:** none.

☐ **NATIONAL PARKS:** Fundy, Kouchibouguac.

☐ **PROVINCIAL DATA: Motto:** *Spem Reduxit:* "Hope was restored." **Flower:** Purple Violet. **Bird:** Black-capped Chickadee. **Tree:** Balsam Fir.

☐ **POLITICS: Premier:** Bernard Lord (Prog. Cons.). **Leaders, opposition parties:** Camille Thériault (Lib.), Elizabeth Weir (NDP). **Date of last general election:** June 7, 1999. **Lt. Governor:** Hon. Marilyn Trenholme Counsell.

Quebec

- **CAPITAL:** Quebec, metro pop. (1999) 688 085. **Date entered Confederation:** July 1, 1867.
- **POPULATION (1999):** 7 345 400; **Pop. density:** 5.4 per sq. km.; **Pop. growth (1996–1999):** 2.8%; **Pop. Urban (1996):** 78.4%; **Official Languages (1996):** 56.1% English; 5.1% French, 37.8% bilingual. **Net interprovincial migration (1999):** -15 008.
- **VITAL STATISTICS:** Rates (per 1 000 pop., 1998-99): **Birth:** 10.1; **Death:** 7.4; **Life expectancy at birth** (1996): male: 75; female: 81.
- **GEOGRAPHY: Total area** 1 540 680 sq. km; **Land area** 1 356 790 sq. km; **Forested land** 940 000 sq. km; **Length of coastline** 10 839 km. **Climate:** varies from subarctic to continental. **Topography:** lowlands along the St. Lawrence R. valley separate the Laurentian Mtns. to the n. and the Appalachian Mtns. to the s.; Canadian Shield landscape dominates north.
- **ECONOMY: Gross Domestic Product** (1998): $193 243 million; **% change GDP** (1997–98): 3.2%; **Per capita GDP** (1998): $26 345. **Employment distrib.** (1999): goods-producing industries (agriculture, primary ind., mfg, construction) 27%; service-producing industries (transpt., trade, finance, service, pub. admin, unclassified) 73%. **Unemployment rate** (1999): 9.3%. **Principal industries:** manufacturing, electric power, mining, pulp and paper, transportation equipment.
- **EDUCATION (1997–98): No. of schools:** 3 055 elem. and sec.; 95 post-sec. **Enrolment:** 1 130 037 elem. and sec.; 405 919 post-sec.
- **INTERNATIONAL AIRPORTS:** Dorval; Mirabel.
- **NATIONAL PARKS:** Forillon, La Mauricie, Mingan Archipelago, Saguenay-St. Lawrence Marine Park.
- **PROVINCIAL DATA: Motto:** *Je me souviens:* "I remember." **Flower:** Lys blanc de jardin (White Garden (Madonna) Lily). **Bird:** Harfang des neiges (Snowy Owl).
- **POLITICS: Premier:** Lucien Bouchard (Parti Québécois). **Leader, opposition parties:** Jean Charest (Lib.), Mario Dumont (A.D.). **Date of last general election:** Nov. 30, 1998. **Lt. Governor:** Hon. Lise Thibault.

Ontario

- **CAPITAL:** Toronto, metro pop. (1999) 4 680 250. **Date entered Confederation:** July 1, 1867.
- **POPULATION (1999):** 11 513 800; **Pop. density:** 12.9 per sq. km.; **Pop. growth (1996–1999):** 6.6%; **Pop. Urban (1996):** 83.3%; **Official Languages (1996):** 85.7% English; 0.4% French, 11.6% bilingual. **Net interprovincial migration (1999):** 17 228.
- **VITAL STATISTICS:** Rates (per 1 000 pop., 1998-99): **Birth:** 11.5; **Death:** 7.3; **Life expectancy at birth** (1996): male: 76; female: 81.
- **GEOGRAPHY: Total area** 1 068 580 sq. km; **Land area** 891 190 sq. km; **Forested land** 807 000 sq. km; **Length of coastline** 1 210 km. **Climate:** ranges from humid continental in south to subarctic in far north; westerly winds bring winter storms; the Great Lakes moderate winter temperatures. **Topography:** Rugged, rocky Canadian Shield plateau is broken by lowlands around Great Lakes, St. Lawrence R. and Hudson Bay.
- **ECONOMY: Gross Domestic Product** (1998): $371 874 million; **% change GDP** (1997–98): 4.3%; **Per capita GDP** (1998): $32 583. **Employment distrib.** (1999): goods-producing industries (agriculture, primary ind., mfg, construction) 27%; service-producing industries (transpt., trade, finance, service, pub. admin, unclassified) 73%. **Unemployment rate** (1999): 6.3%. **Principal industries:** manufacturing, construction, agriculture, forestry, mining.
- **EDUCATION (1997–98): No. of schools:** 5 320 elem. and sec.; 61 post-sec. **Enrolment:** 2 131 871 elem. and sec.; 455 860 post-sec.
- **INTERNATIONAL AIRPORTS:** Pearson (Toronto); Ottawa.
- **NATIONAL PARKS:** Bruce Peninsula, Fathom Five Marine Park, Georgian Bay Islands, Point Pelee, Pukaskwa, St. Lawrence Islands.
- **PROVINCIAL DATA: Motto:** *Ut Incepit Fidelis Sic Permanet:* "Loyal she began, loyal she remains." **Flower:** White trillium. **Bird:** Common Loon. **Tree:** Eastern White Pine. **Gem:** Amethyst.
- **POLITICS: Premier:** Mike Harris (Prog. Cons.). **Leaders, opposition parties:** Dalton McGinty (Lib.); Howard Hampton (NDP). **Date of last general election:** June 21, 1999. **Lt. Governor:** Hon. Hilary Weston.

Manitoba

- **CAPITAL:** Winnipeg, metro pop. (1999) 677 625. **Date entered Confederation:** July 15, 1870.
- **POPULATION (1999):** 1 143 500; **Pop. density:** 2.1 per sq. km.; **Pop. growth (1996–1999):** 2.6%; **Pop. Urban (1996):** 71.8%; **Official Languages (1996):** 89.4% English; 0.1% French, 9.4% bilingual; 1.1% neither English nor French. **Net interprovincial migration (1999):** -950.
- **VITAL STATISTICS: Rates** (per 1 000 pop., 1998-99): **Birth:** 12.6; **Death:** 8.6; **Life expectancy at birth** (1996): male: 75; female: 81.
- **GEOGRAPHY: Total area** 649 950 sq. km; **Land area** 548 360 sq. km; **Forested land** 349 000 sq. km; **Length of coastline** 917 km. **Climate:** continental with seasonal extremes. **Topography:** the land rises gradually south and west from Hudson Bay; flat plateau through south central region; countless lakes, streams and bogs.
- **ECONOMY: Gross Domestic Product** (1998): $29 915 million; **% change GDP** (1997–98): 2.6%; **Per capita GDP** (1998): $26 287. **Employment distrib.** (1999): goods-producing industries (agriculture, primary ind., mfg, construction) 27%; service-producing industries (transpt., trade, finance, service, pub. admin, unclassified) 73%. **Unemployment rate** (1999): 5.6%. **Principal industries:** manufacturing, agriculture, food industry, mining, construction.
- **EDUCATION (1997–98): No. of schools:** 852 elem. and sec.; 11 post-sec. **Enrolment:** 224 136 elem. and sec.; 37 068 post-sec.
- **INTERNATIONAL AIRPORTS:** Winnipeg.
- **NATIONAL PARKS:** Riding Mountain, Wapusk.
- **PROVINCIAL DATA: Motto:** Glorious and Free. **Flower:** Prairie Crocus. **Bird:** Great Gray Owl. **Tartan:** Manitoba Tartan.
- **POLITICS: Premier:** Gary Doer (NDP). **Leaders, opposition parties:** Bonnie Mitchelson (Prog. Cons.), Jon Gerrard (Lib.). **Date of last general election:** Sept. 21, 1999. **Lt. Governor:** Hon. Peter M. Liba.

Saskatchewan

- **CAPITAL:** Regina, metro pop. (1999) 199 163. **Date entered Confederation:** Sept. 1, 1905.
- **POPULATION (1999):** 1 027 800; **Pop. density:** 1.8 per sq. km.; **Pop. growth (1996–1999):** 3.7%; **Pop. Urban (1996):** 63.3%; **Official Languages (1996):** 94.3% English; 5.2% bilingual; 0.5% neither English nor French. **Net interprovincial migration** (1999): -5 916.
- **VITAL STATISTICS: Rates** (per 1 000 pop., 1998-99): **Birth:** 12.4; **Death:** 8.6; **Life expectancy at birth** (1996): male: 75; female: 82.
- **GEOGRAPHY: Total area** 652 330 sq. km; **Land area** 570 700 sq. km; **Forested land** 178 000 sq. km; **Climate:** continental, with cold winters and hot summers. **Topography:** gently rolling plains through south; higher, hilly plateaus in the s.w.; north is rugged Canadian Shield.
- **ECONOMY: Gross Domestic Product** (1998): $28 790 million; **% change GDP** (1997–98): -0.7%; **Per capita GDP** (1998): $28 060. **Employment distrib.** (1999): goods-producing industries (agriculture, primary ind., mfg, construction) 28%; service-producing industries (transpt., trade, finance, service, pub. admin, unclassified) 72%. **Unemployment rate** (1999): 6.1%. **Principal industries:** agriculture, mining, manufacturing, electric power, construction, chemical prod.
- **EDUCATION (1997–98): No. of schools:** 908 elem. and sec.; 8 post-sec. **Enrolment:** 211 062 elem. and sec.; 34 580 post-sec.
- **INTERNATIONAL AIRPORTS:** Saskatoon.
- **NATIONAL PARKS:** Grasslands, Prince Albert.
- **PROVINCIAL DATA: Motto:** *Multis E Gentibus Vires:* "from many peoples strength". **Flower:** Western Red Lily. **Bird:** Prairie sharp-tailed grouse. **Tree:** White Birch. **Tartan:** Saskatchewan Tartan.
- **POLITICS: Premier:** Roy Romanow (NDP). **Leaders, opposition parties:** Elwin Hermanson (Sask.), Jim Melenchuk (Lib.). **Date of last general election:** Sept. 16, 1999. **Lt. Governor:** Hon. Lynda M. Haverstock.

Alberta

- **CAPITAL:** Edmonton, metro pop. (1999) 929 145. **Date entered Confederation:** Sept. 1, 1905.
- **POPULATION (1999):** 2 964 700; Pop. density: 4.6 per sq. km.; **Pop. growth (1996–1999):** 9.0%; **Pop. Urban** (1996): 79.5%; **Official Languages** (1996): 91.9% English; 0.1 French; 6.7% bilingual; 1.3% neither English nor French. **Net interprovincial migration** (1999): 16 602.
- **VITAL STATISTICS: Rates** (per 1 000 pop., 1998-99): Birth: 12.9; Death: 5.9; **Life expectancy at birth** (1996): male: 76; female: 81.
- **GEOGRAPHY: Total area** 661 190 sq. km; **Land area** 644 390 sq. km; **Forested land** 349 000 sq. km. Climate: great variance in temperatures between regions and seasons; summer highs between 16°C and 32°C; winters as low as -45°C. Topography: Rocky Mtns. in s.w. to rolling prairie throughout southern region; far north is a forested plateau.
- **ECONOMY: Gross Domestic Product** (1998): $104 982 million; **% change GDP** (1997–98): -1.4%; **Per capita GDP** (1998): $36 076. **Employment distrib.** (1999): goods-producing industries (agriculture, primary ind., mfg, construction) 27%; service-producing industries (transpt., trade, finance, service, pub. admin, unclassified) 73%. **Unemployment rate** (1999): 5.7%. **Principal industries:** chemical products, mining, agriculture, food, manufacturing, construction, oil prod. and refinement.
- **EDUCATION (1997–98):** No. of schools: 1 901 elem. and sec.; 26 post-sec. **Enrolment:** 563 170 elem. and sec.; 117 556 post-sec.
- **INTERNATIONAL AIRPORTS:** Edmonton; Calgary.
- **NATIONAL PARKS:** Banff, Elk Island, Jasper, Waterton Lakes, Wood Buffalo (shared with Northwest Territories).
- **PROVINCIAL DATA: Motto:** *Fortis et Liber:* "Strong and free." **Flower:** Wild Rose. **Bird:** Great horned owl. **Tree:** Lodge pole pine. **Tartan:** Alberta Tartan. **Stone:** Petrified wood.
- **POLITICS: Premier:** Ralph Klein (Prog. Cons.). **Leaders, opposition parties:** Nancy McBeth (Lib.), Raj Pannu (NDP). **Date of last general election:** March 11, 1997. **Lt. Governor:** Hon. Lois E. Hole.

British Columbia

- **CAPITAL:** Victoria, metro pop. (1999) 316 195. **Date entered Confederation:** July 20, 1871.
- **POPULATION (1999):** 4 023 100; Pop. density: 4.3 per sq. km.; **Pop. growth (1996–1999):** 7.4%; **Pop. Urban** (1996): 82.1%; **Official Languages** (1996): 90.6% English; 6.7% bilingual; 2.6% neither English nor French. **Net interprovincial migration** (1999): -11 285.
- **VITAL STATISTICS: Rates** (per 1 000 pop., 1998-99): Birth: 11.0; Death: 7.2; **Life expectancy at birth** (1996): male: 76; female: 82.
- **GEOGRAPHY: Total area** 947 800 sq. km; **Land area** 929 730 sq. km; **Forested land** 633 000 sq. km; **Length of coastline** 17 856 km. Climate: maritime with mild temperatures and abundant rainfall in the coastal areas; continental climate with temperature extremes in the interior and northeast. Topography: mostly mountainous; deep river valleys and gorges, except for the n.e. area which is an extension of the Great Plains; indented coast with numerous bays and islands.
- **ECONOMY: Gross Domestic Product** (1998): $110 948 million; **% change GDP** (1997–98): -0.2%; **Per capita GDP** (1998): $27 716. **Employment distrib.** (1999): goods-producing industries (agriculture, primary ind., mfg, construction) 21%; service-producing industries (transpt., trade, finance, service, pub. admin, unclassified) 79%. **Unemployment rate** (1999): 8.3%. **Principal industries:** forestry, wood and paper, mining, tourism, agriculture, fishing, manufacturing.
- **EDUCATION (1997–98):** No. of schools: 2 064 elem. and sec.; 30 post-sec. **Enrolment:** 677 270 elem. and sec.; 161 227 post-sec.
- **INTERNATIONAL AIRPORTS:** Vancouver; Victoria.
- **NATIONAL PARKS:** Glacier, Kootenay, Mount Revelstoke, Pacific Rim, Gwaii Haanas (South Moresby), Yoho.
- **PROVINCIAL DATA: Motto:** *Splendor Sine Occasu:* "Splendor without Diminishment." **Flower:** Dogwood. **Bird:** Stellar's Jay.
- **POLITICS: Premier:** Ujjal Dosanjh (NDP). **Leader, opposition parties:** Gordon Campbell (Lib.), Bill Vander Zalm (Reform). **Date of last general election:** May 28, 1996. **Lt. Governor:** Hon. Garde B. Gardom.

Yukon Territory

- **CAPITAL:** Whitehorse, metro pop. (1999) 22 879. **Date entered Confederation:** June 13, 1898.
- **POPULATION (1999):** 30 600; **Pop. density:** 0.06 per sq. km.; **Pop. growth (1996–1999):** -0.5%; **Pop. Urban (1996):** 60.0%; **Official Languages (1996):** 89.2% English; 0.2% French; 10.5% bilingual; 0.2% neither English nor French. **Net interprovincial migration (1999):** -761.
- **VITAL STATISTICS:** Rates (per 1 000 pop., 1998-99): Birth: 13.9; Death: 4.1; **Life expectancy at birth (1996):** male: 71; female: 84.
- **GEOGRAPHY:** Total area 483 450 sq. km; **Land area** 478 970 sq. km; **Forested land** 242 000 sq. km; **Length of coastline** 343 km. Climate: great variance in temperatures; warm summers, very cold winters; low precipitation. Topography: main feature is the Yukon plateau with 21 peaks exceeding 3 300 m; open tundra in the far north.
- **ECONOMY:** Gross Domestic Product (1998): $1 073 million; **% change GDP (1997–98):** -0.7%; **Per capita GDP (1998):** $33 531. **Unemployment rate (1999):** n.a. **Principal industries:** mining, tourism.
- **EDUCATION (1997–98):** No. of schools: 28 elem. and sec.; 1 post-sec. **Enrolment:** 6 370 elem. and sec.; 813 post-sec.
- **INTERNATIONAL AIRPORTS:** Whitehorse.
- **NATIONAL PARKS:** Ivvavik, Kluane, Vuntut.
- **PROVINCIAL DATA:** Flower: Fireweed. Bird: Common Raven.
- **POLITICS:** Govt. Leader: Pat Duncan (Lib). Leader, opposition party: Peter Jenkins (Yukon Party), Trevor Harding (NDP). Date of last general election: April 17, 2000. Commissioner: Hon. Judy Gingell.

Northwest Territories[1]

- **CAPITAL:** Yellowknife, metro pop. (1999) 17 702. **Date entered Confederation:** July 15, 1870.
- **POPULATION (1999):** 41 600; **Pop. density:** 0.01 per sq. km.; **Pop. growth (1996–1999)** [1]: -54.8%; **Pop. Urban (1996):** 42.5%; **Official Languages (1996):** 87.1% English; 6.3% bilingual; 6.5% neither English nor French. **Net interprovincial migration (1999):** 376.
- **VITAL STATISTICS:** Rates (per 1 000 pop., 1998-99): Birth: 17.0; Death: 3.5; **Life expectancy at birth (1996):** male: 70; female: 76.
- **GEOGRAPHY:** Total area 3 426 320 sq. km; **Land area** 3 293 020 sq. km; **Forested land** 615 000 sq. km; **Length of coastline** 111 249 km. Climate: extreme temperatures and low precipitation; arctic and sub-arctic. Topography: mostly tundra plains formed on the rocks of the Canadian Shield; the Mackenzie Lowland is a continuation of the Great Plains; the Mackenzie River Valley is forested.
- **ECONOMY:** Gross Domestic Product (1998): $2 527 million; **% change GDP (1997–98):** -1.3%; **Per capita GDP (1998):** $37 162. **Unemployment rate (1999):** n.a. **Principal industries:** construction, utilities, services, tourism.
- **EDUCATION (1997–98):** No. of schools: 86 elem. and sec.; 2 post-sec. **Enrolment:** 17 534 elem. and sec.; 649 post-sec.
- **INTERNATIONAL AIRPORTS:** none.
- **NATIONAL PARKS:** Aulavik, Nahanni, Tuktut Nogait, Wood Buffalo (shared with Alberta).
- **PROVINCIAL DATA:** Flower: Mountain Avens. Bird: Gyrfalcon. Tree: Jack pine.
- **POLITICS:** Premier: Stephen Kakfwi. Date of last general election: Dec. 6, 1999. Commissioner: Hon. Glenna F. Hansen.

(1) Divided into Nunavut and Northwest Territories April 1, 1999. Some statistics remain combined.

Provinces on the Web

Newfoundland: http://www.gov.nf.ca
Prince Edward Island: http://www.gov.pe.ca
Nova Scotia: http://www.gov.ns.ca
New Brunswick: http://www.gov.nb.ca
Quebec: http://www.gouv.qc.ca
Ontario: http://www.gov.on.ca
Manitoba: http://www.gov.mb.ca
Saskatchewan: http://www.gov.sk.ca
Alberta: http://www.gov.ab.ca
British Columbia: http://www.gov.bc.ca
Nunavut: http://www.gov.nu.ca
Northwest Territories: http://www.gov.nt.ca
Yukon Territory: http://www.gov.yk.ca

Nunavut

☐ **CAPITAL:** Iqaluit, metro pop. (1996): 4220. **Date became province:** April 1, 1999.

☐ **POPULATION (1999):** 27 000; **Pop. density:** 0.01 per sq. km.; **Pop. growth (1996–1999) :** 8.4%; **Pop. Urban** (1996): 25.4%; **Official Languages** (1996): 71.4% Inukitut; 23.6% English; 1.6% French. **Net interprovincial migration** (1999): 82.

☐ **VITAL STATISTICS: Rates** (per 1 000 pop., 1998-99): **Birth:** 27.2; **Death:** 4.6; **Life expectancy at birth** (1996): male: 70; female: 76.

☐ **GEOGRAPHY: Total area:** 2 million sq. km. **Climate:** extreme temperatures and low precipitation; arctic. **Topography:** rocky tundra with stunted vegetation located above the tree-line; snow-covered most of the year.

☐ **ECONOMY: Gross Domestic Product** (1998): n.a.; **% change GDP** (1997–98): n.a.%; **Per capita GDP** (1998): n.a. **Unemployment rate:** 15.4. **Principal industries:** mining, tourism, shrimp and scallop fishing, hunting and trapping, arts and crafts production.

☐ **EDUCATION (1997–98): No. of schools:** 38 elem. and sec.; 1 post-sec. **Enrolment:** 7 770.

☐ **INTERNATIONAL AIRPORTS:** Iqaluit Airport.

☐ **NATIONAL PARKS:** Auyuittuq, Quttinirpaaq (Ellesmere Island), Sirmilik.

☐ **PROVINCIAL DATA:** n.a.

☐ **POLITICS: Premier:** Paul Okalik. **Date of last general election:** Feb. 9, 1999. **Commissioner:** Hon. Peter Irniq.

CANADIAN CITIES

A census metropolitan area (CMA) is a very large urban area (known as the urban core) together with adjacent urban and rural areas (known as urban and rural fringes) that have a high degree of social and economic integration with the urban core. A CMA has an urban core population of at least 100 000 based on the previous census. Once an area becomes a CMA, it is retained as a CMA even if the population of its urban core declines below 100 000. All CMAs are subdivided into census tracts. A CMA may be consolidated with adjacent census agglomerations (CAs) if they are socially and economically integrated. This new grouping is known as a consolidated CMA and the component CMA and CA(s) are known as the primary census metropolitan area (PCMA) and primary census agglomeration(s) [PCA(s)]. A CMA may not be consolidated with another CMA.

Calgary, Alta

Year Incorporated: 1893. **Area:** 5 083 sq. km.

☐ **DEMOGRAPHICS: CMA Population (1999):** 933 748. **Pop. density:** 183.7 per sq. km. **Pop. growth (1996–1999):** 3.4%. **Immigrant pop.** (1996): 170 880, 20.8%. **Age Structure** (1996): Male pop.: under 25: 35.8%, over 65: 7.4%; Female pop.: under 25: 34.1%, over 65: 10.0%.

☐ **OFFICIAL LANGUAGES (1996):** 90.7% English; 0.1% French; 7.3% bilingual; 1.9% neither.

☐ **FAMILIES:** Avg. family size (1996): 3.2. **Lone-parent families** (1996): 13.2% of families.

☐ **INCOME:** Avg. Employment Income (1995): $28 991. **Avg. Family Income** (1995): $63 586. **Incidence of low income** (1995): 19.8%.

☐ **LABOUR FORCE (1999): Employed (000s):** 519.3. **Unemployed (000s):** 30.6. **Unemployment rate:** 5.6%. **Participation rate:** 74.4%. **Employment rate:** 70. 3 %.

☐ **CLIMATE:** Avg. day/night temps.: -3.6°/-15.7° (Jan.); 23.2°/9.5° (July). **Avg. annual sunshine:** 2 395 h. **Avg. annual precip.:** 398.8 mm. **Avg. annual snowfall:** 135.4 cm.

Chicoutimi–Jonquière, Que.

Year Incorporated: 1976. **Area:** 1 723 sq. km.

☐ **DEMOGRAPHICS: CMA Population (1999):** 162 346. **Pop. density:** 94.2 per sq. km. **Pop. growth (1996–1999):** -0.1%. **Immigrant pop.** (1996): 1 165, 0.7%. **Age Structure** (1996): Male pop.: under 25: 36.3%, over 65: 8.8%; Female pop.: under 25: 33.0%, over 65: 12.6%.

☐ **OFFICIAL LANGUAGES (1996):** 0.1% English; 82.5% French; 17.4% bilingual.

☐ **FAMILIES:** Avg. family size (1996): 3.1. **Lone-parent families** (1996): 15.0% of families.

☐ **INCOME:** Avg. Employment Income (1995): $25 127. **Avg. Family Income** (1995): $46 656. **Incidence of low income** (1995): 20.7%.

☐ **LABOUR FORCE (1999): Employed (000s):** 67.5. **Unemployed (000s):** 8.6. **Unemployment rate:** 11.3%. **Participation rate:** 58.0%. **Employment rate:** 51.5%.

☐ **CLIMATE:** Avg. day/night temps.: -10.2°/-21.5° (Jan.); 24.2°/11.8° (July). Avg. annual sunshine: 1 676 h. Avg. annual precip.: 929.7 mm. Avg. annual snowfall: 345 cm.

Edmonton, Alta

Year Incorporated: 1904. **Area:** 9 537 sq. km.

☐ **DEMOGRAPHICS: CMA Population** (1999): 929 145. **Pop. density:** 97.4 per sq. km. **Pop. growth** (1996–1999): 1.6%. **Immigrant pop.** (1996): 158 370, 18.4%. **Age Structure** (1996): Male pop.: under 25: 37.0%, over 65: 8.4%; Female pop.: under 25: 35.1%, over 65: 11.1%.

☐ **OFFICIAL LANGUAGES (1996):** 90.9% English; 0.1% French; 7.5% bilingual; 1.6% neither.

☐ **FAMILIES:** Avg. family size (1996): 3.2. **Lone-parent families (1996):** 15.0% of families.

☐ **INCOME:** Avg. Employment Income (1995): $25 974. Avg. Family Income (1995): $56 090. Incidence of low income (1995): 21.3%.

☐ **LABOUR FORCE (1999): Employed (000s):** 483.1. **Unemployed (000s):** 30.1. **Unemployment rate:** 5.9%. **Participation rate:** 70.7%. **Employment rate:** 66.5%.

☐ **CLIMATE:** Avg. day/night temps.: -8.7°/-19.8° (Jan.); 22.5°/9.4° (July). Avg. annual sunshine: 2 303 h. Avg. annual precip.: 465.8 mm. Avg. annual snowfall: 127.1 cm.

Halifax, NS

Year Incorporated: 1841. **Area:** 2 503 sq. km.

☐ **DEMOGRAPHICS: CMA Population** (1999): 352 594. **Pop. density:** 140.9 per sq. km. **Pop. growth** (1999–1999): 1.1%. **Immigrant pop.** (1996): 23 635, 7.1%. **Age Structure** (1996): Male pop.: under 25: 35.0%, over 65: 8.3%; Female pop.: under 25: 32.4%, over 65: 11.8%.

☐ **OFFICIAL LANGUAGES (1996):** 88.9% English; 0.1% French; 10.7% bilingual; 0.3% neither.

☐ **FAMILIES:** Avg. family size (1996): 3.1. **Lone-parent families (1996):** 15.9% of families.

☐ **INCOME:** Avg. Employment Income (1995): $25 419. Avg. Family Income (1995): $54 241. Incidence of low income (1995): 17.8%.

☐ **LABOUR FORCE (1999): Employed (000s):** 174.8. **Unemployed (000s):** 12.5. **Unemployment rate:** 6.7%. **Participation rate:** 68.5%. **Employment rate:** 63.9%.

☐ **CLIMATE:** Avg. day/night temps.: -1.5°/-10.3° (Jan.); 23.4°/13.2° (July). Avg. annual sunshine: 1 949 h. Avg. annual precip.: 1 473.5 mm. Avg. annual snowfall: 261.4 cm.

Hamilton, Ont.

Year Incorporated: 1846. **Area:** 1 359 sq. km.

☐ **DEMOGRAPHICS: CMA Population** (1999): 665 169. **Pop. density:** 489.5 per sq. km. **Pop. growth** (1996–1999): 1.2%. **Immigrant pop.** (1996): 145 660, 23.3%. **Age Structure** (1996): Male pop.: under 25: 34.2%, over 65: 12.0%; Female pop.: under 25: 31.3%, over 65: 15.7%.

☐ **OFFICIAL LANGUAGES (1996):** 91.7% English; 0.1% French; 6.8% bilingual; 1.5% neither.

☐ **FAMILIES:** Avg. family size (1996): 3.1. **Lone-parent families (1996):** 14.3% of families.

☐ **INCOME:** Avg. Employment Income (1995): $29 455. Avg. Family Income (1995): $60 899. Incidence of low income (1995): 19.0%.

☐ **LABOUR FORCE (1999): Employed (000s):** 325.0. **Unemployed (000s):** 16.7. **Unemployment rate:** 4.9%. **Participation rate:** 64.3%. **Employment rate:** 61.1%.

☐ **CLIMATE:** Avg. day/night temps.: -2.6°/-10.0° (Jan.); 26.4°/15.1° (July). Avg. annual sunshine: 2 079 h. Avg. annual precip.: 890.4 mm. Avg. annual snowfall: 152.4 cm.

Kitchener, Ont.

Year Incorporated: 1912. **Area:** 824 sq. km.

☐ **DEMOGRAPHICS: CMA Population** (1999): 414 957. **Pop. density:** 503.6 per sq. km. **Pop. growth** (1996–1999): 1.6%. **Immigrant pop.** (1996): 82 760, 21.6%. **Age Structure** (1996): Male pop.: under 25: 37.0%, over 65: 8.9%; Female pop.: under 25: 34.5%, over 65: 12.8%.

☐ **OFFICIAL LANGUAGES (1996):** 91.4% English; 0.1% French; 6.9% bilingual; 1.6% neither.

☐ **FAMILIES:** Avg. family size (1996): 3.2. **Lone-parent families (1996):** 13.7% of families.

☐ **INCOME:** Avg. Employment Income (1995): $27 893. Avg. Family Income (1995): $59 658. Incidence of low income (1995): 14.6%.

☐ **LABOUR FORCE (1999): Employed (000s):** 218.8. **Unemployed (000s):** 13.3. **Unemployment rate:** 5.7%. **Participation rate:** 71.1%. **Employment rate:** 67.0%.

☐ **CLIMATE:** Avg. day/night temps.: -3.3°/-11.4° (Jan.); 26.1°/13.6° (July). Avg. annual sunshine: 1 969 h. Avg. annual precip.: 917.0 mm. Avg. annual snowfall: 158.0 cm.

London, Ont.

Year Incorporated: 1855. **Area:** 2 105 sq. km.

☐ **DEMOGRAPHICS: CMA Population** (1999): 418 660. **Pop. density:** 198.9 per sq. km. **Pop. growth** (1996–1999): 0.7%. **Immigrant pop.** (1996): 75 975, 19.1%. **Age Structure** (1996): Male pop.: under 25: 35.9%, over 65: 10.6%; Female pop.: under 25: 32.6%, over 65: 14.5%.

☐ **OFFICIAL LANGUAGES (1996):** 92.2% English; 6.6% bilingual; 1.1% neither.

☐ **FAMILIES:** Avg. family size (1996): 3.1. **Lone-parent families** (1996): 15.5% of families.

☐ **INCOME:** Avg. Employment Income (1995): $27 289. Avg. Family Income (1995): $58 671. Incidence of low income (1995): 17.3%.

☐ **LABOUR FORCE (1999): Employed (000s):** 211.3. **Unemployed (000s):** 15.1. **Unemployment rate:** 6.7%. **Participation rate:** 68.1%. **Employment rate:** 63.5%.

☐ **CLIMATE:** Avg. day/night temps.: -2.8°/-10.7° (Jan.); 26.4°/14.2° (July). Avg. annual sunshine: 1 858 h. Avg. annual precip.: 955.1 mm. Avg. annual snowfall: 212.3 cm.

Montreal, Que.

Year Incorporated: 1832. **Area:** 4 024 sq. km.

☐ **DEMOGRAPHICS: CMA Population** (1999): 3 438 532. **Pop. density:** 854.5 per sq. km. **Pop. growth** (1996–1999): 0.4%. **Immigrant pop.** (1996): 586 470, 17.6%. **Age Structure** (1996): Male pop.: under 25: 33.3%, over 65: 9.8%; Female pop.: under 25: 30.3%, over 65: 14.1%.

☐ **OFFICIAL LANGUAGES (1996):** 8.5% English; 39.8% French; 49.7% bilingual; 1.9% neither.

☐ **FAMILIES:** Avg. family size (1996): 3.1. **Lone-parent families** (1996): 17.4% of families.

☐ **INCOME:** Avg. Employment Income (1995): $26 918. Avg. Family Income (1995): $52 795. Incidence of low income (1995): 27.3%.

☐ **LABOUR FORCE (1999): Employed (000s):** 1 656.2. **Unemployed (000s):** 156.7. **Unemployment rate:** 8.6%. **Participation rate:** 65.3%. **Employment rate:** 59.7%.

☐ **CLIMATE:** Avg. day/night temps.: -5.8°/-14.9° (Jan.); 26.2°/15.4° (July). Avg. annual sunshine: 2 015 h. Avg. annual precip.: 939.7 mm. Avg. annual snowfall: 214.2 cm.

Oshawa, Ont.

Year Incorporated: 1924. **Area:** 894 sq. km.

☐ **DEMOGRAPHICS: CMA Population** (1999): 292 948. **Pop. density:** 327.7 per sq. km. **Pop. growth** (1996–1999): 1.9%. **Immigrant pop.** (1996) 44 105, 16.4%. **Age Structure** (1996): Male pop.: under 25: 37.6%, over 65: 8.4%; Female pop.: under 25: 35.1%, over 65: 11.2%.

☐ **OFFICIAL LANGUAGES (1996):** 92.8% English; 0.1% French; 6.7% bilingual; 0.5% neither.

☐ **FAMILIES:** Avg. family size (1996): 3.2. **Lone-parent families** (1996): 14.1% of families.

☐ **INCOME:** Avg. Employment Income (1995): $31 332. Avg. Family Income (1995): $62 101. Incidence of low income (1995): 12.4%.

☐ **LABOUR FORCE (1999): LABOUR FORCE (1999): Employed (000s):** 147.8. **Unemployed (000s):** 9.3. **Unemployment rate:** 5.9%. **Participation rate:** 69.9%. **Employment rate:** 65.7%.

☐ **CLIMATE:** Avg. day/night temps.: -1.7°/-9.9° (Jan.); 25.2°/15.3° (July). Avg. annual sunshine: 2 025 h. Avg. annual precip.: 880.3 mm. Avg. annual snowfall: 125.7 cm.

Ottawa-Hull, Ont/Que

Year Incorporated: 1854 (Ottawa). **Area:** 5 686 sq. km.

☐ **DEMOGRAPHICS: CMA Population** (1999): 1 065 021. **Pop. density:** 187.3 per sq. km. **Pop. growth** (1996–1999): 0.9%. **Immigrant pop.** (1996): 161 885, 16.0%. **Age Structure** (1996): Male pop.: under 25: 35.1%, over 65: 8.4%; Female pop.: under 25: 32.3%, over 65: 11.9%.

☐ **OFFICIAL LANGUAGES (1996):** 45.8% English; 9.0% French; 44.0% bilingual.

☐ **FAMILIES:** Avg. family size (1996): 3.1. **Lone-parent families** (1996): 15.6% of families.

☐ **INCOME:** Avg. Employment Income (1995): $30 633. Avg. Family Income (1995): $64 243. Incidence of low income (1995): 18.9%.

☐ **LABOUR FORCE (1999): Employed (000s):** 543.8. **Unemployed (000s):** 37.5. **Unemployment rate:** 6.5%. **Participation rate:** 68.7%. **Employment rate:** 64.3%.

☐ **CLIMATE:** Avg. day/night temps.: -6.3°/-15.5° (Jan.); 26.4°/15.1° (July). Avg. annual sunshine: 2 054 h. Avg. annual precip.: 910.5 mm. Avg. annual snowfall: 221.5 cm.

Quebec, Que.

Year Incorporated: 1832. **Area:** 3 150 sq. km.

☐ **DEMOGRAPHICS: CMA Population** (1999): 688 085. **Pop. density:** 218.4 per sq. km. **Pop. growth** (1996–1999): 0.2%. **Immigrant pop.** (1996): 17 390, 2.6%. **Age Structure** (1996): Male pop.: under 25: 33.1%, over 65: 9.1%; Female pop.: under 25: 30.0%, over 65: 14.0%.

☐ **OFFICIAL LANGUAGES (1996):** 0.2% English; 69.6% French; 30.0% bilingual; 0.2% neither.

☐ **FAMILIES:** Avg. family size (1996): 3.0. **Lone-parent families** (1996): 16.1% of families.

☐ **INCOME:** Avg. Employment Income (1995): $26 039. Avg. Family Income (1995): $52 570. Incidence of low income (1995): 22.8%.

☐ **LABOUR FORCE (1999): Employed (000s):** 319.6. **Unemployed (000s):** 29.4. **Unemployment rate:** 8.4%. **Participation rate:** 62.2%. **Employment rate:** 57.0%.

☐ **CLIMATE:** Avg. day/night temps.: -7.7°/-17.3° (Jan.); 24.9°/13.2° (July). Avg. annual sunshine: 1 910 h. Avg. annual precip.: 1 207.7 mm. Avg. annual snowfall: 337.0 cm.

Regina, Sask.

Year Incorporated: 1903. **Area:** 3 422 sq. km.

☐ **DEMOGRAPHICS: CMA Population** (1999): 199 163. **Pop. density:** 58.2 per sq. km. **Pop. growth** (1996–1999): -0.1%. **Immigrant pop.** (1996): 15 230, 7.9%. **Age Structure** (1996): Male pop.: under 25: 38.5%, over 65: 9.8%; Female pop.: under 25: 35.5%, over 65: 13.6%.

☐ **OFFICIAL LANGUAGES (1996):** 93.9% English; 0.1% French; 5.6% bilingual; 0.4% neither.

☐ **FAMILIES:** Avg. family size (1996): 3.2. **Lone-parent families** (1996): 16.6% of families.

☐ **INCOME:** Avg. Employment Income (1995): $25 918. Avg. Family Income (1995): $56 844. Incidence of low income (1995): 17.6%.

☐ **LABOUR FORCE (1999): Employed (000s):** 104.8. **Unemployed (000s):** 5.9. **Unemployment rate:** 5.3%. **Participation rate:** 71.1%. **Employment rate:** 67.3%.

☐ **CLIMATE:** Avg. day/night temps.: -11.0°/-22.1° (Jan.); 26.3°/11.9° (July). Avg. annual sunshine: 2 365 h. Avg. annual precip.: 364.0 mm. Avg. annual snowfall: 107.4 cm.

St. Catharines–Niagara, Ont.

Year Incorporated: 1876. **Area:** 1 400 sq. km.

☐ **DEMOGRAPHICS: CMA Population** (1999): 389 607. **Pop. density:** 278.3 per sq. km. **Pop. growth** (1996–1999): 0.6%. **Immigrant pop.** (1996): 67 290, 18.1%. **Age Structure** (1996): Male pop.: under 25: 33.8%, over 65: 14.2%; Female pop.: under 25: 30.2%, over 65: 18.3%.

☐ **OFFICIAL LANGUAGES (1996):** 90.8% English; 0.2% French; 8.3% bilingual; 0.7% neither.

☐ **FAMILIES:** Avg. family size (1996): 3.0. **Lone-parent families** (1995): 14.8% of families.

☐ **INCOME:** Avg. Employment Income (1995): $25 749. Avg. Family Income (1995): $53 674. Incidence of low income (1995): 16.1%.

☐ **LABOUR FORCE (1999): Employed (000s):** 178.4. **Unemployed (000s):** 13.2. **Unemployment rate:** 6.9%. **Participation rate:** 61.0%. **Employment rate:** 56.8%.

☐ **CLIMATE:** Avg. day/night temps.: -1.3°/-8.4° (Jan.); 27.2°/15.8° (July). Avg. annual sunshine: 2 079 h. Avg. annual precip.: 953.1 mm. Avg. annual snowfall: 163.7 cm.

Saint John, NB

Year Incorporated: 1785. **Area:** 3 509 sq. km.

☐ **DEMOGRAPHICS: CMA Population** (1999): 127 211. **Pop. density:** 36.3 per sq. km. **Pop. growth** (1996–1999): -0.2%. **Immigrant pop.** (1996): 4 915, 3.9%. **Age Structure** (1996): Male pop.: under 25: 36.4%, over 65: 10.4%; Female pop.: under 25: 32.9%, over 65: 14.7%.

☐ **OFFICIAL LANGUAGES (1996):** 87.5% English; 0.1% French; 12.3% bilingual; 0.1% neither.

☐ **FAMILIES:** Avg. family size (1996): 3.1. **Lone-parent families** (1996): 16.9% of families.

☐ **INCOME:** Avg. Employment Income (1995): $24 201. Avg. Family Income (1995): $49 138. Incidence of low income (1995): 20.0%.

☐ **LABOUR FORCE (1999): Employed (000s):** 59.3. **Unemployed (000s):** 4.8. **Unemployment rate:** 7.5%. **Participation rate:** 63.7%. **Employment rate:** 58.9%.

☐ **CLIMATE:** Avg. day/night temps.: -2.8°/-13.6° (Jan.); 22.1°/11.6° (July). Avg. annual sunshine: 1 894 h. Avg. annual precip.: 1 432.8 mm. Avg. annual snowfall: 283.2 cm.

St. John's, Nfld

Year Incorporated: 1888. **Area:** 790 sq. km.

☐ **DEMOGRAPHICS: CMA Population** (1999): 174 509. **Pop. density:** 220.9 per sq. km. **Pop. growth** (1996–1999): -0.5%. **Immigrant pop.** (1996): 5 065, 2.9%. **Age Structure** (1996): Male pop.: under 25: 37.4%, over 65: 8.2%; Female pop.: under 25: 34.4%, over 65: 11.7%.

Canadian Cities

☐ **OFFICIAL LANGUAGES (1996):** 94.5% English; 0% French; 5.4% bilingual; 0.1% neither.

☐ **FAMILIES:** Avg. family size (1996): 3.2. **Lone-parent families** (1996): 16.8% of families.

☐ **INCOME:** Avg. Employment Income (1995): $24 717. **Avg. Family Income** (1995): $52 054. **Incidence of low income** (1995): 19.5%.

☐ **LABOUR FORCE (1999):** Employed (000s): 80.1. **Unemployed (000s):** 8.9. **Unemployment rate:** 10.0. **Participation rate:** 63.3%. **Employment rate:** 56.9%.

☐ **CLIMATE:** Avg. day/night temps.: -0.7°/-7.9° (Jan.); 20.2°/10.5° (July). **Avg. annual sunshine** 1 527 h. **Avg. annual precip.:** 1 481.7 mm. **Avg. annual snowfall:** 322.1 cm.

Saskatoon, Sask.

Year Incorporated: 1906. **Area:** 5 322 sq. km.

☐ **DEMOGRAPHICS:** CMA Population (1999): 231 403. **Pop. density:** 43.5 per sq. km. **Pop. growth** (1996–1999): 0.8%. **Immigrant pop.** (1996): 16 455, 7.5%. **Age Structure** (1996): Male pop.: under 25: 39.5%, over 65: 9.4%; Female pop.: under 25: 37.0%, over 65: 12.8%.

☐ **OFFICIAL LANGUAGES (1996):** 92.9% English; 0.0% French; 6.5% bilingual; 0.5% neither.

☐ **FAMILIES:** Avg. family size (1996): 3.2. **Lone-parent families** (1996): 15.9% of families.

☐ **INCOME:** Avg. Employment Income (1995): $24 033. **Avg. Family Income** (1995): $53 196. **Incidence of low income** (1995): 21.4%.

☐ **LABOUR FORCE (1999):** Employed (000s): 113.3. **Unemployed (000s):** 8.0. **Unemployment rate:** 6.6%. **Participation rate:** 67.8%. **Employment rate:** 63.3%.

☐ **CLIMATE:** Avg. day/night temps.: -12.3°/-22.9° (Jan.); 25.4°/11.7° (July). **Avg. annual sunshine:** 2 381 h. **Avg. annual precip.:** 347.2 mm. **Avg. annual snowfall:** 105.4 cm.

Sherbrooke, Que.

Year Incorporated: 1875. **Area:** 980 sq. km.

☐ **DEMOGRAPHICS:** CMA Population (1999): 153 140. **Pop. density:** 156.3 per sq. km. **Pop. growth** (1996–1999): 0.7%. **Immigrant pop.** (1996): 6 225, 4.2%. **Age Structure** (1996): Male pop.: under 25: 35.7%, over 65: 9.6%; Female pop.: under 25: 32.5%, over 65: 14.7%.

☐ **OFFICIAL LANGUAGES (1996):** 1.9% English; 58.8% French; 39.1% bilingual; 0.3% neither.

☐ **FAMILIES:** Avg. family size (1996): 3.0. **Lone-parent families** (1996): 17.0% of families.

☐ **INCOME:** Avg. Employment Income (1995): $23 410. **Avg. Family Income** (1995): $47 198. **Incidence of low income** (1995): 22.8%.

☐ **LABOUR FORCE (1999):** Employed (000s): 69.6. **Unemployed (000s):** 7.3. **Unemployment rate:** 9.5%. **Participation rate:** 62.4%. **Employment rate:** 56.4%.

☐ **CLIMATE:** Avg. day/night temps.: -5.6°/-17.7° (Jan.); 24.7°/11.2° (July). **Avg. annual sunshine** 1 901 h. **Avg. annual precip.:** 1 108.9 mm. **Avg. annual snowfall:** 288.2 cm.

Sudbury, Ont.

Year Incorporated: 1930. **Area:** 2 612 sq. km.

☐ **DEMOGRAPHICS:** CMA Population (1999): 160 357. **Pop. density:** 61.4 per sq. km. **Pop. growth** (1996–1999): -0.9%. **Immigrant pop.** (1991): 12 840, 8.1%. **Age Structure** (1996): Male pop.: under 25: 35.8%, over 65: 10.4%; Female pop.: under 25: 33.5%, over 65: 13.0%.

☐ **OFFICIAL LANGUAGES (1996):** 58.0% English; 1.5% French; 40.1% bilingual; 0.3% neither.

☐ **FAMILIES:** Avg. family size (1996): 3.1. **Lone-parent families** (1996): 15.2% of families.

☐ **INCOME:** Avg. Employment Income (1995): $28 345. **Avg. Family Income** (1995): $57 109. **Incidence of low income** (1995): 17.3%.

☐ **LABOUR FORCE (1999):** Employed (000s): 72.0. **Unemployed (000s):** 7.8. **Unemployment rate:** 9.8%. **Participation rate:** 61.5%. **Employment rate:** 55.5%.

☐ **CLIMATE:** Avg. day/night temps.: -8.5°/-18.7° (Jan.); 24.8°/13.3° (July). **Avg. annual sunshine:** 1 960 h. **Avg. annual precip.:** 871.8 mm. **Avg. annual snowfall:** 266.6 cm.

Thunder Bay, Ont.

Year Incorporated: 1970. **Area:** 2 295 sq. km.

☐ **DEMOGRAPHICS:** CMA Population (1999): 126 649. **Pop. density:** 55.2 per sq. km. **Pop. growth** (1996–1999): -0.6%. **Immigrant pop.** (1996): 15 275, 12.2%. **Age Structure** (1996): Male pop.: under 25: 34.3%, over 65: 12.2%; Female pop.: under 25: 32.0%, over 65: 15.9%.

☐ **OFFICIAL LANGUAGES (1996):** 91.7% English; 0.1% French; 7.4% bilingual; 0.7% neither.

☐ **FAMILIES:** Avg. family size (1996): 3.1. **Lone-parent families** (1996): 16.0% of families.

☐ **INCOME:** Avg. Employment Income (1995): $27 649. Avg. Family Income (1995): $58 731. Incidence of low income (1995): 14.5%.

☐ **LABOUR FORCE (1999):** Employed (000s): 60.5. Unemployed (000s): 5.1. Unemployment rate: 7.8%. Participation rate: 64.4%. Employment rate: 59.5%.

☐ **CLIMATE:** Avg. day/night temps.: -8.9°/-21.3° (Jan.); 24.4°/11.0° (July). Avg. annual sunshine: 2 183 h. Avg. annual precip.: 703.5 mm. Avg. annual snowfall: 195.5 cm.

Toronto, Ont.

Year Incorporated: 1834. **Area:** 5 568 sq. km.

☐ **DEMOGRAPHICS:** CMA Population (1999): 4 680 250. Pop. density: 840.6 per sq. km. Pop. growth (1996–1999): 2.1%. Immigrant pop. (1996): 1 772 905, 41.6%. Age Structure (1996): Male pop.: under 25: 34.7%, over 65: 9.5%; Female pop.: under 25: 31.6%, over 65: 12.4%.

☐ **OFFICIAL LANGUAGES (1996):** 87.4% English; 0.1% French; 8.0% bilingual; 4.5% neither.

☐ **FAMILIES:** Avg. family size (1996): 3.3. Lone-parent families (1996): 15.5% of families.

☐ **INCOME:** Avg. Employment Income (1995): $31 264. Avg. Family Income (1995): $64 044. Incidence of low income (1995): 21.1%.

☐ **LABOUR FORCE (1999):** Employed (000s): 2 390.8. Unemployed (000s): 155.6. Unemployment rate: 6.1%. Participation rate: 67.9%. Employment rate: 63.7%.

☐ **CLIMATE:** Avg. day/night temps.: -2.5°/-11.1° (Jan.); 26.8°/14.2° (July). Avg. annual sunshine: 2 038 h. Avg. annual precip.: 780.8 mm. Avg. annual snowfall: 124.2 cm.

Trois–Rivières, Que.

Year Incorporated: 1857. **Area:** 872 sq. km.

☐ **DEMOGRAPHICS:** CMA Population (1999): 141 751. Pop. density: 162.6 per sq. km. Pop. growth (1996–1999): -0.1%. Immigrant pop. (1996): 2 220, 1.6%. Age Structure (1996): Male pop.: under 25: 33.2%, over 65: 10.5%; Female pop.: under 25: 30.1%, over 65: 15.6%.

☐ **OFFICIAL LANGUAGES (1996):** 0.1% English; 75.4% French; 24.4% bilingual.

☐ **FAMILIES:** Avg. family size (1996): 3.0. Lone-parent families (1996): 16.1% of families.

☐ **INCOME:** Avg. Employment Income (1995): $24 763. Avg. Family Income (1995): $47 242. Incidence of low income: (1995) 23.4%.

☐ **LABOUR FORCE (1999):** Employed (000s): 61.9. Unemployed (000s): 7.8. Unemployment rate: 11.2%. Participation rate: 59.9%. Employment rate: 53.3%.

☐ **CLIMATE:** Avg. day/night temps.: -7.5°/-17.7° (Jan.); 25.6°/14.1° (July). Avg. annual sunshine: 1 910 h. Avg. annual precip.: 1 046.7 mm. Avg. annual snowfall: 242.0 cm.

Vancouver, BC

Year Incorporated: 1886. **Area:** 2 821 sq. km.

☐ **DEMOGRAPHICS:** CMA Population (1999): 2 016 643. Pop. density: 714.9 per sq. km. Pop. growth (1996–1999): 0.9%. Immigrant pop. (1996) 633 740, 34.6%. Age Structure (1996): Male pop.: under 25: 32.8%, over 65: 10.1%; Female pop.: under 25: 30.6%, over 65: 13.5%.

☐ **OFFICIAL LANGUAGES (1996):** 87.9% English; 0.1% French; 7.4% bilingual; 4.7% neither.

☐ **FAMILIES:** Avg. family size (1996): 3.2. Lone-parent families (1996): 13.9% of families.

☐ **INCOME:** Avg. Employment Income: (1995) $29 122. Avg. Family Income: (1995) $60 438. Incidence of low income: (1995) 23.3%.

☐ **LABOUR FORCE (1999):** Employed (000s): 1 005.4. Unemployed (000s): 84.7. Unemployment rate: 7.8%. Participation rate: 66.0%. Employment rate: 60.9%.

☐ **CLIMATE:** Avg. day/night temps.: 5.7°/0.1° (Jan.); 21.7°/12.7° (July). Avg. annual sunshine: 1 919 h. Avg. annual precip.: 1 167.4 mm. Avg. annual snowfall: 54.9 cm.

Victoria, BC

Year Incorporated: 1862. **Area:** 633 sq. km.

☐ **DEMOGRAPHICS:** CMA Population (1999): 316 195. Pop. density: 499.5 per sq. km. Pop. growth (1996–1999): -0.2%. Immigrant pop. (1996): 57 795, 19.0%. Age Structure (1996): Male pop.: under 25: 30.7%, over 65: 15.1%; Female pop.: under 25: 27.6%, over 65: 20.4%.

☐ **OFFICIAL LANGUAGES (1996):** 90.6% English; 0.0% French; 8.6% bilingual; 0.7% neither.

☐ **FAMILIES:** Avg. family size (1996): 2.9. Lone-parent families (1996): 14.1% of families.

☐ **INCOME:** Avg. Employment Income (1995): $27 038. Avg. Family Income (1995): $59 585. Incidence of low income (1995): 15.4%.

☐ **LABOUR FORCE (1999):** Employed (000s): 154.2. Unemployed (000s): 11.1. **Unemployment rate:** 6.7%. **Participation rate:** 64.7%. **Employment rate:** 60.4%.

☐ **CLIMATE:** Avg. day/night temps.: 6.5°/0.3° (Jan.); 21.8°/10.7° (July). **Avg. annual sunshine:** 2 082 h. **Avg. annual precip.:** 857.9 mm. **Avg. annual snowfall:** 46.9 cm.

Windsor, Ont.

Year Incorporated: 1892. Area: 862 sq. km.

☐ **DEMOGRAPHICS:** CMA Population (1999): 299 966. **Pop. density:** 348.0 per sq. km. **Pop. growth** (1996–1999): 1.4%. **Immigrant pop.** (1996): 56 990, 20.4%. **Age Structure** (1996): Male pop.: under 25: 35.7%, over 65: 10.8%; Female pop.: under 25: 32.9%, over 65: 15.0%.

☐ **OFFICIAL LANGUAGES (1996):** 87.8% English; 0.2% French; 10.5% bilingual; 1.5% neither.

☐ **FAMILIES:** Avg. family size (1996): 3.2. **Lone-parent families** (1996): 16.0% of families.

☐ **INCOME:** Avg. Employment Income (1995): $30 048. **Avg. Family Income** (1995): $62 244. **Incidence of low income** (1995): 15.7%.

☐ **LABOUR FORCE (1999):** Employed (000s): 146.2. Unemployed (000s): 10.2. **Unemployment rate:** 6.5%. **Participation rate:** 65.2%. **Employment rate:** 61.0%.

☐ **CLIMATE:** Avg. day/night temps.: -1.3°/-8.8° (Jan.); 27.7°/17.0° (July). **Avg. annual sunshine:** 2 045 h. **Avg. annual precip.:** 901.6 mm. **Avg. annual snowfall:** 123.3 cm

Winnipeg, Man.

Year Incorporated: 1873. Area: 4 078 sq. km.

☐ **DEMOGRAPHICS:** CMA Population (1999): 667 625. **Pop. density:** 166.2 per sq. km. **Pop. growth** (1996–1999): -0.1%. **Immigrant pop.** (1996): 111 690, 16.7%. **Age Structure** (1996): Male pop.: under 25: 35.4%, over 65: 10.9%; Female pop.: under 25: 32.5%, over 65: 15.6%.

☐ **OFFICIAL LANGUAGES (1996):** 87.9% English; 0.1% French; 10.9% bilingual; 1.1% neither.

☐ **FAMILIES:** Avg. family size (1996): 3.1. **Lone-parent families** (1996): 15.8% of families.

☐ **INCOME:** Avg. Employment Income (1995): $30 048. **Avg. Family Income** (1995): $62 244. **Incidence of low income** (1995): 15.7%.

☐ **LABOUR FORCE (1999):** Employed (000s): 345.7. Unemployed (000s): 21.1. **Unemployment rate:** 5.8%. **Participation rate:** 68.5%. **Employment rate:** 64.6%.

☐ **CLIMATE:** Avg. day/night temps.: -13.2°/-23.6° (Jan.); 26.1°/13.4° (July). **Avg. annual sunshine:** 2 377 h. **Avg. annual precip.:** 504.4 mm. **Avg. annual snowfall:** 114.8 cm.

NATIONAL PARKS

Canada's national parks are protected by law to preserve representative natural areas throughout the country. The parks are maintained to enhance public understanding, appreciation and enjoyment of the country's natural heritage, and increasingly, park management efforts are being directed to protect Canada's wide variety of ecosystems for the long term.

In 1988, the National Parks Act was amended to ensure that each park's management plan would maintain the ecological integrity of the area, that is, that the structure and function of the existing ecosystem would not be harmed by human activity. This amendment was made as it became increasingly clear that many ecological features, such as grizzly bear populations, require very large areas and very long time lines if they are to survive, if not thrive. The host of modern environmental stresses also affect protected areas and their inhabitants, and mere protection is not enough; a co-operative parks management structure—including public, corporate, environmental and Aboriginal interest groups—and an ecosystem management approach is the preferred management model to minimize damage.

The goal of the national parks policy is to create at least one national park in each of Canada's 39 natural regions. Thirty-nine national parks and national park reserves currently exist, however to achieve the goal, 14 more national parks are needed. Once completed, the parks system will preserve just over 3 percent of the country's land mass.

▶

Park	Location	Size (sq. km)	Year est.	Description
Aulavik	northern portion of Banks Is., NWT	12 200	(1992)[1]	Thomsen River forms core of a park marked by deep river canyons and desert-like badlands. Area supports high concentration of musk oxen. The Thomsen River is Canada's most northerly navigable river.
Auyuittuq[2]	Cumberland Peninsula, Baffin Is., NT	21 469	1976	Located on the Arctic Circle; this is an isolated and very rugged wilderness area with mountains, fjords, tundra and permafrost. Park protects part of Northern Davis Strait Natural Region and portions of Baffin Island Shelf Marine region. Contains prehistoric and historic resources from ancient Thule settlements.
Banff	Banff, Alta.	6 641	1885	Our first national park is noted for ice-capped peaks, canyons, glaciers, hot springs, and hoodoos (rock pillars, often in fantastic shapes). Wildlife includes bighorn sheep, black and grizzly bears, elk and caribou. Banff is part of UNESCO's Rocky Mountain Parks World Heritage Site.
Bruce Peninsula, including Fathom Five National Marine Park	299 km northwest of Toronto, between Lake Huron and Georgian Bay	154	(1987)[1]	This park was created to protect the Niagara Escarpment and the limestone cliffs on Georgian Bay; contains mixed forests, wetlands and limestone cliffs. Fathom Five National Marine Park includes 19 islands, over 20 shipwrecks, clear water and distinctive underwater geological features.
Cape Breton Highlands	across northern Cape Breton Is., NS	948	1936	The scenic Cabot Trail is characterized by a rugged shoreline with plunging cliffs.
Elk Island	45 km east of Edmonton, Alta.	194	1913	A large population of plains and wood bison, elk and moose inhabit the rolling woodlands and lakes. Other wildlife include bear, beaver and coyote.
Forillon	northeast tip of Gaspé Peninsula, Que.	244	1970	Protects parts of the Notre-Dame and Mégantic mountains and some of the Gulf of St. Lawrence marine area. Features a rich variety of seabirds and animals, limestone cliffs, Arctic-alpine plants and the highest mountains in eastern Canada.
Fundy	southeastern shore on the Bay of Fundy, NB	206	1948	The giant tides of the Bay of Fundy, among the highest in the world, and a bold, irregular coastline.
Georgian Bay Islands	160 km northwest of Toronto, Ont.	25	1929	59 glacier swept islands are home to endangered species, limestone cliffs, caves and archaeological sites. This area was the inspiration for many of the Group of Seven artists.

National Parks

Park	Location	Size (sq. km)	Year est.	Description
Glacier	45 km east of Revelstoke, BC	1 349	1886	Protects a section of the Columbia Mountains Natural Region that includes habitats for grizzly bear and mountain caribou. Steep angular mountains, deep valleys, icefields, glaciers, waterfalls, avalanche paths and high precipitation characterise the area.
Grasslands	100 km south of Swift Current, Sask.	906	(1975)[1]	Unique natural habitat of short-grass prairie; blacktailed prairie dogs, pronghorn antelope and the prairie falcon are found.
Gros Morne	west coast of Nfld	1 805	(1970)[1]	Park is dominated by a coastal lowland and an alpine plateau that each boast a variety of land mammals, bird species, fish and trees, ferns and flowers. The park has been declared a UNESCO World Heritage Site because of its spectacular geology.
Gwaii Haanas (South Moresby)[2] including Gwaii Haanas, National Marine Conservation Area	southern part of Queen Charlotte Islands, BC	1 495	(1987)[1]	Canada's "Galapagos," home to 39 unique plants, an estimated 750,000 seabirds come to nest, and animals such as black bear, pine marten, deer mice, shrews and weasels. Geography features deep fjords, rugged mountains, and one of the finest old-growth temperate rainforest left on Pacific coast.
Ivvavik	northern tip of Yukon	10 168	1984	Migration route for Porcupine caribou herd; major North American waterfowl area; home to grizzly, black and polar bears. Contains unique non-glaciated landscape.
Jasper	340 km west of Edmonton, Alta.	10 878	1907	Contains the largest icefield in the Canadian Rockies—Columbia Icefield—and preserves the headwaters of major rivers, particularly the Athabasca.
Kejimkujik	central southwestern NS	404	1974	Gently rolling country with many lakes and rivers; provides good canoeing and camping. The earliest inhabitants—Maritime Archaic Indians—arrived about 4,500 years ago.
Kluane[2]	southwest corner of Yukon	22 013	1976	Features Mount Logan, Canada's highest peak, Kluane Lake (Yukon's largest), grizzly bears, dall sheep and whitewater rivers.
Kootenay	1 km east of Radium Hot Springs, BC	1 406	1920	The park contains Rocky Mountain wilderness and is part of UNESCO's Rocky Mountain Parks World Heritage Site. Hot springs, alpine lakes, canyons, glaciers, two river valleys; home to bighorn sheep, mountain goats.
Kouchibouguac	eastern NB	239	1979	Swimming, sunbathing on the beaches and dunes; cycling, hiking trails; windsurfing.
La Mauricie	55 km north of Trois-Rivières, Que.	536	1977	Hilly terrain at the edge of the Canadian Shield with transitional forest vegetation from evergreens to deciduous. Beaver, moose and the common loon; an area filled with brooks, lakes and waterfalls.
Mingan Archipelago[2]	N of Anticosti Is. along the St. Lawrence shore, QC	151	1984	This is a limestone environment that is home to diversified plant species, nesting seabirds and whales, seals and porpoises.

40 The Land

Park	Location	Size (sq. km)	Year est.	Description
Mount Revelstoke	Revelstoke, BC	260	1914	Columbia Mountain ranges. Park is characterised by deep snow accumulation and high annual precipitation. Contains three ecoregions: Interior Alpine Tundra, Interior Sub-alpine Tundra and Interior Cedar Hemlock. Each is packed with their own variety of vegetation and wildlife.
Nahanni[2]	southwestern NWT	4 765	1976	The wild and spectacular South Nahanni river passes through this long, narrow park. The route contains four canyons; the river plunges from twice the height of Niagara Falls at Virginia Falls. Park contains sulphur hotsprings, alpine tundra and vast forests, plus numerous species of birds, mammals and fish.
Pacific Rim [2]	west coast of Vancouver Island	500	(1970)[1]	3 sections—Long Beach, Broken Group Islands and West Coast Trail—offer rainforest, beaches and scenic, rugged hiking. Park contains native archaeological sites that indicate settlement for at least 4,300 years.
Point Pelee	southernmost point of Ont.	15	1918	Extensive marshlands and beaches provide refuge for many migratory birds and butterflies. The temperate climate allows over 70 species of tree to survive, as well as a huge variety of reptiles, birds, amphibians, insects and spiders.
Prince Albert	200 km north of Saskatoon, Sask.	3 875	1927	Mixture of forest land and lakes, home to woodland caribou, bison and a pelican colony. Archaeological digs indicate that the area has been inhabited by Aboriginal cultures for at least 6,000 years.
Prince Edward Island	north shore of PEI	22	1937	40 km of fine saltwater beaches, sand dunes, high coastal cliffs, marshes, ponds and woodlands. Green Gables in located in this park.
Pukaskwa	northeastern shore of Lake Superior	1 878	(1971)[1]	Hilly terrain is characterised by ridges and cliffs, and lakes on rocky shores with shallow soil. Park interior features spruce, fir, cedar, aspen and birch. Wildlife includes moose, wolves, black bears and woodland caribou. This park is also the site of rare Arctic plants.
Quttinirpaaq (Ellesmere Island)	northern tip of Canada	37 775	1988	Vast isolated high Arctic wilderness park. Mountains, glaciers, musk-oxen, Peary's caribou. Fragile permafrost environments. Historic sites and artifacts from early Arctic explorers
Riding Mountain	270 km northwest of Winnipeg, Man.	2 973	1929	Wildlife—wolf, elk, moose, black bear and beaver—abound.
Sirmilik[2]	northern Baffin Is., incl Bylot Is. and Borden Penin	22 200	(1992)	Mountains, snowfields, glaciers, tundra. Sparse vegetation: 50 bird species incl. murres, kittiwakes, snow geese. Caribou, wolf, Artic fox, lemming, seals, whales, walrus, polar bear

National Parks

Park	Location	Size (sq. km)	Year est.	Description
St. Lawrence Islands	Thousand Islands	8	1904	Park includes over 21 islands and 90 islets between Kingston and Brockville, with 100 acres on the mainland at Mallorytown Landing. The area features Thousand Islands landscape and the St. Lawrence River. The Great Lakes moderate the climate, allowing many animals and plants to exist further north than might otherwise be possible.
Terra Nova	east coast of Nfld on Bonavista Bay	400	1957	Rolling forested hills are remnants of the ancient Appalachian Mountains. Rugged cliffs and sheltered inlets are featured on the coast; the interior has spongy bogs, rolling hills covered with forest and inland ponds.
Tuktut Nogait	east of Inuvik in NWT	16 340	1996	Spectacular river canyons and cliffs dotted by hundreds of archaeological sites. Park protects calving grounds of Bluenose caribou and one of the highest concentrations of birds of prey in North America.
Vuntut	Old Crow Flats, northern Yukon	4 345	(1993)[1]	Yukon's most important waterfowl habitat and home to porcupine caribou, grizzly bear, moose, muskrat and several species of fish. Vertebrate fossils found at over 56 sites within park. The area is only 300 m in elevation and features over 2,000 shallow lakes.
Wapusk	northeast corner of Manitoba	11 475	1996	This region of flat inland expanse of tundra, eskers and permafrost includes one of the world's largest known polar bear denning areas.
Waterton Lakes	southwest corner of Alta.	505	1895	Officially renamed the Waterton-Glacier International Peace Park in 1932; the world's first park established by two governments. Protects transition from prairie grasslands to Rocky Mountains and a rich variety of wildlife.
Wood Buffalo	straddles the Alta.-NWT border	44 802	1922	Canada's largest national park is also a UNESCO World Heritage Site. Home to the largest free-roaming herd of bison; only site of naturally nesting whooping cranes, peregrine falcons and red-sided garter snakes. Geography features sinkholes, underground rivers, caves and sunken valleys.
Yoho	25 km east of Golden, BC	1 313	1886	Contains several of the highest peaks in the Rocky Mountains, icefields, waterfalls and a varied plant and animal life.

Source: *Canadian Heritage, Parks Canada*

(1) Park created by federal/provincial/territorial agreement rather than federal enactment and administered by special legislation. (2) Park reserve, set aside for national park and under jurisdiction of National Parks Act, but lands, fish and wildlife are subject to future settlement of native land claims.

Parks Canada on the Web

For an in-depth look at Canada's National Parks, National Historic Sites, Federal Heritage Buildings, Heritage Railway Stations, Marine Conservation Areas, and Heritage Rivers, visit www.parkscanada.pch.gc.ca. The site includes history, detailed geographic highlights, photographs and access information, plus a site for SchoolNet projects, education resources, virtual tours and information on ecosystem conservation.

THE PEOPLE

POPULATION

Population of Provinces and Territories[1]
(thousands)

	Canada	Nfld	PEI	NS	NB	Que	Ont	Man	Sask	Alta	BC	YT	NWT	NVT
1861[2]	3 230	n.a.	81	331	252	1 112	1 396	*	n.a.	n.a.	52	*	7	n.a.
1871	3 689	n.a.	94	388	286	1 192	1 621	25	n.a.	n.a.	36	*	48	n.a.
1881	4 325	n.a.	109	441	321	1 360	1 927	62	n.a.	n.a.	49	*	56	n.a.
1891	4 833	n.a.	109	450	321	1 489	2 114	153	*	*	98	*	99	n.a.
1901	5 371	n.a.	103	460	331	1 649	2 183	255	91	73	179	27	20	n.a.
1911	7 207	n.a.	94	492	352	2 006	2 527	461	492	374	393	9	7	n.a.
1921	8 788	n.a.	89	524	388	2 361	2 934	610	758	588	525	4	8	n.a.
1931	10 377	n.a.	88	513	408	2 875	3 432	700	922	732	694	4	9	n.a.
1941	11 507	n.a.	95	578	457	3 332	3 788	730	896	796	818	5	12	n.a.
1951	14 009	361	98	643	516	4 056	4 598	777	832	940	1 165	9	16	n.a.
1961	18 238	458	105	737	598	5 259	6 236	922	925	1 332	1 629	15	23	n.a.
1971	21 962	531	113	797	643	6 137	7 849	999	932	1 666	2 241	19	36	n.a.
1981	24 820	575	124	855	706	6 548	8 811	1 036	976	2 294	2 824	24	48	n.a.
1986	26 101	577	128	889	725	6 708	9 438	1 092	1 029	2 431	3 004	25	55	n.a.
1991[3]	28 031	580	130	915	746	7 065	10 428	1 110	1 003	2 593	3 373	29	39	22
1996[3]	29 672	561	136	931	753	7 274	11 101	1 134	1 019	2 781	3 882	32	42	26
1999[4]	30 491	541	138	940	755	7 345	11 514	1 144	1 028	2 965	4 023	31	42	27

Source: © Census of Canada, Statistics Canada

(n.a.) Not applicable. (*) Included with the Northwest Territories. (1) As of July 1. Includes data from incompletely enumerated population. Totals may not add up due to rounding. (2) Pre-Confederation. (3) Final postcensal estimates. (4) Updated intercensal estimates.

Age Structure of the Population[1]

	Total (000s)	% Under 5 Years	% 5–19 Years	% 20–44 Years	% 45–64 Years	% 65+ Years
1851	2 436	18.51	37.81	31.65	9.40	2.67
1861	3 230	16.81	37.21	32.66	10.15	3.03
1871	3 689	14.67	38.03	32.58	11.14	3.66
1881	4 325	13.85	36.02	33.94	12.14	4.12
1891	4 833	12.64	34.49	35.40	12.91	4.55
1901	5 371	12.03	32.73	36.19	14.00	5.05
1911	7 207	12.35	30.15	38.81	14.06	4.66
1921	8 788	12.05	31.51	36.63	15.02	4.78
1931	10 377	10.36	31.29	36.07	16.74	5.55
1941	11 507	9.14	28.39	37.19	18.61	6.67
1951	14 009	12.29	25.60	36.63	17.74	7.75
1961	18 238	12.37	29.44	33.19	17.37	7.63
1971	21 568	8.42	30.97	33.87	18.66	8.09
1981	24 343	7.32	24.70	39.14	19.13	9.70
1991	27 297	6.99	20.42	41.33	19.66	11.61
1996	29 672	6.62	20.35	39.63	21.32	12.07
1999[2]	30 491	6.00	20.17	38.64	22.76	12.43

Source: © Census of Canada, Statistics Canada

(1) As of July 1. Total percentage for census year may not equal 100 due to rounding. (2) Updated intercensal estimates.

Male and Female Population by Age Group

(thousands)

		Total Population	Under 5 Years	5–9 Years	10–14 Years	15–24 Years	25–34 Years	35–44 Years	45–54 Years	55–64 Years	65 Years and Over
1851	MALE	1 250	233	173	152	248	168	116	78	46	35
	FEMALE	1 186	218	173	146	252	161	103	67	38	30
1861	MALE	1 660	277	218	203	341	232	156	107	70	54
	FEMALE	1 570	266	211	196	337	222	141	92	59	44
1871	MALE	1 869	276	264	243	374	249	175	132	86	74
	FEMALE	1 820	265	255	233	385	256	171	120	73	61
1881	MALE	2 189	304	284	262	455	302	217	161	111	94
	FEMALE	2 136	295	278	251	464	301	212	153	100	84
1891	MALE	2 460	309	300	282	504	366	263	191	131	115
	FEMALE	2 373	302	292	272	499	354	246	180	122	105
1901	MALE	2 752	326	313	297	543	412	331	234	157	139
	FEMALE	2 620	320	306	285	530	386	299	214	148	133
1911	MALE	3 822	450	396	356	745	687	475	334	209	171
	FEMALE	3 385	440	389	346	653	535	388	286	184	165
1921	MALE	4 530	534	529	462	757	693	630	434	276	215
	FEMALE	4 258	525	521	452	761	650	532	366	246	206
1931	MALE	5 375	543	573	543	990	778	707	590	356	295
	FEMALE	5 002	531	560	531	962	717	627	485	306	281
1941	MALE	5 901	534	529	556	1 083	920	745	649	494	391
	FEMALE	5 606	518	517	545	1 069	891	691	579	421	377
1951	MALE	7 089	879	714	575	1 070	1 066	950	728	557	551
	FEMALE	6 921	843	684	556	1 077	1 108	919	679	520	535
1961	MALE	9 219	1 154	1 064	948	1 316	1 258	1 191	959	655	674
	FEMALE	9 019	1 102	1 016	908	1 301	1 222	1 199	920	635	717
1971	MALE	10 795	930	1 152	1 181	2 016	1 462	1 286	1 132	854	782
	FEMALE	10 773	887	1 102	1 129	1 988	1 428	1 241	1 160	877	963
1981	MALE	12 068	914	912	985	2 356	2 106	1 497	1 256	1 031	1 011
	FEMALE	12 275	869	865	936	2 303	2 110	1 471	1 242	1 128	1 350
1991	MALE	13 455	976	978	963	1 944	2 420	2 176	1 487	1 180	1 330
	FEMALE	13 842	931	930	915	1 887	2 446	2 196	1 479	1 220	1 840
1996[1]	MALE	14 692	1 007	1 033	1 031	2 059	2 400	2 502	1 891	1 253	1 515
	FEMALE	14 980	958	984	978	1 965	2 346	2 499	1 897	1 286	2 067
1999[1]	MALE	15 103	938	1 057	1 041	2 111	2 251	2 645	2 100	1 344	1 617
	FEMALE	15 388	891	1 005	986	2 011	2 201	2 625	2 111	1 385	2 173

Source: © Census of Canada, Statistics Canada (1) Updated postcensal population estimates as of July 1, 1999.

Canadian Population Projections[1] by Age Group

(thousands)

	Total Population	Under 5 Years	5–9 Years	10–14 Years	15–24 Years	25–34 Years	35–44 Years	45–54 Years	55–64 Years	65 Yrs and Over
2006										
MALE	15 931.4	840.3	917.2	1 078.8	2 203.8	2 203.2	2 534.2	2 517.2	1 795.4	1 841.5
FEMALE	16 317.1	797.8	870.9	1 024.3	2 106.9	2 152.9	2 508.0	2 536.4	1 859.7	2 460.5
2011										
MALE	16 482.1	850.8	877.8	955.6	2 251.3	2 280.4	2 346.7	2 691.6	2 129.0	2 098.7
FEMALE	16 886.9	807.2	833.3	905.0	2 152.8	2 227.3	2 323.5	2 687.7	2 210.4	2 739.5
2016										
MALE	17 009.2	872.2	888.4	917.1	2 141.4	2 352.6	2 363.7	2 565.3	2 397.0	2 511.6
FEMALE	17 419.6	827.2	842.8	868.2	2 045.0	2 299.4	2 332.2	2 551.0	2 474.4	3 179.3
2021										
MALE	17 490.3	885.8	909.7	927.6	1 983.8	2 401.4	2 441.1	2 392.8	2 569.8	2 978.2
FEMALE	17 903.5	839.8	862.6	877.6	1 892.1	2 345.4	2 405.6	2 375.4	2 621.8	3 683.2
2026										
MALE	17 892.8	875.4	923.2	948.6	1 956.8	2 295.0	2 511.2	2 413.6	2 459.9	3 509.1
FEMALE	18 312.4	829.8	875.1	897.1	1 865.4	2 240.0	2 474.9	2 385.6	2 493.8	4 250.6

Source: © Statistics Canada (1) Figures represent the medium-growth projection and are based on 1999 population estimates. Due to rounding, the totals may not always add up to the sum of the figures.

Canadian Population by Country of Birth

	1931	1951	1971	1991	1996
Total Population	10 376 786	14 009 429	21 568 310	27 296 855	28 846 760
Total Foreign Born	2 307 525[11]	2 059 911[11]	3 295 530[11]	4 342 885[11]	4 971 070[11]
Afghanistan[1]	—	—	—	5 545	10 915
Africa—Other	—	—	—	26 355	43 160
Algeria[1]	—	—	—	3 900	8 005
Argentina[1]	—	—	—	11 110	11 740
Asia—Other	6 310	6 740	52 795	24 310	47 940
Australia	3 565	4 161	14 335	13 955	14 660
Austria[2]	37 391	37 598	40 450	26 680	24 600
Barbados[3]	—	—	—	14 825	15 225
Belgium	17 033	17 251	25 770	22 480	21 805
Brazil[1]	—	—	—	7 330	9 360
Cambodia[1]	—	—	—	17 960	19 355
Caribbean & Bermuda—Other	—	—	—	25 995	36 965
Central America—Other	—	—	—	5 745	9 025
Chile[1]	—	—	—	22 870	23 880
China	42 037	24 166	57 150	157 405	231 055
Colombia[1]	—	—	—	7 865	9 465
Czech and Slovak Federal Republic, former [12]	22 835	29 546	43 100	42 615	41 225
Denmark[14]	17 217	15 679	28 045	—	—
Ecuador[1]	—	—	—	8 015	9 640
Egypt[1]	—	—	—	28 020	33 930
El Salvador[1]	—	—	—	28 295	39 020
Ethiopia, former[1]	—	—	—	11 060	18 595
Europe—Other[5]	10 657	10 858	87 255	8 665	7 980
Fiji[3]	—	—	—	15 995	20 580
Finland[14]	30 354	22 035	24 930	—	—
France	16 756	15 650	51 655	55 159	62 600
Germany[6]	39 163	42 693	211 060	180 525	181 650
Ghana[1]	—	—	—	6 675	13 085
Greece	5 579	8 594	78 780	83 680	79 695
Guatemala[1]	—	—	—	8 920	13 270
Guyana[3]	—	—	—	66 060	77 700
Haiti[1]	—	—	—	39 880	49 395
Hong Kong[3]	—	—	—	152 405	241 095
Hungary	28 523	32 929	68 495	57 010	54 225
India[3,7]	4 672	3 934	43 645	173 675	235 930
Indonesia	—	—	—	7 610	8 515
Iran[1]	—	—	—	30 710	47 405
Iraq[1]	—	—	—	7 165	16 795
Ireland	—	24 110	38 490	28 405	28 940
Israel (and Palestine/West Bank/Gaza Strip)[1]	—	—	—	16 770	20 390
Italy	42 578	57 789	385 755	351 615	332 110
Jamaica[3]	—	—	—	102 440	115 800
Japan	12 261	6 239	9 485	12 280	14 990
Kenya[3]	—	—	—	16 585	18 005
Korea[4,13]	—	—	—	33 170	46 025
Laos[4]	—	—	—	14 445	14 765
Lebanon[1]	—	—	—	54 600	63 130
Malaysia[4]	—	—	—	16 100	19 460
Malta[3]	—	—	—	10 185	9 445
Mexico[1]	—	—	—	19 400	27 480
Morocco[1]	—	—	—	16 790	20 435
Netherlands	10 736	41 457	133 525	129 615	124 545
Nicaragua[1]	—	—	—	6 460	8 545
Norway[14]	32 679	22 969	16 350	—	—
Oceania—Other[15]	—	—	—	16 305	13 780 ▶

Population

	1931	1951	1971	1991	1996
▶ Pakistan[7]	—	—	—	25 180	39 245
Peru[1]	—	—	—	11 480	15 235
Philippines[4]	—	—	—	123 295	184 550
Poland[8]	171 169	164 474	160 040	184 695	193 375
Portugal[8]	—	—	—	161 180	158 815
Romania[9]	40 322	19 733	24 405	33 785	46 400
Scandanavia	—	—	—	54 980	50 145
Singapore[1]	—	—	—	6 285	7 970
Somalia[1]	—	—	—	5 290	16 740
South America—Other	—	—	—	15 840	19 445
South Africa[3]	2 235	2 057	—	24 730	28 465
Spain[8]	—	—	—	11 170	11 240
Sri Lanka[4]	—	—	—	25 435	67 425
Syria[1]	—	—	—	11 005	13 105
Sweden[14]	34 415	22 635	14 110	—	—
Switzerland[8]	6 076	6 414	13 895	16 330	19 310
Taiwan[4]	—	—	—	17 770	49 290
Tanzania[1]	—	—	—	17 820	18 130
Thailand[1]	—	—	—	5 815	7 710
Trinidad/Tobago[3]	—	—	—	49 385	62 020
Turkey[8]	—	—	—	12 180	14 430
Uganda[1]	—	—	—	8 960	10 755
USSR, former[10]	133 869	188 292	160 120	99 355	108 390
United Kingdom	1 138 942	912 482	933 040	717 750	655 535
UK possessions/dependencies[5]	35 416	10 415	112 120	—	—
United States	344 574	282 010	309 640	249 075	244 695
Viet Nam[4]	—	—	—	113 595	139 325
Yugoslavia, former[8]	17 110	20 912	78 285	88 815	121 975

Source: © Statistics Canada, Census of Canada   (—) Not reported.

(1) Included in "Other countries" until 1986 Census. (2) Includes Hungary (Austria-Hungary) in 1911 Census. (3) British possessions/dependencies (see UK possessions) during various census years could include African, Asian, Caribbean, Mediterranean and Pacific possessions, as well as any territory in British North America prior to Confederation with Canada (in the case of Newfoundland, this was not until 1949); many not reported separately until 1986 Census. (4) Included in "Asia—Other" until 1986 Census. (5) More detailed breakdown given in subsequent census data. (6) Total for Germany includes both East and West Germany. (7) Totals for India before 1986 include Pakistan. (8) Where not reported, included in "Europe—Other." (9) For 1911 Census, also includes Bulgaria. (10) Includes Russia. (11) Totals include those where country unknown or not noted: 1931: 3 051; 1951: 6 089; 1971: 78 805; 1991: 65; 1996: 20. (12) Includes Czech and Slovak Federal Republics. (13) Includes North and South Korea. (14) After 1986, reported as Scandanavia. (15) Includes New Zealand.

Welcome Home Campaign

In Spring 2000, Citizenship and Immigration Canada launched the Welcome Home Campaign for young people aged 5 to 13. The campaign encourages them to welcome new Canadians during 2000 and 2001.

"The best way to make citizenship real for youngsters is to let them know that there are things they can do to be good citizens and contribute to our quality of life," said Elinor Caplan, Minister of Citizenship and Immigration Canada. "Acceptance and understanding—being a good neighbour—are important values in Canadian citizenship. I can't think of a better way to celebrate citizenship than to send messages of welcome to new citizens, especially messages from Canadian children."

A bright, child-friendly campaign poster highlights the message: "Welcome home. People come from all over the world to make Canada their new home. Let's welcome our new friends, neighbours and families." An activity guide encourages children to welcome newcomers in their own communities and to appreciate Canada's rich multicultural fabric. Young people can use the medium of their choice to send messages of welcome. The campaign web site address is www.cic.gc.ca/welcomehome.

Source: Citizenship and Immigration Canada

Top 15 Ethnic Origins in Canada, 1996

Ethnic origin as defined in the Census refers to the ethnic or cultural group(s) to which an individual's ancestors belonged. In other words, it refers to the ancestral roots of the population—not place of birth, citizenship, or nationality.

In the 1996 Census, respondents were given four blank spaces to indicate single or multiple ethnic origins. Over 35 percent of them (10.2 million) reported more than one ethnic origin, reflecting intermarriage among those who have been in Canada for several generations.

The table below shows the 15 most commonly cited ethnic origins, either as the sole ethnic origin or as part of a mixed heritage.

	Total Responses	Single Ethnic Origin	Multiple Ethnic Origins
Total population	28 528 125	18 303 625	10 224 495
Canadian	8 806 275	5 326 995	3 479 285
English	6 832 095	2 048 275	4 783 820
French	5 597 845	2 665 250	2 932 595
Scottish	4 260 840	642 970	3 617 870
Irish	3 767 610	504 030	3 263 580
German	2 757 140	726 145	2 030 990
Italian	1 207 475	729 455	478 025
Aboriginal	1 101 955	477 630	624 330
Ukrainian	1 026 475	331 680	694 790
Chinese	921 585	800 470	121 115
Dutch	916 215	313 880	602 335
Polish	786 735	265 930	520 805
South Asian	723 345	590 145	133 200
Jewish	351 705	195 810	155 900
Norwegian	346 310	47 805	298 500

Source: © Census of Canada, Statistics Canada

Visible Minority Population by Group, 1996

The 1996 Census also gathered information on the number of people in Canada who are members of a visible minority, as defined by the Employment Equity Act: "persons, other than Aboriginal peoples, who are non-Caucasian in race or non-white in colour." According to the 1996 Census, these groups accounted for 11.2 percent of the population (3,197,480 people).

The visible minorities are represented by the following groups:

	Total Number	% of Total Population[1]
Total visible minority population	3 197 480	11.2
Chinese	860 150	3.0
South Asian	670 585	2.4
Black	573 860	2.0
Arab/West Asian	244 665	0.9
Filipino	234 200	0.8
Latin American	176 975	0.6
Southeast Asian	172 765	0.6
Japanese	68 135	0.2
Korean	64 835	0.2
Visible minority not included elsewhere	69 745	0.2
Multiple visible minority	61 570	0.2

Source: © Census of Canada, Statistics Canada

(1) Total population in 1996 was 28 528 125.

Population **47**

Canadian Population by Mother Tongue[1]

As Canada's population has become more diverse, so have the mother tongues reported at census time. The table below shows all languages reported to be the mother tongue of 10,000 Canadians or more in the 1996 Census, with historical comparisons.

(thousands of persons and percent of total population)

	1941	%	1951	%	1961	%	1971	%	1991	%	1996	%
Total Population	11 507		14 009		18 238		21 568		27 297		28 847	
English	6 448	56.0	8 281	59.1	10 661	58.5	12 974	60.2	16 170	59.2	16 891	58.6
French	3 355	29.2	4 069	29.0	5 123	28.1	5 794	26.9	6 503	23.8	6 637	23.0
Chinese	34	0.3	28	0.2	49	0.3	95	0.4	499	1.8	716	2.5
Italian	80	0.7	92	0.7	340	1.9	538	2.5	511	1.9	485	1.7
German	322	2.8	329	2.3	564	3.1	561	2.6	466	1.7	450	1.6
Spanish	1	...	2	...	7	...	24	0.1	177	0.6	213	0.7
Polish	129	1.1	129	0.9	162	0.9	135	0.6	190	0.7	213	0.7
Portuguese	n.a.		n.a.		18	0.1	87	0.4	212	0.8	211	0.7
Punjabi	n.a.		n.a.		n.a.		n.a.	n.a.	136	0.5	202	0.7
Ukrainian	313	2.7	352	2.5	361	2.0	310	1.4	187	0.7.	163	0.6
Arabic	8	0.1	5	...	13	0.1	29	0.1	108	0.4	149	0.5
Dutch	53	0.5	88	0.6	170	0.9	145	0.7	139	0.5	134	0.5
Tagalog (Pilipino)	n.a.		n.a.		n.a.		n.a.		100	0.4	133	0.5
Greek	9	0.1	8	0.1	40	0.2	104	0.5	126	0.5	121	0.4
Vietnamese	n.a.		n.a.		n.a.		n.a.		79	0.3	107	0.4
Hungarian	46	0.4	42	0.3	86	0.5	87	0.4	80	0.3	77	0.3
Cree	n.a.		n.a.		n.a.		n.a.		74	0.3	77	0.3
Tamil	n.a.		n.a.		n.a.		n.a.		31	0.1	67	0.2
Persian (Farsi)	n.a.		n.a.		n.a.		n.a.		41	0.2	60	0.2
Russian	52	0.5	39	0.3	43	0.2	32	0.1	35	0.1	58	0.2
Korean	n.a.		n.a.		n.a.		n.a.		36	0.1	55	0.2
Croatian	n.a.		n.a.		n.a.		n.a.		40	0.1	50	0.2
Gujarati	n.a.		n.a.		n.a.		n.a.		38	0.1	45	0.2
Hindi	n.a.		n.a.		n.a.		n.a.		35	0.1	43	0.2
Urdu	n.a.		n.a.		n.a.		n.a.		25	0.1	40	0.1
Romanian	n.a.		n.a.		n.a.		n.a.		22	0.1	36	0.1
Creoles	n.a.		n.a.		n.a.		n.a.		28	0.1	35	0.1
Japanese	22	0.2	18	0.1	18	0.1	17	0.1	30	0.1	34	0.1
Serbian	n.a.		n.a.		n.a.		n.a.		11	...	29	0.1
Inuktitut	n.a.		n.a.		n.a.		n.a.		24	0.1	27	0.1
Armenian	n.a.		n.a.		n.a.		n.a.		26	0.1	26	0.1
Czech[2]	38	0.3	46	0.3	51	0.3	45	0.2	27	0.1	25	0.1
Finnish	37	0.3	32	0.2	45	0.2	37	0.2	28	0.1	25	0.1
Somali	n.a.		n.a.		n.a.		n.a.		—		25	0.1
Ojibway	n.a.		n.a.		n.a.		n.a.		22	0.1	23	0.1
Yiddish	130	1.1	104	0.7	82	0.4	50	0.2	25	0.1	21	0.1
Danish	19	0.2	16	0.1	35	0.2	27	0.1	22	0.1	20	0.1
Macedonian	n.a.		n.a.		n.a.		n.a.		15	0.1	19	0.1
Serbo-Croatian	n.a.		n.a.		n.a.		n.a.		5	...	18	0.1
Slovak	n.a.		n.a.		n.a.		n.a.		18	0.1	18	0.1
Bengali	n.a.		n.a.		n.a.		n.a.		8	...	16	0.1
Khmer	n.a.		n.a.		n.a.		n.a.		14	...	15	0.1
Slovenian	n.a.		n.a.		n.a.		n.a.		9	...	14	...
Hebrew	n.a.		n.a.		n.a.		n.a.		12	...	13	...
Lao	n.a.		n.a.		n.a.		n.a.		12	...	13	...
Turkish	n.a.		n.a.		n.a.		n.a.		9	...	12	...
Estonian	n.a.		n.a.		n.a.		n.a.		12	...	11	...
Norwegian	60	0.5	44	0.3	40	0.2	27	0.1	13	...	10	...
Swedish	50	0.4	36	0.3	33	0.2	22	0.1	12	...	10	...
Latvian	n.a.		n.a.		n.a.		n.a.		10	...	10	...
Lithuanian	n.a.		n.a.		n.a.		n.a.		11	...	9	...

Source: © *Census of Canada, Statistics Canada*   (n.a.) Not available/not collected. (...) Too small to be included.
(1) The language first spoken in childhood and still understood. (2) Prior to 1996, includes Slovak.

Native Population of Canada

	1991				1996[2]			
	Total Population with Aboriginal Origins[1,4]	Native Indian	Métis	Inuit	Total Aboriginal Population[3]	Native Indian	Métis	Inuit
Canada	1 002 675	783 980	212 650	49 255	799 010	554 290	210 190	41 080
Newfoundland	13 110	5 845	1 605	6 460	14 205	5 430	4 685	4 265
Prince Edward Island	1 880	1 665	185	75	950	825	120	15
Nova Scotia	21 885	19 950	1 590	770	12 380	11 340	860	210
New Brunswick	12 815	11 835	975	450	10 250	9 180	975	120
Quebec	137 615	112 590	19 480	8 480	71 415	47 600	16 075	8 300
Ontario	243 550	220 135	26 905	5 250	141 525	118 830	22 790	1 300
Manitoba	116 200	76 370	45 575	900	128 685	82 990	46 195	360
Saskatchewan	96 580	69 385	32 840	540	111 245	75 205	36 535	190
Alberta	148 220	99 650	56 310	2 825	122 840	72 645	50 745	795
British Columbia	169 035	149 570	22 295	1 990	139 655	113 315	26 750	815
Yukon	6 390	5 870	565	170	6 175	5 530	565	110
Northwest Territories	35 390	11 100	4 310	21 355	39 690	11 400	3 895	24 600
Nunavut[5]	n.a.	n.a.	n.a.	n.a.	20 690	90	80	20 490

Source: © Census of Canada (n.a.) Not applicable.
(1) The 1991 Census question on ethnic or cultural origins gathered information on the number of people who reported North American Indian, Métis or Inuit origin as either a single response or in combination with other origins. (2) The numbers shown may exceed the total population as 6 400 respondents counted themselves as belonging to more than one group. (3) The 1996 data examined the responses to both an ancestry and an identity question, and the resulting information is a compilation of the two. The identity question included a more direct inquiry into whether the person considered him or herself to have an Aboriginal identity in addition to an Aboriginal ancestry. (4) In the 1991 Census, 78 reserves were incompletely enumerated, representing 37 000 individuals. (5) Data from the 1996 Census was used to create a profile for Nunavut.

Status Indian Population[1], 1999

	Number of Bands	On Reserve	On Crown Land	Off Reserve	Total Indian Population
Canada	610	360 707	24 071	275 112	659 890
Atlantic Provinces	31	16 726	20	9 089	25 835
Quebec	39	42 672	1 202	18 417	62 291
Ontario	126	74 322	1 974	73 940	150 236
Manitoba	62	66 918	1 818	35 363	104 099
Saskatchewan	70	51 128	1 751	50 535	103 414
Alberta	43	52 079	2 709	27 911	82 699
British Columbia	197	55 944	769	52 010	108 723
Yukon Territory	16	693	3 145	3 693	7 531
Northwest Territories	26	225	10 683	4 154	15 062

Source: Indian and Northern Affairs Canada
(1) Status Indians are those individuals registered with the Indian and Northern Affairs Canada under the *Indian Act*.

Largest Native Bands in Canada, 1998

Band, Province	Population[1]	Band, Province	Population[1]
Six Nations of the Grand River[2], Ontario	20 435	Lac La Ronge, Saskatchewan	6 955
Mohawks of Akwesasne, Ontario	9 260	Peguis, Manitoba	6 948
Blood, Alberta	8 840	Mohawks of the Bay of Quinte	6 921
Kahnawake, Quebec	8 793	Peter Ballantyne Cree Nation, Saskatchewan	6 601
Saddle Lake, Alberta	7 466	Wikwemikong, Ontario	6 347

Source: Indian and Northern Affairs Canada
(1) Registered Indian population as of December 31, 1998. (2) This Six Nations Band consists of the following 13 registry groups: Bay of Quinte Mohawk, Bearfoot Onondaga, Deleware, Konadaha Seneca, Lower Cayuga, Lower Mohawk, Niharondasa Seneca, Oneida, Onondaga Clear Sky, Tuscarora, Upper Cayuga, Upper Mohawk, Walker Mohawk.

Population **49**

Canadian Urban and Rural Population
(thousands)

Year	Urban Total	%	Rural Non-Farm	%	+	Farm	%	=	Total	%
1871	722	19.6	n.a.	n.a.		n.a.	n.a.		2 967	80.4
1881	1 110	25.7	n.a.	n.a.		n.a.	n.a.		3 215	74.3
1891	1 537	31.8	n.a.	n.a.		n.a.	n.a.		3 296	68.2
1901	2 014	37.5	n.a.	n.a.		n.a.	n.a.		3 357	62.5
1911	3 273	45.4	n.a.	n.a.		n.a.	n.a.		3 934	54.6
1921	4 352	49.5	n.a.	n.a.		n.a.	n.a.		4 436	50.5
1931	5 469	52.7	1 670	16.1		3 238	31.2		4 908	47.3
1941	6 271	54.5	2 123	18.4		3 113	27.1		5 236	45.5
1951	8 817	62.9	2 423	17.3		2 769	19.8		5 192	37.1
1956	10 715	66.6	2 734	17.0		2 632	16.4		5 366	33.4
1961	12 700	69.6	3 465	19.0		2 073	11.4		5 538	30.4
1966	14 727	73.6	3 374	16.9		1 914	9.6		5 288	26.4
1971	16 410	76.1	3 738	17.3		1 420	6.6		5 158	23.9
1976	17 367	75.5	4 591	20.0		1 035	4.5		5 626	24.5
1981	18 436	75.7	4 867	20.0		1 040	4.3		5 907	24.3
1986	19 352	76.5	5 067	20.0		890	3.5		5 957	23.5
1991	20 907	76.6	5 583	20.5		807	3.0		6 390	23.4
1996	22 461	77.9	n.a.	n.a.		n.a.	n.a.		6 386	22.1

Source: © *Census of Canada, Statistics Canada* (n.a.) Not available.

Definitions: Urban: persons living in a built-up area having a population of 1 000 or more, and a population density of 400 or more per sq. km; **Rural:** persons living outside "urban areas"; **Rural Farm:** persons living in rural areas who are members of households of farm operators; **Rural Non-Farm:** persons living in rural areas who are not members of households of farm operators.

Urban and Rural Population by Province

Province	1951 Rural	1951 Urban	1991 Rural	1991 Urban	1996 Rural	1996 Urban
Canada	5 174 555	8 473 458	6 389 724	20 907 135	6 385 551	22 461 210
Newfoundland[1]	n.a.	n.a.	264 023	304 451	237 973	313 819
Prince Edward Island	73 744	24 685	77 952	51 813	75 097	59 460
Nova Scotia	297 753	344 831	418 434	481 508	411 424	497 858
New Brunswick	300 686	215 011	378 686	345 214	377 712	360 421
Quebec	1 358 363	2 697 318	1 544 752	5 351 211	1 541 170	5 597 625
Ontario	1 346 443	3 251 099	1 831 043	8 253 842	1 794 832	8 958 741
Manitoba	336 961	439 580	304 767	787 175	313 835	800 063
Saskatchewan	579 258	252 470	365 531	623 397	363 059	627 178
Alberta	489 826	449 675	514 660	2 030 893	554 011	2 142 815
British Columbia	371 739	793 471	641 922	2 640 139	667 112	3 057 388
Yukon Territory	6 502	2 594	11 462	16 335	12 319	18 447
Northwest Territories	13 280[2]	2 724[2]	36 492[2]	21 157[2]	19 073	20 176
Nunavut[3]	n.a.	n.a.	n.a.	n.a.	17 934	7 219

Source: © *Census of Canada, Statistics Canada*
(1) Newfoundland joined confederation in 1949, and urban/rural split in population was not included in 1951 census data. (2) Includes Nunavut. (3) Nunavut became a province in 1999, but data from the 1996 Census was used to create a profile.

Nunavut Census Divisions

*O*n April 1, 1999 what was known as the Northwest Territories was divided into Nunavut and the Northwest Territories. The five census divisions of Northwest Territories listed in the 1996 Standard Geographical Classification are divided as follows: Baffin Region, Keewatin Region and Kitikmeot Region are part of Nunavut, whereas Fort Smith Region and Inuvik Region remain within the Northwest Territories.

Population of Canadian Towns and Cities

(more than 5,000 inhabitants)

Town or city classification is made according to the official designations adopted by provincial or federal authority. *Indicates a city or *ville* in Quebec; all others are towns.

	POPULATION 1991	POPULATION 1996	AREA (sq. km)
■ NEWFOUNDLAND			
Bay Roberts	5 474	5 472	24.15
Carbonear	5 259	5 168	11.81
Channel-Port aux Basques	5 644	5 243	37.83
Clarenville	4 473	5 335	139.98
Conception Bay South	17 590	19 265	59.40
Corner Brook*	22 410	21 893	147.55
Deer Lake	5 161	5 222	71.75
Gander	10 339	10 364	101.16
Grand Falls-Windsor	14 693	14 160	56.66
Happy Valley-Goose Bay	8 610	8 655	306.42
Labrador City	9 061	8 455	6.47
Marystown	6 739	6 742	59.27
Mount Pearl*	23 676	25 519	15.06
Paradise	7 358	7 960	27.83
Placentia	5 515	5 013	58.00
Portugal Cove-St. Philip's	5 459	5 773	56.43
St. John's*	104 659	101 936	431.75
Stephenville	7 621	7 764	34.80
Torbay	4 707	5 230	36.04
■ PRINCE EDWARD ISLAND			
Charlottetown*	31 541	32 531	42.64
Stratford	5 427	5 869	22.14
Summerside*	13 636	14 525	27.71
■ NOVA SCOTIA			
Amherst	9 742	9 669	16.65
Bedford	11 618	13 638	39.79
Bridgewater	7 248	7 351	13.35
Dartmouth*	67 798	65 629	58.57
Halifax*	114 455	113 910	79.22
Kentville	5 506	5 551	17.12
New Glasgow	9 905	9 812	10.36
Truro	11 683	11 938	38.09
Yarmouth	7 781	7 568	11.14
■ NEW BRUNSWICK			
Bathurst*	14 409	13 815	90.94
Campbellton*	8 699	8 404	17.30
Dieppe	10 650	12 497	51.62
Edmunston*	10 835	11 033	34.58
Fredericton*	46 466	46 507	129.58
Grand Falls (Grand-Sault)	6 083	6 133	17.73
Miramichi	21 165	19 241	175.07
Moncton*	56 823	59 313	142.37
Oromocto	9 325	9 194	22.08
Quispamsis	8 446	8 839	39.98
Riverview	16 270	16 653	34.26
Sackville	5 494	5 393	74.42
Saint John*	74 969	72 494	322.88
Woodstock	4 782	5 092	14.08
■ QUEBEC			
Alma*	25 910	26 127	109.27
Amos*	13 783	13 632	428.72
Amqui*	6 518	6 800	120.82
Anjou*	37 207	37 308	13.64
Asbestos*	6 487	6 271	13.47
Aylmer*	32 244	34 901	91.21
Baie-Comeau*	26 012	25 554	352.27
Beaconsfield*	19 616	19 414	10.64
Beauharnois*	6 449	6 435	40.44
Beauport*	69 158	72 920	71.32
Bécancour*	10 911	11 489	434.29
Beloeil*	18 516	19 294	24.01
Bernieres-Saint-Nicholas	14 431	15 594	94.12
Blainville*	22 679	29 603	55.20
Boisbriand*	21 124	25 227	27.32
Bois-des-Filion*	6 337	7 124	3.92
Boucherville*	33 796	34 989	69.33
Brossard*	64 793	65 927	44.98
Buckingham*	10 548	11 678	14.59
Candiac*	10 765	11 805	16.54
Cap-de-la-Madeleine*	33 716	33 438	17.30
Cap-Rouge*	14 105	14 163	6.39
Carignan*	5 386	5 614	62.35
Chambly*	15 893	19 716	25.06
Charlemagne*	5 598	5 739	1.76
Charlesbourg*	70 792	70 942	67.53
Charny*	10 239	10 661	8.80
Chateauguay*	39 833	41 423	35.40
Chibougamau*	8 855	8 664	754.08
Chicoutimi*	62 670	63 061	156.66
Coaticook*	6 637	6 653	12.60
Cote-Saint-Luc*	30 126	29 705	7.40
Cowansville*	11 986	12 051	49.12
Delson*	6 063	6 703	7.15
Deux-Montagnes*	13 035	15 953	6.05
Dolbeau*	8 181	8 310	46.32 ▶

Population

	POPULATION 1991	1996	AREA (sq. km)		POPULATION 1991	1996	AREA (sq. km)
Dollard-des-Ormeaux*	46 922	47 826	15.05	Mont-Saint-Hilaire*	12 267	13 064	43.39
Donnacona*	5 659	5 739	20.12	Montmagny*	11 861	11 885	125.77
Dorval*	17 249	17 572	20.76	Montréal*	1 017 669	1 016 376	177.10
Drummondville*	43 171	44 882	70.25	Montréal-Nord*	85 516	81 581	11.03
Farnham*	6 146	6 044	25.07	Montréal-Ouest*	5 180	5 254	1.63
Fleurimont*	14 727	16 262	34.77	Outremont*	22 935	22 571	3.68
Gaspé*	16 402	16 517	1 105.11	Pierrefonds*	48 735	52 986	24.39
Gatineau*	92 284	100 702	140.62	Pincourt*	9 749	10 023	9.24
Granby*	42 804	43 316	72.73	Plessisville*	6 952	6 810	4.34
Grand-Mere*	14 287	14 223	70.79	Point-Claire*	27 647	28 435	19.19
Greenfield Park*	17 652	17 337	4.58	Port-Cartier*	7 383	7 070	87.34
Hampstead*	7 219	6 986	1.77	Québec*	167 517	167 264	88.86
Hull*	60 707	62 339	37.35	Repentigny*	49 630	53 824	24.42
Iberville*	9 352	9 635	4.90	Rimouski*	30 873	31 773	76.02
Joliette*	17 396	17 541	22.52	Riviere-du-Loup*	14 017	14 721	16.94
Jonquiere*	57 933	56 503	209.62	Roberval*	11 628	11 640	147.24
Kirkland*	17 495	18 678	10.34	Rock Forest*	14 551	16 604	51.34
L'Ancienne-L'orette*	15 242	15 895	7.87	Rosemere*	11 198	12 025	10.20
L'Assomption*	10 817	11 366	66.44	Rouyn-Noranda*	28 958	28 819	210.79
L'Ile Bizard*	11 352	13 038	22.69	Roxboro*	5 879	5 950	2.23
L'Ile Perrot*	8 065	9 178	4.92	Saint-Antoine*	10 232	10 806	9.90
La Baie*	20 995	21 057	261.69	Saint-Basile-le-Grand*	10 127	11 771	34.84
La Plaine*	10 576	14 413	39.70	Saint-Bruno-de-Montarville*	23 849	23 714	41.79
La Prairie*	15 237	17 128	43.33	Saint-Constant*	18 424	21 993	57.32
La Sarre*	8 513	8 345	148.30	Saint-Emile*	6 916	9 889	8.77
La Tuque*	12 577	12 102	599.07	Saint-Eustache*	37 278	39 848	70.03
Lac-Mégantic*	5 852	5 864	20.97	Saint-Félicien*	9 340	9 599	168.56
Lachenaie*	15 052	18 489	42.75	Saint-Georges*	19 583	20 057	24.94
Lachine*	35 266	35 171	17.38	Saint-Hubert*	74 093	77 042	63.05
Lachute*	11 730	11 493	96.24	Saint-Hyacinthe*	39 292	38 981	36.63
LaSalle*	73 804	72 029	16.42	Saint-Jean-Chrysostome*	12 717	16 161	82.90
Laval*	314 398	330 393	245.40	Saint-Jean-sur-Richelieu*	37 607	36 435	47.42
Le Gardeur*	13 814	16 853	44.00	Saint-Jérome*	23 384	23 916	15.79
LeMoyne*	5 412	5 052	0.96	Saint-Lambert*	20 976	20 971	6.43
Lévis*	39 417	40 407	44.0	Saint-Laurent*	72 402	74 240	46.17
Longueuil*	129 808	127 997	42.85	Saint-Leonard*	73 120	71 327	12.93
Loretteville*	14 219	14 168	6.94	Saint-Louis-de-France	6 747	7 327	61.54
Lorraine*	8 410	8 876	5.46	Saint-Luc*	15 008	18 371	51.20
Louiseville*	8 000	7 911	62.57	Saint-Raymond*	8 126	8 773	671.22
Magog*	14 034	14 050	15.28	Saint-Rédempteur*	5 862	6 358	3.46
Marieville*	5 128	5 510	3.42	Saint-Rémi*	5 768	5 707	79.67
Mascouche*	25 828	28 097	107.95	Saint-Romuald*	9 830	10 604	18.34
Masson-Angers*	5 753	7 989	55.60	Saint-Timothée*	8 292	8 495	68.02
Matane*	12 756	12 364	24.35	Sainte-Agathe-des-Monts*	5 452	5 669	15.58
Mercier*	8 227	9 059	45.89	Sainte-Anne-des-Monts*	5 652	5 617	106.06
Mirabel*	17 971	22 689	492.20	Sainte-Anne-des-Plaines*	10 787	12 908	92.23
Mistassini*	6 842	6 904	248.50	Sainte-Catherine*	9 805	13 724	9.06
Mont-Joli*	6 265	6 267	9.59	Sainte-Foy*	71 133	72 330	83.86
Mont-Laurier*	7 862	8 007	82.05	Sainte-Julie*	20 632	24 030	47.91
Mont-Royal*	18 212	18 282	7.43	Sainte-Marie*	10 513	10 966	105.31

	POPULATION 1991	1996	AREA (sq. km)		POPULATION 1991	1996	AREA (sq. km)
Sainte-Marthe-sur-le-Lac*	7 410	8 295	9.01	Espanola	5 527	5 454	17.66
Sainte-Thérèse*	24 158	23 477	10.09	Essex	6 759	6 785	6.48
Salaberry-de-Valleyfield*	27 598	26 600	27.47	Etobicoke*	309 993	328 718	123.93
Sept-Iles*	24 848	25 224	298.93	Fergus	7 940	8 884	7.23
Shawinigan*	19 931	18 678	26.27	Flamborough	29 616	34 037	489.90
Shawinigan-Sud*	11 584	11 804	51.52	Fort Erie	26 006	27 183	168.30
Sherbrooke*	76 431	76 786	57.77	Fort Frances	8 891	8 790	26.05
Sillery*	12 519	12 003	6.73	Gananoque	5 209	5 219	9.01
Sorel*	24 253	23 248	38.04	Georgina	29 746	34 777	286.27
Terrebonne*	39 700	42 214	73.21	Gloucester*	101 677	104 022	293.86
Thetford Mines*	18 251	17 635	33.91	Goderich	7 452	7 553	6.97
Tracy*	13 181	12 773	19.11	Gravenhurst	9 988	10 030	524.06
Trois-Rivières*	49 426	48 419	77.81	Grimsby	18 520	19 585	68.12
Trois-Rivières-Ouest*	20 076	22 886	28.75	Guelph*	88 444	95 821	87.12
Val-Belair*	17 181	20 176	68.52	Haldimand	20 573	22 128	638.15
Val d'Or*	23 842	24 285	1 206.60	Halton Hills	36 816	42 390	275.86
Vanier*	10 833	11 174	4.66	Hamilton*	318 499	322 352	122.99
Varennes*	14 758	18 842	93.96	Hanover	6 711	6 844	6.49
Vaudreuil-Dorion*	17 109	18 466	73.13	Hawkesbury	9 713	10 162	8.71
Verdun*	61 307	59 714	8.15	Hearst	6 079	6 049	96.85
Victoriaville*	36 392	38 174	83.49	Huntsville	14 997	15 918	700.90
Westmount*	20 239	20 420	3.96	Ingersoll	9 378	9 849	10.21
				Innisfil	21 249	24 711	284.10

■ **ONTARIO**

	POPULATION 1991	1996	AREA (sq. km)
Iroquois Falls	5 999	5 714	689.94
Ajax	57 350	64 430	67.70
Kanata*	37 344	47 909	132.21
Amherstburg	8 921	10 245	11.26
Kapuskasing	10 344	10 036	83.92
Ancaster	21 988	23 403	174.55
Kenora	9 782	10 063	15.33
Arnprior	6 679	7 113	13.63
Kincardine	6 601	6 620	10.25
Aurora	29 454	34 857	49.16
Kingston*	56 597	55 947	29.64
Aylmer	6 244	7 018	5.85
Kingsville	5 716	5 991	4.27
Barrie*	62 278	79 191	76.79
Kirkland Lake	10 440	9 905	270.01
Belleville*	37 243	37 083	29.13
Kitchener*	168 282	178 420	135.15
Bracebridge	12 308	13 223	632.09
LaSalle	16 628	20 566	65.61
Bradford-West Gwillimbury	17 702	20 213	197.26
Leamington	14 140	16 188	10.63
Brampton*	234 285	268 251	265.04
Lincoln	17 149	18 801	163.43
Brantford*	81 997	84 764	71.22
Lindsay	16 696	17 638	15.19
Brockville*	21 582	21 752	20.25
Listowel	5 404	5 467	6.19
Burlington*	129 575	136 976	177.40
London*	311 620	325 646	437.99
Caledon	34 965	39 893	686.16
Markham	153 811	173 383	211.53
Cambridge*	92 772	101 429	115.64
Midland	14 485	15 035	21.75
Carleton Place	7 432	8 450	7.30
Milton	32 075	32 104	367.20
Chatham*	43 632	43 409	30.86
Mississauga*	463 388	544 382	273.86
Clarington	49 479	60 615	607.79
Nanticoke*	22 727	23 485	674.72
Cobourg	15 079	16 027	15.89
Napanee	5 179	5 450	4.41
Collingwood	14 382	15 596	33.60
Nepean*	107 627	115 100	217.00
Cornwall*	47 137	47 403	63.49
New Liskeard	5 431	5 112	6.42
Dryden	6 505	6 711	16.86
New Tecumseth	20 344	22 902	274.83
Dundas	21 868	23 125	24.20
Newmarket	45 474	57 125	35.91
Dunnville	12 131	12 471	302.92
Niagara Falls*	75 399	76 917	212.02
East Gwillimbury	18 637	19 770	245.14
Niagara-on-the-Lake	12 945	13 238	131.11
Elliot Lake*	14 089	13 588	756.79
Nickel Centre	12 332	13 017	378.36

	POPULATION 1991	POPULATION 1996	AREA (sq. km)
North Bay*	55 405	54 332	312.88
North York*	563 270	589 653	176.87
Oakville	114 670	128 405	138.18
Onaping Falls	5 402	5 277	228.98
Orangeville	17 921	21 498	14.07
Orillia*	25 925	27 846	28.55
Oshawa*	129 344	134 364	143.41
Ottawa*	313 987	323 340	110.15
Owen Sound*	21 674	21 390	23.69
Paris	8 600	8 987	13.64
Parry Sound	6 125	6 326	14.98
Pelham	13 328	14 343	124.52
Pembroke*	13 997	14 177	15.33
Penetanguishene	6 862	7 291	12.58
Perth	5 576	5 886	9.18
Peterborough*	68 379	69 535	53.99
Pickering*	68 631	78 989	226.52
Port Colborne*	18 766	18 451	122.82
Port Elgin	6 857	7 041	5.92
Port Hope	11 505	11 698	13.00
Rayside-Balfour	15 039	16 050	328.21
Renfrew	8 134	8 125	12.25
Richmond Hill	80 142	101 725	99.42
Rockland	6 771	8 070	8.49
Sarnia*	74 167	72 738	163.73
Sault Ste. Marie*	81 476	80 054	221.52
Scarborough*	524 598	558 960	187.70
Simcoe	15 539	15 380	40.51
Smiths Falls	9 439	9 131	8.20
St. Catharines*	129 300	130 926	94.43
St. Marys	5 496	5 952	12.14
St. Thomas*	30 332	32 275	32.22
Stoney Creek*	49 968	54 318	98.60
Stratford*	27 666	28 987	20.33
Strathroy	10 566	11 852	13.89
Sturgeon Falls	5 837	6 162	5.79
Sudbury*	92 884	92 059	262.73
Tecumseh	10 495	12 828	6.17
Thorold*	17 542	17 883	84.54
Thunder Bay*	113 496	113 662	322.87
Tillsonburg	12 019	13 211	21.99
Timmins*	47 461	47 499	3 004.39
Toronto*	635 395	653 734	97.15
Trenton*	16 908	17 179	11.68
Valley East	21 939	23 537	518.03
Vanier*	18 150	17 247	2.93
Vaughan*	111 359	132 549	275.34
Walden	9 805	10 292	718.62
Wallaceburg	11 846	11 772	10.71
Wasaga Beach	6 457	8 698	55.62
Waterloo*	71 181	77 949	64.43
Welland*	47 914	48 411	81.23
Whitby	61 281	73 794	142.99
Whitchurch-Stouffville	18 357	19 835	206.85
Windsor*	191 435	197 694	120.29
Woodstock*	30 075	32 086	24.78
York*	139 819	146 534	23.18

■ MANITOBA

	POPULATION 1991	POPULATION 1996	AREA (sq. km)
Brandon*	38 575	39 175	74.85
Dauphin	8 453	8 266	11.94
Flin Flon* (part in Man. balance in Sask.)	7 119	6 572	11.55
Morden	5 273	5 689	12.44
Portage La Prairie*	13 186	13 077	24.03
Selkirk	9 815	9 881	24.71
Steinbach	8 213	8 478	25.24
The Pas	6 166	5 945	28.46
Thompson*	14 977	14 385	16.85
Winkler	6 397	7 241	16.33
Winnipeg*	615 215	618 477	464.13

■ SASKATCHEWAN

Estevan*	10 240	10 752	17.67
Humboldt	4 989	5 074	11.92
Lloydminster*(part in Sask)	7 241	7 636	17.37
Melfort*	5 628	5 759	14.66
Melville*	4 905	4 646	15.41
Moose Jaw*	33 593	32 973	46.64
North Battleford*	14 348	14 051	35.48
Prince Albert*	34 181	34 777	64.98
Regina*	179 183	180 400	114.06
Saskatoon*	186 067	193 647	136.79
Swift Current*	14 824	14 890	22.87
Weyburn*	9 673	9 723	14.04
Yorkton*	15 315	15 154	23.82

■ ALBERTA

Airdrie*	12 456	15 946	21.02
Banff	5 688	6 098	4.86
Beaumont	5 042	5 810	5.59
Bonnyville	5 132	5 100	14.39
Brooks	9 433	10 093	15.81
Calgary*	710 795	768 082	716.79
Camrose*	13 420	13 728	26.10
Canmore	5 681	8 354	67.08
Coaldale	5 310	5 731	7.06
Cochrane	5 267	7 424	16.09
Crowsnest Pass	6 680	6 356	379.19
Drayton Valley	5 983	5 883	7.95
Drumheller*	6 263	6 587	26.24

54 The People

	POPULATION 1991	1996	AREA (sq. km)
Edmonton*	616 741	616 306	670.08
Edson	7 323	7 399	25.89
Fort Saskatchewan*	12 092	12 408	45.10
Grande Prairie*	28 271	31 140	41.83
High River	6 269	7 359	11.58
Hinton	9 046	9 961	22.27
Innisfail	5 700	6 116	9.82
Lacombe	6 934	8 018	12.45
Leduc*	13 970	14 305	25.49
Lethbridge*	60 974	63 053	119.90
Lloydminster (part)*	10 042	11 317	23.93
Medicine Hat*	43 625	46 783	112.96
Morinville	6 104	6 226	12.32
Okotoks	6 723	8 510	15.76
Olds	5 549	5 815	10.14
Peace River	6 717	6 536	21.20
Ponoka	5 861	6 149	10.07
Red Deer*	58 145	60 075	58.18
Rocky Mountain House	5 641	5 805	10.82
Slave Lake	5 607	6 553	18.00
Spruce Grove	12 908	14 271	25.57
St. Albert*	42 146	46 888	33.97
Stettler	4 947	5 220	9 35
Stony Plain	7 226	8 274	26.51
Sylvan Lake	4 210	5 178	8.18
Taber	6 664	7 214	15.66
Vegreville	5 138	5 337	13.86
Wainwright	4 732	5 079	8.16
Wetaskiwin*	10 657	10 959	16.45
Whitecourt	6 938	7 783	25.40
■ BRITISH COLUMBIA			
Abbotsford	86 928	105 403	343.85
Burnaby	158 858	179 209	88.45
Castlegar*	6 579	7 027	16.16
Colwood*	13 468	13 848	17.87
Comox	9 477	11 069	14.47
Coquitlam*	84 021	101 820	123.36
Courtenay*	11 698	17 335	15.49
Cranbrook*	16 447	18 131	17.18
Dawson Creek*	10 981	11 125	20.30
Fort St. John*	14 156	15 021	21.73
Kamloops*	67 057	76 394	296.06
Kelowna*	75 953	89 442	212.57
Kimberley*	6 531	6 738	58.19
Ladysmith	4 875	6 456	7.53
Langley*	19 765	22 523	10.18
Merritt*	6 898	7 631	23.74
Nanaimo*	60 129	70 130	88.19
Nelson*	8 849	9 585	7.71
New Westminster*	43 585	49 350	15.38
North Vancouver*	38 436	41 475	10.77
Parksville	7 381	9 472	15.93
Penticton*	27 258	30 987	40.80
Port Alberni*	18 523	18 468	17.81
Port Coquitlam*	36 773	46 682	28.76
Port Moody*	17 756	20 847	26.21
Prince George*	69 653	75 150	315.94
Prince Rupert*	16 620	16 714	53.56
Qualicum Beach	5 137	6 728	11.14
Quesnel*	8 208	8 468	23.00
Revelstoke*	7 729	8 047	34.09
Richmond*	126 624	148 867	124.20
Sidney	10 082	10 701	5.02
Smithers	5 029	5 624	13.63
Surrey*	245 173	304 477	301.76
Terrace*	11 433	12 779	19.21
Trail*	7 921	7 696	18.74
Vancouver*	471 844	514 008	113.09
Vernon*	27 722	31 817	75.09
Victoria*	71 228	73 504	18.78
View Royal	5 996	6 441	15.42
White Rock*	16 314	17 210	5.05
Williams Lake*	10 395	10 472	23.45
■ YUKON TERRITORY			
Whitehorse*	17 925	19 157	413.48
■ NORTHWEST TERRITORIES			
Yellowknife*	15 179	17 275	102.38

Source: © Census of Canada, Statistics Canada
*Indicates a city or ville in Quebec; all others are towns.

Nunavut Communities

*O*n May 14, 1996, the census counted 24 730 people in what was to be known as the new Nunavut Territory—38 percent of the total population of the current Northwest Territories. Most of Nunavut's population is located in small towns and hamlets spread across a large area. The largest centres are the Baffin Island town of Iqaluit, the new territorial capital, with a population of 4 220, and the hamlet of Rankin Inlet, with a population of 2 058, on the coast of Hudson Bay.

Source: © Statistics Canada

Population of Census Metropolitan Areas[1] in Canada

Statistics Canada defines a census metropolitan area (CMA) as a very large urban area, together with neighbouring urban and rural areas that have a high degree of economic and social integration with that large urban area. The urban area itself (or urbanized core) must have a population of at least 100,000 based on the previous census. For a more detailed look at these cities, see "Canadian Cities" pages 31–37.

	Population (000s)					Land Area (sq. km)
CMA	1966	1976	1986	1996[2]	1999[3]	1996
Calgary, Alta.	330 575	469 917	671 453	845 493	933 748	5 083.28
Chicoutimi, Que.	109 142	128 643	158 468	162 949	162 346	1 723.31
Edmonton, Alta.	401 299	554 228	774 026	885 123	929 145	9 536.63
Halifax, N.S.	198 193	267 991	295 922	341 463	352 594	2 503.10
Hamilton, Ont.	449 116	529 371	557 029	642 729	665 169	1 358.50
Kitchener, Ont.	192 275	272 158	311 195	395 208	414 957	823.64
London, Ont.	207 396	270 383	342 302	410 407	418 660	2 105.07
Montreal, Que.	2 436 817	2 802 485	2 921 357	3 393 739	3 438 532	4 024.21
Oshawa, Ont.	100 255	135 196	203 543	277 073	292 948	894.19
Ottawa-Hull, Ont.-Que.	494 535	693 288	819 263	1 037 853	1 065 021	5 686.45
Quebec, Que.	413 397	542 158	603 267	683 741	688 085	3 149.65
Regina, Sask.	131 127	151 191	186 521	199 527	199 163	3 421.58
St. Catharines-Niagara, Ont.	109 418	301 921	343 258	382 813	389 607	1 399.80
St. John's, Nfld.	101 161	143 390	161 901	177 054	174 509	789.66
Saint John, N.B.	101 192	112 974	121 265	128 029	127 211	3 509.34
Saskatoon, Sask.	115 892	133 750	200 665	225 963	231 403	5 322.09
Sherbrooke, Que.	79 667	104 505	129 960	150 098	153 140	979.94
Sudbury, Ont.	117 075	157 030	148 877	165 009	160 357	2 612.11
Thunder Bay, Ont.	143 673	119 253	122 217	129 089	126 649	2 295.27
Toronto, Ont.	2 158 496	2 803 101	3 431 981	4 403 092	4 680 250	5 867.73
Trois Rivières, Que.	94 476	98 583	128 888	142 234	141 751	871.91
Vancouver, B.C.	892 286	1 166 348	1 380 729	1 912 120	2 016 643	2 820.66
Victoria, B.C.	173 455	218 250	255 225	316 828	316 195	633.44
Windsor, Ont.	211 697	247 582	253 988	287 486	299 966	861.66
Winnipeg, Man.	508 759	578 217	625 304	679 174	677 625	4 077.64

Source: © Census of Canada, Statistics Canada
(1) Total land area considered to be part of CMA varied from census to census. (2) Intercensal revision of total population.
(3) Postcensal estimate of total population as of July 1.

FOCUS ON...

Census 2001

Canada's next census will be conducted on May 15, 2001, marking a 335-year tradition of collecting data in order to build a statistical picture of our country. Jean Talon, the Intendant of New France, conducted the first census in the land in 1666. It enumerated 3,215 people (not counting Aboriginal people or French royal troops) and asked questions on age, sex, marital status and occupation.

Although the census today still asks for this same basic information, it has been expanded to include questions that give us a wealth of facts about the social and economic condition of the country. The census is so valuable that the *Statistics Act* states that one must be carried out every five years.

How is the census carried out?

In the years leading up to the census, many groups and experts discuss what questions will be asked on the census form. Federal and provincial governments, businesses, universities, social action groups and town planners all make suggestions based on their need for information. Questions must be clearly in the public interest with answers that are unavailable from other sources. Cabinet approval of all questions is required.

Many of the questions remain the same from census to census. In this way it is possible to track trends over the years, such as the growth or decline in the population in various areas of the country. However, as times change, new questions are asked and some are deleted. For example, the 1996 Census asked a new question on unpaid work performed around the home.

In most parts of the country, every household will receive a census form a few days before Census Day on May 15th. An adult in each household usually fills in the form for all members of the household, and then mails it back to Statistics Canada.

Not everyone fills in the same form. Four-fifths of households will receive a short form. This form asks seven basic questions including age, sex and marital status. The other one-fifth will receive the long questionnaire, which asks the same questions plus more detailed ones on other subjects such as education, income and employment.

After all the forms have been returned, the results are tabulated and turned into meaningful data.

How confidential is the information I submit?

Under the Statistics Act, all personal information given by respondents on a census form must be kept confidential. Statistics Canada places the highest priority on maintaining this confidentiality during all stages of the census process. Completed census forms are seen by only a limited number of Statistics Canada employees who need them to carry out their work All employees have taken an oath of secrecy and would face fines and imprisonment if they were to release information that could identify any individual. Furthermore, no one outside of Statistics Canada has the right to access such information. Although names and addresses are required on the census form, this is only to ensure that no individual is missed or counted twice. Names and addresses are not entered into the census database.

Who uses census data?

Census information is used for many different purposes by governments, businesses and industries, social agencies, and countless other organizations and individuals. For example:

Representation in Parliament. The number of federal electoral districts in each province and territory is based on population counts from the decennial census (census years ending in the number "1.")

Transfer payments. Census data helps to determine federal transfer payments to the provinces and territories, as well as provincial transfers to the municipalities.

Health Care. Census data is used to forecast health care needs and costs, and select sites for hospitals and clinics.

Social Services. The census provides the statistical information necessary to implement such things as day care, education and training programs, subsidized housing and services for the elderly.

Research. Census data provides reliable background information for researchers and journalists.

Source: © *Statistics Canada*

Census 2001 Questions

As on previous Census surveys, there will be a short questionnaire, filled out by 80 percent of the respondents, and a long one for the other 20 percent of the population. The general questions to be answered by all census respondents concerning all members of their household are the following:

1. Name. _____
2. Sex. _____
3. Birth date. _____
4. Marital status. _____
5. Is this person living with a common-law partner? _____
6. Relationship to person filling out form. _____
7. What is the language that this person first learned at home in childhood and still understands?
_____

Basic Population Information: question 1 asks for the name of each person in the household so that no one is left out or counted twice. The names are not entered into the census database.

Questions 2 to 6 ask about the people living in each household. The answers provide information on living arrangements, family size, number of children living with one parent or two parents, and the number of people who live alone. This information is used for planning social programs and a variety of other services.

Activities of Daily Living: answers are used to help Statistics Canada find out more about what barriers people may face—physically, mentally or health wise.

Sociocultural Information: answers provide a social and cultural profile, including diversity and movement of population. As well, information is collected about citizenship status, number of immigrants and non-permanent residents, and religion. Some of the uses of this data are helping in electoral planning, and deciding on programs and services.

Mobility: answers help provide population estimates between censuses. They are also used to help identify future needs for housing, education, transportation and social services.

Education: answers help determine what training programs are developed and financed.

Place of Birth of Parents: answers are used to assess the socio-economic conditions of second-generation Canadians.

Household Activities: when combined with other data, the answers will provide a picture of how people balance their paid and unpaid work activities.

Labour Market Activities: answers are important for both businesses and governments to plan for training programs, forecast future job opportunities, plan efficient transportation systems, and develop job creation measures.

Income in 2000: answers provides only source of detailed income statistics for all people in Canada, their families and households. Governments use the information to develop income support programs and social services. Businesses use the data to develop new products and services, and determine "good" locations.

Housing: answers are used in the developing of government programs, and housing communities and projects.

Source: © Statistics Canada

VITAL STATISTICS

Births in Canada

Year	Live Births	Birth Rate[1]	Year	Live Births	Birth Rate[1]
1921	264 879	29.3	1960	478 551	26.8
1922	259 825	28.3	1961	475 700	26.1
1923	247 404	26.7	1962	469 693	25.3
1924	251 351	26.7	1963	465 767	24.6
1925	249 365	26.1	1964	452 915	23.5
1926	240 015	24.7	1965	418 595	21.3
1927	241 149	24.3	1966	387 710	19.4
1928	243 616	24.1	1967	370 894	18.2
1929	242 226	23.5	1968	364 310	17.6
1930	250 335	23.9	1969	369 647	17.6
1931	247 205	23.2	1970	371 988	17.5
1932	242 698	22.5	1971	362 187	16.8
1933	229 791	21.0	1972	347 319	15.9
1934	228 296	20.7	1973	343 373	15.5
1935	228 396	20.5	1974	350 650	15.4
1936	227 980	20.3	1975	359 323	15.8
1937	227 869	20.1	1976	359 987	15.7
1938	237 091	20.7	1977	361 400	15.5
1939	237 991	20.6	1978	358 852	15.3
1940	252 577	21.6	1979	366 064	15.9
1941	263 993	22.4	1980	370 709	15.5
1942	281 569	23.5	1981	371 346	15.3
1943	292 943	24.2	1982	373 082	15.0
1944	293 967	24.0	1983	373 689	15.0
1945	300 587	24.3	1984	377 031	15.0
1946	343 504	27.2	1985	375 727	14.8
1947	372 589	28.9	1986	372 913	14.2
1948	359 860	27.3	1987	369 742	13.9
1949	367 092	27.3	1988	376 795	14.0
1950	372 009	27.1	1989[2]	392 625	14.4
1951	381 092	27.2	1990[2]	405 417	14.6
1952	403 559	27.9	1991[2]	402 528	14.4
1953	417 884	28.1	1992[2]	398 642	14.0
1954	436 198	28.5	1993[2]	388 394	13.5
1955	442 937	28.2	1994[2]	385 112	13.3
1956	450 739	28.0	1995[2]	378 011	12.9
1957	469 093	28.2	1996[2]	366 200	12.3
1958	470 118	27.5	1997[2]	348 598	11.6
1959	479 275	27.4	1998[3]	343 371	11.4
			1998-99[4]	340 891	11.2

Source: © Statistics Canada
(1) Per 1 000 population. (2) Final data for Births from 1989 to 1997. (3) Updated data. (4) Updated data at June 30.

Births by Province, 1998–99[1]

	Births	Birth Rate[2]		Births	Birth Rate[2]
Canada	340 891	11.2	Manitoba	14 381	12.6
Newfoundland	5 084	9.4	Saskatchewan	12 776	12.4
Prince Edward Island	1 558	11.3	Alberta	37 779	12.9
Nova Scotia	9 657	10.3	British Columbia	44 076	11.0
New Brunswick	7 704	10.2	Yukon	431	13.9
Quebec	74 205	10.1	Northwest Territories	701	17.0
Ontario	131 812	11.5	Nunavut	727	27.2

Source: © Statistics Canada
(1) Updated data at June 30. (2) Rate per 1 000 population.

Vital Statistics

Expected Years of Life Remaining by Age, 1991

Age	Male % Dying[1]	Male Years of Life Remaining	Female % Dying[1]	Female Years of Life Remaining	Age	Male % Dying[1]	Male Years of Life Remaining	Female % Dying[1]	Female Years of Life Remaining
0	0.71	74.55	0.58	80.89	56	0.84	22.53	0.48	27.42
1	0.05	74.08	0.05	80.36	57	0.93	21.71	0.52	26.55
2	0.04	73.12	0.03	79.40	58	1.03	20.91	0.57	25.69
3	0.03	72.15	0.02	78.42	59	1.15	20.12	0.62	24.83
4	0.03	71.18	0.02	77.44	60	1.13	19.35	0.68	23.98
5	0.02	70.19	0.01	76.46	61	1.41	18.59	0.74	23.15
6	0.02	69.21	0.01	75.47	62	1.56	17.85	0.81	22.31
7	0.02	68.22	0.01	74.48	63	1.71	17.13	0.89	21.49
8	0.01	67.23	0.01	73.48	64	1.87	16.42	0.97	20.68
9	0.01	66.24	0.01	72.49	65	2.04	15.72	1.06	19.88
10	0.02	65.25	0.01	71.50	66	2.23	15.04	1.16	19.09
11	0.02	64.26	0.01	70.51	67	2.44	14.37	1.28	18.31
12	0.02	63.27	0.02	69.52	68	2.68	13.72	1.40	17.54
13	0.03	62.28	0.02	68.53	69	2.93	13.08	1.53	16.78
14	0.05	61.30	0.02	67.54	70	3.20	12.46	1.67	16.03
15	0.07	60.33	0.03	66.56	71	3.50	11.85	1.84	15.30
16	0.08	59.37	0.03	65.58	72	3.84	11.27	2.04	14.57
17	0.09	58.42	0.04	64.60	73	4.22	10.70	2.26	13.87
18	0.10	57.47	0.04	63.62	74	4.62	10.15	2.51	13.18
19	0.11	56.53	0.04	62.64	75	5.06	9.61	2.78	12.50
20	0.11	55.58	0.04	61.67	76	5.54	9.10	3.09	11.85
21	0.11	54.64	0.04	60.69	77	6.08	8.60	3.45	11.21
22	0.11	53.70	0.04	59.71	78	6.67	8.13	3.84	10.59
23	0.12	52.77	0.04	58.73	79	7.31	7.67	4.27	9.99
24	0.12	51.83	0.04	57.75	80	7.99	7.24	4.74	9.42
25	0.11	50.89	0.04	56.77	81	8.73	6.82	5.27	8.86
26	0.11	49.94	0.04	55.80	82	9.53	6.43	5.87	8.32
27	0.11	49.00	0.04	54.82	83	10.39	6.05	6.53	7.81
28	0.12	48.05	0.04	53.84	84	11.31	5.70	7.25	7.32
29	0.12	47.11	0.05	52.86	85	12.28	5.36	8.03	6.85
30	0.12	46.17	0.05	51.89	86	13.32	5.04	8.90	6.41
31	0.13	45.22	0.05	50.91	87	14.43	4.74	9.85	5.99
32	0.13	44.28	0.05	49.94	88	15.60	4.45	10.90	5.59
33	0.14	43.34	0.06	48.96	89	16.84	4.18	12.02	5.21
34	0.14	42.39	0.06	47.99	90	18.15	3.93	13.22	4.85
35	0.15	41.45	0.07	47.02	91	19.52	3.69	14.53	4.51
36	0.16	40.51	0.07	46.05	92	20.98	3.46	15.96	4.20
37	0.16	39.58	0.08	45.09	93	22.52	3.25	17.49	3.90
38	0.17	38.64	0.09	44.12	94	24.12	3.05	19.13	3.62
39	0.18	37.71	0.09	43.16	95	25.80	2.86	20.87	3.35
40	0.19	36.77	0.10	42.20	96	27.57	2.68	22.74	3.11
41	0.20	35.84	0.11	41.24	97	29.42	2.51	24.74	2.87
42	0.21	34.91	0.12	40.28	98	31.36	2.35	26.88	2.66
43	0.23	33.98	0.13	39.33	99	33.37	2.20	29.13	2.45
44	0.25	33.06	0.15	38.38	100	35.48	2.05	31.52	2.25
45	0.28	32.14	0.17	37.44	101	37.67	1.90	34.05	2.05
46	0.31	31.23	0.19	36.50	102	39.96	1.74	36.75	1.85
47	0.34	30.32	0.21	35.57	103	42.34	1.56	39.59	1.64
48	0.37	29.42	0.23	34.64	104	44.82	1.34	42.58	1.39
49	0.41	28.53	0.25	33.72	105	47.38	1.03	45.73	1.04
50	0.45	27.65	0.27	32.80	106	100.00	0.50	100.00	0.50
51	0.50	26.77	0.30	31.89					
52	0.55	25.90	0.33	30.98					
53	0.61	25.04	0.36	30.08					
54	0.68	24.19	0.40	29.19					
55	0.75	23.35	0.43	28.30					

Source: © Census of Canada, Statistics Canada
(1) Represents the percentage of the population that will die before reaching the next age; in some cases totals do not equal 100 percent due to rounding.

Canadian Health Indicators, 1999

The table below contains approximately 100 of the indicators most commonly used to measure health, and the factors that determine the health of Canadians. Use this table to gain a general picture of the health of Canadians only. Caution should be used in drawing any conclusions from this information due to different methods of collecting data for each category. As well, estimates are not age-standardized, unless otherwise noted. For example, "Injuries" includes people of all ages with injuries while "Work injuries" covers only those age 15 and over.

Well-being
Excellent health (self-rated)	25%
High self-esteem	49%

Function
Long-term activity limitation	16%
Disability days (past 2 weeks)	0.85
Very good health (functional status)	88%

Injuries
Injuries (admissions/10 000 pop.)	72.2
Work injuries (per 1 000 workers)	27.6
Traffic deaths (per 100 000 pop.)	10
Traffic injuries (per 100 000 pop.)	762

Miscellaneous Conditions
Low birth weight rate	5.8%
Stillbirths (per 10 000 births)	65.4
Overweight (age 20 to 64)	29%

Mental Health
Depression (probable)	4%
High chronic stress	26%
Psychiatric hospitalization rate	709.1
High work stress	4%

Sexually Transmitted Diseases
HIV positive tests	41 049
Gonorrhea (per 100 000 pop.)	16.8
Chlamydia (per 100 000 pop.)	114.8

Vaccine-Preventable Diseases
Measles (per 100 000 pop.)	1.1
Whooping cough (per 100 000 pop.)	18.0

Enteric, Foodborne and Waterborne Diseases
Campylobacter (per 100 000 pop.)	42.7
Salmonella (per 100 000 pop.)	22.0
Giardia (per 100 000 pop.)	20.3
Hepatitis A (per 100 000 pop.)	8.7
E. coli 0157 (per 100 000 pop.)	4.1

Cancer (new cases per 100 000 population)
Women	346
Men	501

Cancer (deaths per 100 000 population)
Women	151
Men	232

Chronic Conditions
Arthritis/Rheumatism	14%
Asthma	7%
Back problems	14%
Food allergies	7%
Non-food allergies	22%

Deaths (per 100 000 population)
Total	653
Cancer (all)	185
Lung cancer	49
Breast cancer (women only)	29
Cardiovascular disease	226
Coronary heart disease	133
Stroke	47
Respiratory (all)	58
Pneumonia/Influenza	22
Accidents (all)	43
Suicide (all)	13
Infant mortality (per 1 000 live births)	5.6
Perinatal mortality rate (per 1 000 births)	6.7
Early neonatal mortality rate (per 1 000 live births)	3.3
Therapeutic abortions (per 100 live births)	18.7

Potential Years of Life Lost (per 100 000 population)
Total	3 804
Cancer	1 098
Accidents	746
Suicide	417
Respiratory	113
Heart disease	491
Stroke	91
Other	848

Personal Health Practices
Current smoker	28%
Regular drinker	53%
14+ drinks per week	9%
5+ drinks per occasion	42%
Driving after drinking (1+ times)	10%
Currently use cannabis	7%
1+ illicit drugs, lifetime	24%
Physically active	21%
Walk to work	7%
Always use bicycle helmet	29%
Always insist on seatbelt use	86%
Took actions to improve health	47%

Health-Care Services
Influenza vaccination, ever	26%
Pap smear test, ever (women, age 18+)	87%
Screening mammogram, past 2 years (age 50-69)	54%
Blood pressure test, past year	71%
HIV/AIDS test, ever	15%
Visits to health professional (1+)	93%
Visits to a physician (1+)	81%
Visits to a dentist, past year	62%
Dental insurance	55%
Eye examination, past year	42%
Insurance for corrective lenses	47%
1+ medications used, past two days	63%
Insurance for prescription medicines	61%
Unmet health-care needs	5%
Emergency visits (per 1 000 pop.)	433.1
Hospital (average days of stay)	1.1
Health expenditures (% of GDP)	9.2%
Per capita health expenditures	$2,512.72

Sources: © Statistics Canada; Health Canada

Chronic Conditions by Age and Region[1], 1998–99

(percentage)

	Canada	Atlantic	Quebec	Ontario	Prairies	British Columbia
45-64						
Arthritis/Rheumatism	19.9	25.7[2]	14.8[2]	21.4	23.0[2]	18.3
Hypertension	16.2	19.4[2]	15.0	17.2	16.3	13.9
Heart disease	4.8	6.1	4.6	6.1[2]	3.8	2.3[2]
Diabetes	5.1	5.9	4.1	5.7	5.8	4.4
Migraine headaches	7.5	7.1	6.7	7.5	8.0	8.9
Asthma	5.8	5.4	5.7	6.2	4.5[2]	6.6
Bronchitis/Emphysema	2.4	3.4[2]	2.1	2.3	2.5	2.6
Activity limitation	16.2	20.4[2]	13.2[2]	16.7	17.4	16.9
65+						
Arthritis/Rheumatism	41.5	44.5	34.3[2]	45.4[2]	44.1	38.8
Hypertension	35.6	41.0[2]	35.3	37.9	31.3[2]	31.4
Heart disease	17.4	19.7	14.6	18.8	16.1	19.0
Diabetes	11.6	12.7	11.8	12.5	9.6	10.7
Migraine headaches	3.3	2.9	3.1	3.2	2.9	4.7
Asthma	5.7	7.5	4.5	6.0	6.8	4.9
Bronchitis/Emphysema	5.8	6.2	6.4	5.6	4.6	6.5
Activity limitation	29.1	32.3	22.9[2]	31.4	30.4	29.8

Sources: © Health Reports; Statistics Canada
(1) Prevalence of chronic conditions or long-term activity limitation. Data collected from 1978–79 Canada Health Survey; and 1998–99 National Population Health Survey, cross sectional sample. (2) Significantly different from national average.

Canadian Health

Most Canadians enjoy good health in their middle years. Moreover, the prevalence of several chronic conditions, as well as activity limitation due to illness, has declined over the past 20 years. These trends suggest that efforts in disease prevention and health promotion, along with improvements in treatment of disease, have contributed to improved health among those aged 45 to 64, many of whom are "baby boomers."

Nevertheless, as Canadians grow older, they are more likely to perceive a decline in their health. That is, when compared with younger adults aged 25 to 44, Canadians aged 45 to 64 are more likely to report a decline in the state of their health. Such declines in self-perceived health are associated with various factors, including the presence of certain chronic conditions.

While the incidence of many chronic conditions has declined among Canadians aged 45 to 64 over the past 20 years, some chronic conditions, such as diabetes and asthma, are on the rise, with important differences between men and women. The prevalence of diabetes and asthma has increased among men; women are increasingly reporting asthma and migraine headaches.

The increase in diabetes among men is cause for concern since diabetes is a high risk factor for heart disease, stroke, blindness, kidney diseases, disability and premature death. The increased prevalence of migraine headaches among women is also cause for concern. Stress has been identified as a risk factor for migraine headaches, and more Canadian women report work-related stress than men. In addition, women who report migraine headaches have increased odds of experiencing a major depressive episode.

Sources: © Health Reports; Statistics Canada

Expected Years of Life Remaining by Sex

	At Birth		At Age 20		At Age 40		At Age 60		At Age 80	
	Male	Female	Male	Female	Male	Female	Male	Female	Male	Female
1921[1]	n.a.	n.a.	49.1	49.2	32.2	33.0	16.6	17.1	6.0	6.1
1931	60.0	62.1	49.1	49.8	32.0	33.0	16.3	17.2	5.6	5.9
1941	63.0	66.3	49.6	51.8	31.9	34.0	16.1	17.6	5.5	6.0
1951	66.3	70.8	50.8	54.4	32.5	35.6	16.5	18.6	5.8	6.4
1956	67.6	72.9	51.2	55.8	32.7	36.7	16.5	19.3	5.9	6.8
1961	68.4	74.2	51.5	56.7	33.0	37.5	16.7	19.9	6.1	6.9
1966	68.8	75.2	51.5	57.4	33.0	38.2	16.8	20.6	6.4	7.3
1971	69.3	76.4	51.7	58.2	33.2	39.0	17.0	21.4	6.4	7.9
1976	70.2	77.5	52.1	59.0	33.6	39.7	17.2	22.0	6.4	8.2
1981	71.9	79.0	53.4	60.1	34.7	40.7	18.0	22.9	6.9	8.8
1986	73.0	79.7	54.3	60.7	35.5	41.2	18.4	23.2	6.9	8.9
1991	74.6	80.9	55.6	61.7	36.8	42.2	19.4	24.0	7.2	9.4

Source: © Census Canada, Statistics Canada (n.a.) Not available. (1) Excludes Quebec.

Deaths in Canada

	Deaths	Death Rates[1]		Deaths	Death Rates[1]		Deaths	Death Rates[1]
1921[2]	104 531	11.6	1973	164 039	7.4	1986	184 224	7.0
1926[2]	111 055	11.4	1974	166 794	7.3	1987	184 953	7.0
1931[3]	108 446	10.2	1975	167 404	7.2	1988	190 011	7.1
1936[3]	111 111	9.9	1976	167 009	7.1	1989	190 965	7.0
1941[3]	118 797	10.1	1977	167 498	7.0	1990	191 973	6.9
1946	118 785	9.4	1978	168 179	7.0	1991	195 568	7.0
1951	125 823	9.0	1979	168 183	6.9	1992	196 535	6.9
1956	131 961	8.2	1980	171 473	7.0	1993	204 912	7.1
1961	140 985	7.7	1981	171 029	6.9	1994	207 077	7.1
1966	149 863	7.5	1982	174 413	6.9	1995	210 733	7.2
			1983	174 484	6.9	1996	212 859	7.2
1971	157 272	7.3	1984	175 727	6.8	1997	215 669	7.2
1972	62 413	7.4	1985	181 323	7.0	1998[4]	219 834	7.3

Source: © Statistics Canada
(1) Per 1 000 population. (2) Excludes Que., Nfld, Yukon and NWT. (3) Excludes Nfld, Yukon and NWT. (4) Updated data.

Deaths by Province[1], 1998–99

	Deaths	Death Rate[2]		Deaths	Death Rate[2]
Canada	222 425	7.3	Manitoba	9 754	8.6
Newfoundland	4 441	8.2	Saskatchewan	8 866	8.6
Prince Edward Island	1 059	7.7	Alberta	17 424	5.9
Nova Scotia	8 282	8.8	British Columbia	28 758	7.2
New Brunswick	6 143	8.1	Yukon Territory	128	4.1
Quebec	54 141	7.4	Northwest Territories	144	3.5
Ontario	83 163	7.3	Nunavut	122	4.6

Source: © Statistics Canada (1) Updated data at June 30. (2) Rate per 1 000 population.

Vital Statistics

Leading Causes of Male Death

	1977		1997	
	No. of Deaths	Rate[1]	No. of Deaths	Rate[1]
All Causes	96 872	875.5	111 1971	753.8
Diseases of the Circulatory System	45 760	413.6	39 834	268.2
Ischaemic Heart Disease	31 180	281.8	23 822	160.4
Stroke	7 160	64.7	6 673	44.9
Cancer	20 378	184.2	31 550	212.4
Lung	6 142	55.5	9 725	65.5
Prostate	1 833	16.6	3 622	24.4
Respiratory Diseases	6 828	61.7	10 608	71.4
Other Chronic Airway Obstructions	2 584	23.4	4 517	30.4
Pneumonia and Influenza	2 764	25.0	3 747	25.2
External Causes of Injury and Poisoning	11 366	102.7	8 724	58.7
Suicide	2 459	22.2	2 914	19.6
Motor Vehicle Accidents	3 831	34.6	2 110	14.2
Diseases of the Digestive System	3 742	33.8	3 791	25.5
Chronic Liver Disease and Cirrhosis	1 924	17.4	1 310	8.8
Noninfective Enteritis and Colitis	n.a.	n.a.	422	2.8
Endocrine Diseases	1 616	14.6	3 489	23.5
Diabetes Mellitus	1 289	11.7	2 767	18.6
Fluid, Electrolyte and Acid-Base Balance	85	0.8	192	1.3
Diseases of the Nervous System	1 023	9.3	2 843	19.1
Alzheimer's Disease	n.a.	n.a.	928	6.2
Parkinson's Disease	n.a.	n.a.	0.6	4.7
Mental Disorders	763	6.9	2 253	15.2
Senile and Presenile Dementia	n.a.	n.a.	831	5.6
Psychoses, including Alcoholic	154	1.4	511	3.4
All Other Causes	5 396	48.8	8 879	59.8

Source: © Statistics Canada (1) Per 100 000 population by gender.

Leading Causes of Female Death

	1977		1997	
	No. of Deaths	Rate[1]	No. of Deaths	Rate[1]
All Causes	70 626	644.3	103 668	684.3
Diseases of the Circulatory System	35 714	325.8	39 614	261.5
Ischaemic Heart Disease	20 228	184.6	19 699	130.0
Stroke	8 362	76.3	9 375	61.9
Cancer	16 041	146.5	27 142	179.1
Lung	1 519	13.9	5 713	37.7
Breast	3 321	30.3	4 945	32.6
Respiratory Diseases	4 005	36.5	9 425	62.2
Pneumonia and Influenza	2 392	21.8	4 283	28.3
Other Chronic Airway Obstructions	2 213	20.2	3 028	20.0
External Causes of Injury and Poisoning	4 635	43.4	4 324	28.5
Accidental Falls	829	7.6	1 538	10.2
Motor Vehicle Accidents	1 424	13.0	945	6.2
Endocrine Diseases	2 103	19.2	3 839	25.3
Diabetes Mellitus	1 721	15.7	2 932	19.4
Fluid, Electrolyte and Acid-Base Balance	98	0.9	323	2.1
Diseases of the Digestive System	2 388	21.8	3 839	25.3
Chronic Liver Disease and Cirrhosis	838	7.7	720	4.8
Noninfective Enteritis and Colitis	n.a.	n.a.	648	4.3
Diseases of the Nervous System	786	7.2	3 713	24.5
Alzheimer's Disease	n.a.	n.a.	1 885	12.4
Parkinson's Disease	n.a.	n.a.	578	3.8
Mental Disorders	382	3.57	3 601	23.8
Senile and Presenile Dementia	n.a.	n.a.	1 725	11.4
Psychoses, including Alcoholic	161	1.47	161	1.1
All Other Causes	4 572	41.71	8 171	54.1

Source: © Statistics Canada (1) Per 100 000 population by gender.

MIGRATION

How to Become a Canadian Citizen

To become a Canadian citizen, you must be at least 18 years of age, a permanent resident and in Canada legally.

If you are a permanent resident, you must have lived in Canada for at least three of the four years before the date of your application. If you lived in Canada before becoming a permanent resident, that time is counted at half the rate if it was during the four years before your application date.

You must be able to speak and understand spoken English or French, or be able to read and write in simple English or French.

If you are between 18 and 59 years of age, you must learn about Canada before becoming a citizen. When you apply for citizenship, you'll be sent a free publication called *A Look at Canada* on which your citizenship test will be based.

Children under 18 don't need to meet the three-year residency requirement; however, you must already be a Canadian citizen or be applying to become one. Children don't write a citizenship test.

Who Doesn't Qualify

Not everyone can become a Canadian citizen. You cannot become a citizen if

- you were convicted of an indictable offence in the past three years
- you are under a deportation order
- you were in prison, on parole or on probation in the past four years
- you have been charged with an indictable offence
- you are now charged with an offence under the Citizenship Act
- your Canadian citizenship has been revoked in the past five years
- you are under investigation for war crimes or crimes against humanity

Applying

1. **Get the correct application form.** It should be the "Application for Citizenship." Each child for whom you are applying needs a separate form.
2. **Read the form.** The cost to process your forms isn't refundable, so be sure you are ready to become a citizen and fill the form out carefully. The current fee for citizenship for adults is $200, and the fee for children under 18 is $100.
3. **Complete the application and attach necessary documents.** Photocopies of documents are acceptable, but you may need to bring the original when you take the test. The application form comes with detailed instructions.
4. **Mail the completed application.** Check that you have included all documentation and filled in the application completely.
5. **Prepare for your test.** Read the book *A Look at Canada* that will be sent to you. You may want to take a citizenship class if one is being held near you. A notice detailing the date and time of your citizenship test will be sent to you. The test may be oral or written.
6. **Take the oath.** Once you have met all the requirements, you will receive a notice detailing when and where the citizenship ceremony will take place.

Call Centres and Citizenship Offices

You can get more information on any of the topics discussed here by contacting one of the call centres listed below.

Montreal: (514) 496-1010
Toronto: (416) 973-4444
Vancouver: (604) 666-2171
Toll-free: 1-888-242-2100

Case Processing Centre
P.O. Box 7000
Sydney, NS B1P 6V6

Source: *Citizenship and Immigration Canada*

Canadian Immigration Totals

Year	Total	Year	Total	Year	Total	Year	Total
1853*	29 464	1890	75 067	1927	158 886	1964	112 606
1854*	37 263	1891	82 165	1928	166 783	1965[1]	146 758
1855*	25 296	1892	30 996	1929	164 993	1966	194 743
1856*	22 544	1893	29 633	1930	104 806	1967	222 876
1857*	33 854	1894	20 829	1931	27 530	1968	183 974
1858*	12 339	1895	18 790	1932	20 591	1969	161 531
1859*	6 300	1896	16 835	1933	14 382	1970	147 713
1860*	6 276	1897	21 716	1934	12 476	1971	121 900
1861*	13 589	1898	31 900	1935	11 277	1972	122 006
1862*	18 294	1899	44 543	1936	11 643	1973	184 200
1863*	21 000	1900	41 681	1937	15 101	1974	218 465
1864*	24 779	1901	55 747	1938	17 244	1975	187 881
1865*	18 958	1902	89 102	1939	16 994	1976	149 429
1866*	11 427	1903	138 660	1940	11 324	1977	114 914
1867	10 666	1904	131 252	1941	9 329	1978	86 313
1868	12 765	1905	141 465	1942	7 576	1979	112 096
1869	18 630	1906	211 653	1943	8 504	1980	143 117
1870	24 706	1907	272 409	1944	12 801	1981	128 618
1871	27 773	1908	143 326	1945	22 722	1982	121 147
1872	36 578	1909	173 694	1946	71 719	1983	89 157
1873	50 050	1910	286 839	1947	64 127	1984	88 239
1874	39 373	1911	331 288	1948	125 414	1985	84 302
1875	27 382	1912	375 756	1949	95 217	1986	99 219
1876	25 633	1913	400 870	1950	73 912	1987	152 098
1877	27 082	1914	150 484	1951	194 391	1988	161 929
1878	29 807	1915	36 665	1952	164 498	1989	192 001
1879	40 492	1916	55 914	1953	168 868	1990	214 230
1880	38 505	1917	72 910	1954	154 227	1991	232 020
1881	47 991	1918	41 845	1955	109 946	1992	253 345
1882	112 458	1919	107 698	1956	164 857	1993	255 935
1883	133 624	1920	138 824	1957	282 164	1994	223 912
1884	103 824	1921	91 728	1958	124 851	1995	212 463
1885	79 169	1922	64 224	1959	106 928	1996	226 072
1886	69 152	1923	133 729	1960	104 111	1997	216 048
1887	84 526	1924	124 164	1961	71 689	1998[1]	174 190
1888	88 766	1925	84 907	1962	74 586	1999[1]	189 946
1889	91 600	1926	135 982	1963	93 151		

Source: *Citizenship and Immigration Canada*   (*) Pre-Confederation. (1) Preliminary figure.

Business Immigration

Economic immigrants are selected on the basis of their ability to contribute to Canada's economic and social wellbeing. Immigrants in this component bring with them the skills, entrepreneurial spirit and business knowledge that allow them to contribute to Canada's economy soon after arrival. The 2000 Plan established a range of 116,900 to 130,700 for this component. This included 100,500 to 113,300 skilled workers; 15,000 to 16,000 business immigrants, including entrepreneurs, investors and self-employed; and 1,400 provincial nominees.

Citizenship and Immigration Canada is working to modernize its selection processes to ensure economic immigrants have the skills and business experience to allow them to adapt to a rapidly developing economy. Part of this process includes providing the means for provincial and territorial governments to participate directly in the selection of immigrants destined for their regions. Provincial nominee agreements had been struck with five provincial governments by November 1999. This ongoing process was reflected in the 1,400 provincial nominees projected in the Year 2000 Plan.

Source: *Citizenship and Immigration Canada*

Immigration to Canada[1]

	Total Immigrants	United States	Asia[2]	Europe	Caribbean[3]	South America	Africa	Oceania
1956	164 857	9 777	3 537	145 554	1 351	1 551	1 079	1 924
1957	282 164	11 008	3 244	257 540	1 586	2 376	2 970	3 345
1958	124 851	10 846	4 223	102 270	1 519	2 168	1 355	2 344
1959	106 928	11 338	5 368	84 517	1 529	1 750	843	1 512
1960	104 111	11 247	4 002	82 922	1 542	1 823	833	1 657
1961	71 689	11 516	2 706	52 132	1 454	1 301	1 088	1 432
1962	74 586	11 643	2 593	53 790	1 842	1 103	2 171	1 384
1963	93 151	11 736	3 553	69 069	2 611	1 779	2 431	1 692
1964	112 606	12 565	6 121	82 798	2 467	2 257	3 874	2 303
1965	146 758	15 143	11 215	108 285	3 420	2 471	3 196	2 711
1966	194 743	17 514	13 835	148 410	4 357	2 604	3 661	4 057
1967	222 876	19 038	20 740	159 979	9 004	3 090	4 608	6 168
1968	183 974	20 422	21 686	120 702	8 129	2 693	5 204	4 815
1969	161 531	22 785	23 319	88 363	13 908	4 767	3 297	4 411
1970	147 713	24 424	21 170	75 609	13 371	4 943	2 863	4 385
1971	121 900	24 366	22 171	52 031	11 653	5 058	2 841	2 902
1972	122 006	22 618	23 325	51 293	9 218	4 309	8 308	2 143
1973	184 200	25 242	43 193	71 883	20 704	11 057	8 307	2 671
1974	218 465	26 541	50 566	88 694	25 276	12 528	10 450	2 594
1975	187 881	20 155	47 382	72 898	19 483	13 270	9 867	2 174
1976	149 429	17 315	44 328	49 903	16 198	10 628	7 752	1 886
1977	114 914	12 888	31 368	40 748	13 187	7 840	6 372	1 545
1978	86 313	9 945	24 007	30 075	9 240	6 782	4 261	1 233
1979	112 096	9 617	50 540	32 858	7 060	5 898	3 958	1 395
1980	143 117	9 926	71 602	41 168	8 141	5 433	4 330	2 497
1981	128 618	10 559	48 831	46 299	9 625	6 163	4 889	2 253
1982	121 147	9 360	41 686	46 156	10 317	6 871	4 513	2 119
1983	89 157	7 381	36 906	24 312	10 864	4 816	3 659	1 213
1984	88 239	6 922	41 920	20 901	9 706	4 085	3 552	1 151
1985	84 302	6 669	38 597	18 859	11 143	4 356	3 545	1 128
1986	99 219	7 275	41 600	22 709	14 947	6 686	4 770	1 227
1987	152 098	7 967	67 337	37 563	18 100	10 801	8 501	1 827
1988	161 929	6 537	81 136	40 689	15 108	7 255	9 380	1 822
1989	192 001	6 931	93 261	52 105	16 764	8 685	12 199	2 041
1990	213 334	6 057	111 195	51 667	19 459	8 888	13 426	2 642
1991	232 020	20 122[4]	120 736	48 232	12 978	10 632	16 175	3 145[5]
1992	253 345	20 123[4]	139 546	44 933	14 993	10 415	19 669	3 666[5]
1993	255 935	8 025	147 378	46 622	24 315	9 588	16 922	3 085[5]
1994	223 912	6 242	141 600	38 652	13 486	7 919	13 708	2 305[5]
1995	212 463[6]	5 199	128 534	41 127	13 352	7 485	14 560	1 873[5]
1996	226 050[6]	5 896	143 956	40 009	12 958	6 115	14 836	2 058[5]
1997	216 050	5 053	138 018	38 580	8 195	5 682	14 473	2 024
1998	174 191	4 781	101 297	38 482	6 341	4 964	13 672	1 639
1999[7]	189 965[8]	5 531	112 837	38 928	6 716	5 572	15 649	1 377

Source: *Citizenship and Immigration Canada*

(1) By country of last permanent residence. (2) Includes China and Hong Kong. (3) Includes Central America, Greenland and St. Pierre & Miquelon for 1956–76; except for 1991, 1992 when North and Central America were included with U.S. figures (4) Includes North and Central America. (5) Includes Australia and other islands. (6) Includes those whose country of last permanent residence was not stated. (7) Preliminary numbers. (8) Includes those whose last permanent residence was North and Central America and those not stated.

Immigration 2000

A legislative requirement of Canada's immigration policy is to set the number and categories of immigrants who can come to Canada each year. The Year 2000 Immigration Plan set the target range of immigrants to 177,900–195,700, and refugees 22,100–29,300.
The Immigration Plan for 2001 will be tabled in November 2000.

Immigration by Province of Intended Destination

	Total immigrants[1]	Nfld	PEI	NS	NB	Que	Ont	Man	Sask	Alta	BC	YT	NWT
1956	164 857	426	112	1 639	852	31 396	90 662	5 796	2 202	9 959	17 812	n.a.	n.a.
1960	104 111	306	83	1 210	634	23 774	54 491	4 337	2 087	6 949	10 120	n.a.	n.a.
1965	146 758	604	137	1 612	1 074	30 346	79 702	3 948	2 649	8 049	18 502	n.a.	n.a.
1970	147 713	630	185	2 007	1 070	23 261	80 732	5 826	1 709	10 405	21 683	n.a.	n.a.
1975	187 881	1106	235	2 124	2 093	28 042	98 471	7 134	2 837	16 277	29 272	n.a.	n.a.
1980	143 117	541	190	1 616	1 207	22 538	62 257	7 683	3 603	18 839	24 437	n.a.	n.a.
1981	128 618	483	128	1 405	990	21 182	55 032	5 370	2 402	19 330	22 095	n.a.	n.a.
1982	121 147	406	165	1 256	751	21 336	53 049	4 931	2 125	17 949	18 999	n.a.	n.a.
1983	89 157	275	105	833	554	16 374	40 036	3 978	1 735	10 688	14 447	n.a.	n.a.
1984	88 239	299	109	1 034	600	14 641	41 527	3 903	2 150	10 670	13 190	n.a.	n.a.
1985	84 302	325	113	974	609	14 884	40 730	3 415	1 905	9 001	12 239	n.a.	n.a.
1986	99 219	274	168	1 097	641	19 459	49 630	3 749	1 860	9 673	12 552	49	67
1987	152 098	458	159	1 227	642	26 822	84 807	4 799	2 119	11 975	18 913	80	72
1988	161 929	408	153	1 299	679	25 789	88 996	5 009	2 223	14 025	23 204	68	76
1989	192 001	468	159	1 473	905	34 171	104 799	6 138	2 142	16 211	25 335	100	100
1990	214 230	546	176	1 563	842	40 842	113 438	6 637	2 361	18 994	28 723	83	75
1991	232 020	641	150	1 504	685	52 155	119 257	5 659	2 455	17 043	32 263	84	124
1992	253 345	787	151	2 359	754	48 597	138 453	5 084	2 511	17 696	36 709	133	111
1993	255 935	807	165	3 021	702	44 964	134 420	4 874	2 403	18 580	45 724	104	171
1995	212 463	585	167	3 581	639	27 182	115 681	3 603	1 949	14 329	44 541	108	91
1996	226 072	585	154	3 225	717	29 802	119 072	3 928	1 824	13 896	52 026	87	92
1997[2]	216 048	431	150	2 873	631	27 905	117 431	3 799	1 759	12 976	47 880	86	101
1998[2]	174 190	412	136	2 059	750	26 645	92 220	3 015	1 578	11 214	35 998	62	63
1999[2,3]	189 946	432	138	1 609	679	29 208	104 069	3 716	1 723	12 071	36 098	75	61

Source: *Citizenship and Immigration Canada*
(1) Includes those whose destination was not stated. (2) Preliminary figures. (3) Six immigrants reported Nunavut as their destination for 1999.

Persons Granted Canadian Citizenship[1]

Year	Count	Year	Count	Year	Count	Year	Count
1920	3 004	1940	18 207	1960	62 378	1980	118 590
1921	10 507	1941	15 594	1961	56 476	1981	94 457
1922	10 360	1942	14 213	1962	72 082	1982	87 468
1923	7 589	1943	12 533	1963	69 468	1983	90 328
1924	7 659	1944	12 827	1964	64 334	1984	109 504
1925	13 288	1945	13 562	1965	63 844	1985	126 466
1926	15 403	1946	9 047	1966	60 852	1986	103 800
1927	16 917	1947	15 335	1967	59 968	1987	73 638
1928	13 466	1948	11 410	1968	60 055	1988	58 810
1929	13 099	1949	11 991[2]	1969	59 900	1989	87 478
1930	21 221	1950	10 441	1970	57 556	1990	104 267
1931	21 392	1951	10 301	1971	63 669	1991	118 630
1932	32 517	1952	10 888	1972	80 866	1992	115 757
1933	23 613	1953	13 562	1973	104 697	1993	150 543
1934	21 908	1954	19 545	1974	130 278	1994	217 320
1935	20 903	1955	58 711	1975	137 507	1995	227 720
1936	30 679	1956	55 404	1976	117 276	1996	166 627
1937	31 744	1957	95 462	1977	123 655	1997	154 624
1938	27 455	1958	84 183	1978	223 214	1998	134 485
1939	21 418	1959	71 280	1979	156 699	1999	158 743

Source: *Citizenship and Immigration Canada*
(1) For fiscal year ending Mar 31 for 1920 to 1951; calendar years 1952 onwards. (2) Does not include approx 359 000 Newfoundlanders who became Canadian citizens when Newfoundland became Canada's 10th province in 1949.

Refugees to Canada[1]

Year	Count	Year	Count	Year	Count	Year	Count
1960	2 329	1970	1 361	1980	40 638	1990	36 093
1961	1 813	1971	614	1981	15 058	1991	35 891
1962	1 733	1972	5 204	1982	17 000	1992	36 943
1963	2 024	1973	2 381	1983	14 062	1993	24 835
1964	2 279	1974	1 656	1984	15 553	1994	19 739
1965	2 131	1975	6 109	1985	17 000	1995	27 753
1966	2 058	1976	5 576	1986	19 485	1996	28 352
1967	1 499	1977	3 670	1987	21 950	1997	24 221
1968	9 971	1978	3 038	1988	27 230	1998	22 787
1969	3 604	1979	27 894	1989	37 361	1999	24 378

Source: *Refugees Branch, Citizenship and Immigration Canada*
(1) Includes persons admitted from abroad as Convention Refugees or members of Designated Classes, as well as persons recognized in Canada as Convention Refugees or members of the special Backlog Clearance Designated Class. Does not include special humanitarian movements of other persons.

Refugees by Province of Destination[1]

Year	Total[2]	Nfld	PEI	NS	NB	Que	Ont	Man	Sask	Alta	BC	YT	NWT
1980	40 631	145	40	669	422	8 110	15 460	2 829	2 148	5 567	5 185	29	27
1981	14 997	28	11	119	76	3 257	5 544	822	657	2 751	1 722	6	4
1982	16 991	40	28	161	47	3 200	7 013	1 031	644	3 112	1 706	7	2
1983	14 062	11	17	89	61	2 184	6 100	844	574	2 488	1 692	0	2
1984	15 553	40	20	175	85	2 228	6 900	1 032	773	2 446	1 848	1	5
1985	17 000	55	33	206	165	1 906	8 301	1 131	749	2 529	1 919	1	5
1986	19 485	77	43	253	170	2 530	9 580	1 350	777	2 677	2 018	5	5
1987	21 921	87	45	241	192	3 216	11 026	1 366	791	2 673	2 277	3	4
1988	27 230	93	18	290	208	3 690	14 716	1 653	806	3 265	2 453	7	1
1989	37 361	94	49	329	194	5 137	21 585	1 929	815	4 535	2 679	9	6
1990	36 093	94	50	361	182	5 085	20 644	2 325	776	4 118	2 447	6	5
1991	35 891	265	40	337	211	6 284	21 342	1 579	706	2 738	2 382	4	3
1992	36 943	220	28	176	95	7 111	22 894	1 048	568	2 428	2 374	1	0
1993	24 835	243	41	189	100	5 776	14 433	692	375	1 649	1 325	1	11
1994	19 739	225	64	173	137	4 430	10 485	582	515	1 606	1 520	2	0
1995	27 753	208	61	223	179	6 122	16 413	663	575	1 447	1 854	8	0
1996	28 352	173	72	232	189	8 909	13 937	683	547	1 341	2 264	2	3
1997	24 221	133	63	211	150	7 686	11 646	621	558	1 156	1 996	1	0
1998	22 787	113	58	235	162	6 227	11 496	655	532	1 275	2 033	0	1
1999	24 378	157	67	261	154	7 335	11 941	771	510	1 286	1 896	0	0

Source: © *Refugees Branch, Citizenship and Immigration Canada* (1) Includes Refugees Resettled from Abroad, their Dependants and inland Determination where destination is known. (2) Shows only those whose destination was identified.

Canadian Emigration by Province[1]

(number of persons moving from Canada)

	Canada	Nfld	PEI	NS	NB	Que	Ont	Man	Sask	Alta	BC	YT	NWT	NVT
1976–81[1]	278 228	1 812	434	2 509	4 643	46 110	131 672	9 873	4 982	37 891	37 773	384	145	n.a.
1981–86[1]	277 579	2 274	483	2 413	4 651	43 062	125 735	9 305	5 778	42 666	40 540	363	309	n.a.
1986–91[1]	212 532	1 378	283	2 860	4 366	28 496	91 635	10 799	4 527	35 105	32 446	254	383	n.a.
1991–96	229 136	1 353	309	4 228	4 744	30 938	97 178	11 047	4 875	38 639	35 036	332	387	n.a.
1996–97[2]	48 970	208	27	493	192	9 365	24 987	1 288	774	5 563	5 919	48	64	42
1998–99[2]	58 787	262	34	592	182	11 048	30 048	1 563	906	6 728	7 234	64	79	47

Source: © *Statistics Canada* (n.a.) Not applicable. (1) Year end June 30. (2) Revised data.

Where Canadians Move Within Canada

When Canadians move from one province to another, it tends to be directly related to economic conditions. This trend was most apparent during 1977–81 when the resource boom in Alberta caused a large influx from other provinces. But falling international oil prices in the early 1980s led to a reversal of this trend as Canadians moved east, especially to Ontario.

The following table shows net interprovincial migration—the number of persons moving into a province minus the number of persons moving out of that province.

	Nfld	PEI	NS	NB	Que	Ont	Man	Sask	Alta	BC	YT	NWT	NVT[1]
1977–81	-21 086	-1 451	-8 185	-13 680	-156 817	-60 890	-42 115	-11 729	190 719	131 176	-2 363	-3 579	n.a.
1982–86	-14 117	811	7 442	835	-67 235	165 460	-2 395	-7 057	-82 737	3 226	-2 393	-1 840	n.a.
1987–91	-11 355	-65	-607	-2 063	-45 406	28 876	-39 533	-69 397	-13 198	154 126	871	-2 249	n.a.
1992–95	-18 730	1 826	-5 454	-3 015	-37 711	-32 592	-18 977	-19 418	242	135 036	-129	-1 078	n.a.
1996[2]	-8 380	315	-246	-1 263	-14 711	-5 942	-2 638	-1 160	13 902	20 665	168	-710	n.a.
1997[3]	-9 279	-466	-3 555	-1 688	-17 789	5 149	-7 008	-3 288	33 834	5 554	-433	-1 231	n.a.
1998[3]	-7 972	-76	-1 491	-2 847	-15 674	11 118	-2 801	-327	43 381	-20 984	-1 455	-852	-20
1999[4]	-2 794	703	1 418	305	-15 008	17 228	-950	-5 916	16 602	-11 285	-761	376	82

Source: © Statistics Canada (n.a.) Not applicable.
(1) Nunavut became a territory in 1999. (2) Updated postcensal estimates. (3) Updated data. (4) Preliminary data.

Population Growth Components
(thousands)

Population growth is made up of natural increase (births minus deaths) plus net migration (immigration minus emigration). As the birth rate in Canada falls and the death rate continues to rise, the role of immigration becomes an increasingly important factor in population growth. By 2030, natural increase is expected to be close to zero, and immigration will become our sole source of population growth.

	Total Population Growth	Natural Increase		Net Migration	
		Births	Deaths	Immigration	Emigration
1851–1861	793	1 281	670	352	170
1861–1871	459	1 370	760	260	411
1871–1881	636	1 480	790	350	404
1881–1891	508	1 524	870	680	826
1891–1901	538	1 548	880	250	380
1901–11	1 836	1 925	900	1 550	739
1911–21	1 581	2 340	1 070	1 400	1 089
1921–31	1 589	2 415	1 055	1 200	971
1931–41	1 130	2 294	1 072	149	241
1941–51	2 141	3 186	1 214	548	379
1951–56	2 072	2 106	633	783	184
1956–61	2 157	2 362	687	760	278
1961–66	1 777	2 249	731	539	280
1966–71	1 553	1 856	766	890	427
1971–76	1 492	1 755	824	1 053	492
1976–81	1 382	1 820	843	771	366
1981–86	1 304	1 872	885	677	360
1986–91	1 907	1 933	946	1 199	279
1991–96	1 848	1 935	1 027	1 170	230
1997[1]	321	349	216	216	50[2]
1998[1]	237	343	220	174	58
1999[1]	258	339	225	190[2]	61

Source: © Statistics Canada (n.a.) Not applicable.
(1) Updated data. (2) Preliminary data.

FOCUS ON...

Changes in Immigration: The Immigration and Refugee Protection Act

As Canada enters a new century, it needs new immigration and refugee protection legislation that can respond quickly to a rapidly evolving environment and to emerging challenges and opportunities. Immigration has proven to be an essential social, cultural and economic lever for Canada in the past. It will be equally vital in the future.

Main Areas of Reform

The proposed *Immigration and Refugee Protection Act*, Bill C-31, and its regulations carry a dual mandate: closing the door to criminals and others who would abuse the system, while opening the door to genuine refugees and to the immigrants the country needs. New legislative provisions aim to better ensure serious criminals and individuals who are threats to public safety are kept out of Canada and that where they have entered the country, they can be removed as quickly as possible. At the same time, Bill C-31 renews the commitment to family reunification so that Canadian citizens, permanent residents and refugees can be reunited with their families as soon as possible, and provides a fair, efficient and adaptable process for welcoming those immigrants who will help Canada grow.

With this dual mandate in mind, the new legislation focuses on the following main areas of reform:

- **Creating a simpler legislative framework that reflects Canadian values and is responsive to current realities.**
- **Maintaining the safety of Canadian society and respect for Canadian standards of social responsibility.** Reforms cover new inadmissibility provisions; tougher penalties for trafficking and smuggling; penalties for fraud and forged documents, as well as the broader fraud of counselling misrepresentation; simplifying the security certificate process to deal more effectively with criminals and security threats; and clearer detention grounds.
- **Introducing transparent criteria for permanent resident status.** Bill C-31 sets objective, transparent and flexible criteria to assess a person's right to retain permanent resident status when they wish to return to Canada following an absence. These criteria replace a vague, highly subjective and easy to abuse test in the current *Act*.
- **Strengthening refugee protection and the integrity of the refugee determination process.** Reforms include enhancing the overseas resettlement program; making the review process more efficient and faster; and granting more authority and independence to the Immigration and Refugee Board, while requiring reasons for all decisions made by the Board.
- **Improving the effectiveness and integrity of the immigration appeal system.** Improvement to the system would include denying the appeal process to serious criminals (and sponsors) if the applicant has been found to be a serious criminal, security risk, human rights violator or was refused because of misrepresentation of a material fact. As well, the judicial review will be streamlined. Re-opening of appeals will be allowed only if the Appeal Division is satisfied that there has been a breach of natural justice.
- **Modernizing the selection system for skilled workers and business immigrants, and facilitating the entry of highly skilled temporary foreign workers.** Emphasis will be shifted from choosing on occupation-based criteria to assessing the solid transferable skills of workers, and a more objective assessment of business experience. Faster approvals of highly skilled temporary workers will take place, in exchange for employers' commitment to hire and train Canadian workers. As well, a new in-Canada "landing" class will be created for these temporary workers who may ultimately prove that they can fill a permanent need.
- **Strengthening family reunification.** The existence of the family class will be formally acknowledged, while its definition broadened, and the best interest of any children affected by the decision will be taken into account.

Source: *Citizenship and Immigration Canada*
NOTE: A tabled Bill is not enacted and does not have effect in law.

SOCIAL TRENDS

Marriages and Divorces in Canada

	Marriages				Divorces		
	Total	Rate[1]	Average Age at Marriage Brides[3]	Average Age at Marriage Grooms[3]	Total	Rate[1]	Average Length of Marriage[2]
1925	66 378	6.9	25.3	29.8	550	0.1	n.a.
1930	73 341	7.0	25.0	29.2	875	0.1	n.a.
1935	78 908	7.1	25.0	29.0	1 431	0.1	n.a.
1940	125 797	10.8	25.2	28.9	2 416	0.2	n.a.
1945	111 376	9.0	25.5	29.0	5 101	0.4	n.a.
1950	125 083	9.1	25.3	28.5	5 386	0.4	n.a.
1955	128 029	8.2	25.1	28.0	6 053	0.4	n.a.
1960	130 338	7.3	24.7	27.7	6 980	0.4	n.a.
1965	145 519	7.4	24.5	27.2	8 974	0.5	n.a.
1970	188 428	8.8	24.9	27.3	29 775	1.4	n.a.
1975	197 585	8.5	22.0	24.4	50 611	2.2	11.1
1980	191 069	7.8	22.8	25.0	62 019	2.6	11.5
1985	184 096	7.1	24.1	26.2	61 980	2.4	11.6
1986	175 518	6.7	24.3	26.5	78 160	3.1	11.5
1987	182 151	6.9	24.7	26.9	90 985	3.6	11.4
1988	187 728	7.0	25.0	27.1	83 507	3.1	11.3
1989	190 640	7.0	25.2	27.3	80 998	3.0	11.2
1990	187 737	6.8	25.5	27.4	78 463	2.8	11.1
1991	172 251	6.1	25.7	27.7	77 020	2.7	11.0
1992	164 573	5.8	26.0	28.0	79 034	2.8	10.9
1993	159 316	5.6	26.8	28.7	78 226	2.7	10.7
1994	159 959	5.5	26.9	28.8	78 880	2.7	10.7
1995	160 251	5.5	27.1	29.0	77 636	2.6	10.7
1996	156 692	5.3	27.3	29.3	71 528	2.4	10.8
1997	153 306	5.1	26.8	28.8	67 408	2.2	n.a.
1998[4]	153 190	5.0	n.a.	n.a.	68 073	2.3	n.a.

Source: © Statistics Canada (n.a.) Not available.

(1) Rate per 1 000 population. (2) Refers to the average length (in years) of those marriages ending in divorce during the year stated. (3) Data after 1975 represents average age of bride and groom at first marriage. (4) Updated data.

Marriages and Divorces by Province

	Marriages				Divorces			
	1997		1998		1997		1998	
	Total	Rate[1]	Total	Rate[1]	Total	Rate[2]	Total	Rate[2]
Canada	153 306	5.1	153 190	5.0	67 408	2.2	68 073	2.3
Newfoundland	3 227	5.8	3 117	5.5	822	1.5	817	1.5
Prince Edward Island	876	6.4	866	6.4	243	1.8	243	1.8
Nova Scotia	5 177	5.5	5 125	5.5	1 986	2.1	1 993	2.1
New Brunswick	4 089	5.4	4 044	5.4	1 373	1.8	1 376	1.8
Quebec	23 958	3.3	23 746	3.0	17 478	2.4	17 543	2.4
Ontario	64 535	5.7	64 536	5.7	23 629	2.1	23 923	2.1
Manitoba	6 261	5.5	6 218	5.5	2 625	2.3	2 629	2.3
Saskatchewan	5 707	5.6	5 730	5.5	2 198	2.2	2 208	2.2
Alberta	17 254	6.1	17 651	6.1	7 185	2.5	7 353	2.5
British Columbia	21 845	5.5	21 788	5.6	9 692	2.4	9 810	2.5
Yukon Territory	167	5.2	161	5.3	101	3.1	99	3.1
Northwest Territories	144	3.4	142	2.5	51	1.2	51	1.2
Nunavut	66	3.5	66	2.5	28	1.1	28	1.1

Source: © Statistics Canada (1) Rate per 1 000 population. (2) Rate per 100 marriages. (3) Updated data.

Marital Status of the Canadian Population, 1999[1]

Age Group	Total Population Male (000s)	Total Population Female (000s)	Single Male (%)	Single Female (%)	Married Male (%)	Married Female (%)	Widowed Male (%)	Widowed Female (%)	Divorced Male (%)	Divorced Female (%)
Total Population 15+	12 068.0	12 505.9	32.6	25.4	60.1	58.2	2.2	9.9	5.1	6.5
15-19	1 058.4	1 003.5	99.8	99.2	0.2	0.8	...	...	...	...
20-24	1 052.2	1 007.5	91.6	80.3	8.1	19.1	...	0.1	0.2	0.5
25-29	1 069.6	1 043.6	59.8	41.6	38.6	55.8	...	0.2	1.5	2.4
30-34	1 181.6	1 157.0	33.7	20.8	62.5	73.9	0.1	0.3	3.7	5.0
35-39	1 361.8	1 341.7	22.2	14.4	71.9	77.9	0.2	0.6	5.7	7.1
40-44	1 283.7	1 283.2	15.2	10.8	76.9	78.6	0.3	1.2	7.6	9.5
45-49	1 123.4	1 128.1	10.9	8.4	79.5	77.9	0.6	2.2	9.1	11.6
50-54	976.3	982.7	7.9	6.6	81.9	77.1	1.0	4.1	9.2	12.2
55-59	739.7	755.5	6.4	5.6	83.4	75.1	1.7	7.9	8.5	11.4
60-64	604.1	629.6	6.0	5.2	83.4	70.9	3.3	14.5	7.3	9.5
65-69	548.4	592.8	6.1	5.3	82.1	63.2	5.6	23.7	6.2	7.7
70-74	446.3	542.9	6.0	5.6	79.6	52.1	9.6	36.7	4.8	5.6
75-79	325.9	462.6	5.7	6.1	75.9	39.4	15.1	50.6	3.4	3.9
80-84	177.2	299.3	5.4	7.3	68.3	24.6	23.9	65.5	2.5	2.5
85-89	86.5	181.7	5.8	8.5	57.0	13.2	35.3	76.8	1.8	1.5
90+	32.9	94.1	6.4	9.9	37.7	4.3	54.6	85.1	1.3	0.7

Source: © Statistics Canada   (...) Less than 0.1 percent. (1) As of July 1.

Fertility Rates[1] by Age and Province, 1997

The total fertility rate represents the average number of children that a woman would have if throughout her life she experienced the fertility observed in a given year. The total fertility rate has to reach 2.1 children per woman to ensure that replacement levels are maintained.

The rate has remained below replacement level since 1971. Between 1989 and 1995, the rate has fluctuated between 1.72 and 1.67, and dropped in 1996 to 1.62, and 1.55 in 1997.

	Total Fertility Rate	15-19	20-24	25-29	30-34	35-39	40-44	45+
Canada	1.6	20.2	64.0	103.7	84.4	32.5	5.2	0.2
Newfoundland	1.3	22.8	59.2	90.6	61.4	17.3	2.2	0.2
Prince Edward Island	1.6	29.0	76.1	111.8	75.7	27.3	6.1	—[2]
Nova Scotia	1.4	23.9	68.7	98.1	71.5	24.5	3.1	0.2
New Brunswick	1.4	25.7	76.0	101.3	64.7	17.1	2.4	—[2]
Quebec	1.5	15.6	66.9	111.5	79.5	26.5	3.9	0.1
Ontario	1.5	17.2	53.6	98.6	91.3	38.1	6.3	0.2
Manitoba	1.8	36.7	85.4	115.9	87.3	33.2	4.7	0.3
Saskatchewan	1.8	38.1	94.7	123.3	79.4	27.0	4.0	0.4
Alberta	1.7	26.1	75.3	112.4	84.8	32.4	5.6	0.1
British Columbia	1.5	17.6	59.5	94.2	83.1	35.7	6.0	0.3
Yukon	1.8	31.5	90.5	114.7	82.5	37.1	7.7	—[2]
Northwest Territories	2.0	56.0	117.5	102.7	79.2	41.2	7.6	—[2]
Nunavut	3.4	144.1	215.2	164.9	97.4	48.5	8.5	—[2]

Source: © Statistics Canada   (1) Rate per 1 000. (2) Nil or zero.

Lone-Parent Families by Province[1], 1999

Province	Lone-Parent Families	Average Family Size	Male Parent	Average Family Size	Female Parent	Average Family Size
Canada	1 256 877	2.5	208 600	2.4	1 048 277	2.6
Newfoundland	21 676	2.4	3 211	2.4	18 465	2.5
Prince Edward Island	5 817	2.6	991	2.5	4 826	2.6
Nova Scotia	43 575	2.5	6 477	2.3	37 098	2.6
New Brunswick	31 565	2.5	5 096	2.4	26 469	2.5
Quebec	334 806	2.5	62 145	2.3	272 661	2.5
Ontario	476 704	2.6	72 249	2.4	404 455	2.6
Manitoba	43 830	2.6	7 083	2.5	36 747	2.7
Saskatchewan	38 724	2.7	6 020	2.6	32 704	2.7
Alberta	103 424	2.6	18 770	2.4	84 654	2.6
British Columbia	156 756	2.6	26 558	2.4	130 198	2.6

Source: © Statistics Canada
(1) Preliminary intercensal estimates as of July 1.

Lone-Parent Families by Age[1], 1999

	Total Families	Size of Families		
		2 Members	3 Members	4 or more Members
Headed by Male Parent	**208 600**	**141 286**	**52 609**	**14 705**
Age 15-24	1 944	1 648	234	62
25-34	20 839	140 041	5 427	1 371
35-44	66 148	39 504	20 659	5 985
45-54	67 600	44 373	18 140	5 087
55-64	25 209	18 976	4 985	1 248
65+	26 860	22 744	3 164	952
Headed by Female Parent	**1 048 277**	**607 173**	**318 348**	**122 756**
Age 15-24	65 118	47 486	14 787	2 845
25-34	226 157	110 217	79 717	36 223
35-44	336 401	148 904	130 176	57 321
45-54	221 624	134 388	67 123	20 113
55-64	78 956	62 253	13 422	3 281
65+	120 021	103 925	13 123	2 973

Source: © Statistics Canada
(1) Preliminary postcensal estimates as of July 1.

Census Families[1] in Private Households

	1991	1996
Total families	7 355 730	7 837 865
Total husband-wife families	6 402 090	6 700 360
Families of married couples	5 682 815	5 779 720
Families of common-law couples	719 275	920 640
Total lone-parent families	953 640	1 137 510
Male parent	165 240	192 275
Female parent	788 395	945 230
Total persons in families	22 568 125	23 907 975
Average number of persons per family	3.1	3.1
Total persons not in families	4 163 580	4 482 710

Source: © Census of Canada, Statistics Canada
(1) A married or common-law couple living together, with or without never-married sons or daughters; or a lone parent living with at least one never-married son or daughter. Census families in private households exclude families living in institutions or other types of collective dwellings.

Composition of Canadian Families

(thousands)

	1971 No. of Families	1971 %	1981 No. of Families	1981 %	1991 No. of Families	1991 %	1996 No. of Families	1996 %
Total families[1]	5 071	100.0	6 325	100.0	7 356	100.0	7 838	100.0
Without children at home	1 545	30.5	2 013	31.8	2 580	35.1	2 730	35.0
With children at home	3 526	69.5	4 312	68.2	4 776	64.9	5 108	65.2
With one child	1 045	20.6	1 580	25.0	1 945	26.4	2 106	27.0
two children	1 077	21.2	1 648	26.1	1 927	26.2	2 047	26.1
three children	677	13.4	730	11.5	691	9.4	729	9.3
four children	367	7.2	243	3.8	165	2.2	175	2.2
five children or more	360	7.1	112	1.8	48	0.5	51	0.6
Lone parent families	471	9.3	653	10.3	955	13.0	1 137	14.5
lone female parent	371	7.3	541	8.6	786	10.7	945	12.1
lone male parent	100	2.0	112	1.8	168	2.3	192	2.5

Source: © Census of Canada, Statistics Canada

(1) Based on the census family definition: a husband and wife (without children or with children who never married) or a parent with one or more children who never married, living together in the same home.

Size of Families in Canada

(thousands)

	1971 No. of Families	1971 Avg. Size	1981 No. of Families	1981 Avg. Size	1991 No. of Families	1991 Avg. Size	1996 No. of Families	1996 Avg. Size
Canada	5 071	3.7	6 325	3.3	7 356	3.1	7 838	3.1
Newfoundland	108	4.4	135	3.8	151	3.3	156	3.1
Prince Edward Island	24	4.0	30	3.5	34	3.2	36	3.2
Nova Scotia	181	3.8	216	3.3	245	3.1	254	3.0
New Brunswick	140	4.0	177	3.4	198	3.1	207	3.0
Quebec	1 357	3.9	1 672	3.3	1 883	3.0	1 950	3.0
Ontario	1 882	3.6	2 279	3.2	2 727	3.1	2 933	3.1
Manitoba	236	3.6	262	3.2	286	3.1	293	3.1
Saskatchewan	216	3.7	246	3.3	258	3.2	260	3.1
Alberta	382	3.7	566	3.3	668	3.1	718	3.1
British Columbia	534	3.5	728	3.1	888	3.0	1 008	3.0
Yukon	11[1]	4.3[1]	6	3.3	7	3.1	8	3.1
Northwest Territories	11[1]	4.3[1]	9	4.0	13	3.7	15	3.6

Source: © Census of Canada, Statistics Canada

(1) Includes both the Yukon and Northwest Territories.

Estimates of Family Size, 1999[1]

Statistics Canada estimates that the size of Canadian families has continued to drop during the 1990s. Compare these estimates with the chart above:

	No. of Families (000's)	Avg. Size
Canada	8 142 312	3.0
Newfoundland	154 701	3.0
Prince Edward Island	37 235	3.1
Nova Scotia	257 790	3.0
New Brunswick	214 108	3.0
Quebec	1 989 046	3.0
Ontario	3 081 072	3.1
Manitoba	297 803	3.1
Saskatchewan	268 222	3.1
Alberta	783 837	3.1
British Columbia	1 058 498	3.0

Source: © Statistics Canada

(1) Preliminary postcensal estimates as of July 1.

Household Internet Use[1] by Province
(percentage of households)

	Home		Work		School		Public Library		Other		Any Location	
	1997	1999	1997	1999	1997	1999	1997	1999	1997	1999	1997	1999
All provinces	16.0	28.7	19.9	21.9	9.4	14.9	3.7	4.5	2.8	4.1	29.4	41.8
Newfoundland	12.4	18.1	15.7	14.2	12.9	18.0	4.3	5.5	...	4.0	26.6	35.2
Prince Edward Island	10.5	20.1	16.6	19.7	11.4	19.0	2.0	3.6[2]	2.2	3.4[2]	26.0	40.5
Nova Scotia	14.3	26.7	20.7	19.7	14.3	14.5	5.0	3.8	3.1	5.0	32.2	41.1
New Brunswick	12.1	23.6	18.0	19.2	10.7	13.1	2.6	2.4	4.9	4.1	29.1	38.0
Quebec	10.2	21.2	13.1	17.2	5.6	11.2	2.1	3.4	1.8	3.4	20.1	33.1
Ontario	19.3	32.0	23.3	24.2	10.6	16.0	4.4	4.9	3.1	3.5	33.2	44.5
Manitoba	13.7	24.7	20.4	20.2	9.4	14.4	3.3	2.8	3.1	4.1	29.3	38.3
Saskatchewan	12.3	23.6	18.2	19.3	8.9	16.6	2.8	4.1	3.3	5.2	27.2	39.9
Alberta	18.7	34.1	25.8	27.6	11.8	21.2	4.3	5.0	3.4	4.9	34.5	50.8
British Columbia	19.9	35.8	21.2	23.6	9.6	14.6	4.5	6.3	3.1	6.5	33.6	48.1

Source: © Statistics Canada   (...) Not included due to unreliable estimate.
(1) Households with at least one regular user, by point of use. (2) Low reliability estimate due to sample size.

Household Internet Use in 15 Cities[1]
(percentage of households)

	1997	1998	1999
Canada	29.4	35.9	41.8
Calgary, Alta	41.1	52.8	60.1
Ottawa, Ont.[2]	55.6	55.4	59.9
Victoria, B.C.	40.1	48.5	56.4
Halifax, N.S.	39.2	50.3	52.4
Vancouver, B.C.	35.9	45.7	49.7
Edmonton, Alta.	35.9	43.9	48.8
Toronto, Ont.	38.0	42.0	48.5
London, Ont.	31.8	41.2	45.9
Kitchener, Ont.	34.9	42.4	43.7
Hamilton, Ont.	30.4	41.2	43.1
Winnipeg, Man.	33.1	37.8	42.1
Montreal, Que.	24.3	31.6	39.1
St. Catharines-Niagara, Ont.	26.1	29.3	34.4
Quebec, Que.	23.9	28.6	33.9
Windsor	25.7	26.8	33.6

Source: © Statistics Canada   (1) Households in top 15 Census Metropolitan Areas with at least one regular user. Information was collected through the monthly household Labour Force Survey. (2) Data includes the Ontario portion only.

Internet Usage

*C*anadians are logging onto the Internet in growing numbers. In 1999, the proportion of households that contained at least one regular user jumped to 41.8 percent from 35.9 percent in 1998. Internet use, measured by household, was higher from both homes and schools, according to data from the 1999 Household Internet Use Survey, while personal Internet use at work decreased slightly and in public libraries remained unchanged.

For the first time, home was the most popular location for Internet use at 28.7 percent of households in 1999, up from 22.6 percent of households in 1998. This might reflect expansion of Internet services offered to households and lower connection costs.

Regular household Internet use from work dropped into second place at 21.9 percent in 1999 from 23.3 percent in 1998. This could be due in part to the development of workplace policies limiting personal Internet use. The third most popular location was from school, which rose to 14.9 percent from 12.1 percent in 1998. Internet use from public libraries was steady at 4.5 percent in 1999.

Other locations, such as the homes of friends, neighbours and relatives as well as Internet cafés, saw an increase to 4.1 percent in 1999, up from 2.6 percent the previous year.

Alberta continued to lead with the highest proportion of households with regular Internet users, from any location, at 50.8 percent in 1999, up from 45.1 percent in 1998. British Columbia was a close second at 48.1 percent in 1999, compared with 42.0 percent in 1998. The province with the highest proportion of regular home Internet use was British Columbia (35.8 percent), just ahead of Alberta (34.1 percent) in 1999.

Source: © Statistics Canada

Average Annual Income in Canada by Family Type[1]

	1993	1994	1995	1996	1997	1998
Economic families, 2 persons or more[2].	**$45 728**	**$46 300**	**$46 159**	**$46 915**	**$47 838**	**$49 626**
Elderly families[3]	**37 452**	**37 103**	**38 435**	**35 552**	**36 045**	**36 051**
Married couples	34 655	34 553	34 960	34 408	34 894	34 846
All other elderly families	43 938	43 668	47 414	39 932	40 107	40 415
Non-elderly families[4]	**47 177**	**47 929**	**47 580**	**48 665**	**49 681**	**51 776**
Married couples	**45 252**	**45 325**	**45 487**	**46 935**	**48 359**	**49 759**
No earner	22 809	23 619	22 139	24 229	24 304	24 027
One earner	37 451	37 098	36 403	36 153	38 379	40 399
Two earners	50 774	50 943	51 327	53 772	54 344	56 232
Two-parent families with children[5]	**50 650**	**51 311**	**50 945**	**51 229**	**52 590**	**55 074**
No earner	19 476	18 790	17 548	19 156	20 226	19 771
One earner	37 546	38 511	37 076	38 616	37 216	41 860
Two earners	51 393	52 580	52 431	52 959	54 257	56 090
Three or more earners	65 548	65 426	65 116	65 837	67 630	68 316
Married couples with other relatives[6]	**64 237**	**64 820**	**63 231**	**66 831**	**67 411**	**69 130**
Lone-parent families[5]	**23 559**	**23 964**	**24 323**	**24 485**	**24 506**	**26 279**
Male lone-parent families	31 008	30 138	30 793	34 001	33 842	36 180
Female lone-parent families	22 328	22 947	23 233	22 880	22 799	24 424
No earner	15 467	14 964	15 395	14 633	13 491	13 714
One earner	24 063	24 993	24 991	25 761	25 016	25 574
Two or more earners	33 013	35 843	36 757	35 322	36 918	39 882
All other economic families	**38 360**	**39 516**	**38 888**	**44 855**	**44 143**	**47 232**
Unattached Individuals	**20 570**	**20 671**	**20 605**	**20 488**	**20 582**	**21 067**
Elderly male	**19 621**	**21 462**	**21 231**	**21 692**	**22 031**	**22 299**
Non-earner	18 671	19 490	19 604	19 967	20 233	20 089
Earner	26 817	36 985	34 600	33 987	32 091	35 350
Elderly female	**16 533**	**16 782**	**17 526**	**18 224**	**18 282**	**18 095**
Non-earner	16 140	16 492	17 191	17 668	17 709	17 533
Earner	26 116	24 237	25 778	29 857	25 676	25 634
Non-elderly male	**22 846**	**23 263**	**22 541**	**22 480**	**22 540**	**23 429**
Non-earner	10 572	11 106	10 170	9 316	8 976	8 911
Earner	25 575	25 743	25 042	25 279	25 316	26 009
Non-elderly female	**20 247**	**19 388**	**19 821**	**18 941**	**19 048**	**19 464**
Non-earner	10 977	12 320	10 977	8 950	9 613	9 054
Earner	22 672	21 816	22 345	22 059	21 888	22 704

Source: © Statistics Canada (1) 1998 constant dollars. After-tax income which is total income including government transfers less income tax. (2) An economic family is a group of individuals sharing a common dwelling unit who are related by blood, marriage (including common-law relationships) or adoption. (3) Head aged 65 years or over. (4) Head aged less than 65 years. (5) With single children less than 18 years. (Children 18 or over and other relatives may also be present.) (6) Children less than 18 years are not present, but children over 18 may be present.

Average Family Income by Province[1]

	1993	1994	1995	1996	1997	1998
Canada	$45 728	$46 300	$46 159	$46 915	$47 838	$49 626
Newfoundland	37 791	37 899	37 556	37 100	36 761	37 731
Prince Edward Island	40 128	41 741	40 605	41 019	40 796	42 270
Nova Scotia	40 698	40 740	39 412	40 206	40 236	41 499
New Brunswick	40 949	39 696	39 199	40 544	39 792	41 131
Quebec	40 244	41 463	41 248	41 413	41 721	42 787
Ontario	49 941	50 529	50 584	51 681	53 153	55 619
Manitoba	42 632	43 442	44 425	43 017	43 443	45 373
Saskatchewan	40 842	40 741	41 798	41 524	42 364	43 407
Alberta	49 164	48 011	43 201	48 974	50 538	52 388
British Columbia	48 052	48 852	49 121	49 106	50 033	51 424

Source: © Statistics Canada
(1) In 1998 constant dollars. After-tax income of economic families. That is, total income, including government transfers, less income tax, for a group of individuals sharing a common dwelling unit who are related by blood, marriage (including common-law relationships) or adoption.

Average Income by Income Type, 1998

	Average market income	Average government transfers	Average total income	Average income tax	Average income after tax
Economic families[1], 2 persons or more	$55 224	$6 892	$62 116	$12 489	$49 626
Elderly families[2]	23 482	18 878	42 360	6 309	36 051
Married couples	22 542	18 701	41 243	6 398	34 846
All other elderly families	26 886	19 519	46 405	5 990	40 415
Non-elderly families[3]	60 249	4 994	65 243	13 468	51 776
Married couples	60 300	3 661	63 961	14 192	49 769
No earner	17 843	10 145	27 988	3 961	24 027
One earner	44 933	6 304	51 237	10 838	40 399
Two earners	70 929	1 935	72 865	16 632	56 232
Two-parent families with children[4]	65 766	4 277	70 043	14 969	55 074
No earner	4 018	16 306	20 324	553	19 771
One earner	48 206	6 345	54 552	12 691	41 860
Two earners	68 033	3 496	71 530	15 439	56 090
Three or more earners	82 111	3 541	85 652	17 336	68 316
Married couples with other relatives[5]	81 765	5 142	86 907	17 777	69 130
Lone-parent families[4]	22 290	7 597	29 887	3 608	26 279
Male lone-parent families	38 560	5 693	44 253	8 073	36 180
Female lone-parent families	19 242	7 953	27 195	2 771	24 424
No earner	1 662	12 198	13 860	146	13 714
One earner	22 349	6 554	28 903	3 329	25 574
Two or more earners	38 790	6 335	45 125	5 243	39 882
All other economic families	48 017	8 854	56 872	9 639	47 232
Unattached Individuals	20 758	5 027	25 784	4 718	21 067
Elderly male	14 124	12 347	26 471	4 173	22 299
Non-earner	10 528	12 455	22 983	2 894	20 089
Earner	35 366	11 712	47 077	11 727	35 350
Elderly female	8 649	11 724	20 372	2 277	18 095
Non-earner	7 817	11 735	19 552	2 018	17 533
Earner	19 814	11 574	31 388	5 753	25 634
Non-elderly male	27 280	2 376	29 656	6 227	23 429
Non-earner	2 754	6 792	9 546	635	8 911
Earner	31 640	1 591	33 231	7 221	26 009
Non-elderly female	21 406	2 440	23 846	4 382	19 464
Non-earner	3 592	6 221	9 813	759	9 054
Earner	26 951	1 263	28 214	5 510	22 704

Source: © Statistics Canada
(1) An economic family is a group of individuals sharing a common dwelling unit who are related by blood, marriage (including common-law relationships) or adoption. (2) Head aged 65 years or over. (3) Head aged less than 65 years. (4) With single children less than 18 years. (Children 18 or over and other relatives may also be present.) (5) Children less than 18 years are not present, but children over 18 may be present.

Income Distribution by Amount[1]

(percentage)

Income Group	1991	1992	1993	1994	1995	1996	1997
Under $5 000	11.7	12.2	11.6	11.0	11.4	11.7	12.0
$5 000–9 999	14.0	13.2	13.2	13.5	12.7	12.8	12.1
$10 000–14 999	15.2	14.9	15.0	15.1	14.6	14.6	13.8
$15 000–19 999	10.9	10.4	11.4	11.1	11.0	10.5	10.9
$20 000–24 999	9.3	9.5	9.7	9.0	9.4	9.0	9.3
$25 000–29 999	8.8	8.3	8.2	8.2	8.2	8.0	8.2
$30 000–34 999	7.2	7.2	7.2	7.4	7.6	7.4	7.3
$35 000–39 999	5.6	5.9	5.5	5.7	5.6	5.7	5.7
$40 000–44 999	4.4	4.6	4.5	4.7	4.7	4.7	4.9
$45 000–49 999	3.3	3.5	3.4	3.4	3.4	3.5	3.3
$50 000 and over	9.6	10.4	10.1	10.8	11.3	12.0	12.5
Average income ($)	24 173	24 701	24 555	24 981	25 518	25 909	26 042
Median income ($)	19 040	19 677	19 400	19 587	20 134	20 202	20 581

Source: © Census Canada
(1) Current dollars. Total percentage may not equal 100 due to rounding.

Low Income by Family Type[1]

(prevalence of low income in percentage)

	1993	1994	1995	1996	1997	1998
Economic families,[2] 2 persons or more	10.2	9.5	10.0	11.0	10.3	9.1
Elderly families[3]	4.0	2.5	2.1	3.0	3.7	3.6
Married couples	2.6	...	...	1.9	1.9	1.7
All other elderly families	7.3	5.8	3.9	7.2	9.9	10.6
Non-elderly families[4]	11.2	10.8	11.4	12.2	11.4	9.9
Married couples	6.6	6.2	6.7	7.2	6.5	5.6
No earner	33.0	31.9	33.0	30.0	28.0	29.7
One earner	7.6	7.0	10.3	10.5	10.5	6.9
Two earners	2.8	2.4	2.2	3.0	2.7	2.2
Two-parent families with children[5]	8.8	8.4	9.8	10.1	9.5	7.3
No earner	78.8	78.2	82.4	81.3	72.1	75.7
One earner	17.0	17.3	20.7	22.2	23.8	17.9
Two earners	4.7	3.8	5.1	4.8	5.0	3.7
Three or more earners	...	...	2.7	2.8	...	...
Married couples with other relatives[6]	2.7	3.8	3.6	3.7	3.8	3.4
Lone-parent families[5]	41.3	42.2	42.4	45.8	42.3	38.1
Male lone-parent families	18.9	26.4	20.5	23.8	18.1	17.5
Female lone-parent families	45.0	44.8	46.1	49.5	46.8	42.0
No earner	76.3	79.5	80.9	88.3	90.3	85.8
One earner	31.8	29.2	32.1	31.5	30.6	31.1
Two or more earners	19.5	...	...	...	...	...
All other economic families	13.5	14.0	11.9	12.3	12.2	12.6
Unattached Individuals	30.9	30.4	30.5	32.5	32.0	30.3
Elderly male	19.0	12.1	11.9	17.6	16.6	17.4
Non-earner	20.4	13.5	13.1	19.3	19.1	19.2
Earner	...	...	...	...	...	...
Elderly female	28.8	23.6	24.2	25.8	23.5	22.1
Non-earner	29.7	24.4	25.0	26.6	24.6	23.3
Earner	...	...	...	...	...	...
Non-elderly male	30.6	29.9	31.9	33.3	32.7	30.3
Non-earner	77.9	74.2	77.2	81.3	83.1	85.2
Earner	20.1	20.8	22.7	23.0	22.4	20.5
Non-elderly female	35.6	40.1	37.0	39.8	40.9	38.8
Non-earner	71.4	68.4	73.5	81.8	80.4	80.2
Earner	26.3	30.3	26.5	26.7	29.0	25.9

Source: © Statistics Canada   (...) Amount too small to express.

(1) 1992 based. (2) An economic family is a group of individuals sharing a common dwelling unit who are related by blood, marriage (including common-law relationships) or adoption. (3) Head aged 65 years or over. (4) Head aged less than 65 years. (5) With single children less than 18 years. (Children 18 or over and other relatives may also be present.) (6) Children less than 18 years are not present, but children over 18 may be present.

Low Income in Canada, 1998[1]

The table below shows the minimum income level necessary to avoid financial hardship. It varies according to changes in the cost of living, family size and place of residence.

Family Size	Rural Areas	Urban Areas			
		Pop. Under 30 000[2]	Pop. 30 000 to 99 999	Pop. 100 000 to 499 999	Pop. 500 000 or more
1 person	12 142	13 924	14 965	15 070	17 571
2 persons	15 178	17 405	18 706	18 837	21 962
3 persons	18 877	21 647	23 264	23 429	27 315
4 persons	22 849	26 205	28 162	28 359	33 063
5 persons	25 542	29 293	31 481	31 701	36 958
6 persons	28 235	32 379	34 798	35 043	40 855
7 or more persons	30 928	35 467	38 117	38 385	44 751

Source: © Statistics Canada
(1) In dollars. 1992 base. (2) Includes cities with a population between 15 000 and 30 000, and small urban areas (under 15 000).

Low Income[1] by Sex, Age and Family

	Estimated number (000s)			Prevalence of low income (%)		
	1991	1996	1998	1991	1996	1998
All persons	3 385	4 186	3 669	12.2	14.2	12.2
Male	1 535	1 960	1 693	11.2	13.5	11.4
Female	1 850	2 227	1 976	13.3	15.0	13.0
Economic family persons	2 255	2 892	2 381	9.4	11.4	9.3
Elderly persons	50	58	74	2.4	2.5	3.0
Persons under 18 years of age[2]	986	1 176	939	14.4	17.2	13.8
Persons 18-64	1 219	1 610	1 312	8.1	10.0	8.1
Unattached individuals	1 130	1 295	1 288	30.8	32.5	30.3
Elderly persons	265	265	245	26.9	23.7	20.8
Persons under 65 years of age	865	1 029	1 043	32.2	36.0	33.9

Source: © Statistics Canada (1) After tax income. (2) Includes persons under 18 years of age in elderly families.

Average Expenditure Per Household[1]

(dollars)

	1996	1997
Total expenditure	$49 929	$49 947
Food	5 960	5 703
Shelter[2]	9 813	9 869
Household operation	2 266	2 284
Household furnishings and equipment	1 294	1 335
Clothing	2 115	1 919
Gifts of clothing	n.a.	263
Transportation	6 044	6 204
Health care	1 006	1 153
Personal care	835	664
Recreation	2 638	2 780
Reading materials and other printed matter	252	275
Education	555	659
Tobacco products and alcoholic beverages	1 146	1 139
Games of chance (net)	264	247
Miscellaneous[2]	695	795
Non-money gifts	509	n.a.
Total current consumption[2]	35 394	35 290
Personal income taxes	10 746	10 634
Personal insurance payments and pension contributions	2 598	2 783
Gifts of money and contributions to persons outside household[2]	1 191	1 240

Source: © Statistics Canada   NOTE: 1996 data has been adjusted for 1997 survey changes.
(1) Expenditure for the 10 provinces. (2) Prior to 1997, mortgage interest and interest on loans were reported in the categories Shelter and Miscellaneous. For 1997, regular mortgage payments on owned living quarters, including both principal and interest, are included under Shelter.

The Poverty Line

While there is no official definition of "poverty line," as noted in the above table it is generally accepted that those spending more than 54.7 percent of their pre-tax income on food, clothing and shelter are likely to be in financial difficulty.

Another way of defining low income (or the poverty line) is to take 50 percent of the median family income considered to be necessary to cover a family's needs. Defining a family's "needs" is not easy. For the purposes of assessing low income, Statistics Canada has set a figure for the needs of one adult and then assumed that family needs increase in proportion to the size of the family. Each additional adult is assumed to increase the family's needs by 40 percent of the first figure, and each additional child increases the needs by 30 percent. These income figures were then compared to the actual incomes of families and individuals and used to calculate how many Canadians, living as family members or single individuals, failed to generate enough income to cover their basic needs for food, clothing, shelter and other expenses.

EDUCATION

Canadian Population[1] by Highest Level of Schooling

(percentage)

	1976	1981	1986	1991	1996	1999
Less than grade 9	25.4	20.7	17.7	14.3	12.4	11.0
Grades 9 to 13	44.1	43.7	42.5	42.6	40.4	37.7[2]
Some postsecondary education	24.1	27.6	30.2	31.7	33.9	36.6[3]
University degree	6.4	8.0	9.6	11.4	13.3	14.8

Source: © Census of Canada, Statistics Canada (1) Over the age of 15. (2) "Some secondary," and "Graduated from high school" data categories added together. (3) "Some post secondary" and "Post secondary certificate or diploma" data categories added together.

Canadian Population[1] by Highest Level of Schooling and Province, 1996

(percentage)

	Elementary–Secondary Schooling Only	Post secondary, Non-university Education	University Without a Degree	University With a Degree
Canada	**52.8**	**24.2**	**9.7**	**13.3**
Newfoundland	58.2	23.0	10.7	8.1
Prince Edward Island	55.4	22.5	11.5	10.6
Nova Scotia	52.8	23.8	11.2	12.2
New Brunswick	58.3	21.6	9.9	10.2
Quebec	57.5	22.3	8.0	12.2
Ontario	51.1	24.6	9.4	14.9
Manitoba	55.9	21.0	11.5	11.6
Saskatchewan	56.8	21.6	11.8	9.8
Alberta	48.7	27.8	10.2	13.3
British Columbia	47.5	27.0	11.9	13.6
Yukon Territory	40.0	33.5	12.0	14.5
Northwest Territories	53.3	28.7	7.5	10.5

Source: © Census of Canada, Statistics Canada (1) Over the age of 15.

Elementary–Secondary Enrolment by School Type and Province

(thousands)

	Canada[1]	Nfld	PEI	NS	NB	Que	Ont[1]	Man	Sask	Alta	BC	YT	NWT
1993-94	5 327.8	118.6	24.5	169.8	140.4	1 140.4	2 113.8	222.0	212.7	540.2	623.1	5.8	15.9
1994-95	5 362.8	114.4	24.5	168.5	138.3	1 137.6	2 140.1	221.7	212.7	544.6	638.1	5.8	16.3
1995-96	5 430.8	110.9	24.7	168.0	136.8	1 138.7	2 189.0	223.0	213.0	548.5	654.4	6.1	17.6
1996-97	5 414.6	106.5	24.8	167.2	135.3	1 137.1	2 161.5	223.8	212.9	553.7	667.1	6.4	18.0
1997-98	5 386.3	102.1	24.7	164.7	133.2	1 130.0	2 131.9	224.1	211.1	563.2	677.3	6.4	17.5
Public	5 027.4	101.6	24.4	160.9	131.6	1 020.2	2 033.3	194.3	194.3	528.9	613.9	6.4	17.5
Private	288.2	0.4	0.2	2.5	0.7	102.9	83.7	13.8	2.8	22.9	58.2	...	...
Federal	69.1[2]	...	0.0	1.3	0.8	6.3	14.1	15.9	13.9	11.3	5.2	...	...
Visually and hearing impaired	1.6	0.1	...	...	...	0.6	0.7	0.2	...[3]	0.1	...[3]	...	...

Source: © Statistics Canada (...) Nil or zero.
(1) Excludes correctional institutions and hospital schools. (2) Includes DND schools overseas. (3) The "Visually and hearing impaired" category for Saskatchewan and British Columbia is included with the "Public" category.

Post Secondary Enrolment, 1997–98

	Full-time	Part-time
Community college	398 643	91 577
Career programs	291 983	53 764
University transfer programs	106 660	37 813
University	573 099	249 673
Undergraduate programs	497 072	207 900
Bachelor's and first professional	468 392	103 938
Other undergraduate	28 680	103 962
Graduate programs	76 027	41 773
Master's	42 191	27 661
Doctoral	23 006	4 356
Other graduate	10 830	9 756
Total Enrolment	**971 742**	**341 250**

Source: © Statistics Canada

University Graduates by Field of Study, 1997

Field of Study	Bachelor's/First Professional Degree	Diploma and Certificate	Men	Women	Total Undergraduate
Education	20 319	2 937	6 670	16 586	23 256
Fine/applied arts	4 047	514	1 458	3 103	4 561
Humanities	14 869	2 911	6 431	11 349	17 780
Social sciences	47 054	8 684	22 744	32 994	55 738
Agricultural/biological sciences	9 538	586	3 951	6 173	10 124
Engineering/applied sciences	9 030	722	7 691	2 061	9 752
Health professions	8 701	1 752	2 529	7 924	10 453
Mathematics/physical sciences	6 992	559	5 124	2 427	7 551
Other	3 474	1 836	1 663	3 647	5 310
Total	**124 024**	**20 501**	**58 261**	**86 264**	**144 525**

Field of Study	Masters	Doctoral	Graduate Diploma and Certificate	Men	Women	Total Graduate
Education	3 266	326	557	1 241	2 908	4 149
Fine/applied arts	503	47	25	214	361	575
Humanities	2 714	453	243	1 520	1 890	3 410
Social sciences	8 405	674	989	5 322	4 746	10 068
Agricultural/biological sciences	977	469	57	765	738	1 503
Engineering/applied sciences	2 134	673	54	2 313	548	2 861
Health professions	1 576	482	390	896	1 552	2 448
Mathematics/physical sciences	1 320	687	54	1 541	570	2 111
Other	63	25	48	47	89	136
Total	**20 958**	**3 836**	**2 417**	**13 859**	**13 402**	**27 261**

Source: © Statistics Canada

Education Expenditures in Canada

(millions of dollars)

	1976	1981	1986	1991	1996	1999
Total	$15 099.7	$25 373.1	$36 610.8	$53 144.3	$58 125.1[2]	$61 865.1[2]
Elementary–Secondary	10 070.9	16 703.2	22 968.0	33 444.9	36 744.7	37 498.9[1]
Vocational	959.9	1 601.2	3 275.1	4 573.8	5 301.8[2]	6 229.6[1]
College	1 081.5	2 088.1	2 999.0	3 870.7	4 477.9[2]	5 261.7[1]
University	2 987.5	4 980.7	7 368.7	11 254.8	11 600.7[2]	12 874.9[1]
Spending as a % of GDP	7.6	7.1	7.3	7.9	7.1	n.a.
Elementary–Secondary pupil-educator ratio	18.1	17.0	16.5	15.5	16.3[1,2]	16.6[1]

Source: © Statistics Canada (n.a.) Not available.
(1) Estimated. (2) Revised.

How We Compare: Education Spending by G-7 Countries, 1996

(percentage)

	Canada	United States	France	United Kingdom	Germany	Italy	Japan
Education spending as a percentage of total public expenditures	13.6	14.4	11.1	n.a	9.5	9.0	9.8
Public spending as a percentage of GDP	5.8	5.0	5.8	4.6	4.5	4.5	3.6
Participation rate in formal education[1]	68.2	68.8	64.5	66.8	61.8	53.8	57.0
Ratio of secondary school graduates to population	73	72	85	n.a.	86	79	99
Ratio of first university degree to population	32	35	n.a.	34	n.a.	1	23
Labour Force Participation by Education Attainment							
Secondary education							
Men	89	88	90	89	85	80	n.a.
Women	72	72	76	74	69	61	n.a.
University education							
Men	92	93	92	94	93	92	n.a.
Women	85	82	83	86	83	81	n.a.
Unemployment Rate by Level of Educational Attainment							
Upper secondary education							
Men	9	6	8	8	8	6	n.a.
Women	9	4	12	6	10	11	n.a.
University education							
Men	5	2	6	4	5	5	n.a.
Women	6	2	9	3	5	10	n.a.

Source: © Statistics Canada (n.a.) Not available.
(1) Total number of students enrolled in formal education as a percentage of the population aged 5–29.

CRIME AND JUSTICE

Rates[1] of Criminal Code Incidents in Canada

	1988	1989	1990	1991	1992	1993
Population[2](000)	2 6798.3	27 286.2	27 700.6	28 030.9	28 376.6	28 703.1
Violent crime rate	868	911	973	1 059	1 084	1 081
Annual % change	4.6	5.0	6.8	8.9	2.3	–0.3
Property crime rate	5 438	5 289	5 611	6 160	5 902	5 571
Annual % change	–2.1	–2.8	6.1	9.8	–4.2	–5.6
Other criminal code rate	2 612	2 691	2 900	3 122	3 051	2 879
Annual % change	1.5	3.0	7.8	7.7	–2.3	–5.6
Total[3] criminal code rate	8 919	8 891	9 484	10 342	10 036	9 531
Annual % change	–0.4	–0.3	6.7	9.0	–3.0	–5.0
	1994	1995	1996	1997	1998[4]	1999
Population[2](000)	29 036.0	29 353.9	29 671.9	29 987.2	30 246.9	30 491.3
Violent crime rate	1 046	1 007	1 000	990	979	955
Annual % change	–3.2	–3.7	–0.7	–1.0	–1.1	–2.4
Property crime rate	5 250	5 283	5 264	4 867	4 556	4 266
Annual % change	–5.8	0.6	–0.4	–7.5	–6.4	–6.4
Other criminal code rate	2 817	2 702	2 650	2 596	2 602	2 512
Annual % change	–2.2	–4.1	–1.9	–2.1	0.3	–3.5
Total[3] criminal code rate	9 114	8 993	8 914	8 453	8 137	7 733
Annual % change	–4.4	–1.3	–0.9	–5.2	–3.7	–5.0

Source: Uniform Crime Reporting Survey, Canadian Centre for Justice Statistics, © Statistics Canada (1) Rates are calculated per 100 000 people. (2) Population estimates as of July 1. (3) Does not include traffic violations. (4) Revised figures.

Percentage of Persons Charged by Gender and Age, 1999

	Age Group[1] by Gender				Total by Age Group[1]	
	Adults		Youth		Adults	Youth
	Male	Female	Male	Female		
Homicide[2]	91	9	80	20	90	10
Attempted murder	87	13	86	14	90	10
Assaults	84	16	71	29	85	15
Sexual assaults	98	2	96	4	84	16
Other sexual offences	97	3	96	4	85	15
Abduction	60	40	57	43	96	4
Robbery	91	9	84	16	67	33
Total violent crime	**86**	**14**	**75**	**25**	**84**	**16**
Break and enter	94	6	90	10	62	38
Motor vehicle theft	93	7	86	14	60	40
Fraud	71	29	68	32	92	8
Theft over $5,000	78	22	84	16	85	15
Theft $5,000 and under	70	30	68	32	73	27
Total property crime	**78**	**22**	**78**	**22**	**73**	**27**
Mischief	88	12	88	12	68	32
Arson	82	18	82	18	55	45
Prostitution	47	53	18	82	98	2
Offensive weapons	89	11	92	8	80	20
Total criminal code	**82**	**18**	**77**	**23**	**79**	**21**
Impaired driving[3]	89	11	85	15	99	1
Cannabis offences	87	13	89	11	84	16
Cocaine offences	82	18	77	23	94	6
Other drugs offences	83	17	83	17	88	12

Source: Uniform Crime Reporting Survey, Canadian Centre for Justice statistics, © Statistics Canada
(1) Adults are defined as people age 18 and over, Youth between the ages of 12 and 17. (2) Data based on Homicide Survey. (3) Includes impaired operation of a vehicle causing death, causing bodily harm, alcohol rate over 80 mg., failure/refusal to provide a breath/blood sample. Dated based on Incident-based survey.

Selected Criminal Code Incidents by Province, 1999[1]

	Canada	Nfld	PEI	NS	NB	Que	Ont
Population	30 491 294	541 000	137 980	939 791	754 969	7 345 390	11 513 808
Homicide							
Number	536	2	1	13	9	136	161
Rate	1.8	0.4	0.7	1.4	1.2	1.9	1.4
Annual % change in rate	-4.7	-71.2	-0.7	-46.0	79.6	-1.0	2.0
Sexual Assault[2,3]							
Number	23 872	644	105	844	775	3 434	8 270
Rate	78	119	76	90	103	47	72
Annual % change in rate	-7.3	6.4	-33.2	-11.6	-13.7	6.1	-9.3
Assault[2,3]							
Number	221 281	4 084	772	7 495	5 768	32 795	75 439
Rate	726	755	560	798	764	446	655
Annual % change in rate	-2.0	4.7	1.5	2.7	5.5	3.0	-4.3
Robbery							
Number	28 745	64	19	425	162	8 287	8 720
Rate	94	12	14	45	21	113	76
Annual % change in rate	-1.5	-12.8	-21.4	-7.6	-1.4	3.0	-5.8
Total violent crime							
Number	291 330	5 004	945	9 269	7 218	48 934	98 118
Rate	955	925	685	986	956	666	852
Annual % change in rate	-2.4	4.0	-5.7	0.8	2.9	3.4	-4.8
Breaking and Entering							
Number	318 448	4 328	717	9 139	5 475	84 972	92 485
Rate	1 044	800	520	972	725	1 157	803
Annual % change in rate	-9.9	-2.6	1.7	-0.2	-7.2	-13.6	-9.5
Motor Vehicle Theft							
Number	161 405	618	191	2 831	1 631	43 068	50 065
Rate	529	114	138	301	216	586	435
Annual % change in rate	-3.5	-3.3	4.8	0.1	14.5	-9.1	-1.7
Other Theft							
Number	701 573	7 770	2 655	22 017	11 758	124 329	227 005
Rate	2 301	1 436	1 924	2 343	1 557	1 693	1 972
Annual % change in rate	-5.6	3.6	13.6	-1.3	-1.1	-7.5	-8.3
Total property crime							
Number	1 300 650	14 634	4 118	37 711	22 531	273 403	411 456
Rate	4 266	2 705	2 984	4 013	2 984	3 722	3 574
Annual % change in rate	-6.4	1.7	9.1	-1.1	-1.3	-8.9	-7.6
Offensive weapons							
Number	16 043	168	29	469	386	1 136	6 567
Rate	53	31	21	50	51	15	57
Annual % change in rate	-5.1	34.4	-22.2	-4.5	63-2	13.1	-8.6
Mischief							
Number	312 563	4 912	1 784	12 445	7 544	51 194	97 269
Rate	1 025	908	1 293	1 324	999	697	845
Annual % change in rate	-5.2	4.9	25.3	3.8	4.7	-6.7	-9.7
Total other criminal code							
Number	765 791	12 395	4 399	31 093	22 121	113 535	239 697
Rate	2 512	2 291	3 198	3 309	2 930	1 546	2 082
Annual % change in rate	-3.5	2.3	14.4	7.0	4.0	-9.6	-8.2
Total criminal code[5]							
Number	2 357 771	32 033	9 462	78 073	51 870	435 872	749 271
Rate	7 733	5 921	6 858	8 307	6 870	5 934	6 508
Annual % change in rate	-5.0	2.3	9.7	2.2	1.5	-7.8	-7.4 ▶

Crime and Justice

	Man	Sask	Alta	BC	Yukon	NWT[4]	NVT[4]
Population	1 143 509	1 027 780	2 964 689	4 023 100	30 633	41 606	27 039
Homicide							
Number	26	13	61	110	1	1	2
Rate	2.3	1.3	2.1	2.7	3.3	2.4	7.4
Annual % change in rate	-21.6	-60.7	-6.5	21.5	-65.6	-1.3	-51.1
Sexual Assault[2,3]							
Number	1 307	1 375	2 715	3 907	90	202	204
Rate	114	134	92	97	294	486	754
Annual % change in rate	1.1	-9.3	-9.5	-11.6	-13.3	-7.7	-18.6
Assault[2,3]							
Number	13 744	12 938	24 339	40 318	807	1 667	1 115
Rate	1 202	1 259	821	1 002	2 634	4 007	4 124
Annual % change in rate	-2.9	2.1	-2.5	-4.6	12.9	-2.8	-7.1
Robbery							
Number	1 987	887	2 542	5 611	15	19	7
Rate	174	86	86	139	49	46	26
Annual % change in rate	8.6	-8.7	-2.7	-1.6	28.9	-14.7	-54.4
Total violent crime							
Number	17 978	16 334	31 462	51 637	972	2 042	1 417
Rate	1 572	1 589	1 061	1 284	3 173	4 908	5 241
Annual % change in rate	-2.2	-0.8	-3.3	-4.8	9.1	-2.9	-11.1
Breaking and Entering							
Number	15 209	16 869	29 287	58 026	560	882	499
Rate	1 330	1 641	988	1 442	1 828	2 120	1 845
Annual % change in rate	-5.7	-5.4	-4.2	-11.9	-5.0	-13.9	-22.8
Motor Vehicle Theft							
Number	10 723	7 078	14 847	29 731	228	225	169
Rate	938	689	501	739	744	541	625
Annual % change in rate	1.3	-3.0	-6.2	0.8	10.4	-3.8	3.2
Other Theft							
Number	28 697	28 342	79 943	166 296	1 198	1 123	440
Rate	2 510	2 758	2 697	4 134	3 911	2 699	1 627
Annual % change in rate	3.4	-6.0	-2.4	-4.7	0.9	-24.0	-7.7
Total property crime							
Number	58 136	59 140	141 736	272 021	2 212	2 376	1 176
Rate	5 094	5 754	4 781	6 761	7 221	5 711	4 349
Annual % change in rate	-1.6	-5.2	-3.5	-6.1	3.2	-18.6	-12.7
Offensive weapons							
Number	1 164	853	1 666	3 438	59	67	41
Rate	102	83	56	85	193	161	152
Annual % change in rate	8.3	-1.1	-16.8	-7.6	48.4	-9.4	-40.2
Mischief							
Number	22 825	16 833	37 999	55 173	803	2 731	1 051
Rate	1 996	1 638	1 282	1 371	2 621	6 564	3 887
Annual % change in rate	6.5	-3.5	-4.2	-6.1	5.5	7.5	-13.7
Total other criminal code							
Number	44 801	49 452	95 076	142 457	2 887	5 584	2 294
Rate	3 918	4 812	3 207	3 541	9 424	13 421	8 484
Annual % change in rate	1.7	0.3	4.7	-2.5	15.6	3.4	-11.5
Total criminal code[5]							
Number	120 915	124 926	268 274	466 115	6 071	10 002	4 887
Rate	10 574	12 155	9 049	11 586	19 818	24 040	18 074
Annual % change in rate	-0.5	-2.5	-0.7	-4.9	9.7	-4.0	-11.7

Source: © Statistics Canada, Uniform Crime Reporting Survey, Canadian Centre for Justice Statistics
(1) Rates are calculated on the basis of 100 000 population. Population estimates at July 1. (2) Royal Newfoundland constabulary St. John jurisdiction was unable to contribute 1999 crime statistics due to a new Police Information and Management System. As such, 1999 data was substituted with 1998 counts. (3) In 1998, Codiac Regional was unable to provide accurate crime statistics due to a change in police information systems. As such, 1998 data was substituted with 1999 counts. (4) Data for 1998 for the Northwest Territories (without Nunavut) and Nunavut was estimated in order to allow for comparisons with 1999. (5) Without traffic offences.

Change in Rates of Crime for Major CMAs[1]

	Violent Crime			Property Crime		
	1998	1999	% 5-Year Change[2]	1998	1999	% 5 Year Change[2]
Toronto	836	805	-16.3	3 354	7 761	72.7
% change	-2.2	-3.9		-14.8	-5.6	
Montreal	827	847	-11.8	4 922	5 590	5.0
% change	4.9	2.5		-6.8	-2.0	
Vancouver	1 170	1 120	-15.1	8 239	4 802	-49.3
% change	-5.2	-4.1		-7.4	-4.0	
Edmonton	996	869	-9.6	4 984	5 036	-9.9
% change	2.0	-13.1		-5.5	-4.6	
Calgary	849	848	1.9	5 254	4 547	-22.2
% change	0.4	-0.7		-1.7	-7.6	
Ottawa	879	732	-28.2	4 593	3 862	-43.3
% change	-2.6	-16.1		-11.0	-2.6	
Quebec	456	465	-22.6	3 511	3 966	-1.9
% change	-11.4	1.8		-8.3	-13.0	
Winnipeg	1 299	1 232	-4.4	5 717	3 144	-57.4
% change	-10.8	-4.9		-4.3	-6.5	
Hamilton	1 025	982	-11.7	3 958	3 100	-39.0
% change	-7.3	-4.3		-7.5	-11.6	

Source: © Statistics Canada, Uniform Crime Reporting Survey, Canadian Centre for Justice Statistics
(1) Rates are calculated per 100 000 people. Population estimates at July 1 for Census Metropolitan Areas. (2) 5-Year change from 1994 to 1999.

Youth Crime in Canada[1]

	1997	1998[2]	1999
Population[1]			
(12-17)	2 439 553	2 449 216	2 449 610
Homicide			
Number	54	56	45
Rate	2	2	2
Assaults			
Number	15 612	15 862	15 306
Rate	640	648	625
Sexual assaults			
Number	1 494	1 440	1 423
Rate	61	59	58
Robbery			
Number	3 792	3 576	3 189
Rate	155	146	130
Total violent crime			
Number	22 172	22 195	21 081
Rate	909	906	861
Break and enter			
Number	17 092	16 007	13 469
Rate	701	654	550
Motor vehicle theft			
Number	6 468	6 228	5 550
Rate	265	254	227
Theft			
Number	27 060	24 744	22 206
Rate	1 109	1 010	907
Total property crime			
Number	58 340	54 104	48 415
Rate	2 391	2 209	1 976
Mischief			
Number	7 005	6 926	6 645
Rate	287	283	271
Offensive weapons			
Number	1 478	1 457	1 436
Rate	61	59	59
Total other criminal code			
Number	30 329	31 153	30 250
Rate	1 243	1 272	1 235
Total criminal code			
Number	110 841	107 452	99 746
Rate	4 543	4 387	4 072

Source: © Statistics Canada, Uniform Crime Reporting Survey, Canadian Centre for Justice Statistics
(1) Rates are calculated per 100 000 youths. Population estimates at July 1. (2) Revised figures.

THE NATION

The National Anthem: O Canada

The music of *O Canada* was composed by Calixa Lavallée and the lyrics were written in French by Adolphe-Basile Routhier in Quebec City. Originally called *Chant National*, it was first performed at a banquet in Quebec City on June 24, 1880. The anthem grew in popularity in Quebec but was not heard in English until the early 1900s. There have been several English versions of the work, the most popular of which was written in 1908 by Robert Stanley Weir. In 1967 a Special Joint Committee of the Senate and the House of Commons was formed to recommend official versions of Canada's National and Royal Anthems. With a few minor changes, the official English version of *O Canada* is based on Weir's lyrics. On June 27, 1980 the House of Commons passed Bill C-36 designating both the music and lyrics of *O Canada* as Canada's national anthem. It was proclaimed July 1, 1980.

O Canada

O Canada! Terre de nos aïeux,

Ton front est ceint de fleurons glorieux!

Car ton bras sait porter l'épée,

Il sait porter la croix!

Ton histoire est une épopée

Des plus brillants exploits,

Et ta valeur, de foi trempée,

Protégera nos foyers et nos droits,

Protégera nos foyers et nos droits.

O Canada

O Canada! Our home and native land!

True patriot love in all thy sons command.

With glowing hearts we see thee rise,

The True North strong and free!

From far and wide, O Canada,

We stand on guard for thee.

God keep our land glorious and free!

O Canada, we stand on guard for thee.

O Canada, we stand on guard for thee!

The National Flag

The National Flag was adopted by Parliament Dec. 15, 1964 and proclaimed by Queen Elizabeth II. It was inaugurated on Feb. 15, 1965.

It is a red flag of the proportions two by length and one by width, containing in its centre a white square, the width of the flag, bearing a single, red, stylized maple leaf. The maple leaf has been looked upon as an emblem of Canada since the early 1700s. Red and white were declared Canada's official colours by King George V on Nov. 21, 1921.

The National Flag is to be flown daily at all federal government buildings, airports and military bases and establishments within and outside Canada. When flown with other flags, it should be given a place of honour.

The National Coat of Arms

The creation of coats of arms dates back to the Middle Ages. Centuries ago few could read, nor did they have access to print material, pictures or the other means we now use to identify people. Heraldry was developed as a form of picture-writing, used in the Middle Ages to create visual emblems that identified individuals or members of a community or nation, particularly on the field of battle.

Over time, the development of such symbols became quite sophisticated; a coat of arms could identify not only the individual but tell if his father was still alive, his birth order, whether or not he was married and the prestige of his branch of the family. In war, the device was painted on a shield; in peace, it would be embroidered on a coat or banner. Because of its significance, heraldry came to be carefully regulated; colleges of arms controlled the grant and use of them.

At the time of Confederation, Canada did not have a coat of arms and used the Royal Arms of the United Kingdom to identify the offices of the Government of Canada. By 1868, however, a Great Seal was required and the government adopted a design that was also used as the Arms of Canada. The design showed the emblems of the original four provinces of the federation—Nova Scotia, New Brunswick, Quebec and Ontario—on a shield. When new provinces joined the federation, their emblems were added to the shield and the design became fragmented and confusing as the provinces multiplied. In 1919, the governor general convened a special committee to study the question of a Canadian coat of arms; a request for a grant of arms was later submitted to the sovereign.

Canada's Coat of Arms was granted by a royal proclamation of King George V on Nov. 21, 1921. Although simplified in 1957 and augmented in 1994, the coat of arms we have now is faithful to that original design.

The most important part of the design is the shield, which shows the emblems of the four founding peoples (English, Scottish, Irish and French) with an added sprig of distinctly Canadian maple leaves. The shield is supported on one side by the lion of England holding the Royal Union flag and the unicorn of Scotland holding a banner of royalist France on the other. A royal helmet and mantle sit above the shield, with a crest showing a royal lion holding a maple leaf on top of the helmet. (The crest is the symbol used on the Governor General's standard.) The imperial crown above the crest represents the monarch as Canada's head of state.

Below the shield is Canada's motto, "A Mari usque ad Mare" (from sea to sea) which is based on a verse from Psalm 72 of the Bible: "He shall have dominion from sea to sea and from the river unto the ends of the earth." Around the shield is a ribbon with the motto of the Order of Canada: "Desiderantes Meliorem Patriam" (They desire a better country). The floral emblems of the four founding nations are found at the base of the design: the English rose, the Scottish thistle, the French fleur-de-lis and the shamrock of Ireland.

Canada's coat of arms represents national sovereignty and is used on federal government property such as buildings, official seals, money, passports, proclamations and publications as well as badges of some members of the armed forces. This national symbol is protected from unauthorized commercial use by the *Trade Marks Act*.

CANADIAN HISTORY

■ Exploration and First Settlements

The first people who came to North America arrived during the last Ice Age which began about 80,000 years ago and ended about 12,000 years ago. These Native People were hunters who crosssed from Asia via a land bridge that is now submerged beneath the Bering Sea. Although there is continuing debate among archeologists as to how early humans might have settled in what is now Canada, the earliest accepted occupation site is at the Bluefish Caves in the Yukon; artifacts at least 12,000 to 17,000 years old have been found there. As the glaciers of the Ice Age retreated, human settlements spread across Canada and gradually, these first Canadians developed lifestyles based on the environments in which they lived. They obtained their food by hunting, fishing, gathering, and in the case of Eastern Woodland tribes, by farming. By the time explorers from Europe reached Canada, the Native People had well developed trading patterns, arts and crafts, languages, writing, religious beliefs, laws and government.

There has been much conjecture as to who the first Europeans to come to Canada were. The claim that an Irish monk, St. Brendan, arrived about the year 550 has not been proven. However, the theory that Vikings settled in Newfoundland was confirmed by archeological excavations at L'Anse aux Meadows during the 1960s and 1970s.

A burst of European exploration didn't take place until the Age of Discovery in the 15th and 16th centuries. Explorers found what they called a New World while in search of a route to the Far East. In 1497, Giovanni Caboto (John Cabot), an Italian sailing for England, landed on the Canadian coast, likely in Cape Breton or Newfoundland, and claimed the land for Henry VII. Although Cabot probably died on a second expedition in 1498, his voyages helped open up the rich fishing grounds of the Grand Banks.

European navigators and fishermen continued to visit the shores of Canada, but the first serious exploration of the area was undertaken by Jacques Cartier, who discovered the Gulf of St. Lawrence while searching for a passage to Asia, in 1534. The next year he travelled up the St. Lawrence River as far as the native settlements of Stadacona (Quebec) and Hochelaga (Montreal). On this voyage, Cartier picked up the Iroquoian word for village, Kanata (thought to be the origin of "Canada"), and used it to apply to the whole region he had discovered. Cartier's discoveries gave France a claim to Canada and led to the first French settlements.

In 1541–42, Cartier and the Sieur de Roberval established a short-lived settlement at Charlesbourg-Royal just above Quebec. In 1605, the Sieur de Monts and Samuel de Champlain established the colony of Port Royal in what is now Nova Scotia. Champlain went on to establish a settlement at Quebec in 1608, to explore the interior and to draw maps of New France. Champlain also started a fur-trading network (mostly in beaver pelts) with the Algonquins and the Hurons who inhabited the St. Lawrence and Great Lakes regions. This trade relationship became a military alliance as Champlain supported these groups against the Iroquois. This enmity between the French and the Iroquois prevailed throughout most of the history of New France.

Circa 1000 **Leif Ericsson** and other **Vikings** visit Labrador and Newfoundland.

1497 **John Cabot** (Giovanni Caboto) claims Cape Breton Island (or possibly Newfoundland or Labrador) for Henry VII of England (June 24).

1498 **Cabot** makes his second voyage to North America.

1534 **Jacques Cartier** visits the Strait of Belle Isle (Newfoundland), and charts the Gulf of St Lawrence (landing in Gaspé July 14).

1535 **Cartier** sails up the St Lawrence River to **Quebec** and **Montreal**.

1541 Cartier and the Sieur de Roberval found Charlesbourg-Royal, the **first French settlement** in America.

1577 **Martin Frobisher** of England makes the first of his three attempts to find a northwest passage, sailing as far as Hudson Strait.

1600 King Henry IV of France grants a **fur-trading monopoly** in the Gulf of St Lawrence to a group of French merchants.

1605 **Samuel de Champlain** and the Sieur de Monts found Port Royal (Annapolis, NS).

1608 **Champlain** founds Quebec.

1609 Champlain supports the Algonquins against the Iroquois at Lake Champlain.

1610 **Étienne Brûlé** goes to live among the Huron and eventually becomes the first European to see Lakes Ontario, Huron and Superior. **Henry Hudson** explores Hudson Bay.

1617 Louis Hébert, the **first habitant (farmer)**, arrives in Quebec.

1625 Jesuits arrive in Quebec to begin missionary work among the Indians.

1627 The **Company of One Hundred Associates** is founded (Apr. 29) to establish a French empire in North America.

■ The Growth of New France (1627-1660)

The economic foundation of New France was the fur trade. In fact, the French kings were content to let fur-trading companies run the colony. Although these companies expanded the territory's boundaries, they failed to encourage settlement. One of King Louis XIII's most able advisers, Cardinal Richelieu, tried to remedy this problem by granting a fur-trading monopoly to the Company of One Hundred Associates in 1627, on condition that it bring out several hundred settlers each year. However, war between England and France broke out and Quebec was captured in 1629. Even after peace was restored in 1633, the Company of One Hundred Associates failed to honor its commitment to bring out settlers.

Despite the lack of settlers, the colony was expanding in other ways. As governor, Champlain encouraged the expansion of the fur trade. The Jesuits had arrived in 1625 and were vigorously pursuing their missionary work among the Hurons.

Champlain died in 1635, just two years after the colony was restored to France. No leader possessing his vision or drive emerged to replace him. Next, despite their conviction, the French missionaries made few converts among the native people. Even Sainte-Marie among the Hurons, their central mission-post, was abandoned in 1649 in the face of invasion by the Iroquois, who dispersed the Hurons and disrupted the French fur-trading network. Finally, the security of the centre of the fur trade, Montreal (founded in 1642), and the rest of the colony was threatened by the wars against the Iroquois. When the wars were renewed in 1659-1660, after a brief peace, there were still only about 3,000 French settlers in the colony. Clearly, the French king would have to act to secure France's foothold in North America.

1629 **David Kirke** captures Quebec for Britain (July 19).

1632 The **Treaty of Saint-Germain-en-Laye** returns Quebec to France.

1634–40 The **Huron nation** is reduced by half from European diseases (smallpox epidemic, 1639).

1637 **Kirke** is named first governor of Newfoundland.

1642 **Montreal** is founded (May 18) by the Sieur **de Maisonneuve**.

1649 The Jesuit Father **Jean de Brébeuf** is martyred by the **Iroquois** at St-Ignace (Mar. 16). The Iroquois disperse the Huron nation (1648-49).

1659 **François de Laval,** later to become Canada's first bishop, arrives in Quebec (June).

1660 **Adam Dollard des Ormeaux** makes his last stand against the Iroquois at Long Sault (May). The small party of French fights so well that the Iroquois decide not to attack Montreal.

■ Royal Government in New France (1663-1700)

In 1663 King Louis XIV made New France a crown colony. Regular troops were sent out and undertook a successful campaign against the Iroquois, which resulted in the signing of a peace treaty in 1667. Several hundred of these regulars stayed on as settlers, thereby adding to the security of the colony. A system of government headed by a governor, an intendant and a bishop was instituted. The governor, who was the king's representative, was charged with defence. The intendant was responsible for industry, trade and administrative affairs. The bishop looked after religious matters, which included education. In theory, this system provided for a clear separation of powers; but, in practice, there were frequent disputes among the three officials. Still, this system survived intact for the remainder of the colony's history, and it provided New France with some remarkably dynamic officials. Two of these arrived in the first years of the Royal Government.

The first intendant of New France, Jean Talon (1665–1672), introduced innovative measures, including awards for early marriage, to boost the population. As well, he tried to build a diversified economy on the St. Lawrence by promoting crafts, farming and local industry. Few subsequent officials in New France shared Talon's concern for settlement or economic diversity. Most were more interested in profits from the fur trade. Count Frontenac, governor for all but seven years between 1672 and 1698, threw his support behind the fur trade, not only raising profits but also encouraging exploration. Under his rule, French adventurers explored the Mississippi River from its upper reaches to the Gulf of Mexico, greatly expanding the fur-trading boundaries of New France. Frontenac gained more fame when he withstood the attack of an English army which besieged Quebec in 1690.

But Frontenac had not only exceeded his powers in promoting territorial expansion, he had also undermined the security of the colony. With its limited population, New France now found itself competing for the fur trade with the more populous English colonies around them. In the north, there was rivalry with the Hudson's Bay Company, founded in 1670. To the south, there was border warfare between French fur traders and their Indian allies, and the English with their Iroquois allies. New France fared well in the limited warfare of the 1680s and 1690s; but in the 18th century there was a series of major wars which resulted in disaster for the colony.

1663   Quebec becomes a **royal province**.

1665   The Carignan-Salières regiment is sent from France to Quebec to deal with the Iroquois. **Jean Talon** becomes Quebec's intendant.

1666   Canada's **first census** counts 3,215 non-native inhabitants in 668 families.

1670   The **Hudson's Bay Company** is formed and granted trade rights over all territory draining into Hudson Bay (May 2).

1672   Count **Frontenac** becomes Governor of Quebec.

1673   **Marquette** and **Jolliet** explore the Mississippi to its junction with the Arkansas.

1674   **Laval** becomes first Bishop of Quebec.

1678–79 **Dulhut** explores the headwaters of the Mississippi.

1682   **La Salle** explores the Mississippi to its mouth.

1686   **De Troyes** and **D'Iberville** capture the English posts of Moose Fort (June 20), Rupert House (July 3) and Fort Albany (July 26) on James Bay.

1689   The Iroquois kill many French settlers at Lachine.

1690   **Sir William Phips captures Port Royal** (May 11). Frontenac repels Phips's attack on Quebec (Oct.).

1697   The **Treaty of Ryswick** restores the status quo in the struggle between England and France. All captured territory is returned.

■ The Collapse of New France (1701-1763)

In the early years of the 18th century, New France stretched from Hudson Bay to the Gulf of Mexico, and from Newfoundland to the Great Lakes. Its population was thinly scattered in the north, south and west but its fur-trading posts in these regions gave legitimacy to its territorial claims. In the Atlantic region, there were several hundred colonists in Newfoundland and another 1,500 in Acadia. The heartland of New France was the settlement of about 20,000 colonists in Montreal, Quebec and in the small communities along the St. Lawrence. The prosperity of the French settlements was to be hurt by long periods of war.

The first of these was the war of the Spanish Succession fought between France and Austria (and their allies) between 1701-1714. Although the British failed to capture their main objective in the North American campaign, the fortress city of Quebec, they made other gains at the bargaining table. In the Treaty of Utrecht, which ended the conflict, France gave up claims to the Hudson Bay territory, all of Acadia except Cape Breton, and Newfoundland.

During a 30-year period of peace, New France enjoyed limited prosperity. The populaton grew, farm yields increased, some industry was established and furs were still exported. But military expenditure necessary to protect the colony was turning it into a financial burden for France. Much of that expenditure went into the huge fortress of Louisbourg, built on Cape Breton Island to protect the offshore fisheries and guard the St. Lawrence.

Prussia, France, Spain, Naples, Bavaria and Saxony fought Austria and England when the war of Austrian Succession broke out in 1740 and Louisbourg was a natural target. The fortress fell to the British, although it was returned to France at the war's end in 1748. The British established their own military and naval base at Halifax in 1749.

The fragile peace was broken in 1754, when fighting broke out between the English and French colonists in the Ohio Valley. Within two years, Britain and France were officially at war again in what became known as the Seven Years' War. Despite some early victories, the French suffered the loss of Louisbourg in 1758. In the following year, General Wolfe defeated General Montcalm on the Plains of Abraham above the St. Lawrence at Quebec. Although Montreal did not fall until the next year, the loss of Quebec was an irreversible setback. The British army occupied New France, and in 1763 the treaty ending the Seven Years' War confirmed British sovereignty.

New France had fallen because of decisive military defeats at Louisbourg and Quebec, but more significant was the inability of France to supply its colony in the face of British naval supremacy. The British were now masters in North America.

1701 The **War of the Spanish Succession** begins in Europe; the conflict spreads to North America the following year.

1710 Francis Nicholson captures Port Royal for England.

1713 The **Treaty of Utrecht** confirms British possession of Hudson Bay, Newfoundland and Acadia (except Cape Breton Island). France starts building Fort **Louisbourg**.

1739 La Vérendrye expedition explores Lake Winnipeg.

1740 The **War of the Austrian Succession** pits Britain against France; the European conflict spreads to North America (**King George's War**) in **1744**.

1745 Massachusetts Governor William Shirley takes the French fortress of **Louisbourg**.

1748 Louisbourg is returned to France by the **Treaty of Aix-la-Chapelle**.

1749 Britain founds **Halifax** to counter the French presence at Louisbourg.

1752 Canada's **first newspaper**, the Halifax *Gazette,* appears (Mar. 25).

1753 **George Washington**'s military expedition to the Monogahela is defeated by the French.

1754 Beginning of **French and Indian War** in America. Although war is not officially declared for another two years, this marks the final phase in the struggle between France and Britain in North America.

1755 Britain expels the **Acadians** from Nova Scotia, scattering them throughout her other North American colonies.

1756 Beginning of the **Seven Years' War** in Europe pits Britain against France. The Marquis **de Montcalm** assumes command of French troops in North America.

1758 The British under Generals Amherst and Wolfe take Louisbourg.

1759 **Wolfe takes Quebec**, defeating Montcalm on the Plains of Abraham (Sept. 13). Both generals are killed.

1760 General **James Murray** is appointed military governor of Quebec; he becomes civil governor in **1764**.

■ The First Years of British Rule (1763-1812)

The British had been active on the continent during their search for a northwest passage to the far east; however, their victory over the French encouraged a shift from exploration and fur trading to settlement and the strengthening of British customs in the new territory.

In 1763 a Royal Proclamation was imposed by the British government on the newly-acquired territories of New France. The intent of this proclamation was clear. By encouraging the establishment of Protestant schools, by promoting the Church of England, and by stipulating that an assembly be elected, the proclamation aimed at Anglicization. The intent was most visible in the matter of the assembly. Although the French inhabitants were in the majority, under British law no Roman Catholic could hold office. If an assembly were elected, a few hundred British settlers would control about 65,000 Canadiens.

Fortunately for the French in Canada, James Murray, the governor of Quebec from 1760 to 1768, felt that the loyalty of the French colonists could more likely be gained by fair treatment. Murray refused to call elections for the assembly, and allowed French legal practices to continue. Murray's sympathies provoked a storm of protest from the British colonists in Quebec and he was recalled. But his successor, Guy Carleton, also realized that the Royal Proclamation of 1763 would only alienate the recently-defeated colonists. Carleton saw that even if Anglicization were carried out, few colonists from the Thirteen Colonies in America or immigrants from Britain would be lured to the rugged colony of Quebec. Consequently, Carleton advised the government in London to replace the proclamation with more liberal legislation.

The result was the Quebec Act of 1774, which dropped the assembly in favour of an appointed council on which Catholics might serve. As well, the French system of civil law and the seigneurial system of land tenure were both guaranteed. Finally, the Quebec Act expanded the borders of the colony to include the rich lands of the Ohio Valley. The British had acted to win the support of the Canadiens. In doing so, however, the British government angered the citizens of the Thirteen Colonies, who resented the special treatment given to their former enemies. These English colonists were especially upset over the loss of the Ohio Valley, a region into which they expected to expand.

The Quebec Act was not the only cause for complaint in the Thirteen Colonies. Protests over British taxation policies and trade restriction led to talk of revolution. That talk led to action, and in 1775 an invading American army took Montreal. Quebec held out against the American siege until relieved by British forces. Although there was some sympathy for the American cause in both Quebec and Nova Scotia, it was not a strong enough sentiment to cause these two colonies to join the revolution.

During and immediately after the American Revolution, some American colonists who wished to retain their British ties fled from the newly-created United States into the Maritimes and Quebec. The arrival of about 30,000 of these Loyalists in Nova Scotia resulted in the creation of a new colony, New Brunswick, in 1784. Similarly, the influx of 10,000 Loyalists into Quebec led to division of the colony, and in 1791, the western part of the colony became Upper Canada. The remainder of the old colony was known as Lower Canada.

Despite these changes, fur trading remained an important economic activity in the interior of British North America. In fact, there was keen rivalry for furs between the Hudson's Bay Company and the newly-formed (1784) North West Company based in Montreal which led to a flurry of western exploration. Alexander Mackenzie, a partner in the North West Company, explored a river (now known as the Mackenzie) to its mouth on the Beaufort Sea in 1789, and found a route to the Pacific via the Fraser and Bella Coola Rivers in 1793. Two other North West Company employees, Simon Fraser and David Thompson, also carried out voyages of discovery. Fraser followed the river named after him to the Pacific in 1808, and Thompson travelled down the Columbia River to the coast in 1811. These voyages, along with the earlier coastal explorations of James Cook in 1778 and George Vancouver in 1792-1795, helped establish Britain's claim to the northwest part of the continent.

1763 France cedes its North American possessions to Britain by the **Treaty of Paris**. A Royal Proclamation imposes British institutions on Quebec (Oct.). This proclamation also serves as the cornerstone for relations between Canadian aboriginal peoples and the Canadian government, preserving land for their use and giving the government exclusive right to negotiate treaties.

1768 **Guy Carleton** succeeds Murray as governor of Quebec.

1769 Frances Brooke publishes *The History of Emily Montague*, a novel with descriptions of geography, climate and social culture in the New World.

1774 The **Quebec Act** provides for British criminal law but restores French civil law and guarantees religious freedom for Roman Catholic colonists.

1775 Americans under Montgomery capture Montreal (Nov.) and attack Quebec (Dec. 31).

1776 Under Carleton, Quebec withstands American siege until the appearance of a British fleet (May 6).

1778 Captain **James Cook** anchors in Nootka Sound, Vancouver Island (Mar. 29–Apr. 26).

1783 The American Revolutionary War ends; the border between Canada and the US is accepted between the Atlantic Ocean and Lake of the Woods.

1784 **United Empire Loyalists** arrive in Canada. The province of **New Brunswick** is created. The **North West Company** is formed.

1789 **Alexander Mackenzie** journeys to the Beaufort Sea, following what would later be named the Mackenzie River.

1791 **Constitutional Act** divides Quebec into Upper and Lower Canada.

1792 **George Vancouver** begins his explorations of the Pacific coast.

1793 **Alexander Mackenzie** reaches the **Pacific**.

1794 **Jay's Treaty** (Nov. 19) between the US and Britain promises British evacuation of the Ohio Valley forts. The treaty's appointment of officials to settle boundary disputes marks the beginning of international arbitration through its provisions for boundary settlements.

1797 **David Thompson** joins the North West Company as a surveyor and mapmaker.

1806 *Le Canadien*, Quebec nationalist newspaper, is founded.

1808 **Simon Fraser**, a North West Company employee, travels the river named after him to the Pacific.

1811 **David Thompson** charts the Columbia River to the Pacific coast.

■ The War of 1812

Although the British and Americans signed a peace treaty in 1783 to end the American War of Independence, there was still friction between them. One source of conflict was the British fur-trading posts in the Ohio Valley which now belonged to the United States. Although Britain surrendered these posts in 1796 as stipulated by Jay's Treaty (1794), there were still American complaints that the British were arming the local native people. At the same time there was growing American resentment over British interference with shipping. The British, who were at war with France, claimed the right to search American ships for cargoes bound for the enemy. In the process, the British often forced American sailors on these ships to join the British navy. Resentment grew among Americans until June 1812, when the United States declared war on Britain.

In the first year of the war, the Americans under General William Hull crossed the Detroit River to invade Upper Canada. Hull expected Canadian sympathizers to flock to his cause but he was disappointed. Without fighting a major battle, he retreated to Detroit. British General Isaac Brock and the Shawnees, under Chief Tecumseh, moved against Detroit and General Hull surrendered. This British and Canadian victory was followed by a victory at Queenston Heights on the Niagara River. Brock was killed in this battle which nevertheless gave confidence to the defenders of the British colonies.

In 1813, the Americans carried out a successful raid on York (now Toronto), and also gained a foothold in the Niagara district. But by the summer of that year the Americans had been pushed back across the Niagara River by British victories at Stoney Creek and Beaver Dam. Meanwhile, the Americans were building up a large fleet on the Great Lakes, and in September 1813 the Americans won control of Lake Erie at the Battle of Put-in-Bay. This victory prompted the British under General Proctor to abandon Fort Malden on the Detroit River. However, the American General Harrison caught the retreating forces at Moraviantown on the Thames River and defeated Proctor. Tecumseh was killed in this battle. In the east, a two-pronged attack on Montreal was repulsed. The American invaders were defeated on the Chateauguay River and at Crysler's Farm near Cornwall in the fall of 1813.

In 1814, the Americans again invaded the Niagara district but were halted at the Battle of Lundy's Lane. From Halifax, British forces attacked targets in Maine, and occupied most of that state. Another attack from Halifax was launched on the American capital, Washington. The British raiders burned the government buildings there in retaliation for the destruction of York the previous year. Despite these successes, a major British offensive against Plattsburgh on Lake Champlain failed. By now the war was in stalemate and both sides were tired. British and American negotiators signed the Treaty of Ghent in Dec. 1814, to end the war.

In the aftermath of the war, the two sides made an effort to settle outstanding differences. The Rush-Bagot Agreement of 1817 provided for naval disarmament on the Great

Lakes. In the following year Britain and the United States agreed to accept the 49th parallel as the international boundary from the Lake of the Woods to the Rocky Mountains. In addition, they agreed to the joint occupation of the Oregon Territory for 10 years.

1812 The US declares war on Britain (June 18), beginning the **War of 1812**. Americans under General William Hull invade Canada from Detroit (July 11). The Red River settlement is begun in Canada's northwest (Aug.–Oct.). Battle of Queenston Heights (Oct. 13): Canadian victory. British **General Isaac Brock** is killed in this battle.

1813 Americans burn York (Apr. 27). Battle of Stoney Creek (June 5): Canadian victory. Battle of Beaver Dams (June 23): Canadian victory; **Laura Secord**, driving a cow, passes American sentries and walks 32 km through dense bush to warn of American attack. Battle of Put-in-Bay, Lake Erie (Sept. 10): American victory. Battle of Moraviantown (Oct. 5): American victory; the Indian Chief **Tecumseh** is killed. Battle of Chateauguay (Oct. 25): Canadian victory. Battle of Crysler's Farm (Nov. 11): Canadian victory.

1814 Battle of Chippewa (July 5): American victory. Battle of Lundy's Lane (July 25): Canadian victory. A British naval force takes Washington (Aug. 24). Battle of Lake Champlain (Sept. 6–11): American victory. The **Treaty of Ghent** ends the War of 1812 (Dec. 24).

■ Rebellion and Reform (1814-1839)

In the years after the War of 1812, there was considerable growth in British North America. The population increased as immigrants from both the United States and Britain arrived to take up land that was free or inexpensive. The economy became more diversified as lumbering, farming and shipbuilding developed in the Canadas and in the Maritimes. Finally, a sense of nationalism began to grow in parts of British North America. This feeling arose partly out of postwar patriotism and partly out of the shared experiences of a demanding colonial life.

As the colonies became more populous, political interest increased. In both the Canadas and the Maritimes friction between ruling elites and the ordinary colonists developed and was partially fueled by the form of government in each colony. British governors or lieutenant-governors picked their own officials, including the members of legislative or executive councils. There were elected assemblies in each colony, but their powers were limited. Legislation might pass in the assembly but be turned down by the legislative council. The assemblies, the voice of the people, found themselves frustrated by the power of appointed officials.

By the mid-1830s, economic distress increased the discontent that had been building during the 1820s. In Lower Canada, where cultural prejudice against the Canadiens added to the tension, Louis Joseph Papineau emerged as leader of the radical Patriote Party. When the colonial authorities would not grant the reforms called for by Papineau and his followers, rebellion broke out in November 1837. But loyalist forces quickly defeated the badly-organized and poorly-led rebels. Papineau and other leaders fled to the United States.

In Upper Canada, the reform movement was able to gain a majority in the assembly in several elections. Still, the reformers could not turn their program into legislation because of Tory control of the Legislative Council. When an anti-reform lieutenant-governor, Sir Francis Bond Head, took over in 1836, some reformers became more radical. Their leader was William Lyon Mackenzie, a newspaper editor and member of the assembly. The Tories won the election of 1836, when Head directly intervened in the campaign. Mackenzie and his followers, spurred on by events in Lower Canada, took up arms in early December of 1837. Mackenzie's disorganization, and lack of widespread support among the colonists, doomed the rebellion. After a skirmish north of Toronto the main body of rebels fled. An uprising in the western districts of Upper Canada was equally unsuccessful. Throughout the following year some rebels and American sympathizers mounted raids on Upper Canada from the United States, but these received no popular support.

In the aftermath of the rebellions came political change. The British government sent out Lord Durham to act as Governor General of British North America and investigate the rebellion. The Durham Report of 1839 contained two main recommendations: the first called for the union of Upper and Lower Canada as a first step in the eventual assimilation of the French Canadians; the second recommended the granting of responsible government (in which the executive is responsible to the assembly), a key demand of reformers.

1816 Agents of the North West Company kill Robert Semple, governor of the Hudson's Bay Company's Red River colony, and 21 others at White Oaks (June 19).

1817 The **Rush-Bagot** agreement limits the number of battleships on the Great Lakes.

1818 The **49th parallel** is accepted as **Canada's border** with the US from Lake of the Woods to the Rocky Mountains.

1821 The Hudson's Bay Company and the North West Company are amalgamated as the HBC.

1829 The **Lachine** and **Welland Canals** are completed.

1835 **William Lyon Mackenzie** becomes the first mayor of Toronto.

1836 Opening of Canada's **first railway line,** from St. Johns, Que., to La Prairie, Que.

1837 Unsuccessful **rebellions** in Upper and Lower Canada are led by Mackenzie and Louis-Joseph Papineau.

1839 **Lord Durham's Report** recommends union of Upper and Lower Canada and the establishment of responsible government.

■ The Road to Confederation (1840-1867)

The middle years of the 19th century were both satisfying and disturbing for British North Americans. Immigrants from Europe streamed into the colonies, more land was cleared and towns grew. Local industries were started while lumbering and shipbuilding activities increased. Montreal and Toronto became commercial centres and the ports of the Maritimes were prosperous, fuelled by ship building and trade. Transportation improved as roads, canals and, by the 1850s, railways were built. Some British North Americans looked beyond their borders and began to think of a federation of British colonies that included not only Canada and the Maritimes, but the Red River settlement and the colonies in British Columbia.

Despite the prosperity, there were reasons to consider such an alliance. Until the mid-1840s, the colonies had enjoyed a preferential trading relationship whereby Britain reduced tariffs on colonial products. This advantage was lost in 1846 when Britain adopted free trade. At first, the colonies found some advantage in entering into a limited free trade arrangement with the United States. But the Americans allowed this Reciprocity Treaty of 1854 to lapse in 1866. British North Americans would have to look to themselves as trading partners.

There was also concern in British North America about the United States. That country seemed intent on fulfilling its "Manifest Destiny" to take over North America. The threat was especially clear during and after the American Civil War (1861-65). During the war, the Northern States were angered by British support for the South, and after the war, there was a fear that the large Northern army might march into British territory.

As well, there was a serious political problem in the colony of Canada. The union of Upper and Lower Canada in 1841 had resulted in the creation of a single legislature for the new colony, Canada. By the 1860s, however, this legislature was barely functioning. No single party could gain enough support from both Francophones and Anglophones to gain a majority. There had been 12 different governments in 15 years, and Canadian politicians were desperate for a solution.

Three powerful figures in Canada's legislature, John A. Macdonald, George Brown and George-Étienne Cartier formed a coalition and proposed a larger union of British North America as a way to end the political deadlock. In addition, this proposal would solve the problem of trade and provide security against the American threat. Meanwhile, on the east coast there was interest in a union too, a union of the Maritimes. A conference had been called for Charlottetown in September 1864 to discuss that topic. When the leaders of the new Canadian coalition heard of this meeting, they asked for an invitation. At Charlottetown the British North American delegates decided on a federation of all the colonies. A second conference at Quebec in October 1864 resulted in a plan for federal union. A federal government would control defence, trade and other matters of national interest. Provincial governments would have power over local matters such as roads and education. The final details were hammered out at another conference in London, England, in 1866.

The British government, which supported this colonial initiative, passed the British North America Act in March of 1867. On July 1, 1867, the provinces of Nova Scotia, New Brunswick, Ontario (formerly Canada West) and Quebec (formerly Canada East), became the Dominion of Canada.

1841 The **Act of Union** unites Upper and Lower Canada.

1842 The Ashburton-Webster Treaty settles the Maine-New Brunswick border dispute.

1843 **Fort Victoria** is built to bolster Britain's claim to Vancouver Island.

1846 Great Britain ends a preferential trading policy with the British North American colonies and enters into a **limited free trade agreement** with the United States.

1848 **Responsible government** is achieved in the Canadas and in the Maritimes, thanks to the work of **Robert Baldwin** and **Joseph Howe**.

1849 The boundary of the 49th parallel is extended to the Pacific Ocean. The province of Canada adopts both English and French as official languages. All bills of the United Canada Parliament, now Quebec and Ontario, are given assent in both English and French.

1851 Britain transfers control of the colonial postal system to Canada.

1854 The **Reciprocity Treaty** between Canada and the US is signed (June 6).

1857 **Ottawa** is named **Canada's capital** by Queen Victoria.

1860 Cornerstone of the **Parliament Buildings** is laid (Sept. 1).

1861 The **Grand Trunk Railway** through the length of the Province of Canada is completed.

1864 The **Charlottetown Conference** (Sept. 1–9) takes the first steps toward **Confederation**. The **Quebec Conference** (Oct. 10–27) sets out the basis for union.

1866 The **London Conference** (Dec. 4) passes resolutions which are redrafted to become the **British North America Act**. First raid into Canada by the **Fenians**, a radical Irish-American anti-British group, takes place (June 2). The American government allows the **Reciprocity Treaty of 1854** to lapse.

1867 **Confederation**. Britain's North American colonies are united by means of the **BNA Act** to become the **Dominion of Canada** (July 1). **Sir John A. Macdonald** is Canada's first prime minister. The BNA Act, now the **Constitution Act, 1867**, confirms the practice of **official bilingualism**, guaranteeing the use of French and English in the debates of the House of Commons and in the Senate, in federal courts and in publications of federal statutes. The provincial legislature, statutes and courts of Quebec are also made bilingual.

■ The Nation Expands (1867-1885)

Soon after the Confederation of Ontario, Quebec, New Brunswick and Nova Scotia in 1867, the new nation of Canada began to acquire more territory. In 1869, guided by the national vision of Prime Minister John A. Macdonald, the federal government bought Rupert's Land from the Hudson's Bay Company. This was a huge territory which included most of modern Manitoba, as well as parts of Saskatchewan, Alberta and the Northwest Territories. The few Ontario immigrants in the Red River Settlement there welcomed this move; but the far more numerous Métis (descendants of French fur traders and native people) were suspicious, especially because they had not been consulted beforehand. When newly-appointed Lieutenant-Governor William McDougall tried to enter the settlement before the territory had officially been transferred to Canada, the Métis turned him back. In the absence of a legitimate government, the Métis, under their leader Louis Riel, seized Fort Garry on the Red River and proclaimed a provisional government. The Métis demanded the right to vote, land laws, the official use of both French and English, and the provision of both Roman Catholic and Protestant schools. The Métis list of rights became the terms for negotiating Manitoba's entry into Confederation in 1870.

In the same year, representatives from the colony of British Columbia arrived in Ottawa to discuss union. With the promise from Ottawa to build a transcontinental railway, British Columbia entered Confederation in 1871. Canada now stretched from sea to sea, but the work of nation building was still not complete.

In 1868, Nova Scotia elected an anti-Confederation provincial government and sent a delegation, led by veteran politician Joseph

Howe, to London to seek a repeal of the union. But Britain was unsympathetic, and in 1869 Macdonald seized the opportunity to offer Nova Scotia better terms and Howe a cabinet position. With the Nova Scotia situation resolved, Macdonald turned his attention to Prince Edward Island. The Islanders were more attracted to the idea of union after an expensive railway project nearly bankrupted the colony. Macdonald agreed to assume the colony's debts, offered a cash subsidy and promised a steamer service to the mainland. In 1873, Prince Edward Island agreed to the terms and became Canada's 7th province.

In the 1870s and 1880s railways were built to link the provinces of the new nation. The Intercolonial Railway, joining central Canada to the Maritimes, was completed in 1876, but construction of a rail link to British Columbia ran into several delays. First, Macdonald's government was defeated in 1873 over charges of corruption associated with the railway project. The new prime minister, Alexander Mackenzie, refused to fund railway projects because the country was in the midst of a depression. However, after Macdonald's re-election in 1878, railway building began in earnest. In February 1881, the Canadian Pacific Railway Company (CPR) was incorporated, and in November 1885 the last spike was driven at Craigellachie in British Columbia to complete the link to the Pacific.

Even before it was fully completed, the CPR was used to carry troops to quell a rebellion in the spring of 1885. Trouble had started several years earlier when settlers in the North-West Territory (modern Alberta and Saskatchewan) complained to the government about land titles, shipping rates, and their lack of an elected government. Among those who complained were the Métis, some of whom had moved farther west after the Red River troubles of 1870. When the federal government was slow to respond, the Métis, again under Louis Riel, rose up in March 1885 against the territorial council appointed by Ottawa. By late April, 5,000 Canadian soldiers, who had travelled by the new railway, were on the march against Riel and his Métis and native followers. At the Battle of Batoche in May, the forces of General Middleton defeated the rebels. Riel was found guilty of treason by an English-speaking jury and executed.

1868 Confederationist **Thomas D'Arcy McGee** is **assassinated** by a Fenian in Canada's first political assassination.

1869 Canada purchases Rupert's Land from the Hudson's Bay Company for £300,000.

1870 **Louis Riel** leads the Métis in resisting Canadian authority in Canada's northwest. The Métis negotiate with the Canadian government over the right to vote, land laws, the official use of both French and English and the provision of Roman Catholic and Protestant schools. The Manitoba Act creates the province of **Manitoba**.

1871 **British Columbia** joins Confederation upon the promise from Ottawa to build a **transcontinental railway**.

1872 Macdonald's Conservatives win federal re-election.

1873 **Prince Edward Island** joins Confederation. A period of economic depression begins. The North-West Mounted Police are formed. **Alexander Mackenzie** becomes Canada's second prime minister after **Macdonald resigns** over the **Pacific Scandal**.

1874 Liberals win federal election.

1875 The **Supreme Court of Canada** is established.

1876 The **Intercolonial Railway** linking central Canada and the Maritimes is completed (July 1). The **Indian Act of 1876** defines special status for aboriginal people living on land reserves and sets out land regulations. Status Indians have no vote in Canadian elections and are exempted from taxation.

1878 Conservatives under Macdonald win federal election.

1879 Macdonald introduces **protective tariffs** as part of his **National Policy**.

1880 **Emily Stowe** receives her medical licence after practising medicine in Toronto since her graduation from a New York medical school in 1867.

1881 The **Canadian Pacific Railway** is incorporated.

1884 **Riel returns** to Canada.

1885 Métis and the NWMP clash at Duck Lake (Mar. 26). The Métis are defeated at Batoche (May 9–12). The **last spike of the transcontinental railway** is driven at Craigellachie in Eagle Pass, BC, by Donald

Smith (Nov. 7). **Louis Riel** is **hanged** in Regina (Nov. 16).

1887 Conservatives win federal election. Liberals choose **Wilfrid Laurier** as leader. The **first provincial premiers' conference** takes place in Quebec City.

1889 The **Dominion Women's Enfranchisement Association** is created to campaign for female voting rights in Canada.

1890 Manitoba Liberals under Thomas Greenway halt public funding of Catholic schools in Manitoba (Mar.).

1891 Conservatives win federal election. **Sir John A. Macdonald dies. Sir John Abbott** takes office as prime minister (June 16).

1892 Abbott resigns (Nov. 24). **Sir John Thompson** becomes prime minister (Dec. 5). He establishes the **Canadian Criminal Code**.

1894 Thompson dies (Dec. 12). **Sir Mackenzie Bowell** is asked by the governor general, the Earl of Aberdeen, to form the fourth Conservative government since 1891.

■ The Laurier Era (1896-1911)

Conservative Prime Minister John A. Macdonald died in 1891, soon after winning a federal election. The Conservatives could not find a suitable successor and by 1896 there had been four prime ministers—John Abbott, John Thompson, Mackenzie Bowell and Charles Tupper. During this period, the Conservatives had to deal with a crisis over school legislation introduced in Manitoba. The Manitoba legislature had replaced the dual school system (both Protestant and Catholic schools) which had been guaranteed in the terms of union, with a single Protestant system. Francophone Catholics across Canada were already bitter about Louis Riel's execution. Now the Manitoba schools legislation convinced them that English Protestant Canadians wanted to stamp out French Catholic rights. Extremists on both sides inflamed the issue, and the Conservatives' inability to settle the matter hurt them in the election of 1896. The Liberals, under Wilfrid Laurier, formed a government.

Laurier settled the Manitoba school question by adopting a compromise approach. Religious instruction would be allowed within the single system, and instruction in French could take place where numbers warranted. The issue died down, but Laurier remained sensitive to the tensions between Anglophone Protestants and Francophone Catholics. Many English Canadians were swept up in a great wave of pro-imperial sentiment associated with the Diamond Jubilee of Queen Victoria. In Britain the event was seen as an opportunity to strengthen ties within the British Empire. Laurier acknowledged Canada's support for the Empire, but resisted proposals for a closer relationship with Britain and the other colonies. The prime minister did not wish to yield Canadian autonomy, nor did he wish to lose support in French Canada. The issue of Canada's role in the Empire came to a head in 1899 during the Boer War when the South African Republic (Transvaal) and the Orange Free State fought against Britain. Once again steering a middle course, Laurier agreed to equip and transport Canadian volunteers to South Africa, but sent no official troops. Although this compromise did not satisfy all Canadians, it avoided a bitter dispute. For a time, imperial issues were forgotten, as Canadians enjoyed boom times after the turn of the century.

Laurier summed up the nation's mood when he declared that the "twentieth century is Canada's century." Impressive growth in both industrial and agricultural production provided support for his words. Canada's prospects appealed to immigrants who flocked to the industrial cities and to the farmland of the Prairies. Many of them were attracted by an extensive government advertising campaign and by the lure of free land in the west. As a result of this influx, two new provinces, Alberta and Saskatchewan, were created in 1905. The immigrant tide boosted Canada's population from 5,371,315 in 1901 to 7,206,643 in 1911. The mood of the country was so confident that two new transcontinental railway building projects got under way in the early years of the century.

The international scene, however, was not so bright. In 1903, the British sided with the Americans in the Alaska Boundary Dispute, a disagreement over the international boundary near the Klondike gold fields. Canadians were dismayed, but Britain was less concerned about the Canadian claim than for the need to maintain good relations with the United States. Tension in Europe was increasing and Britain found itself outside of the complicated system of alliances which had developed there. This same concern led both the British government and the Canadian pro-imperialists to pressure

Laurier into providing money to build British warships. Again, Laurier staked out a middle position by introducing a Naval Service Act which created a Canadian navy that could help Britain where the need arose.

Laurier's compromise on naval policy satisfied neither side. Some French Canadians supported the views of Quebec nationalist Henri Bourassa who claimed Laurier had betrayed his people. Anglophone pro-imperialists complained that Laurier's "tin pot navy" was not enough. Canada's naval policy became an issue in the 1911 election, as did the Liberal plan for free trade with the United States. Conservative leader Robert Borden was able to use both to characterize Laurier as not only disloyal to Britain but favoring annexation to the United States. The Conservatives won the election. Borden became prime minister and Laurier stayed on as leader of the Opposition, continuing to advocate conciliatory policies when the interests of French and English Canadians clashed.

1896 The economic depression ends. Bowell resigns, calling his cabinet a "nest of traitors" (Apr. 27). **Sir Charles Tupper** leads an interim government until the Liberals under Laurier win federal election on **Manitoba Schools Question** (June 23). Canada's minister of the interior, **Clifford Sifton**, develops an immigration plan that will bring farmers from central and eastern Europe to settle on the Prairies. Gold is discovered in the Klondike (Aug. 16).

1897 **Gold Rush** begins in the Klondike. **Clara Brett Martin** is the first woman admitted to the bar of Ontario.

1898 **Yukon** becomes a separate entity from the Northwest Territories. **Kit Coleman**, the first female Canadian war correspondent, covers the Spanish-American War for a Toronto newspaper.

1899 The first **Canadian troops** ever sent overseas are dispatched to the **Boer War** (Oct. 30).

1901 Marconi receives the **first transatlantic radio message** at St. John's, Newfoundland.

1903 Canada loses the **Alaska Boundary Dispute** when British tribunal representative Lord Alverstone sides with the US (Oct. 20). In northern Ontario, Fred LaRose throws hammer at what he thinks are fox's eyes and hits world's richest silver vein.

1904 Liberals win federal election.

1905 The provinces of **Alberta** and **Saskatchewan** are formed.

1907 The **National Council of Women** calls for "equal pay for equal work."

1908 Liberals win federal election.

1909 The Department of External Affairs is formed. John McCurdy's Silver Dart is first heavier-than-air machine to achieve powered flight in Canada at Baddeck, NS. University of Toronto wins **first Grey Cup** football match.

1910 Laurier creates a Canadian navy via the Naval Service Bill.

1911 **Robert Borden** and the Conservatives win federal election, defeating Laurier on the reciprocity issue.

■ Canada and the First World War (1914-1918)

In August 1914, Britain declared war on Germany and Austria–Hungary. The declaration automatically applied to Canada, as part of the British Empire. At first, there was an enthusiastic response, especially among recent British immigrants. When the minister of militia, Sam Hughes, called for 25,000 volunteers, nearly 33,000 appeared. In 1915, when the government asked the Canadian public to buy $50 million in war bonds, they bought $100 million. But enthusiasm for war began to fade as the casualties mounted and the realities of trench warfare became known.

Canadian troops sailed for Europe in October 1914 and, after training in Britain, went into action at Ypres, Belgium, in April 1915. There they gained a reputation for courage, holding their positions in the face of a poison gas attack, a new weapon at the time. Canadians took part in the costly battles at St. Eloi and Mont Sorrel in 1916. By the Battle of the Somme, in late summer of 1916, Canada had four army divisions in France; in the spring of 1917, all four were deployed in the attack on Vimy Ridge, which resulted in the first real Canadian victory of the war. But by now it was clear that every battle would result in terrible losses. At Passchendaele in October 1917, the Canadians sustained more than 15,000 casualties.

Voluntary recruitment could not keep pace with the high casualty rates. Prime Minister Borden was forced to consider conscription to draft soldiers into the army and took the question to the electorate in 1917, unleashing one of the most bitterly fought campaigns in Canadian history. In Quebec, Henri Bourassa rallied anti-conscription supporters and argued that Canada had done enough. In Ontario, Borden's supporters condemned French-Canadian anti-conscriptionists as traitors. For his part Borden introduced the Wartime Elections Act to help secure victory. This act removed the right to vote from enemy aliens, even though some were Canadian citizens. It also gave the right to vote to women relatives of soldiers. In the election Borden won in every province except Quebec where he was soundly rejected. Conscription had created a deep division between Quebec and the rest of Canada and once in practice, it had little impact on the course of the war. When the first 400,000 conscripts were called up, 90 percent of them appealed for exemption, and by the war's end only about 24,000 conscripts had reached the front.

While the conscription crisis raged at home, Canadian soldiers played a major role in the events leading to an Allied victory. They took part in the successful battle at Amiens in August 1918 and helped to roll the Germans back to Mons by November. The Canadians were still fighting at Mons when the armistice was signed Nov. 11, 1918.

Canadians also served with distinction in other theatres of war. By 1918, Canadians made up almost 25 percent of the pilots in Britain's Royal Flying Corps. Other Canadians served in the Royal Navy or on coastal patrol in Canada's own small navy. Some served in forestry corps overseas and others operated the railways behind the British lines. Some, including women, served as ambulance drivers at the front. Many Canadian women also played key roles as nurses overseas and in the munitions factories in Canada.

Canada's war effort won the country a place in the Imperial War Cabinet during the war, and a seat in the League of Nations afterwards. There were other benefits, too. Women's contributions to the war effort helped them win the right to vote in federal elections and in provincial elections in seven of the provinces by 1919. Yet these advances came at a terrible cost. Overseas, 68,300 Canadians had died. At home, bitterness over the conscription issue had created a division between French and English Canadians that would be remembered for decades.

1914 CP ship *Empress of Ireland* sinks in the St Lawrence in 14 minutes after being rammed in fog, with the loss of 1,014 lives (May 29). **Canada is automatically at war** with Germany when Britain declares war (Aug. 4). The first Canadian troops leave for England (Oct. 3). Parliament passes the **War Measures Act,** allowing suspension of civil rights during periods of emergency. European immigration to Canada increases. Over one million settlers come between 1911 and 1913, bringing total immigration to three million since 1891.

1915 Canadians face German gas attack at **Ypres,** Belgium (Apr. 22). John McCrae writes "In Flanders Fields."

1916 **Nellie McClung** succeeds in persuading the Manitoba government to grant women the right to vote and to hold office (Jan.). The Parliament Buildings are destroyed by fire (Feb. 3). Canadian troops fight in the Battle of the **Somme** (July to Nov.); 24,713 Canadians and Newfoundlanders are killed. The unreliable, Canadian-made Ross rifle is withdrawn from war service (Aug.). **Emily Gowan Murphy** is the first woman magistrate appointed within the British Empire.

1917 **Income tax** is introduced as a "temporary wartime measure." Prime Minister Sir Robert Borden sits as a member of the Imperial War Cabinet (Feb. 23), giving Canada a voice in war policy. The Military Service Bill is introduced (June 11), leading to the **Conscription Crisis** between Quebec and English Canada. Unionist government under Borden wins federal election, in which **women vote** for the first time. **Louise McKinney** is elected to the Alberta legislature, the first woman in the British Commonwealth to hold such office. Canadians capture **Vimy Ridge,** France (Apr. 9–12). Canadians take **Passchendaele,** Belgium, (Nov. 7) in one of the war's worst battles; of the 20,000 Canadian troops sent into the two-week battle, 15,654 are killed or wounded. Explosion of a munitions ship in **Halifax harbour** wipes out two square miles (5.2 sq. km) of Halifax, killing almost 2,000 and injuring 9,000 (Dec. 6).

1918 Canadians break through German trenches at Amiens (Aug. 8), "the black day of the German army." The period from this date until the end of the war becomes known as "Canada's Hundred Days." Armistice ends war (Nov. 11).

■ Canada in the 1920s

As the soldiers returned home, many expected to find a Canada ready to reward them for their sacrifices. What they found was a nation in the midst of painful postwar readjustment. Industry had to convert to peacetime production, but interest rates were so high investment capital was scarce. Jobs were hard to find and wages were low, and tariffs on imported goods kept prices high. By 1921, 300,000 men and women—more than 15% of the work force—were unemployed. Farmers, especially on the Prairies, also suffered. During the war, the west had become the world's breadbasket: wheat prices had soared and many farmers had borrowed heavily to expand their production. But with the war's end, world markets collapsed; wheat prices fell by almost half within two years.

These conditions, along with resentment over wartime profiteering by big business, created unrest. The One Big Union movement, centred in western Canada, attempted to create a single union to represent all workers. The Winnipeg General Strike of 1919 grew out of the organizers' efforts and the general discontent. Although the Winnipeg workers were striking over such issues as the right to collective bargaining, better wages and improved working conditions, the opponents of the general strike characterized it as a communist conspiracy by raising the spectre of a revolution similar to the one in Russia two years earlier. The federal government sided with the anti-strike forces. Immigration laws were amended to deport "alien" labour radicals, the strike leaders were arrested and the Royal North West Mounted Police fired into a rioting crowd on June 21, 1919—"Bloody Sunday"—killing 1 and wounding 30. The six-week strike was over and so was the growth of labor unions. In 1919 alone there were more than 400 strikes, but after the Winnipeg General Strike, the federal government and most governments at the provincial level opposed union activities. Throughout the 1920s there was a decline in union membership.

The reasons for unrest and discontent varied from region to region in the 1920s. The government takeover of five financially troubled railways had led to the creation of the Canadian National Railways in 1919 and railway rates in the Maritimes were raised 40% to bring them up to central Canadian levels. Angry over the rail rates and feeling that Ottawa was making decisions on the basis of central Canada's interests, many Maritimers protested by forming the Maritimes Rights movement, aimed at winning transportation concessions and federal subsidies. At the same time it promoted regional rights and pride.

Canadian farmers, resentful over low prices for farm products, high rail rates and high prices for manufactured goods, formed the United Farmers' movement. United Farmers' parties won provincial elections in Ontario in 1919, in Alberta in 1921, and in Manitoba in 1922. At the federal level, the Progressive Party embraced some of the program of the United Farmers' movement. The Progressives called for free trade, nationalization (especially in the case of railways) and more direct democracy (such as the use of a referendum to decide a controversial issue). Although they were a new party, the Progressives were to play an important role in politics in the 1920s.

The election of 1921 marked new directions in Canadian politics. Both major parties had new leaders: Arthur Meighen had replaced Borden as prime minister; William Lyon Mackenzie King had taken over as Liberal leader after Laurier's death. Of even greater significance was that for the first time, Canadians could vote for one of three parties at the federal level: the Liberals, the Conservatives or the Progressives. The Liberals won the 1921 election, but the Progressives finished second and formed the opposition. Their position in the House of Commons was even more important after the 1925 election in which the Conservatives under Meighen won the most seats, but King remained in power by claiming the support of the Progressives. After 1925 the Progressives declined, and many of their supporters voted Liberal in King's 1926 election victory. But the influence of the Progressive movement was felt as King's government, anxious to keep their support, passed Canada's first Old Age Pension Act in 1927.

In foreign affairs, King made sure that Canada played a cautious role in the League of Nations, because he feared that Canada would be drawn into international disputes. In imperial matters, his insistence on autonomy contributed to a redefinition of the empire at the Imperial Conference of 1926. There it was acknowledged that Canada and the other British dominions were autonomous even in their external affairs. As a result, by 1929, Canada had diplomatic posts in Washington, Paris and Tokyo and Britain had a high commissioner in Ottawa. The Governor General became a symbolic representative of the Crown rather than a representative of the British government.

At home, there were many signs that good times had finally come to Canada. World markets for Canadian manufactured goods had revived, and wheat prices were soaring to new levels. New mining and lumbering areas were developed. By 1928, more than a billion dollars' worth of products were being extracted from the newly-developed primary industries of the Canadian Shield. Immigrants poured into Canada by the hundreds of thousands to provide labour in the growing industrial cities. Cars, radios, telephones, electrical appliances and other consumer goods were being bought, especially by middle-class Canadians, often using credit plans. Credit was also used to buy shares on the stock market, as the country became increasingly optimistic about its future. On both sides of the Canadian-American border, the Roaring Twenties were in full swing and there seemed no end in sight to the good times.

1919 Alcock and Brown take off from St. John's, Nfld, (June 14) on the first successful flight across the Atlantic to Cliften, Ireland. A **general strike paralyzes Winnipeg** (May–June), where an armed charge by the RCMP kills one person and injures 30 (June 21).

1920 Canada joins the **League of Nations** at its inception (Jan. 10). The flow of emigrants from the British Isles and Europe resumes, many going to urban centres. Federal legislation makes **women eligible** to sit in the **House of Commons**. The Northwest Mounted Police became the Royal Canadian Mounted Police (RCMP).

1921 Liberals under **Mackenzie King** defeat Conservatives under Arthur Meighen in federal election; the Progressive Party comes in second. **Agnes Macphail** becomes the first woman elected to Parliament. The world's fastest fishing schooner, the ***Bluenose,*** is launched at Lunenburg, NS. (Mar. 26). **Postwar economic depression** puts 300,000 men and women out of work—more than 15% of the work force.

1922 Canada declines to rally to Britain's side during the Chanak Crisis. Sir Frederick **Banting**, Dr Charles **Best**, Dr J.J.R. MacLeod and J.B. Collip share Nobel Prize for the **discovery of insulin.**

1923 The Canadian Northern and Canadian Transcontinental are merged to form the **Canadian National Railways.** Canada signs the Halibut Treaty with the US without a corroborating British signature. Mackenzie King leads opposition to a common imperial policy ("one voice for the empire") at an Imperial Conference in London.

1924 The Saskatchewan Wheat Pool begins operations.

1925 Although Conservatives win more seats in federal election, Mackenzie King's Liberals remain in power with the support of the Progressives.

1926 King's Liberals win federal election. An Imperial Conference defines British dominions as autonomous (Balfour Report).

1927 Britain's Privy Council awards Labrador to Newfoundland instead of to Quebec (Mar. 1). The Diamond Jubilee of Confederation (July 1) is marked by Canada's first coast-to-coast radio network broadcast. King's government, with the support of the Progressive Party, passes Canada's first **Old Age Pension Act.**

1928 The Supreme Court of Canada rules that, according to the British North America Act, women are not "persons" who could hold public office. This decision is reversed by British Privy Council in 1929.

■ **The Great Depression (1929-1939)**

In 1929, Canadians looked with confidence toward the next decade and that confidence made the effects of the Great Depression of the 1930s even more bitter. The Depression was worldwide, but the effects were especially felt in Canada because about a third of the nation's gross national product was based on exports. The first signs of Canadian economic collapse appeared in October 1929 when wheat prices began to fall. In the same month the stock market collapsed, ruining thousands of shareholders, some of whom, on paper at least, had been millionaires. By 1930, the number of unemployed had doubled and the Conservatives, under R.B. Bennett, won the 1930 federal election decisively as voters hoped a change in government would bring a change in fortune. However by 1933, one in five Canadians was unemployed.

Western Canada was hardest hit in "The Dirty Thirties" because of its reliance on wheat. The Prairie provinces also suffered from a drought which led to crop failure during these hard times. The combined results were devastating. In Saskatchewan, provincial income fell by 90% and two-thirds of the province's population had to go on welfare. In the 1930s, welfare, or "relief" as it was then known, became a burden for municipal and provincial governments across the country. By 1935, 10% of Canadians were on relief.

Bennett's government did not intervene to rebuild the economy. In the 1930s, politicians, economists and business leaders assumed that the Depression, like other downswings in the business cycle, would soon be followed by a recovery. Their experience, and most economic theory at the time, did not encourage them to consider major government spending as a way to stimulate a depressed economy.

One of the few federally financed programs created involved sending single unemployed men to camps where they did manual work in return for their keep and a small allowance. Working in isolated conditions, often at meaningless tasks, did nothing to satisfy the men and those in the British Columbia camps took action. In 1935, about 1,500 camp inmates decided to present their complaints directly to Bennett in Ottawa. They began the "On to Ottawa" trek by taking over freight trains heading east. By the time they reached Regina, there were about 2,000 protesters and the railway refused to provide further transportation. Representatives of the Trekkers met with Prime Minister Bennett in Ottawa, but the talks were inconclusive. When the delegation returned to Regina, Bennett decided to arrest the protest leaders. On July 1, there was a bloody riot in Regina involving the Trekkers, local police and the RCMP, which left one policeman dead and several dozen rioters, constables and local citizens injured. The Trek was over and the protesters returned home over the next few days; but Bennett's handling of the affair hurt his image. In the election of 1935, the people turned to King again, in the hope that this time he could deal with the Depression.

After 1935, economic conditions began to improve slowly, yet federal politicians did little to speed this recovery. The failure of the Liberals and the Conservatives to deal with the Depression led to the rise of reform parties. A socialist party, the Co-operative Commonwealth Federation (CCF) won seven seats in the 1935 election and elected members to several provincial legislatures. Other new parties appeared at the provincial level. In Alberta, the Social Credit Party promised $25 prosperity certificates to each resident; but the plan fell flat because the province did not have the power to issue currency. In Quebec, Maurice Duplessis established the Union Nationale and promised economic reform. But the Union Nationale, like the other parties, could not end the Depression, the effects of which faded only with the outbreak of World War II in 1939.

1929 The **Great Depression** begins.

1930 **Cairine Wilson** is appointed Canada's first woman senator (Feb. 20). The Canadian Federation of Business and Professional Women's Clubs is organized. Conservatives under **R.B. Bennett** win federal election (Aug. 7).

1931 The **Statute of Westminster** (Dec. 11) grants Canada full legislative authority domestically and in external affairs. The Governor General becomes a representative of the Crown.

1932 Ottawa Agreements provide for preferential trade between Canada and other Commonwealth nations. The **Co-operative Commonwealth Federation (CCF)** is founded at Calgary.

1933 One in five Canadians is unemployed.

1934 The Bank of Canada is formed. The **Dionne quintuplets** are born in Callander, Ont.

1935 Ten percent of Canadians rely on welfare or "relief." The **On to Ottawa Trek** by young men from government work camps ends in a riot at Regina (July 1). Liberals under Mackenzie King win federal election. The CCF win seven seats. Social Credit claims 17. **William Aberhart** leads Social Credit into office in Alberta. The Canadian Wheat Board is created.

1936 Union Nationale under **Maurice Duplessis** wins its first election in Quebec.

1937 The **Rowell-Sirois Commission** is appointed to investigate the financial relationship between the federal government and the provinces. First regular flight of **Trans Canada Air Lines** (Sept. 1).

1938 Franklin D. Roosevelt becomes first US President in office to visit Canada, meeting Mackenzie King at Kingston.

■ Canada in World War II (1939-1945)

While most Canadians focused attention on the effects of the Depression at home, events in Europe during the 1930s were moving the world closer to another global conflict. After taking over Austria and Czechoslovakia (present-day Czech and Slovak republics), Germany invaded Poland in 1939; Britain and France responded by declaring war. Following Britain's action, King quickly summoned Parliament. On Sept. 10, one week after Britain had entered the conflict, the Canadian Parliament declared war on Germany and its allies.

Parliamentary support for the war declaration was based in part on King's known preference for a limited Canadian role and his assurance that there would be no conscription. Initially, only one Canadian division was sent to Britain. But by 1940, France had fallen and Britain faced invasion. King abandoned the concept of limited participation and decided to dispatch more troops. By late 1942, Canada had five divisions overseas. Canadian soldiers first saw action in December 1941 during the unsuccessful defence of Hong Kong. In August 1942, 5,000 Canadians took part in the disastrous raid on the French port of Dieppe, suffering casualties of 2,200 killed or captured. Despite these setbacks, the Canadian army played a major role in defeating enemy forces in Italy and took part in the Allied landings at Normandy in June of 1944. After taking key targets in France, Canadian soldiers moved northward to liberate Holland in 1945.

Canadians contributed to the war effort in other important ways. The Royal Canadian Navy grew from six destroyers and less than 2,000 personnel in 1939 to 471 warships, 99,688 men and 6,500 women by the war's end in 1945. The navy helped win the Battle of the Atlantic against German submarines by providing protection to the convoys of merchant ships carrying essential supplies from North America to Britain. (Despite the protection German U-boats sank 5,150 merchant ships.) Canadians also fought in the air as members of Britain's Royal Air Force, and, in increasing numbers throughout the war, in the Royal Canadian Air Force (RCAF). By 1945, there were 48 RCAF squadrons overseas. Other members of the RCAF were involved in the British Commonwealth Air Training Plan. Operating from Canadian airfields, this plan trained 131,000 aircrew from around the Commonwealth.

Canada also produced a wide variety of munitions, and provided important food supplies to the Allied war effort. Much of Canada's war production went directly to Britain, so did more than $3 billion in financial assistance.

While the contributions of Canadian men and women to the war effort were significant, the conflict raised disturbing issues at home. In reversing his earlier stand against conscription, Prime Minister King called for a national plebiscite on the issue in 1942. In all provinces except Quebec the electorate voted for conscription; relations between Quebec and the rest of Canada were strained, although not as severely as in World War I.

In a move that would later become controversial, Japanese–Canadians were interned and their property was confiscated in the name of national security after the Japanese attack on Pearl Harbor in 1941. The interned included Japanese–Canadians who had fought for Canada in World War I and more than 40 years later the Canadian government would officially apologize to the interned and their families.

By the war's end, more than a million Canadians had served in the armed forces and more than 42,000 had died. Canada's war effort enhanced its international image. At the same time, Canada had developed closer ties with the United States as the country's interests shifted away from Britain and Europe.

1939 **Canada declares war** on Germany (Sept. 10) after remaining neutral for a week following the British declaration. Quebec Premier Maurice Duplessis, who opposed Quebec participation in the war, is defeated by the provincial Liberals on that issue (Oct. 26).

1940 **Unemployment insurance** is **introduced.** Liberals win federal election (Mar.

26). The Permanent Joint Board of Defence is formed between Canada and the US. **Thérèse Casgrain** wins women in Quebec the right to vote and to hold provincial office.

1941 Canadians are captured when Hong Kong falls to Japanese (Dec. 25); about 500 of the POWs subsequently die in Japanese camps. Immigration has changed Canadian demographic structure. Canadians of British ancestry now make up 49.7% of the population, of French descent 30.3% and of other ethnic backgrounds 20%.

1942 In the Canadian army's first European war action, many soldiers are captured or killed in the disastrous **Dieppe** raid (Aug. 19). Canadians of Japanese descent are moved inland from the coast of British Columbia as "security risks"; their property is confiscated. A national plebiscite releases Mackenzie King from his pledge of no conscription but reveals deep divisions between Quebec and the rest of Canada.

1943 Canadians participate in the invasion of Sicily (July 10). Canadians win the Battle of Ortona (Dec. 20–28). **Ernest C. Manning** wins first of nine successive elections for the Social Credit in Alberta.

1944 Canadian troops push further inland than any other Allied unit on D-Day (June 6). Canadian forces fight as a separate army (July 23). Saskatchewan elects Tommy Douglas's CCF, the first socialist government in North America. Maurice Duplessis regains office for the Union Nationale in Quebec.

1945 War in Europe ends (May 8). One million Canadians fought in WW II; 42,042 were killed. Canadians killed while fighting for other Allied forces numbered 4,500. Liberals win federal election (June 11). First **family allowance payments are made** (June 20). Canada joins the **United Nations** (June 26). Igor Gouzenko defects from the Soviet Embassy in Ottawa (Sept. 5) and reveals the existence in Canada of a Soviet spy network. Canada's first nuclear reactor begins operations at Chalk River, Ontario.

■ Postwar Canada: 1945-1968

In the years following World War II, Canadians enjoyed a standard of living that was in stark contrast to the Depression years. The economy had boomed during the war and the gross national product had doubled. The war had prompted development in new industries which continued to expand in peacetime. Consumer spending had increased dramatically during the war, and continued to rise with the postwar baby boom. This boom, along with large numbers of European immigrants, resulted in a 40% population increase between the war's end and 1958. In Canada's quickly growing cities and suburbs, home ownership was made easier by the National Housing Act, designed to make mortgages easier to obtain. This example of government involvement in the economy was characteristic of the times. By 1945, unemployment insurance and family allowance legislation had been passed and other social welfare measures were being discussed.

Prime Minister King retired in 1948, and was followed as Liberal leader by Louis St. Laurent. One of St. Laurent's first achievements was the entry of Newfoundland into Confederation in 1949. In 1951, his government increased old age pensions and, in 1957, introduced a hospital insurance plan. St. Laurent negotiated with the United States to build the St. Lawrence Seaway, an impressive feat of engineering completed in 1959. In 1956, however, the government used closure (a limit on debate) to cut off the parliamentary debate concerning the building of the trans-Canada pipeline for oil and gas. In the election the following year, the Conservatives under John Diefenbaker won a minority victory. In 1958, Diefenbaker called another election to consolidate his position. This time the Conservatives swept the country, winning 208 of 265 seats.

Western agriculture found huge new markets when the government arranged wheat sales to China. In 1960, Diefenbaker's government introduced the Bill of Rights to protect the rights of all Canadians, and granted Native Canadians the right to vote in federal elections.

Despite continuing popular support for the British Commonwealth, the government of Canada signed the North American Air Defence Agreement (NORAD) with the United States to increase security during a time of international tension. But it could not deal with an economic recession that led to a devalued dollar and high unemployment. Also, the prime minister dealt Canada's fledgling aircraft industry a serious blow when he cancelled production of the Canadian-made Avro Arrow fighter jet, and his refusal to allow nuclear warheads on the American missiles based in Canada earned him the enmity of the US government. In the election of 1962, his government was returned to power, but in a minority situation that forced another election in 1963. The 1963 election also resulted in a minority government, but this time, the Liberals, under Lester B. Pearson, were in power.

As prime minister, Pearson, a career diplomat, concentrated on domestic matters. His government relied on the support of the New Democratic Party (formerly the CCF) to hold a majority in the House of Commons, and the partnership produced legislation that broadened social welfare by introducing Medicare, the Canada Pension Plan and the Canada Assistance Plan. Canadian nationalism was heightened with the adoption of the maple leaf flag in 1965, and in the same year another federal election produced a Liberal government one seat short of a clear majority. The opening of the world's fair, Expo in Montreal, in Canada's centennial year, 1967, marked a year of celebration across the country.

During the 1960s, Pearson was sensitive to growing nationalism in Quebec. His government established a Royal Commission on Bilingualism and Biculturalism in 1963, to demonstrate that Quebec's interests could be served by federalism, and he encouraged some of those closely associated with the Quiet Revolution to run for federal office. Quebec had been transformed from traditional to modern attitudes towards education, social reform and industrialization, a movement known as the Quiet Revolution, under Premier Jean Lesage. The Quebec government was implementing the ideas of the Quiet Revolution, and championed provincial rights with its slogan *maîtres chez nous* (masters in our own house). This sentiment took centre stage during Centennial celebrations. Visiting French President Charles de Gaulle ended a Montreal speech with the cry *"Vive le Québec libre!"* ("Long live free Quebec") which set off a storm of diplomatic protest and delighted local nationalists. Despite growing nationalist sentiment, many Quebeckers, including Pierre Trudeau, went to Ottawa. Trudeau was elected to the House of Commons in 1965, and was named minister of justice in 1967. In 1968, following Pearson's retirement, Trudeau became Liberal leader.

1947 Imperial Oil discovers the **Leduc oil field** (Feb. 13).

1948 **Louis St. Laurent** succeeds Mackenzie King as prime minister (Nov. 15).

1949 Under Premier **Joey Smallwood, Newfoundland** becomes Canada's 10th province (Mar. 31). Canada joins NATO. Canadian appeals to Britain's Judicial Committee of the Privy Council are abolished: Canada's Supreme Court becomes final court of appeal. Liberals under St Laurent defeat Conservatives under George Drew in federal election (June 3).

1950 The Korean War begins (June 25); Canadian troops participate in the conflict as part of a United Nations force.

1951 The midcentury census reports Canada's population as 14,009,429. **Postwar immigration** to Canada exceeds 100,000 annually during the 1950s, primarily moving from central and eastern Europe to hold manufacturing jobs in urban centres. The Massey Royal Commission reports that Canadian cultural life is dominated by American influences. Revisions to the **Indian Act**, beginning in 1951, limit its coverage of aboriginal people. Indian women married to non-Indian men are excluded from the act. This provision was removed in 1985 after much protest of discrimination. **Charlotte Whitton**, the first woman to be mayor of a major Canadian city, is elected in Ottawa.

1952 **Vincent Massey** becomes the first native-born Governor General of Canada. Canada's **first television** stations begin broadcasting in Montreal (Sept. 6) and Toronto (Sept. 8). **W.A.C. Bennett** begins Social Credit's administration in British Columbia.

1953 Canada's National Library is established in Ottawa (Jan. 1). The Stratford Festival opens (July 13). The **Korean War ends** (July 27); total Canadian casualties are 314 killed and 1,211 wounded. Liberals under St Laurent defeat Conservatives under Drew in federal election (Aug. 10).

1954 An economic slump interrupts the postwar boom. Canada's **first subway** opens in Toronto (Mar. 30). Roger Bannister and John Landy run the "miracle mile" at the British Empire Games in Vancouver (Aug.), the first to run a mile in less than four minutes. Sixteen-year-old Marilyn Bell becomes the first person to swim Lake Ontario (Sept. 9).

Hurricane Hazel hits Toronto, killing 83 people (Oct. 15). The Geneva Conference on the Far East invites Canada to join India and Poland in **supervising peace in Indochina**. This peacekeeping commitment continues for nearly 20 years to 1973.

1955 The Canadian Labour Congress is formed. The suspension of Montreal Canadiens' hockey star Maurice (Rocket) Richard leads to rioting in Montreal (Mar. 17).

1956 The Liberals use closure to limit the **Pipeline Debate** (May 8–June 6), a manoeuvre that contributes to their electoral defeat the following year.

1957 Conservatives under **John Diefenbaker** win federal election (June 10) and form minority government. Ellen Fairclough becomes the first woman federal cabinet minister. The Canada Council is created to help foster Canadian cultural life. **Lester B. Pearson wins Nobel Prize** (Oct. 12) for his role in resolving the Suez Crisis. Canadian supply and services troops are sent to work with a multinational UN force around the **Gulf of Aqaba**. They stay until 1967 and return there in 1973.

1958 Conservatives under Diefenbaker win 208 seats in federal election (Mar. 31). Coal mine disaster at Springhill, NS, results in death of 74 miners.

1959 The **Avro Arrow** project is terminated, with a loss of almost 14,000 jobs (Feb. 20). The **St. Lawrence Seaway** is **opened** (June 26).

1960 Liberals under **Jean Lesage** win provincial election in Quebec (June 22), inaugurating the **Quiet Revolution**. A **Canadian Bill of Rights** is approved by Parliament. Native people get the right to vote in federal elections. During the 1960s French is recognized as a language of instruction in elementary and secondary schools in New Brunswick, Ontario and Manitoba. It is recognized subsequently in other provincial jurisdictions.

1961 The **New Democratic Party** replaces the CCF.

1962 Conservatives are reduced to minority status in federal election (June 18). Social Credit wins 30 seats and NDP take 19 to control the balance of power in the House of Commons. The Saskatchewan NDP introduces the first Canadian **Medicare** plan (July 1), and is opposed by a doctors' strike. **Trans-Canada Highway** officially opens (Sept. 3). Canadian-made satellite *Alouette* is launched (Sept. 29), making Canada the third nation in space. Canada's last execution, the double hanging of Ronald Turpin and Arthur Lucas, takes place (Dec. 11), at the Don Jail in Toronto.

1963 Liberals under Pearson win federal election (Apr. 8), and form a minority government. The Quebec separatist group **Front de libération du Québec (FLQ)** sets off a series of bombs in Montreal (Apr.–May). A TCA flight crashes in Quebec, killing all 118 people aboard (Nov. 29). The **Royal Commission on Bilingualism and Biculturalism** begins its work.

1964 Canadians get social insurance cards (Apr.). Canada ends difficult peacekeeping duties in the Congo (Zaïre) after four years of service with heavy casualties. Canadian troops join UN forces in Cyprus.

1965 Canada gets a new flag (Feb. 15). The **Autopact** between Canada and the US is signed. Canadian Roman Catholic Churches begin to celebrate mass in English (Mar. 7). Liberals win federal election (Nov. 8) to continue as a minority government. Failure of an Ontario Hydro relay device at Queenston plunges eastern North America into a power blackout (Nov. 9).

1966 The Munsinger Affair becomes Canada's first major parliamentary sex scandal (Mar. 4). The **Canada Pension Plan** is established. The CBC begins colour television broadcasting (Oct. 1).

1967 The Canadian army, navy and air forces are **unified** to become the Canadian **Armed Forces** (Apr. 25). Montreal hosts a world's fair, **Expo 67** (opened Apr. 27). Canada celebrates its **Centennial** (July 1). French President Charles **de Gaulle** delivers his "Vive le Québec Libre" speech in Montreal (July 24). The federal Department of Manpower and Immigration establishes the **"points system"** for immigrants. Patterns shift in the 1960s from European to Third World immigration as humanitarian objectives and family reunification policies increase multicultural immigration.

■ The Trudeau Years (1968-1984)

The Liberals won a majority victory in the election of 1968. Trudeau was a strong federalist, determined to show that Ottawa could promote the rights of French Canada. The Official Languages Act of 1969 recognized both English and French as official languages, and required federal institutions to provide services in both languages. Although the legislation was supported by all parties, it was not universally popular, even in Quebec.

In the October Crisis of 1970 separatist extremists belonging to the FLQ (Front de libération du Québec) kidnapped British Trade Commissioner James Cross, and killed Quebec cabinet minister Pierre Laporte. Trudeau used the War Measures Act to apply emergency measures of arrest, detention and martial law. This move was generally accepted but was criticized by advocates of civil rights, especially since the FLQ had little real support and the Act was in effect across the country.

In his early years in power, Trudeau attempted to concentrate decision-making in Ottawa, and his newly created Prime Minister's Office led to western Canadian accusations of an eastern-dominated federal government. At the same time opposition parties charged that Trudeau was undermining both the power of the cabinet and of Parliament. The Liberals were almost defeated in the election of 1972, but retained office through a minority government that saw the New Democrats, under David Lewis, hold the balance of power. During this period the Foreign Investment Review Agency was set up (1973) to protect the Canadian economy against foreign domination; business critics claimed that it discouraged investment.

By 1974, the Liberals had regained a majority; their agenda was dominated by an economy battered by inflation. The government tried a variety of economic measures, including a three-year imposition of wage and price controls under the Anti-Inflation Act of 1975. Although the controls may have had some effect, world conditions, especially the international oil crisis, kept inflation high.

In 1976, the separatist Parti Québécois under René Lévesque defeated the provincial Liberals, led by Robert Bourassa in the Quebec election. This election fueled public uncertainty over the future of Quebec (and Canada), while continuing inflation and western alienation also undermined Liberal support. In the 1979 election, the Liberals lost, and Conservative leader Joe Clark took office as head of a minority government. Clark's government was short-lived as it suffered defeat in the House of Commons that same year.

The Liberals won the election of 1980, and Trudeau, lured out of planned retirement by the sudden election, embarked on an eventful term of office. He and members of his government actively campaigned on the victorious NO side in the 1980 Quebec referendum on sovereignty association. The Liberals brought in the National Energy Program in the same year, again attempting to regulate ownership and control in part of the economy, and again succeeding in alienating foreign and local business interests. Resistance to the NEP, particularly in the west, was deep and persistent.

Then, after a long (18 months) and difficult campaign waged in Parliament, at federal-provincial meetings and in the media, Trudeau succeeded in getting an agreement on patriating the Canadian constitution amongst all provinces except Quebec. Patriation officially took place when Queen Elizabeth II proclaimed the new Constitution Act in Ottawa on Apr. 17, 1982. The Charter of Rights and Freedoms was also proclaimed, entrenching bilingualism in the federal jurisdiction and providing for minority language education rights across Canada.

By 1984 the country was mired in a recession and in no mood for the international interest Trudeau was pursuing; he retired and John Turner became Liberal leader and prime minister for a brief period. The Liberal government was at the end of its mandate and parliament was dissolved. After nearly 16 years of Liberal government, the voters were eager for a change.

1968 Pierre Elliott Trudeau succeeds Pearson as prime minister (Apr. 6), and leads Liberals to majority in federal election (June 25). A Royal Commission on the Status of Women is appointed. Canadian divorce law is reformed.

1969 Saturday postal deliveries end. Abortion law is liberalized (May). English and

French become **official languages** of federal administration (July 9). New Brunswick declares official bilingualism. The breathalizer comes into use as a test for alcohol-impaired drivers (Dec. 1).

1970 The FLQ kidnaps British trade commissioner James Cross (Oct. 5), precipitating the **October Crisis**. Quebec labour and immigration minister Pierre Laporte is kidnapped (Oct. 10), and found murdered (Oct. 17). The federal government invokes the **War Measures Act** (Oct. 16), leading to the arrest of 465 people.

1971 A policy of **multiculturalism** is adopted by the federal government. Canadian Gerhard Herzberg wins the Nobel Prize in chemistry for his studies of chemical reactions that help produce smog.

1972 Canada defeats the USSR in the first hockey series between the Soviets and Canadian professionals (Aug.–Sept.). Liberals win federal election with 109 seats to the Conservatives 107, with the NDP holding the balance of power at 31 (Oct. 30).

1973 The separatist Parti Québécois becomes the official Opposition in Quebec. Canadian troops are sent to the Middle East and serve with the United Nations Emergency Task Force there until 1979.

1974 Liberals under Trudeau win federal election and form majority government (July 8). **Pauline McGibbon** becomes the first female lieutenant-governor (Ontario) in the British Commonwealth.

1975 The **CN Tower**, the world's tallest free-standing structure at 553.339 metres, is completed in Toronto (Apr. 2). Federal government announces (July 18) its intention to screen foreign investment in Canada, via the Foreign Investment Review Agency (FIRA). Television cameras are allowed inside the House of Commons for the first time. Federal government imposes **wage and price controls** in an effort to fight inflation (Oct. 14). Grace Hartman is elected president of the Canadian Union of Public Employees.

1976 Canada announces 200-nautical-mile coastal fishing zone (June 4). **Death penalty** is **abolished** in a free vote (130–124) in Parliament (July 14). Montreal hosts **Olympic Games** (July 17–31). Team Canada wins the first **Canada Cup** hockey series (Sept. 15).

The **Parti Québécois** under René Lévesque wins provincial election in Quebec (Nov. 15).

1977 Quebec government passes Bill 101, restricting English-language schooling to children whose mother or father had attended English elementary school in Quebec (Aug. 26). Highway signs in most of Canada become metric (Sept. 6).

1978 **Soviet nuclear-powered satellite crashes** in Canadian north (Jan. 24). Sun Life Assurance Co. announces a head office move from Montreal to Toronto because of language laws and political instability in Quebec. **Hilda Watson**, first woman to lead a political party in Canada, wins leadership of Yukon Progressive Conservative party.

1979 Conservatives under **Joe Clark** win federal election (May 22). Canada's first gold bullion coin, the Maple Leaf, goes on sale (Sept. 5). Supreme Court of Canada declares Manitoba and Quebec legislation creating unilingual courts and legislatures unconstitutional (Dec. 13). Federal Conservatives lose non-confidence vote on budget (Dec. 13), forcing the government's resignation. **Antonine Maillet** wins the prestigious French literary prize, the Prix Goncourt, for her novel *Pélagie-la-Charette*.

1980 Canada's ambassador to Iran, Ken Taylor, arranges the successful **escape of six American Embassy staff** from Tehran while their colleagues are held hostage (Jan. 28). Liberals win federal election (Feb. 18). Canada boycotts the Olympic Games in Moscow because of the Soviet invasion of Afghanistan. **Jeanne Sauvé** becomes the first female Speaker of the House of Commons (Apr. 14). **Quebec votes "no"** to "sovereignty-association" in a **referendum** (May 22). **"O Canada"** becomes Canada's national anthem (June 27). The Supreme Court awards Rosa Becker half the assets accumulated during a 19-year common-law relationship. **National Energy Program** is created to encourage oil self-sufficiency, increase Canadian ownership in the oil industry and obtain a larger share of Canadian energy revenues.

1981 Quebec bans public signs in English (Sept. 23). The federal government and every province except Quebec reach agreement on a method for patriating Canada's constitution (Nov. 5). The 1981 census indicates significant increases in the percentage of new Canadians from Asia, the Caribbean and Latin America.

1982 Bertha Wilson becomes Canada's first woman to be appointed a justice of the Supreme Court (Mar. 4). The Quebec Court of Appeal rejects the Quebec government's claim of veto power over constitutional change (Apr. 7). Canada gains a new **Constitution** and **Charter of Rights and Freedoms** (Apr. 17). Canada's GNP falls 4.8% in the worst recession since the Great Depression of the 1930s.

1983 Canadian pay-TV channels begin operation (Feb. 1). **Jeanne Sauvé** is Canada's first woman to be appointed Governor General (Dec. 23). Canada approves a US plan to test unarmed **cruise missiles** in western Canada beginning in 1984.

■ Mulroney in Power (1984-1993)

In the 1984 general election, the Conservatives, under Brian Mulroney, won a decisive victory, taking 211 of 282 seats in the House of Commons, including 58 seats in Quebec, a former Liberal stronghold. In contrast to the previous government, the Conservatives sought to strengthen ties with the United States and took steps to attract more foreign investment to Canada. The recession of the early 80s was over and business and government were both ready to expand.

One of the goals of the Mulroney government was to amend the Constitution Act of 1982 to obtain the support of Quebec. The prime minister and 10 provincial premiers reached an agreement, which became known as the Meech Lake Accord, on such an amendment in 1987; the agreement was to be taken to provincial legislatures and to parliament for approval by June 23, 1990. Also in 1987, the government negotiated a Canada-US free trade agreement (FTA) which provided for the elimination of all cross-border tariffs over 10 years. But the deal was rejected by both opposition parties and Liberal leader John Turner announced that the Liberal-dominated Senate would not approve free trade unless the Conservatives obtained public support in a general election. Mulroney called an election for November 1988. The campaign that followed was fractious; emotions ran high and there were wide fluctuations in public opinion. Anti-FTA sentiment was split between the opposition parties and the Conservatives won a second majority government. The FTA was approved in December and took effect Jan. 1, 1989.

As the deadline for ratification of the Meech Lake Accord approached, its confirmation became increasingly uncertain. Provincial governments had changed in the interim and both Manitoba and Newfoundland indicated that they had reservations about the agreement. Despite a last-minute first ministers' conference and a great deal of political pressure, the Manitoba legislature failed to ratify the accord and Newfoundland withdrew its consent; the deal lapsed on June 23, 1990. The following years were marked by numerous federal-provincial conferences, a variety of proposals and pressure from Quebec to include recognition of its distinct society. In August 1992 a new federal-provincial agreement was reached (the Charlottetown Accord) in time to be considered in a referendum Quebec Premier Robert Bourassa had pledged to hold on the future of Quebec. The other provinces also took part in a national referendum on the terms of the accord, which included not only recognition of Quebec as a distinct society, but also provisions to transfer mining, forestry, telecommunications and many other jurisdictions to the provinces. Canadians from all walks of life grappled with the issues raised by the terms of the Charlottetown Accord and the question dominated national media, (aside from the sports pages which were distracted by the prospect of a Canadian team, the Toronto Blue Jays, winning the 1992 World Series). The referendum was held on Oct. 26, 1992 and the deal was rejected by 54.8% of the voters.

The Conservatives' second term of office was also marked by the introduction of the Goods and Services Tax (GST), a tax designed to replace the manufacturers' tax and spread the tax burden more evenly across the economy. This tax was deeply unpopular and the Liberal-appointed members of the Senate vowed to block its passage in the upper chamber. Mulroney responded by temporarily increasing the number of senators to 112, with new appointees who would support the measure. The tax was the subject of heated debate and much protest across the country as Canadians transferred their frustration over the endless constitutional discussion, the now faltering economy and disappointment over the results of FTA to the government.

The GST took effect on Jan. 1, 1991, and the Conservative government continued to pursue wider trade agreements by joining the US and Mexico in negotiations for a North American Free Trade Agreement that would supersede the FTA. Amid much controversy, the deal was signed in December and the government's popularity continued to plumb the depths of the popularity polls. In February, Mulroney announced his decision to step aside as leader; Kim Campbell became the new leader of the Conservatives and the country's first female prime minister after a June leadership convention. As the Conservative mandate drew to a close, Campbell attempted to present herself as a brand-new prime minister at the head of a brand-new government. In the election in October 1993, Canadian voters made it clear they did not accept this stance: the Liberals under Jean Chrétien won a lopsided victory in an election that changed the political map of the country. The new government took office with a record number of rookie MPs, the Loyal Opposition was made up of members of the separatist Bloc Québécois, with the Reform Party from western Canada nearly matching the BQ's number of seats. The Conservatives elected only two members and the NDP also fared poorly at the hands of the electorate.

1984 Trudeau is succeeded as prime minister by **John Turner** (June 30). Conservatives under **Brian Mulroney** win federal election with 211 seats, the largest majority in Canada's history (Sept. 4). The **Pope visits Canada** (Sept. 9–20). **Marc Garneau** becomes the first Canadian in space, aboard US space shuttle *Challenger* (Oct. 5). Council for the Northwest Territories recognizes the use of **aboriginal languages** as well as English and French.

1985 The voyage through the Northwest Passage of US icebreaker *Polar Sea* challenges Canada's **Arctic sovereignty**. Prime Minister Mulroney and US President Reagan declare mutual support for **Star Wars research** and **free trade** between the two nations at "Shamrock Summit" (Mar. 18) in Quebec City. The Quebec provincial Liberals under Robert Bourassa defeat the Parti Québécois (Dec. 2).

1986 The Canadian dollar hits a then all-time low of 70.20 cents US (Jan. 31). The **Expo 86** world's fair is held in Vancouver (May 2–Oct. 13). Canada joins other Commonwealth nations (Aug. 5) in adopting **economic sanctions against South Africa** because of its apartheid policy. Canada receives a United Nations award (Oct. 6) for providing a haven for world refugees. Canadian John Polanyi shares the Nobel Prize for chemistry.

1987 The Bank of Canada rate drops to a 13-year low of 7.49% (Jan. 28); 6-month residential mortgages are as low as 7.5%. The **Meech Lake Accord**, proposing major constitutional amendments, is agreed to by Prime Minister Brian Mulroney and the 10 provincial premiers (Apr. 30). Ontario passes the first **pay equity legislation** for the private sector enacted in North America (June). A free vote in Parliament on restoration of **capital punishment** defeats the proposal 148–127 (June). A **free trade** agreement between Canada and the United States is set out. (Oct. 3). **Stock prices tumble** (Oct. 19) in Canada and throughout the world. The founding assembly of the **Reform Party of Canada** is held (Nov.)

1988 Canada is left without an **abortion law** (Jan. 28) when the Supreme Court rules that existing legislation is unconstitutional. Canadian sprinter **Ben Johnson** sets a world record and wins a gold medal at the Summer Olympics in Seoul (Sept. 24) but is stripped of both (Sept. 26) after testing positive for steroids. Yukon Territory passes language legislation recognizing the use of aboriginal languages. Brian Mulroney's Progressive Conservatives win a second consecutive majority in the **federal election** (Nov. 21), a bitter campaign fought over the free trade agreement with the US. Quebec's **French-only sign law** is struck down by the Supreme Court (Dec. 15) but is re-instated by Quebec (Dec. 21) using the "notwithstanding" clause in the Charter of Rights and Freedoms. Free trade legislation passes the House of Commons (Dec. 24) and the Senate (Dec. 30). The "Kamloops Amendment" to the Indian Act grants band councils jurisdiction over all reserve land, including the power to impose taxes.

1989 The Free Trade Agreement takes effect (Jan. 1). The federal government announces a new **goods and services tax** (GST) to take effect Jan. 1991. Audrey McLaughlin becomes Canada's **first female national party leader** as the NDP chooses a successor to Ed Broadbent (Dec. 2).

1990 Revisions to the Criminal Code provide choice of language in criminal hearings (Jan.). Several Quebec Conservative MPs, led by cabinet minister Lucien Bouchard (May 21), leave the government to form the pro-independence **Bloc Québécois**. The **Meech Lake Accord dies** when both Newfoundland and Manitoba fail to ratify the constitutional agreement by the deadline (June 23). Manitoba MLA **Elijah Harper** refuses the unanimous consent required for debate and a vote on the Meech Lake Accord because the accord does not provide special status for aboriginal peoples as it does for Quebec. Jean Chrétien becomes leader of the federal Liberal party. A land dispute leads to a 78-day armed confrontation between Mohawk warriors and government forces at the Kanesatake reserve near **Oka**, Quebec. **Canada sends warships** to the Persian Gulf as part of the multinational force being assembled to force Iraq to withdraw from occupied Kuwait. Brian Mulroney's Conservative government stacks the Senate (Sept. 27) with new appointees to ensure passage of the federal **goods and services tax (GST)**, which becomes law Dec. 17 to take effect Jan. 1.

1991 Canadian military personnel participate with the Allied forces in the assault against Iraq beginning Jan. 16 (the **Gulf War**). Prime Minister Brian Mulroney and US President George Bush sign an **acid rain accord** with the goal of ending acid rain within 10 years. **Rita Johnston** succeeds BC Premier **William Vander Zalm** as premier, the first woman to enter the provincial premier's office in Canada. Mulroney's government announces a **new constitutional reform package** promising aboriginal self-government within 10 years and guaranteeing aboriginal representation in an elected Senate. **Gun control** bill is passed, imposing tougher controls and banning imported military assault weapons; **Yukon First Nations** sign umbrella agreement on land claims and self-government; agreement reached on creation of Nunavut in Northwest Territories.

1992 A year-long crisis in the Atlantic **fisheries** results in a two-year shutdown of the cod fishery (July 2), a five-year ban on commercial salmon fishing in Newfoundland (Mar. 6) and international negotiations to protect the fish stocks; **Gwich'in Indians** sign a deal with Ottawa, giving them title to nearly 24,000 sq. km of land in the NWT and Yukon (Apr. 22); details of North American Free Trade Agreement (**NAFTA**) are announced Aug. 12, Prime Min. Mulroney signs the deal on Dec. 17; negotiations on **constitutional reform** take place throughout the year and an agreement (the Charlottetown Accord) that has Quebec's approval is announced Aug. 19 (proposals include Senate reform, an enlarged House of Commons and self-government for native people); a national referendum on the accord is held Oct. 26 and No side claims victory, killing the deal.

1993 The **Sahtu Tribe** of the Great Bear Lake region in the NWT settled a land claim to 41,437 sq. km; the **Cree** in northern Quebec win compensation from Hydro-Quebec for damage done around James Bay. Jan. 19 Canadian troops begin the planned pull-out from NATO bases. On Feb. 24 Prime Min. Mulroney announces his resignation, to take effect in June. Four members of the **Canadian Airborne Regiment**, in Somalia since Jan. on a peacekeeping mission, are charged in the death of a Somali civilian. NAFTA legislation passes in the House of Commons on May 27. Yukon's 14 First Nations sign the **Umbrella Final Agreement** in Whitehorse on May 29; the settlement includes 41,400 sq. km of land and $280 million. On June 15, Canada officially ends its role in Cyprus after 29 years of peacekeeping duties on the island. Defence Min. **Kim Campbell** takes over the reins of the Conservative government after a second ballot victory at the leadership convention on June 25. On Oct. 25 the Liberal Party wins a decisive victory in a federal election that sees the emergence of **two new parties**—the Bloc Québécois and the Reform party—and the near demise of the Progressive Conservatives. The cod moratorium of 1992 is extended to include the Gulf of St. Lawrence and is slated to last until the end of the decade.

1994 Most of the country west of the Rockies endures the coldest winter since the 1950s. **Cigarette taxes** are cut federally and provincially in an effort to curb a black market in cigarettes. The Liberals first budget forecasts cuts in defence spending, UI benefits, tax deductions and foreign aid and freezes transfer payments and public sector salaries. The **Canada Pension Plan** posts a deficit for the first time in 28 years. Members of the **Saskatchewan Wheat Pool** vote to transform the organization, formed in 1924, into a public company. The prime minister and provincial premiers sign an agreement to end trade barriers among the provinces. The Inuit of Quebec sign a self-government deal with the Quebec government. **Canadian troops leave CFB Lahr**, officially ending 27 years of Canadian service for NATO in Europe. The **Algonquins** of Gold Lake, Ontario, sign an agreement to begin negotiating an 8.5 million acre land claim in southern Canada. Canadian sports fans are left hockey-less until the new year by a labour dispute and **NHL lock-out**.

1995 The Canadian Airborne Regiment is disbanded (Jan.) after a new scandal compounds damage done by the **Somalia Affair**. Federal fisheries officials seize the Spanish fishing vessel *Estai* in Mar., in a battle over fishing rights on the Grand Banks. A settlement of the dispute in Apr. gives the **North Atlantic Fishing Organization** greater powers; in the same month Canada loses its triple A bond rating courtesy of Moody's Investors Service of New York. In June the worst forest fire season in northern parts of central Canada begins, while torrential rains trigger flooding along major rivers in Alberta. BC's Fraser River salmon run is shut down in Aug., because fish stocks are too low. In Sept., Newfoundland voters approve a proposal to shift control of education from the church to the province. In Oct. **Alexa McDonough** is elected leader of the federal NDP. On Oct. 30, after a bruising campaign that sees federal Opposition Leader Bouchard take over the YES side, the **proposal that Quebec separate from Canada** to form a sovereign state is narrowly defeated in a referendum—49.4% Yes, and 50.6% against. In early Nov., security at 24 Sussex Drive is breached as an intruder armed with a knife accosts the prime minister's wife in the hall outside their bedroom. In Dec. consumer exhaustion and caution make the Christmas retail season one of the poorest on record.

1996 Nfld Prem. **Brian Tobin** was sworn in (Jan. 26). Que. Prem. **Lucien Bouchard** was sworn in (Jan. 29). The Mint unveiled the new $2 coin (Feb. 19). **Glen Clark** was sworn in as BC's premier (Feb. 22). The **ANIK** E-1 satellite suffered irreparable damage (Mar. 26). On May 29, Canada and the US signed a **softwood lumber agreement** after 15 years of controversy. **Bob Thirsk** blasted off on *Columbia* for a 17-day space mission (June 7). On July 9, the **Innu** of Davis Inlet agreed to relocate to Sango Bay. On July 20-21, **devastating floods** hit the Saguenay valley in Que. On July 31, Canada and Israel signed a free trade deal. On Oct. 2, former Que. premier **Robert Bourassa** died. On Oct. 8, Gen. Jean Boyle resigned as head of Canada's armed forces after controversial evidence arose at the **Somalia inquiry**; Vice-Admiral Larry Murray became acting chief of defence. On Oct. 10, Keith Milligan was sworn in as premier of PEI. On Nov. 18, PEI Conservatives, led by **Pat Binns**, scored a major election victory after 10 years of Liberal rule. On the same day, Canada and Chile signed a free trade deal. In Dec., Canada signed a $4 billion contract with China for two **CANDU** reactors.

1997 The federal government announced an out-of-court settlement with former Prime Min. Brian Mulroney in his libel suit over the **Airbus investigation** (Jan. 6). Voters in Alta gave Prem. **Ralph Klein** another majority (Mar. 11). On Mar. 6, the federal government's **anti-smoking bill**, which limited tobacco company funding of arts and sports activities, was passed in the House of Commons. **Gilles Duceppe** was elected leader of the Bloc Québécois (Mar. 15). NS Prem. **John Savage** announced his resignation (Mar. 21). Sask. cut its PST by 2%. Census data taken in 1996 and released on Apr. 15 revealed that Que.'s share of Canada's population had fallen below 25% for the first time since 1867. Prem. **Gary Filmon** declared an emergency in southern Man. as the **Red River** flooded across the US border (Apr. 22). An independent auditor confirmed that the gold in samples from the **Bre-X claim** in Indonesia was "negligible" (May 4). The **Confederation Bridge** officially opened to traffic between PEI and the mainland (May 31). The federal Liberals won re-election but with a reduced majority; the Reform party became the Opposition (June 2). The **Somalia inquiry's report** blamed the military's problems on poor leadership (July 12). **Phil Fontaine** was elected national chief of the Assembly of First Nations (July 30). On Aug. 7, Canadian astronaut **Bjarni Tryggvason** blasted off on the space shuttle *Columbia*. Casting ballots in a second referendum on creating secular schools, Nfld voters supported the change (Sept. 2). NB Prem. **Frank McKenna** resigned (Oct. 13). A judge ruled that the **Red Cross** was negligent in the tainted blood scandal (Oct. 8). A bus crash in Que. killed 43 in the worst road accident in Canadian history (Oct. 13). **Sask. Conservatives** voted to mothball their party for at least two provincial elections (Nov. 9). The annual **APEC conference** was held in Vancouver (Nov. 21-25); the RCMP pepper-sprayed student demonstrators. Canada agreed to the **Kyoto Convention** on greenhouse gas emissions (Dec. 11).

1998 An **ice storm** crippled Que. and eastern Ont., leaving one million people without power and food (Jan. 6). Ottawa apologized to Canada's aboriginals for past mistreatment (Jan. 7). On Feb. 17, **Ontario Hydro** reported a loss of $6.32 billion in 1997–the largest business loss in Canadian history. By Feb. 22, Canadian athletes at the **Nagano Winter Olympics** had won a record 15 medals. Que. Liberal leader **Daniel Johnson** announced his resignation (Mar. 2). After signing a $12 billion deal, Nfld and Que. began talks for a new **Churchill Falls** power project. On Mar. 27, federal Conservative leader **Jean Charest** said he would run for leader of Que.'s Liberal party. On the same day, federal and provincial governments announced $1.1 billion in compensation for victims who contracted hepatitis C from tainted blood in 1986-90. Prime Min. Chrétien visited Cuba (Apr. 26-28). **Macmillan Bloedel** said it would phase out the clearcutting of old-growth forests. Ottawa and Washington agreed to save Pacific salmon. The **Nisga'a** people and the BC government signed a historic land claim treaty (July 15). The **Human Rights Tribunal** endorsed the **Public Service Alliance of Canada**'s claim to $5 billion in pay equity (July 29). The Supreme Court of Canada ruled on **Que.'s proposed secession from Canada:** Canada-Que. talks must begin after a majority in Que. votes for independence in a referendum with an unambiguous question (Aug. 20). On Sept. 1, a new blood collection agency replaced the Canadian Red Cross. **Swissair Flight 111** crashed off the coast of NS, killing all 229 passengers (Sept. 2). Ten thousand gun owners met on Parliament Hill to protest firearm registration (Sept. 22). **Bombardier** won a $1.5 billion contract for building 50 jets (Oct. 1). On Oct. 2, an **RCMP probe** into skirmishes between the Mounties and demonstrators at the 1997 **APEC** summit opened in Vancouver. Alta MLAs increased their salaries by five percent and doubled their severance packages (Oct. 5). Canada won a seat on the UN Security Council (Oct. 8). Canada's first diamond mine opened in NWT (Oct. 14). Statistics Canada reported that inflation had sunk to 1960s levels (Oct. 21). *The National Post* published its first edition (Oct. 27). Ont. passed the **Energy Competition Act** to end Ontario Hydro's monopoly on power provision in 2001 (Oct. 29). Former Prime Min. **Joe Clark** was elected leader of the federal Conservative party (Nov. 14). Canada pledged $100 million in hurricane relief to Central America over four years (Nov. 15). Forestry workers at **Abitibi-Consolidated** returned to work after a five-month strike (Nov. 20). Federal Solicitor General **Andy Scott** resigned on Nov. 23 after weeks of criticism over his comments about the pepper spraying of demonstrators at the 1997 APEC conference. The Sask. Court of Appeal ruled that **Robert Latimer** must serve at least 10 years in prison for the 1993 killing of his disabled daughter (Nov. 23). **Environment Canada** declared 1998 the warmest year globally in 130–140 years (Nov. 30). Prem. **Lucien Bouchard** handily won re-election in Que. (Nov. 30) and promised another referendum on Que.'s sovereignty (Dec. 7). On Dec. 1, federal Justice Min. **Anne McLellan** officially launched Canada's new gun control law three years after Parliament had passed the bill. On Dec. 4, the **International Court of Justice** rejected Spain's attempt to punish Canada for seizing Spanish turbot fishing vessels in 1995. Statistics Canada reported that the national jobless rate fell to 8% in Nov.–the lowest level this decade (Dec. 4). NS Labour Min. **Russell MacKinnon** reneged on a pledge to compensate Westray miners (Dec. 8). **Jim Antoine** was elected NWT's premier (Dec. 10). Finance Min. Paul Martin prohibited Canadian **bank mergers**, saying they would concentrate economic power in the hands of fewer bankers and reduce competition (Dec. 14).

1999 Taras Sokolyk, Man. Prem. Gary Filmon's former chief of staff, admitted lying to investigators about his role in a scheme to split votes in three ridings in the 1995 provincial election (Jan. 11). A Senate report on immigration announced that Ottawa lost track of more than 5,000 former refugee claimants facing deportation (Jan. 14). Toronto's task force on homelessness reported that the fastest growing groups of **homeless people** were youths under age 18 and families with children (Jan. 14). The next day, snowfall in

Toronto surpassed 120 cm for Jan. and broke an 1871 record for snowfall in one month. In BC, Justice **Duncan Shaw** ruled that a ban on possessing child pornography violated freedom of thought and expression guarantees in the Canadian Charter of Rights and Freedoms (Jan. 15). Statistics Canada said the number of self-employed and part-time workers steadily grew in the 1990s (Jan. 27). Ottawa pulled the plug on the **Cape Breton Development Corp.**, announcing the closure of the Phalen coal mine by the year 2000 while putting a second mine up for sale (Jan. 28). **Gordon Wilson** abandoned his party, the Progressive Democratic Alliance, for an NDP cabinet post in BC (Jan. 29). At the **World Economic Forum** in Davos, Switzerland, Prime Min. Chrétien rejected the idea of a Canadian–US dollar (Jan 29). Prime Min. Chrétien got nine premiers to agree to a **social union accord** after promising more healthcare funding for the provinces but failed to secure Que.'s signature (Feb. 4). Nfld's Liberal party won a reduced majority in an election (Feb. 9). Alta Prem. **Ralph Klein** said he felt vindicated (Feb. 10) after Auditor General Peter Valentine concluded a six-month investigation into the $420 million public refinancing of the **West Edmonton Mall** in 1994 and found no evidence of undue political influence. Voters in the eastern Arctic elected 19 members to the first assembly of **Nunavut** (Feb. 15) before the new territory appeared on the map. In his federal budget address, Finance Min. Paul Martin promised an $11.5 billion boost in **health-care transfers** to the provinces over the next five years (Feb. 16). Alta. Prem. **Ralph Klein** declared future Alta budget surpluses will be split 75 percent for debt payment and 25 percent for new spending (Feb. 16). The *Free Press* of Regina and Saskatoon declared bankruptcy (Feb. 17). In Ottawa, **Kurds** hurled a gasoline bomb at a police line outside the Turkish Embassy, setting one officer ablaze (Feb. 17); in Montreal, police and about 100 Kurds clashed outside the Israeli consulate (Feb 22). Reform party leader **Preston Manning** declared his willingness to lead a new national right-wing party if such a party emerged from "United Alternative" talks between Reformers and Conservatives (Feb. 24). Ottawa and all provinces except NS offered $1.5 billion in relief to 45,000 farm families facing financial hardship caused by falling international grain and hog markets (Feb. 24). Sen. **Eric Berntson** became the 15th Conservative convicted in Sask.'s long-running expense fraud scandal (Feb. 25). The RCMP raided the home of BC Prem. **Glen Clark**, searching for evidence that he had helped a friend apply for a casino licence in exchange for backyard decks at Clark's home and cottage (Mar. 2). Health Min. **Allan Rock** approved medical studies on the benefits of **marijuana** use (Mar. 3). The Liberal government moved to bar federal Crown corporations from donating to political parties (Mar. 5). The **Canadian Wheat Board** and the **Canadian Pacific Railway** settled their dispute over who was to blame for the disastrous 1996-97 grain shipping season (Mar. 8). Prime Min. Chrétien condemned Cuba's conviction of four dissidents (Mar. 15). Canada's four **stock exchanges** announced major reforms, including the merger of the Vancouver and Alta exchanges (Mar. 15). BC's **Progressive Democratic Alliance** disbanded (Mar. 20). Atlantic Canada's four telephone companies agreed to merge into **AtlanticCo** (Mar. 22). Canadian **CF-18 fighter-bombers** began taking part in NATO air strikes against **Yugoslavia** (Mar. 24); in Toronto, Serbs threw rocks, paint and Molotov cocktails at the US consulate and police (Mar. 24-25). In Man., an inquiry led by **Alfred Monnin** reported that senior Tories illegally recruited and backed supposedly independent aboriginal candidates in the 1995 provincial election to split popular support for the NDP (Mar. 29). For the first time in Canada, **Mohawks** on Que.'s Kahnawake reserve won the right to collect tax-like levies from non-natives on reserves (Mar. 30). Canada's first legal strike by prison guards ended when Ottawa legislated them back to work (Mar. 30). MPs from all federal parties endorsed Canadian participation in NATO's air war against **Yugoslavia** (Mar. 31). **Nunavut** became Canada's newest territory; **Paul Okalik** became its first premier (Apr. 1). Ont. sold **Highway 407** to a Que.-led consortium for $3.1 billion in the biggest privatization in Canadian history to date (Apr. 13). Statistics Canada reported that the average household was no richer than it was 20 years ago (Apr. 14). **Wayne Gretzky** played his last professional hockey game (Apr. 18). Chinese Prem. **Zhu** ended a visit to Canada (Apr. 20);

protesters condemned China's human rights record in six cities. The Supreme Court of Canada said the courts put too many offenders behind bars, making Canada's incarceration rate one of the highest in the world (Apr. 23). Prime Min. Chrétien announced the departure of 800 soldiers to **Macedonia** to join a larger NATO force for training exercises (Apr. 27). BC Prem. **Glen Clark** signed the **Nisga'a Treaty** after invoking closure on debate (Apr. 27); the treaty gave the Nisga'a about 2,000 sq. km of land, fishing and hunting rights and some self-government. Federal Information Commissioner **John Reid** condemned excessive secrecy in six departments: Revenue, Defence, Health, Citizenship and Immigration, the Privy Council Office and Foreign Affairs (Apr. 28). A 14-year-old killed one student and wounded another in shootings at the W.R. Myers High School in **Taber**, Alta (Apr. 28). Nfld's legislature unanimously voted to change the province's official name to Newfoundland and Labrador (Apr. 29). **Horseback riders** in historic uniforms began a 1,500-km ride west from Fort Dufferin, Man., to recreate the first trek of the North-West Mounted Police across the prairies in 1874 (May 8). Alta's Whaleback landscape, a region with distinct windswept ridges, won protection from drilling, logging and mining (May 11). After a two-year probe, the RCMP said that crimes occurred at **Bre-X Minerals Ltd**, but lack of evidence prevented the laying of charges (May 12). Ottawa approved the construction of a dry storage site for used nuclear fuel at Ont.'s **Bruce Nuclear Power Development** (May 14). **David Milgaard**, who spent 22 years in prison for a murder he did not commit, got a record $10 million in compensation from the Sask. and federal governments (May 17). The Canadian Radio-television and Telecommunications Commission said it would not regulate the Internet or impose Canadian content rules (May 17). The Supreme Court of Canada ruled that the **Ont. Family Law Act**'s definition of spouse—which applies only to heterosexual couples—is unconstitutional because it discriminates against gays; the Court also opened band elections to off-reserve natives for the first time (May 20). Ottawa unanimously passed a law giving victims more voice in the criminal justice system (May 28). Ottawa agreed to liberalize trade with five Andean countries (May 31). **MTS**, Man.'s telephone company, locked out 1,400 unionized employees over fears that a labour dispute was affecting emergency calls (June 3). Prem. **Mike Harris**'s Conservatives won a reduced majority in Ont.'s election (June 3). In Kingston, Ont., the grave of Prime Min. **John A. Macdonald** was designated a national historical site (June 6). **Bernard Lord**'s Conservatives won a landslide victory over the Liberals in NB's election (June 7). The House of Commons passed a Reform party motion that said marriage is a union between man and woman (June 8). The federal NDP disciplined **Svend Robinson** (June 9) for presenting a petition in the House of Commons that called for the removal of God from the Constitution (June 8). **Health Canada** opened a new high-security lab in Winnipeg to study the deadliest human and animal diseases in the world (June 11). BC's NDP government repaid some of the money ($118,000) stolen from charities during the bingo scandal of 1983–84 (June 11). Defence Min. **Art Eggleton** announced the departure of another 500 peacekeepers to **Kosovo** (June 11), two days after Western generals and Yugoslavia signed a peace accord. The Supreme Court of Canada ruled that children's organisations can be liable for sexual abuse if their workplaces make employees' sex crimes easier to commit (June 17). US forestry giant **Weyerhaeuser Co.** announced its intention to buy **MacMillan Bloedel Ltd** for $3.6 billion (June 20). In Toronto, a fire in a **Bell Canada** switching room knocked out bank machines and 100,000 telephone lines for a day (July 16). **Joy MacPhail** resigned as BC's finance minister; **Gordon Wilson** replaced her (July 16). Then **Sue Hammell**, BC's minister for women's equality, resigned (July 19). The **Coast Guard** intercepted a cargo ship filled with 123 Chinese **illegal immigrants** off Vancouver Island (July 20). Statistics Canada reported that Canada's crime rate fell for the seventh year in a row and hit a 19-year low (July 21). **Que. nurses** ended a four-week strike for higher pay (July 26). **John Hamm** led the Conservatives to victory over the Liberals in the NS election (July 27). Canadian goaltender **Steve Vézina** tested positive for banned stimulants at the **Pan American Games**; his roller hockey team was stripped of its gold medals (Aug. 1). In Sarnia, Ont., the grave of **Alexander Mackenzie**, Canada's second prime minister, was designated a national historical site (Aug. 2). The

World Trade Organization gave Canada 90 days to scrap or radically change Technology Partnerships Canada, Ottawa's biggest high-technology development program (Aug. 2). Prime Min. Chrétien shuffled the cabinet (Aug. 3). **Toronto-Dominion Bank** announced plans to buy **Canada Trust** for $7.85 billion (Aug. 3). In Winnipeg, the Pan American Games closed after Canadian athletes won 196 medals, 64 of them gold. Five Cuban athletes defected (Aug. 8). Explosions rocked an oil recycling plant in Calgary (Aug. 9). A second cargo ship dumped 131 Chinese illegal immigrants in the Queen Charlotte Islands (Aug. 11). After 130 years, **Eaton's** filed for bankruptcy protection and announced plans to close its stores (Aug. 20). BC Prem. **Glen Clark** resigned following the revelation that he was under criminal investigation for awarding a casino license to a friend (Aug. 21). **Dan Miller** became BC's new premier (Aug. 25). The NDP met for a national convention in Ottawa; **Alexa McDonough** won support for a policy of balanced budgets and moderate tax cuts (Aug.27-29). The Canadian Forces, RCMP and Coast Guard rescued Chinese immigrants aboard a third ship near Vancouver Island (Aug. 31). The Aboriginal Peoples Television Network aired for the first time (Sept. 1). Seven people died in a **63-vehicle crash** on Ont.'s Highway 401 (Sept. 3). A BC court sentenced **Dave Stupich**, a provincial finance minister in the 1980s, to two years in prison for stealing hundreds of thousands of dollars from an NDP fundraising society in Nanaimo (Sept. 3). A three-day meeting of the world's Francophone leaders ended in Moncton, NB (Sept. 5). The owners of Toronto's **Maple Leaf Gardens** put the 68-year-old hockey arena up for sale (Sept. 8). Prime Min. Chrétien said Canada would send up to 600 peacekeepers to **East Timor** (Sept. 12). Cape Breton's Phalen coal mine shut down ahead of schedule; 400 workers lost their jobs (Sept. 13). **Louise Arbour** was sworn in as the newest justice on the Supreme Court of Canada (Sept. 15). In Sask., Prem. **Roy Romanow** was re-elected to a third term, but his NDP government fell to minority status; the new **Saskatchewan Party** became the Opposition (Sept. 16). **Donald Marshall** won a victory in the Supreme Court of Canada defending historic Micmac fishing rights (Sept. 17). **Gary Doer** led the NDP to power in Man.'s election (Sept. 21).

Fathers of Confederation

Union of the British North American colonies into the Dominion of Canada was discussed and its terms negotiated at three confederation conferences held at Charlottetown (C), Sept. 1, 1864; Quebec (Q), Oct. 10, 1864; and London (L), Dec. 4, 1866. The names of delegates are followed by the provinces they represented; Canada refers to what are now the provinces of Ontario and Quebec.

Delegate	Conferences
Adams G. Archibald, NS	C,Q,L
George Brown, Canada	C,Q
Alexander Campbell, Canada	C,Q
Frederick B.T. Carter, Nfld	Q
George-Étienne Cartier, Canada	C,Q,L
Edward B. Chandler, NB	C,Q
Jean-Charles Chapais, Canada	Q
James Cockburn, Canada	Q
George H. Coles, PEI	C,Q
Robert B. Dickey, NS	Q
Charles Fisher, NB	Q,L
Alexander T. Galt, Canada	C,Q,L
John Hamilton Gray, NB	C,Q
John Hamilton Gray, PEI	C,Q
Thomas Heath Haviland, PEI	Q
William A. Henry, NS	C,Q,L
William P. Howland, Canada	L
John M. Johnson, NB	C,Q,L
Hector L. Langevin, Canada	C,Q,L
Jonathan McCully, NS	C,Q,L
A.A. Macdonald, PEI	C,Q
John A. Macdonald, Canada	C,Q,L
William McDougall, Canada	C,Q,L
Thomas D'Arcy McGee, Canada	C,Q
Peter Mitchell, NB	Q,L
Oliver Mowat, Canada	Q
Edward Palmer, PEI	C,Q
William H. Pope, PEI	C,Q
John W. Ritchie, NS	L
J. Ambrose Shea, Nfld	Q
William H. Steeves, NB	C,Q
Sir Étienne-Paschal Taché, Canada	Q
Samuel Leonard Tilley, NB	C,Q,L
Charles Tupper, NS	C,Q,L
Edward Whelan, PEI	Q
R.D. Wilmot, NB	L

Canadian Disasters

Aug. 29, 1583: Canada's first recorded marine disaster took 85 lives when the *Delight* was wrecked on Sable Island.

Aug. 23, 1711: As many as 950 drowned when ships attached to the British fleet preparing to attack Quebec were grounded and sank on the rocks of Ile-aux-Oeufs.

Oct. 5, 1825: The Miramichi fire, north of New Brunswick's Miramichi River, destroyed the towns of Newcastle and Douglastown, and killed between 200–500 people.

June 10-27, 1832: A cholera epidemic peaked in Montreal when at least 947 people died. The epidemic, which first appeared in Quebec City, killed hundreds more throughout Lower Canada during the summer. A second cholera epidemic broke out in 1834.

May 17, 1841: On this date, several large boulders from Cap Diamant tumbled down the precipitous cliffs above the Lower Town of Quebec City and demolished eight houses, killing 32 people.

Oct. 27, 1854: In one of the earliest Canadian train disasters, a gravel train running near Baptiste Creek, 24 km west of Chatham, Ont., was hit by an express train on the same line. In the collision, 52 persons were killed and 48 seriously injured.

June 29, 1864: Near St-Hilaire, Que., a passenger train was unable to stop for an open drawbridge at the Beloeil bridge on the Richelieu River. The train plunged through the opening onto passing barges, killing 99 and injuring 100 people.

Apr. 1, 1873: Sailing from Liverpool to New York, the steamer *Atlantic* struck Meager's Rock off the coast of Nova Scotia and sank with the loss of 535 people.

May 13, 1873: Sixty men died when a fire and subsequent explosion in a coal mine at Westville, Pictou County, NS, trapped firemen and workers. The mine was eventually sealed to starve the fire of oxygen and it was two years before all the bodies were recovered.

Aug. 25, 1873: The Great Nova Scotia Cyclone swept over Cape Breton Island. The hurricane destroyed 1,200 vessels and 900 buildings, demolished dykes, wharves and bridges and claimed 500 lives.

May 3, 1887: An explosion at the Number One mine in Nanaimo, BC owned by the Vancouver Coal Mining and Land Company, killed 148 miners.

Jan. 24, 1888: Seventy-seven men lost their lives in a fire in the Number Five Mine at Wellington, just outside of Nanaimo, BC.

Feb. 21, 1891: In the first of several major disasters in the coal mines of Springhill, NS, 125 men were killed in an explosion.

May 26, 1896: Fifty-five people were killed when a bridge at Point Ellice in Victoria, BC, collapsed while a streetcar was passing over it. The bridge was too weak to support the weight of a recently built tramline.

Sept. 19, 1899: A massive rockslide from the cliffs above Quebec City's Lower Town demolished most of Champlain St, killing 45 people.

Apr. 29, 1903: Parts of the town of Frank, Alta., were obliterated by a sudden landslide when over 90 million tonnes of limestone came crashing down Turtle Mountain, crossed the four-km-wide valley floor and rolled up the other side of the valley. Approximately 75 people were killed. The landslide also sealed a mine entrance at the foot of the mountain and trapped 17 miners inside. The men were able to escape by digging a new tunnel to the surface.

Aug. 29, 1907: The Quebec Bridge, 11 km north of Quebec City, was the largest cantilevered bridge in the world at the time. As the bridge was nearing completion, the southern cantilever span collapsed, killing 75 workmen.

Aug. 2, 1908: A fire in BC's Kootenay Valley caused $5 million in damages and killed 70 people.

Mar. 5, 1910: A CPR work crew clearing the tracks from a previous snow slide in Rogers Pass, BC, was hit by an avalanche. Sixty-two men were killed; one survived.

June 30, 1912: The worst tornado in Canadian history swept through Regina, Sask., killing 28 residents, injuring hundreds and causing $75 million damage (est. 1990 dollars).

May 29, 1914: The Canadian Pacific liner *Empress of Ireland* collided with a Norwegian coal ship in the St Lawrence River near Rimouski, Que., and sank in only 14 minutes with the loss of 1,014 lives. This was one of the worst naval disasters in history, with the eighth largest loss of life for a naval accident.

June 19, 1914: The worst coal mine disaster in Canadian history occurred at Hillcrest, Alta, when dust explosions killed 189 men.

July 29, 1916: A forest fire in northern Ontario, thought to have been started by lightning and locomotive sparks, engulfed the towns of Cochrane and Matheson, killing at least 233 persons.

Sept. 11, 1916: The Quebec Bridge was the scene of further tragedy when a new centre span being hoisted into position fell into the river below. Thirteen men were killed, bringing the loss of life during construction of the bridge to 88.

Dec. 6, 1917: Halifax was the scene of Canada's worst single disaster when a French munitions ship filled with explosives collided with a freighter in Halifax harbour. The French ship, the *Mont Blanc*, was split to the waterline; fuel oil spilled over its explosive cargo and started a fire in the hold. The crew abandoned ship without attempting to extinguish the fire.

In the explosion that followed, the *Mont Blanc* was tossed more than 1,000 m into the air. The explosion levelled homes and businesses in a large part of the city and set off explosives stockpiled on shore. The blast, heard as far away as Prince Edward Island, is thought to be the largest-ever accidental explosion, and the largest non-nuclear blast in history. More than 1,600 people were killed, 9,000 injured, and 6,000 left homeless. Property damage was estimated at $35 million.

Oct. 23, 1918: The Canadian Pacific steamship *Princess Sophia* ran onto Vanderbilt Reef while sailing from Alaska to Vancouver. The ship sank two days later on Oct. 25. All 343 aboard were drowned.

Jan. 9, 1927: A small fire that broke out in Montreal's Laurier Palace Theatre was quickly extinguished, but in the panic that ensued 12 people were crushed to death and 64 were asphyxiated, including many children.

Apr. 14, 1928: The 18-gun sloop *Acorn* sank near Halifax with 115 men on board.

Nov. 18, 1929: Newfoundland's Burin Peninsula was struck by a 4.5 m tidal wave. Property damage was extensive and 27 were killed.

Dec. 12, 1942: An arsonist set fire to the Knights of Columbus hostel in St John's. Because the hostel had no emergency lighting, the doors opened inwards and exits were restricted, 99 people died and another 100 were seriously injured.

Sept. 17, 1949: Seven hundred people were aboard the Great Lakes excursion ship *Noronic* when it caught fire and burned at its pier in Toronto harbour. The ship's fire hydrants were dry and no alarm was sent to the city fire department until 15 minutes after the blaze was discovered. In the meantime, the single exit became blocked by fire and 118 lives were lost.

Oct. 15, 1954: During the worst inland storm in Canadian history, Hurricane Hazel, over 10 cm of rain fell in Toronto in 12 hours. At that time, many houses in Toronto were built on low-lying flood plains. The storm and resulting floods caused 83 deaths and widespread property damage.

Nov. 1, 1956: A second major tragedy struck the coal mines at Springhill, NS, when an accident killed 39 men.

Dec. 9, 1956: A DC-4 North Star flown by Trans-Canada Airways (later Air Canada) crashed into the east face of Mount Slesse, killing all 62 on board.

June 17, 1958: Design errors in Vancouver's Second Narrows Bridge caused one section to collapse. The accident killed 18 men, including the two engineers that an investigation later determined were responsible for the errors.

Oct. 23, 1958: A third mining accident in Springhill, NS, killed 75 when a tunnel collapsed.

Nov. 19, 1963: A Trans Canada Airlines DC-8F crashed after takeoff from Dorval in Montreal, killing 118.

July 5, 1970: At Toronto International Airport, an Air Canada DC-8 lost one starboard engine during a landing attempt. During the pilot's effort to take off and land again, the remaining starboard engine fell off. The aircraft crashed, killing all 109 persons aboard.

May 4, 1971: During a prolonged rainstorm in St-Jean-Vianney, Que., a giant sinkhole appeared in the ground. The hole swallowed 40 houses, several cars and a bus, and 31 people were killed.

Nov. 10, 1975: The 218-m ore carrier *Edmund Fitzgerald*, based in Sault Ste Marie, broke apart during a storm on Lake Superior and sank in 156 m of water with all 29 members of the crew aboard. Two days later only two rubber rafts and some life preservers from the ship were found.

June 21, 1977: A fire that broke out in the cell block of the city police headquarters of St John, NB, was so hot that the locks on several cell doors were fused. Twenty prisoners were killed and 12 police officers who attempted to rescue the prisoners were injured.

Feb. 11, 1978: A Pacific Western Airlines aircraft crashed at Cranbrook, BC, killing 43 people.

Aug. 4, 1978: The brakes on a chartered bus failed near Eastman, Que. The bus plunged into a lake, and 41 passengers were killed.

Dec. 31, 1979: Forty-four persons were killed during New Year's Eve celebrations at a social club in Chapais, Que., in a fire caused by a man playing with a lighter who set decorations ablaze.

Feb. 15, 1982: The ocean drilling rig *Ocean Ranger* overturned and sank during a storm while operating 265 km east of Newfoundland, killing 84 men. Inadequate safety procedures and equipment were later blamed for the accident.

May 31, 1985: A midafternoon tornado struck Barrie, Ont., killing 12, including four children. Property damage was in the hundreds of millions of dollars.

Dec. 12, 1985: In the worst air crash in Canada, an Arrow Airlines DC-8, after refueling in Gander en route to Hopkinsville, Ky., crashed seconds after takeoff, killing 256 passengers and crew.

Feb. 8, 1986: A 16-unit VIA Rail passenger train slammed head-on into a 118-unit CN freight train near Hinton, Alta. Twenty-six people were killed and dozens were seriously injured.

July 31, 1987: A tornado touched down in Edmonton, Alta, killing 26 people, injuring 250 others and causing an estimated $250 million damage.

Mar. 10, 1989: An Air Ontario jet crashed immediately after takeoff from Dryden, Ont., killing 24 people.

Feb. 12, 1990: One of the worst tire fires in North America broke out near Hagersville, Ont., spewing oil and toxic smoke. The dump, which stored 14 million tires for recycling, burned for 16 days; the blaze was extinguished at a cost of $1.5 million.

May 9, 1992: Twenty-six miners died underground in the Westray coal mine near Plymouth, NS, after a methane gas explosion. Fifteen bodies were recovered but the bodies of the remaining victims could not be reached in the debris.

July 16, 1993: Nineteen people died when a truck towing tanks of diesel fuel collided with a van carrying senior citizens near Lac-Bouchette, Que.

July 19-20, 1996: Ten people died in the Lac-St-Jean Saguenay Region when flash floods from overflowing dams and reservoirs wiped out communities along the Saguenay River.

Oct. 13, 1997: Forty-four passengers were killed when the brakes failed on their sightseeing bus; the vehicle missed a turn at the bottom of a steep hill and crashed into a ravine in Les Eboulements, 110 km northeast of Quebec City.

Sept. 2, 1998: All 229 passengers were killed when a Swissair MD-11 en route from New York to Geneva crashed in the Atlantic near Peggy's Cove, NS. The accident was the second worst in Canadian aviation history.

May 2000: At least seven people died and up to 2,000 people fell ill after drinking tap water infected by *E. coli* bacteria in Walkerton, Ont.

Canadian Crimes

July 17, 1771: Samuel Hearne, an Arctic explorer working for the Hudson's Bay Co., witnessed the unprovoked Chipewyan massacre of an Inuit community at Bloody Fall on the Coppermine River. More than 20 Inuit were killed.

June 19, 1816: Métis raiders massacred Gov. Robert Semple and 21 Anglo-Scottish militiamen at Seven Oaks in the North-Western Territory. Tensions had been growing between Métis hunters and Anglo-Scottish settlers over land use in the Red River region.

Apr. 7, 1868: Thomas D'Arcy McGee, a member of Parliament and a Father of Confederation, was shot at his home in Ottawa. McGee's death was the first political murder in the newly united Canada. James Whelan, an Irish nationalist, was convicted and hanged for the shooting.

Mar. 4, 1870: A Métis firing squad at Fort Garry shot Thomas Scott, an Irish settler, for threatening the life of Louis Riel. The execution, which enraged Protestant Ontarians, prompted Ottawa to draft the *Manitoba Act* and send troops to Fort Garry.

July 1871: Axe murderess Phoebe Campbell chopped up her husband George in their farmhouse near London, Ont. She had been having an affair with another man and sought to inherit her husband's property. Campbell was convicted and hanged in 1872.

Late May 1873: Seeking revenge for a series of horse thefts, a party of white plainsmen attacked an Assiniboine encampment in the Cypress Hills. The resulting massacre left 30 Assiniboine Indians and one white man dead.

Feb. 3, 1880: A mob of at least 31 farmers, including a police constable, massacred five members of the Donnelly clan in their farmhouses in Lucan, Ont. The killings climaxed a blood feud dating back to 1855. No one was convicted for the killings.

Feb. 17, 1890: Reginald Birchall shot and killed Frederick Benwell in a swamp near Woodstock, Ont. Birchall had lured Benwell from Britain with the false promise of making him an investor in a farm. Birchall's trial and hanging received international press coverage.

Apr. 1916: John Mychaluk shot and killed six members of the Manchur family at their farm in Wakaw, Sask. Mychaluk also burned down the Manchur's house and barn before shooting himself dead.

1928-46: Lila and William Young, owners of the Ideal Maternity Home in East Chester, NS, sold about 1,500 babies from unwed mothers to couples in the US and Canada. Between 100 and 400 babies deemed unfit for adoption were allowed to die and buried nearby in wooden butterboxes.

Feb. 17, 1932: A posse of RCMP officers killed Albert Johnson, the Mad Trapper of Rat River, in a shoot-out near Eagle River, YT. Johnson had been wanted for killing an RCMP officer on Jan. 29 and wounding another in Dec. The manhunt was the longest in Canadian Arctic history.

Sept. 9, 1949: All 23 passengers aboard a Quebec Airways DC-3 were killed when a bomb exploded in mid-flight and the plane crashed near St. Joachim, Que. Police uncovered a conspiracy to kill one passenger, Rita Guay. Husband Albert Guay and two accomplices were convicted and hanged.

Mar. 6, 1952: Two members of Edwin Alonzo Boyd's gang shot two police officers, killing one, in Toronto. The shootings climaxed a two-and-a-half-year spree of armed bank robberies in Toronto. All four gang members were caught and imprisoned within the year.

Mar. 1, 1966: Thieves disguised in Air Canada uniforms hijacked 12 crates of gold bullion at Winnipeg airport. The haul, worth $383,497, was the largest gold robbery in Canadian history. The thieves were subsequently caught; most of the gold was recovered.

Aug. 15, 1967: Victor Hoffman shot and killed nine members of the Peterson family–a family he did not know–near Shell Lake, Sask. Hoffman was caught, diagnosed as schizophrenic and confined to a mental hospital.

Sept. 5, 1970: In a drunken rampage, Dale Nelson killed eight people in Creston Valley, BC. His victims were either beaten, stabbed or shot to death; one girl was dismembered in the woods. The RCMP caught Nelson; he was sentenced to life imprisonment.

Oct. 5, 1970: The Front de libération du Quebec (FLQ) kidnapped James Cross, the

British trade commissioner, in Montreal. In Dec., the kidnappers exchanged Cross for safe passage to Cuba. Years later, after returning to Canada, the kidnappers stood trial and were convicted.

Oct. 17, 1970: The FLQ murdered Pierre Laporte, Quebec's labour minister, and left his body in the trunk of a car. Laporte had been kidnapped at his home on Oct. 10. In Dec., the killers were caught at a country house; they received long prison sentences.

Sept. 1, 1972: The Blue Bird Bar in Montreal was torched by three disgruntled patrons who had been ejected from the bar earlier in the evening. The blaze killed 37.

July 1977: Four men participated in the 12-hour rape and eventual drowning of Emanuel Jaques, a 12-year-old shoeshine boy, above a body rub parlour in Toronto. Three were convicted and drew life imprisonment. One man was found not guilty.

1980-82: Clifford Olson, a construction worker from Coquitlam, BC, raped and killed eight girls and three boys aged nine to 18 between Nov. 17, 1980, and Olson's arrest on Aug. 12, 1982. Olson drew life imprisonment, but the government paid $90,000 into a trust fund for Olson's wife and son to learn where Olson had buried the bodies of his victims.

Apr. 27, 1982: Police in Toronto arrested Brian Molony, an employee of the CIBC, for embezzling almost $17 million from the bank in 93 separate frauds beginning in Sept. 1980. Molony had gambled away the money in US casinos. He was convicted in 1983.

Jan. 21, 1983: Colin Thatcher, a wealthy Moose Jaw rancher and former provincial Conservative cabinet minister, had his ex-wife murdered in Regina, Sask. He was convicted of first-degree murder and sentenced to life imprisonment.

Nov. 14, 1983: The body of organized crime boss Paul Volpe was found in the trunk of his wife's car at Toronto International Airport. His throat had been slashed.

May 8, 1984: Outraged by the Parti Québécois, Cpl. Denis Lortie killed three people and injured 13 more with machinegun fire in Quebec's national assembly. Rene Jalbert, the assembly's unarmed sergeant-at-arms, talked Lortie into surrendering. Lortie was sentenced to life in prison in 1987.

Mar. 12, 1985: Three Armenian terrorists carrying shotguns, revolvers and explosives attacked the Turkish embassy in Ottawa. They killed one security guard and held 12 hostages for four hours. All were caught and given life sentences.

June 23, 1985: 280 Canadians were killed when an Air India 747 flying from Toronto to London, England, crashed into the Atlantic Ocean. A bomb on board is thought to have caused the disaster.

May 25, 1986: A Punjabi cabinet minister, Malkiat Singh Sidhu, was shot while visiting Vancouver. Police suspected Sikh militants were responsible for the shooting.

Sept. 30, 1988: Newfoundlanders learned that Christian brothers had been sexually abusing altar boys since the 1970s at the Mount Cashel orphanage near St John's. By 1992, nine sex offenders had been convicted, receiving sentences of one to 13 years imprisonment. A public inquiry revealed a cover-up in 1975 involving public officials.

May-Nov. 1989: Escaped convict Allan Legere terrorized Miramichi, NB, killing victims at random while eluding a massive police search. Legere was eventually caught and convicted for four killings; he drew life imprisonment.

Dec. 6, 1989: Gunman Marc Lepine shot and killed 14 women and wounded 13 others at Montreal's l'école Polytechnique before killing himself. Lepine left a letter claiming he had attacked the students because they were feminists.

1990-92: Paul Bernardo and Karla Homolka, a young couple in Port Dalhousie, Ont., committed the sex-slayings of three girls between Dec. 23, 1990 and Apr. 29, 1992. Both killers were convicted, but Homolka got a lighter sentence in exchange for testimony against her husband. Bernardo also admitted to 14 rapes in Scarborough, Ont., in the 1980s.

Sept. 18, 1992: A bomb exploded underground at the Giant goldmine in Yellowknife, NWT, killing nine workers. Striking workers had been locked out since May; disgruntled miner Roger Warren was convicted of murder and sentenced to 20 years.

Prime Ministers of Canada

■ Sir John A. Macdonald

Canada's first prime minister, Sir John A. Macdonald, was born in Glasgow, Scotland, Jan. 11, 1815. At age five he came to Canada with his parents who settled at Kingston, Upper Canada.

Called to the bar in 1836, Macdonald practised law in Kingston and then in Toronto. He established a reputation as a corporate lawyer, company director and businessman.

He was elected to the Legislative Assembly of the Province of Canada in 1844 and was re- elected in 1848, 1851, 1854, 1857, 1861 and 1863. In 1864, he joined a coalition with George Brown, leader of the Upper Canadian reformers, dedicated to bringing about Confederation. That same year, Macdonald was a delegate to the Charlottetown and Quebec Conferences, and became the principal author of the Confederation resolutions agreed upon in Quebec. He was chairman of the London Conference (1866–67) and played a pivotal role in bringing about Confederation.

Macdonald became Canada's first prime minister when the Conservative party won a majority of seats in Parliament following the first post-Confederation general election in 1867. Though he was re-elected in 1872, Macdonald's second administration was marred by the "Pacific Scandal" in 1873, when the Liberal opposition charged that his government had awarded the CPR contract to Sir Hugh Allan in return for political contributions. An investigation into these charges was held, and the government resigned on Nov. 5, 1873.

Macdonald's Liberal-Conservatives were re-elected Sept. 17, 1878, and Macdonald remained prime minister until his death in Ottawa on June 6, 1891.

During his first administration, the Dominion of Canada expanded to include the provinces of British Columbia, Prince Edward Island and the newly created Manitoba.

The building of the transcontinental railway is the most memorable feature of his second administration, but other accomplishments include the establishment of the "National Policy"—a system of tariff protection to aid the development of Canadian industries (1879)—and the increased settlement of the Western provinces that followed the construction of the railway.

■ Alexander Mackenzie

Alexander Mackenzie was born on Jan. 28, 1822 near Dunkeld, Perthshire, Scotland. He left school and became a stonemason at the age of 14.

He emigrated to Canada in 1842 and became a contractor at Lambton, Ontario, and then editor of the *Lambton Shield*. From 1866–74, he was a major in the 27th Lambton Battalion Volunteer Infantry.

In 1861, Mackenzie was elected to the Legislative Assembly of the Province of Canada, where he gave his support to the Confederation plan. When George Brown was defeated in the 1867 election, Mackenzie became *de facto* leader of the Opposition, though it was not until after the 1872 elections that he formally accepted this title.

It was Mackenzie who led the attack on the Macdonald administration over the "Pacific Scandal"; when Macdonald resigned on Nov. 5, 1873, Mackenzie became prime minister.

During his 5-year term of office, Mackenzie introduced changes to election laws that included the secret ballot and universal male suffrage. The Supreme Court of Canada was established under Mackenzie's rule, and Wilfrid Laurier was brought into Mackenzie's cabinet.

Severe economic depression plagued Canada during the Mackenzie years, and in 1878, his Liberal party was routed at the polls.

Mackenzie retained his own seat, however, and was still a member of Parliament when he died Apr. 17, 1892, in Toronto.

■ Sir John Abbott

Sir John Joseph Caldwell Abbott was born Mar. 12, 1821, at St. Andrews, Lower Canada—the first prime minister to be born on Canadian soil.

After taking his law degree from University of McGill College, he was admitted to the bar in 1847 and practised law in Montreal. From 1855–80 he was dean of the Faculty of Law, McGill University.

Abbott was elected to the Legislative Assembly of the Province of Canada in 1857, re-elected in 1861 and 1863, and sat until Confederation. He was then elected to the House of Commons in 1867, 1872 and 1874. He was last elected in 1882 and appointed to the Senate on May 12, 1887.

When Sir John A. Macdonald died in 1891, Abbott—though a senator—inherited the Conservative leadership. The three other leading Conservatives—Langevin, Tupper and Thompson—were unwilling or unable to assume the post. Abbott held the office of prime minister from June 16, 1891, until his resignation on Nov. 24, 1892. He died in Montreal on Oct. 30, 1893.

■ Sir John Thompson

Sir John Sparrow David Thompson was born in Halifax, NS, on Nov. 10, 1845.

Thompson was called to the Nova Scotia bar in 1865, and was instrumental in founding Dalhousie Law School in 1883, where he eventually became a lecturer.

In May 1882, Thompson became premier of Nova Scotia, but when his government was defeated two months later, he retired from politics and became a judge of the Supreme Court of Nova Scotia.

Prime Minister Macdonald coaxed Thompson back into politics, making him Minister of

Justice in 1885. When Macdonald died in 1891, Thompson declined the leadership, fearing that his conversion to Roman Catholicism in 1870 would hinder his party's fortunes. However, the following year, Thompson changed his mind, and on Dec. 5, 1892, he became prime minister.

Though prime minister for just over 2 years, Thompson was largely responsible for the establishment of the Criminal Code and penetentiary reforms. He very nearly succeeded in bringing Newfoundland into Confederation in 1894, and successfully negotiated fisheries clauses in the Treaty of Washington.

He died while still in office on Dec. 12, 1894.

■ Sir Mackenzie Bowell

Mackenzie Bowell was born at Rickinghall, Suffolk, England, on Dec. 27, 1823, and came to Canada in 1832. In 1834, he became an

apprentice printer at Belleville, Upper Canada and was later editor and proprietor of the Belleville *Intelligencer*. He served in the militia of the United Province of Canada during the American Civil War and the Fenian raids of 1866.

Bowell was elected to the House of Commons in 1867 for Hastings North, Ont., and was re-elected in 1872, 1874, 1878, 1887 and 1891.

As spokesman for the Orange Association of British America, Bowell was instrumental in having Louis Riel expelled from the Commons in 1874.

On Dec. 5, 1892, Bowell was appointed to the Senate and, after Thompson's death in 1894, was invited by the Governor General to form a government.

Perhaps the thorniest problem facing Prime Minister Bowell was the Manitoba Schools question. In 1890, Manitoba legislation had withdrawn school privileges from the Roman Catholic and primarily French minority in that province. By the time Bowell assumed office, attempts were being made to restore those lost school privileges by federal remedial legislation. Bowell was not equal to the political challenges facing him; he lost control of his cabinet ministers, several of whom eventually called for his resignation. Bowell denounced this cabinet rebellion as a "nest of traitors," but eventually he resigned on Apr. 27, 1896. He died in Belleville, Ont., on Dec. 10, 1917, at age 93.

■ Sir Charles Tupper

Charles Tupper was born at Amherst, NS, July 2, 1821. He took a degree in medicine at Edinburgh University. At the age of 22, he began practising medicine in Amherst and became the first president of the Canadian Medical Association (1867–70).

The 1855 election that brought him to the Legislative Assembly of Nova Scotia was declared void on Feb. 24, 1857. He was subsequently re-elected in a by-election that same year and was elected again in 1859 and 1863.

Tupper was active in the Confederation movement, and was a delegate to the

Charlottetown, Quebec and London Conferences. He was elected to the House of Commons in 1867 and re-elected 1870, 1872, 1874, 1878 and 1882. He resigned in 1884 and served as High Commissioner for Canada in the United Kingdom from May 28 of that year to Jan. 26, 1887. In 1887, he was re-elected to the House of Commons, but resigned the following year and again served as High Commissioner from May 23, 1888, to Jan. 14, 1896.

In 1896, following the rebellion of Bowell's cabinet, Tupper became *de facto* leader of the administration until Bowell formally resigned on Apr. 27, 1896. At that time, the Governor General invited Tupper to form the government. Parliament was dissolved shortly thereafter and in the election that followed on June 23, Tupper's Conservatives were defeated. Tupper stayed on as leader of the Opposition until Feb. 5, 1901, then retired from public life. He died Oct. 30, 1915 at Bexley Heath, Kent, England.

■ Sir Wilfrid Laurier

Wilfrid Laurier was born at St-Lin, Canada East, Nov. 20, 1841. He first attended College de l'Assomption and then took his degree from McGill University.

He was called to the bar of Lower Canada in 1865. He practised law at Montreal and at Arthabaskaville, Que.

First elected to the Legislative Assembly of Quebec in 1871, Laurier resigned in Jan. 1874 and later that year was elected to the House of Commons. He became leader of the Liberal Opposition in June 1887. Then, following the 1896 election that gave his party a 23-seat majority, Laurier became Canada's first French-speaking prime minister on July 11, 1896. The Liberals retained power in 1900 and won a landslide election victory in 1904.

Immigration increased during his time in office as Clifford Sifton, Laurier's minister of the interior from 1896–1905, mounted a powerful campaign to attract immigrants from Britain, the United States and Europe. In 1905, Laurier created the provinces of Alberta and Saskatchewan and established the boundaries of Manitoba. During Laurier's years in power the Canadian West became a major world wheat producer. In 1909, Laurier established the External Affairs Department.

His government's controversial support for the creation of a Canadian navy, and his unpopular attempt to enter into a reciprocal trade agreement with the United States (an agreement that would have reduced or eliminated duties on many imported goods) spelled trouble for Laurier in 1911. His party was

defeated in the Sept. 21 election. He remained an Opposition M.P. until his death on Feb. 17, 1919, in Ottawa.

■ Sir Robert Borden

Robert Laird Borden was born at Grand Pré, NS, June 26, 1854. At age 14 he gave up formal schooling to become an assistant master in classical studies. He taught classics and mathematics in New Jersey in 1873, before returning to Nova Scotia to study law. He was admitted to the Nova Scotia bar in 1878 and practised first in Halifax, then in Kentville, NS.

Borden was elected to the House of Commons in 1896 and 1900 and became leader of the Conservative party on Feb. 6, 1901. He served as leader of the Opposition until 1911, when he led his party to victory in the Sept. 21 election.

Borden was prime minister throughout World War I, and during the war years his government was accused of scandal over British munitions contracts and its staunch support of the Ross Rifle—a weapon known to jam in battle. Borden's government introduced the first federal income tax, nationalized Canadian railways and introduced conscription in 1917.

In the election of Dec. 17, 1917, Borden led a re-organized Union Government made up of Conservatives and pro-conscription Liberals to victory. Borden headed the Canadian delegation at the Paris Peace Conference in 1919, where the autonomy of Canada and other dominions within the British Commonwealth was successfully established. He resigned on July 10, 1920, and died in Ottawa June 10, 1937.

■ Arthur Meighen

Arthur Meighen was born at Anderson, Ont., June 16, 1874. Following his graduation from university in 1896, Meighen taught high school for a year, then moved to Winnipeg in 1898 to study law. He was called to the Manitoba bar in 1902, and practised at Portage La Prairie.

He was first elected to the House of Commons in 1908, re-elected in 1911, 1913 and 1917, defeated in 1921, and re-elected in 1922 and 1925.

Meighen first achieved national prominence in 1913 when he helped devise a closure rule which permitted the government to end debate on a bill which was to effect a $35-million contribution to the British navy. Prior to closure, the bill had been obstructed by a fierce and protracted Opposition party blockade.

Prime Minister Borden appointed Meighen his solicitor general on Oct. 2, 1915, and Meighen held this post for two years. A strong supporter of conscription, Meighen essentially drafted Canada's 1917 conscription bill, and put it into operation. He was also the chief draughtsman of the Wartime Elections Act.

When Borden resigned on July 10, 1920, Meighen succeeded him as prime minister. In the general election of Dec. 6, 1921, Meighen's party was defeated. Though his Conservatives won the most seats in the election of Oct. 29, 1925, the Liberals were able to stay in power with the support of Progressive and Labour members.

Following the resignation of William Lyon Mackenzie King's government on June 28, 1926, the Governor General invited Meighen to form a new ministry. This government was less than three months old, however, when it was defeated in the House of Commons (by only one vote) and Canadians again went to the polls.

Following a Liberal victory in the election of Sept. 14, 1926, Meighen resigned as Conservative leader in the House of Commons. He was appointed to the Senate on Feb. 3, 1932, during Richard Bennett's ministry and became government leader in the Senate. Then, following King's victory in 1935, he became Senate Opposition leader.

On Nov. 12, 1941, he once again became leader of the Conservative party, but failed in his bid to win a seat in the Commons in a federal by-election on Feb. 2, 1942. Following this defeat, he retired from politics and resumed his law practice in Toronto where he died Aug. 5, 1960.

Mackenzie King

William Lyon Mackenzie King, grandson of William Lyon Mackenzie, was born in Kitchener (then called Berlin) on Dec. 17, 1874.

He took his B.A. and law degrees from the University of Toronto and also studied at the University of Chicago and Harvard University.

He served as deputy minister of labour from 1900–08.

He was first elected to the House of Commons in 1908, and succeeded Laurier as leader of the Liberal party in 1919. King became prime minister when the Liberals won the general election of Dec. 6, 1921.

Though Meighen's Conservatives won a majority of seats in the general election of Oct. 29, 1925, King stayed in office with the help of Progressive and Labour members who supported his proposed tariff reductions and old-age pension legislation. King had lost his York North seat in the 1925 election but returned to the House of Commons as the member for Prince Albert, Sask., following a by-election on Feb. 15, 1926. King's government was shaken in 1926 by the revelation that the customs department was tainted with corruption and incompetence. In the furor that followed, King lost the support of many members of Parliament and, although never technically defeated in the House of Commons, decided that he could no longer hold his minority government. He appealed to Governor General Lord Byng to dissolve Parliament, even though the government had not been defeated. Byng refused. King subsequently resigned on June 28, 1926, and the Governor General invited Arthur Meighen to form a government which was subsequently defeated in the House of Commons.

In the general election of Sept. 14, 1926, King's Liberals regained power and held it until 1930. But the disastrous fall in the price of wheat and other Canadian exports in 1929 soured Canadians on their government, and King was defeated by R.B. Bennett's Conservatives in the election of July 28, 1930.

Five years later, King was back in the prime minister's office, following the Liberal victory in the general election of Oct. 14, 1935. In the coming years, King, an ardent supporter of Canada's autonomy within the British Commonwealth, was faced with the issue of Canada's participation in an impending European war. To soothe French-Canadian concerns over Canadian support of Great Britain, King promised there would be no conscription; Canada declared war in September 1939. Later, however, heavy casualties in France and Italy in 1944 prompted King to break his promise and send conscripts overseas.

King's government began introducing postwar recovery legislation even before peace was declared. These measures included recon-

struction plans and social security schemes such as mother's allowances.

King resigned as prime minister on Nov. 15, 1948, supporting Louis St Laurent as his successor. In poor health in his final years, King died July 22, 1950, at Kingsmere, his estate in Wright County, Que.

Richard Bennett

Richard Bedford Bennett was born at Hopewell, NB, July 3, 1870. Bennett studied law at Dalhousie University. He read and practised law in Chatham, NB, from 1893–97, before moving to Calgary where he entered a legal partnership with Senator James A. Lougheed.

Bennett was first elected to the House of Commons in 1911. He served as minister of justice in Arthur Meighen's 1921 cabinet, and minister of finance and minister of mines in Meighen's 1926 government.

Bennett was chosen to replace Meighen as Conservative leader at the party convention in

Winnipeg in 1927. He became prime minister following the Conservative victory in the election of July 28, 1930.

Bennett had the task of governing Canada during the worst years of the Depression. Virtually every measure his government attempted ended in failure. High unemployment levels continued despite Bennett's efforts to reduce them. Negotiations for a reciprocity treaty with the United States did not succeed. A plan of preferential tariffs agreed to in 1930 at the Imperial Conference did little to ease Canada's economic woes.

Then, in 1935, near the end of his term, Bennett took an unexpected step to the political left. He proclaimed that "the old order is gone" and that it was time for a new economic system. That new system was to include a state-planned economy, new unemployment and health insurance legislation and old-age pension laws.

In the election of Oct. 14, 1935, Bennett's Conservatives suffered a devastating defeat, winning just 39 seats. Bennett remained in Opposition until 1937, when he retired to England. There he was given the title Viscount Bennett of Mickelham, Hopewell and Calgary.

Despite the overwhelming problems of the Great Depression, Bennett's term saw the creation of the Canadian Radio Broadcasting Corporation (the predecessor to the CBC) and the Bank of Canada. As well, it was during Bennett's tenure that the Statute of Westminster gave Canada increased autonomy in 1931.

Bennett died June 27, 1947.

■ Louis St Laurent

Louis Stephen St Laurent was born at Compton, Que., Feb. 1, 1882. Called to the Quebec bar in 1905, he practised law in Quebec City, and became Professor of Law at Université Laval. He was elected president of the Canadian Bar Association in 1930.

St Laurent became justice minister in Mackenzie King's cabinet on Dec. 10, 1941. On Feb. 9, 1942, he was elected to the House of Commons in a by-election for Quebec East.

Originally planning to hold his cabinet post only during the war, St Laurent was persuaded to stay on. On Dec. 10, 1946, he became secretary of state for external affairs. A firm believer in collective security, St Laurent was one of the architects of the North Atlantic Treaty Organization (NATO). On Aug. 7, 1948, he accepted his party's nomination to be King's successor, and on Nov. 15 became prime minister.

While in power St Laurent ended the practice of appealing court cases to the Judicial Committee of the Privy Council in England, and made the Supreme Court of Canada the final Canadian court of appeal. He won the acceptance of a new apportionment of taxes in 1956 and, in negotiation with President Truman, laid the foundation for a US–Canada agreement to develop the St Lawrence Seaway.

In 1958, he retired and returned to Quebec City to practise law. He died July 25, 1973.

■ John Diefenbaker

John George Diefenbaker was born at Neustadt, Ont., Sept. 18, 1895. He received his B.A. from the University of Saskatchewan in 1915 and his M.A. one year later.

After the outbreak of World War I, he joined the Canadian Officers' Training Corps, and served overseas as a lieutenant with the 105th 'Saskatoon Fusiliers' Regiment from 1916 to 1917.

Returning to Saskatchewan, he took his law degree from the University of Saskatchewan in 1919 and established a law practice at Wakaw. He later moved to Prince Albert.

After several unsuccessful attempts to gain a seat, first in the federal, then in Saskatchewan's provincial parliament, Diefenbaker was finally elected to the House of Commons in 1940. He was a candidate for leadership of the Progressive Conservative Party at the 1942 and 1948 conventions, but did not win the nomination until Dec. 14, 1956.

The PCs won the election of June 10, 1957 by a slim margin, and on June 21, John Diefenbaker officially became prime minister. A year later, he called an election, hoping to turn his Conservative minority government into a clear majority. He was overwhelmingly successful, winning 208 of the 265 seats in the Mar. 31, 1958, election. He fared less well in the 1962 election, when only 116 PCs were elected, and in the general election of 1963, a Liberal victory relegated Diefenbaker to the role of Opposition leader. Diefenbaker remained Conservative leader until Sept. 1967, when he was replaced by Robert Stanfield.

The Diefenbaker years (1957–63) saw the passage of the Canadian Bill of Rights, a "roads-to- resources" program to encourage the development of northern resources, legislation providing support for agriculture, encouragement of technical training and improved health and welfare programs. Regional development was emphasized by significant public works such as construction of the South Saskatchewan Dam, and simultaneous translation was introduced in the House of Commons.

Diefenbaker died Aug. 16, 1979, at his home in Rockliffe Park, Ottawa.

■ Lester Pearson

Lester Bowles Pearson was born at Newtonbrook, Ont., on Apr. 23, 1897. He took his B.A. at the University of Toronto and his M.A. at Oxford University.

After serving overseas in World War I, he became a history professor at the University of Toronto, where he taught from 1924–1928. He joined Canada's foreign service in 1928, became Canada's ambassador to the UN in 1945, was appointed under-secretary of state for external affairs in 1946 and accepted the invitations of King and St Laurent to become minister of external affairs in Sept. 1948.

In 1956, following the Anglo-French-Israeli invasion of Egypt, Pearson's work at the United Nations helped establish a UN Emergency Force which kept peace on the Israeli–Egyptian border for the next decade. His settlement of the Suez crisis brought him the Nobel Peace Prize in 1957—the only time a Canadian has been so honoured.

Pearson was chosen leader of the Liberal party Jan. 15, 1958. In the general election of

Apr. 8, 1963, the Liberals won 129 seats in the House of Commons, and Pearson became the leader of a minority government.

In the 1965 election, the Liberals made slight gains, but were still short of a majority. Pearson announced his resignation in Dec. 1967 and, in Apr. 1968, was succeeded by Pierre Trudeau.

Under Pearson, the old age pension was extended and a national health plan created. He secured the adoption of a national flag and established the Royal Commission on Bilingualism and Biculturalism.

Though he retired in 1968, his international reputation prompted the World Bank to commission him to prepare a report on international aid programs.

He died in Ottawa, Dec. 27, 1972.

■ Pierre Trudeau

Pierre Elliott Trudeau was born in Montreal on Oct. 18, 1919. He attended the University of Montreal, Harvard University, Université de Paris and the London School of Economics. He was called to the Quebec bar in 1943. From 1949–51, he was a member of the Privy Council staff in Ottawa. In 1950, he co-founded the magazine *Cité Libre*. From 1952–62, he practised law and was a journalist and broadcaster in Montreal. From 1962–65, he was a law professor at the University of Montreal.

First elected to the House of Commons in 1965, Trudeau was named justice minister in Lester Pearson's cabinet in 1967. The following year, he won the Liberal leadership and became prime minister Apr. 19, 1968. In the general election of the same year, the Liberals won a solid majority.

During his first four years in power, Trudeau faced the "FLQ Crisis"—the kidnapping of British diplomat James Cross and Quebec cabinet minister Pierre Laporte by the radical separatist organization Front de libération du Québec. (Laporte was later murdered.) In response he invoked the War Measures Act, a statute giving the state broad powers of arrest and detention.

In the general election of 1972, Trudeau returned to power with a minority government. In 1974, he regained a majority.

In the general election of 1979, the Progressive Conservatives under Joe Clark won a narrow victory and were able to form a minority government. Trudeau announced his intention to retire, but when the Clark government fell later that year, Trudeau led the Liberals in the election and won a majority on Feb. 18, 1980.

Trudeau's final term in office was devoted to constitutional reform which, for the first time, allowed Canada's Parliament to amend the constitution without appeal to the UK government. A constitutionally-entrenched Charter of Rights and Freedoms was also introduced.

Trudeau's introduction of a National Energy Program led to bitter disputes between the federal government and the energy-producing provinces, particularly Alberta. The NEP was aimed at increasing Canadian control of the oil industry, promoting energy self-sufficiency and generating more federal revenues in the energy sector.

During his final year as prime minister Trudeau launched a world peace initiative, visiting more than 40 world leaders to appeal for peace and an end to the nuclear arms race.

In June of 1984, Trudeau resigned. He was succeeded by John Turner and left politics, eventually joining a Montreal law firm.

Trudeau died Sept. 28, 2000 at his home in Montreal.

■ Joe Clark

Charles Joseph "Joe" Clark was born at High River, Alta., on June 5, 1939. He was educated at the University of Alberta.

Clark was first elected to the House of Commons in 1972. In 1976 he became leader of the Progressive Conservative party and, in the general election of 1979, won enough seats to form a minority government. At 39, Clark was Canada's youngest prime minister. But his minority government fell in Dec. 1979 on a vote of non-confidence on its proposed budget. In the Feb. 1980 election that followed, the Liberals returned to power.

At a national general meeting of the Conservative party in Jan. 1983, Clark received the support of only two-thirds of the delegates and called for a national party leadership convention. In June 1983, Clark lost the leadership to Brian Mulroney on the 4th ballot. He remained an MP and, when Mulroney became prime minister in 1984, Clark joined the cabinet as secretary of state for external affairs.

In 1991, he was appointed as minister responsible for constitutional affairs and given the task of succeeding where the Meech Lake Accord had failed. Late 1991 and the first half of 1992 were marked by weeks of cross-country constitutional negotiations under Clark's guidance. In August 1992 the Charlottetown Accord—an agreement to amend the Constitution Act of 1982—was agreed upon by all first ministers. The text of the agreement was presented to Canadians and a national referendum was held on Oct. 26, 1992, on the issue of whether or not to approve the deal. The agreement was rejected by the majority of voters across the country.

Clark left federal politics after the 1993 election. In 1998, he re-entered public life when Jean Charest vacated the federal Conservative leadership to run in Quebec's provincial election. On Nov. 14, 1998, Clark was re-elected federal Conservative leader.

■ John Turner

John Napier Turner was born at Richmond, Surrey, England on June 7, 1929. He attended the University of British Columbia, Oxford University and Université de Paris. He was called to the bar in England in 1953 and the bar in Quebec in 1954. He lectured for a time in the Faculty of Commerce at Sir George Williams University.

First elected to the House of Commons in 1962, Turner entered Lester Pearson's cabinet in 1965. He became minister of consumer and corporate affairs in 1967. In 1968, he was a candidate for the Liberal leadership, finishing 3rd on the final ballot.

In 1968, Turner was appointed minister of justice in Pierre Trudeau's cabinet. In 1972, he became minister of finance, a post he held until his resignation in Sept. 1975. In Feb. 1976 he left politics and joined a Toronto law firm.

Turner remained in private practice until Trudeau's retirement in 1984, when he successfully ran for leader of the Liberal party and became prime minister on June 30, though he did not have a seat in the House of Commons. He dissolved Parliament July 9, and in the ensuing general election the Liberals were overwhelmingly defeated by the Progressive Conservatives.

As leader of the Opposition, Turner used the Liberal majority in the Senate to block passage of the Conservatives' free trade legislation and force an election on the issue in 1988. The Conservatives won the election and were able to form another majority government.

Early in 1989, Turner announced plans to step down as leader; in June 1990, he was succeeded by Jean Chrétien.

■ Brian Mulroney

Martin Brian Mulroney was born at Baie Comeau, Que., Mar. 20, 1939. He attended St. Francis Xavier University and Université Laval. Called to the bar of Quebec in 1965, Mulroney practised law in Montreal. In 1976, he joined the Iron Ore Company of Canada as executive vice-president and was elected company president the following year.

Mulroney made an unsuccessful bid for the Progressive Conservative party leadership in 1976. In 1983 he ran again, defeating the incumbent leader, Joe Clark, on the 4th ballot.

A by-election for the Maritime riding of Central Nova brought Mulroney into Parliament as leader of the Opposition. In the general election of 1984, he led the Conservatives to victory, winning the largest number of seats (211) in Canadian history.

Mulroney's major initiatives between 1984 and 1988 were the Meech Lake Accord—a package of constitutional changes designed to end Quebec's boycott of the 1982 constitutional reform—and the negotiation of a free trade agreement with the United States.

In 1988, with free trade the central election issue, Mulroney won a second majority government. The free trade agreement subsequently received final approval and took effect in 1989.

His term from 1988 to 1993 was marked by intense negotiations to bring about a new constitutional agreement to replace the Meech Lake Accord which was not ratified by all provinces by the June 1990 deadline. Agreement was reached amongst federal and provincial officials in what became known as the Charlottetown Accord, but the proposals were rejected in a national referendum held on Oct. 26, 1992.

The Conservatives under Mulroney continued their free trade initiative and finalized a North American free trade deal (NAFTA) with the US and Mexico.

Mulroney announced his intention to retire in February 1993 and on June 25, 1993 he was replaced by Kim Campbell, newly-elected leader of the Conservative party.

Kim Campbell

Avril Phaedra (Kim) Campbell was born Mar. 10, 1947 in Port Alberni, BC. She attended the University of British Columbia, earning an honours degree in political science.

After an academic career in BC, she studied law at UBC. In Sept. 1985, she joined BC Premier William Bennett's office as a policy advisor. In May 1986, Campbell ran in the provincial election and won a seat in the legislature, representing Vancouver/Point Grey. She served in the provincial legislature until October 1988 when she resigned her seat to contest the federal riding of Vancouver Centre. An ardent defender of free trade, Campbell joined Prime Minister Mulroney's cabinet with the Indian Affairs and Northern Development portfolio.

In 1990 Campbell became the first woman promoted to the Attorney General and Justice post. In January of 1993 she became Canada's first female defence minister and a candidate in the Conservative leadership contest that year. On June 13, 1993, she was elected leader on the second ballot; on June 25, she was sworn in as Canada's first female prime minister. In the election of Oct. 1993, however, the Conservatives lost all but two seats in the House of Commons. Campbell's tenure as prime minister ended on Nov. 4; she stepped down as federal Conservative leader on Dec. 14, 1993.

Jean Chrétien

Jean Chrétien was born in Shawinigan, Quebec, on Jan. 11, 1934. He studied law at Laval University and was called to the bar of Quebec in 1958.

Chrétien was first elected to the House of Commons in 1963 and after re-election in 1965 served as parliamentary secretary to the prime minister (1965) and the finance minister (1966). He became minister of national revenue in 1968; after the June 1968 election, he became responsible for Indian affairs and northern development. In 1974, he was appointed president of the treasury board; in 1976, he served as minister of industry, trade and commerce. In 1977, he was named finance minister; in 1980 he became justice minister and attorney general and also served as minister of state for social development. Chrétien played an important role in patriating the Constitution. In 1982, he became minister of energy, mines and resources; in 1984, he became deputy prime minister and secretary of state for external affairs.

In 1986, Chrétien left public life, returning after his election as Liberal leader in 1990. After his re-election to the House in a December by-election in Beausejour, he took his seat as leader of the Opposition. In the federal election of October 1993, Chrétien led his party to a majority victory. In the federal elections of October 1993 and June 1997, Chrétien led his party to majority victories.

Power in Ottawa

Selected politicians, civil servants and judges wield great power in the nation's capital: the prime minister and cabinet ministers, deputy ministers and their assistants, and the nine justices of the Supreme Court.

The **prime minister** is the most powerful figure in government: head of government; leader of the majority party in the House of Commons (when a majority government has been elected); and chair of the Cabinet. The prime minister's authority also derives from unwritten conventions such as those related to party discipline. (Party discipline in particular ensures that all members of the governing party—from cabinet ministers to backbenchers—unanimously support the government's policies and legislative agenda. The prime minister's power to enforce this—and expel members who do not support the government—ensures that majority governments will stay in power during their mandate.)

The prime minister also has the power to fill government posts, including appointments to the Cabinet, the Senate, Canadian embassies and the judiciary. Heads of royal commissions, Crown corporations and federal regulatory agencies are also appointed by the prime minister. In addition, the prime minister recommends candidates for Governor General and the lieutenant-governors to the Queen.

The prime minister and staff set Parliament's legislative agenda, selecting the issues to be addressed. The PM can create, reform and abolish cabinet posts, royal commissions, Crown corporations and federal civil service departments. The prime minister also decides (within a five year period) when to dissolve Parliament and call elections.

Cabinet ministers rank below the prime minister in importance. They act as the chief executives of assigned federal departments and approve all government policies coming from their department. Cabinet ministers direct their staff to write new departmental policies, draft bills for debate in Parliament and pass orders-in-council—laws approved by the Governor General but never debated in Parliament. Collectively, cabinet shapes the federal budget, raising, allocating and spending billions of tax dollars annually. Within the Cabinet, some ministers wield more power than others. These include the heads of the departments that affect all citizens (e.g., finance, industry, justice and national revenue). The **deputy prime minister** stands in for the prime minister when the PM is absent. The **government house leader** ensures the timely passage of bills through the House of Commons and the **whip** supervises the attendance of MPs.

Deputy ministers are the most important federal civil servants. They are appointed career bureaucrats who manage their departments, draft the laws and policy that affect their departments, and advise cabinet ministers on management and policy proposals. Deputy ministers possess years of experience, specialized knowledge and the resources of large organizations. They also control access to their minister.

The chief justice and eight associate justices of the **Supreme Court of Canada** are the most powerful judges in the land. Independent of Parliament's executives and legislators, the Supreme Court interprets and applies the law as set down by the legislators. Since 1875, the justices have ruled on the division of federal and provincial powers; since 1949 they have constituted Canada's highest court of appeal. Before the passage of the Canadian Charter of Rights and Freedoms in 1982, Parliament was supreme and the Supreme Court rarely overturned laws. After 1982, the provisions of the Charter gave the justices the power to interpret and enforce Charter guarantees in relation to federal and provincial legislation. The justices now strike down unconstitutional provisions in federal and provincial laws.

GOVERNMENT OF CANADA

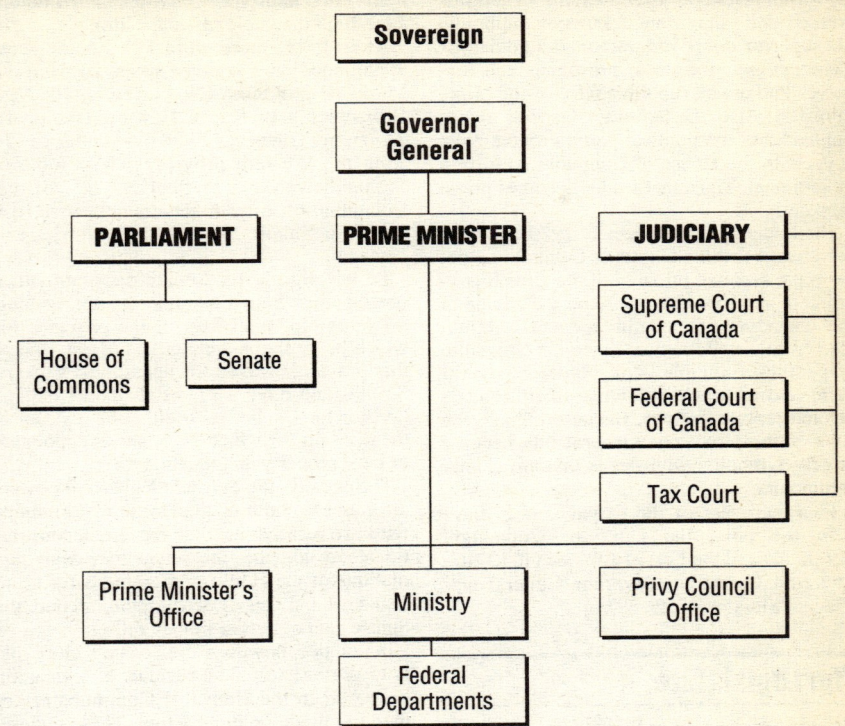

Canada is an independent, self-governing democracy whose form of government is a constitutional monarchy. There are three types of government power: legislative, executive and judicial. In Canada the legislative and executive powers are joined, while the judiciary remains separate. The executive proposes legislation, presents budgets and implements laws; the legislature adopts laws and votes on recommendations for taxes or other revenue; the judiciary interprets the laws.

■ The Monarchy

The Queen (crowned Queen Elizabeth II on June 2, 1953) is Canada's official head of state through which the entire authority of the government is set in motion and in whose name laws are enacted. The Queen's role is set out in the *Constitution Act,* (formerly the *British North America Act, 1867*), and that same act gives the monarch ultimate authority over Canada's armed forces.

In practice, however, the Queen has little or no part to play in Canadian government. She appoints the Governor General, but does so only on the prime minister's recommendation. Once appointed, it is the Governor General who performs the monarch's duties, and these duties have been mainly ceremonial for many years. Only during royal visits does the Queen carry out those functions normally performed in her name by the Governor General, such as the opening of Parliament.

■ The Governor General

The Governor General is selected by the prime minister and formally appointed by the Queen to act as her representative in Canada. The appointment is usually for five years but has sometimes been extended to seven.

Bills passed in the House of Commons and

Senate do not become law until the Governor General has given them royal assent. The Governor General executes all orders-in-council and other state documents, appoints all superior court judges (on the advice of Cabinet) and summons, prorogues and dissolves Parliament (on the advice of the prime minister). Also, the Governor General invites the leader of the political party with the most support in the House of Commons to form a government. Thus, that leader becomes prime minister.

The Imperial Conferences of 1926 and 1930 established that the Governor General was not the representative or agent of the British government and should act only on the advice of the Canadian prime minister and Cabinet. Therefore, the Governor General is obliged to respect the principle of responsible government and to follow the wishes of Canada's elected representatives. Because of this, the role of the Governor General has become largely symbolic, with duties that are chiefly ceremonial.

Two members of the Royal Family have held the post: the Duke of Connaught (1911–16) and the Earl of Athlone (1940–46). The first Canadian Governor General was Vincent Massey (1952–59).

The Legislature

Canada's legislature or Parliament consists of the Queen, an upper house, known as the Senate, and the House of Commons. Senators are appointed by the Governor General on the advice of the prime minister; the seats in the Senate are distributed on a regional basis; originally, there were 72 senators, but through the years the Senate has increased as the number of provinces and the population have grown. In 1975 the Senate was increased to 104 members; in 1990 Prime Minister Brian Mulroney employed a never-before-used section of the *Constitution Act* to increase the number to temporarily 112. The House of Commons is an elected assembly in which each member represents one of 301 electoral districts distributed according to population.

■ The Senate

The Senate is the Upper House of the Canadian Parliament through which all legislation must pass before it becomes law. Its members, appointed by the Governor General on the recommendation of the prime minister, hold office until age 75. (If appointed before June 1965 they hold office for life).

After 1999, there were 105 Senate seats apportioned on a regional basis: 24 from the Maritime provinces (Nova Scotia, 10; New Brunswick, 10; Prince Edward Island, 4); 24 from Quebec; 24 from Ontario; 24 from the Western provinces (Manitoba, 6; Saskatchewan, 6; Alberta, 6; British Columbia, 6); 6 from Newfoundland; 1 each from the Yukon, Northwest Territories and Nunavut.

To be eligible for Senate appointment, a person must be a Canadian citizen, at least 30 years old, a resident of the province for which he or she is appointed, possess land in that province with an unencumbered value of $4 000 and have a net estate of $4 000. A Senator for Quebec must either be resident in the division for which he or she is appointed, or have property qualification there.

Technically, the Senate's legislative powers are equal to those of the House of Commons with two restrictions: first, on certain constitutional amendments, the Senate may delay resolutions of the House of Commons for up to 180 days, but cannot defeat them; second, the Senate cannot initiate money bills.

In practice, however, the Senate's chief role is to provide technical reviews of legislation proposed in the House of Commons rather than to initiate political action. These reviews are done by Senate committees, which inspect each bill clause-by-clause and hear evidence from groups or individuals who may be affected by the proposed legislation.

Historically, the Senate rarely used its powers to impede legislation originating from the elected House of Commons. From 1984 to 1990, however, the Liberal-dominated Senate attempted several times to stall or block legislation approved by the Conservative majority in the House of Commons. In 1990, when the Senate blocked his government's goods and services tax, Mulroney temporarily increased the size of the Senate and added eight new Conservatives, ensuring that the measure would be made law.

In recent years, there have been repeated calls, especially from the West, for constitutional reform which would include an elected Senate with more representation from the Western provinces and Newfoundland. Plans for discussions leading to a Senate overhaul are now part of other constitutional discussions.

■ The House of Commons

The House of Commons is Canada's 301-member elected federal assembly. Its members are chosen in general elections held at least once every five years. By-elections are held if a member dies or resigns between general elections.

All bills governing matters within federal jurisdiction must be passed by a majority of members of Parliament to become law.

Members of Parliament usually belong to a political party and will normally vote with that party on any proposed legislation. Occasionally, members will break with their party on a vote and will sometimes leave the party they were affiliated with when elected to sit as independents or to join another political party within the House. Members of Parliament can also be elected as independent candidates who do not belong to a political party.

The **prime minister** is the leader of the political party able to command the support of a majority of the members of the House of Commons. If no party holds a clear majority of seats, a "minority government" is formed, usually led by the party with the most seats in Parliament, provided it has enough support from the other parties to enable it to pass legislation.

When the House of Commons is in session it convenes at two o'clock daily and 11 o'clock on Fridays when the Speaker of the House takes the chair. After the mace is laid on the table in front of the Speaker and the daily prayer is read, business commences. Members of the government sit to the Speaker's right and the Opposition sits on the left. The leaders of other opposition parties sit on the left farther away from the Speaker's chair.

An important feature of Parliament is the daily question period at which time members question Cabinet ministers about their policies and actions. But most of Parliament's time is spent discussing proposed legislation introduced as "bills". Any member may introduce a bill, although this is usually done by a member of Cabinet. After readings in the House and detailed examination in committee, the bill will go for "third reading" in the House and if passed, will be forwarded to the Senate.

When a major piece of legislation introduced by the government is defeated in the House of Commons, the government is obliged to resign. The Governor General may then call on the leader of the Opposition to form a government but, in most cases, will call a general election so that the electorate can decide which party has the most public support for its policies.

The Executive

■ The Prime Minister

The prime minister is the pre-eminent figure in Canadian politics. The power and authority of the office come from the fact that the prime minister is the leader of the party (or group of parties) that has control of, if not a clear majority of seats in the House of Commons, at least more seats than any of the other parties. The prime minister is an elected member of parliament as well as national party leader and as such has a mandate to govern via programs and policies and to speak on behalf of Canada.

The prime minister has control over appointments, including appointing (and shifting) cabinet members, senior staff in the public service and parliamentary secretaries; and appointing senators, judges, lieutenant governors, privy councillors, provincial administrators, and speakers of the senate. In addition, the prime minister recommends to the monarchy the appointment of the governor general. The prime minister has the authority to dissolve parliament and can therefore control the timing of an election. The prime minister also controls the organization of government, including the power to: create or shut down crown corporations; create, modify or merge cabinet portfolios and bureaucratic agencies; and appoint royal commissions.

■ The Cabinet

The Cabinet is a group of government ministers who, chosen and led by the prime minister, determine executive policies and are responsible for them to the House of Commons. Cabinet members are usually given responsibility for heading specific areas of the government such as finance or foreign policy and will introduce legislation pertaining to them in the House of Commons. They will also explain or defend government actions when questioned in the House.

Cabinet ministers are generally chosen from members of the government's party in the House of Commons, although Senators are sometimes appointed to provide Cabinet representation from all parts of the country. When Senators join the Cabinet they do not usually head a government department because a Senator is constitutionally forbidden to introduce tax or "money bill" legislation.

There are five categories of cabinet ministers:

1. Department Ministers who assume responsibility for running one or more government departments.
2. Ministers with special parliamentary responsibilities.
3. Ministers without portfolios who do not have responsibility for running a department and are often appointed to balance regional representation in the Cabinet.
4. Ministers of state for designated purposes who formulate and develop new policies outside normal departmental responsibilities.
5. Other ministers of state who may assist departmental ministers, though the departmental minister remains legally responsible for the duties and functions performed by the minister of state.

■ The Privy Council Office

The Privy Council Office is directed by the senior member of the public service, the Clerk of the Privy Council, who also serves as the Secretary to the Cabinet. As part of the executive branch of government, the Office staffs the Cabinet secretariat and provides services to ensure the smooth functioning of the Cabinet and Cabinet meetings. In its advisory capacity, the Privy Council Office advises the Prime Minister on government appointments, relations with Parliament and the Monarchy, the roles and responsibilities of ministers and the organization of government. The Office assists in the co-ordination of policy, ensuring that new proposals are compatible both with existing policy and the government's objectives. During a transition period between governments, the Privy Council Office assists in the winding down of outgoing administrations and the startup of the newly-elected government.

The Privy Council Office's primary responsibilities are to ensure the smooth functioning of the machinery of government and the decision-making process, provide support to the Cabinet, monitor developments throughout the government, and act as a broker to resolve governmental problems.

■ The Treasury Board

The Treasury Board is a committee of the Privy Council that reviews planned expenditures and programs proposed by the various government departments, and assigns priorities to each. The Board is responsible for preparing a long-range and comprehensive fiscal plan that projects government income and expenses for up to four years; it also prepares operational plans for departmental programs. The Board's estimates of the costs of existing programs, major statutory payments (such as transfer payments) and public debt charges form the basis of the Main Estimates, which are tabled by the first of March each year for review by various House committees.

The Treasury Board is also responsible for administrative policy; organization of the public service; and financial, expenditure and personnel management. In 1988, the Board was also given responsibility for the policies and programs of the Official Languages Act. The Board's Secretariat negotiates collective agreements with the federal public service, acting as employer on the government's behalf.

■ Departments

Legislation and government policies are administered through departments, departmental branches and corporations, corporations owned or controlled by the government, special boards and various commissions and advisory bodies. Departments and departmental corporations are accountable to a Cabinet minister and ultimately to Parliament; they perform research, administrative, advisory, supervisory or regulatory roles. Crown corporations usually operate in a competitive or commercial environment and some are accountable to Parliament through a minister as well.

The Canadian Judiciary

■ The Supreme Court of Canada

The Supreme Court of Canada is Canada's highest court of law. It was created by federal statute in 1875. Originally, Supreme Court decisions could be appealed to a special tribunal in England, but such appeals were abolished for criminal cases in 1933 and for civil cases in 1949. Since then, the Supreme Court of Canada has been the court of last resort for every case—criminal or civil— commenced in a Canadian court.

The Supreme Court has jurisdiction to hear appeals from the courts of appeal of each province, as well as from the Federal Court of Canada. The Court is also empowered to consider questions referred to it by the federal cabinet, and to rule on the legality of bills submitted by the government.

The *Constitution Act, 1982,* with its new Canadian Charter of Rights and Freedoms, has expanded the role of the courts in general, and of the Supreme Court in particular. Though it has always been within the power of Canadian courts to declare laws or other government actions invalid, this power had narrow limits prior to 1982. Legislation could only be struck down if the government introducing it had exceeded its legislative authority as defined in the *Constitution Act, 1867* (the BNA Act). In other words, the federal government was not permitted to legislate on matters within provincial legislative authority, and the provincial governments were not permitted to legislate on matters within federal legislative authority. As long as the legislation satisfied that test, it was valid.

But since the *Constitution Act* became law in 1982, the courts have had the power to strike down legislation or invalidate other government actions if they infringe or deny any of the fundamental rights and freedoms recognized by the Charter of Rights and Freedoms. This new power has made Supreme Court judges the watchdogs of Parliament and, ultimately, the guardians of our constitutionally-guaranteed rights. As the highest court in the land, it is the Supreme Court of Canada that has the final word on whether laws violate the Constitution.

The Supreme Court consists of 9 judges, including the Chief Justice. Three of the judges must be appointed from Quebec. By convention (although it is not legally required) 3 have usually been appointed from Ontario, 2 from the West and one from Atlantic Canada. All judges are appointed and paid by the federal government, and may hold office until age 75.

■ Federal Court of Canada

This Court consists of a trial division and a court of appeal and has jurisdiction over a small range of specialized areas such as admiralty law, income tax, patents and customs. Once called the Exchequer Court, the Federal Court is administered by the federal government.

■ Appellate Courts

When a decision of the provincial superior courts is to be appealed, these courts hear the appeal and decide upon it. An appeal is not a new trial; there are rarely any witnesses called and the judges do not rehear the whole case. Instead, they examine written transcripts of the trial and listen to legal arguments presented by the parties' lawyers. The appellate courts are provincial institutions and are called either the Court of Appeal, the Supreme Court Appeal Division or Appellate Division; the judges are appointed by the federal government.

■ Superior Court of Original Jurisdiction

This is the highest court at the provincial level, with jurisdiction to hear all civil and criminal cases, unless a statute specifically says otherwise. The name of the superior court differs among provinces. It can be called either the Court of Queen's Bench, the High Court of Justice or the Supreme Court Trial Division. The judges of these courts are appointed and paid by the federal government.

■ District or County Courts

These trial courts hear all but the most serious criminal matters and civil matters up to a certain dollar value. The judges of these courts are also appointed by the federal government.

■ Provincial Courts

This is the lowest rung of the judicial ladder. The jurisdiction of the provincial courts is limited by statute to the less serious criminal matters and civil cases involving relatively small sums of money. These judges are appointed and paid by the province in which they serve.

■ Federal and Provincial Legislative Authority

Because Canada is a federal state, legislative powers are divided between 2 levels of government: federal and provincial. (Municipal governments only exercise powers delegated to them by the provincial government).

Each level of government has a distinct sphere of authority. With a few exceptions, neither level is permitted to encroach on the legislative authority of the other.

The Constitution Act, 1867 (formerly called the British North America Act, 1867), lists the classes of subject over which the federal and provincial governments have exclusive authority. The federal government, in addition to a general power to make laws for the "peace, order and good government of Canada," has exclusive power in a number of areas including criminal law, unemployment insurance, postal service, regulation of trade, external relations, money and banking, transportation, citizenship, Indian affairs and defence. Matters exclusively within provincial legislative authority include property and civil rights, administration of justice, education, health and welfare, municipal institutions and matters of a merely local or private nature.

Many of the subject classes set out in the Constitution Act, 1867, are broadly worded, and considerable debate has arisen over which level of government has authority to pass certain laws. Confusion has also arisen over the proper distribution of powers to regulate matters that could not have been foreseen by the Fathers of Confederation, such as air travel, radio and television broadcasting, etc. These difficulties have led to long political debates and frequently to court challenges which arise when a person adversely affected by a particular law claims that the law is invalid because it is *ultra vires*—beyond the powers of the level of government that enacted it. Prior to the passing of the Constitution Act, 1982, only statutes found to be *ultra vires* could be declared inoperative by the Constitution. Now, there is an additional restraint on the federal parliament and the provincial legislatures to comply with constitutional provisions, including the Canadian Charter of Rights and Freedoms.

■ The Provincial Governments

Canada's provinces have a system of government which parallels that of the federal government in several ways. A premier, like the prime minister, leads the government by virtue of being leader of the party with the most support in the provincial legislature and forms a Cabinet from the elected members of the governing party. Members of a provincial legislature, like members of the federal Parliament, represent constituencies and approve legislation within their constitutional jurisdiction. A lieutenant-governor, like the Governor General, gives royal assent to the laws passed by the legislature.

The major difference between the provincial and federal systems is that the provinces have no equivalent body to Canada's Senate.

■ Government in the Yukon, Northwest Territories and Nunavut

The Yukon, Northwest Territories and Nunavut are governed by elected representatives. Although the administration of each territory is technically in the hands of a commissioner appointed by the federal government, in practice, the commissioners' role has become much like that of the provincial lieutenant-governors' in that they follow the wishes of the territories elected representatives when exercising their authority.

In the Northwest Territories, the legislature consists of 14 elected members who run for office as independents rather than as members of political parties. This assembly selects the territory's political executives: a premier, who must win more than 50 per cent of the vote, and five other cabinet ministers.

In Nunavut, the legislature consists of 19 elected members who also run for office as independents rather than as members of political parties. The territory's executive, which is drawn from this assembly, consists of a premier and seven cabinet ministers.

Yukon has a 17-member legislative assembly which features political parties. The leader of the party supported by a majority of the assembly's elected representatives is named government leader. Executive power is in the hands of an executive council, which functions like a provincial cabinet. Its members are appointed by Yukon's commissioner on the advice of the government leader.

In the territories, the elected bodies have jurisdiction over such areas as education, housing, social services and renewable resources.

In 1990, the Northwest Territories established six aboriginal languages (Dogrib, Chipewyan, Gwich'in, Cree, Slavey and Inuktitut) as Official Languages, in addition to English and French.

■ Mechanics of Government

Formation of Government: General elections to choose House of Commons members occur at least every five years. But they may take place more often if the prime minister decides to call an election or if the governing party loses the support of the majority of members of the House.

Following an election, the Governor General calls upon the leader of the party with the greatest House of Commons support to become prime minister. This is almost always the leader of the party with the most seats in the House but, under unusual circumstances, it could be the leader of another party which is able to gain majority support in Parliament.

The prime minister selects the cabinet, usually from members of his party in the House of Commons. Formally, the prime minister and cabinet act as advisors to the Governor General. In practice, however, they wield executive power and the Governor General's role is mainly ceremonial.

Passage of Legislation: To become law, proposed legislation (known as bills) must be passed by a majority of members in both the House of Commons and the Senate and must then be given royal assent by the Governor General. Most bills are introduced by members of the government in the House of Commons. Typically, a bill is given three "readings" in the House. The first reading is simply to introduce the bill. The second reading is accompanied by debate on the principle of the bill. The bill is then voted on and, if approved, is sent to a House committee composed of representatives of all parties to be considered clause-by-clause. The committee prepares a report and submits it to the House of Commons along with any proposed amendments. These amendments, plus any others moved by any member of Parliament, are debated and usually voted on. A motion is then brought for the bill to be given third reading. If the vote is favorable, the bill is then introduced in the Senate where it undergoes a similar process. After a bill has been approved by both Houses, the Governor General gives it royal assent in a ceremony that takes place in the Senate chamber.

Defeat of a Government: Between elections, a government can be forced to resign if it is defeated in a vote on a major government bill. When this happens the government is considered to have lost the support of the majority of Parliament's elected representatives. This typically occurs only when the party in power has formed a minority government—that is, if it holds more seats than any other single party but fewer seats than the combined Opposition parties. This last happened federally in 1979 when a minority Conservative government, elected earlier that year, introduced a budget which was defeated by the combined votes of the Liberal and New Democratic Party members in the House. Parliament was dissolved, an election was called and the Liberals regained power.

■ The Constitution of Canada

Canada's constitution consists of written documents and unwritten conventions. The written constitution is embodied in the *Constitution Acts 1867–1982*. The 1867 legislation (originally titled the British North America Act) was a British statute that established a federal state with a Parliament modelled on the British system. That Act assembled the colonies of Nova Scotia, New Brunswick and Canada (Ontario and Quebec) into the "Dominion of Canada," created a federal government in Ottawa, and divided the powers of government between Ottawa and the provinces.

The BNA Act gave Ottawa broad jurisdiction over internal matters, including unlimited powers of taxation, while allowing the provinces only a narrow field of local control. In general, the Canadian constitution of the late 19th century was a centralist document.

Under the BNA Act, Britain still had the power to veto Canadian laws or to enact statutes affecting Canada. But the British had no desire to raise revenue in Canada, for example, or to tax Canadians directly. This approach extended to trade and tariffs. Gradually, the practice was established that where money was involved, even in trade treaties, Canada would determine its own policy.

The same was not true of political foreign policy. When Britain declared war on Germany in 1914, Canada, as part of the British Empire, was automatically at war. During this period, British courts also interpreted Canadian statutes, especially those involving the division of power between Ottawa and the provinces. Through this process, the constitution's strong centralist thrust was altered to give more authority to the provinces.

The constitution was also adjusted more directly, through amendments. But because the BNA Act was a British statute, Canada could make formal changes to it only with the consent of the British Parliament. Ottawa tended to seek such amendments only when they did not affect provincial powers or when the provinces agreed with the changes. This process worked at least some of the time: 29 times, in fact, between 1870 and 1975. In 1940, for example, unemployment insurance became a federal responsibility through an amendment to the BNA Act.

In 1931, Britain attempted to tidy up relations with Canada and other self-governing dominions within the Commonwealth by passing the Statute of Westminster. The Statute ceded full powers over foreign affairs and trade to Canada. But because the federal and provincial governments could not agree on a method for amending the BNA Act at home, the British Parliament retained ultimate power over Canada's constitution. Until 1949, British courts continued to review Canadian constitutional cases.

From 1927 until 1982, a succession of federal governments attempted to resolve the problem by getting the provinces to agree to an amending formula. These negotiations failed as the provinces used them as a means to gain concessions from Ottawa.

The catalyst in constitutional discussions during the late 20th century has been the province of Quebec, where provincial governments since 1960 have sought to expand the province's jurisdiction. To protect French culture, the Quebec government requested more powers, over culture itself, and over the economy and social institutions.

Ottawa resisted the move under prime ministers Lester Pearson and Pierre Trudeau. Trudeau argued that without a strong central power a country as sprawling and diverse as Canada would be fatally weakened and might disintegrate.

In lengthy negotiations with the provinces, Trudeau was unable to gain agreement on an amending formula, even when he offered increased powers in return. In 1976, the election of the separatist Parti Québécois in Quebec made constitutional compromise even more unlikely and the matter was set aside.

After Quebec's 1980 referendum on the question of sovereignty association was won by the "No" side, constitutional renewal was back on the agenda. However, federal-provincial discussions became mired in disagreement through the summer of 1980. In September, Trudeau announced that the federal government, with the support of only Ontario and New Brunswick, would ask the British parliament to amend the BNA Act to patriate the constitution and establish a *Charter of Rights and Freedoms* to protect individual liberties. The *Charter* would also protect minority rights in education and the mobility rights of Canadian citizens, and change the name of the constitution: the BNA Act became the *Constitution Act, 1982*.

It took 18 months to get the new amendments approved by the Canadian Parliament, resolve the concerns of eight provincial governments, and get the act through the British Parliament. But, in April 1982, the *Constitution Act* was proclaimed—although the consent of the Quebec government was never given.

The *Constitution Act, 1982*, consolidated all the previous BNA Acts and added an amending formula and a *Charter of Rights and Freedoms*. The Charter, which provided for basic democratic rights, also contained a "notwithstanding" clause that allowed Parliament or any provincial legislature to over-ride its provisions.

The amending formula provided for two types of constitutional change: the division of powers between the federal and provincial governments could be modified with the consent of the federal Parliament and seven provincial legislatures in provinces totalling more than 50 percent of the Canadian population; matters such as the composition of the Supreme Court or the status of English or French, however, required unanimous consent. It also stipulated that no amendment could take longer than three years to be ratified by Ottawa and all 10 provinces.

Government of Canada Primary Internet Site

The Canada Site is the official website of the Canadian government. It provides access to information and services about Canada and Canadian governments. The starting point is http://canada.gc.ca/main_e.html, and the information appears in French and English. Across the top of the site, the following web links appear in red:

WHAT'S NEW?: This link connects you to an archive of government press releases, advisories and reports about politics, health, science, technology, business and other issues. The information is organized by date, archive and website. You can find news bulletins in the *Canada Gazette, The Wire, The Daily* and the published debates from Parliament. Calendars list forthcoming government-sponsored events across Canada.

DIRECTORIES: This link connects you to several directories. The *Government of Canada Employees Directory* lists federal public servants, and its search engine allows you to find them by surname, telephone number, job title and organization. *Government of Canada Internet Addresses* links you to an extensive list of federal institutions ranging from Agriculture and Agri-Food Canada to the Yukon Territory Water Board. *Members of Parliament* organizes information on all MPs by surname, party, province and territory; it also provides contact information. Other directories list Canadian officials working abroad and foreign officials in Canada.

PROGRAMS AND SERVICES: *Subject Categories* links you to sites on business, customs and tariffs, education, employment insurance, the environment, health, immigration, social programs and tourism. *Jobs and Employment* connects you to job information for youth, aboriginals and aspiring civil servants. *On-line Services (E-services)* links you to commonly requested government forms (e.g., pension applications and GST/HST remittance forms), services provided by Canada Post and online forums on public issues.

ABOUT CANADA: This link connects you to sites promoting travel and tourism in Canada. Other links provide access to sites on Canada's geography, history, culture and people. *Ceremonial and Canadian Symbols*, for example, provides information about national, provincial and historical flags and emblems. Other sites include information on museums, libraries, and parks.

ABOUT GOVERNMENT: *Government at a Glance* provides an overview of Canada's federal system including web pages for the Queen, the Governor General, Parliament and the Supreme Court. Some links provide information on orders-in-council and legislative procedures. *Other Governments* connects you to the official websites of the provinces, territories, municipalities and international organizations. *Frequently Requested Acts* provides access to federal laws (e.g., the *Divorce Act*). Other links lead to web pages on linguistic minorities, the auditor general's report and *Info Source*—a researchers' guide to federal publications and databases.

PUBLICATIONS AND FORMS: This site connects you to Canadian Government Publishing. You can find specialized books and CD-ROMs listed by subject or title. You can order online, and some publications are free. The site lists public libraries in Canada and around the world that carry federal government publications; the site also explains Crown copyright.

The Canada Site's home page also features two drop-down menus: one leads to "service access points" (e.g., postal outlets); the second leads to the websites of Canada's provinces and territories. Other icons point to Canadian maps, a search engine, a "frequently asked questions" page and an index to federal programs and services. One link connects you to the most recent Speech from the Throne; another link leads you to a short online survey on the usefulness of the Canada Site. Throughout the site, you can e-mail government officials.

If You're Not on the Internet...

*I*nformation on the Government of Canada is a telephone inquiry service that is available toll-free within Canada. **1 (800) 667–3355** will connect callers to a service that will either supply the necessary information or direct the caller to the department that has the answer.

Text of the Canadian Charter of Rights and Freedoms

Whereas Canada is founded upon principles that recognize the supremacy of God and the rule of law:

■ Guarantee of Rights and Freedoms

1 The Canadian Charter of Rights and Freedoms guarantees the rights and freedoms set out in it subject only to such reasonable limits prescribed by law as can be demonstrably justified in a free and democratic society.

■ Fundamental Freedoms

2 Everyone has the following fundamental freedoms: (a) freedom of conscience and religion; (b) freedom of thought, belief, opinion and expression, including freedom of the press and other media of communication; (c) freedom of peaceful assembly; and (d) freedom of association.

■ Democratic Rights

3 Every citizen of Canada has the right to vote in an election of members of the House of Commons or of a legislative assembly and to be qualified for membership therein.

4 (1) No House of Commons and no legislative assembly shall continue for longer than five years from the date fixed for the return of the writs at a general election of its members. (2) In time of real or apprehended war, invasion or insurrection, a House of Commons may be continued by Parliament and a legislative assembly may be continued by the legislature beyond five years if such continuation is not opposed by the votes of more than one-third of the members of the House of Commons or the legislative assembly, as the case may be.

5 There shall be a sitting of Parliament and of each legislature at least once every twelve months.

■ Mobility Rights

6 (1) Every citizen of Canada has the right to enter, remain in and leave Canada. (2) Every citizen of Canada and every person who has the status of a permanent resident of Canada has the right (a) to move to and take up residence in any province; and (b) to pursue the gaining of a livelihood in any province. (3) The rights specified in subsection (2) are subject to (a) any laws or practices of general application in force in a province other than those that discriminate among persons primarily on the basis of province of present or previous residence; and (b) any laws providing for reasonable residency requirements as a qualification for the receipt of publicly provided social services. (4) Subsections (2) and (3) do not preclude any law, program or activity that has as its object the amelioration in a province of conditions of individuals in that province who are socially or economically disadvantaged if the rate of employment in that province is below the rate of employment in Canada.

■ Legal Rights

7 Everyone has the right to life, liberty and security of the person and the right not to be deprived thereof except in accordance with the principles of fundamental justice.

8 Everyone has the right to be secure against unreasonable search or seizure.

9 Everyone has the right not to be arbitrarily detained or imprisoned.

10 Everyone has the right on arrest or detention (a) to be informed promptly of the reasons therefor; (b) to retain and instruct counsel without delay and to be informed of that right; and (c) to have the validity of the detention determined by way of *habeas corpus* and to be released if the detention is not lawful.

11 Any person charged with an offence has the right (a) to be informed without unreasonable delay of the specific offence; (b) to be tried within a reasonable time; (c) not to be compelled to be a witness in proceedings against that person in respect of the offence; (d) to be presumed innocent until proven guilty according to law in a fair and public hearing by an independent

and impartial tribunal; (e) not to be denied reasonable bail without just cause; (f) except in the case of an offence under military law tried before a military tribunal, to the benefit of trial by jury where the maximum punishment for the offence is imprisonment for five years or a more severe punishment; (g) not to be found guilty on account of any act or omission unless, at the time of the act or omission, it constituted an offence under Canadian or international law or was criminal according to the general principles of law recognized by the community of nations; (h) if finally acquitted of the offence, not to be tried for it again and, if finally found guilty and punished for the offence, not to be tried or punished for it again; and (i) if found guilty of the offence and if the punishment for the offence has been varied between the time of commission and the time of sentencing, to the benefit of the lesser punishment.

12 Everyone has the right not to be subjected to any cruel and unusual treatment or punishment.

13 A witness who testifies in any proceedings has the right not to have any incriminating evidence so given used to incriminate that witness in any other proceedings, except in a prosecution for perjury or for the giving of contradictory evidence.

14 A party or witness in any proceedings who does not understand or speak the language in which the proceedings are conducted or who is deaf has the right to the assistance of an interpreter.

■ Equality Rights

15 (1) Every individual is equal before and under the law and has the right to the equal protection and equal benefit of the law without discrimination and, in particular, without discrimination based on race, national or ethnic origin, colour, religion, sex, age or mental or physical disability. (2) Subsection (1) does not preclude any law, program or activity that has as its object the amelioration of conditions of disadvantaged individuals or groups including those that are disadvantaged because of race, national or ethnic origin, colour, religion, sex, age or mental or physical disability.

■ Official Languages of Canada

16 (1) English and French are the official languages of Canada and have equality of status and equal rights and privileges as to their use in all institutions of the Parliament and government of Canada. (2) English and French are the official languages of New Brunswick and have equality of status and equal rights and privileges as to their use in all institutions of the legislature and government of New Brunswick. (3) Nothing in this Charter limits the authority of Parliament or a legislature to advance the equality of status or use of English and French.

17 (1) Everyone has the right to use English or French in any debates and other proceedings of Parliament. (2) Everyone has the right to use English or French in any debates and other proceedings of the legislature of New Brunswick.

18 (1) The statutes, records and journals of Parliament shall be printed and published in English and French and both language versions are equally authoritative. (2) The statutes, records and journals of the legislature of New Brunswick shall be printed and published in English and French and both language versions are equally authoritative.

19 (1) Either English or French may be used by any person in, or in any pleading in or process issuing from, any court established by Parliament. (2) Either English or French may be used by any person in, or in any pleading in or process issuing from, any court of New Brunswick.

20 (1) Any member of the public in Canada has the right to communicate with, and to receive available services from, any head or central office of an institution of the Parliament or government of Canada in English or French, and has the same right with respect to any other office of any such institution where (a) there is a significant demand for communications with and services from that office in such language; or (b) due to the nature of the office, it is reasonable that communications with and services from that office be available in both English and French. (2) Any member of the public in New Brunswick has the

right to communicate with, and to receive available services from, any office of an institution of the legislature or government of New Brunswick in English or French.

21. Nothing in sections 16 to 20 abrogates or derogates from any right, privilege or obligation with respect to the English and French languages, or either of them, that exists or is continued by virtue of any other provision of the Constitution of Canada.

22. Nothing in sections 16 to 20 abrogates or derogates from any legal or customary right or privilege acquired or enjoyed either before or after the coming into force of this Charter with respect to any language that is not English or French.

■ Minority Language Educational Rights

23. (1) Citizens of Canada (a) whose first language learned and still understood is that of the English or French linguistic minority population of the province in which they reside, or (b) who have received their primary school instruction in Canada in English or French and reside in a province where the language in which they received that instruction is the language of the English or French linguistic minority population of the province, have the right to have their children receive primary and secondary school instruction in that language in that province. (2) Citizens of Canada of whom any child has received or is receiving primary or secondary school instruction in English or French in Canada, have the right to have all their children receive primary and secondary school instruction in the same language. (3) The right of citizens of Canada under subsections (1) and (2) to have their children receive primary and secondary school instruction in the language of the English or French linguistic minority population of a province (a) applies wherever in the province the number of children of citizens who have such a right is sufficient to warrant the provision to them out of public funds of minority language instruction; and (b) includes, where the number of those children so warrants, the right to have them receive that instruction in minority language educational facilities provided out of public funds.

■ Enforcement

24. (1) Anyone whose rights or freedoms, as guaranteed by this Charter, have been infringed or denied may apply to a court of competent jurisdiction to obtain such remedy as the court considers appropriate and just in the circumstances. (2) Where, in proceedings under subsection (1), a court concludes that evidence was obtained in a manner that infringed or denied any rights or freedoms guaranteed by this Charter, the evidence shall be excluded if it is established that, having regard to all the circumstances, the admission of it in the proceedings would bring the administration of justice into disrepute.

■ General

25. The guarantee in this Charter of certain rights and freedoms shall not be construed so as to abrogate or derogate from any aboriginal, treaty or other rights or freedoms that pertain to the aboriginal peoples of Canada including (a) any rights or freedoms that have been recognized by the Royal Proclamation of October 7, 1763; and (b) any rights or freedoms that now exist by way of land claims agreements or may be so acquired. (SI/84-102)

26. The guarantee in this Charter of certain rights and freedoms shall not be construed as denying the existence of any other rights or freedoms that exist in Canada.

27. This Charter shall be interpreted in a manner consistent with the preservation and enhancement of the multicultural heritage of Canadians.

28. Notwithstanding anything in this Charter, the rights and freedoms referred to in it are guaranteed equally to male and female persons.

29. Nothing in this Charter abrogates or derogates from any rights or privileges guaranteed by or under the Constitution of Canada in respect of denominational, separate or dissentient schools.

30. A reference in this Charter to a province or to the legislative assembly or legislature or a province shall be deemed to include a reference to the Yukon Territory and the Northwest Territories, or to the appropriate legislative authority thereof, as the case may be.

31. Nothing in this Charter extends the legislative powers of any body or authority

Application of Charter

32 (1) This Charter applies (a) to the Parliament and government of Canada in respect of all matters within the authority of Parliament including all matters relating to the Yukon Territory and Northwest Territories; and (b) to the legislature and government of each province in respect of all matters within the authority of the legislature of each province. (2) Notwithstanding subsection (1), section 15 shall not have effect until three years after this section comes into force.

33 (1) Parliament or the legislature of a province may expressly declare in an Act of Parliament or of the legislature, as the case may be, that the Act or a provision thereof shall operate notwithstanding a provision included in section 2 or sections 7 to 15 of this Charter. (2) An Act or a provision of an Act in respect of which a declaration made under this section is in effect shall have such operation as it would have but for the provision of this Charter referred to in the declaration. (3) A declaration made under subsection (1) shall cease to have effect five years after it comes into force or on such earlier date as may be specified in the declaration. (4) Parliament or the legislature of a province may re-enact a declaration made under subsection (1). (5) Subsection (3) applies in respect of a re-enactment made under subsection (4).

Citation

34 This Part may be cited as the Canadian Charter of Rights and Freedoms.

Canadian Orders and Decorations

For more information on Canada's orders and decorations, see the website of the Governor General of Canada at http://www.gg.ca/honour_e.html and the website of Veterans Affairs Canada at http://www.vacacc.gc.ca/general/sub.cfm?source=collections/cmdp/mainmenu.

☐ National Orders

■ The Order of Canada

History Creation of the Order of Canada was announced by Prime Minister Lester B. Pearson in 1967. It was instituted on the centennial of Canadian Confederation, July 1, 1967.

Basis of Award To honour Canadians for outstanding achievement and service to their country or humanity. Appointments are announced twice annually, around July 1 and Jan. 1. Investitures occur three times a year, in February, April and October when the awards are given by the Governor General.

Eligibility Every living Canadian is eligible to become a member. Federal and provincial politicians and judges are ineligible while in office.

Membership There are three categories of membership. The first is Companion of the Order of Canada (C.C.). No more than 15 companions may be appointed in any one year, and no more than 165 living companions may hold the order at one time.

The second is Officer of the Order of Canada (O.C.). No more than 52 appointments may be made annually.

The third is Member of the Order of Canada (C.M.), which recognizes service in a locality or a field of activity. No more than 106 appointments may be made annually.

Badge A stylized snowflake bearing the crown with a ribbon in the same proportions of white and red which appear on the Canadian flag and the Latin motto *Desiderantes Meliorem Patriam*—"They Desire a Better Country." Worn at the neck by companions and officers and on the left breast by members.

■ The Order of Military Merit

History The Order of Military Merit was instituted on July 1, 1972.

Basis of Award To recognize exceptional service and conspicuous merit by regular and reserve members of Canada's Armed Forces.

Appointments are made by the Governor General on the recommendation of the Chief of Defence Staff.

Eligibility Active members of the Canadian Armed Forces, regular and reserve. A formula limits the number of annual appointments per year to one-tenth of one per cent of the average number of persons who were members of the Armed Forces during the previous year.

Membership There are three categories of membership. The first is Commander of the Order of Military Merit (C.M.M.). Six percent of annual appointments go to this category of membership.

The second is Officer of the Order of Military Merit (O.M.M.). Thirty percent of annual appointments go to this category of membership.

The third is Member of the Order of Military Merit (M.M.M.). The balance of annual appointments go to this category of membership.

Badge In the form of an enamelled blue cross having expanded arms, with a blue ribbon edged in gold. Bears the words "Merit Merite Canada." Worn at the neck by commanders and on the left breast by officers and members.

☐ Medals for Military Valour

The Military Valour Decorations, consisting of the Victoria Cross (Canadian), the Star of Military Valour and the Medal of Military Valour, enable Canada to recognize members of the Canadian Forces, or members of an allied armed force serving with the Canadian Forces, for deeds of military valour.

■ Victoria Cross (V.C.) (Canadian)

History Approved by Queen Elizabeth II on Feb. 2, 1993. The British Victoria Cross was created by Queen Victoria in 1856 and was awarded to Canadians in all wars until 1945. There have been 93 Canadian recipients of the British V.C. and none of the Canadian version.

Basis of Award In recognition of "the most conspicuous bravery, a daring or pre-eminent act of valour or self-sacrifice or extreme devotion to duty, in the presence of the enemy." The V.C. will be awarded by the Governor General on the advice of the Military Valour Advisory Committee. It is the highest in the order of precedence in Canadian honours.

Eligibility Members of the Canadian Forces or a member of an allied armed force that is serving with or in conjunction with the Canadian Forces on or after Jan. 1, 1993. The V.C. may be awarded posthumously.

Badge The Cross is a bronze straight armed cross, suspended from a crimson ribbon. The face has, in the middle of the cross, a lion guardant standing on the Royal Crown, with the Latin inscription *Pro Valore*—"For Valour". The date of the act for which the decoration is bestowed is engraved in a raised circle on the reverse.

■ The Star of Military Valour (S.M.V.)

History Approved by Queen Elizabeth II on Feb. 2, 1993.

Basis of Award Awarded for distinguished and valiant service in the presence of the enemy.

Eligibility Members of the Canadian Forces or a member of an allied armed force that is serving with or in conjunction with the Canadian Forces on or after Jan. 1, 1993. The S.M.V. may be awarded posthumously.

Badge A gold star with four points with a maple leaf in each of the angles, on the face of which a gold maple leaf is superimposed in the centre of a sanguine field surrounded by a silver wreath of laurel and on the reverse of which the Royal Cypher and Crown and the Latin inscription *Pro Valore*—"For Valour" shall appear. The Star shall be worn, suspended from a crimson ribbon with two white stripes, immediately after any order and before the Star of Courage.

■ The Medal of Military Valour (M.M.V.)

History Approved by Queen Elizabeth II on Feb. 2, 1993.

Basis of Award Awarded for an act of valour or devotion to duty in the presence of the enemy.

Eligibility Members of the Canadian Forces or a member of an allied armed force that is serving with or in conjunction with the Canadian Forces on or after Jan. 1, 1993. The M.M.V. may be awarded posthumously.

Badge A circular gold medal, on the face of which there shall be a maple leaf surrounded by a wreath of laurel and on the reverse of which the Royal Cypher and Crown and the Latin inscription *Pro Valore*—"For Valour" will appear. The medal shall be worn, from a crimson ribbon with three white stripes, immediately after the Meritorious Service Cross and before the Medal of Bravery.

☐ Decorations for Bravery

The Decorations for Bravery, consisting of the Cross of Valour, the Star of Courage and the Medal of Bravery honour those who have risked their lives to save or protect others. These three Canadian decorations replaced the

Government of Canada

following non-combatant Commonwealth medals: the George Cross, the George Medal and the Queen's Gallantry Medal, respectively.

■ The Cross of Valour (C.V.)

History Created in 1972, the Cross of Valour takes precedence before all orders and other decorations except the Victoria Cross.

Basis of Award Awarded for acts of the most conspicuous courage in circumstances of extreme peril.

Eligibility May be awarded to civilians or members of the Armed Forces. Only 19 have been awarded. May be awarded posthumously.

Badge A gold cross bearing the words "Valour Vaillance."

■ The Star of Courage (S.C.)

History Created in 1972.

Basis of Award Awarded for acts of conspicuous courage in circumstances of great peril.

Eligibility May be awarded to civilians or members of the Armed Forces. May be awarded posthumously.

Badge A four-pointed silver star with the word "Courage."

■ The Medal of Bravery (M.B.)

History Created in 1972.

Basis of Award Awarded for acts of bravery in hazardous circumstances.

Eligibility May be awarded to civilians or members of the Armed Forces. May be awarded posthumously.

Badge A circular silver medal with the words "Bravery Bravoure."

■ The Meritorious Service Cross (M.S.C.) (military and civilian)

History Military division created in 1984; civilian division created in 1991.

Basis of Award *Military division*: awarded in recognition of a military deed or activity that has been performed in an outstandingly professional manner, according to a rare high standard that brings considerable benefit or great honour to the Canadian Forces. *Civilian division*: awarded in recognition of the performance of a deed or activity performed in an outstandingly professional manner or according to an uncommonly high standard that brings considerable benefit or great honour to Canada.

Eligibility A member of the Canadian and allied forces, persons serving in conjunction with the Canadian Forces or other persons, Canadian and foreigners.

Badge A Greek cross of silver, ends splayed and convexed, ensigned with the Royal Crown. On the face appear a maple leaf within a circle and a laurel wreath between the arms. Recipients are entitled to use the letters "M.S.C." after their names.

■ The Meritorious Service Medal (M.S.M.) (military and civilian)

History Created in 1991.

Basis of Award *Military division*: awarded in recognition of a military deed or activity that has been performed in a highly professional manner or is of a very high standard that brings benefit or honour to the Canadian Forces. *Civilian division*: awarded in recognition of the performance of a deed or activity performed in a highly professional manner or of a very high standard that brings benefit or honour to Canada.

Eligibility A member of the Canadian and allied forces, persons serving in conjunction with the Canadian Forces or other persons, Canadian and foreigners.

Badge A circular medal of silver ensigned with the Royal Crown. On the face appears the design of the cross. On the reverse appears the Royal Cypher and, within a double circle, the words "Meritorious Service Méritoire." Recipients are entitled to use the letters "M.S.M." after their names.

☐ Other Notable Awards

The Governor General also bestows these awards.

■ The Academic Medal

Created in 1873. Awarded for academic excellence. Medals are distributed in March to colleges and universities and in April to high schools.

■ The Governor General's Caring Canadian Award

Created in 1996. Awarded to unpaid volunteers for their extraordinary contributions, performed behind the scenes and for several years, in support of family, community or humanitarian causes.

Governors General of Canada

Name	Date Appointed	Assumed Office	Term
Sir Charles Stanley, Viscount Monck	June 1, 1867	July 1, 1867	1867–69
Sir John Young, Baron Lisgar	Dec. 29, 1868	Feb. 2, 1869	1869–72
Frederick Temple Hamilton Blackwood, Earl of Dufferin	May 22, 1872	June 25, 1872	1872–78
John Douglas Sutherland Campbell, Marquess of Lorne	Oct. 5, 1878	Nov. 20, 1878	1878–83
Henry Charles Keith Petty-Fitzmaurice, Marquess of Lansdowne	Aug. 18, 1883	Oct. 23, 1883	1883–88
Frederick Arthur Stanley, Baron Stanley of Preston	May 1, 1888	June 11, 1888	1888–93
John Campbell Hamilton-Gordon, Earl of Aberdeen	May 22, 1893	Nov. 18, 1893	1893–98
Gilbert John Elliott Murray-Kynynmound, Earl of Minto	July 30, 1898	Nov. 12, 1898	1898–1904
Albert Henry George Grey, Earl Grey	Sept. 26, 1904	Dec. 10, 1904	1904–11
His Royal Highness The Prince Arthur, Field Marshal Duke of Connaught	Mar. 21, 1911	Oct. 13, 1911	1911–16
Victor Christian William Cavendish, Duke of Devonshire	Aug. 19, 1916	Nov. 11, 1916	1916–21
Julian Byng, General Baron Byng of Vimy and of Thorpe	Aug. 2, 1921	Aug. 11, 1921	1921–26
Freeman Freeman-Thomas, Baron Willingdon of Ratton	Aug. 5, 1926	Nov. 2, 1926	1926–31
Vere Brabazon Ponsonby, Earl of Bessborough	Feb. 9, 1931	Apr. 4, 1931	1931–35
John Buchan, Baron Tweedsmuir	Aug. 10, 1935	Nov. 2, 935	1935–40
Alexander George Cambridge, Major General Earl of Athlone	Apr. 3, 1940	June 21, 1940	1940–46
Sir Harold George Alexander, Field Marshal Viscount Alexander of Tunis	Aug. 1, 1945	Apr. 18, 1946	1946–52
The Right Honourable Vincent Massey	Jan. 24, 1952	Feb. 22, 1952	1952–59
General the Right Honourable Georges P. Vanier	Aug. 1, 1959	Sept. 15, 1959	1959–67
The Right Honourable Daniel Roland Michener	Mar. 25, 1967	Apr. 15, 1967	1967–74
The Right Honourable Jules Léger	Oct. 5, 1973	Jan. 14, 1974	1974–79
The Right Honourable Edward Richard Schreyer	Dec. 7, 1978	Jan. 22, 1979	1979–83
The Right Honourable Jeanne Sauvé	Dec. 23, 1983	May 14, 1984	1984–90
The Right Honourable Ramon John Hnatyshyn	Oct. 6, 1989	Jan. 21, 1990	1990–95
The Right Honourable Roméo LeBlanc	Nov. 22, 1994	Feb. 8, 1995	1995–99
The Right Honourable Adrienne Clarkson	Sept 8, 1999	Oct. 7, 1999	1999–

Prime Ministers of Canada

Prime Minister	Party	Term(s)	Born	P.M. at age	Died
Sir John A. Macdonald	Conservative	July 1, 1867–Nov. 5, 1873 Oct. 9, 1878–June 6, 1891	Jan. 11, 1815	52	June 6, 1891
Alexander Mackenzie	Liberal	Nov. 5, 1873–Oct. 9, 1878	Jan. 28, 1822	51	Apr. 17, 1892
Sir John Abbott	Conservative	June 15, 1891–Nov. 24, 1892	Mar. 12, 1821	70	Oct. 30, 1893
Sir John Thompson	Conservative	Nov. 25, 1892–Dec. 12, 1894	Nov. 10, 1845	48	Dec. 12, 1894
Sir Mackenzie Bowell	Conservative	Dec. 13, 1894–Apr. 27, 1896	Dec. 27, 1823	70	Dec. 10, 1917
Sir Charles Tupper	Conservative	Apr. 27, 1896–July 8, 1896	July 2, 1821	74	Oct. 30, 1915
Sir Wilfrid Laurier	Liberal	July 11, 1896–Oct. 6, 1911	Nov. 20, 1841	54	Feb. 17, 1919
Sir Robert Borden	Conservative/Unionist	Oct. 10, 1911–Oct. 12, 1917 Oct. 12, 1917–July 10, 1920	June 26, 1854	57	June 10, 1937
Arthur Meighen	Unionist/Conservative	July 10, 1920–Dec. 29, 1921 June 29, 1926–Sept. 25, 1926	June 16, 1874	46	Aug. 5, 1960
Mackenzie King	Liberal	Dec. 29, 1921–June 28, 1926 Sept. 25, 1926–Aug. 6, 1930 Oct. 23, 1935–Nov. 15, 1948	Dec. 17, 1874	47	July 22, 1950
Richard B. Bennett	Conservative	Aug. 7, 1930–Oct. 23, 1935	July 3, 1870	60	June 27, 1947
Louis St. Laurent	Liberal	Nov. 15, 1948–June 21, 1957	Feb. 1, 1882	66	July 25, 1973
John Diefenbaker	Prog. Cons.	June 21, 1957–Apr. 22, 1963	Sept. 18, 1895	61	Aug. 16, 1979
Lester Pearson	Liberal	Apr. 22, 1963–Apr. 20, 1968	Apr. 23, 1897	65	Dec. 27, 1972
Pierre Trudeau	Liberal	Apr. 20, 1968–June 4, 1979 Mar. 3, 1980–June 30, 1984	Oct. 18, 1919	48	Sept. 28, 2000
Joe Clark	Prog. Cons.	June 4, 1979–Mar. 3, 1980	June 5, 1939	39	
John Turner	Liberal	June 30, 1984–Sept. 17, 1984	June 7, 1929	55	
Brian Mulroney	Prog. Cons.	Sept. 17, 1984–June 25, 1993	Mar. 20, 1939	45	
Kim Campbell	Prog. Cons.	June 25, 1993–Nov. 4, 1993	Mar. 10, 1947	46	
Jean Chrétien	Liberal	Nov. 4, 1993–	Jan. 11, 1934	59	

Government of Canada **153**

Canadian Cabinet Ministers and Secretaries of State
(as of October 2000)

Cabinet ministers are the most powerful elected officials in government. They are sworn to the Privy Council and are bound by collective responsibility. They work with their staffs to set policies for their ministries and present (or defend) those policies in the House of Commons. They shepherd their bills through various readings and committees before having their bills voted into law.

Secretaries of state, although sworn to the Privy Council and bound by collective responsibility as well, are not members of the Cabinet. Secretaries of state are assigned to support specific Cabinet ministers; they also get smaller staffs and less pay than Cabinet ministers. Prime Minister Jean Chrétien introduced the distinction between these "senior" and "junior" officials on Nov. 4, 1993.

For cabinet updates after October 2000, visit www.cdgbooks.com and look for Almanac FastFacts.

■ The Cabinet

The Prime Minister of Canada
The Right Hon. Jean Chrétien
(Saint-Maurice, Quebec)

The Deputy Prime Minister of Canada
The Hon. Herbert Eser Gray
(Windsor West, Ontario)

The Leader of the Government in the Senate
Represents the Cabinet in the Senate.
The Hon. J. Bernard Boudreau
(Nova Scotia)

The Minister of Agriculture and Agri-Food
Responsible for nearly all aspects of production, processing, marketing and protection of crops and livestock, including research and technology; soil conservation; food processing and inspection; and trade policies and support programs.
The Hon. Lyle Vanclief
(Prince Edward–Hastings, Ontario)

The Minister of Canadian Heritage
Responsible for both Canada's natural heritage (parks) and our historic and cultural heritage, including the arts, sports and multiculturalism.
The Hon. Sheila M. Copps
(Hamilton East, Ontario)

The Minister of Citizenship and Immigration
Administers policies and procedures for citizenship and immigration.
The Hon. Elinor Caplan
(Thornhill, Ontario)

The Minister of the Environment
Protects and conserves Canada's air and water; monitors climate and pollution.
The Hon. David Anderson
(Victoria, British Columbia)

The Minister of Finance
Provides the federal government with an annual budget; provides research and advice on financial issues; regularly monitors the performance of Canada's economy.
The Hon. Paul Martin
(LaSalle–Émard, Quebec)

The Minister of Fisheries and Oceans
Manages Canada's resources in the water, particularly in the ocean, when outside other jurisdictions; oversees public harbours and coastal and inland fisheries.
The Hon. Harbance Singh Dhaliwal
(Vancouver South–Burnaby, British Columbia)

The Minister of Foreign Affairs
Creates foreign policy; promotes and protects Canada's interests abroad; manages Canadian embassies and diplomatic staff; ensures Canadian citizens abroad receive fair treatment under foreign laws.
The Hon. Lloyd Axworthy
(Winnipeg South Centre, Manitoba)

The Minister of Health
Provides funding and policies for a national health care system; sets and enforces health standards.
The Hon. Allan Rock
(Etobicoke Centre, Ontario)

▶

The Minister of Human Resources Development
Fosters an educated and mobile workforce; provides income as necessary for seniors, the unemployed and the disabled.
The Hon. Jane Stewart
(Brant, Ontario)

The Minister of Indian Affairs and Northern Development
Meets the federal government's treaty obligations to Inuit and First Nations people, including the provision of basic services; negotiates and oversees claims settlements.
The Hon. Robert Daniel Nault
(Kenora–Rainy River, Ontario)

The Minister of Industry
Drafts major federal bills and programs for consumer and business groups; provides policy advice, business services and industrial information. The minister is also responsible for Western Economic Diversification.
The Hon. John Manley
(Ottawa South, Ontario)

The Minister for International Cooperation
Administers economic and technical aid to the developing world through CIDA.
The Hon. Maria Minna
(Beaches–East York, Ontario)

The Minister for International Trade
Takes part in international trade talks and institutions to promote Canadian business abroad and to resolve trade disputes.
The Hon. Pierre S. Pettigrew
(Papineau–Saint-Denis, Quebec)

The Minister of Justice and Attorney General of Canada
Provides legal services to all government departments and agencies; supervises the administration of justice.
The Hon. Anne McLellan
(Edmonton West, Alberta)

The Minister of Labour
Enforces the labour code including health and safety in the workplace; promotes fairness and cooperation between labour and management; provides mediation and conciliation in labour disputes.
The Hon. Claudette Bradshaw
(Moncton–Riverview–Dieppe, New Brunswick)

The Minister of National Defence
Administers Canada's armed forces, defends citizens at home and meets Canada's military obligations abroad.
The Hon. Arthur C. Eggleton
(York Centre, Ontario)

The Minister of National Revenue and Secretary of State (Economic Development Agency of Canada for the Regions of Quebec)
Administers the Customs and Excise Acts as well as import and export taxes and permits.
The Hon. Martin Cauchon
(Outremont, Quebec)

The Minister of Natural Resources and Minister responsible for Canadian Wheat Board
Proposes and plans national policies for energy, mines and resources (renewable and nonrenewable); researches conservation and development strategies.
The Hon. Ralph E. Goodale
(Wascana, Saskatchewan)

The Minister of Public Works and Government Services
Buys services to support the daily operation of government; provides office space and maintains public buildings; provides telecommunications and information services; prepares public audits and disburses public monies.
The Hon. Alfonso Gagliano
(Saint-Léonard–Saint Michel, Quebec)

The Minister of State and Leader of the Government in the House of Commons
Plans and manages the government's legislative agenda in its pre-parliamentary and parliamentary stages; maintains relations with the Opposition.
The Hon. Don Boudria
(Glengarry–Prescott–Russell, Ontario)

The Minister of Transport
Oversees national policies to ensure competitive, safe and environmentally sustainable transportation.
The Hon. David Michael Collenette
(Don Valley East, Ontario)

The Minister of Veterans Affairs and Secretary of State (Atlantic Canada Opportunities Agency)
Provides Canadian combat veterans and their families with benefits; preserves the memory veterans' sacrifices and achievements.
The Hon. George S. Baker
(Gander–Grand Falls, Newfoundland)

The President of the Queen's Privy Council for Canada and Minister of Intergovernmental Affairs
Manages federal-provincial relations; provides legal advice on constitutional issues and national unity.
The Hon. Stéphane Dion
(Saint-Laurent–Cartierville, Quebec)

The President of the Treasury Board and Minister responsible for Infrastructure
Functions as the government's chief employer and general manager; responsible for finances, personnel and administration.
The Hon. Lucienne Robillard
(Westmount–Ville Marie, Quebec)

The Solicitor General of Canada
Responsible for prisons, the RCMP, CSIS, parole boards and everything within Parliament's jurisdiction that is not legally assigned somewhere else.
The Hon. Lawrence MacAuley
(Cardigan, Prince Edward Island)

■ **Secretaries of State**

Secretary of State (Amateur Sport)
The Hon. Denis Coderre
(Bourassa, Quebec)

Secretary of State (Asia-Pacific)
The Hon. Raymond Chan
(Richmond, British Columbia)

Secretary of State (Children and Youth)
The Hon. Ethel Blondin-Andrew
(Western Arctic, Northwest Territories)

Secretary of State (Federal Economic Development Initiative for Northern Ontario) (Rural Development)
The Hon. Andrew Mitchell
(Parry Sound–Muskoka, Ontario)

Secretary of State (Francophonie) (Western Economic Diversification)
The Hon. Ronald J. Duhamel
(Saint Boniface, Manitoba)

Secretary of State (International Financial Institutions)
The Hon. James Scott Peterson
(Willowdale, Ontario)

Secretary of State (Latin America and Africa)
The Hon. David Kilgour
(Edmonton Southeast, Alberta)

Secretary of State (Multiculturalism) (Status of Women)
The Hon. Hedy Fry
(Vancouver Centre, British Columbia)

Secretary of State (Science, Research and Development)
The Hon. Gilbert Normand
(Bellechasse–Etchemins–Montmagny–L'Islet, Quebec)

Deputy Prime Ministers of Canada

(as of October 2000)

The title of deputy prime minister is strictly honorary. It is conferred at the prime minister's discretion on a member of the Cabinet. The title has no standing in law and carries no formal duties or tasks. Deputy prime ministers, however, often have other Cabinet portfolios.

Prime Minister Pierre Trudeau named the first deputy prime minister during a press interview after the nomination of his Cabinet on Sept. 16, 1977. Since then only Prime Minister Joe Clark (1979–80) has not named a deputy prime minister.

In 1984, Prime Minister Brian Mulroney began the practice of appointing the deputy prime minister by "instrument of advice." An instrument of advice is a private letter written by the prime minister to the Crown. Since 1984, all deputy prime ministers have been appointed by this method.

Deputy Prime Minister	Date Appointed	Term Ended	Designated by Prime Minister
Allan J. MacEachen	Sept. 16, 1977	June 3, 1979	Pierre Trudeau
Allan J. MacEachen	Mar. 3, 1980	June 29, 1984	Pierre Trudeau
Jean Chrétien	June 30, 1984	Sept. 16, 1984	John Turner
Erik Nielsen	Sept. 17, 1984	June 29, 1986	Brian Mulroney
Donald Mazankowski	June 30, 1986	June 24, 1993	Brian Mulroney
Jean J. Charest	June 25, 1993	Nov. 3, 1993	Kim Campbell
Sheila M. Copps	Nov. 4, 1993	Apr. 30, 1996	Jean Chrétien
Sheila M. Copps	June 19, 1996	June 10, 1997	Jean Chrétien
Herbert E. Gray	June 11, 1997–		Jean Chrétien

Source: Library of Parliament, Information and Documentation Branch

Members of Canada's Senate

(7 vacancies as of Oct. 1, 2000)

The Governor General appoints senators under the Great Seal of Canada on the prime minister's advice.

To be eligible for the Senate, a candidate must be a Canadian citizen and at least 30 years old. A candidate must also live in the region the appointment represents—either Ontario, Quebec, the West, the Maritimes or a territory. He or she must own land in that region with an unencumbered value of at least $4,000 and have a net estate worth at least $4,000. A senator from Quebec must either live in or have land in Quebec. A senator must retire at age 75.

Senator	Birthdate	Date Appointed	Appointed by	Province
Willie Adams	June 22, 1934	Apr. 5, 1977	Trudeau	Nunavut
Raynell Andreychuk	Aug. 14, 1944	Mar. 11, 1993	Mulroney	Sask.
W. David Angus	July 21, 1937	June 10, 1993	Mulroney	Que.
Norm Atkins	June 27, 1934	July 2, 1986	Mulroney	Ont.
Jack Austin	Mar. 2, 1932	Aug. 19, 1975	Trudeau	BC
Lise Bacon	Aug. 25, 1934	Sept. 15, 1994	Chrétien	Que.
Tommy Banks	Dec. 17, 1936	Apr. 7, 2000	Chrétien	Alta
Gérald Beaudoin	Apr. 15, 1929	Sept. 26, 1988	Mulroney	Que.
Eric Arthur Berntson	May 16, 1941	Sept. 27, 1990	Mulroney	Sask.
Roch Bolduc	Sept. 10, 1928	Sept. 26, 1988	Mulroney	Que.
J. Bernard Boudreau	July 25, 1944	Oct. 4, 1999	Chrétien	NS
John G. Bryden	Aug. 25, 1937	Nov. 23, 1994	Chrétien	NB
John Buchanan	Apr. 22, 1931	Sept. 12, 1990	Mulroney	NS
Catherine Callbeck	July 25, 1939	Sept. 23, 1997	Chrétien	PEI
Pat Carney	May 26, 1935	Aug. 30, 1990	Mulroney	BC
Sharon Carstairs	Apr. 26, 1942	Sept. 15, 1994	Chrétien	Man.
Thelma Chalifoux	Feb. 8, 1929	Nov. 26, 1997	Chrétien	Alta
Ione Christensen	Oct. 10, 1933	Sept. 2, 1999	Chrétien	YT
Ethel Cochrane	Sept. 23, 1937	Nov. 17, 1986	Mulroney	Nfld
Erminie J. Cohen	July 23, 1926	June 4, 1993	Mulroney	NB
Gérald J. Comeau	Feb. 1, 1946	Aug. 30, 1990	Mulroney	NS
Joan Cook	Oct. 6, 1934	Mar. 6, 1998	Chrétien	Nfld
Anne C. Cools	Aug. 12, 1943	Jan. 13, 1984	Trudeau	Ont.
Eymard Corbin	Aug. 2, 1934	July 9, 1984	Turner	NB
Jane Marie Cordy	July 2, 1950	June 9, 2000	Chrétien	NB
Pierre De Bané	Aug. 2, 1938	June 29, 1984	Chrétien	NS
Mabel Margaret DeWare	Aug. 9, 1926	Sept. 23, 1990	Mulroney	NB
Consiglio Di Nino	Jan. 24, 1938	Aug. 30, 1990	Mulroney	Ont.
C. William Doody	Feb. 26, 1931	Oct. 3, 1979	Clark	Nfld
John Trevor Eyton	July 12, 1934	Sept. 23, 1990	Mulroney	Ont.
Joyce Fairbairn	Nov. 6, 1939	June 29, 1984	Trudeau	Alta
Marisa Ferretti Barth	Apr. 28, 1931	Sept. 23, 1997	Chrétien	Que.
Sheila Finestone	Jan. 28, 1927	Aug. 11, 1999	Chrétien	Que.
Isobel Finnerty	July 15, 1930	Sept. 2, 1999	Chrétien	Ont.
D. Ross Fitzpatrick	Feb. 4, 1933	Mar. 6, 1998	Chrétien	BC
John Michael Forrestall	Sept. 23, 1932	Sept. 27, 1990	Mulroney	Maritime[1]
Joan Fraser	1945	Sept. 17, 1998	Chrétien	Que.
George Furey	May 12, 1948	Aug. 11, 1999	Chrétien	Nfld
Jean-Robert Gauthier	Oct. 22, 1929	Nov. 23, 1994	Chrétien	Ont.
Aurélien Gill	1933	Sept. 17, 1998	Chrétien	Que.
Jerahmiel S. Grafstein	Jan. 2, 1935	Jan. 13, 1984	Trudeau	Ont.
B. Alasdair Graham	May 21, 1929	Apr. 27, 1972	Trudeau	NS
Leonard J. Gustafson	Nov. 10, 1933	May 26, 1993	Mulroney	Sask.
Daniel Hays	Apr. 24, 1939	June 29, 1984	Trudeau	Alta
Céline Hervieux-Payette	Apr. 22, 1941	Mar. 21, 1995	Chrétien	Que.
Janis Johnson	Apr. 27, 1946	Sept. 27, 1990	Mulroney	Man.
Serge Joyal	Feb. 1, 1945	Nov. 26, 1997	Chrétien	Que.
James Francis Kelleher	Oct. 2, 1930	Sept. 23, 1990	Mulroney	Ont.
Betty Kennedy	Jan. 24, 1926	June 20, 2000	Chrétien	Ont.
Colin Kenny	Dec. 10, 1943	June 29, 1984	Trudeau	Ont.
Wilbert Joseph Keon	May 17, 1935	Sept. 27, 1990	Mulroney	Ont.[1]
Noel A. Kinsella	Nov. 28, 1939	Sept. 12, 1990	Mulroney	NB
Michael Kirby	Aug. 5, 1941	Jan. 13, 1984	Trudeau	NS
E. Leo Kolber	Jan. 18, 1929	Dec. 23, 1983	Trudeau	Que.
Richard H. Kroft	May 22, 1938	June 11, 1998	Chrétien	Man.
Thérèse Lavoie-Roux	Mar. 12, 1928	Sept. 27, 1990	Mulroney	Que.[1]

Name	Born	Appointed	PM	Province
▶ Edward M. Lawson	Sept. 24, 1929	Oct. 7, 1970	Trudeau	BC
Marjory LeBreton	July 4, 1940	June 18, 1993	Mulroney	Ont.
Rose-Marie Losier-Cool	June 18, 1937	Mar. 21, 1995	Chrétien	NB
John Lynch-Staunton	June 19, 1930	Sept. 23, 1990	Mulroney	Que.
Shirley Maheu	Oct. 7, 1931	Feb. 1, 1996	Chrétien	Que.
Frank Mahovlich	Jan. 10, 1938	June 11, 1998	Chrétien	Ont.
Michael Arthur Meighen	Mar. 25, 1939	Sept. 27, 1990	Mulroney	Ont.[1]
Léonce Mercier	Aug. 11, 1926	Aug. 9, 1996	Chrétien	Que.
Lorna Milne	Dec. 13, 1934	Sept. 22, 1995	Chrétien	Ont.
Gildas L. Molgat	Jan. 25, 1927	Oct. 7, 1970	Trudeau	Man.
Wilfred P. Moore	Jan. 14, 1942	Sept. 26, 1996	Chrétien	NS
Lowell Murray	Sept. 26, 1936	Sept. 13, 1979	Clark	Ont.
Pierre Claude Nolin	Oct. 30, 1950	June 18, 1993	Mulroney	Que.
Donald H. Oliver	Nov. 16, 1938	Sept. 7, 1990	Mulroney	NS
Landon Pearson	Nov. 16, 1930	Sept. 15, 1994	Chrétien	Ont.
Lucie Pépin	Sept. 7, 1936	Apr. 8, 1997	Chrétien	Que.
Raymond J. Perrault	Feb. 6, 1926	Oct. 5, 1973	Trudeau	BC
P. Michael Pitfield	June 18, 1937	Dec. 22, 1982	Trudeau	Ont.
Marie-Paul Poulin	June 21, 1945	Sept. 21, 1995	Chrétien	Ont.
Vivienne Poy	1941	Sept. 17, 1998	Chrétien	Ont.
Marcel Prud'homme	Nov. 30, 1934	May 26, 1993	Mulroney	Que.
Jean-Claude Rivest	Jan. 27, 1943	Mar. 11, 1993	Mulroney	Que.
Brenda Mary Robertson	May 23, 1929	Dec. 21, 1984	Mulroney	NB
Fernand Robichaud	Dec. 2, 1939	Sept. 23, 1997	Chrétien	NB
Louis J. Robichaud	Oct. 21, 1925	Dec. 21, 1973	Trudeau	NB
Douglas Roche	1929	Sept. 17, 1998	Chrétien	Alta.
William Rompkey	May 13, 1936	Sept. 22, 1995	Chrétien	Nfld
Eileen Rossiter	July 14, 1929	Nov. 17, 1986	Mulroney	PEI
Gerry St. Germain	Nov. 6, 1937	June 23, 1993	Mulroney	BC
Raymond C. Setlakwe	July 3, 1928	June 20, 2000	Chrétien	Que.
Nick G. Sibbeston	Nov. 21, 1943	Sept. 2, 1999	Chrétien	NWT
Jean-Maurice Simard	June 21, 1931	June 26, 1985	Mulroney	NB
Herbert O. Sparrow	Jan. 4, 1930	Feb. 9, 1968	Pearson	Sask.
Mira Spivak	July 12, 1934	Nov. 17, 1986	Mulroney	Man.
Raymond Squires	Feb. 6, 1926	June 9, 2000	Chrétien	Nfld
Peter A. Stollery	Nov. 29, 1935	July 2, 1981	Trudeau	Ont.
Terrance R. Stratton	Mar. 16, 1938	Mar. 25, 1993	Mulroney	Man.
Nicholas W. Taylor	Nov. 17, 1927	Mar. 7, 1996	Chrétien	Alta.
David Tkachuk	Feb. 18, 1945	June 8, 1993	Mulroney	Sask.
Charlie Watt	June 29, 1944	Jan. 16, 1984	Trudeau	Que.
John (Jack) Wiebe	May 31, 1936	Apr. 7, 2000	Chrétien	Sask.
The Very Rev. Lois Wilson	Apr. 8, 1927	June 11, 1998	Chrétien	Ont.

(1) Represents region rather than a province.

Senate Changes

As of Oct. 1, 2000, one senator is slated to retire in 2000: Louis J. Robichaud on Oct. 21. In the year 2001, six senators are slated to retire: Betty Kennedy on Jan. 4, Raymond J. Perreault on Feb. 6, Raymond Squires on Feb. 6, Erminie J. Cohen on Jul. 23, Mabel M. DeWare on Aug. 9, and Léonce Mercier on Aug. 11. Both Kennedy and Squires were appointed in 2000.

Members of Parliament

(as of October 2000)

Correspondence to Members of Parliament should be addressed individually and may be sent postage free to the following address: (Name of MP), House of Commons, Ottawa, Ontario, K1A 0A6. For general information, call (613) 992-4793.

To contact a government department or minister's office via the Internet, go to http://canada.gc.ca/main_e.html (the website for the Government of Canada) and access "About Government."

In the event of a post-publication election, visit www.cdgbooks.com and look for Almanac FastFacts for an updated list of MPs.

■ Newfoundland

Riding	Member (year of birth)	Party	Occupation	First Elected[1]
Bonavista/Trinity/Conception	Fred Mifflin (1938)	Lib.	Politician	1988
Burin/St. George's	Bill Matthews (1947)	Lib.	Politician	1997
Gander/Grand Falls	George S. Baker (1942)	Lib.	M.P.	1974
Humber/St. Barbe/Baie Verte	Gerry Byrne (1966)	Lib.	Civil Servant	1996*
Labrador	Lawrence O'Brien (1951)	Lib.	Civil Servant	1996*
St. John's East	Norman Doyle (1945)	PC	Politician	1997
St. John's West	Loyola Hearn (1943)	PC	Teacher	2000

■ Prince Edward Island

Riding	Member (year of birth)	Party	Occupation	First Elected[1]
Cardigan	Lawrence MacAulay (1946)	Lib.	M.P.	1988
Egmont	Joe McGuire (1944)	Lib.	M.P.	1988
Hillsborough	George Proud (1939)	Lib.	Property Sup.	1988
Malpeque	Wayne Easter (1949)	Lib.	Farmer	1993

■ Nova Scotia

Riding	Member (year of birth)	Party	Occupation	First Elected[1]
Bras d'Or/Cape Breton	Michelle Dockrill (1960)	NDP	Health-care	1997
Cumberland/Colchester	Bill Casey (1945)	PC	Financial advisor	1997
Dartmouth	Wendy Lill (1950)	NDP	Writer/Soc. worker	1997
Halifax	Alexa McDonough (1945)	NDP	Social worker	1997
Halifax West	Gordon Earle (1943)	NDP	Civil servant	1997
Kings/Hants	Joe Clark (1939)	PC	Politician	2000
Pictou/Antigonish/Guysborough	Peter Mackay (1965)	PC	Crown attorney	1997
Sackville/Musquodoboit Valley/Eastern Shore	Peter Stoffer (1956)	NDP	Customer Serv.	1997
South Shore	Gerald Keddy (1953)	PC	Businessman	1997
Sydney/Victoria	Peter Mancini (1956)	NDP	Legal Aid Lawyer	1997
West Nova	Mark Muise (1957)	PC	Insurance Agent	1997

■ New Brunswick

Riding	Member (year of birth)	Party	Occupation	First Elected[1]
Acadie/Bathurst	Yvon Godin (1955)	NDP	Staff Reprsntative	1997
Beauséjour/Petitcodiac	Angela Vautour (1960)	PC	Parks Canada	1997
Fredericton	Andy Scott (1955)	Lib.	Public Servant	1993
Fundy/Royal	John Herron (1967)	PC	Manager	1997
Madawaska/Restigouche	Jean Dubé (1962)	PC	Businessman	1997
Miramichi	Charles Hubbard (1940)	Lib.	School Principal	1993
Moncton/Riverview/Dieppe	Claudette Bradshaw (1949)	Lib.	Public servant	1997
New Brunswick Southwest	Greg Thompson (1947)	PC	Educator	1997
Saint John	Elsie Wayne (1932)	PC	Retired	1993
Tobique/Mactoguac	Gilles Bernier (1955)	PC	Businessman	1997

▶ ■ Quebec

Riding	Member (year of birth)	Party	Occupation	First Elected[1]
Abitibi/Baie-James/Nunavik	Guy St-Julien (1940)	Lib.	Lawyer	1997
Ahuntsic	Eleni Bakopanos (1954)	Lib.	Political admin.	1993
Anjou/Rivière-des-Prairies	Yvon Charbonneau (1940)	Lib.	Politician	1997
Argenteuil/Papineau/Mirabel	Maurice Dumas (1927)	BQ	Professor	1993
Bas-Richelieu/Nicolet/Bécancour	Louis Plamondon (1943)	BQ	Businessman	1984
Beauce	Claude Drouin (1956)	Lib.	Civil servant	1997
Beauharnois/Salaberry	Daniel Turp (1955)	BQ	Professor	1997
Beauport/Montmorency/ Côte-de-Beaupré/Île-d'Orléans	Michel Guimond (1953)	Lib.	Lawyer	1993
Bellechasse/Etchemins/Montmagny/L'Islet	Gilbert Normand (1943)	Lib.	Doctor	1997
Berthier/Montcalm	Michel Bellehumeur (1963)	BQ	Lawyer	1993
Bonaventure/Gaspé/ Îes-de-la-Madeleine/Pabok	Yvan Bernier (1960)	BQ	Administrator	1993
Bourassa	Denis Coderre (1963)	Lib.	Editor	1997
Brome/Missisquoi	Denis Paradis (1949)	Lib.	Lawyer	1995
Brossard/La Prairie	Jacques Saada (1947)	Lib.	Teacher	1997
Chambly	Ghislain Lebel (1946)	BQ	Notary Public	1993
Champlain	Réjean Lefebvre (1943)	Ind.	Forestry	1993
Charlesbourg	Richard Marceau (1970)	BQ	Lawyer	1997
Charlevoix	Gérard Asselin (1950)	BQ	Foreman	1993
Châteauguay	Maurice Godin (1932)	BQ	Retired	1993
Chicoutimi	André Harvey (1941)	Lib.	School Com.	1997
Compton/Stanstead	David Price (1945)	Lib.	Mayor	1997
Drummond	Pauline Picard (1947)	BQ	Admin. Assistant	1993
Frontenac/Mégantic	Jean-Guy Chrétien (1946)	BQ	Professor	1993
Gatineau	Mark Assad (1940)	Lib.	Professor	1988
Hochelaga/Maisonneuve	Réal Ménard (1962)	BQ	Political Attaché	1993
Hull/Aylmer	Marcel Proulx (1946)	Lib.	Administrator	1999
Joliette	René Laurin (1940)	BQ	Director General	1993
Jonquière	Jocelyne Girard-Bujold (1943)	BQ	Businesswoman	1997
Kamouraska/Rivière-du-Loup/ Témiscouata/Les Basques	Paul Crête (1943)	BQ	Personnel Dir.	1993
Lac-Saint-Jean	Stéphan Tremblay (1973)	BQ	Bush Pilot	1996*
Lac-Saint-Louis	Clifford Lincoln (1928)	Lib.	Consultant	1993
LaSalle/Émard	Paul Martin (1938)	Lib.	M.P.	1988
Laurentides	Monique Guay (1959)	BQ	Businesswoman	1993
Laurier/Sainte-Marie	Gilles Duceppe (1947)	BQ	M.P.	1990*
Laval Centre	Madeleine Dalphond-Guiral (1938)	BQ	Professor	1993
Laval-Est	Maud Debien (1938)	BQ	Retired	1993
Laval-Ouest	Raymonde Folco (1940)	Lib.	Commissioner	1997
Lévis-et-Chutes-de-la-Chaudière	Antoine Dubé (1947)	BQ	Administrator	1993
Longueuil	Caroline St. Hilaire (1969)	BQ	Author agent	1997
Lotbinière	Odina Desrochers (1951)	BQ	Civil servant	1997
Louis-Hébert	Helene Alarie (1941)	BQ	Civil servant	1997
Manicouagan	Ghislain Fournier (1938)	BQ	Businessman	1997
Matapédia/Matane	René Canuel (1936)	BQ	Teacher	1993
Mercier	Francine Lalonde (1940)	BQ	Lecturer	1993
Mont-Royal	Irwin Cotler	Lib.	Professor	1999
Notre-Dame-de-Grâce/Lachine	Marlene Jennings (1951)	Lib.	Public servant	1965
Outremont	Martin Cauchon (1962)	Lib.	Lawyer	1993
Papineau/Saint-Denis	Pierre Pettigrew (1951)	Lib.	Businessman	1996*
Pierrefonds/Dollard	Bernard Patry (1943)	Lib.	Doctor	1993
Pontiac/Gatineau/Labelle	Robert Bertrand (1953)	Lib.	Insurance Agent	1993
Portneuf	Pierre de Savoye (1942)	BQ	Professor	1993
Québec	Christiane Gagnon (1948)	BQ	Real Estate Agent	1993
Québec-Est	Jean-Paul Marchand (1944)	BQ	Writer	1993
Repentigny	Benoît Sauvageau (1963)	BQ	Teacher	1997
Richmond/Arthabaska	André Bachand (1951)	PC	Educator	1997

Riding	Member (year of birth)	Party	Occupation	First Elected[1]
Rimouski/Mitis	Suzanne Tremblay (1937)	BQ	Professor	1993
Rivière-des-Mille-Îles	Gilles–A. Perron (1940)	BQ	Pol. Advisor	1997
Roberval	Michel Gauthier (1950)	BQ	Administrator	1993
Rosemont	Bernard Bigras (1970)	BQ	Civil servant	1997
Saint-Hyacinthe/Bagot	Yvan Loubier (1959)	BQ	Economist	1993
Saint-Léonard/Saint-Michel	Alfonso Gagliano (1942)	Lib.	CGA	1984
Saint-Bruno/Saint-Hubert	Pierrette Venne (1945)	BQ	Notary Public	1988
Saint-Jean	Claude Bachand (1951)	BQ	Educator	1993
Saint-Lambert	Yolande Thibeault (1939)	Lib.	Director (DRO)	1997
Saint-Laurent/Cartierville	Stéphane Dion (1955)	Lib.	Professor	1996*
Saint-Maurice	Jean Chrétien (1934)	Lib.	Lawyer	1963
Shefford	Diane St-Jacques (1953)	Lib.	P.R.	1997
Sherbrooke	Serge Cardin (n.a.)	BQ	Accountant	1998*
Témiscamingue	Pierre Brien (1970)	BQ	Economist	1993
Terrebonne/Blainville	Paul Mercier (1924)	BQ	Mayor	1997
Trois-Rivières	Yves Rocheleau (1944)	BQ	Dev. Consultant	1993
Vaudreuil/Solanges	Nunzio Discepola (1949)	Lib.	Mayor	1993
Verchères/Les-Patriotes	Stéphane Bergeron (1965)	BQ	Political Attaché	1993
Verdun/Saint-Henri	Raymond Lavigne (1945)	Lib.	Consultant	1993
Westmount/Ville-Marie	Lucienne Robillard (1945)	Lib.	Politician	1995

■ Ontario

Riding	Member (year of birth)	Party	Occupation	First Elected[1]
Algoma/Manitoulin	Brent St. Denis (1950)	Lib.	Parl. Assistant	1993
Barrie/Simcoe/Bradford	Aileen Carroll (1944)	Lib.	Businesswoman	1997
Beaches/East York	Maria Minna (1948)	Lib.	Consultant	1993
Bramalea/Gore/Malton/Springdale	Gurbax Singh Malhi (1949)	Lib.	Real Estate Agent	1993
Brampton Centre	Sarkis Assadourian (1948)	Lib.	Businessman	1993
Brampton West/Missisauga	Colleen Beaumier (1944)	Lib.	Businesswoman	1993
Brant	Jane Stewart (1955)	Lib.	Human Resources	1993
Broadview/Greenwood	Dennis Mills (1946)	Lib.	Businessman	1988
Bruce/Grey	Ovid L. Jackson (1939)	Lib.	Teacher	1993
Burlington	Paddy Torsney (1962)	Lib.	Consultant	1993
Cambridge	Janko Peric (1949)	Lib.	Welder	1993
Carleton/Gloucester	Eugène Bellemare (1932)	Lib.	M.P.	1988
Chatham/Kent/Essex	Jerry Pickard (1940)	Lib.	Teacher	1997
Davenport	Charles Caccia (1930)	Lib.	Economist	1968
Don Valley East	David Collenette (1946)	Lib.	Mgmt. Consultant	1993
Don Valley West	John Godfrey (1942)	Lib.	Journalist	1993
Dufferin/Peel/Wellington/Grey	Murray Calder (1951)	Lib.	Poultry Producer	1993
Durham	Alex Shepherd (1946)	Lib.	C.A.	1993
Eglinton/Lawrence	Joseph Volpe (1947)	Lib.	Educator	1988
Elgin/Middlesex/London	Gar Knutson (1956)	Lib.	Manager	1993
Erie/Lincoln	John Maloney (1945)	Lib.	Lawyer	1993
Essex	Susan Whelan (1963)	Lib.	Lawyer	1993
Etobicoke Centre	Allan Rock (1947)	Lib.	Lawyer	1993
Etobicoke North	Roy Cullen (1944)	Lib.	Accountant	1996*
Etobicoke/Lakeshore	Jean Augustine (1937)	Lib.	School Principal	1993
Glengarry/Prescott/Russell	Don Boudria (1949)	Lib.	Civil Servant	1984
Guelph/Wellington	Brenda Chamberlain (1952)	Lib.	Exec. Director	1993
Haldimand/Norfolk/Brant	Bob Speller (1956)	Lib.	M.P.	1988
Haliburton/Victoria/Brock	John O'Reilly (1940)	Lib.	Real Estate Broker	1993
Halton	Julian Reed (1936)	Lib.	Farmer	1993
Hamilton East	Sheila Copps (1952)	Lib.	M.P.	1984
Hamilton Mountain	Beth Phinney (1938)	Lib.	M.P.	1988
Hamilton West	Stan Keyes (1953)	Lib.	M.P.	1988
Hastings/Frontenac/Lennox & Addington	Larry McCormick (1940)	Lib.	Consultant	1993
Huron/Bruce	Paul Steckle (1942)	Lib.	Businessman	1993
Kenora/Rainy River	Robert D. Nault (1955)	Lib.	M.P.	1988
Kingston & the Islands	Peter Milliken (1946)	Lib.	Lawyer	1988
Kitchener Centre	Karen Redman (1953)	Lib.	Councillor	1997
Kitchener/Waterloo	Andrew Telegdi (1946)	Lib.	Mun. Politician	1993
Lambton/Kent/Middlesex	Rose-Marie Ur (1946)	Lib.	Sr. Const. Asst.	1993

Riding	Member	Party	Occupation	Year
▶ Lanark/Carleton	Ian Murray (1951)	Lib.	Govt. Relations	1993
Leeds/Grenville	Joe Jordan (1958)	Lib.	Professor	1997
London North Centre	Joe Fontana (1950)	Lib.	Businessman	1988
London West	Sue Barnes (1952)	Lib.	Lawyer	1993
London/Fanshawe	Pat O'Brien (1948)	Lib.	Teacher	1993
Markham	Jim Jones (1945)	CRCA	Marketing Mgr	1997
Mississauga Centre	Carolyn Parrish (1946)	Lib.	Public servant	1993
Mississauga East	Albina Guarnieri (1953)	Lib.	M.P.	1988
Mississauga South	Paul Szabo (1948)	Lib.	Chartered Acct.	1993
Mississauga West	Steve Mahoney (1947)	Lib.	Bus./Politician	1997
Nepean/Carleton	David Pratt (1955)	Lib.	Mun. Politician	1997
Niagara Centre	Gilbert Parent (1935)	Lib.	Teacher	1997
Niagara Falls	Gary Pillitteri (1936)	Lib.	Farmer	1993
Nickel Belt	Raymond Bonin (1942)	Lib.	Professor	1993
Nipissing	Bob Wood (1940)	Lib.	M.P.	1988
Northumberland	Christine Stewart (1941)	Lib.	M.P.	1988
Oak Ridges	Bryon Wilfert (1952)	Lib.	Ed/Mun. Politics	1997
Oakville	Bonnie Brown (1941)	Lib.	Social Worker	1993
Oshawa	Ivan Grose (1928)	Lib.	Businessman	1993
Ottawa Centre	Mac Harb (1953)	Lib.	M.P.	1988
Ottawa South	John Manley (1950)	Lib.	Lawyer	1988
Ottawa West/Nepean	Marlene Catterall (1939)	Lib.	M.P.	1988
Ottawa/Vanier	Mauril Bélanger (1955)	Lib.	M.P.	1995
Oxford	John Finlay (1929)	Lib.	Retired	1993
Parkdale/High Park	Sarmite Bulte (1953)	Lib.	Lawyer	1997
Parry Sound/Muskoka	Andy Mitchell (1953)	Lib.	Bank Manager	1993
Perth/Middlesex	John Richardson (1932)	Lib.	Self-employed	1993
Peterborough	Peter Adams (1936)	Lib.	Professor	1993
Pickering/Ajax/Uxbridge	Dan McTeague (1962)	Lib.	Media Relations	1993
Prince Edward/Hastings	Lyle Vanclief (1943)	Lib.	Agrologist	1988
Renfrew/Nipissing/Pembroke	Hec Clouthier (1949)	Lib.	Businessman	1997
Sarnia/Lambton	Roger Gallaway (1948)	Lib.	Lawyer	1993
Sault Ste. Marie	Carmen Provenzano (1942)	Lib.	Lawyer	1997
Scarborough Centre	John Cannis (1951)	Lib.	HR Consultant	1993
Scarborough East	John McKay (1948)	Lib.	Lawyer	1997
Scarborough Southwest	Tom Wappel (1950)	Lib.	M.P.	1988
Scarborough/Agincourt	Jim Karygiannis (1955)	Lib.	Ind. Engineer	1988
Scarborough/Rouge River	Derek Lee (1948)	Lib.	Lawyer	1988
Simcoe North	Paul DeVillers (1946)	Lib.	Lawyer	1993
Simcoe/Grey	Paul Bonwick (1964)	Lib.	Businessman	1997
St. Catharines	Walt Lastewka (1940)	Lib.	Plant Manager	1993
St. Paul's	Carolyn Bennett (1950)	Lib.	Doctor	1997
Stoney Creek	Tony Valeri (1957)	Lib.	Insurance	1993
Stormont/Dundas/Charlottenburgh	Bob Kilger (1944)	Lib.	Businessman	1988
Sudbury	Diane Marleau (1943)	Lib.	M.P.	1988
Thornhill	Elinor Caplan (1944)	Lib.	Provincial Politician	1997
Thunder Bay/Atikokan	Stan Dromisky (1931)	Lib.	Retired	1993
Thunder Bay/Superior North	Joe Comuzzi (1933)	Lib.	M.P.	1988
Timiskaming/Cochrane	Benoît Serré (1951)	Lib.	Businessman	1993
Timmins/James Bay	Réginald Bélair (1949)	Lib.	M.P.	1997
Toronto Centre/Rosedale	Bill Graham (1939)	Lib.	Lawyer	1993
Trinity/Spadina	Tony Ianno (1957)	Lib.	Businessman	1993
Vaughan/King/Aurora	Maurizio Bevilacqua (1960)	Lib.	Consultant	1988
Waterloo/Wellington	Lynn Myers (1951)	Lib.	Mayor	1997
Wentworth/Burlington	John Bryden (1943)	Lib.	Journalist	1993
Whitby/Ajax	Judi Longfield (1947)	Lib.	Exec. Assistant	1997
Willowdale	Jim Peterson (1941)	Lib.	Lawyer	1988
Windsor West	Herb Gray (1931)	Lib.	Lawyer	1962
Windsor/St. Clair	Richard Limoges	Lib.	Bank Manager	1999*
York Centre	Arthur C. Eggleton (1943)	Lib.	Consultant	1993
York North	Karen Kraft Sloan (1952)	Lib.	Consultant	1993
York South/Weston	John Nunziata (1955)	Ind.	Lawyer	1984
York West	Judy Sgro (1944)	Lib.	Politician	1999 ▶

▸ ■ Manitoba

Riding	Member (year of birth)	Party	Occupation	First Elected[1]
Brandon/Souris	Rick Borotsik (1950)	PC	Mayor	1997
Charleswood St. James/Assiniboia	John Harvard (1938)	Lib.	Broadcaster	1988
Churchill	Bev Desjarlais (1955)	NDP	School trustee	1997
Dauphin/Swan River	Inky Mark (1947)	CRCA	Mayor	1997
Portage/Lisgar	Jake E. Hoeppner (1936)	Ind.	Farmer	1993
Provencher	David Iftody (1956)	Lib.	Business Adv.	1993
Saint Boniface	Ronald J. Duhamel (n.a.)	Lib.	M.P.	1988
Selkirk/Interlake	Howard Hilstrom (1947)	CRCA	RCMP Officer	1997
Winnipeg Centre	Pat Martin (1955)	NDP	Union Official	1997
Winnipeg North-St. Paul	Rey Pagtakhan (1935)	Lib.	Physician	1988
Winnipeg North	Judy Wasylycia-Leis (1951)	NDP	Provincial Politician	1997
Winnipeg South	Reg Alcock (1948)	Lib.	Politician	1993
Winnipeg South Centre	Lloyd Axworthy (1939)	Lib.	M.P.	1979
Winnipeg/Transcona	Bill Blaikie (1951)	NDP	Clergyman	1979

■ Saskatchewan

Riding	Member (year of birth)	Party	Occupation	First Elected[1]
Battlefords/Lloydminster	Gerry Ritz (1951)	CRCA	Rancher	1997
Blackstrap	Allan Kerpan (1954)	CRCA	Farmer	1997
Churchill River	Rick Laliberte (1958)	Lib.	Education	1997
Cypress Hills/Grasslands	Lee Morrison (1932)	CRCA	Farmer	1993
Palliser	Dick Proctor (1941)	NDP	Journalist	1997
Prince Albert	Derrek Konrad (1943)	CRCA	Surveyor	1997
Regina/Lumsden/Lake Centre	John Solomon (1950)	NDP	Businessman	1993
Regina/Qu'Appelle	Lorne Nystrom (1947)	NDP	Politician	1968
Saskatoon/Humboldt	Jim Pankiw (1966)	CRCA	Chiropractor	1997
Saskatoon/Rosetown/Biggar	Dennis Gruending (1948)	NDP	Journalist	1999
Souris/Moose Mountain	Roy Bailey (1928)	CRCA	School Supt.	1997
Wanuskewin	Maurice Vellacott (1955)	CRCA	Minister	1997
Wascana	Ralph E. Goodale (1949)	Lib.	Business Exec.	1993
Yorkton-Melville	Garry Breitkreuz (1945)	CRCA	Teacher	1993

■ Alberta

Riding	Member (year of birth)	Party	Occupation	First Elected[1]
Athabasca	David Chatters (1946)	CRCA	Farmer	1993
Calgary Centre	Eric Lowther (1954)	CRCA	Mgt. Consultant	1997
Calgary East	Deepak Obhrai (1950)	CRCA	Entrepreneur	1997
Calgary Northeast	Art Hanger (1943)	CRCA	Police Officer	1993
Calgary/Nose Hill	Diane Ablonczy (1949)	CRCA	Lawyer	1993
Calgary Southeast	Jason Kenney (1968)	CRCA	CEO-Taxpyrs.' org.	1997
Calgary Southwest	Preston Manning (1942)	CRCA	Consultant	1993
Calgary West	Rob Anders (1972)	CRCA	Lobbyist	1997
Crowfoot	Jack Ramsay (1937)	Ind.–CRCA	Bus. Consultant	1993
Edmonton East	Peter Goldring (1944)	CRCA	Businessman	1997
Edmonton North	Deborah Grey (1952)	CRCA	Teacher	1989*
Edmonton Southeast	David Kilgour (1941)	Lib.	M.P.	1979
Edmonton/Strathcona	Rahim Jaffer (1971)	CRCA	Entrepreneur	1997
Edmonton Southwest	Ian McClelland (1942)	CRCA	Businessman	1993
Edmonton West	Anne McLellan (1950)	Lib.	Professor	1993
Elk Island	Ken Epp (1939)	CRCA	Instructor	1993
Lakeland	Leon E. Benoit (1950)	CRCA	Civ.servant/ Farmer	1993
Lethbridge	Rick Casson (1943)	CRCA	Manager/Printer	1997
Macleod	Grant Hill (1943)	CRCA	Physician	1993
Medicine Hat	Monte Solberg (1958)	CRCA	Businessman	1993

Riding	Member (year of birth)	Party	Occupation	First Elected[1]
▶ Peace River	Charlie Penson (1942)	CRCA	Farmer	1993
Red Deer	Bob Mills (1941)	CRCA	Businessman	1993
St Albert	John Williams (1946)	CRCA	Accountant	1993
Wetaskiwin	Dale Johnston (1941)	CRCA	Farmer	1993
Wild Rose	Myron Thompson (1936)	CRCA	Retired	1993
Yellowhead	Cliff Breitkreuz (1940)	CRCA	Farmer	1993

■ British Columbia

Riding	Member (year of birth)	Party	Occupation	First Elected[1]
Burnaby/Douglas	Svend J. Robinson (1952)	NDP	M.P.	1979
Cariboo/Chilcotin	Philip Mayfield (1937)	CRCA	Ord. Minister	1993
Delta/South Richmond	John Cummins (1942)	CRCA	Teacher	1993
Dewdney/Alouette	Grant McNally (1962)	CRCA	Teacher	1997
Esquimalt/Juan de Fuca	Keith Martin (1960)	CRCA	Physician	1993
Fraser Valley	Chuck Strahl (1957)	CRCA	Logging Cont.	1993
Kamloops/Thompson/Highland Valleys	Nelson Riis (1942)	NDP	M.P.	1980
Kelowna	Werner Schmidt (1932)	CRCA	Businessman	1993
Kootenay/Boundary/Okanagan	Jim Gouk (1946)	CRCA	Real Estate Agt.	1993
Kootenay-Columbia	Jim Abbott (1942)	CRCA	Businessman	1993
Langley/Abbotsford	Randy White (1948)	CRCA	CMA	1993
Nanaimo/Alberni	Bill Gilmour (1942)	CRCA	Forester	1993
Nanaimo/Cowichan	Reed Elley (1945)	CRCA	Minister	1997
New Westminster/Coquitlam/Burnaby	Paul E. Forseth (1946)	CRCA	Probation Officer	1993
North Vancouver	Ted White (1949)	CRCA	Company Pres.	1993
Okanagan/Coquihalla	Stockwell Day (1950)	CRCA	Politician	2000
Okanagan/Shuswap	Darrel Stinson (1945)	CRCA	Mining	1993
Port Moody/Coquitlam/Port Coquitlam	Lou Sekora (1931)	Lib.	Politician	1998*
Prince George/Bulkley Valley	Richard M. Harris (1944)	CRCA	Retired	1993
Prince George/Peace River	Jay Hill (1952)	CRCA	Farmer	1993
Richmond	Raymond Chan (1951)	Lib.	Research Eng.	1993
Saanich/Gulf Islands	Gary Lunn (1957)	CRCA	Lawyer	1997
Skeena	Mike Scott (1954)	CRCA	Businessman	1993
South Surrey/White Rock/Langley	Val Meredith (1949)	CRCA	Businesswoman	1993
Surrey Central	Gurmant Grewal (1957)	CRCA	Real Estate Agt.	1997
Surrey North	Chuck Cadman (1948)	CRCA	Elec. Eng. Tech.	1997
Vancouver Centre	Hedy Fry (1941)	Lib.	Physician	1993
Vancouver East	Elizabeth Davies (1953)	NDP	Councillor	1997
Vancouver Island North	John Duncan (1948)	CRCA	Forester	1993
Vancouver Kingsway	Sophia Leung (1934)	Lib.	Social Worker	1997
Vancouver Quadra	Ted McWhinney (1924)	Lib.	Professor	1993
Vancouver South/Burnaby	Harbance Singh Dhaliwal (1952)	Lib.	Businessman	1993
Victoria	David Anderson (1937)	Lib.	Env. Consultant	1968
West Vancouver/Sunshine Coast	John Reynolds (1942)	CRCA	Businessman	1997

■ Yukon

Riding	Member (year of birth)	Party	Occupation	First Elected[1]
Yukon	Louise Hardy (1959)	NDP	Social worker	1997

■ Northwest Territories

Riding	Member (year of birth)	Party	Occupation	First Elected[1]
Western Arctic	Ethel Blondin-Andrew (1951)	Lib.	Politician	1988

■ Nunavut

Riding	Member (year of birth)	Party	Occupation	First Elected[1]
Nunavut	Nancy Karetak-Lindell (1957)	Lib.	Businessperson	1997

(1) General election unless * indicating by-election. (n.a.) not available. PC—Progressive Conservative; Lib.—Liberal; NDP—New Democratic Party; CRCA—Canadian Reform Conservative Alliance; Ind.—Independent; Ind. CRCA—Independent Canadian Reform Conservative Alliance.

FOCUS ON...

Federal Watchdogs

Several federal officials monitor Ottawa's politicians and civil servants to ensure that they act responsibly and respect the rights of citizens. Acting independently of the Cabinet and political parties, these officials report to the House of Commons on the government's shortcomings. Three of these watchdogs are the auditor general, the information commissioner and the privacy commissioner.

The Auditor General

Appointed by the Governor in Council to a 10-year term, the auditor general examines the federal government's handling of public funds. Authorized by the *Auditor General Act* and the *Financial Administration Act*, this official ensures that federal institutions keep accurate accounts, collect and spend the authorized amounts of money and spend money in the intended ways. The auditor general also checks for economy and effectiveness in spending and tries to deter and expose fraud. The current auditor general, L. Denis Desautels, has been in office since 1991.

The office of the auditor general employs its own staff, which includes not only accountants but also lawyers, engineers, computer technicians, economists and management experts. The auditor general organizes these specialists into teams and stations them throughout the federal bureaucracy. Because these teams belong to the auditor general, they remain independent of the organizations that they audit. The auditor general can compel civil servants to provide information needed for an investigation. Some investigations involve scores of auditors and last up to 18 months.

The scope of the auditor general's activities is broad. The office investigates about 70 federal departments and agencies ranging in size from small boards to international organizations. It audits about 40 Crown corporations (including the Canadian Broadcasting Corporation and the Royal Canadian Mint), 10 departmental corporations, Canada's territorial governments and 60 other entities. Some investigations, which focus on the use of computers or staff, encompass the entire federal government.

The auditor general presents one major report to the House of Commons annually and may submit up to three smaller reports each year too. Because reports are submitted to the Speaker of the House, Opposition MPs and the news media receive the news at the same time as the governing party. The standing committee on public accounts reviews the auditor general's reports throughout the year and conducts public hearings attended by the auditor general, the audit teams and senior civil servants. The committee reports back to the House of Commons; audited organizations also report to the House of Commons to show how they've solved problems.

The Information Commissioner

Appointed by Parliament to a seven-year term, the information commissioner investigates complaints from people who encounter problems when retrieving information from the federal government. Acting as an ombudsman, the commissioner mediates disputes and recommends solutions to the government; however, the commissioner cannot issue binding orders. The current commissioner, John M. Reid, has been in office since 1998.

The commissioner ensures that the provisions of the *Access to Information Act* are respected. Passed in 1983, this law grants the right to Canadians to obtain copies of most records from the federal government. The law lists 13 specific exemptions including Cabinet documents, some diplomatic records and some records on federal-provincial relations. The law requires the government to respond to formal requests for records within 30 days; most requests should be filled within 60 days.

The commissioner launches investigations when requests for information encounter refusals, delays or demands for exorbitant fees. The commissioner intervenes if the government fails to provide the information in the right official language or if the request violates the privacy of a third party. The office of the commissioner conducts its investigations confidentially, and investigations cost the complainant nothing. If the investigation fails to resolve the dispute, the complainant or the commissioner may take the issue to the Federal Court of Canada.

However, the independence of the information commissioner is not absolute; the office falls under the authority of the justice minister. In legal disputes over access to information, the justice department acts as the commissioner's adversary. The justice department also provides legal advice to federal organizations that face complaints filed with the information commissioner. Yet the commissioner reports that the government fulfills most of the 12,000 annual requests for documents filed under the *Access to Information Act*.

In the spring, the commissioner tables an annual report in Parliament and rates the performance of six federal departments in meeting information requests. The commissioner issues pass or fail grades after monitoring departmental progress over the year. In 2000, the commissioner noted significant improvements in the way Health Canada and the Privy Council Office handled requests. The commissioner failed the departments of National Defence, Canada Customs, Foreign Affairs, and Citizenship and Immigration. In the House of Commons, the standing committee on justice and human rights should review the administration of the *Access to Information Act* but has not done so since 1986. On Aug. 21, 2000, however, the justice minister announced the establishment of a task force to review public access to information.

The Privacy Commissioner

The privacy commissioner is an ombudsman appointed by Parliament to a seven-year term. Authorized by the *Privacy Act*, the commissioner monitors the federal government's collection, use and disclosure of Canadians' personal information. The commissioner also investigates complaints involving the misuse of government-held information. The current commissioner, George Radwanski, has been in office since 2000.

The commissioner ensures that the *Privacy Act* is respected. Passed in 1983, this law grants the right to Canadians to examine information about them held in government files. One hundred and ten federal organizations hold personal documents such as tax records, security clearances, student loans, pension files and unemployment insurance files. The law requires the government to ensure the information is accurate, tell people why the information is held, use the information only for intended purposes and keep the information confidential.

The privacy commissioner launches investigations when requests for personal documents encounter refusals, delays or demands for fees. The commissioner intervenes if the government fails to correct or annotate disputed information or if the government fails to provide the records in the right official language. The commissioner investigates complaints that the government is collecting or using information improperly (e.g., to conduct illegal surveillance). The commissioner also investigates the improper disposal of records, which could jeopardize confidentiality.

The commissioner has the right to enter all federal buildings, examine records and interview staff. After an investigation ends, the commissioner reports to the complainant and the government agency concerned. As an ombudsman, the commissioner resolves disputes by recommending, for example, restrictions on the collection of personal details or changes in procedure. However, the commissioner cannot impose penalties or compel compliance. Thinking a person has been improperly denied access to his or her records, the commissioner may take the case to the Federal Court of Canada.

In May 2000, in his annual report to Parliament, the commissioner warned about the existence of a database kept by Human Resources Development Canada; the database contains as many as 2,000 pieces of information on each of Canada's 30 million citizens. The minister responsible subsequently pledged to dismantle the database. In 2000, Parliament also passed the *Personal Information Protection and Electronic Documents Act*. This law, which takes effect on Jan. 1, 2001, will govern the collection, use and disclosure of information by Canadian businesses.

For more information on the auditor general, phone (613) 995-3708 or visit the website at http://www.oag-bvg.gc.ca. To contact either the information or privacy commissioner, phone 1 (800) 267-0441. The website of the information commissioner is at http://infoweb.magi.com/~accessca; the privacy commissioner's is at http://www.privcom.gc.ca.

Salaries of Federal Political Figures

(as of October 2000)

The **GOVERNOR GENERAL** receives $102 700 per year.
All **LIEUTENANT–GOVERNORS** receive $97 900 per year (taxable).
SENATORS .... $68 200 plus $10 700 tax-free expense allowance and 64 travel points[2] per year.

The following senators receive as *extra* salary on top of their Senate salaries:

Leader of the Government	$49 300 plus $2 122 car allowance.
Leader of the Opposition	$25 000
Speaker of the Senate	$38 100 plus $3 000 residence allowance and $1 061 car allowance.
Speaker pro tempore	$10 900
Deputy Leader of the Government	$15 700
Deputy Leader of the Opposition	$9 700
Government Whip	$7 800
Opposition Whip	$4 800

MEMBERS OF PARLIAMENT—$68 200 plus $22 500 tax-free expense allowance[1] and 64 travel points[2] per year.[3]

The following members of Parliament receive as *extra* salary on top of their MP salaries:

Prime Minister	$74 100 plus $2 122 car allowance
Cabinet Ministers	$49 300 plus $2 122 car allowance
Speaker of the House	$52 000 plus $1 061 car allowance and $3 000 rent allowance
Secretaries of State	$36 975
Deputy Speaker	$27 200 plus $1 500 rent allowance
Official Opposition Leader	$52 000 plus $2 122 car allowance
Other Opposition Party Leaders	$31 200
Official Opposition House Leader	$25 000
Other House Leaders	$10 700
Government and Official Opposition Whips	$13 800
Other Party Whips	$7 800
Government and Opposition Deputy Whips	$7 800
Deputy Chairman, Committees of the Whole House	$11 100
Assistant Deputy Chairman, Committees of the Whole House	$11 100
Parliamentary Secretaries	$11 100

(1) MPs representing large rural districts listed in Schedule III of the Canada Elections Act receive an annual tax-free expense allowance of $27,700; MPs from Nunavut and the Western Arctic receive annual tax-free expense allowances of $29,700 each. (2) One travel point represents a business-class return air trip anywhere in Canada and can be used by representatives or their spouses or a designated family member. (3) Members who travel in Canada on official business and are at least 100 km from their principal residences may claim up to $12,000 in food, accommodation, and incidental expenses.

■ OFFICE BUDGET

Each of the 301 elected members has an office in both Ottawa and their riding, with staff to assist constituents with problems they may encounter when dealing with federal government departments and agencies. Each member's office budget covers staff salaries in Ottawa and constituency offices, as well as individuals or firms hired under contract. The budget is also intended to cover the costs of renting, equipping and maintaining constituency offices, as well as covering the costs of travel within the constituency and within the member's province.

A Member's office budget is set at $194,800; $198,100 or $201,400 according to the size of the constituency and its number of urban and/or rural polling divisions.

Geographic and Elector Supplement: Members receive supplements to the main office budget if they represent large constituencies with over 70,000 voters (e.g. the riding of York North) and/or geographic boundaries over 8,000 sq. km (e.g. the riding of Nunavut). These annual budgetary supplements cover the additional staff, operating and travel expenses required to serve the riding. Based on constituency characteristics, these supplements range from $6,630 to $39,850 and may change after each general election as the riding demographics change. A member may have more than one constituency office should he or she so desire, and many do.

Other Services: To help meet the needs and requests of their constituents, members are also given access to printing, translation, mail and other support services that help them respond to the thousands of letters and requests they receive. (Canadians may write to members of Parliament free of charge from anywhere in Canada.) The services also allow members to keep the public up-to-date on the events in Ottawa through a parliamentary report generally known as a "householder." Finally, members are provided with desks, computers, typewriters, photocopiers and other office supplies and equipment required to run an efficient office in Ottawa.

■ PARLIAMENTARY PENSION PLAN

Members' pensions are provided for by law under the "Members of Parliament Retiring Allowances Act" and, like many pension plans, members must make a financial contribution. Specifically, members must contribute 9% of their annual sessional allowance (salary) of $68,200. For members who are receiving additional salaries for extra duties such as ministers, whips or parliamentary secretaries, they have the option to contribute up to 9% of these salaries as well. The Act also provides that, upon ceasing to be a member of the House of Commons, a former member who retired prior to 1995 is immediately entitled to an annual pension after a minimum of six years of service. This pension is payable at the rate of 4% per year of service (i.e., a minimum of 24%: 6 x 4%) up to a maximum of 75% (18.75 years of service) of the average of the best consecutive six years of earnings. Members who serve less than six years must withdraw their contributions.

Indexing of a former member of the House of Commons' pension begins only when he or she reaches the age of 60, except for extraordinary situations such as disability. Survivors' benefits are payable to spouses and dependent children. If a former member in receipt of a pension is re-elected to the House of Commons or becomes a senator, the pension allowance is suspended for the period in office. In 1995 the pension plan was amended to allow members to opt out; eliminate "double dipping" (drawing more than one pension after holding several positions); and provide that a former member cannot receive a pension until they are at least 55 years old.

Source: *Public Information Office, House of Commons*

The Governor General's Salary

*B*ecause the Governor General represents Queen Elizabeth II, Canada's head of state, the Governor General must remain politically neutral throughout his or her term in office. To protect the Governor General from politically inspired financial pressure, Parliament bestows special status on his or her salary.

The Governor General's Act determines the Governor General's salary. The act includes a formula that ties any salary increase to the annual industrial wage index maintained by Statistics Canada. The formula itself was borrowed from The Judges' Act, which was created to preserve the independence of federal judges.

The Governor General's salary is also set lower than the pre-tax level of other public figures; hence it is not subject to income tax. This tax exemption reflects the tradition that the Crown does not tax monies paid to itself. However, the Governor General does file an annual income tax return and pays taxes on personal holdings and other sources of income.

The Governor General's current salary of $102,700 was set on Jan. 1, 1999. Between 1869 and 1985, the annual sum remained unchanged at $48,666.

Supreme Court Justices of Canada

(as of October 2000)

Name	Date of Birth	Date Appointed	Appointed from
The Rt. Hon. Madam Justice Beverley McLachlin....	Sept. 7, 1943	Mar. 30, 1989[1]	Supreme Court of BC
The Hon. Madam Justice Louise Arbour...........	Feb. 10, 1947	June 10, 1999	Ontario Court of Appeal
The Hon. Mr. Justice Michel Bastarache..........	June 10, 1947	Oct. 1, 1997	NB Court of Appeal
The Hon. Mr. Justice William Ian Corneil Binnie.....	Apr. 14, 1939	Jan. 8, 1998	Private law practice
The Hon. Mr. Justice Charles Doherty Gonthier.....	Aug. 1, 1928	Feb. 1, 1989	Quebec Court of Appeal
The Hon. Mr. Justice Frank Iacobucci.............	June 29, 1937	Jan. 7, 1991	Federal Court of Canada
The Hon. Madam Justice Claire L'Heureux-Dubé....	Sept. 7, 1927	Apr. 15, 1987	Quebec Court of Appeal
The Hon. Mr. Justice Louis LeBel................	Nov. 30, 1939	Jan. 7, 2000	Quebec Court of Appeal
The Hon. Mr. Justice John Charles Major.........	Feb. 20, 1931	Nov. 13, 1992	Alberta Court of Appeal

Source: *Supreme Court of Canada*

(1) Appointed Chief Justice Jan. 7, 2000.

Chief Justices of the Supreme Court of Canada

(as of October 2000)

Name	Date of Birth	Date Appointed Chief Justice	Term Ended
The Hon. Sir William Buell Richards..................	May 2, 1815	Sept. 30, 1875	Jan. 10, 1879
The Hon. Sir William Johnston Ritchie................	Oct. 28, 1813	Jan. 11, 1879	Sept. 25, 1892
The Rt. Hon. Sir Samuel Henry Strong...............	Aug. 13, 1825	Dec. 13, 1892	Nov. 18, 1902
The Rt. Hon. Sir Henri-Elzéar Taschereau............	Oct. 7, 1836	Nov. 21, 1902	May 2, 1906
The Rt. Hon. Sir Charles Fitzpatrick..................	Dec. 19, 1853	June 4, 1906	Oct. 21, 1918
The Rt. Hon. Sir Louis Henry Davies................	May 6, 1845	Oct. 23, 1918	May 1, 1924
The Rt. Hon. Francis Alexander Anglin...............	Apr. 2, 1865	Sept. 16, 1924	Feb. 28, 1933
The Rt. Hon. Sir Lyman Poore Duff..................	Jan. 7, 1865	Mar. 17, 1933	Jan. 7, 1944
The Rt. Hon. Thibaudeau Rinfret.....................	June 22, 1879	Jan. 8, 1944	June 22, 1954
The Hon. Patrick Kerwin.............................	Oct. 25, 1889	July 1, 1954	Feb. 2, 1963
The Rt. Hon. Robert Taschereau.....................	Sept. 10, 1896	Apr. 22, 1963	Sept. 1, 1967
The Rt. Hon. John Robert Cartwright................	Mar. 23, 1895	Sept. 1, 1967	Mar. 23, 1970
The Rt. Hon. Joseph Honoré Gérald Fauteux.........	Oct. 22, 1900	Mar. 23, 1970	Dec. 23, 1973
The Rt. Hon. Bora Laskin............................	Oct. 5, 1912	Dec. 27, 1973	Mar. 26, 1984
The Rt. Hon. Robert George Brian Dickson..........	May 25, 1916	Apr. 18, 1984	June 30, 1990
The Rt. Hon. Antonio Lamer.........................	Jul. 8, 1933	July 1, 1990	Jan. 6, 2000
The Rt. Hon. Beverley McLachlin....................	Sept. 7, 1943	Jan. 7, 2000–	

Source: *Supreme Court of Canada and Canadian Parliamentary Guide*

Contacting the Supreme Court

*F*or information on the Supreme Court of Canada, turn to page 141. Visit the court's website at http://www.scc-csc.gc.ca for more information on judges, history, recent decisions, tours and news. You may also write to the Supreme Court of Canada, 301 Wellington Street, Ottawa, Ontario, K1A 0J1. Phone (613) 947-5651 or fax (613) 996-9138.

Lieutenant-Governors and Commissioners

(as of October 2000)

On the advice of the prime minister, the governor general of Canada appoints 10 provincial lieutenant-governors and three territorial commissioners. Lieutenant-governors and commissioners represent the monarch and perform the same duties at the provincial and territorial levels that the governor general performs at the federal level. They open, prorogue and dissolve legislatures and give royal assent to legislation and orders-in-council.

Lieutenant-governors and commissioners are paid by the federal government and usually serve terms of five years.

Province or Territory	Lieutenant-Governor	Birthdate	Date Sworn in
Newfoundland	Hon. Arthur M. House	Aug. 10, 1926	Feb. 5, 1997
Prince Edward Island	Hon. Gilbert R. Clements	Sept. 11, 1928	Aug. 30, 1995
Nova Scotia	Hon. Myra A. Freeman	May 17, 1949	May 17, 2000
New Brunswick	Hon. Marilyn T. Counsell	Oct. 22, 1933	Apr. 18, 1997
Quebec	Hon. Lise Thibault	Apr. 2, 1939	Jan. 30, 1997
Ontario	Hon. Hilary Weston	Jan. 12, 1942	Jan. 24, 1997
Manitoba	Hon. Peter M. Liba	May 10, 1940	Mar. 2, 1999
Saskatchewan	Hon. Lynda M. Haverstock	Sept. 16, 1948	Feb. 21, 2000
Alberta	Hon. Lois Elsa Hole	1933	Feb. 10, 2000
British Columbia	Hon. Garde B. Gardom	July 17, 1924	Apr. 21, 1995
Nunavut	Hon. Peter Irniq	1947	Apr. 1, 2000
Northwest Territories	Hon. Glenna F. Hansen	Aug. 10, 1956	Mar. 31, 2000
Yukon	Hon. Jack Cable	Aug. 17, 1934	Sept. 30, 2000

n.a. not available

Provincial Premiers: A Historical Listing

(as of October 2000)

■ Newfoundland

Premier	Term	Party	Elected or sworn in
Joseph R. Smallwood	1949–1972	Liberal	Apr. 1, 1949
Frank D. Moores	1972–1979	Conservative	Jan. 18, 1972
A. Brian Peckford	1979–1989	Conservative	Mar. 26, 1979
Tom Rideout	1989	Conservative	Mar. 22, 1989
Clyde Wells	1989–1996	Liberal	May 5, 1989
Brian Tobin	1996–	Liberal	Jan. 26, 1996

■ Prince Edward Island

Premier	Term	Party	Elected or sworn in
C. Pope	1873	Conservative	Apr., 1873
L. C. Owen	1873–76	Conservative	Sept., 1873
L. H. Davies	1876–79	Liberal (Coalition)	Aug.,1876
W. W. Sullivan	1879–89	Conservative	Apr. 25, 1879
N. McLeod	1889–91	Conservative	Nov., 1889
F. Peters	1891–97	Liberal	Apr. 27, 1891
A. B. Warburton	1897–98	Liberal	Oct., 1897
D. Farquharson	1898–1901	Liberal	Aug., 1898
A. Peters	1901–08	Liberal	Dec. 29, 1901
F. L. Haszard	1908–11	Liberal	Feb. 1, 1908
H. James Palmer	1911	Liberal	May 16, 1911
John A. Mathieson	1911–17	Conservative	Dec. 2, 1911
Aubin Arsenault	1917–19	Conservative	June, 21, 1917
J. H. Bell	1919–23	Liberal	Sept. 9, 1919
James D. Stewart	1923–27	Conservative	Sept. 5, 1923
Albert C. Saunders	1927–30	Liberal	Aug. 12, 1927
Walter M. Lea	1930–31	Liberal	May 20, 1930
James D. Stewart	1931–33	Conservative	Aug. 29, 1931
William J. P. MacMillan	1933–35	Conservative	Oct. 14, 1933

Premier	Term	Party	Elected or sworn in
Walter M. Lea	1935–36	Liberal	Aug. 15, 1935
Thane A. Campbell	1936–43	Liberal	Jan. 14, 1936
J. Walter Jones	1943–53	Liberal	May 11, 1943
Alexander W. Matheson	1953–59	Liberal	May 25, 1953
Walter Shaw	1959–66	Prog. Conservative	Sept. 16, 1959
Alexander B. Campbell	1966–78	Liberal	July 28, 1966
William Bennett Campbell	1978–79	Liberal	Sept. 18, 1978
J. Angus MacLean	1979–81	Prog. Conservative	May 3, 1979
James M. Lee	1981–86	Prog. Conservative	Nov. 17, 1981
Joseph A. Ghiz	1986–93	Liberal	May 2, 1986
Catherine Callbeck	1993–96	Liberal	Jan. 25, 1993
Keith Milligan	1996	Liberal	Oct. 10, 1996
Pat Binns	1996–	Prog. Conservative	Nov. 27, 1996

■ Nova Scotia

Premier	Term	Party	Elected or sworn in
H. Blanchard	1867	Conservative	July 4, 1867
William Annand	1867–75	Liberal	Nov. 7, 1867
P. C. Hill	1875–78	Liberal	May 11, 1875
S. H. Holmes	1878–82	Conservative	Oct. 22, 1878
John S. D. Thompson	1882	Conservative	May 25, 1882
W. T. Pipes	1882–84	Liberal	Aug. 3, 1882
W. S. Fielding	1884–96	Liberal	July 28, 1884
George H. Murray	1896–1923	Liberal	July 20, 1896
E. H. Armstrong	1923–25	Liberal	Jan. 24, 1923
E. N. Rhodes	1925–30	Conservative	July 16, 1925
Col. Gordon S. Harrington	1930–33	Conservative	Aug. 11, 1930
Angus L. Macdonald	1933–40	Liberal	Sept. 5, 1933
A. S. MacMillan	1940–45	Liberal	July 10, 1940
Angus L. Macdonald	1945–54	Liberal	Sept. 8, 1945
Harold Connolly	1954	Liberal	Apr. 13, 1954
Henry D. Hicks	1954–56	Liberal	Sept. 30, 1954
Robert L. Stanfield	1956–67	Prog. Conservative	Nov. 20, 1956
George Smith	1967–70	Prog. Conservative	Sept. 13, 1967
Gerald A. Regan	1970–78	Liberal	Oct. 28, 1970
John Buchanan	1978–90	Prog. Conservative	Oct. 5, 1978
Roger Bacon	1990–91	Prog. Conservative	Sept. 12, 1990
Donald Cameron	1991–93	Prog. Conservative	Feb. 9, 1991
John Savage	1993–97	Liberal	June 11, 1993
Russell MacLellan	1997–99	Liberal	July 18, 1997
John Hamm	1999–	Prog. Conservative	July 27, 1999

■ New Brunswick

Premier	Term	Party	Elected or sworn in
Andrew Wetmore	1867–70	Confederation Party	1867
G.E. King	1870–71	Conservative	1870
George Hatheway	1871–72	Conservative	1871
G.E. King	1872–78	Conservative	1872
James Fraser	1878–82	Conservative	1878
D. L. Hanington	1882–83	Conservative	1882
Andrew Blair	1883–96	Liberal	1883
James Mitchell	1896–97	Liberal	July, 1896
Henry Emmerson	1897–1900	Liberal	Oct. 29, 1897
L. J. Tweedie	1900–07	Liberal	Aug. 31, 1900
William Pugsley	1907	Liberal	Mar. 6, 1907
Clifford Robinson	1907–08	Liberal	May 31, 1907
John Douglas Hazen	1908–11	Conservative	Mar. 24, 1908
James K. Flemming	1911–14	Conservative	Oct. 16, 1911
George J. Clark	1914–17	Conservative	Dec. 17, 1914
James Murray	1917	Conservative	Feb. 1, 1917
Walter E. Foster	1917–23	Liberal	Apr. 4, 1917
Peter Veniot	1923–25	Liberal	Feb. 28, 1923
John B. M. Baxter	1925–31	Conservative	Sept. 14, 1925

Government of Canada

Premier	Term	Party	Elected or sworn in
Charles D. Richards	1931–33	Conservative	May 19, 1931
Leonard Tilley	1933–35	Conservative	June 1, 1933
Allison Dysart	1935–40	Liberal	July 16, 1935
John McNair	1940–52	Liberal	Mar. 13, 1940
Hugh J. Flemming	1952–60	Prog. Conservative	Oct. 8, 1952
Louis J. Robichaud	1960–70	Liberal	July 12, 1960
Richard Hatfield	1970–87	Prog. Conservative	Nov. 12, 1970
Frank McKenna	1987–97	Liberal	Oct. 27, 1987
Ray Frenette (interim)	1997–98	Liberal	Oct 14, 1997
Camille Thériault	1998–99	Liberal	May 14, 1998
Bernard Lord	1999–	Prog. Conservative	June 21, 1999

■ Quebec

Premier	Term	Party	Elected or sworn in
Pierre-Joseph-Olivier Chauveau	1867–73	Conservative	July 15, 1867
Gédéon Ouimet	1873–74	Conservative	Feb. 26, 1873
Charles E. Boucher deBoucherville	1874–78	Conservative	Sept. 22, 1874
Henri Joly	1878–79	Liberal	Mar. 8, 1878
J. Adolphe Chapleau	1879–82	Conservative	Oct. 31, 1879
J. Alfred Mousseau	1882–84	Conservative	July 31, 1882
John J. Ross	1884–87	Conservative	Jan. 23, 1884
L. Olivier Taillon	1887	Conservative	Jan. 25, 1887
Honoré Mercier	1887–91	Liberal	Jan. 27, 1887
Charles E. Boucher deBoucherville	1891–92	Conservative	Dec. 21, 1891
L. Olivier Taillon	1892–96	Conservative	Dec. 16, 1892
Edmund J. Flynn	1896–97	Conservative	May 11, 1896
F. Gabriel Marchand	1897–1900	Liberal	May 24, 1897
S. Napoléon Parent	1900–05	Liberal	Oct. 3, 1900
Lomer Gouin	1905–20	Liberal	Mar. 23, 1905
L. Alexandre Taschereau	1920–36	Liberal	July 9, 1920
Adélard Godbout	1936	Liberal	June 11, 1936
Maurice Duplessis	1936–39	Union Nationale	Aug. 26, 1936
Adélard Godbout	1939–44	Liberal	Nov. 8, 1939
Maurice Duplessis	1944–59	Union Nationale	Aug. 30, 1944
Paul Sauvé	1959–60	Union Nationale	Sept. 11, 1959
Antonio Barrette	1960	Union Nationale	Jan. 8, 1960
Jean Lesage	1960–66	Liberal	July 5, 1960
Daniel Johnson	1966–68	Union Nationale	June 16, 1966
Jean-Jacques Bertrand	1968–70	Union Nationale	Oct. 2, 1968
Robert Bourassa	1970–76	Liberal	May 12, 1970
René Lévesque	1976–85	Parti Québécois	Nov. 25, 1976
Pierre-Marc Johnson	1985	Parti Québécois	Oct. 3, 1985
Robert Bourassa	1985–94	Liberal	Dec. 12, 1985
Daniel Johnson	1994–94	Liberal	Jan. 11, 1994
Jacques Parizeau	1994–96	Parti Québécois	Sept. 26, 1994
Lucien Bouchard	1996–	Parti Québécois	Jan. 29, 1996

■ Ontario

Premier	Term	Party	Elected or sworn in
J.S. Macdonald	1867–71	Coalition	July 16, 1867
Edward Blake	1871–72	Liberal	Dec. 20, 1871
Oliver Mowat	1872–96	Liberal	Oct. 25, 1872
Arthur S. Hardy	1896–99	Liberal	July 25, 1896
George William Ross	1899–1905	Liberal	Oct. 21, 1899
Sir James P. Whitney	1905–14	Conservative	Feb. 8, 1905
Sir William Hearst	1914–19	Conservative	Oct. 2, 1914
Ernest C. Drury	1919–23	United Farmers of Ontario	Nov. 14, 1919
George Howard Ferguson	1923–30	Conservative	July 16, 1923
George Stewart Henry	1930–34	Conservative	Dec. 15, 1930
Mitchell F. Hepburn	1934–42	Liberal	July 10, 1934
Gordon Daniel Conant	1942–43	Liberal	Oct. 21, 1942
Harry C. Nixon	1943	Liberal	May 18, 1943
George Drew	1943–48	Prog. Conservative	Aug. 17, 1943
Thomas L. Kennedy	1948–49	Prog. Conservative	Oct. 19, 1948

Premier	Term	Party	Elected or sworn in
Leslie M. Frost	1949–61	Prog. Conservative	May 4, 1949
John P. Robarts	1961–71	Prog. Conservative	Nov. 8, 1961
William G. Davis	1971–85	Prog. Conservative	Mar. 1, 1971
Frank Miller	1985	Prog. Conservative	Feb. 8, 1985
David Peterson	1985–90	Liberal	June 26, 1985
Bob Rae	1990–95	New Democratic	Oct. 1, 1990
Mike Harris	1995–	Prog. Conservative	June 28, 1995

■ Manitoba

Premier	Term	Party	Elected or sworn in
A. Boyd	1870–71	n.a.	Sept. 16, 1870
M. A. Girard	1871–72	Conservative	Dec. 14, 1871
H. H. Clarke	1872–74	n.a.	Mar. 14, 1872
M. A. Girard	1874	Conservative	July 8, 1874
R. A. Davis	1874–78	n.a.	Dec. 3, 1874
John Norquay	1878–87	Conservative	Oct. 16, 1878
D. H. Harrison	1887–88	Conservative	Dec. 26, 1887
T. Greenway	1888–1900	Liberal	Jan. 19, 1888
H. J. Macdonald	1900	Conservative	Jan. 8, 1900
Sir R. P. Roblin	1900–15	Conservative	Oct. 29, 1900
T. C. Norris	1915–22	Liberal	May 12, 1915
John Bracken	1922–43	Coalition[1]	Aug. 8, 1922
S. S. Garson	1943–48	Coalition	Jan. 8, 1943
D. L. Campbell	1948–58	Conservative	Nov. 11, 1948
Duff Roblin	1958–67	Prog. Conservative	June 16, 1958
Walter Weir	1967–69	Prog. Conservative	Nov. 25, 1967
Edward Schreyer	1969–77	New Democratic	July 15, 1969
Sterling Lyon	1977–81	Prog. Conservative	Nov. 24, 1977
Howard Pawley	1981–88	New Democratic	Nov. 30, 1981
Gary Filmon	1988–99	Prog. Conservative	Apr. 26, 1988
Gary Doer	1999–	New Democratic	Oct. 5, 1999

■ Saskatchewan

Premier	Term	Party	Elected or sworn in
Walter Scott	1905–16	Liberal	Sept. 5, 1905
W. M. Martin	1916–22	Liberal	Oct. 20, 1916
C. A. Dunning	1922–26	Liberal	Apr. 5, 1922
J. G. Gardiner	1926–29	Liberal	Feb. 26, 1926
J. T. M. Anderson	1929–34	Conservative	Sept. 9, 1929
J. G. Gardiner	1934–35	Liberal	July 19, 1934
W. J. Patterson	1935–44	Liberal	Nov. 1, 1935
Tommy Douglas	1944–61	C.C.F.[2]	July 10, 1944
W. S. Lloyd	1961–64	C.C.F.—N.D.P.	Nov. 7, 1961
W. Ross Thatcher	1964–71	Liberal	May 22, 1964
Allan E. Blakeney	1971–82	New Democratic	June 30, 1971
Grant Devine	1982–91	Prog. Conservative	May 8, 1982
Roy Romanow[5]	1991–2000	New Democratic	Nov. 1, 1991

■ Alberta

Premier	Term	Party	Elected or sworn in
Alex Rutherford	1905–10	Liberal	Sept. 2, 1905
A. L. Sifton	1910–17	Liberal	May 26, 1910
Charles Stewart	1917–21	Liberal	Oct. 30, 1917
Herbert Greenfield	1921–25	United Farmers of Alberta	Aug. 13, 1921
John E. Brownlee	1925–34	United Farmers of Alberta	Nov. 23, 1925
Richard G. Reid	1934–35	United Farmers of Alberta	July 10, 1934
William Aberhart	1935–43	Social Credit	Sept. 3, 1935
E. C. Manning	1943–68	Social Credit	May 31, 1943
Harry Strom	1968–71	Social Credit	Dec. 12, 1968
Peter Lougheed	1971–85	Prog. Conservative	Sept. 10, 1971
Don Getty	1985–92	Prog. Conservative	Nov. 1, 1985
Ralph P. Klein	1992–	Prog. Conservative	Dec. 14, 1992

■ British Columbia

Premier	Term	Party	Elected or sworn in
J. F. McCreight	1871–72	n.a.	Nov. 13, 1871
Amor De Cosmos	1872–74	n.a.	Dec. 23, 1872
G. A. Walkem	1874–76	n.a.	Feb. 11, 1874
A. C. Elliott	1876–78	n.a.	Feb. 1, 1876
G. A. Walkem	1878–82	n.a.	June 25, 1878
Robert Beaven	1882–83	n.a.	June 13, 1882
William Smithe	1883–87	n.a.	Jan. 29, 1883
A. E. B. Davie	1887–89	n.a.	May 1, 1887
John Robson	1889–92	n.a.	Aug. 2, 1889
Theodore Davie	1892–95	n.a.	July 2, 1892
J. H. Turner	1895–98	n.a.	Mar. 4, 1895
C. A. Semlin	1898–1900	n.a.	Aug. 15, 1898
Joseph Martin	1900	n.a.	Feb. 28, 1900
James Dunsmuir	1900–02	n.a.	June 15, 1900
E. G. Prior	1902–03	n.a.	Nov. 21, 1902
Richard McBride	1903–15	Conservative	June 1, 1903
William J. Bowser	1915–16	Conservative	Dec. 15, 1915
Harlan C. Brewster	1916–18	Liberal	Nov. 23, 1916
John Oliver	1918–27	Liberal	Mar. 6, 1918
John D. MacLean	1927–28	Liberal	Aug. 20, 1927
Simon F. Tolmie	1928–33	Conservative	Aug. 21, 1928
T. D. Pattullo	1933–41	Liberal	Nov. 15, 1933
John Hart	1941–47	Liberal[3]	Dec. 9, 1941
Byron Johnson	1947–52	Liberal[3]	Dec. 29, 1947
W. A. C. Bennett	1952–72	Social Credit	Aug. 1, 1952
David Barrett	1972–75	New Democratic	Sept. 15, 1972
William R. Bennett	1975–86	Social Credit	Dec. 22, 1975
Bill Vander Zalm	1986–91	Social Credit	Aug. 6, 1986
Rita Johnston	1991–91	Social Credit	Apr. 2, 1991
Michael Harcourt	1991–96	New Democratic	Nov. 5, 1991
Glen Clark	1996–99	New Democratic	Feb. 22, 1996
Dan Miller	1999–2000	New Democratic	Aug. 25, 1999
Ujjal Dosanjh	2000–	New Democratic	Feb. 24, 2000

■ Nunavut

Premier	Term	Party	Elected or sworn in
Paul Okalik	1999–	n.a.	Apr. 1, 1999

■ Northwest Territories

Premier	Term	Party	Elected or sworn in
George Braden	1980–83	n.a.	July 25, 1980
Richard Nerysoo	1984–85	n.a.	Jan. 12, 1984
Nick Sibbeston	1985–87	n.a.	Nov. 5, 1985
Dennis Patterson	1987–91	n.a.	Nov. 12, 1987
Nellie Cournoyea	1991–95	n.a.	Nov. 13, 1991
Don Morin	1995–98	n.a.	Nov. 20, 1995
James L. Antoine	1998–2000	n.a.	Dec. 10, 1998
Stephen Kakfwi	2000–	n.a.	Jan. 19, 2000

■ Yukon

Government Leader	Term	Party	Elected or sworn in
Chris Pearson	1978–85	Prog. Conservative	
Willard Phelps	1985	Prog. Conservative	Mar. 20, 1985
Tony Penikett	1985–92[4]	New Democratic	May 29, 1985
John Ostashek	1992–96	Yukon Party	Nov. 7, 1992
Piers McDonald	1996–2000	New Democratic	Oct. 19, 1996
Pat Duncan	2000–	Liberal	May 6, 2000

Source: *Historical Statistics of Canada; Provincial Archives*

(1) United Farmer/Progressive, 1922–27; Coalition, 1927–37; Liberal—Progressive, 1937–43. (2) Co-operative Commonwealth Federation. (3) Coalition. (4) From 1989–92, Government Leader was designated Premier. (n.a.) not available. (5) Roy Romanow resigned Sept 25, 2000. Leadership vote to be held.

Cabinets of the Provinces and Territories

(as of October 2000)

■ Newfoundland

Ministry or Portfolio	Minister
Premier	Brian Tobin
Development and Rural Renewal	Beaton Tulk
Education	Judy Foote
Environment and Labour	Oliver Langdon
Finance	Lloyd Matthews
Fisheries and Aquaculture	John Efford
Forest Resources and Agrifoods	Kevin Aylward
Government Services and Lands	Ernest McLean
Health and Community Services	Roger Grimes
Human Resources and Employment	Julie Bettney
Industry, Trade and Technology	Sandra Kelly
Intergovernmental Affairs	Walter Noel
Justice	Kelvin Parsons
Mines and Energy	Paul Dicks
Municipal and Provincial Affairs	Joan-Marie Aylward
President of Treasury Board	Anna Thistle
Tourism, Culture and Recreation	Chuck Furey
Works, Services and Transportation	Rick Woodford

■ New Brunswick

Ministry or Portfolio	Minister
Premier; Intergovernmental Affairs	Bernard Lord
Deputy Premier; Supply and Services	Dale Graham
Agriculture, Fisheries and Aquaculture	Paul Robichaud
Attorney General; Justice	Bradley Green
Business New Brunswick	Joan MacAlpine
Education	Elvy Robichaud
Environment and Local Government	Kim Jardine
Family and Community Services	Percy Mockler
Finance	Norman Betts
Health and Wellness	Dennis Furlong
Investment and Exports	Peter Mesheau
Natural Resources and Energy	Jeannot Volpé
Public Safety	Milton Sherwood
Training and Employment Development	Norman McFarlane
Transportation	Margaret-Ann Blaney

■ Nova Scotia

Ministry or Portfolio	Minister
Premier; Intergovernmental Affairs	John F. Hamm
Agriculture and Fisheries; Natural Resources	Ernest L. Fage
Attorney General; Justice	Michael G. Baker
Business and Consumer Services; Finance	Neil J. LeBlanc
Community Services	Peter G. Christie
Economic Development	Gordon D. Balser
Education	Jane S. Purves
Environment, Labour and Regulatory Affairs; Service Nova Scotia and Municipal Relations	Angus MacIsaac
Health	Jamie A. Muir
Tourism and Culture	Rodney J. MacDonald
Transportation and Public Works	Ronald S. Russell
Treasury and Policy Board	Vacant

■ Prince Edward Island

Ministry or Portfolio	Minister
Premier; Intergovernmental Affairs	Patrick G. Binns
Agriculture and Forestry	P. Mitchell Murphy
Attorney General; Education	Jeff Lantz

Government of Canada **175**

Community and Cultural Affairs	Gail Shea
Development and Technology	Michael Currie
Fisheries, Aquaculture and Environment	Kevin J. MacAdam
Health and Social Services	Jamie Ballem
Provincial Treasurer	Patricia J. Mella
Tourism	Greg Deighan
Transportation and Public Works	Don MacKinnon

■ Quebec

Ministry or Portfolio	Minister
Premier	Lucien Bouchard
Deputy Premier; Economy and Finance; Industry and Trade	Bernard Landry
Administration and Public Service; Treasury Board	Jacques Léonard
Agriculture, Fisheries and Food	Rémy Trudel
Canadian Intergovernmental Affairs	Joseph Facal
Charter of the French Language; International Relations; Relations with French-speaking Communities	Louise Beaudoin
Child and Family Welfare; Health and Social Services	Pauline Marois
Child and Family Welfare	Nicole Léger
Culture and Communications	Agnès Maltais
Education; Education and Youth	François Legault
Electoral Reform; Native Affairs; Transport; Wildlife and Parks	Guy Chevrette
Environment; Revenue	Paul Bégin
Government House Leader; Natural Resources; Parliamentary Reform	Jacques Brassard
Health, Social Services and Youth Protection	Gilles Baril
Industry and Trade	Guy Julien
Information Highway and Government Services	David Cliche
Justice; Status of Women	Linda Goupil
Labour and Employment	Diane Lemieux
Municipal Affairs and Greater Montreal; Seniors	Louise Harel
Public Security	Serge Ménard
Regions	Jean-Pierre Jolivet
Relations with Citizens and Immigration	Robert Perreault
Research, Science and Technology	Jean Rochon
Social Solidarity	André Boisclair
Tourism	André Arseneau
Transport	Jacques Baril

■ Ontario

Ministry or Portfolio	Minister
Premier	Michael D. Harris
Deputy Premier; Finance	Ernie Eves
Agriculture, Food and Rural Affairs	Ernie Hardeman
Attorney General; Native Affairs	James M. Flaherty
Citizenship, Culture and Recreation; Seniors and Women	Helen Joanne Johns
Community and Social Services; Francophone Affairs	John R. Baird
Consumer and Commercial Relations	Robert Runciman
Correctional Services	Rob Sampson
Economic Development and Trade	Al Palladini
Education	Janet Lynne Ecker
Energy, Science and Technology	Jim Wilson
Environment	Dan Newman
Government House Leader; Intergovernmental Affairs	Norman W. Sterling
Health and Long-Term Care	Elizabeth Witmer
Labour	Chris Stockwell
Management Board of Cabinet	Chris Hodgson
Municipal Affairs and Housing	Tony Clement
Natural Resources	John C. Snobelen
Northern Development and Mines	Timothy Patrick Hudak
Solicitor General	David H. Tsubouchi
Tourism	Cameron D. Jackson
Transportation	David Turnbull
Min. without Portfolio; Children	Margaret Marland
Min. without Porfolio; Chief Government Whip and Deputy House Leader	Frank F. Klees

Manitoba

Ministry or Portfolio	Minister
Premier; Federal-Provincial Relations	Gary Doer
Aboriginal and Northern Affairs	Eric Robinson
Agriculture and Food	Rosann Wowchuk
Conservation	Oscar Lathlin
Consumer and Corporate Affairs	Ron Lemieux
Culture and Tourism; Seniors; Status of Women	Diane McGifford
Education and Training	Drew Caldwell
Family Services and Housing	Tim Sale
Finance; Treasury Board	Gregory Selinger
Health; Sport	David Walter Chomiak
Highways and Government Services	Steve Ashton
Industry, Trade and Mines	MaryAnn Mihychuk
Intergovernmental Affairs	Jean Myfanwy Friesen
Justice and Attorney General	Gord Mackintosh
Labour; Multiculturalism	Becky Barrett

Saskatchewan

Ministry or Portfolio	Minister
Premier	Roy Romanow[1]
Agriculture and Food	Clay Serby
Crown Investments Corporation	John Nilson
Economic and Cooperative Development	Janice MacKinnon
Education	Jim Melenchuk
Energy and Mines	Eldon Lautermilch
Environment and Resource Management	Buckley Belanger
Finance	Eric Cline
Health	Patricia Atkinson
Health (Assoc. Min.); Seniors	Judy Junor
Highways and Transportation	Maynard Sonntag
Intergovernmental and Aboriginal Affairs; Municipal Affairs, Culture and Housing	Jack Hillson
Justice and Attorney General	Chris Axworthy
Labour	Joanne Crofford
Northern Affairs	Keith Goulet
Post-secondary Education and Skills Training	Glenn Hagel
Saskatchewan Property Management Corporation	Doreen Hamilton
Social Services	Harry Van Mulligen

Alberta

Ministry or Portfolio	Minister
Premier	Ralph Klein
Aboriginal Affairs (Assoc. Min.)	Pearl Calahasen
Agriculture, Food and Rural Development	Ty Lund
Children's Services	Iris Evans
Community Development; Seniors' Housing	Stan Woloshyn
Economic Development	Jon Havelock
Environment	Halvar C. Jonson
Gaming	Murray D. Smith
Government Services; Consumer Affairs	Pat L. Nelson
Health and Wellness	Gary Mar
Health and Wellness (Assoc. Min.)	Gene Zwozdesky
Human Resources and Employment	Clint Dunford
Infrastructure; Transportation; Utilities	Ed Stelmach
Innovation and Science	Lorne Taylor
International and Intergovernmental Relations	Shirley McClellan
Justice and Attorney General	Dave Hancock
Learning	Lyle Oberg
Municipal Affairs	Walter Paszkowski
Resource Development; Energy	Mike Cardinal
Treasury	Stephen C. West

Government of Canada

■ British Columbia

Ministry or Portfolio	Minister
Premier; Intergovernmental Relations	Ujjal Dosanjh
Aboriginal Affairs	Dale Lovick
Advanced Education, Training and Technology	Graeme Bowbrick
Agriculture, Food and Fisheries	Corky Evans
Attorney General	Andrew Petter
Children and Families	Gretchen Mann Brewin
Community Development, Cooperatives and Volunteers	Jenny Kwan
Education	Penny Priddy
Employment and Investment	Gordon Wilson
Energy and Mines	Dan Miller
Environment, Lands and Parks	Joan Sawacki
Finance and Corporate Relations	Paul Ramsey
Forests	Jim Doyle
Health	Mike Farnsworth
Labour	Joy MacPhail
Multiculturalism and Immigration	Sue Hammell
Municipal Affairs	Cathy McGregor
Small Business, Tourism and Culture	Ian Waddell
Social Development and Economic Security	Jan Pullinger
Transportation and Highways	Harry Lali
Women's Equality	Joan Smallwood

■ Yukon Territory

Ministry or Portfolio	Minister
Premier; Economic Development; Finance	Pat Duncan
Community and Transportation Services; Justice	Pam Buckway
Education; Renewable Resources	Dale Eftoda
Government Services	Wayne Jim
Health and Social Services	Don Roberts
Tourism; Women's Directorate	Sue Edelman

■ Northwest Territories

Ministry or Portfolio	Minister
Premier; Intergovernmental Affairs	Stephen Kakfwi
Deputy Premier; Health and Social Services	Jane Groenewegen
Aboriginal Affairs; Municipal and Community Affairs; Justice	James L. Antoine
Education, Culture and Employment	Jake Ootes
Finance; Resources, Wildlife and Economic Development	Joe Handley
NWT Housing Corporation; Youth	Roger T. Allen
Public Works and Services; Seniors; Transportation	Vince Steen

■ Nunavut

Ministry or Portfolio	Minister
Premier; Executive and Intergovernmental Affairs	Paul Okalik
Community Government and Transportation; Justice	Jack Anawak
Culture, Language, Elders and Youth	Peter Kattuk
Education	James Arvaluk
Finance and Administration; Human Resources	Kelvin Ng
Health and Social Services	Edward Picco
Public Works, Telecommunications and Technical Services	Manitok Thompson
Sustainable Development	Peter Kilabuk

(1) Resigned Sept 25, 2000. Leadership vote to be held.

Federal Political Parties in Parliament

Five political parties occupy seats in the House of Commons:

Bloc Québécois: Founded in 1991, the BQ consists of Quebec MPs who left the Progressive Conservative and Liberal parties after the federal government failed to pass the Meech Lake Accord. The BQ promotes sovereignty for Quebec.

Canadian Reform Conservative Alliance: Founded in Ottawa in 2000, the CRCA replaced the populist Reform party to broaden its conservative appeal. It seeks to reduce the size, scope and cost of government and to decentralize the federal system. Reform was founded in Winnipeg in 1987.

Liberal Party: Rooted in the movement for responsible government in the 19th century, the Liberal party ruled Canada throughout most of the 20th century. Since the 1930s, Liberals have projected an image of competence and compromise while staying close to the political centre.

New Democratic Party: Founded in Ottawa in 1961, the NDP united the Canadian Labour Congress and the Co-operative Commonwealth Federation (CCF). The NDP promotes the public ownership of key industries and the redistribution of wealth. Its predecessor, the CCF, was founded in Calgary in 1932.

Progressive Conservative Party: One of Canada's oldest parties, the Conservative party initially endorsed British Tory traditions but renamed itself "progressive" in 1942. The Conservatives are the only other party to have formed majority federal governments.

POLITICS AND ELECTIONS

Registered Federal Political Parties
(as of October 2000)

Federal political parties can only be registered at election time, when they qualify for registration by fielding at least 50 candidates by the nomination deadline in a forthcoming election. In between elections, parties can be founded and organized, and can apply for registration to the chief electoral officer.

Bloc Québécois—Rm 055, 1200 Papineau Ave, Montréal, QC H2K 4R5; Tel: (514) 526-3000; Fax: (514) 526-2868; leader: Gilles Duceppe. Website: http://www.blocquebecois.parl.gc.ca

Canadian Action Party—Ste 302, 99 Atlantic Ave, Toronto, ON M6K 3J8; Tel: (416) 535-4144; Fax: (416) 535-6325; leader: The Hon. Paul Hellyer. Website: http://www.canadianactionparty.ca

Canadian Reform Conservative Alliance—600–833 4th Ave SW, Calgary, AB T2P 0K5; Tel.: (403) 269-1990; Fax: (403) 269-4077; leader: Stockwell Day. Website: http://www.canadianalliance.ca/index_e.htm

Christian Heritage Party of Canada—Ste 200, Heritage Pl, 155 Queen St, Ottawa, ON K1P 6L1; Tel: (613) 788-3716; Fax: (819) 457-9242; leader: Ronald O. Gray. Website: http://www.chp.ca

The Green Party—244 Gerrard St E, Toronto, ON M5A 2G2; Tel.: (416) 929-2397; Fax (416) 929-2397; leader: Dr. Joan Russow. Website: http://green.ca

Liberal Party of Canada—Ste 400, 81 Metcalfe St, Ottawa, ON K1P 6M8; Tel: (613) 237-0740; Fax: (613) 235-7208; leader: The Right Hon. Jean Chrétien. Website: http://www.liberal.ca

Marxist-Leninist Party of Canada—Ste 405, 396 Cooper St, Ottawa, ON K2P 2H7; Tel: (613) 565-6446; Fax: (613) 565-8787; leader: Sandra Smith. Website: http://www.cpcml.ca

Natural Law Party of Canada—500 Wilbrod St, Ottawa, ON K1N 6N2; Tel: (613) 565-8517; Fax: (613) 565-1596; leader: Dr. Neil Paterson. Website: http://www.natural-law.ca

New Democratic Party—Ste 900, 81 Metcalfe St, Ottawa, ON K1P 6K7; Tel: (613) 236-3613; Fax: (613) 230-9950; leader: Alexa McDonough. Website: http://www.ndp.ca

Progressive Conservative Party of Canada—5th Flr, Ste 501, 275 Slater St, Ottawa, ON K1P 5H9; Tel: (613) 238-6111; Fax: (613) 238-7429; leader: The Right Hon. Joe Clark. Website: http://www.pcparty.ca

Accepted for registration:

Communist Party of Canada—290A Danforth Ave, Toronto, ON M4K 1N6; Tel: (416) 469-2446; Fax: (416) 469-4063; leader: Miguel Figueroa. Website: http://www.communistparty.ca

Rest of Canada (ROC) Party—210–320 Sioux Rd, Sherwood Park, AB T8A 3X6; Tel.: (780) 464-3560; Fax: (780) 464-3574; leader: Ace Cetinski. Website: http://www.rocparty.ca/home.htm

Source: *Elections Canada*

Federal Election Results, 1867–1997

🍁 1867–1904

	1867	1872	1874	1878	1882	1887	1891	1896	1900	1904
Canada										
Conservative	101	103	73	137	139	123	123	89	80	75
Liberal	80	97	133	69	71	92	92	117	133	139
Other	—	—	—	—	—	—	—	7	—	—
Prince Edward Island[1]										
Conservative	—	—	—	5	4	—	2	3	2	3
Liberal	—	—	6	1	2	6	4	2	3	1
Nova Scotia										
Conservative	3	11	4	14	15	14	16	10	5	—
Liberal	16	10	17	7	6	7	5	10	15	18
New Brunswick										
Conservative	7	7	5	5	10	10	13	9	5	6
Liberal	8	9	11	11	6	6	3	5	9	7
Quebec										
Conservative	45	38	32	45	48	33	30	16	7	11
Liberal	20	27	33	20	17	32	35	49	58	54
Other	—	—	—	—	—	—	—	5	—	—
Ontario										
Conservative	46	38	24	59	54	52	48	44	55	48
Liberal	36	50	64	29	37	40	44	43	37	38
Other	—	—	—	—	—	—	—	5	—	—
Manitoba[2]										
Conservative	—	3	2	3	2	4	4	4	4	3
Liberal	—	1	2	1	3	1	1	2	3	7
Other	—	—	—	—	—	—	—	1	—	—
British Columbia[3]										
Conservative	—	6	6	6	6	6	6	2	2	—
Liberal	—	—	—	—	—	—	—	4	4	7
Yukon[4]										
Conservative	—	—	—	—	—	—	—	—	—	1
Northwest Territories[2]										
Conservative	—	—	—	—	—	4	4	1	—	3
Liberal	—	—	—	—	—	—	—	2	4	7
Other	—	—	—	—	—	—	—	1	—	—

🍁 1908–1940

	1908	1911	1917[7]	1921	1925	1926	1930	1935	1940
Canada									
Conservative	85	133	153	50	116	91	137	39	39
Liberal	133	86	82	117	101	116	88	171	178
Progressive	—	—	—	64	25	—	2	—	—
CCF	—	—	—	—	—	—	—	7	8
Social Credit	—	—	—	—	—	—	—	17	10
Other	3	2	—	4	3	38	18	11	10
Prince Edward Island									
Conservative	1	2	2	—	2	1	3	—	—
Liberal	3	2	2	4	2	3	1	4	4
Nova Scotia									
Conservative	6	9	12	—	11	12	10	—	1
Liberal	12	9	4	16	3	2	4	12	10
CCF	—	—	—	—	—	—	—	—	1

(1) Entered Confederation July 1, 1873. (2) Entered Confederation July 15, 1870. (3) Entered Confederation July 20, 1871. (4) Entered Confederation June 13, 1898. (5) Entered Confederation Mar. 31, 1949. (6) Entered Confederation Sept. 1, 1905. (7) For the 1917 election, Conservative refers to "Unionists," a coalition of Conservatives and pro-conscription Liberals; Liberals, for the 1917 election, are sometimes called "Laurier Liberals" because of their support for Laurier's anti-conscription stand. (8) The New Democratic Party (NDP) replaced the Co-operative Commonwealth Federation (CCF) in Aug. 1961. (9) From 1908–1949 shared one representative. In 1953, the number was increased to two.

180 *The Nation*

❦ 1908–1940	1908	1911	1917[7]	1921	1925	1926	1930	1935	1940
New Brunswick									
Conservative	2	5	7	5	10	7	10	1	5
Liberal	11	8	4	5	1	4	1	9	5
Other	—	—	—	1	—	—	—	—	—
Quebec									
Conservative	11	27	3	—	4	4	24	5	—
Liberal	53	37	62	65	60	60	40	55	61
Other	1	1	—	—	1	1	1	5	4
Ontario									
Conservative	48	72	74	37	68	53	59	25	25
Liberal	36	36	8	21	12	23	22	56	55
Progressive	—	—	—	24	2	4	—	—	—
Other	2	1	—	—	—	2	1	1	2
Manitoba									
Conservative	8	8	14	—	7	—	11	1	1
Liberal	2	2	1	2	1	4	1	12	14
CCF	—	—	—	—	—	—	—	2	1
Progressive	—	—	—	12	7	4	—	—	—
Other	—	—	—	1	2	9	5	2	1
Saskatchewan[6]									
Conservative	1	1	16	—	—	—	8	1	2
Liberal	9	9	—	1	15	16	11	16	12
CCF	—	—	—	—	—	—	—	2	5
Progressive	—	—	—	15	6	5	2	—	—
Social Credit	—	—	—	—	—	—	—	2	—
Other	—	—	—	—	—	—	—	—	2
Alberta[6]									
Conservative	3	1	11	—	3	1	4	1	—
Liberal	4	6	1	—	4	3	3	1	7
Progressive	—	—	—	10	9	—	—	—	—
Social Credit	—	—	—	—	—	—	—	15	10
United Farmers of Alta.	—	—	—	—	—	11	9	—	—
Other	—	—	—	2	—	1	—	—	—
British Columbia									
Conservative	5	7	13	7	10	12	7	5	4
Liberal	2	—	—	3	3	1	5	6	10
CCF	—	—	—	—	—	—	—	3	1
Progressive	—	—	—	2	1	—	—	—	—
Social Credit	—	—	—	—	—	—	—	—	—
Other	—	—	—	1	—	1	2	2	1
Yukon and Northwest Territories[9]									
Conservative	—	1	—	1	1	1	1	—	1
Liberal	1	—	—	—	—	—	—	—	—
Other	—	—	—	—	—	—	—	1	—

❦ 1945–1968	1945	1949	1953	1957	1958	1962	1963	1965	1968
Canada									
Conservative	67	41	51	112	208	116	95	97	72
Liberal	125	190	170	105	48	99	129	131	155
NDP (CCF)[8]	28	13	23	25	8	19	17	21	22
Social Credit	13	10	15	19	—	30	24	5	—
Other	12	8	6	4	1	1	—	11	15
Newfoundland[5]									
Conservative	—	2	—	2	2	1	—	—	6
Liberal	—	5	7	5	5	6	7	7	1
NDP (CCF)	—	—	—	—	—	—	—	—	—
Prince Edward Island									
Conservative	1	1	1	4	4	4	2	4	4
Liberal	3	3	3	—	—	—	2	—	—

Politics and Elections

🍁 1945–1968

	1945	1949	1953	1957	1958	1962	1963	1965	1968
Nova Scotia									
Conservative	3	2	1	10	12	9	7	10	10
Liberal	8	10	10	2	—	2	5	2	1
NDP (CCF)	1	1	1	—	—	1	—	—	—
New Brunswick									
Conservative	3	2	3	5	7	4	4	4	5
Liberal	7	7	7	5	3	6	6	6	5
Other	—	1	—	—	—	—	—	—	—
Quebec									
Conservative	1	2	4	9	50	14	8	8	4
Liberal	54	66	66	63	25	35	47	56	56
NDP (CCF)	—	—	—	—	—	—	—	—	—
Social Credit	—	—	—	—	—	26	20	—	—
Other	10	5	5	3	—	—	—	11	14
Ontario									
Conservative	48	25	33	61	67	35	27	25	17
Liberal	34	56	50	20	14	43	52	51	64
NDP (CCF)	—	—	—	3	3	6	6	9	6
Other	—	2	2	1	1	1	—	—	1
Manitoba									
Conservative	2	1	3	8	14	11	10	10	5
Liberal	10	12	8	1	—	1	2	1	5
NDP (CCF)	5	3	3	5	—	2	2	3	3
Saskatchewan									
Conservative	1	1	1	3	16	16	17	17	5
Liberal	2	14	5	4	—	1	—	—	2
NDP (CCF)	18	5	11	10	1	—	—	—	6
Alberta									
Conservative	2	2	2	3	17	15	14	15	15
Liberal	2	5	4	1	—	—	1	—	4
NDP (CCF)	—	—	—	—	—	—	—	—	—
Social Credit	13	10	11	13	—	2	2	2	—
British Columbia									
Conservative	5	3	3	7	18	6	4	3	—
Liberal	5	11	8	2	—	4	7	7	16
NDP (CCF)	4	3	7	7	4	10	9	9	7
Social Credit	—	—	4	6	—	2	2	3	—
Other	2	1	—	—	—	—	—	—	—
Yukon[9]									
Conservative	1	—	—	—	1	1	1	1	1
Liberal	—	1	2	1	—	—	—	—	—
NDP (CCF)	—	—	—	—	—	—	—	—	—
Northwest Territories[9]									
Conservative	n.a.	n.a.	n.a.	—	—	—	1	—	—
Liberal	n.a.	n.a.	n.a.	1	1	1	—	1	1
NDP (CCF)	n.a.	n.a.	n.a.	—	—	—	—	—	—

🍁 1972–1997

	1972	1974	1979	1980	1984	1988	1993	1997
Canada								
Bloc Québécois	—	—	—	—	—	—	54	44
Conservative	107	95	136	103	211	169	2	20
Liberal	109	141	114	147	40	83	177	155
NDP (CCF)[8]	31	16	26	32	30	43	9	21
Reform	—	—	—	—	—	—	52	60
Social Credit	15	11	6	—	—	—	—	—
Other	2	1	—	—	1	—	1	1
Newfoundland								
Conservative	4	3	2	2	4	2	—	3
Liberal	3	4	4	5	3	5	7	4
NDP (CCF)	—	—	1	—	—	—	—	—
Prince Edward Island								
Conservative	3	3	4	2	3	—	—	—
Liberal	1	1	—	2	1	4	4	4

1972–1997

	1972	1974	1979	1980	1984	1988	1993	1997
Nova Scotia								
Conservative	10	8	8	6	9	5	—	5
Liberal	1	2	2	5	2	6	11	—
NDP (CCF)	—	1	1	—	—	—	—	6
New Brunswick								
Conservative	5	3	4	3	9	5	1	5
Liberal	5	6	6	7	1	5	9	3
NDP	—	—	—	—	—	—	—	2
Other	—	1	—	—	—	—	—	—
Quebec								
Bloc Québécois	—	—	—	—	—	—	54	44
Conservative	2	3	2	1	58	63	1	5
Liberal	56	60	67	74	17	12	19	26
NDP (CCF)	—	—	—	—	—	—	—	—
Social Credit	15	11	6	—	—	—	—	—
Other	1	—	—	—	—	—	1	—
Ontario								
Conservative	40	25	57	38	67	46	—	1
Liberal	36	55	32	52	14	43	98	101
NDP (CCF)	11	8	6	5	13	10	—	—
Reform	—	—	—	—	—	—	1	—
Other	1	—	—	—	1	—	—	1
Manitoba								
Conservative	8	9	7	5	9	7	—	1
Liberal	2	2	2	2	1	5	12	6
NDP (CCF)	3	2	5	7	4	2	1	4
Reform	—	—	—	—	—	—	1	3
Saskatchewan								
Conservative	7	8	10	7	9	4	—	—
Liberal	1	3	—	—	—	—	5	1
NDP (CCF)	5	2	4	7	5	10	5	5
Reform	—	—	—	—	—	—	4	8
Alberta								
Conservative	19	19	21	21	21	25	—	—
Liberal	—	—	—	—	—	—	4	2
NDP (CCF)	—	—	—	—	—	1	—	—
Reform	—	—	—	—	—	—	22	24
British Columbia								
Conservative	8	13	19	16	19	12	—	—
Liberal	4	8	1	—	1	1	6	6
NDP (CCF)	11	2	8	12	8	19	2	3
Reform	—	—	—	—	—	—	24	25
Yukon								
Conservative	1	1	1	1	1	—	—	—
Liberal	—	—	—	—	—	—	—	—
NDP (CCF)	—	—	—	—	—	1	1	1
Northwest Territories								
Conservative	—	—	1	1	2	—	—	—
Liberal	—	—	—	—	—	2	2	2
NDP (CCF)	1	1	1	1	—	—	—	—

Federal Election Districts

*E*very 10 years, after Statistics Canada publishes new national population figures in its census results, the number of seats in the House of Commons changes. The number of seats and the redrawing of electoral boundaries change according to formulas in the Constitution Act and the Electoral Boundaries Readjustment Act.

In 1992, following the release of population figures in the 1991 census, the Canada Gazette published the chief electoral officer's calculations affecting federal representation. The number of seats in the House of Commons subsequently rose from 295 to 301, and the boundaries of federal electoral districts changed to reflect movements in Canada's population.

Statistics Canada's next census is scheduled for 2001; future changes to representation in the House of Commons could be made known as early as 2002.

Federal Election 1997—Total Votes by Province and Party

	Bloc Québécois	Conservative	Liberal	New Democrat	Reform	Other[1]
Newfoundland	—	82 214	84 657	49 125	5 632	1 952
Prince Edward Island	—	26 992	31 584	10 671	1 055	219
Nova Scotia	—	143 754	132 456	142 078	45 165	3 684
New Brunswick	—	139 381	131 215	73 229	52 248	2 518
Quebec	1 386 056	811 381	1 322 320	70 508	10 766	76 623
Ontario	—	871 439	2 244 920	495 091	886 825	134 611
Manitoba	—	84 480	163 214	110 216	112 805	5 193
Saskatchewan	—	34 457	109 196	136 633	159 311	2 741
Alberta	—	162 510	243 549	60 670	577 578	12 376
British Columbia	—	94 809	438 599	276 903	655 279	56 790
Yukon	—	1 928	3 036	4 002	3 493	1 370
Northwest Territories	—	3 425	8 868	4 289	2 413	1 567
Total votes cast	1 368 056	2 456 770	4 913 614	1 433 415	2 512 570	299 644

Source: *Elections Canada* (1) Includes Canada Action, Christian Heritage, Green, Marxist-Leninists, Natural Law and Independents

Federal Election, 1997—% of Popular Vote by Province and Party

	Bloc Québécois	Conservative	Liberal	New Democrat	Reform	Other[1]
Newfoundland	—	36.77	37.86	21.97	2.52	.87
Prince Edward Island	—	38.28	44.79	15.13	1.50	.31
Nova Scotia	—	30.77	28.35	30.41	9.67	.79
New Brunswick	—	34.97	32.92	18.37	13.11	.63
Quebec	37.38	22.17	36.13	1.93	.29	2.09
Ontario	—	18.81	48.46	10.69	19.14	2.91
Manitoba	—	17.75	34.30	23.16	23.70	1.09
Saskatchewan	—	7.79	24.69	30.89	36.02	.62
Alberta	—	15.38	23.05	5.74	54.66	1.17
British Columbia	—	6.23	28.81	18.19	43.04	3.73
Yukon	—	13.94	21.95	28.94	25.26	9.91
Northwest Territories	—	16.66	43.13	20.86	11.74	7.62
Canada	10.39	18.65	37.31	10.88	19.08	2.27
Total seats	44	20	155	21	60	1

Source: *Elections Canada*

Voter Turnout at Canada's Federal Elections, 1867–1997

(percentage of eligible voters casting votes)

Year	Voter turnout[1]	Year	Voter turnout[1]	Year	Voter turnout[1]	Year	Voter turnout[1]
1867	73%	1904	84%	1940	71%	1968	76%
1872	70	1908	79	1945	76	1972	77
1874	75	1911	72	1949	75	1974	71
1878	71	1917	90	1953	68	1979	76
1882	72	1921	71	1957	75	1980	69
1887	70	1925	69	1958	81	1984	75
1891	65	1926	70	1962	80	1988	76
1896	61	1930	76	1963	80	1993	70
1900	79	1935	75	1965	76	1997	67

Source: *Elections Canada*

[1]Percentage of actual votes to eligible voters. In many early general elections, several electoral districts were won by acclamation; hence, no eligible voters nor actual votes were recorded. Furthermore, in some of the more remote districts, votes were cast but no voters' lists had been prepared.

FOCUS ON...

The New Canada Elections Act

On Feb. 28, 2000, Parliament passed the new *Canada Elections Act*. The law introduced changes that will affect election advertising, campaign financing, opinion poll reporting and other issues during the next federal election. The changes aim at providing more information to voters who wish to make informed choices when they cast their ballots.

First, the new law affects **third-party election advertising**. Henceforth, a third party (i.e., an individual or group other than a candidate, a registered political party or a riding association) may spend no more than $150,000 nationally on election advertising; however, a third party may spend no more than $3,000 in any single riding to promote or oppose a candidate. If expenses for election advertising exceed $500 during an election campaign, a third party must register immediately with the chief electoral officer, appoint a financial agent and file an expense report. The report must include the names and addresses of all donors who contributed more than $200; the reporting period begins six months before the election was called and ends on election day. If a numbered company donates more than $200, the report must name the president or chief executive officer. The chief electoral officer will publish this information.

Third-party election ads must identify their sponsors. Third party advertisers cannot issue tax receipts, receive voters' lists or receive reimbursements for expenses.

The new *Canada Elections Act* also requires **greater disclosure of electoral financing**. Registered political parties and candidates must submit more detailed financial reports than they have in the past. Reports must include balance sheets that state all assets, liabilities, loans, securities and sources of income. For each riding, registered political parties must report all transfers of funds made to candidates, riding associations and trust funds created for a candidate's election. Parties, candidates and third parties must report the names and addresses of all donors who give more than $200 to a campaign; again, if a numbered company gives more than $200, the report must name the president or chief executive officer. All reports (including new *audited* reports of trust fund transactions) must be submitted to the chief electoral officer, who will publish the information.

The law also requires higher standards for the **reporting of election surveys**. The first media outlet that releases the results of a new survey, or opinion poll, must publish the survey's methodology at the same time. Other media outlets that broadcast or publish the same results within the next 24 hours must also describe the survey's methodology. Furthermore, the opinion poll's sponsor must provide a detailed description of the survey's methodology to anyone who requests it for no more than 25 cents per page.

The description of the survey's methodology must include the name of the survey's sponsor; the name of the person or organization that conducted the survey; the date or period when the polling was done; the population from which the survey sample was drawn; the number of people contacted to participate; and the margin of error. If the survey was not conducted according to recognized statistical methods, the sponsor's description must say so. In addition, print and Internet publishers must list the survey questions and describe how people can get copies of the report from the poll's sponsor.

Finally, the new *Canada Elections Act* shortens the **bans on election advertising and election-survey publishing**. In the past, the law banned partisan election advertising for one week at the start of a campaign and for two days at the campaign's end. The law also prohibited the publication of new election survey results during the last three days of the election period. Henceforth, the law will ban the broadcasting and publishing of election advertising and new survey results only on election day. The ban will affect all registered political parties, candidates and third parties; it will also affect most media (e.g., print, broadcast, Internet) but not billboards and signs.

Federal Political Party Leaders

■ Progressive Conservative[1] Party

Leader	Term
Sir John A. Macdonald	1854–June 6, 1891
Sir J.J.C. Abbott	June 16, 1891–Dec. 5, 1892
Sir John Thompson	Dec. 5, 1892–Dec. 12, 1894
Sir Mackenzie Bowell	Dec. 21, 1894–Apr. 27, 1896
Sir Charles Tupper	May 1, 1896–Feb. 5, 1901
Sir Robert Borden	Feb. 6, 1901–July 10, 1920
Arthur Meighen	July 10, 1920–Oct. 11, 1926
Hugh Guthrie[2]	Oct. 11, 1926–Oct. 12, 1927
R.B. Bennett	Oct. 12, 1927–July 7, 1938
R.J. Manion	July 7, 1938–May 13, 1940
R.B. Hanson[2]	May 13, 1940–Nov. 12, 1941
Arthur Meighen	Nov. 12, 1941–Dec. 11, 1942
John Bracken	Dec. 11, 1942–Oct. 2, 1948
George A. Drew	Oct. 2, 1948–Dec. 14, 1956
John G. Diefenbaker	Dec. 14, 1956–Sept. 9, 1967
Robert L. Stanfield	Sept. 9, 1967–Feb. 22, 1976
Joe Clark	Feb. 22, 1976–Feb. 8, 1983
Erik Nielsen[2]	Feb. 9, 1983–June 11, 1983
Brian Mulroney	June 11, 1983–June 13, 1993
Kim Campbell	June 13, 1993–Dec. 13, 1993
Jean Charest	Dec. 14, 1993–Apr. 3, 1998
Elsie Wayne	Apr. 6, 1998–Nov. 13, 1998
Joe Clark	Nov. 14, 1998–

■ Liberal Party

Leader	Term
Robert Baldwin	1804–1858
Louis-H. Lafontaine	1807–1864
George Brown	1867–1872
Alexander Mackenzie	Mar. 6, 1873–Apr. 27, 1880
Edward Blake	May 4, 1880–June 2, 1887
Sir Wilfrid Laurier	June 1887–Feb. 17, 1919
Daniel D. McKenzie[2]	Feb. 1919–Aug. 1919
W.L. Mackenzie King	Aug. 7, 1919–Aug. 7, 1948
Louis St. Laurent	Aug. 7, 1948–Jan. 16, 1958
Lester B. Pearson	Jan. 16, 1958–Apr. 2, 1968
Pierre E. Trudeau	Apr. 6, 1968–June 16, 1984
John N. Turner	June 16, 1984–June 23, 1990
Jean Chrétien	June 23, 1990–

■ New Democratic Party[3]

Leader	Term
James S. Woodsworth	Aug. 1932–July 1942
M.J. Coldwell	July 1942–Aug. 1960
Hazen Argue	Aug. 1960–Aug. 1961
Tommy Douglas	Aug. 1961–Apr. 1971
David Lewis	Apr. 24, 1971–July 7, 1975
Ed Broadbent	July 7, 1975–Dec. 2, 1989
Audrey McLaughlin	Dec. 2, 1989–Oct. 1995
Alexa McDonough	Oct. 14, 1995–

■ Bloc Québécois

Leader	Term
Lucien Bouchard	June 15, 1991–Jan. 18, 1996
Michel Gauthier	Feb. 17, 1996–Mar. 15, 1997
Gilles Duceppe	Mar. 16, 1997–

■ Canadian Reform Conservative Alliance[4]

Leader	Term
E. Preston Manning	Nov. 1, 1987–July 8, 2000
Stockwell Day	July 8, 2000–

(1) Name changed from Conservative to Progressive Conservative Dec. 1942. (2) Interim leader appointed to fill a vacancy until a party leadership convention could be held. (3) Prior to Aug. 1961 party was called the Co-operative Commonwealth Federation (CCF). (4) Before Jan. 2000, party was called the Reform Party of Canada

Provincial Election Results

■ Newfoundland

	1971	1972	1975	1979	1982	1985	1989	1993	1996	1999
Liberal	20	9	16	19	8	15	31	35	37	32
Progressive Conservative	21	33	30	33	44	36	21	16	9	14
New Democratic	—	—	—	—	—	1	—	1	1	2
Other	1	—	5	—	—	—	—	—	1	—
Size of legislature	42	42	51	52	52	52	52	52	48	48

■ Prince Edward Island

	1970	1974	1978	1979	1982	1985	1989	1993	1996	2000
Liberal	27	26	17	11	14	21	30	31	8	1
Progressive Conservative	5	6	15	21	18	11	2	1	18	26
New Democratic	—	—	—	—	—	—	—	—	1	—
Size of legislature	32	32	32	32	32	32	32	32	27	27

■ Nova Scotia

	1967	1970	1974	1978	1981	1984	1988	1993	1998	1999
Liberal	6	23	31	17	13	6	21	40	19	11
New Democratic[1]	—	2	3	4	1	3	2	3	19	11
Progressive Conservative[2]	40	21	12	31	37	42	28	9	14	30
Other	—	—	—	—	1	1	1	—	—	—
Size of legislature	46	46	46	52	52	52	52	52	52	52

■ New Brunswick

	1963	1967	1970	1974	1978	1982	1987	1991	1995	1999
Liberal	332	32	26	25	28	18	58	46	48	10
Progressive Conservative[3]	20	26	32	33	30	39	—	3	6	44
New Democratic	—	—	—	—	—	1	—	1	1	1
Confederation of Regions	—	—	—	—	—	—	—	8	—	—
Size of legislature	52	58	58	58	58	58	58	58	55	55

■ Quebec

	1962	1966	1970	1973	1976	1981	1985	1989	1994	1998
Crédit Social	—	—	12	2	1	—	—	—	—	—
Equality	—	—	—	—	—	—	—	4	—	—
Liberal	63	50	72	102	26	42	99	92	47	48
Parti Québécois[4]	—	—	7	6	71	80	23	29	77	76
Union Nationale	31	56	17	—	11	—	—	—	—	—
Other	1	2	—	—	1	—	—	—	1	1
Size of legislature	95	108	108	110	110	122	122	125	125	125

■ Ontario

	1967	1971	1975	1977	1981	1985	1987	1990	1995	1999
Liberal	28	20	36	34	34	48	95	36	30	35
New Democratic[5]	20	19	38	33	21	25	19	74	17	9
Progressive Conservative[3]	69	78	51	58	70	52	16	20	82	59
Independent	—	—	—	—	—	—	—	—	1	—
Size of legislature	117	117	125	125	125	125	130	130	130	103

Politics and Elections

■ Manitoba

	1966	1969	1973	1977	1981	1986	1988	1990	1995	1999
Liberal	14	4	5	1	—	1	20	7	3	1
New Democratic[5]	11	28	31	23	34	30	12	20	23	32
Progressive Conservative[6]	31	22	21	33	23	26	25	30	31	24
Other	1	3	—	—	—	—	—	—	—	—
Size of legislature	57	57	57	57	57	57	57	57	57	57

■ Saskatchewan

	1964	1967	1971	1975	1978	1982	1986	1991	1995	1999
Liberal	33	35	15	15	—	—	1	1	11	4
New Democratic[7]	25	24	45	39	44	8	25	55	42	29
Progressive Conservative[8]	1	—	—	7	17	56	38	10	5	—
Saskatchewan Party	—	—	—	—	—	—	—	—	—	25
Size of legislature	59	59	60	61	61	64	64	66	58	58

■ Alberta

	1963	1967	1971	1975	1979	1982	1986	1989	1993	1997
Liberal	2	3	—	—	—	—	4	8	32[9]	18
New Democratic[1]	—	—	1	1	1	2	16	16	—	2
Progressive Conservative[6]	—	6	49	69	74	75	61	59	51	63
Social Credit	60	55	24	4	4	—	—	—	—	—
Other	1	1	1	1	—	2	2	—	—	—
Size of legislature	63	65	75	75	79	79	83	83	83	83

■ British Columbia

	1963	1966	1969	1972	1975	1979	1983	1986	1991	1996
Liberal	5	6	5	5	1	—	—	—	17	33
New Democratic[5]	14	16	12	38	18	26	21	22	51	39
Progressive Conservative[6]	—	—	—	2	1	—	—	—	—	—
Social Credit	33	33	38	10	35	31	35	47	7	—
Other	—	—	—	—	—	—	—	1	—	3
Size of legislature	52	55	55	55	55	57	57	69	75	75

■ Yukon

	1978	1982	1985	1989	1992	1996	2000
Liberal	2	—	2	—	1	3	10
New Democratic	1	6	8	9	6	11	6
Progressive Conservative	11	10	6	7	—	—	—
Yukon Party	—	—	—	—	7	3	1
Independent	2	—	—	—	3	—	—
Size of Legislature	16	16	16	16	17	17	17

(1) Known as the Co-operative Commonwealth Federation until 1962. (2) Known as the Conservative Party until 1946. (3) Known as the Conservative Party until 1943. (4) Formed in 1968. (5) Known as the Co-operative Commonwealth Federation until 1961. (6) Known as the Conservative Party until 1944. (7) Known as the Co-operative Commonwealth Federation until 1967. (8) Known as the Conservative Party until 1945. (9) One Alberta Liberal became an independent.

Provincial Party Leaders[1]

(as of October 2000)

■ Newfoundland

Progressive Conservative Party	Liberal Party	New Democratic Party
A. Brian Peckford 1979–89	Len Sterling 1982–84	Peter Fenwick 1981–89
Tom Rideout 1989–91	Stephen Neary 1984–85	Cle Newhook 1989–92
Len Simms 1991–95	Leo Barry 1985–87	Jack Harris 1992–
Lynn Verge................. 1995–96	Clyde Wells 1987–96	
Loyola Sullivan............. 1996–98	Brian Tobin............... 1996–	
Ed Byrne.................. 1998–		

■ Prince Edward Island

Progressive Conservative Party	Liberal Party	New Democratic Party
James M. Lee 1981–87	Alex Campbell 1965–78	Douglas Murray 1979–81
Leone Bagnall 1987–88	Bennett Campbell 1978–81	David Burke 1982–83
Melbourne Gass 1988–90	Joseph Ghiz 1981–93	Jim Mayne 1983–89
Pat Mella 1990–96	Catherine Callbeck 1993–96	Larry Duchesne 1991–95
P. Binns 1996–	Keith Milligan 1996–99	Herb Dickieson 1995–
	Wayne Carew 1999–	

■ Nova Scotia

Progressive Conservative Party[2]	Liberal Party	New Democratic Party[3]
George I. Smith 1967–71	Vincent J. MacLean 1985	James Aitchison 1966–68
John M. Buchanan 1971–90	J. William Gillis 1985–86	Jeremy Akerman 1968–80
Donald Cameron 1991–93	Vincent J. MacLean 1986–92	Alexa McDonough 1980–94
Terence R.B. Donahoe 1993–95	John Savage 1992–97	John Holme............... 1994–96
Dr. John Hamm 1995–	Russell MacLellan 1997–2000	Robert Chisholm 1996–2000
	Wayne Gaudet 2000–	Helen MacDonald 2000–

■ New Brunswick

Progressive Conservative Party	Liberal Party	New Democratic Party
Richard B. Hatfield 1969–87	Robert Higgins 1971–78	Elizabeth Weir 1988–
Malcolm MacLeod 1987–89	Joe Daigle 1978–8	
Barbara Baird Filliter..... 1989–91	Doug Young 1982–83	
Dennis Cochrane 1991–95	Frank McKenna 1985–97	
Bernard Valcourt.......... 1995–97	Ray Frenette (interim)..... 1997–98	
Bernard Lord 1997–	Camille Theriault 1998–	

■ Quebec

Parti Québécois	Parti Libéral	Action démocratique
René Lévesque 1968–85	Robert Bourassa 1970–77	Mario Dumont 1994–
Pierre-Marc Johnson 1985–88	Claude Ryan 1978–82	
Jacques Parizeau 1988–96	Robert Bourassa 1983–94	
Lucien Bouchard 1996–	Daniel Johnson 1994–98	
	Jean Charest.............. 1998–	

■ Ontario

Progressive Conservative Party	Liberal Party	New Democratic Party[4]
Frank Miller 1985	Stuart Smith 1977–81	Stephen H. Lewis 1970–78
Larry Grossman 1985–87	David Peterson 1982–90	Michael Cassidy 1978–82
Andrew Brandt 1987–90	Lyn McLeod 1992–96	Bob Rae 1982–96
Mike Harris 1990–	Dalton McGinty 1996–	Howard Hampton 1996–

Manitoba

Progressive Conservative Party	Liberal Party	New Democratic Party [4]
Walter C. Weir ... 1967–70	Paul Edwards ... 1993–96	A. Russell Paulley ... 1960–69
Sidney Spivak ... 1971–75	Ginny Hasselfield ... 1996–98	Edward R. Schreyer ... 1969–79
Sterling Lyon ... 1975–83	Neil Gaudry ... 1998	Howard R. Pawley ... 1979–88
Gary Filmon ... 1983–2000	Jon Gerrard ... 1998–	Gary Doer ... 1988–
Bonnie Mitchelson ... 2000–		

Saskatchewan

Progressive Conservative Party	Liberal Party	New Democratic Party [4]
Party inactive as of Nov. 9, 1997	Ron Osika (interim) ... 1996	John H. Brockelbank ... 1941–44
	Jim Melenchuk ... 1996–	Tommy Douglas ... 1944–61
Saskatchewan Party		Woodrow Lloyd ... 1961–70
Ken Karwetz ... 1997–98		Allan Blakeney ... 1970–78
Elwin Hermanson ... 1998–		Roy Romanow ... 1987–2000[5]

Alberta

Progressive Conservative Party	Liberal Party	New Democratic Party [4]
Milt Harradance ... 1962–64	Laurence Decore ... 1988–94	W. Grant Notley ... 1968–84
Peter Lougheed ... 1965–85	Betty Hewes (interim) ... 1994	Ray Martin ... 1984–94
Donald R. Getty ... 1985–92	Grant Mitchell ... 1994–98	Ross Harvey ... 1994–96
Ralph P. Klein ... 1992–	Nancy MacBeth ... 1998–	Pam Barrett ... 1996–2000
		Raj Pannu ... 2000–

British Columbia

Reform Party of British Columbia	New Democratic Party	Liberal
Ron Gamble ... 1993–95	Dave Barrett ... 1969–84	Jevington Blair Tothill ... 1979–81
Jack Weisgerber ... 1995–97	Bob Skelly ... 1984–87	Shirley McLoughlin ... 1981–83
Wilf Hanni ... 1997–98	Michael Harcourt ... 1987–96	Arthur Lee ... 1984–87
Bill Vander Zalm ... 1998–	Glen Clark ... 1996–99	Gordon Wilson ... 1987–93
	Dan Miller ... 1999–2000	Gordon Campbell ... 1993–
	Ujjal Dosanjh ... 2000–	

Yukon

Progressive Conservative Party	Liberal Party	New Democratic Party
Willard Phelps ... 1985–91	Ron Veale ... 1980–85	Fred Berger ... 1978–81
Chris Young ... 1991	Roger Coles ... 1985–92	Tony Penikett ... 1981–95
	Paul Theriault ... 1992–95	Piers McDonald ... 1995–2000
Yukon Party	Ken Taylor ... 1995–98	Trevor Harding ... 2000–
John Ostashek ... 1991–2000	Pat Duncan ... 1998–	
Peter Jenkins ... 2000–		

(1) Includes up to 5 most recent leaders of the major parties; for years no leader is listed, the leadership was vacant or there was an interim leader.
(2) Known as the Conservative Party until 1946.
(3) Known as the Co-operative Commonwealth Federation until 1962.
(4) Known as the Co-operative Commonwealth Federation until 1961.
(5) Roy Romanow resigned Sept 25, 2000. Leadership vote to be held.

DEFENCE

Canadian security policy is based on three elements: defence and collective security, arms control and disarmament, and the peaceful resolution of disputes. The Department of National Defence and the Canadian Forces support this policy by their contributions to strategic deterrence, conventional defence, sovereignty, peacekeeping and arms control.

In addition, the Department of National Defence provides special support to other government departments in areas such as search and rescue, fisheries patrols, enforcement of drug prohibitions, disaster relief, and aid to civil powers in law enforcement. These tasks are carried out both in emergencies and where it complements military surveillance and control responsibilities.

The Defence Department's website can be found at http://www.dnd.ca.

Canadian Regular Armed Forces Strength

Canada has an all-volunteer Armed Forces which, since 1968, has been a single body composed of what had been a separate army, navy and air force.

	Navy	Army	Air Force	Total Armed Forces
1914	379	3 000	—	3 379
1915	1 255	81 195	—	82 450
1916	1 557	274 194	—	275 751
1917	2 220	304 585	—	306 805
1918	4 792	326 258	—	331 050
1919	5 495	228 292	—	233 787
1920	1 048	4 684	—	5 732
1925	496	3 410	384	4 290
1930	783	3 510	844	5 137
1935	860	3 509	794	5 163
1939	1 585	4 169	2 191	7 945
1940	6 135	76 678	9 483	92 296
1941	17 036	194 774	48 743	260 553
1942	32 067	311 118	111 223	454 408
1943	56 259	460 387	176 307	692 953
1944	81 582	495 804	210 089	787 475
1945	92 529	494 258	174 254	761 041
1950	9 259	20 652	17 274	47 185
1951	11 082	34 986	22 359	68 427
1952	13 505	49 278	32 611	95 394
1953	15 546	48 458	40 423	104 427
1955	19 207	49 409	49 461	118 077
1960	20 675	47 185	51 737	119 597
1965	19 756	46 264	48 144	114 164
1970	—	—	—	93 353
1975	—	—	—	79 817
1980	—	—	—	80 166
1985	—	—	—	83 740
1990	—	—	—	87 976
1991	—	—	—	87 319
1992	—	—	—	84 792
1993	—	—	—	78 376
1994	—	—	—	75 949
1995	—	—	—	72 079
1996	—	—	—	61 336
1997	—	—	—	60 320
1998	—	—	—	60 942
1999	—	—	—	58 567

Source: Department of National Defence

Senior Canadian Military Personnel

(as of Oct. 1, 2000)

Chief of the Defence Staff	Gen. Maurice Baril
Vice-Chief of the Defence Staff	Vice-Admiral Gary L. Garnett
Deputy Chief of the Defence Staff	Lt.-Gen. Ray R. Henault
Chief of the Land Staff	Lt.-Gen. Bill Leach
Chief of the Maritime Staff	Vice-Admiral Greg R. Maddison
Chief of the Air Staff	Lt.-Gen. David N. Kinsman
Canadian Military Representative, North Atlantic Treaty Organization	Vice-Admiral J.A. King
Deputy Commander-in-Chief, North American Aerospace Defence	Lt.-Gen. G.E.C. Macdonald
Commander, Canadian Defence Liaison Staff (London)	Brig.-Gen. Bill Richard
Commander, Canadian Defence Liaison Staff (Washington)	Rear Admiral F.W. Gibson

Source: Department of National Defence

Canadian Military Ranks

Army/Air Force

General Officers: General, Lieutenant-General, Major-General, Brigadier-General
Senior Officers: Colonel, Lieutenant-Colonel, Major
Junior Officers: Captain, Lieutenant, Second Lieutenant, Officer Cadet
Non-commissioned Members: Chief Warrant Officer, Master Warrant Officer, Warrant Officer, Sergeant, Master Corporal, Corporal, Private

Navy

Flag Officers: Admiral, Vice-Admiral, Rear Admiral, Commodore
Senior Officers: Captain (N), Commander, Lieutenant-Commander
Junior Officers: Lieutenant (N), Sub-Lieutenant, Acting Sub-Lieutenant, Officer Cadet
Non-commissioned Members: Chief Petty Officer 1st class, Chief Petty Officer 2nd class, Petty Officer 1st class, Petty Officer 2nd class, Master Seaman, Leading Seaman, Able Seaman

Source: *Department of National Defence*

Canadian Participation in UN Peacekeeping Missions 1947–2000

Location	Year	Mission (Canadian participation)
Korea	1947–8	Supervision of elections (2)
India-Pakistan	1949–96	Supervision of ceasefire between India and Pakistan (39)
Korea	1950–53	Supervision of Armistice Agreement (6 146)
Korea	1953–	Supervise armistice agreement between North and South Korea (1)
Cambodia, Laos, Vietnam	1954–74	Supervision of withdrawal of French forces (133)
Middle East	1954–	UN Truce Supervision of 1949 armistice between Israel and Egypt, Lebanon, Jordan and Syria (11)
Egypt (Sinai)	1956–67	Supervision of withdrawal of French, British and Israeli forces (1 007)
Lebanon	1958	Ensure no infiltration across Lebanese borders (77)
Congo	1960–4	Assist in maintaining law and order (421)
West New Guinea (now West Irian)	1962–3	Maintain peace and security (13)
Yemen	1963–4	Observe withdrawal of Egyptian troops (36)
Cyprus	1964, 1974–	Maintain 1974 ceasefire, preserve peace (2).
Dominican Republic	1965–6	Observe withdrawal of OAS forces (1)
India–Pakistan border	1965–6	Supervise ceasefire (112)
Nigeria	1968–70	Observation of ceasefire (2)
Egypt (Sinai)	1973–9	Supervise redeployment of Israeli and Egyptian forces (1 145)
South Vietnam	1973	Truce supervision (248)
Syria, Israel	1974–	Supervise ceasefire on Golan Heights (185)
Southern Lebanon	1978	Confirm withdrawal of Israeli forces (117)
Sinai, Egypt	1986–	Supervise 1979 peace treaty between Israel, Egypt and US (Camp David Accord) (25)
Afghanistan	1988–90	Confirm withdrawal of Soviet forces (5)
Iran/Iraq	1988–91	Supervise ceasefire and withdrawal of forces (525)
Namibia	1989–90	Assist in transition to independence (301)
Central America	1989–92	Verify compliance with Esquipulas Agreement (174)
Afghanistan, Pakistan	1990–92	Military advisory unit (1)
Haiti	1990–91	Observe 1990 elections (11)
Persian Gulf	1990–91	Air, naval, infantry units to help secure liberation of Kuwait
Iraq-Kuwait	1991	Monitor demilitarized pre-war boundary at end of Persian Gulf War (5)
Iraq	1991–	Supervision of destruction of Iraq's nuclear, biological and chemical weapons (12); periodic enforcement of UN restrictions on Iraq's oil trade; periodic monitoring of no-fly zones over Iraq.
Western Sahara	1991–94	Monitor ceasefire; supervise referendum (34)
Angola	1991–93	Monitor ceasefire (15)
El Salvador	1991–94	Investigate human rights violations and monitor progress

		leading to military reform (55)
Former Yugoslavia and neighbouring states	1991–4	Monitor and report on the implementation of ceasefire (15); report on breaches of Geneva Convention (7)
Red Sea	1992	Naval participation in post Gulf War embargo of Iraq (250)
Cambodia	1992–93	Monitor ceasefire, establish mine awareness and monitor disarmament (240)
Yugoslavia	1992–95	Observation patrols, mine clearance, construction and maintenance of shelters (2 400)
El Salvador	1992–95	Investigate human rights violations; develop process for military reform and elections (55)
Somalia	1992–93	Headquarters personnel (12)
Somalia, Kenya	1992–3	Distribution of relief supplies (1 250)
Mozambique	1993–95	Security, monitor de-mining operations, ceasefire verification (4)
Cambodia	1993–	Assist the Cambodian Mine Action Centre in de-mining the country (7)
Somalia	1993–5	Assist in provision of relief, economic rehabilitation and political reconciliation (9)
Uganda, Rwanda	1993–94	Monitor border to enforce military embargo (3)
Haiti	1993–94	Embargo Enforcement (250)
Rwanda	1993–96	Provide security and protection for refugees and civilians, distribution of relief supplies (112)
Yugoslavia	1993–95	Enforcing no-fly zone (13)
Dominican Republic	1994	Monitor DR-Haitian border, provide technical advice to UN re: enforcement of Haitian trade embargo (15)
Haiti	1994–96	Provide secure and stable environment for training of Haitian armed forces and police and for legislative elections (500)
Haiti	1996, 1997–	Assist government of Haiti in professionalizing the Haitian National Police Force (5)
Bosnia-Herzegovina	1995–	Participate in stabilization force to allow for consolidation of peace as set out in Dayton peace agreement (1,684)
Guatemala	1997–	Verify implementation of Comprehensive Agreement on Human Rights and strengthen institutions for the protection of human rights (1)
Central African Republic	1998–	Maintain and improve security and stability following a series of mutinies, disarmament, police training, advice and technical support (55)
Central Europe	1998–99	Participate in Organization for Security and Cooperation in Europe military inspections in Macedonia and Slovakia and military evaluations in Estonia and Moldova.
Kosovo	1999	Support CF-18 fighter jets in Italy (260); support NATO land forces in Macedonia (800); coordinate humanitarian aid in Albania (10)
Mozambique	1999	Assist UN in demining the country (3)
East Timor	1999	Restore peace and security; protect and support UN assistance mission (650)

Source: *Department of National Defence*

Canadian Forces Units in Canada

National Defence Headquarters in Ottawa oversees a network of military installations across Canada. These installations are classified differently.

Canadian Forces Bases (CFBs), which are designated by the defence minister, support either land, air or naval units. Canadian Forces Stations (CFSs) are smaller than bases. Stations have fewer resources and personnel; they are organized for operations and lack support capability.

Area Support Units (ASUs) provide food, fuel, maintenance and transportation for nearby operational units. Forward Operating Locations (FOLs) are unmanned airstrips stocked with aviation fuel for use in emergencies. All FOLs are in the Arctic.

Defence

Air Force Bases:
CFB Bagotville (Que.)
CFB Cold Lake (Alta)
CFB Comox (BC)
CFB Gander (Nfld)
CFB Goose Bay (Nfld)
CFB Greenwood (NS)
CFB Moose Jaw (Sask.)
CFB North Bay (Ont.)
CFB Shearwater (NS)
CFB Trenton (Ont.)
CFB Winnipeg (Man.)

Land Force Bases:
CFB Edmonton (Alta)
CFB Gagetown (NB)
CFB Kingston (Ont.)
CFB Montreal (Que.)
CFB Petawawa (Ont.)
CFB Shilo (Man.)
CFB Suffield (Alta)

Naval Bases:
CFB Esquimalt (BC)
CFB Halifax (NS)

Training Base:
CFB Borden (Ont.)

Other Units and Locations:
ASU Longue-Pointe (Que.)
ASU Saint-Jean (Que.)
ASU Valcartier (Que.)
CFS Alert (Nunavut)
FOL Inuvik (NWT)
FOL Iqaluit (Nunavut)
FOL Rankin Inlet (Nunavut)

Source: *Department of National Defence*

Note: as of October 2000.

Humanitarian Missions

Canadian Forces have taken part in numerous humanitarian missions since 1947. Recent efforts have included hurricane disaster relief in Florida and the Caribbean; relief after the 1998 mudslides in Sarno, Italy; and aid to Turkish residents following the August 1999 earthquake.

The delivery of such aid has changed since 1947. After the 1994 medical relief mission in Rwanda, it became clear that humanitarian efforts now require a rapid response to be most effective. Canada's Disaster Assistance Response Team (DART) was created to serve as the primary component of such operations.

The four critical needs in most emergencies are medical care, clean drinking water, engineering assistance, and communications. DART was designed to include all these components and to deploy them rapidly during crises that could include natural disasters as well as humanitarian emergencies.

DART consists of 200 highly trained personnel drawn mostly from Canada's Land Force Command. The team can provide up to 40 days of emergency relief in the host country while longer term aid is organized. The medical platoon of 45 people can set up a field hospital to care for a maximum of 250 out-patients and 30 in-patients daily. The engineer troop of 40 people can construct buildings, provide power, distribute fresh water and dispose of explosives. Other members of DART provide leadership, security, transportation, communication, supplies and labour.

Year	Aid was brought to
1947	Japan
1948	British Columbia
1960	Congo, Chile
1965	Zambia
1967	India
1970	Peru
1971	Pakistan
1973	West Africa, Newfoundland
1973–79	Nicaragua
1974–89	Manitoba
1974	Saskatchewan
1979	St. Vincent
1983	Grenada
1988–91	Ethiopia
1989	Monserrat
1989–90–91	Northern Ontario
1991	Iraq
1992	Bahamas, Florida
1992–93	Somalia, CIS
1992–96	Sarajevo
1993–95	Somalia
1994, 1996	Rwanda
1996	Haiti
1996	Quebec (Saguenay floods)
1997	Manitoba
1998	Quebec, Ont., NB, Italy, Carribbean
1999	Turkey

Source: *Department of National Defence*

THE ECONOMY

Understanding the Economy: A Glossary of Terms

Appreciation: the increase in the value of a currency relative to other currencies under free market conditions.

Balance of payments: a measure of all yearly business transactions between one country and the rest of the world. It is the difference between the value of exports and imports, as well as the difference between investment money coming into and leaving the country.

Balanced budget: when a government's budget is balanced, all revenues equal expenditures in a budget year. There is no surplus or deficit, but a national debt may still exist.

Bank of Canada: the sole money-issuing bank in Canada, acting as banker to all other financial institutions and the government. It is responsible for Canada's banking system, sets interest rates and regulates the money supply.

Bank rate: the interest rate at which the Bank of Canada lends money to the chartered banks.

Cartel: a group of companies in a specific industry that band together to restrict output and increase prices to get higher profits. In Canada, cartels are illegal. The best known international cartel is the Organization of Petroleum Exporting Countries (OPEC).

Constant dollars: dollars in a specified base year used to adjust for the effects of inflation.

Consumer price index: an indexed measure of the average prices of household goods to show inflationary trends; compiled monthly by Statistics Canada.

Cost of living: the cost of maintaining a particular standard of living measured in terms of purchased goods and services. The rise in the cost of living is the same as the rate of inflation.

Current dollars: cost of an asset in today's prices.

Deficit spending: the practice whereby a government goes into debt to finance some expenditures.

Deflation: a decline in general price levels, often caused by a reduction in the supply of money or credit.

Depreciation: the decrease in the value of a currency relative to other currencies under free market conditions. This differs from devaluation.

Depression: a long period of little business activity when prices are low, unemployment is high, and purchasing power decreases sharply.

Devaluation: the official lowering of the value of a nation's currency relative to foreign currencies.

Disposable income: income after taxes available to persons for spending and saving.

Equalization payments: transfers of tax revenues from the Canadian government to provinces with a high proportion of lower-income earners as compensation for their lower per capita tax revenues.

Exchange rate: the price of one country's currency relative to another country's currency.

Fiscal policy: the deliberate use of government budget measures (i.e., tax and spending policies) to alleviate economic problems such as low GNP, high unemployment and inflation.

Free trade: a system whereby the free movement of all goods and services, investment money and workers between countries is neither restricted nor encouraged by governments.

Gross domestic product (GDP): the value of all goods and services produced in a country.

Gross national product (GNP): the value of all goods and services produced by citizens of a country both inside and outside the country.

Inflation: a steady rise in the average level of prices in an economy.

Less developed countries (LDCs): also known as Third World countries, these are countries considered economically underdeveloped relative to the western industrialized nations.

Minimum wage: a minimum hourly wage as set by federal or provincial legislation.

Monetary policy: the government's manipulation of interest rates and the money supply to achieve economic growth, employment and price stability.

Money supply: the amount of money in an economy, with money defined as all currency in circulation and in chequing accounts.

National debt: the debt of the central government; in Canada's case, the federal government.

Per capita GNP: also known as per capita income, it is the nation's gross national product divided by its population.

Prime interest rate: the rate charged by chartered banks on short-term loans to large commercial customers with the best credit ratings.

Protectionism: government policies designed to restrict imports to protect domestic industries. These policies include customs duties (tariffs) and restrictions on the quantity of imports (quotas). ▶

Economic Indicators

▶ **Real GNP:** gross national product adjusted for inflation.

Recession: not as severe or as long-lasting as a depression but with the same general characteristics: a decline in real GNP for two consecutive quarters, with resulting unemployment and widespread softening in many sectors of the economy.

Stagflation: a high inflation rate combined with a high unemployment rate.

Supply-side economics: a school of thinking that states that an economy can prosper through policies affecting costs of production—that is, by giving production incentives to labour and greater financial rewards to investors.

Trade balance: the difference between the value of exports and imports.

Transfer payments: government payments to the provinces where no productive return is provided, such as old age pensions, unemployment insurance and welfare.

Wage-price controls: legislation whereby the government sets wage, salary and price increases to curb inflation.

Wage-price spiral: inflation brought about by increased wages that increase costs to the producers, who in turn increase prices. The increase in prices would cause labour to bargain for higher wages, resulting in a spiralling inflation.

ECONOMIC INDICATORS

Canadian Gross Domestic Product

(millions of dollars)

The gross domestic product (GDP) measures the value of all goods and services produced in Canada. The real (adjusted for inflation) change in the GDP shows year-to-year changes in economic activity and is considered a prime indicator of how well the nation's economy is performing.

	Current Dollars		Constant (1986) Dollars			Current Dollars[1]		Constant (1992) Dollars[1]	
	GDP	Annual % Change	Real GDP	Annual % Change		GDP	Annual % Change	Real GDP	Annual % Change
1927	5 777	7.9	48 108	9.4	1963	48 059	7.4	247 944	5.1
1928	6 279	8.7	52 527	9.2	1964	52 653	9.6	264 174	6.5
1929	6 400	1.9	52 997	0.9	1965	58 050	10.3	281 249	6.5
1930	6 009	-6.1	51 262	-3.3	1966	64 943	11.9	299 689	6.6
1931	4 975	-17.2	45 521	-11.2	1967	69 834	7.5	308 639	3.0
1932	4 079	-18.0	41 302	-9.3	1968	76 285	9.2	325 147	5.3
1933	3 723	-8.7	38 331	-7.2	1969	84 006	10.1	342 468	5.3
1934	4 186	12.4	42 318	10.4	1970	90 367	7.6	351 434	2.6
1935	4 514	7.8	45 357	7.2	1971	98 630	9.1	370 859	5.5
1936	4 879	8.1	47 437	4.6	1972	110 124	11.7	390 702	5.4
1937	5 477	12.3	51 635	8.9	1973	129 196	17.3	418 797	7.2
1938	5 523	0.8	52 354	1.4	1974	154 290	19.4	436 151	4.1
1939	5 880	6.5	56 265	7.5	1975	173 893	12.7	445 813	2.2
1940	6 987	18.8	63 722	13.3	1976	200 296	15.2	470 291	5.5
1941	8 532	22.1	72 214	13.3	1977	221 358	10.5	486 562	3.5
1942	10 497	23.0	84 925	17.6	1978	245 526	10.9	506 413	4.1
1943	11 282	7.5	88 164	3.8	1979	280 309	14.2	527 703	4.2
1944	12 068	7.0	91 385	3.7	1980	315 245	12.5	535 007	1.4
1945	12 063	0.0	89 170	-2.4	1981	360 494	14.4	551 305	3.0
1946	12 167	0.9	87 177	-2.2	1982	379 734	5.3	535 113	-2.9
1947	13 940	14.6	91 665	5.1	1983	411 160	8.3	549 843	2.8
1948	15 969	14.6	93 056	1.5	1984	449 249	9.3	581 038	5.7
1949	17 347	8.6	97 234	4.5	1985	485 139	8.0	612 416	5.4
1950	19 125	10.3	104 821	7.8	1986	511 796	5.5	628 575	2.6
1951	22 280	16.5	109 492	4.5	1987	558 106	9.0	654 360	4.1
1952	25 170	13.0	118 627	8.3	1988	611 785	9.6	686 176	4.9
1953	26 395	4.9	124 526	5.0	1989	656 190	7.3	703 577	2.5
1954	26 531	0.5	123 163	-1.1	1990	678 135	3.3	705 464	0.3
1955	29 250	10.2	134 889	9.5	1991	683 239	0.8	692 247	-1.9
1956	32 902	12.5	146 523	8.6	1992	698 544	2.2	698 544	0.9
1957	34 467	4.8	150 179	2.5	1993	724 960	3.8	714 583	2.3
1958	35 689	3.5	153 439	2.2	1994	767 506	5.9	748 350	4.7
1959	37 877	6.1	159 484	3.9	1995	807 088	5.2	769 082	2.8
1960	39 448	4.1	164 126	2.9	1996	833 070	3.2	780 916	1.5
1961	41 253	n.a.	220 816	n.a	1997	877 921	5.4	815 013	4.4
1962	44 755	8.5	235 900	6.8	1998	901 805	2.7	842 002	3.3
					1999	957 911	6.2	880 254	4.5

Source: © Statistics Canada

(n.a.) Not available. (1) New base for constant dollars.

Canadian Consumer Price Index by Year

(1992 = 100)

Year	Index	Year	Index	Year	Index	Year	Index
1915	7.3	1958	18.0	1973	28.1	1988	84.8
1920	13.5	1959	18.3	1974	31.1	1989	89.0
1925	10.9	1960	18.5	1975	34.5	1990	93.3
1930	10.9	1961	18.7	1976	37.1	1991	98.5
1935	8.7	1962	18.9	1977	40.0	1992	100.0
1940	9.5	1963	19.2	1978	43.6	1993	101.8
1945	10.9	1964	19.6	1979	47.6	1994	102.0
1950	14.9	1965	20.0	1980	52.4	1995	104.2
1951	16.4	1966	20.8	1981	58.9	1996	105.9
1952	16.9	1967	21.5	1982	65.3	1997	107.6
1953	16.7	1968	22.4	1983	69.1	1998	108.6
1954	16.8	1969	23.4	1984	72.1	1999	110.5
1955	16.8	1970	24.2	1985	75.0	2000[1]	112.4
1956	17.1	1971	24.9	1986	78.1		
1957	17.6	1972	26.1	1987	81.5		

Source: © Statistics Canada

(1) As of April.

Canadian Consumer Price Index by Item

(1992 = 100)

This table shows the relative costs, as far back as 1950, of categories of purchases made by Canadian consumers. To compare 1997 costs with those of another year, divide the 1997 index by the index for the year you wish to compare it with; then multiply that by your actual cost in the year for which you are making the comparison.

Example: you spent $65 per week on family food purchases in 1985. To calculate what that would be in today's dollars, divide the 1999 food index (110.7) by the 1985 food index (78.8). Now multiply the result by $65. The answer, $91.31, is what you now must spend to buy the same package of groceries that cost $65 in 1985.

	All Items	Food	Housing	Clothing	Transportation	Health and Personal Care	Recreation and Education	Tobacco and Alcohol
1950	14.9	14.2	n.a.	n.a.	14.8	12.0	15.7	11.3
1955	16.8	15.5	n.a.	n.a.	16.6	14.9	18.9	11.8
1960	18.5	16.9	n.a.	n.a.	19.7	18.2	22.3	12.7
1965	20.0	18.8	n.a.	n.a.	20.7	20.6	23.8	13.4
1970	24.2	22.3	n.a.	n.a.	24.6	25.5	29.6	16.2
1975	34.5	36.4	n.a.	n.a.	33.1	34.6	39.3	20.6
1980	52.4	58.6	50.2	n.a.	51.4	51.8	53.0	30.4
1985	75.0	78.8	74.7	74.8	79.6	73.1	72.9	52.9
1986	78.1	82.8	76.8	76.8	82.1	76.1	76.6	59.2
1987	81.5	86.4	80.3	79.8	85.1	80.0	80.4	63.1
1988	84.8	88.7	84.0	84.2	86.7	83.5	84.9	67.8
1989	89.0	92.0	88.9	87.6	91.2	87.1	88.8	74.1
1990	93.3	95.8	93.9	90.0	96.3	91.4	92.5	80.6
1991	98.5	100.4	98.2	99.0	98.0	97.8	98.9	94.4
1992	100.0	100.0	100.0	100.0	100.0	100.0	100.0	100.0
1993	101.8	101.7	101.4	101.0	103.2	102.7	102.4	101.6
1994	102.0	102.1	101.8	101.6	107.8	103.6	105.5	85.0
1995	104.2	104.5	102.9	101.6	113.4	103.5	109.5	84.9
1996	105.9	105.9	103.1	101.3	117.8	104.1	112.1	86.6
1997	107.6	107.6	103.3	102.7[1]	121.5	105.9	114.9	89.3
1998	108.6	109.3	103.7	103.9[1]	120.5	108.1	117.5	92.6
1999	110.5	110.7	105.1	105.3[1]	124.5	110.2	119.6	94.5

Source: © Statistics Canada

(1) Clothing and footwear.

Economic Indicators

Canadian Inflation Rate by Year

This table shows annual inflation rates, as measured by the percentage change in the Consumer Price Index (CPI) from one year to the next. The CPI, determined monthly by Statistics Canada, is a "weighted" average of the cost of a package of goods and services — such as food, clothing, housing and health care — normally purchased by Canadian households. Weighted average means that some items are given more importance according to the proportion of household income spent on them.

Prices increase for several reasons: rising production costs, limited availability of the commodity, unfavourable exchange rates pushing up import prices, excessive consumer demand and too much currency in the economy.

Year	Rate	Year	Rate	Year	Rate	Year	Rate
1915	1.4	1958	2.3	1973	7.7	1988	4.0
1920	16.4	1959	1.7	1974	10.7	1989	5.0
1925	1.9	1960	1.1	1975	10.9	1990	4.8
1930	-0.9	1961	1.1	1976	7.5	1991	5.6
1935	1.2	1962	1.1	1977	7.8	1992	1.5
1940	3.3	1963	1.6	1978	9.0	1993	1.8
1945	0.9	1964	2.1	1979	9.2	1994	0.2
1950	2.8	1965	2.0	1980	10.1	1995	2.2
1951	10.1	1966	4.0	1981	12.4	1996	1.6
1952	3.0	1967	3.4	1982	10.9	1997	1.6
1953	-1.2	1968	4.2	1983	5.8	1998	0.9
1954	0.6	1969	4.5	1984	4.3	1999	1.7
1955	0.0	1970	3.4	1985	4.0	2000[1]	2.1
1956	1.8	1971	2.9	1986	4.1		
1957	2.9	1972	4.8	1987	4.4		

Source: © Statistics Canada

(1) As of April 2000.

Canadian Interest Rates

(average annual)

	Bank Rate	Prime Rate	Savings Rate[1]	Conventional 5 Year Mortgage	Govt of Canada Average Bond Yield (10 yrs and over)
1982	13.96	15.81	11.50	17.89	14.26
1983	9.55	11.17	6.85	13.29	11.79
1984	11.31	12.06	7.69	13.59	12.75
1985	9.65	10.58	6.08	12.13	11.04
1986	9.21	10.52	6.02	11.21	9.52
1987	8.40	9.52	4.81	11.17	9.95
1988	9.69	10.83	5.69	11.65	10.22
1989	12.29	13.33	8.08	12.06	9.92
1990	13.05	14.06	8.77	13.35	10.85
1991	9.03	9.94	4.48	11.13	9.76
1992	6.78	7.48	2.27	9.51	8.77
1993	5.09	6.10	0.77	8.78	7.85
1994	5.79	7.25	0.50	9.53	8.63
1995	7.31	8.65	0.50	9.16	8.28
1996	4.53	6.06	0.50	7.93	7.50
1997	3.52	4.96	0.50	7.07	6.42
1998	5.10	6.60	0.10	6.93	5.47
1999	4.92	6.44	0.10	7.56	5.69
2000[2]	6.00	7.50	0.10[2]	8.75	5.94

Source: Bank of Canada

(1) Non-chequable savings deposit. (2) As of May 2000.

1992 = 100

*A*ll indexes measuring changes over time must have a specified time base. The time base is the reference point against which all levels are compared. Without a common time base, the indexes are meaningless. When quoting an index figure, the time base should always be included [e.g., all-items CPI in 1985 was 75.0 (1992 = 100)].

As of January, 1998, the time base changed from 1986 to 1992. All constant dollar series were converted to 1992 dollars during the process, including historical tables for CPI.

Foreign Currency Exchange Rates

	Canadian Dollars in US Dollars			Foreign Currency Units Per Canadian Dollar (annual averages)				
	High	Low	Average	British Pound	French Franc	German Mark	Swiss Franc	Japanese Yen
1975	1.0095	0.9615	0.9830	0.4426	4.2070	2.4131	2.5368	291.5452
1976	1.0389	0.9588	1.0141	0.5615	4.8379	2.5510	2.5336	300.5711
1977	0.9985	0.8963	0.9403	0.5385	4.6189	2.1805	2.2502	251.2563
1978	0.9170	0.8363	0.8770	0.4568	3.9448	1.7572	1.5547	182.4818
1979	0.8778	0.8320	0.8536	0.4023	3.6311	1.5640	1.4192	186.0465
1980	0.8767	0.8249	0.8554	0.3677	3.6088	1.5518	1.4314	192.9385
1981	0.8506	0.8031	0.8340	0.4117	4.3346	1.8804	1.6335	183.4862
1982	0.8446	0.7680	0.8103	0.4634	5.3050	1.9662	1.6418	201.3693
1983	0.8208	0.7990	0.8114	0.5352	6.1576	2.0687	1.7027	192.6782
1984	0.8038	0.7486	0.7723	0.5780	6.7250	2.1911	1.8093	183.2509
1985	0.7587	0.7107	0.7325	0.5649	6.5232	2.1381	1.7809	173.4004
1986	0.7332	0.6913	0.7197	0.4905	4.9751	1.5564	1.2872	120.5400
1987	0.7721	0.7248	0.7541	0.4603	4.5290	1.3543	1.1230	108.8376
1988	0.8444	0.7688	0.8124	0.4560	4.8263	1.4229	1.1844	104.0150
1989	0.8652	0.8254	0.8445	0.5151	5.3821	1.5863	1.3801	116.1980
1990	0.8859	0.8275	0.8570	0.4806	4.6577	1.3824	1.1862	123.6094
1991	0.8934	0.8573	0.8728	0.4932	4.9044	1.4422	1.2458	117.3709
1992	0.8771	0.7729	0.8276	0.4694	4.3706	1.2892	1.1592	104.7120
1993	0.8065	0.7416	0.7753	0.5162	4.3879	1.2814	1.1449	85.8369
1994	0.7642	0.7097	0.7321	0.4778	4.0502	1.1843	0.9976	74.6826
1995	0.7533	0.7009	0.7285	0.4614	3.6311	1.0426	0.8596	68.0272
1996	0.7474	0.7267	0.7331	0.4701	3.7453	1.0250	0.9049	79.7448
1996	0.7212	0.7526	0.7334	0.4699	3.7495	1.1028	0.9049	79.6813
1997	0.6945	0.7493	0.7223	0.4409	4.2105	1.2509	1.0473	87.3362
1998	0.6311	0.7123	0.6743	0.4067	3.9683	1.1834	0.9748	87.7963
1999	0.6462	0.6935	0.6730	0.4160	4.1391	1.2343	1.0100	76.2777
2000[1]	0.6693	0.6776	0.6742	0.4317	4.8852	1.4567	1.4567	72.9395

Source: Bank of Canada

(1) As of May 3, 2000.

Construction in Canada—Building Permits

(millions of dollars)

	Total	Annual % Change	Residential	Non-Residential Total	Industrial	Commercial	Institutional and Government
1950	958	28.6	531	427	64	241	110
1955	1 805	18.6	1 031	774	196	254	311
1960	2 025	-14.9	944	1 080	184	433	460
1965	3 810	16.6	1 757	2 053	430	783	840
1970	4 700	-4.0	2 312	2 389	498	807	1 084
1975	10 598	14.2	6 129	4 469	876	2 251	1 342
1980	15 452	9.2	7 468	7 984	1 911	4 322	1 751
1985	19 524	25.9	10 883	8 641	1 885	4 640	2 116
1986	24 690	26.5	14 219	10 471	1 899	6 152	2 420
1987	30 981	25.5	18 832	12 148	2 806	7 039	2 303
1988	34 829	12.4	20 119	14 710	3 046	8 756	2 908
1989	39 318	12.9	21 268	18 050	5 492	9 666	2 892
1990	32 131	-18.3	17 424	14 706	3 393	7 975	3 338
1991	28 468	-11.4	16 632	11 836	2 120	5 906	3 811
1992	26 995	-5.2	17 161	9 834	1 643	4 918	3 273
1993	25 586	-5.2	16 433	9 154	1 756	4 268	3 130
1994	27 637	8.0	17 590	10 047	2 250	4 993	2 803
1995	24 595	-11.0	13 242	11 353	2 823	5 441	3 089
1996	26 155	6.3	15 718	10 437	2 643	5 567	2 227
1997	31 249	19.5	18 317	12 931	3 455	6 520	2 956
1998	33 199	6.2	17 953	15 246	3 951	8 100	3 195
1999	35 770	7.7	19 957	15 814	3 631	8 482	3 701

Source: © Statistics Canada

Annual Bankruptcies in Canada

	Personal	Business	Total		Personal	Business	Total
1966	1 903	2 774	4 677	1989	29 202	8 664	37 866
1970	2 732	2 927	5 659	1990	42 782	11 642	54 424
1975	8 335	2 958	11 293	1991	62 277	13 496	75 773
1980	21 025	6 595	27 620	1992	61 822	14 317	76 139
1981	23 036	8 055	31 091	1993	54 456	12 527	66 983
1982	30 643	10 765	41 408	1994	53 802	11 810	65 612
1983	26 822	10 260	37 082	1995	65 432	13 258	78 690
1984	22 022	9 578	31 600	1996	79 631	14 229	93 860
1985	19 752	8 663	28 415	1997	85 297	12 200	97 497
1986	21 765	8 502	30 267	1998	75 465	10 791	86 256
1987	24 384	7 659	32 043	1999	72 997	10 026	83 023
1988	25 817	8 031	33 848				

Source: Bankruptcy Branch, Industry Canada

Business Bankruptcies by Province[1], 1999

	Total Bankruptcies	Total Assets	Total Liabilities	Total Deficiency
Canada	10 026	1 008 015 287	3 045 655 034	2 037 639 747
Newfoundland	73	4 826 073	13 843 494	9 017 421
Nova Scotia	284	45 895 655	92 119 550	46 223 895
Prince Edward Island	38	3 880 518	7 173 885	3 293 367
New Brunswick	183	20 577 377	45 350 488	24 773 111
Quebec	3 281	226 591 410	701 782 523	475 191 113
Ontario	2 885	290 279 678	1 187 799 552	897 519 874
Manitoba	216	22 081 901	46 382 066	24 300 165
Saskatchewan	420	62 416 697	126 737 316	64 320 618
Alberta	1 553	227 030 955	469 339 646	242 308 690
British Columbia	1 077	103 237 141	352 657 374	249 420 233
Yukon	4	313 820	946 520	632 700
Northwest Territories	12	884 061	1 522 621	638 560
Nunavut	0	0	0	0

Source: Bankruptcy Branch, Industry Canada (1) Totals include all reported bankruptcies.

Consumer Bankruptcies by Province[1], 1999

	Total Bankruptcies	Total Assets	Total Liabilities	Total Deficiency
Canada	72 997	2 304 805 797	3 793 618 504	1 488 812 707
Newfoundland	1 330	46 594 950	67 064 790	20 469 840
Nova Scotia	2 647	76 549 447	111 371 800	34 822 353
Prince Edward Island	157	5 129 821	9 354 914	4 225 093
New Brunswick	1 212	34 349 502	52 856 357	18 506 855
Quebec	23 275	524 223 682	1 099 688 174	575 464 492
Ontario	23 231	702 397 013	1 262 700 116	560 303 103
Manitoba	2 466	71 600 890	103 341 941	31 741 051
Saskatchewan	1 616	57 386 170	72 019 500	14 633 330
Alberta	8 783	367 574 579	413 521 965	45 947 386
British Columbia	8 181	414 565 545	595 897 024	181 331 479
Yukon	40	1 397 626	1 940 707	543 081
Northwest Territories	59	3 036 572	3 861 216	824 644
Nunavut	0	0	0	0

Source: Bankruptcy Branch, Industry Canada (1) Totals include all reported bankruptcies.

Canadian Unemployment Rates[1]

	1976	1980	1985	1990	1991	1992	1993	1994	1995	1996	1997	1998	1999
Canada	7.0	7.5	10.7	8.1	10.3	11.2	11.4	10.4	9.4	9.6	9.1	8.3	7.6
Newfoundland	13.3	13.1	20.8	16.9	18.0	20.2	20.4	20.2	18.1	19.3	18.6	18.0	16.9
Prince Edward Island	9.0	10.5	13.5	14.6	16.7	18.1	17.6	17.2	15.0	14.7	15.4	13.8	14.4
Nova Scotia	9.2	9.7	13.6	10.5	12.1	13.2	14.3	13.5	12.1	12.3	12.1	10.5	9.6
New Brunswick	10.9	11.1	15.3	12.1	12.8	13.0	12.5	12.4	11.2	11.6	12.7	12.2	10.2
Quebec	8.7	10.0	12.2	10.4	12.1	12.7	13.3	12.3	11.4	11.9	11.4	10.3	9.3
Ontario	6.1	6.8	8.1	6.2	9.5	10.7	10.9	9.6	8.7	9.0	8.4	7.2	6.3
Manitoba	4.6	5.5	8.4	7.3	8.6	9.2	9.3	8.6	7.2	7.2	6.5	5.5	5.6
Saskatchewan	3.8	4.2	8.3	7.0	7.4	7.9	8.2	6.8	6.6	6.6	5.9	5.7	6.1
Alberta	3.9	3.8	10.0	6.8	8.1	9.4	9.6	8.7	7.8	6.9	5.8	5.6	5.7
British Columbia	8.4	6.6	14.5	8.6	10.1	10.2	9.7	9.0	8.4	8.7	8.4	8.8	8.3

Source: © Statistics Canada
(1) Percentage of labour force.

FEDERAL GOVERNMENT SPENDING

Statement of Assets and Liabilities

as at March 31, 1999 (millions of dollars)

	1998	1999
Assets		
Current Assets		
Cash	10 379	9 306
Cash in transit	4 530	5 432
Less outstanding cheques and warrants	(3 218)	(4 045)
Accounts receivable[1]	4 122	4 580
FOREIGN EXCHANGE ACCOUNTS	28 968	34 668
Loans Investments and Advances		
Enterprise Crown corporations[2]	12 601	11 052
National governments include developing countries and international organizations	6 869	7 555
Provincial and territorial governments and other loans investments and advances	2 591	3 100
Portfolio investments	1 241	1 241
Less allowance for valuation	(9 266)	(9 412)
Total Assets	**58 817**	**63 477**
Accumulated Deficit	579 708	576 824
Liabilities		
Current Liabilities and Allowances		
Accounts payable and accrued liabilities	22 364	24 509
Interest and matured debt	10 419	9 791
Allowance for employee benefits	6 729	6 926
Allowance for loan guarantees and for borrowings of Crown corporations	4 188	4 090
INTEREST-BEARING DEBT		
Unmatured debt payable in Canadian currency		
Marketable bonds	294 583	295 752
Treasury bills	112 300	96 950
Canada savings bonds	29 769	27 662
Bonds for Canada Pension Plan	3 456	4 063
Unmatured debt payable in foreign currencies	27 183	36 000
Public sector pensions	117 457	122 407
Canada Pension Plan (net of securities)	4 205	5 427
Other pension and other accounts	5 872	6 724
Total Liabilities	**638 525**	**640 301**

Source: Finance Canada, Auditor General
(1) Net of allowance for doubtful accounts of $2 461 million in 1998 and $2 432 million in 1999. (2) Also includes other government business enterprises.

Statement of Revenue and Expenditure

for the Year Ended March 31, 1999

(net, millions of dollars)

	1998	1999
Revenue		
Tax revenue		
Income tax		
Personal	70 787	72 488
Corporation	22 496	21 575
Other income tax revenues	2 974	2 901
Employment insurance premiums	18 802	19 363
Excise tax and duties		
Goods and services tax	19 461	20 684
Energy taxes	4 638	4 716
Customs import duties	2 766	2 359
Other excise taxes and duties	3 995	3 640
Non-tax revenue		
Return on investments	4 427	4 991
Other non-tax revenue	2 816	2 954
Total Revenue	**153 162**	**155 671**
Expenditure		
Transfer payments		
Old age security benefits, guaranteed income supplements and spouses' allowances	22 225	22 781
Other levels of government	20 054	25 523
Employment insurance benefits[1]	11 842	11 884
Other transfer payments	20 664	18 735
Crown Corporation expenditures	2 548	3 497
Other program expenditures		
National Defence	8 879	8 781
All other departments and agencies	20 279	20 192
Public debt charges	40 931	41 394
Total Expenditure	**147 422**	**152 787**
Surplus	**3 478**	**2 884**

Source: *Finance Canada, Auditor General*
(1) Employment insurance benefits exclude administration costs of $1 322 million in 1998 and $1 360 million in 1999.

Government Finances

*A*ll three levels of government—federal, provincial and local—recorded financial surpluses in the fiscal year 1999–2000, according to Statistics Canada's Financial Management System (FMS). The overall surplus was estimated at $4.1 billion.

The federal government reported a surplus of almost $2.6 billion, its third consecutive. Provincial and territorial governments, which reduced their deficits throughout the 1990s, had their first overall surplus in decades, $1.1 billion. Local governments recorded a surplus of $367 million, their second consecutive.

Source: *Statistics Canada*
NOTE: FMS standardizes accounts to provide comparable statistics, and therefore numbers may differ from published individual government figures.

Federal Ministry Spending

(millions of dollars)

Department	1977-78	1987-88	1997-98	1998-99
Agriculture and Agri-Food	958.6	3.386.6	1 911.7	1 580.0
Canada Customs and Revenue Agency[7]	522.3	1 328.5	2 441.9	2 757.2
Canadian Heritage (Communications)	89.5	1 706.5	2 619.6	2 722.4
Citizenship and Immigration	—	—	748.8	789.2
Consumer and Corporate Affairs	71.8	533.7	—[1]	—[1]
Energy, Mines & Resources	1 566.4	1 335.8	—[2]	—[2]
Environment	547.3	784.9	557.9	574.4
Finance	9 298.6	35 973.6	64 439.9	70 497.3
Fisheries and Oceans	—	608.5	1 151.5	1 333.7
Foreign Affairs and International Trade (External Affairs)	1 125.6	3 172.8	3 363.8	3 443.3
Governor General (and Lieutenant-Governors)	3.0	8.1	11.2	13.0
Health	—	—	1 884.3	2 270.4
Human Resources Development	—	—	24 943.5	25 961.9
Indian and Northern Affairs	1 169.6	2 824.1	4 555.9	4 926.1
Industry	542.7	—	4 523.2	4 030.8
Justice	101.2	567.9	828.1	986.5
Labour	40.7	222.7	—[3]	—[3]
Manpower/Employment and Immigration	2 638.5	4 622.5	—[3]	—[3]
National Defence	3 771.0	10 650.4	10 187.3	10 256.5
National Health and Welfare	11 172.6	28 973.6	—[4]	—[4]
Natural Resources	—	—	753.3	782.5
Parliament	88.6	225.2	296.5	316.0
Post Office	1 237.2	—	—	—
Privy Council	43.7	88.2	339.4	237.4
Public Works and Government Services	808.4	2 925.1	3 757.0	3 929.1
Regional Economic (Industrial) Expansion	562.2	1 425.7	—[1]	—[1]
Science and Technology	273.6	799.2	—[1]	—[1]
Secretary of State	2 193.5	3 382.7	—[5]	—[5]
Solicitor General	807.3	1 905.3	2 738.0	2 766.7
Supply & Services	127.3	768.8	—[6]	—[6]
Transport	1 470.8	4 758.6	2 256.4	1 094.4
Treasury Board	180.1	417.8	1 150.6	998.5
Urban Affairs and Housing	629.4	—	—	—
Veterans Affairs	840.9	1 611.7	1 934.7	1 996.8
Total	**42 882.3**	**115 110.5**	**141 298.8**	**144 264.0**

Source: *Public Accounts of Canada*
(1) See Industry.
(2) See Natural Resources.
(3) Responsibilities moved to Human Resources Development.
(4) See Health.
(5) Split between Canadian Heritage and Human Resources Development.
(6) See Public Works.
(7) Formerly Revenue

Federal Government Annual Surplus or Deficit

Fiscal Year Ending March 31 (millions of dollars)

	Surplus or Deficit[1]	% of GDP[2]		Surplus or Deficit[1]	% of GDP[2]		Surplus or Deficit[1]	% of GDP[2]
1958	-196	0.6[3]	1972	-1 542	1.6	1986	-34 404	7.2
1959	-877	2.5[3]	1973	-1 675	1.5	1987	-30 733	6.0
1960	-600	1.7[3]	1974	-1 999	1.6	1988	-28 201	5.1
1961	-529	1.4[3]	1975	-2 009	1.3	1989	-28 951	4.8
1962	-948	2.3	1976	-5 737	3.3	1990	-28 996	4.4
1963	-833	1.9	1977	-6 297	3.2	1991	-30 618	4.7
1964	-1 169	2.5	1978	-10 426	4.8	1992	-34 643	5.1
1965	-315	0.6	1979	-12 617	5.2	1993	-41 021	5.8
1966	-303	0.5	1980	-11 501	4.2	1994	-42 012	5.6
1967	-187	0.3	1981	-13 522	4.4	1995	-37 462	4.8
1968	-711	1.0	1982	-14 872	4.2	1996	-28 617	3.6
1969	-400	0.5	1983	-27 816	7.4	1997	-8 897	1.0
1970	332	0.4	1984	-32 399	8.0	1998	3 478	0.4
1971	-780	0.9	1985	-38 324	8.7	1999	2 884	0.3

Source: *Public Accounts of Canada*

(1) A minus (-) sign indicates a deficit. (2) GDP (Gross Domestic Product) represents the value (in current dollars) of all goods and services produced in Canada. (3) Represents percentage of GNP.

Per Capita Accumulated Federal Debt[1]

	(millions of dollars)		(dollars)	
	Net Debt[2]	Interest on Debt	Net Debt Per Capita	Interest Per Capita
1940	3 271	139	288	12
1945	11 298	409	936	34
1950	11 645	440	849	32
1955	11 263	478	718	30
1960	12 089	736	677	41
1965	15 504	1 012	789	52
1970	16 943	1 676	796	79
1975	19 276	3 164	849	139
1980	72 159	8 494	2 853	353
1981	85 681	10 658	3 520	438
1982	100 553	15 114	4 090	615
1983	128 369	16 903	5 179	682
1984	160 768	18 077	6 436	724
1985	199 092	22 445	7 911	892
1986	233 496	25 441	9 210	1 003
1987	264 101	26 658	10 306	1 040
1988	292 184	29 028	11 276	1 120
1989	320 918	33 183	12 240	1 266
1990	357 811	38 820	13 484	1 472
1991	388 429	42 537	14 424	1 590
1992	423 072	41 020	15 469	1 499
1993	466 198	38 825	16 301	1 356
1994	508 210	37 982	17 381	1 299
1995	545 672	42 046	18 435	1 420
1996	574 289	46 905	19 908	1 626
1997	583 186	44 973	19 247	1 484
1998	579 708	40 931	19 166	1 353
1999	576 824	41 394	18 918	1 358

Source: *Public Accounts of Canada*

(1) As of Mar. 31, on a public accounts basis. (2) Accumulated budgetary deficit (net recorded assets minus gross liabilities) since Confederation.

Annual Federal Government Expenditure

(millions of dollars)[1]

Year	Total Expenditure	Expenditure on Goods & Services	Transfer Payments[2]	Interest on Public Debt
1965	8 556	3 093	4 411	1 052
1970	15 058	4 922	8 274	1 862
1975	35 364	9 369	22 290	3 705
1980	60 846	15 335	35 614	9 897
1985	112 362	26 701	60 923	24 738
1986	114 476	27 335	60 925	26 216
1987	120 669	28 434	64 352	27 883
1988	129 012	29 950	67 351	31 711
1989	138 561	31 904	69 233	37 424
1990	151 590	35 067	74 643	41 880
1991	161 314	35 910	84 351	41 053
1992	164 547	36 498	88 491	39 558
1993	167 301	37 690	90 392	39 219
1994	166 003	37 912	87 934	40 157
1995	172 500	37 887	88 359	46 254
1996	166 180	36 704	84 124	45 352
1997	160 619	34 905	81 939	43 775
1998	165 059	36 648	84 453	43 958
1999	172 533	38 810	90 216	43 507

Source: © Statistics Canada
(1) Expressed in constant dollars, 1992 = 100. (2) Includes payments to persons, businesses, non-residents, and provinces and local administrations.

Interest on Public Debt

(millions of dollars)[1]

Year	Mun.	Prov.	Fed.	Total	Year	Mun.	Prov.	Fed.	Total
1962	249	207	865	1 321	1980	1 986	5 150	9 897	17 033
1963	264	238	935	1 437	1981	2 257	6 534	13 739	22 530
1964	290	267	995	1 552	1982	2 544	8 200	16 675	27 419
1965	330	306	1 052	1 688	1983	2 837	9 558	17 463	29 858
1966	373	359	1 151	1 883	1984	3 015	11 126	21 006	35 147
1967	430	435	1 245	2 110	1985	3 298	12 549	24 738	40 585
1968	476	548	1 409	2 433	1986	3 313	13 693	26 216	43 222
1969	517	710	1 589	2 816	1987	3 340	15 056	27 883	46 279
1970	591	856	1 862	3 309	1988	3 365	15 730	31 711	50 806
1971	728	1 049	1 974	3 751	1989	3 495	17 366	37 424	58 285
1972	748	1 243	2 253	4 244	1990	3 722	18 684	41 880	64 286
1973	858	1 534	2 518	4 910	1991	3 886	19 587	41 053	64 526
1974	846	1 681	2 961	5 488	1992	4 089	21 594	39 558	65 241
1975	942	1 992	3 705	6 639	1993	4 295	23 337	39 219	66 851
1976	1 220	2 503	4 519	8 242	1994	4 219	25 221	40 157	69 597
1977	1 443	2 888	5 101	9 432	1995	4 316	26 957	46 254	77 527
1978	1 638	3 693	6 410	11 741	1996	4 176	26 756	45 352	76 284
1979	1 781	4 196	8 080	14 057	1997	4 034	26 431	43 775	74 240
					1998	3 921	28 111	43 958	75 990
					1999	3 769	27 513	43 507	74 789

Source: © Statistics Canada
(1) Expressed in constant dollars, 1992 = 100.

Major Federal Transfer Payments to Provinces and Territories, 1998–99 to 2000–2001

(millions of dollars)

	Newfoundland	Prince Edward Island	Nova Scotia	New Brunswick	Quebec	Ontario
1998–99						
Canada Health and Social Transfer[1]	499	117	819	648	6 882	9 453
Equalization	1040	222	1 255	1 077	4 618	–
Total[2]	**1440**	**317**	**1 960**	**1 619**	**11 018**	**9 453**
1999–2000						
Canada Health and Social Transfer[1]	533	133	910	728	7 284	10 968
Equalization	1 051	241	1 260	1 152	4 589	–
Total[2]	**1 474**	**350**	**2 054**	**1 763**	**11 361**	**10 968**
2000–01						
Canada Health and Social Transfer[1]	547	138	944	754	7 557	11 571
Equalization	1 038	236	1 238	1 127	4 493	–
Total[2]	**1 477**	**350**	**2 067**	**1 765**	**11 540**	**11 571**
2000–01 Per Capita Transfer Payment	2 751	2 544	2 204	2 348	1 566	994
% of 2000–01 Revenue	45	40	42	37	25	20

	Manitoba	Saskatchewan	Alberta	British Columbia	Yukon[3]	Northwest Territories	Nunavut
1998–99							
Canada Health and Social Transfer[1]	980	858	2 324	3 343	29	68	–
Equalization	960	407	–	–	296	886	–
Total[2]	**1 870**	**1 151**	**2 324**	**3 343**	**326**	**954**	–
1999–2000							
Canada Health and Social Transfer[1]	1 102	982	2 791	3 843	30	41	29
Equalization	1 114	388	–	–	306	521	523
Total[2]	**2 114**	**1 230**	**2 791**	**3 843**	**337**	**562**	**552**
2000–01							
Canada Health and Social Transfer[1]	1 146	1 022	2 969	4 049	31	43	30
Equalization	1 074	315	–	–	311	535	558
Total[2]	**2 120**	**1 205**	**2 969**	**4 049**	**342**	**578**	**588**
2000–01 Per Capita Transfer Payment	1 854	1 174	984	996	114 441	36 932	1 327
% of 2000–01 Revenue	35	22	17	20	71	81	94

Source: *Finance Canada*

(1) CHST is a combination of cash and tax transfers.
(2) Equalization associated with CHST tax transfer is included in both CHST and Equalization. Totals have been adjusted to avoid double counting. Totals may not add due to rounding.
(3) Non CHST payment is in the form of formula financing rather than equalization.

Employment Insurance

On July 1, 1996, the Employment Insurance (EI) Act replaced the Unemployment Insurance and the National Training Act. The EI program consists of two parts—Income Benefits (Part 1) and Active Re-employment Benefits (Part 2).

EI Income Benefits provide temporary income support for claimants while they look for work. Under the EI program every hour of work, including part-time, counts towards determining eligibility. There is also a Family Income Supplement that increases benefits for low-income claimants with children.

Active Re-employment Benefits provides assistance to unemployed workers returning to work through a set of active re-employment benefits and support measures. Targeted wage subsidies, self-employment assistance and job creation partnerships are available in all provinces and territories. Skills loans and grants are being implemented with the agreement of provinces and territories.

Eligibility
Most claimants require 420 to 700 insured hours of employment within the last 52 weeks, depending on the local unemployment rate. The higher the rate, the fewer hours of work required. Claimants who are entering the workforce for the first time or re-entering after a two-year absence will require 910 hours of work. To qualify for special benefits (sickness, maternity, parental) all claimants require 700 hours regardless of where they live.

Income Benefits
Claimants will receive 55 percent of their average weekly-insured earnings to a maximum of $413 per week. Claimants who have previously collected EI benefits have their basic rate (55 percent) reduced by 1 percent for every additional 20 weeks of benefits collected after the first 20 weeks in the last 5 years, to a maximum reduction of 5 percent. Claimants in receipt of the Family Income Supplement are exempt from the reduction of the benefit rate.

Claim Period
A claim for benefits lasts a maximum of 1 year or until all benefits have been collected, whichever occurs first. The number of weeks of benefits a claimant is entitled to is determined by the unemployment rate in their region and the number of insured hours used to establish the claim. The more insured hours used, the more weeks of benefits; the higher the unemployment rate, the more weeks of benefits.

Special Benefits
Claimants who are unable to work due to illness or injury are also entitled to benefits. A maximum of 15 weeks of sick benefits can be paid per claim. Claimants who are off work on maternity leave are entitled to a maximum of 15 weeks of benefits. A claimant off work caring for a newly born or adopted child can collect 10 weeks parental benefits. A claimant cannot collect more than a total of 30 weeks of special benefits (sick, maternity, parental) per claim.

Effective December 31, 2000, the Government of Canada will increase the duration of parental benefits to 35 weeks for biological and adoptive parents. A maximum of 50 weeks of combined maternity, parental and sickness benefits will be available. Presently, claimants must accumulate 700 hours of insured employment ($4,200 for fishers) to receive maternity and parental benefits. This requirement will be reduced to 600 hours of insurable employment ($3,762 for fishers) for parents of a child born or placed in their care for adoption on or after December 31, 2000.

Additional information on Employment Insurance can be obtained at
http://www.hrdc-drhc.gc.ca/ei/common/home.shtml.

Source: Human Resources Development Canada

Employment Insurance Program Payments

	Claims[1,2] (000s)	Benefit Payments ($000)[3]	Weeks Paid (000s)[4]	Maximum Weekly Payment	Average Weekly Payment[4]
1945	296.4	$ 14 576	1 224	$ 14.40	$ 11.91
1950	1 150.2	98 994	6 980	21.00	14.18
1955	1 929.8	228 860	12 375	30.00	18.49
1960	2 700.4	481 836	21 592	36.00	22.32
1965	1 628.2	312 110	12 718	36.00	24.54
1970	2 260.8	695 222	19 817	53.00	35.08
1975	2 857.2	3 146 497	37 327	123.00	84.64
1980	2 762.2	4 393 308	36 333	174.00	120.92
1985	3 312.4	10 266 888	59 788	276.00	171.05
1990	3 259.0	13 189 000	57 052	384.00	231.18
1995	3 095.8	13 748 243	50 462	448.00	260.14
1996	2 972.5	13 069 982	47 932	413.00	259.26
1997	2 766.7	12 018 601	40 933	413.00	254.13
1998	2 842.2	11 995 880	39 102	413.00	258.60
1999	2 692.3	11 830 162	36 789	413.00	262.32

Source: Human Resources Development Canada
(1) Refers to the program in place prior to July 1, 1996. (2) Initial and renewal. (3) The Total Benefit Payments include all payments under the EI Act. In addition to Employment Insurance benefits there are labour support measures. The EI benefit payments for 1999 were $9 730 778. (4) The weeks paid and the average weekly payment are for EI benefits.

Canada and Quebec Pension Plans

The Canada and Quebec Pension Plans were instituted in 1966 to provide benefits to Canadians who have contributed to the plan during their working lives. Both plans pay a monthly retirement benefit in addition to a one-time death benefit, survivor benefits for the spouse and dependent children of a deceased contributor and benefits to the severely disabled and their families.

Payments to the plan are made by all workers between the ages of 18 and the time they claim retirement (between the ages of 60 and 70). Payments are based on a contribution rate which in 2000 was 7.8 percent of "pensionable earnings". Employers and employees share this payment equally; self-employed persons must pay the entire amount themselves.

The contribution rate is scheduled to increase steadily, targeted to reach 9.9 percent in 2003. Contributions are not paid if income falls below an annual minimum ($3,500 in 2000) or on income above an annual maximum ($37,600 in 2000).

Retirement benefits from the plan are based on lifetime earnings and generally amount to 25 percent of average annual income, adjusted for inflation. The maximum monthly benefit at age 65 in 2000 was $762.92.

Source: *Human Resources Development Canada*

Spouses in a continuing marriage, and partners in a common-law relationship, may apply to receive an equal share of the retirement pension earned by both parties during their life together.

A provision that allows divorced couples to divide CPP credits earned during marriage was introduced in 1978. On January 1, 1987, the provision was expanded to include legally separated married spouses and those living in a common-law union. In March 1991, a further amendment allowed those previously denied a division due to a property waiver to have their situation remedied.

Since January 1987, Canadians eligible for CPP benefits who retire before age 65 can receive partial pensions beginning as early as age 60. Those who begin collecting at 60 receive 70 percent of the amount they would be entitled to at age 65. For each month past age 60 that a person delays retirement an additional half a percentage point is added (so that someone retiring at age 61 would receive 76 percent of their full (age 65) pension while someone postponing retirement to age 70 would receive 130 percent.

The federal government administers the Canada Pension Plan, while the Government of Quebec's Pension Board administers the Quebec Pension Plan. Essentially the same rules and benefits apply to each.

Canada and Quebec Pension Plans Payments

	Canada Pension				Quebec Pension Plan			
	Beneficiaries[1]	Benefits paid[2] ($000)	Contributors[3] (000s)	Avg. monthly retirement payments[1]	Beneficiaries[1]	Benefits paid[2] ($000s)	Contributors[3] (000s)	Avg. monthly retirement payments[1]
1971	251 853	$ 89 236	6 755	23	79 649	$ 47 576	2 234	25
1976	774 890	587 834	7 561	67	232 815	266 181	2 726	66
1981	1 274 306	2 010 924	8 626	144	406 069	704 798	2 909	148
1986	1 764 604	4 887 134	8 932	247	627 317	1 899 730	2 932	243
1991	2 584 986	10 541 912	9 630	342	809 409	3 182 379	3 149	323
1992	2 713 692	11 792 756	9 429	363	845 846	3 605 378	3 107	341
1993	2 845 059	13 199 084	9 399	370	883 610	3 860 717	3 039	349
1994	2 988 911	14 402 175	9 595	380	919 866	4 217 524	3 019	357
1995	3 116 453	15 256 542	9 726	384	964 116	4 505 435	3 055	354
1996	3 212 847	15 969 269	9 800	393	1 015 819	4 815 659	3 089	359
1997	3 281 603	16 675 314	10 051	400	1 061 569	5 055 947	3 094	360
1998	3 365 808	17 536 907	11 185	409	1 095 971	5 333 715	n.a.	366
1999	3 437 649	18 184 939	n.a.	412	1 127 050	5 575 730	n.a.	368
2000	3 514 482	18 754 816	n.a.	418	1 144 886	5 490 756	n.a.	369

Source: *Human Resources Development Canada*   (n.a.) Not available.
Note: From 1971 to 1978, data is for calendar years; from 1981 to 1988, data is for fiscal years ending Mar. 31.
(1) As of March. (2) For fiscal years ending Mar. 31. (3) Calendar years.

Old Age Security, Guaranteed Income Supplement and Spouse's Allowance

The Old Age Security (OAS) program, introduced in 1952, provides pensions to persons 65 years and older who meet Canadian residence requirements. Full monthly pensions ($424.12 per month as of July 2000) are given to persons who have lived in Canada for 40 years since the age of 18; some persons who have lived in Canada for 10 consecutive years are also eligible for full pensions. Partial pensions, introduced in 1977, are based on the number of years a pensioner has lived in Canada.

Proposed changes to the law will affect same-sex common-law partners who will have the same benefits and obligations as opposite sex common-law partners. As well, proving you are in a common-law relationship will be handled differently. Public representation will no longer be used in determining whether or not a common-law relationship exists.

The Guaranteed Income Supplement (GIS) was introduced in 1966 to assist those with little or no income other than their OAS pension. The amount of income supplement depends upon the pensioner's income, marital status and spouse's income. Generally, the maximum GIS payment is reduced by $1 for every $2 of income a pensioner has above his/her old age security pension. For example, in July 2000 a single pensioner with no personal income received OAS benefits of $424.12 per month and an income supplement of $504.05 per month. If this person had a private pension of $400 per month, the GIS would be reduced $200 to $304.05 per month.

Spouse's Allowance (SPA) benefits are payable to persons aged 60 to 64 whose spouses have died, or those with low income whose spouse receives an Old Age Security pension. Like Guaranteed Income Supplement benefits, the amount of the SPA benefit is dependent on income and marital status. The maximum SPA benefit payable in July 2000 was $830.70 for widows and widowers, and $752.44 for spouses of OAS pensioners.

A proposal has been made to change the programs' names from the Spouse's Allowance, and Widowed Spouse's Allowance, to the Allowance. The change has not been approved yet.

Source: *Human Resources Development Canada*

Old Age Security Program Payments

	Number of Recipients[1] (000s)			Net Payments[2] ($000 000)			Average Yearly[3] Payment per Pensioner		
	OAS	GIS	SPA	OAS	GIS	SPA	OAS	GIS	SPA
1961	905	n.a.	n.a.	$ 592	n.a.	n.a.	n.a.	n.a.	n.a.
1966	1 106	n.a.	n.a.	927	n.a.	n.a.	n.a.	n.a.	n.a.
1971	1 720	860	n.a.	1 627	$ 280	n.a.	$ 956	$ 340	n.a.
1976	1 957	1 087	54	2 976	923	$ 35	1 537	863	$1 788
1981	2 303	1 245	85	5 322	1 918	178	2 338	1 592	2 168
1986	2 652	1 330	142	8 858	3 319	348	3 385	2 555	3 105
1991	3 099	1 346	121	12 705	3 976	450	4 153	3 009	3 759
1992	3 180	1 329	116	13 808	4 139	446	4 386	3 171	3 927
1993	3 264	1 331	113	14 421	4 250	435	4 464	3 268	3 964
1994	3 341	1 355	112	15 027	4 446	429	4 542	3 372	3 984
1995	3 420	1 377	112	15 478	4 604	429	4 570	3 422	3 942
1996	3 500	1 368	106	15 999	4 628	408	4 615	3 464	3 980
1997	3 564	1 376	103	16 576	4 639	396	4 678	3 452	3 951
1998	3 635	1 376	100	17 114	4 729	389	4 745	3 466	3 934
1999	3 694	1 382	99	17 564	4 805	383	4 785	3 532	3 944
2000	3 755	1 375	98	18 038	4 920	390	4 834	3 589	4 031

Source: *Human Resources Development Canada* (n.a.) Not available or not applicable.
OAS = Old Age Security; GIS = Guaranteed Income Supplement; SPA = Spouse's Allowance.
(1) As of March. (2) For fiscal years ending Mar. 31. (3) For fiscal years ending Mar. 31, using annual average number of recipients.

Health Care

Total Health Care Spending by Use of Funds[1]

(millions of dollars)[2]

	Hospitals	Other Institutions	Physicians	Other Professionals[3]	Drugs[4]	Capital	Other[5]	Total	% Change
1975	5 514.3	1 124.3	1 839.9	1 094.6	1 076.2	536.1	1 074.6	12 260.1	n.a.
1980	9 399.2	2 544.9	3 287.5	2 260.0	1 881.5	990.7	2 008.0	22 371.9	82.5
1985	16 413.2	4 106.3	6 046.7	4 131.9	3 793.4	1 657.7	3 836.6	39 985.8	78.7
1990	24 061.9	5 757.5	9 245.2	6 491.7	6 865.9	2 123.4	6 760.0	61 305.7	53.3
1995	25 812.5	7 400.0	10 582.3	8 590.3	9 966.8	2 211.9	10 052.7	74 616.5	21.7
1996	25 704.5	7 563.0	10 642.4	8 991.8	10 258.4	2 104.5	10 337.3	75 601.9	1.3
1997	25 363.4	7 755.6	11 061.8	9 741.2	11 264.7	2 013.0	10 755.9	77 955.5	3.1
1998	26 364.3	8 078.5	11 452.3	10 367.7	12 204.6	2 110.8	11 244.3	81 822.3	5.0
1999	27 217.8	8 381.0	11 967.3	11 049.5	13 035.2	2 274.1	12 088.2	86 013.1	5.1

Source: *Canadian Institute for Health Information* (n.a.) Not available.
(1) Public and private sector. (2) Current dollars. (3) Includes dental services, vision-care services and other. (4) Includes prescription and nonprescriptive drugs. (5) Includes pre-payment administration, public health, health research and other.

Total Health Care Spending Per Capita by Use of Funds[1]

(dollars)[2]

	Hospitals	Other Institutions	Physicians	Other Professionals[3]	Drugs[4]	Capital	Other[5]	Total	% Change
1975	238.28	48.58	79.50	47.30	46.50	23.16	46.44	529.77	n.a.
1980	383.39	103.81	134.09	92.18	76.75	40.41	81.90	912.53	72.3
1985	635.12	158.90	233.98	159.89	146.79	64.15	148.46	1 547.28	69.6
1990	868.64	207.85	333.75	234.35	247.86	76.66	244.04	2 213.13	43.0
1995	879.36	252.10	360.51	292.65	339.54	75.35	342.46	2 541.97	14.9
1996	866.29	254.89	358.67	303.04	345.73	70.93	348.39	2 547.93	0.2
1997	845.34	258.48	368.68	324.66	375.44	67.09	358.48	2 598.18	2.0
1998	870.09	266.61	377.96	342.16	402.79	69.66	371.09	2 700.37	3.9
1999	890.82	274.30	391.68	361.64	426.63	74.43	395.64	2 815.13	4.2

Source: *Canadian Institute for Health Information* (n.a.) Not available.
(1) Public and private sector. (2) Current dollars. (3) Includes dental services, vision-care services and other. (4) Includes prescription and nonprescriptive drugs. (5) Includes pre-payment administration, public health, health research and other.

Percentage Distribution of Health Care Spending by Use of Funds[1]

(millions of dollars)[2]

	Hospitals	Other Institutions	Physicians	Other Professionals[3]	Drugs[4]	Capital	Other[5]
1975	45.0	9.2	15.0	8.9	8.8	4.4	8.8
1980	42.0	11.4	14.7	10.1	8.4	4.4	9.0
1985	41.0	10.3	15.1	10.3	9.5	4.1	9.6
1990	39.2	9.4	15.1	10.6	11.2	3.5	11.0
1995	34.6	9.9	14.2	11.5	13.4	3.0	13.5
1996	34.0	10.0	14.1	11.9	13.6	2.8	13.7
1997	32.5	9.9	14.2	12.5	14.5	2.6	13.8
1998	32.2	9.9	14.0	12.7	14.9	2.6	13.7
1999	31.6	9.7	13.9	12.8	15.2	2.6	14.1

Source: *Canadian Institute for Health Information*
(1) Public and private sector. (2) Current dollars. (3) Includes dental services, vision-care services and other. (4) Includes prescription and nonprescriptive drugs. (5) Includes pre-payment administration, public health, health research and other.

FOREIGN TRADE

Canadian Balance of International Payments
(millions of dollars)

The balance of payments statement provides information about a country's economic transactions with non-residents for a specified time frame. Canada produces balance of payments statistics on a quarterly basis. It is structured under two broad accounts: the Current Account and the Capital and Financial Account.

The current account measures revenues and expenditures arising from transactions in goods and services, investment income and current transfers. The capital and financial account comprises the capital account (capital transfers and non-produced, non-financial assets), and the financial account (transactions in financial instruments). The financial account provides information about the financing and investing activities of Canadian residents with non-residents.

	Current Account			Capital Account[3]			
	Receipts[1]	Payments	Balance[2]	Canadian Assets	Canadian Liabilities	Financial Account[4]	Total Capital and Financial Account[4]
1970	22 436	21 942	494	-4 449	3 944	-504	-314
1971	23 167	24 214	-1 046	-1 888	3 993	2 105	2 352
1972	26 428	27 813	-2 385	-2 216	5 769	3 553	3 834
1973	32 999	35 054	-2 055	-5 988	8 448	2 460	2 805
1974	42 098	46 573	-4 475	-3 209	8 016	4 808	5 346
1975	43 038	51 357	-8 319	-1 954	10 354	8 400	8 895
1976	48 067	55 611	-7 544	-6 303	16 311	10 008	10 531
1977	56 058	63 465	-7 407	-4 356	12 841	8 485	8 941
1978	66 872	76 222	-9 350	-10 021	21 603	11 582	11 714
1979	84 918	94 750	-9 832	-12 064	22 697	10 633	11 177
1980	98 419	105 540	-7 120	-21 411	27 894	6 483	6 979
1981	108 933	123 927	-14 994	-22 459	41 250	18 791	19 423
1982	112 362	110 060	2 302	-9 656	8 070	-1 586	-28
1983	115 409	118 541	-3 132	-9 973	15 141	5 168	6 506
1984	143 435	145 109	-1 673	-12 633	20 228	7 594	8 967
1985	151 338	159 166	-7 828	-7 352	19 556	12 204	13 659
1986	155 323	170 836	-15 514	-20 153	35 746	15 593	17 416
1987	162 736	180 542	-17 806	-17 716	34 868	17 152	20 869
1988	181 791	200 120	-18 328	-17 602	30 599	12 997	17 817
1989	186 280	212 091	-25 812	-19 745	41 882	22 137	27 617
1990	194 972	218 107	-23 135	-19 699	38 664	18 965	25 167
1991	188 719	214 348	-25 629	-15 128	34 509	19 381	25 791
1992	205 455	230 815	-25 360	-14 411	27 727	13 316	21 890
1993	235 576	263 670	-28 093	-26 943	50 706	23 763	34 467
1994	285 601	303 331	-17 730	-49 029	56 550	7 520	17 762
1995	330 978	337 078	-6 099	-38 394	32 905	-5 489	1 294
1996	351 038	346 438	4 600	-73 306	53 116	-20 191	-12 234
1997	381 269	395 205	-13 936	-61 944	70 827	8 884	16 391
1998	407 077	423 331	-16 255	-61 239	67 524	6 285	11 218
1999	449 400	452 846	-3 447	-45 338	33 946	-11 393	-6 301

Source: © *Statistics Canada*

(1) Money received for Canadian exports of goods and services. (2) Receipts minus payments. (3) Net flows. (4) The difference between the Financial Account and Total Capital and Financial Account is the net on Capital Account (not shown). For example, in 1999 the Financial Account was −11 393 and Total Capital and Financial Account was −6 301. Therefore, the net on the Capital Account would be 5 091.

Canadian Trade Balance[1]

(millions of dollars)

	1995	1996	1997	1998	1999
Total[2]	20 837	26 729	7 109	-931	11 063
Australia	-131	-316	-237	-345	-288
Belgium	1 127	679	618	463	904
Brazil	243	202	235	-122	-376
Chile	90	54	53	-31	-69
China	-1 345	-2 060	-3 989	-5 178	-6 403
Colombia	-22	162	118	72	-37
Cuba	-62	-138	-30	98	47
Egypt	112	107	147	118	144
El Salvador	-21	-17	-24	0	-23
France	-1 210	-1 719	-3 530	-3 279	-3 540
Germany	-1 626	-1 657	-2 787	-3 577	-4 694
Hong Kong	76	46	400	71	-358
Hungary	-4	-6	14	-1	-45
India	-107	-257	-261	-484	-606
Iran	308	323	217	109	426
Israel	-23	-50	-84	-203	-166
Italy	-1 493	-1 396	-1 572	-1 942	-2 204
Jamaica	-104	-156	-174	-161	-109
Japan	-188	634	-1 509	-5 448	-6 742
Kenya	-2	15	20	4	30
Malaysia	-1 014	-1 062	-1 305	-1 523	-1 645
Mexico	-4 228	-4 816	-5 802	-6 279	-8 014
Morocco	118	112	134	101	68
Netherlands	616	667	578	615	241
New Zealand	-116	-101	-75	-178	-168
Nigeria	-559	-269	-417	-247	-271
Peru	41	42	175	14	15
Philippines	-171	-265	-308	-710	-756
Poland	-5	17	-5	14	-40
Romania	-39	47	-4	-68	-66
Russia	-308	-137	-260	-454	-436
Saudi Arabia	5	-21	-105	-89	-137
Singapore	-827	-656	-660	-803	-912
South Africa	-95	-214	-136	-204	-249
South Korea	-500	47	148	-1 520	-1 630
Spain	-93	-176	-198	-270	-245
Sweden	-977	-942	-941	-1 028	-1 119
Switzerland	-369	-28	-514	-208	-801
Taiwan (Taipei)	-1 085	-1 483	-1 899	-2 903	-3 506
Turkey	131	105	135	-38	-53
United Kingdom	-1 721	-2 070	-2 860	-2 156	-3 630
United States[3]	43 668	51 853	43 703	47 546	71 136
Venezuela	-291	-265	-464	-408	-612

Source: © *Statistics Canada*

(1) The trade balance is the value of merchandise exports minus the value of merchandise imports; (2) Total includes countries not shown. (3) Includes Puerto Rico and the US Virgin Islands.

Canadian Imports by Country

(millions of dollars)

	1995	%	1996	%	1997	%	1998	%	1999	%
Total[1]	225 553	100.00	232 566	100.00	272 924	100.00	298 382	100.00	320 159	100.00
Australia	1 283	0.57	1 291	0.55	1 186	0.43	1 295	0.43	1 215	0.38
Belgium	728	0.32	818	0.35	846	0.31	958	0.32	932	0.29
Brazil	1 038	0.46	1 134	0.49	1 320	0.48	1 377	0.46	1 359	0.42
Chile	279	0.12	342	0.15	326	0.12	360	0.12	421	0.13
China	4 639	2.06	4 931	2.12	6 344	2.32	7 655	2.57	8 917	2.79
Colombia	372	0.16	297	0.13	314	0.11	364	0.12	281	0.09
Cuba	321	0.14	401	0.17	353	0.13	333	0.11	306	0.10
Egypt	19	0.01	20	0.01	29	0.01	35	0.01	40	0.01
El Salvador	44	0.02	28	0.01	45	0.02	33	0.01	36	0.01
France	3 124	1.39	3 402	1.46	5 137	1.88	4 875	1.63	5 311	1.66
Germany	4 799	2.13	4 824	2.07	5 412	1.98	6 120	2.05	6 947	2.17
Hong Kong	1 305	0.58	1 142	0.49	1 263	0.46	1 255	0.42	1 303	0.41
Hungary	45	0.02	48	0.02	75	0.03	95	0.03	101	0.03
India	541	0.24	604	0.26	743	0.27	899	0.30	1 016	0.32
Iran	122	0.05	238	0.10	506	0.19	154	0.05	112	0.03
Israel	241	0.11	267	0.11	315	0.12	417	0.14	443	0.14
Italy	3 271	1.45	2 719	1.17	3 070	1.12	3 437	1.15	3 597	1.12
Jamaica	200	0.09	239	0.10	258	0.09	256	0.09	201	0.06
Japan	12 094	5.36	10 439	4.49	12 553	4.60	13 999	4.69	15 032	4.70
Kenya	19	0.01	19	0.01	18	0.01	19	0.01	13	...
Malaysia	1 550	0.69	1 579	0.68	1 991	0.73	1 998	0.67	2 058	0.64
Mexico	5 353	2.37	6 035	2.59	7 022	2.57	7 681	2.57	9 541	2.98
Morocco	70	0.03	82	0.04	66	0.02	88	0.03	109	0.03
Netherlands	999	0.44	927	0.40	1 059	0.39	1 164	0.39	1 224	0.38
New Zealand	298	0.13	322	0.14	369	0.14	384	0.13	371	0.12
Nigeria	585	0.26	311	0.13	521	0.19	301	0.10	299	0.09
Peru	96	0.04	126	0.05	135	0.05	171	0.06	150	0.05
Philippines	498	0.22	553	0.24	726	0.27	958	0.32	1 044	0.33
Poland	121	0.05	144	0.06	147	0.05	171	0.06	185	0.06
Romania	60	0.03	50	0.02	69	0.03	122	0.04	99	0.03
Russia	498	0.22	449	0.19	621	0.23	731	0.24	607	0.19
Saudi Arabia	502	0.22	651	0.28	648	0.24	394	0.13	429	0.13
Singapore	1 311	0.58	1 192	0.51	1 174	0.43	1 180	0.40	1 252	0.39
South Africa	419	0.19	439	0.19	497	0.18	514	0.17	488	0.15
South Korea	3 204	1.42	2 729	1.17	2 838	1.04	3 314	1.11	3 574	1.12
Spain	706	0.31	687	0.30	786	0.29	834	0.28	855	0.27
Sweden	1 303	0.58	1 201	0.52	1 316	0.48	1 368	0.46	1 488	0.46
Switzerland	902	0.40	938	0.40	929	0.34	1 111	0.37	1 265	0.40
Taiwan (Taipei)	2 791	1.24	2 852	1.23	3 475	1.27	4 030	1.35	4 593	1.43
Turkey	150	0.07	152	0.07	194	0.07	250	0.08	251	0.08
United Kingdom	5 476	2.43	5 908	2.54	6 501	2.38	6 314	2.12	8 112	2.53
United States[2]	150 682	66.81	156 953	67.49	184 375	67.56	203 548	68.22	215 426	67.29
Venezuela	669	0.30	726	0.31	972	0.36	842	0.28	1 014	0.32

Source: © Statistics Canada (...) Too small to be included.
(1) Total includes countries not shown. (2) Includes Puerto Rico and the U.S. Virgin Islands.

Canadian Exports by Country

(millions of dollars)

	1995	%	1996	%	1997	%	1998	%	1999	%
Total[1]	246 390	100.00	259 295	100.00	280 033	100.00	297 451	100.00	331 222	100.00
Australia	1 152	0.47	974	0.38	949	0.34	950	0.32	927	0.28
Belgium	1 854	0.75	1 497	0.58	1 463	0.52	1 421	0.48	1 836	0.55
Brazil	1 281	0.52	1 336	0.52	1 555	0.56	1 255	0.42	983	0.30
Chile	369	0.15	396	0.15	379	0.14	329	0.11	352	0.11
China	3 294	1.34	2 871	1.11	2 355	0.84	2 477	0.83	2 514	0.76
Colombia	350	0.14	459	0.18	431	0.15	436	0.15	243	0.07
Cuba	259	0.11	263	0.10	323	0.12	432	0.15	353	0.11
Egypt	131	0.05	127	0.05	176	0.06	153	0.05	184	0.06
El Salvador	23	0.01	11	...	21	0.01	33	0.01	14	...
France	1 914	0.78	1 684	0.65	1 608	0.57	1 597	0.54	1 771	0.53
Germany	3 172	1.29	3 167	1.22	2 625	0.94	2 544	0.86	2 253	0.68
Hong Kong	1 381	0.56	1 188	0.46	1 663	0.59	1 326	0.45	945	0.29
Hungary	41	0.02	42	0.02	89	0.03	94	0.03	56	0.02
India	434	0.18	347	0.13	482	0.17	414	0.14	411	0.12
Iran	429	0.17	561	0.22	723	0.26	263	0.09	538	0.16
Israel	218	0.09	217	0.08	231	0.08	214	0.07	276	0.08
Italy	1 778	0.72	1 323	0.51	1 497	0.53	1 494	0.50	1 393	0.42
Jamaica	97	0.04	83	0.03	84	0.03	95	0.03	92	0.03
Japan	11 906	4.83	11 072	4.27	11 044	3.94	8 551	2.87	8 290	2.50
Kenya	17	0.01	33	0.01	38	0.01	24	0.01	43	0.01
Malaysia	536	0.22	517	0.20	686	0.25	474	0.16	413	0.12
Mexico	1 124	0.46	1 218	0.47	1 219	0.44	1 402	0.47	1 526	0.46
Morocco	189	0.08	194	0.07	200	0.07	189	0.06	176	0.05
Netherlands	1 615	0.66	1 594	0.61	1 637	0.58	1 779	0.60	1 465	0.44
New Zealand	182	0.07	221	0.09	294	0.11	206	0.07	202	0.06
Nigeria	26	0.01	42	0.02	104	0.04	55	0.02	29	0.01
Peru	137	0.06	168	0.06	309	0.11	185	0.06	165	0.05
Philippines	326	0.13	287	0.11	418	0.15	248	0.08	288	0.09
Poland	116	0.05	161	0.06	142	0.05	185	0.06	145	0.04
Romania	21	0.01	97	0.04	64	0.02	54	0.02	33	0.01
Russia	190	0.08	312	0.12	361	0.13	276	0.09	172	0.05
Saudi Arabia	507	0.21	630	0.24	543	0.19	304	0.10	292	0.09
Singapore	484	0.20	536	0.21	515	0.18	376	0.13	341	0.10
South Africa	324	0.13	225	0.09	361	0.13	310	0.10	239	0.07
South Korea	2 703	1.10	2 776	1.07	2 985	1.07	1 794	0.60	1 944	0.59
Spain	613	0.25	512	0.20	588	0.21	564	0.19	609	0.18
Sweden	326	0.13	259	0.10	375	0.13	340	0.11	370	0.11
Switzerland	534	0.22	910	0.35	414	0.15	903	0.30	464	0.14
Taiwan (Taipei)	1 706	0.69	1 369	0.53	1 576	0.56	1 127	0.38	1 087	0.33
Turkey	281	0.11	257	0.10	330	0.12	212	0.07	197	0.06
United Kingdom	3 755	1.52	3 838	1.48	3 641	1.30	4 158	1.40	4 482	1.35
United States[2]	194 350	78.88	208 806	80.53	228 078	81.45	251 094	84.42	286 561	86.52
Venezuela	378	0.15	461	0.18	508	0.18	433	0.15	401	0.12

Source: © Statistics Canada (...) Too small to be included.
(1) Total includes countries not shown. (2) Includes Puerto Rico and the U.S. Virgin Islands.

Foreign Investment in Canada

(millions of dollars)

	Total	United States	United Kingdom	Other EU[1]	Japan	Other OECD[2]	All Other
1926	1 782	1 403	336	—	—	—	43
1930	2 427	1 993	392	—	—	—	42
1935	2 284	1 870	373	—	—	—	41
1940	2 477	2 064	362	—	—	—	51
1945	2 831	2 422	348	—	—	—	61
1950	4 098	3 549	468	—	—	—	81
1955	8 010	6 778	905	—	—	—	327
1960	13 583	11 210	1 550	553	—	—	270
1965	17 864	14 408	2 107	968	10	240	131
1970	27 374	22 054	2 641	1 617	103	580	379
1975	38 728	30 506	3 830	2 520	257	987	628
1980	64 708	50 368	5 773	5 168	605	1 524	1 270
1985	90 358	67 874	8 643	6 774	2 250	2 562	2 255
1990	130 932	84 089	17 185	14 339	5 222	5 871	4 227
1991	135 234	86 396	16 224	14 908	5 596	6 803	5 308
1992	137 918	88 161	16 799	15 056	5 962	6 913	5 027
1993	141 493	90 600	15 872	15 732	6 249	7 312	5 727
1994	154 594	102 629	14 693	16 824	6 587	7 989	5 873
1995	168 167	112 948	14 097	21 778	6 987	5 827	6 529
1996	180 418	120 526	14 233	23 911	7 864	6 948	6 936
1997	197 884	132 950	15 375	25 554	8 022	8 680	7 304
1998	219 220	150 194	15 205	30 030	8 337	8 272	7 183
1999	239 972	173 340	14 229	30 931	6 362	7 755	7 355

Source: © Statistics Canada

(1) Other European Union countries (EU) include Belgium, Denmark, Germany, France, Greece, Ireland, Italy, Luxembourg, Netherlands, Portugal, Spain; from January 1995, Austria, Finland and Sweden. (2) Other OECD countries include Australia, Iceland, New Zealand, Norway, Switzerland and Turkey; from July 1994, Mexico; from December 1995, Czech Republic; from May 1996, Hungary, from November 1996, Poland; and up to December 1994, Austria, Finland and Sweden.

Foreign Investment in Canada by Industry

(millions of dollars)

	Total	Wood & Paper	Energy & Metallic Minerals	Machinery & Transportation Equipment	Finance & Insurance	Services & Retailing	Other Industries
1990	130 932	7 599	31 581	18 431	24 766	9 780	38 776
1991	135 234	7 902	31 706	18 212	25 939	10 363	41 112
1992	137 918	8 895	30 062	18 496	26 873	10 807	42 785
1993	141 493	9 109	30 846	20 641	26 685	11 010	43 203
1994	154 594	9 598	29 959	24 638	28 119	14 417	47 864
1995	168 167	10 010	29 061	25 305	29 086	16 885	57 820
1996	180 418	10 193	31 295	25 289	33 310	18 689	61 643
1997	197 884	12 318	34 419	28 033	39 786	19 698	63 630
1998	219 220	13 566	37 722	29 831	47 328	20 547	70 227
1999	239 972	18 417	39 153	27 176	50 125	19 412	85 688

Source: © Statistics Canada

Canadian Investment Abroad

(millions of dollars)

	Total	United States	United Kingdom	Other EU[1]	Japan	Other OECD[2]	All Other
1920	212	132	1	—	1	—	78
1925	246	144	1	—	1	—	100
1930	443	260	14	—	1	—	168
1935	485	266	46	—	—	—	173
1940	681	412	58	—	1	—	210
1945	720	455	54	—	2	—	209
1950	1 043	814	73	—	—	—	156
1955	1 835	1 362	145	—	6	—	322
1960	2 600	1 716	277	46	15	—	546
1965	3 655	2 178	510	125	28	44	769
1970	6 520	3 518	636	304	48	142	1 871
1975	11 091	5 975	1 105	633	74	699	2 605
1980	28 413	17 849	3 080	1 377	109	1 370	4 628
1985	60 292	41 851	4 865	2 868	276	2 293	8 139
1990	98 402	60 049	13 527	7 098	917	3 996	12 815
1991	109 068	63 379	15 262	8 505	2 182	3 548	16 192
1992	111 691	64 502	12 271	9 071	2 521	3 957	19 370
1993	122 427	67 677	12 907	11 478	2 845	4 355	23 165
1994	146 315	77 987	15 038	15 620	3 485	6 635	27 551
1995	161 237	84 562	16 412	18 106	2 739	7 166	32 251
1996	180 616	93 886	17 825	19 193	2 676	8 389	38 647
1997	209 678	105 683	21 828	22 158	2 985	9 306	47 718
1998	246 313	124 405	22 783	28 571	3 404	11 282	55 869
1999	257 408	134 281	22 885	26 033	4 076	11 555	58 679

Source: © Statistics Canada

(1) Other European Union countries (EU) include Belgium, Denmark, Germany, France, Greece, Ireland, Italy, Luxembourg, Netherlands, Portugal, Spain; from January 1995, Austria, Finland and Sweden. (2) Other OECD countries include Australia, Iceland, New Zealand, Norway, Switzerland and Turkey; from July 1994, Mexico; from December 1995, Czech Republic; from May 1996, Hungary, from November 1996, Poland; and up to December 1994, Austria, Finland and Sweden.

Canadian Investment Abroad by Industry

(millions of dollars)

	Total	Wood & Paper	Energy & Metallic Minerals	Machinery & Transportation Equipment	Finance & Insurance	Services & Retailing	Other Industries
1990	98 402	3 498	20 876	3 238	28 575	8 273	33 941
1991	109 068	3 473	22 051	2 794	32 443	10 043	38 264
1992	111 691	3 576	24 198	3 188	32 140	10 263	38 326
1993	122 427	3 727	27 008	4 030	37 353	10 423	39 887
1994	146 315	4 358	32 189	4 681	44 725	12 066	48 297
1995	161 237	5 340	37 219	5 207	48 932	17 892	46 646
1996	180 616	4 710	44 218	5 862	57 947	20 179	47 701
1997	209 678	6 106	51 951	7 662	67 536	22 473	53 950
1998	246 313	6 927	54 485	11 081	77 868	32 999	62 954
1999	257 408	7 125	54 053	12 223	85 323	33 953	64 732

Source: © Statistics Canada

BUSINESS

Mining in Canada
(millions of dollars)

	1950	1960	1970	1980	1990	1997	1998
Total Value[1]	1 045.5	2 492.5	5 722.1	31 841.8	40 778.4	49 843.2	44 315.1
METALS							
Cadmium	1.9	3.3	15.3	7.6	11.6	2.1	1.3
Cobalt	1.0	6.7	10.2	134.7	49.6	150.8	167.7
Copper	123.2	264.8	779.2	1 859.6	2 428.9	2 065.5	1 693.2
Gold	168.9	157.2	88.1	1 165.4	2 407.6	2 510.4	2 322.4
Iron Ore	23.4	175.1	588.6	1 700.9	1 258.8	1 431.2	1 584.1
Lead	47.9	43.9	123.1	273.7	279.3	148.4	118.0
Nickel	112.1	295.6	830.2	1 497.4	2 027.9	1 777.1	1 419.4
Platinum metals	10.3	28.9	43.6	159.1	189.4	152.3	222.9
Silver	18.8	30.2	81.9	828.8	249.7	259.1	293.5
Uranium	n.a.	269.9	n.a.	702.0	887.9	559.2	0.0
Zinc	98.0	108.6	398.9	858.2	2 272.6	1 875.5	1 487.0
NON-METALS							
Asbestos	65.9	121.4	208.1	618.5	272.1	224.0	167.2
Gypsum	6.7	9.5	14.2	39.5	80.1	91.7	88.0
Potash	—	178.7	108.7	1 020.7	964.9	1 465.6	1 667.0
Salt	7.1	19.4	36.1	122.8	240.9	380.7	399.5
Sulphur (elemental)	2.2	4.3	28.4	444.1	368.9	86.6	54.3
STRUCTURAL MATERIALS							
Cement	35.9	93.3	155.7	581.4	991.4	1 022.3	1 126.9
Sand and gravel	36.4	111.2	133.6	508.4	817.3	800.5	819.9
Stone	25.9	60.6	87.9	341.2	663.4	617.7	646.2

Source: © Statistics Canada
(1) Total includes metals, non-metals, structural materials and fuels that are not shown.

Mining by Province, 1998
(millions of dollars)

	Nfld	PEI	NS	NB	Que	Ont	Man	Sask	Alta	BC	YT	NWT
METALS												
Copper	—	—	—	35.8	299.7	553.0	123.4	—	—	681.3	—	—
Gold	19.5	—	—	3.7	530.9	1 175.0	...	...	—	303.9	79.8	53.8
Iron Ore	942.8	—	—	—	...	...	—	—	—	2.2	—	—
Lead	—	—	—	63.6	—	—	—	—	—	24.4	7.3	22.7
Nickel	—	—	—	—	113.3	951.9	354.3	—	—	—	—	—
Zinc	—	—	—	429.6	248.6	144.4	142.7	—	—	231.3	22.6	267.8
NON-METALS												
Asbestos	—	—	—	—	167.2	—	—	—	—	—	—	—
STRUCTURAL MATERIALS												
Cement	...	—	...	—	214.6	477.3	—	—	...	187.5	—	—
Sand & Gravel	11.8	1.0	13.9	...	67.9	342.6	...	154.5	146.2	2.9	3.8	
Stone	17.4	—	34.6	19.3	192.9	307.7	20.0	—	6.3	47.1	—	1.1

Source: © Statistics Canada   (...) Sample too small.

Agriculture in Canada

(millions of dollars)[1]

	1950	1960	1970	1980	1990[2]	1998[2]	1999[2]
Total value of agricultural products	2 135.8	2 811.7	4 250.9	15 958.8	21 997.9	29 648.4	30 311.4
Barley	45.8	69.4	144.7	553.6	545.2	525.9	448.0
Canola	n.a	14.8	96.7	673.6	789.6	2 702.7	1 824.7
Cattle	421.8	469.7	858.9	3 221.4	3 627.1	5 147.6	5 543.0
Corn	7.2	10.1	49.4	467.5	521.5	640.9	707.3
Dairy products	328.2	486.5	678.9	2 015.5	3 154.8	3 844.8	3 923.2
Eggs	86.9	137.8	172.8	407.0	482.3	476.0	482.4
Fruits	33.6	52.1	91.8	137.3	348.1	468.1	546.5
Ginseng	n.a.	n.a.	n.a.	n.a.	30.5	59.2	50.1
Honey	n.a	n.a.	n.a.	44.8	45.0	79.8	73.9
Maple products	8.9	9.5	8.1	34.1	70.8	137.5	153.9
Nurseries	n.a.	n.a.	n.a.	276.2	913.6	1 209.9	1 319.9
Oats	42.6	23.9	20.9	53.5	81.0	218.7	203.6
Pigs	286.9	266.8	484.5	1 404.2	2 021.2	2 230.2	2 397.9
Potatoes	29.9	67.4	90.1	211.9	399.0	613.6	714.8
Poultry[4]	80.1	135.5	262.7	670.2	1 201.6	1 593.7	1 572.4
Sheep	1.3	0.4	0.3	2.9	2.3	3.9	4.0
Soybeans	n.a.	10.0	23.7	183.3	256.6	797.5	612.2
Sugar Beets	13.5	12.8	15.1	73.5	42.9	39.8	30.5
Tobacco	56.7	96.4	154.8	212.5	281.1	354.4	361.0
Vegetables	43.8	68.1	125.1	360.1	706.5	1 036.1	1 098.5
Wheat	377.5	442.7	570.1	2 774.5	2 351.5	1 792.0	1 795.5

Source: © Statistics Canada (1) Not adjusted for inflation. (2) Based on intercensal counts (1991–96).

Canadian Agriculture by Province, 1999

(thousands of dollars)

	Nfld	PEI	NS	NB	Que	Ont	Man	Sask	Alta	BC
Barley	...	4 411	429	1 306	16 613	7 899	39 040	211 330	164 162	2 786
Calves	229	219	2 228	18 761	182 679	86 060	93 806	275 475	8 327	69 740
Canola	...	...	...	...	4 313	8 845	384 177	800 652	611 821	14 911
Cattle	1 948	22 957	28 008	25 554	233 024	895 559	358 702	6 898 031	3 063 173	224 307
Corn	...	...	200	...	257 620	427 308	21 637	...	536	...
Dairy products	25 780	48 995	89 852	69 306	1 486 588	1 273 338	152 288	109 910	327 063	340 102
Eggs	9 532	2 953	19 391	12 044	83 006	188 300	46 946	19 508	36 389	64 287
Fruits	876	2 880	47 996	14 975	85 503	220 401	3 605	2 393	2 217	164 517
Ginseng	...	...	...	...	...	26 720	...	...	...	23 400
Hogs	1 141	21 603	27 446	22 928	747 675	591 091	466 380	142 513	338 743	38 398
Honey	...	135	1 722	570	5 246	9 373	15 415	15 163	20 263	6 043
Maple products	...	...	13 201	4 634	136 953	10 983	...	...	...	...
Nurseries	7 720	1 592	33 574	35 507	171 462	626 893	30 016	15 795	68 517	328 761
Potatoes	1 223	194 818	6 713	97 740	89 009	593 921	121 316	27 237	77 442	39 897
Poultry	21 454	5 161	55 696	42 998	43 1307	517 447	72 433	39 389	135 025	251 383
Sheep	9	9	54	14	718	2 503	106	65	204	305
Soybeans	...	336	...	...	90 652	521 250	...	...	...	...
Sugar beets	...	...	...	...	...	...	...	876	29 651	...
Tobacco	...	...	...	...	21 299	339 662	...	...	...	...
Vegetables	4 015	12 295	23 300	8 046	261 902	495 842	27 919	3 285	60 424	201 445
Wheat	...	2 161	574	220	7 080	92 676	375 358	732 342	576 525	8 601

Source: © Statistics Canada (...) Too small to be included.

Fuel Production in Canada

(millions of dollars)

	1950	1960	1970	1980	1990	1997	1998
Total fuels.............	201.2	565.9	1 717.7	17 943.9	22 989.9	32 721.1	27 770.1
Coal...................	110.1	74.7	86.1	932.0	1 823.7	1 929.5	1 793.2
Natural gas.............	6.4	52.2	315.1	6 148.8	5 692.0	10 109.5	11 196.0
Natural gas by-products[1]..	n.a.	16.1	160.1	1 825.1	2 370.8	2 552.0	1 790.6
Petroleum, crude	84.6	422.9	1 156.5	9 037.9	13 103.4	18 130.2	12 990.3

Source: © Statistics Canada
(1) Incl. butane, propane and pentane plus.

Fuel Production by Province, 1998

(millions of dollars)

	Nfld	PEI	NS	NB	Que	Ont	Man	Sask	Alta	BC	YT	NWT
Total fuels....	454.9	–	263.8	23.1	–	65.7	76.8	2 449.0	21 677.8	2 569.0	17.7	172.4
Coal.........	–	–	138.0	23.1	–	–	–	126.4	519.0	986.7	–	–
Natural gas ...	–	–	–	–	–	39.0	–	377.2	9 616.9	1 132.9	17.7	12.2
Natural gas by-products[1]	–	–	–	–	–	–	–	7.4	1 711.4	71.8	–	–
Crude oil and equivalent ..	454.9	–	125.9	–	–	26.7	76.8	1 937.9	9 830.3	377.6	–	160.2

Source: © Statistics Canada
(1) Incl. butane, propane and pentane plus.

Primary Energy Supply

(annual petajoules)[1]

	Petroleum	Natural Gas[2]	Coal	Hydro-electricity	Nuclear Energy[3]	Steam & Biomass	Total
1988.........	3 878	3 465	1 614	1 096	281	516	11 222
1989.........	3 769	3 654	1 718	1 039	271	507	11 337
1990.........	3 765	3 732	1 673	1 058	248	477	11 343
1991.........	3 765	3 980	1 748	1 099	288	482	11 763
1992.........	3 932	4 415	1 554	1 128	274	483	12 218
1993.........	4 117	4 901	1 651	1 154	319	471	13 098
1994.........	4 300	5 353	1 735	1 176	366	548	13 979
1995.........	4 458	5 648	1 801	1 198	332	554	14 573
1996.........	4 591	5 852	1 832	1 268	315	552	14 999
1997.........	4 843	5 953	1 897	1 250	280	554	15 381
1998.........	5 013	6 135	1 801	1 183	243	569	15 564

Source: © Statistics Canada
(1) A petajoule is one quadrillion joules (10^{15}).
(2) Incl. butane, propane and pentane plus.
(3) 3.6 MJ/kwh.

Television Operating Revenues and Expenses[1]

	1995		1996		1997		1998	
	Private Broadcasters[2]	Cable[3]	Private Broadcasters[2]	Cable[3]	Private Broadcasters[2]	Cable[3]	Private Broadcasters[2]	Cable[3]
Revenues	1 530 515	1 846 052	1 581 024	1 903 555	1 703 298	1 967 920	1 821 868	2 008 990
Expenses								
Program	825 206	85 384	861 944	85 541	917 540	85 236	1 053 939	83 496
Technical services	75 486	605 668	75 946	422 808	73 837	641 833	77 818	665 891
Sales and promotion	168 201	59 512	172 057	69 815	187 962	61 869	202 504	106 880
Administration and general	210 069	409 864	199 434	395 040	200 014	394 190	226 493	470 918
Depreciation	55 674	297 280	58 835	324 139	59 716	368 866	60 352	409 572
Interest expense	103 893	337 638	102 126	409 366	84 945	489 321	80 231	481 919
Net profit after income tax	44 272	226 221	30 168	132 396	85 340	151 682	52 986	199 235
Total subscribers	7 791		7 867		7 957		8 254	

Source: © Statistics Canada
(1) Figures in thousands.
(2) Excludes cable TV, pay TV and non-commercial broadcasting stations operated by religious groups, educational institutions and provincial governments.
(3) Includes all cable TV systems licensed to operate in Canada by the CRTC. Master antenna TV and pay TV (such as First Choice or Superchannel) are not included.

Telephones

	Revenue (millions of dollars)			Lines in service (thousands)		
	Total	Local	Long Distance	Total	Residential	Business
1975	$ 2 788	$ 1 307	$ 1 407	12 328	8 620	3 709
1976	3 296	1 537	1 664	12 975	9 067	3 908
1977	3 766	1 756	1 892	13 695	9 599	4 095
1978	4 391	2 010	2 239	14 337	10 053	4 284
1979	5 080	2 246	2 636	15 071	10 534	4 538
1980	5 775	2 512	3 053	15 844	11 054	4 790
1981	6 828	2 948	3 625	16 375	11 366	5 008
1982	7 708	3 360	4 058	16 503	11 499	5 004
1983	8 363	3 524	4 404	16 296	11 467	4 829
1984	9 099	3 666	4 842	16 174	11 480	4 693
1985	9 814	3 798	5 333	15 555	11 126	4 429
1986	10 455	3 896	5 817	15 524	11 086	4 438
1987	10 954	4 044	6 055	15 383	10 991	4 392
1988	11 704	4 237	6 319	15 392	10 915	4 476
1989	12 659	4 593	6 791	15 497	10 949	4 548
1990	13 251	4 906	7 143	15 472	10 888	4 585
1991	13 267	5 137	7 006	15 187	10 671	4 515
1992	13 536	5 430	6 915	14 690	10 314	4 376
1993	13 838	5 827	6 795	14 182	9 985	4 196
1994	13 988	6 216	6 475	13 696	9 624	4 072
1995	14 106	6 647	5 983	n.a.	n.a.	n.a.
1996	15 889	6 391	5 483	17 781	11 910	5 871
1997	16 845	7 080	5 391	18 101	12 084	6 017
1998	17 367	8 118	4 793	18 688	12 295	6 392

Source: © Statistics Canada (n.a.) Not available.

Transportation and Storage Industries

Gross Domestic Product ($ millions)[1]

	1995	1996	1997	1998	1999
Transportation and storage industries total	30 368	31 132	32 948	33 576	34 916
Transportation industries	26 191	26 875	28 592	29 115	30 442
Air	3 562	3 686	4 084	4 227	4 291
Railway	3 902	3 994	4 328	4 217	4 462
Water	2 128	2 199	2 256	2 287	2 407
Truck	9 482	11 080	11 035	11 532	12 376
Public passenger transit systems	3 275	3 139	3 256	3 275	3 333
Other transport and services	3 842	3 777	3 633	3 577	3 573
Pipeline transport	3 360	3 376	3 430	3 528	3 525
Storage and warehousing industries	817	881	926	933	949

Source: © Statistics Canada (1) At 1992 prices.

Railways

	Total Railway Operating Revenue ($millions)	Freight Revenues ($millions)	Passenger Revenues ($millions)	Passenger (thousands)	Passenger Kilometres (thousands)
1992	$ 6 909 544	$ 5 930 457	$ 158 639	4 241	1 439 122
1993	6 992 827	5 959 792	168 592	4 112	1 412 752
1994	7 510 192	6 584 631	180 033	4 184	1 439 932
1995	7 206 586	6 370 251	179 470	4 082	1 472 620
1996	7 179 537	6 386 605	185 213	3 989	1 513 335
1997	7 898 383	7 076 555	199 069	4 104	1 514 593
1998	7 574 452	6 786 685	207 557	3 980	1 457 832

Source: © Statistics Canada

Major Canadian Airlines

	Total Operating Revenues ($thousands)	Total Operating Expenses ($thousands)	Total Passengers (thousands)	Total Passenger Kilometres (thousands)	Total Goods Transported (thousands of kilograms)	Total Goods Tonne-kilometres (thousands)
1984	$ 4 169 498	$ 4 089 755	22 628	44 665 698	396 632	1 120 391
1985	4 653 924	4 564 665	23 281	47 169 986	403 403	1 169 013
1986	4 889 763	4 599 049	23 188	49 124 261	379 238	1 155 488
1987	4 980 699	4 796 049	23 799	48 628 014	380 907	1 210 285
1988	5 453 507	5 262 624	24 097	54 279 293	403 806	1 323 315
1989	5 608 588	5 535 479	22 482	53 178 429	442 675	1 445 191
1990	5 660 477	5 765 017	21 236	50 091 785	435 224	1 487 833
1991	5 514 264	5 845 917	21 000	43 626 433	390 819	1 315 448
1992	5 498 189	5 820 218	21 261	45 414 285	392 514	1 331 586
1993	5 601 108	5 739 512	21 947	44 806 137	419 838	1 463 995
1994	5 529 198	5 356 713	19 126	45 281 336	395 674	1 537 977
1995	6 114 883	5 932 592	21 428	51 798 045	386 560	1 728 762
1996	6 322 113	6 369 399	23 164	57 016 000	405 975	1 882 803
1997	7 128 654	6 694 766	24 363	62 479 000	449 828	2 058 953
1998	7 463 998	7 382 909	24 571	64 426 000	431 150	2 340 594
1999	8 237 466	7 906 199	24 047	65 711 000	451 801	2 016 503

Source: © Statistics Canada

Manufacturing in Canada

(millions of dollars)[1]

	1985		1995	
	Value of Shipments of Goods Manufactured	Value Added	Value of Shipments of Goods Manufactured	Value Added
All Industries	248 492.6	95 875.3	396 384.3	161 793.0
Food	32 792.9	9 737.6	44 956.6	14 721.4
Beverage	4 863.7	2 735.9	6 808.5	3 893.1
Tobacco products	1 640.9	808.6	2 505.0	1 651.2
Rubber products	2 554.2	1 268.4	3 887.7	1 703.5
Plastic products	3 860.9	1 749.0	8 243.1	3 742.5
Leather and allied products	1 308.2	634.0	958.9	445.8
Primary textile	2 669.7	1 156.7	3 401.0	1 525.1
Textile products	2 650.1	1 145.8	3 286.7	1 480.0
Clothing	5 543.2	2 807.9	6 497.9	3 298.2
Wood	11 121.6	4 623.8	23 257.1	8 865.1
Furniture and fixtures	3 398.6	1 797.1	5 000.1	2 651.7
Paper and allied products	18 074.6	7 555.2	36 393.1	18 032.8
Printing, publishing and allied products	9 534.8	5 982.6	14 637.4	9 109.5
Primary metal	16 971.0	7 006.3	25 861.8	10 926.0
Fabricated metal products	13 971.0	6 638.1	20 226.6	10 319.4
Machinery	7 450.8	3 634.9	14 989.0	7 545.7
Transportation equipment	43 182.3	14 089.5	85 546.3	25 423.6
Electrical and electronic products	13 270.3	6 677.0	28 827.0	11 080.8
Non-metallic mineral products	5 879.1	3 047.1	7 137.2	3 842.6
Refined petroleum and coal products	24 420.8	2 614.2	18 066.7	2 848.2
Chemical and chemical products	18 268.6	7 625.3	28 553.8	14 490.9
Other manufacturing	5 065.4	2 540.6	7 342.7	4 196.0

	1996	1997	% Change
All Industries	406 579.1	434 082.9	6.8
Food	47 987.7	50 468.6	5.2
Beverage	6 857.2	7 183.3	4.8
Tobacco products	2 670.8	2 810.1	5.2
Rubber products	4 092.4	4 406.5	7.7
Plastic products	9 126.2	9 819.8	7.6
Leather and allied products	923.4	950.6	3.0
Primary textile	3 479.9	3 752.0	7.8
Textile products	3 258.1	3 431.9	5.3
Clothing	6 612.6	6 904.9	4.4
Wood	24 665.0	26 810.4	8.7
Furniture and fixtures	5 584.7	6 464.6	15.8
Paper and allied products	31 162.1	30 405.4	-2.4
Printing, publishing and allied products	15 317.8	15 759.1	2.9
Primary metal	25 955.6	27 918.9	7.6
Fabricated metal products	22 045.7	23 783.2	7.9
Machinery	16 008.6	17 930.1	12.0
Transportation equipment	87 180.7	96 052.0	10.2
Electrical and electronic products	28 062.6	30 040.2	7.0
Non-metallic mineral products	7 771.9	8 386.3	7.9
Refined petroleum and coal products	20 976.3	21 036.1	0.3
Chemical and chemical products	28 696.8	31 002.4	8.0
Other manufacturing	8 143.1	8 766.2	7.7

Source: © Statistics Canada

(1) Not adjusted for inflation.

Value of Manufacturing[1] by Province, 1997

(millions of dollars)

	Newfoundland	Prince Edward Island	Nova Scotia	New Brunswick	Quebec
All industries	1 658.2	802.3	6 464.6	8 434.6	102 825.6
Food	621.7	525.3	1 701.5	1 628.1	11 697.7
Beverage	n.a.	n.a.	146.0	192.0	1 867.1
Tobacco products	n.a.	n.a.	n.a.	n.a.	n.a.
Rubber products	n.a.	n.a.	n.a.	n.a.	1 298.6
Plastic products	21.4	n.a.	n.a.	n.a.	2 446.0
Leather and allied products	n.a.	n.a.	n.a.	5.3	437.3
Primary textile	n.a.	n.a.	n.a.	n.a.	1 941.9
Textile products	0.8	4.8	77.7	20.1	1 752.7
Clothing	n.a.	n.a.	55.4	n.a.	4 281.9
Wood	48.0	32.0	266.9	1 055.5	6 561.9
Furniture and fixture	n.a.	n.a.	37.9	n.a.	1 722.0
Paper and allied products	n.a.	5.9	667.1	1 879.9	10 069.0
Printing publishing and allied	67.3	24.5	188.6	124.1	4 337.0
Primary metal	n.a.	n.a.	n.a.	n.a.	9 562.2
Fabricated metal products	72.4	15.3	196.8	189.3	4 882.2
Machinery	3.5	22.0	51.1	97.0	3 122.5
Transportation equipment	34.9	94.9	829.7	127.7	10 581.6
Electrical and electronic products	n.a.	n.a.	119.8	n.a.	9 298.2
Non-metallic mineral products	34.4	10.7	107.8	77.5	1 789.2
Refined petroleum and coal products	n.a.	n.a.	n.a.	n.a.	3 976.4
Chemical and chemical products	25.1	41.5	92.4	105.7	7 284.1
Other manufacturing	21.7	2.5	n.a.	n.a.	n.a.

	Ontario	Manitoba	Saskatchewan	Alberta	British Columbia
All industries	228 505.2	9 969.3	6 114.5	34 675.7	34 582.7
Food	20 271.4	2 162.2	1 526.4	6 682.1	3 652.2
Beverage	3 148.8	202.4	103.3	641.7	775.3
Tobacco products	n.a.	n.a.	n.a.	n.a.	n.a.
Rubber products	2 279.4	n.a.	n.a.	n.a.	n.a.
Plastic products	5 408.0	292.0	72.5	697.4	634.5
Leather and allied products	372.4	66.3	4.0	32.3	11.5
Primary textile	1 442.3	n.a.	n.a.	n.a.	n.a.
Textile products	1 289.3	76.5	25.2	54.6	130.3
Clothing	1 737.5	327.2	24.0	186.9	264.7
Wood	4 520.8	434.5	306.3	2 110.3	11 474.1
Furniture and fixture	3 560.1	319.1	n.a.	540.5	242.0
Paper and allied products	9 139.8	364.7	n.a.	1 656.0	5 674.1
Printing publishing and allied	7 833.4	632.8	257.2	990.7	1 303.5
Primary metal	14 465.0	622.5	n.a.	1 339.8	1 070.8
Fabricated metal products	13 632.5	554.5	290.7	2 135.1	1 814.6
Machinery	9 388.0	1 379.5	590.8	2 168.0	1 107.7
Transportation equipment	80 992.6	1 342.5	196.5	559.1	1 292.5
Electrical and electronic products	16 579.4	410.9	330.6	2 048.6	1 200.6
Non-metallic mineral products	4 003.9	156.3	89.0	1 024.7	992.6
Refined petroleum and coal products	6 763.7	9.3	n.a.	4 989.7	1 373.5
Chemical and chemical products	15 403.5	427.7	562.1	6 045.7	1 014.7
Other manufacturing	n.a.	124.5	48.5	501.0	495.1

Source: © *Statistics Canada*   (n.a.) Not reported.

(1) Value of shipments of goods of own manufacture only. That is, does not include value added.

Retail Merchandising in Canada

(millions of dollars)[1]

	1994	1995	1996	1997	1998	1999
Total	207 841	213 774	220 870	237 837	246 641	260 691
Total excl. motor vehicles	159 096	161 714	165 367	175 089	182 183	191 314
Supermarkets and grocery stores	48 793	49 162	48 918	51 655	53 346	54 500
All other food stores	3 831	4 332	4 417	4 294	4 318	4 389
General merchandise stores	21 679	22 805	24 009	26 183	27 956	29 990
Rec. & motor vehicles	48 745	52 060	55 503	62 768	64 458	69 376
Service stations	14 256	14 766	16 774	16 928	16 187	18 001
Automotive parts and services	11 840	11 321	12 133	13 628	14 336	14 938
Shoe stores	1 751	1 682	1 683	1 650	1 671	1 626
Clothing stores – men's	1 687	1 623	1 516	1 570	1 582	1 536
Clothing stores – women's	4 127	4 229	4 203	4 335	4 406	4 505
Other clothing stores	4 812	5 377	5 522	5 830	6 259	6 667
Furniture and appliance stores	8 749	8 657	8 469	9 306	10 107	11 082
Other household furnishings stores	2 126	2 067	2 079	2 300	2 429	2 572
Drug stores	11 870	11 705	12 107	12 298	12 944	13 335
Other semi-durable goods stores	7 266	7 222	7 519	8 188	8 218	8 493
Other durable goods stores	5 596	5 475	5 551	6 008	6 750	7 060
Other	10 714	11 293	10 469	10 897	11 675	12 621
Volume (1992 $)	204 370	206 339	200 367	221 036	228 715	237 453
% Change	6.6	1.0	1.5	5.6	3.5	3.8

Source: © Statistics Canada

(1) Retail sales estimates exclude the Goods and Services Tax (GST).

Retail Merchandising by Province, 1999

(millions of dollars)

	Nfld	PEI	NS	NB	Que	Ont
Supermarkets, grocery and other food stores[1]	1 101.3	292.9	1 988.7	1 608.1	14 238.9	17 151.9
General merchandise and all other stores	923.6	232.8	1 790.7	1 324.0	10 891.1	24 376.5
Motor vehicle, recreational vehicle, automotive parts and gas stations	1 534.3	428.7	3 026.2	2 607.6	23 942.1	39 589.2
Shoe stores	14.6	—[1]	26.2	62.2	549.9	615.3
Clothing stores	141.8	30.5[1]	306.0	244.5	3 229.5	5 117.7
Household goods	143.1	47.9	302.6	245.9	3 380.2	5 183.1
Drug stores	240.4	71.6	530.6	349.9	2 823.6	5 619.1

	Man	Sask	Alta	BC	YT/NWT/NVT
Supermarkets, grocery and other food stores[1]	2 127.0	1 837.6	6 361.4	7 749.3	209.4
General merchandise and all other stores	1 994.0	1 713.0	6 728.2	7 999.2	329.8
Motor vehicle, recreational vehicle, automotive parts and gas stations	3 734.7	3 062.9	11 554.8	11 878.7	—[1]
Shoe stores	45.9	22.3	130.0	191.5	—[1]
Clothing stores	365.6	306.9	1 369.4	1 561.0	4.7[1]
Household goods	398.5	340.1	1 703.4	1 905.2	22.7
Drug Stores	289.6	388.4	1 292.4	1 795.0	—[1]

Source: © Statistics Canada

(1) Some data may be incomplete or not available in this category.

FOCUS ON...

E-Commerce

A majority of Canadian businesses has embraced the use of technologies such as e-mail and the Internet. One out of 10 companies used the Internet to sell goods and services in 1999, and these sales amounted to 0.2 percent of their total economic activity.

The total value of customer orders received over the Internet, with or without on-line payment, was $4.4 billion in 1999. Of this total, $4.2 billion was generated by the private sector. This amount represents only 0.2 percent of total operating revenues during the year, according to the first-ever national snapshot of electronic commerce and the use of information and communications technologies.

In fact, estimated Internet sales did not rise higher than 1.5 percent of any sector's total sales. Internet-based sales were 1.3 percent of total operating revenue in accommodation and food services, 1.0 percent in information and cultural industries, 0.8 percent in professional, scientific and technical services, and less than 0.5 percent in all other industrial sectors.

Manufacturers received orders worth just over $900.0 million on the Internet, about 22 percent of overall private sector Internet-based sales. This represented 0.2 percent of manufacturing shipments in 1999.

Retailers, who had Internet sales worth $610.6 million in 1999, and who accounted for 15 percent of total Internet sales, were in second place. This represented 0.2 percent of total retail sales in 1999. In the United States, retailers sold US$5.2 billion worth of goods and services on the Internet during the fourth quarter of 1999, according to the Census Bureau of the Department of Commerce. This represented 0.6 percent of total sales in the U.S. retail sector for the fourth quarter of 1999.

Information and cultural industries accounted for 13 percent of all Internet based-sales, the accommodation and food service sector 10 percent, and professional, scientific and technical services sector just under 10 percent. All the other industrial categories combined accounted for the remaining 30 percent of Internet-based sales.

On average, a greater proportion of businesses used the Internet to buy goods and services rather than to sell. In the private sector, 14 percent of businesses used the Internet for purchasing; these firms accounted for 25 percent of total operating revenue. Again, ranking first was the information and cultural industries sector, where half of firms reported using the Internet to buy goods or services.

While 22 percent of private sector firms had a Web site in 1999, some sectors were more likely to have a Web presence. The information and cultural industries sector led the way, with 62 percent of enterprises. About 44 percent of firms in the private educational services sector had a Web site, including private elementary schools, private technical and trade schools, and language schools, followed by just 32 percent of the manufacturing sector.

In the public sector, 69 percent of institutions had a Web site. The public educational services sector led the way; 98 percent of institutions had a site. This sector includes public elementary and secondary schools, community colleges and universities. Eighty-eight percent of institutions in the public administration sector had a Web site.

Source: *Statistics Canada*

Value of Internet Sales, 1999

Private Sector (millions of dollars)

	Internet sales with or without on-line payment	Total operating revenue[1]	Internet sales as % of total operating revenue
Manufacturing	900.0	568 346	0.2%
Retail trade	610.6	231 622	0.3%
Information and cultural industries	552.7	55 910	1.0%
Accommodation and food services	429.3	32 474	1.3%
Professional, scientific and technical services	406.1	52 116	0.8%
Finance and insurance	320.8	222 483	0.1%
Transport and warehousing	164.3	65 268	0.3%
Wholesale trade	156.3	290 440	0.1%
Real estate and rental and leasing	114.8	37 954	0.3%
Other services (except public administration)	27.4	37 439	0.1%
Utilities	15.8	24 499	0.1%
Mining and oil and gas extraction	15	67 517	0%
Health care and social assistance (private sector)	10	11 441	0.1%
Other industry sectors[2]	456.6	104 577	0.4%
All private sector[1]	**4 179.70**	**1 802 086**	**0.2%**

Source: © Statistics Canada

(1) Sum of total operating revenue for each quarter of 1999; excluding Construction. (2) Other industry sectors include: Administration and support; Waste management and remediation services; Arts, entertainment and recreation; Private educational services; Management of companies and enterprises; and Forestry, logging and support activities.

E-Commerce, 1999

Business Use (percentage)

	Use of Internet	Have a Web site	Purchase internet goods or services	Economic activity due to use of Internet to purchase	Sell goods or services on the Internet	Economic activity due to use of Internet to sell
Forestry, logging and support activities	32.8	5.7	7.4	10.6	1.1	0.9
Mining and oil and gas extraction	60.6	27.6	19.3	24.5	7.1	5.2
Utilities	82.4	27.3	24.7	37.7	9.2	9.8
Manufacturing	63.7	31.7	18.9	31.8	14.9	16.3
Wholesale trade	63.0	26.1	13.9	23.2	13.6	17.1
Retail trade	40.5	16.0	10.8	15.7	10.9	21.9
Transport and warehousing	43.8	17.6	10.7	27.8	10.1	21.1
Information and cultural industries	89.1	61.7	49.6	53.6	20.1	44.3
Finance and insurance	65.9	27.2	12.7	39.5	14.7	23.0
Real estate and rental and leasing	46.3	18.4	8.2	11.3	9.5	11.5
Professional, scientific and technical services	77.5	27.6	30.0	39.7	11.5	14.9
Management of companies and enterprises	47.0	9.9	12.9	16.8	8.0	3.7
Administration and support, waste management and remediation services	55.4	29.5	13.4	17.7	17.3	23.3
Educational services (private sector)	74.5	44.0	27.2	35.3	17.3	22.2
Health care and social assistance (private sector)	46.2	10.0	9.5	14.4	3.1	6.3
Arts, entertainment and recreation	51.0	29.7	12.1	16.5	10.1	22.2
Accommodation and food services	32.0	17.4	3.9	8.5	7.9	16.3
Other services (except public administration)	44.5	19.3	6.5	10.3	3.7	5.0
All private sectors	**52.8**	**21.7**	**13.8**	**25.1**	**10.1**	**17.0**
Educational services (public sector)	99.2	97.6	60.6	65.5	32.2	43.4
Health care and social assistance (public sector)	92.8	50.0	34.7	37.2	3.1	3.3
Public administration	98.0	87.8	50.7	59.8	24.7	28.2
All public sectors	**95.4**	**69.2**	**44.2**	**52.0**	**14.5**	**23.1**

Source: © Statistics Canada
Note: Estimates are weighted by revenue for the private sector, and by the number of employees for the public sector.

New Vehicle Sales in Canada

New motor vehicle sales has stabilized since the fall of 1999, after a strong upward movement that began at the end of 1998. Generally, sales were relatively stable in 1998, but with sizable monthly fluctuations.

New passenger car sales have been slowing since the end of 1999, after a period of growth that started in the fall of 1998. Previously, sales of new passenger cars had been generally stable since the summer of 1997.

Source: © Statistics Canada

(thousands of units)

	Total units sold	Total commercial vehicles	Total passenger cars	Passenger cars manufactured in North America	% of total passenger cars	Passenger cars manufactured overseas	% of total passenger cars
1953	466	103	363	337	93	26	7
1954	384	72	312	292	94	20	6
1955	463	78	385	363	94	23	6
1956	495	91	404	370	92	34	8
1957	460	76	384	333	87	50	13
1958	450	69	381	302	79	78	21
1959	500	78	423	310	73	113	27
1960	522	75	446	321	72	126	28
1961	515	75	440	339	77	102	23
1962	577	82	495	420	85	74	15
1963	648	98	550	499	91	51	9
1964	723	108	614	549	89	65	11
1965	828	122	706	631	89	75	11
1966	831	133	698	630	90	68	10
1967	812	136	677	603	89	74	11
1968	887	148	739	636	86	104	14
1969	920	157	763	641	84	122	16
1970	773	134	640	496	78	144	22
1971	935	159	776	588	76	187	24
1972	1 062	207	855	651	76	204	24
1973	1 230	256	973	784	81	190	19
1974	1 249	306	943	796	84	147	16
1975	1 328	328	1 000	844	84	156	16
1976	1 281	343	939	785	84	153	16
1977	1 349	355	994	802	81	192	19
1978	1 365	377	987	816	83	171	17
1979	1 396	393	1 003	862	86	141	14
1980	1 268	332	936	742	79	194	21
1981	1 191	286	906	649	72	256	28
1982	925	207	718	494	69	224	31
1983	1 079	238	841	623	74	218	26
1984	1 283	312	971	724	75	247	25
1985	1 528	393	1 135	795	70	340	30
1986	1 523	422	1 102	765	69	337	31
1987	1 530	469	1 061	698	66	364	34
1988	1 564	508	1 056	724	69	332	31
1989	1 481	496	985	671	68	313	32
1990	1 318	433	885	579	65	306	35
1991	1 288	415	873	573	66	300	34
1992	1 227	429	798	503	63	295	37
1993	1 193	454	739	494	67	245	33
1994	1 260	511	749	573	77	175	23
1995	1 167	496	670	553	83	117	17
1996	1 205	544	661	573	87	88	13
1997	1 424	685	739	629	85	110	15
1998.....	1 428	688	741	591	80	150	20
1999.....	1 542	736	806	625	78	181	22

Source: © Statistics Canada

Operating Profits by Major Industry

(millions of dollars)[1]

Some industries have fared better than others when it comes to making profits in the last fifteen years—or perhaps just not quite as badly. While businesses in industries such as food, computers and electronics, and communications have experienced a measure of stability when it comes to making profits, others—such as wood and paper, construction, metals, motor vehicles and transportation—have come through much more volatile times.

Nineteen ninety-nine saw a growth in profits for most major industries, although the difference in growth varied dramatically for some industries and fell for a couple. Education saw a sharp rise in profit, increasing by 259.8 percent, while the second largest increase was Agriculture at 101.8 percent. Most other industries experienced a profit, ranging from an increase of 68 percent to a mere 1 percent. In contrast, profit for the Construction industry decreased by 33.2 percent in 1999. The only other industry that did not show a profit was Information and Recreation, which fell by 1.7 percent.

	Agriculture & Other Primary	Utilities	Manufacturing	Construction	Transportation	Trade	Finance, Insurance & Real Estate
1988	5 768	1 535	25 448	16 297	1 223	12 370	29 678
1989	5 602	1 552	22 591	21 332	1 116	12 773	34 374
1990	6 545	1 499	14 993	22 464	1 044	10 713	32 868
1991	3 430	1 415	7 258	15 453	927	8 514	34 431
1992	4 637	1 506	8 374	5 595	850	6 148	26 392
1993	6 378	1 565	13 746	2 764	1 421	7 231	34 676
1994	8 669	1 757	24 499	8 212	1 872	10 214	34 226
1995	8 246	1 842	34 786	9 604	2 043	11 487	40 946
1996	10 957	2 094	29 967	8 036	2 058	10 176	48 383
1997	10 420	2 026	34 852	7 606	2 557	12 272	60 231
1998	5 366	1 973	35 039	5 057	2 172	13 040	53 720
1999	10 831	2 633	46 464	3 378	2 198	21 788	58 176

	Health & Social	Managerial & Related	Professional & Related	Educational	Information & Recreation	Accommodation & Food	Other Services
1988	402	22 583	728	286	4 764	2 219	1 026
1989	504	26 041	1 050	-42	5 154	2 352	1 086
1990	591	31 510	821	87	5 071	1 991	934
1991	593	30 144	372	214	5 537	1 488	732
1992	639	23 161	464	235	5 821	1 394	537
1993	843	24 101	574	248	5 500	929	630
1994	881	22 040	912	279	5 802	1 419	917
1995	884	21 107	1 035	123	5 465	2 020	1 082
1996	1 078	17 762	636	35	6 148	2 276	1 136
1997	1 130	20 382	898	73	7 222	2 919	1 437
1998	1 152	12 221	1 084	107	7 165	2 591	1 607
1999	1 382	13 304	1 817	385	7 046	2 811	2 104

Source: © Statistics Canada

LABOUR

Provincial Labour Force by Industry, 1989
(thousands)

	Canada	Nfld	PEI	NS	NB	Que	Ont	Man	Sask	Alta	BC
All Industries	14 046.6	243.9	63.6	423.5	337.1	3 456.0	5 469.8	554.7	492.0	1 347.4	1 658.5
Agriculture	476.3	2.7	6.7	7.7	7.2	75.0	119.8	41.6	83.2	94.6	37.7
Primary industries[1]	342.0	18.6	3.5	19.6	15.9	53.6	66.2	10.2	14.6	76.9	63.0
Utilities	139.6	3.3	0.3	3.6	3.9	29.3	64.5	6.3	4.8	11.9	11.7
Construction	916.3	18.4	5.7	31.6	24.9	204.7	357.1	27.3	29.3	93.8	123.4
Manufacturing	2 272.6	30.1	5.1	52.6	43.0	660.4	1 090.3	65.4	27.1	104.7	193.9
Trade[2]	2 184.8	40.9	9.5	73.0	56.1	541.3	822.0	85.5	73.3	216.1	267.1
Transportation & warehousing	697.7	12.5	2.8	20.6	17.3	172.7	244.0	38.7	21.8	71.2	96.1
Finance, insurance, real estate & leasing	844.9	8.1	2.0	21.5	14.8	193.0	378.4	30.2	23.6	72.8	100.4
Services[3]	578.5	5.9	1.3	12.1	7.9	119.7	254.6	17.7	11.4	61.1	86.7
Management, admin. & other support	345.6	4.1	0.9	8.6	6.3	77.6	150.6	12.1	8.0	35.2	42.1
Educational serv.	863.4	17.8	3.7	28.4	23.1	214.4	329.1	35.0	31.3	90.1	90.4
Health care & social assist.	1 272.4	24.9	5.9	42.2	34.9	322.7	467.6	59.1	50.9	118.9	145.3
Information, culture & rec.	559.7	6.9	2.3	14.1	10.0	122.4	239.4	20.8	17.3	54.0	72.5
Accommodation & food serv.	826.6	13.5	4.5	25.6	21.2	192.5	307.6	34.2	27.8	74.4	125.2
Other services	660.0	11.2	3.4	21.4	18.0	183.0	227.9	24.9	25.6	62.3	82.3
Public administration[4]	844.4	18.8	5.4	33.8	25.7	210.9	301.7	36.4	33.0	90.3	88.4
Unclassified	221.8	6.2	0.7	6.9	7.1	82.8	48.8	9.3	8.8	19.0	32.3

Source: © *Statistics Canada* (1) Primary industries include fishing, trapping, forestry, mining, oil and gas extractions. (2) Trade is the sales and distribution network of merchandise. Includes wholesale and retail. (3) Services refers to professional, scientific and technical occupations in which a service is provided but no goods are produced. (4) Includes municipal, provincial and federal levels.

Provincial Employment by Industry, 1989
(thousands)

	Canada	Nfld	PEI	NS	NB	Que	Ont	Man	Sask	Alta	BC
All Industries	12 986.4	206.2	54.9	382.1	296.3	3 123.7	5 193.4	513.7	456.0	1 251.4	1 508.9
Agriculture	452.2	2.1	5.7	6.7	5.8	68.1	115.6	40.6	81.7	92.9	33.0
Primary industries[1]	308.2	16.4	2.7	16.9	12.9	46.7	62.6	9.4	13.3	72.7	54.5
Utilities	136.7	3.2	0.3	3.5	3.8	28.8	63.4	6.1	4.7	11.7	11.3
Construction	811.8	12.5	4.1	26.4	20.0	178.9	329.6	23.1	24.7	81.9	110.5
Manufacturing	2 129.7	24.2	4.1	47.7	37.8	610.6	1 042.8	61.7	25.1	97.6	178.0
Trade[2]	2 054.3	36.0	8.9	68.3	52.0	497.5	786.0	80.4	69.2	205.1	250.9
Transportation & warehousing	664.3	11.5	2.4	19.1	16.0	164.2	234.8	36.8	20.4	68.1	90.9
Finance, insurance, real estate & leasing	815.6	7.7	2.0	20.1	13.9	184.4	369.8	29.3	22.7	69.2	96.5
Services[3]	554.6	5.4	1.2	11.5	7.2	113.3	246.1	17.0	10.7	58.0	84.0
Management, admin. & other support	310.1	3.5	0.8	7.5	5.3	66.6	141.3	10.6	7.2	31.6	35.8
Educational serv.	832.9	16.8	3.5	27.2	21.9	205.0	321.4	33.7	30.1	86.9	86.4
Health care & social assist.	1 230.4	23.2	5.6	40.4	32.9	313.0	456.1	56.7	49.5	114.7	138.7
Information, culture & rec.	524.7	6.3	2.0	13.0	9.2	110.5	228.7	19.6	16.2	50.9	68.4
Accommodation & food serv.	744.5	11.3	3.4	22.5	18.1	169.6	285.8	30.8	25.1	66.3	111.2
Other services	618.3	9.5	3.0	19.8	16.5	170.2	216.8	23.6	24.3	58.4	76.3
Public administration[4]	797.9	16.6	4.8	31.7	23.1	196.1	292.4	34.1	31.1	85.4	82.6

Source: © *Statistics Canada* (1) Primary industries include fishing, trapping, forestry, mining, oil and gas extractions. (2) Trade is the sales and distribution network of merchandise. Includes wholesale and retail. (3) Services refers to professional, scientific and technical occupations in which a service is provided but no goods are produced. (4) Includes municipal, provincial and federal levels.

Labour 229

Provincial Labour Force by Industry, 1999

(thousands)

	Canada	Nfld	PEI	NS	NB	Que	Ont	Man	Sask	Alta	BC
All Industries	15 721.2	246.7	71.6	452.0	365.7	3 701.6	6 070.8	574.8	511.0	1 647.9	2 079.1
Agriculture	432.4	1.5	5.0	8.2	6.7	67.4	120.8	38.0	68.8	84.0	31.9
Primary industries[1]	305.2	17.8	3.8	17.6	15.0	47.1	40.9	7.5	15.2	83.8	56.6
Utilities	118.3	2.4	0.0	2.2	3.8	26.9	50.5	6.4	3.7	10.7	11.6
Construction	866.1	17.0	5.0	26.0	23.4	153.6	325.6	32.2	27.0	127.6	128.5
Manufacturing	2 344.8	23.5	7.3	49.7	43.8	686.1	1 091.4	68.4	30.1	141.3	203.3
Trade[2]	2 360.7	38.5	10.4	74.9	57.9	548.9	887.5	86.6	79.7	250.5	325.7
Transportation & warehousing	777.7	12.3	2.7	22.2	20.1	172.3	268.0	35.8	26.0	95.7	122.7
Finance, insurance, real estate & leasing	885.5	8.2	2.1	23.6	14.1	182.7	392.3	31.3	25.1	83.2	122.9
Services[3]	938.4	6.7	1.9	18.4	11.5	205.0	408.2	23.1	16.1	106.1	141.4
Management, admin. & other support	556.5	5.5	2.1	16.1	12.9	114.9	243.6	17.8	12.9	60.1	70.5
Educational services	1015.5	18.0	4.3	32.0	23.9	242.7	378.0	39.5	37.5	108.1	131.5
Health care & social assistance	1 478.4	30.1	7.5	49.4	40.0	356.2	529.1	65.0	52.2	148.7	200.2
Information, culture & recreation	669.7	6.5	2.6	16.9	15.2	153.1	269.2	19.9	21.0	68.5	96.8
Accommodation and food services	1 003.0	13.3	5.1	31.5	24.2	217.8	362.6	35.8	33.8	112.0	166.9
Other services	765.0	14.7	3.9	25.0	21.0	191.3	266.8	25.1	26.1	79.7	111.4
Public administration[4]	802.2	19.4	6.5	27.1	24.3	210.8	292.0	33.7	27.4	67.5	93.4
Unclassified	401.9	11.2	1.3	11.3	7.9	124.7	144.3	8.7	8.4	20.4	63.8

Source: © *Statistics Canada* (1) Primary industries include fishing, trapping, forestry, mining, oil and gas extractions. (2) Trade is the sales and distribution network of merchandise. Includes wholesale and retail. (3) Services refers to professional, scientific and technical occupations in which a service is provided but no goods are produced. (4) Includes municipal, provincial and federal levels.

Provincial Employment by Industry, 1999

(thousands)

	Canada	Nfld	PEI	NS	NB	Que	Ont	Man	Sask	Alta	BC
All Industries	14 531.2	204.9	61.3	408.6	328.4	3 357.4	5 688.1	542.7	480.1	1 553.3	1 906.4
Agriculture	410.3	1.1	4.0	6.9	5.8	62.6	114.0	37.3	67.5	82.5	28.6
Primary industries[1]	267.5	15.1	2.6	15.0	12.1	37.6	38.1	6.8	13.5	77.8	49.0
Utilities	115.8	2.3	0.0	2.1	3.7	26.6	49.5	6.4	3.7	10.0	11.5
Construction	774.8	11.6	3.9	21.8	19.3	132.6	300.1	29.3	23.5	117.4	115.3
Manufacturing	2 217.4	18.1	6.2	45.0	39.3	640.7	1 048.7	64.5	28.4	134.3	192.2
Trade[2]	2 248.3	35.0	9.6	70.7	54.5	518.3	850.2	83.4	76.6	241.4	308.5
Transportation & warehousing	744.5	10.8	2.2	21.0	19.0	162.8	260.0	34.7	24.9	91.0	117.9
Finance, insurance, real estate & leasing	862.9	7.9	2.0	23.0	13.6	176.6	384.1	30.7	24.7	80.4	119.9
Services[3]	905.0	6.0	1.8	17.4	10.6	196.1	396.5	22.3	15.2	102.5	136.7
Management, admin. & other support	507.2	4.2	1.8	14.1	11.3	103.0	224.2	16.4	11.8	56.4	64.1
Educational services	982.6	16.8	4.1	30.8	22.5	233.4	368.2	37.9	36.3	105.1	127.5
Health care & social assistance	1 444.4	29.0	7.2	48.0	38.7	347.7	518.3	63.7	51.2	145.4	195.2
Information, culture and recreation	630.0	5.6	2.2	15.3	13.6	142.7	256.6	18.8	20.0	63.5	91.6
Accommodation & food services	924.8	11.7	4.1	28.7	21.7	197.0	340.3	33.2	30.9	104.5	152.7
Other services	721.6	12.3	3.5	23.2	19.7	178.9	253.8	24.2	25.3	75.4	105.2
Public administration[4]	774.2	17.6	6.0	25.6	22.9	200.9	285.5	33.0	26.7	65.8	90.4

Source: © *Statistics Canada* (1) Primary industries include fishing, trapping, forestry, mining, oil and gas extractions. (2) Trade is the sales and distribution network of merchandise. Includes wholesale and retail. (3) Services refers to professional, scientific and technical occupations in which a service is provided but no goods are produced. (4) Includes municipal, provincial and federal levels.

Canadian Labour Force by Province, 1999

(thousands)

	Population 15 Years and Over	Labour Force[1]	Participation Rate[2]	Employed	Employment Population Ratio[3]	Un- employed	% Un- employed[4]
Canada	23 969.0	15 721.2	65.6	14 531.2	60.6	1 190.1	7.6
Newfoundland	438.4	246.7	56.3	204.9	46.7	41.7	16.9
Prince Edward Island	107.9	71.6	66.4	61.3	56.8	10.3	14.4
Nova Scotia	740.8	452.0	61.0	408.6	55.2	43.3	9.6
New Brunswick	599.5	365.7	61.0	328.4	54.8	37.3	10.2
Quebec	5 893.3	3 701.6	62.8	3 357.4	57.0	344.2	9.3
Ontario	9 111.1	6 070.8	66.6	5 688.1	62.4	382.7	6.3
Manitoba	852.0	574.8	67.5	542.7	63.7	32.2	5.6
Saskatchewan	762.8	511.0	67.0	480.1	62.9	31.0	6.1
Alberta	2 270.4	1 647.9	72.6	1 553.3	68.4	94.7	5.7
British Columbia	3 192.9	2 079.1	65.1	1 906.4	59.7	172.8	8.3

Source: © Statistics Canada

(1) The labour force consists of employed workers, and those who are unemployed but actively seeking work. (2) Participation rate is the percent of the total population aged 15 and over that makes up the labour force. (3) The percent of the total population aged 15 and over that is employed. (4) The percent of the labour force that is unemployed.

Labour Force by Age, 1999

(thousands)

	Population 15 Years and Over	Labour Force[1]	Participation Rate[2]	Employed	Employment Population Ratio[3]	Un- employed	% Un- employed[4]
Males	11 768.3	8 534.0	72.5	7 865.8	66.8	6 68.2	7.8
15–19	1 034.3	525.0	50.8	422.2	40.8	102.8	19.6
20–24	1 026.8	821.8	80.0	718.8	70.0	103.1	12.5
25–34	2 184.8	1 999.9	91.5	1 847.7	84.6	152.3	7.6
35–44	2 588.5	2 396.3	92.6	2 244.6	86.7	151.6	6.3
45–54	2 068.0	1 834.9	88.7	1 732.0	83.8	102.9	5.6
55–59	730.1	527.2	72.2	492.4	67.4	34.7	6.6
60–64	594.5	277.1	46.6	260.9	43.9	16.2	5.8
65–69	537.3	91.1	17.0	88.6	16.5	2.5	2.7
70 and over	1004	60.8	6.1	58.7	5.8	2.0	3.3
Females	12 200.8	7187.2	58.9	6 665.3	54.6	521.9	7.3
15–19	985.3	490.7	49.8	408.5	41.5	82.2	16.8
20–24	991.6	728.1	73.4	656.8	66.2	71.3	9.8
25–34	2 170.8	1 718.3	79.2	1 599.0	73.7	119.2	6.9
35–44	2 597.1	2 075.9	79.9	1 943.5	74.8	132.4	6.4
45–54	2 091.7	1 566.9	74.9	1 480.2	70.8	86.7	5.5
55–59	747.7	378.5	50.6	357.8	47.9	20.6	5.4
60–64	620.8	161.1	26.0	153.1	24.7	8.1	5.0
65–69	582.3	41.8	7.2	40.7	7.0	0	0
70 and over	1 413.4	26.0	1.8	25.7	1.8	0	0

Source: © Statistics Canada

(1) The labour force consists of employed workers, and those who are unemployed but actively seeking work. (2) Participation rate is the percent of the total population aged 15 and over that makes up the labour force. (3) The percent of the total population aged 15 and over that is employed. (4) The percent of the labour force that is unemployed.

Average Weekly Earnings[1]

(dollars)

	1996	1997	1998	1999
Average weekly earnings	586.06	598.26	606.31	610.4
Goods producing industries	742.16	762.22	776.46	775.48
Forestry	768.63	793.12	767.91	774.65
Mining	1 039.08	1 057.61	1 111.82	1 112.94
Manufacturing	716.62	736.69	755.92	755.86
Construction	695.67	711.35	697.57	698.8
Services-producing industries	539.29	548.56	553.87	559.19
Transportation, communication and other utilities	735.32	754.55	766.68	772.49
Trade	439.72	451.89	467.77	472.56
Finance, insurance, and real estate	704.59	742.17	754.62	760.73
Services	501.18	506.58	507.09	513.45
Public administration	740.05	739.57	737.53	741.07

Source: © Statistics Canada

(1) Includes overtime.

Labour Income[1]

(millions of dollars)

	1970	1975	1980	1985	1990
Total labour income[2]	215 562	299 915	351 781	368 916	428 291
Agriculture, fishing and trapping	1 809	2 345	2 746	3 115	3 081
Forestry	2 356	2 890	3 333	2 669	2 913
Mines	4 788	6 296	9 206	9 635	8 638
Manufacturing	52 797	63 076	71 172	69 459	71 550
Construction	14 024	24 279	23 009	19 076	26 504
Transportation, communication and other utilities	22 492	28 897	34 427	34 962	36 738
Trade	28 537	39 722	44 190	44 403	55 094
Finance, insurance and real estate	11 093	17 304	22 972	25 476	32 272
Services	49 162	70 146	85 129	95 690	116 982
Public administration	15 258	2 2677	25 751	28 403	31 202

	1995	1996	1997	1998	1999
Total labour income[2]	435 528	428 792	453 103	474 571	498 836
Agriculture, fishing and trapping	3 164	3 511	3 720	3 846	3 767
Forestry	3 202	3 007	3 053	2 984	3 013
Mining	7 881	8 375	9 296	9 802	9 648
Manufacturing	68 729	68 677	72 488	77 562	82 468
Construction	20 876	20 231	22 962	24 335	26 400
Transportation, communication and other utilities	35 864	34 571	35 761	37 332	39 160
Trade	54 089	53 113	57 491	60 633	64 138
Finance, insurance and real estate	40 104	31 460	31 838	35 900	38 137
Services	124 562	122 154	127 580	134 867	141 937
Public administration	29 650	30 244	29 786	29 692	30 743

Source: © Statistics Canada

(1) Figures adjusted for inflation. (2) Total includes income categories not shown.

Employment in Manufacturing by Sector

1989	Number of Manufacturing Establishments	Number of Production and Related Workers	Person Hours Paid
All Industries	39 150	1 495 937	3 124 874
Food	3 385	145 804	296 875
Beverage	274	15 828	33 136
Tobacco products	19	2 874	5 050
Rubber products	193	18 793	39 463
Plastic products	1 257	43 556	90 919
Leather and allied products	353	16 353	33 368
Primary textile	221	18 428	40 097
Textile products	915	30 170	64 574
Clothing	2 686	97 276	194 245
Wood	3 380	106 682	223 850
Furniture and fixtures	1 845	55 784	116 937
Paper and allied products	746	90 781	195 159
Printing, publishing and allied products	5 207	87 002	173 098
Primary metal	523	82 110	173 558
Fabricated metal products	5 926	153 392	319 939
Machinery	2 173	72 519	153 113
Transportation equipment	1 699	188 887	411 579
Electrical and electronic products	1 627	104 259	215 776
Non-metallic mineral products	1 688	46 019	98 861
Refined petroleum and coal products	163	6 973	14 482
Chemical and chemical products	1 443	51 955	110 458
Other manufacturing	3 427	60 492	120 336

1997	Number of Manufacturing Establishments	Number of Production and Related Workers	Person Hours Paid
All industries	34 935	1 409 852	2 924 759
Food	3 072	153 063	307 499
Beverage	199	11 723	24 552
Tobacco products	18	2 363	4 460
Rubber products	216	20 264	43 335
Plastic products	1 294	54 883	114 282
Leather and allied products	211	9 158	17 630
Primary textile	174	1 605	33 674
Textile products	757	23 216	48 305
Clothing	1 665	71 353	145 630
Wood	3 019	111 853	233 055
Furniture and fixture	1 315	49 438	103 312
Paper and allied products	691	81 240	172 959
Printing, publishing and allied	4 748	75 738	152 674
Primary metal	453	71 171	151 177
Fabricated metal products	5 787	143 632	300 073
Machinery	2 068	76 858	160 392
Transportation equipment	1 495	198 009	413 964
Electrical and electronic products	1 516	87 880	181 018
Non-metallic mineral products	1 631	36 208	75 924
Refined petroleum and coal products	186	5 866	12 989
Chemical and chemical products	1 365	51 416	109 305
Other manufacturing	3 055	58 415	118 550

Source: © Statistics Canada

Employment in Retail by Sector

1989	Total Number of Employees	Number of Employees Paid by the Hour	Average Weekly Hours
All Retail[1]	1 434 200	1 011 600	26.8
Food stores	334 000	260 600	25.7
Liquor, wine & beer stores	25 800	17 500	29.3
General merchandise stores	220 900	188 800	23.3
Rec. & motor vehicle dealers	118 400	59 100	35.7
Gasoline service stations	105 200	74 700	30.2
Automotive parts	40 800	27 800	28.5
Shoe stores	19 400	11 800	27.4
Clothing stores - men's	21 100	11 660	22.7
Clothing stores - women's	56 900	43 000	23.8
Other clothing stores	48 400	35 600	22.6
Furniture & appliance stores	63 100	30 800	30.9
Other household furnishing stores	26 800	13 700	30.6
Drug stores	69 100	59 000	24.2
Other retail stores	192 800	123 100	26.4

1999	Total Number of Employees	Number of Employees Paid by the Hour	Average Weekly Hours
All Retail	1 435 100	996 800	26.9
Food stores	374 200	295 700	25.8
Liquor, wine & beer stores	22 500	18 100	24.9
General merchandise stores	179 200	141 500	26.7
Rec. & motor vehicle dealers	129 100	54 800	36.0
Gasoline service stations	58 600	45 800	26.7
Automotive parts	49 300	29 200	31.7
Shoe stores	13 900	10 400	23.5
Clothing stores - men's	13 500	10 000	24.8
Clothing stores - women's	52 900	39 800	23.1
Other clothing stores	47 400	35 300	22.5
Furniture & appliance stores	62 500	29 600	29.9
Other household furnishing stores	20 300	9 500	29.6
Drug stores	91 800	75 800	25.2
Other retail stores	226 900	145 100	25.6

Source: © Statistics Canada

(1) Totals may not add due to rounding or exclusion of some sectors.

Measuring Productivity

*P*roductivity refers to the "efficiency with which the economy transforms inputs into output" according to Statistics Canada. Growth in this area (or lack of) has been a source of concern among economists studying our financial future. How do they measure this?

There are different ways. Labour productivity refers to the amount of output per hour worked; multifactor productivity measures the combined output of labour and capital. Increasing efficiencies mean growth in productivity without having to increase labour or capital investments.

Between 1988 and 1999, multifactor productivity in business grew at an annual average rate of 0.7% compared to 2.3% recorded from 1966 to 1973. Annual average growth between 1973 and 1979 was 0.6%; between 1979 and 1988 the annual average figure was 0.4%.

PERSONAL FINANCE

What's a Dollar Worth?[1]

This table shows how many current (2000) dollars it would take to equal the purchasing power of a single dollar in earlier years. For example, if you spent $30 a week on groceries in 1985 and want to know what that would be by today's standards, multiply $30 times the relative value of a 1985 dollar ($1.52) and you have your answer: $45.60. The relative value of a dollar for the years listed was calculated according to changes in the cost of living in Canada as measured by the Consumer Price Index (CPI).

CPI by Year	Rate	2000	CPI by Year	Rate	2000	CPI by Year	Rate	2000	CPI by Year	Rate	2000
1915	7.3	15.58	1960	18.5	6.15	1974	31.1	3.66	1988	84.7	1.34
1920	13.5	8.42	1961	18.7	6.08	1975	34.5	3.30	1989	89.2	1.27
1925	10.9	10.43	1962	18.9	6.02	1976	37.1	3.06	1990	93.1	1.22
1930	10.9	10.43	1963	19.2	5.92	1977	40.0	2.84	1991	98.9	1.15
1935	8.7	13.07	1964	19.6	5.80	1978	43.6	2.61	1992	100.0	1.14
1940	9.5	11.97	1965	20.0	5.69	1979	47.6	2.39	1993	101.6	1.12
1945	10.9	10.43	1966	20.8	5.47	1980	52.1	2.18	1994	101.6	1.12
1950	14.9	7.63	1967	21.5	5.29	1981	58.9	1.93	1995	104.4	1.09
1955	16.8	6.77	1968	22.4	5.08	1982	65.3	1.74	1996	105.9	1.07
1956	17.1	6.65	1969	23.4	4.86	1983	69.2	1.64	1997	107.7	1.06
1957	17.6	6.46	1970	24.2	4.70	1984	72.1	1.58	1998	108.8	1.05
1958	18.0	6.32	1971	24.9	4.57	1985	75.0	1.52	1999	110.5	1.03
1959	18.3	6.21	1972	26.1	4.36	1986	77.8	1.46	2000	113.7	1.00
			1973	28.1	4.05	1987	81.5	1.40			

Source: © Statistics Canada

(1) Based on Consumer Price Index as of June 30, 2000.

Credit Summary
(millions of dollars)[1]

Year	Household Credit			Business Credit
	Consumer	Mortgage	Total	
1971	11 441	19 520	30 961	58 927
1972	13 334	23 214	36 548	63 890
1973	16 091	28 138	44 229	69 996
1974	18 966	34 269	53 236	80 039
1975	21 746	40 269	62 014	90 702
1976	25 234	48 067	73 302	100 988
1977	29 039	58 538	87 577	113 704
1978	33 362	69 767	103 129	128 391
1979	38 465	81 333	119 798	151 757
1980	42 738	90 543	133 281	180 064
1981	47 464	96 475	143 939	221 426
1982	47 168	97 668	144 836	252 141
1983	47 285	101 932	149 217	257 123
1984	50 191	110 383	160 574	269 664
1985	55 729	117 945	173 673	291 568
1986	62 433	132 801	195 233	317 637
1987	69 929	155 329	225 258	346 740
1988	80 098	182 346	262 445	384 719
1989	89 843	210 578	300 421	428 837
1990	98 656	240 447	339 103	471 198
1991	101 218	259 896	361 114	487 624
1992	102 296	282 976	385 272	495 599
1993	104 683	305 250	409 933	498 961
1994	112 624	325 171	437 795	522 786
1995	120 873	337 274	458 146	548 196
1996	129 092	351 356	480 448	574 228
1997	141 812	370 823	512 634	622 762
1998	156 014	388 662	544 676	682 724
1999	167 009	406 750	573 759	712 346

Source: © Statistics Canada

(1) Not adjusted for inflation.

Total Income, 1998

(millions of dollars)

	Median Income[1] ($)	1997–98 % change		Median Income[1] ($)	1997–98 % change
St. John's	18 300	2.5	Kitchener	23 900	3.0
Halifax	21 800	3.4	London	22 700	2.7
Saint John	18 400	3.6	Windsor	24 200	3.4
Chicoutimi-Jonquière	18 200	3.7	Sudbury	20 800	0.6
Quebec	20 600	2.6	Thunder Bay	22 400	0.5
Sherbrooke	18 500	3.6	Winnipeg	21 100	3.5
Trois-Rivières	17 100	3.3	Regina	22 900	2.2
Montreal	19 500	3.4	Saskatoon	20 800	2.6
Ottawa-Hull	25 200	2.8	Calgary	24 100	4.3
Oshawa	25 900	1.9	Edmonton	21 900	3.4
Toronto	22 400	3.3	Vancouver	20 700	1.1
Hamilton	23 400	3.1	Victoria	23 400	0.8
St. Catharines–Niagara	21 100	3.0			

Source: © *Statistics Canada* (1) Data based on income tax returns filed in Spring 1999.
NOTE: Median income corresponds exactly to the mid-point of income distribution. It is not affected by extreme income values as is average income.

Minimum Hourly Wage by Province

On December 18, 1996, the minimum hourly wage provisions of the Canada Labour Code were amended to align the federal minimum wage with the provincial and territorial general adult minimum wage rates. Minimum wage rates may not apply to registered apprentices who are paid according to a provincial apprenticeship act, to certain employees who are being trained on the job or special types of employees in some provinces (see table).

If an employees is paid through a system based on something besides hours (such as mileage), the employee's pay, if divided by the hours worked, must be equivalent to the appropriate provincial or territorial minimum wage.

	Adult Minimum Wage Rate	Date Effective	Other Categories of Workers	Minimum Wage Rates
Newfoundland	$5.50	October 1999	–	–
Prince Edward Island	5.60[1]	January 2000	–	–
Nova Scotia	5.70	October 2000	For inexperienced workers	$5.25
New Brunswick	5.75	January 2000	–	–
Quebec	6.90	October 1998	For workers receiving gratuities	6.15
Ontario	6.85	January 1995	For students	6.40
			For liquor servers	5.95
Manitoba	6.00	April 1999	–	–
Saskatchewan	6.00	January 1999	–	–
Alberta	5.90	October 1999	–	–
British Columbia	7.60	November 2000	–	–
Yukon	7.20	October 1998	–	–
Northwest Territories	6.50	April 1998	Beyond the NWT Highway System	7.00
			Youth	6.00
			For Youth beyond the NWT Highway System	6.50
Nunavut	7.00	April 1999	–	6.50

Sources: *Manitoba Labour; provincial labour departments* (1) $5.80 as of January 2001.
Note: For workers in federal jurisdiction industries, the federal minimum wage is aligned with the general adult minimum wage rates in each provincial and territorial jurisdiction.

Canadian Income Tax

Income tax was introduced in 1917 as a temporary measure to finance Canada's participation in World War I. The law introducing the tax (the Income War Tax Act) was shorter and much simpler than our current legislation. It imposed tax at graduated rates, ranging from 4 percent on the first $1,500 to 25 percent for income over $100,000.

This "temporary" tax was not repealed when the war ended. But on Jan. 1, 1949, the federal government removed "war" from the title and gave the statute the name it has today—the Income Tax Act. This act has been amended many times—most notably in 1972 when a major overhaul of the tax system broadened the tax base and introduced a tax on capital gains. This is still the basis of our federal income tax laws today.

In 1988, all personal exemptions and many deductions were changed to non-refundable tax credits. Unlike deductions, which reduce taxable income, credits are used to reduce the amount of tax payable. The term "non-refundable" refers to the fact that, although you can use these credits to reduce or eliminate your federal tax payable, any unused portion is not refundable to you. In some cases, however, you may be able to transfer the unused portion of the credits to someone else.

Because the credits are calculated by multiplying eligible amounts by 17 percent—the same as the lowest personal tax rate—the change makes no difference to those whose income falls within the lowest tax bracket. But it increases taxes for most of those with higher incomes.

For 2000, the federal income tax rates for individuals were: 17 percent on income up to $30,004; $5,101 plus 25 percent on the next $30,004 up to $60,009; and $12,602 plus 29 percent on income in excess of $60,009.

Provincial Income Tax

All provinces and territories except Quebec use to compute provincial tax as a percentage of basic federal tax ("tax on tax" systems). Starting in 2000, five provinces are switching to "tax on income" systems, with others to follow in 2001. This allows the provinces to set their own rates, brackets and credits, much as Quebec has done.

Filing Tax Returns

Though corporations must file tax returns each year, individuals need only file if they owe taxes or if they are eligible to claim tax credits such as the Child Tax Credit, or the Goods and Services Tax Credit. Persons owing money must file a return by April 30 of the year following the taxation year. Failure to do so makes the taxpayer liable to a late-filing penalty of 5 percent of unpaid tax plus an additional penalty of 1 percent per month on the amount outstanding, to a maximum of 12 months, plus interest on amounts owing.

Source: Revenue Canada

Taxes Paid by Province, 1997
(millions of dollars)

	Number of Taxable Returns	Total Income Assessed	Net Federal Tax	Net Provincial Tax
Canada	14 069 020	519 010.6	71 484.7	29 534.0
Newfoundland	219 830	6 433.7	764.1	516.9
Prince Edward Island	63 280	1 793.1	202.7	119.8
Nova Scotia	410 720	13 138.7	1 637.7	914.6
New Brunswick	334 950	10 233.3	1 249.2	767.5
Quebec	3 447 500	115 916.8	15 075.4	18.4
Ontario	5 309 190	211 917.7	30 634.9	15 499.9
Manitoba	532 780	17 570.3	2 225.9	1 420.6
Saskatchewan	468 640	15 433.1	1 913.9	1 288.0
Alberta	1 387 840	55 163.9	7 970.3	3 765.9
British Columbia	1 844 090	69 424.5	9 517.9	5 124.9
Yukon	13 980	561.9	67.1	32.6
Northwest Territories	17 580	796.6	108.4	47.2
Nunavut	6 840	289.5	38.3	16.7
Outside Canada	11 800	337.3	78.8	0.9

Source: Taxation Statistics, Revenue Canada

Individual Income Tax Rates, 2000

Federal Components

The federal components of personal income tax rates apply to all taxpayers except in Quebec.

Before Surtaxes and Basic Credit						After Surtaxes and Basic Credit	
Basic Federal Brackets	Marginal Rate[1]	Tax at Bottom of Bracket	Effect of Basic Credit[1]	Brackets After Basic Credit and Surtaxes	Effect of Federal Surtaxes[2]	Total Marginal Rate	Tax at Bottom of Bracket
$60 009	29%	$12 602	0%	$74 241	+1.45%	30.45%	$15 500
				60 009	0%	29%	11 373
30 004	25%	5 101	0%	30 004	0%	25%	3 871
0	17%	0	-17%[3]	7 231	0%	17%	0
				0		0%	

Source: PricewaterhouseCoopers

(1) Marginal rates for the federal component of personal tax in Quebec are adjusted by a factor of 83.5 percent, to 24.215 percent (83.5 percent x 29 percent), 20.875 percent (83.5 percent x 25 percent) and 14.195 percent (83.5 percent x 17 percent). The federal surtax is not affected. The 83.5 percent factor is what remains after the 16.5 percent abatement. (2) For 2000, federal surtax is 5 percent of basic federal tax in excess of $15 500, so taxpayers with basic federal tax of $15 500 or less will pay no federal surtax. (3) The basic personal credit eliminates federal tax for taxable income below $7 231.

Provincial Components (Except Quebec)

All provinces and territories except Quebec use to compute income tax as a percentage of basic federal tax ("tax on tax" systems). Starting in 2000, five provinces are switching to "tax on income" systems, with the others to follow in 2001. This allows the provinces to set their own rates, brackets and credits, much as Quebec has done.

Eight provinces have surtaxes, calculated as a percentage of provincial tax. Five are single-tiered and three are two-tiered. Quebec and Alberta eliminated their surtaxes effective 2000.

	% of Federal Tax	Provincial Surtaxes		Provincial Flat Taxes[1] as % of incomes	Provincial Tax Reduction for Low Incomes[2] (thresholds)	
		% of Prov. Tax	On Prov. Tax Above			
Nfld	62%	6% +10%	$ 250 7 050			
PEI	57.5%	10%	5 200		$ 9 789	$20 000
NS	57.5%	10%	10 000		13 703	21 000
NB	58.5%	8%	13 500			
Ont	38.5% (or 37.5%)[4]	20% +36%	3 561 4 468		9 680	12 129
Man	47%			2%[1] +2%[1]	7 965	21 500
Sask	48%	10%[3] +15%[3]	1 500[3] 4 000[3]	1.5%[1,3]	5 133	15 400
Alta	44%	(Eliminated for 2000)		0.5%[1]	9 545	17 555
BC	49.48% +15	30% +15%	5 300 8 660			
YT	49%	5%	6 000			
NWT & NVT	45%					
Nonresidents	48%					

Source: PricewaterhouseCoopers Note: "Tax on income" jurisdictions (B.C., Manitoba, New Brunswick, Nova Scotia, Ontario and Quebec) set rates independent of federal rates. "Tax on Tax" jurisdictions set rates as the fixed percentage of federal tax.

(1) Flat taxes are calculated as the given percentage of taxable income in Alberta. In Manitoba and Saskatchewan, the percentages apply to net income. Manitoba's 2 percent second-tier flat tax (bringing the total to 4 percent) applies to net income over a threshold of $30 000 (or higher, if certain credits apply). These flat taxes apply from the first dollar of income. However, for low-income taxpayers in Alberta, Manitoba and Saskatchewan, provincial tax reductions may reduce or eliminate flat tax that would otherwise be payable. (2) Provincial tax reductions eliminate provincial tax up to at least the first taxable income figure and reduce provincial tax up to at least the second taxable income figure. (3) Saskatchewan's surtax applies to the flat tax as well as to basic provincial tax. (4) Ontario's personal tax rate is 37.5 percent of the basic federal rate for those in the bottom tax bracket.

Personal Tax Credits, 2000

(dollars)

	Basic Amount	Federal Credit	Quebec Credit
Basic	7 231	1 229	1 298
Married[1]	6 140	1 044	1 298
Disability	4 293	730[3]	484
Age 65[2]	3 531	600	484
Infirm dependant[3]	2 386	406	1 298
Pension income[2]	1 000	170	220
Dependant			
—1st	—	—	572
—Children (Additional)[4]	—	—	528
Single parent	—	—	286
Living alone[2]	—	—	231
Dividends[5]	—	13.33%	10.83%
Charitable donations			
First $200	—	17%	22%
$200–$2 000	—	29%	22%
Education credit[7]	—	17%	22%
CPP/QPP/EI[6]	—	17%	22%
Tuition	—	17%	22%
Union, Professional dues	—	17%	22%

Source: *PricewaterhouseCoopers* (1) The spousal and equivalent credits are reduced when the income of the spouse or qualifying dependant exceeds $614. Any net income of the spouse reduces the Quebec spouse credit. (2) The age credit is reduced if net income exceeds $26 284, except for Quebec, where the total of the age, pension and living alone credits is reduced if net family income exceeds $26 000. (3) Infirm dependants must be over 18 years of age at the end of the year. Dependant's income over $4 845 reduces the federal credit. Any income reduces the Quebec credit. (4) Children must be full-time students or under 19 years of age at the end of the year. (5) Credits for taxable Canadian dividends apply to the grossed-up amount (125 percent) of dividends. (6) For self-employed persons in Quebec, QPP contributions give rise to a tax credit and to a deduction in calculating income, both based on 50 percent of the contributions. (7) The maximum federal education credit is $34 per month, $10 for part-time (Ontario: $13 for full-time, $4 for part-time). For Quebec, the maximum is $363 per term (maximum two terms per year) for a supporting Quebec parent.

Individual Tax Tables, 2000

This table shows the combined federal and provincial (or territorial) income taxes, including surtaxes and flat taxes, payable on the assumption that only the basic personal tax credit is available, and that all income is either interest or ordinary income (such as salary). The political contribution tax credit and provincial credits for homeowners, renters, and children have not been taken into account. Other credits (notably the cost of living in the Northwest Territories and the new sales tax credit in Saskatchewan) have been excluded as well.

Taxable Income

	$20 000	$30 000	$40 000	$50 000	$60 000	$70 000	$80 000	$90 000	$100 000
Newfoundland	3 582	6 400	10 542	14 685	18 828	23 813	28 882	34 013	39 144
Prince Edward Island	3 419	6 096	10 033	13 971	18 042	22 776	27 594	32 473	37 352
Nova Scotia	3 368	6 116	10 111	14 106	18 115	22 682	27 340	32 219	37 098
New Brunswick	3 440	6 156	10 176	14 197	18 233	22 828	27 508	32 249	37 001
Quebec[1]	4 315	7 774	12 111	16 449	20 986	25 907	30 912	35 979	41 045
Ontario	2 984	5 321	8 783	12 245	15 862	20 455	25 179	29 965	34 751
Manitoba[2]	3 562	6 310	10 431	14 553	18 687	23 349	28 096	32 904	37 712
Saskatchewan[2]	3 513	6 259	10 244	14 380	18 568	23 395	28 306	33 278	38 251
Alberta[2]	3 226	5 724	9 373	13 023	16 673	20 899	25 208	29 579	33 950
British Columbia	3 218	5 758	9 498	13 238	17 070	21 835	26 684	31 782	36 908
Yukon	3 234	5 767	9 492	13 217	16 942	21 312	25 788	30 325	34 862
Northwest Territories & Nunavut	3 148	5 613	9 237	12 862	16 487	20 692	24 980	29 330	33 680

Source: *PricewaterhouseCoopers*
(1) In some situations, the calculation of taxable income for federal and Quebec purposes may be different, and the amounts shown may require adjustments. (2) In Manitoba and Saskatchewan, flat taxes are based on net income, rather than taxable income as in Alberta.

Taxable Income by Age and Gender, 1997

	Number of Tax Returns Filed		Total Income Assessed ($millions)		Average Income Assessed	
	Male	Female	Male	Female	Male	Female
Under 20	131 120	79 940	$ 2 947	$ 2 384	$22 476	$29 827
20–24	519 410	394 130	12 383	9 168	23 841	23 261
25–29	753 550	615 000	23 802	16 679	31 586	27 120
30–34	906 960	746 030	37 456	23 817	41 298	31 925
35–39	1 040 790	808 590	48 961	27 519	47 042	34 033
40–44	964 620	827 640	49 891	28 826	51 721	34 829
45–49	829 220	734 730	46 485	26 146	56 059	35 586
50–54	708 590	586 860	41 134	20 434	58 051	34 819
55–59	529 830	397 200	29 106	13 357	54 935	33 627
60–64	447 410	322 200	21 271	10 041	47 542	31 164
65–69	399 900	288 200	17 986	10 375	44 976	35 998
70–74	318 490	269 880	13 296	9 409	41 747	34 863
75 and over	379 000	419 740	16 285	17 927	42 969	42 710
Total	**7 929 750**	**6 490 270**	**361 058**	**216 086**	**45 532**	**33 294**

Source: *Revenue Canada*

Income Taxes Collected, 1997

(millions of dollars)

	Number of Returns[1] (000s)	Taxable Income Assessed	Total Tax Payable	CPP Contributions by Individuals	Employment Insurance Contributions
Canada	20 453 540	$ 491 682.6	$ 101 018.7	$ 6 992.4	$ 7830.6
Newfoundland	372 330	6 400.0	1 281.0	91.5	108.1
Prince Edward Island	92 610	1 762.3	322.6	25.2	29.6
Nova Scotia	624 740	12 847.8	2 552.3	181.4	211.2
New Brunswick	520 780	10 135.6	2 016.7	152.3	174.7
Quebec	5 135 940	110 572.9	15 093.8	1 677.3	1 904.0
Ontario	7 606 110	199 739.7	46 135.4	2 732.2	3 064.6
Manitoba	783 830	16 807.8	3 646.5	245.8	281.3
Saskatchewan	680 330	14 588.5	3 201.9	204.7	228.7
Alberta	1 918 750	51 668.8	11 736.2	732.7	791.4
British Columbia	2 641 540	65 429.4	14 642.9	919.6	1 004.1
Yukon	24 380	679.0	155.6	12.5	13.9
Northwest Territories	18 630	469.5	99.7	9.1	10.0
Nunavut	12 060	251.0	55.0	4.8	5.4
Outside Canada	21 520	330.3	79.0	3.2	36.0

Source: © *Statistics Canada*

(1) All returns, both taxable returns and non-taxable returns.

Mortgage Rates by Year[1]

	One-Year	Three-Year	Five-Year		One-Year	Three-Year	Five-Year
1980	13.98	n.a.	14.52	1990	13.40	13.38	13.35
1981	1812	18.33	18.38	1991	10.08	10.90	11.13
1982	16.85	17.83	18.04	1992	7.87	8.95	9.51
1983	10.98	12.52	13.23	1993	6.91	8.10	8.78
1984	12.00	13.21	13.58	1994[2]	7.83	8.99	9.53
1985	10.31	11.54	12.12	1995[2]	8.38	8.82	9.16
1986	10.15	10.88	11.21	1996[2]	6.19	7.37	7.93
1987	9.85	10.69	11.17	1997[2]	5.54	n.a.	7.07
1988	10.83	11.42	11.65	1998[2]	6.50	n.a.	6.93
1989	12.85	12.15	12.06	1999[2]	6.80	n.a.	7.56

Source: Bank of Canada, CMHC (n.a.) Not available.
(1) Average typical mortgage rates. (2) 1-year and 5-year figures revised.

Average Resale Value of Canadian Homes[1]

The average value of resale homes in Canada decreased by more than $5 000 between 1998 and 1999. Calgary, Alberta and Regina, Saskatchewan tied for the largest increase at 5.6 percent. In contrast, Victoria, B.C. and Greater Vancouver, B.C. increased by 1.5 percent and 0.9 percent respectively.

	1980	1985	1990	1995	1998	1999
Canada	66 951	80 122	139 922	150 321	152 366	158 030
Calgary	93 977	80 462	128 484	132 114	157 353	166 110
Edmonton	84 623	74 309	101 040	110 329	114 527	118 871
Halifax-Dartmouth	53 161	79 350	97 238	103 011	114 025	118 522
Hamilton-Burlington & District	54 835	72 973	165 742	141 109	153 628	158 162
Mississauga	80 341	99 675	224 449	180 295	202 194	213 150
Montreal	49 419	70 564	111 956	109 929	115 573	119 689
Ottawa-Carleton	63 177	107 640	141 562	143 127	143 914	149 626
Regina	48 628	61 403	71 054	76 629	85 425	90 181
Saint John	45 170	57 088	78 041	83 498	87 087	88 731
St. John's	53 247	66 642	88 939	89 655	92 560	95 606
Toronto	75 621	109 094	254 890	203 028	216 815	228 372
Greater Vancouver	100 065	112 852	226 385	307 747	278 659	281 163
Victoria	85 066	88 451	160 743	210 669	217 886	221 126
Winnipeg	50 491	62 478	81 740	82 994	92 090	n.a.

Source: The Canadian Real Estate Association (n.a.) Not available.
(1) Average price of all homes sold on the Multiple Listing Service in constant dollars.

The Effect of Interest Rate Changes on Mortgage Payments

The table below shows the monthly mortgage payment (principal and interest) for each $1,000 of mortgage debt. To calculate your payment at a given interest rate, choose the corresponding amount in the amortization column you select and multiply the amount by the number of thousands of dollars of debt. For example, if you want to know the cost per month to carry an $85,000 mortgage amortized over 25 years at 7.00 percent, multiply 7 by 85 and the result, $595, is your monthly payment. If the same mortgage was coming up for renewal at 8.00 percent, the new payment amount would be $648.66 (7.63 x 85) or $53.56 more each month.

Monthly Payments for Each $1 000 of Mortgage

Interest Rate (%)	\multicolumn{8}{c}{Amortization Period}
	1 Year	2 Years	3 Years	5 Years	10 Years	15 Years	20 Years	25 Years
4.00	$85.13	$43.41	$29.51	$18.40	$10.11	$7.38	$6.04	$5.26
4.25	85.25	43.52	29.62	18.51	10.23	7.50	6.17	5.40
4.50	85.36	43.63	29.73	18.62	10.34	7.63	6.30	5.53
4.75	85.47	43.74	29.84	18.74	10.46	7.75	6.44	5.67
5.00	85.58	43.85	29.95	18.85	10.58	7.88	6.57	5.82
5.25	85.70	43.96	30.06	18.96	10.70	8.01	6.71	5.95
5.50	85.81	44.07	30.17	19.07	10.82	8.14	6.84	6.10
5.75	85.92	44.18	30.28	19.19	10.94	8.27	6.98	6.25
6.00	86.03	44.29	30.39	19.30	11.07	8.40	7.12	6.40
6.25	86.14	44.40	30.50	19.41	11.19	8.53	7.26	6.55
6.50	86.26	44.51	30.61	19.53	11.31	8.66	7.41	6.70
6.75	86.37	44.62	30.72	19.64	11.43	8.80	7.55	6.85
7.00	86.48	44.73	30.83	19.75	11.56	8.93	7.69	7.00
7.25	86.59	44.84	30.94	19.87	11.68	9.07	7.84	7.16
7.50	86.70	44.95	31.05	19.98	11.81	9.21	7.99	7.32
7.75	86.82	45.06	31.16	20.10	11.94	9.34	8.13	7.47
8.00	86.93	45.17	31.28	20.21	12.06	9.48	8.28	7.63
8.25	87.04	45.28	31.39	20.33	12.19	9.62	8.43	7.79
8.50	87.15	45.39	31.50	20.45	12.32	9.76	8.59	7.95
8.75	87.26	45.50	31.61	20.56	12.45	9.90	8.74	8.12
9.00	87.38	45.61	31.72	20.68	12.58	10.05	8.89	8.28
9.25	87.49	45.72	31.84	20.80	12.71	10.19	9.05	8.44
9.50	87.60	45.83	31.95	20.91	12.84	10.33	9.20	8.61
9.75	87.71	45.94	32.06	21.03	12.97	10.48	9.36	8.78
10.00	87.82	46.05	32.17	21.15	13.10	10.62	9.52	8.94
10.25	87.93	46.16	32.28	21.27	13.24	10.77	9.68	9.11
10.50	88.04	46.27	32.40	21.38	13.37	10.92	9.83	9.28
10.75	88.16	46.38	32.51	21.50	13.50	11.06	10.00	9.45
11.00	88.27	46.49	32.62	21.62	13.64	11.21	10.16	9.63
11.25	88.38	46.61	32.74	21.74	13.77	11.36	10.32	9.80
11.50	88.49	46.72	32.85	21.86	13.91	11.51	10.48	9.97
11.75	88.60	46.83	32.96	21.98	14.04	11.66	10.65	10.14
12.00	88.71	46.94	33.08	22.10	14.18	11.82	10.81	10.32
12.25	88.82	47.05	33.19	22.22	14.32	11.97	10.98	10.49
12.50	88.94	47.16	33.30	22.34	14.46	12.12	11.14	10.67
12.75	89.05	47.27	33.42	22.46	14.59	12.28	11.31	10.85
13.00	89.18	47.38	33.53	22.58	14.73	12.43	11.48	11.02

Source: *The Royal Bank of Canada*

Housing Affordability Table

The table below shows how expensive a home an individual or family could likely afford, using various income levels and mortgage interest rates—assuming a down-payment of 25 percent of the purchase price. As income rises, housing becomes more affordable, but it becomes less affordable as interest rates increase.

For example, most couples with a combined annual income of $60,000 would qualify for a mortgage on a home costing $192,170 at an 8 percent interest rate—provided they had a downpayment of $38,094 (25 percent of the purchase price). But at a 10 percent interest rate, the same couple earning the same income could only afford a $163,967 home.

The table assumes that mortgage payments, property taxes, heating costs and 50 percent of condominium fees should not exceed 32 percent of gross income (net income if self-employed). Most lending institutions use this percentage when calculating how large a mortgage you can afford. For this table, we have established annual costs of $2,400 for taxes and $2,400 for taxes and $2,400 for heating. Most lenders will also require that you total debt service ratio (mortgage payments, property taxes, heating cots 50 percent of condo fees and any other liabilities such as car loans or other debts) does not exceed 40 percent of gross income.

Mortgage Interest Rate (%)[1]	\$30 000	\$40 000	\$50 000	\$60 000	\$70 000	\$80 000	\$90 000	\$100 000
4.00	25 348	109 838	194 332	278 823	363 314	439 357	506 951	574 546
4.25	24 707	107 062	189 420	271 776	354 132	428 252	494 138	560 024
4.50	24 090	104 391	184 693	264 993	345 294	417 564	481 806	546 048
4.75	23 497	101 818	180 142	258 464	336 785	407 275	469 934	532 593
5.00	22 925	99 341	175 760	252 176	328 592	397 367	458 501	519 636
5.25	22 374	96 955	171 538	246 119	320 700	387 823	447 489	507 155
5.50	21 844	94 658	167 471	240 283	313 095	378 627	436 878	495 129
5.75	21 333	92 440	163 550	234 658	305 766	369 764	426 652	483 539
6.00	20 840	90 334	159 771	229 236	298 701	361 220	416 793	472 386
6.25	20 364	88 244	156 127	224 007	291 887	352 980	407 285	461 591
6.50	19 906	86 257	152 611	218 863	185 315	345 032	398 115	451 197
6.75	19 463	84 340	149 219	214 096	278 973	337 363	389 265	441 169
7.00	19 036	82 490	145 946	209 399	272 853	329 962	380 726	431 490
7.25	18 624	80 704	142 785	204 865	256 945	322 817	372 482	422 147
7.50	18 226	78 979	139 733	200 486	261 239	315 917	364 520	413 124
7.75	17 842	77 313	136 785	196 257	255 728	309 252	356 830	404 408
8.00	17 470	75 703	133 937	192 170	250 403	302 813	349 400	395 987
8.25	17 111	74 147	131 184	188 220	245 256	296 589	342 219	387 848
8.50	16 764	72 643	128 523	184 402	240 281	290 572	335 276	379 981
8.75	16 428	71 188	125 950	180 170	235 470	284 754	328 583	372 372
9.00	16 103	69 781	123 461	177 138	230 816	279 127	322 070	365 013
9.25	15 789	68 420	121 052	173 683	226 314	273 682	315 787	357 893
9.50	15 485	67 103	118 722	170 339	221 958	268 413	309 707	351 002
9.75	15 191	65 827	116 465	167 102	217 738	263 312	303 822	344 332
10.00	14 906	64 593	114 281	163 967	213 654	258 372	296 122	337 873
10.25	14 630	63 397	112 165	160 932	209 698	253 588	292 602	331 616
10.50	14 363	62 238	110 115	157 990	205 865	248 953	287 254	325 555
10.75	14 104	61 115	108 128	155 139	202 151	244 462	282 072	319 682
11.00	13 852	60 027	106 202	152 376	198 550	240 108	277 048	313 988
11.25	13 609	58 971	104 335	149 697	195 060	235 886	272 177	308 468
11.50	13 373	57 948	102 524	147 099	191 674	231 792	267 453	303 114
11.75	13 144	56 955	100 767	144 579	188 390	227 820	262 870	297 920
12.00	12 921	55 991	99 063	142 133	185 203	223 966	258 423	292 880
12.25	12 705	55 058	97 408	139 759	182 110	220 225	254 107	287 988
12.50	14 496	54 148	95 802	137 454	179 196	216 594	249 917	283 239
12.75	12 292	53 267	94 242	135 216	176 190	213 067	245 847	278 627
13.00	12 095	52 410	92 727	133 042	173 358	209 642	241 895	274 148

Source: *The Royal Bank of Canada*

(1) Compounded semi-annually. Mortgage payments based on a 25-year amortization.

Personal Income and Savings

	Total Personal Income ($millions)	Annual % Change in Personal Income	Total Personal Disposable Income ($millions)	Total Personal Saving ($millions)	Personal Saving Rate
1965	$ 41 881	9.8	$ 37 113	$ 2 306	6.2
1970	67 840	8.3	55 295	3 537	6.4
1971	74 531	9.9	60 462	4 222	7.0
1972	84 423	13.3	68 838	5 902	8.6
1973	98 528	16.7	80 373	8 324	10.4
1974	117 905	19.7	95 304	11 166	11.7
1975	136 921	16.1	111 258	14 052	12.6
1976	156 372	14.2	126 157	15 543	12.3
1977	173 286	10.8	139 752	16 536	11.8
1978	193 519	11.7	158 055	20 292	12.8
1979	217 974	12.6	178 544	23 792	13.3
1980	248 188	13.9	203 161	28 960	14.3
1981	289 797	16.8	235 056	37 349	15.9
1982	320 241	10.5	259 065	48 039	18.5
1983	337 138	5.3	270 794	40 963	15.1
1984	365 056	8.3	294 145	44 020	15.0
1985	395 166	8.2	317 392	44 390	14.0
1986	423 088	7.1	334 854	39 244	11.7
1987	454 736	7.5	356 134	35 928	10.1
1988	499 206	9.8	388 639	40 903	10.5
1989	542 295	8.6	425 566	47 744	11.2
1990	581 741	7.3	449 644	50 030	11.1
1991	600 658	3.3	464 289	52 832	11.4
1992	616 055	2.6	475 645	53 381	11.2
1993	627 885	1.9	486 641	48 618	10.0
1994	640 275	2.0	493 625	39 345	8.0
1995	666 390	4.0	511 378	37 608	7.4
1996	687 708	2.3	529 788	37 106	7.0
1997	714 643	3.9	546 788	25 674	4.7
1998	745 919	4.4	567 960	25 382	4.5
1999	776 120	4.0	590 608	21 492	3.6

Source: © Statistics Canada

(1) As of June 1999.

Consumer Spending

Households spent an estimated average of $51,360 on everything from clothing to car maintenance to travel in 1998, a 3 percent increase from the previous year, exceeding the annual 1998 inflation rate of 1 percent.

Households spent almost 12 percent more on home furnishings and equipment. Spending on recreation, and tobacco products and alcoholic beverages both increased by 6 percent.

Computer ownership rose 13 percent, although the actual amount spent on computer equipment and supplies dropped since 1996 due mostly to the decline in prices. Forty-five percent of households reported having a computer, almost doubling the number compared to five years ago. Spending increased 11 percent from 1997 to an average of $242 for Internet services.

In 1998, ownership of cell phones increased by 4 percent, bringing the total of households using cells to 26 percent. However, spending fell 4 percent to an average of $490 for cellular services.

Source: Statistics Canada

INVESTMENT

Investment: A Glossary of Terms

Annual report: A report issued by a company to its shareholders at the end of the fiscal year. It contains a report on company operations and formal financial statements.

Bankers' acceptance: A commercial draft backed by the guarantee of a bank. The bankers' acceptance promises repayment on a certain date, usually not more than 90 days ahead, and bears a rate of return competitive with other chartered bank securities.

Bear market: A market in which prices are falling.

Bid and ask: The bid price is the highest price anyone is willing to pay to buy a stock; the ask is the lowest price anyone will accept to sell a stock. Together, the bid and ask prices are a quote.

Blue chip stocks: Stocks with good investment qualities, usually common shares of well-established companies with good earnings records and long-time dividend payments.

Board lot: A unit of trading. Board lots on the Toronto Stock Exchange are: under 10 cents each—1000 shares; between 10 cents and 99 cents each—500 shares; at and above $1 each—100 shares.

Bond: A written promise or IOU by the issuer to repay a fixed amount of borrowed money on a specified date, and to pay a set annual rate of interest in the meantime, generally at semi-annual intervals. Bonds are usually considered a safe investment because the borrower (whether a company or the government) must make interest payments before its money is spent on anything else.

Bull market: A market in which prices are rising.

Call: An option to buy a fixed amount of a certain stock at a specified price within a specified time.

Canada Savings Bonds: These are issued each fall, and are popular with small investors because they come in denominations starting at $100. They are not traded. They have a term of several years and a minimum guaranteed rate of interest. However, the government sets an effective rate during the issuing period each year, and adjusts it when necessary to conform with interest rate trends. Interest can be awarded yearly or compounded, depending upon the type of bond.

Capital gain or loss: Profit or loss resulting from the sale of an asset, such as a security. The gain or loss is the difference between the buying and selling price of the security with commissions figured in.

Commercial paper: Short-term negotiable securities issued by corporations that call for the payment of a specific amount of money at a given time.

Common shares: Securities issued by the company that represent part-ownership in the company. Common shares sometimes carry a voting privilege and entitle the holder to a share in the company's profits, usually issued in the form of dividends.

Convertible bond: A corporate bond (see below) that may be converted into a stated number of shares of the corporation's common stock. Its price tends to fluctuate with the price of the stock, as well as with changes in interest rates.

Corporate bonds: Evidence of debt by a corporation. The bond bears interest much like a government bond, and matures at a certain date in the future. Considered safer than the common or preferred stock of the same company.

Day order: An order to buy or sell a security valid only for the day the order is given.

Dividend: A portion of a company's profit paid to the common and preferred shareholders. The amount is decided upon by the company's board of directors, and may be paid in cash or stock.

Equities: Common and preferred stocks that represent a share in the ownership of a company.

Ex-dividend: Without dividend. The buyer of shares quoted ex-dividend is not entitled to receive an already declared dividend. When shares are un-dividend, the purchaser will receive the declared dividend.

Floor trader: A brokerage-firm employee who works on the stock exchange trading floor, and is responsible for executing buy and sell orders on behalf of the firm and its clients.

Futures: Contracts to buy or sell specific quantities of a commodity or financial instrument with delivery delayed until some agreed-upon time in the future.

Government of Canada bonds: These bear a fixed rate of interest and a maturation date in the future, and are traded on the market, with the price rising and falling in response to interest rate trends. ▶

▶ Long-term government bonds are considered a safe investment. Provinces and municipalities may also issue long-term bonds.

Index: Statistical measure of the state of the stock market or economy, based on the performance of stocks or other components. Examples are the TSE 300 Composite Index and the Toronto 35 Index.

Limit order: An order to buy or sell securities in which the client has specified the price. The order can be executed only at the specified price or a better one.

Liquidity: The measure of how quickly an investor can turn securities into cash. A security is liquid if it can be bought and sold quickly with small price changes between transactions.

Long: A term signifying ownership of securities. "I am long 100 XYZ" means that the speaker owns 100 shares of XYZ.

Margin: The amount paid by clients when they use credit to buy a security, the balance being loaned by their brokers.

Market order: An order to buy a security immediately at the best possible price.

Money market: Part of the capital market established for short-term borrowing and lending of funds. Money market dealers conduct business over the telephone, and trade securities such as short-term (three years and less) government bonds, government treasury bills and commercial paper.

Mutual fund: A portfolio, or selection, of professionally bought and managed stocks in which the investor pools money with thousands of others. A share price is based on net asset value, or the value of all the investments owned by the fund, less any debt, divided by the total number of shares. The major advantage is less risk—an investment is spread out over many stocks, and if one or two do badly, the remainder may shield the investor from the losses. Bond funds are mutual funds that deal in the bond market exclusively. Money market mutual funds concentrate on debt instruments sold on the money market. Equity mutual funds place their investments in the common shares of companies.

Odd lot: A number of shares less than a board lot.

Open order: An order to buy or sell a security at a specified price, valid until executed or cancelled.

Over-the-counter: The over-the-counter (OTC) or unlisted market is the market maintained by securities dealers for issues not listed on a stock exchange.

Penny stock: Low-priced, often speculative issues selling at less than $1 a share.

Preferred shares: Shares that carry dividends at fixed rates that must be paid before any dividends are paid to common shareholders.

Price/earnings ratio: A common stock's current market price divided by the company's annual per share earnings.

Prospectus: A legal document describing securities being offered for sale to the public. It must be prepared in accordance with provincial securities commission regulations.

Put: An option to sell a fixed amount of a certain stock at a specified price within a specified time.

Registered representative: A salesperson or broker employed by an investment firm. Salespersons must be registered with the provincial securities commission.

Right: A temporary privilege granted to existing common shareholders to purchase additional shares directly from the company at a stated price.

Settlement date: The date on which a securities buyer must pay for a purchase or a seller must deliver the securities sold. In general, settlement must be made on or before the third business day following the transaction date.

Short sale: The sale of shares that the seller does not own. The seller is speculating that the stock price will fall, in the hope of later purchasing the same number of securities at a lower price, thereby making a profit. Sellers must advise their brokers when they are selling short.

Stock yield: The percentage of the dividend paid in relation to the price of the stock. For example, a stock selling at $40 a share with an annual dividend of $2 a share yields 5 percent.

Transfer agent: A trust company appointed by a company to keep a record of the names, addresses and numbers of shares held by its shareholders. Transfer agents are often responsible for distributing dividend cheques.

Underwriting: The purchase for resale of a new issue of securities by an investment dealer or group of dealers.

Warrant: A certificate giving the holder the right to purchase securities at a stipulated price within a specified period of time. They are often detachable and may be traded separately.

Government of Canada Average Bond Yields

Year	1 to 3 Years	3 to 5 Years	5 to 10 Years	10 Years and Over
1981	15.97	15.68	15.29	15.22
1985	10.12	10.39	10.78	11.04
1990	11.65	11.19	10.82	10.85
1991	8.99	9.16	9.36	9.76
1992	7.03	7.43	8.16	8.77
1993	5.89	6.46	7.24	7.85
1994	7.14	7.79	9.01	8.63
1995	7.26	7.63	7.93	9.49
1996	5.35	5.80	6.88	7.75
1997	4.53	4.98	5.80	6.66
1998	5.05	5.13	5.21	5.45
1999	6.08	6.20	6.15	6.00

Source: Bank of Canada

RRSP Contributors and Contributions

	Nfld	PEI	NS	NB	Que	Ont	Man	Sask	Alta	BC	YT	NWT[3]	NVT[3]
Contributors (000)													
1997	65.9	21.4	145.2	108.5	1 444.5	2 425.2	230.5	211.6	654.6	835.8	6.1	7.4	2.1
1998	64.4	20.8	142.4	104.8	1 415.5	2445.6	231.1	202.3	659.1	820.9	5.8	7.0	2.0
% Change 1997–1998	-2.2	-2.9	-1.9	-3.4	-2.01	0.8	0.2	-4.4	0.7	-1.8	-5.3	-5.3	-1.4
Contributions ($000,000)													
1997[1]	276.8	96.2	622.1	439.6	6 102.9	11393.3	873.9	825.32	955.83	778.4	29.2	39.3	12.3
1998[1]	266.1	80.8	578.3	394.1	5 555.3	11423.9	867.7	762.32	952.73	675.5	26.4	36.7	11.5
% Change 1997–1998[2]	-4.7	-16.7	-7.9	-11.1	-9.8	-0.6	-1.6	-8.5	-1	-3.6	-10.3	-7.4	-7.5

Source: © Statistics Canada. (1) Current dollars. (2) Calculated using 1997 contributions expressed in constant 1998 dollars. (3) Data for the Northwest Territories and Nunavut are based on the current boundaries created when Nunavut officially became a new territory in April 1999.

Toronto and Montreal Stock Exchange Activity

	Montreal Stock Exchange		Toronto Stock Exchange	
Year	Combined volume (millions)	Value of shares traded ($millions)	Combined volume (millions)	Value of shares traded ($millions)
1960	77	$ 481	470	$ 1 223
1965	428	1 251	934	3 199
1970	268	1 205	523	3 654
1975	135	1 385	470	4 089
1980	299	3 857	2 009	29 514
1985	643	10 553	3 298	44 196
1990	1 365	15 405	5 660	64 009
1995	2 881	38 834	15 758	207 665
1996	4 302	50 167	22 341	301 299
1997	4 321	61 912	25 670	423 170
1998	3 532	55 647	26 800	493 212
1999	2 830	42 500	29 300	529 000

Sources: © Monthly Review; Montreal Stock Exchange; Canadian Stock Exchange; Toronto Stock Exchange

GLOBAL INFORMATION

Global Superlatives

Largest continent	Asia	44 485 900 sq. km
Smallest continent	Australia	7 682 300 sq. km
Largest ocean	Pacific	166 241 000 sq. km
Smallest ocean	Arctic	9 485 000 sq. km
Deepest point of any ocean	Mariana Trench, Pacific Ocean	10 924 m
Largest sea	South China Sea	2 974 600 sq. km
Largest lake	Caspian Sea, Russian Fed., Kazakhstan, Turkmenistan, Iran, Azerbaijan	371 000 sq. km
Deepest lake	Lake Baykal, Russia	1 620 m
Largest freshwater lake	Lake Superior, North America	82 100 sq. km
Highest major lake	Lake Titicaca, Bolivia-Peru, South America	3 809 m
Lowest major lake	Caspian Sea, Russian Fed., Kazakhstan, Turkmenistan, Iran, Azerbaijan	-28 m
Largest island	Greenland, Denmark	2 175 600 sq. km
Longest reef	Great Barrier Reef, Australia-Papua New Guinea	2 027 km
Longest river	Nile, Africa	6 671 km
Largest nation	Russia	17 075 272 sq. km
Smallest nation	Vatican City	.44 ha.
Most populous nation	People's Republic of China (July 1999 est)	pop. 1 246 871 951
Oldest city	Damascus, Syria	continuously inhabited since c. 2500 B.C.
Highest point	Mount Everest, Nepal-Tibet	8 848 m
Lowest point	Dead Sea, Israel-Jordan	-400 m
Highest city	La Paz, Bolivia	3 636 m
Coldest city	Norilsk, Russia	average temp. -10.9°C
Hottest city	Djibouti, Djibouti	average temp. 30°C
Coldest place	Plateau Station, Antarctica	-56.7°C
Hottest place	Dalol, Danakil Depression, Ethiopia	35°C avg.
Coldest recorded temperature	Vostok, Antarctica (Australian territory), July 21, 1983	-89.2°C
Hottest recorded temperature (shade)	Al-Aziziyah, Libya, Sept. 13, 1922	58°C
Wettest spot	Mount Waialeale, Kauai, Hawaii	avg. ann. rainfall of 16 800 mm
Driest spot	Atacama Desert, Chile	avg. ann. precipitation barely measurable
Greatest snowfall in 24 hrs	Silver Lake, Colorado, U.S., Apr. 14–15, 1921	193 cm
Greatest rainfall in 24 hrs	Cilaos, Reunion Island, Indian Ocean, Mar. 15–16, 1952	1 870 mm
Largest desert	Sahara, Africa	9 million sq. km
Largest waterfall (by volume)	Khone, Kampuchea-Laos	11 610 cu. m/sec.
Tallest waterfall	Angel Falls, Venezuela	807 m
Largest gorge	Grand Canyon, Colorado River, Arizona	349 km long; 6–20 km wide; 1.6 km deep
Deepest gorge	Colca River Canyon, Peru	3 223 m
Oldest tree	a bristlecone pine, Wheeler's Peak, Nevada	approx. age of 5 100 yrs.
Greatest tides	Bay of Fundy, Nova Scotia	14.5 m
Most devastating volcanic eruption	Tambora, Sumbawa, Indonesia, Apr. 5–7, 1815	92 000 deaths
Longest bridge	Confederation, linking New Brunswick and Prince Edward Island (main span 11 km); bridge between the tip of Florida and Key West is also 11 km.	12.9 km
Largest man-made lake	Owen Falls, Uganda	2 700 000 cu. m
Longest street	Yonge Street, from Toronto, Ont. to Rainy River (at. Man. border)	1 896.2 km
Tallest building	Sears Tower, Chicago, Illinois	110 storeys, 443 m
Tallest free-standing structure	CN Tower, Toronto, Ont.	553.34 m
Most common language	Mandarin	approx. 750 million speakers
Most common religion	Christianity	(approx. 1/3 of world's pop.) 2 025 334 000

GEOGRAPHY

The Continents

Continent	Total Area (sq. km)	% of Earth's Land	Population	% of World Total
Asia	44 485 900	30.0	3 292 337 000	62.4
Africa	30 269 680	20.4	702 013 000	13.2
North and Central America	24 235 280	16.3	441 826 000	8.4
South America	17 820 770	12.0	309 634 000	5.9
Antarctica	13 209 000	8.9	uninhabited	
Europe	10 530 750	7.1	504 925 000	9.6
Oceania	7 830 682	5.3	27 752 000	.5

Source: *National Geographic Atlas of the World (1990), FAO Production Yearbook (1993)*

Highest and Lowest Points on Each Continent

Continent	Highest Point	(metres)	Lowest Point	(metres)
Asia	Everest	8 848	Dead Sea	-400
South America	Aconcagua	6 960	Valdés Peninsula	-40
North America	McKinley (Denali)	6 194	Death Valley	-86
Africa	Kilimanjaro	5 895	Lake Assal	-156
Europe	El'brus	5 642	Caspian Sea	-28
Antarctica	Vinson Massif	4 897	—	-2 538
Australia	Kosciusko	2 228	Lake Eyre	-16

Source: *National Geographic Atlas of the World (1990)*

World's Highest Cities

City	Altitude[1]	City	Altitude[1]
Cerro de Pasco, Peru	4 259 m	Cuaco, Peru	3 400 m
Potosi, Bolivia	4 200 m	Quito, Ecuador	2 811 m
Shigatse, Tibet	3 939 m	Sucre, Bolivia	2 790 m
La Paz, Bolivia	3 665 m	Toluca de Lerdo, Mexico	2 680 m
Lhasa, Tibet	3 606 m	Addis Ababa, Ethiopia	2 450 m

Source: *Global Atlas, Gage Educational Publishing Co., South American Handbook.*
(1) Estimates vary, depending on source.

Oceans' Area and Depth

Ocean	Area (sq. km)	% of Earth's Water Area	Deepest Point	Depth (metres)
Pacific	166 241 000	46.0	Mariana Trench	10 924
Atlantic	86 557 000	23.9	Puerto Rico Trench	8 605
Indian	73 427 000	20.3	Java Trench	7 258
Arctic	9 485 000	2.6	Eurasia Basin	5 122

Source: *National Geographic Atlas of the World (1990)*

Major Seas of the World

Sea	Area (sq. km)	Average Depth (metres)	Sea	Area (sq. km)	Average Depth (metres)
South China	2 974 600	1 464	Sea of Japan	1 012 900	1 667
Caribbean	2 515 900	2 575	Hudson Bay	730 100	93
Mediterranean	2 510 000	1 501	East China	664 600	189
Bering	2 261 100	1 491	Andaman	564 900	1 118
Gulf of Mexico	1 507 600	1 615	Black	507 900	1 191
Sea of Okhotsk	1 392 100	973	Red	453 000	538

Source: *National Geographic Atlas of the World (1990)*

Largest Lakes of the World

Lake	Location	Area sq. mi.	Area sq. km
Caspian (Sea)	Iran/Caspian Sea, Russian Fed., Kazakhstan, Turkmenistan, Iran, Azerbaijan	146 100	378 400
Superior	Canada/U.S.	31 760	82 260
Aral (Sea)	Kazakhstan-Uzbekistan	24 750	64 100
Victoria	Kenya/Tanzania/Uganda	24 300	62 940
Huron	Canada/U.S.	23 000	59 580
Michigan	U.S.	22 400	58 020
20 Tanganyika	Burundi/Tanzania/Zaire/Zambia	12 350	32 000
Baykal	Russia	12 160	31 500
Great Bear	**NWT, Canada**	**12 030**	**31 150**
Great Slave	**NWT, Canada**	**11 030**	**28 570**

Source: *World Facts and Figures, 1989; Victor Showers; John Wiley & Sons, Inc.*

Major Islands of the World

Island	Area (sq. km)	Island	Area (sq. km)
Greenland (Denmark)	2 175 600	Sumatra (Indonesia)	427 300
New Guinea (independent)	792 500	Honshu (Japan)	227 400
Borneo (Indonesia)	725 500	Great Britain (independent)	218 100
Madagascar (independent)	587 000	**Victoria (Canada)**	**217 300**
Baffin (Canada)	**507 500**	**Ellesmere (Canada)**	**196 200**

Source: *National Geographic Atlas of the World (1990)*

Highest Waterfalls in the World

Fall/Country	Height[1] (m)	Fall/Country	Height[1] (m)
Angel, Venezuela	807	Pilao, Brazil	524
Monge, Norway	774	Montoya, Venezuela	505
Itatinga, Brazil	628	Ribbon, United States	491
Ormeli, Norway	563	Great, Guyana	488
Tusse, Norway	533	Vestre Mardals, Norway	468

Source: *World Facts and Figures, 1989; Victor Showers; John Wiley & Sons Inc.*
(1) Height of the greatest individual leap.

Highest Mountains by Continent

Peak	Mountain Range or System	Location	Elevation[1] ft	Elevation[1] m	First Ascent
■ Africa					
Kibo	n.a.	Tanganyika, Tanzania	19 340	5 890	1889
Mawensi	n.a.	Tanganyika, Tanzania	17 100	5 210	1912
Batian	n.a.	Kenya	17 050	5 200	1899
Nelion	n.a.	Kenya	17 020	5 190	1929
Margherita	Ruwenzori	Uganda/D. Rep. of Congo	16 760	5 110	1906
Alexandra	Ruwenzori	Uganda/D. Rep. of Congo	16 700	5 090	1906
Albert	Ruwenzori	Dem. Rep. of Congo	16 690	5 090	1932
Savoia	Ruwenzori	Uganda	16 330	4 980	1906
Elena	Ruwenzori	Uganda	16 300	4 970	1906
Elizabeth	Ruwenzori	Uganda	16 170	4 930	1953
■ Antarctica					
—	Sentinel	Antarctica	16 860	5140	1966
Tyree	Sentinel	Antarctica	16 290	4970	1967
Shinn	Sentinel	Antarctica	15 750	4800	1966
Gardner	Sentinel	Antarctica	15 370	4690	1966
Epperly	Sentinel	Antarctica	15 100	4600	n.a.
Kirkpatrick	Queen Alexandra	Antarctica	14 850	4530	n.a.
Elizabeth	Queen Alexandra	Antarctica	14 700	4480	n.a.
Markham	Queen Elizabeth	Antarctica	14 290	4360	n.a.
Bell	Queen Alexandra	Antarctica	14 120	4300	n.a.
Mackellar	Queen Alexandra	Antarctica	14 100	4300	n.a.
■ Asia					
Everest (alt Qomolangma, Chumulangma)	Nepal Himalaya	China/Nepal	29 030	8 850	1953
K2 (alt Chogori, Dapsang, Godwin Austen)	Karakoram	Pakistan-held Kashmir	28 250	8 610	1954
Kangchenjunga (alt Kanchenjunga): highest peak	Nepal Himalaya	India/Nepal	28 170	8 590	1955
Lhotse (alt E1, Luozi, Lotzu)	Nepal Himalaya	China/Nepal	27 890	8 500	1956
Kangchenjunga: S peak	Nepal Himalaya	India/Nepal	27 800	8 470	n.a.
Makalu I	Nepal Himalaya	China/Nepal	27 790	8 470	1955
Kangchenjunga: W peak	Nepal Himalaya	India/Nepal	27 620	8 420	1973
Lhotse Shar (alt Lhotse: E peak)	Nepal Himalaya	China/Nepal	27 500	8 380	1970
Dhaulagiri I (alt Daulagiri I)	Nepal Himalaya	Nepal	26 810	8 170	1960
Cho Oyu (alt Zhuoaoyu, Choaoyu): highest peak	Nepal Himalaya	China/Nepal	26 750	8 150	1954
■ Europe					
Elbrus (for Elborus): W peak	Caucasus (off Kavkaz)	Russia	18 480	5630	1874
Elbrus: E peak	Caucasus	Russia	18 360	5 590	1829
Shkhara: E peak	Caucasus	Georgia/Russia	17 060	5 200	1888
Dykh(-Tau): W peak	Caucasus	Russia	17 050	5 200	1888
Dykh(-Tau): E peak	Caucasus	Russia	16 900	5 150	1938
Koshtan(-Tau)	Caucasus	Russia	16 880	5 140	1888
Shkhara: W peak	Caucasus	Georgia/Russia	16 880	5 140	n.a.
Pushkina	Caucasus	Russia	16 730	5 100	1938
Dzhangi(-Tau): NW peak	Caucasus	Georgia	16 570	5 050	1903
Kazbek: E peak	Caucasus	Georgia	16 560	5 050	1868 ▶

North America

McKinley: S peak	Alaska	Alaska, U.S.	20 320	6 190	1913
Logan: central peak[2]	Saint Elias	Yukon, Canada	19 520	5 959	1925
Logan: W peak[2]	Saint Elias	Yukon, Canada	19 470	5 930	1925
McKinley: N peak	Alaska	Alaska, U.S.	19 470	5 930	1910
Logan: E peak	Saint Elias	Yukon, Canada	19 420	5 920	1957
Citlaltepetl (alt Orizaba)	Neovolcanica	Puebla-Veracruz, Mexico	18 410	5 610	1848
Logan: N peak	Saint Elias	Yukon, Canada	18 270	5 570	1959
Saint Elias	Saint Elias	Canada/U.S.	18 010	5 490	1897
Popocatepetl	Neovolcanica	Puebla, Mexico	17 930	5 460	1520
Foraker	Alaska	Alaska, U.S.	17 400	5 300	1934

Oceania

Jaya (for Carstensz, Djaja, Sukarno)	Sudirman (for Nassau)	Irian Jaya, Indonesia	16 500	5 030	1936
Daam	Jayawijaya (for Djajawidjaja, Orange)	Irian Jaya, Indonesia	16 150	4 920	n.a.
Pilimsit (for Idenburg)	Sudirman	Irian Jaya, Indonesia	15 750	4 800	1962
Trikora (for Wilhelmina)	Jayawijaya	Irian Jaya, Indonesia	15 580	4 750	1913
Mandala (for Juliana)	Jayawijaya	Irian Jaya, Indonesia	15 420	4 700	1959
Wilhelm	Bismarck	Papua New Guinea	15 400	4 690	n.a.
Wisnumurti (for Jan Pieterszoon Coen)	Jayawijaya	Irian Jaya, Indonesia	15 080	4 590	n.a.
Yamin (for Prins Hendrik)	Jayawijaya	Irian Jaya, Indonesia	14 860	4 530	n.a.
Kubor	Kubor	Papua New Guinea	14 300	4 360	n.a.
Herbert	Bismarck	Papua New Guinea	14 000	4 270	n.a.

South America

Aconcagua	Andes	Mendoza, Argentina	22 840	6 960	1897
Ojos del Salado: SE peak	Andes	Argentina/Chile	22 560	6 870	1937
Bonete	Andes	La Rioja, Argentina	22 550	6 870	1913
Pissis	Andes	Catamarca, La Rioja, Argentina	22 240	6 780	1937
Huascaran: S peak	Blanca (Andes)	Peru	22 210	6 770	1932
Mercedario	Andes	San Juan, Argentina	22 210	6 770	1934
Llullaillaco	Andes	Argentina/Chile	22 100[1]	6 730	bef 1550
Libertador (for Cachi: N peak)	Andes	Salta, Argentina	22 050	6 720	1950
Ojos del Salado: NW peak	Andes	Argentina/Chile	22 050	6 720	1937
Tupungato	Andes	Argentina/Chile	21 900	6 670	1897

Source: World Facts and Figures, 1989; Victor Showers; John Wiley & Sons, Inc.

(1) Rounded figures except from some Canadian peaks from Energy, Mines and Resources Canada. n.a. not available or not applicable.
(2) Name change proposed: Mount Pierre Elliott Trudeau.

Longest Rivers in the World

River	Outflow and Location	Length	
		mi.	km
Nile-Kagera-Ruvuvu-Luvironza	Mediterranean Sea, Egypt	4 140	6 670
Amazon-Ucayali-Tambo-Ene-Apurimac	Atlantic Ocean, Amapa-Para, Brazil	4 080	6 570
Yangtze	East China Sea, Jiangsu, China	3 720	5 980
Mississippi-Missouri-Jefferson-Beaverhead-Red Rock	Gulf of Mexico, Louisiana, U.S.	3 710	5 970
Yenisey-Angara-Selenga-Ider	Yenisey Gulf of Kara Sea, Russia	3 650	5 870
Amur-Argun-Kerulen	Tatar Strait, Russia	3 590	5 780
Ob-Irtysh	Gulf of Ob of Kara Sea, Russia	3 360	5 410
Plata-Parana-Grande	Atlantic Ocean, Argentina-Uruguay	3 030	4 880
Huang	Gulf of Chihli of Yellow Sea, Shandong, China	3 010	4 840
Congo-Lualaba	Atlantic Ocean, Angola-Dem. Rep. of Congo	2 880	4 630

Source: World Facts and Figures, 1989; Victor Showers; John Wiley & Sons, Inc.

WORLD POPULATION

The 30 Largest Countries by Population, 1950

(millions)

Rank	Country	Population	Rank	Country	Population
1	China	555	16	Viet Nam	30
2	India	358	17	Spain	28
3	United States of America	158	18	Mexico	28
4	Russian Federation	102	19	Poland	25
5	Japan	84	20	Egypt	22
6	Indonesia	80	21	Philippines	21
7	Germany	68	22	Turkey	21
8	Brazil	54	23	Republic of Korea	20
9	United Kingdom	51	24	Thailand	20
10	Italy	47	25	Ethiopia	18
11	France	42	26	Myanmar	18
12	Bangladesh	42	27	Argentina	17
13	Pakistan	40	28	Iran (Islamic Republic of)	17
14	Ukraine	37	29	Romania	16
15	Nigeria	33	**30**	**Canada**	**14**

Source: *World Population Prospects: The 1996 Revision, Population Division of the United Nations*

The 30 Largest Countries by Population, 1996

(millions)

Rank	Country	Population	Rank	Country	Population
1	China	1 232	16	Egypt	63
2	India	945	17	Turkey	62
3	United States of America	269	18	Thailand	59
4	Indonesia	200	19	France	58
5	Brazil	161	20	Ethiopia	58
6	Russian Federation	148	21	United Kingdom	58
7	Pakistan	140	22	Italy	57
8	Japan	125	23	Ukraine	52
9	Bangladesh	120	24	The Dem. Republic of the Congo	47
10	Nigeria	115	25	Myanmar	46
11	Mexico	93	26	Republic of Korea	45
12	Germany	82	27	South Africa	42
13	Viet Nam	75	28	Spain	40
14	Iran (Islamic Republic of)	70	29	Poland	39
15	Philippines	69	30	Colombia	36

Source: *World Population Prospects: The 1996 Revision, Population Division of the United Nations*

The 30 Largest Countries by Population, 2050 (projection)

(millions)

Rank	Country	Population	Rank	Country	Population
1	India	1 533	16	Russia Federation	114
2	China	1 517	17	Japan	110
3	Pakistan	357	18	Turkey	98
4	United States of America	348	19	South Africa	91
5	Nigeria	339	20	United Republic of Tanzania	89
6	Indonesia	318	21	Myanmar	81
7	Brazil	243	22	Thailand	73
8	Bangladesh	218	23	Germany	70
9	Ethiopia	213	24	Uganda	66
10	Iran (Islamic Republic of)	170	25	Kenya	66
11	The Dem. Republic of the Congo	165	26	Colombia	62
12	Mexico	154	27	Afghanistan	61
13	Philippines	131	28	Yemen	61
14	Viet Nam	130	29	Sudan	60
15	Egypt	115	30	Saudi Arabia	60

Source: *World Population Prospects: The 1996 Revision, Population Division of the United Nations*

Population Projections by Region and for Selected Countries

(thousands)

Region and Country	2005	2035	Region and Country	2005	2035
World Total	6 490 722	8 669 468	Senegal	10 810	19 809
More developed regions[1]	1 197 344	1 201 271	Sierra Leone	5 432	9 654
Least developed regions[2]	5 293 378	7 168 197	Togo	5 332	10 491
Least developed countries	747 540	1 370 341	**ASIA**	**3 929 031**	**5 107 111**
AFRICA	**930 735**	**1 716 771**	**Eastern Asia**	**1 532 751**	**1 723 222**
Eastern Africa	**293 183**	**577 222**	China	1 321 569	1 510 678
Burundi	7 899	14 402	Dem. People's Republic of Korea	25 416	31 818
Comoros	827	1 562	Hong Kong, China	6 457	6 243
Djibouti	776	1 302	Japan	127 196	116 175
Eritrea	4 286	7 448	Macau	496	562
Ethiopia	77 114	170 478	Mongolia	3 023	4 501
Kenya	34 469	57 161	Republic of Korea	48 594	53 246
Madagascar	20 254	41 606	**South-Central Asia**	**1 627 567**	**2 295 606**
Malawi	12 451	24 731	Afghanistan	29 494	52 943
Mauritius[3]	1 242	1 568	Bangladesh	139 911	197 879
Mozambique	22 137	42 744	Bhutan	2 313	4 328
Reunion	743	968	India	1 082 184	1 430 882
Rwanda	8 640	14 536	Iran (Islamic Republic of)	87 024	146 156
Seychelles	81	100	Kazakstan	17 311	21 086
Somalia	13 511	29 390	Kyrgyzstan	4 742	6 526
Uganda	26 032	54 616	Maldives	355	681
United Republic of Tanzania	38 574	74 222	Nepal	27 439	45 839
Zambia	10 342	18 585	Pakistan	177 590	305 275
Zimbabwe	13 805	21 800	Sri Lanka	19 858	25 410
Middle Africa	**110 000**	**230 414**	Tajikistan	7 036	10 917
Angola	14 882	31 503	Turkmenistan	4 907	7 153
Cameroon	17 340	34 366	Uzbekistan	27 402	40 531
Central African Republic	4 040	6 981	**South-Eastern Asia**	**560 239**	**750 255**
Chad	8 184	15 045	Brunei Darussalam	354	481
Congo	3 416	7 066	Cambodia	12 302	18 760
Democratic Republic of the Congo	60 065	131 776	East Timor	950	1 291
Equatorial Guinea	510	952	Indonesia	226 938	296 252
Gabon	1 396	2 482	Lao People's Democratic Republic	6 547	11 616
Sao Tome and Principe	161	244	Malaysia	24 329	34 683
Northern Africa	**192 485**	**284 501**	Myanmar	53 479	74 032
Algeria	35 186	52 926	Philippines	82 102	117 001
Egypt	74 273	104 958	Singapore	3 778	4 288
Libyan Arab Jamahiriya	7 495	15 613	Thailand	62 612	71 941
Morocco	31 298	43 530	Viet Nam	86 847	119 909
Sudan	33 246	52 253	**Western Asia**	**208 474**	**338 027**
Tunisia	10 657	14 724	Armenia	3 773	4 311
Western Sahara	329	497	Azerbaijan	8 116	10 308
Southern Africa	**58 828**	**93 015**	Bahrain	671	907
Botswana	1 798	2 885	Cyprus	833	988
Lesotho	2 594	4 736	Gaza Strip	1 187	3 306
Namibia	1 949	3 513	Georgia	5 424	5 900
South Africa	51 365	79 975	Iraq	26 668	47 587
Swaziland	1 121	1 905	Israel	6 570	8 538
Western Africa	**276 239**	**531 618**	Jordan	7 371	13 900
Benin	7 193	14 826	Kuwait	2 192	3 140
Burkina Faso	13 857	28 755	Lebanon	3 535	4 811
Cape Verde	490	767	Oman	3 302	8 460
Côte d'Ivoire	17 003	27 442	Qatar	648	808
Gambia	1 379	2 260	Saudi Arabia	25 255	50 146
Ghana	22 818	42 587	Syrian Arab Republic	18 237	29 895
Guinea	9 069	18 703	Turkey	70 456	91 970
Guinea-Bissau	1 302	2 254	United Arab Emirates	2 660	3 463
Liberia	3 830	8 120	Yemen	21 577	49 589
Mali	14 529	30 068	**EUROPE**	**726 474**	**677 763**
Mauritania	2 918	5 165	**Eastern Europe**	**302 633**	**272 532**
Niger	12 659	27 851	Belarus	10 169	9 285
Nigeria	147 610	282 857	Bulgaria	8 110	7 122
St. Helena[4]	7	8	Czech Republic	10 126	9 194

254 Global Data

Hungary		9 541	8 231	Saint Kitts and Nevis		41	51
Poland		39 000	39 875	Saint Lucia		161	216
Republic of Moldova		4 508	4 987	Saint Vincent and Grenadines		122	159
Romania		22 251	20 327	Trinidad and Tobago		1 409	1 794
Russian Federation		143 618	124 238	Turks and Caicos Islands		19	29
Slovakia		5 408	5 400	United States Virgin Islands		112	145
Ukraine		49 903	43 872	**Central America**		**147 221**	**208 425**
Northern Europe		**94 038**	**95 259**	Belize		270	424
Channel Islands		158	178	Costa Rica		4 165	6 196
Denmark		5 307	5 298	El Savador		6 957	10 198
Estonia		1 374	1 185	Guatemala		13 971	25 075
Faeroe Islands		48	50	Honduras		7 346	12 075
Finland		5 216	5 234	Mexico		106 147	141 728
Iceland		295	351	Nicaragua		5 295	8 659
Ireland		3 615	3 758	Panama		3 067	4 069
Isle of Man		84	106	**South America**		**365 293**	**486 618**
Latvia		2 299	2 015	Argentina		39 302	50 514
Lithuania		3 645	3 429	Bolivia		9 275	14 780
Norway		4 467	4 694	Brazil		179 446	230 126
Sweden		8 989	9 545	Chile		16 136	20 844
United Kingdom		58 541	59 414	Colombia		41 877	57 209
Southern Europe		**144 525**	**131 274**	Ecuador		13 798	19 410
Albania		3 616	4 545	Falkland Islands (Malvinas)		2	3
Andorra		95	177	French Guiana		211	327
Bosnia and Herzegovina		4 361	4 129	Guyana		918	1 182
Croatia		4 449	4 123	Paraguay		6 216	10 790
Gibraltar		28	28	Peru		27 804	38 741
Greece		10 643	9 687	Suriname		476	657
Holy See		1	1	Uruguay		3 365	3 841
Italy		56 703	48 339	Venezuela		26 468	38 192
Malta		389	432	**NORTHERN AMERICA**		**319 855**	**377 571**
Portugal		9 751	9 185	Bermuda		67	77
San Marino		28	36	**Canada**		**31 856**	**36 710**
Slovenia		1 894	1 633	Greenland		62	70
Spain		39 748	35 623	St. Pierre and Miquelon		7	8
TFYR Macedonia		2 306	2 598	United States of America		287 863	340 707
Yugoslavia		10 512	10 736	**OCEANIA**		**32 312**	**43 009**
Western Europe		**185 277**	**178 699**	**Australia/New Zealand**		**23 819**	**29 762**
Austria		8 419	8 028	Australia[5]		19 846	24 683
Belgium		10 321	10 113	New Zealand		3 973	5 079
France		59 607	59 808	**Melanesia**		**7 217**	**11 329**
Germany		82 769	77 025	Fiji		917	1 275
Liechtenstein		35	43	New Caledonia		208	274
Luxembourg		446	467	Papua New Guinea		5 357	8 406
Monaco		36	46	Solomon Islands		517	988
Netherlands		16 073	15 786	Vanuatu		217	385
Switzerland		7 571	7 382	**Micronesia**		**601**	**961**
LATIN AMERICA AND CARIBBEAN		**552 315**	**747 242**	Guam		177	233
Caribbean		39 801	52 199	Kiribati		95	145
Anguilla		9	12	Marshall Islands		77	158
Antigua and Barbuda		70	91	Micronesia (Fed. States of)		162	290
Aruba		77	100	Nauru		13	21
Bahamas		324	415	Northern Mariana Islands		57	83
Barbados		269	305	Palau		20	31
British Virgin Islands		24	34	**Polynesia**		**675**	**958**
Cayman Islands		41	61	American Samoa		71	123
Cuba		11 371	11 736	Cook Islands		21	26
Dominica		72	89	French Polynesia		262	368
Dominican Republic		9 123	12 121	Niue		2	1
Grenada		97	123	Pitcairn		0	0
Guadeloupe		485	606	Samoa		189	285
Haiti		8 572	14 827	Tokelau		2	2
Jamaica		2 713	3 640	Tonga		102	118
Martinique		417	500	Tuvalu		11	14
Montserrat		11	13	Wallis and Futuna Islands		16	21
Netherlands Antilles		209	248				
Puerto Rico		4 054	4 884				

Source: *World Population Prospects: The 1996 Revision*, Population Division of the United Nations
(1) More developed regions comprise Northern America, Japan, Europe, Australia-New Zealand. (2) Less developed regions comprise all regions of Africa, Latin America, Asia (excluding Japan), and Melanesia, Micronesia and Polynesia. (3) Including Agalega, Rodrigues and St. Brandon. (4) Including Ascension and Tristan da Cunha. (5) Including Christmas Island, Cocos (Keeling) Islands, and Norfolk Island.

WORLD ECONOMY

International Comparisons[1]

	Canada	United States	France	Italy	United Kingdom	Germany	Japan	Mexico
Area [sq.km ('000)]	9 985[7]	9 372	549	301	245	357	378	1 996
Population (1997) [('000)]	30 287	266 792	58 608	56 868	59 009	82 061	126 166	94 184
Growth rate [1996–97 (%)]	1.1	0.5	0.4	0.2	0.4	0.2	0.2	2.2
Density [persons per sq. km]	3	28	107	189	241	230	334	47
Vital Statisics (1996)								
Infant mortality [% of live births]	0.5	0.8	0.5	0.6	0.6	0.5	0.4	1.7
Life expectancy at birth: males	75.4	72.7	74.1	74.9	74.4	73.6	77.0	70.1
Life expectancy at birth: females	81.5	79.4	82.0	81.3	79.3	79.9	83.6	76.5
Gross domestic product (1998) [$US billion]	584.2	8 178.8	1 435.5	1 171.8	1 362.3	2 142.1	3 797.2	417.3
GDP per capita[2] [$US]	24 468	30 514	22 091	21 739	21 170	22 835	24 109	7 998
Average annual growth over ten years [1988–98 (%)]	1.8	2.8	1.8	1.4	1.7	2.1	1.9	3.4
Sectoral contributions (1997)								
Agriculture [% of GDP]	2.9[4]	1.8[4]	2.3	2.6	1.7[3]	1.1	1.9[4]	5.6[4]
Industry [% of GDP]	32.4[4]	26.8[4]	26.2	30.5	27.5[3]	29.1	37.9[4]	26.1[4]
Services [% of GDP]	64.7[4]	71.4[4]	71.5	66.9	70.8[3]	69.9	60.2[4]	68.4[4]
Consumer Price Index [Dec. 1997–98 (% change) 1990=100]	1.0	1.6	0.3	1.5	2.8	0.5	0.6	18.6
Labour markets (1997)								
Labour force ['000]	15 416	137 282	25 696	23 434	28 716	39 602	67 870	37 222
Total civilian employment ['000]	13 941	129 558	22 016	20 038	26 564	35 351	65 570	35 904
Unemployment rate[5] [%]	9.2	4.9	12.4	12.2	7.1	9.8	3.4	3.5
Female participation rate[6] [%]	67.8	71.3	59.8	44.1	66.8	61.8	63.7	42.8
Energy (1997)								
Total consumption [tonnes of oil equiv. (millions)]	187.52	1 445.25	161.16	125.45	157.21	244.34	340.46	94.86
Consumption per capita [tonnes of oil equiv.]	6.2	5.4	2.7	2.2	2.7	3.0	2.7	1.0
Total production [tonnes of oil equiv. (millions)]	362.70	1 683.81	127.84	29.31	268.99	139.73	106.98	223.13
Health and education (1996)								
Expenditure on health [% of GDP]	9.2	13.6	9.8	7.8	6.9	10.5	7.2	4.6
Expenditure on public education [% of GDP]	7.0	6.7	6.3	4.7	n.a.	5.8	4.7	5.6
Int'l merchandise trade (1997)								
Imports (cost, insurance, freight) [$US billion]	193.2	869.6	270.5	208.1	290.3	445.3	338.8	109.8
Exports (free on board) [$US billion]	202.8	643.2	283.7	238.0	268.4	512.4	421.0	110.2
Currency (exchange rate) [per US $, Dec. 1998]	1.542	1.000	5.600	1 652	0.599	1.669	117.6	9.909

(n.a.) Not available

Sources: © OECD; Statistics Canada
(1) International comparisons should be used to gain a general impression only, as there are differences in definition, data collection, and other factors. (2) At purchasing power parity exchanges rates. (3) 1995. (4) 1996. (5) National definitions. (6) Defined as female labour force of all ages divided by female population aged 15–64. (7) Data from Natural Resources Canada.

Energy Consumption by OECD Countries

	Coal (million short tons)		Natural Gas (billion cubic feet)		Petroleum (thousand barrels per day)		Hydroelectric Power (billion kilowatt hours)	
	1988	1998	1988	1998	1988	1998	1988	1998
Australia	95.83	129.77	555	753	652	831	13.4	15.6
Austria	7.56	6.16	183	279	212	248	35.2	37.0
Belgium	13.96	14.08	337	517	469	601	0.4	0.4
Canada	60.19	65.69	2 331	2 963	1 693	1 873	303.5	329.3
Czech Republic	0.00	77.19	0	333	0	172	0.0	1.6
Denmark	12.43	6.34	56	172	205	229	n.a.	n.a.
Finland	7.28	5.41	58	145	228	212	13.2	14.8
France	24.95	26.10	961	1 338	1 797	2 032	74.0	59.9
Germany	0.00	260.30	0	3 301	0	2 916	0.0	16.8
Greece	56.22	65.87	4	30	285	392	2.4	3.6
Hungary	26.98	17.59	407	432	193	155	0.2	0.2
Iceland	0.10	0.10	n.a.	n.a.	n.a.	n.a.	4.2	5.6
Ireland	3.63	3.20	71	118	78	149	0.9	0.9
Italy	23.37	19.80	1 460	2 203	1 836	2 072	40.2	42.0
Japan	122.58	139.54	1 618	2 446	4 752	5 512	89.9	89.5
Korea	120.14	132.24	94	491[2]	769	2 030	34.7	25.2
Luxembourg	1.76	0.39	15	25	28	42	0.1	0.1
Mexico	8.09	13.16	926	1 283	1 550	1 950	21.0	24.3
Netherlands	12.77	15.94	1 513	1 752	716	812	n.a.	n.a.
New Zealand	2.42	2.65	166	175	95	133	23.1	23.6
Norway	1.61	1.77	71	128	187	228	107.9	114.5
Poland	253.41	161.07	447	465	350	415	4.2	4.3
Portugal	3.71	4.80	0	28	206	330	12.0	12.9
Spain	52.25	46.59	129	438	980	1 385	34.8	34.4
Sweden	4.94	3.26	13	32	359	371	69.0	72.9
Switzerland	0.55	0.08	63	102	261	272	35.4	33.2
Turkey	50.82	78.39	43	370	447	626	28.4	41.8
United Kingdom	122.84	63.16	1 972	3 093	1 697	1 784	4.9	5.1
United States	885.24	1 038.77	18 030	21 338	17 283	18 917	257.8	344.3

	Nuclear Power (billion kilowatt hours)		Total Net Electricity (billion kilowatt hours)		Other[1] (billion kilowatt hours)	
	1988	1998	1988	1998	1988	1998
Australia	n.a.	n.a.	121.4	173.3	0.0	3.4
Austria	n.a.	n.a.	40.8	51.9	n.a.	1.5
Belgium	40.9	43.9	54.7	74.5	n.a.	n.a.
Canada	78.2	67.5	242.8	484.5	0.0	4.4
Czech Republic	0.0	12.5	0.0	54.7	n.a.	n.a.
Denmark	n.a.	n.a.	28.2	33.0	0.3	3.7
Finland	18.4	20.8	48.3	79.3	n.a.	8.4
France	260.3	366.7	307.9	389.3	0.6	2.6
Germany	0.0	152.7	0.0	488.0	0.0	10.4
Greece	n.a.	n.a.	28.0	42.2	0.0	n.a.
Hungary	12.7	13.3	36.9	33.3	n.a.	n.a.
Iceland	n.a.	n.a.	4.1	5.8	0.2	0.6
Ireland	n.a.	n.a.	11.1	18.4	0.0	n.a.
Italy	n.a.	n.a.	193.0	266.7	2.9	6.0
Japan	173.9	318.1	664.2	926.3	1.3	23.9
Korea	37.8	85.2[2]	122.8	235.5	n.a.	n.a.
Luxembourg	n.a.	n.a.	4.3	5.9	n.a.	n.a.
Mexico	0.0	8.8	100.3	164.8	4.7	5.4
Netherlands	3.5	3.6	66.7	94.3	0.0	4.0
New Zealand	n.a.	n.a.	27.2	33.3	1.2	2.5
Norway	n.a.	n.a.	95.2	111.0	0.0	n.a.
Poland	n.a.	n.a.	130.9	121.9	0.0	0.5
Portugal	n.a.	n.a.	21.3	36.2	0.0	1.3
Spain	48.3	56.0	119.3	170.3	0.0	2.5
Sweden	65.6	70.8	128.2	135.1	0.0	3.5
Switzerland	21.5	24.5	43.7	50.8	n.a.	n.a.
Turkey	n.a.	n.a.	43.4	102.2	0.1	n.a.
United Kingdom	55.6	97.7	280.5	331.5	0.0	6.1
United States	527.0	673.7	2 578.1	3 367.4	12.0	75.7

Source: *National Energy Information Center, Energy Information Administration, International Energy Annual* (n.a.) Not available.
(1) Includes geothermal, solar and wind electric power. (2) South Korea only.

INTERNATIONAL ORGANIZATIONS

United Nations

The first United Nations declaration was signed by 22 Allied governments on Jan. 1, 1942, and was an alliance against Germany, Italy and Japan. This anti-Axis coalition was converted into an international body in 1945 when 51 nations signed a United Nations Charter to form an organization that would "save succeeding generations from the scourge of war." The Charter was drawn up at the Conference on International Organization held in San Francisco from Apr. 25 to June 26, 1945, and took effect Oct. 24, 1945. UN membership has since grown to 189.

The UN has six parts, with the General Assembly—the central organ—acting as the main deliberative body. General Assembly meetings have been held at UN Headquarters in New York since 1946. The International Court of Justice in The Hague, Netherlands, is the only major UN organ not based in New York. Specialized agencies are located throughout the world.

General information on the UN may be requested from the Public Inquiries Unit, Dept. of Public Information, Room GA-057A, United Nations, New York, NY 10017; or the United Nations Association in Canada, 900-130 Slater St., Ottawa, Ont., K1P 6E2, or obtained from the UN website at http://www.un.org

■ Structure of the United Nations

General Assembly The General Assembly is the UN's forum for discussing issues, reviewing UN activities and setting the agenda for initiatives. All member states are represented, and each is entitled to one vote. Resolutions require a majority vote before adoption. A president, 21 vice-presidents and six committee chairs head the Assembly, which sits from mid-September to mid-December. The six committees study issues relating to: disarmament and security; economy and finance; social, humanitarian and cultural issues; UN administrative and budgetary matters; legal issues; and political and security issues and report back to a plenary session of the Assembly.

The General Assembly sets UN policies, admits new members on recommendation of the Security Council, approves the budget and receives reports from all other UN bodies.

Security Council The Security Council has the power to act for the maintenance of peace and security. It can enforce military action or economic sanctions, and it can send peace-keeping units (the Blue Berets) to troubled areas. The Security Council may also try to negotiate a ceasefire in the case of conflicts.

The Council has 15 members, five permanent and 10 elected by the General Assembly for two-year terms. Decisions require nine affirmative votes, but all permanent members have the right to veto. The permanent members are: China, France, the United Kingdom, the United States and the Russian Federation. Canada is serving its sixth term as a non-permanent member of the Council (Jan. 1, 1999 to Dec. 31, 2000). The Security Council is permanently in session and representatives are on call 24 hours a day.

Economic and Social Council The Economic and Social Council co-ordinates the economic and social work of the UN and its related agencies. The Council's 54 members hold two month-long sessions each year: one in New York, the other in Geneva. Each member is elected by the General Assembly for a three-year term.

Trusteeship Council The council, created to oversee the independence of trust territories, is now in abeyance.

International Court of Justice (World Court) The Security Council elects 15 judges to the Court for nine-year terms. No two members may be from the same nation. The Court, located in The Hague, only sits in judgement on disputes between states. Both member and non-member states may submit grievances (border disputes, resource access, breach of treaty, etc.).

Countries can opt out of any proceeding, unless required to participate by treaty provisions. But after agreeing to become a party in a case, a nation must comply with the Court's decision, enforced by the Security Council.

Secretariat The Secretariat administers the programs and policies laid out by other UN bodies. The Secretary General is the Chief Administrative Officer of the Secretariat, which administers the work of the UN as directed by the General Assembly, Security Council and other organs.

Glossary of United Nations Acronyms

FAO: Food and Agriculture Organization
IAEA: International Atomic Energy Agency
IBRD: International Bank for Reconstruction and Development
ICAO: International Civil Aviation Organization
IDA: International Development Association
IFAD: International Fund for Agricultural Development
IFC: International Finance Corporation
ILO: International Labour Organization
IMF: International Monetary Fund
INSTRAW: International Research and Training Institute for the Advancement of Women
ITU: International Telecommunications Union
MINURSO: United Nations Mission for the Referendum in Western Sahara
MONUC: United Nations Mission in the Democratic Republic of the Congo
UNCHS/HABITAT: United Nations Centre for Human Settlements
UNCTAD: United Nations Conference on Trade and Development
UNDOF: United Nations Disengagement Observer Force
UNDHA: United Nations Department of Humanitarian Affairs
UNDP: United Nations Development Programme
UNEP: United Nations Environment Programme
UNESCO: United Nations Educational, Scientific and Cultural Organization
UNFICYP: United Nations Peacekeeping Force in Cyprus
UNFPA: United Nations Population Fund
UNHCR: Office of the United Nations High Commissioner for Refugees
UNICEF: United Nations Children's Fund
UNIDO: United Nations Industrial Development Organization
UNIFIL: United Nations Interim Force in Lebanon
UNIKOM: United Nations Iraq-Kuwait Observation Mission
UNITAR: United Nations Institute for Training and Research
UNMIBH: United Nations Mission in Bosnia and Herzegovina
UNMIK: United Nations Interim Administration Mission in Kosovo

UNMOGIP: United Nations Military Observer Group in India and Pakistan
UNMOP: United Nations Mission of Observers in Prevlaka
UNOMIG: United Nations Mission of Observers in Georgia
UNAMSIL: United Nations Mission in Sierra Leone
UNRWA: United Nations Relief and Works Agency for Palestine Refugees in the Near East
UNSMIH: United Nations Support Mission in Haiti
UNTAET: United Nations Transitional Administration in East Timor
UNTSO: United Nations Truce Supervision Organization
UNU: United Nations University
UNV: United Nations Volunteers
UPU: Universal Postal Union
WFP: World Food Programme
WHO: World Health Organization
WIPO: World Intellectual Property Organization
WMO: World Meteorological Organization
WTO: World Trade Organization (formerly General Agreement on Tariffs and Trade)

■ Functional Commissions

Commission for Social Development
Commission of Sustainable Development
Commission on Human Rights
Commission on Narcotic Drugs
Commission on the Status of Women
Population Commission
Statistical Commission

■ Regional Commissions

ESCAP: Economic and Social Commission for Asia and the Pacific
ESCWA: Economic and Social Commission for Western Asia
ECA: Economic Commission for Africa
ECE: Economic Commission for Europe
ECLAC: Economic Commission for Latin America and the Caribbean

International Organizations **259**

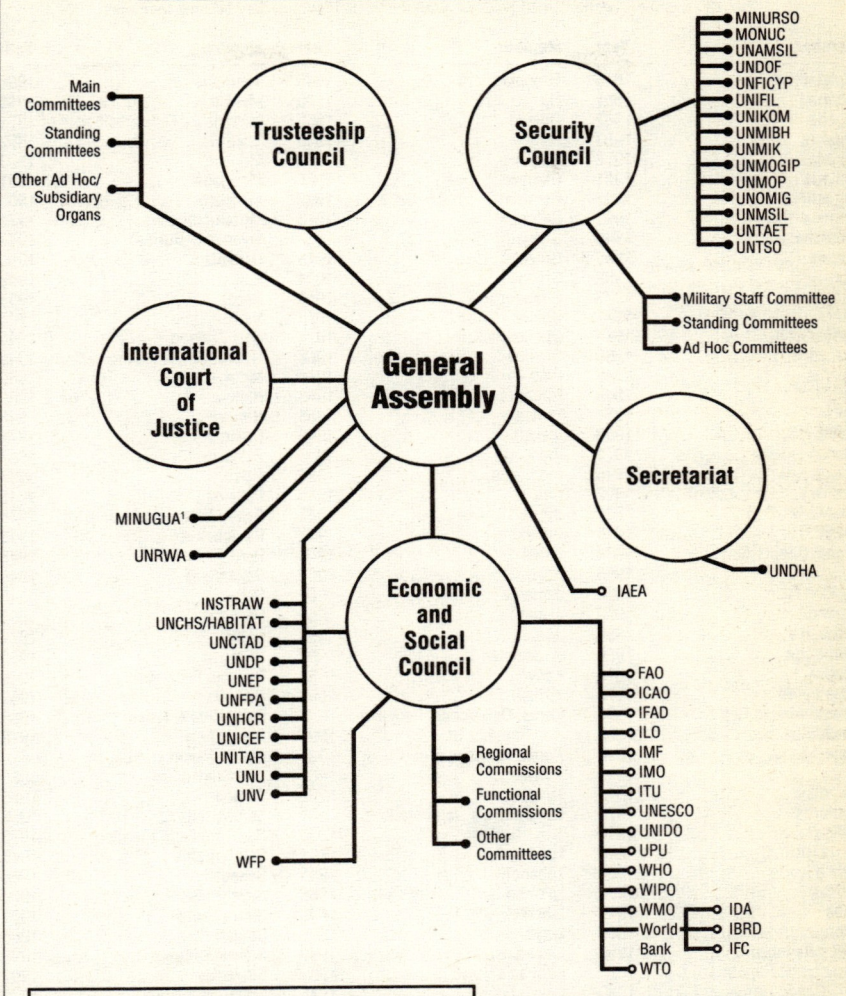

Roster of the United Nations

(As of October 2000)

The 189 members of the United Nations, with the years in which they became members.

Member	Year
Afghanistan	1946
Albania	1955
Algeria	1962
Andorra	1993
Angola	1976
Antigua and Barbuda	1981
Argentina	1945
Armenia	1992
Australia	1945
Austria	1955
Azerbaijan	1992
Bahamas	1973
Bahrain	1971
Bangladesh	1974
Barbados	1966
Belarus	1945
Belgium	1945
Belize	1981
Benin	1960
Bhutan	1971
Bolivia	1945
Bosnia and Herzegovina	1992
Botswana	1966
Brazil	1945
Brunei Darussalam	1984
Bulgaria	1955
Burkina Faso	1960
Burundi	1962
Cambodia	1955
Cameroon	1960
Canada	1945
Cape Verde	1975
Central African Rep.	1960
Chad	1960
Chile	1945
China	1945
Colombia	1945
Comoros	1975
Congo	1960
Costa Rica	1945
Côte d'Ivoire	1960
Croatia	1992
Cuba	1945
Cyprus	1960
Czech Republic	1993
Democratic Republic of the Congo (formerly Zaïre)	1960
Denmark	1945
Djibouti	1977
Dominica	1978
Dominican Rep.	1945
Ecuador	1945
Egypt	1945
El Salvador	1945
Equatorial Guinea	1968
Eritrea	1993
Estonia	1991
Ethiopia	1945
Fiji	1970
Finland	1955
France	1945
Gabon	1960
Gambia	1965
Georgia	1992
Germany	1973
Ghana	1957
Greece	1945
Grenada	1974
Guatemala	1945
Guinea	1958
Guinea-Bissau	1974
Guyana	1966
Haiti	1945
Honduras	1945
Hungary	1955
Iceland	1946
India	1945
Indonesia	1950
Iran	1945
Iraq	1945
Ireland	1955
Israel	1949
Italy	1955
Jamaica	1962
Japan	1956
Jordan	1955
Kazakhstan	1992
Kenya	1963
Kiribati	1999
Korea, Democratic People's Republic of	1991
Korea, Republic of	1991
Kuwait	1963
Kyrgyzstan	1992
Lao People's Democratic Republic	1955
Latvia	1991
Lebanon	1945
Lesotho	1966
Liberia	1945
Libya	1955
Liechtenstein	1990
Lithuania	1991
Luxembourg	1945
Macedonia, Former Yugoslav Republic of	1993
Madagascar	1960
Malawi	1964
Malaysia	1957
Maldives	1965
Mali	1960
Malta	1964
Marshall Islands	1991
Mauritania	1961
Mauritius	1968
Mexico	1945
Micronesia, Federated States of	1991
Moldova	1992
Monaco	1993
Mongolia	1961
Morocco	1956
Mozambique	1975
Myanmar (Burma)	1948
Namibia	1990
Nauru	1999
Nepal	1955
Netherlands	1945
New Zealand	1945
Nicaragua	1945
Niger	1960
Nigeria	1960
Norway	1945
Oman	1971
Pakistan	1947
Palau	1995
Panama	1945
Papua New Guinea	1975
Paraguay	1945
Peru	1945
Philippines	1945
Poland	1945
Portugal	1955
Qatar	1971
Romania	1955
Russian Federation	1945
Rwanda	1962
Saint Kitts & Nevis	1983
Saint Lucia	1979
Saint Vincent and the Grenadines	1980
Samoa	1976
San Marino	1992
Sao Tome and Principe	1975
Saudi Arabia	1945
Senegal	1960
Seychelles	1976
Sierra Leone	1961
Singapore	1965
Slovak Republic	1993
Slovenia	1992
Solomon Islands	1978
Somalia	1960
South Africa	1945
Spain	1955
Sri Lanka	1955
Sudan	1956
Suriname	1975
Swaziland	1968
Sweden	1946
Syria	1945
Tajikistan	1992

International Organizations

Member	Year	Member	Year	Member	Year
Tanzania, United Rep. of	1961	Tuvalu	2000	Vanuatu	1981
Thailand	1946	Uganda	1962	Vietnam	1977
Togo	1960	Ukraine	1945	Venezuela	1945
Tonga	1999	United Arab Emirates	1971	Yemen	1947
Trinidad & Tobago	1962	United Kingdom	1945	Yugoslavia, Federal Republic of, (Serbia and Montenegro)	1945
Tunisia	1956	United States of America	1945	Zambia	1964
Turkey	1945	Uruguay	1945	Zimbabwe	1980
Turkmenistan	1992	Uzbekistan	1992		

Source: *United Nations Association* http://www.un.org

United Nations Secretaries-General

The Secretary-General, heading the Secretariat, is responsible for the UN's administration and for alerting the Security Council to any threats to international peace and security, and acts as spokesperson for the UN. The Secretary-General is elected by the General Assembly on the recommendation of the Security Council and cannot be from one of the five permanent members of the Security Council.

Secretary, Nation	Date Installed
Trygve Lie, Norway	Feb. 1946
Dag Hammarskjold, Sweden	Apr. 1953
U Thant, Burma	Nov. 1961
Kurt Waldheim, Austria	Dec. 1971
Javier Perez de Cuellar, Peru	Dec. 1981
Boutros Boutros-Ghali, Egypt	Jan. 1992
Kofi Annan, Ghana	Jan. 1997 (to Dec. 31, 2001)

Source: *United Nations Association*

Canadian Ambassadors to the United Nations

Ambassador	Date Appointed
Andrew McNaughton	Jan. 1948
John Holmes	Jan. 1950
Gerald Riddell	June 1950
David Johnson	Oct. 1951
Robert MacKay	June 1955
Charles Ritchie	Nov. 1957
Paul Tremblay	May 1962
George Ignatieff	Mar. 1966
Yvon Beaulne	Jan. 1969
Saul Forbes Rae	June 1972
William Barton	May 1976
Michel Dupuy	Mar. 1980
Gérard Pelletier	Aug. 1981
Stephen H. Lewis	Oct. 1984
Yves Fortier	July 1988
Louise Fréchette	Jan. 1992
Robert K. Fowler	Jan. 1995
Paul Heinbecker	June 2000

Source: *Dept. of Foreign Affairs*

Canada's New Ambassador to the UN

On June 26, 2000, Paul Heinbecker became Canada's new ambassador and permanent representative to the United Nations in New York.

Heinbecker is a career diplomat. After joining the Department of External Affairs in 1965, he served with the Permanent Delegation of Canada to the Organization for Economic Co-operation and Development (OECD) in Ankara, Stockholm and Paris. From 1985 to 1989, Heinbecker worked at the Canadian Embassy in Washington DC. In Ottawa, he directed the United States General Relations Division and chaired the Policy Development Secretariat in External Affairs.

From 1989 to 1991, Heinbecker was Prime Minister Brian Mulroney's chief speech writer. From 1991 to 1992, he served as chief foreign policy advisor to the prime minister and as assistant secretary to the Cabinet for foreign and defence policy at the Privy Council Office. In 1992, Heinbecker was named ambassador to Germany; in 1996, at the Department of Foreign Affairs, he became assistant deputy minister for global and security policy.

He replaced Ambassador Robert Fowler, who now represents the Canadian government in Italy.

Other International Organizations in the News

Arab League
(also known as League of Arab States)
Midan Attahrir, Tahrir Square,
P.O. Box 11642, Cairo, Egypt
Established: 22 March 1945
Aim: to promote economic, social, political, and military cooperation among member states
Members: (22) Algeria, Bahrain, Comoros, Djibouti, Egypt, Iraq, Jordan, Kuwait, Lebanon, Libya, Mauritania, Morocco, Oman, Palestine, Qatar, Saudi Arabia, Somalia, Sudan, Syria, Tunisia, United Arab Emirates, Yemen

Arctic Council
Chair of the Arctic Council, Ministry of Foreign Affairs, PO Box 176, 00161 Helsinki, Finland
Website: http://www.dfait-maeci.gc.ca/arctic/menu-e.htm
Established: 19 September 1996
Aim: to promote sustainable development and environmental protection through circumpolar cooperation
Members: (8) Canada, Denmark/Greenland, Finland, Iceland, Norway, Russia, Sweden and the USA; plus 4 international aboriginal organizations with permanent participant status

Association of Southeast Asian Nations (ASEAN)
Jalan Sisingamangaraja 70A, Kebayoran Baru, P.O. Box 2072, Jakarta 12110, Indonesia
Website: http://www.aseansec.org
Established: 9 August 1967
Aim: to encourage regional economic, social and cultural cooperation among member states
Members: (10) Brunei Darussalam, Cambodia, Indonesia, Laos, Malaysia, Myanmar, Philippines, Singapore, Thailand, Vietnam

Commonwealth
Commonwealth Secretariat, Marlborough House, Pall Mall, London SWIY 5HX, United Kingdom
Website: http://www.thecommonwealth.org/home.htm
Established: 11 December 1931
Aim: to promote democracy and cooperation among former members of the British Empire.
Members: 54 including Canada

International Civil Aviation Organization (ICAO)
999 University St., Montreal PQ H3C 5H7, Canada
Website: http://www.icao.int
Established: 7 December 1944
Aim: to promote international cooperation in civil aviation; a UN specialized agency
Members: 185 including Canada

International Criminal Police Organization (Interpol)
BP 6041, F-69411 Lyon CEDEX 06, France
Website: http://www.interpol.int
Established: 13 June 1956
Aim: to promote international cooperation among police authorities in fighting crime
Members: 178 countries including Canada

International Federation of Red Cross and Red Crescent Societies
(formerly Red Cross)
PO Box 372, CH-1211, Geneva 19, Switzerland
Website: http://www.ifrc.org
Established: 1919
Aim: to promote humanitarianism, prepare for disaster relief, provide relief after disasters, and promote health in communities
Members: 176 national societies worldwide, including Canada

International Monetary Fund (IMF)
700 19th Street NW, Washington, DC 20431, USA
Website: http://www.imf.org/external/index.htm
Established: 22 July 1944
Aim: to promote world monetary stability and economic development; a UN specialized agency
Members: 182 including Canada

International Olympic Committee (IOC)
Chateau de Vidy, CH-1007 Lausanne, Switzerland
Website: http://www.olympic.org
Established: 23 June 1894
Aim: to promote the Olympic ideals and administer the Olympic games: 2002 Winter Olympics in Salt Lake City, United States; 2004 Summer Olympics in Athens, Greece
Members: 199 National Olympic Committees including Canada

International Organizations

International Organization for Standardization (ISO)
CP 56, 1 rue de Varembe, CH-1211 Geneva 20, Switzerland
Website: http://www.iso.ch
Established: 23 February 1947
Aim: to promote the development of international standards to aid the international exchange of goods and services and to develop cooperation in intellectual, scientific, technological and economic activity
Members: 130 national standards organizations including Canada

International Organization of Francophones (also known as La Francophonie)
Website: http://www.francophonie.org
Established: 20 March 1970
Aim: to promote peace, democracy and French culture throughout the French-speaking world
Members: 52 including Canada; plus 3 observers

Inter-Parliamentary Union
CP 438, 1211 Geneva 19, Switzerland
Website: http://www.ipu.org
Established: 30 June 1889
Aim: to promote dialogue and cooperation among parliamentarians
Members: 138 national parliaments, including Canada's; five associate (international) parliaments

Liberal International
1 Whitehall Place, London SW1A 2HD United Kingdom
Website: http://www.worldlib.org
Established: 10-14 April 1947
Aim: to strengthen ties among liberal parties and governments worldwide
Members: 84 political parties in 67 countries including Canada

Organization of African Unity
PO Box 3243, Addis Ababa, Ethiopia
Website: http://www.oau-oua.org
Established: 25 May 1963
Aim: to promote the unity of African states, defend members' sovereignty and coordinate socio-economic policies
Members: 51 states plus Western Sahara

Organization of American States (OAS)
Corner of 17th St. and Constitution Ave. NW, Washington, DC 20006, USA
Website: http://www.oas.org
Established: 30 April 1948
Aim: to promote regional peace and security as well as economic and social development
Members: 35 including Canada; plus 46 observers including the European Union. Cuba, although still a member of the OAS, has been barred from participating by a resolution passed in 1962.

Organization of Petroleum Exporting Countries (OPEC)
Obere Donaustrasse 93, A-1020 Vienna, Austria
Website: http://www.opec.org
Established: 14 September 1960
Aim: to coordinate petroleum policies
Members: (11) Algeria, Indonesia, Iran, Iraq, Kuwait, Libya, Nigeria, Qatar, Saudi Arabia, United Arab Emirates, Venezuela

Socialist International
Maritime House, Old Town, Clapham, London SW4 0JW United Kingdom
Website: http://www.socialistinternational.org
Established: 1951 (in its present form)
Aim: to strengthen ties among social democratic, socialist and labour parties
Members: 143 political parties and organizations worldwide

World Council of Churches
PO Box 2100, 1211, Geneva 2, Switzerland
Website: http://www.wcc-coe.org
Established: 23 August 1948
Aim: to promote the visible unity of Christianity
Members: 337 Christian churches in 120 countries including Canada

World Wide Fund for Nature (formerly World Wildlife Fund)
Avenue du Mont-Blanc, CH-1196, Gland, Switzerland
Website: http:www.panda.org/home.cfm
Established: 11 September 1961
Aim: to save wildlife and their habitats from extinction around the world
Members: 24 national organizations including Canada; five associate organizations

The European Union (EU)

The European Union (EU) represents a unique relationship among 15 democratic nations, with the aim of constructing a united Europe. The EU is more than an international organization, but not a full-blown federation. The European Union is the world's largest trading entity, accounting for well over 20% of world trade. Its population totals about 375 million people.

The European Union originated as the European Coal and Steel Community (ECSC), formed in 1951 by France, West Germany, Italy, the Netherlands, Belgium and Luxembourg and became operational in 1952.

The ECSC boosted internal trade in coal and steel by 129% in five years. Its success spurred the Six to apply the same approach to the entire economy. In 1957, the same six countries formed the European Economic Community (EEC), creating a common market for all sectors of the economy. The EEC committed the Six to dismantle trade barriers and to allow the free movement of goods, services, capital and people between member countries. At the same time the Six formed the European Atomic Energy Community (Euratom) to further the use of nuclear energy for peaceful purposes.

In 1967, the institutions of the ECSC, Euratom and the EEC were merged. In 1973, Denmark, Ireland and the United Kingdom became members, as did Greece in 1981, Spain and Portugal in 1986 and Austria, Finland and Sweden in 1995.

From its inception, the EC has been dedicated to reducing the gap in living standards between the various Member States and supporting the development of the poorer regions. To that end, the EC uses four main sources of funding, known as the Structural Funds: The European Regional Development Fund, the European Social Fund, the European Agricultural Guidance and Guarantee Fund, and the Cohesion Fund. Greece, Portugal, Ireland and parts of Spain and Italy have been targeted for aid to bring their standards of living closer to that of the other Member States.

The Europe 1992 project to complete the common market and create one single internal market by dismantling the remaining physical, technical and fiscal barriers among the Member States was part of the Single European Act, which came into force in 1987.

The Maastricht Treaty on European Union was signed in 1992 and came into effect in November 1993. It was one further step on the road to a European constitution and integrated the previous EC structures.

The European Union consists of three pillars. The first pillar is the European Community with its joint supranational institutions. The two new pillars are intergovernmental cooperation in foreign and security policy as well as intergovernmental cooperation in justice and home affairs. While this cooperation is intergovernmental, the European Commission is fully associated with all activities.

The Maastricht Treaty committed the Member States to create an economic and monetary Union. In January 1999, the EURO was introduced as the new single European currency. The Treaty also committed the 15 to political union, by developing a common foreign and security policy, which might lead to a common defence policy.

The Maastricht Treaty committed the Member States to:

- establish a European Central Bank and introduce a common currency;
- develop a common foreign and security policy, notably through joint actions;
- increase the power for the European Parliament; by involvement in the enactment of legislation: in the appointment of the Commission; and assent for major international agreements;
- establish closer cooperation on justice and home affairs, including visa policy and immigration;
- introduce new responsibilities to the European Community in social policy, public health, education, culture, environment and research and development;
- strengthen the Cohesion Fund to increase aid to the Union's less favoured regions;
- give the regions a part to play in the Community, through a Committee of the Regions; and
- introduce the principle of subsidiarity, according to which the EC should deal only with the enactment of matters it is better equipped to deal with, than the Member States.

In 1997, the 15 agreed to revise the Maastricht Treaty by drawing up a new Treaty of Amsterdam. Coming into force in May 1999, the Treaty of Amsterdam contains four major objectives. They are to:

- put employment and citizens' rights at the heart of the Union;
- ensure that citizens can move freely within the Union and live in a secure environment;
- strengthen the Union's objectives in foreign policy, thereby giving the EU a single voice in foreign affairs; and

- make the Union's institutions and decision-making process more effective.

By mid-2000, 13 countries had applied for membership in the EU. Accession negotiations are currently being held with Estonia, Hungary, Poland, the Czech Republic, Slovenia, Cyprus, Bulgaria, Latvia, Lithuania, Romania, the Slovak Republic and Malta. Negotiations have not started with Turkey. The basic principle of the negotiations is that all the applicants must accept existing EU law.

■ INSTITUTIONS OF THE EU

The European Union creates its own laws and policies through the following institutions:

The European Commission proposes legislation, implements policy and enforces the treaties. It has investigative powers and can take legal action. It also represents the EU in trade negotiations. The Commission is headed by 20 Commissioners: France, Germany, Italy, Spain and the UK each appoint two Commissioners while the other Member States appoint one Commissioner each. The Commissioners are appointed for five years.

The European Parliament is directly elected by the citizens of the Union. Its 626 members debate issues, question the Commission and Council, and scrutinize proposed legislation. It can dismiss the Commission and has final approval over the EC budget. Elections take place every five years. The number of MPs from each country are: Germany 99, UK 87, France 87, Italy 87, Spain 64, Netherlands 31, Belgium 25, Portugal 25, Greece 25, Sweden 22, Austria 21, Denmark 16, Finland 16, Ireland 15 and Luxembourg 6. MPs sit according to political affiliation and not nationality.

The Council of the European Union is composed of ministers from the 15 member countries. The Council acts on Commission proposals and is the final decision-making body. Participation in the meetings changes according to the agenda. Agricultural ministers, for instance, decide on agricultural matters and economic and finance ministers on economic and monetary matters. Ministers represent and defend the interest of their countries, while seeking agreements that promote the Union's goals. The presidency of the Council rotates among the Member States every six months. In one of the EC's most important reforms, the Single European Act provided for majority voting in the Council in certain areas that previously required unanimity. Areas for majority voting were extended again in the Maastricht and Amsterdam Treaties.

The European Council is comprised of the heads of state or government of the EU Member States and the Commission president. The group meets at least twice a year to define major internal and foreign policy orientations. The European Council does not legislate, but its written conclusions provide guidance.

The Court of Justice is the EC's supreme court. It interprets EC law and its rulings are binding—also on Member States. The court comprises 15 judges, assisted by nine advocates-general. Both groups are appointed for six years by mutual consent of the Member States.

The Court of Auditors audits the accounts of the EC and EC bodies.

The Committee of the Regions and the **Economic and Social Committee** must be consulted by the Commission and the Council on policies and proposals for legislation.

The European Central Bank governs monetary policy.

Members of the European Union
(As of October 2000)

Member	Year Joined	Member	Year Joined
Austria	1995	Italy	1952
Belgium	1952	Luxembourg	1952
Denmark	1973	Netherlands	1952
Finland	1995	Portugal	1986
France	1952	Spain	1986
Germany	1952	Sweden	1995
Greece	1981	United Kingdom	1973
Ireland	1973		

Source: *Commission of the European Communities*
For Internet information, visit: http://europa.eu.int and http://www.delcan.cec.eu.int

Asia-Pacific Economic Cooperation (APEC)

APEC is an association of 21 Asia-Pacific countries. It promotes economic cooperation, freer trade and greater prosperity throughout the Pacific basin. APEC's members include wealthy countries (e.g., the United States) and poor countries (e.g., Vietnam). Members include capitalist and socialist economies. From 1989 to late 1997, APEC helped turn the Asia-Pacific region into the fastest growing economic region in the world.

APEC was established in 1989 at a conference of trade and foreign ministers in Canberra, Australia. The 12 founding states included Canada. APEC's members agreed to meet annually for informal talks in different member countries. They also agreed to hold alternate ministerial meetings in APEC countries that belonged to the Association of Southeast Asian Nations (ASEAN).

In the first years, talks were held at the ministerial level. In 1990, Singapore hosted the second meeting of ministers which created seven working groups. These groups focussed on trade and investment data, trade promotion, investment and technology transfer, human resource development, regional energy cooperation, marine resource conservation and telecommunications.

In 1991, APEC's members met in Seoul, Korea. They committed themselves to private enterprise and "open regionalism." China, Hong Kong and Taiwan participated for the first time. Three new working groups were created: fisheries, tourism and transportation. In 1992 in Bangkok, Thailand, the ministers decided to create a permanent Secretariat in Singapore and a central fund to cover APEC's administration.

In 1993, the United States hosted ministerial talks in Seattle and, for the first time, the political leaders of APEC's member states met for separate talks on Blake Island. The resulting "Economic Vision Statement" recognized the interdependence of Asia-Pacific economies and the need for freer trade. The talks also produced a Committee on Trade and Investment to increase cooperation in the exchange of goods, services and investment according to the principles of the World Trade Organization.

Separate meetings of APEC's political leaders became annual events. In 1994, after a ministerial meeting in Jakarta, Indonesia, APEC's leaders issued the "Bogor Declaration of Common Resolve." This statement set the goals of total free trade and investment within the region by 2010 for APEC's industrialized economies and by 2020 for its developing economies. The 1995 meetings in Osaka, Japan, and the 1996 meetings in the Philippines discussed how to accomplish these goals. At Osaka, APEC created a Business Advisory Council (ABAC) to enlist more support from private businesses.

The 1997 conferences took place in Vancouver amidst a financial crisis in Southeast Asia. APEC conferees identified 15 economic sectors for early trade liberalization: environmental goods and services, fish, toys, forest products, gems and jewellery, medical equipment, chemicals, energy, food, natural and synthetic rubber, telecommunications, fertilizers, automobiles, oilseeds and civil aircraft. APEC also aimed at streamlining customs procedures by 2002.

In 1998, APEC participants met in Kuala Lumpur, Malaysia. The United States and Japan proposed a US$10 billion aid package to ease the financial crisis which, APEC leaders acknowledged, had spread beyond the Asia-Pacific region. The 1999 summit was in Auckland, New Zealand. The eighth informal meeting of economic leaders will be in Brunei Darussalam on Nov. 15-16, 2000.

The executive director of the APEC Secretariat is Serbini Ali of Brunei Darussalam; he is the eighth executive director since 1993.

Member Economies (date of membership)

Australia (1989)
Brunei Darussalam (1989)
Canada (1989)
Chile (1994)
Chinese Taipei (1991)
Hong Kong (1991)
Indonesia (1989)
Japan (1989)
Malaysia (1989)
Mexico (1993)
New Zealand (1989)
Papua New Guinea (1993)
People's Republic of China (1991)
Peru (1998)
Philippines (1989)
Republic of Korea (1989)
Russia (1998)
Singapore (1989)
Thailand (1989)
United States (1989)
Vietnam (1998)

For more information about APEC, visit the official websites at http://www.apecsec.org.sg and http://dfait-maeci.gc.ca/canada-apec/menu-e.asp

Organization for Economic Co-operation and Development (OECD)

The Organization for Economic Co-operation and Development was launched in 1961 to foster economic growth among the world's major industrialized market economies. The OECD replaced the Organization for European Economic Co-operation (OEEC), which was created in 1948 to administer American Marshall Plan aid to the devastated economies of Western Europe after World War II. Twenty European and North American countries joined the OECD at its inception; today the organization has 29 member states.

The OECD offers, through its many committees and working groups, opportunities for government officials to talk to one another about economic and social policy. These groups meet two-to-four times a year and consist of senior policy-makers. They propose trade and investment policies aimed at reducing conflict among the OECD's member states and at helping the economies of non-member countries to develop.

The OECD has been variously described as a think tank, a monitoring agency and a rich man's club. Its members include the wealthiest countries on earth, which produce approximately two thirds of the world's goods and services. Member states proclaim their commitment to "the principles of the market economy, pluralist democracy and respect for human rights." A few non-member countries also participate in the OECD; often this participation precedes full membership. On July 28, 2000, the OECD invited Slovakia to join; Slovakia is expected to accept the invitation.

OECD headquarters are located on the western edge of Paris at the Château de la Muette, and the Secretariat there facilitates the flow of information and analysis among member countries. Parts of the OECD Secretariat collect data, monitor trends, analyse and forecast economic developments, while other divisions study social changes, trade patterns, agriculture, taxation, technology or the environment. The work is done in consultation with policy-makers from the member governments which use the data, and it also supports international discussion at committee level.

Among the numerous directorates, the most well-known is the Economics Department which publishes the *OECD Economic Outlook* twice a year, in June and December. That publication evaluates trends in the recent past and forecasts economic conditions for the coming 12 months. The economy of each member country (and many non-members) is monitored by the Country Studies Branch and that data is published annually in an *Economic Survey*.

The Statistics Directorate collects and compares economic statistics from across the OECD. The figures appear in electronic and printed form in *Main Economic Indicators*. This monthly journal also publishes statistics on Eastern Europe's newly emerging market economies.

Other directorates focus on environmental issues, aid to developing countries, public management (how governments go about their business), trade, market development, science and technology as it relates to industry, social policy (including education, unemployment and migration), agriculture, energy (including nuclear), and how cities and regions grow and develop.

For more information about the OECD, visit the website at http://www.oecd.org/

Members (date of membership)

Australia (1971)
Austria (1961)
Belgium (1961)
Canada (1961)
Czech Republic (1995)
Denmark (1961)
Finland (1969)
France (1961)
Germany (1961)
Greece (1961)
Hungary (1996)
Iceland (1961)
Ireland (1961)
Italy (1961)
Japan (1964)
Korea, South (1996)
Luxembourg (1961)
Mexico (1994)
Netherlands (1961)
New Zealand (1973)
Norway (1961)
Poland (1996)
Portugal (1961)
Spain (1961)
Sweden (1961)
Switzerland (1961)
Turkey (1961)
United Kingdom (1961)
United States (1961)

The World Trade Organization (WTO)

The World Trade Organization (WTO) was established on January 1, 1995. It was the result of eight years of global trade negotiations, collectively known as the Uruguay Round, among 125 nations. The result of those negotiations–a 22,000-page 385-pound agreement–was signed in Marrakech, Morocco, on April 15, 1994. It created the WTO and established the framework for global commerce.

The WTO is now the only international body dealing with the rules of trade among nations. It succeeds the General Agreement on Tariffs and Trade (GATT) which was established provisionally after the Second World War in the wake of other new institutions dedicated to international economic cooperation–including the forerunners to the World Bank and the International Montary Fund.

■ Promoting fair competition

The WTO is not a true "free trade" institution because it permits tariffs and, in limited circumstances, other forms of economic protection. But the WTO does oversee a system of rules dedicated to open, fair and undistorted competition. All WTO agreements are founded on the basic principles of non-discrimination, freer trade, predictable policy-making, encouragement of competition and providing for less developed countries.

The rules on non-discrimination are designed to secure fair trade conditions; so too are the rules on dumping and subsidies. Previous GATT rules established which governments could impose compensating duties on these two forms of "unfair" competition, but GATT's rules only dealt with goods. WTO agreements have extended and clarified GATT's rules to include services and intellectual property.

At the close of the 20th century, the WTO focuses on five policies that support the organization's main tasks: assisting developing and transitional economies, providing specialized help for export promotion, arranging regional trade, cooperating in global economic policy-making and notifying members when trade measures are introduced or changed.

■ The structure of the WTO

The WTO has 137 member countries, 35 observer countries and seven observer organizations to the General Council. As of June 14, 2000, Georgia was the last country to join; most observer nations are waiting for full membership.

The WTO's highest authority is the Ministerial Conference. It consists of representatives of all WTO members, and it must meet at least once every two years. It decides on all matters that affect any of the trade agreements.

The General Council directs the daily work of the WTO. It consists of all WTO members and reports to the Ministerial Conference. The General Council works regularly for the Conference and convenes two more bodies: the Dispute Settlement Body and the Trade Policy Review Body. The latter regularly reviews the trade policies of individual WTO members. Numerous other councils, committees, working parties and negotiating groups are responsible for specific areas or agreements.

Mike Moore, a New Zealander, is the Director-General of the WTO. His three-year term began on September 1, 1999. He will be succeeded by Dr. Supachai Panitchpakdi of Thailand in 2002.

For more information on the WTO, visit the website at http://www.wto.org or write to the World Trade Organization at 154 Rue de Lausanne, 1211 Geneva 21, Switzerland.

Source: *Information and Media Relations Division, WTO 1997; http://www.DFAIT-maeci.gc.ca*

North Atlantic Treaty Organization (NATO)

The North Atlantic Treaty Organization (NATO) is a political and military alliance, created in Washington on April 4, 1949, when 12 states in Europe and North America signed the North Atlantic Treaty. NATO defends the peace and freedom of its members through collective security without sacrificing members' sovereignty. Headquarters is in Brussels, Belgium.

NATO was created to defend Western and Southern Europe from a perceived threat of invasion by the Soviet Union following World War II. Western leaders began negotiating in 1948, after a Soviet attempt to deny Western access to West Berlin.

Today 19 countries belong, including the original 12: Belgium, Canada, Denmark, France, Iceland, Italy, Luxembourg, the Netherlands, Norway, Portugal, the United Kingdom and the United States, plus Greece and Turkey (1952), Germany (joined as West Germany, 1955) and Spain (1982). On March 12, 1999, NATO admitted its newest members—former members of the Soviet-led Warsaw Pact—Hungary, Poland and the Czech Republic.

The highest authority within NATO is the North Atlantic Council (NAC). It consists of Permanent Representatives, who act as ambassadors for their respective countries, and is directed by a Secretary General. Meetings are weekly; the NAC also convenes less frequent meetings of Foreign or Defence Ministers or Heads of State. Discussions cover political, economic, military and scientific issues. The NAC reaches decisions only after all member states have been consulted. It cannot impose decisions on any of its members, although members can block the wishes of others by withholding consent.

The NAC can create subordinate committees and planning groups. The most important are the Defence Planning Committee and the Nuclear Planning Group. The Defence Planning Committee, which consists of Permanent Representatives and Defence Ministers, deals with collective defence planning. The Nuclear Planning Group, which consists of Defence Ministers, deals with nuclear weapons issues. Both are chaired by the NAC's Secretary General. This post is currently held by Lord George Robertson, who took office on October 14, 1999, and who had previously served as the UK's Secretary of State for Defence.

At the Rome Summit in 1991, NATO outlined a new strategy for Europe in response to the collapse of the Soviet Union: cooperation with the ex-Warsaw Pact states, reduced dependence on nuclear weapons, reductions in the size and readiness of military forces, improvements in military flexibility, greater use of multinational military units and a new focus on peacekeeping.

Also concurrent with the disintegration of the Soviet Union, NATO created a number of mechanisms for consultation and co-operation with former Warsaw Pact states, including the North Atlantic Cooperation Council (NACC) (1991), the Partnership for Peace program (1994) and the Euro-Atlantic Partnership Council (1997). The goal of these organisations was peaceful progress toward a new security environment in Europe. Despite these efforts, the political and economic transformation of many of the former Soviet republics destabilized the area as regional ethnic and political rivalries emerged.

In 1995, NATO first sent land troops outside NATO territory when 60 000 personnel went into Bosnia and Herzegovina under United Nations' authority to enforce the Dayton Peace Accord, negotiated to end armed conflict in the former Yugoslavia. NATO forces and troops from 19 non-NATO countries, including Russia, worked together during the mission, first as part of the Implementation Force (IFOR) and then as the Stabilisation Force (SFOR), which is ongoing.

On March 23, 1999, the NAC authorised air strikes by NATO forces against targets in the Federal Republic of Yugoslavia in an effort to end that country's campaign against ethnic Albanians in Kosovo. The air strike campaign continued until June 10when the withdrawal of Yugoslav forces from the Kosovo region began. As of June 12, 1999, NATO forces joined a UN-mandated peacekeeping force (Kosovo Force or KFOR), to enforce the withdrawal agreement.

For more information about NATO, visit the websites at http://www.nato.int

HISTORY IN HEADLINES

■ Ancient History 5000 BC to AD 476

5000–3501: The earliest known cities are in Mesopotamia—in southwest Asia between the Tigris and Euphrates Rivers—a plain rendered fertile by canals; the Egyptian calendar is regulated by the sun and moon; Sumerian writing exists, in southern Mesopotamia on clay tablets, consisting of 2,000 pictograph signs; the Neolithic period in western Europe is characterized by polished stone weapons and tools and agriculturally-based settlements; Cretan ships appear in the Mediter-ranean Sea; copper alloys are used, and there is smelting of gold and silver in Sumer and Egypt; harps and flutes are played in Egypt; painted pottery appears along the Mediter-ranean; coloured ceramic ware from Russia reaches China.

3500–2001: The Middle Eastern Bronze Age begins (c. 3500 BC); the height of Sumerian civilization (in the region of the Euphrates River valley) is noted for having a numerical system, irrigated agriculture, poetry, potters' wheels, linen, wheeled vehicles, wedge-shaped (cuneiform) script, barley, bread, beer, use of metal coins as legal tender, oil-burning lamps, brick temples and medicine; the dynasty of Pharoahs as god-kings in Egypt begins (2200–525 BC); the Great Sphynx of Gizeh is built; wrestling is the first highly developed sport; glass beads are worn in Egypt; the bow and arrow is first used in warfare; the Yao dynasty is the first recorded in China (2500–2300); the Indus civilization begins in India; the earliest Egyptian mummies are made; equinoxes and solstices are calculated in China; the first library is in Egypt.

2000–1501: The Egyptian height of power and achievement (18th dynasty) features an irrigation system, contraceptives, bathrooms with a water supply, an alphabet of 24 signs, and the oldest form of a novel (*Story of Sinuhe*); the Persian empire begins (1750–1550); the first legal system and laws of a kingdom are set up by Hammurabi, king of Babylonia; the first of seven periods of Chinese literature begins; Stonehenge is built; Abraham, the patriarch of the Jewish religion, lives (c. 1800); Babylonia uses geometry as the basis for astronomical measurements, and describes the signs of the Zodiac; religious dances are performed in Crete.

1500–1001: The Israelites, led by Moses, leave bondage in Egypt (eventually settling in Canaan in 1250), and receive the Ten Commandments and the world's first monotheistic belief at Mt Sinai; the decline of Egyptian power begins (1200–1090); Troy is destroyed during the Trojan War (1193–83) over Helen of Sparta (Greek legend); the Iron Age begins in the Mediterranean area (1000); obelisk structures are used as sundials in Egypt; the first Chinese dictionary is written; silk fabrics appear in China; leprosy spreads in India and Egypt; Phoenicia is the dominant trading power in the Mediterranean; the Mexican Sun Pyramid is built in Teotihuacan.

1000–901: Asiatic and Greek civilizations are linked by Phoenician trading; David is the king of the united kingdom of Judah and Israel (1000–960) with Jerusalem as its capital; David is succeeded by his son Solomon who presides over the height of Israel's ancient civilization (960–25); classical paganism reigns in Greece; pantheistic belief reigns in India (teaching reincarnation and the caste system); the Chou dynasty's rational philosophy reigns in China; Pinto Indians build huts in southwest North America; brush and ink painting appears in China; gold vessels and jewellery are made in northern Europe; the Hebrew alphabet and literature are developed; the Germanic peoples begin to migrate en masse.

900–601: Carthage is founded as a trading centre (813); *Iliad* and *Odyssey* are written and credited to the poet Homer (c. 800); according to legend, Rome is founded by the twins Romulus and Remus (753); the first recorded Olympic Games are held in Greece (776), and every four years thereafter during ancient times; the earliest record of music is a hymn on a Sumerian tablet; arts and crafts flourish in Asia Minor and Greece; a canal between the Nile River and the Red Sea is started under Pharoah Nechos; Etruscan art forms emerge in Tuscany; the Assyrians destroy Babylon and divert the Euphrates River to cover the site of the city; the Babylonians and their allies later destroy the Assyrian empire, which is then divided among the conquerors; the Acropolis, a fortified hill and religious centre, is built in Athens; limestone and marble are used in the construction of Greek temples; flutes and lyres accompany song; Greek choral and lyric poetry use strophe and antistrophe; Zoroaster, a religious teacher and prophet of ancient Persia, lives (c. 628–c. 551).

600–451: The Mayan civilization flourishes in Mexico; Nebuchadnezzer builds what may be the terraced Hanging Gardens of Babylon (600); Babylonian troops destroy the Jewish Temple at Jerusalem and take many Jews as slaves; Jews write the early books of the Bible during the Babylonian Captivity; Siddhartha Gautama, who becomes Buddha, the "enlightened" Indian philosopher and religious teacher, is born (563): at age 29 he renounces world luxuries and searches for enlightenment, which he attains at age 35 while meditating under a pipal tree at Bodh Gaya, and he teaches monks to continue his work; Confucius, the Chinese philosopher and teacher, is born (551); his moral and religious system governs China and is contained in the sayings of *Analects*; Cyrus II the Great of Persia conquers Babylon and surrounding areas and transforms Persia into a vast empire (c. 540): he frees the Jews from Babylon (536) and aids their return to Israel; Darius I divides the Persian empire into 20 provinces and introduces reforms including a common currency, regular taxes and a standing army; Solon's laws are adopted in Athens; Milo of Crotona, a legendary athlete, is crowned six times at the Olympic Games (536); Chinese feudal structure begins to weaken during Chou dynasty (c. 500–451); Greek cities are freed from Persian domination when the Greeks in Cyprus win the Persian Wars (490–49); the marble temple of Apollo is built at Delphi (478); the statue of Zeus, the centrepiece of the temple of Olympia, is built (460); Aeschylus writes *Prometheus Bound* (460); the *Fables of Aesop* is written by a former Phrygian slave.

450–301: The Greek Periclean Age unfolds with the philosophers Socrates and (his pupil) Plato, the dramatists Sophocles and Euripides and historians Thucydides and Herodotus; the beginning of the Indian empire is centred at Magadha (the "cradle of Buddhism"); the Torah becomes the moral code of the Jewish people; Celtic settlements begin in the British Isles; the Spartans use chemicals in warfare (charcoal, sulphur and pitch); the Parthenon, the masterpiece of Greek architecture, is built (447–32); the population of Greece reaches two million citizens and one million slaves; indigenous Indian civilization ends in Mexico; the Peloponnesian Wars between Athens and Sparta (431–04) end when the Spartan navy destroys the Athenian navy at Aegospotami: this leads to the decline of Athens as a great power; the first horoscopes are developed in Mesopotamia (c. 410); Socrates is put to death for state offences (399); Brennus leads the Gauls from northern Italy to sack Rome (390); Rome is rebuilt (387) and city walls are built around it (377); Plato, a Greek philosopher, founds the most influential school in the world, the Academy (c. 387); the use of catapults as weapons of war begins; Aristotle, the Greek philosopher, is born (384); Alexander the Great, son of Philip II of Macedon, is born (356); Shung-tse founds Chinese monist philosophy (the doctrine that the universe can be explained by one principle) (350); Corinth becomes a trading centre (338); Philip II is assassinated (336); Alexander succeeds his father and conquers Persia, Jerusalem and Tyre, extending his empire to the Indus River in India where his generals force him to turn back; Alexander dies in Babylon (323) and his empire is divided among his generals who fight civil wars for a time (beginning in 321); the Hellenistic period of Greek arts begins (330–20) and the leading Greek schools of thought are: Stoics, Epicureans and Cynics; Euclid writes *Elements*, a standard work on geometry (323); Alexandria is the centre of Greek learning.

300–151: The Mexican sun temple Atetello is built at Teotihuacan (300); accurate star maps are compiled by Chinese astronomers (c. 300); full equality between patricians and plebeians is mandated in Rome (287); Archimedes, the Greek mathematician, is born (287); the practical end of the history of Babylon coincides with Babylonian re-establishment in the new city of Seleucia (275); Manetho, the high priest of Egypt, writes a history of Egypt in Greek (275); the Colossus at Rhodes is completed (275); the Lighthouse of Pharos is completed at Alexandria (275); the First Punic War between the Cartha-ginians and the Romans (264–41) arises out of a dispute involving the Sicilian cities of Messana and Syracuse: the Romans win naval battles at Mylae (260) and Cape Ecnomus (256) but lose in Africa (255); a Roman victory of the Aegadian Isles (241) brings a peace treaty that gives Sicily to Rome, but Rome reneges on the treaty and invades Sardinia and Corsica; the leap year is introduced into the Egyptian calendar (239); the Greeks and Romans play ball games, roll dice and play board games; the death of Sun-tsi marks the end of Chinese classical philosophy; the Great Wall of China (2,400 km long) is built to keep out invaders (215); the Second Punic War (218–01) opens when Hannibal and the Carthaginians conquer the Spanish city Saguntum, a Roman ally, and Rome declares war: Hannibal successfully invades Italy from the north (217) and makes an alliance with Philip V of Macedon (216), but is later defeated by the Romans at Zama (202) in Africa; Carthage surrenders its war fleet to Rome as well as its Spanish province; the Second Macedonian War (200–197) ends with the Romans under Flamius defeating Philip V of Macedon; the use of gears leads to the invention of the ox-driven water wheel for irrigation (200); an inscription is engraved on the Rosetta Stone (c. 200); Antiochus IV of Syria persecutes the Jews in Israel and desecrates their Temple of Jerusalem (168); the Jews revolt under Judas Maccabeus and repel the Syrians, then rededicate (Chanukah) the Temple (165); the inventor of trigonometry, Hipparchus of Nicaea, is born (160).

150–1 BC: During the Third Punic War (149–46) the Romans destroy Corinth and massacre the inhabitants of Carthage (due to alleged breach of treaty); the Roman Empire now consists of seven provinces; the Venus of Milo is sculpted (140); Cicero, the greatest Roman orator, is born (106); the first Chinese ships reach the east coast of India (100); the greatest of Roman poets, Virgil, is born (70): he pens the epic *Aeneid*; Horace, the lyric poet, is born (65); Julius Caesar, Roman military commander, organizes the First Trium-virate (60) with Pompey, commander-in-chief of the army, and Marcus Crassus; Caesar conquers the northern Gauls (55) and the Britons; Caesar and Pompey battle for control of Rome after Caesar crosses the Rubicon River and provokes a civil war; Caesar emerges victorious (48); the Julian calendar and leap year are adopted in Rome (46); Cleopatra, the last queen of Egypt, orders the death of Pompey; Caesar, now the dictator of Rome, is murdered by a group headed by Brutus and Cassius Longinus (44); Mark Antony, Octavian and Lepidus form the Second Triumvirate and defeat Brutus and Cassius at Phillipi (42); Mark Antony returns to Egypt (38) where he and Cleopatra commit suicide after being defeated by Octavian at Actium (31); Octavian, retitled Augustus, is a virtual emperor of Rome (30–AD 14); Herod the Great is appointed king of Judea by the Romans (c. 40); the probable date of the birth of Jesus, the Jewish son of Mary, in Bethlehem (AD 4).

AD 1–150: Jesus, who is revered as the Son of God by his followers, the Christians, preaches for three years in Galilee (c. 30); in the third year of his preaching, Jesus is crucified in Jerusalem by Roman authorities at the request of local political and religious leaders; Caligula becomes emperor of Rome (37) and is known for his ruthlessness and insanity: he is assassinated by the Praetorian Guard (42) and is succeeded by Claudius I, who consolidates and reinvigorates the empire despite a paralysis (dies in 54); the apostle Paul sets out on his missionary travels (45) and spreads Christianity; Nero, emperor of Rome, is the first to persecute the Christians, for allegedly burning half of Rome (64); the Gospels according to Matthew, Mark and John are written; Jews revolt against Rome and the Romans destroy the second Temple at Jerusalem and enslave many inhabitants (70); 1,000 Jewish Zealots hold off the 15,000-member Roman legion for three years on the mountaintop fortress of Masada, and the Zealots commit suicide to escape capture (73); under Emperor Trajan, the Roman Empire reaches its greatest geographical extent when he conquers Dacia and much of Parthia (98–116); paper is made by the Chinese, though not for writing (by 100); Hadrian's Wall is built as the northern boundary and defence line of the Roman Empire (122–26); the medical authority up to the 16th century, Greek physician and writer Galen, (c. 130–200) demonstrates that arteries carry blood (not air) and establishes the importance of the spinal cord by correlating earlier medical knowledge with his discoveries based on experiments and animal dissection; the earliest known Sanskrit inscriptions are made in India (150).

151–300: Ptolemy, a Greco-Egyptian thinker, compiles *Almagest*, the 13-volume work on ancient astronomy (earth-centred universe), mathematics, geography and science, which is influential to the 16th century; the oldest known Maya monuments are built (c. 164); the period of Neo-Platonism, the last of the Greek philosophies, begins (c. 200); silkworms are exported from Korea to China and then to Japan (c. 200); citizenship is granted to every freeborn subject in the Roman Empire (212); Afghanistan is invaded by the Huns (200); the

Goths invade Asia Minor and the Balkan Peninsula (220); the end of the Han dynasty in China is followed by four centuries of division (220); the southern part of India breaks into several kingdoms; Rome celebrates its 1,000th anniversary (248); persecution of Christians increases and martyrs are revered as saints (c. 250); the first book of algebra is written by Diophantus of Alexandria (c. 250); the Goths attack the Black Sea area (257) as well as Athens, Sparta and Corinth (268); Pappus of Alex-andria documents use of cogwheel, lever, pulley, screw and wedge (c. 285); Rome is partitioned into a western and an eastern empire; five distinct German dukedoms emerge (Saxons, Franks, Alemanni, Thuringians and Goths) (c. 300).

301–400: Constantine the Great reunites the western and eastern Roman Empires and becomes sole emperor (310–37); Constantine establishes toleration of Christianity with the Edict of Milan (313); the seat of the Roman Empire is moved to Constantinople (c. 331); the Basilican Church of St Peter is erected (330); Emperor Constantine is baptized on his deathbed (337) and is succeeded by his three sons, who again split Rome into two empires; the Huns invade Europe (360) and Russia (376); books begin to replace scrolls (360); Lo-Tsun, a Chinese monk, founds the Caves of the Thousand Buddhas in Kansu (360); Theodosius the Great becomes the last emperor of a united Roman Empire (392); Alaric, king of the Visigoths, invades Greece (396) and plunders Athens and the Balkans (398); the first definite records of Japanese history appear (400), although legend claims Japan was founded in 660 BC.

401–76: The Visigoths invade Italy (401); Alaric sacks Rome (410); Roman legions withdraw from Britain to defend Italy from the Visigoths (410); barbarians settle in Roman provinces (425); Attila becomes ruler of the Huns (433); St Augustine, Christian theologian, writes *The City of God* (411); alchemy begins with the search for the Philosopher's Stone and the Elixir of Life as chief objects; pre-Inca culture develops in Peru; Venice is founded by refugees from Attila's Huns (452); the Vandals sack Rome (455) and destroy the Roman fleet at Cartegena (460); the Huns leave Europe (470); the Mayan civilization flourishes in southern Mexico (c. 470); the first Shinto religious shrines are built in Japan (478): they deal primarily with nature and ancestor worship; the German barbarian Odoacer takes Ravenna and deposes Emperor Romulus Augustulus, thereby ending the Western Roman Empire (476); Aryabhata, Hindu astronomer and mathematician, studies powers and roots of numbers (b. 476).

■ Middle or Dark Ages: 477–1450

477–529: Chi dynasty in southern China (479–502); Clovis, leader of the Franks (since 481), converts to Christianity (496); the first schism between the Western and Eastern Churches occurs when Pope Felix III excommunicates Patriarch Acacius of Constantinople (484–519); Armenian Church separates from Byzantium and Rome (491); the Moshica culture of the Chimic Indians flowers in Peru with agriculture, pottery and textiles; the Vatican Palace in Rome is first planned (500); Tamo carries tea from India to China (c. 500); Clovis kills Alaric II and annexes the Visigoth kingdom of Toulouse (507), and Clovis's realm is divided among his four sons upon his death (511); Emperor Wu-Ti converts to Buddhism and encourages the new religion in central China (517); Justinian I becomes the Byzantine Emperor (527): he is known for heavy taxes, public works and codifying Roman law; the Saxon kingdoms of Essex and Middlesex appear; Chosroes I is king of Persia (531–79) and encourages culture and art.

530–99: Arthur, the semi-legendary king of the Britons, is first mentioned at the Battle of Mt Badon (c. 540); the earliest Chinese roll paintings appear in Tun-huang (landscapes); war breaks out between Persia and the Byzantine Empire (539–62); St Gildas writes the first important source of early British history, *De excido et conquestu Brittaniae* (542); disastrous earthquakes occur around the world (543); the plague of Constantinople, imported by rats from Egypt and Syria, spreads throughout Europe and reaches Britain (547); the Golden Era of Byzantine art begins (550); Poles settle in western Galacia, Ukrainians in eastern Galacia (550); chess begins in India (c. 550); Buddhism is introduced into Japan by Emperor Shotoko Taishi (c.552–621), and the first Buddhist monastery in Japan is founded (587); Japanese prehistory ends and the Asuka period begins; Justinian sends missionaries to China and Ceylon to smuggle out silkworms and the European silk industry becomes a Byzantine state monopoly (553); Mohammed, the founder of Islam, is born (570); war is renewed between Persia and the Byzantine Empire (572–91), and again when Chosroes II ascends the throne of Persia (590–628); the plague ends after killing half the population of Europe (542–94); first verified account of decimal number system in India (595); probably the first English school is established at Canterbury (598); the authoritative Talmud Babli, a compilation of Jewish Oral Law with rabbinical interpretations, is compiled (c. 6th century).

600–749: Books printed in China (600); Czechs and Slovaks take up land in Bohemia and Moravia, Yugoslavs in Serbia (c. 600); smallpox spreads from India, via China and Asia Minor, to southern Europe; the oldest surviving wooden building in the world, the Horyuji temple and hospital, is completed in Japan (607); Mohammed experiences a religious vision on Mt Hira (610); "burning water" (petroleum) is used in Japan (615); orchestras are formed in China (619); porcelain is produced in China (620); the Hegira is named after Mohammed's flight from hostile Mecca to Yathrib (later renamed Medina), and is year one in the Muslim calendar (622); an encyclopedia of arts and sciences is written by Isidore of Seville (622); Shaka Trinity, the famous altarpiece of the Kondo in Japan, is built by Tori (623); Mohammed begins to dictate the Koran (the sacred book of Islam) in Arabic (625); the Byzantines decisively defeat the Persians at Nineveh (627); Mohammed captures Mecca and writes letters to world leaders explaining the Muslim faith (628); cotton is introduced in Arab countries (630); Buddhism becomes the state religion in Tibet (632); Medina is the seat of the first caliph (religious and political leader of Muslims) who is Abu Bekr, Mohammed's father-in-law; the Arabs attack Persia (633); Damascus is the new capital of the caliphs (635–70); Jerusalem is conquered by the Arabs (637); the book-copying industry of the west is destroyed by the Arabs and the Alexandrian school ceases to be the centre of Western culture (641); the Arabs under Omar destroy the Persian Empire: the caliphs rule the area (until 1258), and Islam replaces the religion of Zoroaster; the Eastern Roman Empire is weakened by the Arab conquest of Egypt, Mesopotamia and Syria (642); the Dome of the Rock, a Muslim mosque, is begun in Jerusalem (643); the Muslim fleet destroys the Byzantine fleet at Lycia (655); Croats and Serbs settle in Bosnia (650); Chinese artists invent lamp-black ink and wood block printing (c. 650); Caliphs organize first news service (650); Japanese Buddhism and Shintoism are reconciled by the Korean-born priest Gyogi (c. 668–749); the Byzantines use "Greek Fire," a missile weapon of sulphur, rock, salt, resin and petroleum, against the Arabs at the siege of Constantinople (671–78); glass windows appear in English churches (674); the first Arab coinage is introduced (695); the Arabs destroy Carthage (697); Greek, instead of Latin, becomes the official language of the Eastern Roman Empire (700); the Arabs conquer Algiers (700) and virtually eliminate Christianity in northern Africa; mass migration of European peoples is followed by their subjection at the hands of property owners; China's population grows rapidly (700) and the first large urban developments appear there; the Great Mosque of Damascus is built (705); Buddhist monasteries in Japan become centres of civilization (710); the first written history of Japan, *Kojiki*, is compiled (712); the Lombard kingdom in northern Italy reaches its height (c. 600–c. 799); the Muslim empire now extends from the Pyrenees to China, with Damascus as its capital (715); the earliest Islamic paintings appear (715); Caliph Omar II grants tax exemption to all Muslim believers (717); the Chinese capital Ch'ang-an is the largest city in the world and Constantinople is the second largest (725); Casa Grande, a North American Indian fort and large irrigation works, is built in Arizona (725); Charles Martel (mayor of the Frankish court) wins victory over the Arabs in the battle of Tours and halts their westward advance (732); first printed newspaper published in Beijing (748).

750–849: Pueblos are built in southwest North America (750–900); Spain, under Arab influence, excels in mathematics, optics and chemistry (c. 750); Kiev, Russia, becomes known as a trading centre (750); the Turkish Empire is founded by a Tartar tribe in Armenia (760); Charlemagne becomes ruler of the Franks after the death of his father (Pepin the Short, son of Charles Martel) (768) and brother Carloman (771); Arabic learning flourishes under Harun-al-Rashid (790), peaks during reign of Caliph Mamun (813–33); the Byzantine Empress Irene overthrows her son Constantine (797), an act heralded by the Greek Church; Charlemagne is crowned Holy Roman Emperor (Western Empire) at Rome (800); the earliest records of Persian poetry and literature appear (800); the Vikings dominate Ireland (802); Arabic numerals are created under Indian influence (814); the Arabs conquer Crete, proceed as far as the Greek isles (826) and begin their conquest of Italy and Sardinia (827); Prince Mimir founds the Great Moravian Empire (830) from a confederation of Slavs in Bohemia, Moravia, Slovakia, Hungary and Transylvania; the Treaty of Verdun divides the Frankish Empire into France, Germany and Italy (843); paper currency in China creates inflation and state bankruptcy (845); Abu Tamman writes *Hamasa*, a collection of Arabian legends, proverbs and heroic stories (845); the Arabs sack Rome (846), damage the Vatican and destroy the Venetian fleet.

850–99: Salerno University is founded (850); the discovery of coffee is credited to Arabia (850); Jews settling in Germany develop the Yiddish language (c. 850); the first important Japanese painter, Kudara Kuwanari, dies (853); Norse pirates enter the Mediterranean and sack the coast up to Asia Minor (859); Iceland is discovered by the Northmen (861); Russian Northmen sack parts of France (861) and attack Constantinople (865); Basil I, the Byzantine Emperor, compiles the Basilican code (reforming finance and law and restoring the prestige of the military), and begins the Macedonian dynasty (867); Alfred the Great, king of England, recaptures London from the Danes (878); Emperor Charles III becomes king of France and once more unites the empire of Charlemagne (884), he is deposed (887) and there is a final separation of Germany and France; England's King Alfred establishes a regular militia and navy, extends the power of the king's courts and institutes fairs and markets (890).

900–99: The Vikings discover Greenland (900); the Mayans relinquish their settlements in the lowlands of Mexico and emigrate to the Yucatan peninsula (900); England is divided into shires with county courts in order to safeguard the civil rights of the inhabitants (900); the Arabian tales *A Thousand and One Nights* is begun (900); castles become the seats of the European nobility (900); Cordoba, Spain, is the seat of Arab learning, science, commerce and industry (930); Yenching becomes new capital city of China, later known as Beijing (938); revolts against imperial rule in Japan set off a period of civil war (939–1185); the Arab empire creates advanced postal and news services (942); the earliest record of the existence of a London bridge (963); a Chinese encyclopedia of 1,000 volumes is begun (978–84); the rule of nobles in Rome ends (980); Venice and Genoa carry on a flourishing trade between Asia and Western Europe (983); systematic musical notation develops (990); canonization of Christian saints begins.

1000–99: The heroic poem *Beowulf* is written in Old English by an unknown author (1000); Leif Ericsson, son of Eric the Red, sails to North America (1000); the Chinese invent gunpowder (1000); Mayan culture on the Yucatan peninsula achieves its zenith (1000); Sridhara, Indian mathematician, describes the importance of zero (1000); the Holy Sepulchre in Jerusalem is sacked by Muslims (1009); Danes under Canute control England (1016); Canute conquers Norway (1028); Jaroslav the Wise, Prince of Kiev (1020–54), codifies Russian law and builds cities, schools and churches; Byzantine power begins to decline (1025); Canute dies (1035) and his kingdom of England, Norway and Denmark is divided among his three sons; after murdering Duncan of Scotland, Macbeth becomes king (1040) and is later murdered by Malcolm (1057); time values are given to musical notes (1050); the separation of the Roman and Eastern Churches becomes permanent (1054); Westminster Abbey is consecrated (1065); William of Normandy is crowned William the Conqueror, of England (1066); the comet, later known as Halley's comet, appears (1066); She-tsung, Emperor of China, nationalizes agricultural production and distribution (1068); Constantine the African brings Greek medicine to the Western world (1071); the original Tower of London is built (1078); the Domesday Book, a survey of assessment for tax purposes, is compiled (1086); the start of the First Crusade (1096) is proclaimed by Pope Urban II to recapture the Holy Land from the Turks; Crusaders take Jerusalem (1099).

1100–99: Middle English supercedes Old English (1100); Islamic science begins to decline; secular music first appears; Robert of Normandy is appeased after invading England in the Treaty of Alton (1101); colonization of eastern Germany begins (1105); the earliest record of a miracle play is from Dunstable, England (1110): based on Scriptures and the lives of saints, they are widely performed until the 16th century; Bologna University founded

(1119); the earliest account of a mariner's compass is by Alexander Neckham (1125); the Second Crusade begins (1146) and fails one year later; Paris University is founded (1150); Bologna Medical School is founded (1150); the first recorded fire and plague insurance is in Iceland (1151); the Japanese clans Taira and Minamoto fight each other (1156); Eric of Sweden conquers Finland (1157); Thomas à Becket is elected Archbishop of Canterbury (1162) in an effort to curb church power, but he later quarrels with King Henry II over growing royal power; Becket is murdered by Norman knights (1170) and buried at Canterbury; jails are ordered erected in all English counties and boroughs (1166); Oxford University is founded (1167); rules for the canonization of saints are established by Pope Alexander III (1170); first authenticated influenza epidemics occur (1173); the Campanile ("Leaning Tower") of Pisa is built (1174); Walter Map organizes the Arthurian legends in their present form (1176); all Jews are banished from France (1182); the Third Crusade (1189–93) fails to recapture Jerusalem from the Muslims; Moses Maimonides, Jewish philosopher, introduces Aristotle to modern western philosophy when he attempts to reconcile Aristotle's theories with those of Jewish philosophy in *Guide to the Perplexed* (1190), and he is also credited with organizing all Jewish law for the layman as well as religious educators.

1200–49: Cambridge University founded (1200); Islam takes root in India; the Fourth Crusade begins with crusaders from Venice fighting Constantinople and establishing a Latin Kingdom of Jerusalem (1204); St Francis of Assisi issues the first rules of his brotherhood of educators and missionaries, the Franciscans (1209); in the Children's Crusade (1212), thousands of children from Europe leave for the Holy Land, but most are either sold as slaves or die of hunger or disease; Genghis Khan becomes chief prince of the Mongols (1206) and conquers most of the Chinese empire of north China (1213–15) as well as Turkistan, Afghanistan and Trans-oxania (1218–24), and he raids Persia and Eastern Europe; Genghis Khan's empire is divided among his descendants upon his death (1227); the Council of St Albans is the precursor to the British Parliament (1213); King John puts his seal on England's Magna Carta at Runnymede under compulsion by the barons (1215): it defines the limitations of royal power and sets out basic civil rights; the Fifth Crusade fails in Egypt (1217–21); the oldest national flag in the world, Danneborg, is adopted by Denmark (1218); the form of the sonnet develops in Italian poetry (1221); Thomas Aquinas (1225–74) theorizes philosophical proofs for the existence of God and reconciles Greek ideas with Christian theology; the Sixth Crusade is led by Emperor Frederick II (1228); crusaders bring back leprosy to Europe (1230), and they secure a temporary truce with the Muslims; three later crusades against Muslims in the 13th century fail; coal is mined for the first time in Newcastle, England (1233); the Inquisition begins as the pope makes Dominicans responsible for putting an end to heresy (1233); Alexander Nevski made Grand Duke of Novgorod (1236).

1250–99: Kublai Khan becomes governor of China (1251) and ruler of the Mongol peoples (1259–94); he fails to conquer Japan (1274), southeast Asia and Indonesia, but he defeats the Sung dynasty of China (1279); instruments of torture are first used in the Inquisition (1252); the Sorbonne is founded by Robert de Sorbon as the Paris School of Theology (1254); the House of Commons is established in England (1258); Mongols control Baghdad, end caliphate (1258); Roger Bacon writes *"De computo naturali"* (1264); the glass mirror is invented (1278); Marco Polo, the Venetian explorer, journeys to China (1271–95) and is in the diplomatic service of Kublai Khan (1275–92); Florence, Italy, is the leading European city in commerce and finance (c. 1282); the Teutonic Order, a German military and religious order, conquers Prussia (1283) after killing the native "heathens" and replacing them with Germans; spectacles (eyeglasses) are invented (1290); the crusades end and the Knights of St John of Jerusalem settle in Cyprus (1291).

1300–99: Trade fairs at Bruges, Antwerp, Lyons and Geneva (c. 1300); Edward I of England standardizes the yard and the acre (1305); Dante composes his *Divina Commedia* (1307–21); mechanical clocks are driven by weights in Europe; Salic Law, excluding women from succession to the throne, is adopted in France (1317); No plays originate in Japan (1325); the Aztecs establish Mexico City (1327); the sawmill is invented (1328); weaving at York first documented (1331); the Hundred Years War between

France and England begins (1337) as a dispute over lands held by the English crown in France: it later becomes a dispute over the French crown itself; the first scientific weather forecasts are attempted by William Merlee of Oxford (1337); the Black Death (bubonic plague) devastates Europe, killing about 75 million people, more than one-third of the population (1347–51); Boccaccio writes *Decameron* (1348–53), which is intended to be a diversion from the horrors of the plague; Timur the Lame (Tamerlaine) begins his conquest of Asia (1363); the Aztecs of Mexico build their capital, Tenochtitlan (1364); the Mongol Yüan dynasty in China is overthrown by the national Ming dynasty (1368–1644); the building of the Bastille begins in Paris (1369); "Robin Hood," the legendary hero who robbed the rich to help the poor, appears in English ballads and literature; The Great Schism in the Catholic Church begins (1378–1417) when, after the death of Pope Gregory XI, two popes are elected, one each at Rome and Avignon; Venice wins its Hundred Years War against Genoa (1256–1381); Briton John Wyclif calls for the reform of church practices (1379); he is condemned as a heretic (1380, 1382) and inspires the first English translation of the Latin Bible, the Wyclif Bible; Chaucer writes *The Canterbury Tales*; the rival southern and northern courts of Japan's divided imperial family reunite after 50 years of strife; Denmark, Sweden and Norway unite under Queen Margaret of Denmark (1397) in the Union of Kalmar.

1400–39: Russia's greatest icon painter, Andrei Rublex, creates *Trinity* (1411); England and France sign a perpetual peace treaty upon the marriage of Henry V and Catherine of Valois (1420); Joan of Arc and her French followers defeat the British at Orleans (1429) and march triumphantly to Paris: she is then taken prisoner by the Burgundians (1430) and condemned and executed (1431) in a political inquisition and trial; complete suits of metal armor plate replace chain mail in Europe (1430); China shuts out the western world and bans voyages there (1433) because Confucian doctrine sees little merit in trade; the Portuguese find the way round Cape Bojador (on the west coast of Africa) under Henry the Navigator (1434); the Greek (Eastern or Byzantine) Church unites with the Roman church (1439) in order to save itself from the Turkish threat; Montezuma becomes ruler of the Aztecs in Mexico (1440) and begins to conquer surrounding tribes.

■ Renaissance: 1440–1650

1440–69: The rise of the Italian city-states heralds the Renaissance (1440–50), and the richest families (such as the Medici) vie with each other as patrons of art and learning (mainly in Florence); the first oil painter, Jan van Eyck, dies in Flanders (1441); France defeats England at Castillion, ending the Hundred Years War (1453), and the English give up everything except Calais, thus ending English rule in France; Zimbabwe, the great African kingdom, declines after 200 years of expansion (1450) because of food shortages; Constantinople, the old capital of the Byzantine empire, falls to the Ottomans (1453); a treaty unites rival Italian city-states (1454), requiring them to protect each other from outside aggression; Ming porcelain pottery appears in Europe (1460); the Bible is printed mechanically with metal type faces and oil-based ink by Johann Gutenberg (1455); the Wars of the Roses begin in England (1455) as a struggle for the throne between the houses of York and Lancaster, and end (1485) when Henry VII of the house of Lancaster prevails over Richard III; Plato's writings are translated into Latin at the Platonic Academy in Florence (1469).

1470–99: Music sheets, maps and posters are mechanically printed (1470s); Vlad the Impaler dies in Transylvania (1477) and the mass murderer becomes the source for Dracula legends; Peruvian-centred Inca rule expands to include the entire Andean region (3,200 sq. km) under Pachacuti, and his son Topa Inca (1470), and it is characterized by terracing, irrigation, pantheistic religion with human sacrifice, advanced metalwork, tapestry making and construction; the Spanish Catholic Inquisition begins (1478); King Ferdinand V of Aragón and Queen Isabella I of Castile unite their crowns in Spain to ward off Alfonso V of Portugal (1479); Ivan the Great declares Russian independence (1480) from the Mongols when he refuses to continue paying them tribute; the first European manual of navigation and nautical almanac is prepared in Portugal by mathematical experts (1484) who calculate the latitude of the sun, based on the work of the Jewish astronomer Abraham Zacuto; the spread of witchcraft and heresy in Germany is attacked by Pope Innocent VIII (1484) and he authorizes Dominican inquisitors to torture and burn witches; the publication of an encyclopedia of witchcraft, *Malleus Maleficarum* (1486), adds to witch hunt hysteria; the Genoese seaman Christopher Columbus secures the sponsorship of Queen Isabella of Spain (1486) for his expedition to discover a western route to Asia (he sets sail with his three ships: Santa María, Pinta and Niña in 1492); the Aztecs of Mexico inaugurate the Great Temple of Tenochtitlan (1487) when they ritually sacrifice the hearts of 20,000 people; the Portugese explorer Bartholomew Dias rounds the Cape of Good Hope off South Africa (1488); Leonardo da Vinci is in his prime in Italy (1488) as an artist, scientist, inventor and philosopher, with inventions centuries ahead of their time (e.g., he conceives of flying machines and an apparatus to enable humans to breathe under water); the Great Wall of China is rebuilt by Ming emperors as a defence against attacks by northern Barbarians (1488); the first terrestrial globe is made by Martin Behaim, a German (1492); Jews are ordered by Spain's Catholic rulers to choose between expulsion or forced conversion (1492), and the rulers change the options to conversion or death (1498); Spain conquers Granada (1492), the last Muslim kingdom in Spain; Spain and Portugal sign a treaty dividing lands discovered in the new world, but Spain benefits the most from the treaty (1494); French armies in Italy bring a virus later identified as syphilis to Naples and the epidemic spreads through Europe (1495); Columbus brings tobacco back from the new world (1496); the Chinese invent a toothbrush (1498); Vasco da Gama discovers a sea route round the Cape of Good Hope to India via the Indian Ocean (1498); the Italian navigator Amerigo Vespucci explores the northeast coast of South America (1499) and reports cannibals (1502); Portugal's Pedro Cabral discovers the east coast of Brazil and observes natives using stone to cut wood (1499).

1500–25: The discovery of plays and poems by Hroswitha of Gandersheim, a 10th-century saxoness, makes her the first European playwright since the Classical Age (1500); King Ferdinand of Spain sanctions a system of levying tribute payments from Indians in the new world and using Indians as forced labour (1501); Shi'ism becomes the state religion in Persia (1502) and Sunni Muslim dissenters are executed there; a hand-held timepiece, made possible by the invention of the coiled mainspring, is constructed by German locksmith Peter Henlein (1502); *David*, a 13-foot statue, is completed by Michelangelo Buon-arrotti (1504) in Florence, Italy; Leonardo da Vinci paints the *Mona Lisa* (1505); Venice dominates Mediterranean trade (c. 1507); a map calls the new world "America" after Amerigo Vespucci (1507) and shows it as a distinct continent; the first great German artist, Albrecht Dürer (painter/engraver), creates his *Adam and Eve* oil painting (1507); Michelangelo paints the ceiling of the Sistine Chapel (1508–12); Sebastion Cabot sails around Cuba, proving it is an island (1508) and later reaches Hudson Bay in search of a northwest passage; the first African slaves are brought to the Americas (Cuba) (1510); Erasmus, the Dutch humanist, writes the satirical *In Praise of Folly* (1511); Juan Ponce de Léon claims Florida for Spain (1513) while searching for the Fountain of Youth; Niccolo Machiavelli writes *The Prince* (1513) which discusses the uses and abuses of power; Vasco Núñez de Balboa discovers the "South Sea," or Pacific Ocean, for Spain (1513); Spain orders new world natives to convert to Christianity under threat of enslavement or death (1514); Henry VIII of England puts forth measures to protect peasants from enclosure—the dividing and closing off of common land (1515); Sir Thomas More writes *Utopia*, which depicts an ideal state (1516); Martin Luther, a German Augustinian monk, writes his *95 Theses*, attacking the Catholic church's sale of indulgences granting the forgiveness of sins (1517) and nails it to the door of the Wittenberg church; English sailors complain to King Henry VIII about the growing number of French cod fishermen in Newfoundland (1517); the rule of Suleiman I the Magnificent sees the Ottoman Turks reach the zenith of their empire with the conquest of Egypt, Syria and Hungary (1520); Ferdinand Magellan begins a three-year voyage to circumnavigate the globe (1519); Hernando Cortes lands at Vera Cruz, Mexico, where Montezuma II and the Aztecs surrender (1519); chocolate is introduced to Europe from Mexico (1520); Nicholas Copernicus publishes his "Commentariolus" stating his theory that the earth revolves around the sun (1521); Martin Luther translates the Bible into German (1522).

1526–49: Lutheran German troops sack and burn Rome (1527); Hippocrates' ancient idea of the four humours governing bodily health is first disputed (1528); Henry VIII separates from the Church of Rome and becomes head of the English Church (1534) after he is refused an annulment of his first marriage; the Jesuit order of missionaries is founded by Ignatius Loyola (1534); Jacques Cartier searches for riches in North America along the St Lawrence River (1535); John Calvin, the French leader of the Protestant Refor-mation in Geneva, theorizes the concepts of predestination and God's omniscience (1536); the first mechanical artificial limbs appear for crippled war veterans (1539); the founder of the Sikh religion, Guru Nanak, dies in India (1539); Henry VIII becomes King of Ireland and Head of the Irish Church (1541); John Knox leads the Calvinist Reformation in Scotland (1541); oil is discovered in North America by the Spaniards (1543); Portuguese traders are the first to sell guns to Japan (1543); Nostradamus, the French astrologer, begins making predictions (1547); Ivan IV (the Terrible) is crowned the first czar of Russia (1547): he calls the first national assembly (1549).

1550–99: Jesuit missionaries protect natives in the new world from slavery (1551); Ivan the Terrible defeats the Mongols (1552), and conquers as far as the Caspian Sea (1556); Lady Jane Grey is executed for treason in England by Queen Mary Tudor (1554), who becomes known as "Bloody Mary" after persecuting Protestants (1555); Mary restores papal authority in England and Wales (1554); Charles V relinquishes the Holy Roman Empire and Spain to his brother and son, and goes to a monastery (1556); an influenza epidemic hits Europe (1557); Elizabeth I becomes Queen of England (1558) and rejects papal power in England (1559); the Huguenot (Calvinist French Protestant) conspiracy occurs at Amboise: liberty of worship is promised in France (1560); the Edict of Orleans suspends persecution of Huguenots (1561); the Peace of Amboise ends the first War of Religion in France and the Huguenots are granted limited toleration (1563); Andreas Vesalius, the Flemish founder of modern anatomy, dies (1564); Nobunaga deposes the Japanese shogunate and centralizes the government (1567); the Iroquois Confederacy of five North American nations (Mohawk, Oneida, Onondaga, Cayuga, Seneca) is founded (c. 1570); Huguenots are massacred on St Bartholomew's Day in Paris (1572); the Dutch War of Independence begins (1572); the Union of Utrecht is the foundation of the Dutch Republic (1579); William of Orange accepts the sovereignty of northern Nether-lands and is assassinated (1584); the first English colony in Newfoundland is founded (1582); Elizabeth of England orders Mary Queen of Scots beheaded for treason (1587); Christopher Marlowe completes *Dr. Faustus* (1588); the first Spanish Armada leaves for England and is defeated by the English under Charles Howard (1588); Sir Francis Drake, with 18,000 men, fails to take Lisbon for England (1589); William Shakespeare completes the play *Romeo and Juliet* (1594); the Second Spanish Armada leaves for England but is scattered by storms (1597); an English Act of Parliament calls for convicted criminals to serve their terms in the colonies (1597).

1600–49: France boasts the largest population in central Europe, with 16 million persons (1600); William Shakespeare completes *Hamlet* (1600); Dutch opticians invent the telescope (1600); the first modern public company is founded, the Dutch East India Company (1602); Guy Fawkes is arrested and accused of trying to blow up the House of Lords during James I's state opening of Parliament (The Gunpowder Plot, 1605); Fawkes is sentenced to death (1606); the first English settlement on the American mainland is founded at Jamestown, Virginia (1607); Shakespeare writes his *Sonnets* (1609); the first cheques appear in Netherlands as "cash letters" (1608); the *King James Bible* is published (1611); Peter Paul Rubens paints *Descent from the Cross* (1611); the North American Indian princess Pocahantas marries English colonist John Rolfe (1614); Galileo Galilei, Italian astronomer, faces the Inquisition for the first time for renouncing the Ptolemaic system of the earth-centred universe and embracing the Copernican sun-centred system (1615); the Thirty Years War begins in Prague as Protestants rebel against Catholic oppression (1618); slavery in North America begins when the first Africans are brought to Virginia (1619) and the triangular slave trade starts (British goods are sent to west Africa and are traded for slaves, who are traded for agricultural staples in the new world, which are sent back to Britain); pilgrims arriving on the *Mayflower* found Plymouth Colony, Massachusetts (1620); patent law is created in England to protect inventors (1623); construction begins on the Taj Mahal mausoleum in

Agra, North India (1628); Charles I dissolves the English Parliament for 11 years (1629); Cardinal Richelieu, chief minister of Louis XIII of France, rules France (1630–42); Galileo is forced by the Inquisition to cease promulgating the theories of Copernicus (1633); Japan forbids foreign books, Christianity and any European contacts (1637); René Descartes, called the father of modern philosophy, writes *Discourse on Method* (1637); the Ming dynasty in China ends and the Manchu dynasty takes power (1644–1912); Charles I of England, after a long struggle for power with Parliament (English Civil War 1642–48), is beheaded by Oliver Cromwell for treason (1649).

1650–99: Bishop James Ussher dates the creation of the world at Oct. 23, 4004 BC (1650); the wholesale massacre of North American Indians by European settlers begins (1650); Thomas Hobbes writes *Leviathan*, a defence of absolute monarchy in England (1651); Oliver Cromwell becomes Lord Protector in England, dissolves Parliament, divides England into 11 districts, prohibits Anglican services (1653) and readmits Jews to England after 365 years (1655); Blaise Pascal (French) develops the basic laws of probability (1654); the Portugese drive the Dutch out of Brazil (1654); the first London opera house opens (1656); Dutch peasants (Boers) first settle in South Africa (1660); the Royal Society is founded in London to promote scientific discussion among great thinkers (1660); the earliest condemnation of industrial pollution, *The Inconvenience of the Air and Smoke of London Dissipated*, is written by John Evelyn (1661); Louis XIV (the Sun King) begins to build the palace at Versailles (1662); Jean Baptiste Colbert forms the North American colony of New France with Quebec as its capital (1663); the British annex New Netherlands from the Dutch and rename the main city New York (1664); Isaac Newton begins to experiment with gravity and develops calculus (1664–66); the cell is named and described by Briton Robert Hooke (1665); the French army uses the first hand grenades (1667); Portugal gains independence from Spain through the Treaty of Lisbon (1668); microorganisms are discovered by Anton van Leeuwenhoek (Dutch, 1669) who later observes bacteria (1683) for the first time; the Hudson's Bay Company is incorporated by a British royal charter to trade in the region of North America defined by those rivers which drain into Hudson Bay (1670); Dutch philosopher Baruch Spinoza writes *Ethics* (1675); the poems of Bashu (a pseudonym) popularize Japanese haiku poetry (1675); the *Declaration of the People of Virgina* by Nathaniel Bacon lends support to rebellion against authorities in the colonies (1676); Roman Catholics are excluded from both houses of Parliament in England (1678); the Habeas Corpus Amendment Act in England protects citizens from unjust imprisonment (1679); the French colonial empire of North America, reaching from Quebec to the mouth of the Mississippi River, is organized (1680); the large dodo bird with small, flightless wings becomes extinct (1680); Sir Isaac Newton writes *Principles of Natural Philo-sophy* (1687), which discusses universal gravitation; the Glorious Revolution establishes the constitutional monarchy in England (1688–89) and William of Orange III and Mary II ascend the throne; Peter the Great becomes Czar of Russia (1689); John Locke writes *Essay Concerning Human Understanding* and *Two Treatises on Civil Government* (1690).

1700–49: The War of the Spanish Succession to the childless Charles II, Hapsburg king of Spain, is fought (1701–14) between the French Bourbons and Austrian Hapsburgs; rebellion occurs in Astrakhan against Czar Peter's westernization of Russia (1705); England and Scotland form Great Britain (1707); the Peace of Utrecht is signed between Spain and England: Spain cedes Gibraltar and Minorca to England (1713) and Philip of France retains the Spanish crown; D.G. Fahrenheit constructs a mercury thermometer with a temperature scale (1714); George F. Handel writes *Water Music* for King George I (1717); Daniel Defoe writes *The Life and Strange Surprising Adventures of Robinson Crusoe* (1719); the German composer and virtuoso organist J.S. Bach composes *The Brandenburg Concertos* (1721); Johnathan Swift writes *Gulliver's Travels* (1726); Benjamin Franklin, American statesman, scientist, printer and writer, writes *Poor Richard's Almanack* (1732); John Kay patents the fly shuttle loom, which revolutionizes weaving (1733); Alexander Pope, poet and English verse satirist, writes *Essay on Man* (1733); the modern classification system of plants and animals is introduced by Carolus Linnaeus (Swedish, 1735); Alaska is discovered by Victor Behring (1740); Frederick the Great introduces freedom of the press and freedom of worship in Prussia (1740); sign language for the deaf is created by Rodriguez Pereire (1749).

■ Industrial Revolution: 1750–1850

1750–99: Benjamin Franklin experimented with static electricity and invented the lightning conductor (1752); in the Seven Years War (1756–63) Britain declares war on France and, in the North American colonies, the French drive the British from the Great Lakes area (1756); the French lose Quebec to the British (1759) during the battle on the Plains of Abraham; Voltaire writes the philosophical novel *Candide* (1759); Catherine II (the Great) becomes czarina of Russia (1762); Swiss-French philosopher Jean Jacques Rousseau writes *Social Contract* (1762) which discusses his theory of "natural man"; the Peace of Paris (1763) ends the war between England and France and gives Canada to England; eight-year-old Mozart writes his first symphony (1764); the spinning jenny, which spins up to 120 threads at once is invented by Briton James Hargreaves (1764); the British Parliament passes the Stamp Act for taxing American colonies: Virginia and New York challenge the right of Britain to taxation without representation (1766); the Mason-Dixon Line is drawn by English surveyors between Pennsylvania and Maryland (1767) and is later the boundary between "slave" and "free" states; Daniel Rutherford and Joseph Priestley independently discover nitrogen (1772); the Bolshoi Ballet is founded in Russia (1773); during the Boston Tea Party American colonists protesting British taxes dress as Indians and dump the cargo of three tea ships in the Boston, Mass., harbor (1773); James Watt, Scottish inventor, perfects the steam engine (1775); the American Revolution begins (1775); the Second Continental Congress assembles at Philadelphia and appoints George Washington commander-in-chief of the American forces; the Americans proclaim the *Declaration of Independence* (July 4, 1776); Edward Gibbon writes *Decline and Fall of the Roman Empire* (1776); Adam Smith completes *Wealth of Nations* (1776); after the American victory in the Saratoga Campaign (1777) France entered into an alliance with the Americans (1778); Washington's army suffers at Valley Forge (1778); Hawaii is discovered by James Cook (1778); Franz Mesmer practices mesmerism (hypnotism) (1778); Spain joins the American War of Indepen-dence against Britain (1779); the Dutch support the American side (1780); Sir William Herschel discovers Uranus (1781); British General Cornwallis surrenders to the Ameri-cans (Oct. 1781) at the end of the Yorktown Campaign, and the Treaty of Paris recognizes American independence (1783); John Wesley writes the *Deed of Declaration,* the charter of Wesleyan Methodism (1784); the British colony of Australia is founded (1788); the French Revolution begins (1789); a Paris mob opposing the monarchy storms the Bastille jail; French royalists begin to emigrate; the French revolutionaries proclaim the Decrees of Aug. 4 and the *Declaration of the Rights of Man and of the Citizen;* the government limits the monarchy's power, abolishes the French feudal system, extends religious tolerance to Jews and protestants and reorganizes the Catholic Church; A.L. Lavoisier completes the *Table of Thirty-One Chemical Elements* (1790); the Constitutional Act divides Britain's Canadian colony into Upper Can-ada (English-speaking) and Lower Canada (French-speaking) (1791); Thomas Paine writes *The Rights of Man* in defence of the French Revolution (1791); the French King Louis XIV and Queen Marie Antoinette are beheaded for treason (Jan., 1793); the Reign of Terror (guillotine executions of prisoners) under the Jacobin government ends with the execution of Maximilien Robespierre; Robert Burns' *Auld Lang Syne* is published (1794); Edward Jenner discovers a smallpox vaccine (1796).

1800–09: Ottawa is founded (1800); Eli Whitney makes muskets with interchangeable parts (1800); the Library of Congress is established in Washington, DC by Thomas Jefferson (1800); the first battery is produced from zinc and copper plates by Alessandro Volto (1800); William Herschel discovers the existence of infrared solar rays (1800); the first submarine *Nautilus* is made by American civil engineer Robert Fulton (1801); the atomic theory of chemistry is put forth by John Dalton (1802); the US buys land from France in the Louisiana Purchase (1803); Henry Shrapnel invents the shell used in warfare (1803); Napoleon crowns himself emperor of the French empire (1804) and king of Italy (1805); modern Egypt is established when Mehemet Ali becomes Pasha (1805); morphine is isolated by F.W.A. Satürner (1805); Napoleon wins his greatest victory, at Austerlitz, over the Austrians and Russians allied against him (1805); the American frigate *Chesapeake* is stopped and boarded by British naval officers looking for deserters, almost causing a war (1807); Ludwig van Beethoven, the great German composer who brought together Classical and Romantic styles, performs his *Fifth Symphony* (written for Napoleon) and *Sixth Symphony* (1808); the first part of J.W. von Goethe's *Faust* is published (1808); Washington Irving writes *Rip van Winkle* (1809).

1810–19: Simón Bolívar becomes a leading figure in South American politics (1810) and liberates Greater Colombia (Panama, Venezuela, Ecuador and Colombia) (1819) and Peru (1824) from Spanish rule; a machine for spinning flax is invented by Philippe Girard (1812); German folklorist Jakob Grimm completes *Grimm's Fairy Tales* (1812–15); Napoleon Bonaparte's first military setback is in the Peninsular War (1808–14); and he later retreats from an unsuccessful invasion of Russia; the War of 1812 (1812–14) between Britain and the United States is foreshadowed by the battle at Tippecanoe (1811); Jane Austen writes *Pride and Prejudice* (1813), depicting English country life and mores; Austria, Russia and Prussia form an alliance against Napoleon and defeat him at Leipzig (1813) and recapture Paris (1814); Napoleon abdicates and is exiled to Elba Island; the War of 1812 continues in North America as the British capture Washington, DC (1814) but the Americans win battles at Fort McHenry, Thames (killing Tecumseh, an Indian ally of the British) and at Plattsburgh (1814); the British initiate peace in the Treaty of Ghent (1814) but this news travels too slowly to stop the Battle of New Orleans (1815), won by the Americans; Napoleon escapes from exile and returns to march on Paris; he is defeated at Waterloo (1815), abdicates again and is banished to St Helena Island; the German Confederation, dominated by Austria and Prussia, is created to replace the Holy Roman Empire (1815); Argentina declares its independence from Spain (1816); the classical economist David Ricardo (British) writes *The Principles of Political Economy and Taxation* (1817), discussing the determination of wage and value; Georg Hegel writes his all-embracing *Encyclopedia of the Philosophical Sciences* (1817); Mary Wollstonecraft Shelley writes *Frankenstein* (1818); Lord Byron begins *Don Juan* (1818–23); Chile proclaims its independence from Spain (1818); electromagnetism is discovered by Danish physicist Hans C. Oersted (1819); Greater Colombia (including Panama, Venezuela, Ecuador and Colombia) declares independence from Spain (1819).

1820–29: Andre Ampere (French) writes *Laws of Electrodynamic Action* (1820); Liberia is founded by the Washington Colonization Society, for the repatriation of black slaves (1820); Sir Walter Scott writes *Ivanhoe* (1820); John Keats writes *Ode to a Nightingale* (1820); an electric recording device for sound reproduction is invented by Sir Charles Wheatstone (1821); Peru and Guatemala declare their independence from Spain (1821); the Reign of Terror begins between the Greeks and the Turks (1821); Franz Liszt, the Hungarian pianist who revolutionizes Romantic music and invents the symphonic poem, makes his debut at age 11 in Vienna (1822); Brazil declares itself independent from Portugal (1822); the Monroe Doctrine closes the American continent to colonial settlement by European powers (1823); Spanish are defeated and Paris independence recognized (1824); Simón Bolívar creates his namesake, Bolivia (1825); the first steam-powered railroads carrying freight and passengers, operated by the the Stockton and Darlington Railway, run in England (1825); the Erie Canal opens, linking the Hudson River and the Great Lakes (1825); the first major American author, James Fenimore Cooper, writes *The Last of the Mohicans* (1826); Felix Mendelssohn composes the Overture to *A Midsummer Night's Dream* (1826); the great cholera epidemic begins in India (1826) and spreads from Russia into Central Europe; J. J. Audubon writes *Birds of North America* (1827); Noah Webster writes the *American Dictionary of the English Language* (1828); Uruguay declares independence from Brazil (1828); the Peace of Adrianople ends the Russo-Turkish war and Turkey acknowledges the independence of Greece (1829); Frederic Chopin, the Polish pianist, debuts in Vienna (1829); Venezuela withdraws from Greater Colombia and becomes independent (1829).

1830–39: Charles Lyell of Scotland divides the geological system into three groups: Eocene, Miocene and Pliocene (1830); Ecuador declares independence (1830); mass demonstrations in Swiss cities lead to liberal reforms

(1831); Charles Darwin sails on the HMS *Beagle* as a naturalist, surveying South America, New Zealand and Australia (1831–36); the leading anti-slavery leader in the United States, W. L. Garrison, begins publishing *The Liberator* in Boston (1831); the wealthy middle classes emerging from the Industrial Revolution are enfranchised in Britain, doubling the number of voters (1832); the New England anti-slavery society is founded in Boston (1832); slavery is abolished in the British Empire (1833); the Spanish Inquisition, begun during the 13th century, is finally abolished (1834); France's leading writer, Victor Hugo, writes *The Hunchback of Notre Dame* (1834); the Poor Law Amendment Act decrees that no able-bodied person (displaced by the Industrial Revolution) in Great Britain shall receive assistance unless he or she enters a workhouse (1834); Hans Christian Anderson writes his first stories for children (1835); the American writer Ralph Waldo Emerson writes *Nature* (1836); the People's Charter initiates Britain's first national working-class movement, calling for universal suffrage for men and voting by ballot (1836); the Dutch (Afrikaner) farmers begin "The Great Trek" of emigration across the Orange and Vaal Rivers, South Africa (1836); the first botanical textbook, *The Elements of Botany*, is written by American Asa Gray (1836); Victoria becomes Queen of Great Britain (1837); citizens stage unsuccessful rebellions in Lower and Upper Canada (1837); Louis Braille invents his reading system for the blind (1837); Charles Dickens's *Oliver Twist*, a critique of British industrial society, is a bestseller (1838); the first bicycle is invented by a Scot, Kirkpatrick Macmillan (1839); the cell-growth theory is put forth by Theodor Schwann (1839); ozone is discovered by Christian Schönbein, a German-Swiss chemist (1839); American Charles Goodyear develops the process of vulcanization, making the commercial use of rubber possible (1839); a photograph produced on a silver-coated copperplate treated with iodine vapor, the daguerreotype, is invented by Louis Daguerre and J. Niepce (French) (1839); the First Opium War between Britain and China begins (1839).

1840–49: New Zealand becomes a British colony (1840); philosopher Thomas Carlyle writes *On Heroes, Hero-Worship and the Heroic in History* in support of strong government (1841); the father of the guided tour, Thomas Cook (British), arranges his first trip (1841); showman P.T. Barnum gains fame after opening his American Museum of freak exhibitions (1841); the Webster-Ashburton Treaty between Britain and the US settles American border disputes with Canada (1842); the Treaty of Nanking ends the Opium War between Britain and China and confirms the cession of Hong Kong to Great Britain (1842); riots and strikes erupt in northern England's industrial areas (1842); Richard Wagner (German) finishes the opera *The Flying Dutchman* (1843); the amount of work required to produce a unit of heat, the joule, is determined by English physicist James P. Joule (1843); American social reformer Dorothea Dix reports on the shocking conditions in prisons and asylums, influencing the establishment of state hospitals for the insane in Europe and North America (1843); Samuel Morse's telegraph is used for the first time between Baltimore and Washington (1844); US troops are victorious over the Mexicans at Palo Alto (1846), Congress formally declares war, US forces take Santa Fe and annex New Mexico; the Smithsonian Institution, a research and educational centre, is founded in Washington, DC (1846); ether is first used as an anaesthetic by dentist W.T. Morton (1846); sisters Charlotte and Emily Brontë publish *Jane Eyre* and *Wuthering Heights* respectively (1847); US forces capture Mexico City (1847) and the Treaty of Guadalupe Hidalgo ends the Mexican-US war (1848), the US acquires Texas and much of the surrounding territory in return for $15 million; gold discoveries in California lead to the first gold rush (1848); a revolt in Paris causes Louis Philippe to abdicate (1848); a revolution in Vienna brings Metternich's resignation (1848); revolutions in Venice, Berlin, Milan, Rome and Parma (1848); the first Public Health Act is introduced in Britain (1848); the first women's rights convention, organized by Elizabeth Stanton and Lucretia Mott, is held in Seneca Falls, New York (1848); the *Communist Manifesto* is issued by Germans Karl Marx and Friedrick Engels (1848), championing the working class and establishing socialist theory.

1850–59: Harriet Beecher Stowe writes her anti-slavery novel *Uncle Tom's Cabin* (1852); the Transvaal is granted self-government (1852); the Crimean War (1853–56) begins when Russia occupies Moldavia and Walachia and Turkey declares war, the Russians destroy the Turkish fleet off Sinope, and England, France and Sardinia join Turkey's fight; after a long siege the Russian base Sevastopol falls to the allied forces (1855), and after the allied victory at Balaklava, Russia recognizes the integrity of Turkey (1856); English nurse Florence Nightingale founds modern nursing while tending soldiers during the Crimean War (1853–56); the first hypodermic syringe is used by Alexander Wood (1853); Samuel Colt revolutionizes the manufacture of small arms (1853); Commander Matthew Perry negotiates the first American-Japanese treaty, permitting US ships to use two Japanese ports (1854); the Elgin Reciprocity Treaty between Great Britain and the US implements free trade between Canada and the US (1854); steel making becomes inexpensive when Henry Bessemer introduces a converter into his process for making steel (1855); pure cocaine is extracted from coca leaves (1856); Gustave Flaubert, the French master of realistic novels, writes *Madame Bovary* (1856); Louis Pasteur discovers that fermentation is caused by micro-organisms (1857), and later invents pasteurization and discovers a vaccine for rabies; the first Neanderthal skeleton is found in a cave in Neander Valley (near Düsseldorf, Germany); the Indian Mutiny against British rule (1857) causes the British siege and capture of Delhi; the British Royal Navy destroys the Chinese fleet, and Britain and France take Canton (1857); Guiseppe Garibaldi forms the Italian National Association for the unification of Italy (1857); the Treaty of Tientsin ends the Anglo-Chinese war (1858); Charles Darwin writes *On the Origin of Species by Natural Selection*, explaining his theory of evolution (1859); the German National Association is formed to unite Germany under Prussia (1859); John Stuart Mill (British) writes his essay *On Liberty* (1859).

■ Modern Era

1860–64: Garibaldi and his redshirts sail from Genoa to take Palermo and Naples; Victor Emmanuel II (King of Sardinia) invades the Papal States and defeats the Papal troops, Garibaldi proclaims Emmanuel II king of Italy (1860); Anglo-French troops defeat the Chinese at Pa-li-Chau (1860) and sign the Treaty of Peking; the first Food and Drugs Act is enacted in Britain (1860); Lenoir constructs the first internal-combustion engine (1860); a primitive form of typewriter is created by American Christopher L. Sholes (1860); hundreds of thousands of Irish and British citizens flee their homelands following the potato famine (by 1860); Russian troops fire at anti-Russian demonstrators in Poland during the Warsaw Massacre (1861); the first machine-chilled cold storage unit is built by T. S. Mort (1861); Krupp begins arms production in Essen, Germany (1861); the Archaeopteryx, the skeleton linking reptiles and birds, is discovered at Solnhofen, Germany (1861); the American Civil War (1861–65) begins after Abraham Lincoln, who views slavery as evil, is elected president; South Carolina secedes in protest, followed by 10 other southern states, to form the Confederacy fighting for states' rights and opposing the abolition of slavery; Lincoln issues the Emancipation Proclamation (1862) calling for the freeing of black slaves in Confederate territory; the Red Cross voluntary relief organization is proposed by Jean Henri Dunant, a Swiss humanist (1862); the first form of a machine gun is invented by the American Richard Gatling (1862); Otto von Bismarck becomes the prime minister of Prussia (1862) and begins his system of alliances and alignments that result in German preeminence in Europe; Victor Hugo writes *Les Miserables* (1862); Leo Tolstoy writes *War and Peace* (1864); the Geneva Convention establishes the neutrality of battlefield medical facilities (1864); liberalism, socialism and rationalism are condemned in *Syllabus Errorum*, issued by Pope Pius IX (1864); Cheyenne and Arapahoe Indians are massacred at Sand Creek, Colorado (1864); the First International Workingmen's Association is founded by Karl Marx in London and New York (1864); Confederate forces surrender finally at Appomattox, Virginia (1865) marking the end of the war and victory for the Union; slavery in the US is abolished by the Thirteenth Amendment; US Pres. Lincoln is assassinated by the actor John Wilkes Booth (1865).

1865–69: Lewis Carroll (British) writes *Alice's Adventures in Wonderland* (1865); Joseph Lister initiates antiseptic surgery by using carbolic acid on a compound wound (1865); line geometry is invented by German mathematician Julius Plücker (1865); Gregor Mendel, an Austrian monk, describes his Law of Heredity (1865); Bismarck, the Prussian foreign minister, provoked the brief Austro-Prussian War by invading the duchies of Schleswig-Holstein and overrunning the German states allied with Austria; after seven weeks a peace settlement gave Schleswig-Holstein, Hanover, Hesse, Nasau and Frankfurt to Prussia and excluded Austria from influence in German affairs (1866); *Crime and Punishment* by Feodor Dosto-evsky is published (1866); Alfred Nobel invents dynamite (1866); Johann Strauss popularizes the Viennese waltz with Blue Danube (1866); the underwater torpedo is invented by Robert Whitehead, an English engineer (1866); the fundamental law of biogenetics, *General Morphology,* is published by Ernst Haeckel (1866); Claude Monet, a French founder of Impressionism, paints *Camille* (1866); Russia sells Alaska to the US for $7.2 million (1867); Karl Marx writes *Das Kapital*, volume I (1867); the British North America Act establishes the Dominion of Canada and John A. Macdonald becomes prime minister (1867); Louisa May Alcott describes Victorian American life in *Little Women* (1868); a skeleton of Cro Magnon man from the Upper Paleolithic age (the first Homo sapiens in Europe, successor to the Neanderthal man) is found in France by Louis Lartet (1868); the first regular Trades Union Congress is held at Manchester, England (1868); Dmitri Mendeleyev formulates his periodic law for the classification of the elements (1869); John Stuart Mill writes *On the Subjection of Women* (1869); the major early treatise on eugenics, *Hereditary Genius,* is published by Francis Galton (1869); J.W. Hyatt invents celluloid (plastic) (1869); the First Nihilist Congress is held at Basel, Switzerland (1869); the strategically important Suez Canal opens (1869); the doctrine of papal infallibility is established by Pope Pius IX during Vatican Council I (1869–79).

1870–79: US industrialist John D. Rockefeller founds the Standard Oil Company (1870); T.H. Huxley, English biologist and educator, writes the *Theory of Biogenesis* (1870); the Franco-Prussian War begins (1870) and France under Napoleon III capitulates; William I, king of Prussia, is proclaimed the German Emperor at Versailles, and in the Peace of Frankfurt France cedes Alsace-Lorraine to Germany (1871); the Italian Law of Guarantees allows the Pope possession of the Vatican (1871); labour unions become legal in Britain (1871); Charles Darwin writes *The Descent of Man* (1871); the Great Fire ravages Chicago (1871);

explorer Sir Henry M. Stanley is sent to find David Livingstone in Africa (1871); the first modern luxury liner, SS *Oceanic*, is launched (1871); Civil War in Spain ends with the Carlists' defeat (1872); the Three Emperors League is established in Berlin as an alliance between Germany, Russia and Austria-Hungary (1872); colour photographs are first developed (1873); James C. Maxwell writes *Electricity and Magnetism* (1873); Willhelm Wundt, known for the experimental method, writes *Physiological Psychology* (1873); under the direction of Benjamin Disraeli as prime minister, Britain expands its imperial power by annexing the Fiji islands (1874); Johannes Brahms composes the *Hungarian Dances* (1874); Johann Strauss II performs the operetta *Die Fledermaus* in Vienna (1874); Bosnia and Herzegovina rebel against Turkish rule (1875): Turkish sultan promises reforms (1875); Mary Baker Eddy writes *Science and Health* (1875) and she founds the Christian Science movement (1879); Georges Bizet performs *Carmen* in Paris (1875); British Queen Victoria is crowned empress of India (1876); Britain annexes the Transvaal (1877); US General George Custer is killed along with his cavalry by Cheyenne Indians in the Battle of the Little Bighorn (1876); Alexander Graham Bell constructs a telephone (1876); first national lawn tennis championship played at Wimbledon (1877); German historian Heinrich Treitschke begins a racial anti-semite movement (1878); Gilbert and Sullivan write *HMS Pinafore* (1878); British troops are massacred by Zulus in Isand-hlwana, Africa (1879); the British occupy the Khyber Pass near Afghanistan and are massacred in Kabul (1879); Norwegian Henrik Ibsen completes the play *A Doll's House* (1879); Chile invades Bolivia and its ally Peru after Bolivia cancels a Chilean company's contract to exploit Bolivia's nitrate deposits (1879).

1880–84: Auguste Rodin sculpts *The Thinker* (1880); France annexes Tahiti (1880); Transvaal declares its independence from Britain and the Boers establish a republic after a brief war with Britain (1880–81); the first practical electrical lights are independently made by Thomas Edison and J.W. Swan (1880); the malaria parasite is discovered by Charles Laveran (1880); the first large steel furnace is developed by American steel baron Andrew Carnegie (1880); the Vatican opens its archives to scholars (1881); the first Japanese political parties are founded (1881); violent government-condoned attacks (po-groms) are carried out against Russian Jews (1881–1917) causing large-scale Jewish emigration to North America; the Federation of Organized Trades and Labor Unions of the US and Canada is formed (1881); Germany, Austria and Italy form an alliance (1882); the three-mile limit for territorial waters is agreed upon at the Hague Convention (1882); Peter I. Tchaikovsky composes the *1812 Overture* (1882); psychoanalysis begins when Joseph Breuer (Austrian) uses hypnosis to treat hysteria (1882); Thomas Edison designs the first hydroelectric plant in Wisconsin (1882); the Orient Express train between Paris and Istanbul makes its first run (1883); *On the Size of Atoms* is published by British scientist William Thomson, later Lord Kelvin (1883); peace is restored between Peru and Chile (1883); Friedrich Nietzsche (German philosopher) begins *Thus Spake Zarathustra* (1884–91); gold is discovered in the Transvaal (1884) and this leads to the rise of Johannesburg; a truce is signed between Bolivia and Chile, with Bolivia forced to cede its only coastal territory to Chile (1884); the *Oxford English Dictionary* begins publication (1884–1928); the Berlin Conference of 14 nations on African affairs is held (1884).

1885–89: Karl Benz builds the single-cylinder engine for motor cars (1885); the individuality of fingerprints is proved by Sir Francis Galton (1885); the first Indian National Congress meets (1886); the Statue of Liberty is presented to the US by France (1886); steam is first used to sterilize surgical instruments by Ernst von Bergmann (1886); Irish politician Charles Parnell, the Fenians, and British Prime Min. William Gladstone try unsuccessfully to pass the first Irish Home Rule Bill to give Ireland control over domestic affairs (1886); Sir Arthur Conan Doyle writes the first Sherlock Holmes story, *A Study in Scarlet* (1887); William II (the Kaiser) becomes emperor of Germany (1888); Vincent Van Gogh paints the series of sunflowers (1888) and later, *Starry Night*; the electric motor is first constructed by Nikola A. Tesla and manufactured by George Westinghouse (1888); radio waves are discovered to be of the same family as light waves by the independently working Heinrich Hertz and Oliver Lodge (1888); Kodak box camera produced by George Eastman (1888); "Jack the Ripper" murders six women in London (1888); Alexander G. Eiffel designs the Eiffel Tower for the Paris World Exhibition (1889).

1890–94: The first Japanese general election is held (1890); German Chancellor Bismarck dismissed by Emperor William II (1890); the first moving picture shows appear in New York (1890); Oscar Wilde writes *The Picture of Dorian Gray* (1890); antitoxins are discovered by Emil von Behring (1890); the first entirely steel-framed building is erected in Chicago (1890); the Triple Alliance between Austria, Germany and Italy is renewed for 12 years (1891); Briton Thomas Hardy writes *Tess of the D'Ubervilles* (1891); Henri Toulouse-Lautrec produces his first music hall posters (1891); *Experiments in Aero-dynamics* is published by Samuel P. Langley (1891); the All-Deutschland Verband (Pan-Germany League) is founded (1891); Russia experiences widespread famine (1891); an earthquake in Japan kills ten thousand people (1891); the Java Man (*Pithecanthropus homo erectus*) is discovered by Dutch anthropologist Eugène Dubois, in Java (1891); Paul Gauguin (French) paints *By the Sea* in Tahiti (1892); Rudolph Diesel (German) patents his internal-combustion engine (1892); Tchai-kovsky performs his *The Nutcracker* ballet score in St Petersburg (1892); Karl Benz constructs his four-wheel car (1893); Jewish French army captain Alfred Dreyfus is arrested under controversy and convicted of spying for Germany (1894); Rudyard Kipling writes *The Jungle Book* (1894); after Japan sends troops to Seoul, Korea, Japan declares war on China and defeats the Chinese at Port Arthur (1894); Emil Berliner develops a horizontal gramophone disc, replacing the record cylinder for sound reproduction (1894).

1895–99: The Chinese-Japanese war ends with Japan victorious: Formosa and Port Arthur are first ceded to Japan and later returned to China for payment (1895); H.G. Wells writes *The Time Machine* (1895); William B. Yeats writes *Poems* (1895); x-rays are discovered by William Röntgen (1895); Marchese Marconi invents radio telegraphy (1895); the principle of rocket reaction propulsion is developed by Konstantin Isiolkovski (1895); the first modern Olympics is held in Athens, Greece (1896); Anton Chekhov (Russian) writes *The Sea Gull* (1896); five annual Nobel prizes are established by Alfred Nobel for persons who have contributed the most in the fields of physics, physiology and medicine, chemistry, literature and peace (1896); Wilfrid Laurier becomes the first French Canadian prime minister of Canada (1896–1911); the Klondike gold rush in Bonanza Creek, Canada, begins (1896); Edmond Rostand writes *Cyrano de Bergerac* (1897); Queen Victoria celebrates her Diamond Jubilee (1897); French writer Emile Zola writes an open letter, *J'accuse*, condemning the Dreyfus espionage trial and he is imprisoned (1898), Col. Henry admits forging documents in the case (1898), and Captain Dreyfus is pardoned after a retrial (1899)—the case polarized French politics for a decade; the US declares war on Spain over Cuba and destroys the Spanish fleet at Manila (1898); Spain cedes Cuba, Puerto Rico, Guam and the Philippines to the US for $20 million at the Treaty of Paris; Chinese Boxers, an anti-Western organization, is formed (1898); the Boer War begins as the South African Republic (Transvaal) and the Orange Free State unite against the British (1898); Marie and Pierre Curie discover radium and polonium (1898); German Count Ferdinand von Zeppelin builds his airship (1898); photographs using artificial light are first taken (1898); Marchese Marconi invents the radio (1899).

1900: The Boer War continues and Canadian troops set sail for South Africa to fight for England in their first foreign war; Boxer rebellion against Western influence, supported by the Dowager Empress Tzu-hsi, continues in China against Christian missionaries and foreigners; Sigmund Freud, the founder of psychoanalysis (Austrian), completes *The Interpretation of Dreams*; Wilhelm Wundt writes *Comparative Psychology*; Shintoism is reinstated in Japan to counter Buddhist influence; Commonwealth of Australia is created; Max Planck formulates the quantum theory; human speech is first transmitted via radio waves by the Canadian-born scientist R.A. Fessenden; Holland's senate creates an international arbitration court at The Hague; millions are reported starving in India; botanist Hugo de Vries rediscovers Gregor Mendel's laws of heredity after 30 years; 10,000 Ashanti natives attack a British force of 400 at Cape Coast, Ghana, and are defeated.

1901: Queen Victoria dies and is succeeded by her son Edward VII; the Dutch Boers begin organized guerrilla warfare against the British; the Cuba Convention makes Cuba a US protectorate; US Pres. William McKinley is assassinated and is succeeded by Theodore Roosevelt; a treaty is signed to build the Panama Canal under US supervision; the hormone adrenaline is first isolated; Walter Nernst postulates the "third law of thermodynamics"; John Pierpont Morgan organizes the US Steel Corp., the first billion-dollar corporation; the Peace of Peking ends the Boxer uprising and China is forced to pay an indemnity of $333 million to the Allies to amend commercial treaties in favor of foreign nationals and to allow foreign troops to be posted in Peking; French physicist Henri Becquerel determines that atoms have internal structure; there are racial riots in New Orleans when American black leader Booker T. Washington is invited to the White House; the Trans-Siberian railroad reaches Port Arthur on the east coast of Russia; oil drilling begins in Persia (Iran).

1902: An Anglo-Japanese treaty recognizes the independence of China and Korea; the Treaty of Vereeniging ends the Boer War and the Orange Free State becomes a British colony; the Triple Alliance between Ger-many, Austria and Italy is renewed for another six years; the US acquires perpetual control over the Panama Canal; the Colonial Conference meets in London; the Committee of Imperial Defence meets in London for the first time; Jean Sibelius, Finnish composer and conductor, completes *Symphony No. 2*; Egypt's Aswan Dam is opened.

1903: The "Entente Cordiale" between England and France is established to counter German imperialism; the Russian Social Democratic Party splits into Mensheviks (led by Plechanoff) and Bolsheviks (led by Vladimir Lenin and Leon Trotsky); *The Conduction of Electricity through Gases* is published by Joseph John Thomson; Briton George Bernard Shaw writes *Man and Superman*; Orville and Wilbur Wright successfully fly a powered airplane near Kitty Hawk, North Carolina; the electrocardiograph, which records heart action, is invented by William Einthoven; Briton Emmeline Pankhurst founds the National Women's Social and Political Union and campaigns for women's right to vote; Albert I, Prince of Monaco, founds the International Peace Institute; Henry Ford founds the Ford Motor Company.

1904: The Russo-Japanese War breaks out over Korea and Manchuria; the Japanese besiege Port Arthur and occupy Seoul; the Russian fleet is partially destroyed off Port Arthur; the Russians are defeated at Mukden and Toushima Straits; Max Weber writes *The Protestant Ethic and the Birth of Capitalism*; the first performance of Giacomo Puccini's opera *Madame Butterfly* in Milan; the first radio transmission of music is at Graz, Austria; the general theory of radioactivity is postulated by Ernest Rutherford and Frederick Soddy; W.C. Gorgas eradicates yellow fever in the Panama Canal Zone; silicones are discovered by F.S. Kipping.

1905: Albert Einstein publishes four papers detailing his special theory of relativity, the relationship between mass and energy, the Brownian theory of motion and another formulating the photon theory of light; the Russian city of Port Arthur surrenders to the Japanese; in Russia troops fire at peaceful protest marchers heading for the czar's Winter Palace in St Petersburg, and the event becomes known as "Bloody Sunday"; Wil-liam II of Germany and Nicholas II of Russia sign the Treaty of Bjorko for mutual help in Europe; the Treaty of Portsmouth ends the Russo-Japanese War; a general strike in Russia in response to Bloody Sunday includes a sailors' mutiny on the battleship *Potemkin* and the creation of the first workers soviet in St Petersburg; Czar Nicholas establishes a constitutional government (the Imperial Duma); the Norwegian Parliament decides to separate from Sweden; the Anglo-Japanese alliance is renewed for 10 years; the Sinn Fein nationalist party is formed in Ireland; George Santayana writes his philosophical work *The Life of Reason*.

1906: Reform laws are proposed in Russia and the Imperial Duma is dissolved by the czar to end the radical change; the All India Muslim League is founded by Aga Khan; the term "allergy" is introduced by Clemens von Pirquet; the position of the magnetic North Pole is determined by Norwegian explorer Roald Amundsen; night-shift work for women is forbidden in many countries; the San Francisco earthquake kills 700 people and causes $400 million in property loss; Transvaal and Orange River colonies are granted self-government.

1907: The second Russian Duma meets in March; its radical proposals lead to its dissolution five months later; the US prohibits Japanese immigration; Lenin leaves Russia and founds the newspaper *The Proletarian*; Grigori Rasputin, a Russian mystic, gains influence with the royal family when he treats the hemophiliac son of Nicholas II; New Zealand becomes a dominion within the British Empire; Baden-Powell forms the Boy Scout movement; Korea becomes a Japanese protectorate; Russian artist Marc Chagall paints *Peasant Women*; Gustav Mahler (Austrian) composes *Symphony No. 8*; Ivan Pavlov (Russian) studies conditioned reflexes in dogs; the SS *Lusitania* beats the SS *Mauritania* in a race from Ireland to New York.

1908: Austria occupies Bosnia and Herzegovina; Bulgaria declares independence from Turkey; Isadora Duncan emerges as a popular modern dancer; the Zeppelin airship crashes near Echterdingen; General Motors Corporation is formed in the US; Henry Ford designs the inexpensive, standardized Model T automobile while pioneering assembly line techniques for autos; an earthquake in Sicily and Calabria kills 150,000; American Gertrude Stein writes *Three Lives*; French writer Anatole France completes the political satire *Penguin Island*; Canadian Lucy Maud Montgomery writes *Anne of Green Gables*.

1909: Turkey and Serbia acknowledge Austrian control of Bosnia and Herzegovina; sultan of Turkey is deposed and replaced by his brother; Ezra Pound writes *Exultations*; the first newsreels appear and director D.W. Griffith features Canadian-born Mary Pickford, who becomes the first film star; Sergei Diaghilev presents his *Ballets Russes*, revolutionizing dance, in Paris; Blériot flies from Calais to Dover in 37 minutes, Farman makes the first 100-mile flight; W.E. Du Bois cofounds the National Negro Committee which becomes the National Association for the Advancement of Colored People in 1910; Girl Guides organized in Britain; Thomas Hunt Morgan begins research in genetics; US explorer Robert E. Peary reaches the North Pole.

1910: The Union of South Africa becomes a dominion within the British Empire with Louis Botha as premier; China abolishes slavery; Japan takes over Korea; Montenegro becomes an independent kingdom; Portugal becomes a republic after a revolution ends the monarchy; Albania rebels against Turkish rule; Roger Fry arranges the Post-Impressionist Exhibition in London with works by Cezanne, van Gogh and Matisse; Igor Stravinsky performs his ballet score *The Firebird* in Paris; the South American tango is the dance craze in Europe and North America; the first deep-sea research expedition is undertaken by Murray and Hjort; the five-day work week is instituted in the US, making the "week-end" possible.

1911: US-Japanese and Anglo-Japanese commercial treaties are signed; Diaz surrenders power in Mexico but revolutions continue; the Kaiser's Hamburg speech promises Germany's "Place in the Sun"; war erupts between Turkey and Italy and aircraft are first used for offensive measures; a revolution in Central China is followed by the fall of the Manchu dynasty (in power since 1644) and the proclamation of a Chinese Republic; Sun Yat-sen is elected president and he appoints Chiang Kai-shek as his military adviser; Russian premier, Peter Stolypin, is assassinated; Roald Amundsen reaches the South Pole; Marie Curie is the first person to win a second Noble Prize, in chemistry; Rutherford formulates his theory of atomic structure.

1912: British dock workers, coal miners and transport workers strike; the German-Austro-Italian alliance is renewed again; Lenin becomes editor of *Pravda*; Sun Yat-sen founds Kuomintang (Chinese National Party); Montenegro declares war against Turkey and Bulgaria, Greece and Serbia mobilize; Carl Jung writes *The Theory of Psychoanalysis*; the term "vitamin" is coined by Polish chemist Kasimir Funk; Stefansson and Anderson explore Arctic Canada; Wilson's cloud chamber (particle detector) photographs lead to the detection of protons and electrons; the Royal Flying Corps (later RAF) is established in Britain; SS *Titanic* sinks on its first voyage after colliding with an iceberg: 1,513 people drown.

1913: The London Peace Treaty ending the First Balkan War is signed and Turkey loses all possessions in Europe except E. Thrace; the Second Balkan War breaks out as Bulgaria attacks Serbia and Greece; Russia declares war on Bulgaria, Bulgaria and Turkey settle a peace treaty and Turkey regains Thrace, Serbia invades Albania; Greece and Turkey make peace; police crack down on suffragette demonstrations led by Emmeline Pankhurst in London; Maxim Gorki, the father of Soviet literature, writes *My Childhood*; Charlie Chaplin first stars in movies; Niels Bohr formulates his theory of atomic structure; Albert Schweitzer, medical missionary, opens his famous hospital in Lambaréné, French Congo.

1914: Archduke Francis Ferdinand, heir to the Austrian throne, is assassinated in Sarajevo (capital of the Austro-Hungarian province of Bosnia) by a Serbian nationalist (June 28); Austria-Hungary challenges Serbia and declares war (July 28); Russia and France support Serbia and mobilize troops; Austria's ally Germany declares war on Russia and France in response; the members of the Triple Entente (Britain, France, Russia) declare war on Turkey after Turks attack Russia; Germany, Austria-Hungary and the Ottoman Empire (Turkey) form alliance of Central Powers, they are opposed by UK, members of British Empire, France, Russia, Belgium, Japan and Serbia (Allied Powers); Germany invades Belgium, attacks France, and establishes the Eastern Front against the Russians at Tannenberg and the Masurian Lakes; on the Western Front the Germans are held in check after battles at Marne River, France (Sept. 6); the First Battle of Ypres, Belgium, is waged to prevent the Germans from cutting British supply lines to France; Austria-Hungary fails in three attacks on Serbia and, after the Russians capture the province of Galicia, retreats to its own territory; by Nov. 14, 1914 there is a deadlock along the Western Front (stretching 720 km across Belgium and northeast France to the Swiss border) that remains throughout the war; Irish writer James Joyce writes *Dubliners* (1914); John B. Watson writes *Behavior: an Introduction to Comparative Psychology* (1914); the first successful heart surgery is performed on a dog by Dr. Alexis Carrel (1914); the Panama Canal opens (1914); millions of immigrants leave southern and eastern Europe between 1905 and 1914.

1915: The Allied Gallipoli Campaign to neutralize Turkey fails and Australian and New Zealand troops suffer heavy losses; the first German submarine (U-boat) attack is at Le Havre; the German blockade of England begins; at the Second Battle of Ypres, Canadian forces hold off the German advance while under heavy fire and attacks from chlorine gas and newly-introduced flame throwers; Italy joins the Allied Powers, declares war on Austria-Hungary (May 23) and an Italian Front soon opens; a German submarine sinks the *Lusitania* (May 7); the first Zeppelin air attack takes place on London; Ottoman-controlled Mesopotamia (now Iraq) surrenders to Britain; Italians fight Austria-Hungary in continuous battles at Isonzo (1915–17); Germans invade

Warsaw and Brest-Litovsk; Allied troops land at Salonika; the first fighter airplane is constructed by Hugo Junkers; Henry Ford develops a farm tractor; the dysentery bacillus is isolated by British chemist James Kendall; the first book advocating birth control, by American Margaret Sanger, is published, and the author is sent to jail.

1916: Germany stages a Zeppelin raid on Paris and declares war on Portugal; Portugal and Rumania later join the Allied Powers; in the Middle East, T.E. Lawrence leads an Arab revolt against Turkey; heavy casualties occur at Verdun (Feb. 21); British and German fleets clash at the Battle of Jutland (May 31–June 1); the 1st Newfoundland Regiment is annihilated along with 624,000 Allied troops during the offensive at the Somme (launched July 1); HMS *Hampshire* is sunk; Italy declares war on Germany; the Germans first use gas masks and steel helmets; peace notes are exchanged between Germany and the Allies; Lloyd George becomes British prime minister; blood for transfusion is first refrigerated; the theory of shell shock is put forth by F.W. Mott; an underwater ultrasonic source for submarine detection is built by Paul Langevin; Britain initiates daylight-saving time; US purchases the Virgin Islands for $25 million.

1917: The United States enters the war on the Allied side (Apr. 6); Germans withdraw on the Western Front; the Russian Black Sea fleet mutinies at Sebastopol; there is revolution in Russia in Feb. and the Czar abdicates (Mar. 16); Kerensky becomes Russian premier and continues the war effort; Canadian forces seize Vimy Ridge in northern France; Germany stages air attacks on England; Greece joins the Allies (July); China declares war on Germany and Austria; the British-led offensive at the Third Battle of Ypres (Passchendaele) fails (July 31); the Italian army is defeated at Caporetto by Austria-Hungary; Kerensky's government is overthrown in Petrograd in Oct. and Lenin is appointed Chief Commissar, Trotsky becomes Commissar for Foreign Affairs and Russia seeks peace with Germany; the first tank battle is at Cambrai; starvation sweeps Germany; Finland declares independence from Russia; the Allies execute dancer Mata Hari as a spy; Lord Arthur Balfour, the British Foreign Secretary, issues the Balfour Declaration stating British support for a Jewish national homeland in Palestine; women are arrested for suffrage activities in the US.

1918: Russia, the Ukraine and the Central Powers conclude the Treaties of Brest-Litovsk: the first one establishes the independence of the Ukraine, the second strips Russia of its Baltic and Polish possessions; Turks surrender to British at Jerusalem; US Pres. Wilson puts forth Fourteen Points for world peace (including a proposal for a League of Nations); Rumania signs a peace treaty with the Central Powers; Germany launches three final offensives on the Western Front (Mar. 21); Germans bomb Paris; the Second Battle of the Marne (July 15–Aug. 6) is won by the Allies; the Allies win victories on all fronts in the fall; the Japanese push into Siberia; Germany and Austria agree to retreat to their own territory before an armistice is signed; the Hungarian premier is assassinated; the Turkish and Austro-Hungarian empires and Bulgaria surrender to the Allies (Nov. 3); the German fleet mutinies at Kiel and the emperor flees; an armistice between the Allies and Germany is signed (Nov. 11); Germany agrees to the provisions of the Treaty of Versailles after the Allies threaten to invade; Emperor Charles of Austria loses the throne; the map of Europe is reshaped: Austria becomes a republic and the Serbo-Croatian-Slovene Kingdom of Yugoslavia is proclaimed, Poland and Czechoslovakia are created; Iceland becomes independent state; the Russian Revolution continues as Bolshevik workers take over government buildings, the Winter Palace and later Moscow and other cities; civil war between the Bolshevik (Red) and anti-Bolshevik (White) continues (until 1920); British, French and American troops intervene against the Reds; the British government abandons Home Rule for Ireland; ex-Czar Nicholas II and family are executed by Russian revolutionaries; Hsu-Shih-Chang becomes president of the Chinese Republic; women over 30 get the vote in Britain; controversy rages over the psychology of Freud and Jung; the true dimensions of the Milky Way are discovered by Harlow Shapley, an American astronomer.

1919: US Pres. Woodrow Wilson heads the first League of Nations meeting in Paris; the Peace Conference opens at Versailles; Benito Mussolini founds the Fasci del Combatimento in Italy; socialist governments are founded in Austria and Budapest, Hungary; the Treaty of Versailles is signed with Germany; the final treaty exacts heavy financial penalties on Germany, restricts the German army and navy, blames Germany for provoking the war and establishes the League of Nations; US refusal to ratify the treaty excludes it from League membership; the Allied peace treaty with Austria is signed at St Germain; the Treaty of Neuilly with Bulgaria is signed; the International Labor Congress in Washington endorses the eight-hour workday; the Red (Soviet) forces win successive battles in the Russian civil war; Soviets attack Finland; the first nonstop flight across the Atlantic is made from Newfound-land to Ireland by J.W. Alcock and A. Whitten Brown; Lady Astor is elected to Britain's Parliament, becoming the first female MP.

1920: The League of Nations is founded in Paris and establishes headquarters in Geneva; Russian civil war ends with Soviet victory; Great Britain gains control of Palestine from the Turks; The Hague becomes the International Court of Justice; the Little Entente between Czechoslovakia, Yugoslavia and Rumania is formed; the Treaty of Trianon is signed with Hungary; the Treaty of Sevres is signed with the Ottoman Empire; the 19th Amendment gives American women the vote; 200,000 Chinese die in an earthquake in Kansu province; the world population is 1.8 billion; Britain establishes separate parliaments for Northern and Southern Ireland; Adolph Hitler founds the Nazi party in Munich, Germany, and announces his 25-point program, blaming Germany's war defeat on Jews and Communists; Mohandas (Mahatma) Ghandi becomes India's leader in its struggle for independence from Britain; Prohibition goes into effect in the US, banning the sale and consumption of alcoholic beverages; a worldwide influenza epidemic, which began in 1918, leaves 22 million dead.

1921: The first Indian Parliament meets; German reparations payments totalling $33.3 million are fixed by the Allies at a Paris conference; Hitler's storm troopers (SA) begin to terrorize ideological opponents; Mackenzie King is elected prime minister of Canada; British Broadcasting Company is founded (changed to the British Broadcasting Corporation in 1927); the Spanish prime minister and Japanese premier are assassinated; founder of Portuguese republic is murdered; ex-emperor Charles stages two failed coup attempts to regain Hungarian throne; Britain and Ireland sign a peace treaty; German mark falls and rapid inflation plagues the economy; coal is successfully hydrogenated into oil by Friedrich Bergius; the tuberculosis vaccine (B-C-G) is developed by Albert Calmette and Camille Guerin; the chromosome theory of heredity is put forth by American biologist Thomas Morgan; Albert Einstein wins Nobel Prize for Physics; Ku Klux Klan members terrorize blacks and black sympathizers in the southern US; one of the founders of modern aeronautics, Hermann J. Oberth, writes *The Rocket into Interplanetary Space.*

1922: Gandhi is sentenced to six years imprisonment for civil disobedience; German reconstruction minister Walter Rathenau is assassinated by German nationalists; the Arab Congress at Nablus rejects the British control of Palestine; Austria denounces "Anschluss" (union with Germany); Mussolini stages the March on Rome and forms a Fascist government; Irish Free State is proclaimed; the tomb of Tutankhamen is discovered by Lord Carnarvaron and Howard Carter; a self-winding wristwatch is invented by John Harwood (patented in 1924); a stock market "boom" begins in the US; Soviet states form the USSR; insulin, prepared by Canadian physicians Frederick Banting, Charles Best and John Macleod, is first given to diabetic patients.

1923: An earthquake kills 120,000 people in Tokyo and Yokohama; Adolph Hitler tries (and fails) to overthrow the German government ("Beer Hall Putsch"); Greek army overthrows monarch; Jewish philosopher Martin Buber writes the theological *I and Thou*; the theory of acids and bases is postulated by J.N. Brönsted; Lee de Forest demonstrates the process for motion pictures with sound; the first commercial airline, Aeroflot, is founded in the USSR.

1924: Ramsay MacDonald forms the first Labour government in Britain; Adolph Hitler writes *Mein Kampf* during an eight-month jail term; R.C. Andrews discovers skulls and skeletons of Mesozoic dinosaurs in the Gobi desert; Winston Churchill, having switched from the Liberals to the Conservatives, is named Chancellor of the Exchequer in Britain; in Russia, Lenin dies and Stalin, Zinoviev and Kamenev ally against Trotsky; the "Zinoviev letter," purported to be calling for a communist revolution in Britain, is published by the British Foreign Office; Greece becomes a republic; elections are held in Italy and Mussolini wins support of 65% of the electorate; leader of Italian socialists is murdered; Albanian Republic is founded; Sigmund Freud begins *Collected Writings* (12 vols. 1924–39); Ghandi fasts for 21 days, protesting feuding between Hindus and Muslims in India; British astronomer Arthur Eddington discovers that the luminosity of a star is approximately related to its mass; insecticides are used for the first time; a patent application for iconoscope (television) is filed by Russian-American inventor V.K. Zworkin; Danish polar explorer Knud Ras-mussen completes the longest dog-sled journey ever made across the North American Arctic; British Imperial Airways begins commercial air flights.

1925: Locarno Conference creates a series of treaties between Germany, France, Belgium, Poland, UK, Italy and Czechoslovakia that set up a demilitarized zone in the Rhineland and confirmed borders between Belgium, France and Germany; Mrs Nellie Tayloe Ross of Wyoming becomes the first woman governor in the US; the United Church of Canada is founded; recognizable human features are transmitted by television by Scottish inventor John Logie Baird; Walter P. Chrysler founds the Chrysler Corporation; the (Franz) Fischer and (Hans) Tropsch synthesis leads to the industrial development of synthetic oil; Heisenberg, Bohr and Jordan develop quantum mechanics for atoms; the presence of cosmic rays in the upper atmosphere is discovered by US physicist Robert Andrews Millikan; the "flapper" era takes hold; an international convention condemns the illegal narcotics trade.

1926: Fascist youth organizations appear: "Balilla" in Italy and "Hitlerjugend" in Germany; Josef Pilsudski successfully stages a coup d'état in Poland and begins a military dictatorship; commerce in Britain is stopped by a general strike; Trotsky is expelled from Moscow; Hirohito succeeds his father Taisho as Emperor of Japan; Robert H. Goddard fires the first liquid fuel rocket; vitamin B is isolated by B. Jansen and W. Donath; Kodak produces the first 16mm movie film; British Imperial Chemical Industries (ICI) begins operations; H.L. Mencken writes *Notes on Democracy*; Turkish reforms include the abolition of polygamy, modernization of female attire and adoption of Latin alphabet (1926–28).

1927: The Allied military control of Germany ends; an economic conference in Geneva is attended by 52 nations; the economic system in Germany collapses ("Black Friday"); Trotsky expelled from the Communist Party in the USSR; Nazis on trial in Austria for political murder are acquitted and socialists riot in Venice to protest; the first film with sound, a "talkie," *The Jazz Singer*, stars Al Jolson; Lev Theremin invents the earliest electronic musical instrument; Charles Lindbergh flies the monoplane *Spirit of St Louis* in the first solo transatlantic flight, nonstop from New York to Paris in 33.5 hours; Canadian forests are the first sprayed with insecticides by airplanes; the first vehicular tunnel, the Holland Tunnel, links New York and New Jersey.

1928: The Supreme Court of Canada rules that women may not hold public office because they are not "persons" as defined by the British North America Act, but the British Privy Council overturns the decision in a landmark Commonwealth case in 1929; the Kellogg-Briand Pact outlawing war is signed by 65 states; Josef Stalin emerges as leader of Soviet Union; the first economic five-year plan begins in the USSR; Chiang Kai-Shek is elected president of China; over-production of coffee leads to the collapse of Brazil's economy; penicillin is discovered by Alexander Fleming (Scottish); American anthropologist Margaret Mead writes *Coming of Age in Samoa;* the first colour motion pictures are exhibited by George Eastman in Rochester, New York; J.L. Baird presents colour television; Mickey Mouse makes his Disney debut.

1929: The US Stock Exchange collapses on Oct. 28, Black Friday; the Great Depression, a world economic crisis, begins and is primarily caused by easy credit and stock market over-speculation, overproduction of goods and tariff and war-debt policies; six Chicago-area gangsters are machine-gunned to death in the St Valentine's Day Massacre; a dictatorship is established in Serbo-Croat-Slovene kingdom by the monarch and the country's name is changed to Yugoslavia; Trotsky is exiled from USSR; talks on Indian sovereignty begin beetween Indian leaders and the Viceroy; the Lateran Treaty establishes the independence of Vatican City; precise timekeeping is made possible with the quartz-crystal clocks by W.A. Morrison; the airship *Graf Zeppelin* flies around the world in 21 days.

1930: Austria and Italy sign a treaty of friendship; Britain, the US, Japan, France and Italy sign a treaty on naval disarmament; right-wing coalition comes to power in Germany, Nazis later capture 107 more seats in an election; right-wing government is formed in Poland; Catholic-Fascist units are established in Austria; revolution in Argentina brings new military dictatorship to power; the planet Pluto is discovered by C.W. Tombaugh at Lowell Observatory; a yellow fever vaccine is developed by South African microbiologist Max Theiler; photoflash bulb is introduced; the word "technocracy," meaning the domination of technology, comes into use.

1931: A financial crisis in central Europe is caused by the collapse of Austria's Credit-Anstalt; all German banks close following the bankruptcy of the German Danatbank; Britain abandons the gold standard; Fascist party is formed in Britain; the Statute of Westminster established the British Commonwealth of Nations as a free association of autonomous nations sharing a common allegiance to the British crown, and declared that British Parliament could no longer legislate for any member states unless requested to do so; US Pres. Hoover proposes a one-year moratorium for reparations and war debts; the first trans-African railroad line is completed, Benguella-Katanga; the northern face of the Matterhorn is climbed for the first time by Franz and Toni Schmid.

1932: The Indian National Congress, a nationalist party dedicated to home rule, is declared illegal and its leader, Mahatma Gandhi, is arrested; the US criticizes Japanese aggression in Manchuria; the Nazis sweep the German Reichstag (Parliament) elections while WWI hero Hindenburg wins the Presidential election; Hitler refuses Hinden-burg's offer to become Vice Chancellor, and the Austrian-born Hitler receives German citizenship; Franklin D. Roosevelt wins the US presidential election and proposes domestic reform programs to provide recovery and relief from the Great Depression ("New Deal"); the USSR suffers famine; Zuider Zee, a huge dam and drainage project in Holland, is completed; Amelia Earheart is the first woman to fly solo across the Atlantic; Japan conquers world markets by undercutting prices; about 30 million people are unemployed worldwide; the neutron is discovered by James Chadwick; vitamin D is discovered.

1933: Reichstag building is burned in Berlin and Hitler uses the event to justify banning opposition parties and labour unions; Hitler is appointed German Chancellor and granted dictatorial powers with the Enabling Law; Nazi Hermann Goering is named Prussian prime minister; Parliamentary government is suspended in Austria; starvation spreads in USSR; Paul Joseph Goebbels is named Hitler's Minister of Propaganda; Japan withdraws from the League of Nations; the first concentration camps are built by the Nazis in Germany to hold Jews and ideological opponents; books by non-Nazi and Jewish authors are burned in Germany; Germans begin to boycott and restrict Jewish services; an anti-Nazi treatise, *Judaism-Christendom-Germanism*, is published by Cardinal von Faulhaber in Munich; Assyrian Christians are massacred in Iraq; US goes off the gold standard and tries to stimulate its economy by creating The Tennessee Valley Authority to construct dams and generate electricity.

1934: A revolution in Austria overturns the Social Democrats and Austrian Chancellor is assassinated by the Nazis; a general strike takes place in France; the USSR is admitted to the League of Nations; Winston Churchill warns the British Parliament of the German air menace; Hitler oversees purge of his associates and many are executed; a national vote grants him the title Führer (leader); Stalin's purge of the Soviet Communist party begins and he reportedly oversees the murder of millions of people; German scientist Albert Einstein is persecuted by the Nazis for being Jewish and he flees, settling in the US; Japan renounces the Washington treaties of 1922 and 1930; Mao Tse-tung, leader of the Chinese Communists, heads the Long March.

1935: Nazis repudiate the Treaty of Versailles and reintroduce compulsory military service; the autonomous territory of Saarland votes for reunion with Germany; an Anglo-German Naval Agreement is concluded; Nazis implement the Nuremburg Laws against Jews, stripping them of civic rights and forbidding intermarriage with non-Jews; Mussolini invades Ethiopia, and the League of Nations retaliates by imposing sanctions; the Chaco War, a bitter conflict between Paraguay and Bolivia begun in 1932 and fought over oil-rich but otherwise barren territory, ended after 100,000 lives were lost and both sides were exhausted (treaty not concluded until 1938); radar equipment to detect aircraft is built by Robert Watson Watt; oil pipelines between Iraq, Haifa and Tripoli open; Persia changes its name to Iran.

1936: King George V of England dies and is succeeded by Edward VIII; German troops occupy the Rhineland and Hitler wins the German elections with 99 percent of the vote; Italy, Austria and Hungary sign the Rome Pact; Britain, France and the US sign the London Naval Convention; an Austro-German convention acknowledges Austrian independence; the Spanish Civil War begins and Francisco Franco is appointed Chief of State by the Nationalist insurgents against the government's Loyalist republicans; Franco begins the siege of Madrid, rebels take Malaga and destroy Guernica and Gijon and Franco begins a naval blockade (1937); Heinrich Himmler is appointed head of the Gestapo, responsible for Nazi concentration camps (1936–45); King Edward VIII abdicates in order to marry American divorcee Wallis Simpson; Mussolini and Hitler proclaim the Rome-Berlin Axis; the Anti-Comintern Pact is signed by Germany and Japan; Chiang Kai-shek declares war on Japan; Dr Alexis Carrel develops an artificial heart; the airship *Hindenburg* burns at Lakehurst, New Jersey, after a transatlantic flight; black American athlete Jesse Owens upsets the Nazis when he wins four gold medals at the Olympic Games in Berlin.

1937: Poland refuses to return Danzig to Germany; the first worldwide radio broadcast is heard when George VI is crowned King of Great Britain; Roosevelt signs a US Neutrality Act, intended to keep the US out of a possible European war; Trotsky, exiled from Russia in 1929, is forced to leave Norway and settles in Mexico; aggressive Japanese war policy begins when Prince Konoye is named the Japanese premier, and the Japanese seize major Chinese cities (Beijing, Tianjin, Shanghai, Nanjing and Hangzhou), forcing Chiang Kai-shek and the Communists, under Mao Tse-tung and Chou En-lai, to unite; the Chinese government makes Chungking its capital; the Royal Commission on Palestine recommends the establishment of Arab and Jewish states; Stalin initiates a purge of Soviet generals and show trials of political leaders; Britain signs naval agreements with Germany and the USSR; Germany guarantees Belgian sovereignty; Italy joins the Anti-Comintern Pact and withdraws from the League of Nations; Japanese planes sink US gunboat in Chinese waters; Amelia Earheart disappears during a Pacific flight.

1938: Germany annexes Austria, "Anschluss" (Mar.); France calls up reservists; Great Britain, France and Italy agree to let Germany absorb the Sudetenland, Czechoslovakia, in a policy of appeasement (Munich Pact, Sept.) and Germany promises to cease its aggressive expansion; British foreign minister Anthony Eden resigns in protest against the appeasement policy and Winston Churchill also voices opposition; Franco begins an offensive against the Spanish Loyalists in Catalonia; anti-Jewish legislation is enacted in Italy; Kristallnacht, or "Night of Broken Glass," is a large-scale pogrom by the Nazis against German Jews; the US and Germany recall their respective ambassadors; Japan withdraws from the League of Nations and sets up a puppet Chinese government in Nanking; Howard Hughes flies around the world in less than four days.

1939: US Pres. Roosevelt demands assurances from Hitler and Mussolini that they have no plans to attack other states; Germany breaks the Munich Pact and occupies Bohemia and Moravia; Slovakia is placed under "protection"; Italy invades Albania; Germany renounces the nonaggression pact with Poland and naval agreement with England, and concludes a 10-year alliance with Italy and a nonaggression pact with the USSR, secretly dividing Poland; Germany stages a surprise (blitzkrieg) invasion of Poland, and annexes Danzig (Sept. 1); Britain and France declare war on Germany (Sept. 3); the Allied powers are Britain and France and the Axis powers are led by Germany; Canada declares war (Sept. 10); US Pres. Roosevelt announces US neutrality; Soviets invade Poland from the east (Sept. 17); Germans overrun western Poland and reach Brest-Litovsk and Warsaw; France masses troops along the Maginot Line on the eastern frontier of France and Germany sends troops to its parallel Siegfried Line; the British Expeditionary Force is sent to France; the USSR invades Finland and is expelled from the League of Nations; Japan occupies Hainan and blockades the British at Tientsin; the US renounces the Japanese trade agreement of 1911; the Spanish Civil War ends with Franco's Nationalists (supported by Hitler and Mussolini) victorious over the Loyalists (supported by the USSR); Spain joins the Anti-Comintern Pact and leaves the League of Nations; England and Poland sign a treaty of mutual assistance; women and children are first evacuated from London; the first helicopter is built by Russian-American Igor Sikorsky; the US economy booms from arms sales to Europe.

1940: Food rationing begins in Britain; Finland surrenders (Mar.) and signs a peace treaty with the USSR; Germany invades Norway and Denmark (Apr. 9); Winston Churchill becomes British prime minister (May 10); Norway falls (June); Germany invades Belgium, Luxembourg and the Netherlands (May 10); Holland and Belgium surrender to Germany and 340,000 Allied forces are trapped in Belgium, but most are evacuated from Dunkirk, a French seaport on the English channel (May 29 to June 3); Italy declares war on France and Britain; Germans attack France from the north and enter Paris (June 14); France concludes an armistice with Germany; southern France remains unoccupied until 1942 and is ruled by the Vichy government; USSR seizes Estonia, Latvia and Lithuania (summer); the Royal Navy sinks the French fleet in Oran; the Royal Air Force begins night bombing of Germany; the Battle of Britain in Aug. is the first battle fought completely in the air; Hitler begins bombing England (all-night blitzes) throughout fall and winter; Japan, Germany and Italy sign a military and economic pact; US destroyers are sold to Britain; Germany intensifies U-boat warfare; Italian forces attempt to take Egypt and Libya in order to cut off British access to Middle East oil and the Suez Canal; the British Eighth Army opens an offensive in North Africa and defeats the Italian forces; Trotsky is murdered in Mexico; Batista becomes president of Cuba; wall paintings dating to about 20,000 BC are discovered in France, the Lascaux caves; a giant cyclotron is built at the University of California for producing mesotrons from atomic nuclei.

1941: The British invade Ethiopia and defeat the Italians (by May); Germany opens a counter-offensive in North Africa to aid Italy; German General Rommel regains Libya and Egypt; Germans launch an airborne invasion against Crete, thereby securing an important base in the Mediterranean (by the end of May); England sinks the German battleship *Bismarck* in an effort to protect vital US shipments to Great Britain; Allies develop radar and sonar to track U-boats; German air raids over London continue; US freezes German and Italian assets in that country; Germans invade Russia (Operation Barbarossa, June 22); Churchill and Roosevelt sign the Atlantic charter (Aug. 14); German troops surround Leningrad and Moscow (Nov.), but an early, harsh winter saves the USSR; Marshal Timoshenko launches the Russian counter-offensive; the US ambassador to Japan warns Pres. Roosevelt of possible Japanese attack; Japanese bomb Pearl Harbor (Dec. 7) and the US and Britain declare war on Japan (Dec. 8); China declares war on the Axis (Dec. 9); Japan invades the Philippines; Germany and Italy declare war on the US; the US declares war on Germany and Italy; British Hong Kong surrenders to the Japanese; Henry Moore draws refugees in London air raid shelters while an official war artist; Dmitri Shostakovich writes *Symphony No. 7* during the German siege of Leningrad; German dramatist Bertolt Brecht writes *Mother Courage and Her Children* while in exile from the Nazis.

1942: Hitler's Final Solution, the systematic murder of Jews in the Nazi gas chambers (Holocaust) is in full force at death camps such as Auschwitz and Dachau; the 26 Allied nations agree not to make separate treaties with the Axis powers; Rommel breaks through British lines and reaches El Alamein (320 km from the Suez Canal); Montgomery (British Eighth Army) scores the first decisive defeat of Rommel at El Alamein; Germans reach Stalingrad, Russia; 400,000 American troops land in French North Africa; Rommel, in full retreat, loses Tobruk and Benghazi; Japan invades Burma, the Dutch East Indies, and captures Singapore; the British bomb Cologne and Lübeck; the US and Canada intern residents of Japanese heritage in camps; many American and Philippine prisoners die in the Japanese-forced Bataan Death March; Americans bomb Tokyo; Americans begin successful island-hopping strategy against Japan and win the battles of the Coral Sea and Midway; French navy loses in Toulon; British and Indian troops advance in Burma; Fermi achieves the first controlled nuclear chain reaction when he splits the atom; the Manhattan Project of intensive US atomic research begins; the first electronic brain or automatic computer is developed in the US; a recorder using plastic magnetic recording tape is invented by German engineers; Gandhi demands independence from Britain and is arrested.

1943: German troops surrender at Stalingrad (Feb. 2) and begin to withdraw from the Caucasus; Churchill and Roosevelt meet in Casablanca; the Japanese are driven from Guadalcanal by US troops; the British Eighth Army reaches Tripoli; Axis powers surrender in North Africa (Tunisia, May 13); Russians destroy the German army southwest of Stalingrad; Russians recapture Rostov and Kharkov; the Royal Air Force raids Berlin; US planes sink the 22-ship Japanese convoy in the Battle of the Bismarck Sea; British and US armies in Africa link up and Rommel retreats; an armed Jewish uprising begins in the overcrowded Warsaw ghetto, but it is crushed by German troops (1943–44) who massacre Jewish inhabitants; the RAF bombs Ruhr dams; US forces land in New Guinea; US recaptures Aleutians; Allies land in Sicily (July 10); Churchill, Roosevelt and Mackenzie King meet in Quebec; US troops bomb Ploesti oil fields in Rumania and enter Messina; Allies land in Salerno Bay and invade Italy, which surrenders unconditionally (Sept. 8); Russians take Kiev; Chinese Gen. and Mme Chiang Kai-shek meet with Roosevelt and Churchill in Cairo and pledge to liberate Korea after Japan is defeated; Churchill, Stalin and Roosevelt hold the Teheran Conference; Allied round-the-clock bombing of Germany begins; the first fully electronic computer is used by the British government to crack German military codes; penicillin is used to treat chronic diseases; Bengal is swept by famine; rationing of selected foods begins in the US; major US cities are troubled by race riots.

1944: Germany continues air raids on London; Russian offensives continue in the Ukraine and Crimea; Allies bomb Berlin; Monte Cassino and Rome are liberated by the Allies June 4; D-day landings in Normandy (France, June 6): over 700 ships and 4,000 landing craft are involved and Canadian troops lead the trek from the Normandy beaches; Germans drop first flying bomb (V-1) on London; southern Japan is bombed by the US; US troops take Saipan; Russians capture 100,000 Germans at Minsk; German officers unsuccessfully attempt to assassinate Hitler; Russians reach Brest-Litovsk; Amer-icans capture Guam from the Japanese; the British Eighth Army takes Florence; creation of a United Nations is discussed at the Dunbarton Oaks conference in Washington; Charles De Gaulle leads the Free French into Paris (Aug. 25); Allies liberate Belgium; the first V-2 rockets land in Britain; Churchill and Roosevelt meet in Quebec; Americans cross the German frontier near Trier; British airborne forces land at Eindhoven and Arnheim but have to withdraw; US troops land in the Philippines; Russians and Yugoslavs enter Belgrade; Russian Army occupies Hungary; Japanese suffer heavy losses in Battle of Leyte Gulf; Battle of the Bulge (Ardennes Forest) results in Allied victory; France regains Lorraine; Rommel commits suicide; Vietnam, under Ho Chi Minh, declares independence from France; American playwright Tennessee Williams completes *The Glass Menagerie*; quinine is synthesized; Richard Strauss completes the opera *Die Liebe der Danae* in Austria but its performance is cancelled when the Nazis shut down the theatres; French playwright Jean-Paul Sartre writes the existentialist work *Being and Nothingness*.

1945: Britain begins major offensive in Burma; Russians take Warsaw, Cracow and reach Oder River; Churchill, Roosevelt and Stalin meet at the Yalta Conference; Americans enter Manila; Russians take Budapest; British troops reach the Rhine; US air raids on Tokyo, Cologne and Danzig; Okinawa is captured; the British Second Army crosses the Rhine; the last German V-2 rocket falls on Britain; Franklin D. Roosevelt dies and is succeeded by Harry S. Truman; Russians reach Berlin; Bologna is captured; US and Soviet troops meet at Torgau and both liberate Nazi death camps, finding gas chambers and crematoriums; anti-Axis coalition agrees to set up new international body to replace ineffective League of Nations; new United Nations charter drawn up at conference in San Francisco (Apr.–June); Bremen, Genoa, Verona and Venice are captured by the Allies; the Allies cross the Elbe; Mussolini is killed by Italian partisans; Hitler commits suicide (Apr. 30); the German army on the Italian front surrenders; Berlin surrenders to the Russians (May 2) and Germany capitulates to the Allies (May 7); V-E Day (Victory in Europe) ends the war in Europe (May 8); Germany is divided into four zones by the Allies and the three-power occupation of Berlin begins; Churchill, Truman and Stalin meet at Potsdam; Clement Attlee replaces Churchill as prime minister of Great Britain in a Labour landslide; the first atomic bomb is detonated near Alamogordo, New Mexico after being developed by J. Robert Oppenheimer, Enrico Fermi and others (July 16); the Soviet Union declares war on Japan and occupied Manchuria; the US drops atomic bombs on Hiroshima (Aug. 6) and Nagasaki (Aug. 9); Japan surrenders and World War II ends; war dead are estimated at 35 million plus victims of Nazi concentration camps; the Nuremburg trials of Nazi war criminals begin; the League of Nations holds its final meeting in Geneva and turns over its assets to the UN (Oct.); Charles De Gaulle is elected president of the French provisional government; Tito is chief of state of the newly created Federal People's Republic of Yugoslavia; Nationalists and Communists resume civil war in north China; the Arab League is founded to oppose the creation of a Jewish state; Shintoism is abolished in Japan; vitamin A is synthesized; black markets for food, clothing and cigarettes develop in Europe; the UN World Bank (International Bank for Reconstruction and Development) is founded with authorized share capital of $27 billion.

1946: Albania, Bulgaria, Hungary and Transjordan become sovereign states; the UN General Assembly holds its first session in London (Jan. 7), electing Trygve Lie of Norway as its first Secretary-General, and its permanent headquarters is made in New York; Juan Perón is elected president of Argentina; a Peace Conference of 21 nations is held in Paris; 12 leading Nazis are sentenced to death following the Nuremburg trials and others get life imprisonment; power in Japan is transferred from the Emperor to an elected assembly; the UN Atomic Energy Commission is formed to monitor member nations; after a referendum in Italy, the king abdicates, Italy becomes a republic and de Gasperi becomes head of state; xerography (photocopying) is invented by Chester Carlson; Dr Benjamin Spock writes *Baby and Child Care*, the "baby boom" reference book.

1947: British coal industry is nationalized; *The Diary of Anne Frank* is published by Anne's father, the only member of the German-Jewish Frank family to survive the Holocaust; Burma proclaims its independence; Paris Peace treaties signed; the Dead Sea Scrolls, dating from about 22 BC to AD 100, are discovered in Wadi Qumran, Palestine; American Chuck Yeager flies the first airplane at supersonic speeds; the transistor is invented by Bell Telephone Laboratory scientists; the UN divides Palestine, which is under British mandate, into a Jewish and an Arab state (Nov. 1947) and the British withdraw six months later; India gains independence from Great Britain and is partitioned into India and East and West Pakistan.

1948: Gandhi is assassinated by a Hindu opposing his tolerance of Muslims; a Communist coup d'état takes place in Czechoslovakia (Feb. 25); the Marshall Plan providing $17 billion in aid for Europe is passed by the US Congress; Winston Churchill chairs the Hague Congress for European unity; the Jewish state of Israel is proclaimed with Chaim Weizmann as president and David Ben-Gurion as premier (May 14); neighbouring Arab states declare war (1948–49) on Israel but by the end of the conflict Israel succeeds in increasing its territory; the Berlin airlift by the west begins after the USSR imposes a land and water blockade (1948–Sept. 1949); bread rationing ends in Britain; the World Council of Churches is organized in Amsterdam; American biologist Alfred C. Kinsey writes *Sexual Behavior in the Human Male*; the first World Health Assembly meets in Geneva; the first port radar system is installed in Liverpool, England.

1949: Tianjin, China, falls to the Communists, Chiang Kai-shek resigns as president of China, and removes his Nationalist forces to Formosa; the Communist People's Republic is proclaimed under Mao Tse-tung, with Chou En-lai as premier; the North Atlantic Treaty establishing a defence alliance (NATO) is signed by all parties (Belgium, Canada, Denmark, France, Iceland, Italy, Luxembourg, the Netherlands, Norway, Portugal, UK and US) in Washington; the Berlin blockade by the Soviet Union is lifted; the German Federal Republic (West Germany) comes into being with Bonn as its capital and Konrad Adenauer as Chancellor; republic of Eire is proclaimed with its capital in Dublin; Transjordan is renamed the Hashemite Kingdom of Jordan; the state of Vietnam, under Ho Chi Minh, is established at Saigon; civil war looms in Korea; the apartheid program of official racial discrimination is established in South Africa; the Democratic Republic is established in East Germany with Pieck as president; India becomes a federal republic with Pandit Nehru as prime minister; Indonesia gains sovereignty from Holland; the USSR tests its first atomic bomb; the US launches a guided missile to a height of 400 km, the highest altitude yet; George Orwell publishes *Nineteen Eighty-Four*.

1950: Communist China and Russia sign a treaty of friendship and mutual assistance, Britain also recognizes Communist China; 18 protesters are killed in anti-apartheid riots in South Africa; Vietnam, Laos and Cambodia gain independence from France; North Korea invades South Korea, capturing Seoul and forcing Pres. Syngman Rhee to flee; US Atomic Energy Commission begins work on hydrogen bomb; UN forces under Gen. Douglas MacArthur land in South Korea and push north of the 38th parallel, prompting Communist China to enter the war; US recognizes Vietnam, sends military supplies and instructors and signs pact for military assistance with Vietnam, Laos, Cambodia and France.

1951: North Korean forces reach the 38th parallel and capture Seoul: attempts to negotiate peace fail; Gen. MacArthur is replaced as commander in Korea for threatening massive retaliation against China; Winston Churchill forms the government in Britain; Remington Rand produces UNIVAC, the first large-scale, general-purpose computer; electricity is produced from atomic energy in the US; heart-lung machine devised by J. Andre-Thomas; penicillin and streptomycin available in US.

1952: Dwight D. Eisenhower is elected US president; Britain produces an atomic bomb; Elizabeth II becomes Queen of England; Egypt rocked by anti-British riots: premier resigns and the army seizes power; Mau-maus rebel in Kenya and government declares a state of emergency; first hydrogen bomb at Eniwetok Atoll in the Pacific; British Overseas Airways introduces the world's first jet passenger service from London to Rome; the first pocket-sized transistor radio is marketed by Sony in Japan.

1953: An armistice ending the Korean War is signed at Panmunjom; Soviet leader Joseph Stalin dies and is replaced by Malenkov; Sweden's Dag Hammarskjöld is elected UN secretary-general; the Soviet Union explodes a hydrogen bomb; Yugoslavia proclaims a new constitution and Marshall Tito becomes president; Egyptian generals establish a dictatorship and proclaim a republic; rebels from Vietnam attack Laos; Fidel Castro begins a campaign to overthrow Cuban dictator Fulgencio Batista; Ethel and Julius Rosenberg are executed after being convicted of passing American atomic secrets to the Soviet Union; Edmund Hillary and Tenzing Norgay become the first to scale Mt Everest; the first successful open heart surgery is performed in the US; researchers associate lung cancer with cigarette smoking.

1954: Vietnamese Communists defeat the French at Dien Bien Phu; racial segregation in public schools is banned by the US Supreme Court; Gammal Abdel Nasser becomes leader in Egypt; the US Senate censures Sen. Joseph McCarthy for launching a Communist witch-hunt; Canada and the US plan a joint radar defence system in the north (Distant Early Warning, DEW Line); the US *Nautilus* becomes the first nuclear-powered submarine; Dr Jonas Salk begins inoculating children against polio; the oral contraceptive pill is introduced in the US; the first successful kidney transplant is performed in the US; Roger Bannister becomes the first to run a mile in less than four minutes.

1955: Churchill resigns in Britain and is succeeded by Anthony Eden; Bulganin succeeds Malenkov as Soviet premier; eight east-European Communist bloc countries adopt the Warsaw Pact mutual defence treaty; West Germany joins NATO; border clashes between Israel and Jordan increase; Juan Perón is ousted by a military coup in Argentina; the first optical fibres are produced in Britain.

1956: Nasser elected Egyptian president; Egypt seizes control of the Suez Canal; Israeli troops invade Egypt and push towards the canal; British and French forces invade Egypt; a United Nations force arrives in Egypt, prompting a cease-fire; UN truce proposals for dispute between Jordan and Israel accepted; Soviet Communist leader Nikita Khrushchev denounces Joseph Stalin's "cult of personality"; Soviet tanks and troops crush an anti-Communist rebellion in Hungary; Sudan becomes a democratic republic; Pakistan becomes an Islamic republic; Martin Luther King, Jr, leads the campaign against racial segregation in the US South; trans-atlantic telephone service begins; the first computer programming language (FORTRAN) is developed in the US.

1957: Israeli troops withdraw from Egypt and the Gaza Strip comes under UN jurisdiction; UN reopens the Suez Canal; the space race begins as the USSR launches the first earth-orbiting satellite *Sputnik 1*; Belgium, France, Italy, Luxembourg, the Netherlands and West Germany sign the Rome Treaty to extend the common market established for the steel industry to all sectors of the economy; Pres. Eisenhower warns that the US will oppose Communist takeovers in the Middle East; Harold Macmillan leads the new Conservative government in Britain; John Diefenbaker becomes Canada's prime minister.

1958: Nikita Khrushchev becomes Soviet premier; Charles De Gaulle is elected president of France; Pope Pius XII dies and is succeeded by John XXIII; the first US space satellite, *Explorer I*, is launched; scientists in the USSR send two dogs into space and return them safely; Egypt and Syria form the United Arab Republic; Iraq's King Faisal is assassinated in a military coup; Alaska becomes the 49th US state.

1959: Fidel Castro overthrows Fulgencio Batista and establishes a Communist government in Cuba, expropriating sugar mills owned by the US; Soviet Prem. Khrushchev visits the US; American Vice-Pres. Richard Nixon visits the Soviet Union and has the "kitchen debate" with Khrushchev; the USSR sends a space probe to the moon and photographs its hidden side; the St Lawrence Seaway opens; the first commercial photocopier is introduced; the Dalai Lama flees Tibet; Hawaii becomes the 50th state of the US.

1960: An American U-2 spy plane is shot down over the USSR, prompting Soviet Prem. Nikita Khrushchev to cancel a Soviet-American summit meeting; 50 South African black protesters are massacred at Sharpeville; the Congo (Zaïre) gains independence from Belgium, sparking political instability and UN intervention; Cyprus becomes independent and Archbishop Makarios wins the first presidential election; Israeli agents capture former Gestapo chief Adolf Eichmann in Argentina and smuggle him to Israel for trial; Germany bans Neo-Nazi political groups; John F. Kennedy is elected US president; the first weather and communications satellites are launched in the US; the first heart pacemaker is developed.

1961: Soviet Major Yuri Gagarin becomes the first man in space; US breaks off diplomatic ties with Cuba; the US-backed Bay of Pigs invasion by Cuban exiles fails to topple Cuba's Fidel Castro; astronaut Alan Shepard becomes the first American in space with a sub-orbital flight; East Germany builds the Berlin Wall to stop its citizens from moving to the West; Kuwait becomes independent from Britain, which sends troops to counter Iraqi annexation threats; UN Sec.-Gen. Dag Hammarskjöld dies in a plane crash over Northern Rhodesia; UK applies for membership in the Common Market; the silicon chip is patented by Texas Instruments in the US.

1962: Fearing nuclear war, many North Americans build fallout shelters; John Glenn becomes the first American to orbit the earth; US establishes a military council in South Vietnam; the discovery of Soviet missile bases in Cuba leads to a US naval blockade; the Cuban Missile Crisis ends when Soviet leader Khrushchev agrees to dismantle the bases; UN troops quell rebellion in the Congo's Katanga province; Algeria, Uganda and Jamaica gain independence; the UN votes in favor of economic sanctions against South Africa; Pope John XXIII opens the Second Vatican Council which will modernize the Catholic church; the TV satellite *Telstar* is launched in the US.

1963: US Pres. John Kennedy is assassinated in Dallas and Lyndon Johnson succeeds him; the US, Soviet Union and Britain ban nuclear tests in the atmosphere; South Vietnamese leader Ngo Dinh Diem is assassinated following a military coup; US sends financial aid to South Vietnam; Zanzibar and Kenya gain independence; Dr. Martin Luther King leads the March on Washington seeking equality for US blacks; the "hot line" emergency communications link is established between the White House and the Kremlin; UK application to Common Market rejected after French opposition; British government rocked by the Profumo affair and the scandal forces the resignation of a senior minister; Pope John XXIII dies and is succeeded by Paul VI; archaeologists find the remains of a thousand-year-old Viking settlement in Newfoundland; the first liver and lung transplants are performed; Valentina Tereshkova becomes the first female astronaut.

1964: Harold Wilson becomes prime minister in Britain; Communist China announces it has developed an atomic bomb; the US escalates its military involvement in Vietnam following a reported North Vietnamese attack on US destroyers in the Gulf of Tonkin; the Palestine Liberation Organization (PLO) is formed; Zambia, Malta and Malawi become independent; the sultan of Zanzibar is banished and the country is declared a republic; Zanzibar unites with Tanganyika to form Tanzania; Northern Rhodesia declares independence and adopts the name Zambia; Leonid Brezhnev and Alexei Kosygin become Soviet leaders after Khrushchev is deposed; the first word processor is developed by IBM; the Beatles appear on the Ed Sullivan Show as "Beatlemania" sweeps North America.

1965: Ferdinand Marcos is elected president of the Philippines; Gambia and Rhodesia declare independence from Britain; Rhodesia's declaration is met by an oil embargo; a massive power failure blacks out most of the northeast US and eastern Canada; Pope Paul VI reaffirms the Catholic Church's opposition to birth control; a Soviet cosmonaut is the first to leave a spacecraft and "float" in space; two US Gemini capsules rendezvous in space.

1966: China's Red Guards demonstrate against western influences as Mao launches the Cultural Revolution; Indira Gandhi becomes India's prime minister; floods destroy art treasures in Florence, Italy; De Gaulle asks that NATO forces leave France; South African Pres. Hendrik Verwoerd is stabbed to death during a Parliamentary session; Lesotho and Guyana become independent; civilian protests against the Vietnam War escalate in the US; government in Ghana overthrown by military coup; an artificial heart is successfully implanted for the first time by Dr Michael De Bakey in Houston; the Soviet Union lands an unmanned spacecraft on the moon.

1967: Israel defeats Egypt, Syria and Jordan in the Six Day War and occupies the Sinai Peninsula, Golan Heights, Gaza Strip and the east bank of the Suez Canal; Expo 67 world fair opens in Montreal; a Soviet cosmonaut becomes the first reported casualty of the space race; US manned space flights are suspended after astronauts Grissom, White and Chaffee die in Apollo capsule fire; race riots erupt in US cities during the "long hot summer"; Canada celebrates its centennial; Dr Christiaan Barnard of South Africa performs the world's first successful human heart transplant: the patient survives for 18 days.

1968: The US intelligence ship *Pueblo* is captured by North Korea; US civil rights leader Martin Luther King is assassinated in Memphis; presidential candidate Robert Kennedy is assassinated in Los Angeles; Soviet troops crush liberal reform in Czechoslovakia; a treaty limiting military use of outer space is signed by 62 nations; university student protest movement spreads worldwide; Richard Nixon is elected US president; Pierre Trudeau becomes prime minister in Canada; peace talks between the US and North Vietnam begin in Paris; British colony of Mauritius becomes independent; Pope Paul VI issues an encyclical banning artificial birth control; three US astronauts circle the moon and return to Earth; *Surveyor 7*, uncrewed, lands on moon.

1969: US astronaut Neil Armstrong becomes the first man to walk on the moon as *Apollo 11* lands on the lunar surface; Yasir Arafat becomes PLO chairman; North Vietnamese leader Ho Chi Minh dies at age 79; the International Red Cross estimates that 1.5 million Biafrans have died, mostly by starvation, in the civil war with Nigeria; the US begins withdrawal of troops from Vietnam; Golda Meir becomes Israeli prime minister; the Concorde supersonic airliner makes its first flight; *Mariner* space probes transmit pictures of Mars back to earth.

1970: An earthquake kills about 30,000 people in Peru; US National Guardsmen kill four Kent State University students during anti-war protests at the campus and two students are killed at Jackson State following similar demonstrations; the first complete synthesis of a gene is announced by University of Wisconsin scientists; Arab commandos hijack three jets bound for New York from Europe; the civil wars in Nigeria end when Biafra capitulates to the federal government; the Front de Libération du Québec (FLQ) kidnaps British trade commissioner James Cross, and kidnaps and murders Quebec cabinet minister Pierre Laporte; the Canadian federal government responds to this "October Crisis" by invoking the War Measures Act, temporarily suspending civil liberties in Canada; Israel and United Arab Republic declare a 99-day truce in latest conflict; Gambia becomes a republic; a cyclone and tidal wave hit the offshore islands in the Ganges Delta of East Pakistan, leaving at least 168,000 people dead and about 1 million homeless.

1971: US planes bomb Cambodia, attacking Vietcong supply routes; fighting in Indochina spreads to Laos and Cambodia; the US conducts large-scale bombing raids against North Vietnam; mainland China is admitted to the United Nations; women are granted the right to vote in Switzerland; violence in Northern Ireland escalates after Britain introduces policies of internment without trial; India fights with the Bengali rebels against Pakistan; the US and USSR sign a treaty banning nuclear weapons on the ocean floor; Algeria seizes majority control of all French oil and gas interests within its borders but promises restitution; Idi Amin takes control over Uganda; Mao Zedong's heir-apparent, Lin Piao, dies in a mysterious air crash; the USSR soft-lands a space capsule on Mars; a Los Angeles earthquake kills 60 people and causes $1 billion in damage; the hormone that controls human growth is synthesized by Dr. Choh Hao Li at the University of California.

1972: The world's largest diamond (969.8 carats) is unearthed in Sierra Leone; US Pres. Richard Nixon meets Mao Zedong in China; Britain imposes direct rule on Northern Ireland and 467 people are killed in violence between Catholics and Protestants; Ceylon becomes a republic and changes its name to Sri Lanka; Philippine Pres. Ferdinand Marcos assumes near-dictatorial powers; a Soviet spacecraft soft-lands on Venus; more than 70 nations sign a treaty prohibiting the stockpiling of biological weapons; the US conducts its heaviest B-52 bombing raids of the war against North Vietnam but continues to withdraw troops, despite lack of progress at Paris peace talks; Arab terrorists massacre 11 Israeli Olympic athletes in a stand-off with West German police at the summer Olympic games in Munich; Richard Leakey and Glynn Isaac discover a 2.5-million-year-old human skull in northern Kenya; a US federal grand jury indicts seven persons, including two former White House aids, on charges of conspiracy to break into the Democratic national headquarters (in the Watergate building) in Washington, DC; Richard Nixon is reelected as US president.

1973: A cease-fire agreement, intended to end the Vietnam war, is signed in Paris; fighting in the Middle East between Israeli and Arab forces (Yom Kippur War) is resolved by a shaky ceasefire; Arab oil-producing states cut petroleum exports to the US, western Europe and Japan because of their support of Israel; the US Senate begins televised hearings on the Watergate scandal and it is revealed that Pres. Nixon had secretly taped all conversations in his White House office; US vice-president resigns in an unrelated scandal; US combat involvement in Indochina officially ends as American planes halt their bombing of Cambodia; typhoon "Nora" leaves 800,000 Filipinos homeless on the island of Luzon; Great Britain, Ireland and Denmark formally join the Common Market; the Bahamas are granted independence from Britain after three centuries of colonial rule; Chilean Marxist Pres. Salvadore Allende is overthrown by a CIA-backed military junta which claims Allende commits suicide; Shah of Iran nationalizes foreign-owned oil companies.

1974: Oil-producing nations boost their prices and worldwide inflation accelerates as economic growth slows to near zero in most industrialized nations; the government of China launches a new "Cultural Revolution" program aimed at condemning both the Chinese philosopher Confucius and former Defence Minister Lin Piao; West German Chancellor Willy Brandt resigns after a scandal involving an East German spy; the Tower of London and the British Houses of Parliament are bombed by the Irish Republican Army; Soviet Nobel prize-winning author Aleksandr Solzhenitsyn is stripped of his citizenship and exiled; Portuguese dictatorship ended by military coup and democratic reforms are initiated; rebels supported by Greece overthrow government in Cyprus: Turkish forces invade and take over much of the island; India explodes a nuclear device; Syria and Israel agree to the boundaries of a demilitarized zone in the Golan Heights and they begin troop withdrawals from the region; US Pres. Richard Nixon resigns to avoid impeachment by Congress for his coverup of the Watergate scandal; Gerald Ford is sworn in to replace Nixon; the US and Soviet Union reach a tentative agreement to limit the numbers of strategic offensive nuclear weapons and delivery vehicles; severe drought threatens millions in Africa; scientists warn of the effects of chloroflourocarbons (CFCs) on the ozone layer.

1975: Portugal's new constitution grants most power to the military; Angola, Cape Verde, São Tomé and Principe and Mozambique gain independence from Portugal; Turkish Cypriots declare the establishment of a separate state in the northern half of the island; US evacuates as North Vietnam seizes Saigon; Egypt reopens the Suez Canal, which had been closed since the 1967 Arab-Israeli war; a UN Security Council resolution calling for the imposition of an arms embargo against South Africa is vetoed by the US, Great Britain and France; Generalissimo Franco, Spain's chief of state, dies and is replaced by King Juan Carlos I; Peru's president is ousted in a military coup and replaced by a general; a democratic republic is proclaimed in Laos; Papua

New Guinea and Surinam become independent; civil war breaks out in Beirut between Christians and Muslims; rebels in Eritrea provoke battles with Ethiopian government.

1976: Chinese Prem. Chou En-lai and Communist Chinese leader Mao Zedong die within months of each other; riots against apartheid take place in the all-black township of Soweto outside of Johannesburg and spread to Cape Town in black townships and white areas; first reports surface that Libyan leader Col. Moammar Qaddafi is financing, training and arming a widespread terrorist network; the Parti Québécois wins power in Quebec's provincial election, raising the possibility of Quebec's secession from Canada; worldwide earthquakes kill an estimated 780,000 people; the Gang of Four (Mao Zedong's widow and three others) unsuccessfully attempt a coup in China; Venezuela nationalizes petroleum industry; president of Argentina overthrown by military junta; Spanish Sahara released from Spain's jurisdiction and divided between Morocco and Mauritania; North and South Vietnam reunited under Communist government; a military coup in Thailand topples the government; 9,000 refugees flee Angolan civil war.

1977: Cambodian refugees report economic and social disaster following the Communists' capture of Phnom Penh; Egypt severs diplomatic relations with Syria, Iraq, Libya, Algeria and South Yemen for attempting to disrupt its peace overtures to Israel; over 570 die in the world's worst aviation disaster when two Boeing 747s collide on the runway on the Canary Island of Tenerife; black South African leader Steven Biko dies in jail; French territories of Afars and Issa unite to form independent Republic of Djibouti; government of Pakistan is overthrown and martial law is imposed; Leonid Brezhnev becomes USSR president and Communist Party chief; Somalia-backed Eritrean guerrillas are stopped by Ethiopian army; Thailand government seized by military junta; Rhodesia's white government announces it will begin negotiations with black majority; cyclone in India leaves 20,000 dead and 2 million homeless; US unmanned spacecrafts *Voyager I* and *II* begin journeys to explore the outer solar system; the neutron bomb, which causes great loss of life but little property damage, is developed in the US.

1978: A Soviet-supported military junta takes power in Afghanistan and Soviet troops occupy the country; Lebanon is torn by Christian and Muslim militia activity as well as Palestinian guerrilla activity, and Arab League intervenes to restore peace; Israeli forces withdraw; Syria declares a unilateral cease-fire in and around Beirut, Lebanon; Egyptian Pres. Anwar Sadat and Israeli Prem. Menachem Begin sign peace accords, mediated by US Pres. Jimmy Carter; Shah Mohammed Riza Pahlevi of Iran imposes martial law to suppress anti-government demonstrations; leftist Sandinista guerrillas attempt to overthrow the government of Nicaraguan Pres. Anastasio Somoza; US establishes full diplomatic relations with Communist China; the first peaceful transfer of power takes place in Dominican Republic; Zaïre invaded by secessionist rebels: defence aid comes from other African nations, and France and Belgium after the massacre of Europeans; military junta seizes power in Honduras; army seizes government power in Bolivia; former Italian Prem. Aldo Moro is kidnapped and murdered by the Red Brigades, a revolutionary terrorist group; John Paul II (Karol Wojtyla) of Poland becomes the first non-Italian Pope in four centuries; the first "test-tube baby" (human baby conceived outside the womb) is born in England.

1979: Armed Islamic revolutionary followers of Ayatollah Khomeini overthrow the government of Iran and the Shah flees; students demanding the Shah's return to stand trial seize hostages at US embassy; a malfunction in the cooling system of a nuclear reactor at Three Mile Island in Pennsylvania, US, closes down the reactor and radiation escapes into the air; Conservative Margaret Thatcher becomes Britain's first female prime minister; a black government is formally installed in Rhodesia and its name is changed to Zimbabwe; China and the US establish formal commercial relations for the first time since 1949; Vietnamese army invades Cambodia and installs new government; St Lucia, St Vincent and the Grenadines become independent; coup in Grenada replaces government leader; president of Uganda, Idi Amin, overthrown; Egypt is expelled from Arab League after signing Camp David peace treaty; first elections for European Parliament held; the US-USSR SALT (Strategic Arms Limitation Treaty) Agreement is signed in Vienna; Iran nationalizes remaining privately-owned industries without compensation; sharp oil price increases contribute to high inflation worldwide; South Korean Pres. Park Chung Hee and his chief body guard are assassinated by a government official; emperor of Central African Empire overthrown; president of El Salvador is ousted by military coup.

1980: Soviet dissident Andrei Sakharov, a Nobel prize-winning physicist, is arrested in Moscow; human interferon, a promising natural disease-fighting substance, is made by gene splicing; Mt St Helens erupts in Washington, in a blast that sends debris 20 km up into the atmosphere and is heard over 300 km away; in a political comeback, Indira Gandhi wins a landslide victory in India's parliamentary elections; Soviet war in Afghanistan escalates as the US imposes an embargo on the sale of grain and high technology to the Soviet Union in response to the continued occupation of Afghanistan, and 50 nations boycott the Moscow Olympics in protest; Roman Catholic Archbishop Oscar Arnulfo Romero, an El Salvadoran reformer, is assassinated while saying mass; some 10,800 Cubans seek asylum in Peru's Cuban embassy and more than 125,000 Cubans escape by boat to the US; Liberian Pres. William Tolbert, Jr, is killed in a coup; military coup in Turkey unseats government; Zimbabwe gains independence from Britain; 350 Bengalis are massacred by native tribal people in India; black guerrillas successfully bomb two South African petroleum plants and a refinery; mass labour strikes in Poland force the government to allow independent trade unions, including Solidarity, led by Lech Walesa; 20 terrorist bomb attacks take place in France; the Iran-Iraq war begins when Iraqi fighter-bombers attack Iranian airfields and lay siege to its southwestern cities; 3,000 are killed in earthquakes centred in southern Italy; 20,000 die in two strong earthquakes in Algeria; *Voyager I* sends back the first pictures of Saturn; wreck of the *Titanic* found in North Atlantic.

1981: Aquired Immune Deficiency Syndrome (AIDS) is first recognized, in the US; in El Salvador, heavy fighting occurs between the government and leftist insurgents; the world's first reusable spacecraft, the Space Shuttle *Columbia*, is sent into space; clashes between Syrian troops and Christian militiamen in Lebanon are followed by Israeli bombing in support of Christian forces; artificial bone and skin are developed in the US; Pope John Paul II is shot and seriously wounded outside the Vatican by a Turkish terrorist; Israel is condemned worldwide after Israeli warplanes destroy an Iraqi atomic reactor near Baghdad; Irish prisoners in Belfast stage hunger strikes to force the British government to grant political prisoner status to Irish nationalist inmates, and some die; South African troops invade Angola in pursuit of guerrillas; Belize, formerly British Honduras, becomes independent from Britain; Pres. Anwar el-Sadat of Egypt is assassinated by Muslim extremists during a military parade; Israel formally annexes the Golan Heights; a five-day war between Ecuador and Peru erupts over a border dispute; Greece joins the European Community; Italian government rocked by revelation that nearly 1,000 key government, army and business leaders support a secret outlawed Masonic lodge; president of Bangladesh assassinated; Iranian president, prime minister and 29 others killed in bomb attack; 5,000 die when Indonesian ferry sinks in Java Sea; martial law is instituted in Poland in the face of continued labour unrest; the personal computer is introduced by IBM in the US.

1982: Argentina moves to reclaim Malvinas (the Falkland Islands) from UK by invading the territory; Britain defeats Argentina in the subsequent war; Canada gains the power to amend its own constitution from Britain; Israel withdraws from the Sinai and turns it over to Egypt, fulfilling their 1979 peace treaty; Israel invades Lebanon and the PLO leadership leaves Lebanon under UN protection; Lebanese Christian militiamen massacre Palestinians in refugee camps and Israel is accused of indirectly aiding the attack; Iran invades Iraq, but Iraq claims to have killed 27,000 Iranians in 18 days of battle; a series of IRA bombs explode in London, killing nine and wounding 51; western nations debate a proposed Soviet oil pipeline to western Europe; Lech Walesa, former leader of Solidarity, the outlawed Polish labour union, is freed after 11 months of imprisonment; military coups in Bangladesh and Guatemala force changes in government; Soviet leader Leonid Brezhnev dies and Yuri Andropov succeeds him; in Cambodia, support for Khmer Rouge grows as coalition against Vietnamese-backed government joined by Prince Sihanouk; up to 1,200 Afghan civilians and

Soviet soldiers die in a tunnel explosion caused by the collision of two trucks; the first permanent artificial heart is transplanted into Dr Barney B. Clark, 61, in Utah; Mexican volcano, El Chichón, erupts, blasting debris into the stratosphere.

1983: Klaus Barbie, former chief of the German Gestapo in Lyons, France, during WW II is deported to France from Bolivia to face charges of "crimes against humanity"; Soviet citizens and diplomats accused of espionage are expelled from France, Spain, the US and Britain; the US government is accused of having illegally aided Nicaraguan rebels; anti-government protests increase in Chile, governed by Gen. Pinochet; Ethiopia appeals for aid to 4 million victims of drought and famine; Sri Lankan Sinhalese and Tamil forces clash, killing hundreds and destroying the homes of thousands of others; 1,200 die in an earthquake in Turkey; martial law is formally lifted in Poland; the Organization of Petroleum Exporting Countries (OPEC) agrees to cut crude oil prices for the first time in its 23-year history; all 269 people aboard are killed when the Soviet Union shoots down a South Korean airliner, claiming that the plane had been on a spying mission and strayed into Soviet airspace; Benigno Aquino, opponent of Philippine Pres. Marcos, returns to Manila and is assassinated; 241 US Marines and sailors and 40 French paratroopers, members of a multinational peacekeeping force in Lebanon, are killed by suicide terrorists; the US and France support Chad's government against Libyan-supported guerrillas; Israeli withdrawal from Lebanon is followed by full-scale fighting between Lebanese ethnic and religious groups; US-led forces invade the small island of Grenada; US Cruise missiles in Europe are deployed in Britain despite Soviet and civilian opposition; white South Africans approve a new constitution granting limited political participation for persons of mixed race and Asians, but not for blacks, in a new tricameral legislature; Yasir Arafat and PLO guerrillas are evacuated from Lebanon to Tunis, under UN sponsorship; riots in Assam, India claim 5,000 lives and 300,000 refugees flee; the compact disc is introduced; after an 11-year journey, the *Pioneer 10* spacecraft leaves the solar system.

1984: Cholesterol is linked to heart disease following a 10-year study by US researchers; the Apple Macintosh with mouse enters the personal computer market; Konstantin Chernenko becomes Soviet leader following the death of Yuri Andropov; US astronauts fly free of the space shuttle *Challenger*, the first humans to do so without a tether; US and UN forces are withdrawn from Lebanon; French and American researchers, working separately, report that they have identified viruses which appear to be the cause of AIDS; Saudi, Greek and Swiss tankers are attacked by both Iran and Iraq in the Persian Gulf and Saudi Arabia shoots down two Iranian jets; hundreds die during a battle for the Golden Temple in Amritsar between Sikh militants and police in India; Indian Prime Min. Indira Gandhi is slain by two of her Sikh bodyguards in New Delhi and widespread violence follows; Daniel Ortega, Sandinista leader, wins in Nicaraguan elections; the international community sends aid to starving Ethiopians; in a secret operation, Israel airlifts 25,000 Ethiopian Jews (Falashas) out of the Sudan; Britain and China finalize an agreement on Hong Kong's future, guaranteeing its capitalist system for 50 years after it is turned over to China in 1997; a Union Carbide chemical plant leak kills 2,500 in Bhopal, India; the European Space Agency launches the largest telecommunications satellite in the world.

1985: South African police kill 18 blacks commemorating the Sharpville massacre in 1960, 19 more are killed while participating in a funeral procession and later the government declares a state of emergency; Daniel Ortega becomes president of Nicaragua; US president urges military aid to Nicaraguan opposition forces but only humanitarian aid is approved; Mikhail Gorbachev succeeds Konstantin Chernenko as Soviet leader and he opens disarmament talks with the US; Iraq turns back an Iranian offensive, allegedly killing 30,000 to 50,000 Iranians; Shiite Muslim hijackers release hostages after 17 days of captivity in Beirut, having demanded the release of hundreds of Shiites detained by Israeli forces; Argentine president imposes drastic economic measures to cut 1,010 percent inflation rate; top French officials are linked to the bombing of a ship owned by Greenpeace; two leading Soviet KGB officials defect to Britain and the US, where both name Soviet spies in the two countries; a cyclone and tidal waves hit Bangladesh, killing 10,000; a Mexican earthquake kills more than 7,000 and causes widespread destruction, leaving thousands homeless; border dispute between Mali and Burkina Faso leads to war but is eventually referred to International Court of Justice; Nicaragua suspends civil rights; four Palestinians seize the Italian cruise ship *Achille Lauro* off the coast of Egypt, murdering a wheelchair-bound American; Reagan and Gorbachev meet at the first superpower summit in six years; 95 Colombians die when 60 rebels seize the Palace of Justice in Bogotá and take more than 300 persons hostage; 60 die when Arab gunmen hijack an Egyptian jetliner, in an act allegedly backed by Libya's leader Col. Muammar Qaddafi; a Colombian volcanic eruption kills 20,000 people; Guatemala elects its first civilian president following three decades of military rule; Uruguay's military government replaced by civilian government; Sudanese and Ugandan presidents ousted by military coups; terrorists kill 20 people at two airports (in Rome and Vienna), both at the ticket counters of El Al, Israel's national airline; Live Aid rock concert in London, UK and Philadelphia, US raises over $60 million for African famine relief.

1986: Portugal and Spain join the European Community; Jean-Claude Duvalier, Haiti's "president for life," flees to France in the face of nationwide protest; Portugal elects its first civilian president in 60 years; Gorbachev calls for "radical reform" of Soviet economy and reshapes the leadership of the Communist party; Philippine Pres. Ferdinand Marcos flees to the US after allegations of electoral fraud; his opponent, Corazon Aquino, succeeds Marcos as president; Swedish Prime Min. Olof Palme is assassinated; former UN secretary general Kurt Waldheim is elected president of Austria; US planes bomb Libya citing retaliatory measures after missile attacks; radiation is spread following the meltdown of the Chernobyl nuclear power plant in the USSR; South African forces attack alleged African National Congress (ANC) bases in neighbouring Botswana, Zambia and Zim-babwe; the *New York Times* first links Panama's General Manuel Noriega with drug and arms trafficking; US president acknowledges a secret and illegal arms deal with Iran: the "Iran-Contra Affair" involving the US sale of arms in exchange for hostages is first reported in a Lebanese newspaper; The US space shuttle *Challenger* explodes one minute after liftoff and all seven crew members die instantly; *Voyager 2* spacecraft passes Uranus.

1987: Soviet leader Mikhail Gorbachev begins a campaign for openness (glasnost) and reconstruction (perestroika); Tamil separatists kill hundreds of Sri Lankans, mostly Sinhalese, and clash with government forces; German pilot Mathias Rust, 19, embarrasses Soviets when he lands his single-engine Cessna in Red Square, Moscow; Moscow's Communist Party chief, Boris Yeltsin, is dismissed after criticizing Soviet leader Gorbachev; South Africa withdraws its troops from Angola; an Iraqi warplane's missile kills 37 US sailors in the Persian Gulf, and the US escorts Kuwaiti oil tankers despite danger posed by the Iran-Iraq war; 402 Iranian pilgrims to Mecca die in battles with Saudi police; 24 nations sign a treaty to protect the ozone layer; Portugal and China agree that the Portuguese colony of Macao will be returned to China in 1999; stock market prices plunge worldwide; the Palestinian intifadah (uprising) begins against Israeli authorities in the Gaza Strip and West Bank, and thousands of protesters are imprisoned; Syrian troops enter Beirut in an attempt to bring a cease-fire; Lebanese prime minister dies in a bomb attack; a military coup ousts coalition government in Chad; 2,000 die in the Philippines when a ferry sinks.

1988: Nicaraguan contras and the Sandinista government reach a cease-fire agreement; the US and Soviet Union sign a treaty on intermediate-range nuclear forces (INF); Soviet troops begin to pull out of Afghanistan after a nine-year occupation; nationalist groups in Soviet-controlled Azerbaijan and Armenia clash; Colombian drug cartels defy government attempts to bring them to justice, and fight among themselves; a US navy warship accidentally shoots down a commercial Iranian airliner over the Persian Gulf, killing all 290 persons aboard; the Soviet communist party backs Gorbachev's plan for perestroika; Canadian and US governments ratify a free trade agreement, to take effect Jan. 1, 1989; Iran and Iraq agree on a cease-fire to end their eight-year war; Iraq uses poison gas on its Kurdish minority and razes Kurdish villages; Libya and Chad formally end their war; Thailand and Laos do battle in a brief border dispute; Ethiopia and Somalia end 11 years of disputes over borders with a peace treaty; Solidarity supporters stage widespread strikes in Poland; Vietnamese troops leave Kampuchea; a military coup in Burma causes a change in leadership; Yugoslavia's inflation rate tops 250%, ethnic Albanians in Kosovo province demand freedom from Serbian rule; Benazir Bhutto, daughter of a former Pakistani president, becomes prime minister of Pakistan; 270 people die when a bomb blows up a Pan Am jetliner over Lockerbie, Scotland; 25,000 Armenians die during an earthquake.

1989: Iran's Ayatollah Khomeini calls for the execution of UK author Salman Rushdie for blaspheming the prophet Mohammed; the Soviet Union holds historic multicandidate parliamentary elections and Boris Yeltsin emerges as Russian leader; Japanese Prime Min. Noboru Takeshita is toppled by financial scandal, Emperor Hirohito dies and is succeeded by his son; Chinese students lead more than one million in demonstrations for democratic reforms, but spreading unrest is checked by a government crackdown in Tiananmen Square that is suspected to have killed thousands; Hungary opens its border with Austria and moves toward political and economic reform; anti-Communist forces continue to battle the government in Afghanistan; fighting between Christians and Muslims in Beirut intensifies; 90 people die in ethnic violence in Soviet Uzbekistan; Poles participate in their first open election in 40 years and Solidarity wins a solid victory; the three Baltic states (Estonia, Latvia and Lithuania) protest Soviet domination; a Colombian presidential candidate is slain, prompting a renewed crackdown on illegal drug traffickers; thousands of East Germans flee to West Germany and the East German government proposes political reforms; Vietnamese forces withdraw from Cambodia; East German communist leader Erich Honecker is removed from power, he is later charged with corruption; thousands demonstrate in Czechoslovakia and force the communist government to resign, Vaclav Havel is elected president; the spaceship *Atlantis* is launched on a journey to Jupiter; East Germany opens the Berlin wall after 28 years and lifts visa and emigration restrictions; Panama's General Noriega annuls presidential elections after an opposition party victory, the US invades Panama and Noriega goes into hiding; Romanian Pres. Nicolae Ceausescu is overthrown and executed with his wife for genocide, abuse of power and theft; 80 nations sign an agreement to limit production of chorofluorocarbons (CFCs) to protect the ozone layer; Paraguay's president is toppled by a military coup; the Exxon *Valdez* runs aground in Alaska and spills thousands of litres of oil; *Voyager 2* spacecraft reaches Neptune.

1990: Panama's Manuel Noriega surrenders to US authorities; violence erupts in Soviet Azerbaijan as Azerbaijanis attack Armenians; Bulgaria and Yugoslavia switch to multiparty systems; Violeta Chamorro defeats Sandinista leader Daniel Ortega to become the Nicaraguan president; South African government lifts restrictions on opposition organizations and declares amnesty for political prisoners, black leader Nelson Mandela is freed after 27 years in prison; the US, France, Great Britain and the Soviet Union reach agreement on a reunited Germany; Lithuania proclaims its sovereignty and Soviet troops move in; Namibia gains independence from South Africa; newly-released Soviet documents prove Soviet secret police killed 15,000 Polish military officers in the Katyn forest massacre of 1940; the $1.5-billion Hubble Space Tele-scope is sent into space, but flawed light-gathering mirrors distort transmissions; Iran's worst earthquake kills 40,000; more than 1,400 Muslim pilgrims to Mecca suffocate in a stampede in an overcrowded tunnel; the Ukraine declares its sovereignty within the Soviet Union; the two Germanys reunite, merging their economic, legal and political systems; Czechoslovakia and Romania hold their first free elections in the postwar era (Aug. 2); Iraq invades Kuwait over disagreements regarding oil production levels and appears ready to invade Saudi Arabia; the UN passes sweeping trade and financial sanctions against Iraq, and aid and troops pour into Saudi Arabia; civil war in black South African townships kills hundreds; the first human gene therapy for disease is done by blood transfusion; South Africa bans racial discrimination in public places; following a political challenge from within her own party, British Prime Min. Margaret Thatcher resigns and is succeeded by John Major; Mozambique adopts a constitution allowing for a multiparty democracy; civil war in Chad ends with overthrow of president; a military coup in Bangladesh unseats the president; Soviet Pres. Mikhail Gorbachev proposes Union Treaty to restructure Soviet Union; Helmut Kohl elected Chancellor of Unified Germany; Lech Walesa elected president of Poland; African National Congress (ANC) holds first conference in South Africa in 31 years; Rev. Jean-Bertrand Aristide elected president of Haiti; Edward Shevardnadze resigns as Soviet foreign minister; Slovenia and Croatia initiate secession from Yugoslavian republic.

1991: Iraq ignores Jan. 15 deadline for withdrawal from Kuwait and Allied forces (including the US, Canada, Britain, France, Italy, Japan, Pakistan and members of the Arab League) launch a six-week air attack; Soviets suppress independence movements in Baltic republics; US and Italy begin rescue of foreigners trapped in Somalian civil war; limited integration of schools begins in South Africa and sweeping reforms of apartheid law are proposed; Allies launch ground assault on Iraqi forces and informal cease-fire follows; 1,200 killed in major earthquake in Pakistan and Afghanistan; Lithuanians vote to secede from Soviet Union; Estonia and Latvia vote for independence from the Soviet Union; violent protests held in Belgrade to topple Yugoslavian government; Kuwaiti government forced to resign in wake of failure to establish post-war order; UN cease-fire formally ends Gulf War (Apr.) and Kurds flee from Iraq; Soviet republic of Georgia votes for independence; cease-fire declared in Angola's 16-year civil war; Rajiv Ghandi assassinated during Indian national election campaign; Boris Yeltsin elected president of Russia; Mt Pinatubo volcano erupts in Philippines; Population Registration Act repealed in South Africa; fighting between Yugoslav military and Slovenian nationalists escalates; Soviet hardliners attempt a coup against Mikhail Gorbachev: its failure results in the dissolution of the Communist party; rebels oust Haitian Pres. Jean-Bertrand Aristide; Serbia and Croatia reach political settlement but civil war continues; peace accord signed in El Salvador, paving the way to end of 11-year civil war; failed coup in Soviet Union speeds disintegration of the country as Lithuania, Estonia and Latvia act to enforce their independence; civil war in Croatia escalates; warring factions in Cambodia sign peace accord; talks on new constitution begin in South Africa; rebels fighting in Somalia claim to have taken over Mogadishu and deposed the president; Gorbachev resigns as USSR formally dissolved and Commonwealth of Independent States (CIS) created; fighting escalates in Somalia; Slovenia and Croatia recognized as independent states by Germany; Islamic Salvation Front leads in Algerian elections; by year-end, cholera epidemic has killed 3,500 in Latin America and 12,500 in Africa.

1992: A Jan. military coup in Algeria gives power to a committee which cancels elections in progress; in June the Algerian president is assassinated and the defense minister assumes power. Brazil is the site of the Earth Summit (June), which sees 100 world leaders and 30,000 participants gather in Rio de Janeiro to discuss worldwide environmental protection; the country is rocked by political unrest in Aug., which results in the end of the presidency of President Fernando Collor de Mello over an influence-peddling and bribery scandal. The European Community's Maastricht Treaty is first rejected by Denmark (June), then ratified by Irish (June) and French (Sept.) voters, and the Italian senate (Sept.). Czechoslovakia's president, Vaclav Havel, resigns on July 20 and the Parliament of Slovakia declares its sovereignty. An earthquake on Oct. 12 leaves 300 dead and thousands injured in Egypt. The Uruguay round of the GATT (General Agreement on Tariffs and Trade) negotiations remains stalled over the issue of farm subsidies. Germany is plagued by riots and firebombings staged by right-wing extremists attacking foreign-born workers and refugees. Israel's national election results in a victory for the Labour Party and its leader, Yitzhak Rabin; in Aug., Rabin begins to hint that compromise in the area of peace and territorial disputes might be possible. Italy continues an anti-Mafia crackdown despite the assassination of two prominent judges and a police investigator. A ruptured petrol pipeline in Mexico's working-class district of Guadalajara is blamed for an explosion that kills 200 and injures nearly 1,500 in Apr. Peru's president, Alberto Fujimori, suspends sections of the country's constitution in Apr. and seizes power, citing a need to root out corruption and combat the combined forces of the Shining Path guerrillas and various drug barons. Russia's first experiments with free markets trigger soaring inflation and shortages. Civil war in Somalia brings 4.5 million of its people to the brink of starvation; by Aug. the UN brings in forces to ensure that food is distributed to the hungry, but is unable to restore order. The government in South Africa continues to work towards a power-sharing agreement with the black majority after receiving nearly 70% support in a Mar. whites-only referendum; in Sept. troops from the Ciskei homeland open fire on ANC supporters massed at the border and talks on democratic reform are again delayed. Citizens in Thailand take to the streets in a series of demonstrations that eventually force constitutional reforms and democratic elections. In the United Kingdom, the scandals of the royal family threaten the credibility of the monarchy; uncertainty over the fate of the Maastricht Treaty and pressure on UK currency force a withdrawal from the European Monetary System in Sept. and a devaluation of the UK pound. In the United States, riots in Los Angeles in late Apr./early May leave 42 dead; the US state of Florida is devastated by Hurricane Andrew (Aug.) which does an estimated $15 billion damage; on Oct. 12, the *Pioneer* spacecraft plunges into the scorching atmosphere surrounding the planet Venus and ends a 14-year space mission; in Nov., the Democrats, under Bill Clinton and Al Gore, are elected to a four-year term. Yugoslavia continues to disintegrate: the UN Security Council deploys peacekeepers in Jan.; Croatia and Slovenia are given diplomatic recognition by the European community as well as 20 other countries (including Canada); by Feb., Serbia and Montenegro reach agreement on a common state retaining the Yugoslav flag, anthem and joint parliament; in Mar., citizens of the republic of Bosnia-Hercegovina vote for independence; however, ethnic fighting over Bosnian territory escalates throughout the year amid charges of ethnic cleansing and atrocities, and a series of cease-fires that rarely hold for more than a few days; on Sept. 22, Yugoslavia (Serbia and Montenegro) is expelled from the UN General Assembly.

1993: Both sides in the Bosnia-Hercegovina conflict reject peace plans to settle the conflict. In Burundi an abortive Oct. coup leaves the President and 6 ministers dead before the army decides to back the existing government and order is restored. Despite opposition and active interference by the Khmer Rouge, 90% of registered voters cast their ballots in Cambodia's national election in May. One of the longest civil wars in Africa ends when the separation of Eritrea from Ethiopia is approved in a referendum. After 7 years of negotiation, the latest version of the GATT agreement is approved by 117 countries in late Dec. German military forces took part in missions outside its borders for the first time since WWII; the German parliament bows to right-wing pressures and places limits on their liberal immigration laws. Neither the OAS nor the UN is able to restore Haiti's deposed president Jean-Bertrand Aristide to power despite intense negotiations and increased blockades. On Sept 13, PLO leader Yasser Arafat and Israeli Prime Min. Yitzak Rabin meet in Washington to sign a peace agreement secretly negotiated in Norway; the agreement grants Palestinian autonomy over certain lands and recognized Israel's right to exist. The results of the June election in Nigeria are nullified by the long-time dictator, despite protests which include a 3-day general strike. A battle for power in the Russian parliament sees Pres. Boris Yeltsin strip Vice-Pres. Rutskoi of his powers and dissolve parliament to call Dec. elections; parliamentarians respond by barricading themselves in the building which is then surrounded by government troops; the seige is lifted when the insurgents surrender on Oct. 4; a new parliament is elected in Dec. and a new constitution is approved. Slovakia and the Czech republic declare independence on Jan 1. UK Prime Min. John Major and his Irish counterpart announce a tentative peace plan for Northern Ireland that would allow the people to decide their own fate. US troops in Somalia hands the mission to re-establish order over to a UN force made up of personnel from 20 countries and announces they will pull out at the end of Mar. 1994. In Sept. an agreement is reached in South Africa that paves the way for a multi-party transitional council that includes blacks; in Oct. the United Nations lifts economic sanctions; in Nov. a new constitution is approved and national all-race elections are scheduled; white rule ends officially in Dec. In the United States, a standoff outside the compound of a religious group in Waco Texas ends in tragedy when authorities stormed the area and the buildings erupt in flames. (Apr.); a rainy summer leads to record-breaking floods in nine states along the Mississippi River and in Oct. brush fires devaste six counties in California; in Nov. Pres. Clinton secures approval for NAFTA in the House of Representatives.

1994: Islamic fundamentalists in Algeria continue their fight to oust the government, targetting foreigners, journalists, and intellectuals. In Nov., government and rebel negotiators sign a truce and power sharing arrangement to end the civil war in Angola. In Feb. a Bosnian Serb mortar attack on a Sarajevo marketplace kills 66, injures 200 and prompts NATO to threaten punitive bombing if Serb guns are not pulled back from the city; in Aug. the Bosnian Serb rejection of a peace plan moves the government of Serbia to sever relations; in Dec. Bosnian Serbs kidnap UN peace keepers and use them as human shields to halt NATO airstrikes. In Brazil, radical steps are taken to curb inflation; the currency (cruzeiro) is scrapped and replaced by the real, and severe budget cuts are instituted. Increasing numbers of Cuban citizens flee the country in the face of the effects of the trade embargo. Cairo is the site of a UN-sponsored conference on population in September; in Nov., floods trigger the rupture of two oil storage tanks that unleash a wave of burning oil killing 500 and leaving thousands homeless in the town of Durunka (west of Cairo). A car ferry enroute from Estonia to Finland sinks, killing over 900 passengers and crew. In Dec. Algerian highjackers bring an Air France jet to Marseilles, intending to blow the plane up over Paris, commandos storm the plane, killing the highjackers and freeing the passengers. Throughout the year German officials seize illegal shipments of plutonium apparently smuggled out of the former Soviet Union. A US-led force lands in Haiti on Sept. 19, and president-in-exile Jean Bertrand Aristide returns to Haiti in Oct.. In Sept., an outbreak of pneumonic plague in the city of Surat, India sparks panic among local residents, as well as concern among national and international medical authorities. In Jan. a heavily-armed Jewish settler enters a mosque in Hebron on the West Bank and opens fire on Muslim worshippers; 40 Palestinians die and more than 250 are wounded in the riots that follow; throughout the year Islamic fundamentalists use suicide bombing in an effort to derail the peace talks. In May, Yasser Arafat and Israeli Prime Min. Rabin sign the peace accord that inaugurates Palestinian self-rule on the Gaza Strip and in Jericho; the PLO begins to create a government structure for the areas; in July, Jordan and Israel sign an agreement to normalize relations. Japan suffers a year of political uncertainty as a series of prime ministers are unable to maintain a coalition government. A string of comet fragments known as Shoemaker-Levy 9 collide with Jupiter between July 16-22, causing massive explosions in the planet's atmosphere. The government of North Korea reluctantly agrees to allows nuclear inspectors to visit the majority of their nuclear sites. Ruler Kim Il Sung dies as negotiations end; his son and successor Kim Jong Il appears to have a tenuous grip on power. A New Year's dayrebellion in Mexico sets the stage for a turbulent year—Zapatista rebels in the southern state of Chiapas demand land reforms; in Mar. Luis Colosio, the leading candidate in the national election, was gunned down at an outdoor rally; in Dec., the peso loses 40% of its value over 8 days and trade allies move to prop up the economy. Workers try to bring down the military government in Nigeria by staging a general strike that drags on for six weeks. In Northern Ireland, the political wing of the IRA announces a "complete cessation of military operations" in Sept., paving the way for peace talks. In Oct., economic reforms lead to a steep plunge in the value of the ruble and widespread protests over unemployment; a leaky pipeline spills a massive quantity of oil onto the fragile permafrost and into surrounding rivers; in Dec., 40,000 Russian troops invade the rebel area of Chechnya to end the region's drive for independence. Plagued by racially motivated skirmishes at the beginning of the year, Rwanda dissolves into an ethnic blood bath after the death of the president in a plane crash; tens of thousands of Rwandans, mostly Tutsi, die at the hands of the rival Hutus in a killing spree that lasts for months; Tutsi-led forces eventually regain control of the country and thousands more flee to refugee camps in neighbouring countries to escape feared reprisals. In Somalia, factional fighting reignites as both the US and the UN withdraw the forces policing the area. All race elections are held for the first time in Apr. 26-28, and Nelson Mandela is elected president; South Africa is given full membership to the United Nations in June. In the US, California is rocked by a major earthquake in Jan., in Feb., Aldrich Ames, a mid-level officer in the CIA, is exposed as a spy operating for Moscow since the mid-1980s. By June, the US dollar was in a record-breaking dive. North and South Yemen erupt in civil war as the conservative north and formerly Marxist areas of the south try to gain supremacy; by July, the southern separatists are routed.

1995: The Algerian civil war continued, with Muslim extremists stepping up attacks on foreigners, collaborators, journalists, women who adopted modern ways of life and the families of government officials. In the Atlantic region, a harsh hurricane season brought death and destruction to the Caribbean in the latter part of the year. In the Bosnian war, the blockade of Sarajevo continued for much of the year as truces failed to hold. In May NATO launched two days of airstrikes to break the impasse and Bosnian Serbs seized nearly 400 UN peace keepers; the hostages were slowly freed throughout May and June. In July Bosnian Serbs overran the UN safe areas of Srebrenica and Zepa and cleared the territory of Muslims. By August, NATO had resumed airstrikes in response to the shelling of a marketplace in Sarajevo. The bombing missions continued in Sept. to force the Bosnian Serbs to withdraw from positions around Sarajevo; a ceasefire was finally inaugurated in October. In November, negotiators for all sides in the Bosnian conflict met at the Wright-Patterson Air Force Base outside Dayton, Ohio, for a three-week effort to hammer out a workable peace plan. By Dec. US and British military personnel were arriving in Bosnia to implement the agreement. Burmese officials freed political dissident Aung San Suu Kyi from house arrest in July. In Burundi, murders by members of rival factions raised fears of Rwandan-style massacres; thousands of Rwandan refugees fled to Tanzania to escape the violence. Canada ignited a worldwide protest against EU overfishing when it seized a Spanish fishing vessel at gunpoint on the Grand Banks. In October, the country stepped back from the brink as the referendum on separation held in Quebec resulted in a very narrow victory for the federalists. The UN's Fourth World Conference on Women was held in China in September. In Croatia, Pres. Tudjman allowed the UN peacekeeping mandate to lapse; in August, Croatian troops regained the territory in Krajina that had been lost to Croatian Serbs in 1991. France conducted three nuclear tests around the Muroroa Atoll in the South Pacific during the year, despite international protests and local demonstrations. Haitians went to the polls on Dec. 17 in the first election since exiled Pres. Jean-Bertrand Aristide was returned to power. In Ireland, a bitter campaign over the issue of lifting the ban on divorce ended in narrow approval for liberalizing the laws in November. Israel and the Palestinians struggled with the peace process throughout the year, postponing deadlines as suicide bomb attacks in Israel threatened to derail the process altogether. In October, Israeli forces began to withdraw from parts of the West Bank in accordance with an agreement on Palestinian self rule. On Nov. 4, a 25-year-old militant Jewish law student shot and killed Israeli Prime Min. Yitzak Rabin. On Jan. 17, the port of Kobe in Japan was struck by an earthquake measuring 7.2 on the Richter scale; 5,000 residents were killed, 25,000 were injured and 300,000 were left homeless. Also, in Japan a March nerve-gas attack during Monday morning rush hour in a Tokyo subway left 10 dead and 5,500 injured; two more incidents took place in April in Yokohama; police traced the attacks to a religious cult known as Aum Shinrikyo and arrested its leader Shoko Asahara. The Galileo space probe arrived at Jupiter in December after a 3.7 billion km trip that took six years. Mexico spent the early part of the year grappling with a financial crisis that saw the peso fall to record lows; the US engineered a financial bail-out that was conditional upon stringent austerity measures and the reform of the country's electoral process; loan repayments began in October, ahead of schedule. In November, the military government in Nigeria condemned environmentalist and activist Ken Saro-Wiwa and eight others to death; the sentence was carried out on Nov. 10. Peru and Ecuador engaged in a month-long border war in the early part of the year. In Poland, long-time president Lech Walesa was defeated by a former communist who promised to continue western-style reforms in November. Throughout the year Russia was unable to subdue guerrillas in the breakaway republic of Chechnya; bombing raids on the capital of Grozny reduced the city to rubble. A 7.5 (Richter scale) earthquake struck the Sakhalin Island in Russia's far east in May, killing nearly 2,000. UN forces pulled out of Somalia after a two-year attempt to restore order amid drought, starvation and clan warfare. Sri Lanka's civil war with Tamil rebels continued as the Tamils refused to consider peace proposals. In Singapore, at the 232-year-old Barings Bank, a rogue trader's speculation on the currency market cost the bank more than $1 billion; Barings collapsed.

In the US, on the anniversary of the FBI attack on the Branch Davidians in Waco, Texas, a bomb exploded outside a government building in Oklahoma City. One hundred and sixty-seven were killed and over 400 injured; police arrested Timothy McVeigh, a Gulf War veteran linked to American militia groups. On Oct. 16, Nation of Islam minister Louis Farrakhan rallied nearly a million black men in Washington. The Venezuelan government took over two insolvent banks and covered more than $330 million in bad debts; 16 banks had failed in the past 18 months and accumulated debts of $7 billion paralysed the national economy. In Zaire, the deadly Ebola virus struck Kikwit in May; over 100 people died of incurable fever.

1996: The Algerian civil war continued throughout the year. In Bosnia, prisoners were exchanged, residents were evacuated and Sarajevo was handed over to the Muslim-Croat federation. Bosnian Serb leader Radovan Karadzic withdrew from public life in July. In Sept. elections were held for the Serb Republic and the Muslim-Croat Federation. Bulgaria's currency collapsed in May; hyperinflation paralysed the economy. Rwandan refugees were forcibly repatriated in mid-July; days later the Tutsi-dominated army seized power in a coup. Borders closed as Rwanda's neighbours proclaimed sanctions; the new president pledged a return to democracy after three years. On Aug. 3, top generals of the Khmer Rouge opened amnesty negotiations with the Cambodian government to end decades of bloodshed. Hurricane Bertha hit the Caribbean islands and eastern US in July. In May, unrest in Tibet increased as Chinese authorities forbade demonstrations supporting the Dalai Lama. On July 29, the Chinese tested an underground nuclear device and then declared a moratorium on future testing. On Feb. 24, Cuban fighter planes shot down two civilian US aircraft for violating Cuban air space. An Arab summit held in Cairo in June called for Israeli withdrawal from Palestinian territory, including Arab Jerusalem. France's former Pres. Francois Mitterand died Jan. 8. France conducted a nuclear test on Jan. 27; on Jan. 29, Pres. Chirac announced a permanent end to nuclear tests and cancelled the last two. Haiti got a new president, René Préval, on Feb. 7; the UN extended the mandate of its mission at the end of Feb. and Canada took command as the US prepared to pull out. In India, general elections in Apr. and May failed to produce a clear winner; a ruling coalition finally won a vote of confidence on June 12. Yassir Arafat was sworn in as president of the Palestinian Council's executive in Feb.; on Apr. 24 the PLO revoked the charter clauses that called for the destruction of Israel and the waging of war against the Jewish state. In Israel, a May election resulted in victory for Benjamin Netanyahu and the Likud party. In Sept., an archaeological tunnel bordering on Islam's third-holiest site, the Al Aqsa Mosque, was opened, touching off a wave of violent protest. The Bank of Tokyo and Mitsubishi Bank merged on Apr. 1 to create the world's largest bank. On May 13, the World Food Programme and the FAO issued a joint alert over food shortages in N. Korea. In S. Korea, two former presidents were convicted of accepting bribes during their tenures. In Sept., a N. Korean submarine ran aground in S. Korea; most crew members died on S. Korean soil. On Apr. 6, the Liberian capital city of Monrovia was torn by factional fighting; UN troops took control of Monrovia on Apr. 21. In Nov., Pakistan's president dismissed Prime Min. Benazir Bhutto's government and called for elections in the wake of corruption allegations. In Peru, Tupac Amaru guerrillas took diplomats hostage for several months. In Russia, a ceasefire with Chechnya's rebels held in Sept. In June, Pres. Yeltsin narrowly won elections, and a run-off election in July confirmed the victory. In Rwanda, clashes between Hutu and Tutsi soldiers occurred in Jan.; by Nov. thousands of displaced Hutus (many of whom had been away since 1994) were returning home from Zaire. Serbian Pres. Milosevic ordered the results of local elections annulled in Nov. when opposition parties won; outraged citizens protested well into 1997. On Mar. 29, leaders of Sierra Leone's military government transferred power to a democratically elected government. South Africa's main political parties agreed on a new constitution on May 8; on May 9, F.W. de Klerk took his National Party out of the government coalition. In Spain, Basque separatists detonated four bombs during July, killing at least 35 and prompting demonstrations against the ETA. In the UK, the IRA ended a 17-month cease-fire in Feb.

with three bombings; attacks continued through June. On Mar. 13, a gunman killed 16 kindergarten children and their teacher in Dunblane, Scotland, before killing himself. A "mad-cow disease" scare prompted the banning of British beef by the EC and the eventual destruction of thousands of cattle and embryos to contain the problem. Northern Ireland's July marching season saw renewed violence. In the US, outrage over the Feb. downing of two US civilian aircraft by Cuba cleared the way for the Helms-Burton law. On Apr. 3, an arrest was made in the 17-year-old Unabomber case. The Summer Olympics opened in Atlanta on Jul. 19. US Pres. Clinton was re-elected in November.

1997: In Afghanistan's civil war, the Taliban took control of Kabul and other key cities; by year-end they had imposed strict Islamic rule in many areas. Albania experienced a financial crisis in Jan. which triggered a rebellion in the south. An election in June led to the defeat of the government and order was gradually restored. In Algeria, over 2,000 were killed in nearly 50 massacres as suspected Islamic terrorists continued their war against the government; a June election gave the military-backed regime a clear majority. The worst flooding of the century hit Central Europe in July, leaving hundreds dead as dams broke and power failed. In Bulgaria, anti-government strikes and political paralysis in Jan. led to economic collapse. In Cambodia, in July, Second Prime Min. Hun Sen seized control of Phnom Penh while his co-prime minister was out of the country. Hun Sen later crushed forces loyal to his former co-prime minister and drove them out of the country. Chinese premier Deng Xiaoping died on Feb. 19. In Nov., Egyptian terrorists killed 68 people in Luxor. On July 1, the British colony of Hong Kong returned to China, ending a 99-year lease agreement. In late Oct., Hong Kong's stock market dropped over 10% in four days; global markets followed suit. Indonesia's slash-and-burn farming techniques and a delayed rainy season blanketed much of the country with smoke and threatened the health of more than 20 million people. Iraqi leader Saddam Hussein confronted the U.S. in Nov. by barring American members of a UN weapons-inspection team; Allied mobilization prompted Hussein to allow the inspectors to continue their duties. In Japan, Yamichi Securities, one of the largest brokerages in the country, shut down on Nov. 24 amid the collapse of stock prices and a payoff scandal; the closure left US$24 billion in debts. In Dec., representatives from 150 nations met in Japan to devise controls on greenhouse gases to slow ozone damage and global warming. Liberia's former rebel Charles Taylor, a key figure in the country's seven-year civil war, won 75% of the presidential vote and a legislative majority in the country's general election on July 24. In Pakistan, the Muslim League defeated former Prime Min. Bhutto's party in national elections on Feb. 3. In Russia, Pres. Boris Yeltsin was hospitalized on Jan. 8 with double pneumonia; the Duma began discussing Yeltsin's impeachment. On Apr. 14, the World Bank agreed to loan US$6 billion over two years if Russia's economic reforms continued. Serbian protesters continued to demand that the results of the Nov. election be respected; by Feb., parliament recognized the election results and allowed the victors to take office. In Sierra Leone, in June, the third military coup in six years ended the fledgling civilian government. In Thailand, an economic crisis in Mar. forced the government to halt trading in all bank and financial stocks. The crisis continued as the government propped up the baht, and Asian neighbours offered loans to help maintain foreign currency reserves. The Philippines, Malaysia and Indonesia devalued their currency, and the IMF offered aid throughout the region in exchange for economic reforms. The Turkish army wiped out Kurdish camps in Northern Iraq. In Scotland, embryologist Ian Wilmut and four colleagues at Roslin Institute near Edinburgh revealed that they had cloned a sheep. In Nevada, British pilot Andy Green broke the sound barrier on Oct. 13 by driving a jet-propelled automobile at 1,229.775 kph. In the UK, Tony Blair and the Labour Party ended 18 years of Conservative rule on May 1 in general elections. Historic peace talks in Northern Ireland began on Oct. 7 as all parties, including Sinn Fein, tried to end violence. British Prime Min. Tony Blair and Sinn Fein leader Gerry Adams met at Downing Street on Dec. 11 to discuss Northern Ireland's peace–the first such meeting since the 1920s. Viewers around the world watched pictures sent back from Mars by the Pathfinder mission in July. On Oct. 6, the space shuttle Atlantis docked with the

Mir space station. On Mars, Pathfinder fell silent. On Oct. 15, the space probe Cassini was launched for Saturn. In Zaire, Pres. Mobutu fled from an advancing rebel army on May 16; rebel troops subsequently entered Kinshasa, Laurent Kabila took power, and the country was renamed Democratic Republic of the Congo.

1998: In Jan., China ordered the slaughter of over one million poultry in Hong Kong to end the threat of the chicken flu. In Iran, Pres. Khatami called on the US on Jan. 7 to resume formal relations with his country for the first time since 1979. An earthquake measuring 6.2 on the Richter scale killed 50 and left 540,000 homeless in China's Hebei province. The last US shuttle to Mir was launched Jan. 22 to aid the aging space station. Pope John Paul II visited Catholics and Fidel Castro in Cuba from Jan. 21-25. US Pres. Clinton gave a deposition in the Paula Jones case (Jan. 17) and denied his sexual relationship with Monica Lewinsky (Jan. 26). On Jan. 29, tobacco executives acknowledged that smoking endangered health and agreed to a US$368.5 billion settlement in exchange for immunity from further lawsuits. In Feb., an earthquake in Afghanistan destroyed 15,000 homes and killed an estimated 5,000 people. In Bangladesh, a 22-year-old war in the southeastern part of the country ended when tribal fighters surrendered their weapons for more autonomy for their Buddhist culture. In China, Zhu Rongji was elected premier in Mar. In India, the BJP built a coalition of over 20 parties to form a government in the 545-seat parliament (Mar. 11). On Mar. 19 A.B. Vijpayee was sworn in as prime min. On Mar. 23, Russian Pres.Yeltsin fired Prime Min. Viktor Chernomyrdin and his entire cabinet; Yeltsin then appointed Sergei Kiriyenko as acting prime min. In Mar., in Sri Lanka, suicide bombers using boats packed with explosives rammed a navy convoy transporting troops to the Jaffna peninsula; two vessels went down and at least 40 soldiers died. Mid-month, two bombs exploded in Colombo, killing 32 people. On Mar. 24, two boys, aged 11 and 13, gunned down four classmates and a teacher in a shooting that wounded 10 others in Jonesboro, Arkansas. The drug company Pfizer released Viagra in the US. On Mar. 24, fighting erupted again between ethnic Albanians in Kosovo and Serbian police.

Earlier in the month, a 10-day police action against the Kosovar Liberation Front caused 100 deaths of mostly elderly people, women and children. On Apr. 10, after 22 months of talks, the governments of Ireland and Britain and representatives of the warring factions agreed to permit a referendum on the future of Northern Ireland and the creation of a self-governing Northern Ireland assembly. While the IRA retained its initial ceasefire, dissident groups began a campaign of violence. On Apr. 15, Pol Pot, the Khmer Rouge leader responsible for killing more than two million Cambodians in the 1970s, died. On Apr. 19, 34 leaders from the Western Hemisphere met in Santiago, Chile, to begin talks for a free-trade zone that would include all countries in the hemisphere except Cuba. On May 10, Sinn Fein members voted to support the Easter peace agreement and allow its members to sit in Northern Ireland's new assembly. By the end of the month, most Irish in the north and south supported the Easter pact. On May 12, Suharto's troops fired on student protesters in Indonesia; on May 18, a few hundred students occupied the parliament buildings and thousands of others massed outside. On May 21, Suharto resigned; V. Pres. B.J. Habibie was sworn in as his successor. On May 22, the military peacefully cleared the parliament buildings of 2,000 student occupiers. In May, India and Pakistan exchanged artillery fire along the Kashmiri border. On May 11, India exploded three nuclear devices in underground tests. Two more were detonated on May 13. On May 28, Pakistan announced the successful underground test of five nuclear devices. Ethnic turmoil exploded in Kosovo, an Albanian-dominated province in Yugoslavia, and spilled into Albania. In June, Ethiopia and Eritrea fought a border war. NATO warplanes flew over Kosovo to end Serbia's four-month battle with insurgents that had created 65,000 refugees. In July, monsoons in Bangladesh stranded eight million people near the country's capital. David Trimble, leader of the Ulster Unionist Party, was selected first minister of the new Northern Ireland assembly. Former Italian prime min. Silvio Berlusconi was sentenced for bribing tax inspectors. In Nigeria, Gen. Abubakar released hundreds of prisoners and abolished three discredited electoral bodies. On July 17, Papua New Guinea was devastated by tidal waves that killed at least 3,000 people and left another 3,000 missing. In Russia, as economic woes mounted, the IMF and other foreign lenders offered a US$22.6 billion rescue package on July 13. The remains of Tsar Nicholas and his family were interred in St. Petersburg on July 17. By mid-July, UN officials said 2.4 million Sudanese faced starvation because of a two-year-drought and a 15-year civil war. In Florida more than 120,000 people were evacuated from the paths of wildfires. In mid-July, 110 were killed in Kosovo as Kosovar separatists tried to enter the territory from Albania and clashed with the Yugoslav army. Yugoslavia's army tried to recapture the southern territory from rebels on July 24; it ended in early Aug. In the United States, the Dow Jones nosedived in late July; by Aug. 7, it had lost 10% of its value. Stock markets around the world followed suit. On Aug. 7, a car bomb exploded outside the US embassy in Kenya; 263 were killed and over 4,500 were injured. A second car bomb exploded outside the US embassy in Tanzania. Monica Lewinsky, a former White House intern, testified before a grand jury that she had sex with US Pres. Clinton between Nov. 1995 and May 1997–a relationship Clinton had denied. On Aug. 15, an IRA splinter group that refused to support the ceasefire in Northern Ireland detonated a car bomb in Omagh that killed 29 and injured over 220; all supporters of peace condemned the bombing. On Aug. 15, the Iraqi national assembly voted to suspend co-operation with the UN weapons inspectors to protest over eight years of economic sanctions. On Aug. 20, the US military fired missiles at the camp of suspected terrorist Osama bin Laden in retaliation for the bombing of its embassies in Africa. China suffered its worst flood season in 50 years; 3,600 were killed and over 1.4 million were displaced. By Aug. 27, massive flooding in northern and eastern India stranded some 1.5 million people. As food prices hit record highs, Indonesian students took to the streets in August to demand the resignation of B.J. Habibie. In Russia, Pres. Yeltsin fired his entire cabinet and reappointed Viktor Chernomyrdin as acting prime min. On Aug. 23, the Duma refused to confirm the appointment; on Aug. 29, Yeltsin agreed to give up some powers for the confirmation. Later, Pres. Yeltsin proposed and the Duma confirmed Yevgeni Primakov as prime min. In Sept., Hurricane Georges hit the Dominican Republic, Haiti and other islands killing over 200 people and leaving hundreds of thousands homeless. In Liberia, civil war flared up in the capital; thousands fled during the fighting. Floods in the southern part of Mexico left 1.2 million without homes or food. On Sept. 11, US Pres. Clinton admitted his affair with Lewinsky; the admission prompted calls for his impeachment because he had lied to the public. Special Prosecutor Kenneth Starr delivered his report on Clinton to the US Congress on the same day; his report was posted on the Internet. On Sept. 27, one of Europe's longest serving leaders, German Pres. Helmut Kohl, was defeated at the polls by Social Democrat Gerhard Schroeder. On Oct. 16, John Hume and David Trimble won the 1998 Nobel Peace Prize for their efforts in N. Ireland. On Oct. 29, South African Pres. Mandela received the report of the Truth and Reconciliation Commission on crimes committed during apartheid. On Oct. 16, British authorities arrested Chile's former dictator Augusto Pinochet in London. On Oct. 8, the US House of Representatives asked its judiciary committee to begin an impeachment inquiry against Pres. Clinton for his role in the Monica Lewinsky affair. On Oct. 15, Pres. Clinton began talks with Israeli Prime Min. Binyamin Netanyahu and Palestinian Pres. Yasser Arafat in Wye, Md.; the talks broke a 19-month impasse in Israeli-Palestinian relations over the West Bank. Yugoslav Pres. Milosevic and the West negotiated Yugoslavia's troop withdrawal from Kosovo. On Oct. 17, the Albanian Kosovo Liberation Army ended a ceasefire with the Serbs. On Nov. 1, Hurricane Mitch ended after six days of devastation in Central America, killing more than 10,000 people and leaving about two million homeless. On Nov. 22, 11 EU governments launched "The New European Way," a manifesto for a socialist Europe. On Nov. 6, the USA agreed to send US$600 million in food and food credits to Russia after a poor harvest; the EU agreed to send another US$500 million in food aid. On Nov. 7, US Sen. John Glenn, 77, the oldest person to enter space, and the crew of the US space shuttle *Discovery* returned to earth after nine days in orbit. On Nov. 3, the results of US mid-term elections helped the Democratic Party. On Nov. 13, Pres. Clinton agreed to pay US$850,000 to Paula Jones to settle her sexual harassment suit. On Nov. 19, Independent Prosecutor Kenneth Starr appeared before the house judiciary committee to present his case against Pres. Clinton in the Lewinsky affair. On Nov. 6, the first unarmed international peacekeepers arrived in Kosovo under the command of the Organisation for Security and Co-operation in Europe (OSCE). In Algeria, terrorist violence surged across the country before Ramadan. On Dec. 16-20, the US and UK carried out air strikes to "degrade" Iraqi Pres. Saddam Hussein's military forces; the attacks, prompted by Iraq's refusal to cooperate with UN weapons inspectors, lacked the support of the UN Security Council. On Dec. 6, South African Pres. Mandela ruled out a general amnesty for crimes committed during apartheid but repeated that amnesties were possible for those who applied for them. On Dec. 18, the US House of Representatives approved two articles of impeachment against Pres. Clinton.

1999: On Jan. 1, the euro, the new European single currency, was launched in 11 countries. In Pakistan, a bomb intended for Prime Min. Nawaz Sharif killed four people on Jan. 3 near Lahore; Sharif and his family escaped. In Sierra Leone, fighting between Pres. Kabbah's troops and the Revolutionary United Front caused about 3,000 deaths in Freetown. On Jan. 3, an American rocket carrying the *Polar Lander* spacecraft took off for Mars. On Jan. 23-24, the International Olympic Committee in Switzerland, facing allegations of corruption in its selection of host cities, suspended six of its members. In late Jan., four IOC members resigned. On Jan. 19, US Pres. Clinton delivered his sixth State of the Union Address, concentrating on social security, education and health care. In Yugoslavia, the bodies of 45 Albanians were found in Racak (Jan. 15); NATO and OSCE officials blamed Serbs for the massacre; the Serbs denied responsibility. In Feb., Queensland, Australia, suffered its worst floods in a century. On Feb. 6-23, under threat of NATO air strikes, Yugoslavian Serbs and Albanian Kosovars met in France for unsuccessful talks aimed at ending the fighting in Kosovo. On Feb. 14, about 200,000 ultra-Orthodox Jews prayed near the Supreme Court in Jerusalem to protest the court's alleged religious persecution of them. On Feb. 15, Turkish authorities captured Abdullah Ocalan, leader of the Kurdistan Workers' Party in Kenya; Ocalan's return to Turkey sparked Kurdish protests around the world. On Feb. 22, George Robertson, the UK's secretary of state for defence, said the British army had destroyed its stock of two million landmines. On Feb. 12, the US Senate acquitted Pres. Clinton of perjury and obstruction charges stemming from the Paula Jones sexual harassment case and the Lewinsky scandal. On Mar. 16, the executive 20-member European Commission resigned en masse after an independent committee set up by the European Parliament found the commission guilty of fraud, nepotism and mismanagement. US and UK aircraft hammered Iraqi air defences while patrolling "no-fly zones." Periodic air strikes continued throughout 1999. On Mar. 9-11, Iranian Pres. Mohammad Khatami became the first Iranian leader to visit the West since 1979 during a visit to Italy. On Mar. 12, NATO admitted three former Warsaw Pact states as members: Poland, Hungary and the Czech Republic. On Mar. 30, Russian Pres. Yeltsin condemned NATO air strikes against Yugoslavia. On Mar. 24, after the failure of peace talks in Paris, NATO launched air strikes against Yugoslavia to force Pres. Milosevic to compromise over Kosovo. Serbian forces in Kosovo stepped up the "ethnic cleansing" of Albanian Kosovars, creating tens of thousands of refugees. On Apr. 1, British Prime Min. Blair and Irish Prime Min. Bertie Ahern published the Hillsborough Declaration, aimed at disarming terrorists and bringing Sinn Fein into the power-sharing executive. On Apr. 15, former Pakistani Prime Min. Benazir Bhutto was convicted in absentia of corruption and sentenced to five years in prison. On Apr. 15, US astronomers announced the first discovery of a solar system outside our own orbiting the star Upsilon Andromeda. On Apr. 12, US Pres. Clinton became the first sitting president to be found in contempt of court when a judge declared that Clinton had lied in a 1998 deposition in the Paula Jones case. On Apr. 20, two student gunmen attacked a high school in Littleton, Col., killing 13 people before killing themselves. On May 26, for the first time since 1971, Indian fighter jets attacked Islamic guerrillas in Jammu and Kashmir. On May 27-28, Pakistan shot down three Indian aircraft during border fighting. On May 17, in Israeli prime ministerial elections, Ehud Barak defeated Pres. Netanyahu. On May 8, N. Korean officials said thousands of people had died from famine since 1995. On May 19, the Dutch cabinet resigned over a proposal to allow voter referendums to overturn government decisions. On May 12, Russian Pres. Yeltsin dismissed the government of Prime Min. Primakov; Sergei Stepashin became prime min. On May 17, US Sec. of State Madeleine Albright announced food aid for N. Korea. Throughout May, NATO air forces hit targets in Serbia and Montenegro; on May 7, NATO mistakenly bombed the Chinese Embassy in Belgrade, prompting anti-NATO protests in China. On June 4, more than 70,000 people in Hong Kong commemorated the 1989 massacre in Tiananmen Square in Beijing. On June 15, the North and South Korean navies fought a battle in the Yellow Sea. On June 5, Pope John Paul II spoke to 700,000 people near Gdansk, Poland. On June 2, South Africa's ANC won landslide victories in national elections; on June 16, Pres. Thabo Mbeki was sworn into office. On June 6, the space shuttle *Discovery*, carrying Canadian Julie Payette, returned to earth after a 10-day mission. On June 29, a Turkish court sentenced Abdullah Öcalan to death for leading the Kurdish rebellion. On June 19, UK's Prince Edward and Sophie Rhys-Jones wed at Windsor. On June 12, Gov. George W. Bush, Jr., of Tex. declared his bid for the Republican presidential nomination. On June 16, US V. Pres. Al Gore declared his second bid for the Democratic presidential nomination. On June 3, Yugoslav Pres. Milosevic accepted NATO's peace terms. On June 10, NATO's bombing campaign stopped. On June 11-13, NATO K-FOR and Russian troops entered Kosovo as peacekeepers. By June 20, Yugoslav troops had left Kosovo. In July, floods in Bangladesh displaced almost one million people. In China, the flooding of the Yangtze River and its tributaries displaced 1.84 million people. On July 21, Chinese police arrested about 30,000 members of Falun Gong in 30 cities. On July 8-12, FARC attacked 15 towns in Colombia; about 200 people died. Following the collapse of a ceasefire signed by six African states, the rebel Congolese Rally for Democracy launched a new offensive in the Democratic Republic of Congo and drove tens of thousands of refugees into Tanzania. On July 15, Indonesian officials confirmed the victory of the Indonesian Democratic Party in the June 7 parliamentary elections, the first held in 44 years. On July 7, Sierra Leone's government agreed to share power with the rebel Revolutionary United Front, ending an eight-year war. On Aug. 9, Berlin replaced Bonn as Germany's capital. On Aug. 30, East Timorese voted overwhelmingly for independence from Indonesia. On Aug. 15, more than 10,000 Catholics and Protestants united in Omagh, N. Ireland, to mark the anniversary of Ulster's worst IRA bombing. On Aug. 8, Russian troops launched attacks on Islamic rebels in Dagestan. On Aug. 9, Russian Pres. Yeltsin dismissed Prime Min. Stepashin's cabinet and appointed Vladimir Putin as prime min. On Aug. 17, an earthquake shook Izmit in Turkey; at least 12,000 people died, 30,000 people were injured and 200,000 were left homeless. On Aug. 19, up to 150,000 people in Belgrade peacefully demanded the resignation of Yugoslav Pres. Milosevic. On Sept. 1, 1.5 million unionized workers in Colombia ended a two-day strike to protest the government's austerity measures. On Sept. 7, an earthquake hit Athens, Greece, leaving thousands homeless. In East Timor, pro-Jakarta militias stepped up attacks on East Timor's civilians. By mid-month, the Indonesian army had withdrawn at least 3,500 troops from East Timor while 8,000 UN troops under Australian command prepared to arrive. A series of bombings in Moscow and other Russian cities killed more than 200 people; authorities blamed Islamic rebels from Dagestan. On Sept. 15-17, Hurricane Floyd battered the US east coast, forcing three million people to flee and killing at least six.

NATIONS OF THE WORLD

The statistics shown are intended to present an informative and comparative picture of the various nations of the world and their dependent territories. All data, including the geographic, population and government data, are taken from the latest available sources. The economic and finance/trade data indicate the size of the national economies and the amount of economic activity in the respective countries; the population, health and education data, and communications and transportation data give some evidence of the quality of life and the state of the infrastructure in each nation.

All dollar amounts are in US dollars. International dollar price weights have been used instead of an official currency exchange rate in an attempt to make more equitable comparisons.

The figures for "Number of Physicians" under "Population" have been dropped due to the age of the data available. Instead we have substituted "Total Fertility Rate." This figure represents the number of children born per woman, and indicates the potential for population growth. A high total fertility rate will have an impact on a nation's workforce —women's participation may be limited; it may also have an impact on the amount of education available and the level of education achieved in the general population.

The information contained in this section reflects data available up to and including October 1, 2000. Sources used for information include:

CIA World Fact Book 1998 • "Compendium of Statistics: Illiteracy" (UNESCO) • "Facts on File" • Demographic Yearbook (UN) • Encyclopedia Britannica • Direction of Trade Statistics (International Monetary Fund) • Foreign Affairs Canada • Government Finance Statistics Monthly (International Monetary Fund) • "Human Development Report" (UN Development Programme) • International Financial Statistics Yearbook (International Monetary Fund) • International Financial Statistics (monthly IMF update) • "Keesing's Record of World Events" • Monthly Bulletin of Statistics (UN Statistical Division) • "Population and Vital Statistics Report" (UN Dept. of International Economic and Social Affairs) • Statesman's Yearbook (Macmillan) • UNESCO Statistical Yearbook • World Bank Atlas (World Bank) • World Book Encyclopedia • World Debt Tables • "World Development Report" (World Bank) • "World Motor Vehicle Data" (Motor Vehicle Manufactures Assoc. of the US Inc.) • "World Population" (UNESCO) • "World Population Data Sheet" (Population Reference Bureau Inc.) • World Resources (World Resources Institute) • World Statistics Pocketbook • "World Tables" (Johns Hopkins UP) • Worldwide Government Directory with International Organizations (Belmont Publications) • Year Book of Labour Statistics (International Labour Office, Geneva).

Afghanistan

Long-Form Name: Islamic State of Afghanistan; note: the self-proclaimed Taliban government refers to the country as Islamic Emirate of Afghanistan
Capital: Kabul

■ GEOGRAPHY

Area: 647,500 sq. km
Coastline: none: landlocked
Climate: arid to semi-arid; cold winters and hot summers, considerable snowfall
Environment: damaging earthquakes occur in Hindu Kush mountains; poor soil, flooding, desertification, overgrazing, deforestation (largely due to logging for building materials and fuel), pollution, soil degradation
Terrain: mostly rugged mountains; plains in north and southwest
Land Use: 12% arable land; no permanent crops; 46% meadows and pastures; 3% forest and woodland; 39% other, includes about 30,000 sq. km of irrigated farmland
Location: SW Asia (Middle East)

■ PEOPLE

Population: 25,824,882 (July 1999 est.)
Nationality: Afghan
Age Structure: 0-14 yrs: 43%; 15-64: 54%; 65+: 3% (1999 est.)

Afghanistan

Population Growth Rate: 3.95% (1999 est.)
Net Migration: 14.62 migrants/1,000 population (1999 est.)
Ethnic Groups: 38% Pathan, 25% Tajik, 6% Uzbek, 19% Hazara; minor ethnic groups include Charar Aimaks, Turkoman, Baloch and others
Languages: 35% Pushtu (official), 50% Afghan Persian (Dari), 11% Turkic languages (primarily Uzbek and Turmen), 4% thirty minor languages (primarily Balochi and Pahai); much bilingualism
Religions: Islam (84% Sunni Muslim, 15% Shi'a Muslim), 1% other
Birth Rate: 41.93/1,000 population (1999 est.)
Death Rate: 17.02/1,000 population (1999 est.)
Infant Mortality: 140.55 deaths/1,000 live births (1999 est.)
Life Expectancy at Birth: 47.82 years male, 46.82 years female (1999 est.)
Total Fertility Rate: 5.94 children born/woman (1999 est.)
Literacy: 33.4% (1997)

■ GOVERNMENT

Leader(s): Due to a coup on Sept. 27, 1996 by the Taliban movement of Muslim fundamentalists, there is currently no functioning national government; Taliban Supreme Leader is Mullah Mohammad Omar Mujahid
Government Type: transitional government: a six-member council appointed by the Taliban movement of Muslim fundamentalists
Administrative Divisions: 30 provinces (relayat, sing. & pl.)
Nationhood: Aug. 19, 1919 (from UK)
National Holiday: Victory of the Muslim Nation, Apr. 28; Remembrance Day for Martyrs and the Disabled, May 4; Independence Day, August 19

■ ECONOMY

Overview: a poor country, largely dependent on farming (wheat) and livestock (sheep and goats). The economy is adversely affected by political and military disruptions; much of the population continues to suffer from insufficient food, clothing, housing and medical care; inflation remains a serious problem
GDP: $20 billion, per capita $800; real growth rate n.a. (1998 est.)
Inflation: n.a., but considerable
Industries: accounts for 28.5% of GDP; small-scale production of textiles, soap, furniture, shoes, fertilizer and cement; handwoven carpets; natural gas, oil, coal, copper
Labour Force: 68% agriculture and animal husbandry, 10% industry, 22% services and other
Unemployment: n.a.
Agriculture: largely subsistence farming and nomadic animal husbandry; cash products –wheat, fruit, nuts, karakul pelts, wool, mutton, barley, corn; production is limited due to the shortage of modern machinery, high-grade seed and fertilizer. Accounts for 53% of GDP.
Natural Resources: natural gas, crude oil, copper, coal, salt, talc, barites, sulphur, lead, zinc, iron ore, slate, precious and semi-precious stones, especially lapis lazuli, amethysts, rubies

■ FINANCE/TRADE

Currency: afghani (Af) = 100 puls
International Reserves Excluding Gold: n.a.
Gold Reserves: n.a.
Budget: n.a.
Defence Expenditures: n.a.
Education Expenditures: n.a.
External Debt: n.a.
Exports: exact figures for 1999 unavailable; commodities: natural gas 55%, fruit and nuts 24%, handwoven carpets, wool, cotton, hides; partners: FSU, Pakistan, Iran, Germany, India, UK, Belgium, Luxembourg, Czech and Slovak Republics
Imports: exact figures for 1999 unavailable; commodities: food and petroleum products, most consumer goods; partners: FSU, Pakistan, Iran, Japan, Singapore, India, South Korea, Germany

■ COMMUNICATIONS

Daily Newspapers: 12 (1996 est.)
Televisions: 12/1,000 inhabitants (1996 est.)
Radios: 122/1,000 inhabitants (1996 est.)
Telephones: 4.0 lines/1,000 inhabitants (1998 est.)

■ TRANSPORTATION

Motor Vehicles: 67,000; 35,000 passenger cars (1997 est.)
Roads: 21,000 km; 2,793 km paved
Railway: 9.6 km from Kushka (Turkmenistan) to Towraghondi and 15.0 km from Termez (Uzbekistan) to Kheyrabad
Air Traffic: 90,000 passengers carried (1997)
Airports: 44; 11 have paved runways (1998 est.)

Canadian Embassy: c/o Canadian High Commission, Diplomatic Sector G-5, Islamabad; mailing address: GPO Box 1042, Islamabad, Pakistan. Tel: (011-92-51) 27-91-00. Fax (011-92-51) 27-91-10.
Embassy in Canada: c/o High Commission for the Islamic Republic of Pakistan, Burnside Building, 151 Slater St, Ste 608, Ottawa ON K1P 5H3. Tel: (613) 238-7881. Fax: (613) 238-7296.

Albania

Long-Form Name: Republic of Albania
Capital: Tirana

■ GEOGRAPHY

Area: 28,750 sq. km
Coastline: 362 km
Climate: mild temperate; cool, cloudy, wet winters; hot, clear, dry summers; interior is cooler and wetter, with severe winters
Environment: subject to destructive earthquakes; soil erosion; water pollution; tsunami occur along southwestern coast; deforestation and water pollution are still current issues
Terrain: mostly mountains and hills; small plains along coast
Land Use: 21% arable land; 5% permanent crops; 15% meadows and pastures; 38% forest and woodland, including 30% scrub forest; 21% other; includes 3,410 sq. km irrigated
Location: SE Europe, bordering on Adriatic Sea

■ PEOPLE

Population: 3,364,571 (July 1999 est.)
Nationality: Albanian
Age Structure: 0-14 yrs: 33%; 15-64: 61%; 65+: 6% (1999 est.)
Population Growth Rate: 0.97% (1999 est.)
Net Migration: -2.93 migrants/1,000 population (1999 est.)
Ethnic Groups: 95% Albanian, 3% Greek, 2% others (Vlachs, Gypsies, Serbs and Bulgarians)
Languages: Albanian (Tosk is official dialect, also Gheg dialect), Greek
Religions: 70% Muslim, 20% Albanian Orthodox, 10% Roman Catholic
Birth Rate: 20.74/1,000 population (1999 est.)
Death Rate: 7.35/1,000 population (1999 est.)
Infant Mortality: 42.9 deaths/1,000 live births (1999 est.)
Life Expectancy at Birth: 65.92 male, 72.33 years female (1999 est.)
Total Fertility Rate: 2.50 children born/woman (1999 est.)
Literacy: 85% (1997)

■ GOVERNMENT

Leader(s): Pres. Rexhep Mejdani, Prime Min. Ilir Meta
Government Type: in transition to democracy
Administrative Divisions: 36 districts (rrethe, sing. rreth) and 1 municipality (bashki)
Nationhood: Nov. 28, 1912 (from Ottoman Empire); People's Socialist Republic of Albania declared Jan. 11, 1946
National Holiday: Independence Day, Nov. 28

■ ECONOMY

Overview: the poorest country in Europe, it is a Stalinist-type economy (central planning and state ownership of the means of production). Though largely self-sufficient in food until 1990, the recent break-up of cooperative farms and the general economic decline has forced Albania to rely increasingly on foreign aid. The government has taken strong measures to restore public order and to revive economic activity.
GDP: $5 billion, per capita $1,490; real growth rate +7% (1998 est.)
Inflation: -19.0% (as of December 1999)
Industries: accounts for 21% of GDP; food processing, textiles and clothing, lumber, oil, cement, chemicals, basic metals, hydro-electricity; most industries produce at only fraction of past levels
Labour Force: 2 million (1998); 24.1% agriculture, 35.3% industry, 15.9% service
Unemployment: officially 14% (Oct. 1997), but likely to be as high as 28%
Agriculture: accounts for 56% of GDP; arable land per capita among lowest in Europe; one-half of workforce engaged in farming; produces wide range of temperate-zone crops and livestock; claims self-sufficiency in grain output; 80% of all arable land is now in private ownership
Natural Resources: crude oil, natural gas, coal, chromium, copper, timber, nickel, petroleum

■ FINANCE/TRADE

Currency: lek (L) = 100 quintars
International Reserves Excluding Gold: $375 million (Jan. 2000)
Gold Reserves: 0.120 million fine troy ounces (Jan. 2000)
Budget: n.a.
Defence Expenditures: 4.9% of central government expenditures (1997)
Education Expenditures: 3.1% of central government expenditures (1997)
External Debt: $821 million (1998)
Exports: $288 million (1999 est.); commodities: asphalt, bitumen, petroleum products, metals and metallic ores, electricity, oil, vegetables, fruit, tobacco; partners: Italy, Yugoslavia, Germany, Greece, Czech and Slovak Republics, Poland, Romania, Bulgaria, Hungary
Imports: $1.27 billion (1999 est.); commodities: machinery, machine tools, iron and steel products, textiles, chemicals, pharmaceuticals; partners: Italy, Yugoslavia, Germany, Czech and Slovak Republics, Romania, Poland, Hungary, Bulgaria

■ COMMUNICATIONS

Daily Newspapers: 5 (1996)
Televisions: 109/1,000 inhabitants (1998)
Radios: 217/1,000 inhabitants (1997)
Telephones: 31 lines/1000 persons (1998)

■ TRANSPORTATION

Motor Vehicles: n.a.
Roads: 18,000 km; 5,400 km paved
Railway: 447 km
Air Traffic: 55,000 passengers carried (1997)
Airports: 9; 3 have paved runways (1998 est.)

Canadian Embassy: The Office of the Canadian Embassy, Rruga Deshmoret e 4 Shkurtit, Pallati 7/1, Shkalla 1, Tirana, Albania, Postal Address: P.O. Box 47, Tirana, Albania, Tel: (011-355-42) 57275, Fax: (011-355-42) 57273
Embassy in Canada: c/o Embassy of the Republic of Albania, 2100 S St. NW, Washington DC 20005, USA. Tel: (202) 223-4942. Fax: (202) 628-7342.

Algeria

Long-Form Name: Democratic and Popular Republic of Algeria
Capital: Algiers

■ GEOGRAPHY

Area: 2,381,740 sq. km
Coastline: 998 km
Climate: arid to semi-arid; mild, wet winters with hot, dry summers along coast; drier with cold winters and hot summers on high plateau; sirocco is a hot, dust/sand-laden wind especially common in summer
Environment: mountainous areas subject to severe earthquakes; desertification; industrial and domestic pollution and soil erosion contribute to environmental problems
Terrain: mostly high plateau and desert; some mountains; narrow, discontinuous coastal plain
Land Use: 3% arable land; 0% permanent crops; 13% meadows and pastures; 2% forest and woodland; 82% other; cattle, sheep and goat grazing on grassland and shrub regions, includes 5,550 sq. km irrigated
Location: N Africa, bordering on Mediterranean Sea

■ PEOPLE

Population: 31,133,486 (July 1999 est.)
Nationality: Algerian
Age Structure: 0-14 yrs: 37%; 15-64: 59%; 65+: 4% (1999 est.)
Population Growth Rate: 2.10% (1999 est.)
Net Migration: -0.49 migrants/1,000 population (1999 est.)
Ethnic Groups: 99% Arab-Berber, less than 1% European
Languages: Arabic (official), French, Berber dialects
Religions: 99% Sunni Muslim (state religion); 1% Christian and Jewish
Birth Rate: 27.0/1,000 population (1999 est.)
Death Rate: 5.52/1,000 population (1999 est.)
Infant Mortality: 43.82 deaths/1,000 live births (1999 est.)
Life Expectancy at Birth: 68.07 male, 70.46 years female (1999 est.)
Total Fertility Rate: 3.27 children born/woman (1999 est.)
Literacy: 60.3% (1997 est.)

■ GOVERNMENT

Leader(s): Pres. Abdelaziz Bouteflika, Prime Min. Ahmed Benbitour
Government Type: republic
Administrative Divisions: 48 provinces (wilayas, sing. - wilaya)
Nationhood: July 5, 1962 (from France)
National Holiday: Anniversary of the Revolution, Nov. 1

■ ECONOMY

Overview: the economy is largely based on the exploitation of oil and natural gas products. Dropping oil and gas prices have contributed to Algeria's most serious social and economic crisis since independence. Recently, reforms have been implemented to combat social and economic problems
GDP: $140.2 billion, per capita $4,600; real growth rate 3.2% (1998 est.)
Inflation: 3.6% (as of June 1997)
Industries: petroleum, light industries, natural gas, mining, electrical, petrochemical, food processing. Accounts for 51% of GDP
Labour Force: 10 million (1998 est.); 11% industry, 14% agriculture, 75% services
Unemployment: 30% (1998 estimate)
Agriculture: accounts for 12% of GDP and employs 22% of labour force; products include wheat, barley, grapes, oats, olives, fruit, livestock; must import more than one-third of its food
Natural Resources: crude oil, natural gas, iron ore, phosphates, uranium, lead, zinc, mercury

■ FINANCE/TRADE

Currency: dinar (DA) = 100 centimes
International Reserves Excluding Gold: $4.746 billion (Jan. 2000)

Gold Reserves: 5.583 million fine troy ounces (Jan. 2000)
Budget: revenues $14.4 billion; expenditures $15.7 billion, including capital expenditures $4.4 million (1998 est.)
Defence Expenditures: 12.0% of central government expenditure (1997)
Education Expenditures: 5.1% of central government expenditure (1997)
External Debt: $31.4 billion (1998 est.)
Exports: $12.621 billion (1996); commodities: petroleum and natural gas 98%; partners: Netherlands, Czech and Slovak Republics, Romania, Italy, France, US
Imports: $8.690 billion (1996); commodities: capital goods 35%, consumer goods 36%, food 20%; partners: France 25%, Italy 8%, Germany 8%, US 6–7%

■ COMMUNICATIONS

Daily Newspapers: 5 (1996)
Televisions: 105/1,000 inhabitants (1998)
Radios: 241/1,000 inhabitants (1997)
Telephones: 53 lines/1,000 inhabitants (1998)

■ TRANSPORTATION

Motor Vehicles: 930,000; 500,000 passenger cars (1997 est.)
Roads: 102,424 km; 70,570 km paved
Railway: 4,772 km
Air Traffic: 3,518,000 passengers carried (1997)
Airports: 137; 51 have paved runways (1998 est.)

Canadian Embassy: The Canadian Embassy, 18 Mustapha Khalef Street, Ben Aknoun, Algiers, Algeria; mailing address: P.O. Box 48, Alger-Gare, 1600 Alger, Algeria. Tel: (011-213-2) 914951. Fax: (011-213-2) 914973.
Embassy in Canada: Embassy of the People's Democratic Republic of Algeria, 435 Daly Ave, Ottawa ON K1N 6H3. Tel: (613) 789-8505. Fax: (613) 789-1406.

American Samoa

Long-Form Name: Territory of American Samoa
Capital: Pago Pago (on Tutuila Island)

■ GEOGRAPHY

Area: 199 sq. km
Climate: tropical maritime, plentiful rainfall, temperatures consistent throughout the year
Land Use: 5% arable land, 10% permanent crops, 0% meadows and pastures, 70% forest and woodland, 15% other
Location: S Pacific Ocean, E of Australia and New Zealand

■ PEOPLE

Population: 63,786 (July 1999 est.)
Nationality: American Samoan; nationals of the United States
Ethnic Groups: Samoan (Polynesian) 89%, Caucasian 2%, Tongan 4%, other 5%
Languages: Samoan (a Polynesian dialect), English

■ GOVERNMENT

Colony/Territory of: Dependent Territory of the United States
Leader(s): Pres. W.J. Clinton; Gov. Tauese P. Sunia
Government Type: US dependency with democratically elected governor: unorganized unincorporated territory
National Holiday: Territorial Flag Day, Apr. 17

■ ECONOMY

Overview: agriculture: taro, bread-fruit, yams, bananas, coconuts; livestock includes pigs, goats, poultry; industries: fish (tuna) canning; economic activity is closely tied to US; tourism is slowly developing

■ FINANCE/TRADE

Currency: American dollar (US$) = 100 cents

Canadian Embassy: n.a.
Representative to Canada: c/o Embassy of the United States of America, 490 Sussex Dr., Ottawa ON K1N 1G8. Tel: (613) 238-5335. Fax: (613) 688-3097

Andorra

Long-Form Name: Principality of Andorra
Capital: Andorra-la-Vella

■ GEOGRAPHY

Area: 450 sq. km
Coastline: none: landlocked
Climate: temperate; snowy, cold winters and warm, dry summers
Environment: deforestation, overgrazing, soil erosion; avalanches are a natural hazard
Terrain: rugged mountains separated by narrow valleys
Land Use: 2% arable land; 0% permanent crops; 56% meadows and pastures; 22% forest and woodland; 20% other
Location: SW Europe

PEOPLE

Population: 65,939 (July 1999 est.)
Nationality: Andorran
Age Structure: 0-14 yrs: 14%; 15-64: 73%; 65+: 13% (1999 est.)
Population Growth Rate: 2.24% (1999 est.)
Net Migration: 17.61 migrants/1,000 population (1999 est.)
Ethnic Groups: Catalan stock; 61% Spanish, 30% Andorran, 6% French, 3% other
Languages: Catalan (official); many also speak some French and Spanish
Religions: predominantly Roman Catholic
Birth Rate: 10.27/1,000 population (1999 est.)
Death Rate: 5.46/1,000 population (1999 est.)
Infant Mortality: 4.08 deaths/1,000 live births (1999 est.)
Life Expectancy at Birth: 80.55 years male, 86.55 years female (1999 est.)
Total Fertility Rate: 1.25 children born/woman (1999 est.)
Literacy: n.a.

GOVERNMENT

Leader(s): Co-Heads of State Jacques Chirac (France) and Joan Marti Alanis (Spain), Prem. Marc Forné Molné
Government Type: parliamentary democracy; retains as its heads of state a co-principality of president of France and Spanish bishop of Seo de Urgel, who are represented locally by officials called veguers
Administrative Divisions: 7 parishes (parroquies, sing. -parroquia)
Nationhood: 1278 (from France and Spain)
National Holiday: Mare de Deu de Meritxell, Sept. 8

ECONOMY

Overview: tourism is the backbone of the economy, due to its duty-free status and year-round resorts. Most food is imported due to a scarcity of arable land
GDP: n.a.
Inflation: n.a.
Industries: tourism (particularly skiing), sheep, timber, tobacco, banking
Labour Force: n.a.
Unemployment: 0%
Agriculture: sheep raising, small quantities of tobacco, rye, wheat, barley, buckwheat, maize, oats and some vegetables, especially potatoes
Natural Resources: hydroelectricity, mineral water, timber, iron ore, lead

FINANCE/TRADE

Currency: French Franc = 100 centimes, Spanish peseta (F Ptas) = 100 centimos
International Reserves Excluding Gold: n.a.
Gold Reserves: n.a.
Budget: n.a.
Defence Expenditures: defence is the responsibility of Spain and France
Education Expenditures: n.a.
External Debt: n.a.
Exports: exact figures for 1999 unavailable; commodities: electricity, tobacco products, furniture; partners: France, Spain
Imports: exact figures for 1999 unavailable; commodities: consumer goods, food; partners: France, Spain, US

COMMUNICATIONS

Daily Newspapers: 3 (1996)
Televisions: 370/1,000 inhabitants (1996)
Radios: 217/1,000 inhabitants (1996)
Telephones: 441 lines/1,000 inhabitants (1998 est.)

TRANSPORTATION

Motor Vehicles: 36,000; 35,500 passenger cars (1997 est.)
Roads: 269 km; 198 km paved
Railway: none
Air Traffic: n.a.
Airports: none

Canadian Embassy: The Canadian Embassy to Andorra, Apartado 587, 28080, Madrid, Spain. Tel: (011-34) 91-423-3250. Fax: (011-34) 91-423-3251, or (011-34) 91-423-3252.
Embassy in Canada: c/o Embassy of the Principality of Andorra , 2 United Nations Plaza, 25th Floor, New York NY 10017, USA. Tel: (212) 750-8064. Fax: (212) 750-6630.

Angola

Long-Form Name: Republic of Angola
Capital: Luanda

GEOGRAPHY

Area: 1,246,700 sq. km
Coastline: 1,600 km
Climate: semi-arid in south and along coast to Luanda; north has cool, dry season (May to October) and hot, rainy season (Nov. to Apr.)
Environment: locally heavy rainfall causes periodic flooding on plateau; desertification, especially on coastal plain, soil erosion and water pollution; deforestation
Terrain: narrow coastal plain rises abruptly to vast interior plain
Land Use: 2% arable land; 0% permanent crops; 23% meadows and pastures; 43% forest and woodland; 32% other; includes 750 sq. km irrigated

Location: SW Africa

■ PEOPLE

Population: 11,177,537 (July 1999 est.)
Nationality: Angolan
Age Structure: 0-14 yrs: 45%; 15-64: 52%; 65+: 3% (1999 est.)
Population Growth Rate: 2.84% (1999 est.)
Net Migration: 1.60% migrants/1,000 population (1999 est.)
Ethnic Groups: 37% Ovimbundu, 25% Kimbundu, 13% Bakongo, 2% Mestiço, 1% European, 22% other
Languages: Portuguese (official); Bantu dialects spoken include Ovimbundu, Kimbundu, Bakongo and Chokwe
Religions: 38% Roman Catholic, 15% Protestant, 47% Animist (indigenous beliefs)
Birth Rate: 43.11/1,000 population (1999 est.)
Death Rate: 16.35/1,000 population (1999 est.)
Infant Mortality: 129.19 deaths/1,000 live births (1999 est.)
Life Expectancy at Birth: 46.08 years male, 50.82 years female (1999 est.)
Total Fertility Rate: 6.12 children born/woman (1999 est.)
Literacy: 45% (1997)

■ GOVERNMENT

Leader(s): Pres. José Eduardo dos Santos
Government Type: transitional government, nominally a democracy with strong presidential system
Administrative Divisions: 18 provinces (provincias, sing. -provincia)
Nationhood: Nov. 11, 1975 (from Portugal)
National Holiday: Independence Day, Nov. 11

■ ECONOMY

Overview: subsistence agriculture is the main livelihood of the population, but oil production is the most lucrative activity. Recent internal war has weakened the economy, and food must be imported
GDP: $11 billion, per capita 1,000; real growth rate 0.5% (1998 est.)
Inflation: 356.4% (March 2000)
Industries: accounts for 53% of GDP; petroleum, mining (phosphate rock, uranium, gold, iron ore, bauxite, feldspar, diamonds), fish processing, brewing, tobacco, sugar, textiles, cement, food processing, building construction
Labour Force: 6 million economically active (1998); 74% agriculture, 10% industry, 16% services
Unemployment: extensive unemployment and underemployment affects more than half the population (1997 est.)
Agriculture: accounts for 13% of GDP; cash crops—coffee, sisal, corn, cotton, sugar, manioc, tobacco; food crops—cassava, corn, vegetables, plantains, bananas and other local foodstuffs
Natural Resources: petroleum, diamonds, iron ore, phosphates, copper, feldspar, gold, bauxite, uranium

■ FINANCE/TRADE

Currency: new kwanza (Kz) = 100 lwei
International Reserves Excluding Gold: $486 million (Dec. 1999)
Gold Reserves: n.a.
Budget: n.a.
Defence Expenditures: 25% of GDP (1997-98)
Education Expenditures: n.a.
External Debt: $12.173 billion (1998)
Exports: n.a.; commodities: oil, coffee, diamonds, sisal, fish and fish products, timber, cotton; partners: US, former USSR countries, Cuba, Portugal, Brazil
Imports: n.a.; commodities: capital equipment (machinery and electrical equipment), food, vehicles and spare parts, textiles and clothing, medicines, substantial military deliveries; partners: US, former USSR countries, Cuba, Portugal, Brazil

■ COMMUNICATIONS

Daily Newspapers: 5 (1996)
Televisions: 14/1,000 inhabitants (1998)
Radios: 54/1,000 inhabitants (1997)
Telephones: 6.0 lines/1,000 inhabitants (1998)

■ TRANSPORTATION

Motor Vehicles: 225,000; 200,000 passenger cars (1997 est.)
Roads: 72,626 km; 19,156 km paved
Railway: 2,952 km
Air Traffic: 555,000 passengers carried (1997)
Airports: 252; 32 have paved runways (1998 est.)

Canadian Embassy: Consulate of Canada, Rua Rei Katyavala 113, Luanda, Angola. Tel: (011-244-2) 348-371. Fax: (011-244-2) 34-94-94.
Embassy in Canada: Embassy of the Republic of Angola, 75 Albert St, Ste 900, Ottawa ON K1P 5E7. Tel: (613) 234-1152. Fax: (613) 234-1179.

Anguilla

Long-Form Name: Anguilla
Capital: The Valley

■ GEOGRAPHY

Area: 91 sq. km
Climate: dry and sunny, tropical with moderating northeast trade winds

Land Use: mostly rock, with sparse scrub, few trees, some commercial salt ponds; low rainfall limits agricultural potential
Location: West Indies, E of Puerto Rico

■ PEOPLE

Population: 11,510 (July 1999 est.)
Nationality: Anguillan
Ethnic Groups: of English ancestry, black/mixed-black African
Languages: English (official)

■ GOVERNMENT

Colony/Territory of: Dependent Territory of the United Kingdom
Leader(s): Head of State: Queen Elizabeth II/Gov. Peter Johnstone. Chief Min. Hubert Hughes
Government Type: dependent territory of the U.K.
National Holiday: Anguilla Day, May 30

■ ECONOMY

Overview: agriculture: pigeon peas, corn, sweet potatoes; fishing; livestock includes sheep, goats, cattle, poultry; main trading partner: U.K. There are few natural resources and the economy depends heavily on tourism

■ FINANCE/TRADE

Currency: Eastern Caribbean dollar (EC$) = 100 cents

Canadian Embassy: c/o The Canadian High Commission, Macdonald House 1, Grosvenor Square, London W1X 0AB, England, UK. Tel: (011-44-20) 7258-6600. Fax: (011-44-20) 7258-6333.
Representative to Canada: c/o British High Commission, 80 Elgin St, Ottawa ON K1P 5K7. Tel: (613) 237-1530. Fax: (613) 237-7980.

Antigua and Barbuda

Long-Form Name: Antigua and Barbuda
Capital: Saint John's (on Antigua)

■ GEOGRAPHY

Area: 440 sq. km; includes Redonda (1.3 sq. km)
Coastline: 153 km
Climate: tropical marine; little seasonal temperature variation
Environment: subject to hurricanes and tropical storms (July to Oct.); insufficient freshwater resources are decreased further by clear-cutting of trees, which promotes rain run-off; occasional long periods of drought; deeply indented coastline provides many natural harbours
Terrain: mostly low-lying limestone and coral islands with some higher volcanic areas
Land Use: 18% arable land; 0% permanent crops; 9% meadows and pastures; 11% forest and woodland; 62% other
Location: Caribbean islands, SE of Puerto Rico

■ PEOPLE

Population: 64,246 (July 1999 est.)
Nationality: Antiguan, Barbudan
Age Structure: 0-14 yrs: 26%; 15-64: 69%; 65+: 5% (1999 est.)
Population Growth Rate: 0.36% (1999 est.)
Net Migration: -6.90 migrants/1,000 population (1999 est.)
Ethnic Groups: almost entirely of black African origin; some of British, Portuguese, Lebanese and Syrian origin
Languages: English (official), local dialects
Religions: Anglican (predominant), other Protestant sects, some Roman Catholic
Birth Rate: 16.22/1,000 population (1999 est.)
Death Rate: 5.76/1,000 population (1999 est.)
Infant Mortality: 20.69 deaths/1,000 live births (1999 est.)
Life Expectancy at Birth: 69.06 years male, 73.98 years female (1999 est.)
Total Fertility Rate: 1.72 children born/woman (1999 est.)
Literacy: 95% (1997)

■ GOVERNMENT

Leader(s): Head of State: Queen Elizabeth II/Gov. Gen. James B. Carlisle, Prime Min. Lester Bird
Government Type: parliamentary democracy
Administrative Divisions: 6 parishes, 2 dependencies
Nationhood: Nov. 1, 1981 (from UK)
National Holiday: Independence Day, Nov. 1

■ ECONOMY

Overview: tourism is the backbone of this service-oriented economy, therefore economic downturns, particularly in the US, can have adverse effects. A labour shortage is plaguing some sectors of the economy; agriculture is a minor but growing sector of the economy
GDP: $503 million, per capita $7,900; real growth rate 6% (1998 est.)
Inflation: n.a.
Industries: accounts for 12.5% of GDP; tourism, construction, light manufacturing (clothing, alcohol, household appliances)
Labour Force: n.a.

Unemployment: 9% (1997 est.)
Agriculture: accounts for 4% of GDP; expanding output of cotton, fruit, vegetables and livestock; other crops—bananas, coconuts, sugar cane, cucumbers, mangoes; not self-sufficient in food
Natural Resources: negligible; pleasant climate and beautiful beaches foster tourism

■ FINANCE/TRADE

Currency: East Caribbean dollar ($EC) = 100 cents
International Reserves Excluding Gold: $70 million (Jan. 2000)
Gold Reserves: n.a.
Budget: revenues $122.6 million; expenditures $141.2 million, including capital expenditures $17.3 million (1997 est.)
Defence Expenditures: 0.8% of GDP (1996)
Education Expenditures: n.a.
External Debt: $240 million (1997 est.)
Exports: n.a.; commodities: petroleum products 46%, manufactures 23%, food and live animals 4%, machinery and transport equipment 17%; partners: Trinidad and Tobago 2%, Barbados 15%, US 0.3%, others 26%
Imports: n.a.; commodities: food and live animals, machinery and transport equipment, manufactures, chemicals, oil; partners: US 27%, UK 16%, OECS 3%, Canada 4%, other 50%

■ COMMUNICATIONS

Daily Newspapers: 1 (1996)
Televisions: 457/1,000 inhabitants (1996)
Radios: 522/1,000 inhabitants (1996)
Telephones: 468 lines/1,000 inhabitants (1998)

■ TRANSPORTATION

Motor Vehicles: 14,800; 13,400 passenger cars (1997 est.)
Roads: 250 km
Railway: 77 km
Air Traffic: 1,250,000 passengers carried (1997)
Airports: 3, 2 have paved runways (1998 est.)

Canadian Embassy: c/o The Canadian High Commission, Bishop's Court Hill, St. Michael; mailing address: P.O. Box 404, Bridgetown, Barbados.
Embassy in Canada: High Commission for Antigua and Barbuda, 112 Kent St, Ste 1610, Place de Ville, Tower B, Ottawa ON K1P 5P2. Tel: (613) 236-8952. Fax: (613) 236-3042.

Argentina

Long-Form Name: Argentine Republic
Capital: Buenos Aires

■ GEOGRAPHY

Area: 2,766,890 sq. km
Coastline: 4,989 km
Climate: mostly temperate; arid in southeast; subantarctic in southwest
Environment: Tucumán and Mendoza areas in Andes subject to earthquakes; pamperos are violent windstorms that can strike the Pampas and northeast; irrigated soil degradation; desertification; air and water pollution in Buenos Aires; erosion is a current problem
Terrain: rich plains of the Pampas in northern half, flat to rolling plateau of Patagonia in south, rugged Andes along western border
Land Use: 9% arable land; 1% permanent crops; 52% meadows and pastures; 19% forest and woodland; 19% other, includes 17,000 sq. km irrigated
Location: SE South America

■ PEOPLE

Population: 36,737,664 (July 1999 est.)
Nationality: Argentine or Argentinian
Age Structure: 0-14 yrs: 27%; 15-64: 62%; 65+: 11% (1999 est.)
Population Growth Rate: 1.29% (1999 est.)
Net Migration: 0.65 migrants/1,000 population (1999 est.)
Ethnic Groups: 85% white, 15% mestizo, Indian, or other nonwhite groups
Languages: Spanish (official), English, Italian, German, French
Religions: 90% nominally Roman Catholic (less than 20% practising), 2% Protestant, 2% Jewish, 6% other
Birth Rate: 19.91/1,000 population (1999 est.)
Death Rate: 7.64/1,000 population (1999 est.)
Infant Mortality: 18.41 deaths/1,000 live births (1999 est.)
Life Expectancy at Birth: 71.13 years male, 78.56 years female (1999 est.)
Total Fertility Rate: 2.66 children born/woman (1999 est.)
Literacy: 96.5% (1997)

■ GOVERNMENT

Leader(s): Pres. Fernando De La Rua, V. Pres. Carlos Alvarez
Government Type: republic
Administrative Divisions: 23 provinces (provincias, sing. -provincia) and 1 federal district (distrito federal)
Nationhood: July 9, 1816 (from Spain)
National Holiday: Revolution Day, May 25

■ ECONOMY

Overview: though the country possesses

abundant natural resources and a diversified industrial base, burgeoning debt is weakening the economy; high unemployment rates have been a persistent problem, largely because of rigid labour laws
GDP: $374 billion, per capita $10,300; real growth rate 4.3% (1998 est.)
Inflation: -1.1% (March 2000)
Industries: accounts for 37% of GDP; food processing (especially meat packing), motor vehicles, consumer durables, textiles, chemicals and petrochemicals, printing, metallurgy, steel
Labour Force: 14 million (1998); 13% agriculture, 34% industry, 53% services
Unemployment: 12% (Oct. 1998)
Agriculture: accounts for 7% of GNP (including fishing); produces abundant food for both domestic consumption and exports; among world's top five exporters of grain and beef; principal crops—wheat, corn, sorghum, soybeans, sugar beets
Natural Resources: fertile plains of the Pampas, lead, zinc, tin, copper, iron ore, manganese, crude oil, uranium

■ FINANCE/TRADE

Currency: nuevo peso argentino = 100 centavos
International Reserves Excluding Gold: $24.290 billion (Jan. 2000)
Gold Reserves: 0.338 million fine troy ounces (Jan. 2000)
Budget: revenues $56 billion; expenditures $60 billion, including capital expenditures of $4 billion (1998 est.)
Defence Expenditures: 1.4% of GDP (1998)
Education Expenditures: 5.73% of total govt. expenditure (1997)
External Debt: $144.05 billion (1998)
Exports: $23.19 billion (1999 est.); commodities: meat, wheat, corn, oil seed, hides, wool; partners: US 14%, former USSR countries, Italy, Brazil, Japan, Netherlands
Imports: $24.95 billion (1999 est.); commodities: machinery and equipment, metals, chemicals, fuels and lubricants, agricultural products; partners: US 25%, Brazil, Germany, Bolivia, Japan, Italy, Netherlands

■ COMMUNICATIONS

Daily Newspapers: 181 (1996)
Televisions: 289/1,000 inhabitants (1998)
Radios: 681/1,000 inhabitants (1997)
Telephones: 203 lines/1,000 inhabitants (1998)

■ TRANSPORTATION

Motor Vehicles: 6,100,000; 4,800,000 passenger cars (1997 est.)
Roads: 208,350 km; 47,550 km paved
Railway: 37,830 km
Air Traffic: 8,600,000 passengers carried (1997)
Airports: 1,374; 141 have paved runways (1998 est.)

Canadian Embassy: The Canadian Embassy, 2828 Tagle, 1425 Buenos Aires; mailing address: Casilla de Correo C1000WAP, Buenos Aires, Argentina. Tel: (011-54-1) 4805-3032. Fax: (011-54-1) 4806-1209.

Embassy in Canada: Embassy of the Argentine Republic, Royal Bank Centre, 90 Sparks St, Ste 910, Ottawa ON K1P 5B4. Tel: (613) 236-2351. Fax: (613) 235-2659.

Armenia

Long-Form Name: Republic of Armenia
Capital: Yerevan

■ GEOGRAPHY

Area: 29,800 sq. km
Coastline: none: landlocked
Climate: severe winters; hot summers; dry year-round
Environment: prone to earthquakes; little land suitable for cultivation; air and water pollution; deforestation and drought; soil pollution is a current problem
Terrain: rugged highlands; 70% is mountains; little forest land; fast-flowing rivers; Aras River valley has good soil
Land Use: 17% arable, 3% permanent crops, 24% meadows and pasture, 15% forests and woodland, 41% other, includes 2,870 sq. km irrigated; most farmland lies in the Aras Valley; animal herding predominant in the highlands
Location: SW Asia

■ PEOPLE

Population: 3,409,234 (July 1999 est.)
Nationality: Armenian
Age Structure: 0-14 yrs: 25%; 15-64: 66%; 65+: 9% (1999 est.)
Population Growth Rate: -0.38% (1999 est.)
Net Migration: -8.26 migrants/1,000 population (1999 est.)
Ethnic Groups: 93% Armenians, 2% Russians, 3% Azerbaijanis, 2% other, predominantly Kurds
Languages: Armenian (official), Azerbaijan, Russian
Religions: predominantly Armenian Orthodox
Birth Rate: 13.53/1,000 population (1999 est.)
Death Rate: 9.03/1,000 population (1999 est.)
Infant Mortality: 41.12 deaths/1,000 live births (1999 est.)

Life Expectancy at Birth: 62.21 years male, 71.13 years female (1999 est.)
Total Fertility Rate: 1.68 children born/woman (1999 est.)
Literacy: 98.8% (1997)

■ GOVERNMENT

Leader(s): Pres. Robert Kocharian, Prime Min. Andranik Markaryan
Government Type: republic
Administrative Divisions: 10 provinces (marzer, sing. -marz) and 1 city (k'aghak'ner, sing. -k'aghak')
Nationhood: Sept. 23, 1991 (from Soviet Union)
National Holiday: Referendum Day, Sept. 21

■ ECONOMY

Overview: predominantly manufacturing and agriculture; high inflation weakens the economy and much of Armenia's population remains heavily dependent on remittances from relatives abroad
GDP: $9.2 billion, per capita $2,700; real growth rate 6% (1998 est.)
Inflation: -1.9% per month (Feb. 2000)
Industries: accounts for 30% of GDP; electrical equipment and machinery, chemicals, machine tools, vehicles, textiles
Labour Force: 2 million; 42% industry and construction, 18% agriculture and forestry, 40% other (1998)
Unemployment: 20% (1998 est.)
Agriculture: accounts for approximately 35% of GDP; fruit, grapes, vegetables, tobacco, grains, beetroot, potatoes, geranium oil, cattle and sheep herding
Natural Resources: marble, precious metals, iron, tufa, small deposits of gold, copper, molybdenum, zinc, alumina

■ FINANCE/TRADE

Currency: dram = 100 luma
International Reserves Excluding Gold: $335 million (Jan. 2000)
Gold Reserves: 0.044 million fine troy ounces (Jan. 2000)
Budget: revenues $322 million; expenditures $424 million, including capital expenditures of $80 million (1998 est.)
Defence Expenditures: 4% of GDP (1999)
Education Expenditures: 20% of central government expenditure (1997)
External Debt: $800 million (1998)
Exports: $232 million (1999); commodities include cotton, fruit, olives, pomegranates, machine tools, instruments, shoes
Imports: $800 million (1999); commodities include machinery, energy, consumer goods

■ COMMUNICATIONS

Daily Newspapers: 11 (1996)
Televisions: 218/1,000 inhabitants (1998)
Radios: 224/1,000 inhabitants (1997)
Telephones: 157 lines/1,000 persons (1998)

■ TRANSPORTATION

Motor Vehicles: n.a.
Roads: 8,580 km; 8,580 km paved
Railway: 825 km (does not include industrial lines)
Air Traffic: 368,000 passengers carried (1997)
Airports: 11; 5 have paved runways

Canadian Embassy: The Consulate of Canada, #21, 25 Demirjian St, Yerevan, Armenia. Tel: (011-3741) 401-238. Fax: (011-3742) 56-79-03; mailing address: c/o Starokonyushenny Per 23, Moscow 121002, Russian Federation.
Embassy in Canada: Embassy of the Republic of Armenia, 7 Delaware Ave, Ottawa ON K2P 0Z2. Tel: (613) 234-3710. Fax: (613) 234-3444.

Aruba

Long-Form Name: Aruba
Capital: Oranjestad

■ GEOGRAPHY

Area: 193 sq. km
Climate: tropical marine; little seasonal temperature variation
Land Use: 11% arable land; 0% permanent crops; 0% meadows and pastures; 0% forest and woodland; 89% other
Location: Caribbean island, off N coast of South America

■ PEOPLE

Population: 68,675 (July 1999 est.)
Nationality: Aruban
Ethnic Groups: 80% mixed European/Caribbean Indian
Languages: Dutch (official), Papiamento (a Spanish, Portuguese, Dutch, English dialect), English (widely spoken), Spanish

■ GOVERNMENT

Colony/Territory of: Dependent Territory of the Netherlands
Leader(s): Head of State: Queen Beatrix (Netherlands); Gov. Gen. Olindo Koolman; Prime Min. Jan Hendrik Eman
Government Type: part of the Dutch realm; autonomy in internal affairs obtained in 1986
National Holiday: Flag Day, Mar. 18

ECONOMY

Overview: tourism is the mainstay; banking and oil refinery are also important

FINANCE/TRADE

Currency: Aruban florin (Af) = 100 cents

Canadian Embassy: c/o The Canadian Embassy, Sophialaan 7, 2514JP, The Hague, Netherlands. Tel.: (011-31-70) 311-1600. Fax: (011-31-70) 311-1620.
Representative to Canada: c/o Embassy of the Kingdom of the Netherlands, 350 Albert St, Ste 2020, Ottawa ON K1R 1A4. Tel: (613) 237-5030. Fax: (613) 237-6471.

Australia

Long-Form Name: Commonwealth of Australia
Capital: Canberra

GEOGRAPHY

Area: 7,686,850 sq. km; includes Macquarie Island
Coastline: 25,760 km
Climate: generally arid to semi-arid; temperate in south and east; tropical in north
Environment: subject to severe droughts and floods; cyclones along coast; limited freshwater availability; soil degradation; regular, tropical, invigorating, sea breeze known as "the Doctor" occurs along west coast in summer; desertification. Shipping activities and tourism are threatening the Great Barrier Reef
Terrain: mostly low plateau with deserts; fertile plain in southeast
Land Use: 6% arable land; negligible permanent crops; 54% meadows and pastures; 19% forest and woodland; 21% other, includes 21,070 sq. km irrigated
Location: divides Indian and Pacific Oceans

PEOPLE

Population: 18,783,551 (July 1999 est.)
Nationality: Australian
Age Structure: 0-14 yrs: 21%; 15-64: 66%; 65+: 13% (1999 est.)
Population Growth Rate: 0.90% (1999 est.)
Net Migration: 2.66 migrants/1,000 population (1999 est.)
Ethnic Groups: 95% Caucasian, 4% Asian, 1% Aboriginal and other
Languages: English, native languages
Religions: 26.1% Anglican, 26% Roman Catholic, 24.3% other Christian; most of the rest do not profess a religion
Birth Rate: 13.21/1,000 population (1999 est.)
Death Rate: 6.9/1,000 population (1999 est.)
Infant Mortality: 5.11 deaths/1,000 live births (1999 est.)
Life Expectancy at Birth: 77.22 years male, 83.23 years female (1999 est.)
Total Fertility Rate: 1.81 children born/woman (1999 est.)
Literacy: 100% (1997)

GOVERNMENT

Leader(s): Head of State: Queen Elizabeth II/Gov. Gen. William Deane. Prime Min. John Howard
Government Type: federal parliamentary state
Administrative Divisions: 6 states, 2 territories; dependent areas inc.: Ashmore and Cartier Islands (uninhabited), Australian Antarctic Territory (uninhabited except for scientific staff), Cocos (Keeling) Islands, Coral Sea Islands Territory (uninhabited), Christmas Island, Heard and McDonald Islands (uninhabited), Norfolk Island
Nationhood: Jan. 1, 1901 (federation of UK colonies)
National Holiday: Australia Day, Jan. 26

ECONOMY

Overview: successful Western-style capitalist economy and a major exporter of natural resources and agricultural products. Is looking to increase exports of manufactured goods
GDP: $393.9 billion, per capita $21,200; real growth rate 4.5% (1998 est.)
Inflation: 2.8% (March 2000)
Industries: accounts for 31% of GDP; mining, industrial and transportation equipment, food processing, chemicals, steel, motor vehicles
Labour Force: 10 million (1998); 27.5% community, social and business services, 25.5% trade and tourism, 14.2% manufacturing
Unemployment: 6.7% (Oct. 1999)
Agriculture: accounts for 4% of GDP and 30% of export revenues; world's largest exporter of beef and wool, second largest for mutton, and among top wheat exporters; major crops—wheat, barley, sugar cane, fruit; livestock—cattle, sheep, poultry
Natural Resources: bauxite, coal, iron ore, copper, tin, silver, uranium, nickel, tungsten, mineral sands, lead, zinc, diamonds, natural gas, crude oil

FINANCE/TRADE

Currency: dollar ($A) = 100 cents
International Reserves Excluding Gold: $19.550 billion (Jan. 2000)

Gold Reserves: 2.562 million fine troy ounces (Jan. 2000)
Budget: revenues $90.73 billion; expenditures $89.04 billion, including capital expenditures $n.a. (1998–99 est.)
Defence Expenditures: 7.0% of central government expenditure (1998)
Education Expenditures: 7.64% of govt. expenditure (1998)
External Debt: $156 billion (June 1997)
Exports: $56.082 billion (1999); commodities: wheat, barley, beef, lamb, dairy products, wool, coal, iron ore; partners: Japan 26%, US 11%, New Zealand 6%, S Korea 4%, Singapore 4%, former USSR countries 3%
Imports: $69.113 billion (1999); commodities: manufactured raw materials, capital equipment, consumer goods; partners: US 22%, Japan 22%, UK 7%, Germany 6%, New Zealand 4%

■ COMMUNICATIONS

Daily Newspapers: 65 (1996)
Televisions: 639/1,000 inhabitants (1998)
Radios: 1,376/1,000 inhabitants (1997)
Telephones: 512 lines/1,000 inhabitants (1998)

■ TRANSPORTATION

Motor Vehicles: 10,900,000; 9,000,000 passenger cars (1997 est.)
Roads: 913,000 km; 353,331 km paved
Railway: 38,563 km
Air Traffic: 30,954,000 passengers carried (1997)
Airports: 408; 262 have paved runways (1998 est.)

Canadian Embassy: The Canadian High Commission, Commonwealth Ave, Canberra A.C.T. 2600, Australia. Tel: (011-61-2) 6270-4000. Fax: (011-61-2) 6273-3285.
Embassy in Canada: Australian High Commission, 50 O'Connor St, Ste 710, Ottawa ON K1P 6L2. Tel: (613) 236-0841. Fax: (613) 236-4376.

Austria

Long-Form Name: Republic of Austria
Capital: Vienna

■ GEOGRAPHY

Area: 83,858 sq. km
Coastline: none: landlocked
Climate: temperate; continental, cloudy; cold winter with frequent rain in lowlands and snow in mountains; cool summers with occasional showers
Environment: because of steep slopes, poor soils and cold temperatures, population is concentrated on eastern lowlands; air and soil pollution is due to emissions by coal, and oil-fired power stations and industrial plants
Terrain: mostly mountains with Alps in west and south; flat, with gentle slopes along eastern and northern margins
Land Use: 17% arable land; 1% permanent crops; 23% meadows and pastures; 39% forest and woodland; 20% other, includes 40 sq. km irrigated
Location: C Europe

■ PEOPLE

Population: 8,139,299 (July 1999 est.)
Nationality: Austrian
Age Structure: 0-14 yrs: 17%; 15-64: 68%; 65+: 15% (1999 est.)
Population Growth Rate: +0.09% (1999 est.)
Net Migration: +1.32 migrants/1,000 population (1999 est.)
Ethnic Groups: 99.4% German, 0.3 % Croatian, 0.2% Slovene, 0.1% others
Languages: German (official); Slovene, Hungarian, and a Croatian dialect also spoken
Religions: 85% Roman Catholic, 6% Protestant, 9% other
Birth Rate: 9.62/1,000 population (1999 est.)
Death Rate: 10.04/1,000 population (1999 est.)
Infant Mortality: 5.10 deaths/1,000 live births (1999 est.)
Life Expectancy at Birth: 74.31 years male, 80.82 years female (1999 est.)
Total Fertility Rate: 1.37 children born/woman (1999 est.)
Literacy: 99% (1997 est.)

■ GOVERNMENT

Leader(s): Chanc. Wolfgang Schuessel, Pres. Thomas Klestil
Government Type: federal republic
Administrative Divisions: 9 states (bundeslaender, sing. -bundesland)
Nationhood: Nov. 12, 1918 (from Austro-Hungarian Empire)
National Holiday: National Day, Oct. 26

■ ECONOMY

Overview: prosperous, Western capitalist economy, as well as substantial welfare benefits and extensive nationalized industry. Unemployment is a growing problem
GDP: $184.5 billion, per capita $22,700; real growth rate 2.9% (1998 est.)
Inflation: 1.9% (March 2000)
Industries: accounts for 30.8% of GDP; foods, iron and steel, machines, textiles, chemicals, electrical, paper and pulp, tourism, mining

Labour Force: 4 million (1998); 25.1% manufacture, 24.5% community, social and business services, 19.5% trade and tourism; an estimated 200,000 Austrians are employed in other European countries; foreign labourers in Austria number 177,840, about 6% of labour force
Unemployment: 8.4% (Jan. 2000)
Agriculture: accounts for 1.4% of GDP (including forestry); principal crops and animals—grains, fruit, potatoes, sugar beets, sawn wood, cattle, pigs, poultry; 80–90% self-sufficient in food
Natural Resources: iron ore, crude oil, timber, magnesite, aluminum, lead, coal, lignite, copper, hydroelectricity

■ FINANCE/TRADE

Currency: schilling (S) = 100 groschen [As of Jan. 1, 1999, Government securities are issued in Euros (EUR)]
International Reserves Excluding Gold: $14.950 billion (Jan. 2000)
Gold Reserves: 13.101 million fine troy ounces (Jan. 2000)
Budget: revenues $50.4 billion; expenditures $55.9 billion, capital expenditures n.a. (1998 est.)
Defence Expenditures: 0.82% of GDP (1999 est.)
Education Expenditures: 9.21% of total govt. expenditure (1997)
External Debt: $24.33 billion (1997)
Exports: $63.407 billion (1999); commodities: machinery and equipment, iron and steel, lumber, textiles, paper products, chemicals; partners: Germany 35%, Italy 10%, Eastern Europe 9%, Switzerland 7%, US 4%, OPEC 3%
Imports: $68.775 billion (1999); commodities: petroleum, foodstuffs, machinery and equipment, vehicles, chemicals, textiles and clothing, pharmaceuticals; partners: Germany 44%, Italy 9%, Eastern Europe 6%, Switzerland 5%, US 4%, USSR 2%

■ COMMUNICATIONS

Daily Newspapers: 17 (1996)
Televisions: 516/1,000 inhabitants (1998)
Radios: 753/1,000 inhabitants (1997)
Telephones: 491 lines/1,000 inhabitants (1998)

■ TRANSPORTATION

Motor Vehicles: 5,000,000; 4,000,000 passenger cars (1997 est.)
Roads: 129,061 km, all paved
Railway: 5,849 km
Air Traffic: 5,154,000 passengers carried (1997)
Airports: 55; 22 have paved runways (1998)

Canadian Embassy: The Canadian Embassy, Laurenzerberg 2 A-1010 Vienna, Austria. Tel: (011-43-1) 531-38-3000. Fax: (011-43-1) 531-38-3321.
Embassy in Canada: Embassy of the Republic of Austria, 445 Wilbrod St, Ottawa ON K1N 6M7. Tel: (613) 789-1444. Fax: (613) 789-3431.

Azerbaijan

Long-Form Name: Azerbaijani Republic
Capital: Baku

■ GEOGRAPHY

Area: 86,600 sq. km
Coastline: none; landlocked. Inland coastline (Caspian Sea) approximately 800 km.
Climate: Alpine to subtropical; dry, semi-arid steppe subject to drought
Environment: severe air and water pollution render Aspheron Peninsula, including Baku and Sumgait, the "most ecologically devastated area in the world," according to local scientists
Terrain: fertile central lowlands; large flat Kura-Aras Lowland; Caucasus Mountains in north; western uplands
Land Use: 18% arable, 5% permanent crops, 11% forests and woodland, 25% meadows and pastures, 41% other (includes 10,000 sq. km irrigated); grazing land in the Caucasus mountains; farming in lowlands
Location: SW Asia, bordering on Caspian Sea

■ PEOPLE

Population: 7,908,224 (July 1999 est.)
Nationality: Azerbaijani
Age Structure: 0-14 yrs: 32%; 15-64: 61%; 65+: 7% (1999 est.)
Population Growth Rate: 0.63% (1999 est.)
Net Migration: -5.76 migrants/1,000 population (1999 est.)
Ethnic Groups: 90% Azerbaijani, 2.5% Russians, 2.3% Armenians, 3.2% Daghestanis, 2% other
Languages: Azerbaijani (official), Armenian, Russian, 6% other
Religions: Muslim 93.4%, Russian Orthodox 2.3%, Armenian Orthodox 2.3%, other 1.8%
Birth Rate: 21.58/1,000 population (1999 est.)
Death Rate: 9.5/1,000 population (1999 est.)
Infant Mortality: 82.52 deaths/1,000 live births (1999 est.)
Life Expectancy at Birth: 58.76 years male, 67.63 years female (1999 est.)
Total Fertility Rate: 2.67 children born/woman (1999 est.)
Literacy: 96.3% (1997)

■ GOVERNMENT

Leader(s): Pres. Haydar Aliyev, Prem. Artur Rasizade. Parliamentary election scheduled for November 2000.
Government Type: republic
Administrative Divisions: 59 (rayonlar, sing. - rayon), 11 cities (saharlar, sing. -sahar), 1 autonomous republic (muxtar respublika, rayons)
Nationhood: Aug. 30, 1991 (from Soviet Union)
National Holiday: Independence Day, May 28

■ ECONOMY

Overview: cotton and refining industries are most prominent; Azerbaijan is least industrially developed of the Transcaucasian States, and its economy, weakened by massive inflation, continues to fall
GDP: $12.9 billion, per capita $1,640; real growth rate 10% (1998 est.)
Inflation: n.a.
Industries: accounts for 18% of GDP; oil extraction and refining, steel, cement, textiles, chemicals, petrochemicals
Labour Force: 3 million (1998 est.); 32% agriculture and forestry, 26% industry and construction, 42% other
Unemployment: 20% (1996)
Agriculture: accounts for 22% of GDP; cotton, grain, grapes, tea, citrus fruit, vegetables, sheep and horse breeding
Natural Resources: oil reserves, minerals, iron, aluminum

■ FINANCE/TRADE

Currency: manat = 100 gopik
International Reserves Excluding Gold: $670 million (Jan. 2000)
Gold Reserves: n.a.
Budget: revenues $565 million; expenditures $682 million, including capital expenditures n.a. (1996 est.)
Defence Expenditures: 10.8% of central government expenditure (1997)
Education Expenditures: 3.0 % of central government expenditure (1997)
External Debt: $693 million (1998)
Exports: $781 million (1997) to outside the successor states of the former USSR; oil and gas and related equipment, textiles, cotton. Partners: European and successor states of the former USSR
Imports: $794 million (1997) from outside the successor states of the former USSR; machinery and parts, foodstuffs, textiles, consumer durables

■ COMMUNICATIONS

Daily Newspapers: 6 (1996)
Televisions: 254/1,000 inhabitants (1998)
Radios: 23/1,000 inhabitants (1997)
Telephones: 89 lines/1,000 persons (1998)

■ TRANSPORTATION

Motor Vehicles: n.a.
Roads: 57,770 km; 54,188 km hard-surfaced
Railway: 2,125 km (does not include industrial lines)
Air Traffic: 982,000 passengers carried (1997)
Airports: 69; 29 have paved runways

Canadian Embassy: c/o The Canadian Embassy, Nenehatun Caddesi No. 75, Gaziosmanpasa 06700, Ankara, Turkey. Tel: (011-90-312) 436-1275. Fax: (011-90-312) 446-4437.
Embassy in Canada: Embassy of the Republic of Azerbaijan, 927 15th St NW, Ste 700, Washington DC 20005, USA. Tel: (202) 842-0001. Fax: (202) 842-0004.

Bahamas

Long-Form Name: Commonwealth of The Bahamas
Capital: Nassau

■ GEOGRAPHY

Area: 13,940 sq. km
Coastline: 3,542 km
Climate: tropical marine; moderated by warm waters of Gulf Stream
Environment: subject to hurricanes and other tropical storms that cause extensive flood and wind damage; coral reef decay is a current issue
Terrain: long, flat coral islands with some low, rounded hills
Land Use: 1% arable land; 0% permanent crops; 0% meadows and pastures; 32% forest and woodland; 67% other
Location: Caribbean islands, E of Florida

■ PEOPLE

Population: 283,705 (July 1999 est.)
Nationality: Bahamian
Age Structure: 0-14 yrs: 27%; 15-64: 67%; 65+: 6% (1999 est.)
Population Growth Rate: 1.36% (1999 est.)
Net Migration: -1.55 migrants/1,000 population (1999 est.)
Ethnic Groups: 85% black, 15% white
Languages: English; some Creole among Haitian immigrants
Religions: 32% Baptist, 20% Anglican, 19%

Roman Catholic, smaller groups of other Protestants, Greek Orthodox and Jews
Birth Rate: 20.58/1,000 population (1999 est.)
Death Rate: 5.43/1,000 population (1999 est.)
Infant Mortality: 18.38 deaths/1,000 live births (1999 est.)
Life Expectancy at Birth: 70.94 years male, 77.64 years female (1999 est.)
Total Fertility Rate: 2.31 children born/woman (1999 est.)
Literacy: 95.8% (1997)

■ GOVERNMENT

Leader(s): Head of State: Queen Elizabeth II/Gov. Gen. Orville Turnquest. Prime Min. Hubert Alexander Ingraham
Government Type: commonwealth
Administrative Divisions: 21 districts
Nationhood: July 10, 1973 (from UK)
National Holiday: National Day, July 10

■ ECONOMY

Overview: tourism and offshore banking are features of this stable, middle-income developing nation
GDP: $5.63 billion, per capita $20,100; real growth rate 4% (1998 est.)
Inflation: 1.8% (March 2000)
Industries: accounts for 5% of GDP; banking, tourism, cement, oil refining and transshipment, salt production, rum, aragonite, pharmaceuticals, spiral welded steel pipe
Labour Force: 30% government, 40% hotels and restaurants, 10% business services, 5% agriculture
Unemployment: 9% (1998 est.)
Agriculture: accounts for 3% of GDP; dominated by small-scale producers; principal products—citrus fruit, vegetables, poultry; large net importer of food
Natural Resources: salt, aragonite, timber

■ FINANCE/TRADE

Currency: Bahamian dollar ($B) = 100 cents
International Reserves Excluding Gold: $415 million (Jan. 2000)
Gold Reserves: none (Jan. 2000)
Budget: revenues $766 million; expenditures $845 million, including capital expenditures $97 million (1997–98 est.)
Defence Expenditures: 3.15% of central government expenditure (1998)
Education Expenditures: 19.57% of central government expenditure (1998)
External Debt: $381.7 million (1997)
Exports: $380 million (1999); commodities: pharmaceuticals, cement, rum, crawfish; partners: US 90%, UK 10%
Imports: $1.810 billion (1999); commodities: foodstuffs, manufactured goods, mineral fuels; partners: Nigeria 21%, US 35%, Japan 13%, Angola 11%

■ COMMUNICATIONS

Daily Newspapers: 3 (1996)
Televisions: 232/1,000 inhabitants (1996)
Radios: 739/1,000 inhabitants (1996)
Telephones: 352 lines/1,000 inhabitants (1998)

■ TRANSPORTATION

Motor Vehicles: 59,000; 47,000 passenger cars (1996 est.)
Roads: 2,693 km; 1,546 km paved
Railway: none
Air Traffic: 704,000 passengers carried (1997)
Airports: 62; 32 have paved runways (1998 est.)

Canadian Embassy: Consulate of Canada, Shirley Street Plaza, Nassau; mailing address: Consulate of Canada, P.O. Box SS-6371, Nassau, Bahamas. Tel: (1-242) 393-2123. Fax: (1-242) 393-1305.
Embassy in Canada: High Commission for the Commonwealth of the Bahamas, 50 O'Connor St, Ste 1313, Ottawa ON K1P 6L2. Tel: (613) 232-1724. Fax: (613) 232-0097.

Bahrain

Long-Form Name: State of Bahrain
Capital: Manama

■ GEOGRAPHY

Area: 620 sq. km
Coastline: 161 km
Climate: arid; mild, pleasant winters; very hot, humid summers
Environment: there are no natural fresh water resources; dust storms; desertification; drought; coastal degradation resulting from oil industry
Terrain: mostly low desert plain rising gently to low central escarpment
Land Use: 1% arable land; 1% permanent crops; 6% meadows and pastures; 0% forest and woodland; 92% other; includes 10 sq. km irrigated
Location: Persian Gulf, E of Saudi Arabia

■ PEOPLE

Population: 629,090 (July 1999 est.)
Nationality: Bahraini
Age Structure: 0-14 yrs: 31%; 15-64: 67%; 65+: 2% (1999 est.)
Population Growth Rate: 2.0% (1999 est.)
Net Migration: 1.42 migrants/1,000 population (1999 est.)

Ethnic Groups: 63% Bahraini, 13% Asian, 10% other Arab, 8% Iranian, 6% other
Languages: Arabic (official); English also widely spoken; Farsi, Urdu
Religions: Muslim (70% Shi'a, 30% Sunni)
Birth Rate: 21.86/1,000 population (1999 est.)
Death Rate: 3.24/1,000 population (1999 est.)
Infant Mortality: 14.81 deaths/1,000 live births (1999 est.)
Life Expectancy at Birth: 72.75 years male, 77.96 years female (1999 est.)
Total Fertility Rate: 2.97 children born/woman (1999 est.)
Literacy: 86.2% (1997)

■ GOVERNMENT

Leader(s): Prime Min. Khalifa bin Salman Al Khalifa, Amir Hamad bin Isa Al Khalifa
Government Type: traditional monarchy
Administrative Divisions: 12 municipalities (manatiq, sing. -mintaqah)
Nationhood: Aug. 15, 1971 (from UK)
National Holiday: Independence Day, Dec. 16

■ ECONOMY

Overview: petroleum production and processing are the backbone of the economy and any change in the world oil market affects the economy
GDP: $8.2 billion, per capita $13,100; real growth rate -2% (1998 est.)
Inflation: 1.1% (June 1999)
Industries: accounts for 46% of GDP; petroleum processing and refining, aluminum smelting, offshore banking, ship repairing
Labour Force: 42% of labour force is Bahraini; 78% industry, commerce and services, 21% government, 1% agriculture
Unemployment: 15% (1996 est.)
Agriculture: including fishing, accounts for 1% of GDP; not self-sufficient in food production; heavily subsidized sector produces fruit, vegetables, poultry, dairy products, shrimp and fish
Natural Resources: oil, associated and nonassociated natural gas, fish

■ FINANCE/TRADE

Currency: Bahraini dinar (BD) = 1,000 fils
International Reserves Excluding Gold: $1.348 billion (Jan. 2000)
Gold Reserves: 0.15 million fine troy ounces (Jan. 2000)
Budget: revenues $1.5 billion; expenditures $1.9 billion, capital expenditures n.a.(1999 budget)
Defence Expenditures: 17.25% of total govt. expenditures (1998)
Education Expenditures: 13.23% of govt. expenditure (1998)
External Debt: $2 billion (1997)
Exports: $4.086 billion (1999); commodities: petroleum 80%, aluminum 7%, other 13%; partners: US, United Arab Emirates, Japan, Singapore, Saudi Arabia
Imports: $3.403 billion (1999); commodities: non-oil 59%, crude oil 41%; partners: UK, Saudi Arabia, US, Japan

■ COMMUNICATIONS

Daily Newspapers: 4 (1996)
Televisions: 470/1,000 inhabitants (1996)
Radios: 579/1,000 inhabitants (1996)
Telephones: 245 lines/1,000 inhabitants (1998)

■ TRANSPORTATION

Motor Vehicles: 178,000; 143,000 passenger cars (1997 est.)
Roads: 3,013 km; 2,374 km paved
Railway: none
Air Traffic: 1,165,000 passengers carried (1997)
Airports: 3; 2 have paved runways (1998 est.)

Canadian Embassy: The Canadian Embassy to Bahrain, c/o The Canadian Embassy, P.O. Box 94321, Riyadh 11693, Saudi Arabia. Tel: (011-966-1) 488-2288. Fax: (011-966-1) 488-1997.
Embassy in Canada: The Embassy of the State of Bahrain, 3502 International Dr NW, Washington DC 20008, USA. Tel: (202) 342-0741. Fax: (202) 362-2192.

Bangladesh

Long-Form Name: People's Republic of Bangladesh
Capital: Dhaka

■ GEOGRAPHY

Area: 144,000 sq. km
Coastline: 580 km
Climate: tropical; cool, dry winter (Oct. to Mar.); hot, humid summer (Mar. to June)
Environment: vulnerable to droughts; much of country routinely flooded during summer monsoon season (June to Oct.); overpopulation; deforestation; cyclones
Terrain: mostly flat alluvial plain; hilly in southeast
Land Use: 73% arable land; 2% permanent crops; 5% meadows and pastures; 15% forest and woodland; 5% other, includes 31,000 sq. km irrigated
Location: S Asia, bordering on Bay of Bengal

Bangladesh

■ PEOPLE

Population: 127,117,967 (July 1999 est.)
Nationality: Bangladeshi
Age Structure: 0-14 yrs: 38%; 15-64: 59%; 65+: 3% (1999 est.)
Population Growth Rate: 1.59% (1999 est.)
Net Migration: -0.79 migrants/1,000 population (1999 est.)
Ethnic Groups: 98% Bengali, 250,000 Biharis, less than 1 million tribals
Languages: Bangla (official), English widely used, 5% tribal dialects
Religions: 83% Muslim, 16% Hindu, less than 1% Buddhist, Christian and other
Birth Rate: 25.2/1,000 population (1999 est.)
Death Rate: 8.50/1,000 population (1999 est.)
Infant Mortality: 69.68 deaths/1,000 live births (1999 est.)
Life Expectancy at Birth: 60.73 years male, 60.46 years female (1999 est.)
Total Fertility Rate: 2.86 children born/woman (1999 est.)
Literacy: 38.9% (1997)

■ GOVERNMENT

Leader(s): Pres. Shahabuddin Ahmed, Prime Min. Sheikh Hasina Wazed. A presidential election is scheduled for October 2001.
Government Type: republic
Administrative Divisions: 5 divisions
Nationhood: Dec. 16, 1971 (from Pakistan; Bangladesh formerly known as East Pakistan)
National Holiday: Independence Day, Mar. 26

■ ECONOMY

Overview: one of the poorest nations in the world; the economy is based on a small number of agricultural exports, which are vulnerable to natural disasters. Few natural resources. Frequent cyclones and floods, a rapidly growing labour force that cannot be absorbed by agriculture, a low level of industrialization, government interference with the economy, failure to exploit energy reserves, and inadequate power supplies all contribute to stifling economic growth.
GDP: $175.5 billion, per capita $1,380; real growth rate 4% (1998 est.)
Inflation: 3.8% (Dec. 1999)
Industries: accounts for 17% of GDP, jute manufacturing, food processing, cotton textiles, petroleum, urea fertilizer
Labour Force: 64 million (1998); 56.5% agriculture, 33.7% services, 9.8% industry; extensive export of labour to Saudi Arabia, United Arab Emirates, Oman and Kuwait
Unemployment: 35.2% (1996)
Agriculture: accounts for about 30% of GDP, 65% of employment and 20% of exports; imports 10% of food grain requirements; world's largest exporter of jute; commercial products—jute, rice, wheat, tea, sugar cane, potatoes, beef, milk, poultry
Natural Resources: natural gas, arable land, timber

■ FINANCE/TRADE

Currency: taka (Tk) = 100 poisha
International Reserves Excluding Gold: $1.549 billion (Jan. 2000)
Gold Reserves: 0.106 million fine troy ounces (Jan. 2000)
Budget: revenues $3.8 billion; expenditures $5.5 billion, including capital expenditures of n.a. (1997)
Defence Expenditures: 1.8% of GDP (1996-97)
Education Expenditures: 2.2% of central government expenditure (1997)
External Debt: $16.376 billion (1998)
Exports: $3.922 billion (1999); commodities: jute, tea, leather, shrimp, manufacturing; partners: US 25%, Western Europe 22%, Middle East 9%, Japan 8%, Eastern Europe 7%
Imports: $7.694 billion (1999); commodities: food, petroleum and other energy, nonfood consumer goods, semiprocessed goods and capital equipment; partners: Western Europe 18%, Japan 14%, Middle East 9%, US 8%

■ COMMUNICATIONS

Daily Newspapers: 37 (1996)
Televisions: 6/1,000 inhabitants (1998)
Radios: 50/1,000 inhabitants (1997)
Telephones: 3.0 lines/1,000 inhabitants (1998)

■ TRANSPORTATION

Motor Vehicles: 225,000; 152,000 passenger cars (1997 est.)
Roads: 204,022 km; 25,095 km paved
Railway: 2,745 km
Air Traffic: 1,315,000 passengers carried (1997)
Airports: 16; 15 have paved runways (1998 est.)

Canadian Embassy: The Canadian High Commission, House CWN 16/A, Rd. 48, Gulshan; mailing address: G.P.O. Box 569, Dhaka, Bangladesh. Tel: (011-880-2) 988-7091. Fax: (011-880-2) 88-30-43.
Embassy in Canada: High Commission for the People's Republic of Bangladesh, 275 Bank St, Ste 302, Ottawa ON K2P 2L6. Tel: (613) 236-0138. Fax: (613) 567-3213.

Barbados

Long-Form Name: Barbados
Capital: Bridgetown

■ GEOGRAPHY

Area: 430 sq. km
Coastline: 97 km
Climate: tropical; rainy season (June to Oct.)
Environment: subject to hurricanes, especially June to Oct.; water pollution and soil erosion; landslides
Terrain: relatively flat; rises gently to a central highland region
Land Use: 37% arable land; 0% permanent crops; 5% meadows and pastures; 12% forest and woodland; 46% other
Location: Caribbean islands, N of Venezuela

■ PEOPLE

Population: 259,191 (July 1999 est.)
Nationality: Barbadian
Age Structure: 0-14 yrs: 23%; 15-64: 67%; 65+: 10% (1999 est.)
Population Growth Rate: 0.04% (1999 est.)
Net Migration: -5.86 migrants/1,000 population (1999 est.)
Ethnic Groups: 80% African, 16% mixed, 4% European
Languages: English
Religions: 67% Protestant, 9% Methodist, 4% Roman Catholic, 9% other, including Moravian
Birth Rate: 14.46/1,000 population (1999 est.)
Death Rate: 8.16/1,000 population (1999 est.)
Infant Mortality: 16.74 deaths/1,000 live births (1999 est.)
Life Expectancy at Birth: 72.22 years male, 77.81 years female (1999 est.)
Total Fertility Rate: 1.83 children born/woman (1999 est.)
Literacy: 97.6% (1997)

■ GOVERNMENT

Leader(s): Head of State: Queen Elizabeth II/ Gov. Gen. Sir Clifford Husbands. Prime Min. Owen Seymour Arthur
Government Type: parliamentary democracy
Administrative Divisions: 11 parishes
Nationhood: Nov. 30, 1966 (from UK)
National Holiday: Independence Day, Nov. 30

■ ECONOMY

Overview: has one of the highest standards of living of islands in the region; the tourist industry and traditional sugar cane cultivation are main parts of the economy; manufacturing and tourism have become increasingly important in recent years
GDP: $2.9 billion, per capita $11,200; real growth rate 3% (1998 est.)
Inflation: 2.6% (Feb. 2000)
Industries: accounts for 15% of GDP; tourism, sugar, light manufacturing, component assembly for export
Labour Force: 135,000 (1997 est.); 39.9% community, social and business services, 15.2% trade and tourism, 10.5% manufacturing
Unemployment: 11.8% (Nov. 1998)
Agriculture: accounts for 6% of GDP; major cash crop is sugar cane; other crops—vegetables and cotton; not self-sufficient in food
Natural Resources: crude oil, fishing, natural gas

■ FINANCE/TRADE

Currency: Barbadian dollar ($BDS) = 100 cents
International Reserves Excluding Gold: $368 million (June 1999)
Gold Reserves: none (July 1999)
Budget: revenues $725.5 million; expenditures $750.6 million, including capital expenditures of $126.3 million (1997–98 est.)
Defence Expenditures: n.a.
Education Expenditures: n.a.
External Debt: $359 million (1996)
Exports: $229 million (1999); commodities: sugar and molasses, electrical components, clothing, rum, machinery and transport equipment; partners: US 30%, CARICOM, UK, Puerto Rico, Canada
Imports: $1.021 billion (1999); commodities: foodstuffs, consumer durables, raw materials, crude oil; partners: US 34%, CARICOM, Japan, UK, Canada

■ COMMUNICATIONS

Daily Newspapers: 2 (1996)
Televisions: 287/1,000 inhabitants (1996)
Radios: 904/1,000 inhabitants (1996)
Telephones: 424 lines/1,000 inhabitants (1998)

■ TRANSPORTATION

Motor Vehicles: 48,500; 45,000 passenger cars (1997 est.)
Roads: 1,650 km; 1,582 km paved
Railway: none
Air Traffic: n.a.
Airports: 1, usable and with a paved runway (1998 est.)

Canadian Embassy: The Canadian High Commission, Bishop's Court Hill, St. Michael, Barbados; mailing address: P.O. Box 404, Bridgetown, Barbados. Tel: (246) 429-3550. Fax: (246) 429-3780.
Embassy in Canada: High Commission for

Barbados, 130 Albert St, Ste 1204, Ottawa ON K1P 5G4. Tel: (613) 236-9517. Fax: (613) 230-4362.

Belarus

Long-Form Name: Republic of Belarus
Capital: Minsk

■ GEOGRAPHY

Area: 207,600 sq. km
Coastline: none; landlocked
Climate: mild and moist, transitional between continental and maritime
Environment: southern region is badly contaminated with nuclear fallout from 1986 Chernobyl reactor accident; pesticide use results in extensive soil pollution
Terrain: land of forests, lakes, rivers, and marshes; soil poor, sandy, marshy
Land Use: 29% arable, 1% permanent crops and forest, 34% forests and woodland, 15% meadows and pastures, 21% other; includes 1,000 sq. km irrigated
Location: W Asia, bordering on Poland

■ PEOPLE

Population: 10,401,784 (July 1999 est.)
Nationality: Belarusian
Age Structure: 0-14 yrs: 19%; 15-64: 67%; 65+: 14% (1999 est.)
Population Growth Rate: -0.09% (1999 est.)
Net Migration: 3.13 migrants/1,000 population (1999 est.)
Ethnic Groups: 77.9% Byelorussian, 13.2% Russian, 4.1% Polish, 2.9% Ukrainian, 1.9% other
Languages: Byelorussian, Russian
Religions: predominantly Roman Catholic and Eastern Orthodox
Birth Rate: 9.70/1,000 population (1999 est.)
Death Rate: 13.71/1,000 population (1999 est.)
Infant Mortality: 14.39 deaths/1,000 live births (1999 est.)
Life Expectancy at Birth: 62.04 years male, 74.52 years female (1999 est.)
Total Fertility Rate: 1.32 children born/woman (1999 est.)
Literacy: 99% (1997)

■ GOVERNMENT

Leader(s): Pres. Aleksandr Lukashenko, Prime Min. Vladimir Yermoshin
Government Type: republic
Administrative Divisions: 6 regions (voblastsi, sing. -voblasts), 1 municipality (harady, sing. -horad)

Nationhood: Aug. 25, 1991 (from Soviet Union)
National Holiday: Independence Day, July 3

■ ECONOMY

Overview: strong emphasis on mining and agriculture, with growing manufacturing (heavy machinery, chemicals, fertilizer) and services sector; Belarus is an important transport link for the former Soviet states
GDP: $53.7 billion, per capita $5,200; real growth rate 7% (1998 est.)
Inflation: 211.7% (March 2000)
Industries: accounts for 43% of GDP; machinery, tools, refineries, fertilizer production; about 50% of labour force is employed in industry
Labour Force: 5 million (1998); 27.4% manufacturing, 22.4% community, social and business services, 21.9% agriculture
Unemployment: 2.3%, but large numbers of underemployed (Dec 1998)
Agriculture: accounts for almost 21% of GDP; potatoes, flax, rye, oats, barley, wheat, cattle breeding, milk, vegetables, pigs, potatoes, peat, forest resources
Natural Resources: oil, potassium, forest land, peat deposits

■ FINANCE/TRADE

Currency: Belarusian ruble
International Reserves Excluding Gold: $299 million (Jan 2000)
Gold Reserves: n.a.
Budget: revenues $4 billion; expenditures $4.1 billion, including capital expenditures $180 million (1997 est.)
Defence Expenditures: 4.52% of total govt. expenditures (1998)
Education Expenditures: 4.07% of total govt. expenditures (1998)
External Debt: $1.12 billion (1998)
Exports: $5.922 billion (1999); agricultural and transport machinery, computers, refrigerators, foodstuffs; partners: Russia, Ukraine, Poland, Germany
Imports: $6.664 billion (1999); commodities: fuels, raw materials, textiles, sugar; partners: Russia, Ukraine, Poland, Germany

■ COMMUNICATIONS

Daily Newspapers: 8 (1996)
Televisions: 314/1,000 inhabitants (1998)
Radios: 296/1,000 inhabitants (1997)
Telephones: 241 lines/1,000 inhabitants (1998)

■ TRANSPORTATION

Motor Vehicles: n.a.

Roads: 53,407 km; 52,446 km hard-surfaced
Railway: 5,563 km (does not include industrial lines)
Air Traffic: 231,000 passengers carried (1997)
Airports: 118; 36 have paved runways (1998 est.)

Canadian Embassy: The Canadian Embassy to Belarus, c/o The Canadian Embassy, ul. J. Matejki 1/5, Warsaw 00-481, Poland, Tel: (011-48-22) 629-80-51, Fax: (011-48-22) 629-64-57
Embassy in Canada: Embassy of the Republic of Belarus, 130 Albert St, Ste 600, Ottawa ON K1P 5G4. Tel: (613) 233-9994, Fax: (613) 233-8500.

Belgium

Long-Form Name: Kingdom of Belgium
Capital: Brussels

■ GEOGRAPHY

Area: 30,510 sq. km
Coastline: 64 km
Climate: temperate; mild winters, cool summers; rainy, humid, cloudy
Environment: air and water pollution; acid rain
Terrain: flat coastal plains in northwest central rolling hills, rugged mountains of Ardennes Forest in southeast
Land Use: 24% arable land; 1% permanent crops; 20% meadows and pastures; 21% forest and woodland; 34% other; includes negligible irrigated
Location: NW Europe, bordering on North Sea

■ PEOPLE

Population: 10,182,034 (July 1999 est.)
Nationality: Belgian
Age Structure: 0-14 yrs: 17%; 15-64: 66%; 65+: 17% (1999 est.)
Population Growth Rate: 0.06% (1999 est.)
Net Migration: 1.01 migrants/1,000 population (1999 est.)
Ethnic Groups: 55% Flemish, 33% Walloon, 12% mixed or other
Languages: Dutch or Flemish spoken in north (Flanders), French in south (Wallonia), both languages official; small English-speaking minority in east, German 1%
Religions: 75% Roman Catholic, remainder Protestant or other
Birth Rate: 9.98/1,000 population (1999 est.)
Death Rate: 10.43/1,000 population (1999 est.)
Infant Mortality: 6.17 deaths/1,000 live births (1999 est.)
Life Expectancy at Birth: 74.31 years male, 80.90 years female (1999 est.)
Total Fertility Rate: 1.49 children born/woman (1999 est.)
Literacy: 99% (1997)

■ GOVERNMENT

Leader(s): Head of State: King Albert II. Prime Min. Guy Verhofstadt
Government Type: federal parliamentary democracy under a constitutional monarch
Administrative Divisions: 10 provinces
Nationhood: Oct. 4, 1830 (from the Netherlands)
National Holiday: National Day, July 21

■ ECONOMY

Overview: a small, private-enterprise-based economy possessing few natural resources, it is therefore highly vulnerable to the state of world markets. Burgeoning public debt offsets economic growth
GDP: $236 billion, per capita $23,400; real growth rate 2.8% (1998 est.)
Inflation: 2.0% (April 2000)
Industries: accounts for 27.2% of GDP; engineering and metal products, processed food and beverages, chemicals, basic metals, textiles, glass, petroleum, coal
Labour Force: 4 million (1998); 32.9% community, social and business services, 23.1% manufacturing, 17.5% trade and tourism
Unemployment: 11.3% (Jan. 2000)
Agriculture: accounts for 2.0% of GDP; emphasis on livestock production—beef, veal, pork, milk; major crops are sugar beets, fresh vegetables, fruit, grain and tobacco; net importer of farm products
Natural Resources: coal, natural gas

■ FINANCE/TRADE

Currency: Belgian franc (BF) = 100 centimes [As of Jan. 1, 1999, Government securities are issued in Euros (EUR)]
International Reserves Excluding Gold: $10.913 billion (Jan. 2000)
Gold Reserves: 8.298 million fine troy ounces (Jan. 2000)
Budget: n.a.
Defence Expenditures: 3.2% of central government expenditure (1997)
Education Expenditures: 3.1 of central government expenditure (1997)
External Debt: $22.3 billion (1998 est.)
Exports: $176.198 billion (1999) Belgium-Luxembourg Economic Union; commodities: iron and steel, transportation equipment, tractors, diamonds, petroleum products; partners: European Community 74%, US 5%, Communist countries 2%

Imports: $160.818 billion (1999) Belgium-Luxembourg Economic Union; commodities: fuels, grains, chemicals, foodstuffs; partners: European Community 72%, US 5%, oil-exporting, less-developed countries 4%, Communist countries 3%

■ COMMUNICATIONS
Daily Newspapers: 30 (1996)
Televisions: 510/1,000 inhabitants (1998)
Radios: 793/1,000 inhabitants (1997)
Telephones: 500 lines/1,000 inhabitants (1998)

■ TRANSPORTATION
Motor Vehicles: 5,000,000; 4,450,000 passenger cars (1997 est.)
Roads: 143,175 km, all paved
Railway: 3,380 km
Air Traffic: 6,872,000 passengers carried (1997)
Airports: 42; 24 have paved runways (1998 est.)

Canadian Embassy: The Canadian Embassy, 2, Avenue de Tervuren, 1040 Brussels, Belgium. Tel: (011-32-2) 741-0611. Fax: (011-32-2) 741-0643.
Embassy in Canada: Embassy of the Kingdom of Belgium, 80 Elgin St, 4th Fl, Ottawa ON K1P 1B7. Tel: (613) 236-7267. Fax: (613) 236-7882.

Belize

Long-Form Name: Belize
Capital: Belmopan

■ GEOGRAPHY
Area: 22,960 sq. km
Coastline: 386 km
Climate: tropical; very hot and humid; rainy season (May to Feb.)
Environment: frequent devastating hurricanes (Sept. to Dec.) and coastal flooding, especially in south; deforestation; industrial and agricultural water pollution
Terrain: flat, swampy coastal plain; low mountains in south
Land Use: 2% arable land; 1% permanent crops; 2% meadows and pastures; 92% forest and woodland; 3% other, includes 20 sq. km irrigated
Location: Central (Latin) America, just S of Mexico bordering on Caribbean Sea

■ PEOPLE
Population: 235,789 (July 1999 est.)
Nationality: Belizean
Age Structure: 0-14 yrs: 42%; 15-64: 55%; 65+: 3% (1999 est.)
Population Growth Rate: 2.42% (1999 est.)
Net Migration: -0.67 migrants/1,000 population (1999 est.)
Ethnic Groups: 30% Creole, 44% Mestizo, 11% Maya, 7% Garifuna, 8% other
Languages: English (official), Spanish, Maya, Garifuna (Carib)
Religions: 62% Roman Catholic, 30% Protestant sects, 2% none, 6% other
Birth Rate: 30.22/1,000 population (1999 est.)
Death Rate: 5.39/1,000 population (1999 est.)
Infant Mortality: 31.57 deaths/1,000 live births (1999 est.)
Life Expectancy at Birth: 67.23 years male, 71.26 years female (1999 est.)
Total Fertility Rate: 3.74 children born/woman (1999 est.)
Literacy: 75% (1997)

■ GOVERNMENT
Leader(s): Head of State: Queen Elizabeth II/Gov. Gen. Colville Young. Prime Min. Said Musa
Government Type: parliamentary democracy
Administrative Divisions: 6 districts
Nationhood: Sept. 21, 1981 (from UK; Belize formerly known as British Honduras)
National Holiday: Independence Day, Sept. 21

■ ECONOMY
Overview: economy primarily based on agriculture and merchandising; sugar is the main crop; tourism and construction are becoming increasingly important
GDP: $700 million, per capita $3,000; real growth rate 0.5% (1998 est.)
Inflation: -1.0% (Dec 1999)
Industries: accounts for 22% of GDP; sugar refining, clothing, timber and forest products, furniture, rum, soap, beverages, cigarettes, tourism, garment production, citrus concentrates
Labour Force: 71,000 (1997 est.); 30% agriculture, 16% services, 15.4% government, 11.2% commerce, 27.4% other
Unemployment: 13% (1997 est.)
Agriculture: accounts for 22% of GDP (including fish and forestry) and 75% of export earnings; commercial crops include sugar cane, bananas, cocoa, citrus fruit; expanding output of lumber and cultured shrimp; net importer of basic foods
Natural Resources: arable land potential, timber, fish

■ FINANCE/TRADE
Currency: Belizean dollar ($BZ) = 100 cents
International Reserves Excluding Gold: $70 million (Jan. 2000)

Gold Reserves: n.a.
Budget: revenues $140 million; expenditures $142 million, including capital expenditures of n.a. (1997-98 est.)
Defence Expenditures: 2% of GDP (1997-98)
Education Expenditures: 20.39% of govt. expenditures (1996)
External Debt: n.a.
Exports: $167 million (1999); commodities: sugar, clothing, seafood, molasses, citrus, wood and wood products; partners: US 47%, UK, Trinidad and Tobago, Canada
Imports: $366 million (1999 est.); commodities: machinery and transportation equipment, food, manufactured goods, fuels, chemicals, pharmaceuticals; partners: US 55%, UK, Netherlands Antilles, Mexico

■ COMMUNICATIONS

Daily Newspapers: 0 (1996)
Televisions: 183/1,000 inhabitants (1996)
Radios: 589/1,000 inhabitants (1996)
Telephones: 138 lines/1,000 inhabitants (1998)

■ TRANSPORTATION

Motor Vehicles: 5,600; 2,400 passenger cars (1997 est.)
Roads: 2,248 km; 427 km paved
Railway: none
Air Traffic: n.a.
Airports: 44; 3 have paved runways (1998 est.)

Canadian Embassy: Consulate of Canada, 85 North Front St, P.O. Box 610, Belize City, Belize. Tel: (011-501-2) 33-722. Fax: (011-501-2) 30-060.
Embassy in Canada: c/o High Commission for Belize, 2535 Massachusetts Ave NW, Washington DC, USA. 20008. Tel: (202) 332-9636. Fax: (202) 332-6888.

Benin

Long-Form Name: Republic of Benin
Capital: Porto Novo (official); Cotonou (de facto)

■ GEOGRAPHY

Area: 112,620 sq. km
Coastline: 121 km
Climate: tropical; hot, humid in south; semi-arid in north
Environment: hot, dry, dusty harmattan wind may affect north in winter; deforestation; desertification; recent droughts have severely affected marginal agriculture in north; insufficient safe drinking water
Terrain: mostly flat to undulating plain; some hills and low mountains
Land Use: 13% arable land; 4% permanent crops; 4% meadows and pastures; 31% forest and woodland; 48% other, includes 100 sq. km irrigated
Location: WC Africa, bordering on South Atlantic Ocean

■ PEOPLE

Population: 6,305,567 (July 1999 est.)
Nationality: Beninese (sing. & pl.)
Age Structure: 0-14 yrs: 48%; 15-64: 50%; 65+: 2% (1999 est.)
Population Growth Rate: 3.30% (1999 est.)
Net Migration: 0 migrants/1,000 population (1999 est.)
Ethnic Groups: 99% African (42 ethnic groups, most important being Fon, Adja, Yoruba, Bariba); 5,500 Europeans
Languages: French (official); also Fon, Yoruba, Fulami, Bariba
Religions: majority Animist, 15% Islam, 15% Christian
Birth Rate: 45.37/1,000 population (1999 est.)
Death Rate: 12.4/1,000 population (1999 est.)
Infant Mortality: 97.76 deaths/1,000 live births (1999 est.)
Life Expectancy at Birth: 51.98 years male, 56.24 years female (1998 est.)
Total Fertility Rate: 6.40 children born/woman (1999 est.)
Literacy: 33.9% (1997)

■ GOVERNMENT

Leader(s): Pres. Mathieu Kerekov. A presidential election is scheduled for March 2001.
Government Type: republic under multi-party democratic rule
Administrative Divisions: 6 provinces
Nationhood: Aug. 1, 1960 (from France; Benin formerly Dahomey)
National Holiday: National Day, Aug. 1

■ ECONOMY

Overview: one of the least developed countries in the world; limited natural resources and an underdeveloped infrastructure characterize the economy; agricultural products are a major export
GDP: $7.6 billion, per capita $1,300; real growth rate 4.4% (1998 est.)
Inflation: -0.4% (Feb 2000)
Industries: accounts for 14% of GDP; palm oil and palm kernel oil processing, textiles, beverages, petroleum, cigarettes, construction materials, foodstuffs

Labour Force: 3.1 million (1998); 70.2% agriculture, 23.1% services, 6.6% industry
Unemployment: n.a.
Agriculture: accounts for 34% of GDP; small farms produce 90% of agricultural output; production is dominated by food crops—corn, sorghum, cassava, beans and rice; cash crops include cotton, palm oil and peanuts; poultry and livestock output has not kept up with consumption
Natural Resources: small offshore oil deposits, limestone, marble, timber

■ FINANCE/TRADE

Currency: Communauté financière africaine franc (CFAF) = 100 centimes
International Reserves Excluding Gold: $370 million (Nov. 1999)
Gold Reserves: 0.011 million fine troy ounces (July 1998)
Budget: n.a.
Defence Expenditures: 6.8% of central government expenditure (1997)
Education Expenditures: 3.2% of central government expenditure (1997)
External Debt: $1.647 billion (1998)
Exports: $389 million (1999); partners: Brazil 18%, Portugal 11%, Morocco 10%, Libya 6%, also France
Imports: $643 million (1999); partners: France 21%, UK 9%, Thailand 9%, Hong Kong 8%, also China

■ COMMUNICATIONS

Daily Newspapers: 1 (1996)
Televisions: 10/1,000 inhabitants (1998)
Radios: 108/1,000 inhabitants (1997)
Telephones: 70 lines/1,000 inhabitants (1998)

■ TRANSPORTATION

Motor Vehicles: 56,000; 36,400 passenger cars (1997 est.)
Roads: 6,787 km; 1,357 km paved
Railway: 578 km
Air Traffic: 86,000 passengers carried (1997)
Airports: 5; 2 have paved runways (1998)

Canadian Embassy: c/o The Canadian Embassy, P.O. Box 4104, Abidjan 01, Cote d'Ivoire. Tel: (011-225) 20-21-20-09. Fax: (011-225) 20-21-77-28.
Embassy in Canada: Embassy of the Republic of Benin, 58 Glebe Ave, Ottawa ON K1S 2C3. Tel: (613) 233-4429. Fax: (613) 233-8952.

Bermuda

Long-Form Name: Commonwealth of Bermuda
Capital: Hamilton

■ GEOGRAPHY

Area: 50 sq. km
Climate: subtropical; mild, humid; gales, strong winds common in winter
Land Use: 6% arable land; 0% permanent crops; 0% meadows and pastures; 0% forest and woodland; 94% other
Location: North Atlantic Ocean, E of United States

■ PEOPLE

Population: 62,472 (July 1999 est.)
Nationality: Bermudian
Ethnic Groups: 61% black, 39% white and other
Languages: English

■ GOVERNMENT

Colony/Territory of: Dependent Territory of the United Kingdom
Leader(s): Head of State: Queen Elizabeth II/ Gov. Thorold Masefield. Prem. Jennifer Smith
Government Type: dependent territory of the UK
National Holiday: Bermuda Day, May 24

■ ECONOMY

Overview: a successful tourist industry accounts for its high per capita income; the industrial sector is small, and agriculture is limited by the lack of suitable land; 80% of food must be imported

■ FINANCE/TRADE

Currency: Bermudian dollar ($Ber) = 100 cents

Canadian Embassy: The Canadian Commission to Bermuda, c/o The Canadian Consulate General, 1251 Avenue of the Americas, New York NY, 10020-1175, USA. Tel: (212) 768-2400. Fax: (212) 596-1790.
Representative to Canada: c/o High Commission for the United Kingdom of Great Britain and Northern Ireland, 80 Elgin St, Ottawa ON K1P 5K7. Tel: (613) 237-1530. Fax: (613) 237-7980.

Bhutan

Long-Form Name: Kingdom of Bhutan
Capital: Thimphu

■ GEOGRAPHY

Area: 47,000 sq. km

Bhutan

Coastline: none: landlocked
Climate: varies; tropical in southern plains; cool winters and hot summers in central valleys; severe winters and cool summers in Himalayas
Environment: violent storms coming from the Himalayas were the source of the country's name, which means Land of the Thunder Dragon; soil erosion and limited access to water are ongoing problems
Terrain: mostly mountainous with some fertile valleys and savanna
Land Use: 2% arable land; negligible permanent crops; 6% meadows and pastures; 66% forest and woodland; 26% other; includes 340 sq. km irrigated
Location: S Asia

■ PEOPLE

Population: 1,951,965 (July 1999 est.)
Nationality: Bhutanese (sing. & pl.)
Age Structure: 0-14 yrs: 40%; 15-64: 56%; 65+: 4% (1999 est.)
Population Growth Rate: 2.25% (1999 est.)
Net Migration: 0 migrants/1,000 population (1999 est.)
Ethnic Groups: 50% Bhote, 35% ethnic Nepalese, 15% indigenous or migrant tribes
Languages: Bhotes speak various Tibetan dialects—the most widely spoken dialect is Dzongkha (official); Nepalese speak various Nepalese dialects
Religions: 75% Mahayana Buddhism (state religion), Hinduism (25%, mainly ethnic Nepalese)
Birth Rate: 36.76/1,000 population (1999 est.)
Death Rate: 14.26/1,000 population (1999 est.)
Infant Mortality: 109.33 deaths/1,000 live births (1999 est.)
Life Expectancy at Birth: 53.19 years male, 52.29 years female (1999 est.)
Total Fertility Rate: 5.16 children born/woman (1999 est.)
Literacy: 44.2% (1997 est.)

■ GOVERNMENT

Leader(s): King Jigme Singye Wangchuk
Government Type: monarchy; special treaty relationship with India
Administrative Divisions: 18 districts (dzongkhag, sing. & pl.)
Nationhood: Aug. 8, 1949 (from India)
National Holiday: National Day, Dec. 17

■ ECONOMY

Overview: agriculture and forestry are the bedrock of the economy; it is poorly developed due to omnipresent rugged topography

GDP: adjusted for purchasing power parity: $1.9 billion, per capita $1000; real growth rate 6.5% (1998 est.)
Inflation: 8.5% (Dec 1998)
Industries: accounts for 38% of GDP; cement, chemical products, mining, distilling, food processing, handicrafts, wood products, calcium carbide. Industries are small and technologically underdeveloped
Labour Force: n.a.
Unemployment: n.a.
Agriculture: accounts for 38% of GDP and provides a living for 90% of the population; based on subsistence farming and animal husbandry; self-sufficient in food except for foodgrains; other production—rice, corn, root crops, citrus fruit, dairy and eggs
Natural Resources: timber, hydroelectricity, gypsum, calcium carbide, tourism potential

■ FINANCE/TRADE

Currency: ngultrum (Nu) = 100 chetrum; Indian currency is also legal tender
International Reserves Excluding Gold: $290 million (Nov. 1999)
Gold Reserves: n.a.
Budget: n.a. for 1999; the government of India finances almost 60% of Bhutan's expenditures
Defence Expenditures: negligible
Education Expenditures: 10.92% of govt. expenditure (1998)
External Debt: $87 million (1996)
Exports: $118 million (1997) commodities: cardamom, gypsum, timber, handicrafts, cement, fruit, electricity, precious stones, spices; partners: India, Bangladesh
Imports: $137 million (1997) commodities: fuel and lubricants, grain, machinery and parts, vehicles, fabrics, rice; partners: India, Japan, UK, Germany, US

■ COMMUNICATIONS

Daily Newspapers: 0 (1996)
Televisions: 5.7/1,000 inhabitants (1996)
Radios: 19/1,000 inhabitants (1996)
Telephones: 16 lines/1,000 inhabitants (1998)

■ TRANSPORTATION

Motor Vehicles: n.a.
Roads: 3,285 km; 1,994 surfaced
Railway: none
Air Traffic: 36,000 passengers carried (1996)
Airports: 2; 1 has paved runway (1998)

Canadian Embassy: The Canadian High Commission, 7/8 Shantipath, Chanakyapuri, New Delhi 110021; mailing address: P.O. Box

5207, New Delhi, India. Tel: (011-91-11) 687-6500. Fax: (011-91-11) 687-6579.
Embassy in Canada: c/o High Commission for the Republic of India, 10 Springfield Road, Ottawa ON K1M 1C9. Tel: (613) 744-3751. Fax: (613) 744-0913.

Bolivia

Long-Form Name: Republic of Bolivia
Capital: La Paz (seat of government); Sucre (legal capital and seat of judiciary)

■ GEOGRAPHY

Area: 1,098,580 sq. km
Coastline: none: landlocked
Climate: varies with altitude; humid and tropical to cold and semi-arid
Environment: cold, thin air of high plateau is obstacle to efficient fuel combustion; overgrazing, soil erosion, desertification; deforestation, pollution of drinking water
Terrain: Andes Mountains, high plateau, hills, lowland plains in Amazon basin
Land Use: 2% arable land; negligible permanent crops; 24% meadows and pastures; 53% forest and woodland; 21% other; includes 1,750 sq. km irrigated
Location: C South America

■ PEOPLE

Population: 7,982,850 (July 1999 est.)
Nationality: Bolivian
Age Structure: 0-14 yrs: 39%; 15-64: 56%; 65+: 5% (1999 est.)
Population Growth Rate: 1.96% (1999 est.)
Net Migration: -1.50 migrants/1,000 population (1999 est.)
Ethnic Groups: 30% Quechua, 25% Aymara, 25-30% mixed, 5-15% European
Languages: Spanish, Quechua and Aymara (all official)
Religions: 95% Roman Catholic; 5% Protestant, especially Methodist
Birth Rate: 30.72/1,000 population (1999 est.)
Death Rate: 9.61/1,000 population (1999 est.)
Infant Mortality: 62.02 deaths/1,000 live births (1999 est.)
Life Expectancy at Birth: 58.51 years male, 64.51 years female (1999 est.)
Total Fertility Rate: 3.93 children born/woman (1999 est.)
Literacy: 83.6% (1997)

■ GOVERNMENT

Leader(s): Pres. Hugo Banzer Suarez, V. Pres. Jorge Fernando Quiroga Ramirez

Government Type: republic
Administrative Divisions: 9 departments (departmentos, sing. -departmento)
Nationhood: Aug. 6, 1825 (from Spain)
National Holiday: Independence Day, Aug. 6

■ ECONOMY

Overview: a poor economy vulnerable to price fluctuations for its small number of exports; a major step towards the privatization of the economy was taken in early 1994; market-oriented economic reforms and tighter fiscal discipline are leading to generally improving economic conditions
GDP: $23.4 billion, per capita $3,000; real growth rate 4.7% (1998 est.)
Inflation: 5.8% (April 2000)
Industries: accounts for 26% of GDP; mining, smelting, petroleum, food and beverage, tobacco, handicrafts, clothing; illicit drug industry reportedly produces the largest revenues
Labour Force: 3.1 million (1998); 29.1% trade and tourism, 26.2% community, social and business services, 19.4% manufacturing
Unemployment: 11.4% (1997); with extensive underemployment
Agriculture: accounts for about 17% of GDP (including forestry and fisheries); principal commodities—coffee, coca, cotton, corn, sugar cane, rice, potatoes, timber; self-sufficient in food
Natural Resources: tin, natural gas, crude oil, zinc, tungsten, antimony, silver, iron ore, lead, gold, timber

■ FINANCE/TRADE

Currency: Boliviano ($b) = 100 centavos
International Reserves Excluding Gold: $887 million (Jan. 2000)
Gold Reserves: 0.940 million fine troy ounces (Jan. 2000)
Budget: revenues $2.7 billion; expenditures $2.7 billion (1998)
Defence Expenditures: 9.60% of total govt. expenditure (1998)
Education Expenditures: 19.57% of govt. expenditure (1998)
External Debt: $6.077 billion (1998)
Exports: $1.045 billion (1999); commodities: metals 45%, natural gas 32%, coffee, soyabeans, sugar, cotton, timber; partners: Argentina, UK, US
Imports: $1.755 billion (1999); commodities: food, petroleum, consumer goods, capital goods; partners: US, Brazil, Japan, Argentina

■ COMMUNICATIONS

Daily Newspapers: 18 (1996)
Televisions: 116/1,000 inhabitants (1998)
Radios: 675/1,000 inhabitants (1997)
Telephones: 69 lines/1,000 inhabitants (1998)

■ TRANSPORTATION

Motor Vehicles: 433,000; 200,000 passenger cars (1997 est.)
Roads: 52,216 km; 2,872 km paved
Railway: 3,691 km
Air Traffic: 2,251,000 passengers carried (1997)
Airports: 1,130 airfields; 12 have paved runways (1998 est.)

Canadian Embassy: The Office of Canadian Cooperation, Avenida 20 de Octubre, 2475 Plaza Avaroa Sopocachi, La Paz; mailing address: Casilla Postal 13032, La Paz, Bolivia. Tel: (011-591-2) 432-838. Fax: (011-591-2) 430-250.
Embassy in Canada: Embassy of the Republic of Bolivia, 130 Albert St, Ste 416, Ottawa ON K1P 5G4. Tel: (613) 236-5730. Fax: (613) 236-8237.

Bosnia and Herzegovina

Long-Form Name: Republic of Bosnia and Herzegovina
Capital: Sarajevo

■ GEOGRAPHY

Area: 51,233 sq. km
Coastline: 20 km
Climate: hot summers and cold winters; regions with high elevation have short, cool summers and long, severe winters; mild, rainy winters along the coast
Environment: air pollution; scarce water; waste disposal sites limited; subject to frequent destructive earthquakes
Terrain: mountains and valleys
Land Use: 14% arable, 5% permanent crops, 20% meadows and pastures, 39% forests, 22% other; includes 20 sq. km irrigated
Location: SE Europe

■ PEOPLE

Population: 3,482,495 (July 1999 est.)
Nationality: Bosnian, Herzegovinian
Age Structure: 0-14 yrs: 17%; 15-64: 71%; 65+: 12% (1999 est.)
Population Growth Rate: 3.2% (1999 est.)
Net Migration: 33.42 migrants/1,000 population (1999 est.)
Ethnic Groups: 38% Muslim, 40% Serb, 22% Croat (est. the Croats claim they now make up only 17% of the total population)
Languages: Croatian, Serbian, Bosnian
Religions: 40% Muslim, 31% Orthodox, 15% Catholic, 4% Protestant, 10% other
Birth Rate: 9.36/1,000 population (1999 est.)
Death Rate: 10.81/1,000 population (1999 est.)
Infant Mortality: 24.52 deaths/1,000 live births (1999 est.)
Life Expectancy at Birth: 62.55 years male, 71.71 years female (1999 est.)
Total Fertility Rate: 1.21 children born/woman (1999 est.)
Literacy: n.a.

■ GOVERNMENT

Leader(s): Head of State: Pres. Alija Izetbegovic. Head of gov't. Prime Min. Spasoje Tusevljak. Presidential and parliamentary elections are scheduled for October 8, 2000.
Government Type: in transition to democracy
Administrative Divisions: 2 first-order administrative divisions
Nationhood: Apr. 1992 (from Yugoslavia)
National Holiday: Republic Day, January 9; Independence Day, March 1; Republic Day, November 25

■ ECONOMY

Overview: though farms are almost entirely privately owned, they are small and inefficient, and food must be imported; inter-ethnic warfare has caused sharp decreases in industrial output and soaring unemployment
GDP: $5.8 billion, per capita $1,720; real growth rate 30% (1998 est.)
Inflation: n.a.
Industries: accounts for 23% of GDP; steel production, mining (esp. coal, iron ore, lead, zinc), manufacturing (esp. vehicle assembly, textiles, tobacco products, wood furniture), oil refining
Labour Force: 2 million (1998); 2% agriculture, 45% industry and mining
Unemployment: 40-50% (1996 est.)
Agriculture: accounts for 19% of GDP; regularly produces less than half the region's food needs; foothills of northern Bosnia support orchards, vineyards, livestock and some wheat and corn; long winters and heavy precipitation reduce agricultural output in mountains; farms are generally not very productive
Natural Resources: coal, iron, bauxite, manganese, timber, copper, lead, zinc

■ FINANCE/TRADE

Currency: convertible marka = 100 convertible pfenniga

344 Botswana

International Reserves Excluding Gold: n.a.
Gold Reserves: n.a.
Budget: n.a.
Defence Expenditures: 14.1% of central government expenditure (1997)
Education Expenditures: n.a.
External Debt: n.a.
Exports: $152 million (1997 est.)
Imports: $1.1 billion (1997 est.)

■ COMMUNICATIONS

Daily Newspapers: 3 (1996)
Televisions: 41/1,000 inhabitants (1998)
Radios: 248/1,000 inhabitants (1997)
Telephones: 91 lines/1,000 inhabitants (1998)

■ TRANSPORTATION

Motor Vehicles: n.a.
Roads: 21,846 km; 11,425 km paved
Railway: 1,021 km
Air Traffic: n.a.
Airports: 25; 9 have paved runways (1998 est.)

Canadian Embassy: The Canadian Embassy, Logavina 7, 71000 Sarajevo. Tel: (011-387-71) 447-900. Fax: (011-387-71) 447-901.
Embassy in Canada: Embassy of Bosnia and Herzogovina, 130 Albert St., Ste 805, Ottawa, ON K1P 5G4. Tel: (613) 236-0028. Fax: (613) 236-1139.

Botswana

Long-Form Name: Republic of Botswana
Capital: Gaborone

■ GEOGRAPHY

Area: 600,370 sq. km
Coastline: none: landlocked
Climate: subtropical to semi-arid; warm winters and hot summers
Environment: overgrazing; desertification; limited resources of fresh water, periodic droughts, sand and dust storms
Terrain: predominantly flat to gently rolling tableland; Kalahari Desert in southwest
Land Use: 1% arable land; 0% permanent crops; 46% meadows and pastures; 47% forest and woodland; 6% other; includes 20 sq. km irrigated
Location: S Africa

■ PEOPLE

Population: 1,464,167 (July 1999 est.)
Nationality: Motswana (sing.), Batswana (pl.)
Age Structure: 0-14 yrs: 42%; 15-64: 54%; 65+: 4% (1999 est.)
Population Growth Rate: 1.05% (1999 est.)
Net Migration: 0 migrants/1,000 population (1999 est.)
Ethnic Groups: 95% Batswana; about 4% Kalanga, Basarwa and Kgalagadi; about 1% white
Languages: English (official), Setswana
Religions: 50% indigenous beliefs, 50% Christian
Birth Rate: 31.46/1,000 population (1999 est.)
Death Rate: 21.0/1,000 population (1999 est.)
Infant Mortality: 59.08 deaths/1,000 live births (1999 est.)
Life Expectancy at Birth: 39.42 years male, 40.37 years female (1999 est.)
Total Fertility Rate: 3.91 children born/woman (1999 est.)
Literacy: 74.4% (1997)

■ GOVERNMENT

Leader(s): Pres. Festus Gontebanye Mogae; V. Pres. Seretse Ian Khama
Government Type: parliamentary republic
Administrative Divisions: 10 districts and 4 town councils
Nationhood: Sept. 30, 1966 (from UK; Botswana formerly known as Bechuanaland)
National Holiday: Independence Day, Sept. 30

■ ECONOMY

Overview: economy based on mining (diamonds) and traditionally, cattle raising and crops; exhibits high unemployment
GDP: $5.25 billion, per capita $3,600; real growth rate 3% (1998 est.)
Inflation: 7.0% (April 2000)
Industries: accounts for 45% of GDP; livestock processing; mining of diamonds, copper, nickel, coal, salt, soda ash, potash; tourism
Labour Force: 1 million (1998); 36.6% community, social and business services; 18% trade and tourism, 11.2% manufacturing; 19,000 are employed in various mines in South Africa
Unemployment: 20 - 40% (1997 est.)
Agriculture: plagued by erratic rainfall and poor soil; accounts for only 4% of GDP; subsistence farming predominates; cattle raising supports 50% of the population; must import large share of food needs
Natural Resources: diamonds, copper, nickel, salt, soda ash, potash, coal, iron ore, silver, natural gas

■ FINANCE/TRADE

Currency: pula (P) = 100 thebe
International Reserves Excluding Gold: $6.299 billion (Dec. 1999)

Gold Reserves: n.a.
Budget: revenues $1.6 billion; expenditures $1.8 billion, including capital expenditures of $560 million (1996 - 97 est.)
Defence Expenditures: 1.2% of GDP (1999 - 00)
Education Expenditures: 8.6% of total govt. expenditure (1997)
External Debt: $548 million (1998)
Exports: $1.948 billion (1998); commodities: diamonds 88%, copper and nickel 5%, meat 4%, cattle, animal products; partners: Switzerland, US, UK, other European Community-associated members of Southern African Customs Union
Imports: $2.387 billion (1998); commodities: foodstuffs, vehicles, textiles, petroleum products; partners: Switzerland

■ COMMUNICATIONS
Daily Newspapers: 1 (1996)
Televisions: 20/1,000 inhabitants (1998)
Radios: 156/1,000 inhabitants (1997)
Telephones: 65 lines/1,000 inhabitants (1998)

■ TRANSPORTATION
Motor Vehicles: 100,000; 83,000 passenger cars (1997 est.)
Roads: 18,482 km; 4,343 km paved
Railway: 971 km
Air Traffic: 116,000 passengers carried (1997)
Airports: 92; 12 have paved runways (1998 est.)

Canadian Embassy: The Consulate fo Canada, Vision Hire Building, Plot 182, Queen's Road, Gaborone, Botswana. Tel: (011-267) 30-44-11. Fax: (011-267) 30-44-11.
Embassy in Canada: c/o High Commission for the Republic of Botswana, 1531-1533 New Hampshire Ave. NW, Washington DC 20036, USA. Tel: (202) 244-4990. Fax: (202) 244-4164.

Brazil

Long-Form Name: Federative Republic of Brazil
Capital: Brasilia

■ GEOGRAPHY
Area: 8,511,965 sq. km; includes Arquipélago de Fernando de Noronha, Atol das Rocas, Ilha da Trindade, Ilhas Martin Vaz and Penedos de São Pedro e São Paulo
Coastline: 7,491 km
Climate: mostly tropical, but temperate in south
Environment: recurrent droughts in northeast; floods and frost in south; deforestation in Amazon basin; air and water pollution in Rio de Janeiro and São Paulo and several other large cities
Terrain: mostly flat to rolling lowlands in north; some plains, hills, mountains and narrow coastal belt
Land Use: 5% arable land; 1% permanent crops; 22% meadows and pastures; 58% forest and woodland; 14% other; includes 28,000 sq. km irrigated
Location: E South America

■ PEOPLE
Population: 171,853,126 (July 1999 est.)
Nationality: Brazilian
Age Structure: 0-14 yrs: 30%; 15-64: 65%; 65+: 5% (1999 est.)
Population Growth Rate: 1.16% (1999 est.)
Net Migration: -0.03 migrants/1,000 population (1999 est.)
Ethnic Groups: Portuguese, Italian, German, Japanese, black, Amerindian; 55% white, 38% mixed, 6% black, 1% other
Languages: Portuguese (official), Spanish, English, French
Religions: 70% Roman Catholic (nominal)
Birth Rate: 20.42/1,000 population (1999 est.)
Death Rate: 8.79/1,000 population (1999 est.)
Infant Mortality: 35.37 deaths/1,000 live births (1999 est.)
Life Expectancy at Birth: 59.35 years male, 69.01 years female (1999 est.)
Total Fertility Rate: 2.28 children born/woman (1999 est.)
Literacy: 84% (1997)

■ GOVERNMENT
Leader(s): Pres. Fernando Henrique Cardoso, V. Pres. Marco Maciel
Government Type: federal republic
Administrative Divisions: 26 states (estados, sing. -estado) and 1 federal district (distrito federal)
Nationhood: Sept. 7, 1822 (from Portugal)
National Holiday: Independence Day, Sept. 7

■ ECONOMY
Overview: inflation has dropped sharply and sweeping reforms have boosted the economy, but the domestic debt remains burdensome. Brazil's natural resources remain a major, long-term economic strength
GDP: $1.0352 trillion, per capita $6,100; real growth rate 0.5% (1998 est.)
Inflation: 6.8% (April 2000)
Industries: accounts for 36% of GDP; textiles and other consumer goods, shoes, chemicals, cement, lumber, iron ore, steel, motor vehicles and auto parts, metalworking, capital goods, tin
Labour Force: 76 million (1998); 34.9% community, social and business services, 22.8% agriculture, 15.2% industry

Unemployment: 8.5% (1998 est.)
Agriculture: accounts for 14% of GDP; world's largest producer and exporter of coffee and orange juice concentrate and second-largest exporter of soybeans; self-sufficient in food, except for wheat
Natural Resources: iron ore, manganese, bauxite, nickel, uranium, phosphates, tin, hydro-electricity, gold, platinum, crude oil, timber

■ FINANCE/TRADE

Currency: real (CR$) = 100 centavos
International Reserves Excluding Gold: $36.151 billion (Jan. 2000)
Gold Reserves: 2.749 million fine troy ounces (Jan. 2000)
Budget: revenues $151 billion; expenditures $149 billion, including capital expenditures of $36 billion (1998)
Defence Expenditures: 1.9% of GDP (1998)
Education Expenditures: 5.1% of GDP (1997)
External Debt: $232 billion (1998)
Exports: $51.12 billion (1999); commodities: coffee, metallurgical products, foodstuffs, iron ore, automobiles and parts; partners: US 28%, European Community 26%, Latin America 11%, Japan 6%
Imports: $57.55 billion (1998); commodities: crude oil, capital goods, chemical products, foodstuffs, coal; partners: Middle East and Africa 24%, European Community 22%, US 21%, Latin America 12%, Japan 6%

■ COMMUNICATIONS

Daily Newspapers: 380 (1996)
Televisions: 316/1,000 inhabitants (1998)
Radios: 444/1,000 inhabitants (1997)
Telephones: 121 lines/1,000 inhabitants (1998)

■ TRANSPORTATION

Motor Vehicles: 16,700,000; 13,100,000 passenger cars (1997 est.)
Roads: 1.98 million km; 184.140 km paved
Railway: 28,862 km
Air Traffic: 24,307,000 passengers carried (1997)
Airports: 3,265 airfields; 514 have paved runways (1998 est.)

Canadian Embassy: Setor de Embaixadas Sul, Avenida das Nacoes, Quadra 803, Lote 16, Brasilia DF, 70410-900; mailing address: Caixa Postal 00961, 70359-900 Brasilia DF, Brazil. Tel: (011-55-61) 321-2171. Fax: (011-55-61) 321-4529.
Embassy in Canada: Embassy of the Federative Republic of Brazil, 450 Wilbrod St, Ottawa ON K1N 6M8. Tel: (613) 237-1090. Fax: (613) 237-6144.

British Indian Ocean Territory

Long-Form Name: British Indian Ocean Territory
Capital: None; Victoria (Seychelles) is administrative headquarters

■ GEOGRAPHY

Area: 60 sq. km
Climate: tropical maritime, hot and humid, moderated by trade winds
Land Use: no arable land; 0% permanent crops, meadows or pastures, 100% other
Location: Indian Ocean, the Chagos Archipelago island group E of Madagascar, S of India

■ PEOPLE

Population: no indigenous inhabitants; US and UK military personnel
Nationality: n.a.
Ethnic Groups: n.a. - no indigenous population
Languages: n.a. - no indigenous population

■ GOVERNMENT

Colony/Territory of: Dependent Territory of the United Kingdom
Leader(s): Head of State: Queen Elizabeth II, Comm. C.J.B. White. Admin. L.M. Savill; all reside in the UK
Government Type: dependency of Great Britain
National Holiday: n.a.

■ ECONOMY

Overview: fishing, coconuts, guano fertilizer; all economic activity takes place on the largest island, Diego Garcia, where joint US–UK defence facilities are located; there are no industrial or agricultural activities on the islands

■ FINANCE/TRADE

Currency: pound sterling (£ or £ stg)

Canadian Embassy: c/o of the Canadian High Commission, Macdonald House, 1 Grosvenor Square, London W1X 0AB, England, UK. Tel: (011-44-20) 7258-6600. Fax: (011-44-20) 7258-6333.
Representative to Canada: c/o British High Commission, 80 Elgin St, Ottawa ON K1P 5K7. Tel: (613) 237-1530. Fax: (613) 237-7980.

British Virgin Islands

Long-Form Name: British Virgin Islands
Capital: Road Town

GEOGRAPHY

Area: 150 sq. km; includes the island of Anegada
Climate: subtropical and humid; moderated by trade winds; hurricanes and tropical storms occur from July to Oct.
Land Use: 20% arable; 7% permanent crops; 33% permanent pastures; 3% forests; 33% other
Location: Caribbean islands, E of Puerto Rico

PEOPLE

Population: 19,156 (July 1999 est.)
Nationality: British Virgin Islander
Ethnic Groups: 90% black, 10% white, Asian, and other
Languages: English (official)

GOVERNMENT

Colony/Territory of: Dependent territory of the UK
Leader(s): Head of State: Queen Elizabeth II/Gov. Frank Savage. Chief Min. Ralph Telford O'Neal
Government Type: dependency of Great Britain
National Holiday: Territory Day, July 1

ECONOMY

Overview: one of the most prosperous economies in the Caribbean; highly dependent on tourism

FINANCE/TRADE

Currency: US dollar ($) = 100 cents

Canadian Embassy: c/o The Canadian High Commission, Macdonald House, 1 Grosvenor Square, London, W1X OAB, England, UK. Tel: (011-44-20) 7258-6600. Fax: (011-44-20) 7258-6333.
Representative to Canada: c/o British High Commission, 80 Elgin St, Ottawa ON K1P 5K7. Tel: (613) 237-1530. Fax: (613) 237-7980.

Brunei Darussalam

Long-Form Name: Negara Brunei Darussalam
Capital: Bandar Seri Begawan

GEOGRAPHY

Area: 5,770 sq. km
Coastline: 161 km
Climate: tropical; hot, humid, rainy
Environment: typhoons, earthquakes and severe floods occasionally occur
Terrain: flat coastal plain rises to mountainous east; hilly lowland in west
Land Use: 1% arable land; 1% permanent crops; 1% meadows and pastures; 85% forest and woodland; 12% other, includes 10 sq. km irrigated
Location: Indonesia (island of Borneo), bordering on South China Sea and Malaysia

PEOPLE

Population: 322,982 (July 1999 est.)
Nationality: Bruneian
Age Structure: 0-14 yrs: 33%; 15-64: 63%; 65+: 4% (1998 est.)
Population Growth Rate: 2.38% (1999 est.)
Net Migration: 4.35 migrants/1,000 population (1999 est.)
Ethnic Groups: 64% Malay, 20% Chinese, 16% other
Languages: Malay (official), English and Chinese
Religions: Islam (official, mainly Sunni Muslims); majority of Chinese are Buddhist, Confucian or Taoist
Birth Rate: 24.69/1,000 population (1999 est.)
Death Rate: 5.21/1,000 population (1999 est.)
Infant Mortality: 22.83 deaths/1,000 live births (1999 est.)
Life Expectancy at Birth: 70.35 years male, 73.42 years female (1999 est.)
Total Fertility Rate: 3.33 children born/woman (1999 est.)
Literacy: 90.1% (1997)

GOVERNMENT

Leader(s): Sultan, Prime Min. and Min. of Defence Sir Hassanal Bolkiah
Government Type: constitutional sultanate
Administrative Divisions: 4 districts (daerah-daerah, sing. -daerah)
Nationhood: Jan. 1, 1984 (from UK)
National Holiday: National Day, Feb. 23

ECONOMY

Overview: economy is based on crude oil and natural gas exports and the per capita GDP is one of the highest for underdeveloped nations; almost totally supported by exports of crude oil and natural gas
GDP: $5.4 billion, per capita $17,000; real growth rate -1% (1998 est.)
Inflation: n.a.
Industries: accounts for 46% of GDP; petroleum, liquefied natural gas, construction
Labour Force: 42% production of oil, natural gas and construction; 48% trade, services and other; 4% agriculture, forestry and fishing; 6% other
Unemployment: n.a.
Agriculture: accounts for 5% of GDP; imports

about 80% of its food needs; principal crops and livestock include rice, cassava, bananas, buffalo and pigs
Natural Resources: crude oil, natural gas, timber

■ FINANCE/TRADE

Currency: Bruneian dollar ($B) = 100 cents
International Reserves Excluding Gold: n.a.
Gold Reserves: n.a.
Budget: n.a.
Defence Expenditures: 6.0% of GDP (1997)
Education Expenditures: n.a.
External Debt: none (1998)
Exports: $2.62 billion (1996 est.); commodities: crude oil, liquefied natural gas, petroleum products; partners: Japan 55%
Imports: $2.65 billion (1996 est.); commodities: machinery and transport equipment, manufactured goods, food, beverages, tobacco, consumer goods; partners: Singapore 31%, US 20%, Japan 6%

■ COMMUNICATIONS

Daily Newspapers: 1 (1996)
Televisions: 250/1,000 inhabitants (1996)
Radios: 300/1,000 inhabitants (1996)
Telephones: 247 lines/1,000 inhabitants (1998)

■ TRANSPORTATION

Motor Vehicles: 166,000; 148,000 passenger cars (1997 est.)
Roads: 1,150 km; 399 km paved
Railway: 13 km private line
Air Traffic: 877,000 passengers carried (1997)
Airports: 2; 1 has paved runway (1998 est.)

Canadian Embassy: The High Commission of Canada, Suite 51, Britannia House, Jalan Cator, Bandar Seri Begawan; mailing address: P.O. Box 2808, Bandar Seri, Begawan B58675, Brunei Darussalam. Tel: (011-673-2) 22-00-43. Fax (011-673-2) 22-00-40.
Embassy in Canada: High Commission for Brunei, 395 Laurier Ave E, Ottawa ON K1N 6R4. Tel: (613) 234-5656. Fax: (613) 234-4397.

Bulgaria

Long-Form Name: Republic of Bulgaria
Capital: Sofia

■ GEOGRAPHY

Area: 110,910 sq. km
Coastline: 354 km
Climate: temperate; cold, damp winters; hot, dry summers
Environment: subject to earthquakes, landslides, deforestation, air and water pollution
Terrain: mostly mountains with lowlands in north and south
Land Use: 37% arable land; 2% permanent crops; 16% meadows and pastures; 35% forest and woodland; 10% other, includes 12,370 sq. km irrigated
Location: SE Europe, bordering on Black Sea

■ PEOPLE

Population: 8,194,772 (July 1999 est.)
Nationality: Bulgarian
Age Structure: 0-14 yrs: 16%; 15-64: 68%; 65+: 16% (1999 est.)
Population Growth Rate: -0.52% (1999 est.)
Net Migration: -0.66 migrants/1,000 population (1999 est.)
Ethnic Groups: 85.3% Bulgarian, 8.5% Turk, 2.6% Gypsy, 2.5% Macedonian, 0.3% Armenian, 0.2% Russian, 0.6% other
Languages: Bulgarian (official), Turkish; secondary languages closely correspond to ethnic breakdown
Religions: 85% Bulgarian Orthodox, 13% Muslim (practised by Turkish and Pomak minorities), 0.8% Jewish, 0.7% Roman Catholic, 0.5% Protestant, Gregorian-Armenian and other
Birth Rate: 8.71/1,000 population (1999 est.)
Death Rate: 13.20/1,000 population (1999 est.)
Infant Mortality: 12.37 deaths/1,000 live births (1999 est.)
Life Expectancy at Birth: 68.72 years male, 76.03 years female (1999 est.)
Total Fertility Rate: 1.23 children born/woman (1999 est.)
Literacy: 98.2% (1997)

■ GOVERNMENT

Leader(s): Pres. Petar Stoyanov, Prime Min. Ivan Kostov
Government Type: emerging democracy
Administrative Divisions: 9 provinces (oblasti, sing. -oblast)
Nationhood: Sept. 22, 1908 (from Turkey)
National Holiday: Independence Day, Mar. 3

■ ECONOMY

Overview: heavily in debt with low growth, the economy is also hindered by antiquated industrial plants; continues to adjust to a market economy. The government's structural reform program includes privatization and, where appropriate, liquidation of state-owned enterprises.
GDP: $33.6 billion, per capita $4,100; real growth rate 4% (1998 est.)

Inflation: 9.5% (March 2000)
Industries: accounts for 29% of GDP; food processing, machine building and metal working, electronics, chemicals
Labour Force: 4 million (1998); 33.9% industry, 18% agriculture, 21.9% community, social and business services
Unemployment: 12.2% (1998 est.)
Agriculture: accounts for 26% of GNP; climate and soil conditions support livestock raising and the growing of various grain crops, oilseeds, vegetables, fruit and tobacco; more than one-third of the arable land devoted to grain; world's fourth largest tobacco exporter; surplus food producer
Natural Resources: bauxite, copper, lead, zinc, coal, timber, arable land

■ FINANCE/TRADE

Currency: lev (pl. leva) (Lv) = 100 stotinki
International Reserves Excluding Gold: $2.827 billion (Jan. 2000)
Gold Reserves: 1.031 million fine troy ounces (Jan. 2000)
Budget: revenues $4.1 billion; expenditures $3.8 billion, capital expenditures n.a. (1998 est.)
Defence Expenditures: 8.03% of total govt. expenditure (1998)
Education Expenditures: 4.42% of total govt. expenditure (1998)
External Debt: $9.907 billion (1998)
Exports: $3.925 billion (1999); commodities: machinery and equipment 60.5%, agricultural products 14.7%, manufactured consumer goods 10.6%, fuels, minerals, raw materials and metals 8.5%, other 5.7%; partners: socialist countries 82.5%, developed countries 6.8%, less developed countries 10.7%
Imports: $5.409 billion (1999); commodities: fuels, minerals, raw materials 45.2%, machinery and equipment 39.8%, manufactured consumer goods 4.6%, agricultural products 3.8%, other 6.6%; partners: socialist countries 80.5%, developed countries 15.1%, less developed countries 4.4%

■ COMMUNICATIONS

Daily Newspapers: 17 (1996)
Televisions: 398/1,000 inhabitants (1998)
Radios: 543/1,000 inhabitants (1997)
Telephones: 329 lines/1,000 inhabitants (1998)

■ TRANSPORTATION

Motor Vehicles: 1,990,000; 1,680,000 passenger cars (1997 est.)
Roads: 36,724 km; 33,786 km hard-surfaced
Railway: 4,294 km

Air Traffic: 722,000 passengers carried (1997)
Airports: n.a.

Canadian Embassy: c/o The Canadian Embassy, 36 Nicolae Iorga, 71118 Bucharest, Romania; Postal Address: The Canadian Embassy, P.O. Box 117, Post Office No. 22, Bucharest, Romania, Tel (011-40-1) 222-9845, Fax (011-40-1) 312-9680
Embassy in Canada: Embassy of the Republic of Bulgaria, 325 Stewart St, Ottawa ON K1N 6K5. Tel: (613) 789-3215. Fax: (613) 789-3524.

Burkina Faso

Long-Form Name: Burkina Faso
Capital: Ouagadougou

■ GEOGRAPHY

Area: 274,200 sq. km
Coastline: none: landlocked
Climate: tropical; warm, dry winters; hot, wet summers
Environment: recent droughts and desertification severely affecting marginal agricultural activities, population distribution, economy; overgrazing; desertification
Terrain: mostly flat to dissected, undulating plains; hills in west and southeast
Land Use: 13% arable land; 0% permanent crops; 22% meadows and pastures; 50% forest and woodland; 15% other, includes 200 sq. km irrigated
Location: WC Africa

■ PEOPLE

Population: 11,575,898 (July 1999 est.)
Nationality: Burkinabe (sing. & pl.)
Age Structure: 0-14 yrs: 48%; 15-64: 49%; 65+: 3% (1999 est.)
Population Growth Rate: 2.70% (1999 est.)
Net Migration: -1.25 migrants/1,000 population (1999 est.)
Ethnic Groups: more than 50 tribes; principal tribe is Mossi (about 24% of pop.); other important groups are Gurunsi, Senufo, Lobi, Bobo, Mande and Fulani
Languages: French (official); tribal languages belong to Sudanic family, spoken by 90% of population
Religions: 40% indigenous beliefs, about 50% Muslim, 10% Christian (mainly Roman Catholic)
Birth Rate: 45.84/1,000 population (1999 est.)
Death Rate: 17.56/1,000 population (1999 est.)
Infant Mortality: 107.19 deaths/1,000 live births (1999 est.)

Life Expectancy at Birth: 44.97 years male, 46.84 years female (1999 est.)
Total Fertility Rate: 6.56 children born/woman (1999 est.)
Literacy: 20.7% (1997)

■ GOVERNMENT

Leader(s): Head of State, Head of Government & Chairman: Capt. Blaise Compaoré, Prime Min. Kadre Desire Oudraogo
Government Type: parliamentary democracy
Administrative Divisions: 30 provinces
Nationhood: Aug. 5, 1960 (from France; Burkina Faso formerly known as Upper Volta)
National Holiday: Anniversary of the Revolution, Aug. 4

■ ECONOMY

Overview: a poor economy with high population density and few natural resources, it relies heavily on subsistence agriculture; economic development is hindered by a poor communication network; agriculture provides approximately 35% of national income
GDP: $11.6 billion, per capita $1,000; real growth rate 6% (1998)
Inflation: -0.2% (March 2000)
Industries: accounts for 25% of GDP; agricultural processing plants; brewery, cement and brick plants; soap, cigarettes, textiles, gold mining and extraction; a few other small consumer goods enterprises
Labour Force: 5 million (1998); 86.6% agriculture, 4.3% industry, 9.1% services; 20% of male labour force migrates annually to neighbouring countries for seasonal employment
Unemployment: n.a.
Agriculture: accounts for 35% of GDP; cash crops—peanuts, shea nuts, sesame, cotton; food crops—sorghum, millet, corn, rice; livestock; not self-sufficient in food grains
Natural Resources: manganese, limestone, marble; small deposits of gold, antimony, copper, nickel, bauxite, lead, phosphates, zinc, silver

■ FINANCE/TRADE

Currency: Communauté financière africaine franc (CFAF) = 100 centimes
International Reserves Excluding Gold: $249 million (Nov. 1999)
Gold Reserves: 0.011 million fine troy ounces (June 1998)
Budget: n.a.
Defence Expenditures: 12.3% of central government expenditure (1997)
Education Expenditures: 1.5% of GNP (1997)

External Debt: $1.399 billion (1998)
Exports: $254 million (1999); commodities: oilseeds, cotton, live animals, gold; partners: European Community 42%, Taiwan 17%, Ivory Coast 15%
Imports: $696 million (1999); commodities: grain, dairy products, petroleum, machinery; partners: European Community 37%, Africa 31%, US 15%

■ COMMUNICATIONS

Daily Newspapers: 4 (1996)
Televisions: 9/1,000 inhabitants (1998)
Radios: 33/1,000 inhabitants (1997)
Telephones: 4.0 lines/1,000 inhabitants (1998)

■ TRANSPORTATION

Motor Vehicles: 55,000; 35,600 passenger cars (1997 est.)
Roads: 12,506 km; 2,001 km paved
Railway: 622 km
Air Traffic: 97,000 passengers carried (1997)
Airports: 33; 2 have paved runways (1998 est.)

Canadian Embassy: The Canadian Embassy, rue Agostino Neto, Ouagadougou; mailing address: Office of the Canadian Embassy, P.O. Box 548, Ouagadougou 01, Province du Kadiogo, Burkina Faso. Tel: (011-226) 31-18-95. Fax (011-226) 31-19-00.
Embassy in Canada: Embassy of Burkina Faso, 48 Range Rd, Ottawa ON K1N 8J4. Tel: (613) 238-4796. Fax: (613) 238-3812.

Burundi

Long-Form Name: Republic of Burundi
Capital: Bujumbura

■ GEOGRAPHY

Area: 27,830 sq. km
Coastline: none: landlocked
Climate: temperate; warm; occasional frost in uplands
Environment: soil exhaustion; soil erosion; deforestation; flooding and landslides are natural hazards
Terrain: mostly rolling to hilly highland; some plains
Land Use: 44% arable land; 9% permanent crops; 36% meadows and pastures; 3% forest and woodland; 8% other, includes 140 sq. km irrigated
Location: EC Africa

■ PEOPLE

Population: 5,735,937 (July 1999 est.)

Nationality: Burundian
Age Structure: 0-14 yrs: 47%; 15-64: 50%; 65+: 3% (1999 est.)
Population Growth Rate: 3.54% (1999 est.)
Net Migration: 11.33 migrants/1,000 population (1999 est.)
Ethnic Groups: Africans: 85% Hutu (Bantu), 14% Tutsi (Hamitic), 1% Twa (Pygmy); non-Africans: 3,000 Europeans, 2,000 South Asians
Languages: Kirundi and French (official); Swahili used commercially
Religions: about 67% Christian (62% Roman Catholic, 5% Protestant), 32% indigenous beliefs, 1% Muslim
Birth Rate: 41.27/1,000 population (1999 est.)
Death Rate: 17.23/1,000 population (1999 est.)
Infant Mortality: 99.36 deaths/1,000 live births (1999 est.)
Life Expectancy at Birth: 43.54 years male, 47.41 years female (1999 est.)
Total Fertility Rate: 6.33 children born/woman (1999 est.)
Literacy: 44.6%(1997)

■ GOVERNMENT

Leader(s): Pres. Maj. Pierre Buyoya; First V. Pres. Ferderic Bamvuginyumvira
Government Type: republic
Administrative Divisions: 15 provinces
Nationhood: July 1, 1962 (from UN trusteeship under Belgian administration)
National Holiday: Independence Day, July 1

■ ECONOMY

Overview: economy is heavily dependent on the coffee crop and therefore vulnerable to market conditions; there are only a few basic industries. Massive ethnic-based violence has also interfered with economic activity
GDP: $4.1 billion, per capita $740; real growth rate 4.5% (1998 est.)
Inflation: 19.1% (Dec. 1999)
Industries: accounts for 18% of GDP; light consumer goods such as blankets, shoes, soap; assembly of imports; public works construction; food processing
Labour Force: 4 million (1998); 39.6% community, social and business services, 14.8% manufacturing
Unemployment: n.a.
Agriculture: accounts for 58% of GDP; 90% of population dependent on subsistence farming; marginally self-sufficient in food production; cash crops—coffee, cotton, tea; food crops—corn, sorghum, sweet potatoes, bananas, manioc; livestock—meat, milk, hides and skins
Natural Resources: nickel, uranium, rare earth oxide, peat, cobalt, copper, platinum (not yet exploited), vanadium

■ FINANCE/TRADE

Currency: Burundi franc (FBu) = 100 centimes
International Reserves Excluding Gold: $48 million (Jan. 2000)
Gold Reserves: 0.017 million fine troy ounces (Jan. 2000)
Budget: revenues n.a., expenditures $165 million, including capital expenditures of $42.6 million (1998 est.)
Defence Expenditures: 25.8% of central government expenditure (1998 est.)
Education Expenditures: 13.87% of total govt. expenditure (1997)
External Debt: $1.119 billion (1998)
Exports: $65 million (1998); commodities: coffee 88%, tea, hides and skins; partners: European Community 83%, US 5%, Asia 2%
Imports: $118 million (1999); commodities: capital goods 31%, petroleum products 15%, foodstuffs, consumer goods; partners: European Community 57%, Asia 23%, US 3%

■ COMMUNICATIONS

Daily Newspapers: 1 (1996)
Televisions: 4/1,000 inhabitants (1998)
Radios: 71/1,000 inhabitants (1997)
Telephones: 3 lines/1,000 inhabitants (1998)

■ TRANSPORTATION

Motor Vehicles: 20,000; 8,200 passenger cars (1997 est.)
Roads: 14,480 km; 1,028 km paved
Railway: none
Air Traffic: 9,000 passengers carried (1996)
Airports: 4; 1 has paved runways (1998 est.)

Canadian Embassy: c/o The Canadian High Commission, P.O. Box 30481, Nairobi, Kenya. Tel: (011-254-2) 21-48-04. Fax: (011-254-2) 22-69-87.
Embassy in Canada: Embassy of the Republic of Burundi, 325 Dalhousie St., Suite 815, Ottawa, ON, K1N 7G2, Tel (613) 789-0414, Fax (613) 789-9537

Cambodia

Long-Form Name: Kingdom of Cambodia
Capital: Phnom Penh

■ GEOGRAPHY

Area: 181,040 sq. km
Coastline: 443 km
Climate: tropical; rainy, monsoon season (May

to Oct.); dry season (Dec. to Mar.); little seasonal temperature variation
Environment: a land of paddies and forests dominated by Mekong River and Tonle Sap; deforestation, monsoons; logging and strip mining are resulting in environmental degradation
Terrain: mostly low, flat plains; mountains in southwest and north
Land Use: 13% arable land; 0% permanent crops; 11% meadows and pastures; 66% forest and woodland; 10% other; includes 920 sq. km irrigated
Location: SE Asia, bordering on the Gulf of Siam

■ PEOPLE

Population: 11,626,520 (July 1999 est.)
Nationality: Cambodian
Age Structure: 0-14 yrs: 45%; 15-64: 52%; 65+: 3% (1999 est.)
Population Growth Rate: 2.49% (1999 est.)
Net Migration: 0 migrants/1,000 population (1999 est.)
Ethnic Groups: 90% Khmer (Cambodian), 5% Vietnamese, 1% Chinese, 4% other minorities
Languages: Khmer (official), French
Religions: 95% Theravada Buddhism, 5% Christianity
Birth Rate: 41.05/1,000 population (1999 est.)
Death Rate: 16.2/1,000 population (1999 est.)
Infant Mortality: 105.06 deaths/1,000 live births (1999 est.)
Life Expectancy at Birth: 46.81 years male, 49.75 years female (1999 est.)
Total Fertility Rate: 5.81 children born/woman (1999 est.)
Literacy: 35% (1997)

■ GOVERNMENT

Leader(s): King Norodom Sihanoŭk, Prime Min. Hun Sen
Government Type: liberal democracy under constitutional monarchy
Administrative Divisions: 20 provinces (khett, sing. & pl.) and 3 municipalities (krong, sing. & pl.)
Nationhood: Nov. 9, 1953 (from France)
National Holiday: Independence Day, Nov. 9

■ ECONOMY

Overview: a desperately poor country; the economy has suffered badly due to internal war; the country has not been able to feed its people; economy remains essentially rural, with 90% of the population dependent mainly on subsistence agriculture

GDP: $7.8 billion, per capita $700; real growth rate 0% (1998 est.)
Inflation: 0.2% (March 2000)
Industries: accounts for 15.4% of GDP; rice milling, fishing, wood and wood products, rubber, cement, gem mining
Labour Force: 6 million (1998); 74.4% agriculture, 6.7% industry, 18.9% services
Unemployment: n.a.
Agriculture: accounts for 51% of GDP, mainly subsistence farming except for rubber plantations; main crops—rice, rubber, corn; food shortages—rice, meat, vegetables, dairy products, sugar, flour
Natural Resources: timber, gemstones, some iron ore, manganese, phosphates, hydroelectricity potential

■ FINANCE/TRADE

Currency: new riel (KR) = 100 sen
International Reserves Excluding Gold: $426 million (Jan. 2000)
Gold Reserves: n.a.
Budget: n.a.
Defence Expenditures: 2.4% of GDP (1998)
Education Expenditures: 2.9% of GNP (1997)
External Debt: $2.21 billion total (1998)
Exports: $736 million (1997 est.); commodities: timber, garments, rubber, soybeans, sesame; partners: Singapore, Japan, Thailand, Hong Kong, Indonesia, Malaysia, US
Imports: $1.1 billion (1997 est.); commodities: cigarettes, construction materials, petroleum products, machinery, motor vehicles; partners: Singapore, Vietnam, Japan, Australia, Hong Kong, Indonesia

■ COMMUNICATIONS

Daily Newspapers: 0 (1996)
Televisions: 123/1,000 inhabitants (1998)
Radios: 127/1,000 inhabitants (1997)
Telephones: 2 lines/1,000 inhabitants (1998)

■ TRANSPORTATION

Motor Vehicles: n.a.
Roads: 35,769 km, but some roads are in serious disrepair; 4,165 km paved
Railway: 603 km, much inoperational since 1973
Air Traffic: n.a.
Airports: 20; 7 have paved runways (1998 est.)

Canadian Embassy: The Canadian Embassy, Villa 9, Senei Vinnavaut Oum, Chaktamouk, Daun Penh District, Phnom Penh. Tel: (011-855-23) 213-470. Fax: (011-855-23) 211-389.
Embassy in Canada: c/o Embassy of the Kingdom of Cambodia, 866 UN Plaza, Ste. 420,

New York, NY 10017, USA, Tel (212) 223-0676, Fax (212) 223-0425

Cameroon

Long-Form Name: Republic of Cameroon
Capital: Yaoundé

■ GEOGRAPHY

Area: 475,440 sq. km
Coastline: 402 km
Climate: varies with terrain from tropical along coast to semi-arid and hot in north
Environment: recent volcanic activity with release of poisonous gases; deforestation; overgrazing; desertification; diseases transmitted through the water supply are common
Terrain: coastal plain in southwest, dissected plateau in centre, mountains in west, plains in north
Land Use: 13% arable land; 2% permanent crops; 4% meadows and pastures; 78% forest and woodland; 3% other, includes 210 sq. km irrigated
Location: WC Africa, bordering on South Atlantic Ocean

■ PEOPLE

Population: 15,456,092 (July 1999 est.)
Nationality: Cameroonian
Age Structure: 0-14 yrs: 46%; 15-64: 51%; 65+: 3% (1999 est.)
Population Growth Rate: 2.79% (1999 est.)
Net Migration: n.a. migrants/1,000 population (1999 est.)
Ethnic Groups: over 200 tribes of widely differing background; 31% Cameroon Highlanders, 19% Equatorial Bantu, 11% Kirdi, 10% Fulani, 8% Northwestern Bantu, 7% Eastern Nigritic, 13% other African, less than 1% non-African
Languages: English and French (official), 24 major African language groups, including Fang, Bamileke, Duala
Religions: 51% indigenous beliefs, 33% Christian, 16% Muslim
Birth Rate: 41.84/1,000 population (1999 est.)
Death Rate: 13.95/1,000 population (1999 est.)
Infant Mortality: 75.69 deaths/1,000 live births (1999 est.)
Life Expectancy at Birth: 49.75 years male, 52.94 years female (1999 est.)
Total Fertility Rate: 5.80 children born/woman (1999 est.)
Literacy: 71.7% (1997)

■ GOVERNMENT

Leader(s): Pres. Paul Biya, Prime Min. Peter Mafany Musonge
Government Type: unitary republic; multi-party presidential regime (opposition parties legalized in 1990)
Administrative Divisions: 10 provinces
Nationhood: Jan. 1, 1960 (from UN trusteeship under French administration; Cameroon formerly known as French Cameroon)
National Holiday: National Day, May 20

■ ECONOMY

Overview: an offshore oil industry has boosted the economy but the government is now emphasizing diversification, particularly in agriculture
GDP: $29.6 billion, per capita $2,000; real growth rate 5% (1998 est.)
Inflation: 0.190% (Dec. 1998)
Industries: accounts for 22% of GDP; crude oil products, small aluminum plant, food processing, light consumer goods industries, textiles, sawmills
Labour Force: 6.1 million (1998); 74% agriculture, 4.5% industry, 21.5% services
Unemployment: 30% (1998 est.)
Agriculture: the agriculture and forestry sectors provide employment for the majority of the population, contributing 42% to GDP and providing a high degree of self-sufficiency in staple foods
Natural Resources: crude oil, bauxite, iron ore, timber, hydroelectricity potential

■ FINANCE/TRADE

Currency: Communauté financière africaine franc (CFAF) = 100 centimes
International Reserves Excluding Gold: $4 million (Dec. 1999)
Gold Reserves: 0.03 million fine troy ounces (June 1998)
Budget: revenues $2.23 billion; expenditures $2.23 billion, including capital expenditures of n.a. (1997 est.)
Defence Expenditures: 1.4% of GDP (1998-99)
Education Expenditures: n.a.
External Debt: $9.829 billion (1998)
Exports: $1.861 billion (1997); commodities: petroleum products 56%, coffee, cocoa, timber, manufacturing; partners: European Community 50%, US 3%
Imports: $1.359 million (1997); commodities: machines and electrical equipment, transport equipment, chemical products, consumer goods; partners: France 42%, Japan 7%, US 4%

■ COMMUNICATIONS
Daily Newspapers: 2 (1996)
Televisions: 32/1,000 inhabitants (1998)
Radios: 163/1,000 inhabitants (1997)
Telephones: 5 lines/1,000 inhabitants (1998)

■ TRANSPORTATION
Motor Vehicles: 153,000; 92,000 passenger cars (1997 est.)
Roads: 34,300 km; 4,288 km paved
Railway: 1,104 km
Air Traffic: 279,000 passengers carried (1997)
Airports: 52; 11 have paved runways (1998 est.)

Canadian Embassy: The Consulate of Canada, c/o PRO-PME, 1726 avenue de Gaulle, Bonanjo, Douala. mailing address: P.O. Box 2373, Douala, Cameroon. Tel: (011-237) 23-23-11. Fax: (011-237) 22-10-90.
Embassy in Canada: High Commission for the Republic of Cameroon, 170 Clemow Ave, Ottawa ON K1S 2B4. Tel: (613) 236-1522. Fax: (613) 236-3385.

Canada

Long-Form Name: Canada
Capital: Ottawa

■ GEOGRAPHY
Area: 9,976,140 sq. km
Coastline: 243,791 km
Climate: varies from temperate in south to subarctic and arctic in north
Environment: 80% of population concentrated within 160 km of US border; permafrost in north a serious obstacle to development; acid rain and ocean-water pollution resulting from industrial and agricultural activities are an increasing problem
Terrain: mostly plains with mountains in west and lowlands in southeast
Land Use: 5% arable land; negligible permanent crops; 3% meadows and pastures; 54% forest and woodland; 38% other, includes 7,100 sq. km irrigated
Location: N North America, bordering on North Atlantic Ocean, Arctic Ocean, North Pacific Ocean and United States

■ PEOPLE
Population: 31,006,347 (July 1999 est.)
Nationality: Canadian
Age Structure: 0-14 yrs: 20%; 15-64: 68%; 65+: 12% (1999 est.)
Population Growth Rate: 1.06% (1999 est.)
Net Migration: 5.96 migrants/1,000 population (1999 est.)
Ethnic Groups: 40% British, 27% French, 20% other European, 11.5% other, 1.5% Aboriginal
Languages: English and French (both official)
Religions: 45% Roman Catholic, 12% United Church, 8% Anglican, 35% other
Birth Rate: 11.86/1,000 population (1999 est.)
Death Rate: 7.26/1,000 population (1999 est.)
Infant Mortality: 5.47 deaths/1,000 live births (1999 est.)
Life Expectancy at Birth: 76.12 years male, 82.79 years female (1999 est.)
Total Fertility Rate: 1.65 children born/woman (1999 est.)
Literacy: 99% (1997)

■ GOVERNMENT
Leader(s): Head of State: Queen Elizabeth II/Gov. Gen. Adrienne Clarkson. Prime Min. Jean Chrétien
Government Type: confederation with parliamentary democracy
Administrative Divisions: 10 provinces, 3 territories
Nationhood: July 1, 1867 (from UK)
National Holiday: Canada Day, July 1

■ ECONOMY
Overview: abundant natural resources, skilled labour force, and high-tech industrialization characterize a market-oriented economy. Canada can anticipate solid economic prospects in the future.
GDP: $688.3 billion, per capita $22,400; real growth rate 3% (1998 est.)
Inflation: 3.0% (March 2000)
Industries: accounts for 31% of GDP; processsed and unprocessed minerals, food products, wood and paper products, transportation equipment, chemicals, fish products, petroleum, natural gas
Labour Force: 16.0 million (1998); 31.8% community, social and business services, 23.5% trade and tourism, 14.5% manufacturing
Unemployment: 7.3% (Feb. 2000)
Agriculture: accounts for 3% of GDP; one of the world's major producers and exporters of grain (wheat and barley); key source of US agricultural imports; large forest resources cover 35% of total land area
Natural Resources: nickel, zinc, copper, gold, lead, molybdenum, potash, silver, fish, timber, wildlife, coal, crude oil, natural gas

■ FINANCE/TRADE
Currency: dollar ($ or $Can) = 100 cents
International Reserves Excluding Gold: $28.503 billion (Jan. 2000)

Gold Reserves: 1.645 million fine troy ounces (Jan. 2000)
Budget: revenues $121.3 billion; expenditures $112.6 billion, capital expenditures $1.7 billion (1998)
Defence Expenditures: 1.2% of GDP (1997-98)
Education Expenditures: 6.9% of GNP (1997)
External Debt: $253 billion (1996)
Exports: $238.446 billion (1999); commodities: newsprint, wood pulp, timber, grain, crude petroleum, natural gas, ferrous and nonferrous ores, motor vehicles; partners: US, Japan, UK, Germany, other European Community, former USSR countries
Imports: $220.183 billion (1999); commodities: processed foods, beverages, crude petroleum, chemicals, industrial machinery, motor vehicles, durable consumer goods, electronic computers; partners: US, Japan, UK, Germany, other European Community, Taiwan, S Korea, Mexico

■ COMMUNICATIONS

Daily Newspapers: 107 (1996)
Televisions: 715/1,000 inhabitants (1998)
Radios: 1,077/1,000 inhabitants (1997)
Telephones: 634 lines/1,000 inhabitants (1998)

■ TRANSPORTATION

Motor Vehicles: 17,200,000; 13,600,000 passenger cars (1997 est.)
Roads: 912,200 km; 246,400 km paved
Railway: 67,773 km
Air Traffic: 23,981,000 passengers carried (1997)
Airports: 1,393; 515 have paved runways (1998 est.)

Canadian Embassy: n.a.
Embassy in Canada: n.a.

Cape Verde

Long-Form Name: Republic of Cape Verde
Capital: Praia

■ GEOGRAPHY

Area: 4,030 sq. km
Coastline: 965 km
Climate: temperate; warm, dry, very erratic summer precipitation
Environment: subject to prolonged droughts; harmattan wind can obscure visibility; volcanically and seismically active; deforestation; desertification; overgrazing and overfishing
Terrain: steep, rugged, rocky, volcanic
Land Use: 11% arable land; negligible permanent crops; 6% meadows and pastures; negligible forest and woodland; 83% other, includes 30 sq. km irrigated
Location: Atlantic Ocean W of Africa

■ PEOPLE

Population: 405,748 (July 1999 est.)
Nationality: Cape Verdean
Age Structure: 0-14 yrs: 45%; 15-64: 49%; 65+: 6% (1999 est.)
Population Growth Rate: 1.44% (1999 est.)
Net Migration: -12.35 migrants/1,000 population (1999 est.)
Ethnic Groups: approx. 71% Creole (mulatto), 28% African, 1% European
Languages: Portuguese and Crioulo, a blend of Portuguese and West African tongues
Religions: Roman Catholicism fused with indigenous beliefs
Birth Rate: 33.49/1,000 population (1999 est.)
Death Rate: 6.78/1,000 population (1999 est.)
Infant Mortality: 45.5 deaths/1,000 live births (1999 est.)
Life Expectancy at Birth: 67.66 years male, 74.36 years female (1999 est.)
Total Fertility Rate: 4.95 children born/woman (1999 est.)
Literacy: 71.0% (1997)

■ GOVERNMENT

Leader(s): Pres. Antonio Mascarenhas Monteiro, Prime Min. Carlos Alberto Wahnon de Carvalho Veiga
Government Type: republic
Administrative Divisions: 14 districts (concelhos, sing. -concelho)
Nationhood: July 5, 1975 (from Portugal)
National Holiday: Independence Day, July 5

■ ECONOMY

Overview: a service-oriented economy, which suffers from a poor natural resource base, a high birth rate and a long-term drought
GDP: $581 million, per capita $1,450; real growth rate 7% (1998 est.)
Inflation: 7.6% (March 1999)
Industries: accounts for 18% of GDP, fish processing, salt mining, clothing factories, ship repair, construction materials, food and beverage production
Labour Force: n.a.; 52% agriculture (mostly subsistence), 25% services, 23% industry
Unemployment: n.a.
Agriculture: accounts for 8% of GDP; largely subsistence farming; bananas are the only export crop; annual food imports required; growth potential limited by poor soils and limited

rainfall. Approximately 90% of food needs must be imported
Natural Resources: salt, basalt rock, pozzolana, limestone, kaolin, fish

■ FINANCE/TRADE

Currency: Cape Verdean escudo (C.V. Esc.) = 100 centavos
International Reserves Excluding Gold: $51 million (Jan. 2000)
Gold Reserves: n.a.
Budget: revenues $253.7 million; expenditures $276 million, including capital expenditures of n.a. (1997 est.)
Defence Expenditures: 2.2% of GDP (1997 est.)
Education Expenditures: n.a.
External Debt: $220 million (1998)
Exports: $43 million (1997 est.); commodities: fish, bananas, salt; partners: Portugal, Angola, Algeria, Belgium/Luxembourg, Italy
Imports: $215 million (1997 est.); commodities: petroleum, foodstuffs, consumer goods, industrial products; partners: Portugal, Netherlands, Spain, France, US, Germany

■ COMMUNICATIONS

Daily Newspapers: 0 (1996)
Televisions: 3.7/1,000 inhabitants (1996)
Radios: 179/1,000 inhabitants (1996)
Telephones: 98 lines/1,000 inhabitants (1998)

■ TRANSPORTATION

Motor Vehicles: 18,000; 11,000 passenger cars (1997 est.)
Roads: 1,100 km; 858 km paved
Railway: none
Air Traffic: 237,000 passengers carried (1997)
Airports: 6; all have paved runways (1998 est.)

Canadian Embassy: c/o The Canadian Embassy, P.O. Box 3373, Dakar, Senegal. Tel: (011-221) 823-92-90. Fax: (011-221) 823-87-49.
Embassy in Canada: c/o Embassy of the Republic of Cape Verde, 3415 Massachusetts Ave NW, Washington DC 20007, USA. Tel: (202) 965-6820. Fax: (202) 965-1207.

Cayman Islands

Long-Form Name: Cayman Islands
Capital: George Town (on Grand Cayman Island)

■ GEOGRAPHY

Area: 260 sq. km (three islands: Grand Cayman, Little Cayman, Cayman Brac)
Climate: tropical maritime; warm, rainy summers (May to Oct.); cool season: Nov. to March, hurricane-prone July to Nov.
Land Use: 0% arable, 0% permanent crops; 8% meadows and pastures; 23% forest and woodland; 69% other
Location: Caribbean Sea, S of Cuba

■ PEOPLE

Population: 39,335 (July 1999 est.)
Nationality: Caymanian
Ethnic Groups: 40% mixed, 20% white, 20% black, 20% expatriates of various ethnic groups, various Hispanic strains, descendants of European settlers
Languages: English (official)

■ GOVERNMENT

Colony/Territory of: United Kingdom Crown Colony
Leader(s): Head of State: Queen Elizabeth II. Governor and President of the Executive Council Peter John Smith. Chief Secretary James M. Ryan. Elections scheduled Nov. 8, 2000.
Government Type: United Kingdom Crown Colony
National Holiday: Constitution Day (first Monday in July)

■ ECONOMY

Overview: chiefly tourism (70% of GDP and 75% of export earnings) and financial services; main export turtle products; imports: foodstuffs, (about 90% of food and consumer goods must be imported), manufactured items, textiles, building materials, cars, petroleum products

■ FINANCE/TRADE

Currency: Caymanian dollar (CI$) = 100 cents

Canadian Embassy: c/o The Canadian High Commission, Macdonald House, 1 Grosvenor Square, London W1X 0AB, England, UK. Tel: (011-44-20) 7258-6600. Fax: (011-44-20) 7258-6333.
Representative to Canada: British High Commission, 80 Elgin St, Ottawa ON K1P 5K7. Tel: (613) 237-1530. Fax: (613) 237-7980.

Central African Republic

Long-Form Name: Central African Republic
Capital: Bangui

■ GEOGRAPHY

Area: 622,980 sq. km

Central African Republic

Coastline: none: landlocked
Climate: tropical; hot, dry winters; mild to hot, wet summers
Environment: hot, dry, dusty harmattan winds affect northern areas; poaching has diminished reputation as one of last great wildlife refuges; desertification and flooding; tap water is not safe to drink
Terrain: vast, flat to rolling, monotonous plateau; scattered hills in northeast and southwest
Land Use: 3% arable land; negligible permanent crops; 5% meadows and pastures; 75% forest and woodland; 17% other
Location: C Africa

■ PEOPLE

Population: 3,444,951 (July 1999 est.)
Nationality: Central African
Age Structure: 0-14 yrs: 44%; 15-64: 53%; 65+: 3% (1999 est.)
Population Growth Rate: 2.04% (1999 est.)
Net Migration: -1.45 migrants/1,000 population (1999 est.)
Ethnic Groups: about 80 ethnic groups, the majority of which have related ethnic and linguistic characteristics; 34% Baya, 27% Banda, 10% Sara, 21% Mandjia, 4% Mboum, 4% m'Baka; 6,500 Europeans, of whom 3,600 are French
Languages: French (official); Sangho (lingua franca and national language); Arabic, Hunsa, Swahili
Religions: 25% indigenous beliefs, 25% Protestant, 25% Roman Catholic, 15% Muslim, 10% other; animistic beliefs and practices strongly influence the Christian majority
Birth Rate: 38.28/1,000 population (1999 est.)
Death Rate: 16.46/1,000 population (1999 est.)
Infant Mortality: 103.42 deaths/1,000 live births (1999 est.)
Life Expectancy at Birth: 45.35 years male, 49.09 years female (1999 est.)
Total Fertility Rate: 5.03 children born/woman (1999 est.)
Literacy: 42.4% (1997)

■ GOVERNMENT

Leader(s): Pres. Ange Felix Patassé, Prime Min. Anicet Georges Dologuele
Government Type: republic
Administrative Divisions: 14 prefectures, 2 economic prefectures, 1 capital commune
Nationhood: Aug. 13, 1960 (from France; formerly known as Central African Empire)
National Holiday: National Day (proclamation of the republic), Dec. 1

■ ECONOMY

Overview: subsistence agriculture and forestry are the backbone of the economy. It suffers from a poor transportation infrastructure and a weak human resource base; diamond industry accounts for 54% of export earnings
GDP: $5.5 billion, per capita $1,640; real growth rate 5.5% (1998)
Inflation: -2.7% (June 1999)
Industries: accounts for 21% of GDP; sawmills, breweries, diamond mining, textiles, footwear, assembly of bicycles and motorcycles
Labour Force: 2 million (1997 est.); 32.6% construction industries, 30.5% manufacturing, 17.6% agriculture
Unemployment: n.a.
Agriculture: accounts for 53% of GDP; self-sufficient in food production except for grain; commercial crops—cotton, coffee, tobacco, timber; food crops—manioc, yams, millet, corn, bananas
Natural Resources: diamonds, uranium, timber, gold, oil

■ FINANCE/TRADE

Currency: Communauté financière africaine franc (CFAF) = 100 centimes
International Reserves Excluding Gold: $136 million (Dec. 1999)
Gold Reserves: 0.011 million fine troy ounces (June 1998)
Budget: n.a.
Defence Expenditures: 2.4% of GDP (1996)
Education Expenditures: n.a.
External Debt: $921 million (1998)
Exports: $154 million (1997); commodities: diamonds, cotton, coffee, timber, tobacco; partners: France, Belgium, Italy, Japan, US
Imports: $145 million (1997); commodities: food, textiles, petroleum products, machinery, electrical equipment, motor vehicles, chemicals, pharmaceuticals, consumer goods, industrial products; partners: France, other European Community, Japan, Algeria, former Yugoslavia

■ COMMUNICATIONS

Daily Newspapers: 3 (1996)
Televisions: 5/1,000 inhabitants (1998)
Radios: 83/1,000 inhabitants (1997)
Telephones: 3 lines/1,000 inhabitants (1998)

■ TRANSPORTATION

Motor Vehicles: 20,000; 11,000 passenger cars (1997 est.)
Roads: 23,810 km; 429 km paved
Railway: none
Air Traffic: 86,000 passengers carried (1997)

Airports: 52; 3 have paved runways (1998 est.)

Canadian Embassy: The Canadian High Commission, P.O. Box 572, Yaounde, Cameroon. Tel: (011-236) 61-09-73. Fax: (011-236) 61-40-74.

Embassy in Canada: c/o Embassy of the Central African Republic, 1618-22nd St NW, Washington DC 20008, USA. Tel: (202) 483-7800, Fax: (202) 332-9893

Chad

Long-Form Name: Republic of Chad
Capital: N'Djamena

■ GEOGRAPHY

Area: 1,284,000 sq. km
Coastline: none: landlocked
Climate: tropical in south, desert in north
Environment: hot, dry, dusty harmattan winds occur in north; drought and desertification adversely affecting south; subject to plagues of locusts; unsafe water supply
Terrain: broad, arid plains in centre, desert in north, mountains in northwest, lowlands in south
Land Use: 3% arable land; negligible permanent crops; 36% meadows and pastures; 26% forest and woodland; 35% others, includes 140 sq. km irrigated
Location: NC Africa

■ PEOPLE

Population: 7,557,436 (July 1999 est.)
Nationality: Chadian
Age Structure: 0-14 yrs: 44%; 15-64: 53%; 65+: 3% (1999 est.)
Population Growth Rate: 2.65% (1999 est.)
Net Migration: 0 migrants/1,000 population (1999 est.)
Ethnic Groups: some 200 distinct ethnic groups, most of whom are Muslims in the north and centre, and non-Muslims in the south; some 150,000 non-indigenous, of whom 1,000 are French
Languages: French and Arabic (official); Sara and Sango in south; more than 100 different languages and dialects are spoken
Religions: 50% Muslim, 25% Christian, 25% animism
Birth Rate: 43.06/1,000 population (1999 est.)
Death Rate: 16.57/1,000 population (1999 est.)
Infant Mortality: 115.27 deaths/1,000 live births (1999 est.)
Life Expectancy at Birth: 46.13 years male, 51.09 years female (1999 est.)
Total Fertility Rate: 5.69 children born/woman (1999 est.)
Literacy: 50.3% (1997 est.)

■ GOVERNMENT

Leader(s): Pres. Lt.- Gen. Idriss Deby, Prime Min. Nagoum Yamassoum
Government Type: republic
Administrative Divisions: 14 prefectures
Nationhood: Aug. 11, 1960 (from France)
National Holiday: Independence Day, Aug. 11

■ ECONOMY

Overview: Chad is one of the world's most underdeveloped countries; civil war, drought and food shortages have adversely affected the economy, which is based on subsistence farming and fishing
GDP: $7.5 billion, per capita $1,000; real growth rate 2.9% (1998 est.)
Inflation: -4.7% (Dec. 1999)
Industries: accounts for 15% of GDP, cotton textile mills, slaughterhouses, soap, cigarettes, brewery, natron (sodium carbonate), construction materials
Labour Force: 3.0 million (1998); 42.3% manufacturing, 19.1% community, social and business services, 8.0% transportation and communication
Unemployment: n.a.
Agriculture: accounts for 39% of GDP; largely subsistence farming; cotton most important cash crop; food crops include sorghum, millet, peanuts, rice, potatoes, manioc; livestock—cattle, sheep, goats, camels; self-sufficient in food in years of adequate rainfall
Natural Resources: small quantities of crude oil (unexploited but exploration beginning), uranium, natron, kaolin, fish (Lake Chad)

■ FINANCE/TRADE

Currency: Communauté financière africaine franc (CFAF) = 100 centimes
International Reserves Excluding Gold: $95 million (Dec. 1999)
Gold Reserves: 0.011 million fine troy ounces (June 1998)
Budget: revenues $198 million; expenditures $218 million, including capital expenditures of $146 million (1998 est.)
Defence Expenditures: 12.6% of central government expenditure (1997)
Education Expenditures: 1.7% of GNP (1997)
External Debt: $1.091 billion (1998)
Exports: $261 million (1998); commodities: cotton 43%, cattle 35%, textiles 5%, fish; partners: France, Nigeria, Cameroon

Imports: $264 million (1998); commodities: machinery and transportation equipment 39%, industrial goods 20%, petroleum products 13%, foodstuffs 9%; partners: US, France

■ **COMMUNICATIONS**
Daily Newspapers: 1 (1996)
Televisions: 1/1,000 inhabitants (1998)
Radios: 242/1,000 inhabitants (1997)
Telephones: 1 lines/1,000 inhabitants (1998)

■ **TRANSPORTATION**
Motor Vehicles: 24,600; 10,000 passenger cars (1997 est.)
Roads: 33,400 km; 267 km paved
Railway: none
Air Traffic: 93,000 passengers carried (1997)
Airports: 52; 8 have paved runways (1998 est.)

Canadian Embassy: c/o The Canadian Embassy, Édifice Stamatiades, Place de l'Hôtel de Ville, Yaoundé; mailing address: CP 572, Yaoundé, Cameroon. Tel: (011-237) 23-23-11. Fax: (011-237) 22-12-90.
Embassy in Canada: c/o Embassy of the Republic of Chad, 2002 R St NW, Washington DC 20009, USA. Tel: (202) 462-4009. Fax: (202) 265-1937.

Channel Islands

Long-Form Name: Channel Islands; Guernsey: Bailiwick of Guernsey; Jersey: Bailiwick of Jersey
Capital: St. Helier (Jersey), St. Peter Port (Guernsey)

■ **GEOGRAPHY**
Area: Jersey: 116 sq. km; Guernsey: 194 sq. km
Climate: temperate, with mild winters and cool summers
Land Use: Jersey: 57% arable, remainder n.a.; Guernsey: n.a.
Location: English Channel, off the coast of France

■ **PEOPLE**
Population: Jersey: 89,721; Guernsey: 65,386 (July 1999 est.)
Nationality: Channel Islander
Ethnic Groups: English, French
Languages: English (official), French (official only on Jersey), Norman-French dialect

■ **GOVERNMENT**
Colony/Territory of: Dependent Territory of the United Kingdom

Leader(s): Head of State: Queen Elizabeth II; Jersey: Lt. Gov. and Commander-in-Chief Air Marshal Sir Michael Wilkes, Guernsey: Lt. Gov. and Commander-in-Chief Sir John Coward
Government Type: largely self-governing British Crown dependency
National Holiday: Liberation Day, May 9

■ **ECONOMY**
Overview: Jersey: economy is based chiefly on financial services, agriculture and tourism, vegetable and flower exports, Jersey cattle; Guernsey: tourism, financial services, Guernsey cattle, and tomato and flower exports make up backbone of the economy

■ **FINANCE/TRADE**
Currency: Jersey pound, Guernsey pound, both = 100 pence; both are at par with the British pound

Canadian Embassy: c/o The Canadian High Commission, Macdonald House, 1 Grosvenor Square, London W1X 0AB, England, UK. Tel: (011-44-20) 7258-6600. Fax: (011-44-20) 7258-6333.
Representative to Canada: c/o British High Commission, 80 Elgin St, Ottawa ON K1P 5K7. Tel: (613) 237-1530. Fax: (613) 237-7980.

Chile

Long-Form Name: Republic of Chile
Capital: Santiago

■ **GEOGRAPHY**
Area: 756,950 sq. km
Coastline: 6,435 km
Climate: temperate; desert in north; cool and damp in south
Environment: subject to severe earthquakes, active volcanism, tsunami; Atacama Desert one of world's driest regions; desertification; deforestation; air and water pollution
Terrain: low coastal mountains; fertile central valley; rugged Andes in east
Land Use: 5% arable land; negligible permanent crops; 18% meadows and pastures; 22% forest and woodland; 55% other, includes 12,650 sq. km irrigated
Location: SW South America

■ **PEOPLE**
Population: 14,973,843 (July 1999 est.)
Nationality: Chilean
Age Structure: 0-14 yrs: 28%; 15-64: 65%; 65+: 7% (1999 est.)

Population Growth Rate: 1.23% (1999 est.)
Net Migration: 0 migrants/1,000 population (1999 est.)
Ethnic Groups: 95% European and European-Indian, 3% Indian, 2% other
Languages: Spanish
Religions: 89% Roman Catholic, 11% Protestant and small Jewish population
Birth Rate: 17.81/1,000 population (1999 est.)
Death Rate: 5.53/1,000 population (1999 est.)
Infant Mortality: 10.02 deaths/1,000 live births (1999 est.)
Life Expectancy at Birth: 72.33 years male, 78.75 years female (1999 est.)
Total Fertility Rate 2.25 children born/woman (1999 est.)
Literacy: 95.2% (1997)

■ GOVERNMENT

Leader(s): Pres. Ricardo Lagos Escobar
Government Type: republic
Administrative Divisions: 13 regions (regiones, sing. -region)
Nationhood: Sept. 18, 1810 (from Spain)
National Holiday: Independence Day, Sept. 18

■ ECONOMY

Overview: The Chilean economy remains largely dependent on a few sectors, particularly copper mining (copper is the single largest export product), fishing and forestry.
GDP: $184.6 billion, per capita $12,500; real growth rate 3.5% (1998 est.)
Inflation: 4.5% (April 2000)
Industries: accounts for 33% of GDP; copper (Chile is the world's largest producer and exporter of copper), other minerals, foodstuffs, fish processing, iron and steel, wood and wood products, transport equipment, textiles, cement
Labour Force: 6.0 million (1998); 24.79 community, social and business services, 18.6% trade and tourism, 16.6% agriculture
Unemployment: 8.9% (Nov. 1999)
Agriculture: accounts for about 6% of GDP (including fishing and forestry); major exporter of fruit, fish and timber products; major crops—wheat, corn, grapes, beans, sugar beets, potatoes, fruit; net agricultural importer
Natural Resources: copper, timber, iron ore, nitrates, precious metals, molybdenum

■ FINANCE/TRADE

Currency: peso ($CH) = 100 centavos
International Reserves Excluding Gold: $13.920 billion (Jan. 2000)
Gold Reserves: 1.220 million fine troy ounces (Jan. 2000)

Budget: revenues $17 billion; expenditures $17 billion, including capital expenditures n.a. (1996 est.)
Defence Expenditures: 2.7% of GDP (1998)
Education Expenditures: 20.49% of govt. expenditure (1998)
External Debt: $36.302 billion (1998)
Exports: $15.616 billion (1999); commodities: copper 48%, industrial products 33%, molybdenum, iron ore, wood pulp, fishmeal, fruit; partners: European Community 34%, US 22%, Japan 10%, Brazil 7%
Imports: $15.137 billion (1999); commodities: petroleum, wheat, capital goods, spare parts, raw materials; partners: European Community 23%, US 20%, Japan 10%, Brazil 9%

■ COMMUNICATIONS

Daily Newspapers: 52 (1996)
Televisions: 232/1,000 inhabitants (1998)
Radios: 354/1,000 inhabitants (1997)
Telephones: 205 lines/1,000 inhabitants (1998)

■ TRANSPORTATION

Motor Vehicles: 1,375,000; 900,000 passenger cars (1997 est.)
Roads: 79,800 km; 11,012 km paved
Railway: 6,782 km
Air Traffic: 4,610,000 passengers carried (1997)
Airports: 378; 58 have paved runways (1998 est.)

Canadian Embassy: The Canadian Embassy, 12th Fl., Nueva Tajamar 481, Santiago, Chile; mailing address: Casilla 139-10, Santiago, Chile. Tel: (011-56-2) 362-9660. Fax: (011-56-2) 362-9661.
Embassy in Canada: Embassy of the Republic of Chile, 50 O'Connor St, Ste 1413, Ottawa ON K1P 6L2. Tel: (613) 235-9940. Fax: (613) 235-1176.

China

Long-Form Name: People's Republic of China
Capital: Beijing

■ GEOGRAPHY

Area: 9,596,960 sq. km
Coastline: 14,500 km
Climate: extremely diverse; tropical in south to subarctic in north
Environment: frequent typhoons (about five times per year along southern and eastern coasts), damaging floods, tsunamis, earthquakes; deforestation; soil erosion; industrial pollution; water and air pollution; desertification; lack of safe drinking water

Terrain: mostly mountains, high plateaus, deserts in west; plains, deltas and hills in east
Land Use: 10% arable land; negligible permanent crops; 43% meadows and pastures; 14% forest and woodland; 33% other; includes 498,720 sq. km irrigated
Location: SE Asia, bordering on South China Sea, Yellow Sea

■ PEOPLE

Population: 1,246,871,951 (July 1999 est.)
Nationality: Chinese
Age Structure: 0-14 yrs: 26%; 15-64: 68%; 65+: 6% (1998 est.)
Population Growth Rate: 0.77% (1999 est.)
Net Migration: -0.41 migrants/1,000 population (1999 est.)
Ethnic Groups: 91.9% Han Chinese; 8.1% Zhuang, Uigur, Hui, Yi, Tibetan, Miao, Manchu, Mongol, Buyi, Korean and other nationalities
Languages: Standard Chinese (Putonghua) or Mandarin (based on the Beijing dialect), Yue (Cantonese), Wu (Shanghainese), Minbei (Fuzhou), Minnan. The Tibetans, Uigurs, Mongols, and others have their own languages
Religions: officially atheist, but traditionally pragmatic and eclectic; Confucianism, Taoism and Buddhism; approx. 2-3% Muslim, 1% Christian
Birth Rate: 15.10/1,000 population (1999 est.)
Death Rate: 6.98/1,000 population (1999 est.)
Infant Mortality: 43.31 deaths/1,000 live births (1999 est.)
Life Expectancy at Birth: 68.57 years male, 71.48 years female (1999 est.)
Total Fertility Rate: 1.8 children born/woman (1999 est.)
Literacy: 82.9% (1997)

■ GOVERNMENT

Leader(s): Pres. Jiang Zemin, Prem. Hu Jintao
Government Type: Communist Party-led state
Administrative Divisions: 23 provinces (sheng, sing. & pl.), 5 autonomous regions (zizhigu, sing. & pl.), 4 government-controlled municipalities (shi, sing. & pl.)
Nationhood: People's Republic established Oct. 1, 1949
National Holiday: National Day, Oct. 1

■ ECONOMY

Overview: the Soviet-style, centrally planned economy has been recently altered to include increased local authority, which has led to greater production; population control is vital, but has been weakened by popular resistance and loss of authority by rural cadres. Decentralization of the economic system is slowly progressing
GDP: $4.42 trillion, per capita $3,600; real growth rate 7.8% (1998 est.)
Inflation: -0.2% (March 2000)
Industries: accounts for 49% of GDP; iron, steel, coal, machine building, armaments, textiles, petroleum, chemical fertilizer, cement, consumer durables, food processing
Labour Force: 743 million (1998); 60% agriculture, 17.1% industry, 6.9% community, social and business services
Unemployment: 6.5% (August 1999)
Agriculture: accounts for almost 20% of GDP; among the world's largest producers of rice, potatoes, sorghum, peanuts, tea, millet, barley and pork; commercial crops include cotton, other fibres and oilseeds; produces variety of livestock products; self-sufficient in food
Natural Resources: coal, iron ore, crude oil, mercury, tin, tungsten, antimony, manganese, molybdenum, vanadium, magnetite, aluminum, lead, zinc, uranium, world's greatest hydroelectricity potential

■ FINANCE/TRADE

Currency: yuan (¥), pl. yen; = 10 jiao
International Reserves Excluding Gold: $159.039 billion (Jan. 2000)
Gold Reserves: 12.7 million fine troy ounces (Jan. 2000)
Budget: n.a.
Defence Expenditures: 13.60% of total govt. expenditure (1997)
Education Expenditures: 2.04% of govt. expenditure (1997)
External Debt: $154.599 billion (1998)
Exports: $195.150 billion (1999); commodities: manufactured goods, agricultural products, oilseeds, grain (rice and corn), oil, minerals; partners: US, Japan, former USSR countries, Singapore, Germany
Imports: $165.788 billion (1999); commodities: grain (mostly wheat), chemical fertilizer, steel, industrial raw materials, machinery, equipment; partners: Japan, US, Germany, former USSR countries

■ COMMUNICATIONS

Daily Newspapers: 39 (1996)
Televisions: 272/1,000 inhabitants (1998)
Radios: 333/1,000 inhabitants (1997)
Telephones: 70 lines/1,000 inhabitants (1998)

■ TRANSPORTATION

Motor Vehicles: 11,450,000; 4,700,000 passenger cars (1997 est.)

Roads: 1,210,000 km; 271,300 km paved
Railway: 64,900 km
Air Traffic: 52,277,000 passengers carried (1997)
Airports: 206; 192 have paved runways

Canadian Embassy: The Canadian Embassy, 19 Dong Zhi Men Wai St, Chao Yang District, Beijing 100600, People's Republic of China. Tel: (011-86-10) 6532-3536. Fax (011-86-10) 6532-4311.
Embassy in Canada: Embassy of the People's Republic of China, 515 St. Patrick St, Ottawa ON K1N 5H3. Tel: (613) 789-3434. Fax: (613) 789-1911.

Christmas Island

Long-Form Name: Territory of Christmas Island
Capital: The Settlement

■ GEOGRAPHY

Area: 135 sq. km (land area); includes one of the largest coral islands in the Pacific
Climate: tropical, with little seasonal variation; heat and humidity moderated by trade winds
Land Use: dry sandy soil does not permit much cultivation
Location: SE Asia, between Australia and Indonesia

■ PEOPLE

Population: 2,373 (July 1999 est.)
Nationality: Christmas Islander
Ethnic Groups: 61% Chinese, 25% Malay, 11% European, 3% other. There is no indigenous population
Languages: English, Chinese, Oriental and European-speaking minorities

■ GOVERNMENT

Colony/Territory of: Dependent Territory of Australia
Leader(s): Head of State: Queen Elizabeth II. Administrator Graham Nicholls appointed by Australian Commonwealth govt.
Government Type: dependency of Australia
National Holiday: n.a.

■ ECONOMY

Overview: extraction and export of rock phosphate dust was the only significant economic activity until 1987, when the mine was closed. It was reopened in 1990.

■ FINANCE/TRADE

Currency: Australian dollar = 100 cents
Canadian Embassy: c/o The Canadian High Commission, Commonwealth Ave, Canberra A.C.T. 2600, Australia. Tel: (011-61-2) 6270-4000 Fax: (011-61-2) 6273-3285
Representative to Canada: c/o Australian High Commission, 50 O'Connor St, Ste 710, Ottawa ON K1P 6L2. Tel: (613) 236-0841. Fax: (613) 236-4376.

Cocos (Keeling) Islands

Long-Form Name: Territory of Cocos (Keeling) Islands
Capital: West Island

■ GEOGRAPHY

Area: 14 sq. km
Climate: tropical maritime modified by southeast trade wind for 9 months of the year; moderate rainfall
Land Use: primarily subsistence agriculture
Location: Indian Ocean, SW of Sumatra

■ PEOPLE

Population: 636 (July 1999 est.)
Nationality: Cocos Islander
Ethnic Groups: West Island: Europeans; Home Island: Cocos Malays
Languages: English, Malay

■ GOVERNMENT

Colony/Territory of: Dependent Territory of Australia
Leader(s): Head of State: Queen Elizabeth II. Administrator Maureen Ellis (appointed by Gov. Gen. of Australia)
Government Type: territory of Australia; dependency placed under Australian govt. authority by Cocos (Keeling) Islands Act of 1955
National Holiday: n.a.

■ ECONOMY

Overview: little industrial activity; agriculture limited to copra and coconut cultivation

■ FINANCE/TRADE

Currency: Australian dollar = 100 cents
Canadian Embassy: c/o The Canadian High Commission, Commonwealth Ave, Canberra A.C.T. 2600, Australia. Tel: (011-61-2) 6270-4000 Fax: (011-61-2) 6273-3285
Representative to Canada: c/o Australian High Commission, 50 O'Connor St, Ste 710, Ottawa ON K1P 6L2. Tel: (613) 236-0841. Fax: (613) 236-4376.

Colombia

Long-Form Name: Republic of Colombia
Capital: Bogotá

■ GEOGRAPHY

Area: 1,138,910 sq. km; includes Isla de Malpelo, Roncador Cay, Serrana Bank, and Serranilla Bank
Coastline: 3,208 km
Climate: tropical along coast and eastern plains; cooler in highlands
Environment: highlands subject to volcanic eruptions; deforestation; soil damage from overuse of pesticides; periodic droughts; air pollution
Terrain: mixture of flat coastal lowlands, plains in east, central highlands, some high mountains (Andes)
Land Use: 4% arable land; 1% permanent crops; 39% meadows and pastures; 48% forest and woodland; 8% other; includes 5,300 sq. km irrigated
Location: NW South America, bordering on Caribbean Sea, Pacific Ocean

■ PEOPLE

Population: 39,309,422 (July 1999 est.)
Nationality: Colombian
Age Structure: 0-14 yrs: 33%; 15-64: 62%; 65+: 5% (1999 est.)
Population Growth Rate: 1.85% (1999 est.)
Net Migration: -0.34 migrants/1,000 population (1999 est.)
Ethnic Groups: 58% mestizo, 20% white, 14% mulatto, 4% black, 4% Indian
Languages: Spanish
Religions: 95% Roman Catholic
Birth Rate: 24.45/1,000 population (1999 est.)
Death Rate: 5.59/1,000 population (1999 est.)
Infant Mortality: 24.3 deaths/1,000 live births (1999 est.)
Life Expectancy at Birth: 66.54 years male, 74.54 years female (1999 est.)
Total Fertility Rate: 2.87 children born/woman (1999 est.)
Literacy: 90.9% (1997)

■ GOVERNMENT

Leader(s): Pres. Andrés Pastrana Arango; V. Pres. Gustavo Bell
Government Type: republic; executive branch dominates government structure
Administrative Divisions: 32 departments (departmentos, sing. -department), 1 capital district (distrito capital)
Nationhood: July 20, 1810 (from Spain)
National Holiday: Independence Day, July 20

■ ECONOMY

Overview: traditionally coffee has been the main export, though other industries such as oil and coal are developing; drug-related violence is an increasing threat to economic growth
GDP: $254.7 billion, per capita $6,600; real growth rate 0.2% (1998 est.)
Inflation: 10.7% (April 2000)
Industries: accounts for 26% of GDP; textiles, food processing, oil, clothing and footwear, beverages, chemicals, metal products, cement; mining—gold, coal, emeralds, iron, nickel, silver, salt
Labour Force: 18 million (1998); 28.6% community, social and business services, 23.5% industry, 7.1% finance
Unemployment: 15.7% (1998)
Agriculture: accounts for 19% of GDP; crops make up two-thirds and livestock one-third of agricultural output; climate and soils permit a wide variety of crops, such as coffee, rice, tobacco, corn, sugar cane, cocoa beans, oilseeds, vegetables; forest products and shrimp farming are increasing in importance
Natural Resources: crude oil, natural gas, coal, iron ore, nickel, gold, copper, emeralds

■ FINANCE/TRADE

Currency: peso ($Col) = 100 centavos
International Reserves Excluding Gold: $7.644 billion (Dec. 1999)
Gold Reserves: 0.328 million fine troy ounces (Dec. 1999)
Budget: revenues $27 billion; expenditures $30 billion, including capital expenditures n.a. (1997 est.)
Defence Expenditures: 4.2% of GDP (1998)
Education Expenditures: 4.1 % of GNP (1997)
External Debt: $33.263 billion (1998)
Exports: $11.576 billion (1999); commodities: coffee 30%, petroleum 24%, coal, bananas, fresh cut flowers; partners: US 36%, European Community 21%, Japan 5%, Netherlands 4%, Sweden 3%
Imports: $10.659 billion (1999); commodities: industrial equipment, transportation equipment, foodstuffs, chemicals, paper products; partners: US 34%, European Community 16%, Brazil 4%, Venezuela 3%, Japan 3%

■ COMMUNICATIONS

Daily Newspapers: 37 (1996)
Televisions: 217/1,000 inhabitants (1998)
Radios: 581/1,000 inhabitants (1997)
Telephones: 173 lines/1,000 inhabitants (1998)

Comoros

■ TRANSPORTATION

Motor Vehicles: 1,700,000; 1,150,000 passenger cars (1997 est.)
Roads: 115,564 km; 13,868 km paved
Railway: 3,380 km
Air Traffic: 9,189,000 passengers carried (1997)
Airports: 1,120; 89 have paved runways (1998 est.)

Canadian Embassy: The Canadian Embassy, Carrera 7, No. 115-23, Bogotá, Colombia; mailing address: Apartado Aereo 110067, Bogotá 2, Colombia. Tel: (011-57-1) 657-9800. Fax (011-57-1) 657-9912.
Embassy in Canada: Embassy of the Republic of Colombia, 360 Albert St, Ste 1002, Ottawa ON K1R 7X7. Tel: (613) 230-3760. Fax: (613) 230-4416.

Comoros

Long-Form Name: Federal Islamic Republic of the Comoros
Capital: Moroni

■ GEOGRAPHY

Area: 2,170 sq. km
Coastline: 340 km
Climate: tropical marine; rainy season (Nov. to May)
Environment: soil degradation and erosion, resulting from crop cultivation on slopes without proper terracing; deforestation; cyclones possible during rainy season
Terrain: volcanic islands, interiors vary from steep mountains to low hills
Land Use: 35% arable; 10% permanent; 7% meadows; 18% forest; 30% other
Location: E of Africa, Indian Ocean/Mozambique Channel

■ PEOPLE

Population: 562,723 (July 1999 est.)
Nationality: Comoran
Age Structure: 0-14 yrs: 43%; 15-64: 54%; 65+: 3% (1999 est.)
Population Growth Rate: 3.11% (1999 est.)
Net Migration: 0 migrants/1,000 population (1999 est.)
Ethnic Groups: Antalote, Cafre, Makoa, Oimatsaha, Sakalava
Languages: French and Arabic (both official), Shaafi Islam (a Swahili dialect), Malagasy; majority speaks Comoran
Religions: 86% Sunni Muslim, 14% Roman Catholic
Birth Rate: 40.29/1,000 population (1999 est.)
Death Rate: 9.23/1,000 population (1999 est.)
Infant Mortality: 81.63 deaths/1,000 live births (1999 est.)
Life Expectancy at Birth: 58.39 years male, 63.38 years female (1999 est.)
Total Fertility Rate: 5.43 children born/woman (1999 est.)
Literacy: 55.4% (1997)

■ GOVERNMENT

Leader(s): Head of State: Col. Assumani Azzali. Prime Min. Tarmidi Bianrifi
Government Type: independent republic
Administrative Divisions: 3 islands
Nationhood: July 6, 1975 (from France)
National Holiday: Independence Day, July 6

■ ECONOMY

Overview: agriculture is the main sector of the economy though it does not feed citizens adequately; lack of natural resources makes Comoros one of the world's poorest countries
GDP: $400 million, per capita $700; real growth rate 3.5% (1997)
Inflation: n.a.
Industries: accounts for 14% of GDP; perfume distillation, textiles, furniture, jewelry, soft drinks, construction materials
Labour Force: 144,500 (1996 est.); 80% agriculture, 6% industry, 14% services
Unemployment: 20% (1996 est.)
Agriculture: accounts for 40% of GDP; most of population works in subsistence agriculture and fishing; plantations produce cash crops for export—vanilla, cloves, perfume essences and copra; principal food crops—coconuts, bananas, cassava; large net food importer
Natural Resources: negligible

■ FINANCE/TRADE

Currency: Comoran franc (CFAF) = 100 centimes
International Reserves Excluding Gold: $38 million (Oct. 1999)
Gold Reserves: 0.001 million fine troy ounces (June 1998)
Budget: revenues $48 million; expenditures $53 million, including capital expenditures of n.a. (1997)
Defence Expenditures: n.a.
Education Expenditures: n.a.
External Debt: $206 million (1996)
Exports: $11.4 million (1996 est.); commodities: vanilla, cloves, perfume oil, copra; partners: US 53%, France 41%, Africa 4%, Germany 2%
Imports: $70 million (1996 est.); commodities:

rice and other foodstuffs, cement, petroleum products, consumer goods; partners: Europe 62% (France 22%, other 40%), Africa 5%, Pakistan, China

■ COMMUNICATIONS
Daily Newspapers: 0 (1996)
Televisions: 1.6/1,000 inhabitants (1996)
Radios: 138/1,000 inhabitants (1996)
Telephones: 9 lines/1,000 inhabitants (1998)

■ TRANSPORTATION
Motor Vehicles: n.a.
Roads: 880 km; 673 km paved
Railway: none
Air Traffic: 27,000 passengers carried (1996)
Airports: 4; all have paved runways (1998 est.)

Canadian Embassy: Canadian Embassy to the Comoros, c/o The Canadian High Commission, P.O. Box 1022, Dar-es-Salaam, Tanzania. Tel: (011-255-51) 112-832. Fax: (011-255-51) 116-896.
Embassy in Canada: Embassy of the Islamic Federal Republic of Comoros, c/o Permanent Mission of the Comoros to the UN, 420 East 50th Street, New York, NY, 10022, Tel: (212) 972-8010, Fax: (212) 983-4712

Congo

Long-Form Name: Republic of the Congo
Capital: Brazzaville

■ GEOGRAPHY
Area: 342,000 sq. km
Coastline: 169 km
Climate: tropical; rainy season (Mar. to June); dry season (June to Oct.); constant high temperatures and humidity; particularly enervating climate astride the Equator
Environment: deforestation; air and water pollution; unsafe water supply; about 70% of the population lives in Brazzaville, Pointe Noire or along the railroad between them
Terrain: coastal plain, southern basin, central plateau, northern basin
Land Use: 0% arable land; negligible permanent; 29% meadows; 62% forest; 9% other; includes 10 sq. km irrigated
Location: WC Africa, bordering on South Atlantic Ocean

■ PEOPLE
Population: 2,716,814 (July 1999 est.)
Nationality: Congolese (sing. & pl.)
Age Structure: 0-14 yrs: 42%; 15-64: 54%; 65+: 4% (1999 est.)
Population Growth Rate: 2.16% (1999 est.)
Net Migration: 0 migrants/1,000 population (1999 est.)
Ethnic Groups: about 15 ethnic groups divided into some 75 tribes, almost all Bantu; most important ethnic groups are Kongo (48%) in south, Sangha (20%) and M'Bochi (12%) in the north, Teke (17%) in the centre; about 8,500 Europeans, mostly French
Languages: French (official); many African languages with Lingala and Kikongo most widely used
Religions: 50% Christian, 48% animist, 2% Muslim
Birth Rate: 37.96/1,000 population (1999 est.)
Death Rate: 16.33/1,000 population (1999 est.)
Infant Mortality: 100.58 deaths/1,000 live births (1999 est.)
Life Expectancy at Birth: 45.42 years male, 48.92 years female (1999 est.)
Total Fertility Rate: 4.89 children born/woman (1999 est.)
Literacy: 76.9% (1997)

■ GOVERNMENT
Leader(s): Pres. Denis Sassou-Nguesso
Government Type: republic
Administrative Divisions: 9 regions, 1 commune
Nationhood: Aug. 15, 1960 (from France; formerly known as Congo/Brazzaville)
National Holiday: Congolese National Day, Aug. 15

■ ECONOMY
Overview: oil revenues are responsible for one of the highest growth rates in Africa, though the country faces increasing foreign debt and is vulnerable to the oil market. Recent efforts at economic reform are beginning to show results
GDP: $3.9 billion, per capita $1,500; real growth rate 2.5% (1998 est.)
Inflation: -9.2% (Mar. 1997)
Industries: accounts for 59% of GDP; petroleum, lumbering, cement, sawmills, brewery, sugar mills, palm oil, soap, cigarettes
Labour Force: 1 million (1998); 62.4% agriculture, 25.6% services, 11.9% industry
Unemployment: n.a.
Agriculture: accounts for 10% of GDP (including fishing and forestry); cassava accounts for 90% of food output; other crops—rice, corn, peanuts, vegetables; cash crops include coffee and cocoa; forest products important export earner; imports over 90% of food needs
Natural Resources: petroleum, timber, potash, lead, zinc, uranium, copper, phosphate, natural gas

■ FINANCE/TRADE

Currency: Communauté financière africaine franc (CFAF) = 100 centimes
International Reserves Excluding Gold: $39 million (Dec. 1999)
Gold Reserves: 0.011 million fine troy ounces (June 1998)
Budget: revenues $870 million; expenditures $970 million including capital expenditures of n.a. (1997 est.)
Defence Expenditures: 1.9% of GDP (1996)
Education Expenditures: 6.1% of GNP (1997)
External Debt: $5.119 billion (1998)
Exports: $1.664 billion (1997); commodities: crude petroleum 72%, lumber, plywood, coffee, cocoa, sugar, diamonds; partners: US, France, other European Community
Imports: $1.551 billion (1996); commodities: foodstuffs, consumer goods, intermediate manufactures, capital equipment; partners: France, Italy, other European community members, U.S., Germany, Spain, Japan, Brazil

■ COMMUNICATIONS

Daily Newspapers: 6 (1996)
Televisions: 12/1,000 inhabitants (1998)
Radios: 124/1,000 inhabitants (1997)
Telephones: 8 lines/1,000 inhabitants (1998)

■ TRANSPORTATION

Motor Vehicles: 47,000; 30,000 passenger cars (1997 est.)
Roads: 12,800 km; 1,242 km paved
Railway: 795 km
Air Traffic: 245,000 passengers carried (1997)
Airports: 36; 4 have paved runways (1998 est.)

Canadian Embassy: The Canadian Embassy to the Republic of the Congo, P.O. Box 4037, Libreville, Gabon. Tel: (011-241) 73-73-54. Fax: (011-241) 73-73-88.
Embassy in Canada: c/o Embassy of the Republic of the Congo, 4891 Colorado Ave NW, Washington DC 20011, USA. Tel: (202) 726-5500. Fax: (202) 726-1860.

Cook Islands

Long-Form Name: Cook Islands
Capital: Avarua (on Rarotonga Island)

■ GEOGRAPHY

Area: 240 sq. km
Climate: mild year-round, moderated by trade winds
Land Use: 9% arable, 13% permanent crops, negligible meadows and pastures, negligible forest and woodland, 78% other
Location: S Pacific Ocean, NE of New Zealand

■ PEOPLE

Population: 20,200 (July 1999 est.)
Nationality: Cook Islander
Ethnic Groups: Polynesian 81.3%, Polynesian-European mixture 7.7%, Polynesian-other mixture 7.7%, European 2.4%, other 0.9%
Languages: English (official), Cook Islands Maori

■ GOVERNMENT

Colony/Territory of: Territory in free association with New Zealand
Leader(s): Head of State: Queen Elizabeth II. Prime Min. Sir Geoffrey A. Henry
Government Type: self-governing territory in free association with New Zealand; Cook Island is fully responsible for internal affairs; New Zealand retains responsibility for external affairs, in consultation with the Cook Islands
National Holiday: Constitution Day, Aug. 4

■ ECONOMY

Overview: agriculture provides the backbone of the economy: copra, fruits, tomatoes; livestock: pigs, goats; fishing; manufacturing is limited

■ FINANCE/TRADE

Currency: New Zealand dollar (NZ$) = 100 cents

Canadian Embassy: c/o The Canadian High Commission, 3rd Fl, 61 Molesworth St, Thorndon, Wellington, New Zealand; postal address: c/o Box 12-049, Thorndon, Wellington, New Zealand. Tel: (011-64-4) 473-9577. Fax: (011-64-4)471-2082
Representative to Canada: c/o New Zealand High Commission, Clarica Centre, 99 Bank St, Ste 727, Ottawa ON K1P 6G3. Tel: (613) 238-5991. Fax: (613) 238-5707.

Costa Rica

Long-Form Name: Republic of Costa Rica
Capital: San José

■ GEOGRAPHY

Area: 51,100 sq. km; includes Isla del Coco
Coastline: 1,290 km
Climate: tropical; dry season (Dec. to Apr.); rainy season (May to Nov.)
Environment: subject to occasional earthquakes, hurricanes along Atlantic coast; frequent

flooding of lowlands at onset of rainy season; active volcanoes; deforestation; soil erosion
Terrain: coastal plains separated by rugged mountains
Land Use: 6% arable; 5% permanent; 46% meadows; 31% forest; 12% other, includes 1,200 sq. km irrigated
Location: Central (Latin) America, bordering on Caribbean Sea, Pacific Ocean

■ PEOPLE

Population: 3,674,490 (July 1999 est.)
Nationality: Costa Rican
Age Structure: 0-14 yrs: 33%; 15-64: 62%; 65+: 5% (1999 est.)
Population Growth Rate: 1.89% (1999 est.)
Net Migration: 0.62 migrants/1,000 population (1999 est.)
Ethnic Groups: 96% white (including mestizo), 2% black, 1% Indian, 1% Chinese
Languages: Spanish (official), English is spoken around Puerto Limon
Religions: 95% Roman Catholic
Birth Rate: 22.46/1,000 population (1999 est.)
Death Rate: 4.16/1,000 population (1999 est.)
Infant Mortality: 12.89 deaths/1,000 live births (1999 est.)
Life Expectancy at Birth: 73.60 years male, 78.61 years female (1999 est.)
Total Fertility Rate: 2.76 children born/woman (1999 est.)
Literacy: 95.1% (1997)

■ GOVERNMENT

Leader(s): Pres. Miguel Angel Rodríquez Echeverría
Government Type: democratic republic
Administrative Divisions: 7 provinces (provincias, sing. -provincia
Nationhood: Sept. 15, 1821 (from Spain)
National Holiday: Independence Day, Sept. 15

■ ECONOMY

Overview: inflation and external debt are high, many people are underemployed; coffee and banana crops are vital
GDP: $24billion, per capita $6,700; real growth rate 5.5% (1998 est.)
Inflation: 10.9% (Feb. 2000)
Industries: accounts for 24% of GDP; food processing, textiles and clothing, plastics products, construction materials, fertilizer, tourism
Labour Force: 1 million (1998); 24.1% community, social and business services, 24.1% agriculture, 18.9% industry
Unemployment: 5.6% (1998 est.), but there is much underemployment

Agriculture: accounts for 15% of GDP and 70% of exports; cash commodities—coffee, beef, bananas, sugar; normally self-sufficient in food except for grain; depletion of forest resources resulting in lower timber output
Natural Resources: hydroelectricity potential

■ FINANCE/TRADE

Currency: colón (pl. colones) (C/) = 100 centimes
International Reserves Excluding Gold: $1.414 billion (Jan. 2000)
Gold Reserves: 0.002 million fine troy ounces (Jan. 2000)
Budget: n.a.
Defence Expenditures: 3.1% of central government expenditure (1997)
Education Expenditures: 5.4% of GNP (1997)
External Debt: $3.971 billion (1998)
Exports: $6.557 billion (1999); commodities: coffee, bananas, textiles, sugar; partners: US 75%, Germany, Guatemala, Netherlands, UK, Japan
Imports: $6.320 billion (1999); commodities: petroleum, machinery, consumer durables, chemicals, fertilizer, foodstuffs; partners: US 35%, Japan, Guatemala, Germany

■ COMMUNICATIONS

Daily Newspapers: 6 (1996)
Televisions: 387/1,000 inhabitants (1998)
Radios: 271/1,000 inhabitants (1997)
Telephones: 172 lines/1,000 inhabitants (1998)

■ TRANSPORTATION

Motor Vehicles: 121,000; 49,600 passenger cars (1997 est.)
Roads: 35,597 km; 6,051 km paved
Railway: 950 km
Air Traffic: 992,000 passengers carried (1997)
Airports: 156; 28 have paved runways (1998 est.)

Canadian Embassy: The Canadian Embassy, Oficentro Ejecutivo La Sabana-detrás de la Contraloría, Sabana Sur, San José; mailing address: Canadian Embassy, P.O. Box 351-1007, Centro Colon, San José, Costa Rica. Tel: (011-506) 296-4149. Fax: (011-506) 296-4270.
Embassy in Canada: Embassy of the Republic of Costa Rica, 325 Dalhousie St., Suite 407, Ottawa ON K1N 7G2. Tel: (613) 562-2855. Fax: (613) 562-2582.

Côte d'Ivoire (Ivory Coast)

Long-Form Name: Republic of Côte d'Ivoire
Capital: Yamoussoukro

Côte d'Ivoire (Ivory Coast)

■ GEOGRAPHY

Area: 322,460 sq. km
Coastline: 515 km
Climate: tropical along coast, semi-arid in far north; three seasons: warm and dry (Nov. to Mar.), hot and dry (Mar. to May), hot and wet (June to Oct.)
Environment: coast has heavy surf and no natural harbours; severe deforestation; water pollution; heavy flooding is possible during rainy season
Terrain: mostly flat to undulating plains; mountains in northwest
Land Use: 8% arable; 4% permanent; 41% permanent pastures; 22% forest; 25% other; includes 680 sq. km irrigated
Location: WC Africa, bordering on South Atlantic Ocean

■ PEOPLE

Population: 15,818,068 (July 1999 est.)
Nationality: Ivorian
Age Structure: 0-14 yrs: 47%; 15-64: 51%; 65+: 2% (1999 est.)
Population Growth Rate: 2.35% (1999 est.)
Net Migration: -2.08 migrants/1,000 population (1999 est.)
Ethnic Groups: over 60 ethnic groups; most important are the Baoule 23%, Bete 18%, Senoufou 15%, Malinke 11% and Agni; about 2 million foreign Africans mostly Burkinabe; about 130,000 to 330,000 non-Africans (30,000 French and 100,000-300,000 Lebanese)
Languages: French (official), 60 native dialects, of which Dioula is the most widely spoken
Religions: 28% indigenous, 60% Muslim, 12% Christian
Birth Rate: 41.76/1,000 population (1999 est.)
Death Rate: 16.17/1,000 population (1999 est.)
Infant Mortality: 94.17 deaths/1,000 live births (1999 est.)
Life Expectancy at Birth: 44.48 years male, 47.67 years female (1999 est.)
Total Fertility Rate: 5.89 children born/woman (1999 est.)
Literacy: 42.6% (1997)

■ GOVERNMENT

Leader(s): Head of State: Brig. Gen. Robert Guei. Premier Seydou Elimane Diarra. Presidential election scheduled for October 8, 2000.
Government Type: republic; multi-party presidential regime
Administrative Divisions: 50 departments (departements, sing. -departement)
Nationhood: Aug. 7, 1960 (from France)
National Holiday: National Day, Aug. 7

■ ECONOMY

Overview: despite attempts to diversify, the economy is largely dependent on agriculture and related industries; highly sensitive to fluctuations in world prices for coffee and cocoa and to weather conditions
GDP: $24.2 billion, per capita $1,680; real growth rate 6% (1998 est.)
Inflation: 1.6% (Dec. 1999)
Industries: accounts for 20% of GDP; foodstuffs, wood processing, oil refinery, automobile assembly, textiles, fertilizer, beverages
Labour Force: 6 million (1998); 45.4% community, social and business services, 15.6% industry, 13.8% agriculture
Unemployment: n.a.
Agriculture: most important sector, contributing 31% to GDP and 80% to exports; cash crops include coffee, cocoa beans, timber, bananas, palm kernels, rubber; food crops; not self-sufficient in bread grain and dairy products
Natural Resources: crude oil, diamonds, manganese, iron ore, cobalt, bauxite, copper

■ FINANCE/TRADE

Currency: Communauté financière africaine franc (CFAF) = 100 centimes
International Reserves Excluding Gold: $542 million (Nov. 1999)
Gold Reserves: 0.045 million fine troy ounces (July 1998)
Budget: revenues $2.3 billion; expenditures $2.6 billion, including capital expenditures of $640 million (1997 est.)
Defence Expenditures: 4.0% of central government expenditure (1997)
Education Expenditures: 5.0% of GNP (1997)
External Debt: $14.852 billion (1998)
Exports: $4.077 million (1999) commodities: cocoa 30%, coffee 20%, tropical woods 11%, cotton, bananas, pineapples, palm oil; partners: France, Germany, Netherlands, US, Belgium, Spain
Imports: $3.270 million (1999) commodities: manufactured goods and semifinished products 50%, consumer goods 40%, raw materials and fuels 10%; partners: France, other European Community, Nigeria, US, Japan

■ COMMUNICATIONS

Daily Newspapers: 12 (1996)
Televisions: 70/1,000 inhabitants (1998)
Radios: 164/1,000 inhabitants (1997)
Telephones: 12 lines/1,000 inhabitants (1998)

■ TRANSPORTATION

Motor Vehicles: 255,000; 160,000 passenger cars (1997 est.)

Roads: 50,400 km; 4,889 km paved
Railway: 660 km
Air Traffic: 158,000 passengers carried (1997)
Airports: 36; 7 have paved runways (1998 est.)

Canadian Embassy: The Canadian Embassy, Immeuble Trade-Center, 23 rue Nogues, Le Plateau, Abidjan; mailing address: BP 4104, Abidjan 01, Côte d'Ivoire. Tel: (011-225) 20-21-20-09. Fax: (011-225) 20-21-77-28.
Embassy in Canada: Embassy of the Republic of Côte d'Ivoire, 9 Marlborough Ave, Ottawa ON K1N 8E6. Tel: (613) 236-9919. Fax: (613) 563-8287.

Croatia

Long-Form Name: Republic of Croatia
Capital: Zagreb

■ GEOGRAPHY

Area: 56,538 sq. km
Coastline: 5,790 km
Climate: hot summers and cold winters; along coast, mild winters and dry summers
Environment: air pollution (including acid rain), damaged forests, coastal pollution; subject to frequent and destructive earthquakes
Terrain: flat plains along Hungarian border, low mountains and highlands along Adriatic coast, coastline, and islands
Land Use: 21% arable, 2% permanent crops, 20% meadows and pastures, 38% forest and woodland, 19% other; includes 30 sq. km irrigated
Location: S Europe, bordering on Adriatic Sea

■ PEOPLE

Population: 4,676,865 (July 1999 est.)
Nationality: Croat
Age Structure: 0-14 yrs: 17%; 15-64: 68%; 65+: 15% (1999 est.)
Population Growth Rate: 0.10% (1999 est.)
Net Migration: 1.81 migrants/1,000 population (1999 est.)
Ethnic Groups: 78% Croat, 12% Serb, 0.9% Muslim, 0.5% Hungarian, 0.5% Slovenian, 8.1% other
Languages: Croatian 96%, other 4% (including Italian, Hungarian, Czech, Slovak and German)
Religions: 76.5% Catholic, 11.1% Orthodox, 1.2% Slavic Muslim, 0.4% Protestant, 10.8% others and unknown
Birth Rate: 10.34/1,000 population (1999 est.)
Death Rate: 11.14/1,000 population (1999 est.)
Infant Mortality: 7.84 deaths/1,000 live births (1999 est.)
Life Expectancy at Birth: 70.69 years male, 77.52 years female (1999 est.)
Total Fertility Rate: 1.52 children born/woman (1999 est.)
Literacy: 97.7% (1997)

■ GOVERNMENT

Leader(s): Pres. Stipe Mesic, Prime Min. Ivica Racan
Government Type: parliamentary democracy
Administrative Divisions: 21 counties (zvpanije, sing. -zvpanija)
Nationhood: June 25, 1991, secession from federal Yugoslavia
National Holiday: Statehood Day, May 30

■ ECONOMY

Overview: tourism, manufacturing including chemicals, food products, petroleum, ships and textiles. War and internal strife have severely disrupted economy
GDP: $23.6 billion, per capita $5,100; real growth rate 3% (1998 est.)
Inflation: 4.3% (April 2000)
Industries: accounts for 24% of GDP; mining, fertilizers, plastics, chemicals, fabricated metal, pig iron and rolled steel products, paper, wood products, shipbuilding, food processing, beverages, sugar, cotton fabrics, machinery
Labour Force: 2 million (1998); 33.6% industry, 22.7% community, social and business services, 15.8% trade and tourism
Unemployment: 18.6% (year-end 1998)
Agriculture: accounts for 12% of GDP; Croatia normally produces a food surplus, but much land has been put out of production by fighting; products include wheat, maize, potatoes, plums, fish, livestock, esp. cattle, sheep, pigs, poultry, cereal grains, citrus fruit, vegetables
Natural Resources: oil, salt, coal, bauxite, brown coal and lignite, iron ore, china clay

■ FINANCE/TRADE

Currency: Croatian kuna = 100 lipas
International Reserves Excluding Gold: $2.853 billion (Jan. 2000)
Gold Reserves: none (Jan. 2000)
Budget: revenues $5.3 billion, expenditures $6.3 billion, including capital expenditures of $78.5 million (1997 est.)
Defence Expenditures: 5% of GNP (1999)
Education Expenditures: 6.48% of total govt. expenditure (1998)
External Debt: $8.297 billion (1998)
Exports: $4.280 billion (1999); machinery and transportation equipment and other manufactured goods; partners: mostly Italy,

Germany, United States, successor states of the former USSR
Imports: $7.777 billion (1999); machinery and transportation equipment, chemicals, raw materials

■ COMMUNICATIONS
Daily Newspapers: 10 (1996)
Televisions: 272/1,000 inhabitants (1998)
Radios: 336/1,000 inhabitants (1997)
Telephones: 348 lines/1,000 inhabitants (1998)

■ TRANSPORTATION
Motor Vehicles: n.a.
Roads: 27,840 km; 22,690 km paved
Railway: 2,296 km; railway service disrupted due to territorial dispute (1997)
Air Traffic: 767,000 passengers carried (1997)
Airports: 72; 21 have paved runways (1998 est.)

Canadian Embassy: The Canadian Embassy, Prilaz Gjure Dezelica #4, 10000 Zagreb. Tel: (011-385-1) 488-1200. Fax: (011-385-1) 488-1230.
Embassy in Canada: Embassy of the Republic of Croatia, 229 Chapel St., Ottawa, ON, K1N 7Y6, Tel: (613) 562-7820, Fax: (613) 562-7821

Cuba

Long-Form Name: Republic of Cuba
Capital: Havana

■ GEOGRAPHY
Area: 110,860 sq. km
Coastline: 3,735 km
Climate: tropical; moderated by trade winds; dry season (Nov. to Apr.); rainy season (May to Oct.)
Environment: averages one hurricane every two years; water pollution and deforestation
Terrain: mostly flat to rolling plains with rugged hills and mountains in the southeast
Land Use: 24% arable; 7% permanent; 27% pasture; 24% forest; 18% other, including 9,100 sq. km irrigated
Location: West Indies, bordering on Caribbean Sea, Atlantic Ocean

■ PEOPLE
Population: 11,096,395 (July 1999 est.)
Nationality: Cuban
Age Structure: 0-14 yrs: 22%; 15-64: 69%; 65+: 9% (1999 est.)
Population Growth Rate: 0.40% (1999 est.)
Net Migration: -1.52 migrants/1,000 population (1999 est.)
Ethnic Groups: 51% mulatto, 37% white, 11% black, 1% Chinese
Languages: Spanish
Religions: Christianity (majority Roman Catholic)
Birth Rate: 12.90/1,000 population (1999 est.)
Death Rate: 7.38/1,000 population (1999 est.)
Infant Mortality: 7.81 deaths/1,000 live births (1999 est.)
Life Expectancy at Birth: 73.41 years male, 78.30 years female (1999 est.)
Total Fertility Rate: 1.58 children born/woman (1999 est.)
Literacy: 95.9% (1997)

■ GOVERNMENT
Leader(s): Pres. of the Council of State: Fidel Castro Ruz
Government Type: communist state
Administrative Divisions: 14 provinces (provincias, sing. -provincia) and 1 special municipality (municipio especial)
Nationhood: May 20, 1902 (from Spain Dec. 10, 1898; administered by the US from 1898 to 1902)
National Holiday: Rebellion Day, July 26; Liberation Day, Jan. 1

■ ECONOMY
Overview: The state plays the primary role in the economy and controls practically all foreign trade. Recent government reforms aim at alleviating serious shortages of food, consumer goods, and services. Tourism plays a key role in foreign currency earnings.
GDP: $17.3 billion, per capita $1,560; real growth rate 1.2% (1998 est.)
Inflation: n.a.
Industries: accounts for 36.5% of GDP; sugar milling, petroleum refining, food and tobacco processing, textiles, chemicals, paper and wood products, metals (particularly nickel), cement, fertilizers, consumer goods, agricultural machinery
Labour Force: 5.0 million (1998); 47.7% services, 28.5% industry, 23.8% agriculture
Unemployment: 6.8% (1997 est.)
Agriculture: accounts for 7.4% of GDP (including fishing and forestry); key commercial crops—sugar cane, tobacco and citrus fruit; other products—coffee, rice, potatoes, meat, beans; world's largest sugar exporter; not self-sufficient in food
Natural Resources: cobalt, nickel, iron ore, copper, manganese, salt, timber, silica, petroleum

■ FINANCE/TRADE

Currency: peso ($) = 100 centavos
International Reserves Excluding Gold: n.a.
Gold Reserves: n.a.
Budget: revenues $12.3 billion, expenditures $13 billion, inc. capital expenditures of n.a. (1998 est.)
Defence Expenditures: n.a.
Education Expenditures: 6.7% of GNP (1997)
External Debt: $10.1 billion (1997)
Exports: $2.015 billion (1996); commodities: sugar, nickel, shellfish, citrus, tobacco, coffee; partners: Russia 30%, China 9%, Canada 10%, Japan 6%, Spain 4%
Imports: $3.205 billion (1996); commodities: capital goods, industrial raw materials, food, petroleum; partners: Russia 10%, China 9%, Spain 9%, Mexico 5%, Italy 5%, Canada 4%, France 4%

■ COMMUNICATIONS

Daily Newspapers: 17 (1996)
Televisions: 239/1,000 inhabitants (1998)
Radios: 353/1,000 inhabitants (1997)
Telephones: 35 lines/1,000 inhabitants (1998)

■ TRANSPORTATION

Motor Vehicles: n.a.
Roads: 27,700 km; 15,484 km paved
Railway: 4,807 km
Air Traffic: 1,117,000 passengers carried (1997)
Airports: 170; 77 have paved runways (1998 est.)

Canadian Embassy: The Canadian Embassy, Calle 30, No. 518 Esquina 7a, Avenida Miramar, Havana, Cuba. Tel: (011-53-7) 24-25-16. Fax: (011-53-7) 24-20-44.
Embassy in Canada: Embassy of the Republic of Cuba, 388 Main St, Ottawa ON K1S 1E3. Tel: (613) 563-0141. Fax: (613) 563-0068.

Cyprus

Long-Form Name: Republic of Cyprus
Capital: Nicosia

■ GEOGRAPHY

Area: 9,250 sq. km
Coastline: 648 km
Climate: temperate, Mediterranean with hot, dry summers and cool, wet winters
Environment: moderate earthquake activity; water resource problems (no natural reservoir catchments, seasonal disparity in rainfall and most potable resources concentrated in the Turkish-Cypriot area)
Terrain: central plain with mountains to north and south, plain along south coast
Land Use: 12% arable; 5% permanent; negligible permanent pastures; 13% forest; 70% other, including 390 sq. km irrigated
Location: Middle East, in the Mediterranean Sea

■ PEOPLE

Population: 754,064 (July 1999 est.)
Nationality: Cypriot
Age Structure: 0-14 yrs: 24%; 15-64: 65%; 65+: 11% (1999 est.)
Population Growth Rate: 0.67% (1999 est.)
Net Migration: 0.44 migrants/1,000 population (1999 est.)
Ethnic Groups: 78% Greek; 18% Turkish; 4% other
Languages: 80% Greek, Turkish, English
Religions: 78% Greek Orthodox; 18% Muslim; 4% Maronite, Armenian, Apostolic and other
Birth Rate: 13.64/1,000 population (1999 est.)
Death Rate: 7.42/1,000 population (1999 est.)
Infant Mortality: 7.68 deaths/1,000 live births (1999 est.)
Life Expectancy at Birth: 74.91 years male, 79.39 years female (1999 est.)
Total Fertility Rate: 2.00 children born/woman (1999 est.)
Literacy: 95.9% (1997)

■ GOVERNMENT

Leader(s): Pres. Glafkos Ioannou Klirides
Government Type: republic; Greek Cypriots control the only internationally recognized government, however the country is divided by a UN-patrolled buffer zone. The northern portion of the island (approx. 40%) is a Turkish-Cypriot administered area. (In 1983 this area was declared the Turkish Republic of Northern Cyprus, but Turkey is the only nation to recognize this jurisdiction.)
Administrative Divisions: 6 districts
Nationhood: Aug. 16, 1960 (from UK)
National Holiday: Independence Day, Oct. 1 (Nov. 15 is celebrated as Independence Day in the Turkish area)

■ ECONOMY

Overview: Cyprus remains heavily dependent on agriculture and government service, which together empty about 50% of the workforce.
GDP: $10 billion, per capita $13,000; real growth rate 2.3% (1997)
Inflation: 4.8% (April 2000)
Industries: accounts for 23% of GDP; mining (iron pyrites, gypsum, asbestos); manufactured products—beverages, footwear, clothing and

cement—are principally for local consumption, tourism
Labour Force: 287,700 (1996); 67.4% services, 18.9% industry, 13.7% agriculture
Unemployment: 9.8% (Apr. 1998)
Agriculture: accounts for 4.5-10% of GDP; employs 25% of labour force; major crops—potatoes, vegetables, barley, grapes, olives and citrus fruit; vegetables and fruit provide 25% of export revenues
Natural Resources: copper, pyrites, asbestos, gypsum, timber, salt, marble, clay earth pigment

■ FINANCE/TRADE

Currency: Cypriot pound (£ or £C) = 100 cents and Turkish lira (TL) = 100 kurus
International Reserves Excluding Gold: $1.396 billion (Nov. 1999)
Gold Reserves: 0.464 million fine troy ounces (Nov. 1999)
Budget: Greek area: revenues $2.9 billion; expenditures $3.4 billion, including capital expenditures of $345 million; Turkish area: revenues $171 million; expenditures $306 million, including capital expenditures of $56.8 million (1997 est.)
Defence Expenditures: 5.4% of GDP (1996)
Education Expenditures: 11.87% of govt. expenditures (1997)
External Debt: Greek Cypriot area: $1.56 billion; Turkish Cypriot: n.a. (1997)
Exports: $997 million (1999); commodities: citrus, potatoes, grapes, wine, cement, clothing and shoes; partners: Middle East and North Africa 37%, UK 27%, other European Community 11%, US 2%
Imports: $3.618 billion (1999); commodities: consumer goods 23%, petroleum and lubricants 12%, food and feed grains, machinery; partners: European Community 60%, Middle East and North Africa 7%, US 4%

■ COMMUNICATIONS

Daily Newspapers: 9 (1996)
Televisions: 323/1,000 inhabitants (1996)
Radios: 397/1,000 inhabitants (1996)
Telephones: 585 lines/1,000 inhabitants (1998)

■ TRANSPORTATION

Motor Vehicles: 340,000; 230,000 passenger cars (1997 est.)
Roads: 12,765 km; 7,317 km paved
Railway: none
Air Traffic: 1,278,000 passengers carried (1997)
Airports: 15; 12 have paved runways (1998 est.)

Canadian Embassy: The High Commission for Canada to Cyprus, c/o the Canadian Embassy, P.O. Box 3394, Damascus, Syria. Tel and fax c/o the Consulate of Canada in Nicosia: Tel (011-357-2) 775-508. Fax: (011-357-2) 779-939.
Embassy in Canada: c/o Embassy of the Republic of Cyprus, 2211 R St NW, Washington DC 20008, USA. Tel: (202) 462-5772. Fax: (202) 483-6710.

Czech Republic

Long-Form Name: Czech Republic
Capital: Prague

■ GEOGRAPHY

Area: 78,703 sq. km
Coastline: none: landlocked
Climate: temperate; cool summers; cold, cloudy, humid winters
Environment: air and water pollution and acid rain, which also damages the forests; recently there has been severe flooding
Terrain: Bohemia in the west consists of rolling plains, hills and plateaus surrounded by low mountains; Moravia in east consists of very hilly country
Land Use: 41% arable; 2% permanent crops; 11% permanent pastures; 34% forests and woodland; 12% other; includes 240 sq. km irrigated
Location: C Europe

■ PEOPLE

Population: 10,280,513 (July 1999 est.)
Nationality: Czech
Age Structure: 0-14 yrs: 17%; 15-64: 69%; 65+: 14% (1999 est.)
Population Growth Rate: -0.01% (1999 est.)
Net Migration: 0.91 migrants/1,000 population (1999 est.)
Ethnic Groups: 94% Czech, 3% Slovak, 0.2% Hungarian, 0.5% German, 0.6% Polish, 0.3% Ukrainian, 0.1% Russian, 0.3% Gypsy, 1% other
Languages: Czech and Slovak
Religions: 39.8% atheist, 39.2% Roman Catholic, 4.6% Protestant, 3% Orthodox, 13.4% other
Birth Rate: 9.84/1,000 population (1999 est.)
Death Rate: 10.86/1,000 population (1999 est.)
Infant Mortality: 6.67 deaths/1,000 live births (1999 est.)
Life Expectancy at Birth: 71.01 years male, 77.88 years female (1999 est.)
Total Fertility Rate: 1.28 children born/woman (1999 est.)

Literacy: 99% (1997)

■ GOVERNMENT
Leader(s): Pres. Vaclav Havel, Prem. Milos Zeman
Government Type: parliamentary democracy
Administrative Divisions: 73 districts (okresi, sing. -okres) and 4 municipalities (mesta, sing. -mesto)
Nationhood: Jan. 1, 1993 (from Czechoslovakia)
National Holiday: National Liberation Day, May 8; Founding of the Republic, Oct. 28

■ ECONOMY
Overview: economy is beginning the transition from a command to a market economy; economic growth is less important at this point than economic restructuring
GDP: $116.7 billion, per capita $11,300; real growth rate -1.5% (1998 est.)
Inflation: 3.9% (March 2000)
Industries: accounts for 33.8% of GDP; fuels, ferrous metallurgy, machinery and equipment, coal, motor vehicles, glass, armaments
Labour Force: 6 million (1998 est.); 37.9% industry, 8.1% agriculture, 8.8% construction, 45.2% communications and other
Unemployment: 9% (Nov. 1999)
Agriculture: accounts for 5% of GDP; largely self-sufficient in food production; diversified crop and livestock production, including grains, sugar beets, potatoes, hops, fruit, hogs, cattle and poultry
Natural Resources: hard coal, kaolin, clay, graphite

■ FINANCE/TRADE
Currency: koruna (pl. koruny) (Kcs) = 100 haleru
International Reserves Excluding Gold: $12.779 billion (Jan. 2000)
Gold Reserves: 0.446 million fine troy ounces (Jan. 2000)
Budget: revenues $14.2 billion; expenditures $14.6 billion, including capital expenditures n.a. (1997)
Defence Expenditures: 1.8% of GDP (1998)
Education Expenditures: 9.65% of total govt. expenditure (1998)
External Debt: $25.301 billion (1998)
Exports: $26.861 billion (1999); commodities: machinery and equipment 58.5%, industrial consumer goods 15.2%, fuels, minerals and metals 10.6%, agricultural and forestry products 6.1%, other products 15.2%; partners: former USSR countries, Germany, Poland, Hungary, former Yugoslavia, Austria, Bulgaria, Romania, US
Imports: $30.258 billion (1998); commodities: machinery and equipment 41.6%, fuels, minerals, metals 32.2%, agricultural and forestry products 11.5%, industrial consumer goods 6.7%, other products 8%; partners: former USSR countries, Germany, Poland, Hungary, former Yugoslavia, Austria, Bulgaria, Romania, US

■ COMMUNICATIONS
Daily Newspapers: 21 (1996)
Televisions: 447/1,000 inhabitants (1998)
Radios: 803/1,000 inhabitants (1997)
Telephones: 364 lines/1,000 inhabitants (1998)

■ TRANSPORTATION
Motor Vehicles: 5,000,000; 4,600,000 passenger cars (1997 est.) (includes data for Slovakia)
Roads: 55,489 km; all paved
Railway: 9,440 km
Air Traffic: 1,448,000 passengers carried (1997)
Airports: 69; 35 have paved runways (1998 est.)

Canadian Embassy: The Canadian Embassy, Mickiewiczova 6, 125 33 Prague 6, Czech Republic. Tel: (011-420-2) 7210-1800. Fax: (011-420-2) 7210-1890.
Embassy in Canada: Embassy of the Czech Republic, 251 Cooper St. Ottawa, ON, K2P 0G2. Tel: (613) 562-3875. Fax: (613) 562-3878.

Democratic Republic of the Congo

Long-Form Name: Democratic Republic of the Congo
Capital: Kinshasa

■ GEOGRAPHY
Area: 2,345,410 sq. km
Coastline: 37 km
Climate: tropical; hot and humid in equatorial river basin; cooler and drier in southern highlands; cooler and wetter in eastern highlands
Environment: dense tropical rainforest in central river basin and eastern highlands; periodic droughts in south; water pollution, deforestation; poaching negatively affects wildlife populations
Terrain: vast central basin is a low-lying plateau; mountains in east
Land Use: 3% arable; negligible permanent; 7% meadows; 77% forest; 13% other; includes 100 sq. km irrigated
Location: C Africa, just barely bordering on South Atlantic Ocean

Democratic Republic of the Congo

■ PEOPLE

Population: 50,481,305 (July 1999 est.)
Nationality: Congolese (sing. & pl.)
Age Structure: 0-14 yrs: 48%; 15-64: 49%; 65+: 3% (1999 est.)
Population Growth Rate: 2.96% (1999 est.)
Net Migration: -1.78 migrants/1,000 population (1999 est.)
Ethnic Groups: over 200 African ethnic groups, the majority are Bantu; four largest tribes—Mongo, Luba, Kongo (all Bantu) and the Mangbetu-Azande (Hamitic)—make up 45% of the population
Languages: French (official), Lingala, Swahili, Kinggwana, Kikongo, Tshiluba
Religions: 50% Roman Catholic, 20% Protestant, 10% Kimbanguist, 10% Muslim, 10% other syncretic sects and traditional beliefs
Birth Rate: 46.37/1,000 population (1999 est.)
Death Rate: 14.99/1,000 population (1999 est.)
Infant Mortality: 99.45 deaths/1,000 live births (1999 est.)
Life Expectancy at Birth: 47.28 years male, 51.67 years female (1999 est.)
Total Fertility Rate: 6.45 children born/woman (1999 est.)
Literacy: 77.0% (1997)

■ GOVERNMENT

Leader(s): Pres. Laurent Desire Kabila
Government Type: dictatorship; presumably undergoing a transition to representative government
Administrative Divisions: 10 provinces and 1 town
Nationhood: June 30, 1960 (from Belgium; formerly known as Belgian Congo, then Congo/Leopoldville, then Congo/Kinshasa)
National Holiday: Anniversary of independence from Belgium, June 30

■ ECONOMY

Overview: Despite its vast potential wealth, the Democratic Republic of the Congo continues to suffer from a decline in the national economy. Tight fiscal policies have curbed inflation and currency depreciation. A barter economy flourishes in all but the largest cities.
GDP: $34.9 billion, per capita $710; real growth rate -3.5% (1998 est.)
Inflation: -10% (Feb. 1998)
Industries: accounts for 15% of GDP; mining, mineral processing, consumer products (including textiles, footwear and cigarettes), processed foods and beverages, cement, diamonds
Labour Force: 20 million (1998); 71.5% agriculture, 12.9% industry, 15.6% services
Unemployment: n.a.
Agriculture: accounts for 59% of GDP; cash crops: coffee, palm oil, rubber, quinine; food crops: cassava, bananas, root crops, corn
Natural Resources: cobalt, copper, cadmium, crude oil, industrial and gem diamonds, gold, silver, zinc, manganese, tin, germanium, uranium, radium, bauxite, iron ore, coal, hydroelectric potential

■ FINANCE/TRADE

Currency: Congolese franc
International Reserves Excluding Gold: $83 million (Dec. 1996)
Gold Reserves: 0.05 million fine troy ounces (Dec. 1997)
Budget: revenues $479 million; expenditures $479 million, capital expenditures n.a. (1996 est.)
Defence Expenditures: 4.6% of GDP (1997)
Education Expenditures: 0.18% of total govt. expenditure (1997)
External Debt: $12.929 billion (1998)
Exports: $269 million (1997 est.); commodities: copper 37%, coffee 24%, diamonds 12%, cobalt, crude oil; partners: US, Belgium, France, Germany, Italy, UK, Japan
Imports: $220 million, adjusted for purchasing power parity (1997 est.); commodities: consumer goods, foodstuffs, mining and other machinery, transport equipment, fuels; partners: US, Belgium, France, Germany, Italy, Japan, UK

■ COMMUNICATIONS

Daily Newspapers: 9 (1996)
Televisions: 3.2/1,000 inhabitants (1996)
Radios: 375/1,000 inhabitants (1997)
Telephones: 1 lines/1,000 inhabitants (1998)

■ TRANSPORTATION

Motor Vehicles: 530,000; 330,000 passenger cars (1997 est.)
Roads: 145,000 km; 2,500 km paved
Railway: 5,138 km
Air Traffic: n.a.
Airports: 233; 23 have paved runways (1998 est.)

Canadian Embassy: The Canadian Embassy to the Democratic Republic of Congo, 17 avenue Pumbu, Commune de Gombe, Democratic Republic of Congo; mailing address: P.O. Box 8431, Kinshasa 1, Democratic Republic of Congo. Tel: (011-243) 884-1276. Fax: (011-243) 884-1277.
Embassy in Canada: Embassy of the Democratic

Republic of Congo, 18 Range Rd, Ottawa ON K1N 8J3. Tel: (613) 230-6391. Fax: (613) 230-1945.

Denmark

Long-Form Name: Kingdom of Denmark
Capital: Copenhagen

■ GEOGRAPHY

Area: 43,094 sq. km; includes the island of Bornholm in the Baltic Sea and the rest of metropolitan Denmark, but excludes the Faroe Islands and Greenland
Coastline: 7,314 km (inc. fjords, etc.)
Climate: temperate; humid and overcast; mild, windy winters and cool summers
Environment: air and water pollution; pollution of drinking water
Terrain: low and flat to gently rolling plains
Land Use: 60% arable land; negligible permanent; 5% meadows; 10% forest; 25% other, includes 4,350 sq. km irrigated
Location: N Europe, bordering on North Sea, Baltic Sea

■ PEOPLE

Population: 5,356,845 (July 1999 est.)
Nationality: Dane
Age Structure: 0-14 yrs: 18%; 15-64: 67%; 65+: 15% (1999 est.)
Population Growth Rate: 0.38% (1999 est.)
Net Migration: 3.22 migrants/1,000 population (1999 est.)
Ethnic Groups: Scandinavian, Eskimo, Faroese, German
Languages: Danish, Faroese, Greenlandic (an Eskimo dialect); small German-speaking minority
Religions: 91% Evangelical Lutheran, 2% other Protestant and Roman Catholic, 7% other
Birth Rate: 11.57/1,000 population (1999 est.)
Death Rate: 10.97/1,000 population (1999 est.)
Infant Mortality: 5.11 deaths/1,000 live births (1999 est.)
Life Expectancy at Birth: 73.83 years male, 79.33 years female (1999 est.)
Total Fertility Rate: 1.62 children born/woman (1999 est.)
Literacy: 99% (1997)

■ GOVERNMENT

Leader(s): Head of State: Margrethe II. Prime Min. Poul Nyrup Rasmussen
Government Type: constitutional monarchy
Administrative Divisions: 14 counties (amter, sing. -amt) and 2 kommunes; dependent areas inc.: Faroe Islands, Greenland (see Greenland entry for details)
Nationhood: became a constitutional monarchy in 1849
National Holiday: Birthday of the Queen, Apr. 16

■ ECONOMY

Overview: advanced agriculture and industry; extensive government welfare measures; highly dependent on foreign trade
GDP: $124.4 billion, per capita $23,300; real growth rate 2.6% (1998 est.)
Inflation: 3.2% (March 2000)
Industries: accounts for 27% of GDP; food processing, machinery and equipment, textiles and clothing, chemical products, electronics, construction, furniture and other wood products
Labour Force: 3 million (1998); 36% community, social and business services, 20.2% industry, 14.4% trade and tourism
Unemployment: 6.2% (Jan. 2000)
Agriculture: accounts for 4% of GNP and employs 5.6% of labour force (includes fishing); farm products account for nearly 15% of export revenues; principal products—meat, dairy, grain, potatoes, rape, sugar beets, fish; self-sufficient in food production
Natural Resources: crude oil, natural gas, fish, salt, limestone

■ FINANCE/TRADE

Currency: krone (pl. kroner) (DKr) = 100 oere
International Reserves Excluding Gold: $18.961 billion (Jan. 2000)
Gold Reserves: 2.141 million fine troy ounces (Jan. 2000)
Budget: revenues $62.1 billion; expenditures $66.4 billion, including capital expenditures n.a. (1996 est.)
Defence Expenditures: 1.6% of GDP (1999)
Education Expenditures: 8.1% of GNP (1997)
External Debt: $44 billion (1996)
Exports: $48.152 billion (1999); commodities: meat and meat products, dairy products, transport equipment, fish, chemicals, industrial machinery; partners: US 6%, Germany, Norway, Sweden, UK, other European Community, Japan
Imports: $43.882 billion (1999); commodities: petroleum, machinery and equipment, chemicals, grain and foodstuffs, textiles, paper; partners: US 7%, Germany, Netherlands, Sweden, UK, other European Community

■ COMMUNICATIONS

Daily Newspapers: 37 (1996)
Televisions: 585/1,000 inhabitants (1998)

Radios: 1,141/1,000 inhabitants (1997)
Telephones: 660 lines/1,000 inhabitants (1998)

■ TRANSPORTATION

Motor Vehicles: 2,200,000; 1,830,000 passenger cars (1997 est.)
Roads: 71,600 km; all paved
Railway: 3,358 km
Air Traffic: 6,236,000 passengers carried (1997)
Airports: 118; 28 have paved runways (1998 est.)

Canadian Embassy: The Canadian Embassy, Kr. Bernikowsgade 1, 1105 Copenhagen K, Denmark. Tel: (011-45) 33-48-32-00. Fax: (011-45) 33-48-32-20.
Embassy in Canada: Embassy of the Kingdom of Denmark, 47 Clarence St, Ste 450, Ottawa ON K1N 9K1. Tel: (613) 562-1811. Fax: (613) 562-1812.

Djibouti

Long-Form Name: Republic of Djibouti
Capital: Djibouti

■ GEOGRAPHY

Area: 22,000 sq. km
Coastline: 314 km
Climate: desert; torrid, dry
Environment: vast wasteland; desertification; droughts and earthquakes; occasional cyclones; inadequate safe drinking water
Terrain: coastal plain and plateau separated by central mountains
Land Use: 0% arable; 0% permanent; 9% permanent pastures; negligible forest; 91% other
Location: E Africa, bordering on Gulf of Aden

■ PEOPLE

Population: 447,439 (July 1999 est.)
Nationality: Djiboutian
Age Structure: 0-14 yrs: 43%; 15-64: 54%; 65+: 3% (1999 est.)
Population Growth Rate: 1.51% (1999 est.)
Net Migration: -11.73 migrants/1,000 population (1999 est.)
Ethnic Groups: 60% Somali (Issa), 35% Afar, 5% French, Arab, Ethiopian and Italian
Languages: French and Arabic (both official); Somali and Afar widely used
Religions: 94% Muslim, 6% Christian
Birth Rate: 41.23/1,000 population (1999 est.)
Death Rate: 14.41/1,000 population (1999 est.)
Infant Mortality: 100.24 deaths/1,000 live births (1999 est.)
Life Expectancy at Birth: 49.48 years male, 53.67 years female (1999 est.)
Total Fertility Rate: 5.87 children born/woman (1999 est.)
Literacy: 48.3% (1997)

■ GOVERNMENT

Leader(s): Pres. Ismail Omar Guelleh, Prime Min. Gourad Hamadou Barkat
Government Type: republic
Administrative Divisions: 5 districts (cercles, sing. -cercle)
Nationhood: June 27, 1977 (from France; formerly known as French Territory of the Afars and Issas)
National Holiday: Independence Day, June 27

■ ECONOMY

Overview: based on service activities related to country's strategic location and status as a free trade zone; Djibouti is heavily dependent on foreign aid
GDP: $530 million, per capita $1,200; real growth rate 0.6% (1998 est.)
Inflation: 6.7% (Feb. 1997)
Industries: accounts for 20% of GDP; limited to a few small-scale enterprises, such as dairy products and mineral-water bottling
Labour Force: n.a.; 75% agriculture, 11% industry, 14% services
Unemployment: 40–50% (1996 est.)
Agriculture: accounts for only 3% of GDP; scanty rainfall limits crop production to mostly fruit and vegetables; half of population pastoral nomads herding goats, sheep and camels; imports bulk of food needs
Natural Resources: geothermal areas

■ FINANCE/TRADE

Currency: Djiboutian franc (DF) = 100 centimes
International Reserves Excluding Gold: $69 million (Jan. 2000)
Gold Reserves: n.a.
Budget: revenues $156 million; expenditures $175 million, including capital expenditures of n.a. (1997 est.)
Defence Expenditures: 4.5% of GDP (1997)
Education Expenditures: n.a.
External Debt: $241 million (1996)
Exports: 39.6 million (1996 est.); commodities: hides and skins, coffee (in transit); partners: Middle East 50%, Africa 43%, Western Europe 7%
Imports: $200.5 million (1996 est.); commodities: foods, beverages, transport equipment, chemicals, petroleum products; partners: European Community 36%, Africa 21%, Bahrain 14%, Asia 12%, US 2%

■ COMMUNICATIONS
Daily Newspapers: 0 (1996)
Televisions: 44/1,000 inhabitants (1996)
Radios: 81/1,000 inhabitants (1996)
Telephones: 13 lines/1,000 inhabitants (1998)

■ TRANSPORTATION
Motor Vehicles: 16,500; 13,500 passenger cars (1997 est.)
Roads: 2,890 km; 364 km paved
Railway: 97 km
Air Traffic: n.a.
Airports: 11; 2 have paved runways (1998 est.)

Canadian Embassy: The Canadian Embassy to Djibouti, c/o The Canadian Embassy, P.O. Box 1130, Addis Ababa, Ethiopia. Tel: (011-251-1) 71-30-22. Fax: (011-251-1) 71-30-33.

Embassy in Canada: Embassy of the Republic of Djibouti, 1156 15th St. NW, Ste 515, Washington DC 20005, USA. Tel: (202) 331-0270. Fax: (202) 331-0302.

Dominica

Long-Form Name: Commonwealth of Dominica
Capital: Roseau

■ GEOGRAPHY
Area: 750 sq. km
Coastline: 148 km
Climate: tropical; moderated by northeast trade winds; heavy rainfall
Environment: flash floods a constant hazard; occasional hurricanes
Terrain: rugged mountains of volcanic origin
Land Use: 9% arable; 13% permanent; 3% meadows; 67% forest and woodland; 8% other
Location: Caribbean islands, northern end of the Windward Islands

■ PEOPLE
Population: 64,881 (July 1999 est.)
Nationality: Dominican
Age Structure: 0-14 yrs: 27%; 15-64: 64%; 65+: 9% (1999 est.)
Population Growth Rate: -1.41% (1999 est.)
Net Migration: -24.69 migrants/1,000 population (1999 est.)
Ethnic Groups: mostly black; some Carib Indians
Languages: English (official); French patois widely spoken
Religions: 77% Roman Catholic; 15% Protestant, 2% none, 1% unknown, 5% other
Birth Rate: 16.92/1,000 population (1999 est.)
Death Rate: 6.35/1,000 population (1999 est.)
Infant Mortality: 8.75 deaths/1,000 live births (1999 est.)
Life Expectancy at Birth: 75.15 years male, 81.01 years female (1999 est.)
Total Fertility Rate: 1.89 children born/woman (1999 est.)
Literacy: 94% (1997)

■ GOVERNMENT
Leader(s): Pres. Vernon Shaw, Prime Min. Pierre Charles
Government Type: parliamentary democracy
Administrative Divisions: 10 parishes
Nationhood: Nov. 3, 1978 (from UK)
National Holiday: Independence Day, Nov. 3

■ ECONOMY
Overview: dependent on agriculture and vulnerable to climatic conditions; tourist potential (undeveloped)
GDP: $216 million, per capita $3,300; real growth rate 1.8% (1997 est.)
Inflation: -0.3% (March 2000)
Industries: agricultural processing, tourism, soap and other coconut-based products, cigars, pumice mining, cement blocks, shoes. Industries account for 16% of GDP.
Labour Force: n.a.; agriculture 40%, industry and commerce 32%, services 28%
Unemployment: n.a.
Agriculture: accounts for 20% of GDP; principal crops—bananas, citrus fruit, coconuts, root crops; bananas provide the bulk of export earnings; forestry and fisheries potential not exploited
Natural Resources: timber

■ FINANCE/TRADE
Currency: East Caribbean dollar ($EC) = 100 cents
International Reserves Excluding Gold: $32 million (Dec. 1999)
Gold Reserves: n.a.
Budget: revenues $72 million; expenditures $79.9 million, including capital expenditures of $11.5 million (1997–98)
Defence Expenditures: n.a.
Education Expenditures: n.a.
External Debt: $105 million (1997 est.)
Exports: $54 million (1999); commodities: bananas, coconuts, grapefruit, soap, galvanized sheets; partners: UK 72%, Jamaica 10%, OECS 6%, US 3%, other 9%
Imports: $141 million (1999); commodities: food, oils and fats, chemicals, fuels and lubricants, manufactured goods, machinery and equipment; partners: US 23%, UK 18%,

CARICOM 15%, OECS 15%, Japan 5%, Canada 3%, other 21%

■ COMMUNICATIONS

Daily Newspapers: 0 (1996)
Televisions: 77/1,000 inhabitants (1996)
Radios: 634/1,000 inhabitants (1996)
Telephones: 252 lines/1,000 inhabitants (1998)

■ TRANSPORTATION

Motor Vehicles: 5,700; 2,800 passenger cars (1997 est.)
Roads: 780 km; 393 km paved
Railway: none
Air Traffic: n.a.
Airports: 2; both have paved runways (1998 est.)

Canadian Embassy: c/o The Canadian High Commission, Bishop's Court Hill, St. Michael, Barbados; mailing address: P.O. Box 404, Bridgetown, Barbados. Tel: (246) 429-3550. Fax: (246) 429-3780.
Embassy in Canada: c/o High Commission for the Countries of the Organization of Eastern Caribbean States, 112 Kent St, Ste 1610, Place de Ville, Tower B, Ottawa ON K1P 5P2. Tel: (613) 236-8952. Fax: (613) 236-3042.

Dominican Republic

Long-Form Name: Dominican Republic
Capital: Santo Domingo

■ GEOGRAPHY

Area: 48,730 sq. km
Coastline: 1,288 km
Climate: tropical maritime; little seasonal temperature variation
Environment: subject to occasional hurricanes (July to Oct.); deforestation; erosion and water shortage
Terrain: rugged highlands and mountains interspersed with fertile valleys
Land Use: 21% arable; 9% permanent; 43% meadows; 12% forest; 15% other, includes 2,300 sq. km irrigated
Location: West Indies, bordering on Haiti, Caribbean Sea, Atlantic Ocean

■ PEOPLE

Population: 8,129,734 (July 1999 est.)
Nationality: Dominican
Age Structure: 0-14 yrs: 35%; 15-64: 61%; 65+: 4% (1999 est.)
Population Growth Rate: 1.62% (1999 est.)
Net Migration: -4.14 migrants/1,000 population (1999 est.)

Ethnic Groups: 73% mixed, 16% white, 11% black
Languages: Spanish
Religions: 95% Roman Catholic
Birth Rate: 25.97/1,000 population (1999 est.)
Death Rate: 5.66/1,000 population (1999 est.)
Infant Mortality: 42.52 deaths/1,000 live births (1999 est.)
Life Expectancy at Birth: 67.86 years male, 72.40 years female (1999 est.)
Total Fertility Rate: 3.03 children born/woman (1999 est.)
Literacy: 82.6% (1997)

■ GOVERNMENT

Leader(s): Pres. Rafael Hipolita Mejia Dominguez
Government Type: republic
Administrative Divisions: 29 provinces (provincias, sing. -provincia) and 1 district (distrito)
Nationhood: Feb. 27, 1844 (from Haiti)
National Holiday: Independence Day, Feb. 27

■ ECONOMY

Overview: agriculture is the backbone of the economy (sugar cane); tourism and a free trade zone help. Hurricane damage has adversely affected agriculture and infrastructure.
GDP: $39.8 billion, per capita $5,000; real growth rate 7% (1998 est.)
Inflation: 5.7% (Mar. 2000)
Industries: accounts for 25% of GDP; tourism, sugar processing, ferronickel and gold mining, textiles, cement, tobacco
Labour Force: 4 million (1998); 45.7% agriculture, 38.8% services, 15.5% industry
Unemployment: 15.9% (1997)
Agriculture: accounts for 19% of GDP and employs almost half of labour force; sugar cane most important commercial crop, followed by coffee, cotton and cocoa; food crops; animal output; not self-sufficient in food
Natural Resources: nickel, bauxite, gold, silver

■ FINANCE/TRADE

Currency: Dominican peso ($RD) = 100 centavos
International Reserves Excluding Gold: $621 million (Jan. 2000)
Gold Reserves: 0.062 million fine troy ounces (Jan. 2000)
Budget: revenues $2.3 billion; expenditures $2.9 billion, including capital expenditures of $867million (1999 est.)
Defence Expenditures: 4.69% of total govt. expenditure (1997)

Education Expenditures: 14.26% of govt. expenditure (1997)
External Debt: $4.451billion (1998)
Exports: $795 million (1998); commodities: sugar, coffee, cocoa, gold, ferronickel; partners: US (including Puerto Rico) 74%
Imports: $5.631 billion (1998); commodities: foodstuffs, petroleum, cotton and fabrics, chemicals and pharmaceuticals; partners: US (including Puerto Rico) 36%

■ COMMUNICATIONS

Daily Newspapers: 12 (1996)
Televisions: 95/1,000 inhabitants (1998)
Radios: 178/1,000 inhabitants (1997)
Telephones: 93 lines/1,000 inhabitants (1998)

■ TRANSPORTATION

Motor Vehicles: 209,000; 114,200 passenger cars (1997 est.)
Roads: 12,600 km; 6,224 km paved
Railway: 757 km
Air Traffic: 34,000 passengers carried (1997)
Airports: 36; 14 have paved runways (1998 est.)

Canadian Embassy: The Canadian Embassy, Captain Eugenio de Marchena, No. 39, La Esperilla, Santo Domingo; mailing address: Apartado 2054, Santo Domingo 1, Dominican Republic. Tel: (809) 689-1136. Fax: (809) 682-2691.
Embassy in Canada: Embassy of the Dominican Republic, 130 Albert St., Suite 418, Ottawa, ON, K1P 5G4, Tel: (613) 569-9893, Fax: (613) 569-8673

East Timor

Long-Form Name: Timor Leste
Capital: Dili

■ GEOGRAPHY

Area: 14,874 sq. km
Coastline: n.a.
Climate: tropical with little seasonal temperature variation
Environment: There is a lack of safe drinking water. Water is mainly underground and often far from villages.
Terrain: extremely mountainous
Land Use: n.a.
Location: eastern half of the island of Timor, which lies between Indonesia and Australia

■ PEOPLE

Population: est. 800,000 (2000)
Nationality: East Timorese
Age Structure: n.a.
Population Growth Rate: n.a.
Net Migration: n.a.
Ethnic Groups: 12 ethnic groups including 78% Timorese, Indonesian, Chinese, other
Languages: 9 Austronesian language groups: Tetum (spoken by about 60% of the population), Mambai, Tokodede, Kemak, Galoli, Idate, Waima'a, Naueti and 3 Papuan langauge groups (Bunak, Makasae, Fatuluku)
Religions: Catholic 91%; Other (Muslim, Protestant, Hindu, Buddhist) 9%
Birth Rate: 36.5/1,000 population
Death Rate: 17.4/1,000 population
Infant Mortality: 135 deaths/1,000 live births
Life Expectancy at Birth: 46.7 years male; 48.2 years female
Total Fertility Rate: n.a.
Literacy: n.a.

■ GOVERNMENT

Leader(s): Transitional Administrator: Sergio Vieira de Mello (Brazil). Xanana Gusmao, President of the National Council of Timorese Resistance; José Ramos-Horta, V. Pres. National Council of Timorese Resistance
Government Type: United National Transitional Administration in East Timor (UNTAET) empowered with all legislative and executive authority. After August 30, 1999 pro-independence referendum and October 1999 support from Indonesia's legislature, Indonesian militias mounted a violent reprisal against vote which sparked international intervention.
Administrative Divisions: 13 districts
Nationhood: October 25, 1999 (declared from Indonesia)
National Holiday: Independence Day, August 30

■ ECONOMY

Overview: fierce fighting in struggle for independence has damaged or destroyed most of East Timor's infrastructure. East Timor hopes to revive its economy by export profits from its high quality, organically grown coffee crop.
GDP: n.a.; estimated per capita income is $225, half of what it was before independence
Inflation: n.a.
Industries: n.a.
Labour Force: 341,887 (est.)
Unemployment: 5,397 (est.)
Agriculture: Agriculture is the cornerstone of East Timorese economy. It employs over 80% of the population and is the major source of foreign exchange revenue. While paddy and rainfed rice is the leading cash crop, other principal crops include food crops 51%,

plantations 25.8%, livestock 20.5%, forestry 1% and fisheries 1%. High quality arabica coffee is also being produced.
Natural Resources: extremely rich in oil, natural gas and manganese

■ FINANCE/TRADE

Currency: Indonesian rupiah = 100 sen
International Reserves Excluding Gold: n.a.
Gold Reserves: n.a.
Budget: $584.1 million (proposed for 2000-2001)
Defence Expenditures: n.a.
Education Expenditures: n.a.
External Debt: n.a.
Exports: n.a.
Imports: n.a.

■ COMMUNICATIONS

Daily Newspapers: n.a.
Televisions: n.a.
Radios: n.a.
Telephones: n.a.

■ TRANSPORTATION

Motor Vehicles: n.a.
Roads: n.a.
Railway: n.a.
Air Traffic: n.a.
Airports: n.a.

Canadian Embassy: c/o The Canadian Embassy, Fir 5 Wisma Metropolitan, Jalan Jendral Sudirman, Jakarta 12920; mailing address: P.O.Box 8324/JKS.MP, Jakarta 12084, Indonesia. Tel: (011-62-21) 525-0709. Fax: (011-62-21) 571-2251.
Embassy in Canada: c/o Embassy of the Republic of Indonesia, 55 Parkdale Ave, Ottawa On K1Y 1E5. Tel: (613) 724-1100. Fax: (613) 724-1105.

Ecuador

Long-Form Name: Republic of Ecuador
Capital: Quito

■ GEOGRAPHY

Area: 283,560 sq. km
Coastline: 2,237 km
Climate: tropical along coast becoming cooler inland
Environment: subject to frequent earthquakes, landslides, volcanic activity; deforestation; desertification; soil erosion; periodic droughts
Terrain: coastal plain, inter-Andean central highlands and flat to rolling eastern jungle
Land Use: 6% arable; 5% permanent; 18% meadows; 56% forest; 15% other, includes 5,560 sq. km irrigated
Location: NW South America, bordering on Pacific Ocean

■ PEOPLE

Population: 12,562,496 (July 1999 est.)
Nationality: Ecuadorian
Age Structure: 0-14 yrs: 35%; 15-64: 60%; 65+: 5% (1999 est.)
Population Growth Rate: 1.78% (1999 est.)
Net Migration: 0.55 migrants/1,000 population (1999 est.)
Ethnic Groups: 55% mestizo (mixed Indian and Spanish), 25% Indian, 10% Spanish, 10% black
Languages: Spanish (official), Indian languages, especially Quechua
Religions: 95% Roman Catholic
Birth Rate: 22.26/1,000 population (1999 est.)
Death Rate: 5.06/1,000 population (1999 est.)
Infant Mortality: 30.69 deaths/1,000 live births (1999 est.)
Life Expectancy at Birth: 69.54 years male, 74.90 years female (1999 est.)
Total Fertility Rate: 2.63 children born/woman (1999 est.)
Literacy: 90.7% (1997)

■ GOVERNMENT

Leader(s): Pres. Gustavo Noboa Bejarano, V. Pres. Pedro Pinto Rubianes
Government Type: republic
Administrative Divisions: 21 provinces (provincias, sing. -provincia)
Nationhood: May 24, 1822 (from Spain; Battle of Pichincha)
National Holiday: Independence Day, Aug. 10

■ ECONOMY

Overview: vulnerable to international oil prices; the banana crop, second in importance only to oil, has been hurt by EC import quotas and banana blight; strict austerity program has resulted in economic stabilization
GDP: $58.7 billion, per capita $4,800; real growth rate 1% (1998 est.)
Inflation: 88.9% (April 2000)
Industries: accounts for 37% of GDP; food processing, textiles, metal works, paper products, chemicals, fishing, timber, petroleum
Labour Force: 5 million (1998); 29.7% trade and tourism, 27.7% community, social and business services, 17.5% industry
Unemployment: 12%, with widespread underemployment (Nov. 1998 est.)
Agriculture: accounts for 12% of GDP and 35% of labour force (including fishing and forestry);

leading producer and exporter of bananas and balsawood; crop and livestock sector; net importer of food-grain, dairy products and sugar
Natural Resources: petroleum, fish, timber

■ FINANCE/TRADE

Currency: sucre (S/) = 100 centavos
International Reserves Excluding Gold: $1.630 billion (Jan. 2000)
Gold Reserves: 0.414 million fine troy ounces (Jan. 2000)
Budget: revenues $5.1 billion; expenditures $5.1 billion, including capital expenditures (1999)
Defence Expenditures: 3.4% of GDP (1998)
Education Expenditures: 3.5% of GNP (1997)
External Debt: $15.14 billion (1998)
Exports: $4.451 billion (1999); commodities: petroleum 47%, coffee, bananas, cocoa products, shrimp, fish products; partners: US 58%, Latin America, Caribbean, European Community countries
Imports: $3.017 billion (1999); commodities: transport equipment, vehicles, machinery, chemicals, petroleum; partners: US 28%, Latin America, Caribbean, European Community, Japan

■ COMMUNICATIONS

Daily Newspapers: 29 (1996)
Televisions: 293/1,000 inhabitants (1998)
Radios: 419/1,000 inhabitants (1997)
Telephones: 78 lines/1,000 inhabitants (1998)

■ TRANSPORTATION

Motor Vehicles: 684,000; 258,000 passenger cars (1997 est.)
Roads: 42,874 km; 5,752 km paved
Railway: 965 km
Air Traffic: 1,791,000 passengers carried (1997)
Airports: 183; 56 have paved runways (1998 est.)

Canadian Embassy: The Canadian Embassy, Avenida 6 de Diciembre, 2816 y Paul Rivet, Edificio Josueth Gonzalez, 4th Fl., Quito, Ecuador; mailing address: P.O. Box 17-11-6512, Quito, Ecuador. Tel: (011-593-2) 564-795. Fax: (011-593-2) 503-108.
Embassy in Canada: Embassy of the Republic of Ecuador, 50 O'Connor St, Ste 316, Ottawa ON K1P 6L2. Tel: (613) 563-8206. Fax: (613) 235-5776.

Egypt

Long-Form Name: Arab Republic of Egypt
Capital: Cairo

■ GEOGRAPHY

Area: 1,001,450 sq. km
Coastline: 2,450 km
Climate: desert; hot, dry summers with moderate winters
Environment: Nile is only perennial water source; increasing soil salinization below Aswan High Dam; hot, driving windstorm called khamsin occurs in spring; water pollution; desertification; urbanization and erosion are decreasing the arable land available
Terrain: vast desert plateau interrupted by Nile valley and delta
Land Use: 2% arable; 0% permanent; 0% meadows; negligible forest; 98% other, includes 32,460 sq. km irrigated
Location: NE Africa, bordering on Mediterranean Sea, Red Sea

■ PEOPLE

Population: 67,273,906 (July 1999 est.)
Nationality: Egyptian
Age Structure: 0-14 yrs: 36%; 15-64: 61%; 65+: 3% (1999 est.)
Population Growth Rate: 1.82% (1999 est.)
Net Migration: -0.35 migrants/1,000 population (1999 est.)
Ethnic Groups: 99% Eastern Hamitic stock; 1% Greek, Italian, Syro-Lebanese, Armenian
Languages: Arabic (official); English and French
Religions: 94% Muslim (mostly Sunni), 6% Coptic Christian and other
Birth Rate: 26.8/1,000 population (1999 est.)
Death Rate: 8.27/1,000 population (1999 est.)
Infant Mortality: 67.46 deaths/1,000 live births (1999 est.)
Life Expectancy at Birth: 60.39 years male, 64.49 years female (1999 est.)
Total Fertility Rate: 3.33 children born/woman (1999 est.)
Literacy: 52.7% (1997)

■ GOVERNMENT

Leader(s): Pres. Mohammad Hosni Mubarak, Prime Min. Atef Mohamed Ebeid
Government Type: republic
Administrative Divisions: 26 governorates (muhafazat, sing. -muhafazah)
Nationhood: Feb. 28, 1922 (from UK; formerly known as United Arab Republic)
National Holiday: Anniversary of the Revolution, July 23

■ ECONOMY

Overview: urban population growth puts pressure on the agricultural sector; having difficulty with its debt servicing; vulnerable to oil prices; unemployment has become a growing problem

GDP: $188 billion, per capita $2,850; real growth rate 5% (1998 est.)
Inflation: 3.0% (Feb. 2000)
Industries: accounts for 31% of GDP, textiles, food processing, tourism, chemicals, petroleum, construction, cement, metals
Labour Force: 23 million (1998); 31.3% agriculture, 22.2% community, social and business services, 15.4% industry
Unemployment: 10% (1998 est.)
Agriculture: accounts for 16% of GDP and employs more than one-third of labour force; dependent on irrigation water from the Nile; world's fifth largest cotton exporter; other crops include rice, corn, wheat, beans, fruit, vegetables; not self-sufficient in food
Natural Resources: crude oil, natural gas, iron ore, phosphates, manganese, limestone, gypsum, talc, asbestos, lead, zinc

■ FINANCE/TRADE

Currency: Egyptian pound (LE) = 100 piasters
International Reserves Excluding Gold: $14.484 billion (Dec. 1999)
Gold Reserves: 2.432 million fine troy ounces (Dec. 1999)
Budget: revenues $20 billion; expenditures $20.8 billion, including capital expenditures of $4.4 billion (1997-98 est.)
Defence Expenditures: 9.43% of central government expenditure (1997)
Education Expenditures: 14.76% of central government expenditure (1997)
External Debt: $31.964 billion (1998)
Exports: $3.41 billion (1999 est.); commodities: raw cotton, crude and refined petroleum, cotton yarn, textiles; partners: US, European Community, Japan, Eastern Europe
Imports: $16.289 billion (1999 est.); commodities: foods, machinery and equipment, fertilizers, wood products, durable consumer goods, capital goods; partners: US, European Community, Japan, Eastern Europe

■ COMMUNICATIONS

Daily Newspapers: 17 (1996)
Televisions: 122/1,000 inhabitants (1998)
Radios: 324/1,000 inhabitants (1997)
Telephones: 60 lines/1,000 inhabitants (1998)

■ TRANSPORTATION

Motor Vehicles: 1,711,000; 1,300,000 passenger cars (1997 est.)
Roads: 64,000 km; 49,984 km paved
Railway: 4,751 km
Air Traffic: 4,416,000 passengers carried (1997)
Airports: 89; 70 have paved runways (1998 est.)

Canadian Embassy: The Canadian Embassy, Arab International Bank Building, 5 Midan El Saraya el Kobra, Garden City, Cairo, Egypt; mailing address: P.O. Box 1667, Cairo, Egypt. Tel: (011-20-2) 794-3110. Fax: (011-20-2) 796-3548.
Embassy in Canada: Embassy of the Arab Republic of Egypt, 454 Laurier Ave E, Ottawa ON K1N 6R3. Tel: (613) 234-4931. Fax: (613) 234-9347.

El Salvador

Long-Form Name: Republic of El Salvador
Capital: San Salvador

■ GEOGRAPHY

Area: 21,040 sq. km
Coastline: 307 km
Climate: tropical; rainy season (May to Oct.), dry season (Nov. to Apr.)
Environment: the Land of Volcanoes; subject to frequent and sometimes very destructive earthquakes; deforestation; soil erosion and pollution; water pollution
Terrain: mostly mountains with narrow coastal belt and central plateau
Land Use: 27% arable; 8% permanent; 29% meadows; 5% forest; 31% other, includes 1,200 sq. km irrigated
Location: Central (Latin) America, bordering on Pacific Ocean

■ PEOPLE

Population: 5,839,079 (July 1999 est.)
Nationality: Salvadoran
Age Structure: 0-14 yrs: 37%; 15-64: 58%; 65+: 5% (1999 est.)
Population Growth Rate: 1.53% (1999 est.)
Net Migration: -4.66 migrants/1,000 population (1999 est.)
Ethnic Groups: 94% mestizo, 5% Indian, 1% white
Languages: Spanish, Nahua spoken among some Indians
Religions: approx. 75% Roman Catholic, with activity by Protestant groups throughout the country
Birth Rate: 26.19/1,000 population (1999 est.)
Death Rate: 6.20/1,000 population (1999 est.)
Infant Mortality: 28.38 deaths/1,000 live births (1999 est.)
Life Expectancy at Birth: 66.7 years male, 73.50 years female (1999 est.)
Total Fertility Rate: 2.99 children born/woman (1999 est.)
Literacy: 77.0% (1997)

GOVERNMENT

Leader(s): Pres. Francisco Flores Perez, V. Pres. Carlos Quintanilla
Government Type: republic
Administrative Divisions: 14 departments (departmentos, sing. -departmento)
Nationhood: Sept. 15, 1821 (from Spain)
National Holiday: Independence Day, Sept. 15

ECONOMY

Overview: In recent years inflation has fallen to unprecedented levels and exports have grown considerably. Even so, sizeable fiscal deficits persist.
GDP: $17.5 billion, per capita $3,000; real growth rate 3.7% (1998)
Inflation: 1.1% (April 2000)
Industries: accounts for 24% of GDP; food processing, textiles, non-metallic products, tobacco, beverages, clothing, petroleum products, cement
Labour Force: 3 million (1998); 35.8% agriculture, 19.6% community, social and business services, 17.4% trade and tourism
Unemployment: 7.7% (1997 est.)
Agriculture: accounts for 15% of GDP and 40% of labour force (including fishing and forestry); coffee most important commercial crop; other products—sugar cane, corn, rice, beans, oilseeds, beef, dairy products, shrimp; not self-sufficient in food
Natural Resources: hydroelectricity and geothermal power, crude oil

FINANCE/TRADE

Currency: colón (pl. colones) (C/) = 100 centavos
International Reserves Excluding Gold: $2.017 billion (Jan. 2000)
Gold Reserves: 0.469 million fine troy ounces (Jan. 2000)
Budget: revenues $1.75 billion, expenditures $1.82 billion, including capital expenditures of $317 million (1997 est.)
Defence Expenditures: 7.09% of total govt. expenditure (1997)
Education Expenditures: 19.64% of govt. expenditure (1997)
External Debt: $3.663 billion (1998)
Exports: $1.164 billion (1999); commodities: coffee 60%, sugar, cotton, shrimp; partners: US 49%, Germany 24%, Guatemala 7%, Costa Rica 4%, Japan 4%
Imports: $3.130 billion (1999); commodities: petroleum products, consumer goods, foodstuffs, machinery, construction materials, fertilizer; partners: US 40%, Guatemala 12%, Venezuela 7%, Mexico 7%, Germany 5%, Japan 4%

COMMUNICATIONS

Daily Newspapers: 5 (1996)
Televisions: 675/1,000 inhabitants (1998)
Radios: 464/1,000 inhabitants (1997)
Telephones: 80 lines/1,000 inhabitants (1998)

TRANSPORTATION

Motor Vehicles: 80,100; 35,300 passenger cars (1997 est.)
Roads: 10,029 km; 1,986 km paved
Railway: 602 km
Air Traffic: 1,701,000 passengers carried (1997)
Airports: 86; 4 have paved runways (1998 est.)

Canadian Embassy: Office of the Canadian Embassy, 111 Avenida Las Palmas, Colonia San Benito, San Salvador, El Salvador. Tel: (011-503) 279-4655. Fax: (011-503) 279-0765.
Embassy in Canada: Embassy of the Republic of El Salvador, 209 Kent St, Ottawa ON K2P 1Z8. Tel: (613) 238-2939. Fax: (613) 238-6940.

Equatorial Guinea

Long-Form Name: Republic of Equatorial Guinea
Capital: Malabo

GEOGRAPHY

Area: 28,050 sq. km
Coastline: 296 km
Climate: tropical; always hot, humid
Environment: subject to violent windstorms; desertification; unsafe drinking water
Terrain: coastal plains rise to interior hills; islands are volcanic
Land Use: 5% arable; 4% permanent; 4% meadows; 46% forest; 41% other
Location: WC Africa, bordering on South Atlantic Ocean

PEOPLE

Population: 465,746 (July 1999 est.)
Nationality: Equatorial Guinean or Equatoguinean
Age Structure: 0-14 yrs: 43%; 15-64: 53%; 65+: 4% (1999 est.)
Population Growth Rate: 2.55 (1999 est.)
Net Migration: 0 migrants/1,000 population (1999 est.)
Ethnic Groups: indigenous population of Bioko, primarily Bubi, some Fernandinos; Rio Muni, primarily Fang; less than 1,000 Europeans, mostly Spanish
Languages: Spanish (official), pidgin English,

Fang, Bubi, Ndowe, Bujeba, Anobones and Corisqueño
Religions: natives all nominally Christian and predominantly Roman Catholic; some pagan practices retained (5%)
Birth Rate: 38.49/1,000 population (1999 est.)
Death Rate: 12.98/1,000 population (1999 est.)
Infant Mortality: 91.18 deaths/1,000 live births (1999 est.)
Life Expectancy at Birth: 52.03 years male, 56.83 years female (1999)
Total Fertility Rate: 5.00 children born/woman (1999 est.)
Literacy: 79.9% (1997)

■ GOVERNMENT

Leader(s): Pres. Teodoro Obiang Nguema Mbasogo, Prime Min. Serafin Seriche Dougan
Government Type: republic in transition to multi-party democracy
Administrative Divisions: 7 provinces (provincias, sing. -provincia)
Nationhood: Oct. 12, 1968 (from Spain; formerly Spanish Guinea)
National Holiday: Independence Day, Oct. 12

■ ECONOMY

Overview: the economy is recovering from destruction by a past regime; subsistence agriculture, forestry and fishing predominate; little industry; many undeveloped natural resources, but increased exploitation of recently discovered natural gas resources is boosting the economy
GDP: $660 million, per capita $1,500; real growth rate n.a. (1997)
Inflation: n.a.
Industries: accounts for 33% of GDP; fishing, sawmilling
Labour Force: n.a.; 66% agriculture, 23% services, 11% industry
Unemployment: 30% (1998)
Agriculture: accounts for 46% of GDP; cash crops—timber and coffee from Rio Muni, cocoa from Bioko; food crops—rice, yams, cassava, bananas, oil, palm nuts, manioc, livestock
Natural Resources: timber, crude oil, small unexploited deposits of gold, manganese, uranium

■ FINANCE/TRADE

Currency: Communauté financière africaine franc (CFAF) = 100 centimes
International Reserves Excluding Gold: $3 million (Dec. 1999)
Gold Reserves: n.a.
Budget: revenues $47 million, expenditures $43 million, including capital expenditures of $7 million (1996 est.)
Defence Expenditures: 1.0% of GDP (1996)
Education Expenditures: n.a.
External Debt: $282 million (1996)
Exports: $423 million (1998); commodities: coffee, timber, cocoa beans; partners: Spain 44%, Germany 19%, Italy 12%, Netherlands 11%
Imports: $32 million (1998); commodities: petroleum, food, beverages, clothing, machinery; partners: Spain 34%, Italy 16%, France 14%, Netherlands 8%

■ COMMUNICATIONS

Daily Newspapers: 1 (1996)
Televisions: 9.6/1,000 inhabitants (1996)
Radios: 427/1,000 inhabitants (1996)
Telephones: 13 lines/1,000 persons (1998)

■ TRANSPORTATION

Motor Vehicles: 10,500; 6,500 passenger cars (1997 est.)
Roads: 2,880 km, none paved
Railway: none
Air Traffic: 21,000 passengers carried (1997)
Airports: 3; 2 have paved runways (1998 est.)

Canadian Embassy: The Canadian Embassy to Equatorial Guinea, c/o P.O. Box 4037, Libreville, Gabon. Tel: (011-241) 73-73-54. Fax (011-241) 73-73-88.
Embassy in Canada: Embassy of Equatorial Guinea, 1712 I Street NW, Suite 410, Washington, DC, 20006, Tel: (202) 347-3950, Fax: (202) 296-4195

Eritrea

Long-Form Name: State of Eritrea
Capital: Asmara (formerly Asmera)

■ GEOGRAPHY

Area: 121,320 sq. km
Coastline: 1,151 km mainland coast; 2,234 km including island coastlines
Climate: hot, dry desert along Red Sea coast, cooler and wetter in central highlands, semi-arid in west
Environment: frequent droughts, famine, deforestation, soil erosion, overgrazing
Terrain: highlands descending to coastal desert in east, hilly in northwest, flat to rolling plains in southwest
Land Use: 12% arable, 1% permanent crops, 48% meadows and pastures, 20% forests and woodland, 19% other; includes 280 sq. km irrigated

Location: E Africa

■ PEOPLE

Population: 3,984,723 (July 1999)
Nationality: Eritrean
Age Structure: 0-14 yrs: 43%; 15-64: 54%; 65+: 3% (1999 est.)
Population Growth Rate: 3.88% (1999 est.)
Net Migration: 8.53 migrants/1,000 population (1999 est.)
Ethnic Groups: 50% ethnic Tigrinya, 40% Tigre and Kunama, 4% Afar, 3% Saho, 3% other
Languages: Afar, Amharic, Tigre and Kunama, Cushitic dialects, Tigrinya, Nora Bana, Arabic
Religions: Muslim, Coptic Christian, Roman Catholic, Protestant
Birth Rate: 42.56/1,000 population (1999 est.)
Death Rate: 12.32/1,000 population (1999 est.)
Infant Mortality: 76.84 deaths/1,000 live births (1999 est.)
Life Expectancy at Birth: 53.61 years male, 57.95 years female (1999 est.)
Total Fertility Rate: 5.96 children born/woman (1999 est.)
Literacy: 25% (1997)

■ GOVERNMENT

Leader(s): Pres. Isaias Afworki, V. Pres. Ahmed Sherifo Mahmud
Government Type: transitional govt.
Administrative Divisions: 8 provinces (awraja)
Nationhood: May 24, 1993 (from Ethiopia)
National Holiday: National Day (independence from Ethiopia), May 24

■ ECONOMY

Overview: with independence from Ethiopia, Eritrea faces the bitter economic problems of a small and desperately poor nation; subsistence farming will continue to be the people's economic mainstay; production is augmented by remittances from abroad, and there are long-term prospects for revenue from offshore oil development, offshore fishing, and tourism; Ethiopia is largely dependent on Eritrean ports for foreign trade
GDP: $2.5 billion, per capita $660; real growth rate 5% (1998 est.)
Inflation: n.a.
Industries: accounts for 20% of GDP; food processing, beverages, textiles, clothing manufacture
Labour Force: 2.0 million (1998)
Unemployment: n.a.
Agriculture: accounts for 18% of GDP; livestock, fish, vegetables, sorghum, cotton, coffee and tobacco
Natural Resources: gold, potash, copper, zinc, salt, fish

■ FINANCE/TRADE

Currency: nafka = 100 cents
International Reserves Excluding Gold: n.a.
Gold Reserves: n.a.
Budget: revenues $226 million; expenditures $453 million, including capital expenditures of $88 million (1996)
Defence Expenditures: 28.6% of GDP (1997)
Education Expenditures: 1.8% of GNP (1997)
External Debt: $149 million (1998)
Exports: $71 million (1996 est.); commodities: livestock, sorghum, textiles, food, small manufactures; partners: Ethiopia, Sudan, Saudi Arabia, US, Italy, Yemen
Imports: $499 million (1996 est.); commodities: processed goods, machinery, petroleum products; partners: Ethiopia, Saudi Arabia, Italy, United Arab Emirates

■ COMMUNICATIONS

Daily Newspapers: 0 (1996)
Televisions: 14/1,000 inhabitants (1998)
Radios: 91/1,000 inhabitants (1997)
Telephones: 7 lines/1,000 inhabitants (1998)

■ TRANSPORTATION

Motor Vehicles: n.a.
Roads: 4,010 km, 874 km paved
Railway: 307 km; not operational
Air Traffic: n.a.
Airports: 20; 2 have paved runways (1998 est.)

Canadian Embassy: The Canadian Embassy to Eritrea, c/o P.O. Box 1130, Addis Ababa, Ethiopia. Tel: (011-251-1) 71-30-22. Fax: (011-251-1) 71-30-33.
Embassy in Canada: Embassy of the State of Eritrea, 75 Albert St., Suite 610, Ottawa, ON K1P 5E7. Tel: (613) 234-3989. Fax: (613) 234-6213

Estonia

Long-Form Name: Republic of Estonia
Capital: Tallinn

■ GEOGRAPHY

Area: 45,226 sq. km
Coastline: 3,794 km
Climate: wet, moderate winter; long windy autumn; warm sunny summer; late and short spring
Environment: severe air pollution, soil and ground water contamination (chemicals and

petroleum products), radioactive waste; frequent spring floods are a natural hazard
Terrain: marshy, lowlands, sloping coastal plain; islands account for 10% of the region
Land Use: 25% arable, negligible permanent crops; 11% meadows and pastures; 44% forest and woodland; 20% other; includes 110 sq. km irrigated
Location: NE Europe, bordering on Baltic Sea

■ PEOPLE

Population: 1,408,523 (July 1999)
Nationality: Estonian
Age Structure: 0-14 yrs: 18%; 15-64: 67%; 65+: 15% (1999 est.)
Population Growth Rate: -0.82% (1999 est.)
Net Migration: -3.08 migrants/1,000 population (1999 est.)
Ethnic Groups: 64.2% Estonian, 28.7% Russian, 2.7% Ukrainian, 1.5% Byelorussian, 1.9% other
Languages: Estonian (official), Russian, Latvian, Lithuanian, English and German also spoken
Religions: Lutheran, Orthodox Christian
Birth Rate: 9.05/1,000 population (1999 est.)
Death Rate: 14.21/1,000 population (1999 est.)
Infant Mortality: 13.83 deaths/1,000 live births (1999 est.)
Life Expectancy at Birth: 62.61 years male, 75.00 years female (1999 est.)
Total Fertility Rate: 1.28 children born/woman (1999 est.)
Literacy: 99% (1997)

■ GOVERNMENT

Leader(s): Pres. Lennart Meri, Prime Min. Mart Laar
Government Type: parliamentary democracy
Administrative Divisions: 15 counties (maakonnad, sing. -maakond)
Nationhood: Sept. 6, 1991 (from Soviet Union)
National Holiday: Independence Day, Feb. 24

■ ECONOMY

Overview: market reforms and stabilizing measures are rapidly transforming the economy; living standards and incomes are rising, but so are unemployment and inflation. Estonia expects to join the World Trade Organization soon.
GDP: $7.8 billion, per capita $5,500; real growth rate 5.5% (1998 est.)
Inflation: 3.1% (March 2000)
Industries: accounts for approximately 25% of GDP; electronics, electrical engineering, textiles, clothing, footwear, shipbuilding
Labour Force: 1 million (1998); 24.6% industry, 25.1% community, social and business services, 12.9% trade and tourism
Unemployment: 9.6% (1998); large numbers of underemployed
Agriculture: contributes 6.2% to GDP, and employs 20% of labour force; dairy products, pork, poultry, eggs, fruit, vegetables; net exports of meat, fish, dairy products, potatoes
Natural Resources: fish, shale, phosphorites, amber, limestone, peat, dolomite

■ FINANCE/TRADE

Currency: kroon (pl. kroons) = 100 cents
International Reserves Excluding Gold: $731 million (Jan. 2000)
Gold Reserves: 0.008 million fine troy ounces (Jan. 2000)
Budget: revenues $1.37 billion; expenditures $1.37 billion, including capital expenditures of n.a. (1997 est.)
Defence Expenditures: 4.02% of govt. expenditure (1998)
Education Expenditures: 8.57% of govt. expenditure (1998)
External Debt: $782 million (1998)
Exports: $2.939 billion (1999); dairy products, fish, furniture, electrical power, meat; partners: Russia and other former Soviet republics 50%, West 50%
Imports: $4.093 billion (1999); machinery 45%, oil 13%, chemicals 12%; partners: Finland, Russia

■ COMMUNICATIONS

Daily Newspapers: 15 (1996)
Televisions: 480/1,000 inhabitants (1998)
Radios: 693/1,000 inhabitants (1997)
Telephones: 343 lines/1,000 inhabitants (1998)

■ TRANSPORTATION

Motor Vehicles: n.a.
Roads: 16,437 km; 8,343 km paved
Railway: 1,018 km (does not include industrial lines)
Air Traffic: 231,000 passengers carried (1997)
Airports: 5; all have paved runways (1997 est.)

Canadian Embassy: Office of the Canadian Embassy, Toom Kooli 13, 2nd Fl, 15186 Tallinn, Estonia. Tel: (011-372) 627-3311. Fax: (011-372) 627-3312.
Embassy in Canada: c/o Embassy of the Republic of Estonia, 2131 Massachusetts Ave NW, Washington DC 20008, USA. Tel: (202) 588-0101. Fax: (202) 588-0108.

Ethiopia

Long-Form Name: Federal Democratic Republic of Ethiopia

Ethiopia

Capital: Addis Ababa

■ GEOGRAPHY

Area: 1,127,127 sq. km
Coastline: none; landlocked
Climate: tropical with wide topographic-induced variation; prone to extended droughts
Environment: geologically active Great Rift Valley susceptible to earthquakes, volcanic eruptions; deforestation; overgrazing; soil erosion; desertification; frequent droughts; famine
Terrain: high plateau with central mountain range divided by Great Rift Valley
Land Use: 12% arable; 1% permanent; 40% meadows; 25% forest; 22% other; includes 1,900 sq. km irrigated
Location: E Africa, between Somalia and Sudan

■ PEOPLE

Population: 59,680,383(July 1999 est.)
Nationality: Ethiopian
Age Structure: 0-14 yrs: 46%; 15-64: 51%; 65+: 3% (1999 est.)
Population Growth Rate: 2.16% (1999 est.)
Net Migration: -1.30 migrants/1,000 population (1999 est.)
Ethnic Groups: 40% Oromo, 32% Amhara and Tigrean, 9% Sidamo, 6% Shankella, 6% Somali, 4% Afar, 2% Gurage, 1% other
Languages: Amharic (official), Tigrinya, Orominga, Guaraginga, Somali, Arabic, English (major foreign language taught in schools)
Religions: 45-50% Muslim, 35-40% Ethiopian Orthodox, 12% animist, 5% other
Birth Rate: 44.34/1,000 population (1999 est.)
Death Rate: 21.43/1,000 population (1999 est.)
Infant Mortality: 124.57 deaths/1,000 live births (1999 est.)
Life Expectancy at Birth: 39.22 years male, 41.73 years female (1999 est.)
Total Fertility Rate: 6.81 children born/woman (1999 est.)
Literacy: 35.4% (1997)

■ GOVERNMENT

Leader(s): Pres. Negasso Ghidada, Prem. Zenawi Meles. Presidential election scheduled for December 2000.
Government Type: federal republic
Administrative Divisions: 9 states and 2 chartered cities
Nationhood: oldest (at least 2,000 years) independent country in Africa and one of the oldest in the world
National Holiday: National Day, May 28

■ ECONOMY

Overview: Ethiopia remains one of the poorest and least developed countries in the world. Its economy is based on agriculture and suffers from recent periods of drought, poor cultivation practices, and the deterioration of internal security conditions.
GDP: $32.9 billion, per capita $560; real growth rate 6% (1998 est.)
Inflation: 0.1% (1997)
Industries: accounts for 12% of GDP, cement, textiles, food processing, beverages, chemicals, metals processing, oil refinery
Labour Force: 26.7 million (1998 est.); 80% agriculture, 12% services, 8% industry
Unemployment: n.a.
Agriculture: accounts for 55% of GDP even though frequent droughts, poor cultivation practices and state economic policies keep farm output low; famines not uncommon; estimated 50% of agricultural production at subsistence level
Natural Resources: small reserves of gold, platinum, copper, potash

■ FINANCE/TRADE

Currency: birr (Br) = 100 cents
International Reserves Excluding Gold: $411 million (Jan. 2000)
Gold Reserves: 0.030 million fine troy ounces (Jan. 2000)
Budget: revenues $1 billion; expenditures $1.48 billion, including capital expenditures of $415 million (1997 est.)
Defence Expenditures: 2.5% of GDP (1998-99)
Education Expenditures: 4.0% of GNP (1997)
External Debt: $10.352 billion (1998)
Exports: $560 million (1998); commodities: coffee 60%, hides; partners: US, Germany, Djibouti, Japan, Yemen, France, Italy
Imports: $1.401 billion (1996); commodities: food, fuels, capital goods; partners: former USSR countries, Italy, Germany, Japan, UK, US, France

■ COMMUNICATIONS

Daily Newspapers: 4 (1996)
Televisions: 5/1,000 inhabitants (1998)
Radios: 195/1,000 inhabitants (1997)
Telephones: 3 lines/1,000 inhabitants (1998)

■ TRANSPORTATION

Motor Vehicles: 69,000; 46,400 passenger cars (1997 est.)
Roads: 28,500 km; 4,275 km paved
Railway: 681 km
Air Traffic: 772,000 passengers carried (1996)

Airports: 84; 11 have paved runways (1998 est.)

Canadian Embassy: The Canadian Embassy, Old Airport Area, Higher 23, Kebele 12, House Number 122, Addis Ababa; mailing address: P.O. Box 1130, Addis Ababa, Ethiopia. Tel: (011-251-1) 71-30-22. Fax: (011-251-1) 71-30-33.

Embassy in Canada: Embassy of the Federal Democratic Republic of Ethiopia, 151 Slater St, Ste 210, Ottawa ON K1P 5H3. Tel: (613) 235-6637. Fax: (613) 235-4638.

Falkland Islands

Long-Form Name: Colony of the Falkland Islands
Capital: Stanley (on East Falkland)

■ GEOGRAPHY

Area: numerous islands covering 12,173 sq. km
Climate: damp, cool, temperate; strong winds, esp. in spring; occasional snow all year
Land Use: 99% pastureland
Location: S South America, in the South Atlantic Ocean

■ PEOPLE

Population: 2,758 (July 1999 est.)
Nationality: Falkland Islander
Ethnic Groups: almost 100% British descent
Languages: English

■ GOVERNMENT

Colony/Territory of: Dependent Territory of the United Kingdom
Leader(s): Head of State: Queen Elizabeth II. Governor Donald Lamont, Chief Executive Michael Blanch
Government Type: dependent territory of the UK, although in 1990 Argentina declared the Falklands and other British-held South Atlantic Islands part of new Argentine province Tierra del Fuego
National Holiday: Liberation Day, June 14

■ ECONOMY

Overview: heavily agricultural, esp. sheep farming, with wool main product; fishing: illex squid; exports tend to outweigh imports in value; chief trading partner: United Kingdom

■ FINANCE/TRADE

Currency: Falkland Islands pound (FKP) = 100 pence, at parity with the British pound sterling

Canadian Embassy: c/o The Canadian High Commission, Macdonald House, 1 Grosvenor Square, London W1X 0AB, England, UK. Tel: (011-44-20) 7258-6600. Fax: (011-44-20) 7445-3302.
Representative to Canada: c/o British High Commission, 80 Elgin St, Ottawa ON K1P 5K7. Tel: (613) 237-1530. Fax: (613) 237-7980.

Faroe Islands

Long-Form Name: Faroe Islands
Capital: Tórshavn (island of Stremoy)

■ GEOGRAPHY

Area: 1,399 sq. km (total of 18 islands and some reefs)
Climate: cold and windy; mild winters, cool summers; foggy
Land Use: 6% arable; 94% other
Location: Norwegian Sea (N Atlantic Ocean), N of Scotland

■ PEOPLE

Population: 41,059 (July 1999 est.)
Nationality: Faroese (sing. & pl.)
Ethnic Groups: Scandinavian
Languages: Faroese (derived from Old Norse), Danish

■ GOVERNMENT

Colony/Territory of: Dependent Territory of Denmark
Leader(s): Queen Margrethe II of Denmark, represented by High Comm. Bente Klinte
Government Type: dependency with some degree of self-rule
National Holiday: Birthday of the Queen, Apr. 16

■ ECONOMY

Overview: fishing main industry, now in decline, which poses great danger to the economy; steep coastline and treacherous currents make trading by sea difficult; exports: fish and fish products; partners: Denmark, Norway, Sweden, Germany, United States

■ FINANCE/TRADE

Currency: Danish krone (kr) = 100 oere

Canadian Embassy: c/o The Canadian Embassy, Kr. Bernikowsgade 1, 1105 Copenhagen K, Denmark. Tel: (011-45) 33-48-32-00. Fax: (011-45) 33-48-32-20.
Representative to Canada: c/o Embassy of the Kingdom of Denmark, 47 Clarence St, Ste 450, Ottawa ON K1N 9K1. Tel: (613) 562-1811. Fax: (613) 562-1812.

Fiji

Long-Form Name: Republic of the Fiji Islands
Capital: Suva

■ GEOGRAPHY

Area: 18,270 sq. km; includes 332 islands of which approx. 110 are inhabited
Coastline: 1,129 km
Climate: tropical marine; only slight seasonal temperature variation
Environment: subject to hurricanes from Nov. to Jan.; deforestation and soil erosion
Terrain: mostly mountains of volcanic origin
Land Use: 10% arable; 4% permanent; 10% meadows; 65% forest; 11% other; includes 10 sq. km irrigated
Location: Pacific Ocean, N of New Zealand

■ PEOPLE

Population: 812,918 (July 1999 est.)
Nationality: Fijian
Age Structure: 0-14 yrs: 33%; 15-64: 63%; 65+: 4% (1999 est.)
Population Growth Rate: 1.28% (1999 est.)
Net Migration: -3.78 migrants/1,000 population (1999 est.)
Ethnic Groups: 46% Indian, 49% Fijian, 5% European, other Pacific Islanders, overseas Chinese and others
Languages: English (official); Fijian; Hindi
Religions: Christianity 52%, Hinduism 38%, Muslim 8%, other 2%
Birth Rate: 22.76/1,000 population (1999 est.)
Death Rate: 6.21/1,000 population (1999 est.)
Infant Mortality: 16.3 deaths/1,000 live births (1999 est.)
Life Expectancy at Birth: 64.19 years male, 69.11 years female (1999 est.)
Total Fertility Rate: 2.70 children born/woman (1999 est.)
Literacy: 91.8% (1997)

■ GOVERNMENT

Leader(s): Pres. Ratu Josefa Iloilo, Prime Min. Laisenia Qarase (interim)
Government Type: republic. The government was destabilized by a coup and hostage taking that began May 19, 2000; it ended with the release of final hostages of deposed elected government on July 13, 2000. A new president was elected by the Great Council of Chiefs on July 13.
Administrative Divisions: 4 divisions and 1 dependency
Nationhood: Oct. 10, 1970 (from UK)
National Holiday: Independence Day, Oct. 10

■ ECONOMY

Overview: the economy, based on agriculture, has recovered from military coups, droughts and a drop in tourism; sugar exports are a major source of income
GDP: $5.4 billion, per capita $6,700; real growth rate 2.4% (1998 est.)
Inflation: -1.0% (Jan. 2000)
Industries: accounts for 22% of GDP; sugar, copra, tourism, gold, silver, fishing, clothing, lumber, small cottage industries
Labour Force: n.a. 29.3% community, social and business services, 24.9% industry, 14.5% trade and tourism
Unemployment: 6% (1997 est.)
Agriculture: accounts for 19% of GDP; principal cash crop is sugar cane; coconuts, cassava, rice, sweet potatoes and bananas; small livestock sector includes cattle, pigs, horses and goats; annual fish catch is significant
Natural Resources: timber, fish, gold, copper, offshore oil potential

■ FINANCE/TRADE

Currency: Fijian dollar ($F) = 100 cents
International Reserves Excluding Gold: $428 million (Jan. 2000)
Gold Reserves: 0.001 million fine troy ounces (Jan. 2000)
Budget: revenues $540.65 million; expenditures $742.65 million, including capital expenditures n.a. (1997 est.)
Defence Expenditures: 5.0% of GDP (1997)
Education Expenditures: 18.19% of govt. expenditure (1996)
External Debt: $333.8 million (1996 est.)
Exports: $510 million (1998); commodities: sugar 49%, copra, processed fish, lumber; partners: UK 45%, Australia 21%, US 4.7%
Imports: $721 million (1998); commodities: food 15%, petroleum products, machinery, consumer goods; partners: US 48%, New Zealand, Australia, Japan

■ COMMUNICATIONS

Daily Newspapers: 1 (1996)
Televisions: 25/1,000 inhabitants (1996)
Radios: 615/1,000 inhabitants (1996)
Telephones: 97 lines/1,000 inhabitants (1998)

■ TRANSPORTATION

Motor Vehicles: 59,000; 30,000 passenger cars (1997 est.)
Roads: 3,440 km; 1,692 km paved
Railway: 597 km
Air Traffic: 517,000 passengers carried (1997)
Airports: 24; 3 have paved runways (1998 est.)

Canadian Embassy: The Canadian Embassy to Fiji, c/o The Canadian High Commission, P.O. Box 12-049, Thorndon, Wellington, New Zealand. Tel: (011-679) 721-936. Fax: (011-679) 750-666.
Embassy in Canada: Embassy of the Republic of Fiji, 630 Third Ave, 7th Fl, New York NY 10017, USA. Tel: (212) 687-4130. Fax: (212) 687-3963.

Finland

Long-Form Name: Republic of Finland
Capital: Helsinki

■ GEOGRAPHY

Area: 337,030 sq. km
Coastline: 1,126 km excluding islands and coastal indentations
Climate: cold temperate; potentially subarctic, but comparatively mild because of moderating influence of the North Atlantic Current, Baltic Sea and more than 60,000 lakes
Environment: permanently wet ground covers approx. 30% of land; air and water pollution
Terrain: mostly low, flat to rolling plains interspersed with lakes and low hills
Land Use: 8% arable; 0% permanent; 0% meadows; 76% forest; 16% other; includes 640 sq. km irrigated
Location: N Europe, bordering on Baltic Sea

■ PEOPLE

Population: 5,158,372 (July 1999 est.)
Nationality: Finn
Age Structure: 0-14 yrs: 18%; 15-64: 67%; 65+: 15% (1999 est.)
Population Growth Rate: 0.15% (1999 est.)
Net Migration: 0.40 migrants/1,000 population (1999 est.)
Ethnic Groups: 93% Finn, 6% Swede, 0.11% Lapp, 0.12% Gypsy, 0.02% Tatar
Languages: 93.5% Finnish, 6.3% Swedish (both official); small Lapp-and Russian-speaking minorities; business language is English
Religions: 89% Evangelical Lutheran, 9% atheist, 1% Eastern Orthodox, 1% other
Birth Rate: 10.77/1,000 population (1999 est.)
Death Rate: 9.67/1,000 population (1999 est.)
Infant Mortality: 3.80 deaths/1,000 live births (1999 est.)
Life Expectancy at Birth: 73.81 years male, 80.98 years female (1999 est.)
Total Fertility Rate: 1.68 children born/woman (1999 est.)
Literacy: 99% (1997)

■ GOVERNMENT

Leader(s): Pres. Tarja Halonen, Prime Min. Paavo Lipponen
Government Type: republic
Administrative Divisions: 6 provinces (laanit, sing. -laani)
Nationhood: Dec. 6, 1917 (from Soviet Union)
National Holiday: Independence Day, Dec. 6

■ ECONOMY

Overview: the manufacturing sector and trade are vital to this highly industrialized, largely free market economy; because of the climate, agricultural development is limited to maintaining self-sufficiency in basic products. Unemployment is a continuing problem
GDP: $103.6 billion, per capita $20,100; real growth rate 5.1% (1998 est.)
Inflation: 3.1% (March 2000)
Industries: accounts for 32% of GDP; metal manufacturing and shipbuilding, forestry and wood processing (pulp, paper), copper refining, foodstuffs, textiles, clothing
Labour Force: 3 million (1998); 33.9% community, social and business services, 19.2% industry, 14.6% trade and tourism
Unemployment: 9.1% (Dec. 1999)
Agriculture: accounts for 5% of GDP (including forestry); livestock production, especially dairy cattle, predominates; forestry is an important export earner; main crops—cereals, sugar beets, potatoes; 85% self-sufficient, but short of food and fodder grains
Natural Resources: timber, copper, zinc, iron ore, silver

■ FINANCE/TRADE

Currency: markkaa, or Finmark = 100 pennia [As of Jan. 1, 1999, Government securities are issued in Euros (EUR)]
International Reserves Excluding Gold: $8.116 billion (Jan. 2000)
Gold Reserves: 1.577 million fine troy ounces (Jan. 2000)
Budget: revenues $33 billion; expenditures $40 billion, including capital expenditures of n.a. (1996 est.)
Defence Expenditures: 2.0% of GDP (1999)
Education Expenditures: 7.5% of GNP (1997)
External Debt: n.a.
Exports: $40.665 billion (1999); commodities: timber, paper and pulp, ships, machinery, clothing and footwear; partners: European Community 44.2% (UK 13%, Germany 10.8%), former USSR countries 14.9%, Sweden 14.1%, US 5.8%
Imports: $30.726 billion (1999); commodities:

foodstuffs, petroleum and petroleum products, chemicals, transport equipment, iron and steel, machinery, textile yarn and fabrics, fodder grains; partners: European Community 43.5% (Germany 16.9%, UK 6.8%), Sweden 13.3%, former USSR countries 12.1%, US 6.3%

■ COMMUNICATIONS

Daily Newspapers: 56 (1996)
Televisions: 640/1,000 inhabitants (1998)
Radios: 1,496/1,000 inhabitants (1997)
Telephones: 554 lines/1,000 inhabitants (1998)

■ TRANSPORTATION

Motor Vehicles: 2,270,000; 2,000,000 passenger cars (1997 est.)
Roads: 77,796 km; 49,789 km paved
Railway: 5,895 km
Air Traffic: 6,002,000 passengers carried (1997)
Airports: 157; 68 have paved runways (1998 est.)

Canadian Embassy: The Canadian Embassy, Pohjois Esplanadi 25B, 00100 Helsinki; mailing address: Box 779, 00101 Helsinki, Finland. Tel: (011-358-9) 17-11-41. Fax (011-358-9) 60-10-60.
Embassy in Canada: Embassy of Finland, 55 Metcalfe St, Ste 850, Ottawa ON K1P 6L5. Tel: (613) 236-2389. Fax: (613) 238-1474.

France

Long-Form Name: French Republic
Capital: Paris

■ GEOGRAPHY

Area: 547,030 sq. km; includes Corsica and the rest of metropolitan France, but excludes the overseas administrative divisions
Coastline: 3,427 km (includes Corsica, 644 km)
Climate: generally cool winters and mild summers, but mild winters and hot summers along the Mediterranean
Environment: most of large urban areas and industrial centres in Rhône, Garonne, Seine or Loire River basins; occasional warm, tropical winds known as mistrals are in central south; air and water pollution; acid rain
Terrain: mostly flat plains or gently rolling hills in north and west; remainder is mountainous, especially Pyrenees in south and Alps in east
Land Use: 33% arable; 2% permanent; 20% meadows; 27% forest; 18% other, includes 16,300 sq. km irrigated
Location: W Europe, bordering on Atlantic Ocean, Mediterranean Sea

■ PEOPLE

Population: 58,978,172 (July 1999 est.)
Nationality: French
Age Structure: 0-14 yrs: 19%; 15-64: 65%; 65+: 16% (1999 est.)
Population Growth Rate: 0.27% (1999 est.)
Net Migration: 0.53 migrants/1,000 population (1999 est.)
Ethnic Groups: Celtic and Latin with Teutonic, Slavic, North African, Indochinese and Basque minorities
Languages: French (100% of population); rapidly declining regional dialects (Provençal, Breton, Alsatian, Corsican, Catalan, Basque, Flemish)
Religions: 90% Roman Catholic, 2% Protestant, 1% Jewish, 1% Muslim (North African workers), 6% unaffiliated
Birth Rate: 11.38/1,000 population (1999 est.)
Death Rate: 9.17/1,000 population (1999 est.)
Infant Mortality: 5.62 deaths/1,000 live births (1999 est.)
Life Expectancy at Birth: 74.76 years male, 82.71 years female (1999 est.)
Total Fertility Rate: 1.61 children born/woman (1999 est.)
Literacy: 99% (1997)

■ GOVERNMENT

Leader(s): Pres. Jacques Chirac, Prime Min. Lionel Jospin
Government Type: republic
Administrative Divisions: 22 regions; dependent areas inc.: French Polynesia, Guadeloupe, Guiana (French Guiana), Martinique, Mayotte, New Caledonia, Réunion, St. Pierre and Miquelon, Southern and Antarctic Territories, Wallis and Futuna Islands
Nationhood: unified by Clovis in 486, First Republic proclaimed in 1792
National Holiday: Taking of the Bastille, July 14

■ ECONOMY

Overview: one of the world's most developed economies; largely self-sufficient in agricultural products; the leading agricultural producer in Western Europe; highly diversified industrial sector; economic integration into the European Community has unknown consequences; unemployment is rising rapidly
GDP: $1.32 trillion, per capita $22,600; real growth rate 3% (1998 est.)
Inflation: 1.3% (April 2000)
Industries: accounts for 28.4% of GDP; steel, machinery, chemicals, automobiles, metallurgy, aircraft, electronics, mining, textiles, food processing, tourism

French Guiana

Labour Force: 26.1 million (1998); 34.3% community, social and business services, 16.6% trade and tourism, 10.1% finance
Unemployment: 11.5% (1998)
Agriculture: accounts for 2.4% of GNP (including fishing and forestry); one of the world's top five wheat producers; self-sufficient for most temperate-zone foods; shortages include fats and oils and tropical produce, but overall net exporter of farm products
Natural Resources: coal, iron ore, bauxite, fish, timber, zinc, potash

■ FINANCE/TRADE

Currency: franc (F or FF) = 100 centimes [As of Jan. 1, 1999, Government securities are issued in Euros (EUR)]
International Reserves Excluding Gold: $39.452 billion (Jan. 2000)
Gold Reserves: 97.240 million fine troy ounces (Jan. 2000)
Budget: revenues $222 billion; expenditures $265 billion, including capital expenditures of n.a. (1998 est.)
Defence Expenditures: 6.4% of central government expenditure (1997)
Education Expenditures: 6.0% of GNP (1997)
External Debt: $117.6 billion (1996 est.)
Exports: $300.170 billion (1999); commodities: machinery and transport equipment, chemicals, foodstuffs, agricultural products, iron and steel products, textiles and clothing; partners: Germany 15.8%, Italy 12.2%, UK 9.8%, Belgium/Luxembourg 8.9%, Netherlands 8.7%, US 6.7%, Spain 5.6%, Japan 1.8%, former USSR countries 1.3%
Imports: $289.941 billion (1999); commodities: crude oil, machinery and equipment, agricultural products, chemicals, iron and steel products; partners: Germany 19.4%, Italy 11.5%, Belgium/Luxembourg 9.2%, US 7.7%, UK 7.2%, Netherlands 5.2%, Spain 4.4%, Japan 4.1%, former USSR countries 2.1%

■ COMMUNICATIONS

Daily Newspapers: 117 (1996)
Televisions: 601/1,000 inhabitants (1998)
Radios: 937/1,000 inhabitants (1997)
Telephones: 570/1,000 inhabitants (1998)

■ TRANSPORTATION

Motor Vehicles: 30,755,000; 25,500,000 passenger cars (1997 est.)
Roads: 892,900 km; all paved
Railway: 32,027 km
Air Traffic: 43,401,000 passengers carried (1997)
Airports: 474; 267 have paved runways (1998 est.)

Canadian Embassy: The Canadian Embassy, 35-37 avenue Montaigne, 75008, Paris, France. Tel: (011-33-1) 44-43-29-00. Fax: (011-33-1) 44-43-29-99.
Embassy in Canada: Embassy of France, 42 Sussex Dr, Ottawa ON K1M 2C9. Tel: (613) 789-1795. Fax: (613) 562-3735.

French Guiana

Long-Form Name: Department of Guiana
Capital: Cayenne

■ GEOGRAPHY

Area: 91,000 sq. km
Climate: tropical, warm and humid, little seasonal temperature variation
Land Use: 83% forest and woodland; interior is uncultivated wilderness, with mineral and forest resources that have not been tapped; 31,000 acres under cultivation; 20 sq. km are irrigated
Location: N South America, bordering on Atlantic Ocean

■ PEOPLE

Population: 167,982 (July 1999 est.)
Nationality: French Guianese
Ethnic Groups: 66% black or mulatto, 12% Caucasian, 12% East Indian, Chinese, Amerindian, 10% other
Languages: French (official), Creole patois

■ GOVERNMENT

Colony/Territory of: Overseas Department of France
Leader(s): Prefect Henri Masse, Pres. of General Council Andre Lecante
Government Type: overseas department of France
National Holiday: Taking of the Bastille, July 14

■ ECONOMY

Overview: economy is closely tied to that of France through subsidies and imports; agriculture: rice, manioc, sugar cane, livestock; forestry, fisheries, food processing industry; chief trading partners: France, EC countries, Japan, US. Unemployment is particularly serious among younger workers

■ FINANCE/TRADE

Currency: French franc = 100 centimes

Canadian Embassy: c/o The Canadian Embassy, 35-57 avenue Montaigne, Paris 75008, France. Tel: (011-33-1) 44-43-29-00. Fax: (011-3-1) 44-43-29-99.

Representative to Canada: c/o Embassy of France, 42 Sussex Dr, Ottawa ON K1M 2C9. Tel: (613) 789-1795. Fax: (613) 562-3735.

French Polynesia

Long-Form Name: Territory of French Polynesia
Capital: Papeete (Windward Islands)

■ GEOGRAPHY

Area: 4,167 sq. km, consisting of five island archipelagoes scattered widely over Eastern Pacific; uninhabited Clipperton Territory is a dependency of French Polynesia but does not form part of the territory
Climate: warm and humid; tropical but moderate
Land Use: 1% arable, 6% permanent crops, 5% meadows and pastures, 31% forest and woodland, 57% other
Location: south Pacific Ocean, NE of New Zealand

■ PEOPLE

Population: 242,073 (July 1999 est.)
Nationality: French Polynesian
Ethnic Groups: 78% Polynesian, 12% Chinese, 6% local French, 4% metropolitan French
Languages: French and Tahitian (both official)

■ GOVERNMENT

Colony/Territory of: Overseas Territory of France
Leader(s): Pres. Jacques Chirac (France), represented by High Commissioner of the Republic Paul Ronciere. Head of government: Pres. of the Territorial Government Gaston Flosse, Pres. of the Territorial Assembly Justin Arapari
Government Type: French overseas territory
National Holiday: Taking of the Bastille, July 14

■ ECONOMY

Overview: agriculture: copra, tropical fruits grown for local consumption; tourism accounts for approximately 20% of GDP and is primary source of revenue; trading partners: France, UK, US

■ FINANCE/TRADE

Currency: CFP franc = 100 centimes

Canadian Embassy: c/o The Canadian Embassy, 35-37 avenue Montaigne, Paris 75008, France. Tel: (011-33-1) 44-43-29-00. Fax: (011-33-1) 44-43-29-99.
Representative to Canada: c/o Embassy of France, 42 Sussex Dr, Ottawa ON K1M 2C9. Tel: (613) 789-1795. Fax: (613) 562-3735.

Gabon

Long-Form Name: Gabonese Republic
Capital: Libreville

■ GEOGRAPHY

Area: 267,670 sq. km
Coastline: 885 km
Climate: tropical; always hot, humid
Environment: deforestation and poaching
Terrain: narrow coastal plain; hilly interior; savanna in east and south
Land Use: 1% arable; 1% permanent; 18% meadows; 77% forest; 3% other; includes 40 sq. km irrigated
Location: WC Africa, bordering on South Atlantic Ocean

■ PEOPLE

Population: 1,225,853 (July 1998 est.)
Nationality: Gabonese (sing. & pl.)
Age Structure: 0-14 yrs: 33%; 15-64: 61%; 65+: 6% (1999 est.)
Population Growth Rate: 1.48% (1999 est.)
Net Migration: 0 migrants/1,000 population (1999 est.)
Ethnic Groups: about 40 Bantu tribes, including four major tribal groupings (Fang, Eshira, Bapounou, Bateke); approx. 100,000 expatriate Africans and Europeans, including 27,000 French
Languages: French (official), Fang, Myene, Bateke, Bapounou/Eschira, Bandjabi
Religions: 55–75% Roman Catholic, 1% Muslim, remainder animist
Birth Rate: 27.89/1,000 population (1999 est.)
Death Rate: 13.07/1,000 population (1999 est.)
Infant Mortality: 83.1 deaths/1,000 live births (1999 est.)
Life Expectancy at Birth: 53.98 years male, 60.08 years female (1999 est.)
Total Fertility Rate: 3.77 children born/woman (1998 est.)
Literacy: 66.2% (1997)

■ GOVERNMENT

Leader(s): Pres. El Hadj Omar Bongo, Prem. Jean-François Ntoutoume-Emane
Government Type: republic; multi-party presidential regime (opposition parties legalized in 1990)
Administrative Divisions: 9 provinces
Nationhood: Aug. 17, 1960 (from France)
National Holiday: Independence Day, Aug. 17

ECONOMY

Overview: economy is dependent on oil, which has contributed to an increase in per capita income; agricultural and industrial sectors are relatively underdeveloped
GDP: $7.7 billion, per capita $6,400; real growth rate 1.7% (1998 est.)
Inflation: 4.4% (Mar. 1997)
Industries: accounts for 67% of GDP; sawmills, cement, petroleum, food and beverages; mining of increasing importance (especially manganese and uranium)
Labour Force: 1 million (1998); 75.5% agriculture, 10.8% industry, 13.7% services
Unemployment: 21% (1997 est.)
Agriculture: accounts for 8% of GDP (including fishing and forestry); cash crops—cocoa, coffee, palm oil; livestock not developed; importer of food; okoume (a tropical softwood) is the most important timber product
Natural Resources: crude oil, manganese, uranium, gold, timber, iron ore

FINANCE/TRADE

Currency: Communauté financière africaine franc (CFAF) = 100 centimes
International Reserves Excluding Gold: $18 million (Dec. 1999)
Gold Reserves: 0.013 million fine troy ounces (June 1998)
Budget: revenues $1.5 billion; expenditures $1.3 billion, including capital expenditures of $302 million (1996 est.)
Defence Expenditures: 7.0% of central government expenditure (1997)
Education Expenditures: 2.9% of GNP (1997)
External Debt: $4.425 billion (1998)
Exports: $3.110 billion (1997); commodities: crude oil 70%, manganese 11%, wood 12%, uranium 6%; partners: France 53%, US 22%, Germany, Japan
Imports: $1.104 billion (1997); commodities: foodstuffs, chemical products, petroleum products, construction materials, manufacturers, machinery; partners: France 48%, US 2.6%, Germany, Japan, UK

COMMUNICATIONS

Daily Newspapers: 2 (1996)
Televisions: 55/1,000 inhabitants (1998)
Radios: 183/1,000 inhabitants (1997)
Telephones: 33 lines/1,000 inhabitants (1998)

TRANSPORTATION

Motor Vehicles: 39,500; 23,800 passenger cars (1997 est.)
Roads: 7,670 km; 629 km paved
Railway: 649 km
Air Traffic: 469,000 passengers carried (1997)
Airports: 62; 10 have paved runways (1998 est.)

Canadian Embassy: The Canadian Embassy, P.O. Box 4037 Libreville, Gabon. Tel: (011-241) 73-73-54 Fax: (011-241) 73-73-88.
Embassy in Canada: Embassy of the Gabonese Republic, 4 Range Rd, Ottawa ON K1N 8J5. Tel: (613) 232-5301. Fax: (613) 232-6916.

Gambia

Long-Form Name: Republic of the Gambia
Capital: Banjul

GEOGRAPHY

Area: 11,300 sq. km
Coastline: 80 km
Climate: tropical; hot, rainy season (June to Nov.); cooler, dry season (Nov. to May)
Environment: deforestation and desertification; diseases spread through the water supply are common
Terrain: flood plain of the Gambia River flanked by some low hills
Land Use: 18% arable; 0% permanent; 9% meadows; 28% forest; 45% other; includes 150 sq. km irrigated
Location: W Africa, bordering on Atlantic Ocean

PEOPLE

Population: 1,336,320 (July 1999 est.)
Nationality: Gambian
Age Structure: 0-14 yrs: 46%; 15-64: 52%; 65+: 2% (1999 est.)
Population Growth Rate: 3.35% (1999 est.)
Net Migration: 3.34 migrants/1,000 population (1999 est.)
Ethnic Groups: 99% African (42% Mandinka, 18% Fula, 16% Wolof, 10% Jola, 9% Serahuli, 4% other); 1% non-Gambian
Languages: English (official); Mandinka, Wolof, Fula, other indigenous vernaculars
Religions: 90% Muslim, 9% Christian, 1% indigenous beliefs
Birth Rate: 42.76/1,000 population (1999 est.)
Death Rate: 12.57/1,000 population (1999 est.)
Infant Mortality: 75.33 deaths/1,000 live births (1999 est.)
Life Expectancy at Birth: 52.02 years male, 56.83 years female (1999 est.)
Total Fertility Rate: 5.83 children born/woman (1999 est.)
Literacy: 33.1% (1997)

■ GOVERNMENT

Leader(s): Pres. Yahya Jammeh; V. Pres. Isatou Njie Saidy. Presidential election scheduled for October 2001.
Government Type: republic
Administrative Divisions: 5 divisions and 1 city (Banjul)
Nationhood: Feb. 18, 1965 (from UK)
National Holiday: Independence Day, Feb. 18

■ ECONOMY

Overview: a poor country, lacking in natural resources and possessing a limited agricultural base of peanut products; the recent rebound in tourism has helped the economy.
GDP: $1.3 billion, per capita $1,000; real growth rate 3.8% (1998 est.)
Inflation: 2.2% (Jan. 2000)
Industries: accounts for 13% of GDP; peanut processing, tourism, beverages, agricultural machinery assembly, woodworking, metalworking, clothing
Labour Force: 1 million (1998); 35.4% community, social and business services, 17% trade and tourism, 11.7% transportation and communication
Unemployment: n.a.
Agriculture: accounts for 23% of GDP and employs about 75% of the population; imports one-third of food requirements; major export crop is peanuts; forestry and fishing resources not fully exploited
Natural Resources: fish

■ FINANCE/TRADE

Currency: dalasi (D) = 100 butut
International Reserves Excluding Gold: $104 million (Nov. 1999)
Gold Reserves: n.a.
Budget: revenues $88.6 million; expenditures $98.2 million, including capital expenditures n.a. (1997 est.)
Defence Expenditures: 2.0% of GDP (1996-97)
Education Expenditures: 4.9% of GNP (1997)
External Debt: $477 million (1998)
Exports: $7 million (1999); commodities: peanuts and peanut products, fish, cotton lint, palm kernels; partners: Ghana 49%, Europe 27%, Japan 12%, US 1%
Imports: $192 million (1999); commodities: foodstuffs, manufacturers, raw materials, fuel, machinery and transport equipment; partners: Europe 55%, (European Community 39%, other 16%), Asia 20%, US 11%, Senegal 4%

■ COMMUNICATIONS

Daily Newspapers: 1 (1996)
Televisions: 3/1,000 inhabitants (1998)
Radios: 168/1,000 inhabitants (1997)
Telephones: 21 lines/1,000 inhabitants (1998)

■ TRANSPORTATION

Motor Vehicles: 9,000; 8,000 passenger cars (1997 est.)
Roads: 2,700 km; 956 km paved
Railway: none
Air Traffic: n.a.
Airports: 1, with paved runway (1998 est.)

Canadian Embassy: The Canadian High Commission to the Gambia, c/o The Canadian Embassy, P.O. Box 3373, Dakar, Senegal. Tel: (011-221) 823-92-90. Fax: (011-221) 823-87-49.
Embassy in Canada: High Commission for the Republic of the Gambia, 1155 15th St NW, Ste 1000, Washington DC, 20005-2 USA. Tel: (202) 785-1399. Fax: (202) 785-1430.

Gaza Strip

■ GEOGRAPHY

Area: 360 sq. km
Climate: temperate, mild winters, dry and warm to hot summers
Land Use: 24% arable; 39% permanent crops; 0% permanent pastures; 11% forests and woodland; 26% other; includes 120 sq. km irrigated
Location: Middle East, bordering on Mediterranean Sea, Egypt and Israel.

■ PEOPLE

Population: 1,112,654 (July 1999 est.)
Nationality: n.a.
Ethnic Groups: Palestinian Arab and other 99.4%, Jewish 0.6%
Languages: Arabic, Hebrew (spoken by Israeli settlers and many Palestinians), English (widely understood)

■ GOVERNMENT

Colony/Territory of: claimed and occupied by Israel
Leader(s): local Palestinian authority is headed by Yasser Arafat, subject to Israeli authority
Government Type: Palestinian Legislative Council (Jan. 1996) has limited powers under interim self-governing agreements with Israel. Originally designated as a five-year interim

arrangement in 1993, permanent status still under negotiation.
National Holiday: n.a.

■ ECONOMY

Overview: Economic conditions in the Gaza Strip, under the responsibility of the Palestinian Authority since the Cairo Agreement of May 1994, have deteriorated since the early 1990s. The most serious negative social effect has been the emergence of chronic unemployment, which has risen to over 20%.

■ FINANCE/TRADE

Currency: 1 new Israeli shekel = 100 new agorot

Canadian Embassy: n.a.
Representative to Canada: n.a.

Georgia

Long-Form Name: Republic of Georgia
Capital: T'bilisi

■ GEOGRAPHY

Area: 69,700 sq. km
Coastline: 310 km
Climate: Alpine to subtropical with warm, humid coastlands
Environment: soil, air and water pollution from toxic chemicals
Terrain: largely mountainous in north and south; lowlands open to Black Sea in west; Kura River Basin in east; good soils in river valley, flood plains and lowlands
Land Use: 34% forests and woodlands; 9% arable; 4% permanent crops; 25% meadows and pastures; 28% other, includes 4,000 sq. km irrigated
Location: SW Asia, bordering on Black Sea

■ PEOPLE

Population: 5,066,499 (July 1999 est.)
Nationality: Georgian
Age Structure: 0-14 yrs: 21%; 15-64: 67%; 65+: 12% (1999 est.)
Population Growth Rate: -0.74% (1999 est.)
Net Migration: -4.69 migrants/1,000 population (1999 est.)
Ethnic Groups: 70.1% Georgian, 8.1% Armenian, 6.3% Russian, 5.7% Azerbaijani, 3% Ossetian, 1.9% Greek, 1.8% Abkhazian, 1% Ukrainian, 2.1% other
Languages: Armenian 7%, Azeri 6%, Georgian 71% (official), Russian 9%, other 7%
Religions: Christian Orthodox 75%, Muslim 11%, Armenian Apostolic 8%, unknown 6%

Birth Rate: 11.64/1,000 population (1999 est.)
Death Rate: 14.30/1,000 population (1999 est.)
Infant Mortality: 52.01 deaths/1,000 live births (1999 est.)
Life Expectancy at Birth: 61.13 years male, 68.32 years female (1999 est.)
Total Fertility Rate: 1.53 children born/woman (1999 est.)
Literacy: 99% (1997)

■ GOVERNMENT

Leader(s): Pres. Eduard A. Shevardnadze
Government Type: republic
Administrative Divisions: 53 rayons (raionebi, sing. -raioni), 9 cities (k'alak'ebi, sing. - k'alak'i) and 2 autonomous regions (avtomnoy respubliki, sing. -avtom respublika)
Nationhood: April 9, 1991 (from Soviet Union)
National Holiday: Independence Day, May 26

■ ECONOMY

Overview: steel processing and light industry predominate; agriculture hindered by extensive wooded areas; international transportation services through key ports are Georgia's main hope for the future
GDP: $11.2 billion, per capita $2,200; real growth rate 4% (1998 est.)
Inflation: 22.8% (Nov. 1999)
Industries: accounts for 16% of GDP; coal and non-ferrous metals refining, machinery and instruments, electrical engineering, chemical production, food processing, cloth, hosiery, shoes, vehicles, mining, esp. manganese, coal, baryta
Labour Force: 3 million (1998); 31% industry and construction, 25% agriculture and forestry, 44% other
Unemployment: 16% (1996 est.)
Agriculture: accounts for 29% of GDP; grapes, tobacco, bay leaves, tea, citrus fruit, sugar, vegetables, grains, tobacco, tung, silk, orchard fruit
Natural Resources: manganese deposits; sulphur and other medicinal springs, forest resources, hydropower, coal and oil

■ FINANCE/TRADE

Currency: lari
International Reserves Excluding Gold: n.a.
Gold Reserves: 0.002 million fine troy ounces (Jan. 2000)
Budget: revenues $364 million; expenditures $568 million, including capital expenditures of n.a. (1998)
Defence Expenditures: 9.10% of total govt. expenditure (1998)

Education Expenditures: 4.89% of total govt. expenditure (1998)
External Debt: $1.674 billion (1998)
Exports: $192 million (1998); grain, fruit, vegetables, tea, electric mine cars, seamless pipes
Imports: $887 million (1998); fuel, foodstuffs, machinery, equipment

■ COMMUNICATIONS
Daily Newspapers: n.a.
Televisions: 473/1,000 inhabitants (1998)
Radios: 555/1,000 inhabitants (1997)
Telephones: 115 lines/1,000 inhabitants (1998)

■ TRANSPORTATION
Motor Vehicles: n.a.
Roads: 20,700 km; 19,354 km hard-surfaced
Railway: 1,583 km
Air Traffic: 110,000 passengers carried (1997)
Airports: 28; 14 have paved runways

Canadian Embassy: The Canadian Embassy to Georgia, c/o The Canadian Embassy, Nenehatun Caddesi No. 75, Gaziosmanpasa 06700, Ankara, Turkey. Tel: (011-90-312) 436-1275. Fax: (011-90-312) 446-4437.

Embassy in Canada: Embassy of the Republic of Georgia, 1615 New Hampshire Ave. NW, Suite 300, Washington DC, 20009, Tel: (202) 387-2390, Fax: (202) 393-4537

Germany

Long-Form Name: Federal Republic of Germany
Capital: Berlin

■ GEOGRAPHY
Area: 356,910 sq. km
Coastline: 2,389 km
Climate: temperate; cool, wet summers; cool to cold, cloudy winters with frequent rain and snow; occasional warm, tropical föhn wind; high relative humidity
Environment: air and water pollution; significant deforestation in mountain regions due to environmental pollution
Terrain: flat plains; lowlands in north; central uplands; Bavarian Alps in southwest
Land Use: 33% arable land; 1% permanent crops; 15% meadows and pastures; 31% forest and woodland; 20% other, includes 4,750 sq. km irrigated
Location: NC Europe, bordering on North Sea, Baltic Sea

■ PEOPLE
Population: 82,087,361 (July 1999 est.)
Nationality: German
Age Structure: 0-14 yrs: 15%; 15-64: 69%; 65+: 16% (1999 est.)
Population Growth Rate: 0.01% (1999 est.)
Net Migration: 2.12 migrants/1,000 population (1999 est.)
Ethnic Groups: German 91.5%, Turkish 2.4%, Italian 0.7%, Greek 0.4%. Polish 0.4%, other 4.6%
Languages: German (official)
Religions: 45% Protestant, 37% Roman Catholic, 18% unaffiliated
Birth Rate: 8.68/1,000 population (1999 est.)
Death Rate: 10.76/1,000 population (1999 est.)
Infant Mortality: 5.14 deaths/1,000 live births (1999 est.)
Life Expectancy at Birth: 74.01 years male, 80.50 years female (1999 est.)
Total Fertility Rate: 1.26 children born/woman (1999 est.)
Literacy: 99% (1997)

■ GOVERNMENT
Leader(s): Chanc. Gerhard Schroeder, Pres. Johannes Rau
Government Type: federal republic
Administrative Divisions: 16 states (Laender, sing. -Land)
Nationhood: January 18, 1871 (unification of German Empire); West Germany and East Germany were unified on Oct. 3, 1990
National Holiday: German Unity Day, Oct. 3

■ ECONOMY
Overview: Former W Germany: highly urbanized with advanced market economy and strong exports; manufacturing and service industries dominate with imported raw materials and semimanufactured products. As the world's third-most powerful economy, the former W Germany faces unique problems in bringing the eastern areas up to standard after 45 years of Communist rule. Former E Germany: outmoded economy, slow pace of economic reform deters outside investors; former W Germany's legal, social welfare and economic systems have been extended to the east. Unified Germany: slight nation-wide post-reunification recession.
GDP: $1.813 trillion, per capita $22,100; real growth rate 2.7% (1998 est.)
Inflation: 1.9% (March 2000)
Industries: accounts for 33.1% of GDP; iron, steel, coal, chemicals, vehicles, ships, machinery, food and beverages, electronics, brown coal, shipbuilding, textiles, petroleum refining
Labour Force: 41 million (1998); 30.8% industry, 28.2% community, social and business services,

14.9% trade and tourism
Unemployment: 11.5% (Dec. 1999)
Agriculture: agriculture, including fishing and forestry, accounts for about 1.1% of GDP; diversified crop and livestock farming, including wheat, potatoes, barley, sugar beets, fruit, livestock products; net importer of food
Natural Resources: iron ore, coal, potash, natural gas, salt, nickel, timber

■ FINANCE/TRADE

Currency: Deutsche Mark (DM) = 100 Pfennige [As of Jan. 1, 1999, Government securities are issued in Euros (EUR)]
International Reserves Excluding Gold: $59.622 billion (Jan. 2000)
Gold Reserves: 111.519 million fine troy ounces (Jan. 2000)
Budget: revenues $977 billion; expenditures $1.024 trillion, including capital expenditures n.a. (1998)
Defence Expenditures: 1.5% of GDP (1998)
Education Expenditures: 4.8% of GNP (1997)
External Debt: exact figures n.a., but very high
Exports: $541.076 billion (1999); manufactured goods 88%, agricultural products 5%, raw materials 2.3%, other 4.7%; partners: EU 58%, Eastern Europe 8%, other West European countries 7.5%, US 7%, Japan 2.5%, other 17%
Imports: $472.161 billion (1999); manufactured goods 74%, agricultural products 10%, fuels 6.4%, raw materials 6%, other 3.6%; partners: EU 56%, Eastern Europe 9%, other West European countries 7%, US 7%, Japan 5%, China 2.5%, other 13.5%

■ COMMUNICATIONS

Daily Newspapers: 375 (1996)
Televisions: 580/1,000 inhabitants (1998)
Radios: 948/1,000 inhabitants (1997)
Telephones: 567 lines/1,000 inhabitants (1998)

■ TRANSPORTATION

Motor Vehicles: 47,000,000; 42,800,000 passenger cars (1997 est.)
Roads: 656,074 km; 650,169 km paved
Railway: 46,300 km
Air Traffic: 45,805,000 passengers carried (1997)
Airports: 618; 319 have paved runways (1998 est.)

Canadian Embassy: The Canadian Embassy, Friedrichstrasse 95, 10117, Berlin, Germany, Tel: (011-49-30) 20-312-0, Fax: (011-49-30) 20-312-590
Embassy in Canada: Embassy of the Federal Republic of Germany, 1 Waverley St, Ottawa ON K2P 0T8. Tel: (613) 232-1101. Fax: (613) 594-9330.

Ghana

Long-Form Name: Republic of Ghana
Capital: Accra

■ GEOGRAPHY

Area: 238,540 sq. km
Coastline: 539 km
Climate: tropical; warm and comparatively dry along southeast coast; hot and humid in southwest; hot and dry in north
Environment: recent drought in north severely affecting marginal agricultural activities; deforestation; overgrazing; soil erosion; dry, northeasterly harmattan wind (Jan. to Mar.); water pollution and insufficient safe drinking water
Terrain: mostly low plains with dissected plateau in south-central area
Land Use: 12% arable; 7% permanent crops; 22% meadows; 35% forest; 24% other; includes 60 sq. km irrigated
Location: WC Africa, bordering on South Atlantic Ocean

■ PEOPLE

Population: 18,887,626 (July 1999 est.)
Nationality: Ghanaian
Age Structure: 0-14 yrs: 42%; 15-64: 54%; 65+: 4% (1999 est.)
Population Growth Rate: 2.05% (1999 est.)
Net Migration: -0.88% migrants/1,000 population (1999 est.)
Ethnic Groups: 99.8% black African (major tribes—44% Akan, 16% Moshi-Dagomba, 13% Ewe, 8% Ga, 18.8% other), 0.2% European and other
Languages: English (official); African languages include Akan, Moshi-Dagomba, Ewe and Ga
Religions: 38% indigenous beliefs, 30% Muslim, 24% Christian, 8% other
Birth Rate: 31.79/1,000 population (1999 est.)
Death Rate: 10.40/1,000 population (1999 est.)
Infant Mortality: 76.15 deaths/1,000 live births (1999 est.)
Life Expectancy at Birth: 55.08 years male, 59.27 years female (1999 est.)
Total Fertility Rate: 4.11 children born/woman (1999 est.)
Literacy: 66.4% (1997)

■ GOVERNMENT

Leader(s): Pres. Flt. Lt. (Ret.) Jerry John Rawlings; V. Pres. John Evans Atta Mills.

Presidential election scheduled for December 8, 2000.
Government Type: constitutional democracy
Administrative Divisions: 10 regions
Nationhood: Mar. 6, 1957 (from UK, formerly known as Gold Coast)
National Holiday: Independence Day, Mar. 6

■ ECONOMY

Overview: heavily dependent on cocoa, gold and timber exports; international assistance boosts this economy, which depends on good harvests; population growth is a burden
GDP: $33.6 billion, per capita $1,800; real growth rate 3% (1998 est.)
Inflation: 14.6% (Dec. 1998)
Industries: accounts for 14% of GDP; mining, lumbering, light manufacturing, fishing, aluminum, food processing
Labour Force: 9 million (1998); 59.3% agriculture, 11.1% industry, 29.6% services
Unemployment: 20% (1997 est.)
Agriculture: accounts for almost 41% of GDP; major cash crop is cocoa; other crops: rice, coffee, cassava, peanuts, corn; normally self-sufficient in food
Natural Resources: gold, timber, industrial diamonds, bauxite, manganese, fish, rubber

■ FINANCE/TRADE

Currency: cedi (C/) = 100 pesewas
International Reserves Excluding Gold: $436 million (Nov. 1999)
Gold Reserves: 0.279 million fine troy ounces (Dec. 1999)
Budget: revenues $1.39 billion; expenditures $1.47 billion, including capital expenditures of $370 million (1996 est.)
Defence Expenditures: 0.7% of GDP (1999)
Education Expenditures: 4.2% of GNP (1997)
External Debt: $6.884 billion (1998)
Exports: $1.795 billion (1998); commodities: cocoa 60%, timber, gold, tuna, bauxite, and aluminum; partners: US 23%, UK, other European Community
Imports: $3.505 billion (1999); commodities: petroleum 16%, consumer goods, foods, intermediate goods, capital equipment; partners: US 10%, UK, Germany, France, Japan, S Korea

■ COMMUNICATIONS

Daily Newspapers: 4 (1996)
Televisions: 99/1,000 inhabitants (1998)
Radios: 238/1,000 inhabitants (1997)
Telephones: 8 lines/1,000 inhabitants (1998)

■ TRANSPORTATION

Motor Vehicles: 135,000; 90,000 passenger cars (1997 est.)
Roads: 39,409 km; 11,653 km hard-surfaced
Railway: 953 km
Air Traffic: 211,000 passengers carried (1997)
Airports: 12; 6 have paved runways (1998 est.)

Canadian Embassy: Canadian High Commission, 42 Independence Ave, Accra, Ghana; P.O. Box 1639, Accra, Ghana. Tel: (011-233-21) 77-37-91. Fax: (011-233-21) 77-37-92.
Embassy in Canada: High Commission for the Republic of Ghana, 1 Clemow Ave, Ottawa ON K1S 2A9. Tel: (613) 236-0871. Fax: (613) 236-0874.

Gibraltar

Long-Form Name: Gibraltar
Capital: Gibraltar

■ GEOGRAPHY

Area: 6.5 sq. km
Climate: warm, temperate, low precipitation, mild winters, warm summers
Land Use: almost 100% bare limestone (Rock of Gibraltar) and/or built up; no farmland
Location: Iberian Peninsula of S Spain, bordering on Mediterranean Sea

■ PEOPLE

Population: 29,165 (July 1999 est.)
Nationality: Gibraltarian
Ethnic Groups: Portuguese, Maltese, Spanish, Italian, English
Languages: English (used in schools and for official purposes), Spanish, Italian, Portuguese, Russian

■ GOVERNMENT

Colony/Territory of: Dependent Territory of United Kingdom
Leader(s): Head of State: Queen Elizabeth II. Gov. David Durie; Chief Min. Peter Caruana
Government Type: dependent territory of the UK
National Holiday: Commonwealth Day (second Monday in March)

■ ECONOMY

Overview: tourism most important; industries: construction materials, beverage bottling; re-exports: tobacco, petroleum, wine; exports of local products negligible; must import all food; more than 70% of the economy is in the public sector

■ FINANCE/TRADE
Currency: Gibraltar pound = 100 pence

Canadian Embassy: c/o The Canadian High Commission, Macdonald House, 1 Grosvenor Square, London W1X 0AB, England, UK. Tel: (011-44-20) 7258-6600. Fax: (011-44-20) 7258-6333.

Representative to Canada: c/o British High Commission, 80 Elgin St, Ottawa ON K1P 5K7. Tel: (613) 237-1530. Fax: (613) 237-7980.

Greece

Long-Form Name: Hellenic Republic
Capital: Athens

■ GEOGRAPHY
Area: 131,940 sq. km
Coastline: 13,676 km
Climate: temperate; mild, wet winter; hot, dry summer
Environment: subject to severe earthquakes; air pollution; archipelago of 2,000 islands; water pollution
Terrain: mostly mountainous with ranges extending into sea as peninsulas or chains of islands
Land Use: 19% arable; 8% permanent crops; 41% meadows; 20% forest; 12% other, includes 13,140 sq. km irrigated
Location: S Europe, bordering on Adriatic Sea

■ PEOPLE
Population: 10,707,135 (July 1999 est.)
Nationality: Greek
Age Structure: 0-14 yrs: 16%; 15-64: 67%; 65+: 17% (1999 est.)
Population Growth Rate: 0.41% (1999 est.)
Net Migration: 4.04 migrants/1,000 population (1999 est.)
Ethnic Groups: 98% Greek, 2% others
Languages: Greek (official); English, German and French widely understood
Religions: 98% Greek Orthodox, 1.3% Muslim, 0.7% other
Birth Rate: 9.54/1,000 population (1999 est.)
Death Rate: 9.44/1,000 population (1999 est.)
Infant Mortality: 7.13 deaths/1,000 live births (1999 est.)
Life Expectancy at Birth: 75.87 years male, 81.18 years female (1999 est.)
Total Fertility Rate: 1.30 children born/woman (1999 est.)
Literacy: 96.6% (1997)

■ GOVERNMENT
Leader(s): Pres. Konstandinos Stefanopoulos, Prime Min. Konstandinos Simitis
Government Type: presidential parliamentary government
Administrative Divisions: 51 prefectures (nomoi, singular–nomós) and 1 autonomous region
Nationhood: 1829 (from the Ottoman Empire)
National Holiday: Independence Day (proclamation of the war of independence), Mar. 25

■ ECONOMY
Overview: a large commodity trade deficit is offset by the successful tourism industry; economy is characterized by low GDP growth, and high inflation and national debt
GDP: $143 billion, per capita $13,400; real growth rate 3% (1998 est.)
Inflation: 2.6% (April 2000)
Industries: accounts for 23.5% of GDP; food and tobacco processing, textiles, chemicals, metal products, tourism, mining, petroleum
Labour Force: 5 million (1998); 21.9% agriculture, 20.1% community, social and business services, 19% industry
Unemployment: 10% (1998 est.)
Agriculture: accounts for 8.5% of GDP (including fishing and forestry); self-sufficient in food; principal products—wheat, corn, barley, sugar beets, olives, tomatoes, wine, tobacco, potatoes, beef, mutton, pork, dairy products
Natural Resources: bauxite, lignite, magnesite, crude oil, marble

■ FINANCE/TRADE
Currency: drachma (Dr) = 100 lepta
International Reserves Excluding Gold: $16.641 billion (Jan. 2000)
Gold Reserves: 4.239 million fine troy ounces (Jan. 2000)
Budget: revenues $37 billion; expenditures $45 billion, capital expenditures n.a. (1998 est.)
Defence Expenditures: 6.69% of total govt. expenditure (1997)
Education Expenditures: 9.28% of total govt. expenditure (1997)
External Debt: $33 billion (1997 est.)
Exports: $8.603 billion (1997); commodities: manufactured goods, food and live animals, fuels and lubricants, raw materials; partners: Germany 24%, Italy 14%, non-oil-developing countries 11.8%, France 9.5%, US 7.1%, UK 6.8%
Imports: $27.717 billion (1997); commodities: machinery and transport equipment, light manufactures, fuels and lubricants, foodstuffs,

chemicals; partners: Germany 22%, non-oil-developing countries 14%, oil-exporting countries 13%, Italy 12%, France 8%, US 3.2%

■ COMMUNICATIONS

Daily Newspapers: 156 (1996)
Televisions: 466/1,000 inhabitants (1998)
Radios: 477/1,000 inhabitants (1997)
Telephones: 522 lines/1,000 inhabitants (1998)

■ TRANSPORTATION

Motor Vehicles: 3,500,000; 2,440,000 passenger cars (1997 est.)
Roads: 117,000 km; 107,406 km paved
Railway: 2,548 km
Air Traffic: 7,061,000 passengers carried (1997)
Airports: 78; 63 have paved runways (1998 est.)

Canadian Embassy: The Canadian Embassy, 4 Ioannou Gennadiou St, Athens 115 21, Greece. Tel: (011-30-1) 727-3400. Fax: (011-30-1) 727-3460.
Embassy in Canada: Embassy of the Hellenic Republic, 76-80 MacLaren St, Ottawa ON K2P 0K6. Tel: (613) 238-6271. Fax: (613) 238-5676.

Greenland

Long-Form Name: Grønland
Capital: Nuuk (Godthab)

■ GEOGRAPHY

Area: 2,175,600 sq. km
Climate: arctic to subarctic; cool summers, cold winters
Land Use: 1% meadow and pastures; negligible forest and woodland; 99% bare rock, snow and ice
Location: N North America, bordering on Atlantic Ocean, Greenland Sea, Arctic Ocean, Baffin Bay

■ PEOPLE

Population: 59,827 (July 1999 est.)
Nationality: Greenlander
Ethnic Groups: 87% Greenlander (Inuit and Greenland-born Caucasians), 13% Danish
Languages: Inuit dialects, Danish

■ GOVERNMENT

Colony/Territory of: Dependent Territory of Denmark
Leader(s): Queen Margrethe II of Denmark, represented by High Comm. Gunnar Martens; Prem. Jonathan Motzfeldt
Government Type: part of the Danish realm; self-governing overseas administrative division
National Holiday: Birthday of the Queen, Apr. 16

■ ECONOMY

Overview: dependent on annual subsidy from the Danish government; unemployment is on the increase; fishing is the most important industry; mineral resource exploitation is limited to lead and zinc

■ FINANCE/TRADE

Currency: Danish krone (DKr) = 100 oere

Canadian Embassy: c/o Kr. Bernikowsgade 1, 1105 Copenhagen K, Denmark. Tel: (011-45) 33-48-32-00. Fax: (011-45) 33-48-32-20.
Representative to Canada: c/o Royal Danish Embassy, 47 Clarence St., Ste. 450, Ottawa ON K1N 9K1. Tel: (613) 562-1811. Fax: (613) 562-1812.

Grenada

Long-Form Name: Grenada
Capital: Saint George's

■ GEOGRAPHY

Area: 340 sq. km
Coastline: 121 km
Climate: tropical; tempered by northeast trade winds
Environment: lies on edge of hurricane belt; hurricane season lasts from June to Nov.
Terrain: volcanic in origin with central mountains
Land Use: 15% arable; 18% permanent crops; 3% meadows; 9% forest; 55% other
Location: Caribbean islands, just north of Venezuela

■ PEOPLE

Population: 97,008 (July 1999 est.)
Nationality: Grenadian
Age Structure: 0-14 yrs: 43%; 15-64: 53%; 65+: 4% (1999 est.)
Population Growth Rate: 0.87% (1999 est.)
Net Migration: -13.74 migrants/1,000 population (1999 est.)
Ethnic Groups: mainly of black African descent
Languages: English (official); some French patois
Religions: largely Roman Catholic; Anglican; other Protestant sects
Birth Rate: 27.62/1,000 population (1999 est.)
Death Rate: 5.15/1,000 population (1999 est.)
Infant Mortality: 11.13 deaths/1,000 live births (1999 est.)

Life Expectancy at Birth: 68.97 years male, 74.29 years female (1999 est.)
Total Fertility Rate: 3.57 children born/woman (1999 est.)
Literacy: 96% (1997)

■ GOVERNMENT

Leader(s): Head of State: Queen Elizabeth II/Gov. Gen. Daniel Williams. Prime Min. Keith Mitchell
Government Type: parliamentary democracy
Administrative Divisions: 6 parishes and 1 dependency
Nationhood: Feb. 7, 1974 (from UK)
National Holiday: Independence Day, Feb. 7

■ ECONOMY

Overview: the economy is based on agriculture (spices, tropical plants) and tourism; unemployment is high
GDP: $340 million, per capita $3,500; real growth rate 5% (1998 est.)
Inflation: 0.3% (Dec. 1999)
Industries: accounts for 15% of GDP; food and beverage, textiles, light assembly operations, tourism, construction
Labour Force: n.a.; services 31%, agriculture 24%, construction 8%, manufacturing 5%, other 32%
Unemployment: 20% (Oct. 1996)
Agriculture: accounts for 9.7% of GDP, 80% of exports and employs 24% of the labour force; bananas, cocoa, nutmeg and mace are major crops; small-scale farms predominate
Natural Resources: timber, tropical fruit, deepwater harbours

■ FINANCE/TRADE

Currency: East Caribbean dollar ($EC) = 100 cents
International Reserves Excluding Gold: $51 million (Dec. 1999)
Gold Reserves: n.a.
Budget: revenues $75.7 million; expenditures $126.7 million, including capital expenditures of $51 million (1996 est.)
Defence Expenditures: n.a.
Education Expenditures: n.a.
External Debt: $74 million (1997 est.)
Exports: $23 million (1997); commodities: nutmeg 35%, cocoa beans 15%, bananas 13%, mace 7%, textiles; partners: US 4%, UK, Germany, Netherlands, Trinidad and Tobago
Imports: $171 million (1997); commodities: machinery 24%, food 22%, manufactured goods 19%, petroleum 8%; partners: US 32%, UK, Trinidad and Tobago, Japan, Canada

■ COMMUNICATIONS

Daily Newspapers: n.a.
Televisions: 351/1,000 inhabitants (1996)
Radios: 652/1,000 inhabitants (1996)
Telephones: 263 lines/1,000 inhabitants (1998)

■ TRANSPORTATION

Motor Vehicles: n.a.
Roads: 1,040 km; 638 km paved
Railway: none
Air Traffic: n.a.
Airports: 3; 2 have paved runways (1998 est.)

Canadian Embassy: The Canadian High Commission to Grenada, c/o The Canadian High Commission, P.O. Box 404, Bridgetown, Barbados. Tel: (246) 429-3550. Fax: (246) 429-3780.
Embassy in Canada: c/o High Commission for the Countries of the Organization of Eastern Caribbean States, 112 Kent St, Ste 1610, Place de Ville, Tower B, Ottawa ON K1P 5P2. Tel: (613) 236-8952. Fax: (613) 236-3042.

Guadeloupe

Long-Form Name: Department of Guadeloupe
Capital: Basse-Terre (seat of govt.); each of the 7 inhabited islands has its own chief town

■ GEOGRAPHY

Area: 1,780 sq. km (2 main islands, 5 small islands, one small island group called Iles des Saintes)
Climate: subtropical tempered by trade winds; hot and humid May–Dec., cool and dry Dec.–April
Land Use: 14% arable, 4% permanent crops, 14% meadows and pastures, 39% forest and woodland, 29% other; includes 30 sq. km irrigated
Location: Caribbean, halfway along the Lesser Antilles arch between Puerto Rico and S America

■ PEOPLE

Population: 420,943 (July 1999 est.)
Nationality: Guadeloupian
Ethnic Groups: 90% black or mulatto, 5% white, less than 5% East Indian, Lebanese, Chinese
Languages: French, Creole dialect

■ GOVERNMENT

Colony/Territory of: Dependency of France
Leader(s): Head of State: Pres. Jacques Chirac

(France). Prefect Jean Fedini, Pres. General Council Marcellin Lubeth, Pres. Regional Council Lucette Michaux-Cherry
Government Type: overseas department of France
National Holiday: Taking of the Bastille, July 14

■ ECONOMY

Overview: economy depends on agriculture, tourism, light industry and services; unemployment is especially high among youth; agriculture: includes bananas, sugar cane, rum, flowers, livestock; vegetables and tobacco grown for local consumption; forestry, fisheries, tourism, food processing; partners: France, Martinique

■ FINANCE/TRADE

Currency: French franc = 100 centimes

Canadian Embassy: c/o The Canadian Embassy, 35-37 avenue Montaigne, Paris, 75008, France. Tel: (011-331) 44-43-29-00. Fax: (011-331) 44-43-29-99.
Representative to Canada: c/o Embassy of France, 42 Sussex Dr, Ottawa ON K1M 2C9. Tel: (613) 789-1795. Fax: (613) 562-3735.

Guam

Long-Form Name: Territory of Guam
Capital: Hagatna (Agana)

■ GEOGRAPHY

Area: 541.3 sq. km
Climate: tropical maritime, with little seasonal variation, but typhoon-prone and suffers from earthquakes; wet all year
Land Use: 11% arable, 11% permanent crops, 15% meadows and pastures, 18% forest and woodland, 45% other; interior is mountainous and volcanic hills dominate the south, but many forests in northern Guam have been cleared for farming and the construction of airfields; coconut trees grow throughout the island
Location: N Pacific Ocean, E of the Philippines

■ PEOPLE

Population: 151,716 (July 1999 est.)
Nationality: Guamanian
Ethnic Groups: 47% Chamorro, 25% Filipino, 10% Caucasian, 18% Chinese, Japanese, Korean and other
Languages: English (official), Chamorro, Japanese

■ GOVERNMENT

Colony/Territory of: Unincorporated Outlying Territory of the United States
Leader(s): Head of State: Pres. William Clinton (US) (to Jan. 20, 2001); Gov. Carl T.C. Gutierrez
Government Type: unincorporated outlying territory of the US; executive powers of the legislature similar to those of an American state legislature
National Holiday: Guam Discovery Day (first Monday in March); also Liberation Day, July 21

■ ECONOMY

Overview: economy depends mainly on US military spending and on tourism; agriculture: corn, coconuts, sweet potatoes, cucumbers, watermelons, beans, livestock, esp. cattle and pigs, fruit, vegetables, fish; industry: textile manufacture, cement, petroleum, printing, plastics, ship repair; tourism of growing importance

■ FINANCE/TRADE

Currency: American dollar = 100 cents

Canadian Embassy: c/o The Canadian Embassy, 501 Pennsylvania Avenue NW, Washington DC 20001, USA. Tel: (202) 682-1740. Fax: (202) 682-7726.
Representative to Canada: c/o Embassy of the United States of America, 490 Sussex Drive, Ottawa, ON, K1N 1G8 Tel: (613) 238-5335. Fax: (613) 688-3097.

Guatemala

Long-Form Name: Republic of Guatemala
Capital: Guatemala

■ GEOGRAPHY

Area: 108,890 sq. km
Coastline: 400 km
Climate: tropical; hot, humid in lowlands; cooler in highlands
Environment: numerous volcanoes in mountains, with frequent violent earthquakes; Caribbean coast subject to hurricanes and other tropical storms; deforestation; soil erosion; water pollution
Terrain: mostly mountainous with narrow coastal plains and rolling limestone plateau (Petén)
Land Use: 12% arable; 5% permanent; 24% permanent pastures; 54% forest; 5% other; includes 1,250 sq. km irrigated
Location: northernmost Central (Latin) America, bordering on Caribbean Sea, Pacific Ocean

■ PEOPLE
Population: 12,335,580 (July 1999 est.)
Nationality: Guatemalan
Age Structure: 0-14 yrs: 43%; 15-64: 54%; 65+: 3% (1999 est.)
Population Growth Rate: 2.68% (1999 est.)
Net Migration: -1.93 migrants/1,000 population (1999 est.)
Ethnic Groups: 56% Ladino (mestizo-mixed Indian and European ancestry), 44% Indian
Languages: 60% Spanish, but 40% of the population speaks an Indian language as a primary tongue (23 Indian dialects, including Quiche, Cakchiquel, Kekchi)
Religions: predominantly Roman Catholic; also Protestant, traditional Mayan
Birth Rate: 35.57/1,000 population (1999 est.)
Death Rate: 6.80/1,000 population (1999 est.)
Infant Mortality: 46.15 deaths/1,000 live births (1999 est.)
Life Expectancy at Birth: 63.78 years male, 69.24 years female (1999 est.)
Total Fertility Rate: 4.74 children born/woman (1999 est.)
Literacy: 66.6% (1997)

■ GOVERNMENT
Leader(s): Pres. Alfonso Portillo Cabrera; V. Pres. Juan Francisco Reyes Lopez
Government Type: republic
Administrative Divisions: 22 departments (departamento, pl. departamentos)
Nationhood: Sept. 15, 1821 (from Spain)
National Holiday: Independence Day, Sept. 15

■ ECONOMY
Overview: the inflation rate has dropped significantly as a result of government economic reforms, but political uncertainty casts a shadow over the agriculturally based economy
GDP: $45.7 billion, per capita $3,800; real growth rate 5% (1998 est.)
Inflation: 9.1% (April 2000)
Industries: accounts for 21% of GDP; sugar, textiles and clothing, furniture, chemicals, petroleum, metals, rubber, tourism
Labour Force: 4.0 million (1998); 36.9% community, social and business services, 26.1% agriculture, 16.6% industry
Unemployment: 5.2% (1997 est.)
Agriculture: accounts for 24% of GDP and employs 60% of the labour force; principal crops—sugar cane, corn, bananas, coffee, beans, cardamom; livestock—cattle, sheep, pigs, chickens; food importer
Natural Resources: crude oil, nickel, rare woods, fish, chicle

■ FINANCE/TRADE
Currency: quetzal (pl. quetzalas) (Q) = 100 centavos
International Reserves Excluding Gold: $1.182 billion (Jan. 2000)
Gold Reserves: 0.215 million fine troy ounces (Jan. 2000)
Budget: revenues $1.6 billion; expenditures $1.88 billion, including capital expenditures of $570 million (1996 est.)
Defence Expenditures: 0.7% of GDP (1998)
Education Expenditures: 1.7% of GNP (1997)
External Debt: $4.565 billion (1998)
Exports: $2.398 billion (1999); commodities: coffee 38%, bananas 7%, sugar 7%, cardamon 4%; partners: US 29%, El Salvador, Germany, Costa Rica, Italy
Imports: $4.382 billion (1999); commodities: fuel and petroleum products, machinery, grain, fertilizers, motor vehicles; partners: US 38%, Mexico, Germany, Japan, El Salvador

■ COMMUNICATIONS
Daily Newspapers: 7 (1996)
Televisions: 126/1,000 inhabitants (1998)
Radios: 79/1,000 inhabitants (1997)
Telephones: 41 lines/1,000 inhabitants (1998)

■ TRANSPORTATION
Motor Vehicles: 199,000; 102,000 passenger cars (1997 est.)
Roads: 13,100 km; 3,616 km paved
Railway: 884 km
Air Traffic: 508,000 passengers carried (1997)
Airports: 478; 12 have paved runways (1998 est.)

Canadian Embassy: The Canadian Embassy, 13 Calle 8-44, Zone 10, Guatemala City; mailing address: P.O. Box 400, Guatemala City, Guatemala, C.A. Tel: (011-502) 333-61-02. Fax: (011-502) 333-61-61.
Embassy in Canada: Embassy of the Republic of Guatemala, 130 Albert St, Ste 1010, Ottawa ON K1P 5G4. Tel: (613) 233-7237. Fax: (613) 233-0135.

Guinea

Long-Form Name: Republic of Guinea
Capital: Conakry

■ GEOGRAPHY
Area: 245,860 sq. km
Coastline: 320 km
Climate: generally hot and humid; monsoonal-type rainy season (June to Nov.) with south-

Guinea

westerly winds; dry season (Dec. to May) with northeasterly harmattan winds
Environment: hot, dry, dusty harmattan haze may reduce visibility during dry season; deforestation; insufficient safe drinking water
Terrain: generally flat coastal plain, hilly to mountainous interior
Land Use: 2% arable; negligible permanent; 22% permanent pastures; 59% forest; 17% other; includes 930 sq. km irrigated
Location: W Africa, bordering on Atlantic Ocean

■ PEOPLE

Population: 7,538,953 (July 1999 est.)
Nationality: Guinean
Age Structure: 0-14 yrs: 44%; 15-64: 54%; 65+: 2% (1999 est.)
Population Growth Rate: 0.82% (1999 est.)
Net Migration: -15.12 migrants/1,000 population (1999 est.)
Ethnic Groups: 40% Peuhl, 30% Malinke, 20% Sousou, 10% smaller tribes
Languages: French (official); each tribe has its own language; 8 official languages are taught in schools, including Fulani, Malinke, Soussou
Religions: 85% Muslim, 7% indigenous beliefs, 8% Christian
Birth Rate: 40.62/1,000 population (1999 est.)
Death Rate: 17.30/1,000 population (1999 est.)
Infant Mortality: 126.32 deaths/1,000 live births (1999 est.)
Life Expectancy at Birth: 44.02 years male, 49.06 years female (1999 est.)
Total Fertility Rate: 5.53 children born/woman (1999 est.)
Literacy: 37.9% (1997)

■ GOVERNMENT

Leader(s): Pres. Gen. Lansana Conté, Premier Lamine Sidime
Government Type: republic
Administrative Divisions: 4 administrative regions (regions administrative, sing. -region administrative) and 1 special zone (zone speciale)
Nationhood: Oct. 2, 1958 (from France; formerly known as French Guinea)
National Holiday: Anniversary of the Second Republic, Apr. 3

■ ECONOMY

Overview: although possessing numerous natural resources and potential for agricultural development, it is one of the poorest countries in the world; mining accounts for the bulk of Guinea's exports and apart from the bauxite industry, foreign investment remains low
GDP: $8.8 billion, per capita $1,180; real growth rate 4.9% (1998 est.)
Inflation: n.a.
Industries: accounts for 31% of GDP; bauxite mining, alumina, diamond mining, light manufacturing and agricultural processing industries
Labour Force: 3.1 million (1998); 78.1% agriculture, 1.3% industry, 20.6% services
Unemployment: n.a.
Agriculture: accounts for 24% of GDP and employs 80% of the workforce, (including fishing and forestry); mostly subsistence farming; principal products—rice, coffee, pineapples, palm kernels, cassava, sweet potatoes, timber; livestock—cattle, sheep and goats
Natural Resources: bauxite, iron ore, diamonds, gold, uranium, hydroelectricity, fish

■ FINANCE/TRADE

Currency: Guinean franc = 100 centimes
International Reserves Excluding Gold: $192 million (July 1998)
Gold Reserves: n.a.
Budget: n.a.
Defence Expenditures: 8.0% of central government expenditure (1997)
Education Expenditures: 1.9% of GNP (1997)
External Debt: $3.546 billion (1998)
Exports: $695 million (1998 est.); commodities: alumina, bauxite, diamonds, coffee, pineapples, bananas, palm kernels; partners: US 33%, European Community 33%, Eastern Europe 20%, Canada
Imports: $560 million (1998 est.); commodities: petroleum products, metals, machinery, transport equipment, foodstuffs, textiles and grain; partners: US 16%, France, Brazil

■ COMMUNICATIONS

Daily Newspapers: 0 (1996)
Televisions: 41/1,000 inhabitants (1998)
Radios: 47/1,000 inhabitants (1997)
Telephones: 5 lines/1,000 inhabitants (1998)

■ TRANSPORTATION

Motor Vehicles: 33,000; 13,700 passenger cars (1997 est.)
Roads: 30,500 km; 5,033 km paved
Railway: 1,086 km
Air Traffic: 36,000 passengers carried (1997)
Airports: 15; 5 have paved runways (1998 est.)

Canadian Embassy: The Canadian Embassy, P.O. Box 99, Conakry, Guinea. Tel: (011-224) 46-23-95. Fax: (011-224) 46-42-35.

Embassy in Canada: Embassy of the Republic of Guinea, 483 Wilbrod St, Ottawa ON K1N 6N1. Tel: (613) 789-8444. Fax: (613) 789-7560.

Guinea-Bissau

Long-Form Name: Republic of Guinea-Bissau
Capital: Bissau

■ GEOGRAPHY

Area: 36,120 sq. km
Coastline: 350 km
Climate: tropical; generally hot and humid; monsoon-type rainy season (June to Nov.) with southwesterly winds; dry season (Dec. to May) with northeasterly harmattan winds
Environment: hot, dry, dusty harmattan haze may reduce visibility during dry season; deforestation, soil erosion
Terrain: mostly low coastal plain rising to savanna in east
Land Use: 11% arable; 1% permanent; 38% meadows; 38% forest; 12% other; includes 17 sq. km irrigated
Location: W Africa, bordering on Atlantic Ocean

■ PEOPLE

Population: 1,234,555 (July 1999 est.)
Nationality: Guinean
Age Structure: 0-14 yrs: 42%; 15-64: 55%; 65+: 3% (1999 est.)
Population Growth Rate: 2.31% (1999 est.)
Net Migration: 0 migrants/1,000 population (1999 est.)
Ethnic Groups: approx. 99% African (including 30% Balanta, 20% Fula, 14% Manjaca, 13% Mandinga, 7% Papel); less than 1% European and mulatto
Languages: Portuguese (official); Crioulo (a Portuguese-based Creole), Balante and numerous African languages
Religions: 65% indigenous beliefs, 30% Muslim, 5% Christian
Birth Rate: 38.23/1,000 population (1999 est.)
Death Rate: 15.13/1,000 population (1999 est.)
Infant Mortality: 109.50 deaths/1,000 live births (1999 est.)
Life Expectancy at Birth: 47.91 years male, 51.28 years female (1999 est.)
Total Fertility Rate: 5.09 children born/woman (1999 est.)
Literacy: 33.6% (1997)

■ GOVERNMENT

Leader(s): Pres. Koumba Yala, Prime Min. Caetano N'tchama
Government Type: republic; multi-party since 1991
Administrative Divisions: 9 regions (regiões, singular–região)
Nationhood: Sept. 10, 1974 (from Portugal; formerly known as Portuguese Guinea)
National Holiday: Independence Day, Sept. 24

■ ECONOMY

Overview: this poor country is focusing on agricultural development; exploitation of mineral deposits is hampered by a weak infrastructure and high costs. The heavy foreign debt is a burden
GDP: $1.2 billion, per capita $1,000; real growth rate 3.5% (1998 est.)
Inflation: -5.1% (Sept. 1999)
Industries: accounts for 11% of GDP, agricultural processing, beer, soft drinks
Labour Force: 1 million (1998); 82% agriculture, 4% industry, 14% services
Unemployment: n.a.
Agriculture: accounts for 54% of GDP; nearly 100% of exports and 90% of employment; rice is the staple; not self-sufficient in food; fishing and forestry not fully exploited; crops include corn, beans, cassava, cashew nuts, peanuts, palm kernels and cotton
Natural Resources: unexploited deposits of petroleum, bauxite, phosphates; fish, timber

■ FINANCE/TRADE

Currency: Communauté financière africaine (CFAF) franc = 100 centimes
International Reserves Excluding Gold: $16 million (Mar. 1997)
Gold Reserves: n.a.
Budget: n.a.
Defence Expenditures: 13.0% of central government expenditure (1997)
Education Expenditures: n.a.
External Debt: $964 million (1998)
Exports: $49 million (1999); commodities: cashews, fish, peanuts, palm kernels; partners: Portugal, Spain, Switzerland, Cape Verde, China
Imports: $95 million (1999); commodities: capital equipment, consumer goods, semiprocessed goods, foods, petroleum; partners: Portugal, former USSR countries, European Community, other European, Senegal, US

■ COMMUNICATIONS

Daily Newspapers: 1 (1996)
Televisions: n.a.
Radios: 44/1,000 inhabitants (1997)
Telephones: 7 lines/1,000 inhabitants (1998)

■ TRANSPORTATION
Motor Vehicles: 6,900; 4,000 passenger cars (1997 est.)
Roads: 4,400 km; 453 km paved
Railway: none
Air Traffic: 21,000 passengers carried (1997)
Airports: 30; 3 have paved runways (1998 est.)

Canadian Embassy: The Canadian Embassy to Guinea-Bissau, c/o The Canadian Embassy, P.O. Box 3373, Dakar, Senegal. Tel: (011-221) 823-92-90. Fax: (011-221) 823-87-49.
Embassy in Canada: Embassy of the Republic of Guinea-Bissau, 918 16th St. NW, Washington, DC, 20006, Tel./Fax. n.a.

Guyana

Long-Form Name: Co-operative Republic of Guyana
Capital: Georgetown

■ GEOGRAPHY
Area: 214,970 sq. km
Coastline: 459 km
Climate: tropical; hot, humid, moderated by northeast trade winds; two rainy seasons (May to mid-Aug., mid-Nov. to mid-Jan.)
Environment: flash floods a constant threat during rainy seasons; water pollution; deforestation
Terrain: mostly rolling highlands; low coastal plain; savanna in south
Land Use: 2% arable; negligible permanent; 6% meadows; 84% forest; 8% other; includes 1,300 sq. km irrigated
Location: N South America, bordering on Atlantic Ocean

■ PEOPLE
Population: 705,156 (July 1999 est.)
Nationality: Guyanese
Age Structure: 0-14 yrs: 30%; 15-64: 65%; 65+: 5% (1999 est.)
Population Growth Rate: -0.32% (1999 est.)
Net Migration: -12.43 migrants/1,000 population (1999 est.)
Ethnic Groups: 51% East Indian, 43% black and mixed, 4% Amerindian, 2% European and Chinese
Languages: English, Hindi, Urdu, Amerindian dialects
Religions: 57% Christian, 33% Hindu, 9% Muslim, 1% other
Birth Rate: 18.23/1,000 population (1999 est.)
Death Rate: 9.04/1,000 population (1999 est.)
Infant Mortality: 48.64 deaths/1,000 live births (1999 est.)
Life Expectancy at Birth: 59.15 years male, 64.61 years female (1999 est.)
Total Fertility Rate: 2.09 children born/woman (1999 est.)
Literacy: 98.1% (1997)

■ GOVERNMENT
Leader(s): Pres. Bharrat Jagdeo, Prime Min. Samuel Hinds
Government Type: republic
Administrative Divisions: 10 regions
Nationhood: May 26, 1966 (from UK; formerly known as British Guyana)
National Holiday: Republic Day, Feb. 23

■ ECONOMY
Overview: Guyana is one of the world's poorest countries, with a per capita income less than one-fifth the South American average; electricity has been in short supply and constitutes a major barrier to production
GDP: $1.8 billion, per capita $2,500; real growth rate -1.8% (1998 est.)
Inflation: 9.1% (Nov. 1999)
Industries: accounts for 22% of GDP; bauxite mining, sugar, rice milling, timber, fishing (shrimp), textiles, gold mining
Labour Force: n.a.; 26% industry, 27% agriculture, 47% services
Unemployment: n.a.
Agriculture: most important sector, accounting for 37% of GDP; sugar and rice are main crops; not self-sufficient in food; development potential exists for fishing and forestry
Natural Resources: bauxite, gold, diamonds, hardwood timber, shrimp, fish

■ FINANCE/TRADE
Currency: Guyanese dollar ($G) = 100 cents
International Reserves Excluding Gold: $274 million (Jan. 2000)
Gold Reserves: n.a.
Budget: revenues $253.7 million; expenditures $304.1 million, including capital expenditures of $108.8 million (1997 est.)
Defence Expenditures: n.a.
Education Expenditures: n.a.
External Debt: $1.5 billion (1997)
Exports: $484 million (1998); commodities: bauxite, sugar, rice, shrimp, gold, molasses, timber, rum; partners: UK 37%, US 12%, Canada 10.6%, CARICOM 4.8%
Imports: $629 million (1997); commodities: manufactures, machinery, food, petroleum; partners: CARICOM 41%, US 18%, UK 9%, Canada 3%

COMMUNICATIONS

Daily Newspapers: 2 (1996)
Televisions: 54/1,000 inhabitants (1996)
Radios: 495/1,000 inhabitants (1996)
Telephones: 70 lines/1,000 inhabitants (1998)

TRANSPORTATION

Motor Vehicles: 33,000; 24,000 passenger cars (1997 est.)
Roads: 7,970 km; 590 km paved
Railway: 88 km; no public railroads
Air Traffic: 126,000 passengers carried (1997)
Airports: 48; 4 have paved runways (1998 est.)

Canadian Embassy: Canadian High Commission, High and Young Streets, Georgetown; mailing address: P.O. Box 10880, Georgetown, Guyana. Tel: (011-592-2) 72081. Fax: (011-592-2) 58380.
Embassy in Canada: High Commission for the Co-operative Republic of Guyana, Burnside Bldg, 151 Slater St, Ste 309, Ottawa ON K1P 5H3. Tel: (613) 235-7249. Fax: (613) 235-1447.

Haiti

Long-Form Name: Republic of Haiti
Capital: Port-au-Prince

GEOGRAPHY

Area: 27,750 sq. km
Coastline: 1,771 km
Climate: tropical; semi-arid where mountains in east cut off trade winds
Environment: lies in the middle of the hurricane belt and subject to severe storms from June to Oct.; occasional flooding and earthquakes; deforestation; soil erosion, insufficient safe drinking water
Terrain: mostly rough and mountainous
Land Use: 20% arable; 13% permanent; 18% meadows; 5% forest; 44% other; includes 750 sq. km irrigated
Location: West Indies, bordering on Caribbean Sea, Atlantic Ocean

PEOPLE

Population: 6,884,264 (July 1999 est.)
Nationality: Haitian
Age Structure: 0-14 yrs: 42%; 15-64: 54%; 65+: 4% (1999 est.)
Population Growth Rate: 1.53% (1999 est.)
Net Migration: -3.26 migrants/1,000 population (1999 est.)
Ethnic Groups: 95% black, 5% mulatto and European
Languages: French (official) spoken by only 10% of population; all speak Creole
Religions: 80% Roman Catholic (of which an overwhelming majority also practice Voodoo), 16% Protestant, 4% other
Birth Rate: 32.55/1,000 population (1999 est.)
Death Rate: 13.97/1,000 population (1999 est.)
Infant Mortality: 97.64 deaths/1,000 live births (1999 est.)
Life Expectancy at Birth: 49.53 years male, 53.88 years female (1999 est.)
Total Fertility Rate: 4.59 children born/woman (1999 est.)
Literacy: 45.8% (1997)

GOVERNMENT

Leader(s): Pres. Rene Préval, Prem. Jacques-Edouard Alexis. Presidential election scheduled for December 2000.
Government Type: republic
Administrative Divisions: 9 départments (départements, sing. -département)
Nationhood: Jan. 1, 1804 (from France)
National Holiday: Independence Day, Jan. 1

ECONOMY

Overview: about 75% of the population live in absolute poverty, and do not have access to safe drinking water, medical care or sufficient food; agriculture based on small-scale subsistence farming; trade sanctions have further damaged the economy
GDP: $8.9 billion, per capita $1,300; real growth rate 3% (1998 est.)
Inflation: 12.0% (March 2000)
Industries: accounts for 14% of GDP; sugar refining, textiles, flour milling, cement manufacturing, bauxite mining, tourism, light assembly industries based on imported parts
Labour Force: 3 million (1998); 50.4% agriculture, 43.9% services, 5.7% industry
Unemployment: 60% (1996 est.)
Agriculture: accounts for 42% of GDP and employs 70% of workforce; mostly small-size subsistence farms; commercial crops include coffee and sugar cane; staple crops include rice, corn, sorghum and mangoes
Natural Resources: bauxite

FINANCE/TRADE

Currency: gourde (G) = 100 centimes
International Reserves Excluding Gold: $81 million (Aug. 1998)
Gold Reserves: 0.001 million fine troy ounces (Jan. 2000)
Budget: revenues $323 million; expenditures $363 million, including capital expenditures n.a. (1997-98 est.)

Defence Expenditures: n.a.
Education Expenditures: n.a.
External Debt: $1.048 billion (1998)
Exports: $196 million (1999); commodities: light manufactures 65%, coffee 17%, other agriculture 8%, other products 10%; partners: US 77%, France 5%, Italy 4%, Germany 3%, other industrial 9%, less developed countries 2%
Imports: $1.025 billion (1999); commodities: machines and manufactures 36%, food and beverages 21%, petroleum products 11%, fats and oils 12%, chemicals 12%; partners: US 65%, Netherlands Antilles 6%, Japan 5%, France 4%, Canada 2%, Asia 2%

■ COMMUNICATIONS

Daily Newspapers: 4 (1996)
Televisions: 5.0/1,000 inhabitants (1998)
Radios: 55/1,000 inhabitants (1997)
Telephones: 8 lines/1,000 inhabitants (1998)

■ TRANSPORTATION

Motor Vehicles: 53,000; 32,000 passenger cars (1997 est.)
Roads: 4,160 km; 1,011 km paved
Railway: 40 km
Air Traffic: n.a.
Airports: 13; 3 have paved runways (1998 est.)

Canadian Embassy: The Canadian Embassy, Édifice Banque de Nova Scotia, route de Delmas, Port-au-Prince, Haiti; mailing address: C.P. 826, Port-au-Prince, Haiti. Tel: (011-509) 249-7327 Fax: (011-509) 249-5618.
Embassy in Canada: Embassy of the Republic of Haiti, 112 Kent St, Ste 205, Place de Ville, Tower B, Ottawa ON K1P 5P2. Tel: (613) 238-1628. Fax (613) 238-2986.

Honduras

Long-Form Name: Republic of Honduras
Capital: Tegucigalpa

■ GEOGRAPHY

Area: 112,090 sq. km
Coastline: 820 km
Climate: subtropical in lowlands, temperate in mountains
Environment: subject to frequent, but generally mild, earthquakes; damaging hurricanes along Caribbean coast; deforestation; soil erosion; mining pollution of freshwater resources
Terrain: mostly mountainous in interior, narrow coastal plains
Land Use: 15% arable; 3% permanent; 14% permanent pastures; 54% forest and woodlands; 14% other; includes 740 sq. km irrigated
Location: Central (Latin) America, bordering on Caribbean Sea, Pacific Ocean

■ PEOPLE

Population: 5,997,327 (July 1999 est.)
Nationality: Honduran
Age Structure: 0-14 yrs: 41%; 15-64: 55%; 65+: 4% (1999 est.)
Population Growth Rate: 2.24% (1999 est.)
Net Migration: -1.46 migrants/1,000 population (1999 est.)
Ethnic Groups: 90% mestizo (mixed Indian and European), 7% Indian, 2% black, 1% white
Languages: Spanish, Indian dialects
Religions: about 97% Roman Catholic; small Protestant minority
Birth Rate: 30.98/1,000 population (1999 est.)
Death Rate: 7.14/1,000 population (1999 est.)
Infant Mortality: 40.84 deaths/1,000 live births (1999 est.)
Life Expectancy at Birth: 63.16 years male, 66.27 years female (1999 est.)
Total Fertility Rate: 3.97 children born/woman (1999 est.)
Literacy: 70.7% (1997)

■ GOVERNMENT

Leader(s): Pres. Carlos Roberto Flores Facusse. Presidential election scheduled for November 2001.
Government Type: republic
Administrative Divisions: 18 departments (departamentos, sing. -departamento, plus 1 probable central district)
Nationhood: Sept. 15, 1821 (from Spain)
National Holiday: Independence Day, Sept. 15

■ ECONOMY

Overview: one of the poorest countries in the Western hemisphere, with a high population growth rate, a high unemployment rate, a lack of basic services, and an export sector vulnerable to world prices (coffee, bananas)
GDP: $14.4 billion, per capita $2,400; real growth rate 3% (1998 est.)
Inflation: 11.0% (March 2000)
Industries: accounts for 19% of GDP; agricultural processing (sugar and coffee), textiles, clothing, wood products
Labour Force: 2.0 million (1998); 38.2% agriculture, 19.9% community, social and business services, 37.4% undefined
Unemployment: 6.3%, with 30% underemployment (1997 est.)
Agriculture: accounts for 20% of GDP, over 60%

of the labour force and 20% of exports; main products include bananas, coffee, timber, beef, citrus fruit, shrimp; importer of wheat
Natural Resources: timber, gold, silver, copper, lead, zinc, iron ore, antimony, coal, fish

■ FINANCE/TRADE
Currency: lempira (L) = 100 centavos
International Reserves Excluding Gold: $1.288 billion (Jan. 2000)
Gold Reserves: 0.021 million fine troy ounces (Jan. 2000)
Budget: revenues $655 million; expenditures $850 million, including capital expenditures of $150 million (1997 est.)
Defence Expenditures: 0.6% of GDP (1998)
Education Expenditures: 3.6% of GNP (1997)
External Debt: $5.002 billion (1998)
Exports: $940 million (1999); commodities: bananas, coffee, shrimp, lobster, minerals, lumber; partners: US 52%, Germany 11%, Japan, Italy, Belgium
Imports: $2.728 billion (1999); commodities: machinery and transport equipment, chemical products, manufactured goods, fuel and oil, foodstuffs; partners: US 39%, Japan 9%, CACM, Venezuela, Mexico

■ COMMUNICATIONS
Daily Newspapers: 7 (1996)
Televisions: 90/1,000 inhabitants (1998)
Radios: 386/1,000 inhabitants (1997)
Telephones: 38 lines/1,000 inhabitants (1998)

■ TRANSPORTATION
Motor Vehicles: 185,000; 80,000 passenger cars (1997 est.)
Roads: 14,173 km; 3,126 km paved
Railway: 595 km
Air Traffic: 474,000 passengers carried (1996 est.)
Airports: 122; 11 have paved runways (1998 est.)

Canadian Embassy: The Office of the Canadian Embassy, Centro Financiero BANEXPO, 3rd Floor, Bulevar San Juan Bosco, Colonia Payaqui, Tegucigalpa, Honduras, Postal Address: The Office of the Canadian Embassy, P.O. Box 3552, Tegucigalpa, Honduras, Tel: (011 504) 232-4551, Fax: (011 504) 232-8767
Embassy in Canada: Embassy of the Republic of Honduras, 151 Slater St, Ste 805, Ottawa ON K1P 5H3. Tel: (613) 233-8900. Fax: (613) 232-0193.

Hong Kong

Long-Form Name: Hong Kong Special Administrative Region
Capital: Victoria

■ GEOGRAPHY
Area: 1,092 sq. km
Climate: tropical monsoon; cool and humid in winter, hot and rainy from spring through summer, warm and sunny in fall
Land Use: 6% arable land; 1% permanent; 1% meadows; 20% forest; 72% other, includes 20 sq. km irrigated
Location: SE Asia, bordering on South China Sea

■ PEOPLE
Population: 6,847,125 (July 1999 est.)
Nationality: Chinese
Ethnic Groups: 95% Chinese, 5% other
Languages: Chinese (Cantonese), English

■ GOVERNMENT
Colony/Territory of: Special Administrative Region (SAR) of the People's Republic of China
Leader(s): Pres. of China, Jiang Zemin; Chief Exec. Tung Chee-hwa
Government Type: reverted to China July 1, 1997
National Holiday: National Day, Oct. 1-2

■ ECONOMY
Overview: manufacturing and services (finance, business and professional) are the basis of the economy; natural resources are limited and food and raw materials must be imported

■ FINANCE/TRADE
Currency: Hong Kong dollar (HK$) = 100 cents

Canadian Embassy: c/o The Canadian Embassy, 19 Dong Zhi Men Wai, Chao Yang District, Beijing, PDR China. Tel: (011-86-10) 6532-3536. Fax: (011-86-10) 6532-4311.
Representative to Canada: c/o Embassy of the People's Republic of China, 515 St. Patrick St, Ottawa ON K1N 5H3. Tel: (613) 789-3434. Fax: (613) 789-1911.

Hungary

Long-Form Name: Republic of Hungary
Capital: Budapest

■ GEOGRAPHY
Area: 93,030 sq. km
Coastline: none: landlocked
Climate: temperate; cold, cloudy, humid winter; warm summer
Environment: levees are common along many

streams, but flooding occurs almost every year; pollution of air, soil and underground water resources
Terrain: mostly flat to rolling plains
Land Use: 51% arable; 2% permanent crops; 13% permanent pastures; 19% forest; 15% other, includes 2,060 sq. km irrigated
Location: C Europe

■ PEOPLE

Population: 10,186,372 (July 1999 est.)
Nationality: Hungarian
Age Structure: 0-14 yrs: 17%; 15-64: 68%; 65+: 15% (1999 est.)
Population Growth Rate: -0.20% (1999 est.)
Net Migration: 0.50 migrants/1,000 population (1999 est.)
Ethnic Groups: 89.9% Hungarian, 4% Gypsy, 2% Serb, 2.6% German, 0.8% Slovak, 0.7% Romanian
Languages: Hungarian (Magyar, official), 1.8% other
Religions: 67.5% Roman Catholic, 20% Calvinist, 5% Lutheran, 7.5% atheist and other
Birth Rate: 10.80/1,000 population (1999 est.)
Death Rate: 13.29/1,000 population (1999 est.)
Infant Mortality: 9.46 deaths/1,000 live births (1999 est.)
Life Expectancy at Birth: 66.85 years male, 75.74 years female (1999 est.)
Total Fertility Rate: 1.45 children born/woman (1999 est.)
Literacy: 99% (1997)

■ GOVERNMENT

Leader(s): Pres. Ferenc Madl; Prime Min. Victor Orban
Government Type: republic
Administrative Divisions: 19 counties (megyek, sing. -megye) and 1 capital city (fovaros)
Nationhood: 1001 (unification by King Stephen I)
National Holiday: St. Stephen's Day, Aug. 20 (National Day)

■ ECONOMY

Overview: Hungary has consolidated its stabilization program and undergone enough restructuring to become an established market economy. It appears to have entered a period of sustainable growth, gradually falling inflation, and stable external balances. The government's main economic priorities are to complete structural reforms, particularly in pension, taxation, and healthcare reforms.
GDP: $75.4 billion, per capita $7,400; real growth rate 5% (1998 est.)
Inflation: 10.1% (March 2000)
Industries: accounts for 30.3% of GDP; mining, metallurgy, engineering industries, processed foods, textiles, chemicals (especially pharmaceuticals)
Labour Force: 5 million (1998); 29.1% industry, 28.4% community, social and business services, 13.2% agriculture
Unemployment: 10.8% (1998)
Agriculture: accounts for about 3% of GDP (including forestry) and 16% of employment; highly diversified crop-livestock farming; main crops—wheat, corn, sunflowers, potatoes, sugar beets; livestock—hogs, cattle, poultry and dairy products; self-sufficient in food
Natural Resources: bauxite, coal, natural gas, fertile soils

■ FINANCE/TRADE

Currency: forint (Ft) = 100 filler
International Reserves Excluding Gold: $11.245 billion (Jan. 2000)
Gold Reserves: 0.067 million fine troy ounces (Jan. 2000)
Budget: revenues $11.2 billion; expenditures $13.2 billion, including capital expenditures of n.a. (1998 est.)
Defence Expenditures: 2.29% of total govt. expenditure (1998)
Education Expenditures: 8.57% of total govt. expenditure (1998)
External Debt: $28.58 billion (1998)
Exports: $24.950 billion (1999); commodities: capital goods 36%, foods 24%, consumer goods 18%, fuels and minerals 11%, other 11%; partners: EU nations 65%, former USSR and Eastern Europe 35%
Imports: $27.923 billion (1999); commodities: machinery and transport 28%, fuels 20%, chemical products 14%, manufactured consumer goods 16%, agriculture 6%, other 16%; partners: former USSR countries 43%, Eastern Europe 28%, less developed countries 23%, US 3%

■ COMMUNICATIONS

Daily Newspapers: 40 (1996)
Televisions: 437/1,000 inhabitants (1998)
Radios: 689/1,000 inhabitants (1997)
Telephones: 336 lines/1,000 inhabitants (1998)

■ TRANSPORTATION

Motor Vehicles: 2,810,000; 2,310,000 passenger cars (1997 est.)
Roads: 188,203 km; 81,680 km paved
Railway: 7,606 km
Air Traffic: 1,635,000 passengers carried (1997)
Airports: 25; 15 have paved runways (1998 est.)

Canadian Embassy: The Canadian Embassy, Budakeszi ut 32, 1121 Budapest, Hungary. Tel.: (011-36-1) 275-1200. Fax: (011-36-1) 275-1210.
Embassy in Canada: Embassy of the Republic of Hungary, 299 Waverley St, Ottawa ON K2P 0V9. Tel: (613) 230-2717. Fax: (613) 230-7560.

Iceland

Long-Form Name: Republic of Iceland
Capital: Reykjavik

■ GEOGRAPHY

Area: 103,000 sq. km
Coastline: 4,988 km
Climate: temperate; moderated by North Atlantic Current; mild, windy winters; damp, cool summers
Environment: subject to earthquakes and volcanic activity; water pollution
Terrain: mostly plateau interspersed with mountain peaks, ice fields; coast deeply indented by bays and fjords
Land Use: 0% arable; 0% permanent; 23% meadows; 1% forest; 76% other
Location: NW Europe, island in Norwegian Sea, Atlantic Ocean

■ PEOPLE

Population: 272,512 (July 1999 est.)
Nationality: Icelander
Age Structure: 0-14 yrs: 23%; 15-64: 65%; 65+: 12% (1999 est.)
Population Growth Rate: 0.57% (1999 est.)
Net Migration: -2.17 migrants/1,000 population (1999 est.)
Ethnic Groups: homogeneous mixture of descendants of Norwegians and Celts
Languages: Icelandic
Religions: Christianity (predominantly Protestant)
Birth Rate: 14.87/1,000 population (1999 est.)
Death Rate: 7.01/1,000 population (1999 est.)
Infant Mortality: 5.22 deaths/1,000 live births (1999 est.)
Life Expectancy at Birth: 76.85 years male, 81.19 years female (1999 est.)
Total Fertility Rate: 2.03 children born/woman (1999 est.)
Literacy: 99% (1997)

■ GOVERNMENT

Leader(s): Pres. Olafur Ragnar Grimsson, Prime Min. David Oddsson
Government Type: constitutional republic
Administrative Divisions: 23 counties (syslar, sing. -sysla) and 14 independent towns (kaupstadhir, sing. -kaupstadhur)
Nationhood: June 17, 1944 (from Denmark)
National Holiday: Anniversary of the Establishment of the Republic, June 17

■ ECONOMY

Overview: Iceland's economy is basically capitalistic, but it has an extensive welfare system, low unemployment, and an unusually even distribution of income. The economy depends heavily on the fishing industry and is vulnerable to changing world fish prices.
GDP: $6.06 billion, per capita $22,400; real growth rate 5.1% (1998 est.)
Inflation: 6.0% (April 2000)
Industries: accounts for 24% of GDP; fish processing, aluminum smelting, ferro-silicon production, hydroelectricity
Labour Force: 139,500 (1997); 55% commerce, finance and services, 14% other manufacturing, 6% agriculture, 8% fish processing, 5% fishing
Unemployment: 3.1% (April 1999)
Agriculture: accounts for about 13% of GDP (including fishing); fishing is the most important economic activity, contributing nearly 75% to export earnings; principal crops include potatoes and turnips; livestock—cattle, sheep; self-sufficient in crops
Natural Resources: fish, hydroelectric and geothermal power, diatomite

■ FINANCE/TRADE

Currency: króna (pl. krónur) (ISK) = 100 aurar
International Reserves Excluding Gold: $421 million (Jan. 2000)
Gold Reserves: 0.560 million fine troy ounces (Jan. 2000)
Budget: revenues $1.9 billion; expenditures $2.1 billion, including capital expenditures of $146 million (1996 est.)
Defence Expenditures: none
Education Expenditures: 10.15% of govt. expenditure (1997)
External Debt: $2.2 billion (1996 est.)
Exports: $2.005 billion (1999); commodities: fish and fish products, animal products, aluminum, diatomite; partners: European Community 58.9% (UK 23.3%, Germany 10.3%), US 13.6%, former USSR countries 3.6%
Imports: $2.503 billion (1999); commodities: machinery and transportation equipment, petroleum, foodstuffs, textiles; partners: European Community 58% (Germany 16%, Denmark 10.4%, UK 9.2%), US 8.5%, former USSR countries 3.9%

■ COMMUNICATIONS
Daily Newspapers: 5 (1996)
Televisions: 354/1,000 inhabitants (1996)
Radios: 923/1,000 inhabitants (1996)
Telephones: 646 lines/1,000 inhabitants (1998)

■ TRANSPORTATION
Motor Vehicles: 144,000; 125,300 passenger cars (1997 est.)
Roads: 12,691 km; 3,262 km paved
Railway: none
Air Traffic: 1,334,000 passengers carried (1997)
Airports: 87; 10 have paved runways (1998 est.)

Canadian Embassy: The Consulate General of Canada, Suörlandsbraut 10, 108 Reykjavik, Iceland, Postal Address: The Consulate General of Canada, P.O. Box 8094, 128 Reykjavik, Iceland, Tel: (011 354) 5 68-08-20, Fax: (011 354) 5 68-08-99
Embassy in Canada: Embassy of the Republic of Iceland, 1156 15th St NW, Ste 1200, Washington DC 20005-1, USA. Tel: (202) 265-6653. Fax: (202) 265-6656.

India

Long-Form Name: Republic of India
Capital: New Delhi

■ GEOGRAPHY
Area: 3,287,590 sq. km
Coastline: 7,000 km
Climate: varies from tropical monsoon in south to temperate in north
Environment: deforestation; soil erosion; overgrazing; air and water pollution; desertification, droughts, flash floods, severe thunderstorms common; earthquakes are a hazard
Terrain: upland plain (Deccan Plateau) in south, flat to rolling plain along the Ganges, deserts in west, Himalayas in north
Land Use: 56% arable; 1% permanent; 4% meadows; 23% forest; 16% other, includes 480,000 sq. km irrigated
Location: S Asia, bordering on Arabian Sea, Indian Ocean, Bay of Bengal

■ PEOPLE
Population: 1,000,848,550 (July 1999 est.)
Nationality: Indian
Age Structure: 0-14 yrs: 34%; 15-64: 61%; 65+: 5% (1999 est.)
Population Growth Rate: 1.68% (1999 est.)
Net Migration: -0.08 migrants/1,000 population (1999 est.)
Ethnic Groups: 72% Indo-Aryan, 25% Dravidian, 3% Mongoloid and other
Languages: Hindi (official, spoken by 30%); English; 19 regional languages, including Bengali, Tlegu, Marathi, Tamil, Urdu, Gujarati, Malayalam, Kannada, Oriya, Punjabi, Assamese, Kashmiri, Sindhi and Sanskrit; 24 languages spoken by a million or more persons each; numerous other languages
Religions: 80% Hindu, 14% Muslim, 2.4% Christian, 2% Sikh, 0.7% Buddhist, 0.5% Jains, 0.4% other
Birth Rate: 25.39/1,000 population (1999 est.)
Death Rate: 8.50/1,000 population (1999 est.)
Infant Mortality: 60.81 deaths/1,000 live births (1999 est.)
Life Expectancy at Birth: 62.54 years male, 64.29 years female (1999 est.)
Total Fertility Rate: 3.18 children born/woman (1999 est.)
Literacy: 53.5% (1997)

■ GOVERNMENT
Leader(s): Pres. Kocheril Raman Narayanan, Prime Min. Atal Behari Vajpayee
Government Type: federal republic
Administrative Divisions: 25 states and 7 union territories
Nationhood: Aug. 15, 1947 (from UK)
National Holiday: Anniversary of the Proclamation of the Republic, Jan. 26

■ ECONOMY
Overview: a mixture of traditional village farming and handicrafts, modern agriculture, old and new branches of industry and a multitude of support services; millions still live in poverty, hoping to benefit from modern farming techniques
GDP: $1.689 trillion, per capita $1,720; real growth rate 5.4% (1998 est.)
Inflation: 3.6% (Feb. 2000)
Industries: accounts for 30% of GDP, textiles, food processing, steel, machinery, transportation equipment, cement, jute manufactures, mining, petroleum, power, chemicals, pharmaceuticals, electronics
Labour Force: 431 million (1998); 62.6% agriculture, 10.8% industry, 26.6% services
Unemployment: 10.9% (1996)
Agriculture: accounts for 25% of GDP and employs 65% of labour force; self-sufficient in food grains; main crops—rice, wheat, oilseeds, cotton, jute, tea, sugar cane, potatoes; livestock— cattle, buffalo, sheep, goats and poultry; in top 10 of fishing nations
Natural Resources: coal, iron ore, manganese,

mica, bauxite, titanium ore, chromite, natural gas, diamonds, crude oil, limestone

■ FINANCE/TRADE

Currency: rupee (Rs) = 100 paise
International Reserves Excluding Gold: $32.612 billion (Jan. 2000)
Gold Reserves: 11.502 million fine troy ounces (Jan. 2000)
Budget: revenues $42.12 billion; expenditures $63.79 billion, including capital expenditures of $13.8 billion (1998-99 est.)
Defence Expenditures: 15.76% of govt. expenditure (1998)
Education Expenditures: 2.97% of govt. expenditure (1998)
External Debt: $98.232 billion (1998)
Exports: $36.562 billion (1999); commodities: tea, coffee, iron ore, fish products, manufactures; partners: European Community 25%, former USSR countries and Eastern Europe 17%, US 19%, Japan 10%
Imports: $44.598 billion (1999); commodities: petroleum, edible oils, textiles, clothing, capital goods; partners: European Community 33%, Middle East 19%, Japan 10%, US 9%, former USSR countries and Eastern Europe 8%

■ COMMUNICATIONS

Daily Newspapers: n.a.
Televisions: 69/1,000 inhabitants (1998)
Radios: 121/1,000 inhabitants (1997)
Telephones: 22 lines/1,000 inhabitants (1998)

■ TRANSPORTATION

Motor Vehicles: 6,990,000; 4,300,000 passenger cars (1997 est.)
Roads: 3,319,644 km; 1,517,077 km hard-surfaced
Railway: 62,915 km
Air Traffic: 16,040,000 passengers carried (1997 est.)
Airports: 341; 230 have paved runways (1998 est.)

Canadian Embassy: The Canadian High Commission, 7/8 Shantipath, Chanakyapuri, New Delhi 110021; mailing address: The Canadian High Commission, P.O. Box 5207, New Delhi 110021, India. Tel: (011-91-11) 687-6500. Fax: (011-91-11) 687-6579.
Embassy in Canada: High Commission for the Republic of India, 10 Springfield Rd, Ottawa ON K1M 1C9. Tel: (613) 744-3751. Fax: (613) 744-0913.

Indonesia

Long-Form Name: Republic of Indonesia
Capital: Jakarta

■ GEOGRAPHY

Area: 1,919,440 sq. km (13,677 islands)
Coastline: 54,716 km
Climate: tropical; hot, humid; more moderate in highlands
Environment: archipelago of more than 13,500 islands (6,000 inhabited); occasional floods, severe droughts and tsunamis; deforestation; environmental pollution
Terrain: mostly coastal lowlands; larger islands have interior mountains
Land Use: 10% arable; 7% permanent crops; 7% meadows; 62% forest; 14% other, includes 45,970 sq. km irrigated
Location: SE Asia, bordering on Indian Ocean

■ PEOPLE

Population: 216,108,345 (July 1999 est.)
Nationality: Indonesian
Age Structure: 0-14 yrs: 30%; 15-64: 65%; 65+: 5% (1999 est.)
Population Growth Rate: 1.46% (1999 est.)
Net Migration: 0 migrants/1,000 population (1999 est.)
Ethnic Groups: majority of Malay stock comprising 45% Javanese, 14% Sundanese, 7.5% Madurese, 7.5% coastal Malays, 26% other
Languages: Bahasa Indonesia (modified form of Malay; official); English and Dutch leading foreign languages; 25 local dialects, the most widely spoken of which is Javanese
Religions: 87% Muslim, 6% Protestant, 3% Roman Catholic, 2% Hindu, 1% Buddhist, 1% other
Birth Rate: 22.78/1,000 population (1999 est.)
Death Rate: 8.14/1,000 population (1999 est.)
Infant Mortality: 57.30 deaths/1,000 live births (1999 est.)
Life Expectancy at Birth: 60.67 years male, 65.29 years female (1999 est.)
Total Fertility Rate: 2.57 children born/woman (1999 est.)
Literacy: 85.0 (1997)

■ GOVERNMENT

Leader(s): Pres. Abdurrahman Wahid, V. Pres. Sukarnoputri Megawati
Government Type: republic
Administrative Divisions: 24 provinces (propinsi-propinsi, sing. -propinsi), 2 special regions (daerah-daerah istimewa, sing. -daerah istimewa) and 1 special capital city district (daerah khusus ibukota)

Nationhood: Aug. 17, 1945 (from Netherlands; formerly known as Netherlands or Dutch East Indies)
National Holiday: Independence Day, Aug. 17

■ ECONOMY

Overview: a mixed economy with many socialist institutions and central planning but with a recent emphasis on deregulation and private enterprise; hampered by large population growth; possesses abundant natural wealth
GDP: $602 billion, per capita $2,830; real growth rate -13.7% (1998 est.)
Inflation: -1.2% (Mar. 2000)
Industries: accounts for 40% of GDP; petroleum, textiles, mining, cement, chemical fertilizer production, timber, food, rubber
Labour Force: 98 million (1998); 54.1% agriculture, 10.3% industry, 37.6% services
Unemployment: 15%; 50% underemployment (1998 est.)
Agriculture: accounts for 19% of GDP; subsistence food production; small-holder and plantation production for export; rice, cassava, peanuts, rubber, cocoa, coffee, copra, other tropical products; the staple crop is rice; once the world's largest rice importer, Indonesia is now nearly self-sufficient
Natural Resources: crude oil, tin, natural gas, nickel, timber, bauxite, copper, fertile soils, coal, gold, silver

■ FINANCE/TRADE

Currency: rupiah (Rp)
International Reserves Excluding Gold: $26.445 billion (Dec. 1999)
Gold Reserves: 3.101 million fine troy ounces (Jan. 2000)
Budget: revenues $35 billion; expenditures $35 billion, including capital expenditures of $12 billion (1998-99 est.)
Defence Expenditures: 5.28% of central government expenditure (1998)
Education Expenditures: 6.88% of gov't expenditure (1998)
External Debt: $150.875 billion (1998)
Exports: $48.665 billion (1999); commodities: petroleum and liquefied natural gas 40%, timber 15%, textiles 7%, rubber 5%, coffee 3%; partners: Japan 42%, US 16%, Singapore 9%, European Community 11%
Imports: $24.004 billion (1999); commodities: machinery 39%, chemical products 19%, manufactured goods 16%; partners: Japan 26%, European Community 19%, US 13%, Singapore 7%,

■ COMMUNICATIONS

Daily Newspapers: 69 (1996)
Televisions: 67/1,000 inhabitants (1996)
Radios: 156/1,000 inhabitants (1997)
Telephones: 27 lines/1,000 inhabitants (1998)

■ TRANSPORTATION

Motor Vehicles: 4,600,000; 2,500,000 passenger cars (1997 est.)
Roads: 342,700 km; 158,670 km paved
Railway: 6,458 km
Air Traffic: 12,650,000 passengers carried (1997)
Airports: 443; 125 have paved runways (1998 est.)

Canadian Embassy: The Canadian Embassy, Flr 5 Wisma Metropolitan, Jalan Jendral Sudirman, Jakarta 12920; mailing address: P.O. Box 8324/JKS.MP, Jakarta 12084, Indonesia. Tel: (011-62-21) 525-0709. Fax: (011-62-21) 571-2251.
Embassy in Canada: Embassy of the Republic of Indonesia, 55 Parkdale Ave, Ottawa ON K1Y 1E5. Tel: (613) 724-1100. Fax: (613) 724-1105.

Iran

Long-Form Name: Islamic Republic of Iran
Capital: Tehran

■ GEOGRAPHY

Area: 1,648,000 sq. km
Coastline: 2,440 km
Climate: mostly arid or semi-arid, subtropical along Caspian coast
Environment: deforestation; overgrazing; desertification; air and water pollution; periodic droughts and floods
Terrain: rugged mountainous rim; high, central basin with deserts, mountains; small, discontinuous plains along both coasts
Land Use: 10% arable; 1% permanent crops; 27% meadows; 7% forest; 55% other, includes 94,000 sq. km irrigated
Location: SW Asia (Middle East), bordering on Persian Gulf

■ PEOPLE

Population: 65,179,752 (July 1999 est.)
Nationality: Iranian
Age Structure: 0-14 yrs: 36%; 15-64: 60%; 65+: 4% (1999 est.)
Population Growth Rate: 1.07% (1999 est.)
Net Migration: -4.60 migrants/1,000 population (1999 est.)
Ethnic Groups: 51% Persian, 24% Azerbaijani,

7% Kurd, 8% Gilaki and Mazandarani, 2% Lur, 2% Baloch, 3% Arab, 2% Turkmen, 1% other
Languages: Farsi (Persian) (official) 58%, Turkic and Turkic dialects 26%, Kurdish 9%, Luri 2%, Balochi 1%, Turkish 1%, Arabic 1%, 2% other
Religions: Muslim (89% Shia, 10% Sunni), Christianity, Judaism, Zoroastrianism 1%
Birth Rate: 20.71/1,000 population (1999 est.)
Death Rate: 5.39/1,000 population (1999 est.)
Infant Mortality: 29.73 deaths/1,000 live births (1999 est.)
Life Expectancy at Birth: 68.43 years male, 71.16 years female (1999 est.)
Total Fertility Rate: 2.45 children born/woman (1999 est.)
Literacy: 73.3% (1997)

■ GOVERNMENT

Leader(s): Pres. Mohammed Khatami, Supreme Religious Leader Ayatollah Mohammed Ali Hoseini Khamenei. Presidential election scheduled for May 2001.
Government Type: theocratic republic
Administrative Divisions: 25 provinces (ostanha, sing. -ostan)
Nationhood: Apr. 1, 1979, Islamic Republic of Iran proclaimed
National Holiday: Islamic Republic Day, Apr. 1

■ ECONOMY

Overview: Iran's economy is a mixture of central planning, state ownership of oil and other large enterprises, village agriculture, and small-scale private trading and service ventures. Soaring external debt and high unemployment impede progress towards recovery from the economic devastation of the war with Iraq
GDP: $339.7 billion, per capita $5,000; real growth rate -2.1% (1998 est.)
Inflation: 19.3% (Dec. 1999)
Industries: accounts for 37% of GDP; petroleum, petrochemicals, textiles, cement and other building materials, food processing (particularly sugar refining and vegetable oil production), metal fabricating (steel and copper)
Labour Force: 19.5 million (1998); 36.4% agriculture, 32.8% industry, 30.8% services
Unemployment: over 30% (1998 est.)
Agriculture: accounts for 21% of GDP; principal products—rice, other grains, sugar beets, fruits, nuts, cotton, dairy products, wool, caviar; not self-sufficient in food
Natural Resources: petroleum, natural gas, coal, chromium, copper, iron ore, lead, manganese, zinc, sulphur

■ FINANCE/TRADE

Currency: 10 rials (RIs) = 1 toman
International Reserves Excluding Gold: n.a.
Gold Reserves: 5.42 million fine troy ounces (Mar. 1996)
Budget: revenues $34.6 billion; expenditures $34.9 billion, including capital expenditures of $11.8 billion (1996-97)
Defence Expenditures: 8.50% of govt. expenditure (1998)
Education Expenditures: 15.99% of govt. expenditure (1998)
External Debt: $14.391 billion (1998)
Exports: $18.381 billion (1997); commodities: petroleum 90%, carpets, fruit, nuts, hides; partners: Japan, Turkey, Italy, Netherlands, Spain, France, Germany
Imports: $14.165 billion (1997); commodities: machinery, military supplies, metal works, foodstuffs, pharmaceuticals, technical services, refined oil products; partners: Germany, Japan, Turkey, UK, Italy

■ COMMUNICATIONS

Daily Newspapers: 32 (1996)
Televisions: 157/1,000 inhabitants (1998)
Radios: 265/1,000 inhabitants (1997)
Telephones: 112 lines/1,000 inhabitants (1998)

■ TRANSPORTATION

Motor Vehicles: 2,239,000; 1,630,000 passenger cars (1997 est.)
Roads: 162,000 km; 81,000 km paved
Railway: 7,286 km
Air Traffic: 9,804,000 passengers carried (1997)
Airports: 288; 110 have paved runways (1998 est.)

Canadian Embassy: The Canadian Embassy to the Islamic Republic of Iran, 57 Shahid Javad-e-Sarafraz, Ostad-Motahari Ave, 15868 Tehran; mailing address: P.O. Box 11365-4647, Tehran, Iran. Tel: (011-98-21) 873-2623. Fax: (011-98-21) 873-3202.
Embassy in Canada: Embassy of the Islamic Republic of Iran, 245 Metcalfe St, Ottawa ON K2P 2K2. Tel: (613) 235-4726. Fax: (613) 232-5712.

Iraq

Long-Form Name: Republic of Iraq
Capital: Baghdad

■ GEOGRAPHY

Area: 437,072 sq. km

Iraq

Coastline: 58 km
Climate: desert; mild to cool winters with dry, hot, cloudless summers
Environment: development of Tigris-Euphrates river systems contingent upon agreements with upstream riparians (Syria and Turkey); air and water pollution; soil degradation (salinization) and erosion; desertification
Terrain: mostly broad plains; reedy marshes in southeast; mountains along borders with Iran and Turkey
Land Use: 12% arable; 0% permanent; 9% meadows; 0% forest; 79% other, includes 25,500 sq. km irrigated
Location: SW Asia (Middle East), bordering on Persian Gulf

■ PEOPLE

Population: 22,427,150 (July 1999 est.)
Nationality: Iraqi
Age Structure: 0-14 yrs: 44%; 15-64: 53%; 65+: 3% (1999 est.)
Population Growth Rate: 3.19% (1999 est.)
Net Migration: 0 migrants/1,000 population (1999 est.)
Ethnic Groups: 75–80% Arab, 15–20% Kurdish, 5% Turkoman and other
Languages: Arabic (official), Kurdish (official in Kurdish region), Assyrian, Armenian
Religions: 97% Muslim (60–65% Shi'a, 32–37% Sunni), 3% Christian or other
Birth Rate: 38.42/1,000 population (1998 est.)
Death Rate: 6.56/1,000 population (1998 est.)
Infant Mortality: 62.41 deaths/1,000 live births (1999)
Life Expectancy at Birth: 65.54 years male, 67.56 years female (1999 est.)
Total Fertility Rate: 5.12 children born/woman (1999 est.)
Literacy: 58% (1997)

■ GOVERNMENT

Leader(s): Pres. and Prem. Saddam Hussein at-Takriti; Deputy Premiers: Tariq Aziz, Hikmat Mizban Ibrahim al-Azzawi, Mohammed Hamsa al-Zubaydi
Government Type: republic
Administrative Divisions: 18 provinces (muhafazat, sing. -muhafazah)
Nationhood: Oct. 3, 1932 (from League of Nations mandate under British administration)
National Holiday: Anniversary of the Revolution, July 17

■ ECONOMY

Overview: industrial production and foreign trade is centrally planned and managed while some small-scale industry and services and most agriculture is left to private enterprise. Oil exports are at about 3/4 of their pre-war level. Per capita food imports have increased significantly.
GDP: $52.3 billion, per capita $2,400; real growth rate 10% (1998 est.)
Inflation: n.a.
Industries: petroleum, chemicals, textiles, construction materials, food processing
Labour Force: 6.0 million (1998); 79.7% services, 12.5% agriculture, 7.8% industry
Unemployment: n.a.
Agriculture: accounted for 11% of GNP and 30% of labour force before the Gulf War; principal products— wheat, barley, rice, vegetables, dates, other fruit, cotton, wool; livestock— cattle, sheep; not self-sufficient in food output
Natural Resources: crude oil, natural gas, phosphates, sulphur

■ FINANCE/TRADE

Currency: dinar = 1,000 fils
International Reserves Excluding Gold: n.a.
Gold Reserves: n.a.
Budget: n.a.
Defence Expenditures: n.a.
Education Expenditures: n.a.
External Debt: precise figures n.a., but a considerable portion of the GDP (1998)
Exports: $5 billion (1998 est.); commodities: crude oil and refined products, machinery, chemicals, dates; partners: US, Brazil, former USSR countries, Italy, Turkey, France, Japan, former Yugoslavia
Imports: $3 billion (1998 est.); commodities: manufactures, food; partners: Turkey, US, Germany, UK, France, Japan, Romania, former Yugoslavia, Brazil

■ COMMUNICATIONS

Daily Newspapers: 4 (1996)
Televisions: 83/1,000 inhabitants (1998)
Radios: 229/1,000 inhabitants (1997)
Telephones: 31 lines/1,000 inhabitants (1998)

■ TRANSPORTATION

Motor Vehicles: 1,040,000; 672,000 passenger cars (1997 est.)
Roads: 47,400 km; 40,764 km paved
Railway: 2,032 km
Air Traffic: n.a.
Airports: 109; 77 have paved runways (1998 est.)

Canadian Embassy: The Canadian Embassy to Iraq, c/o The Canadian Embassy, P.O. Box 815403, Amman, Jordan. 11180. Tel: (011-962-6) 566-61-24. Fax: (011-962-6) 568-92-27.

Embassy in Canada: Embassy of the Republic of Iraq, 215 McLeod St, Ottawa ON K2P 0Z8. Tel: (613) 236-9177. Fax: (613) 567-1101.

Ireland

Long-Form Name: Ireland
Capital: Dublin

■ GEOGRAPHY

Area: 70,280 sq. km
Coastline: 1,448 km
Climate: temperate maritime; modified by North Atlantic Current; mild winters, cool summers; consistently humid; overcast about half the time
Environment: deforestation and water pollution from agricultural runoff
Terrain: mostly level to rolling interior plains surrounded by rugged hills and low mountains; sea cliffs on west coast
Land Use: 13% arable; negligible permanent; 68% meadows; 5% forest; 14% other; includes n.a. sq. km irrigated
Location: NW Europe, (British Isles), bordering on Atlantic Ocean and Irish Sea

■ PEOPLE

Population: 3,632,944 (July 1999 est.)
Nationality: Irish
Age Structure: 0-14 yrs: 21%; 15-64: 67%; 65+: 12% (1999 est.)
Population Growth Rate: 0.38% (1999 est.)
Net Migration: -1.31 migrants/1,000 population (1999 est.)
Ethnic Groups: Celtic, with English minority
Languages: Irish (official first language, but use is limited) and English; English is the language generally used, with Gaelic spoken in a few areas, mostly along the western seaboard
Religions: 93% Roman Catholic, 3% Anglican, 1% atheist, 3% other
Birth Rate: 13.58/1,000 population (1999 est.)
Death Rate: 8.43/1,000 population (1999 est.)
Infant Mortality: 5.94 deaths/1,000 live births (1999 est.)
Life Expectancy at Birth: 73.64 years male, 79.32 years female (1999 est.)
Total Fertility Rate: 1.81 children born/woman (1999 est.)
Literacy: 99% (1997)

■ GOVERNMENT

Leader(s): Pres. Mary McAleese, Prime Min. Bertie Ahern
Government Type: republic
Administrative Divisions: 26 counties
Nationhood: Dec. 6, 1921 (from UK)

National Holiday: St. Patrick's Day, Mar. 17

■ ECONOMY

Overview: a small, open economy that is trade dependent; unemployment is high but inflation has been considerably lowered and the deficit burden relieved
GDP: $67.1 billion, per capita $18,600; real growth rate 9.5% (1998 est.)
Inflation: 4.6% (March 2000)
Industries: account for 39% of GDP, 80% of exports and employs almost 30% of the workforce; food products, brewing, textiles, clothing, chemicals, pharmaceuticals, machinery, transportation equipment, glass and crystal
Labour Force: 2 million (1998); 25.4% community, social and business services, 19.7% industry, 17.7% trade and tourism
Unemployment: 7.7% (1998 est.)
Agriculture: accounts for 7% of GDP and 13% of the labour force; principal crops include turnips, barley, potatoes, sugar, beets, wheat; livestock— meat and dairy products; 85% self-sufficient in food; food shortages include bread grain, fruits, vegetables
Natural Resources: zinc, lead, natural gas, crude oil, barite, copper, gypsum, limestone, dolomite, peat, silver

■ FINANCE/TRADE

Currency: Irish pound (£ or £Ir) = 100 pence [As of Jan. 1, 1999, Government securities are issued in Euros (EUR)]
International Reserves Excluding Gold: $5.210 billion (Jan. 2000)
Gold Reserves: 0.193 million fine troy ounces (Jan. 2000)
Budget: revenues $23.5 billion; expenditures $20.6 billion, including capital expenditures of n.a.(1998)
Defence Expenditures: 3.3% of total govt. expenditure (1997)
Education Expenditures: 13.09% of total govt. expenditure (1996)
External Debt: $11 billion (1998)
Exports: $70.281 billion (1999); commodities: live animals, animal products, chemicals, data processing equipment, industrial machinery; partners: European Community 74% (U.K. 35%, Germany 11%, France 9%), US 8%
Imports: $46.030 billion (1999; commodities: food, animal feed, chemicals, petroleum and petroleum products, machinery, textiles, clothing; partners: European Community 66% (U.K. 42%, Germany 9%, France 4%), US 16%

■ COMMUNICATIONS
Daily Newspapers: 6 (1996)
Televisions: 403/1,000 inhabitants (1998)
Radios: 699/1,000 inhabitants (1997)
Telephones: 435 lines/1,000 inhabitants (1998)

■ TRANSPORTATION
Motor Vehicles: 1,320,000; 1,100,00 passenger cars (1997 est.)
Roads: 92,500 km; 87,042 km paved
Railway: 1,947 km
Air Traffic: 8,964,000 passengers carried (1997)
Airports: 44; 16 have paved runways (1998 est.)

Canadian Embassy: The Canadian Embassy, 65 St Stephen's Green, Dublin, Ireland. Tel: (011-353-1) 478-1988. Fax: (011-353-1) 478-1285.
Embassy in Canada: Embassy of Ireland, 130 Albert St, Ste 1105, Ottawa ON K1P 5G4. Tel: (613) 233-6281. Fax: (613) 233-5835.

Isle of Man

Long-Form Name: Isle of Man
Capital: Douglas

■ GEOGRAPHY
Area: 588 sq. km
Climate: temperate maritime, cool summers and mild winters, humid, overcast about half the time
Land Use: 12% arable; 0% permanent crops; 56% permanent pastures; 32% forests and woodland; 0% other; includes n.a. sq. km irrigated
Location: Irish Sea, between Great Britain and Northern Ireland

■ PEOPLE
Population: 75,686 (July 1999 est.)
Nationality: Manxman, Manxwoman
Ethnic Groups: Manx (Norse-Celtic descent), Briton
Languages: English, Manx, Gaelic

■ GOVERNMENT
Colony/Territory of: Dependency of United Kingdom
Leader(s): Head of State: Queen Elizabeth II. Lt.-Gov. Ian David Macfadyen, Chief Min. Donald James Gelling
Government Type: Crown dependency administered in accordance with its own laws
National Holiday: Tynwald Day, July 5

■ ECONOMY
Overview: Offshore banking, manufacturing, and tourism are key sectors of the economy. The government's policy of offering incentives to high-technology companies and financial institutions to locate on the island has paid off in expanding employment opportunities in high-income industries.

■ FINANCE/TRADE
Currency: Manx pound = 100 pence; on a par with British pound sterling

Canadian Embassy: c/o The Canadian High Commission, Macdonald House, 1 Grosvenor Square, London W1X 0AB, England, UK. Tel: (011-44-20) 7258-6600. Fax: (011-44-20) 7258-6333.
Representative to Canada: c/o British High Commission, 80 Elgin St, Ottawa ON K1P 5K7. Tel: (613) 237-1530. Fax: (613) 237-7980.

Israel

Long-Form Name: State of Israel
Capital: Jerusalem

■ GEOGRAPHY
Area: 20,770 sq. km
Coastline: 273 km
Climate: temperate; hot and dry in desert areas
Environment: sandstorms may occur during spring and summer; limited arable land and natural water resources pose serious constraints; deforestation
Terrain: Negev desert in the south; low coastal plain; central mountains; Jordan Rift Valley
Land Use: 17% arable; 4% permanent; 7% permanent pastures; 6% forest; 66% other; includes 1,800 sq. km irrigated
Location: SW Asia (Middle East), bordering on Mediterranean Sea

■ PEOPLE
Population: 5,749,760 (July 1999 est.)
Nationality: Israeli
Age Structure: 0-14 yrs: 28%; 15-64: 62%; 65+: 10% (1999 est.)
Population Growth Rate: 1.81% (1999 est.)
Net Migration: 4.42 migrants/1,000 population (1999 est.)
Ethnic Groups: 82% Jewish, 18% non-Jewish (mostly Arab)
Languages: Hebrew (official); Arabic used officially for Arab minority; European languages (mostly English)

Religions: 82% Judaism, 14% Islam (mostly Sunni Muslim), 2% Christian and Druze, 2% other
Birth Rate: 19.83/1,000 population (1999 est.)
Death Rate: 6.16/1,000 population (1999 est.)
Infant Mortality: 7.78 deaths/1,000 live births (1999 est.)
Life Expectancy at Birth: 76.71 years male, 80.61 years female (1999 est.)
Total Fertility Rate: 2.68 children born/woman (1999 est.)
Literacy: 95.4% (1997)

■ GOVERNMENT

Leader(s): Prime Min. Ehud Barak, Pres. Moshe Katzav
Government Type: republic
Administrative Divisions: 6 districts (mehozot, sing. -mehoz)
Nationhood: May 14, 1948 (from League of Nations mandate under British administration)
National Holiday: Independence Day, May 14; the Jewish calendar is lunar and the holiday may occur in Apr. or May

■ ECONOMY

Overview: a market economy with government participation; despite limited natural resources, this country has strong agriculture and industry sectors; transfer payments and foreign loans offset the deficit; the Palestinian uprising and Russian immigration stifle growth; high Jewish immigration from the former Soviet states has created massive housing problems
GDP: $101.9 billion, per capita $18,100; real growth rate 1.9% (1998 est.)
Inflation: 1.5% (March 2000)
Industries: accounts for 17% of GDP; food processing, diamond cutting and polishing, textiles, clothing, chemicals, metal products, military equipment, transport equipment, electrical equipment, miscellaneous machinery, potash mining, high-technology electronics, tourism
Labour Force: 3 million (1998); 36.1% community, social and business services, 14.3% trade and tourism, 20.9% industry
Unemployment: 8.8% (Nov. 1999)
Agriculture: accounts for 2% of GDP; largely self-sufficient in food production, except for bread grains; principal products—citrus and other fruit, vegetables, cotton; livestock products—beef, dairy and poultry
Natural Resources: copper, phosphates, bromide, potash, clay, sand, sulphur, asphalt, manganese, small amounts of natural gas and crude oil

■ FINANCE/TRADE

Currency: new Israeli shekel (NIS) = 100 new agorot
International Reserves Excluding Gold: $22.090 billion (Jan. 2000)
Gold Reserves: none (Jan. 2000)
Budget: revenues $55 billion; expenditures $58 billion, capital expenditures n.a. (1998 est.)
Defence Expenditures: 9.5% of GDP (1999)
Education Expenditures: 7.6% of GNP (1997)
External Debt: $18.7 billion (1997)
Exports: $25.794 billion (1999); commodities: polished diamonds, citrus and other fruit, textiles and clothing, processed foods, fertilizer and chemical products, military hardware, electronics; partners: US, UK, Germany, France, Belgium, Luxembourg, Italy
Imports: $33.160 billion (1999); commodities: military equipment, rough diamonds, oil, chemicals, machinery, iron and steel, cereals, textiles, vehicles, ships, aircraft; partners: US, Germany, UK, Switzerland, Italy, Belgium, Luxembourg

■ COMMUNICATIONS

Daily Newspapers: 34 (1996)
Televisions: 318/1,000 inhabitants (1998)
Radios: 520/1,000 inhabitants (1997)
Telephones: 471 lines/1,000 inhabitants (1998)

■ TRANSPORTATION

Motor Vehicles: 1,600,000; 1,220,000 passenger cars (1997 est.)
Roads: 15,464 km, all paved
Railway: 610 km
Air Traffic: 3,754,000 passengers carried (1997)
Airports: 54; 31 have paved runways (1998)

Canadian Embassy: The Canadian Embassy, 3 Nirim St., 4th Fl, Tel Aviv, 67060; mailing address: P.O. Box 9442, Tel Aviv, Israel. Tel: (011-972-3) 636-3300.
Embassy in Canada: Embassy of Israel, 50 O'Connor St, Ste 1005, Ottawa ON K1P 6L2. Tel: (613) 567-6450. Fax: (613) 237-8865.

Italy

Long-Form Name: Italian Republic
Capital: Rome

■ GEOGRAPHY

Area: 301,230 sq. km; includes Sardinia and Sicily
Coastline: 7,600 km
Climate: predominantly Mediterranean; Alpine

in far north; hot, dry in south
Environment: regional risks include landslides, mudflows, snowslides, earthquakes, volcanic eruptions, flooding; land sinkage in Venice; serious air and water pollution
Terrain: mostly rugged and mountainous; some plains, coastal lowlands
Land Use: 31% arable; 10% permanent; 15% meadows; 23% forest; 21% other, includes 27,100 sq. km irrigated
Location: S Europe, bordering on Adriatic Sea, Mediterranean Sea

■ PEOPLE

Population: 56,735,130 (July 1999 est.)
Nationality: Italian
Age Structure: 0-14 yrs: 14%; 15-64: 68%; 65+: 18% (1999 est.)
Population Growth Rate: -0.08% (1999 est.)
Net Migration: 0.17 migrants/1,000 population (1999 est.)
Ethnic Groups: primarily Italian but population includes small clusters of German-, French- and Slovene-Italians in the north and Albanian-Italians in the south; Sicilians; Sardinians
Languages: Italian; parts of Trentino-Alto Adige region are predominantly German-speaking; significant French-speaking minority in Valle d'Aosta region; Slovene-speaking minority in the Trieste-Gorizia area
Religions: almost 100% nominally Roman Catholic
Birth Rate: 9.27/1,000 population (1999 est.)
Death Rate: 10.28/1,000 population (1999 est.)
Infant Mortality: 6.30 deaths/1,000 live births (1999 est.)
Life Expectancy at Birth: 75.40 years male, 81.82 years female (1999 est.)
Total Fertility Rate: 1.22 children born/woman (1999 est.)
Literacy: 98.3% (1997)

■ GOVERNMENT

Leader(s): Pres. Carlo Azeglio Ciampi, Prime Min. Guiliano Amato
Government Type: republic
Administrative Divisions: 20 regions (regioni, sing. -regione)
Nationhood: Mar. 17, 1861, Kingdom of Italy proclaimed
National Holiday: Anniversary of the Republic, June 2

■ ECONOMY

Overview: country is divided into a developed industrial north, and an undeveloped agricultural south; an inadequate communications system, high pollution and economic integration into the European Union pose continuing challenges
GDP: $1.181 trillion, per capita $20,800; real growth rate 1.5% (1997 est.)
Inflation: 2.3% (April 2000)
Industries: accounts for 33% of GDP; machinery and transportation equipment, iron and steel, chemicals, food processing, textiles, motor vehicles
Labour Force: 25.0 million (1998); 21.7% industry, 21.4% trade and tourism, 28.5% community, social and business services
Unemployment: 12.5% (1998 est.)
Agriculture: accounts for about 3% of GDP and 10% of the workforce; self-sufficient in foods other than meat and dairy products; principal crops—fruit, vegetables, grapes, potatoes, sugar beets, soybeans, grain, olives
Natural Resources: mercury, potash, marble, sulphur, dwindling natural gas and crude oil reserves, fish, coal

■ FINANCE/TRADE

Currency: lira (Lit) = 100 centesimi [As of Jan. 1, 1999, Government securities are issued in Euros (EUR)]
International Reserves Excluding Gold: $21.899 billion (Jan. 2000)
Gold Reserves: 78.829 million fine troy ounces (Jan. 2000)
Budget: revenues $559 billion; expenditures $589 billion, including capital expenditures n.a. (1998 est.)
Defence Expenditures: 4.1% of central government expenditure (1997)
Education Expenditures: 4.9% of GNP (1997)
External Debt: $45 billion (1996 est.)
Exports: $242.337 billion (1998); commodities: textiles, wearing apparel, metals, transportation equipment, chemicals; partners: European Community 57%, US 9%, OPEC 4%
Imports: $215.899 billion (1998); commodities: petroleum, industrial machinery, chemicals, metals, foods, agricultural products; partners: European Community 57%, OPEC 6%, US 6%

■ COMMUNICATIONS

Daily Newspapers: 78 (1996)
Televisions: 486/1,000 inhabitants (1998)
Radios: 878/1,000 inhabitants (1997)
Telephones: 451 lines/1,000 inhabitants (1998)

■ TRANSPORTATION

Motor Vehicles: 34,000,000; 31,000,000 passenger cars (1997 est.)
Roads: 317,000 km; all paved
Railway: 19,272 km

Air Traffic: 28,184,000 passengers carried (1997)
Airports: 136; 97 have paved runways (1998 est.)

Canadian Embassy: The Canadian Embassy, Via G.B. de Rossi 27, 00161 Rome, Italy. Tel: (011-39-06) 445981. Fax: (011-39-06) 445 98750.
Embassy in Canada: Embassy of the Italian Republic, 275 Slater St, 21st Fl, Ottawa ON K1P 5H9. Tel: (613) 232-2401. Fax: (613) 233-1484.

Jamaica

Long-Form Name: Jamaica
Capital: Kingston

■ GEOGRAPHY

Area: 10,990 sq. km
Coastline: 1,022 km
Climate: tropical; hot, humid; temperate interior
Environment: subject to hurricanes (especially July to Nov.); deforestation; water pollution
Terrain: mostly mountainous with narrow, discontinuous coastal plain
Land Use: 14% arable; 6% permanent; 24% meadows; 17% forest; 39% other, includes 350 sq. km irrigated
Location: West Indies, island in Caribbean Sea, just south of Cuba

■ PEOPLE

Population: 2,652,443 (July 1999 est.)
Nationality: Jamaican
Age Structure: 0-14 yrs: 31%; 15-64: 62%; 65+: 7% (1999 est.)
Population Growth Rate: 0.64% (1999 est.)
Net Migration: -8.39 migrants/1,000 population (1999 est.)
Ethnic Groups: 76.3% African, 15.1% Afro-European, 3% East Indian and Afro-East Indian, 3.2% white, 1.2% Chinese and Afro-Chinese, 1.2% other
Languages: English (official), Creole
Religions: 55.9% Protestant, 5% Roman Catholic, 39.1% other
Birth Rate: 20.22/1,000 population (1999 est.)
Death Rate: 5.39/1,000 population (1999 est.)
Infant Mortality: 13.93 deaths/1,000 live births (1999 est.)
Life Expectancy at Birth: 73.22 years male, 78.13 years female (1999 est.)
Total Fertility Rate: 2.26 children born/woman (1999 est.)
Literacy: 85.5% (1997)

■ GOVERNMENT

Leader(s): Head of State: Queen Elizabeth II/Gov. Gen. Howard Cooke. Prime Min. Percival J. Patterson
Government Type: parliamentary democracy
Administrative Divisions: 14 parishes
Nationhood: Aug. 6, 1962 (from UK)
National Holiday: Independence Day, first Monday in Aug.

■ ECONOMY

Overview: Key sectors in this island economy are bauxite and tourism. Continued tight fiscal policies have helped slow inflation and stabilize the exchange rate, but have resulted in the slowdown of economic growth.
GDP: $8.8 billion, per capita $3,300; real growth rate -2% (1998 est.)
Inflation: 6.6% (Jan. 2000)
Industries: accounts for 42% of GDP; tourism, bauxite mining, textiles, food processing, light manufactures
Labour Force: 1 million (1998); 26.1% agriculture, 29.9% community, social and business services, 16.2% finance
Unemployment: 16.5% (1997 est.)
Agriculture: accounts for about 7.4% of GDP, 22% of workforce and 17% of exports; principal crops—sugar cane, bananas, coffee, citrus, potatoes and vegetables; not self-sufficient in grain, meat and dairy products
Natural Resources: bauxite, gypsum, limestone

■ FINANCE/TRADE

Currency: Jamaican dollar ($J) = 100 cents
International Reserves Excluding Gold: $636 million (Sept. 1999)
Gold Reserves: n.a.
Budget: revenues $2.27 billion; expenditures $3.66 billion, including capital expenditures of $1.265 billion (1998-99 est.)
Defence Expenditures: 2.4% of central government expenditure (1997)
Education Expenditures: 7.4% of GNP (1997)
External Debt: $3.995 billion (1998)
Exports: $1.131 billion (1999); commodities: bauxite, alumina, sugar, bananas; partners: US 40%, UK, Canada, Trinidad and Tobago, Norway
Imports: $2.587 billion (1999); commodities: petroleum, machinery, food, consumer goods, construction goods; partners: US 46%, UK, Venezuela, Canada, Japan, Trinidad and Tobago

■ COMMUNICATIONS

Daily Newspapers: 3 (1996)
Televisions: 182/1,000 inhabitants (1998)
Radios: 480/1,000 inhabitants (1997)
Telephones: 166 lines/1,000 inhabitants (1998)

■ TRANSPORTATION
Motor Vehicles: 58,900; 43,500 passenger cars (1997 est.)
Roads: 18,700; 13,100 km paved
Railway: 370 km
Air Traffic: 1,400,000 passengers carried (1997)
Airports: 36; 11 have paved runways (1998 est.)

Canadian Embassy: The Canadian High Commission, 3 West Kings House Road, Kingston 10; mailing address: The Canadian High Commission, P.O. Box 1500, Kingston 10, Jamaica. Tel: (876) 926-1500. Fax: (876) 511-3494.
Embassy in Canada: Jamaican High Commission, 275 Slater St, Ste 800, Ottawa ON K1P 5H9. Tel: (613) 233-9311. Fax: (613) 233-0611.

Japan

Long-Form Name: Japan
Capital: Tokyo

■ GEOGRAPHY
Area: 377,835 sq. km; includes Bonin Islands (Ogasawara-gunto), Daito-shoto, Minamijima, Okinotori-shima, Ryukyu Islands (Nansei-shoto) and Volcano Islands (Kazan-retto)
Coastline: 29,751 km
Climate: varies from tropical in south to cool temperate in north
Environment: many dormant and some active volcanoes; about 1,500 seismic occurrences (mostly tremors) every year; subject to tsunamis; acid rain caused by industrial emissions
Terrain: mostly rugged and mountainous
Land Use: 11% arable; 1% permanent crops; 2% permanent pastures; 67% forest and woodland; 19% other, includes 27,820 sq. km irrigated
Location: E Asia, bordering on Sea of Japan, North Pacific Ocean

■ PEOPLE
Population: 126,182,077 (July 1999 est.)
Nationality: Japanese
Age Structure: 0-14 yrs: 15%; 15-64: 68%; 65+: 17% (1999 est.)
Population Growth Rate: 0.2% (1999 est.)
Net Migration: -0.34 migrants/1,000 population (1999 est.)
Ethnic Groups: 99.4% Japanese, 0.6% other (mostly Korean)
Languages: Japanese
Religions: most Japanese observe both Shinto and Buddhist rites; about 16% belong to other faiths, including 0.8% Christian
Birth Rate: 10.48/1,000 population (1999 est.)
Death Rate: 8.12/1,000 population (1999 est.)
Infant Mortality: 4.07 deaths/1,000 live births (1999 est.)
Life Expectancy at Birth: 77.02 years male, 83.35 years female (1999 est.)
Total Fertility Rate: 1.48 children born/woman (1999 est.)
Literacy: 99% (1997)

■ GOVERNMENT
Leader(s): Emperor Tsegu no Miya Akihito; Prime Min. Yoshiro Mori (acting)
Government Type: constitutional monarchy
Administrative Divisions: 47 prefectures
Nationhood: 660 BC, traditional founding by Emperor Jimmu; May 3, 1947 constitutional monarchy established
National Holiday: Birthday of the Emperor, Dec. 23

■ ECONOMY
Overview: impressive economic growth and status as the second largest industrial economy in the world is due to government-industry cooperation and a strong work ethic; known for high-tech industry. the crowding of habitable land and the aging population are two major long-term problems.
GDP: $2.903 trillion, per capita $23,100; real growth rate -2.6% (1998 est.)
Inflation: -0.5% (March 2000)
Industries: accounts for 38% of GDP, metallurgy, engineering, electrical and electronic, textiles, chemicals, automobiles, fishing
Labour Force: 68 million (1998); 22.3% community, social and business services, 23.7% industry; 7.1% agriculture
Unemployment: 5.0% (Oct. 1999)
Agriculture: accounts for 2% of GDP; highly subsidized and protected sector, with crop yields among highest in the world; main crops—rice, sugar beets, vegetables, fruit; animal products include pork, poultry, dairy and eggs; about 50% self-sufficient in food
Natural Resources: negligible mineral resources, fish

■ FINANCE/TRADE
Currency: yen (pl. yen) (¥)
International Reserves Excluding Gold: $292.006 billion (Jan. 2000)
Gold Reserves: 24.227 million fine troy ounces (Jan. 2000)
Budget: revenues $528 billion; expenditures

$673 billion, including capital expenditures of $75 billion (1998 est.)
Defence Expenditures: 0.9% of GDP (1998–99)
Education Expenditures: 3.6% of GNP (1997)
External Debt: n.a.
Exports: $419.367 billion (1999); commodities: manufactures 97% (including machinery 38%, motor vehicles 17%, consumer electronics 10%); partners: US 34%, Southeast Asia 22%, Western Europe 21%, Communist countries 5%, Middle East 5%
Imports: $311.262 billion (1999); commodities: manufactures 42%, fossil fuels 30%, foodstuffs 15%, nonfuel raw materials 13%; partners: Southeast Asia 23%, US 23%, Middle East 15%, Western Europe 16%, communist countries 7%

■ COMMUNICATIONS

Daily Newspapers: 122 (1996)
Televisions: 707/1,000 inhabitants (1998)
Radios: 955/1,000 inhabitants (1997)
Telephones: 503 lines/1,000 inhabitants (1998)

■ TRANSPORTATION

Motor Vehicles: 69,700,000; 47,000,000 passenger cars (1997 est.)
Roads: 1,160,000 km; 859,560 km paved
Railway: 23,671 km
Air Traffic: 94,998,000 passengers carried (1997)
Airports: 170; 140 have paved runways (1998 est.)

Canadian Embassy: The Canadian Embassy, 3-38 Akasaka 7-chome, Minato-ku, Tokyo 107, Japan. Tel: (011-81-3) 5412-6200. Fax: (011-81-3) 5412-6303.

Embassy in Canada: Embassy of Japan, 255 Sussex Dr, Ottawa ON K1N 9E6. Tel: (613) 241-8541. Fax: (613) 241-2232.

Jordan

Long-Form Name: Hashemite Kingdom of Jordan
Capital: Amman

■ GEOGRAPHY

Area: 89,213 sq. km
Coastline: 26 km
Climate: mostly arid desert; rainy season in west (Nov. to Apr.)
Environment: lack of natural water resources; deforestation; overgrazing; soil erosion; desertification
Terrain: mostly desert plateau in east, highland area in west; Great Rift Valley separates East and West Banks of the Jordan River
Land Use: 4% arable land; 1% permanent; 9% permanent pastures; 1% forest; 85% other; includes 630 sq. km irrigated
Location: SW Asia (Middle East), on Arabian Peninsula

■ PEOPLE

Population: 4,561,147 (July 1999 est.)
Nationality: Jordanian
Age Structure: 0-14 yrs: 43%; 15-64: 54%; 65+: 3% (1999 est.)
Population Growth Rate: 3.05% (1999 est.)
Net Migration: 0 migrants/1,000 population (1999 est.)
Ethnic Groups: 98% Arab, 1% Circassian, 1% Armenian
Languages: Arabic (official); English widely understood among upper and middle classes
Religions: Islam (92% Sunni Muslim, Shia minority), 8% Christianity
Birth Rate: 34.31/1,000 population (1999 est.)
Death Rate: 3.85/1,000 population (1999 est.)
Infant Mortality: 32.70 deaths/1,000 live births (1999 est.)
Life Expectancy at Birth: 71.15 years male, 75.08 years female (1999 est.)
Total Fertility Rate: 4.64 children born/woman (1999 est.)
Literacy: 87.2% (1997)

■ GOVERNMENT

Leader(s): King Abdullah II, Prem. Ali Abu al-Ragheb
Government Type: constitutional monarchy
Administrative Divisions: 12 governorates (muhafazat, sing. -muhafazah)
Nationhood: May 25, 1946 (from League of Nations mandate under British administration; formerly known as Trans-Jordan)
National Holiday: Independence Day, May 25

■ ECONOMY

Overview: imports are outweighing exports and foreign aid makes up the difference; droughts are a potential threat; debt, poverty and unemployment remain problems; economic recovery is unlikely without substantial foreign aid, debt relief and economic reform
GDP: $15.5 billion, per capita $3,500; real growth rate 2.2% (1998 est.)
Inflation: 4.4% (Dec. 1998)
Industries: accounts for 30% of GDP; phosphate mining, petroleum refining, cement, potash, light manufacturing
Labour Force: 1.1 million (1997 est.); 9.1% transportation and communication industries, 57.7% services, 16.1% industry

Unemployment: official rate 15%, but actually 25-30% (1998 est.)
Agriculture: accounts for 6% of GDP; principal products are wheat, barley, citrus fruit, tomatoes, melons, olives; livestock—sheep, goats, poultry; large net importer of food
Natural Resources: phosphates, potash, shale oil

■ FINANCE/TRADE

Currency: Jordanian dinar (JD) = 1,000 fils
International Reserves Excluding Gold: $3.194 billion (Jan. 2000)
Gold Reserves: 0.420 million fine troy ounces (Jan. 2000)
Budget: revenues $2.8 billion; expenditures $3 billion, including capital expenditures of $672 million (1999 est.)
Defence Expenditures: 7.8% of GDP (1997)
Education Expenditures: 6.8% of GNP (1997)
External Debt: $8.484 billion (1998)
Exports: $1.802 billion (1998); commodities: fruit and vegetables, phosphates, fertilizers; partners: Iraq, Saudi Arabia, India, Kuwait, Japan, China, former Yugoslavia, Indonesia
Imports: $3.828 billion (1998); commodities: crude oil, textiles, capital goods, motor vehicles, foodstuffs; partners: European Community, US, Saudi Arabia, Japan, Turkey, Romania, China, Taiwan

■ COMMUNICATIONS

Daily Newspapers: 4 (1996)
Televisions: 86/1,000 inhabitants (1998)
Radios: 287/1,000 inhabitants (1997)
Telephones: 86 lines/1,000 inhabitants (1998)

■ TRANSPORTATION

Motor Vehicles: 265,000; 175,000 passenger cars (1997 est.)
Roads: 8,000 km, all paved
Railway: 677 km
Air Traffic: 1,353,000 passengers carried (1997)
Airports: 17; 14 have paved runways (1998 est.)

Canadian Embassy: The Canadian Embassy, Pearl of Shmeisani Bldg, Shmeisani, Amman, Jordan; mailing address: P.O. Box 815403, Amman, Jordan 11180. Tel: (011-962-6) 566-61-24. Fax: (011-962-6) 568-92-27.
Embassy in Canada: Embassy of the Hashemite Kingdom of Jordan, 100 Bronson Ave, Ste 701, Ottawa ON K1R 6G8. Tel: (613) 238-8090. Fax: (613) 232-3341.

Kazakhstan

Long-Form Name: Republic of Kazakhstan
Capital: Astana

■ GEOGRAPHY

Area: 2,717,300 sq. km
Coastline: none; landlocked; Kazakhstan borders the Aral Sea (1,015 km) and the Caspian Sea (1,894 km)
Climate: dry desert climate; arid and semi-arid; hot summers and cold winters
Environment: drought and desertification; lack of fresh water; drying up of Aral Sea is causing increased concentrations of chemical pesticides and natural salts; industrial pollution, including radioactive or toxic chemical sites
Terrain: desert and steppe; plains in western Siberia to oasis and desert in Central Asia
Land Use: 12% arable; 11% permanent crops; 57% meadows and pastures; 4% forests; 16% other; includes 22,000 sq. km irrigated
Location: C Asia, bordering on Caspian Sea

■ PEOPLE

Population: 16,824,852 (July 1999 est.)
Nationality: Kazakhstani
Age Structure: 0-14 yrs: 28%; 15-64: 65%; 65+: 7% (1999 est.)
Population Growth Rate: -0.09% (1999 est.)
Net Migration: -7.73 migrants/1,000 population (1999 est.)
Ethnic Groups: 46% Kazakh, 34.7% Russian, 4.9% Ukrainian, 3.1% German, 2.3% Uzbek, 1.9% Tatar, 7.1% other
Languages: Kazakh (official, spoken by over 40% of population), Russian (official, spoken by two-thirds of population), German, Ukrainian
Religions: primarily Sunni Muslim (47%) and Eastern Orthodox (44%), Protestant (2%), other 7%
Birth Rate: 17.16/1,000 population (1999 est.)
Death Rate: 10.34/1,000 population (1999 est.)
Infant Mortality: 58.82 deaths/1,000 live births (1999 est.)
Life Expectancy at Birth: 57.92 years male, 69.13 years female (1999 est.)
Total Fertility Rate: 2.09 children born/woman (1999 est.)
Literacy: 99% (1997)

■ GOVERNMENT

Leader(s): Pres. Nursultan A. Nazarbayev, Prem. Kasymzhomart Tokayev
Government Type: republic
Administrative Divisions: 14 oblasts (oblystar, sing. -oblysy) and 3 cities (gala, sing. -galasy)
Nationhood: Dec. 16, 1991 (from Soviet Union)
National Holiday: Independence Day, Oct. 25; Republic Day, Dec. 16

■ ECONOMY

Overview: predominantly mining and

manufacturing; agriculture possible only with irrigation; serious pollution problems, lack of modern technology, and little experience in foreign markets hamper economic progress
GDP: $52.9 billion, per capita $3,100; real growth rate -2.5% (1998 est.)
Inflation: 20.2% (Feb. 2000)
Industries: accounts for 33% of GDP; coal refining, oil and natural gas extraction, mining, agricultural machinery, electric motors, construction materials
Labour Force: 7 million (1998) 25.9% community, social and business services, 23.9% agriculture, 15.8% industry
Unemployment: 13.7%; large numbers of underemployed (1998 est.)
Agriculture: accounts for 11.5% of GDP, and employs one quarter of labour force; wheat, cotton, rice, vineyard and orchard crops, sheep, cattle
Natural Resources: fish, oil, natural gas, zinc, coal, lead, iron ore, rare metals, tungsten, copper, zinc, manganese

■ FINANCE/TRADE

Currency: tenge = 100 tiyn
International Reserves Excluding Gold: $1.426 billion (Jan. 2000)
Gold Reserves: 1.732 million fine troy ounces (Jan. 2000)
Budget: revenues $2.9 billion; expenditures $4.2 billion, including capital expenditures of n.a.(1998 est.)
Defence Expenditures: 5.12% of central government expenditure (1998)
Education Expenditures: 4.78% of central government expenditure (1998)
External Debt: $5.714 billion (1998)
Exports: $5.592 billion (1999): fuels, karakul fleece, wool, industrial products
Imports: $3.683 billion (1999): fuel, industrial products; partners: mostly Asian countries

■ COMMUNICATIONS

Daily Newspapers: 3 (1996)
Televisions: 231/1,000 inhabitants (1998)
Radios: 384/1,000 inhabitants (1997)
Telephones: 104 lines/1,000 inhabitants (1998)

■ TRANSPORTATION

Motor Vehicles: n.a.
Roads: 141,076 km; 113,566 km hard-surfaced
Railway: 14,400 km
Air Traffic: 568,000 passengers carried (1997)
Airports: 10; 9 have paved runways (1997 est.)

Canadian Embassy: The Canadian Embassy, 34 Karasai Batir, St, Almaty 480100, Kazakhstan. Tel: (011-7-327) 50-11-51. Fax: (011-7-327) 582-493.
Embassy in Canada: c/o The Embassy of the Republic of Kazhakstan, 1401 16th Street NW, Washington, DC 20036, USA. Tel: (202) 232-5488. Fax: (202) 232-5845.

Kenya

Long-Form Name: Republic of Kenya
Capital: Nairobi

■ GEOGRAPHY

Area: 582,650 sq. km
Coastline: 536 km
Climate: varies from tropical along coast to arid in interior
Environment: unique physiography supports abundant and varied wildlife of scientific and economic value, but poaching is a continuing problem; deforestation; soil erosion; desertification; glaciers on Mt. Kenya; deteriorating water quality
Terrain: low plains rise to central highlands bisected by Great Rift Valley; fertile plateau in west
Land Use: 7% arable; 1% permanent; 37% permanent pastures; 30% forest; 25% other; includes 660 sq. km irrigated
Location: E Africa, bordering on Indian Ocean

■ PEOPLE

Population: 28,808,658 (July 1999 est.)
Nationality: Kenyan
Age Structure: 0-14 yrs: 43%; 15-64: 54%; 65+: 3% (1999 est.)
Population Growth Rate: 1.59% (1999 est.)
Net Migration: -0.34 migrants/1,000 population (1999 est.)
Ethnic Groups: 22% Kikuyu, 14% Luhya, 13% Luo, 12% Kalenjin, 11% Kamba, 6% Kisii, 6% Meru, 1% Asian, European and Arab, 15% other
Languages: English and Swahili (official); Kikuyu and Luo are widely spoken; numerous indigenous languages
Religions: 28% Roman Catholic, 26% indigenous beliefs, 38% Protestant, 8% other
Birth Rate: 30.8/1,000 population (1999 est.)
Death Rate: 14.58/1,000 population (1999 est.)
Infant Mortality: 59.07 deaths/1,000 live births (1999 est.)
Life Expectancy at Birth: 46.56 years male, 47.49 years female (1999 est.)
Total Fertility Rate: 3.88 children born/woman (1999 est.)

Literacy: 79.3% (1997)

■ GOVERNMENT
Leader(s): Pres. Daniel T. arap Moi, V. Pres. George Saitoti
Government Type: republic
Administrative Divisions: 7 provinces and 1 area
Nationhood: Dec. 12, 1963 (from UK; formerly known as British East Africa)
National Holiday: Independence Day, Dec. 12

■ ECONOMY
Overview: a large annual population growth, a deteriorating infrastructure and a shortage of arable land threaten economic growth; vulnerable to weather conditions
GDP: $43.9 billion, per capita $1,550; real growth rate 1.6% (1998 est.)
Inflation: 5.1% (Feb. 2000)
Industries: accounts for 17% of GDP; small-scale consumer goods (plastic, furniture, batteries, textiles, soap, cigarettes, flour), agricultural processing, oil refining, cement, tourism
Labour Force: 15 million (1998); 43.2% community, social and business services, 18.9% agriculture, 13.1% industry
Unemployment: 50% in urban areas (1998 est.)
Agriculture: accounts for 29% of GDP and 65% of exports; cash crops include coffee, tea, sisal, pineapple; food products—corn, wheat, sugar cane, fruit, vegetables, dairy products; food output not sufficient for existing population
Natural Resources: gold, limestone, diatomite, salt barytes, magnesite, feldspar, sapphires, fluorspar, garnets, wildlife

■ FINANCE/TRADE
Currency: Kenya shilling (KSh) = 100 cents
International Reserves Excluding Gold: $699 million (Oct. 1999)
Gold Reserves: none (Jan. 2000)
Budget: revenues $2.6 billion; expenditures $2.7 billion, including capital expenditures of n.a. (1997 est.)
Defence Expenditures: 1.9% of GDP (1998-99)
Education Expenditures: 6.5% of GNP (1997)
External Debt: $7.01 billion (1998)
Exports: $2.008 billion (1998); commodities: coffee 20%, tea 18%, manufactures 15%, petroleum products 10%; partners: Western Europe 45%, Africa 22%, Far East 10%, US 4%, Middle East 3%
Imports: $3.197 billion (1998); commodities: machinery and transportation equipment 36%, raw materials 33%, fuels and lubricants 20%, food and consumer goods 11%; partners: Western Europe 49%, Far East 20%, Middle East 19%, US 7%

■ COMMUNICATIONS
Daily Newspapers: 4 (1996)
Televisions: 21/1,000 inhabitants (1998)
Radios: 104/1,000 inhabitants (1997)
Telephones: 9 lines/1,000 inhabitants (1998)

■ TRANSPORTATION
Motor Vehicles: 364,900; 271,000 passenger cars (1997 est.)
Roads: 63,800 km; 8,868 km paved
Railway: 2,652 km
Air Traffic: 836,000 passengers carried (1997)
Airports: 232; 21 have paved runways (1998 est.)

Canadian Embassy: The Canadian High Commission, Comcraft House, Hailé Sélassie Ave, Nairobi; mailing address: The Canadian High Commission, P.O. Box 30481, Nairobi, Kenya. Tel: (011-254-2) 21-48-04. Fax: (011-254-2) 22-69-87.
Embassy in Canada: High Commission for the Republic of Kenya, 415 Laurier Ave E, Ottawa ON K1N 6R4. Tel: (613) 563-1773. Fax: (613) 233-6599.

Kiribati

Long-Form Name: Republic of Kiribati
Capital: Tarawa

■ GEOGRAPHY
Area: 717 sq. km
Coastline: 1,143 km
Climate: tropical; marine, hot and humid, moderated by trade winds
Environment: typhoons can occur anytime, but usually Nov. to Mar.
Terrain: mostly low-lying coral atolls surrounded by extensive reefs
Land Use: negligible arable; 51% permanent; 0% meadows; 3% forest; 46% other; includes n.a. sq. km irrigated
Location: SW Pacific Ocean, NE of Australia

■ PEOPLE
Population: 85,501 (July 1999 est.); 20 of Kiribati's 33 islands are inhabited
Nationality: I-Kiribati (sing. & pl.)
Age Structure: n.a.
Population Growth Rate: 1.78% (1999 est.)
Net Migration: -0.77 migrants/1,000 population (1999 est.)
Ethnic Groups: Micronesian
Languages: English (official), Gilbertese

Religions: 52.6% Roman Catholic, 40.9% Protestant (Congregational), some Seventh-Day Adventist and Baha'i
Birth Rate: 26.13/1,000 population (1999 est.)
Death Rate: 7.53/1,000 population (1999 est.)
Infant Mortality: 48.22 deaths/1,000 live births (1999 est.)
Life Expectancy at Birth: 61.02 years male, 64.98 years female (1999 est.)
Total Fertility Rate: 3.09 children born/woman (1999 est.)
Literacy: 90.6% (1997 est.)

■ GOVERNMENT

Leader(s): Pres. Teburoro Tito, V. Pres. Tewareka Tentoa
Government Type: republic
Administrative Divisions: 3 units
Nationhood: July 12, 1979 (from UK; formerly known as Gilbert Islands)
National Holiday: Independence Day, July 12

■ ECONOMY

Overview: the economy has fluctuated widely in recent years and copra production and a good fish catch have provided a boost; at present there is a moderate but steady growth trend
GDP: $62 million, per capita $800; real growth rate 1.9% (1997 est.)
Inflation: n.a.
Industries: accounts for 7% of GDP; fishing, handicrafts
Labour Force: n.a.
Unemployment: n.a., but massive underemployment
Agriculture: accounts for 14% of GDP (including fishing); copra and fish contribute 65% to exports; subsistence farming predominates; food crops—taro, breadfruit, sweet potatoes, vegetables; not self-sufficient in food
Natural Resources: tuna fishing, phosphates

■ FINANCE/TRADE

Currency: Australian dollar ($A) = 100 cents
International Reserves Excluding Gold: n.a.
Gold Reserves: n.a.
Budget: revenues $33.3 million; expenditures $47.7 million, including capital expenditures n.a. (1996 est.)
Defence Expenditures: n.a.
Education Expenditures: n.a.
External Debt: $7.2 million (1996 est.)
Exports: $8 million (1998); commodities: fish 55%, copra 42%; partners: European Community 20%, Marshall Islands 12%, US 8%, American Samoa 4%
Imports: $40 million (1998); commodities: foodstuffs, fuel, transportation equipment; partners: Australia 39%, Japan 21%, New Zealand 6%, UK 6%, US 3%

■ COMMUNICATIONS

Daily Newspapers: 0 (1996)
Televisions: 13/1,000 inhabitants (1996)
Radios: 213/1,000 inhabitants (1996)
Telephones: 35 lines/1,000 inhabitants (1998)

■ TRANSPORTATION

Motor Vehicles: n.a.
Roads: 670 km; n.a. km paved
Railway: none
Air Traffic: 28,000 passengers carried (1997)
Airports: 21; 4 have paved runways (1998 est.)

Canadian Embassy: The Canadian High Commission to Kiribati, c/o The Canadian High Commission, P.O. Box 12-049, Thorndon, Wellington, New Zealand. Tel: (011-64-4) 473-9577. Fax: (011-64-4) 471-2082.
Embassy in Canada: c/o New Zealand High Commission, Clarica Centre, 99 Bank St, Ste 727, Ottawa, ON K1P 6G3. Tel: (613) 238-5991. Fax: (613) 238-5707.

Korea (North)

Long-Form Name: Democratic People's Republic of Korea
Capital: Pyongyang

■ GEOGRAPHY

Area: 120,540 sq. km
Coastline: 2,495 km
Climate: temperate with rainfall concentrated in summer
Environment: isolated mountainous interior, nearly inaccessible and sparsely populated; late spring droughts often followed by severe flooding
Terrain: mostly hills and mountains separated by deep, narrow valleys; coastal plains wide in west, discontinuous in east
Land Use: 14% arable; 2% permanent; negligible meadows; 61% forest; 23% other, includes 14,600 sq. km irrigated
Location: E Asia, bordering on Yellow Sea, Sea of Japan

■ PEOPLE

Population: 21,386,109 (July 1999 est.)
Nationality: Korean
Age Structure: 0-14 yrs: 26%; 15-64: 68%; 65+: 6% (1999 est.)
Population Growth Rate: +1.45% (1999 est.)

Net Migration: 0 migrants/1,000 population (1999 est.)
Ethnic Groups: Korean (racially homogeneous)
Languages: Korean
Religions: Buddhism and Confucianism; Taoism, Shamanism, Chonodogyu; autonomous religious activities are now almost nonexistent; government-sponsored religious groups exist to provide an illusion of religious freedom
Birth Rate: 21.37/1,000 population (1999 est.)
Death Rate: 6.92/1,000 population (1999 est.)
Infant Mortality: 25.52 deaths/1,000 live births (1999 est.)
Life Expectancy at Birth: 67.41 years male, 72.86 years female (1999 est.)
Total Fertility Rate: 2.30 children born/woman (1999 est.)
Literacy: 99% (1997)

■ GOVERNMENT

Leader(s): Chairman National Defense Commission Kim Jong Il, Chairman Standing Committee of Supreme People's Assembly Kim Yong Nam, Prime Min. Hong Song-man
Government Type: communist state; one-person dictatorship
Administrative Divisions: 9 provinces (do, sing. & pl.) and 3 special cities si, sing. & pl.)
Nationhood: Sept. 9, 1948
National Holiday: Independence Day (DPRK Foundation Day), Sept. 9

■ ECONOMY

Overview: a command economy that is almost completely socialized, with state-owned industry, and collectivization of agriculture; state control over economic affairs is unusually tight even for a communist country; six consecutive years of crop failure and severe summer floods in 1995 have resulted in severe food shortages
GDP: $21.8 billion, per capita $1,000; real growth rate -5% (1998 est.)
Inflation: n.a.
Industries: accounts for 60% of GDP; machine building, military products, electric power, chemicals, mining, metallurgy, textiles, food processing
Labour Force: 12 million (1998); 42.8% agricultural, 26.9% services, 30.3% industry
Unemployment: n.a.
Agriculture: accounts for about 25% of GNP and 36% of workforce; principal crops—rice, corn, potatoes, soybeans, pulses; fish; livestock and livestock products—cattle, hogs, pork, eggs; not self-sufficient in grain
Natural Resources: coal, lead, tungsten, zinc, graphite, magnesite, iron ore, copper, gold, pyrites, salt, fluorspar, hydroelectricity

■ FINANCE/TRADE

Currency: North Korean won (Wn) = 100 chon
International Reserves Excluding Gold: n.a.
Gold Reserves: n.a.
Budget: n.a.
Defence Expenditures: 25% to 33% of GDP (1997 est.)
Education Expenditures: n.a.
External Debt: $12 billion (1996 est.)
Exports: n.a.; commodities: minerals, metallurgical products, agricultural products, manufactures; partners: former USSR countries, China, Japan, Germany, Hong Kong, Singapore
Imports: n.a.; commodities: petroleum, machinery and equipment, coking coal, grain; partners: former USSR countries, Japan, China, Germany, Hong Kong, Singapore

■ COMMUNICATIONS

Daily Newspapers: 3 (1996)
Televisions: 53/1,000 inhabitants (1998)
Radios: 147/1,000 inhabitants (1997)
Telephones: 47 lines/1,000 inhabitants (1998)

■ TRANSPORTATION

Motor Vehicles: n.a.
Roads: 31,200 km; 1,997 km paved
Railway: 5,000 km
Air Traffic: 280,000 passengers carried (1997)
Airports: 49; 22 have paved runways

Canadian Embassy: none
Embassy in Canada: none

Korea (South)

Long-Form Name: Republic of Korea
Capital: Seoul

■ GEOGRAPHY

Area: 98,480 sq. km
Coastline: 2,413 km
Climate: temperate, with rainfall heavier in summer than winter
Environment: occasional typhoons bring high winds and floods; earthquakes in southwest; air and water pollution in large cities
Terrain: mostly hilly and mountainous; wide coastal plains in west and south
Land Use: 19% arable; 2% permanent; 1% meadows; 65% forest; 13% other, includes 13,350 sq. km irrigated
Location: E Asia, bordering on Yellow Sea, Sea of Japan

■ PEOPLE

Population: 46,884,800 (July 1999 est.)
Nationality: Korean
Age Structure: 0-14 yrs: 22%; 15-64: 71%; 65+: 7% (1999 est.)
Population Growth Rate: 1.00% (1999 est.)
Net Migration: -0.30 migrants/1,000 population (1999 est.)
Ethnic Groups: homogeneous; small Chinese minority (about 20,000)
Languages: Korean; English widely taught in high school
Religions: 48.6% Christianity, 47.4% Buddhism, 3% Confucianism, 1% other
Birth Rate: 15.95/1,000 population (1999 est.)
Death Rate: 5.68/1,000 population (1999 est.)
Infant Mortality: 7.57 deaths/1,000 live births (1999 est.)
Life Expectancy at Birth: 70.75 years male, 78.32 years female (1999 est.)
Total Fertility Rate: 1.79 children born/woman (1999 est.)
Literacy: 97.2% (1997)

■ GOVERNMENT

Leader(s): Pres. Kim Dae-jung, Prime Min. Lee Hang Dong
Government Type: republic
Administrative Divisions: 9 provinces (do, sing. & pl.) and 6 special cities (gwangyoksi, sing. & pl.)
Nationhood: Aug. 15, 1948
National Holiday: Independence Day, Aug. 15

■ ECONOMY

Overview: dynamic growth is attributed to the planned development of an export-oriented economy in a strongly entrepreneurial society; labour unrest has hurt its record of non-inflationary growth; economic growth has slowed somewhat in recent years
GDP: $584.7 billion, per capita $12,600; real growth rate -6.8% (1998 est.)
Inflation: 1.0% (April 2000)
Industries: accounts for 43% of GDP; textiles, clothing, footwear, food processing, chemicals, steel, electronics, automobile production, ship building
Labour Force: 23 million (1998); 25.1% trade and tourism, 23.9% industry, 14.8% agriculture
Unemployment: 5.3% (Jan. 2000)
Agriculture: accounts for 6% of GDP and 21% of workforce (including fishing and forestry); main crops—rice, root crops, barley, vegetables, fruit; livestock and livestock products—cattle, hogs, chickens, milk, eggs; self-sufficient in food, except for wheat; fish catch is seventh largest in the world
Natural Resources: coal, tungsten, graphite, molybdenum, lead, hydroelectricity

■ FINANCE/TRADE

Currency: South Korean won (W) = 100 chun
International Reserves Excluding Gold: $76.721 billion (Jan. 2000)
Gold Reserves: 0.437 million fine troy ounces (Jan. 2000)
Budget: revenues $100.4 billion; expenditures $100.5 billion, including capital expenditures of n.a. (1997 est.)
Defence Expenditures: 16.29% of govt. expenditure (1997)
Education Expenditures: 19.56% of govt. expenditure (1997)
External Debt: $139.097 billion (1998)
Exports: $144.745 billion (1999); commodities: textiles, clothing, electronic and electrical equipment, footwear, machinery, steel, automobiles, ships, fish; partners: US 33%, Japan 21%
Imports: $119.75 billion (1999); commodities: machinery, electronics and electronic equipment, oil, steel, transport equipment, textiles, organic chemicals, grains; partners: Japan 28%, US 25%

■ COMMUNICATIONS

Daily Newspapers: 60 (1996)
Televisions: 346/1,000 inhabitants (1998)
Radios: 1,033/1,000 inhabitants (1997)
Telephones: 433/1,000 inhabitants (1998)

■ TRANSPORTATION

Motor Vehicles: 10,000,000; 7,000,000 passenger cars (1997 est.)
Roads: 63,500 km; 46,800 km paved
Railway: 6,240 km
Air Traffic: 35,506,000 passengers carried (1997)
Airports: 103; 68 have paved runways (1997 est.)

Canadian Embassy: The Canadian Embassy, Fl. 10 & 11, Kolon Building, 45 Mugyo-Dong, Jung-Ku, Seoul 100-170; mailing address: P.O. Box 6299, Seoul 100-662 Korea. Tel: (011-82-2) 3455-6000. Fax: (011-82-2) 755-0686.
Embassy in Canada: Embassy of the Republic of Korea, 150 Boteler St, Ottawa ON K1A 5A6. Tel: (613) 244-5010. Fax: (613) 244-5043.

Kuwait

Long-Form Name: State of Kuwait
Capital: Kuwait

■ GEOGRAPHY

Area: 17,820 sq. km

Coastline: 499 km
Climate: dry desert; intensely hot summers; short, cool winters
Environment: large and sophisticated desalination plants are required for adequate drinking water supply; air and water pollution; desertification
Terrain: flat to slightly undulating desert plain
Land Use: negligible arable; 0% permanent; 8% meadows; negligible forest; 92% other; includes 20 sq. km irrigated
Location: SW Asia (Middle East), on Arabian Peninsula, bordering on Persian Gulf

■ PEOPLE

Population: 1,991,115 (July 1999 est.)
Nationality: Kuwaiti
Age Structure: 0-14 yrs: 32%; 15-64: 66%; 65+: 2% (1999 est.)
Population Growth Rate: 3.88% (1999 est.)
Net Migration: 20.65 migrants/1,000 population (1999 est.)
Ethnic Groups: 45% Kuwaiti, 35% other Arab, 9% South Asian, 4% Iranian, 7% other
Languages: Arabic (official); Kurdish, Farsi, English (commercial) widely spoken
Religions: 85% Muslim (30% Shi'a, 45% Sunni, 10% other), 15% Christian, Hindu, Parsi and other
Birth Rate: 20.45/1,000 population (1999 est.)
Death Rate: 2.31/1,000 population (1999 est.)
Infant Mortality: 10.26 deaths/1,000 live births (1999 est.)
Life Expectancy at Birth: 75.11 years male, 79.30 years female (1999 est.)
Total Fertility Rate: 3.34 children born/woman (1999 est.)
Literacy: 80.4% (1997)

■ GOVERNMENT

Leader(s): Prime Min. Shaikh Saad al-Abdullah al-Salim al-Sabah; Emir: Shaikh Jabir al-Ahmad al-Jabir al-Sabah
Government Type: nominal constitutional monarchy
Administrative Divisions: 5 governorates (muhafazat, sing. -muhafazah)
Nationhood: June 19, 1961 (from UK)
National Holiday: National Day, Feb. 25

■ ECONOMY

Overview: Kuwait is a small and relatively open economy with crude oil reserves of about 10% of world reserves. Kuwait lacks water and has practically no arable land, thus preventing development of agriculture. With the exception of fish, it depends almost wholly on food imports.
GDP: $43.7 billion, per capita $22,700; real growth rate -5% (1998 est.)
Inflation: 3.5% (Sept. 1999)
Industries: petroleum (accounts for 53% of GDP and 90% of export revenues), petrochemicals, desalination, food processing, salt, construction
Labour Force: 1 million (1998); 45% services, 20% construction, 12% trade, 9% manufacturing, 3% finance and real estate, 2% agriculture, 2% power and water, 1% mining and quarrying
Unemployment: 1.8% (1996 est.)
Agriculture: virtually none; dependent on imports for food; about 75% of potable water (adversely affected by the Gulf War) must be distilled or imported
Natural Resources: petroleum, fish, shrimp, natural gas

■ FINANCE/TRADE

Currency: dinar (KD) = 1,000 fils
International Reserves Excluding Gold: 4.789 billion (Jan. 2000)
Gold Reserves: 2.539 million fine troy ounces (Jan. 2000)
Budget: revenues $8.1 billion; expenditures $14.5 billion, including capital expenditures n.a. (1998-99 est.)
Defence Expenditures: 20.26% of govt. expenditure (1998)
Education Expenditures: 11.94% of govt. expenditure (1998)
External Debt: $7.3 billion (1997 est.)
Exports: $9.554 billion (1998); commodities: oil 90%; partners: Japan, Italy, Germany, US
Imports: $7.617 billion (1999); commodities: food, construction material, vehicles and parts, clothing; partners: Japan, US, Germany, UK

■ COMMUNICATIONS

Daily Newspapers: 8 (1996)
Televisions: 491/1,000 inhabitants (1998)
Radios: 660/1,000 inhabitants (1997)
Telephones: 236 lines/1,000 inhabitants (1998)

■ TRANSPORTATION

Motor Vehicles: 693,000; 538,000 passenger cars (1997 est.)
Roads: 4,450 km; 3,587 km paved
Railway: none
Air Traffic: 2,114,000 passengers carried (1997)
Airports: 8; 4 have paved runways (1998 est.)

Canadian Embassy: The Canadian Embassy, Villa 24, Area 4, 24 Mutawakel St, Da Aiyah, Kuwait; mailing address: P.O. Box 25281, 13113, Safat, Kuwait City, Kuwait. Tel: (011-

965) 256-3025. Fax: (011-965) 256-0173.
Embassy in Canada: Embassy of the State of Kuwait, 80 Elgin St, Ottawa, ON K1P 1C6. Tel: (613) 780-9999. Fax: (613) 780-9905.

Kyrgyzstan

Long-Form Name: Kyrgyz Republic
Capital: Bishkek

■ GEOGRAPHY

Area: 198,500 sq. km
Coastline: none: landlocked
Climate: dry continental to polar in high Tien Shan; subtropical in south; glacial Alpine; moderate in valley regions
Environment: frequent severe earthquakes; water pollution and water-borne diseases are widespread
Terrain: mountainous; 75% of land covered by snow and glaciers; peaks of Tien Shan rise to 7,000 meters, and associated valleys and basins encompass the entire nation
Land Use: land is cultivated mainly in valleys; 7% arable; negligible permanent crops, 44% meadows and pastures; 4% forest and woodland; 45% other; includes 9,000 sq. km irrigated
Location: C Asia, bordering on China

■ PEOPLE

Population: 4,546,055 (July 1999 est.)
Nationality: Kyrgyzstani
Age Structure: 0-14 yrs: 35%; 15-64: 59%; 65+: 6% (1999 est.)
Population Growth Rate: 0.68% (1999 est.)
Net Migration: -6.28 migrants/1,000 population (1999 est.)
Ethnic Groups: 52.4% Kirghiz, 18% Russian, 12.9% Uzbeks, 2.5% Ukrainian, 2.4% German, 1.6% Tatars, 10.2% other
Languages: Kirghiz and Russian (both official) and Dungan
Religions: 75% Muslim, 20% Eastern Orthodox, 5% other
Birth Rate: 21.83/1,000 population (1999 est.)
Death Rate: 8.74/1,000 population (1999 est.)
Infant Mortality: 75.92 deaths/1,000 live births (1999 est.)
Life Expectancy at Birth: 59.25 years male, 68.10 years female (1999 est.)
Total Fertility Rate: 2.63 children born/woman (1999 est.)
Literacy: 97% (1997)

■ GOVERNMENT

Leader(s): Pres. Askar Akayev; Prime Min. Amangeldy Muraliyev. Presidential election scheduled October 29, 2000.
Government Type: republic
Administrative Divisions: 6 oblasttar (sing. -oblast) and 1 city (sing. -shaar)
Nationhood: August 31, 1991 (from Soviet Union)
National Holiday: National Day, Dec. 2; also Independence Day, Aug. 31

■ ECONOMY

Overview: Kyrgyzstan is a small, poor, mountainous country with a predominantly agricultural economy. Kyrgyzstan has been one of the most progressive countries of the former Soviet Union in carrying out market reforms. Foreign assistance played a substantial role in the country's recent economic turnaround.
GDP: $9.8 billion, per capita $2,200; real growth rate 1.8% (1998 est.)
Inflation: 35.4% (March 2000)
Industries: accounts for 12% of GDP; small machinery, cement, shoes, furniture and appliances, electronics, electrical engineering, silk making
Labour Force: 2 million (1998); 33% agriculture and forestry, 28% industry and construction, 39% other
Unemployment: 6%; large numbers of underemployed (1998 est.)
Agriculture: accounts for 47% of GDP; wheat, barley, beets, cotton, fruit, vegetables, yaks, potatoes, cotton, grain, tobacco, livestock (mainly sheep); irrigation required
Natural Resources: mercury, antimony, zinc, tungsten deposits, coal, natural gas, oil, nepheline, bismuth

■ FINANCE/TRADE

Currency: Kyrgyzstani som = 100 tyiyn
International Reserves Excluding Gold: $248 million (Jan. 2000)
Gold Reserves: 0.083 million fine troy ounces (Jan. 2000)
Budget: revenues $225 million; expenditures $308 million, including capital expenditures of $11 million (1996 est.)
Defence Expenditures: 6.52% of central government expenditure (1998)
Education Expenditures: 22.33% of central government expenditure (1998)
External Debt: $1.148 billion (1998)
Exports: $611 million (1997); agricultural products, antimony, silk, carpets, nonferrous metals, electrical equipment, cotton, wool, meat, tobacco, gold, mercury, hydropower, machinery, consumer goods; partners: China, UK

Imports: $694 million (1997); grain, lumber, industrial products, metals, fuel, machinery, consumer goods; partners: Turkey, Cuba, US, Germany

■ COMMUNICATIONS
Daily Newspapers: 3 (1996)
Televisions: 45/1,000 inhabitants (1998)
Radios: 112/1,000 inhabitants (1997)
Telephones: 76 lines/1,000 inhabitants (1998)

■ TRANSPORTATION
Motor Vehicles: n.a.
Roads: 18,560 km; 16,890 km paved or graveled
Railway: 370 km, plus industrial lines
Air Traffic: 423,000 passengers carried (1997)
Airports: 54; 14 have paved runways

Canadian Embassy: The Canadian Embassy, 34 Karasai Batir St, Almaty 480100, Kazakhstan. Tel: (011-7-3272) 50-11-51. Fax: (011-7-3272) 582-493.
Embassy in Canada: c/o Embassy of the Kyrgyz Republic, 1732 Wisconsin Ave NW, Washington DC 20007, USA. Tel: (202) 338-5141. Fax: (202) 338-5139.

Laos

Long-Form Name: Lao People's Democratic Republic
Capital: Vientiane

■ GEOGRAPHY
Area: 236,800 sq. km
Coastline: none: landlocked
Climate: tropical monsoon; rainy season (May to Nov.); dry season (Dec. to Apr.)
Environment: deforestation; soil erosion; subject to floods; limited safe drinking water
Terrain: mostly rugged mountains; some plains and plateaus
Land Use: 3% arable land; negligible permanent crops; 3% meadows; 54% forest; 40% other; includes 1,250 sq. km irrigated
Location: SE Asia

■ PEOPLE
Population: 5,407,453 (July 1999 est.)
Nationality: Laotian or Lao
Age Structure: 0-14 yrs: 45%; 15-64: 52%; 65+: 3% (1999 est.)
Population Growth Rate: 2.74% (1999 est.)
Net Migration: 0 migrants/1,000 population (1999 est.)
Ethnic Groups: mostly Laotian; Vietnamese, Kha, Thai, Meo, Hmong, Yao, Chinese, European, Indian and Pakistani minorities
Languages: Lao (official), French, English, tribal languages
Religions: 60% Buddhist, 40% animist and other
Birth Rate: 39.93/1,000 population (1999 est.)
Death Rate: 12.56/1,000 population (1999 est.)
Infant Mortality: 89.32 deaths/1,000 live births (1999 est.)
Life Expectancy at Birth: 52.63 years male, 55.87 years female (1999 est.)
Total Fertility Rate: 5.55 children born/woman (1999 est.)
Literacy: 58.6% (1997)

■ GOVERNMENT
Leader(s): Pres. Khamtai Siphandon, Prime Min. Gen. Sisavat Keobounphan
Government Type: communist state
Administrative Divisions: 16 provinces (khoueng, sing. & pl.) and 1 municipality (kampheng nakhon, sing. & pl.) and 1 special zone (khetphiset, sing. & pl.)
Nationhood: July 19, 1949 (from France)
National Holiday: National Day (proclamation of the Lao People's Democratic Republic), Dec. 2

■ ECONOMY
Overview: one of the world's poorest nations, landlocked with a primitive infrastructure; while traditionally a communist centrally planned economy with government ownership and control of productive enterprises, the government is now decentralizing control and encouraging some private enterprise; heavily dependent on foreign aid
GDP: $6.6 billion, per capita $1,260; real growth rate 4% (1998 est.)
Inflation: 86.7% (Dec. 1999)
Industries: accounts for 21% of GDP; tin mining, timber, electric power, agricultural processing
Labour Force: 2 million (1997 est.); 75.7% agriculture, 7.1% industry, 17.2% services
Unemployment: 5.7% (1997 est.)
Agriculture: accounts for 51% of GDP and employs most of the labour force; subsistence farming predominates; normally self-sufficient; principal crops—rice (80% of cultivated land), potatoes, vegetables, coffee, sugar cane, cotton
Natural Resources: timber, hydroelectricity, gypsum, tin, gold, gemstones

■ FINANCE/TRADE
Currency: new kip (NK) = 100 at
International Reserves Excluding Gold: $101 million (Dec. 1999)
Gold Reserves: 0.100 million fine troy ounces

(Dec. 2000)
Budget: revenues $218 million; expenditures $379 million, capital expenditures n.a. (1996 est.)
Defence Expenditures: 17.5% of central government expenditure (1997)
Education Expenditures: 2.1% of GNP (1997)
External Debt: $2.437 billion (1998)
Exports: $311 million (1999); wood products, electricity, tin, consumer goods; partners: Vietnam, Thailand, Germany, France
Imports: $525 million (1999); machinery and equipment, fuel, vehicles; partners: Thailand, Japan, Vietnam, China, Singapore

■ COMMUNICATIONS

Daily Newspapers: 3 (1996)
Televisions: 4/1,000 inhabitants (1998)
Radios: 143,1,000 inhabitants (1997)
Telephones: 6 lines/1,000 inhabitants (1998)

■ TRANSPORTATION

Motor Vehicles: 21,000; 10,000 passenger cars (1997 est.)
Roads: 22,321 km; 3,502 km paved
Railway: none
Air Traffic: 125,000 passengers carried (1997)
Airports: 52; 9 have paved runways (1998 est.)

Canadian Embassy: The Canadian Embassy to Laos, c/o P.O. Box 2090, Bangkok 10501 Thailand. Tel: (011-66-2) 636-0540. Fax: (011-66-2) 636-0565.
Embassy in Canada: Embassy of the Lao People's Democratic Republic, 2222 S St NW, Washington DC 20008, USA. Tel: (202) 332-6416. Fax: (202) 332-4923.

Latvia

Long-Form Name: Republic of Latvia
Capital: Riga

■ GEOGRAPHY

Area: 64,589 sq. km
Coastline: 531 km
Climate: maritime, wet, moderate winters
Environment: air and water pollution, soil and groundwater contaminated with chemicals and petroleum products at military bases
Terrain: hilly, forested land with many lakes and shallow valleys
Land Use: 27% arable, negligible permanent crops, 13% meadows and pastures, 46% forest, 14% other; includes 160 sq. km irrigated
Location: NE Europe, bordering on Baltic Sea

■ PEOPLE

Population: 2,353,874 (July 1999 est.)
Nationality: Latvian
Age Structure: 0-14 yrs: 18%; 15-64: 67 %; 65+: 15% (1999 est.)
Population Growth Rate: -1.25% (1999 est.)
Net Migration: -4.75 migrants/1,000 population (1999 est.)
Ethnic Groups: 51.8% Latvian, 33.8% Russian, 4.5% Belorussian, 3.4% Ukrainian, 2.3% Polish, 4.2% other
Languages: Lettish (official), Lithuanian, Russian, some others
Religions: Lutheran, Catholic, Russian Orthodox
Birth Rate: 8.10/1,000 population (1999 est.)
Death Rate: 15.82/1,000 population (1999 est.)
Infant Mortality: 17.19 deaths/1,000 live births (1999 est.)
Life Expectancy at Birth: 61.24 years male, 73.66 years female (1999 est.)
Total Fertility Rate: 1.18 children born/woman (1999 est.)
Literacy: 99% (1997)

■ GOVERNMENT

Leader(s): Pres. Vaira Vike-Freiberga, Prime Min. Andris Berzins (acting)
Government Type: parliamentary democracy
Administrative Divisions: 26 counties (sing. - rajons) and 7 municipalities
Nationhood: Sept. 6, 1991 (from Soviet Union)
National Holiday: Independence Day, Nov. 18

■ ECONOMY

Overview: Latvia lacks natural resources, aside from its arable land and small forests; its most valuable economic asset is its workforce, which is better educated and disciplined than in most of the former Soviet republics. Latvia is rapidly moving towards a dynamic market economy, but the transition has seen dramatic declines in both GDP and industrial production
GDP: $9.7 billion, per capita $4,100; real growth rate 3.6% (1998 est.)
Inflation: 3.2% (March 2000)
Industries: accounts for 28% of GDP and 31% of labour force; manufacturing of railroad cars, paper, woolen goods, electronics and engineering, food processing
Labour Force: 1.0 million (1998); 41% industry, 16% forestry and agriculture, 43% services
Unemployment: 9.2% (1998), but large numbers of underemployed
Agriculture: accounts for 7% of GDP, employs 9% of labour force and has become largely privatized; poor soil hinders agriculture products including grain, beets, potatoes, cattle

and dairy farming, poultry, fishing
Natural Resources: forests, peat deposits, amber, dolomite

■ FINANCE/TRADE

Currency: lat = 100 santims
International Reserves Excluding Gold: $816 million (Jan. 2000)
Gold Reserves: 0.249 milllion fine troy ounces (Jan. 2000)
Budget: revenues $1.33 billion, expenditures $1.27 billion, including capital expenditures of n.a. (1998 est.)
Defence Expenditures: 2.60% of total govt. expenditure (1998)
Education Expenditures: 5.35% of govt. expenditure (1998)
External Debt: $756 million (1998)
Exports: $1.723 billion (1999); vehicles, household appliances, electric power; partners: Russia 21%, Germany 14%, UK 14%, Sweden 8%
Imports: $2.945 billion (1999): fuels, cars, chemicals and metal products; partners: Russia 16%, Germany 16%, Finland 10%, Sweden 8%

■ COMMUNICATIONS

Daily Newspapers: 24 (1996)
Televisions: 492/1,000 inhabitants (1998)
Radios: 710/1,000 inhabitants (1997)
Telephones: 302 lines/1,000 inhabitants (1998)

■ TRANSPORTATION

Motor Vehicles: n.a.
Roads: 55,942 km; 21,426 km paved
Railway: 2,412 km
Air Traffic: 229,000 passengers carried (1997)
Airports: 50; 36 have paved runways

Canadian Embassy: The Canadian Embassy, Doma Laukums 4, 4th Fl, Riga LV-1977. Tel. (011-371) 783-0141. Fax: (011-371) 783-1040.
Embassy in Canada: Embassy of the Republic of Latvia, 280 Albert St., Suite 300, Ottawa, ON, K1P 5G8. Tel: (613) 238-6014. Fax: (613) 238-7044.

Lebanon

Long-Form Name: Lebanese Republic
Capital: Beirut

■ GEOGRAPHY

Area: 10,400 sq. km
Coastline: 225 km
Climate: Mediterranean; mild to cool, wet winters with hot, dry summers
Environment: deforestation; soil erosion; air and water pollution; desertification
Terrain: narrow coastal plain; al Biqa' separates Lebanon and Anti-Lebanon Mountains; rugged terrain historically helped isolate, protect and develop numerous factional groups based on religion, clan and ethnicity.
Land Use: 21% arable; 9% permanent; 1% meadow; 8% forest; 61% other, includes 860 sq. km irrigated
Location: SW Asia (Middle East), bordering on Mediterranean Sea

■ PEOPLE

Population: 3,562,699 (July 1999 est.)
Nationality: Lebanese (sing. & pl.)
Age Structure: 0-14 yrs: 30%; 15-64: 64%; 65+: 6% (1999 est.)
Population Growth Rate: 1.61% (1999 est.)
Net Migration: 0 migrants/1,000 population (1999 est.)
Ethnic Groups: 95% Arab, 4% Armenian, 1% other
Languages: Arabic and French (both official); Armenian, English, Kurdish
Religions: Muslim 70% (Sunni, Shia and Druse), Christian 30% (mainly Maronite; also, Armenian, Greek and Syrian sects and Protestants)
Birth Rate: 22.50/1,000 population (1999 est.)
Death Rate: 6.45/1,000 population (1999 est.)
Infant Mortality: 30.53 deaths/1,000 live births (1999 est.)
Life Expectancy at Birth: 68.34 years male, 73.66 years female (1999 est.)
Total Fertility Rate: 2.25 children born/woman (1999 est.)
Literacy: 84.4% (1997)

■ GOVERNMENT

Leader(s): Pres. Emile Jamil Lahud; Prime Min. Salim Ahmad al-Huss
Government Type: republic
Administrative Divisions: 5 governorates (muhafazat, sing. -muhafazah)
Nationhood: Nov. 22, 1943 (from League of Nations mandate under French administration)
National Holiday: Independence Day, Nov. 22

■ ECONOMY

Overview: factional infighting has led to deterioration of the infrastructure and disrupted normal economic activity in what used to be the centre for Middle Eastern banking; high unemployment; growing shortages; international aid is vital
GDP: $15.8 billion, per capita $4,500; real

growth rate 3% (1998 est.)
Inflation: 13.8% (Feb. 1997)
Industries: accounts for 23% of GDP; banking, food processing, textiles, cement, oil refining, chemicals, jewelry, some metal fabricating
Labour Force: 1 million (1998); 27.4% industry, 58.4% services, 14.3% agriculture
Unemployment: 18% (1997 est.)
Agriculture: accounts for about 4% of GDP; principal products—citrus fruit, vegetables, potatoes, olives, tobacco, hemp (hashish), sheep and goats; not self-sufficient in grain
Natural Resources: limestone, iron ore, salt; water-surplus state in a water-deficit region

■ FINANCE/TRADE

Currency: Lebanese pound (£L) = 100 piasters
International Reserves Excluding Gold: $7.625 billion (Jan. 2000)
Gold Reserves: 9.222 milllion fine troy ounces (Jan. 2000)
Budget: revenues $4.9 billion; expenditures $7.9 billion, including capital expenditures of n.a. (1998 est.)
Defence Expenditures: 9.66% of total govt. expenditure (1998)
Education Expenditures: 8.30% of total govt. expenditure (1998)
External Debt: $6.725 billion (1998)
Exports: $677 million (1999); commodities: agricultural products, chemicals, textiles, metals and jewelry; partners: 21% Saudi Arabia, 9.5% Switzerland, 6% Jordan, 12% Kuwait, 5% US
Imports: $6.207 billion (1999); commodities: consumer goods, machinery and transport equipment, petroleum products; partners: 14% Italy, 12% France, 6% US, 5% Turkey, 3% Saudi Arabia

■ COMMUNICATIONS

Daily Newspapers: 15 (1996)
Televisions: 352/1,000 inhabitants (1998)
Radios: 906/1,000 inhabitants (1997)
Telephones: 194 lines/1,000 inhabitants (1998)

■ TRANSPORTATION

Motor Vehicles: n.a.
Roads: 6,270 km; all paved
Railway: 222 km; railroad system in disrepair, considered inoperable
Air Traffic: 857,000 passengers carried (1997)
Airports: 9; 7 have paved runways (1998 est.)

Canadian Embassy: The Canadian Embassy, Coolrite Building, 434 Autostrade, Jal-ed-Dib, Lebanon; mailing address: P.O. Box 60163, Jal-el-Dib, Beirut, Lebanon. Tel: (011-961-4) 713-900. Fax: (011-961-4) 710-595.
Embassy in Canada: Embassy of the Lebanese Republic, 640 Lyon St, Ottawa ON K1S 3Z5. Tel: (613) 236-5825. Fax: (613) 232-1609.

Lesotho

Long-Form Name: Kingdom of Lesotho
Capital: Maseru

■ GEOGRAPHY

Area: 30,350 sq. km
Coastline: none: landlocked
Climate: temperate; cool to cold, dry winters; hot, wet summers
Environment: population pressure forcing settlement in marginal agricultural areas results in overgrazing, severe soil erosion, soil exhaustion; desertification
Terrain: mostly highland with some plateaus, hills and mountains
Land Use: 11% arable; 0% permanent; 66% meadows; 0% forest; 23% other; includes 30 sq. km irrigated
Location: S Africa

■ PEOPLE

Population: 2,128,950 (July 1999 est.)
Nationality: Mosotho (sing.), Basotho (pl.)
Age Structure: 0-14 yrs: 40%; 15-64: 56%; 65+: 4% (1999 est.)
Population Growth Rate: 1.80% (1999 est.)
Net Migration: 0 migrants/1,000 population (1998 est.)
Ethnic Groups: 99.7% Sotho; 1,600 Europeans, 800 Asians
Languages: Sesotho (southern Sotho) and English (official); also Zulu and Xhosa
Religions: 80% Christian, indigenous beliefs
Birth Rate: 31.26/1,000 population (1999 est.)
Death Rate: 13.23/1,000 population (1999 est.)
Infant Mortality: 77.58 deaths/1,000 live births (1999 est.)
Life Expectancy at Birth: 51.37 years male, 54.65 years female (1999 est.)
Total Fertility Rate: 4.03 children born/woman (1999 est.)
Literacy: 71.3% (1997)

■ GOVERNMENT

Leader(s): King Letsie III, Prime Min. Pakalitha Mosisili. Election scheduled March 2001.
Government Type: parliamentary constitutional monarchy
Administrative Divisions: 10 districts
Nationhood: Oct. 4, 1966 (from UK: formerly known as Basutoland)

National Holiday: Independence Day, Oct. 4

ECONOMY

Overview: the economy is hampered by the geography of the country (small, landlocked and mountainous) and the lack of natural resources other than water; subsistence farming is the main occupation; labourers in South Africa make remittances; industry is growing in importance
GDP: $5.1 billion, per capita $2,400; real growth rate 10% (1997)
Inflation: 6.3% (March 2000)
Industries: accounts for 42% of GDP; light manufacturing, milling, canning, leather, jute production, textiles, clothing, light engineering, food, beverages, handicrafts, tourism
Labour Force: 1 million (1998); 23.3% agriculture, 33.1% industry, 43.6% services
Unemployment: substantial unemployment and underemployment
Agriculture: accounts for 14% of GDP; very primitive, mostly subsistence farming and livestock; principal crops are corn, wheat, pulses, sorghum and barley
Natural Resources: some diamonds and other minerals, water, agricultural and grazing land

FINANCE/TRADE

Currency: loti, maloti (pl.) = 100 lisente
International Reserves Excluding Gold: $493 million (Jan. 2000)
Gold Reserves: n.a.
Budget: revenues $507 million; expenditures $487 million, including capital expenditures of $170 million (1996-97 est.)
Defence Expenditures: 6.54% of central government expenditure (1998)
Education Expenditures: 26.71% of central government expenditure (1998)
External Debt: $692 million (1998)
Exports: $194 million (1998); commodities: wool, mohair, wheat, cattle, peas, beans, corn, hides, skins, baskets; partners: South Africa 53%, European Community 30%, North and South America 13%
Imports: $863 million (1998).; commodities: corn, building materials, clothing, vehicles, machinery, medicines, petroleum, oil and lubricants; partners: South Africa 95%, European Community 2%

COMMUNICATIONS

Daily Newspapers: 2 (1996)
Televisions: 25/1,000 inhabitants (1998)
Radios: 49/1,000 inhabitants (1997)
Telephones: 10 lines/1,000 inhabitants (1998)

TRANSPORTATION

Motor Vehicles: n.a.
Roads: 4,955 km; 887 km paved
Railway: 2.6 km, owned, operated by, and included in the statistics for South Africa
Air Traffic: 10,000 passengers carried (1997)
Airports: 29; 4 have paved runways (1998 est.)

Canadian Embassy: The Canadian High Commission to Lesotho, c/o Canadian Embassy, Private Bag X13, Hatfield 0028, Pretoria, South Africa. Also, consulate in Maseru: Canadian Consulate, 1st Floor, Maseru Book Centre, Kingsway, Box 1165, Maseru, Lesotho. Tel: (011-266) 316-435. Fax: (011-266) 310-462.
Embassy in Canada: c/o High Commission for the Kingdom of Lesotho, 2511 Massachusetts Ave NW, Washington DC 20008, USA. Tel: (202) 797-5533. Fax: (202) 234-6815.

Liberia

Long-Form Name: Republic of Liberia
Capital: Monrovia

GEOGRAPHY

Area: 111,370 sq. km
Coastline: 579 km
Climate: tropical; hot, humid; dry winters with hot days and cool to cold nights; wet, cloudy summers with frequent heavy showers
Environment: West Africa's largest tropical rain forest, subject to deforestation; soil erosion is increasingly a problem; river pollution
Terrain: mostly flat to rolling coastal plains rising to rolling plateau and low mountains in northeast
Land Use: 1% arable; 3% permanent; 59% permanent pastures; 18% forest; 19% other; includes 20 sq. km irrigated
Location: W Africa, bordering on South Atlantic Ocean

PEOPLE

Population: 2,923,725 (July 1999 est.)
Nationality: Liberian
Age Structure: 0-14 yrs: 45%; 15-64: 52%; 65+: 3% (1999 est.)
Population Growth Rate: 4.92% (1999 est.)
Net Migration: 18.77 migrants/1,000 population (1999 est.)
Ethnic Groups: 95% indigenous African tribes, including Kpelle, Bassa, Gio, Kru, Grego, Mano, Krahn, Gola, Gbandi, Lom, Kissi, Vai and Bella; 5% descendants of repatriated slaves known as Americo-Liberians

Languages: English (official); 20 local languages of the Niger-Congo language group; English used by approx. 20%
Religions: 70% traditional, 20% Muslim, 10% Christian
Birth Rate: 41.49/1,000 population (1999 est.)
Death Rate: 11.03/1,000 population (1999 est.)
Infant Mortality: 100.63 deaths/1,000 live births (1999 est.)
Life Expectancy at Birth: 57.20 years male, 62.64 years female (1999 est.)
Total Fertility Rate: 6.02 children born/woman (1999 est.)
Literacy: 48.4% (1997)

■ GOVERNMENT

Leader(s): Pres. Charles Taylor
Government Type: republic
Administrative Divisions: 13 counties
Nationhood: July 26, 1847
National Holiday: Independence Day, July 26

■ ECONOMY

Overview: Civil war since 1990 has destroyed much of Liberia's economy, especially the infrastructure in and around Monrovia. Many business people have fled the country, taking capital and expertise with them. The government must encourage foreign investment to restore the infrastructure and to raise incomes.
GDP: $2.8 billion, per capita $1,000; real growth rate n.a. (1998 est.)
Inflation: n.a.
Industries: accounts for 36% of GDP; rubber processing, food processing, construction materials, furniture, palm oil processing, mining (iron ore, diamonds)
Labour Force: n.a; 74.2% agriculture, 16.4% services, 9.4% industry
Unemployment: 70%
Agriculture: accounts for 30% of GDP (including fishing and forestry); principal products—rubber, timber, coffee, cocoa, rice, cassava, palm oil, sugar cane, bananas, sheep and goats; not self-sufficient in food, imports 25% of rice consumption
Natural Resources: iron ore, timber, diamonds, gold

■ FINANCE/TRADE

Currency: Liberian dollar ($L) = 100 cents
International Reserves Excluding Gold: n.a.
Gold Reserves: n.a.
Budget: n.a.
Defence Expenditures: 29% of GDP (1998)
Education Expenditures: n.a.
External Debt: $2 billion (1997 est.)
Exports: $1.1 billion (1998 est.); commodities: diamonds, iron ore, rubber, timber, coffee; partners: US, EU, Netherlands, Singapore
Imports: $3.65 billion (1998 est.); commodities: mineral fuels, chemicals, machinery, foodstuffs; partners: EU, US, Japan, China, Netherlands

■ COMMUNICATIONS

Daily Newspapers: 6 (1996)
Televisions: 27/1,000 inhabitants (1996)
Radios: 318/1,000 inhabitants (1996)
Telephones: 2 lines/1,000 inhabitants (1998)

■ TRANSPORTATION

Motor Vehicles: 28,700; 17,800 passenger cars (1997 est.)
Roads: 10,037 km; 603 km paved
Railway: 480 km
Air Traffic: n.a.
Airports: 45; 2 have paved runways (1998 est.)

Canadian Embassy: The Canadian Embassy to Liberia, c/o Canadian Embassy, P O Box 4104, Abidjan 01, Cote d'Ivoire. Tel: (011-225) 20-21-20-09. Fax: (011-225) 20-21-77-28.
Embassy in Canada: consular address: Consulate of Liberia, 18 Old Yonge St., Toronto, ON, M2P 1P7, Tel: (416) 385-0194. Fax: (416) 322-4996.

Libya

Long-Form Name: Socialist People's Libyan Arab Jamahiriya
Capital: Tripoli

■ GEOGRAPHY

Area: 1,759,540 sq. km
Coastline: 1,770 km
Climate: Mediterranean along coast; dry, extreme desert interior
Environment: hot, dry, dust-laden ghibli is a southern wind lasting one to four days in spring and fall; desertification; dust storms; sparse natural surface-water resources
Terrain: mostly barren, flat to undulating plains, plateaus, depressions
Land Use: 1% arable; 0% permanent; 8% meadows; 0% forest; 91% other; includes 4,700 sq. km irrigated
Location: N Africa, bordering on Mediterranean Sea

■ PEOPLE

Population: 4,992,838 (July 1999 est.)
Nationality: Libyan

Age Structure: 0-14 yrs: 36%; 15-64: 60%; 65+: 4% (1999 est.)
Population Growth Rate: 2.40% (1999 est.)
Net Migration: 0 migrants/1,000 population (1999 est.)
Ethnic Groups: 97% Berber and Arab; some Greeks, Maltese, Italians, Egyptians, Pakistanis, Turks, Indians and Tunisians
Languages: Arabic (official); Italian and English widely understood in major cities, Berber
Religions: 97% Sunni Muslim, 3% Christian and other
Birth Rate: 27.33/1,000 population (1999 est.)
Death Rate: 3.35/1,000 population (1999 est.)
Infant Mortality: 28.15 deaths/1,000 live births (1999 est.)
Life Expectancy at Birth: 73.81 years male, 77.74 years female (1999 est.)
Total Fertility Rate: 3.79 children born/woman (1999 est.)
Literacy: 76.5% (1997)

■ **GOVERNMENT**

Leader(s): Leader Col. Mu'ammar Abu Minyar al-Qadhafi. Sec. of Gen. People's Congress Muhammad al-Zanati
Government Type: Jamahiriya (a state of the masses); in theory, governed by the populace through local councils; in fact, a military dictatorship
Administrative Divisions: 25 municipalities (baladiyat, sing. -baladiyah)
Nationhood: Dec. 24, 1951 (from Italy)
National Holiday: Revolution Day, Sept. 1

■ **ECONOMY**

Overview: a socialist-oriented economy that depends largely on revenues from the oil sector; cutbacks on imports due to declining oil revenues have led to shortages of foodstuffs and basic goods; must import 75% of its food needs, as poor soil and climate limit agricultural production
GDP: $38 billion, per capita $6,700; real growth rate -1% (1998 est.)
Inflation: n.a.
Industries: accounts for 55% of GDP; petroleum, food processing, textiles, handicrafts, cement
Labour Force: 2 million (1998); 28.9% industry, 53% services, 18.1% agriculture
Unemployment: 30% (1998 est.)
Agriculture: accounts for 5% of GDP; cash crops— wheat, barley, olives, dates, citrus fruit, peanuts; 75% of food is imported
Natural Resources: crude oil, natural gas, gypsum

■ **FINANCE/TRADE**

Currency: Libyan dinar (LD) = 1,000 dirhams
International Reserves Excluding Gold: $7.040 billion (Jan. 2000)
Gold Reserves: n.a.
Budget: revenues $3.6 billion; expenditures $5.1 billion, including capital expenditures of n.a. (1998 est.)
Defence Expenditures: 19.7% of central government expenditure (1997)
Education Expenditures: n.a.
External Debt: $4 billion (1998 est.)
Exports: $6.659 billion (1998); commodities: petroleum, peanuts, hides; partners: Italy, former USSR countries, Germany, Spain, France, Belgium/Luxembourg, Turkey
Imports: $5.466 billion (1998); commodities: machinery, transport equipment, food, manufactured goods; partners: Italy, former USSR countries, Germany, UK, Japan

■ **COMMUNICATIONS**

Daily Newspapers: 4 (1996)
Televisions: 126/1,000 inhabitants (1998)
Radios: 233/1,000 inhabitants (1997)
Telephones: 84 lines/1,000 inhabitants (1998)

■ **TRANSPORTATION**

Motor Vehicles: 904,000; 592,000 passenger cars (1997 est.)
Roads: 83,200 km; 47,590 km paved
Railway: no railroads in operation since 1965
Air Traffic: 571,000 passengers carried (1997)
Airports: 143; 60 have paved runways (1998 est.)

Canadian Embassy: The Canadian Embassy to Libya, c/o Canadian Embassy, CP 31, Belvédère, 1002, Tunis-Belvedere, Tunisia. Tel: (011-216-1) 796-577. Fax: (011-216-1) 792-371.
Embassy in Canada: Embassy of the Socialist People's Libyan Arab Jamahiriya, 309–315 East 48th St, New York NY 10017, USA. Tel: (212) 752-5775. Fax: (212) 593-4787.

Liechtenstein

Long-Form Name: Principality of Liechtenstein
Capital: Vaduz

■ **GEOGRAPHY**

Area: 160 sq. km
Coastline: none: landlocked
Climate: continental; cold, cloudy winters with frequent snow or rain; cool to moderately warm, cloudy, humid summers

Environment: variety of microclimatic variations based on elevation
Terrain: mostly mountainous (Alps) with Rhine Valley in western third
Land Use: 24% arable; 0% permanent; 16% meadows; 35% forest; 25% other; includes n.a. sq. km irrigated
Location: C Europe, bordering on Switzerland and Austria

■ PEOPLE

Population: 32,057 (July 1999 est.)
Nationality: Liechtensteiner
Age Structure: 0-14 yrs: 19%; 15-64: 70%; 65+: 11% (1999 est.)
Population Growth Rate: 1.08% (1999 est.)
Net Migration: 5.9 migrants/1,000 population (1999 est.)
Ethnic Groups: 95% Alemannic, 5% Italian and other
Languages: German (official), also Alemannic dialect
Religions: 87.3% Roman Catholic, 8.3% Protestant, 2.8% other, 1.6% unknown
Birth Rate: 12.23/1,000 population (1999 est.)
Death Rate: 7.33/1,000 population (1999 est.)
Infant Mortality: 5.23 deaths/1,000 live births (1999 est.)
Life Expectancy at Birth: 75.64 years male, 80.69 years female (1999 est.)
Total Fertility Rate: 1.60 children born/woman (1999 est.)
Literacy: 100% (1997)

■ GOVERNMENT

Leader(s): Head of State: Prince Hans Adam II von und zu Liechtenstein. Prime Min. Mario Frick
Government Type: hereditary constitutional monarchy
Administrative Divisions: 11 communes (gemeinden, sing. -gemeinde)
Nationhood: Jan. 23, 1719, Imperial Principality of Liechtenstein established
National Holiday: Assumption Day, Aug. 15

■ ECONOMY

Overview: a prosperous economy based mainly on small-scale light industry and some farming; economy closely tied to that of Switzerland in a customs union; known for low business taxes and easy incorporation rules
GDP: $730 million, per capita $23,000; real growth rate n.a. (1998 est.)
Inflation: n.a.
Industries: electronics, metal manufacturing, textiles, ceramics, pharmaceuticals, food products, precision instruments, tourism

Labour Force: 22,891 (1996 est.), of which 13,847 are foreigners; 46% industry, trade and building, 52% services, 2% agriculture, fishing, forestry and horticulture
Unemployment: 1.6% (1997 est.)
Agriculture: livestock, vegetables, corn, wheat, potatoes, grapes
Natural Resources: hydroelectric potential

■ FINANCE/TRADE

Currency: Swiss franc, franken, or franco (SwF) = 100 centimes, rappen, or centesimi
International Reserves Excluding Gold: n.a.
Gold Reserves: n.a.
Budget: revenues $455 million; expenditures $435 million, including capital expenditures n.a. (1996 est.)
Defence Expenditures: defence is the responsibility of Switzerland
Education Expenditures: n.a.
External Debt: none (1996)
Exports: $2.47 billion (1996); small speciality machinery, dental products, stamps, hardware, pottery; partners: EU and EFTA countries, especially Switzerland
Imports: $917.3 million (1996); commodities: machinery, metal goods, textiles, foodstuffs, motor vehicles; partners: EU countries, Switzerland

■ COMMUNICATIONS

Daily Newspapers: 2 (1996)
Televisions: 342/1,000 inhabitants (1996)
Radios: 668/1,000 inhabitants (1996)
Telephones: 630 lines/1,000 inhabitants (1998)

■ TRANSPORTATION

Motor Vehicles: n.a.
Roads: 250 km; all paved
Railway: 18.5 km, owned, operated, and included in statistics for Austria
Air Traffic: n.a.
Airports: none

Canadian Embassy: The Canadian Embassy to Liechtenstein, c/o the Canadian Embassy, P.O. Box 3000, Berne 6, Switzerland. Tel: (011-41-31) 357-32-00. Fax: (011-41-31) 357-32-10.
Embassy in Canada: Embassy of Liechtenstein, c/o Embassy of Switzerland, 5 Marlborough Ave, Ottawa ON K1N 8E6. Tel: (613) 235-1837. Fax: (613) 563-1394.

Lithuania

Long-Form Name: Republic of Lithuania
Capital: Vilnius

Lithuania

■ GEOGRAPHY

Area: 65,200 sq. km
Coastline: 99 km
Climate: transitional, between maritime and continental; mild, with moderate precipitation
Environment: risk of accidents from the two Chernobyl-type reactors; at military bases, contamination of soil and groundwater with chemicals and petroleum products
Terrain: undulating glacial terrain; rivers, lakes, and swamps predominate
Land Use: 35% arable; 12% permanent crops; 7% permanent pastures; 31% forest; 15% other; includes 430 sq. km irrigated
Location: NE Europe, bordering on Baltic Sea

■ PEOPLE

Population: 3,584,966 (July 1999 est.)
Nationality: Lithuanian
Age Structure: 0-14 yrs: 20%; 15-64: 67%; 65+: 13% (1999 est.)
Population Growth Rate: -0.40% (1999 est.)
Net Migration: -1.58 migrants/1,000 population (1999 est.)
Ethnic Groups: 80.1% Lithuanian, 8.6% Russian, 7.7% Polish, 1.5% Byelorussian, 2.1% other
Languages: Lithuanian (official), Russian, Polish
Religions: predominantly Protestant, Roman Catholic, Russian Orthodox
Birth Rate: 10.52/1,000 population (1999 est.)
Death Rate: 12.93/1,000 population (1999 est.)
Infant Mortality: 14.71 deaths/1,000 live births (1999 est.)
Life Expectancy at Birth: 62.91 years male, 75.31 years female (1999 est.)
Total Fertility Rate: 1.45 children born/woman (1999 est.)
Literacy: 99% (1997)

■ GOVERNMENT

Leader(s): Pres. Valdas Adamkus, Prime Min. Andrius Kubilius
Government Type: parliamentary democracy
Administrative Divisions: 44 regions (rajonai, sing. -rajonas) and 11 municipalities
Nationhood: Sept. 6, 1991 (from Soviet Union)
National Holiday: Statehood Day, Feb. 16

■ ECONOMY

Overview: arable land and strategic location are Lithuania's only important natural resources; Lithuania remains highly dependent on Russia for energy, raw materials, grains and markets for its products
GDP: $17.6 billion, per capita $4,900; real growth rate 4.5% (1998 est.)
Inflation: 0.3% (Dec. 1999)
Industries: accounts for 32% of GDP and employs 42% of labour force; heavy engineering, shipbuilding, production of building materials, nuclear and electric power production; electric motors, television sets, appliances, refining, fertilizer
Labour Force: 2 million (1998); 26.9% industry, 22% community, social and business services, 19% agriculture
Unemployment: 8.4% (Sept. 1999); large numbers of underemployed
Agriculture: accounts for 13% of GDP and employs approximately 18% of labour force; beef and dairy cattle and related products, pigs, poultry, grains, flax, potatoes and other vegetables, eggs, fish, dairy products; net exporter of meat, milk and eggs
Natural Resources: amber, oil reserves, peat

■ FINANCE/TRADE

Currency: litas (pl. litai) = 100 centas
International Reserves Excluding Gold: $1.133 billion (Jan. 2000)
Gold Reserves: 0.186 million fine troy ounces (Jan. 2000)
Budget: revenues $1.5 billion; expenditures $1.7 billion, including capital expenditures of n.a. (1997 est.)
Defence Expenditures: 3.10% of govt. expenditure (1998)
Education Expenditures: 6.05% of govt. expenditure (1998)
External Debt: $1.95 billion (1998)
Exports: $3.711 billion (1998); 18% electronics, 5% petroleum products, 10% food, 6% chemicals; partners: 40% Russia, 16% Ukraine, 32% other former Soviet republics, 12% West
Imports: $5.794 billion (1998); 24% oil, 14% machinery, 8% chemicals, grain; partners: 62% Russia, 18% Belarus, 10% other former Soviet republics, 10% West (1989)

■ COMMUNICATIONS

Daily Newspapers: 19 (1996)
Televisions: 459/1,000 inhabitants (1998)
Radios: 513/1,000 inhabitants (1997)
Telephones: 300 lines/1,000 inhabitants (1998)

■ TRANSPORTATION

Motor Vehicles: n.a.
Roads: 68,161 km; 60,527 km paved
Railway: 2,002 km
Air Traffic: 237,200 passengers carried (1997)
Airports: 96; 25 have paved runways

Canadian Embassy: Office of the Canadian Embassy, Gedimino pr. 64, 2001 Vilnius,

Lithuania. Tel: (011-370-2) 220-898. Fax: (011-370-2) 220-884.
Embassy in Canada: Embassy of the Republic of Lithuania, 130 Albert St, Ste 204, Ottawa, ON K1P 5G4. Tel: (613) 567-5458. Fax: (613) 567-5315.

Luxembourg

Long-Form Name: Grand Duchy of Luxembourg
Capital: Luxembourg

■ GEOGRAPHY

Area: 2,586 sq. km
Coastline: none: landlocked
Climate: modified continental with mild winters, cool summers
Environment: deforestation; air and water pollution in urban areas
Terrain: mostly gently rolling uplands with broad, shallow valleys; uplands to slightly mountainous in the north; steep slope down to Moselle floodplain in the southeast
Land Use: 24% arable; 1% permanent; 20% meadows; 21% forest; 34% other; including 10 sq. km irrigated shared with Belgium
Location: NC Europe, bordering on Belgium, France and Germany

■ PEOPLE

Population: 429,080 (July 1999 est.)
Nationality: Luxembourger
Age Structure: 0-14 yrs: 18%; 15-64: 67%; 65+: 15% (1999 est.)
Population Growth Rate: 0.88% (1999 est.)
Net Migration: 7.78 migrants/1,000 population (1999 est.)
Ethnic Groups: Celtic base, with French and German blend; also guest and worker residents
Languages: Luxembourgisch (official), German (written language of commerce and press), French (administrative), English
Religions: 97% Roman Catholic, 3% Protestant and Jewish
Birth Rate: 10.35/1,000 population (1999 est.)
Death Rate: 9.32/1,000 population (1999 est.)
Infant Mortality: 4.99 deaths/1,000 live births (1999 est.)
Life Expectancy at Birth: 74.58 years male, 80.83 years female (1999 est.)
Total Fertility Rate: 1.57 children born/woman (1999 est.)
Literacy: 99% (1997)

■ GOVERNMENT

Leader(s): Head of State: Jean, Grand Duke of Luxembourg. Prime Min. Jean-Claude Juncker

Government Type: constitutional monarchy
Administrative Divisions: 3 districts
Nationhood: 1839 (Grand Duchy)
National Holiday: National Day (public celebration of the Grand Duke's birthday), June 23

■ ECONOMY

Overview: a stable economy featuring moderate growth, low inflation and negligible unemployment; is in an economic union with Belgium for trade and most financial matters and is also closely connected economically with the Netherlands; financial sector is strong; industrial sector is becoming increasingly diversified
GDP: $13.9 billion, per capita $32,700; real growth rate 2.9% (1998 est.)
Inflation: 2.8% (March 2000)
Industries: accounts for 22% of GDP; banking, iron and steel, food processing, chemicals, metal products, engineering, tires, glass, aluminum
Labour Force: 171,600 (1996); 14% community, social and business services, 20% trade and tourism, mining and manufacturing 16%, construction 11%, transportation and communication 8%, other 42%
Unemployment: 3.0% (Jan. 2000)
Agriculture: accounts for only 1% of GDP (including forestry); principal products—barley, oats, potatoes, wheat, fruits, wine grapes; cattle-raising widespread
Natural Resources: iron ore (no longer exploited)

■ FINANCE/TRADE

Currency: Luxembourg franc (LuxF) = 100 centimes [As of Jan. 1, 1999, Government securities are issued in Euros (EUR)]
International Reserves Excluding Gold: $77 million (Jan. 2000)
Gold Reserves: 0.076 million fine troy ounces (Jan. 2000)
Budget: revenues $5.46 billion; expenditures $5.44 billion, including capital expenditures n.a. (1997 est.)
Defence Expenditures: n.a.
Education Expenditures: n.a
External Debt: n.a.
Exports: $7.887 billion (1999); commodities: finished steel products, chemicals, rubber products, glass, aluminum, other industrial products; partners: European Community 75%, US 6%
Imports: $2.989 billion (1999); commodities: minerals, metals, foodstuffs, quality consumer goods; partners: Germany 40%, Belgium 35%, France 15%, US 3%

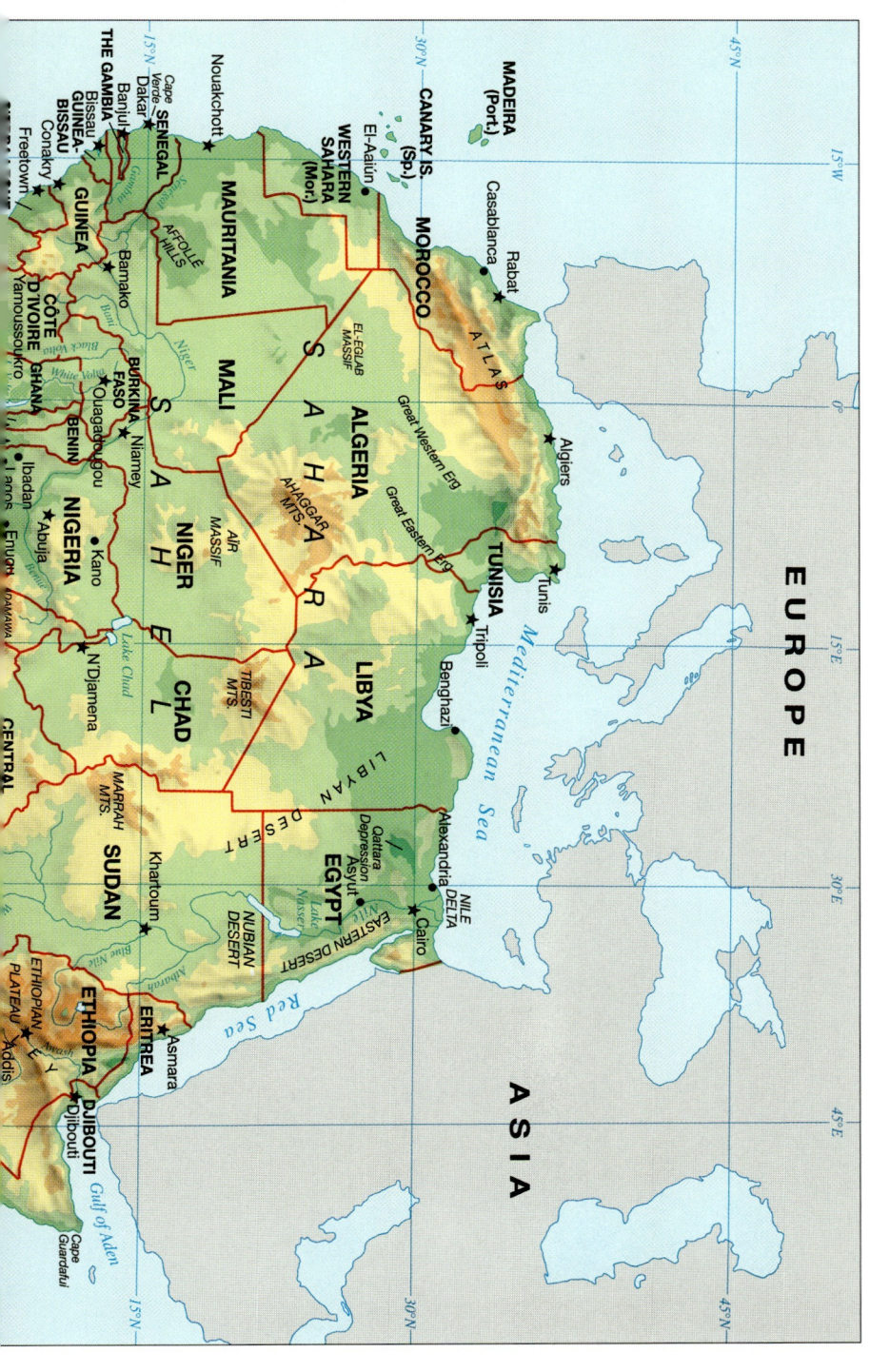

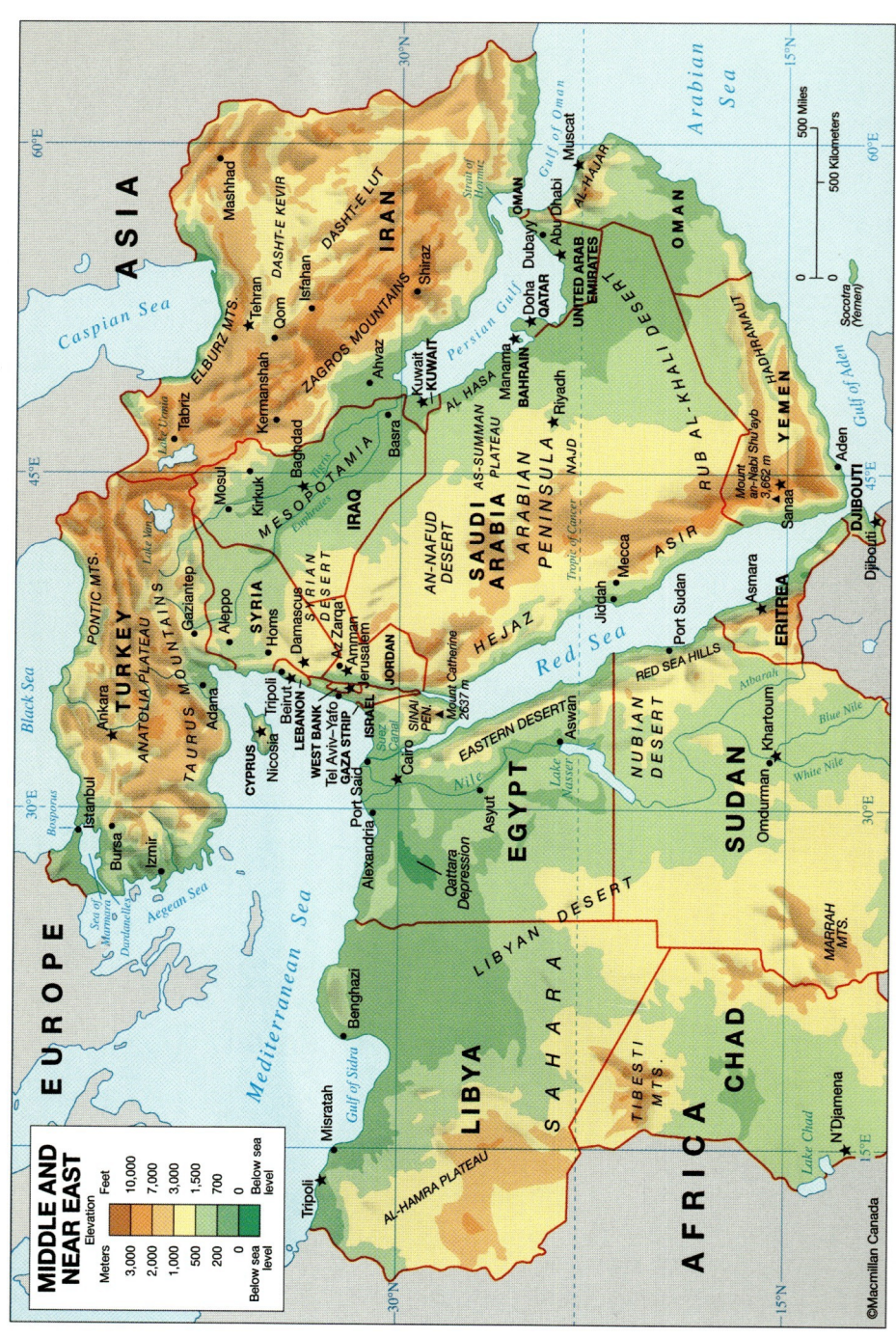

COMMUNICATIONS

Daily Newspapers: 5 (1996)
Televisions: 387/1,000 inhabitants (1996)
Radios: 678/1,000 inhabitants (1996)
Telephones: 692 lines/1,000 inhabitants (1998)

TRANSPORTATION

Motor Vehicles: 251,000; 233,000 passenger cars (1997 est.)
Roads: 5,137 km; 5,086 km paved
Railway: 275 km
Air Traffic: 560,000 passengers carried (1997)
Airports: 2; 1 has paved runways (1998 est.)

Canadian Embassy: The Canadian Embassy to Luxembourg, c/o 2, Avenue de Tervuren, 1040 Brussels, Belgium. Tel: (011-32-2) 741-0611. Fax: (011-32-2) 741-0643. Office: The Consulate of Canada, c/o Price Waterhouse and Co., 400 Route d'Esch, L-1471 Luxembourg Tel: (011-35-2) 40-24-20201. Fax: (011-35-2) 40-24-206155.
Embassy in Canada: Embassy of the Grand Duchy of Luxembourg, 2200 Massachusetts Ave NW, Washington DC 20008, USA. Tel: (202) 265-4171. Fax: (202) 328-8270.

Macau

Long-Form Name: Macau
Capital: Macau

GEOGRAPHY

Area: 21 sq. km (a peninsula and three small islands)
Climate: subtropical maritime; marine with cool winters, warm summers
Land Use: almost 100% built-up; almost no agricultural lands or fresh water resources
Location: SE coast of China, bordering on South China Sea

PEOPLE

Population: 437,312 (July 1999 est.)
Nationality: Macanese (sing. & pl.)
Ethnic Groups: Chinese 95%, Portuguese 3%, other 2%
Languages: Portuguese (official), Cantonese, English widely spoken

GOVERNMENT

Colony/Territory of: Special Administrative Region of China (as of Dec. 1999)
Leader(s): Pres. (China) Jiang Zemin, Prem. (China) Hu Jintao
Government Type: overseas territory of Portugal scheduled to revert to China in 1999
National Holiday: Day of Portugal, June 10

ECONOMY

Overview: gambling and tourism; industry confined to textiles, fireworks, toy-making, plastics; imports almost all energy, food and water from China

FINANCE/TRADE

Currency: pataca (pl. patacas) = 100 avos

Canadian Embassy: The Canadian Consulate General, c/o The Office of the Consulate General for Canada, P.O. Box 11142, Hong Kong Special Administrative Region, PR China. Tel: (011-86-10) 6532-3536. Fax: (011-86-10) 6532-4311.
Representative to Canada: none

Macedonia

Long-Form Name: The Former Yugoslav Republic of Macedonia
Capital: Skopje

GEOGRAPHY

Area: 25,333 sq. km
Coastline: none: landlocked
Climate: hot, dry summers and autumns; winters relatively cold with heavy snowfall
Environment: high earthquake hazard; air pollution from metallurgical plants
Terrain: mountainous, with deep valleys and basins; three large lakes
Land Use: 24% arable land, 2% permanent crops, 25% permanent pastures, 39% forests, 10% other; includes 830 sq. km irrigated
Location: SE Europe

PEOPLE

Population: 2,022,604 (July 1999 est.)
Nationality: Macedonian
Age Structure: 0-14 yrs: 23%; 15-64: 67%; 65+: 10% (1999 est.)
Population Growth Rate: 0.64% (1999 est.)
Net Migration: -.0.83 migrants/1,000 population (1999 est.)
Ethnic Groups: 65% Macedonian, 22% Albanian, 4% Turkish, 2% Serb, 3% Gypsies, 4% other
Languages: 70% Macedonian, 21% Albanian, 3% Turkish, 3% Serbo-Croatian, 3% other
Religions: 67% Eastern Orthodox, 30% Muslim, 3% other
Birth Rate: 15.21/1,000 population (1999 est.)
Death Rate: 8.03/1,000 population (1999 est.)

Infant Mortality: 18.68 deaths/1,000 live births (1999 est.)
Life Expectancy at Birth: 70.93 years male, 75.34 years female (1999 est.)
Total Fertility Rate: 2.00 children born/woman (1999 est.)
Literacy: 94% (1997)

■ GOVERNMENT

Leader(s): Pres. Boris Trajkovski, Prime Min. Ljubco Georgievski
Government Type: emerging democracy
Administrative Divisions: 34 counties (opstinas, sing. -opstina)
Nationhood: Sept. 17, 1991 (from Yugoslavia)
National Holiday: Sept. 8

■ ECONOMY

Overview: although it is the poorest of the six republics of the dissolved Yugoslav federation, Macedonia can meet its basic food requirements; new economic ties are necessary, however, to keep living standards from falling to a bare subsistence level; all oil, gas, modern machinery and parts must be imported; continued political upheaval prevents return to settled economic conditions. An important supplement to GDP is the remittances from thousands of Macedonians working in Germany and other West European countries. Continued recovery depends on Macedonia's ability to attract investment, to redevelop trade ties with Greece and Serbia and Montenegro, and to maintain its commitment to economic liberalization.
GDP: $2.1 billion, per capita $1,050; real growth rate 4.5% (1998 est.)
Inflation: -3.1% (March 1999)
Industries: accounts for 39% of GDP; level of technology is generally low; basic liquid fuels, coal, metallic chromium, lead, zinc; Macedonia is one of the seven legal cultivators of the opium poppy for the world pharmaceutical industry
Labour Force: 1 million (1998); 35.2% industry, 20.2% community, social and business services, 11.6% trade and tourism
Unemployment: 30% (1998 est.)
Agriculture: highly labour-intensive; accounts for 20% of GDP. Rice, tobacco, corn, millet and wheat are the chief crops
Natural Resources: chromium, lead, zinc, manganese, tungsten, nickel, timber

■ FINANCE/TRADE

Currency: denar = 100 deni
International Reserves Excluding Gold: $415 million (Jan. 2000)
Gold Reserves: 0.102 million fine troy ounces (Jan. 2000)
Budget: revenues $1.06 billion; expenditures $1.06 billion, including capital expenditures of n.a. (1996 est.)
Defence Expenditures: 2.2% of GDP (1998)
Education Expenditures: 5.1% of GNP (1997)
External Debt: $2.392 billion (1998)
Exports: $1.315 billion (1999 est.); manufactured goods, machinery and transportation equipment, raw materials, food and livestock, tobacco and beverages, chemicals; partners: mostly the former Yugoslav republics, Germany, Albania, Greece
Imports: $1.934 billion (1999 est.); fuel and lubricants, machinery and transport equipment, food and livestock, chemicals, raw materials, manufactures; partners: other former Yugoslav republics, Germany, Albania, Greece, Bulgaria

■ COMMUNICATIONS

Daily Newspapers: 3 (1996)
Televisions: 250/1,000 inhabitants (1998)
Radios: 200/1,000 inhabitants (1997)
Telephones: 199 lines/1,000 inhabitants (1998)

■ TRANSPORTATION

Motor Vehicles: n.a.
Roads: 10,591 km; 5,500 km paved
Railway: 922 km
Air Traffic: 229,000 passengers carried (1997)
Airports: 16; 10 have paved runways (1998 est.)

Canadian Embassy: Office of the Canadian Embassy, 12-ta Udarna Brigada 2-a, 91000 Skopje, Former Yugoslav Republic of Macedonia, Tel: (011-389-91) 125-228. Fax: (011-389-91) 122-681.
Embassy in Canada: Embassy of the Former Yugoslav Republic of Macedonia, 130 Albert St., Ste. 1006, Ottawa, ON, K1P 5G4. Tel: (613) 234-3882. Fax: (613) 233-1852.

Madagascar

Long-Form Name: Republic of Madagascar
Capital: Antananarivo

■ GEOGRAPHY

Area: 587,040 sq. km
Coastline: 4,828 km
Climate: tropical along coast, temperate inland, arid in south
Environment: subject to periodic cyclones; deforestation; overgrazing; soil erosion; desertification; water pollution
Terrain: narrow coastal plain; high plateau and mountains in centre
Land Use: 4% arable; 1% permanent crops; 41%

Madagascar

permanent pastures; 40% forest; 14% other; includes 10,870 sq. km irrigated
Location: island in the Indian Ocean, E of Africa

■ PEOPLE

Population: 14,873,387 (July 1999 est.)
Nationality: Malagasy
Age Structure: 0-14 yrs: 45%; 15-64: 52%; 65+: 3% (1999 est.)
Population Growth Rate: 2.80% (1999 est.)
Net Migration: 0 migrants/1,000 population (1999 est.)
Ethnic Groups: basic split between highlanders of predominantly Malayo-Indonesian origin (Merina and Betsileo) and coastal tribes, collectively termed the Côtiers, with mixed African, Malayo-Indonesian and Arab ancestry (Betsimisaraka, Tsimihety, Antaiska, Sakalava)
Languages: French and Malagasy (both official)
Religions: 52% indigenous beliefs; approx. 41% Christian, 7% Muslim
Birth Rate: 41.52/1,000 population (1999 est.)
Death Rate: 13.56/1,000 population (1999 est.)
Infant Mortality: 89.10 deaths/1,000 live births (1999 est.)
Life Expectancy at Birth: 52.01 years male, 54.51 years female (1999 est.)
Total Fertility Rate: 5.70 children born/woman (1999 est.)
Literacy: 47% (1997)

■ GOVERNMENT

Leader(s): Pres. Didier Ratsiraka, Prime Min. Tantely Andrianarivo
Government Type: republic
Administrative Divisions: 6 provinces (faritany)
Nationhood: June 26, 1960 (from France; formerly known as Malagasy Republic)
National Holiday: Independence Day, June 26

■ ECONOMY

Overview: a poor country, hampered by high population growth and a GDP growth rate that is not keeping pace; agriculture is the basis of the economy; industrial development is hurt by government policies restricting imports of equipment and spare parts
GDP: $10.3 billion, per capita $730; real growth rate 3% (1997 est.)
Inflation: 14.4% (Dec. 1999)
Industries: accounts for 13% of GDP; agricultural processing (meat canneries, soap factories, breweries, tanneries, sugar refining), light consumer goods industries (textiles, glassware), cement, automobile assembly plant, paper, petroleum
Labour Force: 7.0 million (1998); 59.2% community, social and business services, 26.7% agriculture
Unemployment: n.a.
Agriculture: accounts for 32% of GDP; cash crops—coffee, vanilla, sugar cane, cloves, cocoa; food crops—rice, cassava, beans, bananas, peanuts; almost self-sufficient in rice
Natural Resources: graphite, chromite, coal, bauxite, salt, quartz, tar sands, semi-precious stones, mica, fish

■ FINANCE/TRADE

Currency: Malagasy franc (FMG) = 100 centimes
International Reserves Excluding Gold: $158 million (Nov. 1999)
Gold Reserves: n.a.
Budget: revenues $477 million; expenditures $706 million, including capital expenditures of $264 million (1996 est.)
Defence Expenditures: 8.5% of govt. expenditure (1997)
Education Expenditures: 1.9% GNP (1997)
External Debt: $4.394 billion (1998)
Exports: $243 million (1999); commodities: coffee 45%, vanilla 15%, cloves 11%, sugar, petroleum products; partners: France, Japan, Italy, Germany, US
Imports: $514 million (1998); commodities: intermediate manufactures 30%, capital goods 28%, petroleum 15%, consumer goods 14%, food 13%; partners: France, Germany, UK, other European Community, US

■ COMMUNICATIONS

Daily Newspapers: 5 (1996)
Televisions: 21/1,000 inhabitants (1998)
Radios: 192/1,000 inhabitants (1997)
Telephones: 3 lines/1,000 inhabitants (1998)

■ TRANSPORTATION

Motor Vehicles: 74,700; 58,900 passenger cars (1997 est.)
Roads: 49,837 km; 5,781 km paved
Railway: 883 km
Air Traffic: 575,000 passengers carried (1997)
Airports: 133; 29 have paved runways (1998 est.)

Canadian Embassy: The Canadian Embassy to Madagascar, P.O. Box 1022, Dar-es-Salaam, Tanzania. Tel: (011-255-51) 112-831. Fax: (011-255-51) 116-896.
Embassy in Canada: Embassy of the Republic of Madagascar, 649 Blair Rd, Gloucester, ON K1J 7M4. Tel: (613) 744-7995. Fax: (613) 744-2530.

Malawi

Long-Form Name: Republic of Malawi
Capital: Lilongwe

■ GEOGRAPHY

Area: 118,480 sq. km
Coastline: none: landlocked
Climate: tropical; rainy season (Nov. to May); dry season (May to Nov.)
Environment: deforestation; water pollution; soil degradation
Terrain: narrow elongated plateau with rolling plains, rounded hills, some mountains
Land Use: 18% arable; 0% permanent; 20% meadows; 39% forest; 23% other; includes 280 sq. km irrigated
Location: SE Africa

■ PEOPLE

Population: 10,000,416 (July 1999 est.)
Nationality: Malawian
Age Structure: 0-14 yrs: 45%; 15-64: 52%; 65+: 3% (1999 est.)
Population Growth Rate: 1.57% (1999 est.)
Net Migration: 0 migrants/1,000 population (1999 est.)
Ethnic Groups: Chewa, Nyanja, Tumbuko, Yao, Lomwe, Sena, Tonga, Ngoni, Ngonde, Asian, European
Languages: English and Chichewa (both official); other languages important regionally
Religions: 55% Protestant, 20% Roman Catholic, 25% Muslim, traditional indigenous beliefs
Birth Rate: 39.54/1,000 population (1999 est.)
Death Rate: 23.84/1,000 population (1999 est.)
Infant Mortality: 132.14 deaths/1,000 live births (1999 est.)
Life Expectancy at Birth: 36.49 years male, 36.11 years female (1999 est.)
Total Fertility Rate: 5.48 children born/woman (1999 est.)
Literacy: 57.7% (1997)

■ GOVERNMENT

Leader(s): Pres. Bakili Muluzi; Prime Min. Justin Malewezi
Government Type: multi-party democracy
Administrative Divisions: 24 districts
Nationhood: July 6, 1964 (from UK; formerly known as Nyasaland)
National Holiday: Independence Day, July 6; Republic Day, July 6

■ ECONOMY

Overview: one of the world's least developed countries; the economy is predominantly agricultural, with about 90% of the population living in rural areas; economy depends heavily on foreign aid
GDP: $8.9 billion, per capita $940; real growth rate 3.2% (1998 est.)
Inflation: 30.7% (Feb. 2000)
Industries: accounts for 30% of GDP; agricultural processing (tea, tobacco, sugar), sawmilling, cement, consumer goods
Labour Force: 5.1 million (1998); 54% agriculture, 12.9% industry, 12.7% services
Unemployment: n.a.
Agriculture: 45% of GDP; crops: tobacco, sugar cane, cotton, tea, corn; subsistence crops: cattle and goats
Natural Resources: limestone; unexploited deposits of uranium, coal and bauxite

■ FINANCE/TRADE

Currency: kwacha (K) = 100 tambala
International Reserves Excluding Gold: $252 million (Jan. 2000)
Gold Reserves: 0.013 million fine troy ounces (Jan. 2000)
Budget: n.a.
Defence Expenditures: 0.8% of GDP (1996-97)
Education Expenditures: 5.4% of GNP (1997)
External Debt: $2.444 billion (1998)
Exports: $517 million (1998); commodities: tobacco, tea, sugar, coffee, peanuts; partners: US, UK, Zambia, South Africa, Germany
Imports: $382 million (1998); commodities: food, petroleum, semimanufactures, consumer goods, transportation equipment; partners: South Africa, Japan, US, UK, Zimbabwe

■ COMMUNICATIONS

Daily Newspapers: 5 (1996)
Televisions: 2/1,000 inhabitants (1998)
Radios: 249/1,000 inhabitants (1997)
Telephones: 3 lines/1,000 inhabitants (1998)

■ TRANSPORTATION

Motor Vehicles: 54,300; 25,400 passenger cars (1997 est.)
Roads: 28,400 km; 5,254 km paved
Railway: 789 km
Air Traffic: 158,000 passengers carried (1997)
Airports: 45; 5 have paved runways (1998 est.)

Canadian Embassy: The Canadian High Commission to Malawi, c/o The Canadian High Commission, 5199 United Nations Ave, Lusaka; mailing address: P.O. Box 31313 Lusaka, Zambia. Tel: (011-260-1) 25-08-33. Fax: (011-260-1) 25-41-76.

Embassy in Canada: High Commission for the Republic of Malawi, 7 Clemow Ave, Ottawa ON K1S 2A9. Tel: (613) 236-8931. Fax: (613) 236-1054.

Malaysia

Long-Form Name: Malaysia
Capital: Kuala Lumpur

■ GEOGRAPHY

Area: 329,750 sq. km; includes Sabah and Sarawak
Coastline: 4,675 km total (2,068 km Peninsular Malaysia, 2,607 km East Malaysia)
Climate: tropical; annual southwest (Apr. to Oct.) and northeast (Oct. to Feb.) monsoons
Environment: subject to flooding; air and water pollution; deforestation
Terrain: coastal plains rising to hills and mountains
Land Use: 3% arable; 12% permanent crops; negligible meadows; 68% forest; 17% other, includes 2,941 sq. km irrigated
Location: SE Asia, bordering on South China Sea

■ PEOPLE

Population: 21,376,066 (July 1999 est.)
Nationality: Malaysian
Age Structure: 0-14 yrs: 35%; 15-64: 61%; 65+: 4% (1999 est.)
Population Growth Rate: 2.08% (1999 est.)
Net Migration: 0 migrants/1,000 population (1999 est.)
Ethnic Groups: 59% Malay and other indigenous, 32% Chinese, 9% Indian
Languages: Peninsular Malaysia: Malay (official), English, Chinese dialects, Tamil; State of Sabah: English, Malay, numerous tribal dialects; Chinese State of Sarawak: English, Malay, Mandarin, numerous tribal languages
Religions: Peninsular Malaysia: Muslim (Malays), Buddhist (Chinese), Hindu (Indians); State of Sabah: 38% Muslim, 17% Christian, 45% other; Chinese State of Sarawak: 35% tribal religions, 24% Buddhist and Confucianist, 20% Muslim, 16% Christian, 5% other
Birth Rate: 26.05/1,000 population (1999 est.)
Death Rate: 5.29/1,000 population (1999 est.)
Infant Mortality: 21.68 deaths/1,000 live births (1999 est.)
Life Expectancy at Birth: 67.62 years male, 73.90 years female (1999 est.)
Total Fertility Rate: 3.35 children born/woman (1999 est.)
Literacy: 85.7% (1997)

■ GOVERNMENT

Leader(s): Paramount Ruler (King) Tuanku Jaafar ibni Al-Marhum Abdul Rahman, Prime Min. Mahathir bin Mohamad
Government Type: constitutional monarchy nominally headed by the paramount ruler (king) and a bicameral parliament
Administrative Divisions: 13 states (negeri-negeri, sing. -negeri) and 2 federal territories (wilaya-wilaya persekutuan, sing. -wilayah persekutuan)
Nationhood: Aug. 31, 1957 (from UK)
National Holiday: National Day, Aug. 31

■ ECONOMY

Overview: the economy is vulnerable to recession or a fall in world commodity prices because of its high export dependence; the world's largest producer of semiconductor devices; the majority of the rural population subsists at the poverty level but recent increases in economic output have improved living standards and real income. Foreign investment has increased significantly in recent years
GDP: $215.4 billion, per capita $10,300; real growth rate -7% (1998 est.)
Inflation: 1.5% (March 2000)
Industries: accounts for 46% of GDP; rubber and oil palm processing and manufacturing, light manufacturing industries, electronics, tin mining and smelting, logging and processing timber, logging, petroleum production, agriculture processing, petroleum production and refining, logging`
Labour Force: 9 million (1998); 26% agriculture, 19.9% industry, 19.9% services
Unemployment: 2.6% (1996 est.)
Agriculture: accounts for 13% of GDP; Peninsular Malaysia—natural rubber, palm oil, rice; Sabah—mainly subsistence; main crops—rubber, timber, coconut, rice; Sarawak—main crops—rubber, timber, pepper; there is a deficit of rice in all areas
Natural Resources: tin, crude oil, timber, copper, iron ore, natural gas, bauxite

■ FINANCE/TRADE

Currency: ringgit ($M) = 100 sen
International Reserves Excluding Gold: $32.179 billion (Jan. 2000)
Gold Reserves: 1.190 million fine troy ounces (Dec. 2000)
Budget: revenues $22.6 billion; expenditures $22 billion, including capital expenditures of $5.3 billion (1996 est.)
Defence Expenditures: 2.1% of GDP (1998)
Education Expenditures: 4.9% of GNP (1997-98)
External Debt: $44.773 billion (1998)

Exports: $84.455 billion (1999); commodities: natural rubber, palm oil, tin, timber, petroleum, electronics, light manufactures; partners: Singapore, Japan, former USSR countries, European Community, Australia, US
Imports: $64.966 billion (1999); commodities: food, crude oil, consumer goods, intermediate goods, capital equipment, chemicals; partners: Japan, Singapore, Germany, UK, Thailand, China, Australia, US

■ COMMUNICATIONS

Daily Newspapers: 42 (1996)
Televisions: 166/1,000 inhabitants (1998)
Radios: 420/1,000 inhabitants (1997)
Telephones: 198 lines/1,000 inhabitants (1998)

■ TRANSPORTATION

Motor Vehicles: 3,100,000; 3,050,000 passenger cars (1997 est.)
Roads: 94,500 km; 70,970 km paved
Railway: Peninsular Malaysia: 1,672 km; Sabah: 134 km; Sarawak: none
Air Traffic: 15,592,000 passengers carried (1997)
Airports: 115; 32 have paved runways (1998 est.)

Canadian Embassy: The Canadian High Commission, Flr 7, Plaza OSK, 172 Jalan Ampang, 50450 Kuala Lumpur, Malaysia; mailing address: P.O. Box 10890, 50732 Kuala Lumpur, Malaysia. Tel: (011-60-3) 2718-3333. Fax: (011-60-3) 2718-3315.
Embassy in Canada: High Commission for Malaysia, 60 Boteler St, Ottawa ON K1N 8Y7. Tel: (613) 241-5182. Fax: (613) 241-5214.

Maldives

Long-Form Name: Republic of Maldives
Capital: Malé

■ GEOGRAPHY

Area: 300 sq. km; 1,190 coral islands grouped in 26 atolls
Coastline: 644 km
Climate: tropical; hot, humid; dry, northeast monsoon (Nov. to Mar.); rainy, southwest monsoon (June to Aug.)
Environment: future rise in ocean level could obliterate large parts of the country; freshwater supplies are limited
Terrain: flat with elevations of only 2.5 metres
Land Use: 10% arable; 0% permanent; 3% meadows; 3% forest; 84% other; includes n.a. sq. km irrigated
Location: islands in the Indian Ocean, S of India

■ PEOPLE

Population: 300,220 (July 1999 est.)
Nationality: Maldivian
Age Structure: 0-14 yrs: 47%; 15-64: 50%; 65+: 3% (1999 est.)
Population Growth Rate: 3.37% (1999 est.)
Net Migration: 0 migrants/1,000 population (1999 est.)
Ethnic Groups: mixtures of Sinhalese, Dravidian, Arab and African
Languages: Dhivehi (Maldivian dialect of Sinhara; script derived from Arabic); English spoken by most government officials
Religions: Sunni Muslim
Birth Rate: 39.30/1,000 population (1999 est.)
Death Rate: 5.63/1,000 population (1999 est.)
Infant Mortality: 38.14 deaths/1,000 live births (1999 est.)
Life Expectancy at Birth: 66.53 years male, 70.15 years female (1999 est.)
Total Fertility Rate: 5.73 children born/woman (1999 est.)
Literacy: 95.7% (1997)

■ GOVERNMENT

Leader(s): Pres. Maumoun Abdul Gayoom
Government Type: republic
Administrative Divisions: 19 atolls (atolhu, sing. & pl.) and 1 other first-order administrative division
Nationhood: July 26, 1965 (from UK)
National Holiday: Independence Day, July 26

■ ECONOMY

Overview: based on fishing, tourism and shipping; fishing is the largest industry; tourism has become one of the largest and most important sources of revenue
GDP: $500 million, per capita $1,840; real growth rate 5.8% (1998 est.)
Inflation: 3.3% (Dec. 1999)
Industries: accounts for 15% of GDP; fishing and fish processing, tourism, shipping, boat building, some coconut processing, garments, woven mats, coir (rope), handicrafts
Labour Force: n.a.; 25% agriculture, 21% industry, 21% services, transportation and communication 10%, other 23%
Unemployment: negligible
Agriculture: accounts for almost 22% of GDP (including fishing); fishing more important than farming; limited production of coconuts, corn, sweet potatoes; most staple foods must be imported
Natural Resources: fish

■ FINANCE/TRADE

Currency: rufiyaa (Rf) = 100 laari

International Reserves Excluding Gold: $130 million (Jan. 2000)
Gold Reserves: 0.002 million fine troy ounces (Jan. 2000)
Budget: n.a.
Defence Expenditures: 18.33% of govt. expenditure (1997)
Education Expenditures: 19.00% of govt. expenditure (1998)
External Debt: $167 million (1996)
Exports: $64 million (1999); commodities: fish 57%, clothing 39%; partners: Thailand, Western Europe, Sri Lanka
Imports: $402 million (1999); commodities: intermediate and capital goods 47%, consumer goods 42%, petroleum products 11%; partners: Japan, Western Europe, Thailand

■ COMMUNICATIONS

Daily Newspapers: 2 (1996)
Televisions: 27/1,000 inhabitants (1996)
Radios: 122/1,000 inhabitants (1996)
Telephones: 71 lines/1,000 inhabitants (1998)

■ TRANSPORTATION

Motor Vehicles: n.a.
Roads: Malé has 9.6 km of coral highways within the city
Railway: none
Air Traffic: 189,000 passengers carried (1997)
Airports: 5; 2 have paved runways (1998 est.)

Canadian Embassy: The Canadian High Commission to Maldives, c/o The Canadian High Commission, P.O. Box 1006, Colombo 7, Sri Lanka. Tel: (011-94-1) 69-58-41. Fax: (011-94-1) 68-70-49.
Embassy in Canada: Embassy of the Maldives, c/o High Commission for the Democratic Socialist Republic of Sri Lanka, 333 Laurier Ave W, Ste 1204, Ottawa ON K1P 1C1. Tel: (613) 233-8449. Fax: (613) 238-8448.

Mali

Long-Form Name: Republic of Mali
Capital: Bamako

■ GEOGRAPHY

Area: 1,240,000 sq. km
Coastline: none: landlocked
Climate: subtropical to arid; hot and dry Feb. to June; rainy, humid and mild June to Nov.; cool and dry Nov. to Feb.
Environment: hot, dust-laden harmattan haze common during dry seasons; soil erosion; desertification; deforestation
Terrain: mostly flat to rolling northern plains covered by sand; savanna in south, rugged hills in northeast
Land Use: 2% arable; 0% permanent; 25% meadows; 6% forest; 67% other; includes 780 sq. km irrigated
Location: NW Africa

■ PEOPLE

Population: 10,429,124 (July 1999 est.)
Nationality: Malian
Age Structure: 0-14 yrs: 47%; 15-64: 49%; 65+: 4% (1999 est.)
Population Growth Rate: 3.01% (1999 est.)
Net Migration: 0.87 migrants/1,000 population (1999 est.)
Ethnic Groups: 50% Mande (Bambara, Malinke, Sarakole), 17% Peul, 12% Voltaic, 6% Songhai, 10% Tuareg and Moor, 5% other
Languages: French (official); Bambara spoken by about 80% of the population; numerous African languages
Religions: 90% Muslim, 9% indigenous beliefs, 1% Christian
Birth Rate: 49.50/1,000 population (1999 est.)
Death Rate: 18.56/1,000 population (1999 est.)
Infant Mortality: 119.44 deaths/1,000 live births (1999 est.)
Life Expectancy at Birth: 46.09 years male, 48.96 years female (1999 est.)
Total Fertility Rate: 6.96 children born/woman (1999 est.)
Literacy: 35.5% (1997)

■ GOVERNMENT

Leader(s): Pres. Alpha Oumar Konare, Prime Min. Mande Sidibe
Government Type: republic
Administrative Divisions: 8 regions
Nationhood: Sept. 22, 1960 (from France; formerly French Sudan)
National Holiday: Anniversary of the Proclamation of the Republic, Sept. 22

■ ECONOMY

Overview: Mali is among the poorest countries in the world, with 65% of its land area desert or semidesert. Economic activity is largely confined to the area irrigated by the Niger. Industrial activity is concentrated on processing farm commodities.
GDP: $8 billion, per capita $790; real growth rate 4.6% (1998 est.)
Inflation: -0.9% (March 2000)
Industries: accounts for 17% of GDP; small local consumer goods and processing, construction, phosphate, gold, fishing
Labour Force: 5.1 million (1998); 85.5% agriculture, 12.5% services, 2% industry

Unemployment: n.a.
Agriculture: accounts for 49% of GDP; most production based on small subsistence farms; cotton and livestock products account for over 70% of exports; other crops—millet, rice, corn, vegetables, peanuts; livestock—cattle, sheep and goats
Natural Resources: gold, phosphates, kaolin, salt, limestone, uranium; bauxite, iron ore, manganese, tin and copper deposits are known but not exploited

■ FINANCE/TRADE

Currency: Communauté financière africaine franc (CFAF) = 100 centimes
International Reserves Excluding Gold: $300 million (Nov. 1999)
Gold Reserves: 0.19 million fine troy ounces (July 1998)
Budget: revenues $730 million; expenditures $770 million, including capital expenditures of n.a. (1997 est.)
Defence Expenditures: 7.2% of central government expenditure (1997)
Education Expenditures: 2.2% of GNP (1997)
External Debt: $3.201 billion (1998)
Exports: $536 million (1999); commodities: livestock, peanuts, dried fish, cotton, skins; partners: mostly franc zone and Western Europe
Imports: $751 million (1999); commodities: textiles, vehicles, petroleum products, machinery, sugar, cereals; partners: mostly franc zone and Western Europe

■ COMMUNICATIONS

Daily Newspapers: 3 (1996)
Televisions: 12/1,000 inhabitants (1998)
Radios: 54/1,000 inhabitants (1997)
Telephones: 3 lines/1,000 inhabitants (1998)

■ TRANSPORTATION

Motor Vehicles: 41,800; 24,700 passenger cars (1997 est.)
Roads: 15,100 km; 1,827 km paved
Railway: 641 km
Air Traffic: 86,000 passengers carried (1997)
Airports: 28; 6 have paved runways (1998 est.)

Canadian Embassy: The Canadian Embassy, P.O. Box 198, Bamako, Mali. Tel: (011-223) 21-22-36. Fax: (011-223) 21-43-62.
Embassy in Canada: Embassy of the Republic of Mali, 50 Goulburn Ave, Ottawa ON K1N 8C8. Tel: (613) 232-1501. Fax: (613) 232-7429.

Malta

Long-Form Name: Republic of Malta
Capital: Valletta

■ GEOGRAPHY

Area: 320 sq. km
Coastline: 140 km
Climate: Mediterranean with mild, rainy winters and hot, dry summers
Environment: numerous bays provide good harbours; fresh water very scarce, increasing reliance on desalination
Terrain: mostly low, rocky, flat to dissected plains; many coastal cliffs
Land Use: 38% arable; 3% permanent; 0% meadows; 0% forest; 59% other, includes 10 sq. km irrigated
Location: Mediterranean Sea, S of Sicily

■ PEOPLE

Population: 381,603 (July 1999 est.)
Nationality: Maltese (sing. & pl.)
Age Structure: 0-14 yrs: 20%; 15-64: 68%; 65+: 12% (1999 est.)
Population Growth Rate: 0.49% (1999 est.)
Net Migration: 1.24 migrants/1,000 population (1999 est.)
Ethnic Groups: mixture of Arab, Sicilian, Norman, Spanish, Italian, English
Languages: Maltese and English (both official), Italian widely spoken
Religions: 98% Roman Catholic
Birth Rate: 11.02/1,000 population (1999 est.)
Death Rate: 7.37/1,000 population (1999 est.)
Infant Mortality: 7.42 deaths/1,000 live births (1999 est.)
Life Expectancy at Birth: 75.43 years male, 80.23 years female (1999 est.)
Total Fertility Rate: 1.63 children born/woman (1999 est.)
Literacy: 91.1% (1997)

■ GOVERNMENT

Leader(s): Pres. Guido De Marco, Prime Min. Eddie Fenech Adami
Government Type: parliamentary democracy
Administrative Divisions: none
Nationhood: Sept. 21, 1964 (from UK)
National Holiday: Independence Day, Sept. 21

■ ECONOMY

Overview: manufacturing and tourism are important; economy is dependent on foreign trade and services (food, water and energy); Malta produces only 20% of its food needs, has a limited supply of fresh water and lacks domestic energy sources

GDP: $5 billion, per capita $13,000; real growth rate 4% (1998 est.)
Inflation: 2.7% (Feb. 2000)
Industries: accounts for 26% of GDP; tourism, ship repair yard, clothing, construction, food manufacturing, textiles, footwear, clothing, beverages, tobacco
Labour Force: 22% industry, 66% services, other 12%
Unemployment: 7.4% (year-end 1998)
Agriculture: accounts for 3% of GDP; 20% self-sufficient overall; main products—potatoes, cauliflower, grapes, wheat, barley, tomatoes, citrus, cut flowers, green peppers, hogs, poultry, eggs; adequate supplies of vegetables, poultry, milk, pork products; seasonal or periodic shortages
Natural Resources: limestone, salt

■ FINANCE/TRADE

Currency: Maltese lira (LM) = 100 cents
International Reserves Excluding Gold: $1.875 million (Oct. 1999)
Gold Reserves: 0.006 million fine troy ounces (Oct. 1999)
Budget: revenues $1.32 billion; expenditures $1.76 billion, including capital expenditures of n.a. (1998 est.)
Defence Expenditures: 2.7% of GDP (1996–97)
Education Expenditures: 12.18% of govt. expenditure (1997)
External Debt: $130 million (1997)
Exports: $1.989 million (1999); commodities: clothing, textiles, footwear, ships; partners: Germany 31%, UK 14%, Italy 14%
Imports: $2.860 billion (1999); commodities: food, petroleum, nonfood raw materials; partners: Germany 19%, UK 17%, Italy 17%, US 11%

■ COMMUNICATIONS

Daily Newspapers: 2 (1996)
Televisions: 751/1,000 inhabitants (1996)
Radios: 678/1,000 inhabitants (1996)
Telephones: 499 lines/1,000 inhabitants (1998)

■ TRANSPORTATION

Motor Vehicles: 141,200; 122,100 passenger cars (1997 est.)
Roads: 1,582 km; 1,471 km paved
Railway: none
Air Traffic: 1,054,000 passengers carried (1997)
Airports: 1, with a paved runway (1998 est.)

Canadian Embassy: The Canadian High Commission to Malta, c/o The Canadian Embassy, Via G.B. Rossi; 27, 00161, Rome, Italy. Tel: (011-39-06) 445981. Fax: (011-39-06) 445 989750
Embassy in Canada: High Commission for Malta, 2017 Connecticut Ave NW, Washington DC 20008, USA. Tel: (202) 462-3611. Fax: (202) 387-5470.

Marshall Islands

Long-Form Name: Republic of the Marshall Islands
Capital: Majuro

■ GEOGRAPHY

Area: 181.3 sq. km; 2 island chains of 30 atolls and 1,152 islands
Coastline: 370.4 km
Climate: islands border typhoon belt; wet season, May to Nov.; hot and humid
Environment: occasional typhoons; insufficient fresh water
Terrain: low coral limestone and sand islands
Land Use: 0% arable, 60% permanent crops, 0% meadows or forests, 40% other; includes n.a. sq. km irrigated
Location: Oceania, in North Pacific Ocean, SW of Hawaii

■ PEOPLE

Population: 65,507 (July 1999 est.)
Nationality: Marshallese (sing. & pl.)
Age Structure: 0-14 yrs: 50%; 15-64: 48%; 65+: 2% (1999 est.)
Population Growth Rate: 3.86% (1999 est.)
Net Migration: 0 migrants/1,000 population (1999 est.)
Ethnic Groups: Micronesian
Languages: English (official), two major Marshallese dialects, Japanese
Religions: Christian (predominantly Protestant)
Birth Rate: 45.31/1,000 population (1999 est.)
Death Rate: 6.73/1,000 population (1999 est.)
Infant Mortality: 43.38 deaths/1,000 live births (1999 est.)
Life Expectancy at Birth: 63.21 years male, 66.50 years female (1999 est.)
Total Fertility Rate: 6.67 children born/woman (1999 est.)
Literacy: 93% (1997)

■ GOVERNMENT

Leader(s): Pres. Kessai Note
Government Type: constitutional government in free association with the US
Administrative Divisions: 33 municipalities
Nationhood: Oct. 21, 1986 (from US-administered UN trusteeship)

National Holiday: Proclamation of the Republic of the Marshall Islands, May 1

■ ECONOMY

Overview: agriculture and tourism are the backbone of the economy; industry is on a small scale, limited to handicrafts, copra and fish processing; imports far exceed exports; foreign aid is vital
GDP: $91 million, per capita $1,450; real growth rate -5% (1998 est.)
Inflation: n.a.
Industries: accounts for 13% of GDP; copra, fish, tourism, crafts; offshore banking is in its infancy
Labour Force: n.a.
Unemployment: n.a.
Agriculture: accounts for 15% of GDP; coconuts, taro, cacao, breadfruit, fruits, poultry, tomatoes, melons, cattle
Natural Resources: phosphate, marine products, minerals

■ FINANCE/TRADE

Currency: US currency is used
International Reserves Excluding Gold: n.a.
Gold Reserves: n.a.
Budget: n.a.
Defence Expenditures: defence is the responsibility of the US
Education Expenditures: n.a.
External Debt: $125 million (1996-97)
Exports: $17.5 million (1996 est.); fish, coconut oil, trochus shells; partners: US, Japan, Australia
Imports: $71.8 million (1996 est.); foodstuffs, machinery, equipment, fuels, beverages, tobacco; partners: US, Japan, Australia, New Zealand

■ COMMUNICATIONS

Daily Newspapers: n.a.
Televisions: n.a.
Radios: n.a.
Telephones: 62 lines/ 1,000 inhabitants (1998)

■ TRANSPORTATION

Motor Vehicles: n.a.
Roads: paved roads on major islands only
Railway: none
Air Traffic: 33,000 passengers carried (1997)
Airports: 16; 4 have paved runways (1998 est.)

Canadian Embassy: The Canadian Embassy to the Marshall Islands, c/o The Canadian High Commission, Commonwealth Ave., Canberra A.C.T., Australia. Tel: (011-61-2) 6270-4000.

Fax: (011-61-2) 6273-3285.
Embassy in Canada: c/o Embassy of the Republic of the Marshall Islands, 2433 Massachusetts Ave NW, Washington DC, USA. Tel: (202) 234-5414. Fax: (202) 232-3236.

Martinique

Long-Form Name: Department of Martinique
Capital: Fort-de-France

■ GEOGRAPHY

Area: 1,100 sq. km
Climate: tropical, moderated by trade winds; rainy season (June to Oct.)
Land Use: 8% arable; 8% permanent crops; 17% permanent pastures; 44% forest; 23% other, includes 40 sq. km irrigated
Location: Caribbean Islands, halfway along the Lesser Antilles arch between Puerto Rico and Venezuela

■ PEOPLE

Population: 411,539 (July 1999 est.)
Nationality: Martiniquais
Ethnic Groups: majority black, remainder a mix of black African and Latin ancestry, Caucasian 5%
Languages: French (official), majority speak Creole

■ GOVERNMENT

Colony/Territory of: Overseas Department of France
Leader(s): Pres. Jacques Chirac (France), Prefect Michel Cadot
Government Type: overseas department of France
National Holiday: Taking of the Bastille, National Day, July 14

■ ECONOMY

Overview: most of the meat, vegetable and grain requirements must be imported; industry: food processing, oil refining, chemical engineering; agriculture: pineapples, tobacco, cotton, bananas, sugar, rum, livestock; forest products; fishing; chief trading partners: France, UK, Guadeloupe

■ FINANCE/TRADE

Currency: French franc (F) = 100 centimes

Canadian Embassy: c/o The Canadian Embassy 35-37 avenue Montaigne, 75008 Paris, France. Tel: (011-33-1) 44-43-29-00. Fax: (011-33-1) 44-43-29-99.

Representative to Canada: c/o Embassy of France, 42 Sussex Dr, Ottawa ON K1M 2C9. Tel: (613) 789-1795. Fax: (613) 562-3735.

Mauritania

Long-Form Name: Islamic Republic of Mauritania
Capital: Nouakchott

■ GEOGRAPHY

Area: 1,030,700 sq. km
Coastline: 754 km
Climate: desert; constantly hot, dry, dusty
Environment: hot, dry, dust/sand-laden sirocco wind blows primarily in Mar. and Apr.; desertification; only perennial river is the Senegal; overgrazing and insufficient fresh water
Terrain: mostly barren, flat plains of the Sahara; some central hills
Land Use: 0% arable; 0% permanent crops; 38% meadows; 4% forest; 58% other; includes 490 sq. km irrigated
Location: NW Africa, bordering on Atlantic Ocean

■ PEOPLE

Population: 2,581,738 (July 1999 est.)
Nationality: Mauritanian
Age Structure: 0-14 yrs: 47%; 15-64: 51%; 65+: 2% (1999 est.)
Population Growth Rate: 2.99% (1999 est.)
Net Migration: 0 migrants/1,000 population (1999 est.)
Ethnic Groups: 30% Maur, 40% mixed Maur-black, 30% black
Languages: Hasaniya Arabic and Wolof (both official), Pular, Soninke
Religions: nearly 100% Muslim
Birth Rate: 44.10/1,000 population (1999 est.)
Death Rate: 14.20/1,000 population (1999 est.)
Infant Mortality: 76.46 deaths/1,000 live births (1999 est.)
Life Expectancy at Birth: 47.39 years male, 53.65 years female (1999 est.)
Total Fertility Rate: 6.35 children born/woman (1999 est.)
Literacy: 38.4% (1997)

■ GOVERNMENT

Leader(s): Pres. Maaouya Ould Sid Ahmed Taya; Prime Min. Cheikh El Afia Ould Mohamed Khouna
Government Type: republic
Administrative Divisions: 12 regions and 1 capital district
Nationhood: Nov. 28, 1960 (from France)
National Holiday: Independence Day, Nov. 28

■ ECONOMY

Overview: most of the population is engaged in agricultural and livestock production; substantial iron ores; threatened by foreign overexploitation of fishing areas; in recent years, droughts, conflicts with Senegal, rising energy costs and economic mismanagement have resulted in a substantial build-up of foreign debt. Short-term growth prospects are dismal
GDP: $4.7 billion, per capita $1,890; real growth rate 4.2% (1998 est.)
Inflation: 7.4% (May 1998)
Industries: accounts for 31% of GDP; fishing, fish processing, mining of iron ore and gypsum
Labour Force: 1 million (1998); 69.4% agriculture, 21.7% services, 8.9% industry
Unemployment: n.a.
Agriculture: accounts for 26% of GDP (including fishing); largely subsistence farming, nomadic cattle and sheep herding except in Senegal river valley; crops—dates, millet, sorghum, root crops; fish products number-one export; large food deficit in years of drought
Natural Resources: iron ore, gypsum, fish, copper, phosphate

■ FINANCE/TRADE

Currency: ouguiya (UM) = 5 Khoums
International Reserves Excluding Gold: $209 million (Jan. 2000)
Gold Reserves: 0.012 million fine troy ounces (Jan. 2000)
Budget: revenues $329 million; expenditures $265 million, including capital expenditures of $75 million (1996 est.)
Defence Expenditures: 2.9% of GDP (1996)
Education Expenditures: 5.1% of GNP (1997)
External Debt: $2.589 billion (1998)
Exports: $562 million (1997); commodities: iron ore, processed fish, small amounts of gum arabic and gypsum, unrecorded but numerically significant cattle exports to Senegal; partners: European Community 57%, Japan 39%, Ivory Coast 2%
Imports: $552 million (1997); commodities: foodstuffs, consumer goods, petroleum products, capital goods; partners: European Community 79%, Africa 5%, US 4%, Japan 2%

■ COMMUNICATIONS

Daily Newspapers: 2 (1996)
Televisions: 25/1,000 inhabitants (1996)
Radios: 151/1,000 inhabitants (1997)
Telephones: 6 lines/1,000 inhabitants (1998)

Mauritius

■ TRANSPORTATION
Motor Vehicles: 27,000; 17,800 passenger cars (1997 est.)
Roads: 7,660 km; 866 km paved
Railway: 704 km
Air Traffic: 245,000 passengers carried (1997)
Airports: 26; 8 have paved runways (1998 est.)

Canadian Embassy: The Canadian Embassy to Mauritania, c/o The Canadian Embassy, P.O. Box 3373, Dakar, Senegal. Office: The Consulate of Canada, Abass Commercial Centre, 1st Floor, Suite 2, Charles de Gaulle Ave., Plot o, No. 34, Nouakchott, Mauritania. Tel: (011-2222) 515-42. Fax: (011-2222) 576-10.
Embassy in Canada: Embassy of the Islamic Republic of Mauritania, 249 McLeod St, Ottawa, ON K2P 1A1. Tel: (613) 237-3283. Fax: (613) 237-3287.

Mauritius

Long-Form Name: Republic of Mauritius
Capital: Port Louis

■ GEOGRAPHY
Area: 1,860 sq. km; includes Agalega Islands, Cargados Carajos Shoals (St. Brandon) and Rodriques
Coastline: 177 km
Climate: tropical modified by southeast trade winds; warm, dry winter (May to Nov.); hot, wet, humid summer (Nov. to May)
Environment: subject to cyclones (Nov. to Apr.); almost completely surrounded by reefs; water pollution is a growing problem
Terrain: small coastal plain rising to discontinuous mountains encircling central plateau
Land Use: 49% arable; 3% permanent crops; 3% meadows; 22% forest; 23% other, includes 170 sq. km irrigated
Location: Indian Ocean, E of Africa (E of Madagascar)

■ PEOPLE
Population: 1,182,212 (July 1999 est.)
Nationality: Mauritian
Age Structure: 0-14 yrs: 26%; 15-64: 68%; 65+: 6% (1999 est.)
Population Growth Rate: 1.18% (1999 est.)
Net Migration: 0 migrants/1,000 population (1999 est.)
Ethnic Groups: 68% Indo-Mauritian, 27% Creole, 3% Sino-Mauritian, 2% Franco-Mauritian
Languages: English (official), Creole, French, Hindi, Urdu, Hakka, Bojpoori
Religions: 52% Hindu, 28% Christian (mostly Roman Catholic with a few Anglicans), 17% Muslim, 3% other
Birth Rate: 18.49/1,000 population (1999 est.)
Death Rate: 6.70/1,000 population (1999 est.)
Infant Mortality: 16.20 deaths/1,000 live births (1999 est.)
Life Expectancy at Birth: 67.21 years male, 74.96 years female (1999 est.)
Total Fertility Rate: 2.21 children born/woman (1999 est.)
Literacy: 83.0% (1997)

■ GOVERNMENT
Leader(s): Pres. Cassam Uteem, Prime Min. Sir Navinchandra Ramgoolam
Government Type: parliamentary democracy
Administrative Divisions: 9 administrative districts and 3 dependencies
Nationhood: Mar. 12, 1968 (from UK)
National Holiday: Independence Day, Mar. 12

■ ECONOMY
Overview: based on sugar, manufacturing (textiles) and tourism; features low unemployment and a high real growth rate; industrialization programs stress increasing exports
GDP: $11.7 billion, per capita $10,000; real growth rate 5% (1998 est.)
Inflation: 4.6% (April 2000)
Industries: accounts for 29% of GDP; food processing (largely sugar milling), textiles, wearing apparel, chemical and chemical products, metal products, transport equipment, nonelectrical machinery, tourism
Labour Force: 500,000 (1996 est.); 14% agriculture, 36% industry, 24% community, social and business services, 26% other
Unemployment: 9.8% (1997 est.)
Agriculture: accounts for 8% of GDP; about 90% of cultivated land in sugar cane (which accounts for 40% of export earnings); other products—tea, corn, potatoes, bananas, pulses, cattle, goats, fish; net food importer, especially rice and fish
Natural Resources: arable land, fish

■ FINANCE/TRADE
Currency: rupee (Mau Rs) = 100 cents
International Reserves Excluding Gold: $747 million (Jan. 2000)
Gold Reserves: 0.062 million fine troy ounces (Jan. 2000)
Budget: n.a.

Defence Expenditures: 0.88% of total govt. expenditure (1998)
Education Expenditures: 16.89% of govt. expenditure (1998)
External Debt: $2.482 billion (1998)
Exports: $1.645 billion (1998); commodities: textiles 44%, sugar 40%, light manufactures 10%; partners: European Community 77%, US 15%
Imports: $2.073 billion (1998); commodities: manufactured goods 50%, capital equipment 17%, foodstuffs 13%, petroleum products 8%, chemicals 7%; partners: European Community, US, South Africa, Japan

■ COMMUNICATIONS

Daily Newspapers: 6 (1996)
Televisions: 226/1,000 inhabitants (1998)
Radios: 368/1,000 inhabitants (1997)
Telephones: 214 lines/1,000 inhabitants (1998)

■ TRANSPORTATION

Motor Vehicles: 83,050; 70,000 passenger cars (1997 est.)
Roads: 1,860 km; 1,732 km paved
Railway: none
Air Traffic: 804,000 passengers carried (1997)
Airports: 5; 2 have paved runways (1998 est.)

Canadian Embassy: The Canadian High Commission to Mauritius, c/o The Canadian High Commission, Private Bag X13, Hatfield 0028, Pretoria, South Africa. Office: The Canadian Consulate, P.O. Box 209, Port Louis, Mauritius. Tel: (011-230) 212-5500. Fax: (011-230) 208-3391.
Embassy in Canada: c/o Embassy of Mauritius, 4301 Connecticut Avenue NW, Ste 441, Washington DC 20008, USA. Tel: (202) 244-1491. Fax: (202) 966-0983.

Mayotte

Long-Form Name: Territorial Collectivity of Mayotte
Capital: Mamoutzou

■ GEOGRAPHY

Area: 375 sq. km
Climate: tropical maritime; hot, humid rainy season during northeastern monsoon (Nov. to May), dry season is cooler (May to Nov.)
Land Use: 20,000 acres under agricultural cultivation
Location: Mozambique Channel, off E coast of Africa

■ PEOPLE

Population: 149,336 (July 1999 est.)
Nationality: Mahorais (sing. & pl.)
Ethnic Groups: Antalote, Cafre, Makoa, Oimatsaha, Sakalava
Languages: French (official), Mahorian (a Swahili dialect)

■ GOVERNMENT

Colony/Territory of: Territorial Collectivity of France
Leader(s): Pres. Jacques Chirac (France), Prefect Philippe Boisadam; Head of government: Pres. of the General Council Younoussa Bamana
Government Type: territorial collectivity
National Holiday: Taking of the Bastille, July 14

■ ECONOMY

Overview: industry: lobster, shrimp; agriculture: pineapples, bananas, mangoes, breadfruit, cassava, ylang-ylang, vanilla, coffee, spices; Mayotte must import a large portion of its food requirements, mainly from France; chief trading partners: France, UK, South Africa, Bahrain, Thailand, Réunion

■ FINANCE/TRADE

Currency: French franc (F) = 100 centimes

Canadian Embassy: c/o The Canadian Embassy, 35-37 avenue Montaigne, 75008 Paris, France. Tel: (011-33-1) 44-43-29-00. Fax: (011-33-1) 44-43-29-99.
Representative to Canada: c/o Embassy of France, 42 Sussex Dr., Ottawa ON K1M 2C9. Tel: (613) 789-1795. Fax: (613)562-3735.

Mexico

Long-Form Name: United Mexican States
Capital: Mexico

■ GEOGRAPHY

Area: 1,972,550 sq. km
Coastline: 9,330 km
Climate: varies from tropical to desert
Environment: subject to tsunamis along the Pacific coast and destructive earthquakes in the centre and south; natural water resources scarce and polluted; deforestation; erosion widespread; desertification; serious air pollution
Terrain: high, rugged mountains, low coastal plains, high plateaus and desert
Land Use: 12% arable, 1% permanent; 39% meadows; 26% forest; 22% other, includes

Mexico

61,000 sq. km irrigated
Location: Central (Latin) America, bordering on United States, Gulf of Mexico, Pacific Ocean

■ PEOPLE

Population: 100,294,036 (July 1999 est.)
Nationality: Mexican
Age Structure: 0-14 yrs: 35%; 15-64: 61%; 65+: 4% (1999 est.)
Population Growth Rate: 1.73% (1999 est.)
Net Migration: -2.84 migrants/1,000 population (1999 est.)
Ethnic Groups: 60% mestizo (Indian-Spanish), 30% Amerindian or predominantly Amerindian, 9% white or predominantly white, 1% other
Languages: Spanish, also indigenous (Mayan) languages
Religions: 89% Roman Catholic, 6% Protestant, 5% other
Birth Rate: 24.99/1,000 population (1999 est.)
Death Rate: 4.83/1,000 population (1999 est.)
Infant Mortality: 24.62 deaths/1,000 live births (1999 est.)
Life Expectancy at Birth: 68.98 years male, 75.17 years female (1999 est.)
Total Fertility Rate: 2.85 children born/woman (1999 est.)
Literacy: 90.1% (1997)

■ GOVERNMENT

Leader(s): Pres. Ernesto Zedillo Ponce de Léon. Pres. Elect Vicente Fox Quesada (takes office Dec. 1, 2000)
Government Type: federal republic operating under a centralized government
Administrative Divisions: 31 states (estados, sing. -estado) and 1 federal district (distrito federal)
Nationhood: Sept. 16, 1810 (from Spain)
National Holiday: Independence Day, Sept. 16

■ ECONOMY

Overview: The outlook for Mexico remains positive, but this country still needs to overcome many structural problems as it strives to modernize its economy and raise living standards. Income distribution is very unequal, with the top 20% of income earners accounting for 55% of income. Trade with the US and Canada has nearly doubled since NAFTA was implemented in 1994.
GDP: $815.3 billion, per capita $8,300; real growth rate 4.8% (1998 est.)
Inflation: 10.1% (March 2000)
Industries: accounts for 26% of GDP; food and beverages, tobacco, chemicals, iron and steel, petroleum, mining, textiles, clothing, transportation equipment, tourism
Labour Force: 38.0 million (1998); 57% services, 22.9% agriculture, 20.1% industry
Unemployment: 2.6% (1998 est.); plus considerable underemployment
Agriculture: accounts for 6% of GDP and over 25% of labour force; large number of small farms at subsistence level; major food crops—corn, wheat, rice, beans; cash crops—cotton, coffee, fruit, tomatoes
Natural Resources: crude oil, silver, copper, gold, lead, zinc, natural gas, timber

■ FINANCE/TRADE

Currency: peso ($Mex) = 100 centavos
International Reserves Excluding Gold: $33.643 billion (Jan. 2000)
Gold Reserves: 0.151 million fine troy ounces (Jan. 2000)
Budget: revenues $117 billion; expenditures $123 billion, capital expenditures n.a. (1998 est.)
Defence Expenditures: 1.3% of GDP (1998)
Education Expenditures: 4.9% of GNP (1997)
External Debt: $159.959 billion (1998)
Exports: $136.703 billion (1999); commodities: crude oil, oil products, coffee, shrimp, engines, cotton; partners: US 66%, European Community 16%, Japan 11%
Imports: $148.741 billion (1999); commodities: grain, metal manufactures, agricultural machinery, electrical equipment; partners: US 62%, European Community 18%, Japan 10%

■ COMMUNICATIONS

Daily Newspapers: 295 (1996)
Televisions: 261/1,000 inhabitants (1998)
Radios: 325/1,000 inhabitants (1997)
Telephones: 104 lines/1,000 inhabitants (1998)

■ TRANSPORTATION

Motor Vehicles: 12,330,000; 8,200,000 passenger cars (1997 est.)
Roads: 252,000 km; 94,248 km paved
Railway: 31,048 km
Air Traffic: 17,266,000 passengers carried (1997)
Airports: 1,805; 232 have paved runways (1998 est.)

Canadian Embassy: The Canadian Embassy, Calle Schiller no. 529, Rincon del Bosque, Colonia Polanco, 11580 Mexico; mailing address: Apartado Postal 105-05, 11580 Mexico, Mexico. Tel: (011-52-5) 724-7900. Fax: (011-52-5) 724-7980.
Embassy in Canada: Embassy of the United Mexican States, 45 O'Connor St, Ste 1500, Ottawa ON K1P 1A4. Tel: (613) 233-8988. Fax: (613) 235-9123.

Micronesia

Long-Form Name: Federated States of Micronesia
Capital: Palikir

■ GEOGRAPHY

Area: 702 sq. km.; 4 major island groups totalling 607 islands
Coastline: 6,112 km
Climate: tropical; heavy rainfall all year long, particularly in the eastern islands
Environment: occasional severe typhoons mostly from June to Dec.
Terrain: varies from high, mountainous islands to low coral atolls; volcanic outcroppings
Land Use: n.a.
Location: Oceania, in the N Pacific Ocean, NE of Australia

■ PEOPLE

Population: 131,500 (July 1999 est.)
Nationality: Micronesian
Age Structure: n.a.
Population Growth Rate: 3.30% (1999 est.)
Net Migration: 11.65 migrants/1,000 population (1999 est.)
Ethnic Groups: 9 Micronesian and Polynesian groups
Languages: English (offical and common), local languages including Pohnpeian, Yapese, Trukese and Kosrean
Religions: Roman Catholic 50%, Protestant 47%, other or none 3%
Birth Rate: 27.32/1,000 population (1999 est.)
Death Rate: 6.01/1,000 population (1999 est.)
Infant Mortality: 33.99 deaths/1,000 live births (1999 est.)
Life Expectancy at Birth: 66.52 years male, 70.48 years female (1999 est.)
Total Fertility Rate: 3.87 children born/woman (1999 est.)
Literacy: 89% (1998 est.)

■ GOVERNMENT

Leader(s): Pres. Leo Falcom; V. Pres. Redley Killion
Government Type: constitutional government in free association with the United States
Administrative Divisions: 4 states
Nationhood: Nov. 3, 1986 (from US-administered UN Trusteeship)
National Holiday: Proclamation of the Federated States of Micronesia, May 10

■ ECONOMY

Overview: mostly subsistence farming and fishing; few economically viable mineral deposits; region's remote location and lack of adequate facilities hinders development of the tourism potential. The islands are considerably dependant on financial assistance from the US
GDP: $220 million, per capita $1,760; real growth rate 1% (1997 est.)
Inflation: n.a.
Industries: fish processing, crafts, tourism, construction
Labour Force: n.a.; two-thirds are government employees
Unemployment: n.a.
Agriculture: pepper, tropical fruits and vegetables, coconuts, pigs, chickens
Natural Resources: forests, marine products, deep-sea minerals

■ FINANCE/TRADE

Currency: US dollar ($) = 100 cents
International Reserves Excluding Gold: $63 million (Sept. 1999)
Gold Reserves: n.a.
Budget: n.a.
Defence Expenditures: n.a.
Education Expenditures: n.a.
External Debt: $129 million
Exports: $73 million (1996 est.); commodities: fish, garments, bananas, pepper; partners: Japan, US, Guam
Imports: $168 million (1996 est.); commodities: food, manufactures, machinery and equipment, beverages; partners: US, Japan, Australia

■ COMMUNICATIONS

Daily Newspapers: n.a.
Televisions: n.a.
Radios: n.a.
Telephones: 80 lines/1,000 inhabitants (1998)

■ TRANSPORTATION

Motor Vehicles: n.a.
Roads: 240 km; 42 km paved
Railway: none
Air Traffic: n.a.
Airports: 6; 5 have paved runways (1998 est.)

Canadian Embassy: Canadian Embassy to the Federated States of Micronesia, c/o The Canadian High Commission, Commonwealth Avenue, Canberra ACT 2600, Australia, Tel: (011 61 2) 6270-4000. Fax: (011 61 2) 6273-3285.
Embassy in Canada: c/o The Embassy of the Republic of the Philippines, 130 Albert St, Suite 606, Ottawa, ON K1P 5G4. Tel: (613) 233-1121. Fax: (613) 233-4165.

Moldova

Long-Form Name: Republic of Moldova
Capital: Chisinau

■ GEOGRAPHY

Area: 33,843 sq. km
Coastline: none: landlocked
Climate: mild sunny winters; warm rainy summers; long dry autumns
Environment: heavy use of agricultural chemicals, including banned pesticides such as DDT, has contaminated ground water and soil; erosion severe due to poor farming methods
Terrain: hilly plains in north; southern steppe
Land Use: 53% arable, 14% permanent crops, 13% permanent pastures, 13% forest, 7% other, includes 3,110 sq. km irrigated
Location: E Europe, bordering on Ukraine and Romania

■ PEOPLE

Population: 4,460,838 (July 1999 est.)
Nationality: Moldovan
Age Structure: 0-14 yrs: 24%; 15-64: 66%; 65+: 10% (1999 est.)
Population Growth Rate: 0.10% (1999 est.)
Net Migration: -0.92 migrants/1,000 population (1999 est.)
Ethnic Groups: 64.5% Moldavian, 13.8% Ukrainian, 13% Russian, 3.5% Gagauz, 1.5% Jews, 3.7% other
Languages: Moldavan (official), Russian, Ukrainian, Gagauz (a Turkish dialect)
Religions: 98.5% Eastern Orthodox, 1.5% Jewish, minority Baptists (note that almost all churchgoers are ethnic Moldovan; the Slavic population are not churchgoers)
Birth Rate: 14.43/1,000 population (1999 est.)
Death Rate: 12.50/1,000 population (1999 est.)
Infant Mortality: 43.52 deaths/1,000 live births (1999 est.)
Life Expectancy at Birth: 59.76 years male, 69.24 years female (1999 est.)
Total Fertility Rate: 1.86 children born/woman (1999 est.)
Literacy: 98.3% (1997)

■ GOVERNMENT

Leader(s): Pres. Petru Lucinschi, Prime Min. Dumitru Braghi. Presidential election scheduled for December 3, 2000.
Government Type: republic
Administrative Divisions: previously divided into 40 rayons; to be divided into fewer, larger districts at unspecified future date
Nationhood: Aug. 27, 1991 (from Soviet Union)

National Holiday: Independence Day, Aug. 27

■ ECONOMY

Overview: predominantly agricultural, with important manufacturing sector; Moldova has a climate favourable to agriculture, and this is where the bulk of economic development has taken place
GDP: $10 billion, per capita $2,200; real growth rate -8.6% (1998 est.)
Inflation: 39.4% (March 2000)
Industries: accounts for 29% of GDP; machinery and appliances, hosiery, refined sugar, vegetable oil, canned food, shoes, textiles
Labour Force: 2 million (1998); 40.5% agriculture, 20.6% services, 19.2% industry
Unemployment: 2%; also large numbers of underemployed (Sept. 1998)
Agriculture: accounts for 30% of GDP; grapes and other fruits, vegetables, sugar, wheat and cereal grains, tobacco, oil, essential oil crops
Natural Resources: lignite, phosphorites, gypsum

■ FINANCE/TRADE

Currency: leu (pl. lei)
International Reserves Excluding Gold: $184 million (Jan. 2000)
Gold Reserves: n.a.
Budget: revenues $536 million; expenditures $594 million, including capital expenditures of n.a. (1998 est.)
Defence Expenditures: 1% of GDP (1999)
Education Expenditures: 10.6% of GNP (1997)
External Debt: $1.035 billion (1998)
Exports: $414 million (1999 est.); wine, grapes, other agricultural products, machinery, pumps
Imports: $520 million (1999 est.); fuels, metals and metal products, consumer products, foodstuffs

■ COMMUNICATIONS

Daily Newspapers: 4 (1996)
Televisions: 297/1,000 inhabitants (1998)
Radios: 740/1,000 inhabitants (1997)
Telephones: 150 lines/1,000 inhabitants (1998)

■ TRANSPORTATION

Motor Vehicles: n.a.
Roads: 12,300 km; 10,738 km hard-surfaced
Railway: 1,328 km, which does not include industrial lines
Air Traffic: 46,000 passengers carried (1997)
Airports: 26; 8 have paved runways

Canadian Embassy: The Canadian Embassy to Moldova, c/o The Canadian Embassy, P.O. Box 117, Post Office No. 22, 71118 Bucharest,

Romania. Tel: (011-40-1) 222-9845. Fax: (011-40-1) 312-9680.
Embassy in Canada: Embassy of the Republic of Moldova, 2101 S. Street NW, Washington DC 20008, USA. Tel: (202) 667-1130. Fax: (202) 667-1204.

Monaco

Long-Form Name: Principality of Monaco
Capital: Monaco

■ GEOGRAPHY

Area: 1.95 sq. km
Coastline: 4.1 km
Climate: Mediterranean with mild, wet winters and hot, dry summers
Environment: almost entirely urban
Terrain: hilly, rugged, rocky
Land Use: almost 100% urban
Location: W Europe, bordering on France and Mediterranean Sea

■ PEOPLE

Population: 32,149 (July 1999 est.)
Nationality: Monegasque or Monacan
Age Structure: 0-14 yrs: 17%; 15-64: 64%; 65+: 19% (1999 est.)
Population Growth Rate: 0.31% (1999 est.)
Net Migration: 4.17 migrants/1,000 population (1999 est.)
Ethnic Groups: 47% French, 16% Monegasque, 16% Italian, 21% other
Languages: French (official), English, Italian, Monegasque
Religions: 95% Roman Catholic
Birth Rate: 10.70/1,000 population (1999 est.)
Death Rate: 11.79/1,000 population (1999 est.)
Infant Mortality: 6.47 deaths/1,000 live births (1999 est.)
Life Expectancy at Birth: 75.00 years male, 82.35 years female (1999 est.)
Total Fertility Rate: 1.71 children born/woman (1999 est.)
Literacy: 99% (1997 est.)

■ GOVERNMENT

Leader(s): Prince Rainier III, Min. of State Patrick Leclercq
Government Type: constitutional monarchy
Administrative Divisions: 4 districts (quartiers, sing. -quartier)
Nationhood: 1419, rule by the House of Grimaldi
National Holiday: National Day, Nov. 19

■ ECONOMY

Overview: a popular resort, attracting tourists to its casinos and pleasant climate; no income tax and low business taxes make it a tax haven; no data is published on the economy
GDP: $800 million, per capita $25,000; real growth rate n.a. (1996 est.)
Inflation: n.a.
Industries: pharmaceuticals, food processing, precision instruments, glassmaking, printing, tourism
Labour Force: n.a.
Unemployment: negligible (1996)
Agriculture: none
Natural Resources: none

■ FINANCE/TRADE

Currency: French franc (F) = 100 centimes
International Reserves Excluding Gold: n.a.
Gold Reserves: n.a.
Budget: n.a.
Defence Expenditures: defence is the responsibility of France
Education Expenditures: n.a.
External Debt: n.a.
Exports: n.a.; full customs integration with France, which collects and rebates Monegasque trade duties
Imports: n.a.; full customs integration with France, which collects and rebates Monegasque trade duties

■ COMMUNICATIONS

Daily Newspapers: 1 (1996)
Televisions: 727/1,000 inhabitants (1996)
Radios: 1,021/1,000 inhabitants (1996)
Telephones: n.a.

■ TRANSPORTATION

Motor Vehicles: 21,000; 17,000 passenger cars (1997 est.)
Roads: 50 km paved city streets only
Railway: 1.7 km
Air Traffic: 44,000 passengers carried (1997)
Airports: Monaco is linked to the airport in Nice, France, by helicopter service

Canadian Embassy: The Canadian Consulate General, c/o The Canadian Embassy, 35 av Montaigne, 75008 Paris, France. Tel: (011-33-1) 44-43-22-51. Fax: (011-33-1) 44-43-29-99.
Embassy in Canada: Consulate of Monaco, 1000 Sherbrooke St W, Ste 2200, Montreal PQ H3A 2W1. Tel: (514) 849-0589. Fax: (514) 631-2771.

Mongolia

Long-Form Name: Mongolia
Capital: Ulan Bator

Mongolia

■ GEOGRAPHY

Area: 1,565,000 sq. km
Coastline: none: landlocked
Climate: desert; continental (large daily and seasonal temperature ranges)
Environment: harsh and rugged; water resources are severely limited; deforestation is a problem; spring dust storms are a natural hazard
Terrain: vast semidesert and desert plains; mountains in west and southwest; Gobi desert in southeast
Land Use: 1% arable; 0% permanent; 80% meadows; 9% forest; 10% other; includes 800 sq. km irrigated
Location: EC Asia, bordering China and Russia

■ PEOPLE

Population: 2,617,379 (July 1999 est.)
Nationality: Mongolian
Age Structure: 0-14 yrs: 36%; 15-64: 60%; 65+: 4% (1999 est.)
Population Growth Rate: 1.45% (1999 est.)
Net Migration: 0 migrants/1,000 population (1999 est.)
Ethnic Groups: 90% Mongol, 4% Kazakh, 2% Chinese, 2% Russian, 2% other
Languages: Kazakh and Khalkha Mongol is spoken by over 90% of population; minor languages include Turkic, Russian, Chinese and English
Religions: no state religion; predominantly Buddhist Lamaism and Shamanism, Islam 4%
Birth Rate: 22.51/1,000 population (1999 est.)
Death Rate: 7.97/1,000 population (1999 est.)
Infant Mortality: 64.63 deaths/1,000 live births (1999 est.)
Life Expectancy at Birth: 59.71 years male, 64.02 years female (1999 est.)
Total Fertility Rate: 2.60 children born/woman (1999 est.)
Literacy: 84.0% (1997)

■ GOVERNMENT

Leader(s): Pres. Natsagiin Bagabandi, Prime Min. Nambaryn Enkhbayar. Presidential election scheduled June 2001.
Government Type: republic
Administrative Divisions: 18 provinces (aymguud, sing. -aymag) and 3 municipalities (hotuud, sing. -hot)
Nationhood: Mar. 13, 1921 (from China; formerly known as Outer Mongolia)
National Holiday: National Day, July 11

■ ECONOMY

Overview: severe climate, widely dispersed population and largely unproductive land have hindered economic development; one-quarter of the population lives below the poverty line; traditionally based on agriculture and the breeding of livestock (has highest number of livestock per person in the world); recently extensive mineral resources have been developed
GDP: $5.8 billion, per capita $2,250; average real growth rate 3.5% (1998 est.)
Inflation: 10.0% (Dec. 1999)
Industries: accounts for 35% of GDP; processing of animal products, building materials, food and beverage, mining (particularly coal), copper
Labour Force: 1.1 million (1998); 39.9% agriculture, 21% industry, 39.2% services
Unemployment: 4.5% (1998 est.)
Agriculture: accounts for 31% of GDP; 90% of exports, and provides livelihood for about 50% of the population; livestock raising predominates (sheep, goats, horses); crops—wheat, barley, potatoes, forage
Natural Resources: coal, copper, molybdenum, tungsten, phosphates, tin, nickel, zinc, wolfram, fluorspar, gold

■ FINANCE/TRADE

Currency: tughrik (Tug) = 100 mongos
International Reserves Excluding Gold: $122 million (Jan. 2000)
Gold Reserves: 0.001 million fine troy ounces (Jan. 2000)
Budget: n.a.
Defence Expenditures: 8.32% of central government expenditure (1998)
Education Expenditures: 8.03% of central government expenditure (1998)
External Debt: $739 million (1998)
Exports: $763 million (1999); commodities: livestock, animal products, wool, hides, fluorspar, nonferrous metals, minerals; partners: former USSR countries 80%
Imports: $1.010 billion (1999); commodities: machinery and equipment, fuels, food products, industrial consumer goods, chemicals, building materials, sugar, tea; partners: former USSR countries 80%

■ COMMUNICATIONS

Daily Newspapers: 4 (1996)
Televisions: 63/1,000 inhabitants (1998)
Radios: 151/1,000 inhabitants (1997)
Telephones: 37 lines/1,000 inhabitants (1998)

■ TRANSPORTATION

Motor Vehicles: n.a.
Roads: 46,470 km; 3,730 km paved
Railway: 1,928 km

Air Traffic: 240,000 passengers carried (1997)
Airports: 34; 8 have paved runways

Canadian Embassy: The Canadian Embassy to Mongolia, c/o The Canadian Embassy, 19 Dong Zhi Men Wai St, Chao Yang District, Beijing 100600, China. Tel: (011-976-1) 327-586. Fax: (011-976-1) 325-530.
Embassy in Canada: Embassy of Mongolia, 2833 M St NW, Washington DC 20007, USA. Tel: (202) 333-7117. Fax: (202) 298-9327.

Montserrat

Long-Form Name: Montserrat
Capital: Plymouth (abandoned in 1997 due to volcanic activity) Interim government buildings are located in Brades

■ GEOGRAPHY

Area: 100 sq. km
Climate: tropical, no well-defined rainy season; June to Nov. hottest; prone to hurricanes
Land Use: 20% arable, 0% permanent crops, 10% meadows and pastures, 40% forests, 30% other; includes n.a. sq. km irrigated
Location: Caribbean island, SE of Puerto Rico

■ PEOPLE

Population: 12,853 (July 1999 est.)
Nationality: Montserratian
Ethnic Groups: descendants of British, French, Irish settlers; also black
Languages: English (official)

■ GOVERNMENT

Colony/Territory of: Crown Colony of the United Kingdom
Leader(s): Head of State: Queen Elizabeth II. Gov. Martin Williams, Chief Min. David Brandt
Government Type: dependent territory of the UK
National Holiday: Celebration of the Birthday of the Queen, second Saturday in June

■ ECONOMY

Overview: manufacturing accounts for 85% of exports: leather goods, cotton clothing, electronics, plastic bags, herbal teas, ornamental plants, tropical fruit; the economy is heavily dependent on imports, making it vulnerable to fluctuations in world prices. Ongoing major volcanic activity is hindering economic activity

■ FINANCE/TRADE

Currency: Eastern Caribbean dollar = 100 cents

Canadian Embassy: c/o Macdonald House, 1 Grosvenor Square, London WIX OAB, England, UK. Tel: (011-44-20) 7258-6600. Fax: (011-44-20) 7258-6333.
Representative to Canada: c/o High Commission for the Countries of the Organization of Eastern Caribbean States, 112 Kent St, Ste 1610, Place de Ville, Tower B, Ottawa ON K1P 5P2. Tel: (613) 236-8952. Fax: (613) 236-3042.

Morocco

Long-Form Name: Kingdom of Morocco
Capital: Rabat

■ GEOGRAPHY

Area: 446,550 sq. km
Coastline: 1,835 km
Climate: Mediterranean, becoming more extreme in the interior
Environment: northern mountains geologically unstable and subject to earthquakes; desertification; unsafe water supply; land degradation
Terrain: mostly mountains with rich coastal plains
Land Use: 21% arable; 1% permanent crops; 47% permanent pastures; 20% forest; 11% other, includes 12,580 sq. km irrigated
Location: NW Africa, bordering on Atlantic Ocean

■ PEOPLE

Population: 29,661,636 (July 1999 est.)
Nationality: Moroccan
Age Structure: 0-14 yrs: 36%; 15-64: 60%; 65+: 4% (1999 est.)
Population Growth Rate: 1.84% (1999 est.)
Net Migration: -1.27 migrants/1,000 population (1999 est.)
Ethnic Groups: 99.1% Arab-Berber, 0.7% non-Moroccan, 0.2% Jewish
Languages: Arabic (official); several Berber dialects; French is language of business, government, diplomacy and post-primary education
Religions: 98.7% Sunni Muslim, 1.1% Christian, 0.2% Jewish
Birth Rate: 25.78/1,000 population (1999 est.)
Death Rate: 6.12/1,000 population (1999 est.)
Infant Mortality: 50.96 deaths/1,000 live births (1999 est.)
Life Expectancy at Birth: 66.85 years male, 70.99 years female (1999 est.)
Total Fertility Rate: 3.24 children born/woman (1999 est.)
Literacy: 45.9% (1997)

■ GOVERNMENT

Leader(s): King Sidi Mohammed VI, Prime Min. Abderrahmane Youssoufi
Government Type: constitutional monarchy
Administrative Divisions: 37 provinces and 2 municipalities (wilayas)
Nationhood: Mar. 2, 1956 (from France)
National Holiday: National Day (anniversary of King Hassan II's accession to the throne), Mar. 3

■ ECONOMY

Overview: Morocco faces the problems typical of developing countries: restraining government spending, reducing constraints on private activity and foreign trade, and keeping inflation manageable.
GDP: $107 billion, per capita $3,200; real growth rate 6.8% (1998 est.)
Inflation: 1.8% (Feb. 1999)
Industries: accounts for 33% of GDP, phosphate rock mining and processing, food processing, leather goods, textiles, construction, tourism
Labour Force: 11.3 million (1998); 45.6% agriculture, 29.4% services, 25% industry
Unemployment: 19% (1998 est.)
Agriculture: accounts for 14% of GDP; 50% of employment and 30% of export value; not self-sufficient in food; cereal farming and livestock raising predominate; barley, wheat, citrus fruit, wine, vegetables, olives
Natural Resources: phosphates, iron ore, manganese, lead, zinc, fish, salt

■ FINANCE/TRADE

Currency: dirham (DH) = 100 centimes
International Reserves Excluding Gold: $5.420 billion (Jan. 2000)
Gold Reserves: 0.705 million fine troy ounces (Jan. 2000)
Budget: revenues $8.4 billion; expenditures $10 billion, including capital expenditures $1.8 billion (1997-98 est.)
Defence Expenditures: 3.8% of GDP (1997-98)
Education Expenditures: 5.0% of GNP (1997)
External Debt: $20.687 billion (1998)
Exports: $7.367 billion (1999); commodities: food and beverages 30%, semiprocessed goods 23%, consumer goods 21%, phosphates 17%; partners: European Community 58%, India 7%, Japan 5%, former USSR countries 3%, US 2%
Imports: $10.788 billion (1999); commodities: capital goods 24%, semi-processed goods 22%, raw materials 16%, fuel and lubricants 16%, food and beverages 13%, consumer goods 10%; partners: European Community 53%, US 11%, Canada 4%, Iraq 3%, former USSR countries 3%, Japan 2%

■ COMMUNICATIONS

Daily Newspapers: 22 (1996)
Televisions: 160/1,000 inhabitants (1998)
Radios: 241/1,000 inhabitants (1997)
Telephones: 54 lines/1,000 inhabitants (1998)

■ TRANSPORTATION

Motor Vehicles: 1,380,000; 1,040,000 passenger cars (1997 est.)
Roads: 60,626 km; 30,556 km paved
Railway: 1,907 km
Air Traffic: 2,638,000 passengers carried (1997)
Airports: 69; 26 have paved runways (1998 est.)

Canadian Embassy: The Canadian Embassy, 13 bis, rue Jaafar As-Sadik; Rabat-Agdal; mailing address: CP 709, Rabat-Agdal, Morocco. Tel: (011-212-7) 68-74-00. Fax: (011-212-7) 67-21-87.
Embassy in Canada: Embassy of the Kingdom of Morocco, 38 Range Rd, Ottawa ON K1N 8J4. Tel: (613) 236-7391. Fax: (613) 236-6164.

Mozambique

Long-Form Name: Republic of Mozambique
Capital: Maputo

■ GEOGRAPHY

Area: 801,590 sq. km
Coastline: 2,470 km
Climate: tropical to subtropical
Environment: severe drought and floods occur in south; desertification; water pollution; danger of cyclones
Terrain: mostly coastal lowlands, uplands in centre, high plateaus in northwest, mountains in west
Land Use: 4% arable; negligible permanent; 56% meadows; 18% forest; 22% other; includes 1,180 sq. km irrigated
Location: SE Africa, bordering on Mozambique Channel

■ PEOPLE

Population: 19,124,335 (July 1999 est.)
Nationality: Mozambican
Age Structure: 0-14 yrs: 45%; 15-64: 53%; 65+: 2% (1999 est.)
Population Growth Rate: 2.54% (1999 est.)
Net Migration: 0 migrants/1,000 population (1999 est.)
Ethnic Groups: majority from indigenous tribal groups; about 0.06% Europeans, 0.2% Euro-Africans, 0.08% Indians
Languages: Portuguese (official); English; many indigenous dialects

Religions: 50% indigenous beliefs, 30% Christian, 20% Muslim
Birth Rate: 42.75/1,000 population (1999 est.)
Death Rate: 17.31/1,000 population (1999 est.)
Infant Mortality: 117.56 deaths/1,000 live births (1999 est.)
Life Expectancy at Birth: 44.73 years male, 47.09 years female (1999 est.)
Total Fertility Rate: 5.88 children born/woman (1999 est.)
Literacy: 40.5% (1997)

■ GOVERNMENT

Leader(s): Pres. Joaquím Alberto Chissano, Prime Min. Pascoal Manuel Mocumbi
Government Type: republic
Administrative Divisions: 10 provinces (provincias, sing. -provincia)
Nationhood: June 25, 1975 (from Portugal)
National Holiday: Independence Day, June 25

■ ECONOMY

Overview: internal disorder, lack of government administrative control and a growing foreign debt have contributed to the country's failure to exploit the economic potential of its agricultural, hydropower and transportation resources; depends on much foreign aid; industry operates at only 20–40% of capacity
GDP: $16.8 billion, per capita $900; real growth rate 11% (1998 est.)
Inflation: 1.6% (Mar. 1998)
Industries: accounts for 13% of GDP; food, beverages, chemicals (fertilizer, soap, paints), petroleum products, textiles, nonmetallic mineral products (cement, glass, asbestos), tobacco
Labour Force: 9.0 million (1998); 84.5% agriculture, 7.4% industry, 8.1% services
Unemployment: n.a.
Agriculture: accounts for 35% of GDP, over 90% of labour force and about 90% of exports; cash crops—cotton, cashew nuts, sugar cane, tea, shrimp; other crops—cassava, corn, rice, tropical fruit; not self-sufficient in food
Natural Resources: coal, titanium

■ FINANCE/TRADE

Currency: metical (pl. meticais) (Mt) = 100 centavos
International Reserves Excluding Gold: $654 million (Dec. 1999)
Gold Reserves: n.a.
Budget: revenues $402 million; expenditures $799 million, including capital expenditures n.a. (1997 est.)
Defence Expenditures: 4.7% of GDP (1997)
Education Expenditures: n.a.
External Debt: $8.209 billion (1998)
Exports: $295 million (1998 est.); commodities: shrimp 48%, cashews 21%, sugar 10%, copra 3%, citrus 3%; partners: US, Western Europe, Germany, Japan
Imports: $965 million (1998 est.); commodities: food, clothing, farm equipment, petroleum; partners: US, Western Europe, former USSR countries

■ COMMUNICATIONS

Daily Newspapers: 2 (1996)
Televisions: 5/1,000 inhabitants (1998)
Radios: 40/1,000 inhabitants (1997)
Telephones: 4 lines/1,000 inhabitants (1998)

■ TRANSPORTATION

Motor Vehicles: 88,800; 67,600 passenger cars (1997 est.)
Roads: 30,400 km; 5,685 km paved
Railway: 3,131 km
Air Traffic: 188,000 passengers carried (1997)
Airports: 174; 22 have paved runways (1998 est.)

Canadian Embassy: The Canadian Embassy, avenida Julius Nyerere, No. 1128, Maputo; mailing address: P.O. Box 1578, Maputo, Mozambique. Tel: (011-258-1) 492-623. Fax: (011-258-1) 492-667.
Embassy in Canada: High Commission for the Republic of Mozambique, 1900 M St NW, Ste 570, Washington DC 20036, USA. Tel: (202) 293-7146. Fax: (202) 835-0245.

Myanmar

Long-Form Name: Union of Myanmar (formerly Burma)
Capital: Rangoon

■ GEOGRAPHY

Area: 678,500 sq. km
Coastline: 1,930 km
Climate: tropical monsoon; cloudy, rainy, hot, humid summers (southwest monsoon, June to Sept.); less cloudy, scant rainfall, mild temperatures, lower humidity during winter (northeast monsoon, Dec. to Apr.)
Environment: subject to destructive earthquakes and cyclones; flooding and landslides common during rainy season (June to Sept.); deforestation
Terrain: central lowlands ringed by steep, rugged highlands
Land Use: 15% arable land; 1% permanent crops; 1% meadows and pastures; 49% forest

and woodland; 34% other, includes 10,680 sq. km irrigated
Location: SE Asia, bordering on Bay of Bengal

■ PEOPLE

Population: 48,081,302 (July 1999 est.)
Nationality: Burmese
Age Structure: 0-14 yrs: 36%; 15-64: 60%; 65+: 4% (1999 est.)
Population Growth Rate: 1.61% (1999 est.)
Net Migration: 0 migrants/1,000 population (1999 est.)
Ethnic Groups: 68% Burmese, 9% Shan, 7% Karen, 4% Rakhine, 3% Chinese, 2% Mon, 2% Indian, 5% other
Languages: Myanmar (Burmese); minority ethnic groups have their own languages
Religions: 89% Buddhist, 11% animist beliefs, Muslim, Christian or other
Birth Rate: 28.48/1,000 population (1999 est.)
Death Rate: 12.39/1,000 population (1999 est.)
Infant Mortality: 76.25 deaths/1,000 live births (1999 est.)
Life Expectancy at Birth: 53.24 years male, 56.32 years female (1999 est.)
Total Fertility Rate: 3.63 children born/woman (1999 est.)
Literacy: 83.6% (1997)

■ GOVERNMENT

Leader(s): Chairman and Prime Min. General Than Shwe
Government Type: military regime
Administrative Divisions: 7 divisions yin-mya, sing. -yin), 7 states (pyine-mya, sing. pyine)
Nationhood: Jan. 4, 1948 (from UK)
National Holiday: Independence Day, Jan. 4

■ ECONOMY

Overview: economy is dependent on agriculture and is vulnerable to world market conditions (especially for rice); Myanmar has been unable to achieve much improvement in export earnings due to falling prices for many of its export commodities
GDP: $56.1 billion, per capita $1,200; real growth rate 1.1% (1998 est.)
Inflation: 9.3% (Dec. 1999)
Industries: accounts for 11% of GDP; agricultural processing; textiles and footwear; wood and wood products; petroleum refining; mining of copper, tin, tungsten, iron; construction materials; pharmaceuticals; fertilizer
Labour Force: 24 million (1998); 69.1% agriculture, 8.9% trade and tourism, 7.2% industry
Unemployment: n.a.
Agriculture: accounts for 59% of GDP; self-sufficient in food; principal crops: rice, corn, oilseed, sugar cane, pulses; world's largest stand of hardwood trees; rice and teak account for 55% of exports; world's largest producer of opium poppies
Natural Resources: crude oil, timber, tin, antimony, zinc, copper, tungsten, lead, coal, some marble, limestone, precious stones, natural gas

■ FINANCE/TRADE

Currency: kyat (K) = 100 pyas
International Reserves Excluding Gold: $399 million (Dec. 1999)
Gold Reserves: 0.231 million fine troy ounces (Dec. 1999)
Budget: revenues $7.9 billion; expenditures $12.2 billion, including capital expenditures $5.7 billion (1996-97 est.)
Defence Expenditures: 30.62% of govt. expenditure (1997)
Education Expenditures: 9.35% of govt. expenditure (1997)
External Debt: $5.68 billion (1998)
Exports: $1.125 billion (1999); commodities: teak, rice, oilseed, metals, rubber, gems; partners: Southeast Asia, India, China, European Community, Africa
Imports: $2.300 billion (1999); commodities: machinery, transport equipment, chemicals, food products; partners: Japan, European Community, CEMA, China, Southeast Asia

■ COMMUNICATIONS

Daily Newspapers: 5 (1996)
Televisions: 7/1,000 inhabitants (1998)
Radios: 95/1,000 inhabitants (1997)
Telephones: 5 lines/1,000 inhabitants (1998)

■ TRANSPORTATION

Motor Vehicles: 69,000; 35,000 passenger cars (1997 est.)
Roads: 28,200 km; 3,440 km paved
Railway: 3,740 km
Air Traffic: 334,000 passengers carried (1997)
Airports: 80; 11 have paved runways (1998 est.)

Canadian Embassy: The Canadian Embassy to Myanmar, c/o The Canadian Embassy, 11th Floor, Boonmitr Bldg, 138 Silom Rd, Bangkok 10501; mailing address: P.O. Box 2090, Bangkok 10500, Thailand. Tel: (011-66-2) 636-0540. Fax: (011-66-2) 636-0565.
Embassy in Canada: Embassy of the Union of Myanmar, 85 Range Rd, Ste 902, Ottawa ON

K1N 8J6. Tel: (613) 232-6434. Fax: (613) 232-6435.

Namibia

Long-Form Name: Republic of Namibia
Capital: Windhoek

■ GEOGRAPHY

Area: 825,418 sq. km
Coastline: 1,572 km
Climate: desert; hot, dry; rainfall sparse and erratic
Environment: inhospitable with very limited natural water resources; drought and desertification
Terrain: mostly high plateau; Namib Desert along coast; Kalahari Desert in east
Land Use: 1% arable; 0% permanent crops; 46% permanent pastures; 22% forest; 31% other; includes 60 sq. km irrigated
Location: SW Africa, bordering on South Atlantic Ocean

■ PEOPLE

Population: 1,648,270 (July 1999 est.)
Nationality: Namibian
Age Structure: 0-14 yrs: 44%; 15-64: 52%; 65+: 4% (1999 est.)
Population Growth Rate: 1.57% (1999 est.)
Net Migration: 0 migrants/1,000 population (1999 est.)
Ethnic Groups: 86% black, 6% white, 8% mixed; about 50% of the population belong to the Ovambo tribe and 9% to the Kavangos tribe
Languages: white population: 60% Afrikaans, 33% German, 7% English (all official); several indigenous languages
Religions: 90% Christian, 10% traditional religions
Birth Rate: 35.63/1,000 population (1999 est.)
Death Rate: 19.92/1,000 population (1999 est.)
Infant Mortality: 65.94 deaths/1,000 live births (1999 est.)
Life Expectancy at Birth: 41.64 years male, 40.87 years female (1999 est.)
Total Fertility Rate: 4.94 children born/woman (1999 est.)
Literacy: 38% (1997)

■ GOVERNMENT

Leader(s): Pres. Sam Nujoma, Prime Min. Hage Geingob
Government Type: republic
Administrative Divisions: 13 regions
Nationhood: Mar. 21, 1990 (from South Africa)
National Holiday: Independence Day, Mar. 21

■ ECONOMY

Overview: economy is very dependent on the mining industry to extract and process minerals for export; world's fifth largest producer of uranium; rich diamond deposits; more than 50% of the population depends on subsistence agriculture
GDP: $6.6 billion, per capita $4,100; real growth rate 2% (1998 est.)
Inflation: 6.2% (Dec. 1998)
Industries: meat packing, fish processing, dairy products; mining accounts for 20% of GDP (copper, lead, zinc, diamonds, uranium)
Labour Force: 1 million (1998); 43.5% agriculture, 21.9% industry, 34.8% services
Unemployment: 30-40%, including under-employment (1997 est.)
Agriculture: accounts for 11% of GDP (including fishing); mostly subsistence farming; livestock raising major source of cash income; crops: millet, sorghum, peanuts; large unfulfilled fish catch potential; needs to import food
Natural Resources: diamonds, copper, uranium, gold, lead, tin, zinc, salt, vanadium, natural gas, fish; suspected deposits of coal and iron ore

■ FINANCE/TRADE

Currency: Namibian dollar = 100 cents
International Reserves Excluding Gold: $351 million (Jan. 2000)
Gold Reserves: none (Jan. 2000)
Budget: revenues $1.1 billion; expenditures $1.2 billion, including capital expenditures of $193 million (1996–97 est.)
Defence Expenditures: 2.6% of GDP (1997-98)
Education Expenditures: 9.1% of GNP (1997)
External Debt: about $315 million (1996 est.)
Exports: $1.44 billion (1998 est.); commodities: diamonds, uranium, zinc, copper, meat, processed fish, karakul skins; partners: South Africa, UK, Spain, Japan
Imports: $1.48 billion (1998 est.); commodities: foodstuffs, manufactured consumer goods, machinery and equipment; partners: South Africa, Germany, US, Japan

■ COMMUNICATIONS

Daily Newspapers: 4 (1996)
Televisions: 37/1,000 inhabitants (1998)
Radios: 144/1,000 inhabitants (1997)
Telephones: 69 lines/1,000 inhabitants (1998)

■ TRANSPORTATION

Motor Vehicles: 129,000; 62,500 passenger cars (1997 est.)
Roads: 64,799 km; 7,841 km paved
Railway: 2,382 km

Air Traffic: 214,000 passengers carried (1997)
Airports: 135; 22 have paved runways (1998 est.)

Canadian Embassy: The Canadian High Commission to Namibia, c/o The Canadian High Commission, 1103 Arcadia St, Hatfield 0083, Pretoria; mailing address: Private Bag X13, Hatfield 0083, Pretoria, South Africa. Tel: (011-27-12) 422-3000. Fax: (011-27-12) 422-3052.
Embassy in Canada: High Commission for the Republic of Namibia, 1605 New Hampshire Ave NW, Washington DC 20009, USA. Tel: (202) 986-0540. Fax: (202) 986-0443.

Nauru

Long-Form Name: Republic of Nauru
Capital: no capital city as such; government offices in Yaren

■ GEOGRAPHY

Area: 21 sq. km
Coastline: 30 km
Climate: tropical; monsoonal; rainy season (Nov. to Feb.)
Environment: only 53 km south of equator; periodic droughts; water supply limited and unreliable
Terrain: sandy beach rises to fertile ring around raised coral reefs with phosphate plateau in centre
Land Use: 0% arable; 0% permanent; 0% meadows; 0% forest; 100% other
Location: island in the Pacific Ocean, NE of Australia

■ PEOPLE

Population: 10,605 (July 1999 est.)
Nationality: Nauruan
Age Structure: n.a.
Population Growth Rate: 0.00% (1999 est.)
Net Migration: 0.0 migrants/1,000 population (1999 est.)
Ethnic Groups: 58% Nauruan, 26% other Pacific Islander, 8% Chinese, 8% European
Languages: Nauruan, a distinct Pacific Island language (official); English widely understood, spoken and used for most government and commercial purposes
Religions: Christian (two-thirds Nauruan Protestant, one-third Roman Catholic)
Birth Rate: 18.03/1,000 population (1998 est.)
Death Rate: 5.1/1,000 population (1998 est.)
Infant Mortality: 40.6 deaths/1,000 live births (1998 est.)
Life Expectancy at Birth: 64.3 years male, 69.18 years female (1998 est.)
Total Fertility Rate: 2.08 children born/woman (1998 est.)
Literacy: n.a.

■ GOVERNMENT

Leader(s): Pres. Bernard Dowiyogo
Government Type: republic
Administrative Divisions: 14 districts
Nationhood: Jan. 31, 1968 (from UN trusteeship under Australia, New Zealand and UK; formerly known as Pleasant Island)
National Holiday: Independence Day, Jan. 31

■ ECONOMY

Overview: most other resources are imported; has one of the highest per capita incomes in the Third World; the rehabilitation of mined land and the replacement of income from phosphates are serious long-term considerations
GDP: n.a.
Inflation: n.a.
Industries: phosphate mining, financial services, coconuts
Labour Force: n.a.
Unemployment: 0%
Agriculture: coconuts; other agricultural activities are negligible; almost completely dependent on imports for food and water
Natural Resources: phosphates

■ FINANCE/TRADE

Currency: Australian dollar ($A) = 100 cents
International Reserves Excluding Gold: n.a.
Gold Reserves: n.a.
Budget: revenues $23.4 million; expenditures $64.8 million, capital expenditures n.a. (1996)
Defence Expenditures: no formal defence structure
Education Expenditures: n.a.
External Debt: $33.3 million
Exports: n.a.; commodities: phosphates; partners: Australia, New Zealand
Imports: n.a.; commodities: food, fuel, manufacturers, building materials, machinery; partners: Australia, UK, New Zealand, Japan

■ COMMUNICATIONS

Daily Newspapers: 0 (1996)
Televisions: n.a.
Radios: 582/1,000 inhabitants (1996)
Telephones: n.a.

■ TRANSPORTATION

Motor Vehicles: n.a.
Roads: 30 km; 24 km paved
Railway: 3.9 km
Air Traffic: 137,000 passengers carried (1997)

Airports: 1, with a paved runway (1998 est.)

Canadian Embassy: c/o The Canadian High Commission, Commonwealth Ave, Canberra A.C.T. 2600, Australia. Tel: (011-61-2) 6270-4000. Fax: (011-61-2) 6273-3285.
Embassy in Canada: c/o Australian High Commission, 50 O'Connor St, Ste 710, Ottawa ON K1P 6L2. Tel: (613) 236-0841. Fax: (613) 236-4376.

Nepal

Long-Form Name: Kingdom of Nepal
Capital: Kathmandu

■ GEOGRAPHY

Area: 140,800 sq. km
Coastline: none: landlocked
Climate: varies from cool summers and severe winters in north to subtropical summers and mild winters in south
Environment: contains eight of the world's 10 highest peaks; flooding, drought, landslides; deforestation; soil erosion; water pollution
Terrain: flat river plain of the Ganges in south, central hilly region, rugged Himalayas in north
Land Use: 17% arable; negligible permanent crops; 15% meadows; 42% forest; 26% other, includes 8,500 sq. km irrigated
Location: SC Asia, bordering on India and Tibet

■ PEOPLE

Population: 24,302,653 (July 1999 est.)
Nationality: Nepalese
Age Structure: 0-14 yrs: 41%; 15-64: 55%; 65+: 4% (1999 est.)
Population Growth Rate: 2.51% (1999 est.)
Net Migration: 0 migrants/1,000 population (1999 est.)
Ethnic Groups: Newars, Indians, Tibetans, Gurungs, Magars, Tamangs, Bhotias, Rais, Limbus, Sherpas, as well as many smaller groups
Languages: Nepali (official); 20 languages divided into numerous dialects
Religions: 90% Hindu, 5% Buddhist, 3% Muslim, 2% other; only official Hindu state in the world, although no sharp distinction between many Hindu and Buddhist groups; small groups of Muslims and Christians
Birth Rate: 35.32/1,000 population (1999 est.)
Death Rate: 10.18/1,000 population (1999 est.)
Infant Mortality: 73.58 deaths/1,000 live births (1999 est.)
Life Expectancy at Birth: 58.47 years male, 58.36 years female (1999 est.)
Total Fertility Rate: 4.78 children born/woman (1999 est.)
Literacy: 38.1% (1997)

■ GOVERNMENT

Leader(s): King Bir Bikram Shah Dev Birendra, Prime Min. Girija Prasad Koirala
Government Type: parliamentary democracy as of May 12, 1991
Administrative Divisions: 14 zones (anchal, sing. & pl.)
Nationhood: 1768, unified by Prithvi Narayan Shah
National Holiday: Birthday of His Majesty the King, Dec. 28

■ ECONOMY

Overview: one of the poorest and most underdeveloped countries in the world; agriculture provides the backbone of the economy, employing more than 80% of the population. There have been attempts to expand into other economic sectors
GDP: $26.2 billion, per capita $1,100; real growth rate 4.9% (1998 est.)
Inflation: 1.8% (Dec. 1999)
Industries: accounts for 22% of GDP; small rice, jute, sugar and oilseed mills, cigarettes, textiles, cement, brick; tourism, carpet production
Labour Force: 11 million (1998); 93% agriculture, 6.5% services, 0.6% industry
Unemployment: n.a., but substantial rate of underemployment
Agriculture: accounts for 41% of GDP and 80% of workforce; farm products—rice, corn, wheat, sugar cane, root crops, milk, buffalo meat; not self-sufficient in food, particularly in drought years
Natural Resources: quartz, water, timber, hydroelectric potential, scenic beauty; small deposits of lignite, copper, cobalt, iron ore

■ FINANCE/TRADE

Currency: rupee (NRs) = 100 paisa
International Reserves Excluding Gold: $809 million (Nov. 1999)
Gold Reserves: 0.153 million fine troy ounces (Dec. 1999)
Budget: revenues $536 million; expenditures $818 million, including capital expenditures n.a. (1996-97 est.)
Defence Expenditures: 4.53% of govt. expenditure (1998)
Education Expenditures: 13.98% of govt. expenditure (1998)
External Debt: $2.646 billion (1998)
Exports: $474 million (1998); commodities:

clothing, carpets, leather goods, grain; partners: India 38%, US 23%, UK 6%, other Europe 9%
Imports: $1.246 billion (1998); commodities: petroleum products 20%, fertilizer 11%, machinery 10%; partners: India 36%, Japan 13%, Europe 4%, US 1%

■ COMMUNICATIONS
Daily Newspapers: 29 (1996)
Televisions: 6/1,000 inhabitants (1998)
Radios: 38/1,000 inhabitants (1997)
Telephones: 8 lines/1,000 inhabitants (1998)

■ TRANSPORTATION
Motor Vehicles: n.a.
Roads: 7,700 km; 3,196 km paved
Railway: 101 km
Air Traffic: 755,000 passengers carried (1997)
Airports: 45; 5 have paved runways (1998 est.)

Canadian Embassy: The Canadian Embassy to Nepal, c/o The Canadian High Commission, 7/8 Shantipath, Chanakyapuri, New Delhi 110 021; mailing address: The Canadian High Commission, P.O. Box 5207, New Delhi, India. Tel: (011-9771) 415-193. Fax: (011-9771) 687-6579.
Embassy in Canada: Embassy of the Kingdom of Nepal, 2131 Leroy Place NW, Washington DC 20008, USA. Tel: (202) 667-4550. Fax: (202) 667-5534.

Netherlands

Long-Form Name: Kingdom of the Netherlands
Capital: Amsterdam; seat of government: The Hague

■ GEOGRAPHY
Area: 41,532 sq. km
Coastline: 451 km
Climate: temperate; marine; cool summers and mild winters
Environment: nearly half of the land area is below sea level and protected from the North Sea by dikes; water and air pollution
Terrain: mostly coastal lowland and reclaimed land (polders); some hills in southeast
Land Use: 25% arable; 3% permanent; 25% permanent pastures; 8% forest; 39% other, includes 6,000 sq. km irrigated
Location: NW Europe, bordering on North Sea

■ PEOPLE
Population: 15,807,641 (July 1999 est.)
Nationality: Dutch
Age Structure: 0-14 yrs: 18%; 15-64: 68%; 65+: 14% (1999 est.)
Population Growth Rate: 0.47% (1999 est.)
Net Migration: 1.99 migrants/1,000 population (1999 est.)
Ethnic Groups: 96% Dutch, 4% Moroccans, Turks and others
Languages: Dutch, Frisian
Religions: 62% Christianity, of which 34% is Roman Catholic and 25% is Protestant; most of the rest do not profess a religion
Birth Rate: 11.36/1,000 population (1999 est.)
Death Rate: 8.69/1,000 population (1999 est.)
Infant Mortality: 5.11 deaths/1,000 live births (1999 est.)
Life Expectancy at Birth: 75.28 years male, 81.17 years female (1999 est.)
Total Fertility Rate: 1.49 children born/woman (1999 est.)
Literacy: 99% (1997)

■ GOVERNMENT
Leader(s): Head of State: Queen Beatrix. Prem. Willem (Wim) Kok
Government Type: constitutional monarchy
Administrative Divisions: 12 provinces (provincien, sing. provincie); dependent areas: Aruba, Netherland Antilles
Nationhood: 1579 (from Spain)
National Holiday: Queen's Day, Apr. 30

■ ECONOMY
Overview: a highly developed and affluent economy based on private enterprise; numerous government-backed welfare programs; trade and financial sectors are the strongest part of the economy
GDP: $348.6 billion, per capita $22,200; real growth rate 3.7% (1998 est.)
Inflation: 1.9% (March 2000)
Industries: contributes 27.5% to the GDP; agro-industries, metal and engineering products, electrical machinery and equipment, chemicals, petroleum, fishing, construction, microelectronics
Labour Force: 7.1 million (1998); 35.4% community, social and business services, 19.2% trade and tourism, 18% industry
Unemployment: 2.9% (Jan. 2000)
Agriculture: accounts for 3.2% of GDP and 4% of labour force; animal production predominates; crops—grains, potatoes, sugar beets, fruits, vegetables; shortages of grain, fats and oils
Natural Resources: natural gas, crude oil, fertile soil

■ FINANCE/TRADE
Currency: guilder, gulden or florin (f.) = 100 cents [As of Jan. 1, 1999, Government securities are issued in Euros (EUR)]

International Reserves Excluding Gold: $9.552 billion (Jan. 2000)
Gold Reserves: 30.452 million fine troy ounces (Jan. 2000)
Budget: revenues $163 billion; expenditures $170 billion, including capital expenditures of n.a. (1999 est.)
Defence Expenditures: 3.86% of govt. expenditures (1997)
Education Expenditures: 9.97% total govt. expenditures (1997)
External Debt: none
Exports: $200.286 billion (1999); commodities: agricultural products, processed foods and tobacco, natural gas, chemicals, metal products, textiles, clothing; partners: European community 74.9% (Germany 28.3%, Belgium-Luxembourg 14.2%, France 10.7, UK 10.2%), US 4.7%
Imports: $187.525 billion (1999); commodities: raw materials and semifinished products, consumer goods, transportation equipment, crude oil, food products; partners: European Community 63.8% (Germany 26.5%, Belgium-Luxembourg 23.1%, UK 8.1%), US 7.9%

■ COMMUNICATIONS

Daily Newspapers: 38 (1996)
Televisions: 543/1,000 inhabitants (1998)
Radios: 978/1,000 inhabitants (1997)
Telephones: 593 lines/1,000 inhabitants (1998)

■ TRANSPORTATION

Motor Vehicles: 6,490,000; 5,750,000 passenger cars (1997 est.)
Roads: 127,000 km; 114,427 km paved
Railway: 2,813 km
Air Traffic: 17,890,000 passengers carried (1997)
Airports: 28; 19 have paved runways (1998 est.)

Canadian Embassy: The Canadian Embassy, Sophialaan 7, 2514JP, The Hague, Netherlands. Tel: (011-31-70) 311-1600. Fax: (011-31-70) 311-1620.
Embassy in Canada: Embassy of the Kingdom of the Netherlands, 350 Albert St, Ste 2020, Ottawa ON K1R 1A4. Tel: (613) 237-5030. Fax: (613) 237-6471.

Netherlands Antilles

Long-Form Name: Netherlands Antilles
Capital: Willemstad

■ GEOGRAPHY

Area: 960 sq. km, 2 island groups
Climate: tropical maritime, moderated by northeasterly trade winds, short rainy season

Land Use: islands mostly too rocky for agriculture; only 10% is arable land; 0% permanent crops, 0% meadows and pastures, 0% forest, 90% other; includes n.a. sq. km irrigated
Location: West Indies, just north of Venezuela

■ PEOPLE

Population: 207,827 (July 1999 est.)
Nationality: Netherlands Antillean
Ethnic Groups: mixed African 85%, Carib Indian, European, Latin, Oriental
Languages: Dutch (official), Papiamento (derived from Dutch, Spanish, Portuguese), English

■ GOVERNMENT

Colony/Territory of: Dependent Territory of the Netherlands
Leader(s): Chief of State: Queen Beatrix/Gov. Jaime M. Saleh. Prime Min. Miguel Pourier
Government Type: dependency with internal self-government
National Holiday: Queen's Day, Apr. 30

■ ECONOMY

Overview: unlike many Latin American countries, the Netherlands Antilles has avoided crushing external debt; Curaçao has one of the largest ship-repair dry docks in the western hemisphere; almost all consumer goods must be imported; chief trading partner: UK

■ FINANCE/TRADE

Currency: Netherlands Antilles guilder, gulden or florin = 100 cents

Canadian Embassy: c/o The Canadian Embassy, 7, 2514JP The Hague, Netherlands. Tel: (011-31-70) 311-1600. Fax: (011-31-70) 311-1620.
Representative to Canada: c/o Embassy of the Kingdom of the Netherlands, 350 Albert St, Ste 2020, Ottawa ON K1R 1A4. Tel: (613) 237-5030. Fax: (613) 237-6471.

New Caledonia

Long-Form Name: Territory of New Caledonia and Dependencies
Capital: Nouméa

■ GEOGRAPHY

Area: 19,060 sq. km (a peninsula and three small islands)
Climate: humid, subtropical maritime, modified by southeast trade winds

Land Use: 0% arable, 0% permanent crops, 12% meadow and pasture, 39% forest and woodland, 49% other; includes n.a. sq. km irrigated
Location: SW Pacific Ocean (Melanesia), E of Australia

■ PEOPLE

Population: 197,361 (July 1999 est.)
Nationality: New Caledonian
Ethnic Groups: 42.5% Melanesian, 37.1% European, 8.4% Wallisian, 3.8% Polynesian, 3.6% Indonesian, 1.6% Vietnamese, 3% other
Languages: French (official), 28 Melanesian and Polynesian languages

■ GOVERNMENT

Colony/Territory of: Overseas Territory of France
Leader(s): Pres. Jacques Chirac (France), High Commissioner Dominique Bur; Pres. of the Territorial Congress Simon Loueckhote
Government Type: overseas territory of France since 1956
National Holiday: Taking of the Bastille, July 14

■ ECONOMY

Overview: only a negligible portion of the land is arable, and most food must be imported; the backbone of the economy is nickel export

■ FINANCE/TRADE

Currency: CFP franc = 100 centimes

Canadian Embassy: c/o The Canadian Embassy, 35-37 avenue Montaigne 75008 Paris, France. Tel: (011-33-1) 44-43-29-00. Fax: (011-33-1) 44-43-29-99.
Representative to Canada: c/o Embassy of France, 42 Sussex Dr, Ottawa ON K1M 2C9. Tel: (613) 789-1795. Fax: (613) 562-3735.

New Zealand

Long-Form Name: New Zealand
Capital: Wellington

■ GEOGRAPHY

Area: 268,680 sq. km
Coastline: 15,134 km
Climate: temperate with sharp regional contrasts
Environment: earthquakes are common though usually not severe; deforestation and soil degradation are increasing; occasional volcanic activity
Terrain: predominantly mountainous with some large coastal plains
Land Use: 9% arable; 5% permanent crops; 50% meadows and pastures; 28% forest and woodland; 8% other; includes 2,850 sq. km irrigated
Location: SE of Australia, bordering on Tasman Sea, Pacific Ocean

■ PEOPLE

Population: 3,662,265 (July 1999 est.)
Nationality: New Zealander
Age Structure: 0-14 yrs: 23%; 15-64: 65%; 65+: 12% (1999 est.)
Population Growth Rate: 0.99% (1999 est.)
Net Migration: 3.01 migrants/1,000 population (1999 est.)
Ethnic Groups: 88% European, 8.9% Maori, 2.9% Pacific Islander, 0.2% other
Languages: English (official), Maori
Religions: 75% Christian, 18% unspecified, 7% Hindu, Confucian, other
Birth Rate: 14.42/1,000 population (1999 est.)
Death Rate: 7.53/1,000 population (1999/ est.)
Infant Mortality: 6.22 deaths/1,000 live births (1999 est.)
Life Expectancy at Birth: 74.55 years male, 81.27 years female (1999 est.)
Total Fertility Rate: 1.85 children born/woman (1999 est.)
Literacy: 99% (1997)

■ GOVERNMENT

Leader(s): Head of State: Queen Elizabeth II/Gov. Gen. Sir Michael Hardie-Boyes. Prime Min. Helen Clark
Government Type: parliamentary democracy
Administrative Divisions: 93 counties, 9 districts, 3 town districts; dependent areas inc.: the Cook Islands, the Kermadec Islands, Niue, the Ross Dependency (uninhabited except for scientific personnel), Tokelau
Nationhood: Sept. 26, 1907 (from UK)
National Holiday: Waitangi Day, Feb. 6

■ ECONOMY

Overview: government has been reorienting from an agrarian to an open, free-market economy that can compete in the global community; inflation has been reduced; growth has been sluggish, unemployment has been at an all-time high
GDP: $61.1 billion, per capita $17,000; real growth rate -0.2% (1998 est.)
Inflation: 1.5% (March 2000)
Industries: accounts for 25% of GDP; food processing, wool production, wood and paper products, textiles, machinery, transportation equipment, banking and insurance, tourism, mining

Labour Force: 2 million (1998); 28.7% community, social and business services, 21.1% trade and tourism, 17% industry
Unemployment: 7.5% (Jan. 1999)
Agriculture: accounts for 9% of GDP and 11% of workforce; livestock predominates: wool, meat, dairy products; crops: wheat, barley, potatoes, pulses, fruit and vegetables; fish; surplus producer of farm products
Natural Resources: natural gas, iron ore, sand, coal, timber, hydroelectricity, gold, limestone

■ FINANCE/TRADE

Currency: New Zealand dollar (NZ$) = 100 cents
International Reserves Excluding Gold: $4.179 billion (Jan. 2000)
Gold Reserves: none (Jan. 2000)
Budget: revenues $24.9 billion; expenditures $23.7 billion, including capital expenditures n.a. (1997–98 est.)
Defence Expenditures: 3.27% of total govt. expenditure (1998)
Education Expenditures: 16.18% of total govt. expenditure (1998)
External Debt: $53.2 billion (March 1998)
Exports: $12.452 billion (1999); commodities: wool, lamb, mutton, beef, fruit, fish, cheese, manufactures, chemicals, forestry products; partners: European Community 18.3%, Japan 17.9%, Australia 17.5%, US 13.5%
Imports: $14.301 billion (1999); commodities: petroleum, consumer goods, motor vehicles, industrial equipment; partners: Australia 19.7%, Japan 16.9%, European Community 16.9%, US 15.3%, Taiwan 3%

■ COMMUNICATIONS

Daily Newspapers: 23 (1996)
Televisions: 508/1,000 inhabitants (1998)
Radios: 990/1,000 inhabitants (1997)
Telephones: 479 lines/1,000 inhabitants (1998)

■ TRANSPORTATION

Motor Vehicles: 2,110,000; 1,770,000 passenger cars (1997 est.)
Roads: 92,306 km; 53,568 km paved
Railway: 3,973 km
Air Traffic: 9,435,000 passengers carried (1997)
Airports: 111; 44 have paved runways (1998 est.)

Canadian Embassy: The Canadian High Commission, 61 Molesworth St, 3rd Floor, Thorndon, Wellington; mailing address: P.O. Box 12049, Thorndon, Wellington, New Zealand. Tel: (011-64-4) 473-9577. Fax: (011-64-4) 471-2082.
Embassy in Canada: New Zealand High Commission, Clarica Centre, 99 Bank St, Ste 727, Ottawa ON K1P 6G3. Tel: (613) 238-5991. Fax: (613) 238-5707.

Nicaragua

Long-Form Name: Republic of Nicaragua
Capital: Managua

■ GEOGRAPHY

Area: 129,494 sq. km
Coastline: 910 km
Climate: tropical in lowlands, cooler in highlands
Environment: subject to destructive earthquakes, volcanoes, landslides and occasional severe hurricanes; deforestation; soil erosion; water pollution
Terrain: extensive Atlantic coastal plains rising to central interior mountains; narrow Pacific coastal plain interrupted by volcanoes
Land Use: 9% arable; 1% permanent; 46% meadows; 27% forest; 17% other; includes 880 sq. km irrigated
Location: Central (Latin) America, bordering on Caribbean Sea, Pacific Ocean

■ PEOPLE

Population: 4,717,132 (July 1999 est.)
Nationality: Nicaraguan
Age Structure: 0-14 yrs: 44%; 15-64: 54%; 65+: 2% (1999 est.)
Population Growth Rate: 2.84% (1999 est.)
Net Migration: -1.06 migrants/1,000 population (1999 est.)
Ethnic Groups: 69% mestizo, 17% white, 9% black, 5% Indian
Languages: Spanish (official); English- and Indian-speaking minorities on Atlantic coast
Religions: 95% Roman Catholic, 5% Protestant
Birth Rate: 35.04/1,000 population (1999 est.)
Death Rate: 5.60/1,000 population (1999 est.)
Infant Mortality: 40.47 deaths/1,000 live births (1999 est.)
Life Expectancy at Birth: 64.70 years male, 69.56 years female (1999 est.)
Total Fertility Rate: 4.14 children born/woman (1999 est.)
Literacy: 63.4% (1997)

■ GOVERNMENT

Leader(s): Pres. José Arnoldo Aleman Lacayo, V. Pres. Enriqué Bolanos Geyer
Government Type: republic
Administrative Divisions: 15 departments (departamentos, sing. -departamento) and 2 autonomous regions (regiones autonomistas, sing. -region autonomista)

Nationhood: Sept. 15, 1821 (from Spain)
National Holiday: Independence Day, Sept. 15

■ ECONOMY

Overview: the economy is based on the export of coffee and cotton; government control is extensive, including the financial system, wholesale purchasing, production, sales, foreign trade and distribution of goods; many shortages; high inflation
GDP: $11.6 billion, per capita $2,500; real growth rate 4% (1998 est.)
Inflation: 7.2% (Dec. 1999)
Industries: accounts for 24% of GDP; food processing, chemicals, metal products, textiles, clothing, petroleum refining and distribution, beverages, footwear
Labour Force: 2.1 million (1998); 37.7% services, 46.5% agriculture, 15.8% industry
Unemployment: 14%; underemployment approximately 36% (1997 est.)
Agriculture: accounts for 32% of GDP; cash crops—coffee, bananas, sugar cane, cotton; food crops—rice, corn, cassava, citrus fruit, beans; variety of animal products—beef, veal, pork, poultry, dairy; war has lowered self-sufficiency in food
Natural Resources: gold, silver, copper, tungsten, lead, zinc, timber, fish

■ FINANCE/TRADE

Currency: gold córdoba ($C) = 100 centavos
International Reserves Excluding Gold: $510 million (Dec. 1999)
Gold Reserves: n.a.
Budget: revenues $389 million; expenditures $551 million, including capital expenditures n.a. (1996 est.)
Defence Expenditures: 1.2% of GDP (1998)
Education Expenditures: 3.9% of GNP (1997)
External Debt: $5.968 billion (1998)
Exports: $544 million (1999); commodities: coffee, cotton, sugar, bananas, seafood, meat, chemicals; partners: CEMA 15%, OECD 75%, others 10%
Imports: $1.846 billion (1999); commodities: petroleum, food, chemicals, machinery, clothing; partners: CEMA 55%, European Community 20%, Latin America 10%, others 10%

■ COMMUNICATIONS

Daily Newspapers: 4 (1996)
Televisions: 190/1,000 inhabitants (1998)
Radios: 285/1,000 inhabitants (1997)
Telephones: 31 lines/1,000 inhabitants (1998)

■ TRANSPORTATION

Motor Vehicles: 148,000; 73,000 passenger cars (1997 est.)
Roads: 16,382 km; 1,818 km paved
Railway: none
Air Traffic: 51,000 passengers carried (1997)
Airports: 184; 13 have paved runways (1998 est.)

Canadian Embassy: The Office of the Canadian Embassy, Costado Oriental de la Casa Nazareth, Una Quadra Arriba, Calle Noval, Managua. Mailing address: The Office of the Canadian Embassy, Apartado Postal 25, Managua, Nicaragua. Tel: (011-505-2) 68-0433. Fax: (011-505-2) 68-0437.
Embassy in Canada: Embassy of the Republic of Nicaragua, 1627 New Hampshire Ave NW, Washington DC 20009, USA. Tel: (202) 939-6537. Fax: (202) 939-6545.

Niger

Long-Form Name: Republic of Niger
Capital: Niamey

■ GEOGRAPHY

Area: 1,267,000 sq. km
Coastline: none: landlocked
Climate: mostly hot, dry, dusty; tropical in extreme south
Environment: recurrent drought and desertification severely affecting marginal agricultural activities; overgrazing; soil erosion
Terrain: desert and sand dunes; hills in north
Land Use: 3% arable land; 0% permanent; 7% meadows; 2% forest; 88% other; includes 660 sq. km irrigated
Location: WC Africa

■ PEOPLE

Population: 9,962,242 (July 1999 est.)
Nationality: Nigerian
Age Structure: 0-14 yrs: 48%; 15-64: 50%; 65+: 2% (1999 est.)
Population Growth Rate: 2.95% (1999 est.)
Net Migration: 0 migrants/1,000 population (1999 est.)
Ethnic Groups: 56% Hausa; 22% Djerma; 9% Fula; 8% Tuareg; 4% Beri Beri (Kanouri); 1% Arab, Toubou and Gourmantche; about 4,000 French expatriates
Languages: French (official); Hausa (50%), Djerma, also Tuareg, Fulani
Religions: 80% Muslim, remainder indigenous beliefs and Christians
Birth Rate: 52.31/1,000 population (1999 est.)

Death Rate: 22.78/1,000 population (1999 est.)
Infant Mortality: 112.79 deaths/1,000 live births (1999 est.)
Life Expectancy at Birth: 42.22 years male, 41.70 years female (1999 est.)
Total Fertility Rate: 7.24 children born/woman (1999 est.)
Literacy: 14.3% (1997)

■ GOVERNMENT

Leader(s): Pres. Mamadou Tandja, Prime Min. Hama Amadou
Government Type: republic
Administrative Divisions: 7 departments (departements, sing. -departement); 1 capital district (capitale district)
Nationhood: Aug. 3, 1960 (from France)
National Holiday: Republic Day, Dec. 18

■ ECONOMY

Overview: about 90% of the population is engaged in livestock rearing and farming; depends heavily on exploitation of uranium deposits, thus vulnerable to demand for uranium; increasing external debt is a problem. GDP growth can barely keep pace with the rapid population growth
GDP: $9.4 billion, per capita $970; real growth rate 4.5% (1998 est.)
Inflation: 0.3% (Feb. 2000)
Industries: accounts for 18% of GDP; cement, brick, rice mills, small cotton gins, textiles, chemicals, oilseed presses, slaughterhouses and a few other small light industries; uranium production began in 1971
Labour Force: 5 million (1998); 85% agriculture, 2.7% industry, 12.3% services
Unemployment: n.a.
Agriculture: accounts for 40% of GDP and 90% of labour force; cash crops—cowpeas, cotton, peanuts; food crops—millet, sorghum, cassava, rice; livestock—cattle, sheep, goats; self-sufficient in food except in drought years
Natural Resources: uranium, coal, iron ore, tin, phosphates

■ FINANCE/TRADE

Currency: Communauté financière africaine franc (CFAF) = 100 centimes
International Reserves Excluding Gold: $39 million (Nov. 1999)
Gold Reserves: 0.011 million fine troy ounces (July 1998)
Budget: revenues $370 million; expenditures $370 million, including capital expenditures of $186 million (1998 est.)
Defence Expenditures: 6.9% of central government expenditure (1997)
Education Expenditures: 2.3% of GNP (1997)
External Debt: $1.659 billion (1998)
Exports: $276 million (1999); commodities: uranium 76%, livestock, cowpeas, onions, hides, skins; partners: n.a.
Imports: $396 million (1999); commodities: petroleum products, primary materials, machinery, vehicles and parts, electronic equipment, pharmaceuticals, chemical products, cereals, foodstuffs; partners: n.a.

■ COMMUNICATIONS

Daily Newspapers: 1 (1996)
Televisions: 27/1,000 inhabitants (1998)
Radios: 69/1,000 inhabitants (1997)
Telephones: 2 lines/1,000 inhabitants (1998)

■ TRANSPORTATION

Motor Vehicles: 51,600; 37,500 passenger cars (1997 est.)
Roads: 10,100 km; 798 km paved
Railway: none
Air Traffic: 86,000 passengers carried (1997)
Airports: 27; 9 have paved runways (1998 est.)

Canadian Embassy: Office of the Canadian Embassy, Boulevard Mali Béro, Niamey; mailing address: Box 362, Niamey, Niger. Tel: (011-227) 75-36-86. Fax: (011-227) 75-31-01.
Embassy in Canada: Embassy of the Republic of Niger, 38 Blackburn Ave, Ottawa ON K1N 8A3. Tel: (613) 232-4291. Fax: (613) 230-9808.

Nigeria

Long-Form Name: Federal Republic of Nigeria
Capital: Abuja

■ GEOGRAPHY

Area: 923,770 sq. km
Coastline: 853 km
Climate: varies; equatorial in south, tropical in centre, arid in north
Environment: recent droughts in north severely affecting marginal agricultural activities; desertification; soil degradation, rapid deforestation
Terrain: southern lowlands merge into central hills and plateaus; mountains in southeast, plains in north
Land Use: 33% arable; 3% permanent crops; 44% permanent pastures; 12% forest; 8% other; includes 9,570 sq. km irrigated
Location: WC Africa, bordering on South Atlantic Ocean

Nigeria

■ PEOPLE

Population: 113,828,587 (July 1999 est.)
Nationality: Nigerian
Age Structure: 0-14 yrs: 45%; 15-64: 52%; 65+: 3% (1999 est.)
Population Growth Rate: 2.92% (1999 est.)
Net Migration: 0.31 migrants/1,000 population (1999 est.)
Ethnic Groups: more than 250 tribal groups; Hausa and Fulani of the north, Yoruba of the southwest and Ibos of the southeast make up 65% of the population; about 27,000 non-Africans
Languages: English (official); Hausa, Yoruba, Ibo, Fulani and several other languages also widely used
Religions: 50% Muslim, 40% Christian, 10% indigenous beliefs
Birth Rate: 41.84/1,000 population (1999 est.)
Death Rate: 12.98/1,000 population (1999 est.)
Infant Mortality: 69.46 deaths/1,000 live births (1999 est.)
Life Expectancy at Birth: 52.55 years male, 54.06 years female (1999 est.)
Total Fertility Rate: 6.02 children born/woman (1999 est.)
Literacy: 59.5% (1997)

■ GOVERNMENT

Leader(s): Pres. Olusegun Obasanjo; V. Pres. Atiku Abubakar
Government Type: military government since Dec. 1983; the present regime has announced democratization beginning Oct. 1998
Administrative Divisions: 30 states and 1 territory
Nationhood: Oct. 1, 1960 (from UK)
National Holiday: Independence Day, Oct. 1

■ ECONOMY

Overview: the economy is dependent on oil and vulnerable to oil prices; agricultural production cannot keep pace with rapid population growth and Nigeria, once a large exporter of food, must now import foodstuffs; high inflationary pressures are a concern; government efforts to reduce Nigeria's dependence on oil exports and to sustain noninflationary economic growth have been hampered by inadequate new investment and endemic corruption
GDP: $106.2 billion, per capita $960; real growth rate 1.6% (1998 est.)
Inflation: 0.2% (Dec.1999)
Industries: accounts for 42% of GDP; crude oil, natural gas, coal, tin, columbite; palm oil, peanut, cotton, rubber, petroleum, wood, hides and skins; textiles, cement, building materials, food products, footwear, chemicals, printing, ceramics, steel
Labour Force: 48 million (1998); 44.6% agriculture, 51.2% services, 4.2% industry
Unemployment: n.a.
Agriculture: accounts for 33% of GDP and half of labour force; inefficient small-scale farming dominates; once a large net exporter of food and now an importer; cash crops—cocoa, peanuts, palm oil, rubber; food crops—corn, rice, sorghum, millet, cassava, yams, fishing and forestry
Natural Resources: crude oil, tin, columbite, iron ore, coal, limestone, lead, zinc, natural gas

■ FINANCE/TRADE

Currency: naira (N) = 100 kobo
International Reserves Excluding Gold: $4,075 million (Dec. 1996)
Gold Reserves: 0.69 million fine troy ounces (Jan. 1997)
Budget: adjusted for purchasing power parity: revenues $13.9 billion; expenditures $13.9 billion, including capital expenditures of n.a. (1998 est.)
Defence Expenditures: 0.7% of GDP (1999)
Education Expenditures: 0.7% of GNP (1997)
External Debt: $30.315 billion (1998)
Exports: $9.729 billion (1998); commodities: oil 95%, cocoa, palm kernels, rubber; partners: European Community 51%, US 32%
Imports: $10.002 billion (1998); commodities: consumer goods, capital equipment, chemicals, raw materials; partners: European Community, US

■ COMMUNICATIONS

Daily Newspapers: 25 (1996)
Televisions: 66/1,000 inhabitants (1998)
Radios: 223/1,000 inhabitants (1997)
Telephones: 4 lines/1,000 inhabitants (1998)

■ TRANSPORTATION

Motor Vehicles: 970,000; 590,200 passenger cars (1997 est.)
Roads: n.a. km; 26,005 km paved
Railway: 3,557 km
Air Traffic: 318,000 passengers carried (1997)
Airports: 72; 36 have paved runways (1998 est.)

Canadian Embassy: The Canadian High Commission, 3A Bobo St, Abuja FCT, Nigeria. Tel: (011-234-9) 413-9910. Fax: (011-234-9) 413-9911.
Embassy in Canada: High Commission for the Federal Republic of Nigeria, 295 Metcalfe St, Ottawa, ON K2P 1R9. Tel: (613) 236-0522. Fax: (613) 236-0529.

Niue

Long-Form Name: Niue
Capital: Alofi

■ GEOGRAPHY

Area: 260 sq. km, world's largest uplifted coral island
Climate: tropical maritime, modified by southeasterly trade winds
Land Use: 19% arable, 8% permanent crops, 4% meadows and pastures, 19% forest, 50% other; includes n.a. sq. km irrigated
Location: Pacific Ocean, NE of New Zealand

■ PEOPLE

Population: 2,103 (July 1999 est.)
Nationality: Niuean
Ethnic Groups: Polynesian
Languages: English, Polynesian closely related to Tongan and Samoan

■ GOVERNMENT

Colony/Territory of: Territory of New Zealand
Leader(s): Head of State: Queen Elizabeth II, High Comm. John Bryan; Prem. Sani Lakatani
Government Type: self-governing territory in free association with New Zealand
National Holiday: Waitangi Day, Feb. 6

■ ECONOMY

Overview: heavily dependent on aid from New Zealand; govt. expenditures regularly exceed revenues; agriculture includes coconuts, honey, limes, root crops, livestock; chief trading partner: New Zealand

■ FINANCE/TRADE

Currency: New Zealand dollar = 100 cents

Canadian Embassy: c/o The Canadian High Commission, 3rd Fl, 61 Molesworth St, Thorndon, Wellington, New Zealand; Mailing address: c/o P.O. Box 12-049, Thorndon, Wellington, New Zealand. Tel: (011-64-4) 473-9577. Fax: (011-64-4) 471-2082.
Representative to Canada: c/o New Zealand High Commission, Clarica Centre, 99 Bank St, Ste 727, Ottawa ON K1P 6G3. Tel: (613) 238-5991. Fax: (613) 238-5707.

Norfolk Island

Long-Form Name: Territory of Norfolk Island
Capital: Kingston (administrative centre), Burnt Pine (commercial centre)

■ GEOGRAPHY

Area: 34.6 sq. km
Climate: subtropical, mild, little seasonal variation
Land Use: 0% arable, 0% permanent crops, 25% meadows and pastures, 0% forests, 75% other; includes no irrigated land
Location: S Pacific Ocean, E of Australia

■ PEOPLE

Population: 1,905 (July 1999 est.)
Nationality: Norfolk Islander
Ethnic Groups: majority descendants of Polynesians and British (the latter crew members of the British naval ship Bounty)
Languages: English (official), Norfolk (a mixture of 18th-century English and ancient Tahitian)

■ GOVERNMENT

Colony/Territory of: Dependent Territory of Australia
Leader(s): Queen Elizabeth II, represented by Admin. Anthony J. Messner; Chief Min. Ronald Coane Nobbs
Government Type: a largely self-governing dependency, territory of Australia
National Holiday: Pitcairners' Arrival Day Anniversary, June 8

■ ECONOMY

Overview: tourism is backbone of economy; revenues from tourism have helped the agricultural sector become self-sufficient in beef, poultry and eggs; export of indigenous fruit and vegetables

■ FINANCE/TRADE

Currency: Australian dollar = 100 cents

Canadian Embassy: c/o The Canadian High Commission, Commonwealth Ave, Canberra, A.C.T. 2600, Australia. Tel: (011-61-2) 6270-4000. Fax: (011-61-2) 6273-3285.
Representative to Canada: c/o Australian High Commission, 50 O'Connor St, Ste 710, Ottawa ON K1P 6L2. Tel: (613) 236-0841. Fax: (613) 236-4376.

Northern Marianas

Long-Form Name: The Commonwealth of the Northern Mariana Islands
Capital: Saipan

■ GEOGRAPHY
Area: 477 sq. km (combined land area of 16 islands)
Climate: tropical maritime, moderated by northeasterly trade winds; little seasonal temperature variation
Land Use: 21% arable on Saipan island; volcanic islands too mountainous for cultivation; chief agricultural use is grazing; 19% meadows and pastures; no irrigated land
Location: Pacific Ocean, E of the Philippines

■ PEOPLE
Population: 69,398 (July 1999 est.)
Nationality: no descriptive term; American citizenship
Ethnic Groups: Chamorro, Carolinians and other Micronesians, Caucasian, Japanese, Chinese, Korea
Languages: English (official), Chamorro, Carolinian, Japanese; 86% of the population speaks a language other than English at home

■ GOVERNMENT
Colony/Territory of: Outlying Territory of the United States
Leader(s): Head of State: Pres. William Clinton (US) to Jan. 20, 2001; Head of Government: Pedro P. Tenorio
Government Type: commonwealth in political union with the US; self-governing with locally elected governing body
National Holiday: Commonwealth Day, Jan. 8

■ ECONOMY
Overview: economy benefits from US financial assistance, but the rate of funding has declined as local revenues have increased; tourism is growing in importance and now employs approximately 50% of the workforce; agriculture: cattle, coconuts, breadfruit, vegetables

■ FINANCE/TRADE
Currency: American dollar = 100 cents

Canadian Embassy: c/o The Canadian Embassy, 501 Pennsylvania Ave. NW, Washington DC 20001, USA. Tel: (202) 682-1740. Fax: (202) 456-7726.
Representative to Canada: c/o Embassy of the United States of America, 490 Sussex Dr., Ottawa, ON, K1N 1G8. Tel: (613) 238-5335. Fax: (613) 688-3097.

Norway

Long-Form Name: Kingdom of Norway
Capital: Oslo

■ GEOGRAPHY
Area: 324,220 sq. km
Coastline: 21,925 km (3,491 km mainland; 2,413 km large islands; 16,093 km long fjords; numerous small islands and minor indentations); one of the longest and most rugged coastlines in the world
Climate: temperate along coast, modified by North Atlantic Current; colder interior; rainy year-round on west coast
Environment: air and water pollution; acid rain damages forests and adversely affects lakes
Terrain: glaciated; mostly high plateaus and rugged mountains broken by fertile valleys; small, scattered plains; coastline deeply indented by fjords; arctic tundra in north
Land Use: 3% arable; 0% permanent crops; negligible meadows, 27% forest; 70% other; includes 970 sq. km irrigated
Location: N Europe, bordering on Norwegian Sea, North Sea

■ PEOPLE
Population: 4,438,547 (July 1999 est.)
Nationality: Norwegian
Age Structure: 0-14 yrs: 20%; 15-64: 65%; 65+: 15% (1999 est.)
Population Growth Rate: 0.40% (1999 est.)
Net Migration: 1.62 migrants/1,000 population (1999 est.)
Ethnic Groups: Germanic (Nordic, Alpine, Baltic) and racial-cultural minority of 20,000 Lapps
Languages: Norwegian (official); small Lapp- and Finnish-speaking minorities
Religions: Lutheran (88%, state church), other Protestant and Roman Catholic 4%, none 3.2%, other 4.8%
Birth Rate: 12.54/1,000 population (1999 est.)
Death Rate: 10.12/1,000 population (1999 est.)
Infant Mortality: 4.96 deaths/1,000 live births (1999 est.)
Life Expectancy at Birth: 75.55 years male, 81.35 years female (1999 est.)
Total Fertility Rate: 1.77 children born/woman (1999 est.)
Literacy: 99% (1997)

■ GOVERNMENT
Leader(s): King Harald V, Prime Min. Jens Stoltenberg
Government Type: constitutional monarchy

Administrative Divisions: 19 provinces (fylker, sing. -fylke); dependent areas inc.: Bouvet Island (uninhabited), Jan Mayen (uninhabited), Peter I Island (uninhabited), Queen Maud Land (uninhabited), Svalbard
Nationhood: Oct. 26, 1905 (from Sweden)
National Holiday: Constitution Day, May 17

■ ECONOMY

Overview: a small country with high dependence on international trade; a prosperous capitalist nation that has extensive welfare measures; concerns are the aging population, increased economic integration with Europe and the balance between private and public influence in economic decisions
GDP: $109 billion, per capita $24,700; real growth rate 2.4% (1998 est.)
Inflation: 2.6% (April 2000)
Industries: accounts for 30% of GDP; petroleum and gas, food processing, shipbuilding, pulp and paper products, metal, chemicals, timber, mining, textiles, fishing
Labour Force: 2 million (1998); 38.7% community, social and business services, 17.4% trade and tourism, 14.6% industry
Unemployment: 3.0% (Dec. 1999)
Agriculture: accounts for 2% of GDP and 6% of labour force; among world's top 10 fishing nations; livestock output exceeds value of crops; over half of food needs imported
Natural Resources: rich in natural resources: crude oil, copper, natural gas, pyrites, nickel, iron ore, zinc, lead, fish, timber, hydropower

■ FINANCE/TRADE

Currency: krone (pl. kroner) (NKr) = 100 oere
International Reserves Excluding Gold: $19.947 billion (Jan. 2000)
Gold Reserves: 1.184 million fine troy ounces (Jan. 2000)
Budget: n.a.
Defence Expenditures: 6.77% of total govt. expenditure (1997)
Education Expenditures: 6.93% of total govt. expenditure (1997)
External Debt: none
Exports: $44.884 billion (1999); commodities: petroleum and petroleum products 25%, natural gas 11%, fish 7%, aluminum 6%, ships 3.5%, pulp and paper; partners: UK 26%, EFTA 16.3%, less developed countries 14%, Sweden 12%, Germany 12%, US 6%, Denmark 5%
Imports: $34.041 billion (1999); commodities: machinery, fuels and lubricants, transportation equipment, chemicals, foodstuffs, clothing, ships; partners: Sweden 18%, less developed countries 18%, Germany 14%, Denmark 8%, UK 7%, Japan 5%

■ COMMUNICATIONS

Daily Newspapers: 83 (1996)
Televisions: 579/1,000 inhabitants (1998)
Radios: 915/1,000 inhabitants (1997)
Telephones: 660 lines/1,000 inhabitants (1998)

■ TRANSPORTATION

Motor Vehicles: 2,210,000; 1,700,000 passenger cars (1997 est.)
Roads: 91,180 km; 67,473 km paved
Railway: 4,012 km
Air Traffic: 13,759,000 passengers carried (1997)
Airports: 103; 66 have paved runways (1998 est.)

Canadian Embassy: The Canadian Embassy, Wergelandsveien #7, 0244 Oslo, Norway. Tel: (011-47) 22-99-53-00. Fax: (011-47) 22-99-53-01.
Embassy in Canada: Embassy of the Kingdom of Norway, Royal Bank Centre, 90 Sparks St, Ste 532, Ottawa ON K1P 5B4. Tel: (613) 238-6571. Fax: (613) 238-2765.

Oman

Long-Form Name: Sultanate of Oman
Capital: Masqat or Muscat

■ GEOGRAPHY

Area: 212,460 sq. km
Coastline: 2,092 km
Climate: dry desert; hot, humid along coast; hot, dry interior; strong southwest summer monsoon (May to Sept.) in far south
Environment: summer winds often raise large sandstorms and dust storms in interior; sparse natural freshwater resources are threatened by increasing soil salinity
Terrain: vast central desert plain, rugged mountains in north and south
Land Use: 0% arable; negligible permanent; 5% meadows; 0% forest; 95% other; includes 580 sq. km irrigated
Location: SW Asia (Middle East), bordering on Arabian Sea

■ PEOPLE

Population: 2,446,645 (July 1999 est.)
Nationality: Omani
Age Structure: 0-14 yrs: 41%; 15-64: 57%; 65+: 2% (1999 est.)
Population Growth Rate: 3.45% (1998 est.)
Net Migration: 0.84 migrants/1,000 population (1999 est.)

Ethnic Groups: almost entirely Arab, with small Balochi, Zanzibari, Pakistani and Indian groups
Languages: Arabic (official); English, Balochi, Urdu, Indian dialects
Religions: 75% Ibadhi Muslim; remainder Sunni Muslim, Shi'a Muslim, Hindu minority
Birth Rate: 37.98/1,000 population (1999 est.)
Death Rate: 4.29/1,000 population (1999 est.)
Infant Mortality: 24.71 deaths/1,000 live births (1999 est.)
Life Expectancy at Birth: 69.31 years male, 73.39 years female (1999 est.)
Total Fertility Rate: 6.11 children born/woman (1999 est.)
Literacy: 67.1 (1997)

■ GOVERNMENT

Leader(s): Sultan and Prime Min. Qaboos bin Sa'id Al Said
Government Type: absolute monarchy; independent, with residual UK influence
Administrative Divisions: 6 regions (mintaqat, sing. -mintaqah) and 2 governorates (muhafazat, sing. -muhafazah)
Nationhood: 1650, expulsion of the Portuguese
National Holiday: National Day, Nov. 18

■ ECONOMY

Overview: economy depends on the success of its oil industry which has 20 years' supply at the current rate of extraction; subsistence agriculture is the major employment, and the general populace relies on imported food
GDP: $18.6 billion, per capita $7,900; real growth rate -8.5% (1998 est.)
Inflation: -0.6% (Feb. 2000)
Industries: accounts for 50% of GDP; crude oil production and refining, natural gas production, construction, cement, copper
Labour Force: 1 million (1998); 50% agriculture, 21.8% industry, 28.6% services; 58% of labour force are non-Omani
Unemployment: n.a.
Agriculture: accounts for 2% of GDP and 40% of labour force (including fishing); less than 2% of land cultivated; largely subsistence farming (dates, limes, bananas, alfalfa, vegetables, camels, cattle); not self-sufficient in food
Natural Resources: crude oil, copper, asbestos, some marble, limestone, chromium, gypsum, natural gas

■ FINANCE/TRADE

Currency: Omani rial (RO) = 1,000 baiza
International Reserves Excluding Gold: $1.163 billion (Jan. 1999)
Gold Reserves: 0.291 million fine troy ounces (Jan. 2000)
Budget: revenues $4 billion; expenditures $5.6 billion, including capital expenditures of n.a. (1999 est.)
Defence Expenditures: 32.43% of govt. expenditure (1998)
Education Expenditures: 15.58% of govt. expenditure (1998)
External Debt: $3.629 billion (1998)
Exports: $5.508 billion (1998); commodities: petroleum, re-exports, processed copper, dates, nuts, fish; partners: Japan, S Korea, Thailand
Imports: $4.674 billion (1999); commodities: machinery, transportation equipment, manufactured goods, food, livestock, lubricants; partners: Japan, United Arab Emirates, UK, Germany, US

■ COMMUNICATIONS

Daily Newspapers: 4 (1996)
Televisions: 595/1,000 inhabitants (1998)
Radios: 598/1,000 inhabitants (1997)
Telephones: 92 lines/1,000 inhabitants (1998)

■ TRANSPORTATION

Motor Vehicles: 300,000; 209,000 passenger cars (1997 est.)
Roads: 32,800 km; 9,840 km paved
Railway: none
Air Traffic: 1,678,000 passengers carried (1997)
Airports: 143; 6 have paved runways (1998 est.)

Canadian Embassy: The Canadian Embassy to Oman, c/o The Canadian Embassy, P.O. Box 94321, Riyadh 11693, Saudi Arabia. Tel: (011-966-1) 488-2288. Fax: (011-966-1) 488-1997.
Embassy in Canada: c/o Embassy of the Sultanate of Oman, 2535 Belmont Rd. NW, Washington DC 20008, USA. Tel: (202) 387-1980. Fax: (202) 745-4933.

Pakistan

Long-Form Name: Islamic Republic of Pakistan
Capital: Islamabad

■ GEOGRAPHY

Area: 803,940 sq. km
Coastline: 1,046 km along Gulf of Oman and Arabian Sea
Climate: mostly hot, dry desert; temperate in northwest; arctic in north
Environment: frequent earthquakes, occasionally severe especially in north and west; flooding along the Indus after heavy rains (July and Aug.); deforestation; soil erosion; desertification; water pollution from raw sewage
Terrain: flat Indus plain in east; mountains in north and northwest; Balochistan plateau in west

Pakistan

Land Use: 27% arable; 1% permanent crops; 6% meadows; 5% forest; 61% other, includes 171,100 sq. km irrigated
Location: SW Asia (Middle East), bordering on Arabian Sea

■ PEOPLE

Population: 138,123,359 (July 1999 est.)
Nationality: Pakistani
Age Structure: 0-14 yrs: 41%; 15-64: 55%; 65+: 4% (1999 est.)
Population Growth Rate: 2.18% (1999 est.)
Net Migration: -1.30 migrants/1,000 population (1999 est.)
Ethnic Groups: Punjabi, Sindhi, Pashtun (Pathan), Baloch, Muhajir (immigrants from India and their descendants)
Languages: Urdu (official), Punjab (spoken by majority), Sindhi, Pushto, English
Religions: 97% Muslim (77% Sunni, 20% Shi'a), 3% Christian, Hindu and other
Birth Rate: 33.51/1,000 population (1999 est.)
Death Rate: 10.45/1,000 population (1999 est.)
Infant Mortality: 91.86 deaths/1,000 live births (1999 est.)
Life Expectancy at Birth: 58.49 years male, 60.30 years female (1999 est.)
Total Fertility Rate: 4.73 children born/woman (1999 est.)
Literacy: 40.9% (1997)

■ GOVERNMENT

Leader(s): Pres. Rafiq Mohammad Tarar. Chief Exec. Lt.-Gen Pervez Musharraf
Government Type: federal republic
Administrative Divisions: 4 provinces, 1 territory and 1 capital territory
Nationhood: Aug. 14, 1947 (from UK; formerly West Pakistan)
National Holiday: Pakistan Day (proclamation of the republic), Mar. 23

■ ECONOMY

Overview: long-standing economic weaknesses such as indebtedness, a small tax base, large population and dependence on cotton exports hamper the economy
GDP: $270 billion, per capita $2,000; real growth rate 5% (1998 est.)
Inflation: 3.9% (April 2000)
Industries: accounts for 26% of GDP; textiles, food processing, beverages, petroleum products, construction materials, clothing, paper products, international finance, shrimp
Labour Force: 49.4 million (1998); 47.4% agriculture, 12.4% industry, 13.3% community, social and business services
Unemployment: n.a.

Agriculture: 24% of GDP, over 50% of labour force; world's largest continuous irrigation system; cotton, wheat, rice, sugar cane, fruits, vegetables, livestock (milk, beef, mutton, eggs); self-sufficient in food grain
Natural Resources: land, extensive natural gas reserves, limited crude oil, poor quality coal, iron ore, copper, salt, limestone

■ FINANCE/TRADE

Currency: Pakistani rupee (PRs) = 100 paisa
International Reserves Excluding Gold: $1.560 billion (Jan. 2000)
Gold Reserves: 2.088 million fine troy ounces (Jan. 2000)
Budget: revenues $9.6 billion; expenditures $13.6 billion, including capital expenditures n.a. (1996-97)
Defence Expenditures: 4.4% of GDP (1998-99)
Education Expenditures: 2.7% of GNP (1997)
External Debt: $32.229 billion (1998)
Exports: $8.997 billion (1999); commodities: rice, cotton, textiles, clothing; partners: European Community 31%, US 11%, Japan 11%
Imports: $9.775 billion (1999); commodities: petroleum, petroleum products, machinery, transportation, equipment, vegetable oils, animal fats, chemicals; partners: European Community 26%, Japan 15%, US 11%

■ COMMUNICATIONS

Daily Newspapers: 264 (1996)
Televisions: 21/1,000 inhabitants (1996)
Radios: 98/1,000 inhabitants (1997)
Telephones: 19 lines/1.000 inhabitants (1998)

■ TRANSPORTATION

Motor Vehicles: 1,100,000; 800,000 passenger cars (1997 est.)
Roads: 224,774 km; 128,121 km paved
Railway: 8,163 km
Air Traffic: 5,883,000 passengers carried (1997 est.)
Airports: 116; 80 have paved runways (1998 est.)

Canadian Embassy: The Canadian High Commission, Diplomatic Enclave, Sector G-5, Islamabad; mailing address: The Canadian High Commission, G.P.O. Box 1042, Islamabad, Pakistan. Tel: (011-92-51) 27-91-00. Fax: (011-92-51) 27-91-88.
Embassy in Canada: High Commission for the Islamic Republic of Pakistan, Burnside Bldg, 151 Slater St, Ste 608, Ottawa ON K1P 5H3. Tel: (613) 238-7881. Fax: (613) 238-7296.

Palau

Long-Form Name: Republic of Palau
Capital: Koror (on Koror Island); a new capital is being built 20 km northeast

■ GEOGRAPHY

Area: 458 sq. km (26 islands and 300+ islets)
Coastline: 1,519 km
Climate: tropical, warm year-round; wet season, May to Dec.; dry season, Jan. to April; typhoon-prone with violent winds and heavy rain, esp. in July
Environment: inadequate facilities for waste management; typhoons
Terrain: about 200 islands; topography varies from high and mountainous to low coral reef islands; northern islands of volcanic origin, fertile and extensively cultivated; southern islands too rugged for habitation
Land Use: n.a.
Location: W Pacific Ocean (Micronesia), E of the Philippines

■ PEOPLE

Population: 18,467 (July 1999 est.)
Nationality: Palauan
Age Structure: 0-14 yrs: 27%; 15-64: 68%; 65+: 5% (1999 est.)
Population Growth Rate: 1.94% (1999 est.)
Net Migration: 5.63 migrants/1,000 population (1999 est.)
Ethnic Groups: Polynesian, Malayan, Melanesian, mixtures
Languages: English (official in all states), Sonsorolese, Angaur, Japanese, Tobi, Palauan
Religions: Christian, Modekngei, a religion indigenous to Palau
Birth Rate: 21.55/1,000 population (1999 est.)
Death Rate: 7.74/1,000 population (1999 est.)
Infant Mortality: 18.50 deaths/1,000 live births (1999 est.)
Life Expectancy at Birth: 64.69 years male, 70.98 years female (1999 est.)
Total Fertility Rate: 2.66 children born/woman (1999 est.)
Literacy: 92% (1997)

■ GOVERNMENT

Leader(s): Pres. Kuniwo Nakamura, V. Pres. Tommy Remengesau
Government Type: constitutional government in free association with the US
Administrative Divisions: 16 states
Nationhood: Oct. 1, 1994 (from US-administered UN trusteeship)
National Holiday: Constitution Day, July 9

■ ECONOMY

Overview: subsistence agriculture and fishing; some tourism; government is main employer; phosphate deposits on northern islands; largely dependent on imports from the US
GDP: $160 million, per capita $8,800; real growth rate 10% (1997 est.)
Inflation: n.a.
Industries: some fishing and agriculture, tourism, crafts
Labour Force: n.a.
Unemployment: 7%
Agriculture: subsistence-level cultivation of coconuts, copra, yams, cassava
Natural Resources: marine resources, minerals, forests

■ FINANCE/TRADE

Currency: American dollar (US$) = 100 cents
International Reserves Excluding Gold: n.a.
Gold Reserves: n.a.
Budget: revenues $52.9 million; expenditures $59.9 million, including capital expenditures of n.a. (1997 est.)
Defence Expenditures: defence is the responsibility of the US
Education Expenditures: n.a.
External Debt: n.a.
Exports: $14.3 million (1996); fish, copra, handicrafts; partners: US, Japan
Imports: $72.4 million (1996): partners: US

■ COMMUNICATIONS

Daily Newspapers: n.a.
Televisions: n.a.
Radios: n.a.
Telephones: n.a.

■ TRANSPORTATION

Motor Vehicles: n.a.
Roads: 61 km; 36 km paved
Railway: none
Air Traffic: n.a.
Airports: 3; 1 has a paved runway (1998 est.)

Canadian Embassy: c/o The Canadian Embassy, 501 Pennsylvania Ave NW, Washington DC 20001, USA. Tel: (202) 682-1740. Fax: (202) 456-7726.
Embassy in Canada: c/o Embassy of the United States of America, 490 Sussex Drive, Ottawa, ON, K1N 1G8, Tel: (613) 238-5335. Fax: (613) 688-3097.

Panama

Long-Form Name: Republic of Panama
Capital: Panama

■ GEOGRAPHY

Area: 78,200 sq. km
Coastline: 2,490 km
Climate: tropical; hot, humid, cloudy; prolonged rainy season (May to Jan.), short dry season (Jan. to May)
Environment: dense tropical forest in east and northwest is threatened by deforestation; water pollution and soil degradation
Terrain: interior mostly steep, rugged mountains and dissected, upland plains; coastal areas largely plains and rolling hills
Land Use: 7% arable; 2% permanent crops; 20% meadows; 44% forest; 27% other; includes 320 sq. km irrigated
Location: Central (Latin) America, bordering on S America, Caribbean Sea, Pacific Ocean

■ PEOPLE

Population: 2,778,526 (July 1999 est.)
Nationality: Panamanian
Age Structure: 0-14 yrs: 32%; 15-64: 63%; 65+: 5% (1999 est.)
Population Growth Rate: 1.53% (1999 est.)
Net Migration: -1.22 migrants/1,000 population (1999 est.)
Ethnic Groups: 70% mestizo (mixed Indian and European ancestry), 14% West Indian, 10% white, 6% Indian
Languages: Spanish (official), 14% English; many Panamanians are bilingual
Religions: 85% Roman Catholic, 15% Protestant
Birth Rate: 21.69/1,000 population (1999 est.)
Death Rate: 5.13/1,000 population (1999 est.)
Infant Mortality: 23.35 deaths/1,000 live births (1999 est.)
Life Expectancy at Birth: 71.91 years male, 77.51 years female (1999 est.)
Total Fertility Rate: 2.54 children born/woman (1999 est.)
Literacy: 91.1% (1997)

■ GOVERNMENT

Leader(s): Pres. Mireya Elisa Moscoso de Gruber, First V. Pres. Arturo Ulises Vallarino
Government Type: constitutional republic
Administrative Divisions: 9 provinces (provincias, sing. provincia) and 2 territories (comarca)
Nationhood: Nov. 3, 1903 (from Colombia; became independent from Spain Nov. 28, 1821)
National Holiday: Independence Day, Nov. 3

■ ECONOMY

Overview: political instability, lack of credit and the erosion of business confidence have drastically hurt the economy; exports are stagnant; unemployment and economic reform are two of the greatest challenges the government must face
GDP: $19.9 billion, per capita $7,300; real growth rate 2.7% (1998 est.)
Inflation: 6.9% (Jan. 2000)
Industries: accounts for 18% of GDP; manufacturing and construction activities, petroleum refining, brewing, cement and other construction materials, sugar mills
Labour Force: 1 million (1998); 26.9% community, social and business services; 26.3% agriculture, 9.5% industry
Unemployment: 13.1% (1997 est.)
Agriculture: accounts for 8% of GDP and 27% of labour force; bananas, rice, corn, coffee, sugar cane, livestock, fishing, importer of food grain, vegetables, milk products
Natural Resources: copper, mahogany forests, shrimp

■ FINANCE/TRADE

Currency: balboa (B) = 100 centesimos
International Reserves Excluding Gold: $886 million (Jan. 2000)
Gold Reserves: n.a.
Budget: revenues $2.4 billion; expenditures $2.4 billion, including capital expenditures of $341 million (1997 est.)
Defence Expenditures: 5.04% of total govt. expenditure (1997)
Education Expenditures: 18.33% of govt. expenditure (1997)
External Debt: $6.689 billion (1998)
Exports: $822 million (1999); commodities: bananas 40%, shrimp 27%, coffee 4%, sugar, petroleum products; partners: US 90%, Central America and Caribbean, European Community
Imports: $3.516 billion (1999); commodities: foodstuffs 16%, capital goods 9%, crude oil 16%, consumer goods, chemicals; partners: US 35%, Central America and Caribbean, European Community, Mexico, Venezuela

■ COMMUNICATIONS

Daily Newspapers: 7 (1996)
Televisions: 187/1,000 inhabitants (1998)
Radios: 299/1,000 inhabitants (1997)
Telephones: 151 lines/1,000 inhabitants (1998)

■ TRANSPORTATION

Motor Vehicles: 226,800; 144,000 passenger cars (1997 est.)

Roads: 11,100 km; 3,730 km paved
Railway: 335 km
Air Traffic: 772,000 passengers carried (1997)
Airports: 110; 43 have paved runways (1998 est.)

Canadian Embassy: The Canadian Embassy, World Trade Center, 1st Floor, Calle 53 Este y Calle 5 B Sur, Urbanización Marbella City, Panama; Postal Address: The Canadian Embassy, Apartado Postal 0832-2446, Estafeta World Trade Center, Panama City, Panama. Tel: (011-507) 264-9731. Fax: (011-507) 263-8083.
Embassy in Canada: Embassy of the Republic of Panama, 130 Albert St, Ste 300, Ottawa ON K1P 5G4. Tel: (613) 236-7177. Fax: (613) 236-5775.

Papua New Guinea

Long-Form Name: Independent State of Papua New Guinea
Capital: Port Moresby

■ GEOGRAPHY

Area: 462,840 sq. km
Coastline: 5,152 km
Climate: tropical; northwest monsoon (Dec. to Mar.), southeast monsoon (May to Oct.); slight seasonal temperature variation
Environment: one of the world's largest swamps along southwest coast; some active volcanos; frequent earthquakes and mudslides; pollution and deforestation
Terrain: mostly mountains with coastal lowlands and rolling foothills
Land Use: 0.1% arable; 1% permanent crops; negligible meadows; 92.9% forest; 6% other; includes n.a. sq. km irrigated
Location: Pacific Ocean, Coral Sea N of Australia

■ PEOPLE

Population: 4,705,126 (July 1999 est.)
Nationality: Papua New Guinean
Age Structure: 0-14 yrs: 39%; 15-64: 58%; 65+: 3% (1999 est.)
Population Growth Rate: 2.26% (1999 est.)
Net Migration: 0 migrants/1,000 population (1999 est.)
Ethnic Groups: predominantly Melanesian and Papuan; some Negrito, Micronesian and Polynesian
Languages: pidgin, English, Motu (all official); also 715 local languages
Religions: 22% Roman Catholic, 16% Lutheran, 8% Presbyterian/Methodist/London Missionary Society, 5% Anglican, 4% Evangelical Alliance, 1% Seventh-Day Adventists, 10% other Protestant sects, 34% indigenous beliefs
Birth Rate: 32.04/1,000 population (1999 est.)
Death Rate: 9.47/1,000 population (1999 est.)
Infant Mortality: 55.58 deaths/1,000 live births (1999 est.)
Life Expectancy at Birth: 57.58 years male, 59.40 years female (1999 est.)
Total Fertility Rate: 4.17 children born/woman (1999 est.)
Literacy: 73.7% (1997)

■ GOVERNMENT

Leader(s): Head of State: Queen Elizabeth II/Gov. Gen. Silas Atopare. Prime Min. Mekere Morauta
Government Type: parliamentary democracy
Administrative Divisions: 20 provinces
Nationhood: Sept. 16, 1975 (from UN trusteeship under Australian administration)
National Holiday: Independence Day, Sept. 16

■ ECONOMY

Overview: country has abundant natural resources but exploitation has been hampered by the rugged terrain and the high cost of developing an infrastructure; subsistence agriculture is the livelihood for 85% of the population; mining accounts for about 60% of export earnings
GDP: $11.1 billion, per capita $2,400; real growth rate 1.6% (1998 est.)
Inflation: 13.2% (Dec. 1999)
Industries: accounts for 34.5% of GDP; copra crushing, oil palm processing, plywood processing, wood chip production, gold, silver, copper, construction, tourism
Labour Force: 2 million (1998); 85% agriculture, 10.2% industry,
Unemployment: n.a.
Agriculture: 28.2% of GDP; fertile soils and favourable climate permits cultivating a wide variety of crops; cash crops: coffee, cocoa, coconuts, palm kernels; other products: tea, rubber, sweet potatoes, fruit, vegetables, poultry, pork; net importer of food for urban centres
Natural Resources: gold, copper, silver, natural gas, timber, oil potential

■ FINANCE/TRADE

Currency: kina (K) = 100 toea
International Reserves Excluding Gold: $205 million (Dec. 1999)
Gold Reserves: 0.063 million fine troy ounces (Dec. 1999)
Budget: revenues $1.5 billion; expenditures $1.35 billion, including capital expenditures (1997 est.)

Defence Expenditures: 1.0% of GDP (1998)
Education Expenditures: n.a.
External Debt: $2.692 billion (1998)
Exports: $1.877 billion (1999); commodities: gold, copper ore, coffee, copra, palm oil, timber, lobster; partners: Germany, Japan, Australia, UK, Spain, US
Imports: $1.188 billion (1999); commodities: machinery and transport equipment, fuels, food, chemicals, consumer goods; partners: Australia, Singapore, Japan, US, New Zealand, UK

■ COMMUNICATIONS
Daily Newspapers: 2 (1996)
Televisions: 24/1,000 inhabitants (1998)
Radios: 97/1,000 inhabitants (1997)
Telephones: 11 lines/1,000 inhabitants (1998)

■ TRANSPORTATION
Motor Vehicles: 99,300; 21,600 passenger cars (1997 est.)
Roads: 19,600 km; 686 km paved
Railway: none
Air Traffic: 1,114,000 passengers carried (1997)
Airports: 492; 19 have paved runways (1998 est.)

Canadian Embassy: The Canadian High Commission to Papua New Guinea, c/o The Canadian High Commission, Commonwealth Ave, Canberra A.C.T. 2600, Australia. Office: The Consulate of Canada, P.O. Box 851, Port Moresby, NCD, Papua New Guinea. Tel: (011-675) 6270-4000. Fax: (011-675) 322-4824.
Embassy in Canada: c/o High Commission for Papua New Guinea, 1779 Massachusetts Ave. NW, Ste. 805, Washington DC 20036, USA. Tel: (202) 745-3680. Fax: (202) 745-3679.

Paraguay

Long-Form Name: Republic of Paraguay
Capital: Asunción

■ GEOGRAPHY
Area: 406,750 sq. km
Coastline: none: landlocked
Climate: subtropical; varies from temperate in east to semi-arid in far west
Environment: local flooding in southeast (early Sept. to June); poorly drained plains may become boggy (early Oct. to June); deforestation and water pollution are increasing
Terrain: grassy plains and wooded hills east of Río Paraguay; Gran Chaco region west of Río Paraguay mostly low, marshy plain near the river and dry forest and thorny scrub elsewhere
Land Use: 6% arable; 0% permanent crops; 55% permanent pastures; 32% forest; 7% other; includes 670 sq. km irrigated
Location: C South America

■ PEOPLE
Population: 5,434,095 (July 1999 est.)
Nationality: Paraguayan
Age Structure: 0-14 yrs: 39%; 15-64: 56%; 65+: 5% (1999 est.)
Population Growth Rate: 2.65% (1999 est.)
Net Migration: -0.09 migrants/1,000 population (1999 est.)
Ethnic Groups: 95% mestizo (Spanish and Indian), 5% white and Indian
Languages: Spanish (official), Guarani
Religions: 90% Roman Catholic; 10% Mennonite and other Protestant denominations
Birth Rate: 31.87/1,000 population (1999 est.)
Death Rate: 5.23/1,000 population (1999 est.)
Infant Mortality: 36.35 deaths/1,000 live births (1999 est.)
Life Expectancy at Birth: 70.47 years male, 74.49 years female (1999 est.)
Total Fertility Rate: 4.22 children born/woman (1999 est.)
Literacy: 92.4% (1997)

■ GOVERNMENT
Leader(s): Pres. Luis Angel Gonzalez Macchi
Government Type: republic
Administrative Divisions: 18 departments (departamentos, sing.-departamento)
Nationhood: May 14, 1811 (from Spain)
National Holiday: Independence Days, May 14-15

■ ECONOMY
Overview: in the absence of significant mineral or petroleum resources, the economy is based on agriculture; has a large hydropower potential; is vulnerable to climatic conditions and international commodity prices for agricultural exports. Nontraditional exports are growing rapidly
GDP: $19.8 billion, per capita $3,700; real growth rate -0.5% (1998 est.)
Inflation: 9.6% (March 2000)
Industries: accounts for 30% of GDP; meat packing, oilseed crushing, milling, brewing, textiles, other light consumer goods, cement, construction
Labour Force: 2 million (1998); 26.8% trade and tourism, 17.7% industry, 33.1% services
Unemployment: 8.2% (1997 est.)
Agriculture: accounts for 27% GDP and 45% of labour force; cash crops: cotton, sugar cane; other crops: corn, wheat, tobacco, soybeans,

cassava, fruit and vegetables; animal products: beef, pork, eggs, milk; surplus producer of timber; self-sufficient in most foods
Natural Resources: iron ore, manganese, limestone, hydropower, timber

■ FINANCE/TRADE
Currency: guaraní (pl. guaraníes) (G/) = 100 centimos
International Reserves Excluding Gold: $930 million (Jan. 2000)
Gold Reserves: 0.035 million fine troy ounces (Jan. 2000)
Budget: n.a.
Defence Expenditures: 1.4% of GDP (1998)
Education Expenditures: 4.0% of GNP (1997)
External Debt: $2.304 billion (1998)
Exports: $1.089 billion (1997); commodities: cotton, soybeans, timber, vegetable oils, coffee, tung oil, meat products; partners: European Community 37%, Brazil 25%, Argentina 10%, Chile 6%, US 6%
Imports: $3.403 billion (1997); commodities: capital goods 35%, consumer goods 20%, fuels and lubricants 19%, raw materials 16%, foodstuffs, beverages and tobacco 10%; partners: Brazil 30%, European Community 20%, US 18%, Argentina 8%, Japan 7%

■ COMMUNICATIONS
Daily Newspapers: 5 (1996)
Televisions: 101/1,000 inhabitants (1998)
Radios: 182/1,000 inhabitants (1997)
Telephones: 55 lines/1,000 inhabitants (1998)

■ TRANSPORTATION
Motor Vehicles: 121,000; 71,000 passenger cars (1997 est.)
Roads: 29,500 km; 2,803 km paved
Railway: 971 km
Air Traffic: 196,000 passengers carried (1997)
Airports: 941; 10 have paved runways (1998 est.)

Canadian Embassy: The Canadian Embassy to Paraguay, 1598 Casilla de Correo, 1425 Buenos Aires, Argentina. Office: The Consulate of Canada, Professor Ramirez c/Juan de Salazar, Asunción, Paraguay. Tel: (011-595-21) 227-207. Fax: (011-595-21) 227-208.
Embassy in Canada: Embassy of the Republic of Paraguay, 151 Slater St, Ste 501, Ottawa, ON K1P 5H3. Tel: (613) 567-1283. Fax: (613) 567-1679.

Peru

Long-Form Name: Republic of Peru
Capital: Lima

■ GEOGRAPHY
Area: 1,285,220 sq. km
Coastline: 2,414 km
Climate: varies from tropical in east to dry desert in west
Environment: subject to earthquakes, tsunamis, landslides, mild volcanic activity; deforestation; overgrazing; soil erosion; desertification; air pollution in Lima; shares control of Lago Titicaca, world's highest navigable lake, with Bolivia
Terrain: western coastal plain (costa), high and rugged Andes in centre (sierra), eastern lowland jungle of Amazon Basin (selva)
Land Use: 3% arable: negligible permanent; 21% meadows; 66% forest; 10% other, includes 12,800 sq. km irrigated
Location: W South America, bordering on Pacific Ocean

■ PEOPLE
Population: 26,624,582 (July 1999 est.)
Nationality: Peruvian
Age Structure: 0-14 yrs: 35%; 15-64: 60%; 65+: 5% (1999 est.)
Population Growth Rate: 1.93% (1999 est.)
Net Migration: -1.13 migrants/1,000 population (1999 est.)
Ethnic Groups: 45% Indian; 37% mestizo (mixed Indian and European ancestry); 15% white; 3% black, Japanese, Chinese and other
Languages: Spanish and Quechua (official), Aymara
Religions: predominantly Roman Catholic
Birth Rate: 26.09/1,000 population (1999 est.)
Death Rate: 5.70/1,000 population (1999 est.)
Infant Mortality: 38.97 deaths/1,000 live births (1999 est.)
Life Expectancy at Birth: 68.08 years male, 72.78 years female (1999 est.)
Total Fertility Rate: 3.23 children born/woman (1999 est.)
Literacy: 88.7% (1997)

■ GOVERNMENT
Leader(s): Pres. Alberto Kenyo Fujimori, Prime Min. Frederico Salas Guevara. Elections scheduled March 2001.
Government Type: republic
Administrative Divisions: 24 departments (departamentos, sing. -departamento) and 1 constitutional province (provincia constitucional)
Nationhood: July 28, 1821 (from Spain)
National Holiday: Independence Day, July 28

■ ECONOMY
Overview: revival of growth in GDP continues to

be restricted by the large amount of public and private resources being devoted to strengthening internal security; deficit spending and poor relations with international lenders are problems; labour unrest has cut production; food shortages; world's largest producer of coca (for cocaine)
GDP: $111.8 billion, per capita $4,300; real growth rate 1.8% (1998 est.)
Inflation: 3.8% (April 2000)
Industries: accounts for 37% of GDP, mining of metals, petroleum, fishing, textiles, clothing, food processing, cement, auto assembly, steel, shipbuilding, metal fabrication
Labour Force: 9.2 million (1998); 34.1% trade and tourism, 28.6% community, social and business services, 6% finance
Unemployment: 7.7%, plus extensive underemployment (1997)
Agriculture: accounts for 7% of GDP and 35% of labour force; commercial crops: coffee, cotton, sugar cane; other crops: rice, wheat, potatoes, plantains, coca; animal products: poultry, meats, dairy, wool; not self-sufficient in grain or vegetable oil; fish catch of 6.9 million metric tons
Natural Resources: copper, silver, gold, petroleum, timber, fish, iron ore, coal, phosphate, potash

■ FINANCE/TRADE

Currency: nuevo sol (pl. soles) (S/.) = 100 centimos
International Reserves Excluding Gold: $9.082 billion (Jan. 2000)
Gold Reserves: 1.100 million fine troy ounces (Jan. 2000)
Budget: revenues $8.5 billion; expenditures $9.3 billion, including capital expenditures n.a. (1996 est.)
Defence Expenditures: 1.4% of GDP (1998)
Education Expenditures: 2.9% of GNP (1997)
External Debt: $32.397 billion (1998)
Exports: $6.814 billion (1997); commodities: fishmeal, cotton, sugar, coffee, copper, iron ore, refined silver, lead, zinc, crude petroleum and by-products; partners: European Community 22%, US 20%, Japan 11%, Latin America 8%, former USSR countries 4%
Imports: $10.263 billion (1997); commodities: foodstuffs, machinery, transport equipment, iron and steel semimanufactures, chemicals, pharmaceuticals; partners: US 23%, Latin America 16%, European Community 12%, Japan 7%, Switzerland 3%

■ COMMUNICATIONS

Daily Newspapers: 74 (1996)
Televisions: 144/1,000 inhabitants (1998)
Radios: 273/1,000 inhabitants (1997)
Telephones: 67 lines/1,000 inhabitants (1998)

■ TRANSPORTATION

Motor Vehicles: 775,000; 500,000 passenger cars (1997 est.)
Roads: 72,800 km; 7,353 km paved
Railway: 2,041 km
Air Traffic: 2,725,000 passengers carried (1997)
Airports: 244; 44 have paved runways (1998 est.)

Canadian Embassy: The Canadian Embassy, Calle Libertad 130, Miraflores, Lima; mailing address: Casilla 18-1126, Correo Miraflores, Lima, Peru. Tel: (011-51-1) 444-4015. Fax: (011-51-1)242-4050
Embassy in Canada: Embassy of the Republic of Peru, 130 Albert St, Ste 1901, Ottawa ON K1P 5G4. Tel: (613) 238-1777. Fax: (613) 232-3062.

Philippines

Long-Form Name: Republic of the Philippines
Capital: Manila

■ GEOGRAPHY

Area: 300,000 sq. km
Coastline: 36,289 km
Climate: tropical marine; northeast monsoon (Nov. to Apr.); southwest monsoon (May to Oct.)
Environment: astride typhoon belt, usually affected by 15 and struck by five to six cyclonic storms per year; subject to landslides, active volcanoes, destructive earthquakes, tsunami; deforestation; soil erosion; water pollution
Terrain: mostly mountains with narrow to extensive coastal lowlands
Land Use: 19% arable; 12% permanent crops; 4% meadows; 46% forest; 19% other, includes 15,800 sq. km irrigated
Location: SE of China, bordering on South China Sea, Pacific Ocean

■ PEOPLE

Population: 79,345,812 (July 1999 est.)
Nationality: Filipino
Age Structure: 0-14 yrs: 37%; 15-64: 59%; 65+: 4% (1999 est.)
Population Growth Rate: 2.04% (1999 est.)
Net Migration: -1.03 migrants/1,000 population (1999 est.)
Ethnic Groups: 91.5% Christian Malay, 4% Muslim Malay, 1.5% Chinese, 3% other
Languages: Pilipino (native national language based on Tagalog) and English (both official);

Spanish also spoken, also 76 indigenous languages including Cebuano, Tagalog, Iloco, Ifugao
Religions: 83% Roman Catholic, 9% Protestant, 5% Muslim, 3% Buddhist and other
Birth Rate: 27.88/1,000 population (1999 est.)
Death Rate: 6.45/1,000 population (1999 est.)
Infant Mortality: 33.89 deaths/1,000 live births (1999 est.)
Life Expectancy at Birth: 63.79 years male, 69.50 years female (1999 est.)
Total Fertility Rate: 3.46 children born/woman (1999 est.)
Literacy: 94.6% (1997)

■ GOVERNMENT

Leader(s): Pres. Joseph Estrada, V. Pres. Gloria Macapagal-Arroyo
Government Type: republic
Administrative Divisions: 14 regions, divided into 72 provinces and 61 chartered cities
Nationhood: July 4, 1946 (from US)
National Holiday: Independence Day (from Spain), June 12

■ ECONOMY

Overview: drought and power supply problems have hampered production; world's largest exporter of coconuts and coconut products
GDP: $270.5 billion, per capita $3,500; real growth rate -0.5% (1997 est.)
Inflation: 3.7% (April 2000)
Industries: accounts for 32% of GDP; textiles, pharmaceuticals, chemicals, wood products, food processing, electronics assembly, petroleum refining, fishing
Labour Force: 32 million (1998); 45.8% agriculture, 17.1% community, social and business services, 9.5% industry
Unemployment: 9.6% (Oct. 1998)
Agriculture: accounts for about 20% of GDP and 45% of labour force; major crops: rice, coconuts, corn, sugarcane, bananas, pineapples, mangoes; animal products: pork, eggs, beef: net exporter of farm products: fish catch of 2 million metric tons annually
Natural Resources: timber, crude oil, nickel, cobalt, silver, gold, salt, copper

■ FINANCE/TRADE

Currency: peso (P) = 100 centavos
International Reserves Excluding Gold: $12.897 billion (Jan. 2000)
Gold Reserves: 6.474 million fine troy ounces (Jan. 2000)
Budget: revenues $14.5 billion; expenditures $12.6 billion, including capital expenditures n.a. (1998 est.)
Defence Expenditures: 7.98% of total govt. expenditure (1997)
Education Expenditures: 20.41% of total govt. expenditure (1997)
External Debt: $47.817 billion (1998)
Exports: $35.763 billion (1999); commodities: electrical equipment 19%, textiles 16%, minerals and ores 11%, farm products 10%, coconut 10%, chemicals 5%, fish 5%, forest products 4%; partners: US 36%, European Community 19%, Japan 18%, ESCAP 9%, ASEAN 7%
Imports: $31.771 billion (1999); commodities: raw materials 53%, capital goods 17%, petroleum products 17%; partners: US 25%, Japan 17%, ESCAP 13%, European Community 11%, ASEAN 10%, Middle East 10%

■ COMMUNICATIONS

Daily Newspapers: 47 (1996)
Televisions: 108/1,000 inhabitants (1998)
Radios: 159/1,000 inhabitants (1997)
Telephones: 37 lines/1,000 inhabitants (1998)

■ TRANSPORTATION

Motor Vehicles: n.a.
Roads: n.a.
Railway: 897 km; 499 km operational
Air Traffic: 7,475,000 passengers carried (1997)
Airports: 260; 75 have paved runways (1998 est.)

Canadian Embassy: The Canadian Embassy, 9th and 11th Fl, Allied Bank Centre, 6754 Ayala Ave, Makati, Manila, Philippines; mailing address: P.O. Box 2168, Makati CPO 1261 Makati, Metro Manila, Philippines. Tel: (011-63-2) 867-0001. Fax: (011-63-2) 810-8839.
Embassy in Canada: Embassy of the Republic of the Philippines, 130 Albert St, Ste 606, Ottawa ON K1P 5G4. Tel: (613) 233-1121. Fax: (613) 233-4165.

Pitcairn Islands

Long-Form Name: Pitcairn, Henderson, Ducie and Oeno Islands
Capital: Adamstown

■ GEOGRAPHY

Area: 47 sq. km (Pitcairn and 3 small uninhabited islands)
Climate: tropical, hot, humid, modified by southeasterly trade winds; rainy season from Nov. to March
Land Use: rugged but fertile interior
Location: S Pacific Ocean, E of French Polynesia

■ PEOPLE

Population: 49 (July 1999 est.)

Nationality: Pitcairn Islander
Ethnic Groups: descendants of Polynesians and British (the latter crew members of the British naval ship Bounty)
Languages: English (official), Tahitian-English dialect

■ GOVERNMENT

Colony/Territory of: Dependent Territory of the United Kingdom
Leader(s): Queen Elizabeth II (UK), Gov. Robert John Alston
Government Type: dependency of the UK
National Holiday: Celebration of the Birthday of the Queen, second Saturday in June

■ ECONOMY

Overview: inhabitants subsist on fishing and farming; fertile soil of the valleys produces wide variety of fruit and vegetables; bartering is an important part of the economy; imports: fuel oil, machinery, building materials; no exports other than small tourist trade with passing ships

■ FINANCE/TRADE

Currency: New Zealand dollar = 100 cents

Canadian Embassy: c/o The Canadian High Commission, Macdonald House, 1 Grosvenor Square, London, W1X 0AB. Tel: (011-44-20) 7258-6600. Fax: (011-44-20) 7258-6333.
Representative to Canada: c/o British High Commission, 80 Elgin St, Ottawa ON K1P 5K7. Tel: (613) 237-1530. Fax: (613) 237-7980.

Poland

Long-Form Name: Republic of Poland
Capital: Warsaw

■ GEOGRAPHY

Area: 312,683 sq. km
Coastline: 491 km along Baltic Sea
Climate: temperate with cold, cloudy, moderately severe winters with frequent precipitation; mild summers with frequent showers and thundershowers
Environment: plain crossed by a few meandering streams; severe air and water pollution in south; flat terrain; lack of natural barriers; recently there has been severe flooding
Terrain: mostly flat plain, mountains along southern border
Land Use: 47% arable; 1% permanent crops; 13% meadows; 29% forest; 10% other; includes 1,000 sq. km irrigated
Location: NE Europe, bordering on Baltic Sea

■ PEOPLE

Population: 38,608,929 (July 1999 est.)
Nationality: Polish, Pole
Age Structure: 0-14 yrs: 20%; 15-64: 68%; 65+: 12% (1999 est.)
Population Growth Rate: +0.05 (1999 est.)
Net Migration: -0.4 migrants/1,000 population (1999 est.)
Ethnic Groups: 97.6% Polish, 1.3% German, 0.6% Ukrainian, 0.5% Byelorussian
Languages: Polish
Religions: 95% Roman Catholic (about 75% practising), 5% Russian Orthodox, Protestant and other
Birth Rate: 10.61/1,000 population (1999 est.)
Death Rate: 9.72/1,000 population (1999 est.)
Infant Mortality: 12.76 deaths/1,000 live births (1999 est.)
Life Expectancy at Birth: 68.93 years male, 77.41 years female (1999 est.)
Total Fertility Rate: 1.45 children born/woman (1999 est.)
Literacy: 99% (1997)

■ GOVERNMENT

Leader(s): Pres. Aleksander Kwasniewski, Prem. Jerzy Buzek. Presidential election scheduled October 8, 2000.
Government Type: democratic state
Administrative Divisions: 16 provinces (wojewodztwa, sing. -wojewodztwo)
Nationhood: Nov. 11, 1918, independent republic proclaimed
National Holiday: Constitution Day, May 3; Independence Day, Nov. 11

■ ECONOMY

Overview: Poland continues to make good progress in the difficult transition to a free-market economy. In contrast to the vibrant expansion of private non-farm activity, the large agricultural component remains handicapped by structural problems, surplus labour, inefficient small farms, and lack of investment.
GDP: $263 billion, per capita $6,800; real growth rate 5.6% (1998 est.)
Inflation: 10.3% (March 2000)
Industries: accounts for 26.6% of GDP, machine building, iron and steel, extractive industries, chemicals, shipbuilding, food processing, glass, beverages, textiles
Labour Force: 20 million (1998); 26.7% agriculture, 24.3% industry, 18.7% community, social and business services
Unemployment: 13.6% (Jan. 2000)
Agriculture: accounts for 5.1% GDP and 27% of labour force; 75% of output from private farms, 25% from state farms; low productivity; leading

European producer of rye, rapeseed and potatoes; wide variety of other crops and livestock; major exporter of pork products
Natural Resources: coal, sulphur, copper, natural gas, silver, lead, salt

■ FINANCE/TRADE

Currency: zloty (pl. zlotych) (Zl) = 100 groszy
International Reserves Excluding Gold: $24.535 billion (Dec. 1999)
Gold Reserves: 3.306 million fine troy ounces (Jan. 2000)
Budget: revenues $33.8 billion; expenditures $35.5 billion, including capital expenditures n.a. (1997 est.)
Defence Expenditures: 4.00% of total govt. expenditure (1998)
Education Expenditures: 6.38% of total govt. expenditure (1998)
External Debt: $47.708 billion (1998)
Exports: $27.397 billion (1999); commodities: machinery and equipment 63%, fuels, minerals and metals 14%, manufactured consumer goods 14%, agricultural and forestry products 5%; partners: former USSR countries 25%, Germany 12%, Czech and Slovak Republics 6%
Imports: $45.903 billion (1999); commodities: machinery and equipment 36%, fuels, minerals and metals 35%, manufactured consumer goods 9%, agricultural and forestry products 12%; partners: former USSR countries 23%, Germany 13%, Czech and Slovak Republics 6%

■ COMMUNICATIONS

Daily Newspapers: 55 (1996)
Televisions: 413/1,000 inhabitants (1998)
Radios: 523/1,000 inhabitants (1997)
Telephones: 228 lines/1,000 inhabitants (1998)

■ TRANSPORTATION

Motor Vehicles: 9,120,000; 7,580,000 passenger cars (1997 est.)
Roads: 377,048 km; 247,721 km paved
Railway: 24,313 km
Air Traffic: 1,998,000 passengers carried (1997)
Airports: 92; 74 have paved runways (1998 est.)

Canadian Embassy: The Canadian Embassy, Ulica Jana Matejki 1/5, 00-481, Warsaw, Poland. Tel: (011-48-22) 629-80-51. Fax: (011-48-22) 629-64-57.
Embassy in Canada: Embassy of the Republic of Poland, 443 Daly Ave, Ottawa ON K1N 6H3. Tel: (613) 789-0468. Fax: (613) 789-1218.

Portugal

Long-Form Name: Portuguese Republic
Capital: Lisbon

■ GEOGRAPHY

Area: 92,391 sq. km; includes Azores and Madeira Islands
Coastline: 1,793 km
Climate: maritime temperature; cool and rainy in north, warmer and drier in south
Environment: air pollution and soil degradation are accelerating; coastal water pollution; Azores subject to severe earthquakes
Terrain: mountainous north, rolling plains in south
Land Use: 26% arable; 9% permanent crops; 9% meadows; 36% forest; 20% other, includes 6,300 sq. km irrigated
Location: SW Europe, bordering on North Atlantic Ocean

■ PEOPLE

Population: 9,918,040 (July 1999 est.)
Nationality: Portuguese
Age Structure: 0-14 yrs: 17%; 15-64: 68%; 65+: 15% (1999 est.)
Population Growth Rate: -0.13% (1999 est.)
Net Migration: -1.51 migrants/1,000 population (1999 est.)
Ethnic Groups: homogeneous Mediterranean stock in mainland, Azores and Madeira Islands; citizens of black African descent who immigrated to mainland during decolonization number less than 100,000
Languages: Portuguese (official), English, French
Religions: 97% Roman Catholic, 1% Protestant, 2% other
Birth Rate: 10.49/1,000 population (1999 est.)
Death Rate: 10.25/1,000 population (1999 est.)
Infant Mortality: 6.73 deaths/1,000 live births (1999 est.)
Life Expectancy at Birth: 72.51 years male, 79.46 years female (1999 est.)
Total Fertility Rate: 1.34 children born/woman (1999 est.)
Literacy: 90.8% (1997)

■ GOVERNMENT

Leader(s): Pres. Jorge Sampaio, Prem. Antonio Guterres
Government Type: parliamentary democracy
Administrative Divisions: 18 districts (distritos, sing. -distrito) and 2 autonomous regions (regioes autonomas, sing. -regiao autonoma)
Nationhood: 1140; independent republic proclaimed Oct. 5, 1910

National Holiday: Day of Portugal, June 10

■ ECONOMY

Overview: the economy has grown recently due to strong domestic consumption and investment spending; government is promoting privatization measures; the global slowdown and tight financial policies to combat inflation have caused economic growth to slow
GDP: $144.8 billion, per capita $14,600; real growth rate 4.2% (1998 est.)
Inflation: 1.5% (March 2000)
Industries: accounts for 36% of GDP; textiles and footwear; wood pulp, paper and cork; metalworking; oil refining; chemicals; fish canning; wine; tourism
Labour Force: 5 million (1998); 24.8% community, social and business services, 23.4% industry, 19.5% trade and tourism
Unemployment: 5% (Aug. 1998)
Agriculture: accounts for 4% of GDP and 20% of labour force; small inefficient farms; imports more than half of food needs; major crops: grain, potatoes, olives, grapes; livestock sector: sheep, cattle, goats, poultry, meat, dairy products
Natural Resources: fish, forests (cork), tungsten, iron ore, uranium ore, marble

■ FINANCE/TRADE

Currency: escudo (Esc) = 100 centavos [As of Jan. 1, 1999, Government securities are issued in Euros (EUR)]
International Reserves Excluding Gold: $8.496 billion (Jan. 2000)
Gold Reserves: 19.506 million fine troy ounces (Jan. 2000)
Budget: revenues $48 billion; expenditures $52 billion, including capital expenditures of $7.4 billion (1996 est.)
Defence Expenditures: 2.6% of GDP (1997)
Education Expenditures: 5.8% of GNP (1997)
External Debt: $13.1 billion (1997 est.)
Exports: $23.864 billion (1999); commodities: cotton textiles, cork and cork products, canned fish, wine, timber and timber products, resin, machinery, appliances; partners: European Community 72%, other developed countries 13%, US 6%
Imports: $38.461 billion (1999); commodities: petroleum, cotton, foodgrains, industrial machinery, iron and steel, chemicals; partners: European Community 67%, other developed countries 13%, less developed countries 15%, US 4%

■ COMMUNICATIONS

Daily Newspapers: 27 (1996)
Televisions: 542/1,000 inhabitants (1998)
Radios: 304/1,000 inhabitants (1997)
Telephones: 413 lines/1,000 inhabitants (1998)

■ TRANSPORTATION

Motor Vehicles: 3,680,700; 2,750,000 passenger cars (1997 est.)
Roads: 68,732 km; 59,110 km surfaced
Railway: 3,072 km
Air Traffic: 6,281,000 passengers carried (1997)
Airports: 66; 40 have paved runways (1998 est.)

Canadian Embassy: The Canadian Embassy, Avenida da Liberdade, 196-200, 3rd Floor, 1269-121 Lisbon, Portugal. Tel: (011-351) 21-316-46-00. Fax: (011-351) 21-316-46-91.
Embassy in Canada: Embassy of Portugal, 645 Island Park Dr, Ottawa ON K1Y 0B8. Tel: (613) 729-0883. Fax: (613) 729-4236.

Puerto Rico

Long-Form Name: Commonwealth of Puerto Rico
Capital: San Juan

■ GEOGRAPHY

Area: 9,104 sq. km
Climate: tropical marine, mild, little seasonal temperature variation
Land Use: 4% arable; 5% permanent; 26% permanent pastures; 16% forest; 49% other, includes 390 sq. km irrigated
Location: West Indies, bordering on Caribbean Sea, Atlantic Ocean

■ PEOPLE

Population: 3,887,652 (July 1999 est.)
Nationality: Puerto Rican (US citizens)
Ethnic Groups: almost entirely Hispanic
Languages: Spanish (official); English is widely understood

■ GOVERNMENT

Colony/Territory of: Commonwealth associated with the US
Leader(s): Pres. William Clinton (to Jan. 20, 2001), Gov. Pedro J. Rossello. Gubernatorial election scheduled November 7, 2000.
Government Type: commonwealth associated with the US
National Holiday: US Independence Day, July 4

■ ECONOMY

Overview: economy (one of the most dynamic in the Caribbean region) has benefited from heavy

US investment; new industries include pharmaceuticals and electronics; tourism is important; sugar production has lost out to dairy production and other livestock products as the main facet of the agricultural sector

■ FINANCE/TRADE

Currency: American dollar ($US) = 100 cents

Canadian Embassy: c/o The Canadian Embassy, 501 Pennsylvania Ave NW, Washington DC 20001, USA. Tel: (202) 682-1740. Fax: (202) 456-7726.
Representative to Canada: c/o Embassy of the United States of America, 490 Sussex Drive, Ottawa, ON, K1N 1G8. Tel: (613) 238-5335. Fax: (613) 688-3097.

Qatar

Long-Form Name: State of Qatar
Capital: Doha

■ GEOGRAPHY

Area: 11,437 sq. km
Coastline: 563 km
Climate: desert; hot, dry; humid and sultry in summer
Environment: haze, dust storms, sandstorms common; limited freshwater resources mean increasing dependence on large-scale desalination facilities
Terrain: mostly flat and barren desert covered with loose sand and gravel
Land Use: 1% arable; 0% permanent crops; 5% meadows; 0% forest; 94% other; includes 80 sq. km irrigated
Location: SW Asia (Middle East, Arabian Peninsula), bordering on Persian Gulf

■ PEOPLE

Population: 723,542 (July 1999 est.)
Nationality: Qatari
Age Structure: 0-14 yrs: 27%; 15-64: 71%; 65+: 2% (1999 est.)
Population Growth Rate: 3.62% (1999 est.)
Net Migration: 23.03 migrants/1,000 population (1999 est.)
Ethnic Groups: 40% Arab, 18% Pakistani, 18% Indian, 10% Iranian, 14% other
Languages: Arabic (official); English is commonly used as second language
Religions: Islam (native Qataris—less than one-third of the population—principally adhere to orthodox Wahhabi sect of Sunni Muslims)
Birth Rate: 16.75/1,000 population (1999 est.)
Death Rate: 3.57/1,000 population (1999 est.)
Infant Mortality: 17.25 deaths/1,000 live births (1999 est.)
Life Expectancy at Birth: 71.70 years male, 76.89 years female (1999 est.)
Total Fertility Rate: 3.42 children born/woman (1999 est.)
Literacy: 80.0% (1997)

■ GOVERNMENT

Leader(s): Amir Shaykh Hamad bin Khalifa Al Thani. Prime Min. Shaykh 'Abd Allah ibn Khalifa Al Thani
Government Type: traditional monarchy
Administrative Divisions: 9 municipalities (baladiyah, sing. -baladiyah)
Nationhood: Sept. 3, 1971 (from UK)
National Holiday: Independence Day, Sept. 3

■ ECONOMY

Overview: has one of the highest per capita GDP's in the world, due to oil revenues; reserves should not be completely depleted for about 20 years; production and export of natural gas is becoming increasingly important. Oil has given Qatar a per capita GDP comparable to the leading West European industrial countries.
GDP: $12 billion, per capita $17,100; real growth rate -3% (1998 est.)
Inflation: 2.8% (1997)
Industries: accounts for 49% of GDP; crude oil production and refining, fertilizers, petrochemicals, steel, cement
Labour Force: n.a.; 3% agriculture, 28% industry, 69% services; 83% of labour force in private sector is non-Qatari
Unemployment: n.a.
Agriculture: farming and grazing on small scale, less than 1% of GDP; commercial fishing increasing in importance; most food imported
Natural Resources: crude oil, natural gas, fish

■ FINANCE/TRADE

Currency: Qatari riyal (QR) = 100 dirhams
International Reserves Excluding Gold: n.a.
Gold Reserves: 0.019 million fine troy ounces (Nov. 1999)
Budget: revenues $3.4 billion; expenditures $4.3 billion, including capital expenditures of $700 million (1998-99 est.)
Defence Expenditures: 9.6% of GDP (1998-99)
Education Expenditures: n.a.
External Debt: $11 billion (1997 est.)
Exports: $5.6 billion (1997 est.) commodities: petroleum products 90%, steel, fertilizers; partners: France, Germany, Italy, Japan, Spain
Imports: $3.322 billion (1997 est.) commodities: foodstuffs, beverages, animal and vegetable oils, chemicals, machinery and equipment; partners:

European Community, Japan, Arab countries, US, Australia

■ **COMMUNICATIONS**
Daily Newspapers: 5 (1996)
Televisions: 403/1,000 inhabitants (1996)
Radios: 448/1,000 inhabitants (1996)
Telephones: 260 lines/1,000 inhabitants (1998)

■ **TRANSPORTATION**
Motor Vehicles: 184,000; 97,000 passenger cars (1997 est.)
Roads: 1,230 km; 1,107 km paved
Railway: none
Air Traffic: 1,165,000 passengers carried (1997)
Airports: 4; 2 have paved runways (1998 est.)

Canadian Embassy: The Canadian Embassy to Qatar, c/o The Canadian Embassy, Villa 24, Area 4, Plot 121, Al-Mutawakel St, Da Aiyah, Kuwait City, Kuwait; mailing address: P.O. Box 25281, 13113, Safat, Kuwait City, Kuwait. Tel: (011-965) 256-3025. Fax: (011-965) 256-0173.
Embassy in Canada: c/o Embassy of the State of Qatar, 809 UN Plaza, First Ave. 4th Floor, New York NY 10017, USA. Tel: (212) 486-9335. Fax: (212) 758-4952.

Réunion

Long-Form Name: Department of Réunion
Capital: Saint-Denis

■ **GEOGRAPHY**
Area: 2,510 sq. km; uninhabited islands of Juan de Nova, Europa, Bassas da India, Iles Glorieuses, Tromelin administered by Réunion but do not form part of the territory; Mauritius and the Seychelles claim Tromelin, Madagascar claims all 5 islands
Climate: tropical, but more moderate at higher elevations; May to Nov.: cool and dry; Nov. to April: hot and rainy
Land Use: volcanic island; some cultivation of indigenous plants and cash crops such as corn; 17% arable, 2% permanent crops, 5% meadows and pastures, 35% forest, 41% other; includes 60 sq. km irrigated
Location: Indian Ocean, E of Africa (E of Madagascar)

■ **PEOPLE**
Population: 717,723 (July 1999 est.)
Nationality: Réunionese
Ethnic Groups: French Creoles, African, Malagasy, Pakistani, Indian and Chinese minorities
Languages: French (official), Creole vernacular

■ **GOVERNMENT**
Colony/Territory of: Overseas Department of France
Leader(s): Pres. Jacques Chirac (France); Prefect Robert Pommies
Government Type: overseas department of France
National Holiday: Taking of the Bastille, July 14

■ **ECONOMY**
Overview: agriculture-based economy, of which sugar cane is the backbone; government is promoting the development of the tourist industry; socioeconomic tensions between classes with widely disparate living standards; economy heavily depends on financial assistance from France

■ **FINANCE/TRADE**
Currency: French franc = 100 centimes

Canadian Embassy: c/o The Canadian Embassy, 35-37 avenue Montaigne, 75008, Paris, France. Tel: (011-33-1) 44-43-29-00. Fax: (011-33-1) 44043-29-99.
Representative to Canada: c/o Embassy of France, 42 Sussex Dr, Ottawa ON K1M 2C9. Tel: (613) 789-1795. Fax: (613) 562-3735.

Romania

Long-Form Name: Romania
Capital: Bucharest

■ **GEOGRAPHY**
Area: 237,500 sq. km
Coastline: 225 km
Climate: temperate; cold, cloudy winters with frequent snow and fog; sunny summers with frequent showers and thunderstorms
Environment: frequent earthquakes most severe in south and southwest; geologic structure and climate promotes landslides; water pollution; air pollution in south; soil degradation
Terrain: central Transylvanian Basin is separated from the plain of Moldavia on the east by the Carpathian Mountains and separated from the Walachian Plain on the south by the Transylvanian Alps
Land Use: 41% arable; 3% permanent; 21% meadows; 29% forest; 6% other, includes 31,020 sq. km irrigated
Location: SE Europe, bordering on Black Sea

■ **PEOPLE**
Population: 22,334,312 (July 1999 est.)
Nationality: Romanian
Age Structure: 0-14 yrs: 19%; 15-64: 68%; 65+: 13% (1999 est.)

Population Growth Rate: -0.23% (1999 est.)
Net Migration: -0.87 migrants/1,000 population (1999 est.)
Ethnic Groups: 89.1% Romanian; 8.9% Hungarian; 0.4% German; 1.6% Ukrainian, Serb, Croat, Russian, Turk and Gypsy
Languages: Romanian (official), Hungarian, German; French and English also spoken
Religions: 70% Romanian Orthodox; 6% Roman Catholic; 24% Calvinist, Lutheran, Jewish, Baptist, unaffiliated
Birth Rate: 10.09/1,000 population (1999 est.)
Death Rate: 11.55/1,000 population (1999 est.)
Infant Mortality: 18.12 deaths/1,000 live births (1999 est.)
Life Expectancy at Birth: 67.05 years male, 74.81 years female (1999 est.)
Total Fertility Rate: 1.27 children born/woman (1999 est.)
Literacy: 97.8% (1997)

■ GOVERNMENT

Leader(s): Pres. Emil Constantinescu, Prime Min. Mugur Isarescu. Presidential election scheduled September 2000.
Government Type: republic
Administrative Divisions: 40 counties (judete, sing. -judet) and 1 municipality (municipiu)
Nationhood: 1881 (from Turkey); republic proclaimed Dec. 30, 1947
National Holiday: National Day of Romania, Dec. 1

■ ECONOMY

Overview: industry suffers from an aging capital plant and shortages of energy; agriculture sector has suffered from drought and mismanagement; private enterprise is increasing in importance. Growing budget deficit, inflation, unemployment and a deteriorating infrastructure hamper economic progress
GDP: $90.6 billion, per capita $4,050; real growth rate -7.3% (1998 est.)
Inflation: 49.0% per month (March 2000)
Industries: accounts for 41% of GDP; mining, timber, construction materials, metallurgy, chemicals, machine building, food processing, petroleum
Labour Force: 11 million (1998); 27.4% industry, 33% agriculture, 10.1% community, social and business services
Unemployment: 11.9% (Jan. 2000)
Agriculture: 19% of GDP and 28% of labour force; major wheat and corn producer, sugar beets, sunflower seeds, potatoes, milk, eggs, meat
Natural Resources: crude oil (reserves being exhausted), timber, natural gas, coal, iron ore, salt

■ FINANCE/TRADE

Currency: leu (pl. lei) = 100 bani
International Reserves Excluding Gold: $2.674 billion (Jan. 2000)
Gold Reserves: 3.327 million fine troy ounces (Jan. 2000)
Budget: revenues $10 billion; expenditures $11.7 billion, including capital expenditures of $1.3 billion (1997 est.)
Defence Expenditures: 7.25% of GDP (1997)
Education Expenditures: 9.42% of total govt. expenditure (1997)
External Debt: 9.513 billion (1998)
Exports: $8.505 billion (1999); commodities: machinery and equipment 34.7%, fuels, minerals and metals 24.7%, manufactured consumer goods 16.9%, agricultural materials and forestry products 11.9%, other 11.6%; partners: former USSR countries 27%, Eastern Europe 23%, European Community 15%, US 5%, China 4%
Imports: $10.392 billion (1999); commodities: fuels, minerals and metals 51%, machinery and equipment 26.7%, agricultural and forestry products 11%, manufactured consumer goods 4.2%; partners: Communist countries 60%, non-communist countries 40%

■ COMMUNICATIONS

Daily Newspapers: 106 (1996)
Televisions: 233/1,000 inhabitants (1998)
Radios: 319/1,000 inhabitants (1997)
Telephones: 162 lines/1,000 inhabitants (1998)

■ TRANSPORTATION

Motor Vehicles: 3,000,000; 2,460,000 passenger cars (1997 est.)
Roads: 153,358 km; 78,213 km paved
Railway: 11,376 km
Air Traffic: 995,000 passengers carried (1997)
Airports: 27; 21 have paved runways (1998 est.)

Canadian Embassy: The Canadian Embassy, 36, Nicolae Iorga, Bucharest 71118; mailing address: P.O. Box 117, Post Office No. 22, Bucharest, Romania. Tel: (011-40-1) 222-9845. Fax: (011-40-1) 312-9680.
Embassy in Canada: Embassy of Romania, 655 Rideau St, Ottawa ON K1N 6A3. Tel: (613) 789-3709. Fax: (613) 789-4365.

Russia

Long-Form Name: Russian Federation
Capital: Moscow

Russia

■ GEOGRAPHY

Area: 17,075,200 sq. km
Coastline: 37,653 km
Climate: ranges from steppes in south through humid continental, subarctic in Siberia to tundra in polar north; winters vary—cool along Black Sea, frigid in Siberia; summers—warm in the steppes to cool along Arctic coast
Environment: cold desert in north; volcanic activity; only small percentage of land is arable—much is too far north; permafrost over much of Siberia; severe land, air and water pollution; deforestation and soil erosion
Terrain: rolling western plains, north-south ridge of Ural Mountains, central plateau, rugged eastern uplands
Land Use: 8% arable; 46% forests and woodland; 4% meadows and pastures; 42% steppe and cold desert; includes 40,000 sq. km irrigated
Location: E Europe and N Asia, bordering on Barents Sea, Baltic Sea, Black Sea, Caspian Sea

■ PEOPLE

Population: 146,393,569 (July 1999 est.)
Nationality: Russian
Age Structure: 0-14 yrs: 19%; 15-64: 68%; 65+: 13% (1999 est.)
Population Growth Rate: -0.33% (1999 est.)
Net Migration: 2.05 migrants/1,000 population (1999 est.)
Ethnic Groups: 81.5% Russians; 3.8% Tatars, 1.2% Chuvash, 0.9% Bashkir, 0.8% Belorussian, 3% Ukrainian, remainder inc. Chechens, Germans, Udmurts, Mari, Kazakhs, Avars, Jews, Moldavians and Armenians
Languages: Russian (official), Tartar, Ukrainian
Religions: Christianity (Russian Orthodox) with substantial Muslim populations and other religious minorities
Birth Rate: 9.64/1,000 population (1999 est.)
Death Rate: 14.96/1,000 population (1999 est.)
Infant Mortality: 23.00 deaths/1,000 live births (1999 est.)
Life Expectancy at Birth: 58.83 years male, 71.72 years female (1999 est.)
Total Fertility Rate: 1.34 children born/woman (1999 est.)
Literacy: 99.0% (1997)

■ GOVERNMENT

Leader(s): Pres. Vladimir V. Putin; Prem. Mikhail Kasyanov
Government Type: federation
Administrative Divisions: 49 oblasts (oblastey, sing. -oblast), 21 autonomous republics (avtonomnyk respublik, sing. -avtonomnaya respublika), 10 autonomous okrugs (avtonomnykh okrugov, sing. -avtonomnyy okrug), 6 krays (krayer, sing. -kray), 2 federal cities (gorod) and 1 autonomous oblast (avtonomnaya oblast)
Nationhood: Aug. 24, 1991 (from Soviet Union)
National Holiday: Independence Day, June 12

■ ECONOMY

Overview: a vast country with a great many natural resources, a well-educated population, and a diverse but declining industrial base; 25% of the population lives below the poverty line and the country continues to experience formidable difficulties in moving from its old centrally planned economy to a modern market economy. The severity of Russia's economic problems is dramatized by the large annual decline in population.
GDP: $593.4 billion, per capita $4,000; real growth rate -5% (1998 est.)
Inflation: 22.5% (March 2000)
Industries: accounts for 39% of GDP; natural gas refining, steel and coal production and processing, all forms of machine building, shipbuilding, transportation equipment, consumer durables, communications and agricultural equipment, medical and scientific instruments
Labour Force: 78.1 million (1998); 25.9% industry, 25.9% community, social and business services, 15.4% agriculture
Unemployment: 12.4% (July 1999); substantial underemployment
Agriculture: accounts for 7% of GDP; grain, sugar beets, sunflower seeds, meat, milk, vegetables, fruit
Natural Resources: iron ore, coal, oil, gold, platinum, copper, zinc, lead, tin, rare metals; climate, terrain and distance hinder exploitation

■ FINANCE/TRADE

Currency: ruble (rbl.) = 100 kopeks
International Reserves Excluding Gold: $8.912 billion (Jan. 2000)
Gold Reserves: 13.452 million fine troy ounces (Jan. 2000)
Budget: revenues $40 billion; expenditures $63 billion, including capital expenditures n.a. (1998 est.)
Defence Expenditures: 30.9% of total govt. expenditure (1997)
Education Expenditures: 3.5% of GNP (1997)
External Debt: $183.601 billion (1998)
Exports: $74.142 billion (1999); commodities: fuels, wood products, metals, chemicals, wide range of manufactured products
Imports: $40.895 billion (1999); commodities: machinery, medicine, foodstuffs, consumer products

Rwanda

■ COMMUNICATIONS
Daily Newspapers: 285 (1996)
Televisions: 420/1,000 inhabitants (1998)
Radios: 418/1,000 inhabitants (1997)
Telephones: 197 lines/1,000 inhabitants (1998)

■ TRANSPORTATION
Motor Vehicles: 24,000,000; 14,100,000 passenger cars (1997 est.)
Roads: 948,000 km; 336,000 km paved
Railway: 154,000 km
Air Traffic: 20,419,000 passengers carried (1997)
Airports: 2,517; 630 have paved runways

Canadian Embassy: The Canadian Embassy, 23 Starokonyushenny Per, Moscow, 121002 Russia. Tel: (011-7-095) 956-6666. Fax: (011-7-095) 232-9948.
Embassy in Canada: Embassy of the Russian Federation, 285 Charlotte St, Ottawa ON K1N 8L5. Tel: (613) 235-4341. Fax: (613) 236-6342.

Rwanda

Long-Form Name: Rwandese Republic
Capital: Kigali

■ GEOGRAPHY
Area: 26,340 sq. km
Coastline: none: landlocked
Climate: temperate; two rainy seasons (Feb. to Apr., Nov. to Jan.); mild in mountains with frost and snow possible
Environment: deforestation; overgrazing; soil exhaustion; soil erosion; periodic droughts
Terrain: mostly grassy uplands and hills; mountains in west
Land Use: 35% arable; 13% permanent crops; 18% meadows; 22% forest; 12% other; includes 40 sq. km irrigated
Location: EC Africa

■ PEOPLE
Population: 8,154,933 (July 1999 est.)
Nationality: Rwandan
Age Structure: 0-14 yrs: 44%; 15-64: 53%; 65+: 3% (1999 est.)
Population Growth Rate: 2.43% (1999 est.)
Net Migration: 4.91 migrants/1,000 population (1999 est.)
Ethnic Groups: 80% Hutu, 19% Tutsi, 1% Twa (Pygmoid)
Languages: Kinyarwanda, French, English (all official); Kiswahili used in commercial centres
Religions: 65% Christian (mostly Roman Catholic), 9% Protestant, 1% Muslim, 25% indigenous beliefs and other
Birth Rate: 38.97/1,000 population (1999 est.)
Death Rate: 19.53/1,000 population (1999 est.)
Infant Mortality: 112.86 deaths/1,000 live births (1999 est.)
Life Expectancy at Birth: 40.84 years male, 41.80 years female (1999 est.)
Total Fertility Rate: 5.80 children born/woman (1999 est.)
Literacy: 63.0% (1997)

■ GOVERNMENT
Leader(s): Pres. Paul Kagame, Prime Min. Bernard Makuza
Government Type: republic; presidential system in which military leaders hold key offices
Administrative Divisions: 12 prefectures
Nationhood: July 1, 1962 (from UN trusteeship under Belgian administration)
National Holiday: Independence Day, July 1

■ ECONOMY
Overview: a poor nation whose economy is severely hampered by civil war, which has damaged infrastructure and economic prospects; agricultural sector dominates, with coffee and tea making up 80–90% of total exports; manufacturing is largely restricted to the processing of agricultural products
GDP: $5.5 billion, per capita $690; real growth rate 10.5% (1996 est.)
Inflation: 1.3% (Jan. 2000)
Industries: accounts for 24% of GDP mining of cassiterite (tin ore) and wolframite (tungsten ore), tin, cement, agricultural processing, small-scale beverage production, soap, furniture, shoes, plastic goods, textiles, cigarettes
Labour Force: 4.1 million (1998); 92.8% agriculture, 4.3% services, 3% industry and commerce
Unemployment: n.a.
Agriculture: accounts for 36% of GDP and about 90% of labour force; cash crops: coffee, tea, pyrethrum (insecticide made from chrysanthemums); main food crops: bananas, beans, sorghum, potatoes; stock raising; self-sufficiency declining; country imports foodstuffs as farm production fails to keep up with population growth; coffee and tea constitute 80–90% of total exports
Natural Resources: gold, cassiterite (tin ore), wolframite (tungsten ore), natural gas, hydropower

■ FINANCE/TRADE
Currency: Rwandan franc (RF) = 100 centimes
International Reserves Excluding Gold: $164 million (Jan. 2000)
Gold Reserves: none (Jan. 2000)

Budget: revenues $231 million; expenditures $319 million, including capital expenditures of $13 million (1996 est.)
Defence Expenditures: 3.8% of GDP (1999)
Education Expenditures: n.a.
External Debt: $1.226 billion (1998)
Exports: $60 million (1998); commodities: coffee 85%, tea, tin, cassiterite, wolframite, pyrethrum; partners: Germany, Belgium, Italy, Uganda, UK, France, US
Imports: $285 million (1998); commodities: textiles, foodstuffs, machines and equipment, capital goods, steel, petroleum products, cement and construction material; partners: US, Belgium, Germany, Kenya, Japan

■ COMMUNICATIONS
Daily Newspapers: 1 (1996)
Televisions: 0/1,000 inhabitants (1998)
Radios: 102/1,000 inhabitants (1997)
Telephones: 2 lines/1,000 inhabitants (1998)

■ TRANSPORTATION
Motor Vehicles: 27,800; 11,900 passenger cars (1997 est.)
Roads: 12,000 km; 1,000 km paved
Railway: none
Air Traffic: n.a.
Airports: 7; 4 have paved runways (1998 est.)

Canadian Embassy: Office of the Canadian Embassy, rue Akagera, P.O. Box 1177, Kigali, Rwanda. Tel: (011-250) 73210. Fax: (011-250) 72719.
Embassy in Canada: Embassy of the Republic of Rwanda, 121 Sherwood Dr, Ottawa ON K1Y 3V1. Tel: (613) 722-5835. Fax: (613) 722-4052.

Saint Helena

Long-Form Name: Saint Helena
Capital: Jamestown

■ GEOGRAPHY
Area: 410 sq. km
Climate: tropical marine; little seasonal variation
Land Use: 6% arable; 0% permanent crops; 6% meadows and pastures; 6% forests; 82% other; includes n.a. sq. km irrigated
Location: S Atlantic Ocean, SW of Africa

■ PEOPLE
Population: 7,145 (July 1999 est.)
Nationality: Saint Helenian
Ethnic Groups: Europeans, East Indians, Africans
Languages: English (official)

■ GOVERNMENT
Colony/Territory of: Dependent Territory of the United Kingdom
Leader(s): Head of State: Queen Elizabeth II; Gov. and Commander-in-Chief David Hollamby
Government Type: dependent territory of the UK
National Holiday: Celebration of the Birthday of the Queen, second Saturday in June

■ ECONOMY
Overview: depends primarily on financial assistance from UK; fishing, livestock raising and sale of handicrafts provide income for local population; due to the lack of jobs, many inhabitants have emigrated

■ FINANCE/TRADE
Currency: Saint Helenian pound = 100 pence (at par with British pound)

Canadian Embassy: c/o The Canadian High Commission, Macdonald House, 1 Grosvenor Square, London W1X 0AB, England, UK. Tel: (011-44-20) 7258-6600. Fax: (011-44-20) 7258-6333.
Representative to Canada: c/o British High Commission, 80 Elgin St, Ottawa ON K1P 5K7. Tel: (613) 237-1530. Fax: (613) 237-7980.

Saint Kitts and Nevis

Long-Form Name: Federation of St. Kitts and Nevis
Capital: Basseterre

■ GEOGRAPHY
Area: 269 sq. km
Coastline: 135 km
Climate: subtropical tempered by constant sea breezes; little seasonal temperature variation; rainy season (May to Nov.)
Environment: subject to hurricanes (July to Oct.)
Terrain: volcanic with mountainous interiors
Land Use: 22% arable; 17% permanent; 3% meadows; 17% forest; 41% other; includes n.a. sq. km irrigated
Location: Caribbean islands E of Puerto Rico

■ PEOPLE
Population: 42,838 (July 1999 est.)
Nationality: Kittsian or Kittitian, Nevisian
Age Structure: 0-14 yrs: 33%; 15-64: 61%; 65+: 6% (1999 est.)
Population Growth Rate: 1.34% (1999 est.)
Net Migration: -1.05 migrants/1,000 population (1999 est.)

Saint Lucia

Ethnic Groups: mainly of black African descent
Languages: English
Religions: Anglican, other Protestant sects, Roman Catholic
Birth Rate: 22.60/1,000 population (1999 est.)
Death Rate: 8.15/1,000 population (1999 est.)
Infant Mortality: 17.39 deaths/1,000 live births (1999 est.)
Life Expectancy at Birth: 64.87 years male, 71.21 years female (1999 est.)
Total Fertility Rate: 2.42 children born/woman (1999 est.)
Literacy: 90.0% (1997)

■ GOVERNMENT

Leader(s): Head of State: Queen Elizabeth II/Gov. Gen. Cuthbert Montraville Sebastian. Prime Min. Denzil Douglas
Government Type: constitutional monarchy
Administrative Divisions: 14 parishes
Nationhood: Sept. 19, 1983 (from UK)
National Holiday: Independence Day, Sept. 19

■ ECONOMY

Overview: traditionally dependent on the growing and processing of sugar cane and on remittances from overseas workers; tourism and export-oriented manufacturing are increasing
GDP: $235 million, per capita $6,000; real growth rate 6.3% (1997 est.)
Inflation: 6.3% (Feb. 1998)
Industries: accounts for 22.5% of GDP; sugar processing, tourism, cotton, salt, copra, clothing, footwear, beverages
Labour Force: n.a.
Unemployment: 4% (1997 est.)
Agriculture: accounts for 5.5% of GDP; cash crop: sugar cane; subsistence crops: rice, yams, vegetables, bananas; fishing potential but not fully exploited; most food imported
Natural Resources: negligible

■ FINANCE/TRADE

Currency: East Caribbean dollar ($EC) = 100 cents
International Reserves Excluding Gold: $50 million (Dec. 1999)
Gold Reserves: n.a.
Budget: revenues $64.1 million; expenditures $73.3 million, including capital expenditures of $10.4 million (1997 est.)
Defence Expenditures: n.a.
Education Expenditures: n.a.
External Debt: $58 million (1996)
Exports: $36 million (1997); commodities: sugar, manufactures, postage stamps; partners: US 53%, UK 22%, Trinidad and Tobago 5%, OECS 5%
Imports: $148 million (1997); commodities: foodstuffs, intermediate manufactures, machinery, fuels; partners: US 36%, UK 12%, Trinidad and Tobago 6%, Canada 3%, Japan 3%, OECS 4%

■ COMMUNICATIONS

Daily Newspapers: 0 (1996)
Televisions: 251/1,000 inhabitants (1996)
Radios: 671/1,000 inhabitants (1996)
Telephones: 418 lines/1,000 inhabitants (1998)

■ TRANSPORTATION

Motor Vehicles: n.a.
Roads: 320 km; 136 km paved
Railway: 58 km
Air Traffic: n.a.
Airports: 2, both with paved runways (1998 est.)

Canadian Embassy: The Canadian High Commission to Saint Kitts and Nevis, c/o The Canadian High Commission, Bishop's Court Hill, St. Michael, Barbados; mailing address: P.O. Box 404, Bridgetown, Barbados. Tel: (246) 429-3550. Fax: (246) 429-3780.
Embassy in Canada: c/o High Commission for the Countries of the Organization of Eastern Caribbean States, 112 Kent St, Ste 1610, Place de Ville, Tower B, Ottawa, ON K1P 5P2. Tel: (613) 236-8952. Fax: (613) 236-3042.

Saint Lucia

Long-Form Name: Saint Lucia
Capital: Castries

■ GEOGRAPHY

Area: 620 sq. km
Coastline: 158 km
Climate: tropical, moderated by northeast trade winds; dry season from Jan. to Apr., rainy season from May to Aug.
Environment: subject to hurricanes and volcanic activity; deforestation; soil erosion
Terrain: volcanic and mountainous with some broad, fertile valleys
Land Use: 8% arable; 21% permanent; 5% meadow; 13% forest; 53% other; includes 10 sq. km irrigated
Location: Caribbean islands, N of Venezuela

■ PEOPLE

Population: 154,020 (July 1999 est.)
Nationality: Saint Lucian
Age Structure: 0-14 yrs: 33%; 15-64: 61%; 65+: 6% (1999 est.)
Population Growth Rate: 1.09% (1999 est.)

Net Migration: -5.19 migrants/1,000 population (1999 est.)
Ethnic Groups: 90.3% African descent, 5.5% mixed, 3.2% East Indian, 1% Caucasian
Languages: English (official), French patois
Religions: 90% Roman Catholic, 7% Protestant, 3% Anglican
Birth Rate: 21.63/1,000 population (1999 est.)
Death Rate: 5.58/1,000 population (1999 est.)
Infant Mortality: 16.55 deaths/1,000 live births (1999 est.)
Life Expectancy at Birth: 68.14 years male, 75.74 years female (1999 est.)
Total Fertility Rate: 2.27 children born/woman (1999 est.)
Literacy: 82.0% (1997)

■ GOVERNMENT

Leader(s): Head of State: Queen Elizabeth II/Gov. Gen. Calliopa Pearlette Louisy. Prime Min. Kenny Anthony
Government Type: constitutional monarchy
Administrative Divisions: 11 quarters
Nationhood: Feb. 22, 1979 (from UK)
National Holiday: Independence Day, Feb. 22

■ ECONOMY

Overview: depends on strong agricultural (bananas) and tourist industry sectors; expanding industrial base supported by foreign investment in manufacturing and activities such as data processing; vulnerable to droughts and tropical storms
GDP: $625 million, per capita $4,100; real growth rate 2.2% (1997 est.)
Inflation: -1.7% (June 1997)
Industries: accounts for 32% of GDP; clothing, electronic component assembly, beverages, tourism, lime and coconut processing
Labour Force: n.a.
Unemployment: 15% (1996 est.)
Agriculture: accounts for 11% GDP and 43% of labour force; crops: bananas, coconuts, vegetables, citrus fruit, root crops, cocoa; imports food for the tourist industry
Natural Resources: forests, sandy beaches, minerals (pumice), mineral springs, geothermal potential

■ FINANCE/TRADE

Currency: EC dollar (EC$) = 100 cents
International Reserves Excluding Gold: $75 million (Dec. 1999)
Gold Reserves: n.a.
Budget: revenues $141.2 million; expenditures $146.7 million, including capital expenditures of $25.1 million (1997-98 est.)
Defence Expenditures: n.a.
Education Expenditures: n.a.
External Debt: $159 million (1997)
Exports: $61 million (1997); commodities: bananas 67%, cocoa, vegetables, fruit, coconut oil, clothing; partners: UK 55%, CARICOM 21%, US 18%, other 6%
Imports: $335 million (1998); commodities: manufactured goods 22%, machinery and transportation equipment 21%, food and live animals 20%, mineral fuels, foodstuffs, machinery and equipment, fertilizers, petroleum products; partners: US 33%, UK 16%, CARICOM 14.8%, Japan 6.5%, other 29.7%

■ COMMUNICATIONS

Daily Newspapers: 0 (1996)
Televisions: 217/1,000 inhabitants (1996)
Radios: 765/1,000 inhabitants (1996)
Telephones: 268 lines/1,000 inhabitants (1998)

■ TRANSPORTATION

Motor Vehicles: 12,300; 11,400 passenger cars (1997 est.)
Roads: 1,210 km; 63 km paved
Railway: none
Air Traffic: n.a.
Airports: 2, both with paved runways (1998 est.)

Canadian Embassy: The Canadian High Commission to Saint Lucia, c/o The Canadian High Commission, Bishop's Court Hill, St. Michael, Barbados; mailing address: P.O. Box 404, Bridgetown, Barbados. Tel: (246) 429-3550. Fax: (246) 429-3780.
Embassy in Canada: c/o High Commission for the Countries of the Organization of Eastern Caribbean States, 112 Kent St, Ste 1610, Place de Ville, Tower B, Ottawa ON K1P 5P2. Tel: (613) 236-8952. Fax: (613) 236-3042.

Saint Pierre and Miquelon

Long-Form Name: Territorial Collectivity of Saint Pierre and Miquelon
Capital: Saint-Pierre

■ GEOGRAPHY

Area: 242 sq. km, 8 small islands
Climate: cold and wet, misty and foggy, windy spring and autumn, moist, temperate summers, cold and snowy winters
Land Use: 13% arable, 0% permanent crops, 0% meadows and pastures, 4% forest, 83% other; includes n.a. km irrigated
Location: N Atlantic Ocean, S of Newfoundland

■ PEOPLE
Population: 6,966 (July 1999 est.)
Nationality: French
Ethnic Groups: descendants of French settlers, Basques and Bretons (French fishermen)
Languages: French, English

■ GOVERNMENT
Colony/Territory of: Territorial Collectivity of France
Leader(s): Pres. Jacques Chirac (France); Prefect Francis Spitzer
Government Type: territorial collectivity with internal self-government
National Holiday: Taking of the Bastille, July 14

■ ECONOMY
Overview: fishing, and the servicing of fishing fleets operating off the coast of Newfoundland, have long been an important part of the economy; agriculture: some vegetables and livestock for local consumption; partners: UK, Canada, EEC

■ FINANCE/TRADE
Currency: French franc = 100 centimes

Canadian Embassy: c/o The Canadian Embassy, 35-37 avenue Montaigne, 75008 Paris, France. Tel: (011-33-1) 44-43-29-00. Fax: (011-33-1) 44-43-29-99.
Representative to Canada: c/o Embassy of France, 42 Sussex Dr, Ottawa ON K1M 2C9. Tel: (613) 789-1795. Fax: (613) 562-3735.

Saint Vincent and the Grenadines

Long-Form Name: Saint Vincent and the Grenadines
Capital: Kingstown

■ GEOGRAPHY
Area: 340 sq. km
Coastline: 84 km
Climate: tropical; little seasonal temperature variation; rainy season (May to Nov.)
Environment: subject to hurricanes; Soufrière volcano is a constant threat; water pollution along coasts
Terrain: volcanic, mountainous; Soufrière volcano on the island of Saint Vincent
Land Use: 10% arable; 18% permanent crops; 5% meadows; 36% forest; 31% other; includes 10 sq. km irrigated
Location: Caribbean islands, N of Venezuela

■ PEOPLE
Population: 120,519 (July 1999 est.)
Nationality: Saint Vincentian or Vincentian
Age Structure: 0-14 yrs: 30%; 15-64: 65%; 65+: 5% (1999 est.)
Population Growth Rate: 0.57% (1999 est.)
Net Migration: -7.43 migrants/1,000 population (1999 est.)
Ethnic Groups: mainly of black African descent; remainder mixed, with some white, East Indian, Carib Indian
Languages: English (official), some French patois
Religions: Anglican, Methodist, Roman Catholic, Seventh-Day Adventist
Birth Rate: 18.34/1,000 population (1999 est.)
Death Rate: 5.23/1,000 population (1999 est.)
Infant Mortality: 15.16 deaths/1,000 live births (1999 est.)
Life Expectancy at Birth: 72.29 years male, 75.36 years female (1999 est.)
Total Fertility Rate: 1.94 children born/woman (1999 est.)
Literacy: 82.0% (1997)

■ GOVERNMENT
Leader(s): Head of State: Queen Elizabeth II/Gov. Gen. David Jack. Prime Min. James F. Mitchell
Government Type: constitutional monarchy
Administrative Divisions: 6 parishes
Nationhood: Oct. 27, 1979 (from UK)
National Holiday: Independence Day, Oct. 27

■ ECONOMY
Overview: overdependence on the weather-plagued banana crop as a major export earner has caused high unemployment; has been unsuccessful in diversifying into new industries
GDP: $289 million, per capita $2,400; real growth rate 4% (1998 est.)
Inflation: 0.4% (March 2000)
Industries: accounts for 18% of GDP; food processing (sugar, flour), cement, furniture, rum, starch, sheet metal, beverage
Labour Force: n.a.
Unemployment: n.a.
Agriculture: accounts for 11% of GDP and 60% of labour force; provides bulk of exports; products: bananas, arrowroot (world's largest producer), coconuts, sweet potatoes, spices; small numbers of cattle, sheep, hogs, goats; small fish catch used locally
Natural Resources: negligible

■ FINANCE/TRADE
Currency: EC dollar ($EC) = 100 cents

International Reserves Excluding Gold: $43 million (Dec. 1999)
Gold Reserves: n.a.
Budget: revenues $85.7 million; expenditures $98.6 million, including capital expenditures of $25.7 million (1997 est.)
Defence Expenditures: n.a.
Education Expenditures: 12.83% of govt. expenditure (1998)
External Debt: $83.6 million (1997)
Exports: $49 million (1999); commodities: bananas, eddoes and dasheen (taro), arrowroot starch, copra; partners: CARICOM 37%, UK 43%, US 15%
Imports: $201 million (1999); commodities: foodstuffs, machinery and equipment, chemicals and fertilizers, minerals and fuels; partners: US 42%, CARICOM 19%, UK 15%

■ COMMUNICATIONS
Daily Newspapers: 0 (1996)
Televisions: 159/1,000 inhabitants (1996)
Radios: 673/1,000 inhabitants (1996)
Telephones: 188 lines/1,000 inhabitants (1998)

■ TRANSPORTATION
Motor Vehicles: 8,200; 5,000 passenger cars (1997 est.)
Roads: 1,040 km; 320 km paved
Railway: none
Air Traffic: n.a.
Airports: 6, 5 with paved runways (1998 est.)

Canadian Embassy: The Canadian High Commission to Saint Vincent and the Grenadines, c/o The Canadian High Commission, Bishop's Court Hill, St. Michael, Barbados; mailing address: P.O. Box 404, Bridgetown, Barbados. Tel: (246) 429-3550. Fax: (246) 429-3780.
Embassy in Canada: c/o High Commission for the Countries of the Organization of Eastern Caribbean States, 112 Kent St, Ste 1610, Place de Ville, Tower B, Ottawa, ON K1P 5P2. Tel: (613) 236-8952. Fax: (613) 236-3042.

Samoa

Long-Form Name: Independent State of Samoa
Capital: Apia

■ GEOGRAPHY
Area: 2,860 sq. km
Coastline: 403 km
Climate: tropical; rainy season lasts from Oct. to March, dry season from May to Oct.
Environment: volcanism and typhoons are natural hazards; soil erosion
Terrain: interior is rocky, with volcanic mountains; narrow coastal plain
Land Use: 19% arable, 24% permanent crops, 0% meadows and pastures, 47% forest and woodland, 10% other; includes n.a. sq. km irrigated
Location: South Pacific Ocean, E of Australia and NE of New Zealand

■ PEOPLE
Population: 229,979 (July 1999 est.)
Nationality: Samoan
Age Structure: 0-14 yrs: 39%; 15-64: 57%; 65+: 4% (1999 est.)
Population Growth Rate: 2.30% (1999 est.)
Net Migration: -0.39 migrants/1,000 population (1999 est.)
Ethnic Groups: 92.6% Samoan, 7% European-Polynesian; 0.4% Europeans
Languages: Samoan (Polynesian), also English
Religions: almost 100% Christianity
Birth Rate: 28.81/1,000 population (1999 est.)
Death Rate: 5.40/1,000 population (1999 est.)
Infant Mortality: 30.50 deaths/1,000 live births (1999 est.)
Life Expectancy at Birth: 67.43 years male, 72.33 years female (1999 est.)
Total Fertility Rate: 3.61 children born/women (1999 est.)
Literacy: 98% (1997)

■ GOVERNMENT
Leader(s): Head of State Tanumafili II Malietoa, Prime Min. Tuialepa Sailele Malielegaoi
Government Type: constitutional monarchy under a native chief
Administrative Divisions: 11 districts
Nationhood: Jan. 1, 1962
National Holiday: National Day, June 1

■ ECONOMY
Overview: economy is heavily agriculture-oriented, and disease and pests have done much damage in recent years; tourism has become the most important growth industry. The flexibility of the labor market is a basic strength for future economic gains.
GDP: $470 million; per capita $2,100, real growth rate 3.4% (1997 est.)
Inflation: 2.2% (Dec. 1999)
Industries: accounts for 25% of GDP; fishing, timber, food processing, tourism
Labour Force: n.a.; 65% agriculture, 30% services, 5% industry
Unemployment: n.a.
Agriculture: makes up 40% of GDP; mostly coconuts and fruit

Natural Resources: fish, forest resources

■ FINANCE/TRADE

Currency: tala ($WS) = 100 sene
International Reserves Excluding Gold: $67 million (Jan. 2000)
Gold Reserves: n.a.
Budget: revenues $118 million; expenditures $128 million, including capital expenditures n.a. (1997 est.)
Defence Expenditures: n.a.
Education Expenditures: n.a.
External Debt: $167 million (1996)
Exports: $20 million (1999); commodities: coconut oil and cream, copra, fish, beer; partners: New Zealand, American Samoa, Australia, Germany, US
Imports: $115 million (1999); commodities: intermediate goods, food, capital goods; partners: New Zealand, Australia, Fiji, US

■ COMMUNICATIONS

Daily Newspapers: 0 (1996)
Televisions: 60/1,000 inhabitants (1996)
Radios: 1,054/1,000 inhabitants (1996)
Telephones: 49 lines/1,000 inhabitants (1998)

■ TRANSPORTATION

Motor Vehicles: 2,600; 1,200 passenger cars (1997 est.)
Roads: 790 km; 332 km paved
Railway: none
Air Traffic: 75,000 passengers carried (1997)
Airports: 3; 1 has paved runways (1998 est.)

Canadian Embassy: The Canadian High Commission to Western Samoa, c/o The Canadian High Commission, P.O. Box 12049, Thorndon, Wellington, New Zealand. Tel: (011-64-4) 473-9577. Fax: (011-64-4) 471-2082.
Embassy in Canada: c/o Samoa High Commission, 800 Second Ave, Ste 400D, New York NY 10017, USA. Tel: (212) 599-6196. Fax: (613) 599-0797.

San Marino

Long-Form Name: Republic of San Marino
Capital: San Marino

■ GEOGRAPHY

Area: 60 sq. km
Coastline: none: landlocked
Climate: Mediterranean; mild to cool winters; warm, sunny summers
Environment: dominated by the Appenines
Terrain: rugged mountains
Land Use: 17% arable; 0% permanent; 0% meadows; 0% forest; 83% other; includes n.a. sq. km irrigated
Location: S Europe (E Italy)

■ PEOPLE

Population: 25,061 (July 1999 est.)
Nationality: Sammarinese
Age Structure: 0-14 yrs: 16%; 15-64: 67%; 65+: 17% (1999 est.)
Population Growth Rate: 0.64% (1999 est.)
Net Migration: 4.23 migrants/1,000 population (1999 est.)
Ethnic Groups: Sammarinese, Italian
Languages: Italian
Religions: Roman Catholic
Birth Rate: 10.41/1,000 population (1999 est.)
Death Rate: 8.22/1,000 population (1999 est.)
Infant Mortality: 5.39 deaths/1,000 live births (1999 est.)
Life Expectancy at Birth: 77.59 years male, 85.35 years female (1999 est.)
Total Fertility Rate: 1.51 children born/woman (1999 est.)
Literacy: 96% (1997)

■ GOVERNMENT

Leader(s): Captains-Regent: Maria Domenica Michelotti and Gian Marco Marcucci
Government Type: republic
Administrative Divisions: 9 municipalities (castelli, sing. -castello)
Nationhood: 301 (by tradition)
National Holiday: Anniversary of the Foundation of the Republic, Sept. 3

■ ECONOMY

Overview: tourism and the sale of postage stamps are vital to the economy; tourism itself contributes more than 50% to the GDP; key industries are clothing, electronics, ceramics, agricultural products, wine and cheese
GDP: $500 million, per capita $20,000; real growth rate 4.8% (1997 est.)
Inflation: n.a.
Industries: wine, olive oil, cement, leather, textiles, tourism
Labour Force: n.a.
Unemployment: 3.7% (May. 1999)
Agriculture: employs 3% of labour force; products: wheat, grapes, corn, olives, meat, cheese, hides; small numbers of cattle, pigs, horses; depends on Italy for food imports
Natural Resources: building stone

■ FINANCE/TRADE

Currency: Italian lire (Lit) = 100 centesimi; San Marino also mints its own coins

International Reserves Excluding Gold: n.a.
Gold Reserves: n.a.
Budget: n.a.
Defence Expenditures: n.a.
Education Expenditures: n.a.
External Debt: n.a.
Exports: n.a.; trade data are included in the statistics for Italy
Imports: n.a.; see exports

■ COMMUNICATIONS

Daily Newspapers: 3 (1996)
Televisions: 358/1,000 inhabitants (1996)
Radios: 620/1,000 inhabitants (1996)
Telephones: n.a.

■ TRANSPORTATION

Motor Vehicles: 30,000; 25,000 passenger cars (1997 est.)
Roads: 220 km
Railway: none
Air Traffic: n.a.
Airports: none

Canadian Embassy: The Canadian Consulate to San Marino, c/o The Canadian Embassy, Via G.B. de Rossi, 27, 00161 Rome, Italy. Tel: (011-39-06) 445981. Fax: (011-39-06) 445 98750.

Embassy in Canada: c/o Consulate of San Marino, 15 McMurrich St, Ste 1104, Toronto, ON, M5R 3M6. Tel: (416) 925-7777. Fax: (416) 971-4849.

São Tomé and Príncipe

Long-Form Name: Democratic Republic of São Tomé and Príncipe
Capital: São Tomé

■ GEOGRAPHY

Area: 1,000 sq. km
Coastline: 209 km
Climate: tropical; hot, humid; one rainy season (Oct. to May)
Environment: deforestation; soil degradation
Terrain: volcanic, mountainous
Land Use: 2% arable; 36% permanent crops; 1% meadows; n.a. forest; 61% other; includes 100 sq. km irrigated
Location: S Atlantic Ocean, off W African Coast

■ PEOPLE

Population: 154,878 (July 1999 est.)
Nationality: São Toméan
Age Structure: 0-14 yrs: 48%; 15-64: 48%; 65+: 4% (1999 est.)
Population Growth Rate: 3.14 (1999 est.)
Net Migration: -3.88 migrants/1,000 population (1999 est.)
Ethnic Groups: mestiço, angolares (descendants of Angolan slaves), forros (descendants of freed slaves), servicais (contract labourers from Angola, Mozambique and Cape Verde), tongas (children of servicais born on the islands) and European (primarily Portuguese)
Languages: Portuguese (official), Crioulo
Religions: Roman Catholic, Evangelical Protestant, Seventh-Day Adventist
Birth Rate: 43.31/1,000 population (1999 est.)
Death Rate: 8.08/1,000 population (1999 est.)
Infant Mortality: 52.93 deaths/1,000 live births (1999 est.)
Life Expectancy at Birth: 63.18 years male, 66.28 years female (1999 est.)
Total Fertility Rate: 6.14 children born/woman (1999 est.)
Literacy: 75% (1997)

■ GOVERNMENT

Leader(s): Pres. Miguel Trovoada, Prime Min. Guilherme Posser da Costa
Government Type: republic
Administrative Divisions: 2 provinces
Nationhood: July 12, 1975 (from Portugal)
National Holiday: Independence Day, July 12

■ ECONOMY

Overview: the economy is hampered by overdependence on cocoa production, which has substantially declined in recent years because of drought and mismanagement; imports 90% of food needs as well as all fuels and most manufactured goods; government is attempting to restructure economy and reduce debt burden
GDP: $164 million, per capita $1,100; real growth rate 2.5% (1998 est.)
Inflation: n.a.
Industries: accounts for 19% of GDP; light construction, shirts, soap, beer, fisheries, shrimp processing
Labour Force: n.a.; most of population engaged in subsistence agriculture and fishing. There are shortages of skilled workers.
Unemployment: 50% (1998 est.)
Agriculture: 23% of GDP; primary source of exports; cash crops: cocoa (85%), coconuts, palm kernels, coffee; food products: bananas, papayas, beans, poultry, fish; not self-sufficient in food grain and meat
Natural Resources: fish

■ FINANCE/TRADE

Currency: dobra (Db) = 100 centimos
International Reserves Excluding Gold: $6 million

Saudi Arabia

(June 1998)
Gold Reserves: n.a.
Budget: n.a.
Defence Expenditures: n.a.
Education Expenditures: n.a.
External Debt: $267 million (1997)
Exports: $5.3 million (1997 est.) ; commodities: cocoa 85%, copra, coffee, palm oil; partners: Germany, Netherlands, China
Imports: $19.2 million (1997 est.); commodities: machinery and electrical equipment 54%, food products 23%, other 23%; partners: Portugal, Germany, Angola, China

■ COMMUNICATIONS
Daily Newspapers: 0 (1996)
Televisions: 166/1,000 inhabitants (1996)
Radios: 272/1,000 inhabitants (1996)
Telephones: 22 lines/1,000 inhabitants (1998)

■ TRANSPORTATION
Motor Vehicles: n.a.
Roads: 320 km; 218 km paved
Railway: none
Air Traffic: 25,000 passengers carried (1997)
Airports: 2, both with paved runways (1998 est.)

Canadian Embassy: The Canadian Embassy to São Tomé and Príncipe, c/o The Canadian Embassy, P.O. Box 4037 Libreville, Gabon. Tel: (011-241) 73-73-54. Fax: (011-241) 73-73-88.
Embassy in Canada: Embassy of São Tomé and Príncipe, 400 Park Ave., 7th Floor, New York, NY 10022. Tel: (212) 317-0533. Fax: (212) 317-0580.

Saudi Arabia

Long-Form Name: Kingdom of Saudi Arabia
Capital: Riyadh (royal); Jeddah (administrative)

■ GEOGRAPHY
Area: 1,960,582 sq. km
Coastline: 2,640 km
Climate: harsh, dry desert with great extremes of temperature
Environment: no perennial rivers or permanent water bodies; developing extensive coastal seawater desalination facilities; desertification; coastal pollution; frequent dust and sand storms
Terrain: mostly uninhabited, sandy desert
Land Use: 2% arable; 0% permanent crops; 56% permanent pastures; 1% forest; 41% other; includes 4,350 sq. km irrigated
Location: SW Asia (Middle East), bordering on Persian Gulf, Arabian Sea, Red Sea

■ PEOPLE
Population: 21,504,613 (July 1999 est.)
Nationality: Saudi
Age Structure: 0-14 yrs: 43%; 15-64: 54%; 65+: 3% (1999 est.)
Population Growth Rate: 3.39% (1999 est.)
Net Migration: 1.40 migrants/1,000 population (1999 est.)
Ethnic Groups: 90% Arab, 10% Afro-Asian
Languages: Arabic (official); English (business language)
Religions: Muslim (85% Sunni, 15% Shia)
Birth Rate: 37.38/1,000 population (1999 est.)
Death Rate: 4.86/1,000 population (1999 est.)
Infant Mortality: 38.80 deaths/1,000 live births (1999 est.)
Life Expectancy at Birth: 68.67 years male, 72.53 years female (1999 est.)
Total Fertility Rate: 6.34 children born/woman (1999 est.)
Literacy: 73.4% (1997)

■ GOVERNMENT
Leader(s): King and Prime Min. Fahd bin 'Abd al-'Aziz Al Sa'ud
Government Type: monarchy
Administrative Divisions: 13 provinces (mintaqat, sing. -mintaqah)
Nationhood: Sept. 23, 1932 (unification)
National Holiday: Unification of the Kingdom, Sept. 23

■ ECONOMY
Overview: has the largest reserves of petroleum in the world and is the largest exporter of petroleum; the government is working toward the privatization of the economy; 4 million foreign workers
GDP: $186 billion, per capita $9,000; real growth rate -10.8% (1998 est.)
Inflation: -1.4% (March 2000)
Industries: accounts for 53% of GDP; crude oil production, petroleum refining, basic petrochemicals, cement, small steel-rolling mill, construction, fertilizer, plastic
Labour Force: 7 million (1998); 34% government, 28% industry, 22% services, 16% agriculture
Unemployment: n.a.
Agriculture: accounts for 6% of GDP; fastest growing economic sector; subsidized by government; products: wheat, barley, tomatoes, melons, dates, citrus fruit, mutton, chickens, eggs, milk; approaching self-sufficiency in food
Natural Resources: crude oil, natural gas, iron ore, gold, copper

■ FINANCE/TRADE

Currency: riyal (SR) = 100 halalah
International Reserves Excluding Gold: $16.238 billion (Jan. 2000)
Gold Reserves: 4.596 million fine troy ounces (Jan. 2000)
Budget: revenues $32.3 billion; expenditures $44 billion, including capital expenditures n.a. (1999 est.)
Defence Expenditures: 12% of GDP (1997 est.)
Education Expenditures: 7.5% of GNP (1997)
External Debt: n.a.
Exports: $39.775 billion (1998); commodities: petroleum and petroleum products 89%; partners: Japan 26%, US 26%, France 6%, Bahrain 6%
Imports: $30.013 billion (1998); commodities: manufactured goods, transportation equipment, construction materials, processed food products; partners: US 20%, Japan 18%, UK 16%, Italy 11%

■ COMMUNICATIONS

Daily Newspapers: 13 (1996)
Televisions: 262/1,000 inhabitants (1998)
Radios: 321/1,000 inhabitants (1997)
Telephones: 143 lines/1,000 inhabitants (1998)

■ TRANSPORTATION

Motor Vehicles: 3,000,000; 1,710,000 passenger cars (1997 est.)
Roads: 162,000 km; 69,174 km paved
Railway: 1,390 km
Air Traffic: 11,738,000 passengers carried (1997)
Airports: 205; 70 have paved runways (1998 est.)

Canadian Embassy: The Canadian Embassy, Diplomatic Quarter, Riyadh; mailing address: P.O. Box 94321, Riyadh 11693, Saudi Arabia. Tel: (011-966-1) 488-2288. Fax: (011-966-1) 488-1997.
Embassy in Canada: Royal Embassy of Saudi Arabia, 99 Bank St, Ste 901, Ottawa ON K1P 6B9. Tel: (613) 237-4100. Fax: (613) 237-0567.

Senegal

Long-Form Name: Republic of Senegal
Capital: Dakar

■ GEOGRAPHY

Area: 196,190 sq. km
Coastline: 531 km
Climate: tropical; hot, humid; rainy season (Dec. to Apr.) has strong southeast winds; dry season (May to Nov.) dominated by hot, dry harmattan wind
Environment: lowlands seasonally flooded; deforestation; overgrazing; soil degradation; wildlife populations are endangered by poaching
Terrain: generally low, rolling, plains rising to foothills in southeast
Land Use: 12% arable; 0% permanent; 16% permanent pastures; 54% forest; 18% other, includes 710 sq. km irrigated
Location: W Africa, bordering on Atlantic Ocean

■ PEOPLE

Population: 10,051,930 (July 1999 est.)
Nationality: Senegalese (sing. & pl.)
Age Structure: 0-14 yrs: 48%; 15-64: 49%; 65+: 3% (1999 est.)
Population Growth Rate: 3.32% (1999 est.)
Net Migration: 0 migrants/1,000 population (1999 est.)
Ethnic Groups: 36% Wolof, 17% Fulani, 17% Serer, 9% Toucouleur, 9% Diola, 9% Mandingo, 1% European and Lebanese, 2% other
Languages: French (official); Wolof, Pulaar, Diola, Mandingo
Religions: 92% Muslim, 6% indigenous beliefs, 2% Christian (mostly Roman Catholic)
Birth Rate: 43.88/1,000 population (1999 est.)
Death Rate: 10.71/1,000 population (1999 est.)
Infant Mortality: 59.81 deaths/1,000 live births (1999 est.)
Life Expectancy at Birth: 54.95 years male, 60.78 years female (1999 est.)
Total Fertility Rate: 6.11 children born/woman (1999 est.)
Literacy: 34.6% (1997)

■ GOVERNMENT

Leader(s): Pres. Abdoulaye Wade, Prime Min. Niasse Moustapha
Government Type: republic under multi-party democratic rule
Administrative Divisions: 10 regions
Nationhood: April 4, 1960 (from France)
National Holiday: Independence Day, Apr. 4

■ ECONOMY

Overview: tourism has emerged as a great boon to the economy; fishing is the main economic resource; mining (phosphate) has been hurt by reduced worldwide demand for fertilizers in recent years. Limited resource base, environmental degradation and very high population growth continue to delay improvements
GDP: $15.6 billion, per capita $1,600; real growth rate 5.7% (1998 est.)

Inflation: 0.6% (Jan. 2000)
Industries: accounts for 17% of GDP; fishing, agricultural processing, phosphate mining, petroleum refining, building materials
Labour Force: 4.1 million (1998); 80.6% agriculture, 6.2% industry, 13.1% services
Unemployment: n.a.; urban youth 40%
Agriculture: including fishing, accounts for 19% of GDP; major products: peanuts (cash crop), millet, corn, sorghum, rice, cotton, tomatoes, green vegetables; estimated two-thirds self-sufficient in food; fish catch of 354,000 metric tons
Natural Resources: fish, phosphates, iron ore

■ FINANCE/TRADE

Currency: Communauté financière africaine franc (CFAF) = 100 centimes
International Reserves Excluding Gold: $396 million (Nov. 1999)
Gold Reserves: 0.029 million fine troy ounces (July 1998)
Budget: revenues $876 million; expenditures $1.977 billion, including capital expenditures n.a. (1996 est.)
Defence Expenditures: 1.4% of GDP (1997)
Education Expenditures: 3.7% of GNP (1997)
External Debt: $3.861 billion (1998)
Exports: $968 million (1998); commodities: manufactures 30%, fish products 27%, peanuts 11%, petroleum products 11%, phosphates 10%; partners: US, France, other European Community, Ivory Coast, India
Imports: $1.437 billion (1998); commodities: semimanufactures 30%, food 27%, durable consumer goods 17%, petroleum 12%, capital goods 14%; partners: US, France, other European Community, Nigeria, Algeria, China, Japan

■ COMMUNICATIONS

Daily Newspapers: 1 (1996)
Televisions: 41/1,000 inhabitants (1998)
Radios: 142/1,000 inhabitants (1997)
Telephones: 16 lines/1,000 inhabitants (1998)

■ TRANSPORTATION

Motor Vehicles: 160,000; 110,000 passenger cars (1997 est.)
Roads: 14,580 km; 4,271 km paved
Railway: 904 km
Air Traffic: 166,000 passengers carried (1997)
Airports: 20; 10 have paved runways (1998 est.)

Canadian Embassy: The Canadian Embassy, 45 av. de la République; mailing address: P.O. Box 3373, Dakar, Senegal. Tel: (011-221) 823-92-90. Fax: (011-221) 823-87-49.

Embassy in Canada: Embassy of the Republic of Senegal, 57 Marlborough Ave, Ottawa ON K1N 8E8. Tel: (613) 238-6392. Fax: (613) 238-2695.

Serbia and Montenegro

Long-Form Name: Federal Republic of Yugoslavia (self-proclaimed)
Capital: Belgrade (Serbia), Podgorica (Montenegro)

■ GEOGRAPHY

Area: 102,350 sq. km (Serbia 88,412 sq. km, Montenegro 13,938 sq. km)
Coastline: 199 km (Montenegro 199 km, Serbia 0 km)
Climate: continental in north; continental and Mediterranean in central region; south—Adriatic climate along coast, hot and dry summers, relatively cold winters, with heavy snowfall inland
Environment: coastal water pollution from sewage outlets, esp. in tourist-related areas; air and water pollution; subject to earthquakes
Terrain: varied: rich fertile plain in north, limestone ranges and basins in east, mountains and hills in southeast, high shoreline with no islands in southwest
Land Use: 30% arable, 5% permanent crops, 20% meadows and pastures, 25% forests, 20% other
Location: S Europe, bordering Adriatic Sea

■ PEOPLE

Population: 11,206,847 (July 1999 est.)
Nationality: Serb, Montenegrin
Age Structure: Serbia: 0-14 yrs: 20%; 15-64: 67%; 65+: 13% (1999 est.) Montenegro 0-14 yrs: 2%; 15-64: 68%; 65+: 11% (1999 est.)
Population Growth Rate: Serbia: -0.02% Montenegro: 0.07% (1999 est.)
Net Migration: Serbia: -2.65 migrants/1,000 population (1999 est.) Montenegro: -5.09 migrants/1,000 population (1999 est.)
Ethnic Groups: 63% Serb, 14% Albanian, 6% Montenegrin, 4% Hungarian, 13% other
Languages: 95% Serbian, 5% Albanian
Religions: 65% Orthodox, 19% Muslim, 4% Roman Catholic, 1% Protestant, 11% other
Birth Rate: 12.54/1,000 population (Serbia); 13.19/1,000 population (Montenegro) (1999 est.)
Death Rate: 9.68/1,000 population (Serbia); 7.44/1,000 population (Montenegro) (1999 est.)
Infant Mortality: 16.49 deaths/1,000 live births (Serbia); 10.99 deaths/1,000 live births (Montenegro) (1999 est.)

Life Expectancy at Birth: 71.03 years male, 76.05 years female (Serbia); 72.87 years male, 80.07 years female (Montenegro) (1999 est.)
Total Fertility Rate: 1.74 children born/woman (Serbia); 1.76 children born/woman (Montenegro) (1999 est.)
Literacy: n.a.

■ GOVERNMENT

Leader(s): Pres. Vojislav Kostunica
Government Type: republic
Administrative Divisions: 2 republics (republike, sing. -republika) and 2 nominally autonomous provinces (autonomna pokrajine, sing. -autonomna pokrajina)
Nationhood: April 11, 1992 (from Yugoslavia)
National Holiday: St. Vitus Day, June 28

■ ECONOMY

Overview: bloody ethnic warfare has caused destabilization of republic boundaries and the break-up of important inter-republic trade connections; The economic boom anticipated by the government after the suspension of UN sanctions has failed to take place.
GDP: $25.4 billion, per capita $2,300; real growth rate 3.5% (1998 est.)
Inflation: n.a.
Industries: accounts for 50% of GDP; machine building, metallurgy, mining, consumer goods, electronics, petroleum products, chemicals, pharmaceuticals
Labour Force: 5 million (1998); 41% industry, 35% services, 12% trade and tourism, 7% transportation and communication, 5% agriculture
Unemployment: n.a.
Agriculture: accounts for 25% of GDP; cereals, cotton, oilseed plants, chicory, fodder crops, fruit, vegetables, tobacco, olives, citrus, rice, livestock (sheep, goats)
Natural Resources: oil, gas, coal, antimony, copper, lead, gold, chrome

■ FINANCE/TRADE

Currency: Yugoslav New Dinar (YD) = 100 paras
International Reserves Excluding Gold: $2.549 billion (Jan. 1998)
Gold Reserves: n.a.
Budget: n.a.
Defence Expenditures: 6.5% of GDP (1999)
Education Expenditures: n.a.
External Debt: $13.742 billion (1998)
Exports: $1.500 million (1999 est.); manufactured goods, food, live animals, raw materials; partners: Russia, Italy, Germany
Imports: $2.804 million (1999 est.); machinery, transport equipment, fuels and lubricants, manufactured goods, chemicals, food, live animals, raw materials; partners: Germany, Italy, Russia

■ COMMUNICATIONS

Daily Newspapers: 18 (1996)
Televisions: 259/1,000 inhabitants (1998)
Radios: 297/1,000 inhabitants (1997)
Telephones: 218 lines/1,000 inhabitants (1998)

■ TRANSPORTATION

Motor Vehicles: 1,333,000; 1,002,000 passenger cars (1997 est.)
Roads: 50,414 km; 45,020 km paved
Railway: 3,987 km
Air Traffic: n.a.
Airports: 48; 18 have paved runways (1998 est.)

Canadian Embassy: The Canadian Embassy, 75 Kneza Milosa, 11000 Belgrade, Yugoslavia. Tel: (011-381-11) 64-46-66. Fax: (011-381-11) 64-14-80.
Embassy in Canada: Embassy of the Federal Republic of Yugoslavia, 17 Blackburn Ave, Ottawa ON K1N 8A2. Tel: (613) 233-6289. Fax: (613) 233-7850.

Seychelles

Long-Form Name: Republic of Seychelles
Capital: Victoria

■ GEOGRAPHY

Area: 455 sq. km
Coastline: 491 km
Climate: tropical marine; humid; cooler season during southeast monsoon (late May to Sept.); warmer season during northwest monsoon (Mar. to May)
Environment: lies outside the cyclone belt, so severe storms are rare; short droughts possible; no fresh water, catchments collect rain
Terrain: 40 granitic and about 50 coralline islands; Mahé Group is granitic, narrow coastal strip, rocky, hilly; others are coral, flat, elevated reefs
Land Use: 2% arable; 13% permanent crops; 0% meadows; 11% forest; 74% other; includes n.a. sq. km irrigated
Location: Indian Ocean, NE of Madagascar

■ PEOPLE

Population: 79,164 (July 1999 est.)
Nationality: Seychellois sing. & pl.)

Age Structure: 0-14 yrs: 29%; 15-64: 64%; 65+: 7% (1999 est.)
Population Growth Rate: 0.65% (1999 est.)
Net Migration: -6.32 migrants/1,000 population (1999 est.)
Ethnic Groups: Seychellois (mixture of Asians, Africans, Europeans)
Languages: English, French (both official), Creole
Religions: 90% Roman Catholic, 8% Anglican, 2% other
Birth Rate: 19.39/1,000 population (1999 est.)
Death Rate: 6.56/1,000 population (1999 est.)
Infant Mortality: 16.65 deaths/1,000 live births (1999 est.)
Life Expectancy at Birth: 66.61 years male, 75.42 years female (1999 est.)
Total Fertility Rate: 1.97 children born/woman (1999 est.)
Literacy: 58% (1997)

■ GOVERNMENT

Leader(s): Pres. France Albert René
Government Type: republic
Administrative Divisions: 23 administrative districts
Nationhood: June 29, 1976 (from UK)
National Holiday: National Day, June 18 (1993 adoption of a new constitution)

■ ECONOMY

Overview: the government is moving to reduce the high dependence on tourism by promoting the development of farming, fishing and small-scale manufacturing, yet it is also encouraging foreign investment in order to upgrade hotels and other services
GDP: $550 million, per capita $7,000; real growth rate 4.3% (1997 est.)
Inflation: 6.0% (June 1999)
Industries: accounts for 15% of GDP; tourism employs 30% of labour force; mostly subsistence farming; cash crops: coconuts, cinnamon, vanilla; other products: sweet potatoes, cassava, bananas, broiler chickens; large share of food needs imported; expansion of tuna fishing under way
Labour Force: n.a.; 19% industry, 57% services, 14% government, 10% agriculture
Unemployment: n.a.
Agriculture: accounts for 4% of GDP, mostly subsistence farming; cash crops: coconuts, cinnamon, vanilla; large share of food needs to be imported; tuna fishing is increasing in importance
Natural Resources: fish, copra, cinnamon trees

■ FINANCE/TRADE

Currency: Seychelles rupee (SRe) = 100 cents
International Reserves Excluding Gold: $27 million (Oct. 1999)
Gold Reserves: n.a.
Budget: n.a.
Defence Expenditures: 2.88% of total govt. expenditure (1998)
Education Expenditures: 8.57% of govt. expenditure (1998)
External Debt: $148 million (1996)
Exports: $113 million (1997); commodities: fish, copra, cinnamon bark, petroleum products (re-exports); partners: France 63%, Pakistan 12%, Réunion 10%, UK 7%
Imports: $403 million (1998); commodities: manufactured goods, food, tobacco, beverages, machinery and transportation equipment, petroleum products; partners: UK 20%, France 14%, South Africa 13%, PDRY 13%, Singapore 8%, Japan 6%

■ COMMUNICATIONS

Daily Newspapers: 1 (1996)
Televisions: 145/1,000 inhabitants (1996)
Radios: 541/1,000 inhabitants (1996)
Telephones: 244 lines/1,000 inhabitants (1998)

■ TRANSPORTATION

Motor Vehicles: 8,500; 6,800 passenger cars (1997 est.)
Roads: 280 km; 176 km paved
Railway: none
Air Traffic: 384,000 passengers carried (1997)
Airports: 14; 6 have paved runways (1998 est.)

Canadian Embassy: The Canadian High Commission to Seychelles, c/o The Canadian High Commission, 38 Mirambo St, Dar-es-Salaam; mailing address: P.O. Box 1022, Dar-es-Salaam, Tanzania. Tel: (011-255-51) 112-832. Fax: (011-255-51) 116-896.
Embassy in Canada: High Commission for the Republic of Seychelles, 800 Second Ave, Ste 400C, New York NY 10017, USA. Tel: (212) 972-1785. Fax: (212) 972-1786.

Sierra Leone

Long-Form Name: Republic of Sierra Leone
Capital: Freetown

■ GEOGRAPHY

Area: 71,740 sq. km
Coastline: 402 km
Climate: tropical; hot, humid; summer rainy season (May to Dec.); winter dry season (Dec. to Apr.)

Sierra Leone

Environment: extensive mangrove swamps hinder access to sea; sand and dust storms; deforestation; soil degradation; population pressure negatively affects land
Terrain: coastal belt of mangrove swamps, wooded hill country, upland plateau, mountains in east
Land Use: 7% arable; 1% permanent crops; 31% meadows; 28% forest; 33% other; includes 290 sq. km irrigated
Location: W Africa, bordering on North Atlantic Ocean

■ PEOPLE

Population: 5,296,651 (July 1999 est.)
Nationality: Sierra Leonean
Age Structure: 0-14 yrs: 45%; 15-64: 52%; 65+: 3% (1999 est.)
Population Growth Rate: 4.34% (1999 est.)
Net Migration: 14.50 migrants/1,000 population (1999 est.)
Ethnic Groups: 99% native African (30% Temne, 39% Mende, other 30%); 1% Creole, European, Lebanese and Asian
Languages: English (official); regular use limited to literate minority; principal vernaculars are Mende in south and Temne in north; Krio is the language of the resettled ex-slave population of the Freetown area and is lingua franca
Religions: 60% Muslim, 10% Christian, 30% traditional beliefs
Birth Rate: 45.62/1,000 population (1999 est.)
Death Rate: 16.77/1,000 population (1999 est.)
Infant Mortality: 126.23 deaths/1,000 live births (1999 est.)
Life Expectancy at Birth: 46.07 years male, 52.27 years female (1999 est.)
Total Fertility Rate: 6.16 children born/woman (1999 est.)
Literacy: 37.2% (1997)

■ GOVERNMENT

Leader(s): Pres. Ahmad Tejan Kabbah
Government Type: constitutional democracy
Administrative Divisions: 3 provinces and 1 area
Nationhood: Apr. 27, 1961 (from UK)
National Holiday: Republic Day, Apr. 27

■ ECONOMY

Overview: the economic and social infrastructure is underdeveloped; subsistence agriculture is the backbone of the economy; problems include unemployment, rising inflation, large trade deficits; diamond mining is an important source of national income
GDP: $2.7 billion, per capita $530; real growth rate 0.7% (1998 est.)
Inflation: 36.7% (Dec. 1999)
Industries: accounts for 16% of GDP; mining (diamonds, bauxite, rutile), small-scale manufacturing (beverages, textiles, cigarettes, footwear), petroleum refinery
Labour Force: 2 million (1998); 69.6% agriculture, 14.1% industry, 16.4% services
Unemployment: n.a.
Agriculture: accounts for 52% of GDP and two-thirds of the labour force, largely subsistence farming; cash crops: coffee, cocoa, palm kernels; harvest of food staple rice meets 80% of domestic needs; annual fish catch averages 53,000 metric tons
Natural Resources: diamonds, titanium ore, bauxite, iron ore, gold, chromite

■ FINANCE/TRADE

Currency: leone (Le) = 100 cents
International Reserves Excluding Gold: $45 million (Jan. 2000)
Gold Reserves: n.a.
Budget: revenues $96 million; expenditures $150 million, including capital expenditures n.a. (1996 est.)
Defence Expenditures: 33.0% of central government expenditure (1997)
Education Expenditures: n.a.
External Debt: $1.243 billion (1998)
Exports: $6 million (1999); commodities: rutile 50%, bauxite 17%, cocoa 11%, diamonds 3%, coffee 3%; partners: US, UK, Belgium, Germany, (Western Europe)
Imports: $81 million (1999); commodities: capital goods 40%, food 32%, petroleum 12%, consumer goods 7%, light industrial goods; partners: US, European Community, Japan, China, Nigeria

■ COMMUNICATIONS

Daily Newspapers: 1 (1996)
Televisions: 13/1,000 inhabitants (1998)
Radios: 253/1,000 inhabitants (1997)
Telephones: 4 lines/1,000 inhabitants (1998)

■ TRANSPORTATION

Motor Vehicles: 42,500; 21,000 passenger cars (1997 est.)
Roads: 11,700 km; 1,287 km paved
Railway: 84 km
Air Traffic: 15,000 passengers carried (1996)
Airports: 10; 2 have paved runways (1998 est.)

Canadian Embassy: The Canadian High Commission to Sierra Leone, c/o The Canadian Embassy, PO Box 99, Conakry, Guinea. Tel: (011-224) 46-23-95. Fax: (011-224) 46-42-35.
Embassy in Canada: c/o High Commission for the Republic of Sierra Leone, 1701-19th St NW,

Washington DC 20009, USA. Tel: (202) 939-9261. Fax: (202) 483-1793.

Singapore

Long-Form Name: Republic of Singapore
Capital: Singapore

■ GEOGRAPHY

Area: 647.5 sq. km
Coastline: 193 km
Climate: tropical; hot, humid, rainy; no pronounced rainy or dry seasons; thunderstorms occur on 40% of all days (67% of days in Apr.)
Environment: mostly urban and industrialized; water supply is limited
Terrain: lowland; gently undulating central plateau contains water catchment area and nature preserve
Land Use: 2% arable; 6% permanent; 0% meadows; 5% forest; 87% other; includes n.a. sq. km irrigated
Location: SE Asia (southern tip of Malaysia), bordering on South China Sea

■ PEOPLE

Population: 3,531,600 (July 1999 est.)
Nationality: Singaporean
Age Structure: 0-14 yrs: 21%; 15-64: 72%; 65+: 7% (1999 est.)
Population Growth Rate: 1.15% (1999 est.)
Net Migration: 2.83 migrants/1,000 population (1999 est.)
Ethnic Groups: 76.4% Chinese, 14.9% Malay, 6.4% Indian, 2.3% other
Languages: Chinese (Mandarin), Malay, Tamil and English (all official); Malay (national)
Religions: majority of Chinese are Buddhists or atheists; Malays nearly all Muslim (minorities are Christians, Hindus, Sikhs, Taoists, Confucianists)
Birth Rate: 13.38/1,000 population (1999 est.)
Death Rate: 4.69/1,000 population (1999 est.)
Infant Mortality: 3.84 deaths/1,000 live births (1999 est.)
Life Expectancy at Birth: 75.79 years male, 82.14 years female (1999 est.)
Total Fertility Rate: 1.47 children born/woman (1999 est.)
Literacy: 91.4% (1997)

■ GOVERNMENT

Leader(s): Pres. Sellapan Rama Nathan, Prime Min. Goh Chok Tong
Government Type: republic within Commonwealth
Administrative Divisions: none

Nationhood: Aug. 9, 1965 (from Malaysia)
National Holiday: National Day, Aug. 9

■ ECONOMY

Overview: has an open entrepreneurial economy with strong service and manufacturing sectors and good international trading links; growth has traditionally run at high rates; per capita GDP is among the highest in Asia; rising labour costs continue to adversely affect Singapore's competitiveness
GDP: $91.7 billion, per capita $26,300; real growth rate 1.3% (1998 est.)
Inflation: -7.2% (Feb. 2000)
Industries: accounts for 28% of GDP; petroleum refining, electronics, oil drilling equipment, rubber processing and rubber products, processed food and beverages, ship repair, entrepôt trade, financial services, biotechnology
Labour Force: 2 million (1998); 27% industry, 22.8% trade and tourism, 21.6% community, social and business services
Unemployment: 5.4% (Jan. 2000)
Agriculture: minor importance in the economy; self-sufficient in poultry and eggs; must import most other food; major crops: rubber, copra, fruit, vegetables
Natural Resources: fish, deepwater ports

■ FINANCE/TRADE

Currency: Singapore dollar ($S) = 100 cents
International Reserves Excluding Gold: $75.874 billion (Jan. 2000)
Gold Reserves: n.a.
Budget: revenues $16.3 billion; expenditures $13.6 billion, including capital expenditures n.a. (1997-98 est.)
Defence Expenditures: 28.9% of central government expenditure (1997)
Education Expenditures: 18.82% of central government expenditure (1997)
External Debt: n.a.
Exports: $107.215 billion (1999); commodities (includes transshipments to Malaysia): petroleum products, rubber electronics, manufactured goods; partners: US 24%, Malaysia 14%, Japan 9%, Thailand 6%, Hong Kong 5%, Australia 3%, Germany 3%
Imports: $100.171 billion (1999); commodities (includes transshipments from Malaysia): capital equipment, petroleum, chemicals, manufactured goods, foodstuffs; partners: Japan 22%, US 16%, Malaysia 15%, European Community 12%, Kuwait 1%

■ COMMUNICATIONS

Daily Newspapers: 8 (1996)

Televisions: 348/1,000 inhabitants (1998)
Radios: 822/1,000 inhabitants (1997)
Telephones: 562 lines/1,000 inhabitants (1998)

■ TRANSPORTATION
Motor Vehicles: 545,000; 390,000 passenger cars (1997 est.)
Roads: 3,010 km; 2,932 km paved
Railway: 38.6 km
Air Traffic: 12,981,000 passengers carried (1997)
Airports: 9; all have paved runways (1998 est.)

Canadian Embassy: Canadian High Commission, IBM Towers, 14th & 15th Fls, 80 Anson Rd, Singapore 079907; mailing address: Robinson Rd, P.O. Box 845, Singapore 901645. Tel: (011-65) 325-3200. Fax: (011-65) 325-3297.
Embassy in Canada: c/o High Commission for the Republic of Singapore, 231 East 51st St, New York NY 10022, USA. Tel: (212) 826-0840. Fax: (212) 826-2964.

Slovakia

Long-Form Name: Slovak Republic
Capital: Bratislava

■ GEOGRAPHY
Area: 48,845 sq. km
Coastline: none: landlocked
Climate: temperate: cool summers, cold, cloudy, humid winters
Environment: severe damage to forests from acid rain; industrial air pollution from metallurgical plants
Terrain: rugged mountains in central region and north, lowlands in south
Land Use: 31% arable; 3% permanent crops; 17% permanent pastures; 41% forests; 8% other; includes 800 sq. km irrigated
Location: C Europe

■ PEOPLE
Population: 5,396,193 (July 1999 est.)
Nationality: Slovak
Age Structure: 0-14 yrs: 20%; 15-64: 69%; 65+: 11% (1999 est.)
Population Growth Rate: 0.04% (1999 est.)
Net Migration: 0.29 migrants/1,000 population (1999 est.)
Ethnic Groups: 85.7% Slovak, 10.7% Hungarian, 1.5% Gypsy, 19% Czech, 0.3% Ruthenian, 0.3% Ukrainian, 0.1% German, 0.1% Polish, 0.3% other
Languages: Slovak (official), Hungarian
Religions: 60.3% Roman Catholic, 9.7% atheist, 8.4% Protestant, 4.1% Orthodox, 17.5% other
Birth Rate: 9.52/1,000 population (1999 est.)
Death Rate: 9.43/1,000 population (1999 est.)
Infant Mortality: 9.48 deaths/1,000 live births (1999 est.)
Life Expectancy at Birth: 69.71 years male, 77.40 years female (1999 est.)
Total Fertility Rate: 1.20 children born/woman (1999 est.)
Literacy: 99.0% (1997)

■ GOVERNMENT
Leader(s): Pres. Rudolf Schuster, Prime Min. Mikulas Dzurinda
Government Type: parliamentary democracy
Administrative Divisions: 8 departments (kraje, sing. -kraj)
Nationhood: Jan. 1, 1993 (from Czechoslovakia)
National Holiday: Slovak Constitution Day, Sept. 1; Anniversary of Slovak National Uprising, Aug. 29

■ ECONOMY
Overview: Slovakia continues the difficult transition from a centrally controlled economy to a modern market-oriented economy. Private activity now makes up more than two-thirds of GDP. Slovakia continues to experience difficulty in attracting foreign investment.
GDP: $44.5 billion, per capita $8,300; real growth rate 5% (1998 est.)
Inflation: 16.4% (Feb. 2000)
Industries: accounts for 33.4% of GDP; mining, chemicals, metalworking, consumer appliances, plastics, armaments
Labour Force: 3 million (1998); 29.3% industry, 26.4% community, social and business services, 12.4% agriculture
Unemployment: 14% (1998 est.)
Agriculture: accounts for 4.8% of GDP; very diversified crop and livestock production including grains, livestock, poultry; mostly self-sufficient in food
Natural Resources: brown coal and lignite, iron ore, copper, manganese, salt, gas

■ FINANCE/TRADE
Currency: koruna (pl. koruny) (Kc) = 100 halierov
International Reserves Excluding Gold: $3.339 billion (Jan. 2000)
Gold Reserves: 1.290 million fine troy ounces (Jan. 2000)
Budget: revenues $5.4 billion; expenditures $6.5 billion, including capital expenditures n.a. (1997)
Defence Expenditures: 5.0% of central government expenditure (1998)

Education Expenditures: 10.26% of central government expenditure (1998)
External Debt: $9.893 billion (1998)
Exports: $9.567 billion (1999 est.); machinery and transport equipment, chemicals, fuels, minerals, agricultural products; partners: Czech Republic, successor states of the former USSR, Germany, Poland, Austria, France, US, UK
Imports: $10.587 billion (1999 est.); machinery and transport equipment, fuels, lubricants, manufactured goods, chemicals, agricultural products

■ COMMUNICATIONS
Daily Newspapers: 19 (1996)
Televisions: 402/1,000 inhabitants (1998)
Radios: 580/1,000 inhabitants (1997)
Telephones: 286 lines/1,000 inhabitants (1998)

■ TRANSPORTATION
Motor Vehicles: included in the data for the Czech Republic
Roads: 38,000 km; 37,500 km paved
Railway: 3,660 km
Air Traffic: 81,000 passengers carried (1997)
Airports: 15; 10 have paved runways (1998 est.)

Canadian Embassy: The Canadian Embassy to Slovakia, c/o The Canadian Embassy, Mickiewiczova 6, 125 33 Prague 6, Czech Republic. Tel: (011-420-2) 7210-1800. Fax: (011-420-2) 7210-1890.
Embassy in Canada: Embassy of the Slovak Republic, 50 Rideau Terrace, Ottawa ON K1M 2A1. Tel: (613) 749-4442. Fax: (613) 749-4989.

Slovenia

Long-Form Name: Republic of Slovenia
Capital: Ljubljana

■ GEOGRAPHY
Area: 20,256 sq. km
Coastline: 46.6 km
Climate: Mediterranean climate on the coast, continental climate with mild to hot summers and cold winters in the plateaus and eastern valleys
Environment: pollution of Sava River; heavy metals and toxic chemicals along coast; forest damage from air pollution; subject to flooding and earthquakes
Terrain: short coastal strip, alpine mountain region, mixed mountains and valleys and numerous rivers in east
Land Use: 12% arable; 3% permanent crops; 24% meadows and pastures; 54% forests and woodland; 7% other includes 20 sq. km irrigated
Location: southern Europe, bordering on Adriatic Sea

■ PEOPLE
Population: 1,970,570 (July 1999 est.)
Nationality: Slovene
Age Structure: 0-14 yrs: 16%; 15-64: 70%; 65+: 14% (1999 est.)
Population Growth Rate: -0.04% (1999 est.)
Net Migration: 0.23 migrants/1,000 population (1999 est.)
Ethnic Groups: 91% Slovene, 3% Croat, 2% Serb, 1% Muslim, 3% other
Languages: 91% Slovenian, 6% Serbo-Croatian, 3% other
Religions: 71% Roman Catholic, 1% Lutheran, 1% Muslim, 4.3% athiest, 23% other
Birth Rate: 8.97/1,000 population (1999 est.)
Death Rate: 9.62/1,000 population (1999 est.)
Infant Mortality: 5.28 deaths/1,000 live births (1999 est.)
Life Expectancy at Birth: 71.71 years male, 79.21 years female (1999 est.)
Total Fertility Rate: 1.23 children born/woman (1999 est.)
Literacy: 99% (1997)

■ GOVERNMENT
Leader(s): Pres. Milan Kucan, Prime Min. Andrej Bajuk
Government Type: parliamentary democratic republic
Administrative Divisions: 136 municipalities (obcine, sing. -obcina) and 11 urban municipalities (obcine mestne, sing. -obcina mestna)
Nationhood: June 25, 1991 (from Yugoslavia)
National Holiday: National Statehood Day, June 25

■ ECONOMY
Overview: tourism has suffered due to internal strife; destruction of trade channels and the influx of tens of thousands of refugees have interfered with economic recovery after secession from Yugoslavia; there are efforts toward the privatization of major industrial firms; inflation and unemployment rates are gradually beginning to drop; chief trading partners: Germany, Italy, former Soviet countries, France, Austria, US
GDP: $20.4 billion, per capita $10,300; real growth rate 3.6% (1998 est.)
Inflation: 10.5% (March 2000)
Industries: accounts for 35% of GDP; metallurgy, furniture, sports equipment, steel, cars, sugar, cement, textiles, machine tools

Labour Force: 1 million (1998); 39.3% industry, 23.1% community, social and business services, 11.1% trade and tourism
Unemployment: 7.9% (1998)
Agriculture: accounts for 5% of GDP; products include wheat, maize, sugar beets, potatoes, cabbages, livestock (esp. cattle, sheep, pigs, poultry); fishing, forestry; many other agricultural products must be imported
Natural Resources: brown coal and lignite deposits, lead, zinc, mercury, uranium

■ FINANCE/TRADE

Currency: Slovenian tolar = 100 stotins (at parity with Yugoslav dinar)
International Reserves Excluding Gold: $3.080 billion (Jan. 2000)
Gold Reserves: none (Jan. 2000)
Budget: revenues $8.48 billion; expenditures $8.53 billion, including capital expenditures (1996 est.)
Defence Expenditures: 12.5% of central government expenditure (1997)
Education Expenditures: 5.7% of GNP (1997)
External Debt: $4.4 billion (1998 est.)
Exports: $8.604 billion (1999); machinery, semifinished goods, raw materials, electric motors, transportation equipment, clothing, foodstuffs
Imports: $9.952 billion (1999); raw materials, semifinished goods, machinery, foodstuffs

■ COMMUNICATIONS

Daily Newspapers: 7 (1996)
Televisions: 356/1,000 inhabitants (1998)
Radios: 406/1,000 inhabitants (1997)
Telephones: 375 lines/1,000 inhabitants (1998)

■ TRANSPORTATION

Motor Vehicles: n.a.
Roads: 14,830 km; 12,309 km paved
Railway: 1,201 km
Air Traffic: 404,000 passengers carried (1997)
Airports: 14; 6 have paved runways (1998 est.)

Canadian Embassy: The Canadian Embassy to Slovenia, c/o The Canadian Embassy Budakeszi ut 32, 1121 Budapest, Hungary. Tel.: (011-36-1) 275-1200; (011-36-1) 275-1210.
Embassy in Canada: Embassy of the Republic of Slovenia, 150 Metcalfe St, Ste 2101, Ottawa, ON K2P 1P1. Tel: (613) 565-5781. Fax: (613) 565-5783.

Solomon Islands

Long-Form Name: Solomon Islands
Capital: Honiara (on island of Guadalcanal)

■ GEOGRAPHY

Area: 28,450 sq km
Coastline: 5,313 km
Climate: tropical monsoon; few extremes of temperature and weather
Environment: subject to typhoons, which are rarely destructive; geologically active region with frequent earth tremors; soil degradation and deforestation; deterioration of coral reefs
Terrain: mostly rugged mountains with some low coral atolls
Land Use: 1% arable; 1% permanent; 1% meadows; 88% pastures; 9% other; includes n.a. sq. km irrigated
Location: Melanesia, Pacific Ocean, E of New Guinea

■ PEOPLE

Population: 455,429 (July 1999 est.)
Nationality: Solomon Islander
Age Structure: 0-14 yrs: 45%; 15-64: 52%; 65+: 3% (1999 est.)
Population Growth Rate: 3.18% (1999 est.)
Net Migration: 0 migrants/1,000 population (1999 est.)
Ethnic Groups: 93% Melanesian, 4% Polynesian, 1.5% Micronesian, 0.8% European, 0.3% Chinese, 0.4% other
Languages: English (official), Pidgin, 120 local languages
Religions: 34% Anglican, 19% Roman Catholic, 17% South Seas Evangelical, 25% other Protestant, 5% other
Birth Rate: 35.92/1,000 population (1999 est.)
Death Rate: 4.11/1,000 population (1999 est.)
Infant Mortality: 23.00 deaths/1,000 live births (1999 est.)
Life Expectancy at Birth: 69.55 years male, 74.75 years female (1999 est.)
Total Fertility Rate: 4.96 children born/woman (1999 est.)
Literacy: 62.0% (1997)

■ GOVERNMENT

Leader(s): Head of State: Queen Elizabeth II/Gov. Gen. John Lapli. Prime Min. Manasseh Sogavare
Government Type: parliamentary democracy
Administrative Divisions: 7 provinces and 1 town
Nationhood: July 7, 1978 (from UK; formerly known as British Solomon Islands)
National Holiday: Independence Day, July 7

■ ECONOMY

Overview: about 90% of the population depend

on subsistence agriculture, fishing and forestry for at least part of their livelihood; possesses an abundance of undeveloped mineral resources; little manufacturing activity — most manufactured goods must be imported. Uncontrolled government spending is leading to national financial ruin despite a rich natural resource base
GDP: $1.15 billion, per capita $2,600; real growth rate -10% (1998 est.)
Inflation: 12.4% (Dec. 1998)
Industries: copra, fish (tuna)
Labour Force: n.a.; 41.5% community, social and business services, 23.7% agriculture, 11.9% trade and tourism
Unemployment: n.a.
Agriculture: including fishing and forestry, accounts for approx. 31% of GDP; mostly subsistence farming; cash crops: cocoa, beans, coconuts, palm kernels, timber; other products: rice, potatoes, vegetables, fruit, cattle, pigs; not self-sufficient in food grains; 90% of fish catch is exported
Natural Resources: fish, forests, gold, bauxite, phosphates

■ FINANCE/TRADE

Currency: Solomon Islands dollar ($SI) = 100 cents
International Reserves Excluding Gold: $53 million (Jan. 2000)
Gold Reserves: n.a.
Budget: revenues $147 million; expenditures $168 million, including capital expenditures n.a. (1997 est.)
Defence Expenditures: negligible
Education Expenditures: n.a.
External Debt: $145 million (1996)
Exports: $173 million (1997); commodities: fish 46%, timber 31%, copra 5%, palm oil 5%; partners: Japan 51%, UK 12%, Thailand 9%, Netherlands 8%, Australia 2%, US 2%
Imports: $170 million (1997); commodities: plant and machinery 30%, fuel 19%, food 16%; partners: Japan 36%, US 23%, Singapore 9%, UK 9%, New Zealand 9%, Australia 4%, Hong Kong 4%, China 3%

■ COMMUNICATIONS

Daily Newspapers: 0 (1996)
Televisions: 6.1/1,000 inhabitants (1996)
Radios: 141/1,000 inhabitants (1996)
Telephones: 19 lines/1,000 inhabitants (1998)

■ TRANSPORTATION

Motor Vehicles: n.a.
Roads: 1,360 km; 32 km paved
Railway: none
Air Traffic: 94,000 passengers carried (1997)

Airports: 32; 2 have paved runways (1998 est.)

Canadian Embassy: The Canadian High Commission to Solomon Islands, c/o The Canadian High Commission, Commonwealth Ave, Canberra A.C.T. 2600, Australia. Tel: (011-61-2) 6270-4000. Fax: (011-61-2) 6273-3285.
Embassy in Canada: c/o High Commission for the Solomon Islands, 800-2nd Ave, Ste 400L, New York NY 10017, USA. Tel: (212) 599-6192. Fax: (212) 661-8925.

Somalia

Long-Form Name: Somalia
Capital: Mogadishu

■ GEOGRAPHY

Area: 637,660 sq. km
Coastline: 3,025 km
Climate: desert; northeast monsoon (Dec. to Feb.), cooler southwest monsoon (May to Oct.); irregular rainfall; hot, humid periods (tangambili) between monsoons
Environment: recurring droughts; frequent dust storms over eastern plains in summer; deforestation; overgrazing; soil erosion; desertification
Terrain: mostly flat to undulating plateau rising to hills in north
Land Use: 2% arable; negligible permanent crops; 69% permanent pastures; 26% forest; 3% other; includes 1,800 sq. km irrigated
Location: E Africa, bordering on Gulf of Aden, Indian Ocean

■ PEOPLE

Population: 7,140,643 (July 1999 est.)
Nationality: Somali
Age Structure: 0-14 yrs: 44%; 15-64: 53%; 65+: 3% (1999 est.)
Population Growth Rate: 4.13% (1999 est.)
Net Migration: 11.90 migrants/1,000 population (1999 est.)
Ethnic Groups: 85% Somali, rest mainly Bantu; 30,000 Arabs, 3,000 Europeans, 800 Asians
Languages: Somali (official); Arabic, Italian, English
Religions: almost entirely Sunni Muslim, small Christian community
Birth Rate: 47.98/1,000 population (1999 est.)
Death Rate: 18.62/1,000 population (1999 est.)
Infant Mortality: 125.68 deaths/1,000 live births (1999 est.)
Life Expectancy at Birth: 44.66 years male, 47.85 years female (1999 est.)

Total Fertility Rate: 7.25 children born/woman (1999 est.)
Literacy: 24% (1997)

■ GOVERNMENT

Leader(s): Pres. Abidiqasim Salad Hassan appointed by interim-parliament of 245 clan chiefs in 2000. Not supported by Somaliland or Puntland. State of anarchy continues; government structures absent.
Government Type: n.a.
Administrative Divisions: 18 regions (plural n.a., sing. -gobolka)
Nationhood: July 1, 1960 (from a merger of British Somaliland, which became independent from the UK on June 26, 1960, and Italian Somaliland, which became independent from the Italian-administered UN trusteeship on July 1, 1960, to form the Somali Republic)
National Holiday: Anniversary of the Revolution, Oct. 21

■ ECONOMY

Overview: nomads or semi-nomads who are dependent upon livestock for their livelihoods make up about 50% of the population; one of the world's least developed countries, possessing few resources; problems include high external debt, double-digit inflation and bitter civil war which has devastated much of the economy
GDP: $4 billion, per capita $600; real growth rate n.a.% (1998 est.)
Inflation: n.a.
Industries: accounts for 10% of GDP; based on processing of agricultural products; sugar refining, textiles, petroleum refining
Labour Force: n.a.; 75.6% agriculture, 8.4% industry, 16% services
Unemployment: n.a.
Agriculture: livestock accounts for 59% of GDP and 65% of export revenue: cattle, sheep, goats; fishing potential largely unexploited; crops: bananas, sorghum, corn, mangoes, sugar cane; not self-sufficient in food
Natural Resources: uranium and largely unexploited reserves of iron ore, tin, gypsum, bauxite, copper, salt

■ FINANCE/TRADE

Currency: Somali shilling (So.Sh.) = 100 cents
International Reserves Excluding Gold: n.a.
Gold Reserves: n.a.
Budget: n.a.
Defence Expenditures: n.a.
Education Expenditures: n.a.
External Debt: $2.643 billion (1996)
Exports: n.a.; commodities: livestock, hides, skins, bananas, fish; partners: US 0.5%, Saudi Arabia, Italy, Germany
Imports: n.a.; commodities: textiles, petroleum products, foodstuffs, construction materials; partners: US 13%, Italy, Germany, Kenya, UK, Saudi Arabia

■ COMMUNICATIONS

Daily Newspapers: 2 (1996)
Televisions: 13/1,000 inhabitants (1996)
Radios: 46/1,000 inhabitants (1996)
Telephones: 1 line/1,000 inhabitants (1998)

■ TRANSPORTATION

Motor Vehicles: 20,000; 10,000 passenger cars (1997 est.)
Roads: 22,100 km; 2,700 km paved
Railway: none
Air Traffic: n.a.
Airports: 61; 7 have paved runways (1998 est.)

Canadian Embassy: The Canadian Embassy to Somalia, c/o The Canadian High Commission, Comcraft House, Hailé Sélassie Ave, Nairobi; mailing address: The Canadian High Commission, P.O. Box 30481, Nairobi, Kenya. Tel: (011-254-2) 21-48-04. Fax: (011-254-2) 22-69-87.
Embassy in Canada: c/o The High Commission for the Republic of Kenya, 415 Laurier Ave E, Ottawa ON K1N 6R4. Tel: (613) 563-1773. Fax: (613) 233-6599.

South Africa

Long-Form Name: Republic of South Africa
Capital: Pretoria (administrative), Cape Town (legislative), Bloemfontein (judicial)

■ GEOGRAPHY

Area: 1,219,912 sq. km; includes Walvis Bay, Marion Island, and Prince Edward Island
Coastline: 2,798 km
Climate: mostly semi-arid; subtropical along coast; sunny days, cool nights
Environment: lack of important arterial rivers or lakes requires extensive water conservation and control measures; prolonged droughts and increasing water pollution exacerbate the problem
Terrain: vast interior plateau rimmed by rugged hills and narrow coastal plain
Land Use: 10% arable; 1% permanent; 67% meadows; 7% forest; 15% other, includes 12,700 sq. km irrigated
Location: S Africa, bordering on Indian Ocean, South Atlantic Ocean

South Africa

■ PEOPLE

Population: 43,426,386 (July 1999 est.)
Nationality: South African
Age Structure: 0-14 yrs: 34%; 15-64: 61%; 65+: 5% (1999 est.)
Population Growth Rate: 1.32% (1999 est.)
Net Migration: 0.08 migrants/1,000 population (1999 est.)
Ethnic Groups: 75.2% black, 13.6% white, 8.6% coloured, 2.6% Indian
Languages: 11 official languages: Afrikaans, English, Ndebele, Pedi, Sotho, Swazi, Tsonga, Tswana, Venda, Xhosa, Zulu
Religions: most of whites, coloureds and approx. 60% of blacks are Christian; approx. 60% of Indians are Hindu, 20% Muslim
Birth Rate: 25.94/1,000 population (1999 est.)
Death Rate: 12.81/1,000 population (1999 est.)
Infant Mortality: 51.99 deaths/1,000 live births (1999 est.)
Life Expectancy at Birth: 52.68 years male, 56.90 years female (1999 est.)
Total Fertility Rate: 3.09 children born/woman (1999 est.)
Literacy: 84.0% (1997)

■ GOVERNMENT

Leader(s): Pres. Thabo Mvuyelwa Mbeki
Government Type: republic
Administrative Divisions: 9 provinces; after the election bringing Mandela to power, all 10 black homelands and 4 provinces existing earlier were dissolved
Nationhood: May 31, 1910 (from UK)
National Holiday: Freedom Day, April 27

■ ECONOMY

Overview: there is great disparity in living standards between the white minority (favoured) and the black majority; international embargoes against the country (because of its policy of apartheid) hurt the economy; burgeoning unemployment; has rich mineral resources (diamonds)
GDP: $290.6 billion, per capita $6,800; real growth rate 0.3% (1998 est.)
Inflation: 2.2% (Dec. 1999)
Industries: accounts for 39% of GDP; mining (world's largest producer of platinum, gold, chrome), automobile assembly, metalworking, machinery, textile, iron and steel, chemical, fertilizer, foodstuffs
Labour Force: 16 million (1998); 28.3% industry, 26.5% community, social and business services, 15.4% trade and tourism
Unemployment: 30.0%, with high underemployment (1998 est.)
Agriculture: accounts for 5% of GDP and 30% of labour force; diversified agriculture, with emphasis on livestock; products: cattle, poultry, sheep, wool, milk, beef, corn, wheat; sugar cane, fruit, vegetables; self-sufficient in food
Natural Resources: gold, chromium, antimony, coal, iron ore, manganese, nickel, phosphates, tin, uranium, gem diamonds, platinum, copper, vanadium, salt, natural gas

■ FINANCE/TRADE

Currency: rand (R) = 100 cents
International Reserves Excluding Gold: $6.345 billion (Jan. 2000)
Gold Reserves: 3.940 million fine troy ounces (Jan. 2000)
Budget: revenues $30.5 billion; expenditures $38 billion, including capital expenditures of $2.6 billion (1996 est.)
Defence Expenditures: 5.6% of central government expenditure (1997)
Education Expenditures: 7.9% of GNP (1997)
External Debt: $24.711 billion (1998)
Exports: $26.707 billion (1999); commodities: gold 40%, minerals and metals 23%, food 6%, chemicals 3%; partners: Germany, Japan, UK, US, other European Community, Hong Kong
Imports: $26.696 billion (1999); commodities: machinery 27%, chemicals 11%, vehicles and aircraft 11%, textiles, scientific instruments, base metals; partners: US, Germany, Japan, UK, France, Italy, Switzerland

■ COMMUNICATIONS

Daily Newspapers: 17 (1996)
Televisions: 125/1,000 inhabitants (1998)
Radios: 317/1,000 inhabitants (1997)
Telephones: 115 lines/1,000 inhabitants (1998)

■ TRANSPORTATION

Motor Vehicles: 6,280,000; 4,120,000 passenger cars (1997 est.)
Roads: 331,265 km; 137,475 km paved
Railway: 21,431 km
Air Traffic: 7,274,000 passengers carried (1997)
Airports: 749; 144 have paved runways (1998 est.)

Canadian Embassy: The Canadian High Commission, 1103 Arcadia, Hatfield 0028, Pretoria; mailing address: Private Bag X13, Hatfield 0028, South Africa. Tel: (011-27-12) 422-3000. Fax: (011-27-12) 422-3052.
Embassy in Canada: Embassy of the Republic of South Africa, 15 Sussex Dr, Ottawa ON K1M 1M8. Tel: (613) 744-0330. Fax: (613) 741-1639.

Spain

Long-Form Name: Kingdom of Spain
Capital: Madrid

■ GEOGRAPHY

Area: 504,750 sq. km; includes Balaeric Islands, Canary Islands, Ceuta, Melilla, Islas Chafarinas, Peñón de Vélez de la Gomera
Coastline: 4,964 km
Climate: temperate; clear, hot summers in interior, more moderate and cloudy along coast; cloudy, cold winters in interior, partly cloudy and cool along coast
Environment: deforestation; air and water pollution; soil degradation; desertification; periodic droughts
Terrain: large, flat to dissected, rugged hills; Pyrenees in north
Land Use: 30% arable; 9% permanent crops; 21% meadows; 32% forest; 8% other, includes 34,530 sq. km irrigated
Location: SW Europe, bordering on Mediterranean Sea and N Atlantic Ocean

■ PEOPLE

Population: 39,167,744 (July 1999 est.)
Nationality: Spanish
Age Structure: 0-14 yrs: 15%; 15-64: 68%; 65+: 17% (1999 est.)
Population Growth Rate: 0.10% (1999 est.)
Net Migration: 0.66 migrants/1,000 population (1999 est.)
Ethnic Groups: composite of Mediterranean and Nordic types
Languages: Castilian Spanish; second languages include 17% Catalan (northeast), 7% Galician (northwest), 2% Basque (north)
Religions: 99% Roman Catholic, 1% other sects
Birth Rate: 9.99/1,000 population (1999 est.)
Death Rate: 9.69/1,000 population (1999 est.)
Infant Mortality: 6.41 deaths/1,000 live births (1999 est.)
Life Expectancy at Birth: 73.97 years male, 81.71 years female (1999 est.)
Total Fertility Rate: 1.24 children born/woman (1999 est.)
Literacy: 97.2% (1997)

■ GOVERNMENT

Leader(s): King Juan Carlos I, Pres. Jose Maria Aznar
Government Type: parliamentary monarchy
Administrative Divisions: 17 autonomous communities (comunidades autonomas, sing. - comunidad autonoma)
Nationhood: 1492 (expulsion of the Moors and unification)
National Holiday: National Day, Oct. 12

■ ECONOMY

Overview: Spain advocates liberalization, privatization, and deregulation of the economy, and has introduced some tax reforms to that end. Adjustment to the monetary and other economic policies of an integrated Europe will pose difficult challenges in the next few years.
GDP: $645.6 billion, per capita $16,500; real growth rate 3.5% (1998 est.)
Inflation: 3.0% (April 2000)
Industries: accounts for 33% of GDP; textiles and apparel (including footwear), food and beverages, metals and metal manufacturing, chemicals, shipbuilding, automobiles, machine tools
Labour Force: 17 million (1998); 64% services, 28% manufacturing and mining, 8% agriculture
Unemployment: 20% (1998 est.)
Agriculture: accounts for 3% of GDP and 14% of labour force; major products: grain, vegetables, olives, wine grapes, sugar beets, citrus fruit, beef, pork, poultry, dairy; largely self-sufficient in food; fish catch of 1.4 million metric tons
Natural Resources: coal, lignite, iron ore, uranium, mercury, pyrites, fluorspar, gypsum, zinc, lead, tungsten, copper, kaolin, potash, hydropower

■ FINANCE/TRADE

Currency: peseta (Pta) = 100 centimos [As of Jan. 1, 1999, Government securities are issued in Euros (EUR)]
International Reserves Excluding Gold: $34.042 billion (Jan. 2000)
Gold Reserves: 16.830 million fine troy ounces (Jan. 2000)
Budget: n.a.
Defence Expenditures: 6.0% of central government expenditure (1997)
Education Expenditures: 5.0% of GNP (1997)
External Debt: n.a.
Exports: $109.964 billion (1999); commodities: foodstuffs, live animals, wood, footwear, machinery, chemicals; partners: European Community 66%, US 8%, other developed countries 9%
Imports: $144.436 billion (1999); commodities: petroleum, footwear, machinery, chemicals, grain, soybeans, coffee, tobacco, iron and steel, timber, cotton, transport equipment; partners: European Community 57%, US 9%, other developed countries 13%, Middle East 3%

■ COMMUNICATIONS

Daily Newspapers: 87 (1996)
Televisions: 506/1,000 inhabitants (1998)

Radios: 333/1,000 inhabitants (1997)
Telephones: 414 lines/1,000 inhabitants (1998)

■ TRANSPORTATION
Motor Vehicles: 18,300,000; 14,900,000 passenger cars (1997 est.)
Roads: 346,858 km; 343,389 km paved
Railway: 15,079 km
Air Traffic: 30,316,000 passengers carried (1997)
Airports: 99; 66 have paved runways (1998 est.)

Canadian Embassy: The Canadian Embassy, Calle Nunez de Balboa, 35, 28001 Madrid; mailing address: Apartado 587, 28080 Madrid, Spain. Tel: (011-34) 91-423-3252. Fax: (011-34) 91-423-3251.
Embassy in Canada: Embassy of the Kingdom of Spain, 74 Stanley Ave, Ottawa ON, K1M IP4. Tel: (613) 747-2252. Fax: (613) 744-1224.

Sri Lanka

Long-Form Name: Democratic Socialist Republic of Sri Lanka
Capital: Colombo

■ GEOGRAPHY
Area: 65,610 sq. km
Coastline: 1,340 km
Climate: tropical; monsoonal; northeast monsoon (Dec. to Mar.); southwest monsoon (June to Oct.)
Environment: occasional cyclones, tornados; deforestation; soil erosion; pollution of fresh water resources
Terrain: mostly low, flat to rolling plain; mountains in south-central interior
Land Use: 14% arable; 15% permanent crops; 7% meadows; 32% forest; 32% other, includes 5,500 sq. km irrigated
Location: Indian Ocean, S of India

■ PEOPLE
Population: 19,144,875 (July 1999 est.)
Nationality: Sri Lankan
Age Structure: 0-14 yrs: 27%; 15-64: 67%; 65+: 6% (1999 est.)
Population Growth Rate: 1.10% (1999 est.)
Net Migration: -1.13 migrants/1,000 population (1999 est.)
Ethnic Groups: 74% Sinhalese; 18% Tamil; 7% Moor; 1% Burgher, Malay and Veddha
Languages: Sinhala (official); Sinhala and Tamil are the national languages; Sinhala spoken by about 74% of population, Tamil spoken by about 18%; English commonly used in government and spoken by about 10% of the population
Religions: 69% Buddhist, 15% Hindu (Tamil speakers), 8% Christian, 8% Muslim
Birth Rate: 18.16/1,000 population (1999 est.)
Death Rate: 6.02/1,000 population (1999 est.)
Infant Mortality: 16.12 deaths/1,000 live births (1999 est.)
Life Expectancy at Birth: 69.89 years male, 75.59 years female (1999 est.)
Total Fertility Rate: 2.10 children born/woman (1999 est.)
Literacy: 90.7% (1997)

■ GOVERNMENT
Leader(s): Pres. Chandrika Bandaranaike Kumaratunga, Prime Min. Ratnasiri Wickramanayake
Government Type: republic
Administrative Divisions: 8 provinces
Nationhood: Feb. 4, 1948 (from UK; formerly known as Ceylon)
National Holiday: Independence and National Day, Feb. 4

■ ECONOMY
Overview: Sustained economic growth, coupled with low population growth, has pushed Sri Lanka from the ranks of the poorest countries in the world up to the threshold of the middle income countries.
GDP: $48.1 billion, per capita $2,500; real growth rate 4.7% (1998 est.)
Inflation: 1.9% (Feb. 2000)
Industries: accounts for 31% of GDP; processing of rubber, tea, coconuts and other agricultural commodities; cement, petroleum refining, textiles, tobacco. The apparel industry has surpassed all other kinds of manufacturing
Labour Force: 8.2 million (1998); 38.7% agriculture, 18.3% community, social and business services, 12.7% industry
Unemployment: 11.3% (1997)
Agriculture: accounts for 18.4% of GDP and almost 45% of labour force; most important staple crop is paddy rice; other field crops: sugar cane, grains, pulses, oilseeds, roots; spices; cash crops: tea, rubber, coconuts; animal products: milk, eggs, hides, meat; not self-sufficient in rice production
Natural Resources: limestone, graphite, mineral sands, gems, phosphates, clay

■ FINANCE/TRADE
Currency: rupee (SL Re) = 100 cents
International Reserves Excluding Gold: $1.558 billion (Jan. 2000)
Gold Reserves: 0.063 million fine troy ounces (Jan. 2000)

Budget: revenues $3 billion; expenditures $4.2 billion, including capital expenditures of $1 billion (1997)
Defence Expenditures: 16.74% of total govt. expenditure (1998)
Education Expenditures: 10.52% of govt. expenditure (1998)
External Debt: $8.526 billion (1998)
Exports: $4.599 billion (1999); commodities: tea, textiles and garments, petroleum products, coconut, rubber, agricultural products, gems and jewelry, marine products; partners: US 26%, Egypt, Iraq, UK, Germany, Singapore, Japan
Imports: $5.893 billion (1999); commodities: petroleum, machinery and equipment, textiles and textile materials, wheat, transportation equipment, electrical machinery, sugar, rice; partners: Japan, Saudi Arabia, US 5.6%, India, Singapore, Germany, UK, Iran

■ **COMMUNICATIONS**

Daily Newspapers: 9 (1996)
Televisions: 92/1,000 inhabitants (1998)
Radios: 209/1,000 inhabitants (1997)
Telephones: 28 lines/1,000 inhabitants (1998)

■ **TRANSPORTATION**

Motor Vehicles: 468,900; 220,000 passenger cars (1997 est.)
Roads: 99,200 km; 39,680 km paved
Railway: 1,501 km
Air Traffic: 1,232,000 passengers carried (1997)
Airports: 13, 12 have paved runways (1998 est.)

Canadian Embassy: The Canadian High Commission, 6 Gregory's Rd, Cinnamon Gardens, Colombo 7; mailing address: P.O. Box 1006, Colombo 7, Sri Lanka. Tel: (011-94-1) 69-58-41. Fax: (011-94-1) 68-70-49.
Embassy in Canada: High Commission for the Democratic Socialist Republic of Sri Lanka, 333 Laurier Ave W, Ste 1204, Ottawa ON K1P 1C1. Tel: (613) 233-8449. Fax: (613) 238-8448.

Sudan

Long-Form Name: Republic of the Sudan
Capital: Khartoum

■ **GEOGRAPHY**

Area: 2,505,810 sq. km
Coastline: 853 km
Climate: tropical in south; arid desert in north; rainy season (Apr. to Oct.)
Environment: dominated by the Nile and its tributaries; dust storms; desertification; unsafe drinking water resources; overhunting threatens wildlife population
Terrain: generally flat, featureless plain; mountains in east and west
Land Use: 5% arable; negligible permanent; 46% permanent pastures; 19% forest; 30% other; includes 19,460 sq. km irrigated
Location: NE Africa, bordering on Red Sea

■ **PEOPLE**

Population: 34,475,690 (July 1999 est.)
Nationality: Sudanese
Age Structure: 0-14 yrs: 45%; 15-64: 52%; 65+: 3% (1999 est.)
Population Growth Rate: 2.71% (1999 est.)
Net Migration: -1.68 migrants/1,000 population (1999 est.)
Ethnic Groups: 52% black, 39% Arab, 6% Beja, 2% foreigners, 1% other
Languages: Arabic (official), Nubian, Ta Bedawie, diverse dialects of Nilotic, Nilo-Hamatic and Sudanic languages, English; program of Arabization in process
Religions: 70% Sunni Muslim (in north), 25% indigenous beliefs, 5% Christian (mostly in south and Khartoum)
Birth Rate: 39.34/1,000 population (1999 est.)
Death Rate: 10.60/1,000 population (1999 est.)
Infant Mortality: 70.94 deaths/1,000 live births (1999 est.)
Life Expectancy at Birth: 55.41 years male, 57.44 years female (1999 est.)
Total Fertility Rate: 5.58 children born/woman (1999 est.)
Literacy: 53.3% (1997)

■ **GOVERNMENT**

Leader(s): Pres. Omar Hassan Ahmed al-Bashir. Presidential and parliamentary elections scheduled October 2000.
Government Type: transitional; government was civilianized after the ruling military junta was dissolved on Oct. 16, 1993
Administrative Divisions: 26 states (wilayat, sing. -wilayah)
Nationhood: Jan. 1, 1956 (from Egypt and UK; formerly known as Anglo-Egyptian Sudan)
National Holiday: Independence Day, Jan. 1

■ **ECONOMY**

Overview: a very poor country, hurt by civil war, chronic political instability, adverse weather and counterproductive governmental economic policies; agriculture is the economic base. It employs 80% of the labour force and focuses chiefly on processing agricultural produce; international aid is helping the country manage a high foreign debt, but creditors want economic reform

Suriname

GDP: $31.2 billion, per capita $930; real growth rate 6.1% (1998 est.)
Inflation: 14.1% (March 1999)
Industries: accounts for 17% of GDP; cotton ginning, textiles, cement, edible oils, sugar, soap distilling, shoes, petroleum refining
Labour Force: 11 million (1998); 63.4% agriculture, 4.3% industry, 32.3% services
Unemployment: n.a.
Agriculture: accounts for 33% of GDP and 80% of labour force; untapped potential for higher farm production; water shortages; two-thirds of land area suitable for crops and livestock; major products: cotton, oilseeds, sorghum, millet, wheat, gum arabic, sheep; marginally self-sufficient in most foods
Natural Resources: modest reserves of crude oil, iron ore, copper, chromium ore, zinc, tungsten, mica, silver, crude oil

■ FINANCE/TRADE

Currency: Sudanese pound (LSd) = 100 piastres
International Reserves Excluding Gold: $174 million (Oct. 1999)
Gold Reserves: n.a.
Budget: revenues $482 million; expenditures $1.5 billion, including capital expenditures of $30 million (1996)
Defence Expenditures: 53.8% of central government expenditure (1997)
Education Expenditures: 0.9% of GNP (1997)
External Debt: $16.843 billion (1998)
Exports: $596 million (1998); commodities: cotton 43%, sesame, gum arabic, peanuts; partners: Western Europe 46%, Saudi Arabia 14%, Eastern Europe 9%, Japan 9%, US 3%
Imports: $1.915 billion (1998); commodities: petroleum products, manufactured goods, machinery and equipment, medicines and chemicals; partners: Western Europe 32%, Africa and Asia 15%, US 13%, Eastern Europe 3%

■ COMMUNICATIONS

Daily Newspapers: 5 (1996)
Televisions: 87/1,000 inhabitants (1998)
Radios: 271/1,000 inhabitants (1997)
Telephones: 6 lines/1,000 inhabitants (1998)

■ TRANSPORTATION

Motor Vehicles: 75,000 registered vehicles, including 35,000 passenger cars (1996)
Roads: 11,900 km; 4,320 km paved
Railway: 5,516 km
Air Traffic: 333,000 passengers carried (1997)
Airports: 63; 12 have paved runways (1998 est.)

Canadian Embassy: The Canadian Embassy to the Sudan, c/o The Canadian Embassy, Old Airport Area, Higher 23, Kebele 12, House Number 122, Addis Ababa; mailing address: P.O. Box 1130, Addis Ababa, Ethiopia. Tel: (011-251-1) 71-30-22. Fax: (011-251-1) 71 30 33.
Embassy in Canada: Embassy of the Republic of the Sudan, 354 Stewart St., Ottawa ON K1N 6K8. Tel: (613) 235-4000. Fax: (613) 235-6880.

Suriname

Long-Form Name: Republic of Suriname
Capital: Paramaribo

■ GEOGRAPHY

Area: 163,270 sq. km
Coastline: 386 km
Climate: tropical; moderated by trade winds
Environment: mostly tropical rain forest; deforestation resulting from logging for export
Terrain: mostly rolling hills; narrow coastal plain with swamps
Land Use: 0% arable; 0% permanent; 0% meadows; 96% forest; 4% other; includes 600 sq. km irrigated
Location: N South America, bordering on Atlantic Ocean

■ PEOPLE

Population: 431,156 (July 1999 est.)
Nationality: Surinamer
Age Structure: 0-14 yrs: 33%; 15-64: 62%; 65+: 5% (1998 est.)
Population Growth Rate: 0.71% (1999 est.)
Net Migration: -8.92 migrants/1,000 population (1999 est.)
Ethnic Groups: 37% Hindustani (East Indian), 31% Creole (black and mixed), 15% Javanese, 10% Bush black, 3% Amerindian, 2% Chinese, 1% European, 1% other
Languages: Dutch (official), Hindustani 32%, Javanese 15%; the majority can speak the native language Sranang Tongo (Taki-Taki); English is also widely spoken
Religions: 27.4% Hindu, 19.6% Muslim, 22.8% Roman Catholic, 25.2% Protestant (predominantly Moravian), about 5% indigenous beliefs
Birth Rate: 21.75/1,000 population (1999 est.)
Death Rate: 5.75/1,000 population (1999 est.)
Infant Mortality: 26.52 deaths/1,000 live births (1999 est.)
Life Expectancy at Birth: 68.32 years male, 73.59 years female (1999 est.)
Total Fertility Rate: 2.55 children born/woman (1999 est.)

Literacy: 93.5% (1997)

■ GOVERNMENT

Leader(s): Pres. Ronald Venetiaan, V. Pres. and Prime Min. Jules Ajodhia
Government Type: republic
Administrative Divisions: 10 districts (distrikten, sing. distrikt)
Nationhood: Nov. 25, 1975 (from Netherlands; formerly known as Netherlands Guiana or Dutch Guiana)
National Holiday: Independence Day, Nov. 25

■ ECONOMY

Overview: the economy is vulnerable to world prices for its bauxite, which provides more than 15% of the GDP and 65+% of export earnings. Guerrilla activity has targeted the economic infrastructure; high inflation, high unemployment, widespread black-market activity and hard currency shortfalls continue to characterize the economy
GDP: $1.48 billion, per capita $3,500; real growth rate 2% (1998 est.)
Inflation: 21.0% (June 1998)
Industries: accounts for 32% of GDP; bauxite mining, alumina and aluminum production, lumbering, food processing, fishing
Labour Force: n.a.; 20% agriculture, 8.9% industry, 49.4% services, 15.2% trade and tourism
Unemployment: 20% (1997)
Agriculture: accounts for 10% of GDP and 25% of export earnings; paddy rice planted on 85% of arable land and represents 60% of total farm output; other products: bananas, palm kernels, coconuts, plantains, peanuts, beef, chicken; shrimp and forestry products of increasing importance
Natural Resources: timber, hydropower potential, fish, shrimp, bauxite, iron ore and modest amounts of nickel, copper, platinum, gold

■ FINANCE/TRADE

Currency: Surinamese guilder, gulden or florin (Sf) = 100 cents
International Reserves Excluding Gold: $70 million (May 1999)
Gold Reserves: 0.373 million fine troy ounces (May. 1999)
Budget: adjusted for purchasing power parity: revenues $317 million; expenditures $333 million, including capital expenditures of $52 million (1997 est.)
Defence Expenditures: 1.6% of GDP (1997 est.)
Education Expenditures: n.a.
External Debt: $216 million (1996 est.)

Exports: $436 million (1998); commodities: alumina, bauxite, aluminum, rice, wood and wood products, shrimp and fish, bananas; partners: Netherlands 28%, US 22%, Norway 18%, Japan 11%, Brazil 10%, UK 4%
Imports: $552 million (1998); commodities: capital equipment, petroleum, foodstuffs, cotton, consumer goods; partners: US 34%, Netherlands 20%, Trinidad and Tobago 8%, Brazil 5%, UK 3%

■ COMMUNICATIONS

Daily Newspapers: 2 (1996)
Televisions: 144/1,000 inhabitants (1996)
Radios: 683/1,000 inhabitants (1996)
Telephones: 152 lines/1,000 inhabitants (1998)

■ TRANSPORTATION

Motor Vehicles: 66,000; 46,900 passenger cars (1997 est.)
Roads: 4,530 km; 1,178 km paved
Railway: 166 km
Air Traffic: 279,000 passengers carried (1997)
Airports: 46; 5 have paved runways (1998 est.)

Canadian Embassy: The Canadian Embassy to Suriname, c/o Canadian High Commission, High and Young Streets, Georgetown; mailing address: P.O. Box 10880, Georgetown, Guyana. Office: Canadian Consulate, Wagenwagstraat 50 bov Paramaribo, Suriname. Tel. (011-597) 424-527. Fax: (011-597) 425-962.
Embassy in Canada: c/o Embassy of the Republic of Suriname, Van Ness Center, 4301 Connecticut Ave NW, Ste 460, Washington DC 20008, USA. Tel: (202) 244-7488. Fax: (202) 244-5878.

Svalbard

Long-Form Name: Svalbard
Capital: Longyearbyen

■ GEOGRAPHY

Area: 62,049 sq. km, 5 large islands, many smaller ones
Climate: arctic, tempered by mild Atlantic winds, cool suumers, cold winters
Land Use: undeveloped except for mining establishments; no trees—the only bushes are crowberry and cloudberry
Location: Arctic Ocean, midway between Norway and the North Pole

■ PEOPLE

Population: 2,503 (July 1999 est.)
Nationality: Norwegian

Ethnic Groups: 62% Russian and Ukrainian; 38% Norwegian
Languages: Norwegian, Russian

■ GOVERNMENT

Colony/Territory of: Dependent Territory of Norway
Leader(s): Head of State: King Harald V (Norway). Governor Ann-Kristin Olsen, Ass't Gov. Jan-Atle Hansen
Government Type: Territory of Norway
National Holiday: n.a.

■ ECONOMY

Overview: tourism most important; coal mining only industry (the Norwegian state-owned company employs almost 60% of the population); some trapping of seal, polar bear, fox and walrus

■ FINANCE/TRADE

Currency: Norwegian krone = 100 oere

Canadian Embassy: c/o The Canadian Embassy, Wergelandsveien 7, 0244 Oslo, Norway. Tel: (011-47) 22-99-53-00. Fax: (011-47) 22-99-53-01.
Representative to Canada: c/o Embassy of the Kingdom of Norway, Royal Bank Centre, 90 Sparks St, Ste 532, Ottawa ON K1P 5B4. Tel: (613) 238-6571. Fax: (613) 238-2765.

Swaziland

Long-Form Name: Kingdom of Swaziland
Capital: Mbabane (administrative); Lobamba (legislative)

■ GEOGRAPHY

Area: 17,360 sq. km
Coastline: none: landlocked
Climate: varies from tropical to near temperate
Environment: overhunting and overgrazing; soil degradation; soil erosion; limited safe drinking water
Terrain: mostly mountains and hills; some moderately sloping plains
Land Use: 11% arable; 0% permanent; 62% meadows; 7% forest; 20% other; includes 670 sq. km irrigated
Location: S Africa

■ PEOPLE

Population: 985,335 (July 1999 est.)
Nationality: Swazi
Age Structure: 0-14 yrs: 46%; 15-64: 51%; 65+: 3% (1999 est.)
Population Growth Rate: 1.91% (1999 est.)
Net Migration: 0 migrants/1,000 population (1999 est.)
Ethnic Groups: 97% African, 3% European
Languages: English and siSwati (official); government business conducted in English
Religions: 60% Christian, 40% indigenous beliefs
Birth Rate: 40.80/1,000 population (1999 est.)
Death Rate: 21.72/1,000 population (1999 est.)
Infant Mortality: 101.87 deaths/1,000 live births (1999 est.)
Life Expectancy at Birth: 36.86 years male, 39.40 years female (1999 est.)
Total Fertility Rate: 5.92 children born/woman (1999 est.)
Literacy: 77.5% (1997)

■ GOVERNMENT

Leader(s): King Mswati III; Premier Barnabas Sibusiso Dlamini
Government Type: monarchy; independent member of Commonwealth
Administrative Divisions: 4 districts
Nationhood: Sept. 6, 1968 (from UK)
National Holiday: Somhlolo (Independence) Day, Sept. 6

■ ECONOMY

Overview: the economy is based on subsistence agriculture and is closely tied to that of its neighbour, South Africa, from which it receives 90% of its imports and to which it sends about half of its exports; manufacturing focuses on the processing of agricultural products; mining is becoming less important. Overgrazing, soil deterioration and recurrent droughts are persistent problems
GDP: $4 billion, per capita $4,200; real growth rate 2.6% (1998 est.)
Inflation: 5.1% (Dec. 1999)
Industries: accounts for 42% of GDP; mining (coal and asbestos), wood pulp, sugar; asbestos is declining in importance
Labour Force: 135,000 (1996); 74% agriculture, 17% services, 9% industry; 24,000–29,000 employed in South Africa
Unemployment: n.a.
Agriculture: accounts for 10% of GDP and over 60% of labour force; mostly subsistence agriculture; cash crops: sugar cane, citrus fruit, cotton, pineapple; other crops and livestock: corn, sorghum, peanuts, cattle, goats, sheep; not self-sufficient in grain
Natural Resources: asbestos, coal, clay, tin, hydroelectric power, forests and small gold and diamond deposits

■ FINANCE/TRADE

Currency: lilangeni (pl. emalangeni) (E) = 100 cents
International Reserves Excluding Gold: $369 million (Sept. 1999)
Gold Reserves: n.a.
Budget: revenues $400 million; expenditures $450 million, including capital expenditures of $115 million (1996-97)
Defence Expenditures: n.a.
Education Expenditures: n.a.
External Debt: $175 million (1998)
Exports: $893 million (1996); commodities: sugar, asbestos, wood pulp, citrus, canned fruit, soft drink concentrates; partners: South Africa, UK, US
Imports: $1.286 billion (1997); commodities: motor vehicles, machinery, transport equipment, chemicals, petroleum products, foodstuffs; partners: South Africa, US, UK

■ COMMUNICATIONS

Daily Newspapers: 3 (1996)
Televisions: 23/1,000 inhabitants (1996)
Radios: 170/1,000 inhabitants (1996)
Telephones: 30 lines/1,000 inhabitants (1998)

■ TRANSPORTATION

Motor Vehicles: 36,755; 28,523 passenger cars (1997 est.)
Roads: 3,810 km; 814 km paved
Railway: 297 km, including 71 km disused
Air Traffic: 41,000 passengers carried (1997)
Airports: 18; 1 has paved runways (1998 est.)

Canadian Embassy: The Canadian High Commission to Swaziland, c/o The Canadian Embassy, 1103 Arcadia St, Hatfield 0028, Pretoria; mailing address: Private Bag X13, Hatfield 0028, Pretoria, South Africa. Tel: (011-27-12) 422-3000. Fax (011-27-12) 422-3052.

Embassy in Canada: High Commission for the Kingdom of Swaziland, 3400 International Dr. NW, Suite 3M, Washington DC, 20008, Tel: (202) 362-6683, Fax: (202) 244-8059.

Sweden

Long-Form Name: Kingdom of Sweden
Capital: Stockholm

■ GEOGRAPHY

Area: 449,960 sq. km
Coastline: 3,218 km
Climate: temperate in south with cold, cloudy winters and cool, partly cloudy summers, subarctic in north
Environment: water pollution; acid rain; ice floes in coastal waters hinder navigation
Terrain: mostly flat or gently rolling lowlands; mountains in west
Land Use: 7% arable; 0% permanent crops; 1% meadows; 68% forest; 24% other; includes 1,250 sq. km irrigated
Location: N Europe, bordering on Baltic Sea

■ PEOPLE

Population: 8,911,296 (July 1999 est.)
Nationality: Swedish, Swede
Age Structure: 0-14 yrs: 19%; 15-64: 64%; 65+: 17% (1999 est.)
Population Growth Rate: 0.29% (1999 est.)
Net Migration: 1.68 migrants/1,000 population (1999 est.)
Ethnic Groups: homogeneous white population; small Lappish minority; about 12% foreign born or first-generation immigrants (Finns, Yugoslavs, Danes, Norwegians, Greeks, Turks)
Languages: Swedish (official), small Lapp- and Finnish-speaking minorities; immigrants speak native languages
Religions: 94% Evangelical Lutheran, 1.5% Roman Catholic, 4.5% other
Birth Rate: 12.00/1,000 population (1999 est.)
Death Rate: 10.77/1,000 population (1999 est.)
Infant Mortality: 3.91 deaths/1,000 live births (1999 est.)
Life Expectancy at Birth: 76.61 years male, 82.11 years female (1999 est.)
Total Fertility Rate: 1.83 children born/woman (1999 est.)
Literacy: 99% (1997)

■ GOVERNMENT

Leader(s): King Carl XVI Gustaf, Prime Min. Goran Persson
Government Type: constitutional monarchy
Administrative Divisions: 21 counties (lan, sing. & pl.)
Nationhood: June 6, 1809, constitutional monarchy established
National Holiday: Day of the Swedish Flag, June 6

■ ECONOMY

Overview: a mixed system of high-tech capitalism and extensive welfare benefits; has benefited from neutrality in world wars; economy is heavily oriented toward foreign trade; has excellent communications systems but faces loss of competitive edge as inflation and unemployment rates rise
GDP: $175 billion, per capita $19,700; real growth rate 2.9% (1998 est.)

Switzerland

Inflation: 0.8% (April 2000)
Industries: accounts for 30.5% of GDP; iron and steel, precision equipment (bearings, radio and telephone parts, armaments), wood pulp and paper products, processed foods, motor vehicles
Labour Force: 5 million (1998); 40.4% community, social and business services, 18.3 industry, 14.3 % trade and tourism
Unemployment: 5.7% (Jan. 2000)
Agriculture: accounts for 2% of GDP; animal husbandry predominates, with milk and dairy products accounting for 37% of farm income; main crops: grains, sugar beets, potatoes; 100% self-sufficient in grains and potatoes, 85% self-sufficient in sugar beets
Natural Resources: zinc, iron ore, lead, copper, silver, timber, uranium, hydropower potential

■ FINANCE/TRADE

Currency: krona (pl. kronor) (Skr) = 100 oere
International Reserves Excluding Gold: $14.950 billion (Jan. 2000)
Gold Reserves: 5.961 million fine troy ounces (Jan. 2000)
Budget: revenues $109.4 billion; expenditures $146.1 billion, including capital expenditures n.a. (1995–96)
Defence Expenditures: 5.51% of govt. expenditure (1998)
Education Expenditures: 6.85% of govt. expenditure (1998)
External Debt: n.a.
Exports: $84.776 billion (1999); commodities: machinery, motor vehicles, paper products, pulp and wood, iron and steel products, chemicals, petroleum and petroleum products; partners: European Community 52.1%, (Germany 12.1%, UK 11.2%, Denmark 6.8%), US 9.8%, Norway 9.3%
Imports: $68.416 billion (1999); commodities: machinery, petroleum and petroleum products, chemicals, motor vehicles, foodstuffs, iron and steel, clothing; partners: European Community 55.8%, (Germany 21.2%, UK 8.6%, Denmark 6.6%), US 7.5%, Norway 6%

■ COMMUNICATIONS

Daily Newspapers: 94 (1996)
Televisions: 531/1,000 inhabitants (1998)
Radios: 932/1,000 inhabitants (1997)
Telephones: 674 lines/1,000 inhabitants (1998)

■ TRANSPORTATION

Motor Vehicles: 4,00,000; 3,800,000 passenger cars (1997 est.)
Roads: 138,000 km; 105,018 km paved
Railway: 13,415 km

Air Traffic: 11,327,000 passengers carried (1997)
Airports: 255; 145 have paved runways (1998 est.)

Canadian Embassy: The Canadian Embassy, Tegelbacken 4 (Flr 7), Stockholm; mailing address: P.O. Box 16129; S-10323 Stockholm, Sweden. Tel: (011-46-8) 453-3000. Fax: (011-46-8) 24-24-91.
Embassy in Canada: Embassy of Sweden, Mercury Court, 377 Dalhousie St, Ottawa ON K1N 9N8. Tel: (613) 241-8553. Fax: (613) 241-2277.

Switzerland

Long-Form Name: Swiss Confederation
Capital: Bern

■ GEOGRAPHY

Area: 41,290 sq. km
Coastline: none: landlocked
Climate: temperate, but varies with altitude; cold, cloudy, rainy/snowy winters; cool to warm, cloudy, humid summers with occasional showers
Environment: dominated by Alps; air and water pollution; avalanches, flash floods and landslides are natural hazards
Terrain: mostly mountains (Alps in south, Jura in northwest) with a central plateau of rolling hills, plains and large lakes
Land Use: 10% arable; 2% permanent; 28% permanent pastures; 32% forest; 28% other; includes 250 sq. km irrigated
Location: C Europe

■ PEOPLE

Population: 7,275,467 (July 1999 est.)
Nationality: Swiss (sing. & pl.)
Age Structure: 0-14 yrs: 17%; 15-64: 68%; 65+: 15% (1998 est.)
Population Growth Rate: 0.20% (1999 est.)
Net Migration: 0.49 migrants/1,000 population (1999 est.)
Ethnic Groups: total population: 65% German, 18% French, 10% Italian, 1% Romansch, 6% other; Swiss nationals: 74% German, 20% French, 4% Italian, 1% Romansch, 1% other
Languages: 65% German, 18% French, 12% Italian, 1% Raeto-Romansch (all official), 4% other
Religions: 47.6% Roman Catholic, 44.3% Protestant, 8.1% other
Birth Rate: 10.53/1,000 population (1999 est.)
Death Rate: 9.06/1,000 population (1999 est.)
Infant Mortality: 4.87 deaths/1,000 live births (1999 est.)

Life Expectancy at Birth: 75.83 years male, 82.32 years female (1999 est.)
Total Fertility Rate: 1.46 children born/woman (1999 est.)
Literacy: 99% (1997)

■ GOVERNMENT

Leader(s): Pres. Ruth Dreifuss
Government Type: federal republic
Administrative Divisions: 26 cantons
Nationhood: Aug. 1, 1291
National Holiday: Anniversary of the Founding of the Swiss Confederation, Aug. 1

■ ECONOMY

Overview: country has the highest per capita output, general living standards, education and science, healthcare and diet standards in Europe; important banking and tourist sectors; low inflation and negligible unemployment is due partly to government policies; has rejected membership in the European Economic Community
GDP: $191.8 billion, per capita $26,400; real growth rate 2% (1998 est.)
Inflation: 1.3% (April 2000)
Industries: accounts for 31% of GDP; machinery, chemicals, watches, textiles, precision instruments
Labour Force: 4 million (1998); 24.3% industry, 23.6% community, social and business services, 20.3% trade and tourism
Unemployment: 2.6% (Jan. 2000)
Agriculture: accounts for 3% of GDP; dairy farming predominates; less than 50% self-sufficient; food shortages: fish, refined sugar, fats and oils (other than butter), grains, eggs, fruit, vegetables, meat
Natural Resources: hydropower potential, timber, salt; scenic beauty

■ FINANCE/TRADE

Currency: Swiss franc, franken, or franco (SwF) = 100 centimes, rappen, or centesimi
International Reserves Excluding Gold: $32.173 billion (Jan. 2000)
Gold Reserves: 83.277 million fine troy ounces (Jan. 2000)
Budget: revenues $32.66 billion; expenditures $34.89 billion, including capital expenditures of $2.3 billion (1998 est.)
Defence Expenditures: 5.21% of total govt. expenditure (1997)
Education Expenditures: 2.33% of total govt. expenditure (1997)
External Debt: n.a.
Exports: $76.122 billion (1999); commodities: machinery and equipment, precision instruments, metal products, foodstuffs, textiles and clothing; partners: Europe 64% (European Community 56%, other 8%), US 9%, Japan 4%
Imports: $75.438 billion (1999); commodities: agricultural products, machinery and transportation equipment, chemicals, textiles, construction materials; partners: Europe 79% (European Community 72%, other 7%), US 5%

■ COMMUNICATIONS

Daily Newspapers: 88 (1996)
Televisions: 535/1,000 inhabitants (1998)
Radios: 1,000/1,000 inhabitants (1997)
Telephones: 675 lines/1,000 inhabitants (1998)

■ TRANSPORTATION

Motor Vehicles: 3,700,000; 3,300,000 passenger cars (1997 est.)
Roads: 71,048 km; all paved
Railway: 4,479 km
Air Traffic: 12,482,000 passengers carried (1997)
Airports: 67; 42 have paved runways (1998 est.)

Canadian Embassy: Canadian Embassy, Kirchenfeldstrasse 88, 3005 Berne, Switzerland; mailing address: Box 3000, Berne 6, Switzerland. Tel: (011-41-31) 357-32-00. Fax: (011-41-31) 357-32-10.
Embassy in Canada: Embassy of Switzerland, 5 Marlborough Ave, Ottawa ON K1N 8E6. Tel: (613) 235-1837. Fax: (613) 563-1394.

Syria

Long-Form Name: Syrian Arab Republic
Capital: Damascus

■ GEOGRAPHY

Area: 185,180 sq. km; including 1,295 sq. km of Israeli-occupied territory
Coastline: 193 km
Climate: mostly desert; hot, dry, sunny summers (June to Aug.) and mild, rainy winters (Dec. to Feb.) along coast
Environment: deforestation; overgrazing; soil erosion; desertification; unsafe drinking water
Terrain: primarily semi-arid and desert plateau; narrow coastal plain; mountains in west
Land Use: 28% arable; 4% permanent crops; 43% meadows; 3% forest; 22% other; includes 9,060 sq. km irrigated
Location: SW Asia (Middle East), bordering on Mediterranean Sea

■ PEOPLE

Population: 17,213,871 (July 1999 est.)

Nationality: Syrian
Age Structure: 0-14 yrs: 46%; 15-64: 51%; 65+: 3% (1999 est.)
Population Growth Rate: 3.15% (1999 est.)
Net Migration: 0 migrants/1,000 population (1999 est.)
Ethnic Groups: 90.3% Arab; 9.7% Kurds, Armenians and other
Languages: Arabic (official), Kurdish, Armenian, Aramaic, Circassian; English and French widely understood
Religions: 74% Sunni, 16% Alawite, Druze and other Muslim sects, 10% Christian
Birth Rate: 36.95/1,000 population (1999 est.)
Death Rate: 5.40/1,000 population (1999 est.)
Infant Mortality: 36.42 deaths/1,000 live births (1999 est.)
Life Expectancy at Birth: 66.75 years male, 69.48 years female (1999 est.)
Total Fertility Rate: 5.37 children born/woman (1999 est.)
Literacy: 71.6% (1997)

■ GOVERNMENT

Leader(s): Pres. Bashar al-Asad, V.Pres. Abd al-Halim ibn Said Khaddam. Prime Min. Muhammad Mustafa Mero
Government Type: republic under leftwing military regime
Administrative Divisions: 14 provinces (muhafazat, sing. -muhafazah)
Nationhood: Apr. 17, 1946 (from League of Nations mandate under French administration; formerly known as United Arab Republic)
National Holiday: National Day, Apr. 17

■ ECONOMY

Overview: economic difficulties are due, in part, to severe drought in several recent years, costly but unsuccessful attempts to match Israel's military strength, a fall-off in Arab aid and insufficient foreign exchange earnings to buy needed imports; agricultural output is poor; a major long-term concern is the additional drain of upstream Euphrates water by Turkey once its vast dam and irrigation projects are completed
GDP: $41.7 billion, per capita $2,500; real growth rate 2% (1998 est.)
Inflation: -1.6% (Sept. 1999)
Industries: accounts for 21% of GDP, textiles, food processing, beverages, tobacco, phosphate rock mining, petroleum
Labour Force: 5 million (1998); 62.9% services, 22% agriculture, 15.1% industry
Unemployment: 12-15% (1998 est.)
Agriculture: accounts for 26% of GDP; all major crops (wheat, barley, cotton, lentils, chickpeas) grown on rain-fed land causing wide swings in yields; animal products: beef, lamb, eggs, poultry, milk; not self-sufficient in grain or livestock products
Natural Resources: crude oil, phosphates, chrome and manganese ores, asphalt, iron ore, rock salt, marble, gypsum

■ FINANCE/TRADE

Currency: Syrian pound (£S) = 100 piastres
International Reserves Excluding Gold: n.a.
Gold Reserves: 0.833 million fine troy ounces (Jan. 2000)
Budget: revenues $3.5 billion; expenditures $4.2 billion, including capital expenditures of n.a. (1997 est.)
Defence Expenditures: 23.58% of govt. expenditure (1997)
Education Expenditures: 9.22% of govt. expenditure (1997)
External Debt: $22.435 billion (1998)
Exports: $3.464 billion (1999); commodities: petroleum, textiles, fruit and vegetables, phosphates; partners: Italy, Romania, former USSR countries, US, Iran, France
Imports: $3.832 billion (1999); commodities: petroleum, machinery, base metals, foodstuffs and beverages; partners: Iran, Germany, former USSR countries, France, Libya, US

■ COMMUNICATIONS

Daily Newspapers: 8 (1996)
Televisions: 70/1,000 inhabitants (1998)
Radios: 278/1,000 inhabitants (1997)
Telephones: 95 lines/1,000 inhabitants (1998)

■ TRANSPORTATION

Motor Vehicles: 352,900; 134,000 passenger cars (1997 est.)
Roads: 41,451 km; 9,575 km paved
Railway: 1,998 km
Air Traffic: 694,000 passengers carried (1997)
Airports: 104; 24 have paved runways (1998 est.)

Canadian Embassy: The Canadian Embassy, Lot 12, Mezzah Autostrade, Damascus; mailing address: P.O. Box 3394, Damascus, Syria. Tel: (011-963-11) 611-6692. Fax: (011-963-11) 611-4000.
Embassy in Canada: Embassy of the Syrian Arab Republic, 151 Slater St., Suite 1000, Ottawa, ON, K1P 5H3, Tel: (613) 569-5556, Fax: (613) 569-3800.

Taiwan

Long-Form Name: Taiwan
Capital: Taipei

Taiwan

■ GEOGRAPHY

Area: 35,980 sq. km; includes the Pescadores, Matsu and Quemoy
Coastline: 1,448 km
Climate: tropical; marine; rainy season during southwest monsoon (June to Aug.)
Environment: subject to earthquakes and typhoons; water and air pollution
Terrain: eastern two-thirds mostly rugged mountains; flat to gently rolling plains in west
Land Use: 24% arable; 1% permanent; 5% meadows; 55% forest; 15% other; includes n.a. sq. km irrigated
Location: island, SE of China, bordering on South and East China Seas, Pacific Ocean

■ PEOPLE

Population: 22,113,250 (July 1999 est.)
Nationality: Chinese
Age Structure: 0-14 yrs: 22%; 15-64: 70%; 65+: 8% (1999 est.)
Population Growth Rate: 0.93% (1999 est.)
Net Migration: -0.02 migrants/1,000 population (1999 est.)
Ethnic Groups: 84% Taiwanese, 14% mainland Chinese, 2% aborigine
Languages: Mandarin Chinese (official); Taiwanese and Hakka dialects also used
Religions: 93% mixture of Buddhist, Islam, Confucian and Taoist, 5% Christian, 3% other
Birth Rate: 14.63/1,000 population (1999 est.)
Death Rate: 5.32/1,000 population (1999 est.)
Infant Mortality: 6.01 deaths/1,000 live births (1999 est.)
Life Expectancy at Birth: 74.38 years male, 80.85 years female (1999 est.)
Total Fertility Rate: 1.77 children born/woman (1999 est.)
Literacy: 94% (1998 est.)

■ GOVERNMENT

Leader(s): Pres. Chen Shui-bian, V. Pres.-elect Annette Lu. Prime Min. Tang Fei
Government Type: multi-party democratic regime
Administrative Divisions: 16 counties (hsien, sing. & pl.), 5 municipalities (shih, sing. & pl.), 2 special municipalities (chuan-shih, sing. & pl.)
Nationhood: n.a.
National Holiday: National Day (Anniversary of the Revolution), Oct. 10

■ ECONOMY

Overview: Taiwan has a dynamic capitalist economy with gradually decreasing guidance of investment and foreign trade by government authorities and partial government ownership of some large banks and industrial firms.
GDP: $362 billion, per capita $16,500; real growth rate 4.8% (1998 est.)
Inflation: n.a.
Industries: accounts for 35% of GDP, textiles, clothing, chemicals, electronics, food processing, plywood, sugar milling, cement, shipbuilding, petroleum
Labour Force: 9.4 million (1997 est.); 52% services, 38% industry, 10% agriculture
Unemployment: 2.7% (1998)
Agriculture: accounts for 3% of GDP; heavily subsidized sector; major crops: rice sugar cane, sweet potatoes, fruit, vegetables; livestock: hogs, poultry, beef, milk, cattle; not self-sufficient in wheat, soybeans, corn; fish catch expanding, 1.4 million metric tons
Natural Resources: small deposits of coal, natural gas, limestone, marble and asbestos

■ FINANCE/TRADE

Currency: New Taiwan dollar (NT$) = 100 cents
International Reserves Excluding Gold: $61.888 billion (Dec. 1997)
Gold Reserves: n.a.
Budget: revenues $40 billion; expenditures $55 billion, including capital expenditures of n.a. (1998 est.)
Defence Expenditures: 2.8% of GDP (1998–99)
Education Expenditures: n.a.
External Debt: $80 million (1997 est.)
Exports: $121.528 billion (1999); commodities: textiles 16%, electrical machinery 19%, general machinery and equipment 14%, telecommunications equipment 9%, basic metals and metal products 5%, foodstuffs 0.9%, plywood and wood products 1.3%; partners: US 36.2%, Japan 13.7%
Imports: $110.961 billion (1999); commodities: machinery and equipment 15.9%, crude oil 5%, chemical and chemical products 11.1%, basic metals 7.4%, foodstuffs 2%; partners: Japan 31%, US 23%, Saudi Arabia 8.6%

■ COMMUNICATIONS

Daily Newspapers: n.a.
Televisions: n.a.
Radios: n.a.
Telephones: n.a.

■ TRANSPORTATION

Motor Vehicles: 5,225,000; 4,300,000 passenger cars (1997 est.)
Roads: 19,701 km; 17,238
Railway: 4,600 km
Air Traffic: n.a.
Airports: 39; 36 have paved runways (1998 est.)

Canadian Embassy: none

Tajikistan

Embassy in Canada: none

Long-Form Name: Republic of Tajikistan
Capital: Dushanbe

■ GEOGRAPHY

Area: 143,100 sq. km
Coastline: none; landlocked
Climate: continental; severe winters in east; extremely hot summers; wet spring; semi-arid to polar in Pamir mountains
Environment: lack of fresh water; little land suitable for cultivation; industrial pollution
Terrain: mountains and glaciers constitute 93% of land area, predominantly herding and nonagricultural
Land Use: 6% arable, negligible permanent crops, 25% meadows and pastures, 4% forest and woodland, 65% other, includes 6,390 sq. km irrigated
Location: C Asia, bordering on China and Afghanistan

■ PEOPLE

Population: 6,102,854 (July 1999 est.)
Nationality: Tajik, Tajikistani
Age Structure: 0-14 yrs: 41%; 15-64: 55%; 65+: 4% (1999 est.)
Population Growth Rate: 1.43% (1999 est.)
Net Migration: -5.34 migrants/1,000 population (1999 est.)
Ethnic Groups: 64.9% Tajik, 25% Uzbek, 3.5% Russian (declining due to emigration), 6.6% other
Languages: Tajik (official), Uzbek, Russian
Religions: 80% Sunni Muslim, 5% Shia Muslim, 15% other
Birth Rate: 27.46/1,000 population (1999 est.)
Death Rate: 7.85/1,000 population (1999 est.)
Infant Mortality: 114.78 deaths/1,000 live births (1999 est.)
Life Expectancy at Birth: 61.15 years male, 67.57 years female (1999 est.)
Total Fertility Rate: 3.48 children born/woman (1999 est.)
Literacy: 98.9% (1997)

■ GOVERNMENT

Leader(s): Pres. Emomali Rahmonov, Prime Min. Oqil Oqilov
Government Type: republic
Administrative Divisions: 2 oblasts (viloyatho, sing. -viloyat) and 1 autonomous oblast (viloyati mukhtori)
Nationhood: Sept. 9, 1991 (from Soviet Union)
National Holiday: National Day, Sept. 9

■ ECONOMY

Overview: mostly mining and manufacturing with strong agricultural sector; industry and agriculture have been producing at reduced capacity due to civil unrest. Currency incompatibility with neighbouring countries is straining trade relations
GDP: $6 billion, per capita $990; real growth rate 5.3% (1998 est.)
Inflation: n.a.
Industries: accounts for 35% of GDP; aluminum and electrochemical plants, textile machinery, silk and carpet mills; zinc, lead, chemicals and fertilizers, cement, vegetable oil, refrigerators and freezers
Labour Force: 2 million (1998); 43% agriculture and forestry, 22% industry and construction, 35% other
Unemployment: 5.7% (Dec. 1998); also large numbers of underemployed
Agriculture: accounts for 25% of GDP; cotton, grapes, fruit, grains, silkworm farming, cattle breeding, sheep, goats, pigs
Natural Resources: coal, oil, rare metals, rock crystal, mica, gold, hydropower potential, uranium, mercury, zinc

■ FINANCE/TRADE

Currency: Tajik ruble (R) = 100 tanga
International Reserves Excluding Gold: n.a.
Gold Reserves: n.a.
Budget: n.a.
Defence Expenditures: 10.6% of central government expenditure (1997)
Education Expenditures: 2.2% of GNP (1997)
External Debt: $1.07 billion (1998)
Exports: $758 million (1999 est.); commodities: fruit, plant products, aluminum; partners: other Central Asian countries
Imports: $798 million (1999 est.); commodities: fuel, machinery, foodstuffs; partners: other Central Asian countries

■ COMMUNICATIONS

Daily Newspapers: 2 (1996)
Televisions: 285/1,000 inhabitants (1998)
Radios: 142/1,000 inhabitants (1997)
Telephones: 37 lines/1,000 inhabitants (1998)

■ TRANSPORTATION

Motor Vehicles: n.a.
Roads: n.a.
Railway: 480 km, not including industrial lines
Air Traffic: 594,000 passengers carried (1997)
Airports: 59; 14 have paved runways (1998 est.)

Canadian Embassy: The Canadian Embassy to Tajikistan, c/o The Canadian Embassy, 34 Kasarai Batir St, Almaty 480100, Kazakhstan. Tel: (011-7-3272) 50-11-51. Fax: (011-7-327) 582-493.
Embassy in Canada: n.a.

Tanzania

Long-Form Name: United Republic of Tanzania
Capital: Dar es Salaam

■ GEOGRAPHY

Area: 945,090 sq. km
Coastline: 1,424 km
Climate: varies from tropical along coast to temperate in highlands
Environment: deforestation; lack of water limits agriculture; recent droughts affected marginal agriculture
Terrain: plains along coast; central plateau; highlands in north, south; Kilimanjaro is highest point in Africa
Land Use: 3% arable; 1% permanent; 40% meadows; 38% forest; 18% other; includes 1,500 sq. km irrigated
Location: E Africa, bordering on Indian Ocean

■ PEOPLE

Population: 31,270,820 (July 1999 est.)
Nationality: Tanzanian
Age Structure: 0-14 yrs: 44%; 15-64: 53%; 65+: 3% (1999 est.)
Population Growth Rate: 2.14% (1999 est.)
Net Migration: -2.24 migrants/1,000 population (1999 est.)
Ethnic Groups: 99% native African consisting of well over 100 tribes; 1% Asian, European and Arab
Languages: Swahili and English (official); English primarily language of commerce, administration and higher education; Swahili widely understood and generally used for communication between ethnic groups
Religions: mainland: 45% Christian, 35% Muslim, 20% indigenous beliefs; Zanzibar: almost all Muslim
Birth Rate: 40.37/1,000 population (1999 est.)
Death Rate: 16.75/1,000 population (1999 est.)
Infant Mortality: 95.27 deaths/1,000 live births (1999 est.)
Life Expectancy at Birth: 43.85 years male, 48.57 years female (1999 est.)
Total Fertility Rate: 5.40 children born/woman (1999 est.)
Literacy: 71.6% (1997)

■ GOVERNMENT

Leader(s): Pres. Benjamin William Mkapa, Prem. Frederick Sumaye. Presidential election scheduled October 28, 2000.
Government Type: republic
Administrative Divisions: 25 regions
Nationhood: April 26, 1964; Tanganyika became independent on Dec. 9, 1961 (from UN trusteeship under British administration); Zanzibar became independent Dec. 19, 1963 (from UK); Tanganyika united with Zanzibar Apr. 26, 1964 to form the political unit that was renamed Tanzania on Oct. 29, 1964
National Holiday: Union Day, Apr. 26

■ ECONOMY

Overview: world aid is increasing the availability of imports and providing funds to rehabilitate this country's deteriorated economic infrastructure; this poor economy is heavily dependent on agriculture; industry is largely confined to processing agricultural products; mining is increasing in importance. Recent banking reforms have helped increase private sector growth and investment.
GDP: $22.1 billion, per capita $730; real growth rate 3.8% (1998 est.)
Inflation: 6.2% (March 2000)
Industries: accounts for 15% of GDP; primarily agricultural processing (sugar, beer, cigarettes, sisal twine), diamond mines, oil refineries, shoes, cement, textiles, wood products, fertilizer
Labour Force: 16.1 million (1998); 90% agriculture, 10% industry and commerce
Unemployment: n.a.
Agriculture: accounts for 56% of GDP, 85% of exports and employs 90% of workforce; topography and climatic conditions limit cultivated crops to only 5% of land area; cash crops: coffee, sisal, tea, cotton, pyrethrum (insecticide made from chrysanthemums), cashews, tobacco, cloves (Zanzibar); corn, wheat, beans, fruit and vegetables grown for local consumption
Natural Resources: hydropower potential, tin, phosphates, iron ore, coal, diamonds, gemstones, gold, natural gas, nickel

■ FINANCE/TRADE

Currency: Tanzania shilling (TSh) = 100 cents
International Reserves Excluding Gold: $756 million (Jan. 2000)
Gold Reserves: n.a.
Budget: revenues $700 million; expenditures $1.0 billion, including capital expenditures of n.a. (1998-99 est.)
Defence Expenditures: 10.7% of central government expenditure (1997)

Education Expenditures: n.a.
External Debt: $7.603 billion (1998)
Exports: $541 million (1999); commodities: coffee, cotton, sisal, cashew nuts, meat, tobacco, tea, diamonds, coconut products, pyrethrum, cloves; partners: Germany, UK, US, Netherlands, Japan
Imports: $1.836 billion (1999); commodities: manufactured goods, machinery and transportation equipment, cotton piece goods, crude oil, foodstuffs; partners: Germany, UK, US, Iran, Japan, Italy

■ COMMUNICATIONS

Daily Newspapers: 3 (1996)
Televisions: 21/1,000 inhabitants (1998)
Radios: 279/1,000 inhabitants (1997)
Telephones: 4 lines/1,000 inhabitants (1998)

■ TRANSPORTATION

Motor Vehicles: 133,800; 55,000 passenger cars (1997 est.)
Roads: 88,200 km; 3,704 paved
Railway: 3,569 km
Air Traffic: 218,000 passengers carried (1997)
Airports: 129; 10 have paved runways (1998 est.)

Canadian Embassy: The Canadian High Commission, 38 Mirambo St, Dar-es-Salaam; mailing address: P.O. Box 1022, Dar-es-Salaam, Tanzania. Tel: (011-255-51) 112-832. Fax: (011-255-51) 116-896.
Embassy in Canada: High Commission for the United Republic of Tanzania, 50 Range Rd, Ottawa ON, K1N 8J4. Tel: (613) 232-1500. Fax: (613) 232-5184.

Thailand

Long-Form Name: Kingdom of Thailand
Capital: Bangkok

■ GEOGRAPHY

Area: 514,000 sq. km
Coastline: 3,219 km
Climate: tropical; rainy, warm, cloudy southwest monsoon (mid-May to Sept.); dry, cool, northeast monsoon (Nov. to mid-Mar.); southern isthmus always hot and humid
Environment: air and water pollution; land subsidence in Bangkok area; deforestation; soil erosion; illegal hunting threatens wildlife populations
Terrain: central plain; eastern plateau (Khorat); mountains elsewhere
Land Use: 34% arable; 6% permanent crops; 2% permanent pastures; 26% forest; 32% other; includes 44,000 sq. km irrigated

Location: SE Asia, bordering on Gulf of Siam and Andaman Sea

■ PEOPLE

Population: 60,609,046 (July 1999 est.)
Nationality: Thai (sing. & pl.)
Age Structure: 0-14 yrs: 24%; 15-64: 70%; 65+: 6% (1999 est.)
Population Growth Rate: 0.93% (1999 est.)
Net Migration: 0 migrants/1,000 population (1999 est.)
Ethnic Groups: 75% Thai, 14% Chinese, 11% other
Languages: Thai; English is the secondary language of the elite; small minorities speak Chinese, Malay, indigenous languages
Religions: 95% Buddhist (Theravada), 3.8% Muslim, 0.5% Christianity, 0.1% Hinduism, 0.6% other
Birth Rate: 16.46/1,000 population (1999 est.)
Death Rate: 7.16/1,000 population (1999 est.)
Infant Mortality: 29.54 deaths/1,000 live births (1999 est.)
Life Expectancy at Birth: 65.58 years male, 73.01 years female (1999 est.)
Total Fertility Rate: 1.82 children born/woman (1999 est.)
Literacy: 94.7% (1997)

■ GOVERNMENT

Leader(s): King Phumiphon Adulyadej (Rama IX), Prem. Chuan Likphai
Government Type: constitutional monarchy
Administrative Divisions: 76 provinces (changwat, sing. & pl.)
Nationhood: 1238 (traditional founding date); never colonized
National Holiday: Birthday of His Majesty the King, Dec. 5

■ ECONOMY

Overview: With the currency depreciation and the collapse of domestic demands; imports have fallen by more than a third recently. Foreign investment for new projects, the long-time catalyst of Thailand's economic growth, has also slowed.
GDP: $369 billion, per capita $6,100; real growth rate -8.5% (1998 est.)
Inflation: 0.7% (Dec. 1999)
Industries: accounts for 39% of GDP, tourism is the largest source of foreign exchange; textiles and garments, agricultural processing, beverages, tobacco, cement, other light manufacturing, such as jewelry; electric appliances and components, integrated circuits, furniture, plastics

Labour Force: 37 million (1998); 60.3% agriculture, 11.2% trade and tourism, 11.1% industry
Unemployment: 4.5% (1998)
Agriculture: accounts for 12% of GDP and 57% of labour force; leading producer and exporter of rice and cassava; other crops: rubber, corn, sugar cane, coconuts, soybeans; self-sufficient in food except for wheat
Natural Resources: tin, rubber, natural gas, tungsten, tantalum, timber, lead, fish, gypsum, lignite, fluorite

■ FINANCE/TRADE

Currency: baht (pl. baht) (B) = 100 satang
International Reserves Excluding Gold: $31.912 billion (Jan. 2000)
Gold Reserves: 2.474 million fine troy ounces (Jan. 2000)
Budget: revenues $24 billion; expenditures $25 billion, including capital expenditures of $8 billion (1996–97)
Defence Expenditures: 10.34% of govt. expenditure (1998)
Education Expenditures: 23.13% of govt. expenditure (1998)
External Debt: $86.172 billion (1998)
Exports: $58.392 billion (1999); commodities: textiles 12%, fishery products 12%, rice 8%, tapioca 8%, jewelry 6%, manufactured gas, corn, tin; partners: US 18%, Japan 14%, Singapore 9%, Netherlands, Malaysia, Hong Kong, China
Imports: $41.526 billion (1999); commodities: machinery and parts 23%, petroleum products 13%, chemicals 11%, iron and steel, electrical appliances; partners: Japan 26%, US 14%, Singapore 7%, Germany, Malaysia, UK

■ COMMUNICATIONS

Daily Newspapers: 30 (1996)
Televisions: 189/1,000 inhabitants (1996)
Radios: 232/1,000 inhabitants (1997)
Telephones: 84 lines/1,000 inhabitants (1998)

■ TRANSPORTATION

Motor Vehicles: 5,700,000; 1,550,000 passenger cars (1997 est.)
Roads: 64,600 km; 62,985 km paved
Railway: 4,623 km
Air Traffic: 14,236,000 passengers carried (1997)
Airports: 107; 56 have paved runways (1998 est.)

Canadian Embassy: The Canadian Embassy, 11th Fl, Boonmitr Bldg, 138 Silom Rd, Bangkok 10501; mailing address: P.O. Box 2090, Bangkok 10500, Thailand. Tel: (011-66-2) 636-0540. Fax: (011-66-2) 636-0565.
Embassy in Canada: The Royal Thai Embassy, 180 Island Park Dr, Ottawa ON K1Y 0A2. Tel: (613) 722-4444. Fax: (613) 722-6624.

Togo

Long-Form Name: Togolese Republic
Capital: Lomé

■ GEOGRAPHY

Area: 56,790 sq. km
Coastline: 56 km
Climate: tropical; hot, humid in south; semi-arid in north
Environment: hot, dry harmattan wind; recent droughts affecting agriculture; deforestation
Terrain: gently rolling savanna in north; low coastal plain with extensive lagoons and marshes
Land Use: 38% arable; 7% permanent crops; 4% meadows; 17% forest; 34% other; includes 70 sq. km irrigated
Location: WC Africa, bordering on South Atlantic Ocean

■ PEOPLE

Population: 5,081,413 (July 1999 est.)
Nationality: Togolese (sing. & pl.)
Age Structure: 0-14 yrs: 48%; 15-64: 50%; 65+: 2% (1999 est.)
Population Growth Rate: 3.51% (1999 est.)
Net Migration: 0 migrants/1,000 population (1999 est.)
Ethnic Groups: 37 tribes; largest and most important are Ewe, Mina and Kabyè; under 1% European and Syrian-Lebanese
Languages: French, both official and language of commerce; major African languages are Ewe and Mina in the south and Dagomba and Kabyè in the north
Religions: about 70% indigenous beliefs, 20% Christian, 10% Muslim
Birth Rate: 44.78/1,000 population (1999 est.)
Death Rate: 9.69/1,000 population (1999 est.)
Infant Mortality: 77.55 deaths/1,000 live births (1999 est.)
Life Expectancy at Birth: 56.93 years male, 61.64 years female (1999 est.)
Total Fertility Rate: 6.53 children born/woman (1999 est.)
Literacy: 53.2% (1997)

■ GOVERNMENT

Leader(s): Pres. Gen. Gnassingbé Eyadéma, Prime Min. Eugene Koffi Adoboli
Government Type: republic; one-party

presidential regime under transition to multiparty democratic rule
Administrative Divisions: 5 regions
Nationhood: Apr. 27, 1960 (from UN trusteeship under French administration; formerly known as French Togo)
National Holiday: Independence Day, Apr. 27

■ ECONOMY

Overview: an underdeveloped country that is heavily dependent on subsistence agriculture and phosphate mining; self-sufficient in basic foodstuffs when harvests are normal; political unrest and widespread strikes have interfered with economic activity
GDP: $8.2 billion, per capita $1,670; real growth rate 3.8% (1998 est.)
Inflation: 5.7% (Jan. 2000)
Industries: accounts for 23% of GDP; phosphate mining, agricultural processing, cement, handicrafts, textiles, beverages
Labour Force: 2 million (1998); 64.3% agriculture, 6.3% industry, 29.4% services
Unemployment: n.a.
Agriculture: accounts for 32% of GDP and 64% of labour force; cash crops: coffee, cocoa, cotton; food crops: yams, cassava, corn, beans, rice, millet, sorghum, fish
Natural Resources: phosphates, limestone, marble

■ FINANCE/TRADE

Currency: Communauté financière africaine franc (CFAF) = 100 centimes
International Reserves Excluding Gold: $107 million (Nov. 1999)
Gold Reserves: 0.013 million fine troy ounces (July 1998)
Budget: revenues $242 million; expenditures $262 million, including capital expenditures n.a. (1997 est.)
Defence Expenditures: 11.6% of central government expenditure (1997)
Education Expenditures: 4.5% of GNP (1997)
External Debt: $1.448 billion (1998)
Exports: $411 million (1998); commodities: phosphates, cocoa, coffee, cotton, manufactures, palm kernels; partners: European Community 70%, Africa 9%, US 2%, other 19%
Imports: $631 million (1998); commodities: food, fuels, durable consumer goods, other intermediate goods, capital goods; partners: European Community 69%, Africa 10%, Japan 7%, US 4%, other 10%

■ COMMUNICATIONS

Daily Newspapers: 1 (1996)

Televisions: 18/1,000 inhabitants (1998)
Radios: 218/1,000 inhabitants (1997)
Telephones: 7 lines/1,000 inhabitants (1998)

■ TRANSPORTATION

Motor Vehicles: 110,000; 75,000 passenger cars (1997 est.)
Roads: 7,520 km; 2,376 km paved
Railway: 525 km
Air Traffic: 86,000 passengers carried (1997)
Airports: 9; 2 have paved runways (1998 est.)

Canadian Embassy: The Canadian Embassy to Togo, c/o Canadian High Commission, 42 Independence Ave, Accra, Ghana; P.O. Box 1639, Accra. Tel: (011-233-21) 77-37-91. Fax: (011-233-21) 77-37-92.
Embassy in Canada: Embassy of the Republic of Togo, 12 Range Rd, Ottawa ON K1N 8J3. Tel: (613) 238-5916. Fax: (613) 235-6425.

Tokelau

Long-Form Name: Tokelau
Capital: none; each atoll has its own administrative centre

■ GEOGRAPHY

Area: 10 sq. km, 3 atolls
Climate: tropical maritime, moderated by trade winds (April–Nov.)
Land Use: 0% arable, permanent crops, meadows/pastures or forests; 100% other; includes no irrigated land
Location: S Pacific Ocean, NE of Australia

■ PEOPLE

Population: 1,471 (July 1999 est.)
Nationality: Tokelauan
Ethnic Groups: Polynesian
Languages: Tokelauan, English

■ GOVERNMENT

Colony/Territory of: Overseas Territory of New Zealand
Leader(s): Head of State: Queen Elizabeth II, Admin. Lindsay Watt; Head of government: Aliki Faipule Falimateao
Government Type: territory of New Zealand
National Holiday: Waitangi Day, Feb. 6

■ ECONOMY

Overview: Tokelau's small size, great distance from markets and lack of resources greatly hinder economic development; copra is only agricultural product of significance; the people rely on aid from New Zealand, supplemented by revenue from postage stamps, souvenir coins, and handicrafts

■ FINANCE/TRADE

Currency: New Zealand dollar = 100 cents

Canadian Embassy: c/o The Canadian High Commission, 3rd Fl, 61 Molesworth St. Thorndon, Wellington, New Zealand. Tel: (011-64-4) 6270-4000. Fax: (011-64-4) 471-2082.
Representative to Canada: c/o New Zealand High Commission, Clarica Centre, 99 Bank St, Ste 727, Ottawa ON K1P 6G3. Tel: (613) 238-5991. Fax: (613) 238-5707.

Tonga

Long-Form Name: Kingdom of Tonga
Capital: Nuku'alofa

■ GEOGRAPHY

Area: 748 sq. km; archipelago of 170 islands, of which 36 are inhabited
Coastline: 419 km
Climate: tropical; modified by trade winds; warm season (Dec. to May), cool season (May to Dec.)
Environment: subject to cyclones (Oct. to Apr.); deforestation and overhunting of native animals
Terrain: most islands have limestone base formed from uplifted coral formation; others have limestone overlying volcanic base
Land Use: 24% arable; 43% permanent; 6% meadows; 11% forest; 16% other; includes n.a. sq. km irrigated
Location: Pacific Ocean, NW of New Zealand

■ PEOPLE

Population: 109,082 (July 1999 est.)
Nationality: Tongan
Age Structure: n.a.
Population Growth Rate: 0.80% (1999 est.)
Net Migration: -1.19 migrants/1,000 population (1999 est.)
Ethnic Groups: Polynesian; about 300 Europeans
Languages: Tongan, English
Religions: Christian; Free Wesleyan Church claims over 30,000 adherents
Birth Rate: 25.92/1,000 population (1999 est.)
Death Rate: 6.00/1,000 population (1999 est.)
Infant Mortality: 37.93 deaths/1,000 live births (1999 est.)
Life Expectancy at Birth: 67.73 years male, 72.22 years female (1999 est.)
Total Fertility Rate: 3.56 children born/woman (1999 est.)
Literacy: n.a.

■ GOVERNMENT

Leader(s): King Taufa'ahau Tupou IV, Prince and Prime Min. Prince Lavaka ata Ulukalala
Government Type: hereditary constitutional monarchy
Administrative Divisions: three island groups
Nationhood: June 4, 1970 (from UK; formerly known as Friendly Islands)
National Holiday: Emancipation Day, June 4

■ ECONOMY

Overview: the economy's base is agriculture though the country must import a high proportion of its food, for the most part from New Zealand; tourism is the main source of hard currency; the country also remains dependent on sizeable external aid and remittances to offset its trade deficit.
GDP: $232 million, per capita $2,100; real growth rate -1.5% (1998 est.)
Inflation: 4.6% (Nov. 1999)
Industries: accounts for 10% of GDP; tourism, fishing
Labour Force: n.a.; 70% agriculture, 30% mining
Unemployment: n.a.
Agriculture: 32% of GDP and 70% of labour force; dominated by coconut, copra and banana production; vanilla beans, cocoa, coffee, ginger, black pepper
Natural Resources: fish, fertile soil

■ FINANCE/TRADE

Currency: pa'anga ($T) = 100 seniti
International Reserves Excluding Gold: $26 million (Nov. 1999)
Gold Reserves: n.a.
Budget: revenues $49 million; expenditures $120 million, including capital expenditures of $75 million (1996-97 est.)
Defence Expenditures: n.a.
Education Expenditures: n.a.
External Debt: $62 million (1998)
Exports: $0.6 million (1997 est.); commodities: coconut oil, desiccated coconut, copra, bananas, taro, vanilla beans, fruit, vegetables, fish; partners: New Zealand 54%, Australia 30%, US 8%, Fiji 5%
Imports: $61 million (1997 est.); commodities: food products, beverages, tobacco, fuels, machinery, transport equipment, chemicals, building materials; partners: New Zealand 39%, Australia 25%, Japan 9%, US 6%, European Community 5%

■ COMMUNICATIONS

Daily Newspapers: 1 (1996)

Televisions: 20/1,000 inhabitants (1996)
Radios: 612/1,000 inhabitants (1996)
Telephones: 79 lines/1,000 inhabitants (1998)

■ TRANSPORTATION

Motor Vehicles: n.a.
Roads: 680 km; 184 km paved
Railway: none
Air Traffic: 49,000 passengers carried (1997)
Airports: 6; 1 have paved runways (1998 est.)

Canadian Embassy: The Canadian High Commission to Tonga, c/o The Canadian High Commission, 61 Molesworth St, 3rd Floor, Thorndon, Wellington; mailing address: P.O. Box 12-049, Thorndon, Wellington, New Zealand. Tel: (011-64-4) 473-9577. Fax: (011-64-4) 471-2082.
Embassy in Canada: Embassy of the Kingdom of Tonga, 800 Second Ave., Suite 400B, New York, NY, 10017, Tel: (212) 972-9686, Fax: (212) 490-0534.

Trinidad and Tobago

Long-Form Name: Republic of Trinidad and Tobago
Capital: Port of Spain

■ GEOGRAPHY

Area: 5,130 sq. km
Coastline: 362 km
Climate: tropical; rainy season (June to Dec.)
Environment: outside usual path of hurricanes and other tropical storms; water pollution and soil deterioration; oil pollution of beaches
Terrain: mostly plains with some hills and low mountains
Land Use: 15% arable; 9% permanent crops; 2% meadows; 46% forest; 28% other, includes 220 sq. km irrigated
Location: West Indies, off N coast of South America

■ PEOPLE

Population: 1,102,096 (July 1999 est.)
Nationality: Trinidadian, Tobagonian
Age Structure: 0-14 yrs: 27%; 15-64: 66%; 65+: 7% (1999 est.)
Population Growth Rate: -1.35% (1999 est.)
Net Migration: -19.8 migrants/1,000 population (1999 est.)
Ethnic Groups: 40% black, 40% East Indian, 14% mixed, 1% white, 1% Chinese, 4% other
Languages: English (official), Hindi, French, Spanish, Chinese
Religions: Christianity 61%, Hinduism 24%, Islam 6%, 9% other

Birth Rate: 14.46/1,000 population (1999 est.)
Death Rate: 8.14/1,000 population (1999 est.)
Infant Mortality: 18.56 deaths/1,000 live births (1999 est.)
Life Expectancy at Birth: 68.19 years male, 73.19 years female (1999 est.)
Total Fertility Rate: 2.06 children born/woman (1999 est.)
Literacy: 97.8% (1997)

■ GOVERNMENT

Leader(s): Pres. Arthur Napoleon Raymond Robinson, Prime Min. Basdeo Panday. Presidential and parlimentary elections scheduled November 2000.
Government Type: parliamentary democracy
Administrative Divisions: 8 counties, 3 municipalities and 1 ward
Nationhood: Aug. 31, 1962 (from UK)
National Holiday: Independence Day, Aug. 31

■ ECONOMY

Overview: the economy has suffered in recent years because of the sharp decline in the price of oil; the unemployment rate has risen due to the government's austerity programs; the government is seeking to diversify the country's export base
GDP: $8.85 billion, per capita $8,000; real growth rate 4.3% (1998 est.)
Inflation: 2.0% (Sept. 1999)
Industries: accounts for 44% of GDP; petroleum, chemicals, tourism, food processing, cement, beverage, cotton textiles
Labour Force: 1 million (1998); 30.4% community, social and business services, 11.3% agriculture, 10.9% construction
Unemployment: 14.0% (June 1998)
Agriculture: accounts for approx. 2% of GDP; highly subsidized sector; major crops: cocoa and sugar cane; sugar cane acreage is being shifted into rice, citrus, coffee, vegetables; must import large share of food needs
Natural Resources: crude oil, natural gas, asphalt

■ FINANCE/TRADE

Currency: Trinidad and Tobago dollar ($TT) = 100 cents
International Reserves Excluding Gold: $854 million (Nov. 1999)
Gold Reserves: 0.058 million fine troy ounces (Nov. 1999)
Budget: revenues $1.7 billion; expenditures $1.6 billion, including capital expenditures of $243 million (1997 est.)
Defence Expenditures: 5.4% of central government expenditure (1997)
Education Expenditures: 3.6% of GNP (1997)

External Debt: $2.193 billion (1998)
Exports: $2.258 billion (1998); commodities (including re-exports): petroleum and petroleum products 70%, fertilizer, chemicals 15%, steel products, sugar, cocoa, coffee, citrus; partners: US 61%, European Community 15%, CARICOM 9%, Latin America 7%, Canada 3%
Imports: $2.999 billion (1998); commodities: raw materials 41%, capital goods 30%, consumer goods 29%; partners: US 42%, European Community 21%, Japan 10%, Canada 6%, Latin America 6%, CARICOM 4%

■ COMMUNICATIONS
Daily Newspapers: 4 (1996)
Televisions: 334/1,000 inhabitants (1998)
Radios: 534/1,000 inhabitants (1997)
Telephones: 206 lines/1,000 inhabitants (1998)

■ TRANSPORTATION
Motor Vehicles: 155,000; 128,000 passenger cars (1997 est.)
Roads: 8,320 km; 4,252 km paved
Railway: minimal agricultural railway system near San Fernando
Air Traffic: 807,000 passengers carried (1997)
Airports: 6; 3 have paved runways (1998 est.)

Canadian Embassy: The Canadian High Commission, Maple House, 3-3A Sweet Briar Road, St. Clair, Port-of-Spain; mailing address: P.O. Box 1246, Port-of-Spain, Trinidad and Tobago. Tel: (868) 622-6232. Fax: (868) 628-1830.
Embassy in Canada: High Commission for the Republic of Trinidad and Tobago, 75 Albert St, Ste 508, Ottawa ON K1P 5E7. Tel: (613) 232-2418. Fax: (613) 232-4349.

Tunisia

Long-Form Name: Republic of Tunisia
Capital: Tunis

■ GEOGRAPHY
Area: 163,610 sq. km
Coastline: 1,148 km
Climate: temperate in north with mild, rainy winters and hot, dry summers; desert in south
Environment: deforestation; overgrazing; soil erosion; desertification; ineffective disposal of toxic and hazardous wastes
Terrain: mountains in north; hot, dry central plain; semi-arid south merges into the Sahara
Land Use: 19% arable; 13% permanent; 20% meadows; 4% forest; 44% other, includes 3,850 sq. km irrigated
Location: N Africa, bordering on Mediterranean Sea

■ PEOPLE
Population: 9,513,603 (July 1999 est.)
Nationality: Tunisian
Age Structure: 0-14 yrs: 31%; 15-64: 63%; 65+: 6% (1999 est.)
Population Growth Rate: 1.39% (1999 est.)
Net Migration: -0.74 migrants/1,000 population (1999 est.)
Ethnic Groups: 98% Arab-Berber, 1% European, less than 1% Jewish
Languages: Arabic (official); Arabic and French (commerce)
Religions: 98% Muslim, 1% Christian, less than 1% Jewish
Birth Rate: 19.72/1,000 population (1999 est.)
Death Rate: 5.05/1,000 population (1999 est.)
Infant Mortality: 31.38 deaths/1,000 live births (1999 est.)
Life Expectancy at Birth: 71.95 years male, 74.86 years female (1999 est.)
Total Fertility Rate: 2.38 children born/woman (1999 est.)
Literacy: 67.0% (1997)

■ GOVERNMENT
Leader(s): Pres. Gen. Zine El Abidine Ben Ali, Prime Min. Mohamed Ghannouchi
Government Type: republic
Administrative Divisions: 23 governorates
Nationhood: Mar. 20, 1956 (from France)
National Holiday: National Day, Mar. 20

■ ECONOMY
Overview: Tunisia has a diverse economy, with important agriculture, mining, energy, tourism, and manufacturing sectors. Governmental control of economic affairs has gradually lessened over the past decade with increasing privatization of trade and commerce, simplification of the tax structure, and a prudent approach to debt.
GDP: $49 billion, per capita $5,200; real growth rate 5% (1998 est.)
Inflation: 3.4% (Feb. 2000)
Industries: accounts for 28% of GDP; petroleum, mining (particularly phosphate and iron ore), textiles, footwear, food, beverages, tourism
Labour Force: 4 million (1998); 21.6% agriculture, 16.3% industry, 62.1% services
Unemployment: 15.6% (1998 est.)
Agriculture: accounts for 14% of GDP; output subject to severe fluctuations because of frequent droughts; export crops: olives, dates, oranges, almonds; other products: grain, sugar beets, wine grapes, poultry, beef, dairy; not self-sufficient in food
Natural Resources: crude oil, phosphates, iron ore, lead, zinc, salt

■ FINANCE/TRADE

Currency: Tunisian dinar (D) = 1,000 millimes
International Reserves Excluding Gold: $2.322 billion (Jan. 2000)
Gold Reserves: 0.022 million fine troy ounces (Jan. 2000)
Budget: revenues $5.8 billion; expenditures $6.5 billion, including capital expenditures of $1.4 billion (1998 est.)
Defence Expenditures: 5.3% of govt. expenditure (1997)
Education Expenditures: 7.7% of GNP (1997)
External Debt: $11.078 billion (1998)
Exports: $5.973 billion (1999 est.); commodities: hydrocarbons, agricultural products, phosphates and chemicals; partners: European Community 73%, Middle East 9%, US 1%, Turkey, former USSR countries
Imports: $8.309 billion (1999 est.); commodities: industrial goods and equipment 57%, hydrocarbons 13%, food 12%, consumer goods; partners: European Community 68%, US 7%, Canada, Japan, former USSR countries, China, Saudi Arabia, Algeria

■ COMMUNICATIONS

Daily Newspapers: 8 (1996)
Televisions: 198/1,000 inhabitants (1998)
Radios: 223/1,000 inhabitants (1997)
Telephones: 81 lines/1,000 inhabitants (1998)

■ TRANSPORTATION

Motor Vehicles: 531,000; 248,000 passenger cars (1997 est.)
Roads: 23,100 km; 18,226 km paved
Railway: 2,260 km
Air Traffic: 1,779,000 passengers carried (1997)
Airports: 32; 14 have paved runways (1998 est.)

Canadian Embassy: Canadian Embassy, 3, rue du Sénégal, Place d'Afrique, 1002 Tunis-Belvedere, Tunisia; mailing address: CP 31, Le Belvédère, 1002, Tunis-Belvedere, Tunisia. Tel: (011-216-1) 796-577. Fax: (011-216-1) 792-371.
Embassy in Canada: Embassy of the Republic of Tunisia, 515 O'Connor St, Ottawa ON, K1S 3P8. Tel: (613) 237-0330. Fax: (613) 237-7939.

Turkey

Long-Form Name: Republic of Turkey
Capital: Ankara

■ GEOGRAPHY

Area: 780,580 sq. km
Coastline: 7,200 km
Climate: temperate; hot, dry summers with mild, wet winters; harsher in interior
Environment: subject to severe earthquakes, especially along major river valleys in west; water and air pollution; desertification
Terrain: mostly mountains; narrow coastal plain; high central plateau (Anatolia)
Land Use: 32% arable; 4% permanent; 16% meadows; 26% forest; 22% other, includes 36,740 sq. km irrigated
Location: SW Asia (Near East), bordering on Mediterranean Sea, Black Sea, Aegean Sea

■ PEOPLE

Population: 65,599,206 (July 1999 est.)
Nationality: Turk
Age Structure: 0-14 yrs: 30%; 15-64: 64%; 65+: 6% (1999 est.)
Population Growth Rate: 1.57% (1999 est.)
Net Migration: 0 migrants/1,000 population (1999 est.)
Ethnic Groups: 80% Turkish, 20% Kurd
Languages: Turkish (official), Kurdish 7%, Arabic; English (business language)
Religions: 99.8% Muslim (mostly Sunni), 0.2% other (mostly Christian and Jewish)
Birth Rate: 20.92/1,000 population (1999 est.)
Death Rate: 5.27/1,000 population (1999 est.)
Infant Mortality: 35.81 deaths/1,000 live births (1999 est.)
Life Expectancy at Birth: 70.81 years male, 75.88 years female (1999 est.)
Total Fertility Rate: 2.41 children born/woman (1999 est.)
Literacy: 83.2% (1997)

■ GOVERNMENT

Leader(s): Pres. Ahmet Necdet Sezer, Prime Min. Bulent Ecevit
Government Type: republican parliamentary democracy
Administrative Divisions: 80 provinces (iller, sing. -il)
Nationhood: Oct. 29, 1923 (successor state to the Ottoman Empire)
National Holiday: Anniversary of the Declaration of the Republic, Oct. 29

■ ECONOMY

Overview: Turkey has a strong and rapidly growing private sector, yet the state still plays a major role in basic industry, banking, transport, and communication. Its most important industry and largest exporter is textiles and clothing, which is almost entirely in private hands. Note: Major economic disruption in August 1999 due to a massive earthquake.

GDP: $425.4 billion, per capita $6,600; real growth rate 2.8% (1998 est.)
Inflation: 63.8% (April 2000)
Industries: accounts for 29% of GDP; textiles, food processing, mining (coal, chromite, copper, boron minerals), steel, petroleum, construction, lumber, paper
Labour Force: 30 million (1998); 43.6% agriculture, 15% industry, 14% community, social and business services; about 1,000,000 Turks work abroad
Unemployment: 10% (1998 est.)
Agriculture: accounts for 14% of GDP and 46% the labour force; products: tobacco, cotton, grain, olives, sugar beets, pulses, citrus fruit, variety of animal products; self-sufficient in food most years
Natural Resources: antimony, coal, chromium, mercury, copper, borate, sulphur, iron ore

■ FINANCE/TRADE

Currency: Turkish lira (TL)
International Reserves Excluding Gold: $22.930 billion (Jan. 2000)
Gold Reserves: 3.744 million fine troy ounces (Jan. 2000)
Budget: revenues $44.4 billion; expenditures $58.5 billion, including capital expenditures of $3.7 billion (1998)
Defence Expenditures: 14.7% of govt. expenditure (1997)
Education Expenditures: 2.2% of GNP (1997)
External Debt: $102.074 billion (1998)
Exports: $25.938 billion (1998); commodities: industrial products 70%, crops and livestock products 25%; partners: Germany 18.4%, Iraq 8.5%, Italy 8.2%, US 6.5%, UK 4.9%, Iran 4.7%
Imports: $45.369 billion (1998); commodities: crude oil, machinery, transport equipment, metals, pharmaceuticals, dyes, plastics, rubber, mineral fuels, fertilizers, chemicals; partners: Germany 14.3%, US 10.6%, Iraq 10.0%, Italy 7.0%, France 5.8%, UK 5.2%

■ COMMUNICATIONS

Daily Newspapers: 57 (1996)
Televisions: 286/1,000 inhabitants (1998)
Radios: 180/1,000 inhabitants (1997)
Telephones: 254 lines/1,000 inhabitants (1998)

■ TRANSPORTATION

Motor Vehicles: 4,400,000; 3,300,000 passenger cars (1997 est.)
Roads: 382,397; 95,599 km paved
Railway: 10,386 km
Air Traffic: 9,380,000 passengers carried (1997)

Airports: 117; 81 have paved runways (1998 est.)
Canadian Embassy: The Canadian Embassy, Nenehatun Caddesi 75, Gaziosmanpasa, 06700 Ankara, Turkey. Tel: (011-90-312) 436-1275. Fax: (011-90-312) 446-4437.
Embassy in Canada: Embassy of the Republic of Turkey, 197 Wurtemburg St, Ottawa ON K1N 8L9. Tel: (613) 789-4044. Fax: (613) 789-3442.

Turkmenistan

Long-Form Name: Turkmenistan
Capital: Ashkhabad

■ GEOGRAPHY

Area: 488,100 sq. km
Coastline: landlocked; 1,768 km coastline along Caspian Sea
Climate: subtropical desert; long, extremely hot summers; short and cold winters; rainfall occurs only in the mountains
Environment: soil and groundwater contaminated with chemicals and pesticides; salinization and waterlogging of soil due to poor irrigation methods; desertification in some areas; prone to earthquakes
Terrain: flat to rolling sandy desert; Caspian Sea in west
Land Use: 3% arable, 0% permanent crops, 63% pastures and meadows, 8% forests, 26% other; includes 13,000 sq. km irrigated
Location: WC Asia, bordering on Caspian Sea

■ PEOPLE

Population: 4,366,383 (July 1999 est.)
Nationality: Turkmen
Age Structure: 0-14 yrs: 38%; 15-64: 58%; 65+: 4% (1999 est.)
Population Growth Rate: 1.58% (1999 est.)
Net Migration: -1.35 migrants/1,000 population (1999 est.)
Ethnic Groups: 77% Turkmen, 6.7% Russian, 9.2% Uzbek, 2% Kazakh, 5.1% other
Languages: 72% Turkmen (official), 12% Russian, 9% Uzbek, 7% other
Religions: 89% Muslim, 9% Eastern Orthodox, 2% unknown
Birth Rate: 25.91/1,000 population (1999 est.)
Death Rate: 8.77/1,000 population (1999 est.)
Infant Mortality: 73.10 deaths/1,000 live births (1999 est.)
Life Expectancy at Birth: 75.48 years male, 64.91 years female (1999 est.)
Total Fertility Rate: 3.21 children born/woman (1999 est.)
Literacy: 98% (1997)

Turks and Caicos

■ GOVERNMENT
Leader(s): Pres. Saparmurad Niyazov
Government Type: republic
Administrative Divisions: 5 regions (welayatlar, sing. -welayat)
Nationhood: Oct. 27, 1991 (from Soviet Union)
National Holiday: Independence Day, Oct. 27

■ ECONOMY
Overview: mining produces the greatest part of Turkmenistan's economic production value, but agriculture is the chief occupation; industry leans heavily toward the energy sector (gas, oil), but the lack of pipeline access to hard currency markets limits expansion. Efforts at gas and oil export expansion will take many more years to pay off
GDP: $7 billion, per capita $1,630; real growth rate 5% (1998 est.)
Inflation: n.a.
Industries: accounts for 50% of GDP; oil production and refining, natural gas extraction, chemicals, electrical engineering, fertilizer, carpets, textiles and clothing, food processing
Labour Force: 2.1 million (1998); 42% agriculture and forestry, 21% industry and construction, 37% other
Unemployment: n.a.
Agriculture: accounts for 18% of GDP; irrigation is mandatory for agriculture; products include cotton, grains, fruit, livestock, fish, vegetables
Natural Resources: extensive mineral deposits, including the world's largest sulfur deposits; oil, natural gas, potassium, salts, sulphur

■ FINANCE/TRADE
Currency: manat = 100 tenesi
International Reserves Excluding Gold: n.a.
Gold Reserves: n.a.
Budget: revenues $521 million; expenditures $548 million, including capital expenditures of $83 million (1996 est.)
Defence Expenditures: 15.6% of central government expenditure (1997)
Education Expenditures: n.a.
External Debt: $2.266 billion (1998)
Exports: $1.7 billion (1996); oil, natural gas, electric power, clothing and textiles, petroleum products, carpets; partners: Hong Kong, Switzerland, US, FSU, Germany, Turkey
Imports: $1.5 billion (1996); machinery, foodstuffs, consumer products, plastics and rubber, textiles; partners: US, FSU, Turkey, Germany, Cyprus

■ COMMUNICATIONS
Daily Newspapers: n.a.
Televisions: 201/1,000 inhabitants (1998)
Radios: 276/1,000 inhabitants (1997)
Telephones: 82 lines/1,000 inhabitants (1998)

■ TRANSPORTATION
Motor Vehicles: n.a.
Roads: 24,000 km; 19,488 km paved
Railway: 2,187 km
Air Traffic: 523,000 passengers carried (1997)
Airports: 64; 22 have paved runways (1998 est.)

Canadian Embassy: c/o The Canadian Embassy, Nenehatun Caddesi 75, Gaziosmanpasa 06700, Ankara, Turkey. Tel: (011-90-312) 436-1275. Fax: (011-90-312) 446-4437.
Embassy in Canada: c/o Embassy of the Republic of Turkmenistan, 2207 Massachusetts Ave NW, Washington DC 20008, USA. Tel: (202) 588-1500. Fax: (202) 588-0697.

Turks and Caicos

Long-Form Name: The Turks and Caicos Islands
Capital: Grand Turk (Cockburn Town)

■ GEOGRAPHY
Area: 430 sq. km; 30+ small cays, of which only 8 are inhabited
Climate: sunny, relatively dry, equable climate with moderating winds; occasional hurricanes
Land Use: 2% arable, 0% permanent crops, meadows, forests, 98% other; includes n.a. sq. km irrigated
Location: West Indies (S Atlantic Ocean), N of Dominican Republic

■ PEOPLE
Population: 16,863 (July 1999 est.)
Nationality: none (British citizens)
Ethnic Groups: black majority
Languages: English (official)

■ GOVERNMENT
Colony/Territory of: Colony of the United Kingdom
Leader(s): Head of State: Queen Elizabeth II/Gov. Mervyn Jones. Head of government: Chief Min. Derek H. Taylor
Government Type: dependent territory of the United Kingdom
National Holiday: Constitution Day, Aug. 30

■ ECONOMY
Overview: fishing is the most important activity; exports include lobster, conch, other fish products; imports include food and drink,

tobacco, maufactured goods; tourism; offshore banking; chief trading partner: US

■ FINANCE/TRADE

Currency: US currency is used

Canadian Embassy: c/o The Canadian High Commission, Macdonald House, 1 Grosvenor Square, London W1X 0AB, England, UK. Tel: (011-44-20) 7258-6600. Fax: (011-44-20) 7258-6333.

Representative to Canada: c/o British High Commission, 80 Elgin St, Ottawa ON K1P 5K7. Tel: (613) 237-1530. Fax: (613) 237-7980.

Tuvalu

Long-Form Name: Tuvalu
Capital: Funafuti

■ GEOGRAPHY

Area: 26 sq. km
Coastline: 24 km
Climate: tropical; moderated by easterly trade winds (Mar. to Nov.); westerly gales and heavy rain (Nov. to Mar.)
Environment: severe tropical storms are rare; no natural safe drinking water resources
Terrain: very low-lying and narrow coral atolls
Land Use: the 9 coral atolls have just enough soil to allow for subsistence agriculture; there are also coconut groves
Location: S Pacific Ocean, NE of Australia

■ PEOPLE

Population: 10,588 (July 1999 est.)
Nationality: Tuvaluan
Age Structure: 0-14 yrs: 35%; 15-64: 61%; 65+: 4% (1999 est.)
Population Growth Rate: 1.34% (1999 est.)
Net Migration: 0 migrants/1,000 population (1999 est.)
Ethnic Groups: 96% Polynesian
Languages: Tuvaluan, English
Religions: 97% Congregationalist (Church of Tuvalu), 1.4% Seventh Day Adventists, 1% Baha'i, 0.6% other
Birth Rate: 21.91/1,000 population (1999 est.)
Death Rate: 8.50/1,000 population (1999 est.)
Infant Mortality: 25.53 deaths/1,000 live births (1999 est.)
Life Expectancy at Birth: 63.01 years male, 65.34 years female (1999 est.)
Total Fertility Rate: 3.11 children born/woman (1999 est.)
Literacy: n.a.

■ GOVERNMENT

Leader(s): Head of State: Queen Elizabeth II/Gov. Gen. Sir Tomasi Puapua. Prime Min. Ionatana Ionatana
Government Type: constitutional monarchy with a parliamentary democracy
Administrative Divisions: none
Nationhood: Oct. 1, 1978 from UK (formerly known as Ellice Islands)
National Holiday: Independence Day, Oct. 1

■ ECONOMY

Overview: scattered group of 9 coral atolls with poor soil; a small economy, no known mineral resources and few exports; receives money from the sale of stamps and coins and worker remittances as well as an international trust fund; subsistence farming and fishing are the primary economic activities
GDP: n.a.
Inflation: n.a.
Industries: fishing, tourism, copra
Labour Force: n.a.
Unemployment: n.a.
Agriculture: coconuts, copra
Natural Resources: fish

■ FINANCE/TRADE

Currency: Australian dollar ($A) or Tuvaluan dollar ($T) = 100 cents
International Reserves Excluding Gold: n.a.
Gold Reserves: n.a.
Budget: n.a.
Defence Expenditures: n.a.
Education Expenditures: n.a.
External Debt: n.a.
Exports: n.a.; commodities: copra; partners: Fiji, Australia, New Zealand
Imports: n.a.; commodities: food, animals, fuels, machinery, manufactures; partners: Fiji, Australia, New Zealand

■ COMMUNICATIONS

Daily Newspapers: 0 (1996)
Televisions: 13.2/1,000 inhabitants (1996)
Radios: 400/1,000 inhabitants (1996)
Telephones: n.a.

■ TRANSPORTATION

Motor Vehicles: n.a.
Roads: 8 km gravel roads
Railway: none
Air Traffic: n.a.
Airports: 1; no paved runway (1998 est.)

Canadian Embassy: The Canadian High Commission to Tuvalu, c/o The Canadian High

Commission, 61 Molesworth St, 3rd Fl, Thorndon, Wellington; mailing address: P.O. Box 12-049, Thorndon, Wellington, New Zealand. Tel: (011-64-4) 473-9577. Fax: (011-64-4) 471-2082.
Embassy in Canada: c/o New Zealand High Commission, Clarica Centre, 99 Bank St, Ste 727, Ottawa, ON K1P 6G3. Tel: (613) 238-5991. Fax: (613) 238-5707.

U.S. Virgin Islands

Long-Form Name: Virgin Islands of the United States
Capital: Charlotte Amalie

■ GEOGRAPHY

Area: 352 sq. km
Climate: subtropical, tempered by easterly trade winds, relatively low humidity, little seasonal temperature variation; rainy season May to Nov.
Land Use: 15% arable; 6% permanent; 26% meadows; 6% forest; 47% other; includes n.a. sq. km irrigated
Location: Caribbean islands, just E of Puerto Rico

■ PEOPLE

Population: 119,827 (July 1999 est.)
Nationality: Virgin Islander
Ethnic Groups: 74% West Indian (45% born in the Virgin Islands and 29% born elsewhere in the West Indies), 13% US mainland, 5% Puerto Rican, 8% other (80% black, 15% white, 5% other); 14% of Hispanic origin
Languages: English (official), but Spanish and Creole are widely spoken

■ GOVERNMENT

Colony/Territory of: Dependent Territory of the United States
Leader(s): Head of State: Pres. William Clinton (US) (to Jan. 20, 2001). Gov. Dr. Charles Wesley Turnbull
Government Type: organized, unincorporated territory of the US
National Holiday: Transfer Day, Mar. 31 (1917, from Denmark to the US)

■ ECONOMY

Overview: tourism is the primary economic activity accounting for more than 70% of GDP and 70% of employment; some manufacturing; small agricultural sector (most food is imported); international business and financial services are a small but growing sector

■ FINANCE/TRADE

Currency: US dollar ($) = 100 cents

Canadian Embassy: c/o The Canadian Embassy, 501 Pennsylvania Ave NW, Washington DC 20001, USA. Tel: (202) 682-1740. Fax: (202) 456-7726.
Representative to Canada: c/o Embassy of the United States of America, 490 Sussex Dr., Ottawa, ON, K1N 1G8. Tel: (613) 238-5335. Fax: (613) 688-3097.

Uganda

Long-Form Name: Republic of Uganda
Capital: Kampala

■ GEOGRAPHY

Area: 236,040 sq. km
Coastline: none: landlocked
Climate: tropical; generally rainy with two dry seasons (Dec. to Feb., June to Aug.); semi-arid in northeast
Environment: straddles equator; deforestation; overgrazing; soil erosion; widespread poaching
Terrain: mostly plateau with rim of mountains
Land Use: 25% arable; 9% permanent crops; 9% permanent pastures; 28% forest; 29% other; includes 90 sq. km irrigated
Location: EC Africa

■ PEOPLE

Population: 22,804,973 (July 1999 est.)
Nationality: Ugandan
Age Structure: 0-14 yrs: 51%; 15-64: 47%; 65+: 2% (1999 est.)
Population Growth Rate: 2.83% (1999 est.)
Net Migration: -1.84 migrants/1,000 population (1999 est.)
Ethnic Groups: 17% Baganda, 12% Karamojong, 8% Basogo, 8% Iteso, 6% Langi, 6% Rwanda, 5% Bagisu, 4% Acholi, 4% Lugbara, 3% Bunyro, 27% other
Languages: English (official); Luganda and Swahili widely used; other Bantu and Nilotic languages
Religions: 33% Roman Catholic, 33% Protestant, 16% Muslim, rest indigenous beliefs
Birth Rate: 48.54/1,000 population (1999 est.)
Death Rate: 18.43/1,000 population (1999 est.)
Infant Mortality: 90.68 deaths/1,000 live births (1999 est.)
Life Expectancy at Birth: 42.20 years male, 43.94 years female (1999 est.)
Total Fertility Rate: 7.03 children born/woman (1999 est.)

Literacy: 64.0% (1997)

■ GOVERNMENT

Leader(s): Pres. Yoweri Kaguta Museveni, Prime Min. Apollo Nsibambi
Government Type: republic
Administrative Divisions: 39 districts
Nationhood: Oct. 9, 1962 (from UK)
National Holiday: Independence Day, Oct. 9

■ ECONOMY

Overview: despite substantial natural resources, the economy has been ruined by years of political instability, mismanagement and civil war; the government has started a reform program which is partly aimed at lowering high inflation and increasing export earnings; agriculture is the most important economic sector
GDP: $22.7 billion, per capita $1,020; real growth rate 5.5% (1998 est.)
Inflation: 7.2% (Feb. 2000)
Industries: accounts for 17% of GDP; sugar, brewing, tobacco, cotton textile, cement
Labour Force: 10.1 million (1998); 85.9% agriculture, 4.4% industry, 9.7% services
Unemployment: n.a.
Agriculture: accounts for 44% of GDP and 86% of labour force; coffee, tea and tobacco are the main export crops
Natural Resources: copper, cobalt, limestone, salt

■ FINANCE/TRADE

Currency: Ugandan shilling (USh) = 100 cents
International Reserves Excluding Gold: $763 million (Dec. 1999)
Gold Reserves: n.a.
Budget: revenues $869 million; expenditures $985 million, including capital expenditures of $69 million (1995-96)
Defence Expenditures: 23.9% of central government expenditure (1997)
Education Expenditures: 2.6% of GNP (1997)
External Debt: $3.935 billion (1998)
Exports: $517 million (1999); commodities: coffee 97%, cotton, tea; partners: US 25%, UK 18%, France 11%, Spain 10%
Imports: $1.341 billion (1999); commodities: petroleum products, machinery, cotton piece goods, metals, transportation equipment, food; partners: Kenya 25%, UK 14%, Italy 13%

■ COMMUNICATIONS

Daily Newspapers: 2 (1996)
Televisions: 27/1,000 inhabitants (1998)
Radios: 128/1,000 inhabitants (1997)
Telephones: 3 lines/1,000 inhabitants (1998)

■ TRANSPORTATION

Motor Vehicles: 51,000; 24,400 passenger cars (1997 est.)
Roads: 27,000 km; 1,800 km paved
Railway: 1,241 km
Air Traffic: 100,000 passengers carried (1997)
Airports: 27; 4 have paved runways (1998 est.)

Canadian Embassy: The Canadian High Commission to Uganda, c/o The Canadian High Commission, Comcraft House, Hailé Sélassie Ave, Nairobi; mailing address: The Canadian High Commission, P.O. Box 30481, Nairobi, Kenya. Tel: (011-254-2) 21-48-04. Fax: (011-254-2) 22-69-87.
Embassy in Canada: High Commission for the Republic of Uganda, 231 Cobourg St, Ottawa ON K1N 8J2. Tel: (613) 789-7797. Fax: (613) 789-8909.

Ukraine

Long-Form Name: Ukraine
Capital: Kiev

■ GEOGRAPHY

Area: 603,700 sq. km
Coastline: 2,782 km
Climate: temperate continental; subtropical on southern Crimean coast; moderate rainfall in north; drier in southern regions
Environment: air and water pollution, unsafe drinking water, deforestation, radiation contamination around Chernobyl nuclear power plant
Terrain: Carpathian mountains in west, marshy in north, remainder flat fertile plains (steppes) and plateaus
Land Use: 58% arable, 2% permanent crops, 13% meadows and pastures, 18% forest, 9% other, includes 26,050 sq. km irrigated
Location: E Europe, bordering on Black Sea

■ PEOPLE

Population: 49,811,174 (July 1999 est.)
Nationality: Ukrainian
Age Structure: 0-14 yrs: 18%; 15-64: 68%; 65+: 14% (1999 est.)
Population Growth Rate: -0.62% (1999 est.)
Net Migration: 0.63 migrants/1,000 population (1999 est.)
Ethnic Groups: 73% Ukrainian, 22% Russian, 1% Jewish, 4% other
Languages: Ukrainian, Russian, Romanian, Polish
Religions: predominantly Eastern Orthodox and Roman Catholic; Uniate Church re-legalized in

1991; also, Autocephalous Orthodox Church, Greek rite Catholic
Birth Rate: 9.54/1,000 population (1999 est.)
Death Rate: 16.38/1,000 population (1999 est.)
Infant Mortality: 21.73 deaths/1,000 live births (1999 est.)
Life Expectancy at Birth: 60.23 years male, 71.87 years female (1999 est.)
Total Fertility Rate: 1.34 children born/woman (1999 est.)
Literacy: 99.0% (1997)

■ GOVERNMENT

Leader(s): Pres. Leonid Kuchma, Prime Min. Viktor Yushchenko
Government Type: republic
Administrative Divisions: 24 oblasts (oblasti, sing. -oblast), 1 autonomous republic (avtomnaya respublika), 2 municipalities (mista, sing. -misto) with oblast status
Nationhood: Dec. 1, 1991 (from Soviet Union)
National Holiday: Independence Day, Aug. 24

■ ECONOMY

Overview: mining and heavy industry, with very strong agricultural sector; food surplus area of former USSR; internal political disputes are hobbling economic progress
GDP: $108.5 billion, per capita $2,200; real growth rate -1.7% (1998 est.)
Inflation: 9.9% (1997)
Industries: accounts for 30% of GDP and 33% of labour force; industries include: mining, manufacturing of machinery, food processing, chemicals, electric and electronic equipment, coal, electric power, food processing (esp. sugar)
Labour Force: 25 million (1998); 32% industry and construction, 24% agriculture and forestry, 17% health and cultural services, 27% other
Unemployment: 3.7% (Dec. 1998) officially registered, but there is extensive unregistered unemployment or underemployment
Agriculture: accounts for about 14%; corn, wheat, sugar beets, sunflower seeds, barley, tobacco; livestock includes cattle, pigs, goats, sheep, vegetables, milk, sugar beets
Natural Resources: coal, manganese, oil, gypsum, iron, lead, zinc, titanium, natural gas, oil, salt, sulphur, graphite

■ FINANCE/TRADE

Currency: hryvnia (pl. hryvni), as of Sept. 2, 1996; 1 hryrnia = 100,000 karbovantsi (old currency)
International Reserves Excluding Gold: $963 million (Jan. 2000)
Gold Reserves: 0.168 million fine troy ounces (Jan. 2000)
Budget: revenues $18 billion; expenditures $21 billion, including capital expenditures n.a. (1997 est.)
Defence Expenditures: 8.4% of central government expenditure (1997)
Education Expenditures: 7.3% of GNP (1997)
External Debt: $12.718 billion (1998)
Exports: $12.637 billion (1998): minerals, agricultural products, heavy machinery, vehicles, airplanes
Imports: $14.676 billion (1998): machinery and equipment, chemicals, textiles, energy

■ COMMUNICATIONS

Daily Newspapers: 44 (1996)
Televisions: 490/1,000 inhabitants (1998)
Radios: 884/1,000 inhabitants (1997)
Telephones: 191 lines/1,000 inhabitants (1998)

■ TRANSPORTATION

Motor Vehicles: n.a.
Roads: 172,565 km; 163,937 km paved
Railway: 23,350 km
Air Traffic: 1,190,000 passengers carried (1997)
Airports: 706; 163 have paved runways

Canadian Embassy: The Canadian Embassy, 31 Yaroslaviv Val St, Kiev 01901, Ukraine. Tel: (011-380-44) 464-1144. Fax: (011-380-44) 464-1133.
Embassy in Canada: Embassy of Ukraine, 310 Somerset St W, Ottawa ON K2P 0J9. Tel: (613) 230-2961. Fax: (613) 230-2400.

United Arab Emirates

Long-Form Name: United Arab Emirates
Capital: Abu Dhabi

■ GEOGRAPHY

Area: 82,880 sq. km
Coastline: 1,318 km
Climate: desert; cooler in eastern mountains
Environment: frequent dust and sand storms; lack of natural freshwater resources being overcome by desalination plants; desertification
Terrain: flat, barren coastal plain; desert wasteland; mountains in east
Land Use: 2% permanent pastures; 98% other; includes 50 sq. km irrigated
Location: SW Asia (Middle East), Arabian Peninsula bordering on Persian Gulf

■ PEOPLE

Population: 2,344,402 (July 1999 est.)

Nationality: Emiri
Age Structure: 0-14 yrs: 31%; 15-64: 67%; 65+: 2% (1999 est.)
Population Growth Rate: 1.78% (1999 est.)
Net Migration: 2.03 migrants/1,000 population (1999 est.)
Ethnic Groups: 19% Emiri, 23% other Arab, 50% South Asian (fluctuating), 8% other expatriates (includes Westerners and East Asians); less than 20% of the population are United Arab Emirates citizens
Languages: Arabic (official); Farsi and English widely spoken in major cities; Hindi, Urdu
Religions: 96% Muslim (16% Shi'a); 4% Christian, Hindu and other
Birth Rate: 18.86/1,000 population (1999 est.)
Death Rate: 3.13/1,000 population (1999 est.)
Infant Mortality: 14.10 deaths/1,000 live births (1999 est.)
Life Expectancy at Birth: 73.83 years male, 76.72 years female (1999 est.)
Total Fertility Rate: 3.50 children born/woman (1999 est.)
Literacy: 74.8% (1997)

■ GOVERNMENT

Leader(s): Pres. Zayid bin Sultan Al Nuhayyan, V. Pres. and Prime Min. Maktum bin Rashid al-Maktum
Government Type: federation with specified powers delegated to the United Arab Emirates central government and other powers reserved to member emirates
Administrative Divisions: 7 emirates (imarat, sing. -imarah)
Nationhood: Dec. 2, 1971 (from UK; formerly known as Trucial States)
National Holiday: National Day, Dec. 2

■ ECONOMY

Overview: has an open economy tied to the world prices for oil and gas; currently has a high standard of living; crude oil reserves should last for over 100 years at present levels of production. The government is encouraging privatization measures
GDP: $40 billion, per capita $17,400; real growth rate -5% (1998 est.)
Inflation: n.a.
Industries: accounts for 52% of GDP; petroleum, fishing, petrochemicals, construction materials, some boat building, handicrafts, pearling
Labour Force: 1 million (1998): 38% industry, 4.5% agriculture, 57.3% services
Unemployment: n.a.
Agriculture: accounts for 3% of GDP and 6% of labour force; cash crop: dates; food products: vegetables, watermelons, poultry, eggs, dairy, fish; only 25% self-sufficient in food
Natural Resources: crude oil and natural gas

■ FINANCE/TRADE

Currency: Emirian dirham (Dh) = 100 fils
International Reserves Excluding Gold: $10.675 billion (Dec. 1999)
Gold Reserves: 0.397 million fine troy ounces (Dec. 1999)
Budget: revenues $5.4 billion; expenditures $5.8 billion, including capital expenditures $350 million (1998 est.)
Defence Expenditures: 31.46% of central government expenditure (1998)
Education Expenditures: 17.73% of central government expenditure (1998)
External Debt: $14 billion (1996 est.)
Exports: $43.307 billion (1999); commodities: crude oil 75%, natural gas, re-exports, dried fish, dates; partners: US, European Community, Japan, Singapore, Korea
Imports: $34.745 billion (1999); commodities: food, consumer and capital goods; partners: European Community, Japan, US

■ COMMUNICATIONS

Daily Newspapers: 7 (1996)
Televisions: 133/1,000 inhabitants (1996)
Radios: 345/1,000 inhabitants (1997)
Telephones: 389 lines/1,000 inhabitants (1998)

■ TRANSPORTATION

Motor Vehicles: 400,000; 320,000 passenger cars (1997 est.)
Roads: 4,835 km, all paved
Railway: none
Air Traffic: 4,720,000 passengers carried (1997)
Airports: 41; 21 have paved runways (1998 est.)

Canadian Embassy: The Canadian Embassy, Villa No. 440, 26th St, Rowdah District, Abu Dhabi; mailing address: P.O. Box 6970, Abu Dhabi, UAE. Tel: (011-971-2) 445-6969. Fax: (011-971-2) 445-8787.
Embassy in Canada: c/o Embassy of the United Arab Emirates, 45 O'Connor St., Suite 1800 World Exchange Plaza, Ottawa, ON, K1P 1A4, Tel: (613) 565-7272, Fax: (613) 565-8007.

United Kingdom

Long-Form Name: United Kingdom of Great Britain and Northern Ireland
Capital: London

■ GEOGRAPHY

Area: 244,820 sq. km

United Kingdom

Coastline: 12,429 km
Climate: temperate; moderated by prevailing southwest winds over the North Atlantic Current; more than half of the days are overcast
Environment: pollution control measures improving air, water quality; because of heavily indented coastline, no location is more than 125 km from tidal waters
Terrain: mostly rugged hills and low mountains; level to rolling plains in east and southeast
Land Use: 25% arable; negligible permanent crops; 46% meadows; 10% forest; 19% other; includes 1,080 sq. km irrigated
Location: NW Europe, bordering on North Sea, Atlantic Ocean

■ PEOPLE

Population: 59,113,439 (July 1999 est.)
Nationality: British
Age Structure: 0-14 yrs: 19%; 15-64: 65%; 65+: 16% (1999 est.)
Population Growth Rate: 0.24% (1999 est.)
Net Migration: 1.11 migrants/1,000 population (1999 est.)
Ethnic Groups: 81.5% English, 9.6% Scottish, 2.4% Irish, 1.9% Welsh, 1.8% Ulster, 2.8% West Indian, Indian, Pakistani and other
Languages: English, Welsh (about 26% of population of Wales), Scottish form of Gaelic (about 60,000 in Scotland)
Religions: 73% Anglican, 23% Roman Catholic, 3% Muslim, 0.1% Sikh, 0.2% Presbyterian, 0.5% Methodist, 0.2% Jewish
Birth Rate: 11.90/1,000 population (1999 est.)
Death Rate: 10.64/1,000 population (1999 est.)
Infant Mortality: 5.78 deaths/1,000 live births (1999 est.)
Life Expectancy at Birth: 74.73 years male, 80.15 years female (1999 est.)
Total Fertility Rate: 1.71 children born/woman (1999 est.)
Literacy: 99% (1997)

■ GOVERNMENT

Leader(s): Head of State: Queen Elizabeth II. Prime Min. Tony Blair
Government Type: constitutional monarchy
Administrative Divisions: 47 counties, 7 metropolitan counties, 26 districts, 9 regions and 3 island areas; dependent areas include: Anguilla, Bermuda, British Antarctic Territory (uninhabited except for variable population of research stations – about 300 persons), British Indian Ocean Territory, British Virgin Islands, Cayman Islands, Channel Islands, Falkland Islands, Gibraltar, Guernsey, Isle of Man, Jersey, Montserrat, Pitcairn, Saint Helena, South Georgia (uninhabited except for scientific station and 500 persons in a whaling/sealing settlement), South Sandwich Islands (uninhabited), Turks and Caicos Islands
Nationhood: Jan. 1, 1801, United Kingdom established
National Holiday: Celebration of the Birthday of the Queen, second Saturday in June

■ ECONOMY

Overview: economy is essentially capitalist; intensive agricultural practices produce 60% of domestic food needs with only 1% of the labour force; strong service sector; industry is declining in importance
GDP: $1.252 trillion, per capita $21,200; real growth rate 2.6% (1998 est.)
Inflation: 2.6% (March 2000)
Industries: accounts for 31% of GDP and 25% of labour force; machinery and transportation equipment, metals, food processing, paper and paper products, textiles, chemicals, clothing, other consumer goods, motor vehicles, aircraft, shipbuilding, petroleum, coal
Labour Force: 30 million (1998); 62.8% services, 1.2% agriculture, 1.9% energy, 25% manufacturing and construction, 9.1% government
Unemployment: 4.2% (Sept. 1999)
Agriculture: accounts for only 1.5% of GDP; highly mechanized and efficient farms; wide variety of crops and livestock products produced; about 60% self-sufficient in food and feed needs
Natural Resources: coal, crude oil, natural gas, tin, limestone, iron ore, salt, clay, chalk, gypsum, lead, silica

■ FINANCE/TRADE

Currency: pound sterling (£ or £ stg) = 100 pence
International Reserves Excluding Gold: $29.388 billion (April 1999)
Gold Reserves: 22.978 million fine troy ounces (April 1999)
Budget: revenues $487.7 billion; expenditures $492.6 billion, including capital expenditures $23.1 billion (1996 est.)
Defence Expenditures: 7.14% of central government expenditure (1998)
Education Expenditures: 4.05% of total govt. expenditure (1998)
External Debt: n.a.
Exports: $268.208 billion (1999); commodities: manufactured goods, machinery, fuels, chemicals, semifinished goods, transport equipment; partners: European Community 50.4% (Germany 11.7%, France 10.2%,

Netherlands 6.8%), US 13%, Communist countries 2.3%
Imports: $317.971 billion (1999); commodities: manufactured goods, machinery, semifinished goods, foodstuffs, consumer goods; partners: European Community 52.5% (Germany 16.6%, France 8.8%, Netherlands 7.8%), US 10.2%, Communist countries 2.1%

■ COMMUNICATIONS

Daily Newspapers: 99 (1996)
Televisions: 645/1,000 inhabitants (1998)
Radios: 1,436/1,000 inhabitants (1997)
Telephones: 557 lines/1,000 inhabitants (1998)

■ TRANSPORTATION

Motor Vehicles: 28,800,000; 25,000,000 passenger cars (1997 est.)
Roads: 372,000 km, all paved
Railway: 16,878 km
Air Traffic: 62,763,000 passengers carried (1997)
Airports: 497; 356 have paved runways (1998 est.)

Canadian Embassy: The Canadian High Commission, Macdonald House, 1 Grosvenor Square, London W1X OAB, England, UK. Tel: (011-44-20) 7258-6600. Fax: (011-44-20) 7258-6333.
Embassy in Canada: British High Commission, 80 Elgin St, Ottawa ON K1P 5K7. Tel: (613) 237-1530. Fax: (613) 237-7980.

United States

Long-Form Name: United States of America
Capital: Washington, D.C.

■ GEOGRAPHY

Area: 9,629,091 sq. km; includes only the 50 states and District of Columbia
Coastline: 19,924 km
Climate: mostly temperate, but varies from tropical (Hawaii) to arctic (Alaska); arid to semi-arid in west with occasional warm, dry chinook wind
Environment: pollution control measures improving air and water quality; acid rain; agricultural fertilizer and pesticide pollution; management of sparse natural water resources in west; desertification; tsunamis, volcanoes and earthquake activity around Pacific; permafrost in Alaska
Terrain: vast central plain, mountains in west, hills and low mountains in east; rugged mountains and broad river valleys in Alaska; rugged, volcanic topography in Hawaii

Land Use: 19% arable; negligible permanent crops; 25% meadows; 30% forest; 26% other, includes 207,000 sq. km irrigated
Location: North America, bordering on Canada, Mexico, Pacific Ocean, Atlantic Ocean

■ PEOPLE

Population: 272,639,608 (July 1999 est.)
Nationality: American
Age Structure: 0-14 yrs: 22%; 15-64: 66%; 65+: 12% (1999 est.)
Population Growth Rate: 0.85% (1999 est.)
Net Migration: 3.0 migrants/1,000 population (1999 est.)
Ethnic Groups: 83.4% white, 12.4% black, 3.3% Asian, 0.7% other
Languages: predominantly English; sizable Spanish-speaking minority
Religions: 56% Protestant (including 21% Baptist, 12% Methodist, 8% Lutheran, 4% Presbyterian, 3% Episcopalian), 28% Roman Catholic, 2% Jewish, 4% other, 10% none
Birth Rate: 14.30/1,000 population (1999 est.)
Death Rate: 8.80/1,000 population (1999 est.)
Infant Mortality: 6.33 deaths/1,000 live births (1999 est.)
Life Expectancy at Birth: 72.95 years male, 79.67 years female (1999 est.)
Total Fertility Rate: 2.07 children born/woman (1999 est.)
Literacy: 99.0% (1997)

■ GOVERNMENT

Leader(s): Pres. William Jefferson Clinton, V. Pres. Albert Arnold Gore. Presidential election to be held on November 7, 2000; Inauguration Jan. 20, 2001.
Government Type: federal republic
Administrative Divisions: 50 states and 1 district; dependent areas include: American Samoa, Baker Island, Federated States of Micronesia, Guam, Howland Island, Jarvis Island, Johnston Atoll, Kingman Reef, Marshall Islands, Midway Islands (inhabited by U.S. military personnel), Northern Marianas, Palau, Palymyra Atoll, Puerto Rico (for details see Puerto Rico entry), Virgin Islands (for details see Virgin Islands entry), Wake Island (military base)
Nationhood: July 4, 1776 (from England)
National Holiday: Independence Day, July 4

■ ECONOMY

Overview: market-oriented economy with a very large private sector; a powerful and diversified economy, with high per capita GNP; problems include the significant budget and trade deficits, large medical costs for the aging population and

inadequate investment in industry and infrastructure
GDP: $8.511 trillion, per capita $31,500; real growth rate 3.9% (1998 est.)
Inflation: 3.0% (April 2000)
Industries: accounts for 23% of GDP and 25.3% of labour force; highly diversified industry; petroleum, steel, motor vehicles, aerospace, telecommunications, chemicals, electronics, food processing, consumer goods, fishing, lumber, mining
Labour Force: 138 million (1998); 35.5% community, social and business services, 20.8% trade and tourism, 16.4% industry
Unemployment: 4.4% (Feb. 2000)
Agriculture: accounts for 2% of GDP and 2.8% of labour force; favourable climate and soils support a wide variety of crops and livestock production; world's second largest producer and top exporter of grain; surplus food producer; fish catch of 4.4 million metric tons
Natural Resources: coal, copper, lead, molybdenum, phosphates, uranium, bauxite, gold, iron, mercury, nickel, potash, silver, tungsten, zinc, crude oil, natural gas, timber

■ FINANCE/TRADE

Currency: US dollar ($ or $US) = 100 cents
International Reserves Excluding Gold: $58.850 billion (Jan. 2000)
Gold Reserves: 261.680 million fine troy ounces (Jan. 2000)
Budget: revenues $1.722 trillion; expenditures $1.653 trillion, including capital expenditures n.a. (1998)
Defence Expenditures: 15.36% of govt. expenditure (1998)
Education Expenditures: 1.80% of govt. expenditure (1998)
External Debt: n.a.
Exports: $695.215 billion (1999); commodities: capital goods, automobiles, industrial supplies and raw materials, consumer goods, agricultural products; partners: Canada 22.9%, Japan 11.8%
Imports: $1.059120 trillion (1999); commodities: crude and partly refined petroleum, machinery, automobiles, consumer goods, industrial raw materials, food and beverages; partners: Japan 19.6%, Canada 19.1%

■ COMMUNICATIONS

Daily Newspapers: 1,520 (1996)
Televisions: 847/1,000 inhabitants (1998)
Radios: 2,146/1,000 inhabitants (1997)
Telephones: 661 lines/1,000 inhabitants (1998)

■ TRANSPORTATION

Motor Vehicles: 212,000,000; 137,000,000 passenger cars (1997 est.)
Roads: 6,420,000 km; 3,903,360 km paved
Railway: 247,440 km
Air Traffic: 590,571,000 passengers carried (1997)
Airports: 14,459; 5,167 have paved runways (1998 est.)

Canadian Embassy: The Canadian Embassy, 501 Pennsylvania Ave, NW, Washington DC 20001, USA. Tel: (202) 682-1740. Fax: (202) 682-7726.
Embassy in Canada: Embassy of the United States of America, 490 Sussex Dr., Ottawa, ON, K1N 1G8. Tel: (613) 238-5335. Fax: (613) 688-3097.

Uruguay

Long-Form Name: Oriental Republic of Uruguay
Capital: Montevideo

■ GEOGRAPHY

Area: 176,220 sq. km
Coastline: 660 km
Climate: warm temperate; freezing temperatures almost unknown
Environment: subject to seasonally high winds, droughts, floods; industrial pollution from Brazil
Terrain: mostly rolling plains and low hills; fertile coastal lowland
Land Use: 7% arable; negligible permanent crops; 77% meadows; 6% forest; 10% other; includes 7,700 sq. km irrigated
Location: SE South America, bordering on Atlantic Ocean

■ PEOPLE

Population: 3,308,523 (July 1999 est.)
Nationality: Uruguayan
Age Structure: 0-14 yrs: 24%; 15-64: 63%; 65+: 13% (1999 est.)
Population Growth Rate: 0.73% (1999 est.)
Net Migration: -0.78 migrants/1,000 population (1999 est.)
Ethnic Groups: 88% white, 8% mestizo, 4% black
Languages: Spanish, Brazilero
Religions: 66% nominally Roman Catholic, 2% Protestant, 2% Jewish, 30% other
Birth Rate: 16.84/1,000 population (1999 est.)
Death Rate: 8.81/1,000 population (1999 est.)
Infant Mortality: 13.49 deaths/1,000 live births (1999 est.)

Life Expectancy at Birth: 72.69 years male, 79.15 years female (1999 est.)
Total Fertility Rate: 2.27 children born/woman (1999 est.)
Literacy: 97.5% (1997)

■ GOVERNMENT

Leader(s): Pres. Jorge Batlle Ibanez, V. Pres Luis Herrera
Government Type: republic
Administrative Divisions: 19 departments (departamentos, sing. -departamento)
Nationhood: Aug. 25, 1828 (from Brazil)
National Holiday: Independence Day, Aug. 25

■ ECONOMY

Overview: a small economy with favourable climate, good soils and considerable hydropower potential; problems include high inflation rates, a large domestic debt and frequent strikes; growth in the agriculture and fishing sectors has spurred recovery; inflation continues to drop but unemployment is on the rise and hobbles economic progress
GDP: $28.4 billion, per capita $8,600; real growth rate 3% (1998 est.)
Inflation: -89.6% (March 2000)
Industries: accounts for 26% of GDP and 19% of labour force; meat packing, oil refining, manufacturing, foodstuffs, engineering, transport equipment, sugar, textiles, leather apparel, tires
Labour Force: 1 million (1998); 36.6% community, social and business services, 21.1% industry, 17.9% trade and tourism, 15.3% agriculture
Unemployment: 10.5% (Nov. 1998)
Agriculture: accounts for 8% of GDP and 11% of labour force; meat processing, wool and hides, sugar, textiles, footwear, leather apparel, tires, cement, fishing, petroleum refining, wine, wheat, rice, corn, sorghum; self-sufficient in most basic foods
Natural Resources: soil, hydropower potential, minor minerals

■ FINANCE/TRADE

Currency: new peso (N$Ur) = 100 centesimos
International Reserves Excluding Gold: $2.011 billion (Nov. 1999)
Gold Reserves: 1.800 million fine troy ounces (Nov. 1999)
Budget: revenues $4 billion; expenditures $4.3 billion, including capital expenditures of $385 million (1997 est.)
Defence Expenditures: 3.92% of total govt. expenditure (1998)
Education Expenditures: 6.96% of govt. expenditure (1998)
External Debt: $7.6 billion (1998)
Exports: $2.232 billion (1999); commodities: hides and leather goods 17%, beef 10%, wool 9%, fish 7%, rice 4%; partners: Brazil 17%, US 15%, Germany 10%, Argentina 10%
Imports: $3.357 billion (1999); commodities: fuels and lubricants 15%, metals, machinery, transportation equipment, industrial chemicals; partners: Brazil 24%, Argentina 14%, US 8%, Germany 8%

■ COMMUNICATIONS

Daily Newspapers: 36 (1996)
Televisions: 241/1,000 inhabitants (1998)
Radios: 607/1,000 inhabitants (1997)
Telephones: 250 lines/1,000 inhabitants (1998)

■ TRANSPORTATION

Motor Vehicles: 525,000; 475,000 passenger cars (1997 est.)
Roads: 8,420 km; 7,578 km paved
Railway: 2,998 km
Air Traffic: 544,000 passengers carried (1997)
Airports: 65; 15 have paved runways (1998 est.)

Canadian Embassy: The Canadian Embassy, Edificio Torre Libertad, Plaza Cagancha, 1335, off. 1105, 11100 Montevideo, Uruguay. Tel: (011-598-2) 902-20-30. Fax: (011-598-2) 902-20-29.
Embassy in Canada: Embassy of the Eastern Republic of Uruguay, 130 Albert St, Ste 1905, Ottawa ON K1P 5G4. Tel: (613) 234-2727. Fax: (613) 233-4670.

Uzbekistan

Long-Form Name: Republic of Uzbekistan
Capital: Tashkent

■ GEOGRAPHY

Area: 447,400 sq. km
Coastline: landlocked; 420 km coastline along Aral Sea
Climate: dry continental; warm to hot summers; cool to cold winters; semi-arid grassland in east
Environment: drying up of the Aral Sea is resulting in increasing concentrations of chemical pesticides and natural salts; water and soil pollution
Terrain: flat to rolling deserts and semideserts, mountains, shrinking Aral Sea in west
Land Use: 9% arable, 1% permanent crops, 46% meadows and pastures, 3% forest, 41% other, includes 40,000 sq. km irrigated
Location: C Asia

PEOPLE

Population: 24,102,473 (July 1999 est.)
Nationality: Uzbekistani
Age Structure: 0-14 yrs: 37%; 15-64: 58%; 65+: 5% (1999 est.)
Population Growth Rate: 1.32% (1999 est.)
Net Migration: -2.44 migrants/1,000 population (1999 est.)
Ethnic Groups: 80% Uzbek, 5.5% Russian, 1.5% Tartars, 5% Tajiks, 3% Kazakhs, 2.5% Kara-Kalpaks, 2.5% other
Languages: 74.3% Uzbek (official), 14.2% Russian, 4.4% Tajik, 7.1% other
Religions: predominantly Sunni Muslim and Eastern Orthodox
Birth Rate: 23.43/1,000 population (1999 est.)
Death Rate: 7.75/1,000 population (1999 est.)
Infant Mortality: 71.58 deaths/1,000 live births (1999 est.)
Life Expectancy at Birth: 60.29 years male, 67.71 years female (1999 est.)
Total Fertility Rate: 2.82 children born/woman (1999 est.)
Literacy: 99.0% (1997)

GOVERNMENT

Leader(s): Pres. Islam A. Karimov, Prem. Otkir Sultonov
Government Type: republic
Administrative Divisions: 12 (wiloyatlar, sing. - wiloyat), 1 autonomous republic (respublikasi), 1 city (shahri)
Nationhood: Aug. 31, 1991 (from Soviet Union)
National Holiday: Independence Day, Sept. 1

ECONOMY

Overview: despite the need for irrigation, agriculture is the predominant economic sector; small industrial sector, mining. Inflation is skyrocketing and economic problems are numerous. More than 60% of the population is living in overcrowded rural villages
GDP: $59.2 billion, per capita $2,500; real growth rate 1% (1998 est.)
Inflation: n.a.
Industries: accounts for 27% of GDP; chemicals and gas, machine building, metalmaking, textile manufacture, clothing, butter, preserves, vegetable oil, textiles
Labour Force: 10 million (1998); 39% agriculture and forestry, 24% industry and construction, 37% other
Unemployment: 0.4% (1997); also large numbers of underemployed
Agriculture: accounts for 26% of GDP; vegetables, cotton, grains, almonds, fruit, livestock; 97% of all crops are grown on irrigated land
Natural Resources: gold, nonferrous metals, coal, natural gas, petroleum, uranium, silver, copper

FINANCE/TRADE

Currency: som
International Reserves Excluding Gold: n.a.
Gold Reserves: n.a.
Budget: revenues $4.4 billion, expenditures $4.7 billion, including capital expenditures of $1.1 billion (1997 est.)
Defence Expenditures: 6.1% of central government expenditure (1997)
Education Expenditures: 7.7% of GNP (1997)
External Debt: $3.162 billion (1998)
Exports: $3.094 billion (1999 est.): cotton, agricultural products, machinery; partners: Russia, Ukraine, Eastern and Western Europe
Imports: $2.884 billion (1999 est.): foodstuffs, machinery, consumer products; partners: principally other former Soviet states, Czech Republic, Western Europe

COMMUNICATIONS

Daily Newspapers: 3 (1996)
Televisions: 275/1,000 inhabitants (1998)
Radios: 465/1,000 inhabitants (1997)
Telephones: 65 lines/1,000 inhabitants (1998)

TRANSPORTATION

Motor Vehicles: n.a.
Roads: 81,600 km; 71,237 km hard-surfaced
Railway: 3,380 km, plus industrial lines
Air Traffic: 1,566,000 passengers carried (1997)
Airports: 3; all have paved runways (1997 est.)

Canadian Embassy: c/o The Canadian Embassy, 23 Starokonyushenny Pereulok, Moscow 121002, Russia. Tel: (011-7-095) 956-6666. Fax: (011-7-095) 232-9948.
Embassy in Canada: c/o The Embassy of the Republic of Uzbekistan, 1746 Massachusetts Ave. NW, Washington, DC 20036. Tel: (202) 887-5300. Fax: (202) 293-6804.

Vanuatu

Long-Form Name: Republic of Vanuatu
Capital: Port Vila

GEOGRAPHY

Area: 14,760 sq. km
Coastline: 2,528 km
Climate: tropical; moderated by southeast trade winds

Vanuatu

Environment: subject to tropical cyclones or typhoons (Jan. to Apr.); volcanism causes minor earthquakes; lack of safe drinking water
Terrain: mostly mountains of volcanic origin; narrow coastal plains
Land Use: 2% arable; 10% permanent crops; 2% meadows; 75% forests and woodlands; 11% other; includes n.a. sq. km irrigated
Location: South Pacific Ocean, NE of Australia

■ PEOPLE

Population: 189,036 (July 1999 est.)
Nationality: Ni-Vanuatu (sing. & pl.)
Age Structure: 0-14 yrs: 39%; 15-64: 58%; 65+: 3% (1999 est.)
Population Growth Rate: 2.02% (1999 est.)
Net Migration: 0 migrants/1,000 population (1999 est.)
Ethnic Groups: 94% indigenous Melanesian, 4% French, remainder Vietnamese, Chinese and various Pacific Islanders
Languages: English and French (both official); pidgin (known as Bislama or Bichelama)
Religions: 36.7% Presbyterian, 15% Anglican, 15% Catholic, 7.6% indigenous beliefs, 6.2% Seventh-Day Adventist, 3.8% Church of Christ, 15.7% other
Birth Rate: 28.49/1,000 population (1999 est.)
Death Rate: 8.26/1,000 population (1999 est.)
Infant Mortality: 59.58 deaths/1,000 live births (1999 est.)
Life Expectancy at Birth: 59.41 years male, 63.57 years female (1999 est.)
Total Fertility Rate: 3.61 children born/woman (1999 est.)
Literacy: 64.0% (1997)

■ GOVERNMENT

Leader(s): Pres. John Bani, Prime Min. Barak Sope
Government Type: republic
Administrative Divisions: 6 provinces
Nationhood: July 30, 1980 (from France and UK; formerly known as New Hebrides)
National Holiday: Independence Day, July 30

■ ECONOMY

Overview: economy is based on subsistence farming, fishing and tourism; few mineral deposits; a small light industry sector sees to local needs; tax revenues come largely from import duties
GDP: $240 million, per capita $1,300; real growth rate n.a.% (1997)
Inflation: -0.1% (Sept. 1999)
Industries: accounts for 13% of GDP; food and fish freezing, meat canning, wood processing
Labour Force: n.a.; 65% agriculture, 32% services, 3% industry
Unemployment: n.a.
Agriculture: accounts for 23% of GDP and 65% of labour force; export crops: cocoa, coffee and fish; subsistence crops: copra, taro, yams, coconuts, fruit and vegetables
Natural Resources: manganese, hardwood forests, fish

■ FINANCE/TRADE

Currency: vatu (VT) = 100 centimes
International Reserves Excluding Gold: $41 million (Jan. 2000)
Gold Reserves: n.a.
Budget: revenues $94.4 million; expenditures $99.8 million, including capital expenditures of $30.4 million (1996 est.)
Defence Expenditures: negligible
Education Expenditures: n.a.
External Debt: $47 million (1996)
Exports: $34 million (1998); commodities: copra 37%, cocoa 11%, meat 9%, fish 8%, timber 4%; partners: Netherlands 34%, France 27%, Japan 17%, Belgium 4%, New Caledonia 3%, Singapore 2%
Imports: $88 million (1998); commodities: machines and vehicles 25%, food and beverages 23%, basic manufactures 18%, raw materials and fuels 11%, chemicals 6%; partners: Australia 36%, Japan 13%, New Zealand 10%, France 8%, Fiji 5%

■ COMMUNICATIONS

Daily Newspapers: 0 (1996)
Televisions: 13/1,000 inhabitants (1996)
Radios: 345/1,000 inhabitants (1996)
Telephones: 28 lines/1,000 inhabitants (1998)

■ TRANSPORTATION

Motor Vehicles: 6,300; 4,000 passenger cars (1997 est.)
Roads: 1,070 km; 256 km paved
Railway: none
Air Traffic: 75,000 passengers carried (1997)
Airports: 32; 3 have paved runways (1998 est.)

Canadian Embassy: The Canadian High Commission to Vanuatu, c/o The Canadian High Commission, Commonwealth Ave, Canberra A.C.T. 2600, Australia. Tel: (011-61-2) 6270-4000. Fax: (011-61-2) 6273-3285.
Embassy in Canada: c/o Australian High Commission, 50 O'Connor St, Ste 710, Ottawa, ON K1P 6L2. Tel: (613) 236-0841. Fax: (613) 236-4376.

Vatican City

Long-Form Name: State of the Vatican City, or the Holy See
Capital: Vatican City

■ GEOGRAPHY

Area: 0.438 sq. km
Coastline: none: landlocked
Climate: temperate; mild, rainy winters (Sept. to mid-May) with hot, dry summers (May to Sept.)
Environment: urban
Terrain: low hill
Land Use: 100% built-up
Location: S Europe (W Italy)

■ PEOPLE

Population: 870 (July 1999 est.)
Nationality: n.a.
Age Structure: n.a.
Population Growth Rate: 1.15% (1999 est.)
Net Migration: n.a.

Ethnic Groups: primarily Italians and Swiss but also many other nationalities
Languages: Italian, Latin and various other languages
Religions: Roman Catholic
Birth Rate: n.a.
Death Rate: n.a.
Infant Mortality: n.a.
Life Expectancy at Birth: n.a.
Total Fertility Rate: n.a.
Literacy: 100%

■ GOVERNMENT

Leader(s): Head, Roman Catholic Church, Pope John Paul II (Karol Wojtyla)
Government Type: monarchical-sacerdotal state
Administrative Divisions: none
Nationhood: Feb. 11, 1929 (from Italy)
National Holiday: Installation Day of the Pope (John Paul II), Oct. 22; also Christmas, Easter, Feast of Saints Peter and Paul (June 29), and other holy days of obligation

■ ECONOMY

Overview: economy is supported financially by contributions (known as Peter's Pence) from Roman Catholics throughout the world, the sale of postage stamps, tourist mementos, fees for admission to museums and the sale of publications
GDP: n.a.
Inflation: n.a.
Industries: printing and production of a small amount of mosaics and staff uniforms; worldwide banking and financial activities
Labour Force: approximately 1,500 Vatican City employees divided into three categories: executives, office workers, salaried employees
Unemployment: n.a.
Agriculture: none
Natural Resources: none

■ FINANCE/TRADE

Currency: Vatican Lira (Lit) = 100 centesimi (at par with Italian lira)
International Reserves Excluding Gold: n.a.
Gold Reserves: n.a.
Budget: n.a.
Defence Expenditures: defence is the responsibility of Italy
Education Expenditures: n.a.
External Debt: n.a.
Exports: n.a.
Imports: n.a.

■ COMMUNICATIONS

Daily Newspapers: 1 (1996)
Televisions: n.a.
Radios: n.a.
Telephones: n.a.

■ TRANSPORTATION

Motor Vehicles: n.a.
Roads: no highways, all city streets
Railway: 862 m
Air Traffic: none
Airports: none

Canadian Embassy: The Canadian Embassy, Via G.B. de Rossi, 27, 00161 Rome, Italy. Tel. (011-39-06) 445981. Fax: (011-39-06) 445 98750.
Embassy in Canada: Apostolic Nunciature, 724 Manor Ave, Rockcliffe Park, Ottawa ON K1M 0E3. Tel: (613) 746-4914. Fax: (613) 746-4786.

Venezuela

Long-Form Name: Republic of Venezuela
Capital: Caracas

■ GEOGRAPHY

Area: 912,050 sq. km
Coastline: 2,800 km
Climate: tropical; hot, humid; more moderate in highlands
Environment: subject to floods, rockslides, mud slides; periodic droughts; increasing industrial pollution in Caracas and Maracaibo
Terrain: Andes Mountains and Maracaibo lowlands in northwest; central plains (llanos);

Guyana highlands in southwest
Land Use: 4% arable; 1% permanent crops; 20% meadows; 34% forest; 41% other; includes 1,900 sq. km irrigated
Location: N South America, bordering on Caribbean Sea

■ PEOPLE

Population: 23,203,466 (July 1999 est.)
Nationality: Venezuelan
Age Structure: 0-14 yrs: 33%; 15-64: 62%; 65+: 5% (1999 est.)
Population Growth Rate: 1.71% (1999 est.)
Net Migration: -0.23 migrants/1,000 population (1999 est.)
Ethnic Groups: 67% mestizo, 21% white, 10% black, 2% Indian
Languages: Spanish (official); Indian dialects spoken by approximately 200,000 Amerindians in the remote interior
Religions: 96% nominally Roman Catholic, 2% Protestant, 2% other
Birth Rate: 22.25/1,000 population (1999 est.)
Death Rate: 4.93/1,000 population (1999 est.)
Infant Mortality: 26.51 deaths/1,000 live births (1999 est.)
Life Expectancy at Birth: 69.97 years male, 76.16 years female (1999 est.)
Total Fertility Rate: 2.61 children born/woman (1999 est.)
Literacy: 92.0% (1997)

■ GOVERNMENT

Leader(s): Pres. Lt. Col. Hugo Chavez Frias, V. Pres. Isaias Rodriguez
Government Type: republic
Administrative Divisions: 22 states (estados, sing. -estado), 1 federal district (distrito federal) and 1 federal dependency (dependencia federal)
Nationhood: July 5, 1811 (from Spain)
National Holiday: Independence Day, July 5

■ ECONOMY

Overview: petroleum is the backbone of the economy, accounting for 27% of GDP, 78% of total exports and more than half of government revenue. It is likely to become even more important as the state petroleum company plans to double its production over the next 10 years.
GDP: $194.5 billion, per capita $8,500; real growth rate -0.9% (1998 est.)
Inflation: 18.0% (Apr. 2000)
Industries: accounts for 63% of GDP; petroleum, iron-ore mining, construction materials, food processing, textiles, steel, aluminum, motor vehicle assembly
Labour Force: 9.2 million (1998); 27.5% community, social and business services, 22.2% trade and tourism, 15.5% industry (1993)
Unemployment: 10.3% (1997)
Agriculture: accounts for 4% GDP; products: corn, sorghum, sugar cane, rice, bananas, vegetables, coffee, beef, pork, milk, eggs, fish; not self-sufficient in food other than meat
Natural Resources: crude oil, natural gas, iron ore, gold, bauxite, other minerals, hydropower, diamonds

■ FINANCE/TRADE

Currency: bolívar (Bs) = 100 centimos
International Reserves Excluding Gold: $12.347 billion (Jan. 2000)
Gold Reserves: 9.870 million fine troy ounces (Jan. 2000)
Budget: revenues $11.99 billion; expenditures $11.48 billion, including capital expenditures of $2.3 billion (1996 est.)
Defence Expenditures: 9.8% of central government expenditure (1997)
Education Expenditures: 5.2% of GNP (1997)
External Debt: $37.003 billion (1998)
Exports: $19.852 billion (1999); commodities: petroleum 81%, bauxite and aluminum, iron ore, agricultural products, basic manufactures; partners: US 50.3%, Germany 5.3%, Japan 4.1%
Imports: $14.789 billion (1999); commodities: foodstuffs, chemicals, manufactures, machinery and transport equipment; partners: US 44%, Germany 8.5%, Japan 6%, Italy 5%, Brazil 4.4%

■ COMMUNICATIONS

Daily Newspapers: 86 (1996)
Televisions: 185/1,000 inhabitants (1998)
Radios: 468/1,000 inhabitants (1997)
Telephones: 117 lines/1,000 inhabitants (1998)

■ TRANSPORTATION

Motor Vehicles: 2,025,000; 1,500,000 passenger cars (1997 est.)
Roads: 84,300 km; 33,214 km paved
Railway: 584 km
Air Traffic: 4,020,000 passengers carried (1997)
Airports: 371; 122 have paved runways (1998 est.)

Canadian Embassy: The Canadian Embassy, 6a Av. Entre 3a y 5a, Transv. de Altamira, Altamira, Edificio Omni, Caracas, Venezuela. mailing address: Apartado 62302, Caracas 1060A, Venezuela. Tel: (011-58-2) 264-0833. Fax: (011-58-2) 261-8741.
Embassy in Canada: Embassy of the Republic of

Venezuela, 32 Range Rd, Ottawa ON K1N 8J4.
Tel: (613) 235-5151. Fax: (613) 235-3205.

Vietnam

Long-Form Name: Socialist Republic of Vietnam
Capital: Hanoi

■ GEOGRAPHY

Area: 329,560 sq. km
Coastline: 3,444 km (excluding islands)
Climate: tropical in south; monsoonal in north with hot, rainy season (mid-May to mid-Sept.) and warm, dry season (mid-Oct. to mid-Mar.)
Environment: occasional typhoons (May to Jan.) with extensive flooding; soil deterioration; inadequate supply of safe drinking water
Terrain: low, flat delta in south and north; central highlands; hilly, mountainous far north and northwest
Land Use: 17% arable; 4% permanent crops; 1% meadows; 30% forest; 48% other, includes 18,600 sq. km irrigated
Location: SE Asia, bordering on South China Sea

■ PEOPLE

Population: 77,311,210 (July 1999 est.)
Nationality: Vietnamese (sing. & pl.)
Age Structure: 0-14 yrs: 34%; 15-64: 61%; 65+: 5% (1999 est.)
Population Growth Rate: 1.37% (1999 est.)
Net Migration: -0.53 migrants/1,000 population (1999 est.)
Ethnic Groups: 85–90% predominantly Vietnamese; 3% Chinese; more than 60 ethnic minorities including Muong, Thai, Meo, Khmer, Man, Cham; other mountain tribes
Languages: Vietnamese (official), French, Chinese, English, Khmer, tribal languages (Mon-Khmer and Malayo-Polynesian)
Religions: Buddhist, Confucian, Taoist, Roman Catholic, indigenous beliefs, Islamic, Protestant
Birth Rate: 20.78/1,000 population (1999 est.)
Death Rate: 6.56/1,000 population (1999 est.)
Infant Mortality: 34.84 deaths/1,000 live births (1999 est.)
Life Expectancy at Birth: 65.71 years male, 70.64 years female (1999 est.)
Total Fertility Rate: 2.41 children born/woman (1999 est.)
Literacy: 91.9% (1997)

■ GOVERNMENT

Leader(s): Pres. Tran Duc Luong, Prime Min. Phan Van Khai
Government Type: communist state
Administrative Divisions: 58 provinces (tinh, sing. & pl.), 3 municipalities (thu do, sing. & pl.)
Nationhood: Sept. 2, 1945 (from France)
National Holiday: Independence Day, Sept. 2

■ ECONOMY

Overview: centrally planned, developing economy with extensive government ownership and control of production facilities; dependent on foreign aid; high rate of population growth and high unemployment combine to form the economy's most serious problem
GDP: $134.8 billion, per capita $1,770; real growth rate 4% (1998 est.)
Inflation: n.a.
Industries: accounts for 30% of GDP; food processing, textiles, machine building, mining, cement, chemical fertilizer, glass, tires, oil, fishing
Labour Force: 39 million (1998); 65% agriculture, 11.8% industry, 20.7% services
Unemployment: n.a.
Agriculture: accounts for 28% of GDP; rice, corn, potatoes make up 50% of farm output; commercial crops (rubber, soybeans, coffee, tea, bananas) and animal products other 50%; not self-sufficient in rice
Natural Resources: phosphates, coal, manganese, bauxite, chromate, offshore oil deposits, forests

■ FINANCE/TRADE

Currency: dong (pl. dong) (D) = 100 xu
International Reserves Excluding Gold: $1.365 billion (June 1999)
Gold Reserves: n.a.
Budget: adjusted for purchasing power parity: revenues $5.6 billion; expenditures $6 billion, including capital expenditures $1.7 billion (1996 est.)
Defence Expenditures: 11.1% of central government expenditure (1997)
Education Expenditures: 3.0% of GNP (1997)
External Debt: $22.359 billion (1998)
Exports: $9.4 billion (1998 est.); commodities: agricultural and handicraft products, coal, minerals, ores; partners: former USSR countries, Eastern Europe, Japan, Singapore
Imports: $11.4 billion (1998 est.); commodities: petroleum, steel products, railroad equipment, chemicals, medicines, raw cotton, fertilizer, grain; partners: former USSR countries, Eastern Europe, Japan, Singapore

■ COMMUNICATIONS

Daily Newspapers: 10 (1996)
Televisions: 47/1,000 inhabitants (1998)
Radios: 107/1,000 inhabitants (1997)
Telephones: 26 lines/1,000 inhabitants (1998)

TRANSPORTATION

Motor Vehicles: 178,000; 80,000 passenger cars (1997 est.)
Roads: 93,300 km; 23,418 km paved
Railway: 2,835 km
Air Traffic: 2,527,000 passengers carried (1997)
Airports: 48; 36 have paved runways

Canadian Embassy: The Canadian Embassy, 31 Hung Vuong Street, Hanoi, Vietnam, Tel: (011 84 4) 823-5500, Fax: (011 84 4) 823-5333
Embassy in Canada: Embassy of the Socialist Republic of Vietnam, 470 Wilbrod St, Ottawa, ON K1N 6M8. Tel: (613) 236-0772. Fax: (613) 236-2704.

Wallis and Futuna

Long-Form Name: Territory of the Wallis and Futuna Islands
Capital: Mata-Utu

GEOGRAPHY

Area: 274 sq. km
Climate: tropical maritime, rainy season (Nov. to April); cool, dry season (May to Oct.)
Land Use: 5% arable, 20% permanent crops, 0% meadows and pasture, 0% forests, 75% other; includes n.a. sq. km irrigated
Location: SW Pacific Ocean, E of Australia

PEOPLE

Population: 15,129 (July 1999 est.)
Nationality: Wallisian, Futunan, or Wallis and Futuna Islanders
Ethnic Groups: Polynesians, and descendants of French settlers
Languages: Wallisian, Futunian (Polynesian languages), French

GOVERNMENT

Colony/Territory of: Overseas Territory of France
Leader(s): Head of State: Pres. Jacques Chirac (France); represented by High Administrator Claude Pierret. Head of government Pres. of the Territorial Assembly Victor Brial
Government Type: overseas territory of France
National Holiday: n.a.

ECONOMY

Overview: agriculture includes copra, cassava, yams, taro roots, bananas; livestock includes pigs and goats; considerable imports, negligible exports

FINANCE/TRADE

Currency: CFP franc = 100 centimes

Canadian Embassy: c/o The Canadian Embassy, 35-37 avenue Montaigne, 75008, Paris, France. Tel: (011-33-1) 44-43-29-00. Fax: (011-33-1) 44-43-29-99.
Representative to Canada: c/o Embassy of France, 42 Sussex Dr, Ottawa ON K1M 2C9. Tel: (613) 789-1795. Fax: (613) 562-3735.

West Bank

GEOGRAPHY

Area: 5,860 sq. km
Climate: temperate, temperature and precipitation vary with altitude, warm to hot summers, cool to mild winters
Land Use: 27% arable; 0% permanent crops; 32% permanent pastures; 1% forests and woodland; 40% other; includes n.a. sq. km irrigated
Location: Middle East, between Israel and Jordan

PEOPLE

Population: 1,611,109 (July 1999 est.)
Nationality: n.a.
Ethnic Groups: Palestinian Arab and other 83%, Jewish 17%
Languages: Arabic, Hebrew (spoken by Israeli settlers and many Palestinians), English (widely understood)

GOVERNMENT

Colony/Territory of: claimed and occupied by Israel
Leader(s): local Palestinian authority is headed by Yasser Arafat, subject to Israeli authority
Government Type: Palestinian Legislative Council (Jan. 1996) has limited powers under interim self-governing agreements with Israel. Originally designated as a five-year interim arrangement in 1993, permanent status still under negotiation.
National Holiday: n.a.

ECONOMY

Overview: as for Gaza Strip

FINANCE/TRADE

Currency: 1 new Israeli shekel= 100 new agorot; 1 Jordanian dinar = 1,000 fils.

Canadian Embassy: n.a.
Representative to Canada: n.a.

Western Sahara

Long-Form Name: Western Sahara
Capital: none

■ GEOGRAPHY

Area: 266,000 sq. km
Coastline: 1,110 km
Climate: Mediterranean to arid; hot, dry desert; rain is rare; cold offshore air currents produce fog and heavy dew
Environment: desertification, sparse water and arable land; hot and dry and dust/sand-laden sirocco wind; harmattan haze
Terrain: mostly barren rocky desert; small mountains in south and northeast
Land Use: 0% arable; 0% permanent crops, 19% permanent pastures, 0% forests, 81% other; includes n.a. sq. km irrigated
Location: NW Africa, bordering on Atlantic Ocean

■ PEOPLE

Population: 239,333 (July 1999 est.)
Nationality: Sahrawi, Sahraoui
Age Structure: n.a.
Population Growth Rate: 2.34% (1999 est.)
Net Migration: -5.41 migrants/1,000 population (1999 est.)
Ethnic Groups: Arabs, Berbers
Languages: Hassaniya Arabic, Moroccan Arabic
Religions: Islam (almost 100% Sunni Muslim)
Birth Rate: 45.42/1,000 population (1999 est.)
Death Rate: 16.58/1,000 population (1999 est.)
Infant Mortality: 136.67 deaths/1,000 live births (1999 est.)
Life Expectancy at Birth: 47.98 years male, 50.57 years female (1999 est.)
Total Fertility Rate: 6.70 children born/woman (1999 est.)
Literacy: n.a.

■ GOVERNMENT

Leader(s): under de facto control of Morocco
Government Type: under Moroccan occupation; legal status and matters of sovereignty remain unresolved
Administrative Divisions: none (under de facto control of Morocco)
Nationhood: n.a.
National Holiday: n.a.

■ ECONOMY

Overview: economy severely disrupted by Moroccan occupation and ongoing guerrilla warfare; poor in natural resources and with inadequate rainfall, most food must be imported; all aspects of the economy are controlled by the Moroccan government
GDP: n.a.
Inflation: n.a.
Industries: phosphate mining, fishing, handicrafts
Labour Force: n.a.; 50% of the people are engaged in subsistence farming and animal husbandry
Unemployment: n.a.
Agriculture: limited to subsistence agriculture; some grain production, livestock (esp. sheep, goats, camels); cash economy exists largely for the garrison forces
Natural Resources: rich phosphate deposits, iron ore

■ FINANCE/TRADE

Currency: Moroccan dirham (DH) = 100 centimes
International Reserves Excluding Gold: n.a.
Gold Reserves: n.a.
Budget: n.a.
Defence Expenditures: n.a.
Education Expenditures: n.a.
External Debt: n.a.
Exports: phosphates main export product; Morocco claims and administers Western Sahara, so trade partners are included in overall Moroccan accounts
Imports: fuel for fishing fleet; most of the country's food supply must be imported; partners, see exports

■ COMMUNICATIONS

Daily Newspapers: n.a.
Televisions: 24/1,000 inhabitants (1996)
Radios: 211/1,000 inhabitants (1996)
Telephones: n.a.

■ TRANSPORTATION

Motor Vehicles: n.a.
Roads: 6,200 km; 1,350 km surfaced
Railway: none
Air Traffic: n.a.
Airports: 12; 3 have paved runways (1998 est.)

Canadian Embassy: none
Embassy in Canada: none

Yemen

Long-Form Name: Republic of Yemen
Capital: Sana'a (political capital); Aden (commercial capital)

■ GEOGRAPHY

Area: 527,970 sq. km

Yemen

Coastline: 1,906 km
Climate: hot, dry desert in the south to temperate in central region and north; harsh desert in the east
Environment: desertification, overgrazing, lack of natural fresh water, soil erosion, summer dust and sand storms
Terrain: narrow coastal plain; western mountains, northern desert interior
Land Use: 3% arable land; 0% permanent crops; 30% meadows and pasture; 4% forest and woodland; 63% other; includes 3,600 sq. km irrigated
Location: SW Asia (Middle East), bordering on Red Sea

■ PEOPLE

Population: 16,942,230 (July 1999 est.)
Nationality: Yemeni
Age Structure: 0-14 yrs: 48%; 15-64: 49%; 65+: 3% (1999 est.)
Population Growth Rate: 3.34% (1999 est.)
Net Migration: 0 migrants/1,000 population (1999 est.)
Ethnic Groups: predominantly Arab; Afro-Arab, Indian, Somali and European minorities
Languages: Arabic
Religions: predominantly Muslim; Christian and Hindu minorities in the south
Birth Rate: 43.31/1,000 population (1999 est.)
Death Rate: 9.88/1,000 population (1999 est.)
Infant Mortality: 69.82deaths/1,000 live births (1999 est.)
Life Expectancy at Birth: 58.17 years male, 61.88 years female (1999 est.)
Total Fertility Rate: 7.06 children born/woman (1999 est.)
Literacy: 42.5% (1997)

■ GOVERNMENT

Leader(s): Pres. Ali Abdallah Salih, Prime Min. Abd al-Karim Iryani
Government Type: republic
Administrative Divisions: 17 governorates (muhafazat, sing. -muhafazah)
Nationhood: May 22, 1990
National Holiday: Proclamation of the Republic, May 22

■ ECONOMY

Overview: future economic level depends heavily on Western assistance. North: low level of domestic industry once self-sufficient in food but now dependent on imports; South: economic growth among the slowest of all Arab countries
GDP: $12.1 billion, per capita $740; real growth rate 1.8% (1998 est.)
Inflation: 7.9% (Dec. 1998)
Industries: accounts for 46% of GDP; petroleum, cotton, textiles, leather goods, food processing, handicrafts, cement, small aluminum products factory
Labour Force: 5.1 million (1998)
Unemployment: 27% (1996 est.)
Agriculture: in the north, agriculture accounts for 16% GDP; main crops include fruit (grapes) and cotton; in the south, agriculture accounts for 17% GDP and 45% of the labour force; the main agricultural product is livestock (cattle, camels, sheep, goats, poultry)
Natural Resources: salt deposits, petroleum, fish, marble, coal, gold, lead

■ FINANCE/TRADE

Currency: Yemeni rial (YR)
International Reserves Excluding Gold: $1.311 billion (Oct. 1999)
Gold Reserves: 0.050 million fine troy ounces (Oct. 1999)
Budget: revenues $2.6 billion; expenditures $2.7 billion, including capital expenditures of $1.1 billion (1998 est.)
Defence Expenditures: 18.77% of total govt. expenditure (1999)
Education Expenditures: 21.81% of govt. expenditure (1999)
External Debt: $4.138 billion (1998)
Exports: $1.496 billion (1998); crude oil, cotton, coffee, vegetables, cotton, animal hides, fish; partners: US, Japan, Singapore
Imports: $2.167 billion (1998); textiles and other manufactured consumer goods, petroleum products, sugar, grain, flour, other foodstuffs, cement, grain, consumer goods, crude oil, machinery, chemicals; partners: nations of the former Soviet Union, UK, Ethiopia

■ COMMUNICATIONS

Daily Newspapers: 3 (1996)
Televisions: 29/1,000 inhabitants (1998)
Radios: 64/1,000 inhabitants (1997)
Telephones: 13 lines/1,000 inhabitants (1998)

■ TRANSPORTATION

Motor Vehicles: 516,000; 230,000 passenger cars (1997 est.)
Roads: 64,725 km; 5,243 km paved
Railway: none
Air Traffic: 707,000 passengers carried (1997)
Airports: 48; 12 have paved runways (1998 est.)

Canadian Embassy: The Canadian Embassy to Yemen, c/o Canadian Embassy, Diplomatic Quarter, P.O. Box 94321, Riyadh 11693, Saudi

Arabia. Tel: (011-966-1) 488-2288. Fax: (011-966-1) 488-1997.
Embassy in Canada: Embassy of the Republic of Yemen, 788 Island Park Drive, Ottawa ON K1Y 0C2. Tel: (613) 729-6627. Fax: (613) 729-8915

Yugoslavia

Long-Form Name: see Serbia and Montenegro

Zaire

Long-Form Name: see Democratic Republic of Congo

Zambia

Long-Form Name: Republic of Zambia
Capital: Lusaka

■ GEOGRAPHY

Area: 752,610 sq. km
Coastline: none: landlocked
Climate: tropical; modified by altitude; rainy season (Oct. to Apr.)
Environment: deforestation; soil erosion; desertification; air pollution and resultant acid rain; tropical storms are a natural hazard from Nov. to Apr.
Terrain: mostly high plateau with some hills and mountains
Land Use: 7% arable; 0% permanent crops; 40% meadows; 39% forest; 14% other; includes 460 sq. km irrigated
Location: SC Africa

■ PEOPLE

Population: 9,663,535 (July 1999 est.)
Nationality: Zambian
Age Structure: 0-14 yrs: 49%; 15-64: 49%; 65+: 2% (1999 est.)
Population Growth Rate: 2.12% (1999 est.)
Net Migration: -0.78 migrants/1,000 population (1999 est.)
Ethnic Groups: 98.7% African, 1.1% European, 0.2% other
Languages: English (official); about 70 indigenous languages
Religions: 50–75% Christian, 24–49% Muslim and Hindu, remainder indigenous beliefs
Birth Rate: 44.51/1,000 population (1999 est.)
Death Rate: 22.56/1,000 population (1999 est.)
Infant Mortality: 91.85 deaths/1,000 live births (1999 est.)
Life Expectancy at Birth: 36.72 years male, 37.21 years female (1999 est.)
Total Fertility Rate: 6.35 children born/woman (1999 est.)
Literacy: 75.1% (1997)

■ GOVERNMENT

Leader(s): Pres. Frederick Chiluba, V. Pres. Christon Tembo. Presidential election scheduled October 2001.
Government Type: republic
Administrative Divisions: 9 provinces
Nationhood: Oct. 24, 1964 (from UK; formerly known as Northern Rhodesia)
National Holiday: Independence Day, Oct. 24

■ ECONOMY

Overview: economy continues to decline due to a sustained drop in copper production and ineffective economic policies; problems include a high inflation rate, high population growth and severe drought
GDP: $8.3 billion, per capita $880; real growth rate -2% (1998 est.)
Inflation: 19.1% (Jan. 1998)
Industries: accounts for 40% of GDP; copper mining and processing, transport, construction, foodstuffs, beverages, chemicals, textiles and fertilizer
Labour Force: 4.1 million (1998); 37.9% agriculture, 7.8% industry, 54.9% services
Unemployment: n.a.
Agriculture: accounts for 23% of GDP and 85% of labour force; food production is insufficient for country's needs; crops: corn (food staple), sorghum, rice, peanuts, sunflower, tobacco, cotton, sugar cane, cassava; cattle, goats, beef, eggs produced; marginally self-sufficient in corn
Natural Resources: copper, cobalt, zinc, lead, coal, emeralds, gold, silver, uranium, hydropower potential

■ FINANCE/TRADE

Currency: kwacha (K) = 100 ngwee
International Reserves Excluding Gold: $45 million (Dec. 1999)
Gold Reserves: n.a.
Budget: revenues $888 million; expenditures $835 million, including capital expenditures of $110 million (1995 est.)
Defence Expenditures: 3.93% of govt. expenditure (1999)
Education Expenditures: 14.45% of govt. expenditure (1999)
External Debt: $6.865 billion (1998)
Exports: $901 million (1997); commodities: copper, zinc, cobalt, lead, tobacco; partners: European Community, Japan, South Africa, US

Imports: $806 million (1997); commodities: machinery, transportation equipment, foodstuffs, fuels, manufactures; partners: European Community, Japan, South Africa, US

■ COMMUNICATIONS

Daily Newspapers: 3 (1996)
Televisions: 42/1,000 inhabitants (1996)
Radios: 121/1,000 inhabitants (1997)
Telephones: 9 lines/1,000 inhabitants (1998)

■ TRANSPORTATION

Motor Vehicles: 215,500; 142,000 passenger cars (1997 est.)
Roads: 39,700 km; 7,265 km paved
Railway: 2,164 km
Air Traffic: 50,000 passengers carried (1997)
Airports: 112; 12 have paved runways (1998 est.)

Canadian Embassy: The Canadian High Commission, 5199 United Nations Ave, Lusaka; mailing address: P.O. Box 31313, 10101 Lusaka, Zambia. Tel: (011-260-1) 25-08-33. Fax: (011-260-1) 25-41-76.
Embassy in Canada: High Commision for the Republic of Zambia, c/o Embassy of Zambia, 2419 Massachusetts Ave NW, Washington DC 20008, USA. Tel: (202) 265-9717. Fax: (202) 332-0826.

Zimbabwe

Long-Form Name: Republic of Zimbabwe
Capital: Harare

■ GEOGRAPHY

Area: 390,580 sq. km
Coastline: none; landlocked
Climate: tropical; moderated by altitude; rainy season (Nov. to Mar.)
Environment: recurring droughts; floods and severe storms are rare; deforestation; soil erosion; air and water pollution; desertification; poaching has significantly reduced the black rhinoceros population, which was once the largest concentration of the species anywhere in the world
Terrain: mostly high plateau with higher central plateau (high veld); mountains in east
Land Use: 7% arable; less than 1% permanent crops (coffee plantations); 13% meadows; 23% forest and woodland; 57% other; includes 1,930 sq. km irrigated
Location: S Africa

■ PEOPLE

Population: 11,163,160 (July 1999 est.)
Nationality: Zimbabwean
Age Structure: 0-14 yrs: 43%; 15-64: 54%; 65+: 3% (1999 est.)
Population Growth Rate: 1.02% (1999 est.)
Net Migration: n.a.
Ethnic Groups: 98% African (71% Shona, 16% Ndebele, 11% other), 1% white, 1% mixed and Asian
Languages: English (official); Shona and Sindebele, numerous minor tribal dialects
Religions: 50% syncretic (part Christian, part indigenous beliefs), 25% Christian, 24% indigenous beliefs, a few Muslim
Birth Rate: 30.64/1,000 population (1999 est.)
Death Rate: 20.43/1,000 population (1999 est.)
Infant Mortality: 61.21 deaths/1,000 live births (1999 est.)
Life Expectancy at Birth: 38.77 years male, 38.94 years female (1999 est.)
Total Fertility Rate: 3.71 children born/woman (1999 est.)
Literacy: 90.9% (1997)

■ GOVERNMENT

Leader(s): Pres. Robert Mugabe
Government Type: parliamentary democracy
Administrative Divisions: 8 provinces and 2 cities with provincial status
Nationhood: Apr. 18, 1980 (from UK; formerly known as Southern Rhodesia)
National Holiday: Independence Day, Apr. 18

■ ECONOMY

Overview: severe droughts have adversely affected this agriculture-based economy in recent years. The government is working to consolidate earlier progress in developing a market-oriented economy.
GDP: $26.2 billion, per capita $2,400; real growth rate 1.5% (1998 est.)
Inflation: 31.8% (Dec. 1998)
Industries: accounts for 32% of GDP; mining (minerals and metals account for 40% of exports), steel, clothing and footwear, chemicals, foodstuffs, fertilizer, beverages, transportation equipment, wood products
Labour Force: 5.1 million (1998); 29.9% community, social and business services, 25.9% agriculture, 15.1% industry (1992)
Unemployment: n.a.
Agriculture: accounts for 28% of GDP; 40% of land area divided into 4,500 large commercial farms and 42% in communal lands; crops: corn (food staple), cotton, tobacco, wheat, coffee, sugar cane, peanuts; livestock: cattle, sheep, goats, pigs; self-sufficient in food
Natural Resources: coal, chromium ore, asbestos,

gold, nickel, copper, iron ore, vanadium, lithium, tin

■ FINANCE/TRADE

Currency: Zimbabwean dollar ($Z) = 100 cents
International Reserves Excluding Gold: $237 million (Jan. 2000)
Gold Reserves: 0.648 million fine troy ounces (Jan. 2000)
Budget: revenues $2.5 billion; expenditures $2.9 billion, including capital expenditures of $29 million (1997 est.)
Defence Expenditures: 7.09% of central government expenditure (1997)
Education Expenditures: 24.20% of central government expenditure (1997)
External Debt: $4.716 billion (1998)
Exports: $1.864 billion (1998); commodities: agriculture 34% (tobacco 21%, other 13%), manufactures 19%, gold 11%, ferrochrome 11%, cotton 6%; partners: Europe 55% (European Community 41%, Netherlands 6%, other 8%), Africa 22% (South Africa 12%, other 10%), US 8%, Japan 4%
Imports: $2.701 billion (1998); commodities: machinery and transportation equipment 37%, other manufactures 22%, chemicals 16%, fuels 15%; partners: European Community 31%, Africa 29% (South Africa 21%, other 8%), US 8%, Japan 4%

■ COMMUNICATIONS

Daily Newspapers: 2 (1996)
Televisions: 30/1,000 inhabitants (1998)
Radios: 93/1,000 inhabitants (1997)
Telephones: 17 lines/1,000 inhabitants (1998)

■ TRANSPORTATION

Motor Vehicles: 358,000; 250,000 passenger cars (1997 est.)
Roads: 18,338 km; 8,692 km paved
Railway: 2,759 km
Air Traffic: 790,000 passengers carried (1997)
Airports: 468; 18 have paved runways (1998 est.)

Canadian Embassy: The Canadian High Commission, 45 Baines Ave, Harare; mailing address: P.O. Box 1430, Harare, Zimbabwe. Tel: (011-263-4) 252-181. Fax: (011-263-4) 252-186.
Embassy in Canada: High Commission for the Republic of Zimbabwe, 332 Somerset St W, Ottawa ON K2P 0J9. Tel: (613) 237-4388. Fax: (613) 563-8269.

World Internet Links for Students

*T*he World Bank Group, with help from corporate and government partners, has sponsored a learning web site in English, French and Spanish. Called World Links For Development (WorLD), the program links secondary school students and teachers in developing countries with their counterparts in industrialized countries. During the period from 1997 to 2001, the WorLD program hopes to connect 1,200 secondary schools in 40 developing countries with partner schools in Australia, Canada, Europe, Japan and the U.S.

As of late 1999, 280 pilot schools were connected in 18 developing countries and partnered with schools in 24 other countries. Canadian students at Don Mills Collegiate Institute and St. Patrick's High School were partnered with students in South Africa and Uganda in a dialogue which examined and compared respective living conditions and environment. Students at Univeristy of Toronto Schools and École secondaire des Sources joined in a dialogue with students in Ghana, Senegal and the U.S. about the world in the 21st century; Canada's SchoolNet played a large role in co-ordinating this project.

For more information about WorLD program (or to join a project), visit http://www.worldbank.org/worldlinks

SCIENCE AND NATURE

ASTRONOMY AND SPACE

Astronomy has taught us that the universe is more complex than the ancients thought. Though less dependent on the "patterns" in the sky, we continue the exploration. The skies act not simply as a guide, but also as a frontier to be explored.

Our Solar System

Our solar system consists of our sun, at least nine planets and smaller bodies such as asteroids, comets and moons. The dominant member of this family is the sun, our nearest star. The sun is an enormous ball of hot, glowing gas, mostly hydrogen and helium. Its powerful pull of gravity holds the planets, asteroids and comets in orbit around it.

The planets have been known since people first turned their gaze skyward. The ancient Greeks called them "wanderers" because they moved through the sky relative to the fixed stars. Five planets can be seen without a telescope: Mercury, Venus, Mars, Jupiter and Saturn. They are visible because they reflect the light of the sun.

In order of distance from the sun, the planets are Mercury, Venus, Earth, Mars, Jupiter, Saturn, Uranus, Neptune and Pluto.

All the planets revolve (orbit) around the sun in the same counter-clockwise direction. The closer to the sun, the greater their speed. Except for Pluto, all the orbits lie in nearly the same plane in space, like marbles rolling on a table top.

Our Place in the Universe Although the solar system seems enormous, it is quite small compared to the whole universe. Our sun is only one star among the hundreds of billions that make up our spiral-shaped galaxy, the **Milky Way**. It takes our sun, with planets in tow, about 250 million years to orbit around the Milky Way just once. All the stars that we see at night are in a small, nearby portion of our galaxy. There may be billions of galaxies in the universe, each containing billions of stars of its own. **The Birth of our Solar System** Approximately 4.6 billion years ago, (billions of years after the galaxies were formed), astronomers believe that a vast cloud of gas and dust collapsed and formed a spinning disk. Gravitation compacted so much material in the centre that extremely high pressures and temperatures lit a nuclear fire—our sun began to shine. Meanwhile, any remaining lumps of hot solids and gases slowly collected to become the planets, moons, asteroids and comets.

Our Solar System The planets of the solar system can be divided into two groups. The inner planets, Mercury, Venus, Earth and Mars, are the **terrestrial**, or Earth-like, planets. These are small rocky worlds with metal cores and thin atmospheres, except for airless Mercury. Jupiter, Saturn, Uranus and Neptune make up the realm of the **gas giants**. These planets do not have a solid surface, but are made up of layers of gases and clouds, possibly with rocky cores the size of Earth. The gas giants are huge: a thousand Earths could easily fit inside Jupiter. Saturn's rings may be the most famous feature of the solar system but rings are also found around Jupiter, Uranus and Neptune.

Pluto is unique and does not fit into either of these two groups. It is a tiny world of rock and ice, smaller than the Earth's moon, and with an extremely thin atmosphere.

Separating the terrestrial planets from the gas giants is the **asteroid belt**, a region of space between Mars and Jupiter where as many as 50,000 rocky objects may orbit the sun. Asteroids, often called minor planets, range from gravel-size, or smaller, to the 1,000-km-wide Ceres. They may be the remains of a small, shattered planet.

Over 60 moons, or satellites, are found in the solar system. All the planets, except for Mercury and Venus, have at least one moon orbiting them. Some of these moons are fascinating worlds in their own right: **Phobos** and **Deimos**, the moons of Mars, may be captured asteroids; **Io**, one of Jupiter's moons, has many active volcanoes; **Europa**, another one of Jupiter's moons, may have a subterranean ocean; **Titan**, a moon of Saturn, has an atmosphere thicker than

Earth's. Jupiter with its 16 known moons, Saturn with its 18 and Uranus with its 17 are like miniature solar systems.

Exploring the Solar System Most of the planets have been visited by space probes from Earth: Mercury was visited in 1974 by *Mariner 10*, Soviet *Venera* spacecraft landed on Venus several times in the 1970s while *Viking 1* and *2* landed on Mars in 1976. The best spacecraft views of Jupiter and Saturn were obtained by *Voyager 1* and *2* in 1979 and 1980–81 respectively. *Voyager 2* went on to Uranus in 1986 and Neptune in August 1989. These spacecraft made discoveries not possible from the Earth: craters on Mercury, volcanoes and great valleys on Mars, Jupiter's ring and 10 new moons of Uranus were only a few.

Recent missions include the *Ulysses* mission, launched in 1990, which finished its second orbit of the sun in 1997-8. The spacecraft will do a south polar pass of the sun from September 2000 to January 2001. The combined NASA/ESA (European Space Agency) *Cassini* mission to Saturn was launched in October 1997. *Cassini* will enter orbit around Saturn July 2004.

On July 4, 1997, the Pathfinder mission to Mars made a successful landing, sending back data and pictures. In Novovember 1996 the Mars Global Surveyor (MGS) was launched on a mapping and photography mission. Mapping began in March 1999 and pictures taken in June 2000 showed features resembling water erosion in over 200 places. Scientists had previously thought that the red planet was too cold and the atmosphere too thin to allow water to exist. For the latest releases from the MGS, visit http://www.mars.jpl.nasa.gov/mgs. In April 2001, Mars Surveyor 2001 Orbiter will launch, on another mapping mission.

Our Solar System at a Glance

	Distance from Sun (million km)	Equatorial diameter (km)	Gravity (Earth=1)	Mass (Earth=1)	Period of Orbit about the Sun	Period of Rotation on Axis (days)	Number of known Moons
Sun	—	1 392 000	27.90	332 830	—	25.38	—
Mercury	57.9	4 878	0.38	0.06	88.0 days	58.60	0
Venus	108.2	12 104	0.91	0.8	224.7 days	243.00	0
Earth	149.6	12 756	1.00	1.0	365.3 days	0.99	1
Mars	227.9	6 787	0.38	0.1	1.88 years	1.02	2
Jupiter	778.4	142 800	2.54	317.8	11.86 years	0.41	16
Saturn	1 423.8	120 000	1.08	95.2	29.63 years	0.42	18
Uranus	2 868.7	51 200	0.91	14.5	83.97 years	0.45	21
Neptune	4 492.1	48 680	1.19	17.2	164.80 years	0.67	8
Pluto	5 926.5	2 300	0.06	0.002	248.63 years	6.38	1

Source: *Global Atlas*, Gage Educational Publishing Co.; *Observer's Handbook, 1991*, The Royal Astronomical Society of Canada

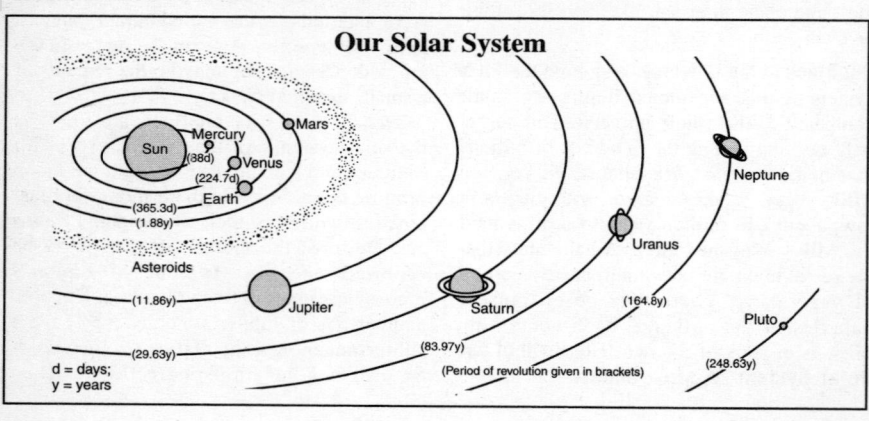

Astronomy and Space

The Canadian Space Program Quiz

When did Canada launch its first satellite?
September 9, 1962. *Alouette 1* was the first satellite to return useful information on the ionosphere (the layer of the upper atmosphere that affects long-distance radio transmissions). Designed to last one year, *Alouette 1* successfully transmitted data for over a decade. (Canada was the third country into space, after the USSR and the US.)

How many communications satellites has Telsat Canada owned and operated?
Twelve. With *Anik A-1*, Canada was the first country to launch a satellite for use in domestic communications. Sent into orbit on November 9, 1972, *Anik A-1* made nationwide, real-time television possible. It also brought reliable telephone service to the North for the first time. Despite a setback in 1994—both operational satellites were knocked out by solar storms—*Anik* satellites have continued to provide telephone and communications services and allow a national newspaper to transmit copy to a number of printing plants across the country. *Anik* A1, A2 and A3 gave way to *Anik* B1 (December 15, 1978 to December 1, 1986), three satellites in the *Anik* C series and two in the D series. *Anik* E1 and E2 have been operational since 1991 and are expected to continue providing service until 2003. The *Nimiq* satellite was launched May 20, 1999 and will operate for 12 years. *Anik F1* is under construction and will be designed to last for 15 years.

What is MOPITT?
It's an instrument that went into space aboard NASA's *Terra* satellite and the acronym stands for Measurement of Pollution in the Troposphere. Launched in the spring of 2000, MOPITT is now taking measurements to determine the amount of carbon monoxide and methane present in the layer of the atmosphere closest to the Earth (from the surface to about 6 to ten km up). The portion of the atmosphere not only holds the oxygen we need to breathe, it also distributes the gases that surround us and filters out harmful ultraviolet radiation. MOPITT will not only monitor the health of this portion of the atmosphere, it will warn us if there are any sudden or serious changes.

MOPITT was designed and financed by Canada, but scientists from around the world with have access to its data for the five years that the instrument will operate.

What are we going to do with SCISAT-1?
SCISAT-1 is Canada's first scientific satellite since 1971 (when we launched ISIS II, which studied the upper section of the ionosphere). Its primary scientific mission will be the Atmospheric Chemistry Experiments, designed to "measure and understand the chemical processes that control the distribution of ozone in high altitudes in the Earth's atmosphere." Scientists have been measuring ozone in the atmosphere over Canada since the 1930s, but the depletion of the layer during the last 20 years has lead to increased concern over the health hazards this poses to Canadians. SCISAT-1 will circle the Earth 15 times each day, witnessing 30 sunrises and sunsets.

And: Did you know... we have an observatory in Hawaii?
The Canada-France-Hawaii Telescope (CFHT) celebrated its 21st anniversary in 2000. CFHT headquarters are in Wiamea and the actual telescope operates at the summit of Mauna Kea, a 4,200 meter, dormant volcano located on the island of Hawaii. Canada (through the National Research Council) and France each contribute about 45 percent of the annual budget, with the University of Hawaii making up the difference. The CFHT has state-of-the-art telescopes and equipment that can produce images that rival those from the Hubble Space Telescope. (You can visit the facility at http://www.cfht.hawaii.edu/.)

2001: A Space Reality

*I*n 1968, renowned producer and director Stanley Kubrick released the movie **2001: A Space Odyssey**. *The film was based on a short story by Arthur C. Clark entitled "The Sentinel." What did* **2001** *predict? People living in a space station, a colony on the moon, regular shuttles into space and a manned mission to Jupiter. And what do we have in 2001? A crew living in a space station, regular shuttles into space (the US space shuttle fleet celebrated its 100th flight with the November 2000 mission to the ISS), and active missions to the Sun (***Ulysses***), Mars (**Global Surveyor**), Jupiter (**Galileo**), Saturn (**Cassini**) and the outer planets and beyond our solar system (**Voyager**).*

International Space Station (ISS)

Sixteen countries have been contributing to the International Space Station (ISS), a project that first got serious attention (and funding) in 1993. That project is now a reality that orbits 400 km above the Earth, at an inclination of 51.6° to the equator.

The actual assembly of the ISS began in December 1998, when the first stage—the Functional Cargo Block—was launched from Kazakstan. That first launch put the propulsion, command and control systems in place with the Zarya module. A six-man crew went up in December 1998 to do some assembly of the space station in orbit—they added the Unity module. In June 1999, tools and a crane were added to assist in construction. On May 19, 2000 a seven-member crew began to ready the space station for residents. On July 25, 2000 the third big component of the station, Zvezda, docked with the ISS. A NASA mission in mid-September took supplies up after a Russian supply ship with oxygen generators, toilet components and other gear had made Zvezda habitable. The September NASA mission installed equipment such as power and data cables as well as bringing supplies. Crew members also tested air filters and heaters aboard the unit. The first permanent crew (two Russians and an American) were scheduled to begin a five-month residence in early November 2000.

Canada's Marc Garneau was scheduled to go to the ISS at the end of November to install solar panels, and Col. Chris Hadfield will visit the ISS in Spring 2001 to perform a space walk (the first for a Canadian astronaut) and install a robotic arm for use in assembly and maintenance. The expected completion date for the station is in 2005.

Other contributions to the project include a pressurized lab and logistics transport vehicles (European Space Agency); a lab with "attached exposed facility" and logistics transport vehicles (Japan); and research modules, a service module with its own life support and habitation system, a science power platform to supply electrical power, more logistics transport vehicles and a Soyuz spacecraft for emergency crew return and transfer (Russia).

When completed, the station will weigh nearly 454,000 kg. It will be 108.5 m by 88 m and it will be able to accommodate up to seven people at a time. Its orbit was chosen because it could be reached by launch vehicles from any of the international partners. The orbit also provides an observation position that covers 85 percent of the globe and 95 percent of the Earth's population.

The ISS was originally planned to establish a permanent laboratory where gravity, temperature and air pressure could be manipulated to create conditions that would be impossible to achieve in Earth-bound labs. The site will be used for testing scientific and engineering hypotheses, and for conducting research in biology, chemistry, physics, ecology and medicine. The space station will also serve as a test site for new technologies for advanced industrial materials, medical research and new communications technology.

The participants in the ISS program are the United States; Canada; European Space Agency partners Belgium, Denmark, France, Germany, Italy, the Netherlands, Norway, Spain, Sweden, Switzerland, and the United Kingdom; plus Japan, Russia and Brazil. Each partner will contribute astronauts to crew the finished station, and have access to its labs for research and experiments.

The International Space Station is the largest scientific cooperative program in history. For more news and information, visit NASA at http://www.nasa.gov/station/.

Some Astronomical Terms

Asteroid Any of the thousands of small, rocky objects that orbit the Sun. Some pass closer to the Sun than Earth does and others have orbits that take them well beyond Jupiter. The largest asteroid is one called Ceres.

Big Bang The primeval explosion that most astronomers think gave rise to the universe as we see it today, in which clusters of galaxies are moving apart from one another. Astronomers calculate the Big Bang happened about 15 to 20 billion years ago.

Black Hole An object whose gravitational pull is so strong that—within a certain distance of it— nothing can escape, not even light. Black holes are thought to result from the collapse of certain very massive stars, but other kinds have been postulated as well: **mini black holes**, for example, which might have been formed in the turbulence shortly after the Big Bang. **Supermassive black holes**—with masses millions of times the Sun's—may exist in the cores of large galaxies.

Comet A small chunk of ice, dust and rocky material (a few kilometres across) which, when it comes close enough to the Sun, can develop a tenuous "tail." The tail of a comet is made of gas and dust that have been driven off the comet's surface by the Sun's energy. The tail always points away from the Sun (no matter in what direction the comet is moving).

Eclipse The blocking of all or part of the light from one object by another.

Galaxy A large assemblage of stars (and sometimes interstellar gas and dust), typically containing millions to hundreds of billions of member stars. A galaxy is held together by the gravitational attraction of its member stars (and other material) to one another.

Light-Year The distance light travels in one year in a vacuum. Since light travels at a speed of about 300 000 km per second, a light-year is roughly 9.5 trillion km long.

Magnitude A way of expressing the brightness of astronomical objects, inherited from the Greeks. In the magnitude system, a lower number indicates a brighter object (for example, a 1st-magnitude star is brighter than a 3rd-magnitude star). Each step in magnitude corresponds to a brightness difference of about 2.5. Stars of the 6th magnitude are the faintest the unaided human eye can see.

Meteor A bit of solid debris from space, burning up in the Earth's atmosphere because of friction with the air. Before entering Earth's atmosphere, the body is called a meteoroid. If any of the object survives its fiery passage through the air, the parts that hit the ground are called **meteorites**.

Milky Way Galaxy A spiral galaxy, with a disk approximately 100 000 light-years across, containing roughly 400 billion stars. Our Sun is in the disk about two-thirds of the way from the centre. It takes about 200 million years to orbit the centre of the Milky Way once.

Neutron Star A crushed remnant left over when a very massive star explodes. Some neutron stars are known to spin very rapidly, at least at the beginning, and can be detected as **pulsars**: rapidly flashing sources of radio radiation or visible light. The pulses are produced by the spinning of a neutron star, much as a lighthouse beacon appears to flash off, on and off.

Nova A star that abruptly and temporarily increases its brightness by a factor of hundreds of thousands.

Orbit The path of one body around another (such as the Moon around the Earth) or around the centre of gravity of a number of objects (such as the Sun's 200-million-year path around the centre of our galaxy).

Planet A major object that orbits around a star.

Quasar One of a class of very distant (typically billions of light years away), extremely bright, and very small objects. Quasar means "quasi-star"— that is, something that looks like a star but can't actually be a star.

Red Giant A very large distended, and relatively cool star in the final stages of its life.

Solar System The Sun and all things orbiting it, including the nine major planets, their satellites, and all the asteroids and comets.

Supernova An explosion that marks the end of a very massive star's life. When it occurs, the star can outshine all the other stars in a galaxy in total for several days, and may leave behind a crushed core (perhaps a neutron star or a black hole).

White Dwarf The collapsed remnant of a relatively low-mass star (roughly one and a half times the Sun's mass and less), which has exhausted the fuel for its nuclear reactions and shines only by radiating its stored up heat.

Source: *The Astronomical Society of the Pacific, San Francisco, CA*

Are There Other Earth-like Planets?

In 2000, much of the news in astronomy was about the discovery of new planets outside our solar system. By August, the total was up to 44, but astronomers were confident that there were more. Many of these planets appear to be about the size of Jupiter, many of them were described as "hot" or else have orbits that send them so close and then so far away from their star that habitation would be impossible. However, there *are* other stars like our sun—Upsilon Andromedae is one that has multiple planets. (All of which appear to be massive gas giants.) Another is Epsilon Eridani, which is located only 10 light years away from us and has at least one planet.

The technology used to detect these new planets is becoming more and more sophisticated, which is why astronomers are suddenly finding so many more of these orbiting bodies. What else is in store?

■ Terrestrial Planet Finder (TPF)

The TPF is an ambitious NASA-sponsored program that will study planets from their formation and development in the disks of dust and gas around newly created or embryonic stars, as well as existing planets that can be assessed for the possibility of life forms. The TPF will use both space telescopes with high sensitivity and an interferometer. The combined technology will reduce the glare of the parent stars by a factor of more than one-hundred-thousand, thus enabling us to see planetary systems up to 50 light years away—and take pictures.

Some of the technology that is required by the TPF is still under development. The interferometer that needs to be built is expected to be as long as a football field. If a longer one is required, NASA may use several telescopes on spacecraft flying in a precise formation to form a "virtual" interferometer. The projected launch date of the TPF is 2010 or 2011 and the expected end date is sometime beyond 2015.

■ What will they find?

With the huge orbiting telescope—which should be able to provide images 100 times clearer than those from the Hubble Space Telescope—astronomers expect to examine 1,000 of our closest star neighbours. They also expect to be able to measure the temperature, size and placement of planets as small as the Earth—something that was impossible before. They will be able to establish whether or not those planets exist in a "habitable zone"—that is whether their orbit keeps them at a relatively even temperature. (Scientists look for the existence of water and whether or not the temperature would allow it to be liquid.) Chemists and biologists will also be using the TPF; the system's spectroscopy will tell them the relative amounts of atmospheric gasses (carbon dioxide, water vapour, methane and ozone). If there is carbon dioxide, it means that the planet would have an atmosphere, while an ozone band would indicate the existence of oxygen. These are all indications of whether a planet could support life forms (or if it does already).

■ Why the TPF?

Technologies such as the Space Interferometery Mission can indirectly detect the existence of planets of Earth-size or larger, but better technology is needed to actually assess what's out there. In the years before the launch of TPF, ground and space-based observatories will be taking a census of planets, setting the stage for analysis of the findings by the more powerful instruments that will be in place by then.

In addition to studying the planets, the TPF will also allow scientists to study other mysteries in the universe(like the black hole at the centre of the Milky Way. For more information visit: http://tpf.jpl.nasa.gov or http://origins.jpl.nasa.gov

Phases of the Moon, 2001

(Eastern Standard Time)

New Moon	First Quarter	Full Moon	Last Quarter
Jan 24–8:07 am	Jan 2–5:31 pm	Jan 9–3:24 pm	Jan 16–7:35 am
Feb 23–3:21 am	Feb 1–9:02 am	Feb 8–2:12 am	Feb 14–10:23 pm
Mar 24–8:21 pm	Mar 2–9:03 pm	Mar 9–12:23 pm	Mar 16–3:45 pm
Apr 23–10:26 am	Apr 1–5:49 am	Apr 7–10:22 pm	Apr 15–10:31 am
May 22–9:46 pm	Apr 30–12:08 pm	May 7–8:53 am	May 15–5:11 am
June 21–6:58 am	May 29–5:09 pm	June 5–8:39 pm	June 14–10:28 pm
July 20–2:44 pm	June 27–10:20 pm	July 5–10:04 am	July 13–1:45 pm
Aug 18–9:55 pm	July 27–5:08 am	Aug 4–12:56 am	Aug 12–2:53 am
Sept 17–5:27 am	Aug 25–2:55 pm	Sept 2–4:43 pm	Sept 10–1:59 pm
Oct 16–2:23 pm	Sept 24–4:31 am	Oct 2–8:49 am	Oct 9–11:20 pm
Nov 15–1:40 am	Oct 24–9:58 pm	Nov 1–12:41 am	Nov 8–7:21 am
Dec 14–3:47 pm	Nov 22–6:21 pm	Nov 30–3:49 pm	Dec 7–2:52 pm
	Dec 22–3:56 pm	Dec 30–5:40 am	

Daylight Saving Time (Summer Time) is kept in most places across Canada. It starts at 2 a.m. on Sunday, April 1, 2001 when clocks go forward one hour. Clocks return to Standard Time at 2 a.m. on Sunday, October 28 when clocks go back one hour. To get wristwatch time in the Eastern Time Zone between April 1 and October 28 *add* one hour to the times listed.

Across Canada, there are six Standard Time Zones. To adjust to wristwatch time in another time zone, add or subtract the following to the times listed in the table: Newfoundland (+1hr 30m), Atlantic (+1hr), Central (-1hr), Mountain (-2hr), Pacific (-3hr).

Organizations

Canadian Astronomical Society:
An organization of professional astronomers. Contact: Serge Demers, CASCA Secretary, Département de Physique, Université de Montréal, Montreal, Quebec H3C 3J7.
Business office: R. Hayes
Dept. of Physics, Queen's University,
Kingston, ON K7L 3N6
Tel: (613) 533-6000 x74431; Fax: (613) 533-6463
Web site: http://www.casca.ca

Royal Astronomical Society of Canada (RASC):
The Society is an organization of amateur and professional astronomers open to anyone interested in astronomy. The Society publishes the annual *Observer's Handbook* as well as other publications. It has over 3 000 members in 23 clubs across Canada. National Headquarters is located at 136 Dupont Street, Toronto, Ontario M5R 1V2 Tel: (416) 924-7973
Web site: http://www.rasc.ca

It Came From Outer Space

*I*n September 2000, a UK report on Near-Earth Objects (NEOs) noted that although a major asteroid only hits the Earth once every 100,000 years, we should be prepared.

Space debris rains down regularly: about 200 tonnes of ice, dust and tiny meteorites enter the Earth's atmosphere daily; every few days a meteoroid disintegrates above. About once a century, a much larger object—up to 50 m wide—hits the Earth. (The last one was in 1908 when an asteroid exploded 10 km up over Siberia. The force of the explosion decimated area wildlife and flattened trees.) After years of speculation, a Canadian geologist found a crater off the coast of Mexico that suggests a 15-km-wide asteroid hit the Earth about 65 million years ago; the resulting destruction and dust eradicated 65 percent of existing animal species (including dinosaurs). There are 160 big asteroid craters in the world; 26 are in Canada.

There is a team out there watching for asteroids: members of a worldwide group who swap data about NEOs, speeds and trajectories. There are 182 catalogued asteroids under scrutiny because they may cross our orbit in a significant way and they are big enough to do some damage.

Events in the 2001 Sky

January

Comet 41P/Tuttle-Giacombini-Kresak at perihelion on January 6—156.9 million km from the Sun. It will be at its peak brightness at the beginning of 2001. Although it will be south of the celestial equator, it will be north of the Sun, therefore visibility in the Northern hemisphere is favoured.

Mid-January to late February, a favourable appearance of Mercury in low WSW, at far lower right of Venus (SW). Four planets (Venus SW, Jupiter ESE, Saturn ESE, Mercury WSW) visible at once.

- 3   Earth at perihelion (closest point to sun for year)—146.5 million km.
- 3   Peak of Quadrantid meteor shower (3:28 p.m. EST).
- 9-10   Total lunar eclipse visible from northeastern Canada and US. (See Eclipses page 565)

February

Comet 24P/Schaumasse will reach perihelion May 2, 2001—179.4 million km. It is expected to become visible in the northern hemisphere in February or March, with peak brightness in May.

March

Venus (WSW) is at its most brilliant this month.

- 20   Sun reaches the March (or vernal) equinox at 8:27 a.m. EST. First day of spring in northern hemisphere.

April

- 1   Daylight Savings Time begins at 2 a.m.; clocks are advanced by one hour.
- 21   Peak of Lyrid meteor shower at 6:08 p.m. EDT.

May

Comet C/2000 OF8 (Spacewatch) will reach peak brightness in May and June, but is best placed for observers in the southern hemisphere. (It will be at perihelion on August 5—324.4 million km.)

Mercury passes Saturn (setting WNW) on May 6 and Jupiter (low WNW) on May 16

- 4   Peak of Eta Aquarid meteor shower at 11:20 p.m. EDT. (Moonlight interference)

June

- 13   Mars (low SE) is visible throughout the night
- 20   Sun reaches June solstice at 3:34 a.m. EDT. Official start of summer in northern hemisphere.
- 21   Total solar eclipse visible in the southern hemisphere. (See Eclipses page 565)

July

- 4   Earth at aphelion (furthest point from sun for year)—152.5 million kilometres.
- 5   Partial lunar eclipse visible from Australia, southeast Asia and the western Pacific region. (See Eclipses page 565)
- 28   Peak of delta-Aquarids meteor shower at 11:36 p.m. EDT (No interference from the moon)

August

- 11   Uranus at opposition
- 12   Peak of Perseid meteor shower at 4:04 a.m. EDT. (No interference from the moon.)

September

- 22   Sun reaches the September equinox at 7:01 p.m. EDT. Official start of the autumn season in the northern hemisphere.

October

- 21   Peak of Orion meteor shower at 7:24 a.m. EDT
- 28   Standard Time begins. Clocks go back one hour at 2 a.m.

November

- 17   Peak of Leonid meteor shower at 10:08 a.m. EST.

December

- 3   Saturn (ENE) is visible throughout the night.
- 13   Peak of Geminid meteor shower at 7:28 a.m. EST.
- 14   Partial solar eclipse: annular eclipse. Late phases may be visible in southern Canada (See Eclipses, page 565)
- 21   The Sun reaches the December solstice at 2:19 p.m. EST. The winter season officially begins in the Northern Hemisphere.
- 30   Partial penumbral lunar eclipse across North America. (See Eclipses page 565)
- 31   Jupiter (rising ENE) is visible throughout the night.

Eclipses in 2001

2001 features two eclipses of the Sun and three eclipses of the Moon. Of the five, the January 9 total lunar eclipse and the December 30 partial lunar eclipse are the ones with the best visibility for North American observers.

January 9-10
Total Lunar Eclipse: This eclipse will only be visible in its final phases as the moon rises on the evening of December 9th, and then only to viewers in northeastern Canada and the US. Mid-eclipse is at 2:20 p.m. with the eclipse waning with the day. The best viewing will be in Europe, Africa and Asia. (Australians will be able to watch its progress before January 10 dawns.) No equipment is needed to observe this event.

June 21
Total Solar Eclipse: The only total solar eclipse of the year will take place in the southern hemisphere, visible in Angola, Zambia, Zimbabwe, Mozambique and southern Madagascar. The five-minute period of maximum darkness will be visible at sea, about 1,100 km west of Angola.

July 5
Partial Lunar Eclipse: The second lunar eclipse of the year is a partial one, only visible in Australia, southeast Asia and the western Pacific region.

December 14
Partial Solar Eclipse: This will be an annular (ring-shaped) eclipse that will be visible mostly over the Pacific Ocean. Costa Ricans and Nicaraguans will see it around 4:30 in the afternoon. Late phases may be visible in southern Canada.

December 30
Partial Lunar Eclipse: The final eclipse of the year is considered to be a "deep penumbral" eclipse that will be visible across North America. A subtle shading will be detectable across the southern part of the moon around mid-eclipse—4:30 a.m. EDT.

WARNING: SPECIAL PRECAUTIONS MUST BE TAKEN TO OBSERVE THE SUN AT ALL TIMES. AT NO TIME DURING A PARTIAL SOLAR ECLIPSE CAN THE SUN BE OBSERVED SAFELY WITH THE UNPROTECTED HUMAN EYE.

Space Information on the World Wide Web

NASA Home Page *http://www.nasa.gov*
NASA provides links to the massive amount of information the agency has placed on the Web, as well as links to other space-related sites in the United States and other countries.

Space Telescope Science Institute *http://www.stsci.edu*
This is the site for the Hubble Telescope.

Cassini Mission to Saturn: *http://www.jpl.nasa.gov/cassini/*
Images, mission status, student activities.

Canadian Space Agency *(see page 566)* has a home page dedicated to our Space Science Program, including an overview that goes back to our first observatory in 1839, and details of current work being done in Space Life Sciences, Atmospheric Sciences, Space Astronomy, Microgravity Sciences and Solar Terrestrial Relations. Review news releases, research opportunities, the special student section or the image gallery. Each program page includes links to major projects and advisory committees (visit the Meteorite and Impacts Advisory Committee) and newsletters. The Microgravity site includes a guide to Microgravity Science. *http://www.science.sp-agency.ca* is the home of the Space Science Program.

The Canadian Space Agency (CSA)

The CSA was created by an act of Parliament on December 14, 1990; its mission is to "promote the peaceful use and development of space for the social and economic benefit of Canadians." Its more immediate job is to co-ordinate Canada's space programs and manage our space-related activities.

Canadian experience in space predates the creation of the CSA: Canadians designed and built the first Canadian satellite in time for a launch on Sept. 9, 1962. *Alouette I* made us the third country in space (after Russia and the US), and was the first satellite to return useful information on the ionosphere, (the layer of the upper atmosphere that affects long-distance radio transmissions).

In 1972, Canada launched *Anik A1* and became the first country to have a commercial communications satellite network. It made nation-wide, real-time television possible. It also brought reliable telephone service to the North for the first time. *Anik E-2* still provides services to television networks and telephone systems, and facilitates activities such as the transmission of newspaper copy to five printing plants across the country.

In 1976, Canada and the United States launched a joint venture communications satellite, *Hermes*, which became the prototype for direct broadcast satellites. In 1981, the Canadian-designed and built Remote Manipulator System or CANADARM, was used on the Space Shuttle *Colombia*. Operated by two hand controls from the comfort of the space shuttle's cabin, the Canadarm allows astronauts to take satellites from the cargo bay and position them in space; it is also designed to snare satellites already in orbit and place them into the cargo bay for a return to Earth.

The Canadian Astronaut Program has been in operation since 1983; see page 567 for details.

Canada and the International Space Station: Canada's contribution is the Mobile Servicing System (MSS), consisting of equipment and facilities on the ISS and on the ground. A very sophisticated "space arm" is part of this system, as is a robotic hand (known formally as a Special Purpose Dexterous Manipulator or SPDM). These pieces and the CANADARM will be used for assembly and maintenance tasks on the space station. The arm, together with the hand, can manipulate delicate objects; the CANADARM can work with large objects. The CSA is working on a Canadian Space Vision System to assist those using the equipment. Ground support for the devices will be at CSA headquarters in St. Hubert, Quebec. Training, logistics support and other resources will be used to monitor the condition of the equipment and train personnel to use it.

RadarSat, launched in 1995, is the country's first Earth Observation satellite. This remote sensing satellite is in a near-polar orbit 800 km above the Earth. RadarSat produces images of the Earth's surface using a microwave Synthetic Aperture Radar (SAR) system. (Similar devices use optical sensors; unlike them, Radarsat can function night or day, and through clouds, fog or smoke.)

RadarSat II, to be launched in 2002, will be an advanced SAR satellite. Personnel in fields as diverse as ice navigation, cartography, geological exploration, maritime surveillance, disaster relief operations, and agriculture and forestry surveillance will be able to use the data images as the markets served by RadarSat I expand. Visit http://www.space.gc.ca/about/csagla/earthenvir/ for updates on Canada's Earth Observation technology.

Canadian Space Agency

Canadian Space Agency (CSA) http://www.space.gc.ca
Information on Canada's contribution to space research and Canada's astronauts, including regular updates on the International Space Station.

Canadian Astronaut Office http://www.space.gc.ca/csa_sectors/human_presence

Canada's Astronauts

The Canadian Astronaut Program began in 1983 when Canada was invited to send an astronaut on the U.S. space shuttle. A permanent corps of Canadian astronauts who could co-ordinate and conduct Canadian experiments in space was created as a result.

The first recruiting drive for the astronaut program resulted in 4,300 applications. Six were successful. In 1992, a second invitation for recruits went out and another 5,000 applications poured in. Four more candidates were selected, based on a combination of academic background, professional experience, health and communication skills.

The first Canadian astronaut to fly in space was **Dr. Marc Garneau**. He conducted a set of experiments in space science, space technology, and life sciences during Mission 41-G, from October 5-13, 1984, aboard the Space Shuttle *Challenger*. **Dr. Steve MacLean** flew on the Space Shuttle mission STS-52, aboard *Columbia*, from October 22 to November 1, 1992, and conducted a second set of these experiments.

January 22-30, 1992, **Dr. Roberta Bondar** flew aboard *Discovery* during Mission STS-42. She served as the prime Canadian Payload Specialist for the first International Microgravity Laboratory mission; she conducted more than 43 experiments on behalf of 13 countries.

In November 1995, **Col. Chris Hadfield** was the first Canadian Mission Specialist to participate in a Space Shuttle mission as a crew member and the first Canadian on board the Russian Space Station *Mir* when he flew aboard *Atlantis* during Mission STS-74, from November 12-20, 1995.

In May 1996, **Dr. Marc Garneau** made his second space flight, as a Mission Specialist aboard Space Shuttle *Endeavor*. This Mission, STS-77, was a rendezvous and proximity mission using the SPARTAN-207 satellite. Once again, the CANADARM played a large role in this run-up to the assembly of the International Space Station (ISS). This mission also carried the commercial SPACEHAB module and two Canadian experiments, one in material processing and one in biology.

Dr. Robert Thirsk flew as a Payload Specialist on Mission STS-78, also known as the Life and Microgravity Spacelab flight, launched on June 20, 1996. During the 17-day mission, Dr. Thirsk conducted a series of 43 life and microgravity experiments aboard the Spacelab—a fully-equipped international space laboratory carried in the Shuttle's cargo bay.

On August 7, 1997, **Bjarni Tryggvason** was Payload Specialist for flight on STS-85. He tested the Microgravity Vibration Isolation Mount (MIM) and performing material science and fluid physics experiments designed to examine sensitivity to spacecraft vibrations. This work was directed at developing better understanding of the need for systems such as the MIM on the International Space Station (ISS) and on the effect of vibrations on the many experiments to be performed on the ISS.

The CSA's **Dr. Dave Williams** was one of seven astronauts to participate in the STS-90 mission on board the Space Shuttle *Columbia* from April 17 to May 3, 1998. Dr. Williams and his fellow crew members conducted a total of 26 life science experiments designed to study the effects of microgravity on the brain and parts of the central nervous system.

During this mission Williams served as official crew medical officer. On July 21, 1998, Dr. Williams was appointed Director of the Space and Life Sciences Directorate at NASA's Johnson Space Centre in Houston.

In August 1996, **Julie Payette** began mission specialist training at the Johnson Space Centre, working for the Astronaut Office's Robotics branch. Initial astronaut training was completed in April 1999; Payette visited the ISS in May 1999 as part of STS-96, a 10-day logistics and resupply mission.

Dr. Marc Garneau was scheduled to fly his third mission on November 30, 2000. He will be installing solar panels for the ISS. **Col. Chris Hadfield** will return to space in April 2001 to install a Remote Manipulator System and become the first Canadian to take a space walk.

Source: *Canadian Space Agency* http://www.space.gc.ca

Constellations

Astronomers have divided the sky into 88 well-defined areas called constellations. They are named after people, animals or objects. The pattern of bright stars in some constellations (such as Orion or Scorpius) resembles the person, animal, or object they are named after but in most constellations it is difficult to see a pattern among the stars. The largest constellation is Hydrus, followed by Virgo and Ursa Major. The smallest is Crux.

Constellation	Meaning
Andromeda	Daughter of Cassiopeia
Antlia	The Air Pump
Apus	Bird of Paradise
Aquarius	The Water-bearer
Aquila	The Eagle
Ara	The Altar
Aries	The Ram
Auriga	The Charioteer
Bootes	The Herdsman
Caelum	The Chisel
Camelopardalis	The Giraffe
Cancer	The Crab
Canes Venatici	The Hunting Dogs
Canis Major	The Big Dog
Canis Minor	The Little Dog
Capricornus	The Horned Goat
Carina	The Keel
Cassiopeia	The Queen
Centaurus	The Centaur
Cepheus	The King
Cetus	The Whale
Chamaeleon	The Chameleon
Circinus	The Compasses
Columba	The Dove
Coma Berenices	Berenice's Hair
Corona Australis	The Southern Crown
Corona Borealis	The Northern Crown
Corvus	The Crow
Crater	The Cup
Crux	The Cross
Cygnus	The Swan
Delphinus	The Dolphin
Dorado	The Goldfish
Draco	The Dragon
Equuleus	The Little Horse
Eridanus	A River
Fornax	The Furnace
Gemini	The Twins
Grus	The Crane (bird)
Hercules	The Son of Zeus
Horologium	The Clock
Hydra	The Water Snake (f)
Hydrus	The Water Snake (m)
Indus	The Indian
Lacerta	The Lizard
Leo	The Lion
Leo Minor	The Little Lion
Lepus	The Hare
Libra	The Balance
Lupus	The Wolf
Lynx	The Lynx
Lyra	The Lyre
Mensa	Table Mountain
Microscopium	The Microscope
Monoceros	The Unicorn
Musca	The Fly
Norma	The Square
Octans	The Octant
Ophiuchus	The Serpent-bearer
Orion	The Hunter
Pavo	The Peacock
Pegasus	The Winged Horse
Perseus	Rescuer of Andromeda
Phoenix	The Phoenix
Pictor	The Painter
Pisces	The Fishes
Piscis Austrinus	The Southern Fish
Puppis	The Stern
Pyxis	The Compass
Reticulum	The Reticle
Sagitta	The Arrow
Sagittarius	The Archer
Scorpius	The Scorpion
Sculptor	The Sculptor
Scutum	The Shield
Serpens	The Serpent
Sextans	The Sextant
Taurus	The Bull
Telescopium	The Telescope
Triangulum	The Triangle
Triangulum Australe	The Southern Triangle
Tucana	The Toucan
Ursa Major	The Great Bear [1]
Ursa Minor	The Little Bear [2]
Vela	The Sails
Virgo	The Maiden
Volans	The Flying Fish
Vulpecula	The Fox

(1) Commonly known as the Big Dipper. (2) Commonly known as The Little Dipper.

Observatories in Canada

Maritime Region:

☐ **Burke-Gaffney Observatory**

Department of Astronomy and Physics, Saint Mary's University, Halifax, NS B3H 3C3. Open: Nov. to Mar. at 7 pm and April to June at 9 pm, every 1st and 3rd Sat. From June to Sept. open every Sat. Tel: (902) 496-8257. Web site: http://mnbsun.stmarys.ca/bgo/bgo.html

☐ **University of New Brunswick**

Brydon Jack Observatory Museum, P.O. Box 4400, Fredericton, NB E3A 5A3. Oldest observatory in Canada, 1851. No charge. Summer (by appointment).

Central Canada:

☐ **David Dunlap Observatory**

University of Toronto, P.O. Box 360, Richmond Hill, Ont. L4C 4Y6. Open Wednesday mornings from 10 to 11:30 am. From April to Sept. Open also on Saturday evenings. Reservations required. Tel: (905) 884-2112.

Astronomy and Space

☐ **Helen B. Hogg Observatory**
Canada Science and Technology Museum. 1867 St. Laurent Blvd. Ottawa, Ont. K1G 5A3. Tel: (613) 991-3044.

☐ **Hume Cronyn Memorial Observatory**
University of Western Ontario, London, Ont. N6A 3K7. Late Oct. to early April by reservation. From June to Aug. on Saturday evenings at 8:30 pm. Tel: (519) 661-3183. Web site: phobos.astro.uwo.ca/~dfgray/pub-nit.html.

☐ **Science North Solar Observatory** 100 Ramsey Lake Rd., Sudbury, Ont. P3A 2K3. Viewing of the solar spectrum and the Sun in hydrogen-alpha and white light in a darkened theatre. Open most days. Tel: (705) 522-3701.

Western Canada:

☐ **Climenhaga Observatory**
Dept. of Physics and Astronomy, University of Victoria, P.O. Box 3055 Stn Csc, Victoria, BC V8W 3P6. Tel: (250) 721-7700. Open daily. Web site: http://astrowww.phys.uvic.ca/climenhaga/obs/telescope.html

☐ **Rothney Astrophysical Observatory**
Physics and Astronomy Dept., University of Calgary, Calgary, Alta. T2N 1N4. Tel: (403) 220-5385. Web site: http://www.ucalgary.ca/~milone/rao.html.

☐ **Dominion Astrophysical Observatory** RR #5, 5071 West Saanich Rd., Victoria, BC V8X 4M6. Open throughout the year Mon. to Fri. 9:15 am to 4:30 pm. In summer, May to Aug., open from 9:00 am until 8 pm Sun. to Fri., as well as on Sat from 9:30 am to 11:00 pm.

☐ **Dominion Radio Astrophysical Observatory**
P.O. Box 248, Penticton, BC V2A 6K3. Conducted tours. Sun., July–Aug. only, 2–5 pm. Visitors' centre open year-round during daytime. Tel: (250) 493-2277.

☐ **H.R. Macmillan Planetarium and Gordon Southam Observatory**
1100 Chestnut St., Vancouver, B.C. V6J 3J9. Open Fri.-Sun., and statutory holidays 12 pm -5 pm and 7 pm-11 pm, weather and volunteer staff permitting. Tel: (604) 763-4431.

☐ **Devon Observatory** Dept. of Physics, University of Alberta, Edmonton, Alta T6G 2J1.

☐ **University of Saskatchewan Observatory**
108 Wiggins Road, Saskatoon, Sask. S7N 5E6. Tel: (306) 966-6434.

☐ **University of British Columbia Observatory**
2219 Main Mall, Van., BC V6T 1W5. Free public observing on clear Sat. eve. Tel: (604) 224-6186 (observing) or (604) 228-2802 (tours).

Planetariums

Maritime Region:

☐ **Burke-Gaffney Planetarium**
Saint Mary's University, Department of Astronomy, Halifax, NS B3H 3C3.

☐ **The Halifax Planetarium**
The education section of the Nova Scotia Museum of Natural History. 1747 Summer St., Halifax, NS B3H 3A6. Tel: (902) 424-7370. Located in the Sir James Dunn Building, Dalhousie Univeristy. The education section of the Nova Scotia Museum of Natural History. Open on Tuesday evenings at 7 pm. Free. Tel: (902) 424-7353.

Central Canada:

☐ **Doran Planetarium**
Laurentian University, Ramsey Lake Rd., Sudbury, Ont. P3E 2C6. Tel: (705) 675-1151, ext. 2222. Web site: http://www.laurentian.ca/.

☐ **Planetarium de Montréal** 1000 St. Jacques St. W., Montreal, Que. H3C 1G7. Tel: (514) 872-4530. Live shows in French and English. Open daily. Web site: http://www.planetarium.montreal.qc.ca/.

☐ **McLaughlin Planetarium**
Royal Ontario Museum: 100 Queen's Park, Toronto, Ont. M5S 2C6. Tel: (416) 586-5549 (switchboard). On-going astronomy program using STARLAB planetariums for school and public programming only. Phone (416) 586-5801 for information. Recorded astronomy information line (416) 586-5736.

☐ **William J. McCallion Planetarium**
Department of Physics and Astronomy, McMaster University, 1280 Main Street, Hamilton, ON L8S 4M1. Tel: (905) 525-9140.

Western Canada:

☐ **Calgary Centennial Planetarium**
Alberta Science Centre, 701-11 St. S.W., P.O. Box 2100, Stn. M. Calgary, Alta. T2P 2M5. Tel: (403) 221-3700.

☐ **Edmonton Space Sciences Centre**
Coronation Park, 1121-142 St., Edmonton. Alta T5M 4A1. Tel: (780) 452-9100 or (780) 451-3344. Features planetarium Star Theatre, IMAX film theatre, exhibit galleries, telescope shop and bookstore. Open daily.

☐ **H.R. MacMillan Planetarium**
1100 Chestnut St., Vancouver, B.C. V6J 3J9. Tel: (604) 738-7827.Web site: http://pacific-space-centre.bc.ca/.

☐ **Manitoba Planetarium**
Museum of Man and Nature. 190 Rupert Ave., Winnipeg, Man. R3B 0N2. Tel: (204) 956-2830 (switchboard). Shows daily except some Mondays. Museum gift shop has scientific books and equipment. Web site: http://portal.mbnet.mb.ca/Manitoba Museum. Also worth a visit is the section on the Manitoba Centre for UFO Studies.

EARTH SCIENCES

The earth sciences include **geology** (the study of earth's origin and composition), **oceanography** (the study of ocean water, currents, life-forms and the ocean floor), **paleontology** (the study of fossils and ancient life-forms), and **meteorology** (the study of earth's atmosphere, including weather and climate). This section includes material on geology and paleontology. Meteorology can be found in the section on Climate (see pages 9–23).

The Geological Survey of Canada

The Geological Survey of Canada (GSC) is Canada's first scientific agency, and one of the first of its kind in the world. The agency was created to survey and map mineral deposits in Canada's nearly 1 million square kilometres of land and freshwater lakes, and more than 6 million square kilometres of coastal boundaries.

The Survey began life in Montreal in 1842. Under the first director William Edmond Logan, a Canadian businessman turned geologist, its initial task was a search for coal, the main industrial fuel at the time. The search, throughout Upper and Lower Canada, was unsuccessful, but Logan did find mineable deposits of copper and other metallic minerals.

Soon Survey geologists were undertaking expeditions westward. In the 1880s another director, George Mercer Dawson, became a noted ethnologist in Western Canada, as well as pioneer geologist. His reports included observations of the Haida people of British Columbia. During his expeditions he took many photographs of settlements and totem poles, capturing a glimpse of a vanishing landscape.

In 1992 the Geological Survey marked its 150th anniversary. While the task of mapping Canada's geology remains its central focus, the computerized Survey of the 1990s is very different from the one started by Sir William Logan. The Survey now undertakes an ever-expanding range of research—from exploring questions related to global change to those concerning natural hazards such as earthquakes, landslides, volcanoes, floods and ground instability.

For more information on the Geological Survey and its programs, contact: Communications Office, Geological Survey of Canada, 601 Booth Street, Ottawa, Ontario K1A OE5.

Geological Cyberspace Connections

The Web address http://www.nrcan.gc.ca will get you to Natural Resources Canada's web site; add /gsc and you will find the Geoscience Information Centre. http://www.atlas.gc.ca will take you to the National Atlas of Canada Online, where the 6th edition of The National Atlas of Canada *is available.*

EarthNet is a web site developed by the Atlantic Geoscience Society, the Canadian Geological Foundation, Canada's Geoscience Education Network, the Canadian Society of Petroleum Geologists and the Geological Survey of Canada. EarthNet is a virtual resource centre for teachers, home educators and students. Check it out at http://agcwww.bio.ns.ca/schools/EarthNet/English/start_contact.html.

Common Geological Terms

Continental shelf: Submerged edge of continent, extending to depths of less than 200 metres, and largely made up of sedimentary rock.

Earthquake: A sudden motion or trembling in the earth caused by the release of slowly accumulated strain along a fault line or through volcanic activity.

Echo Sounding: A determination of water depth by measuring the time required for a sonic or ultrasonic signal to travel to the bottom of a body of water and back to the ship emitting the signal.

Epicentre: Point on the earth's surface directly above the focus of an earthquake, usually the location of the most severe damage.

Erosion: Breakdown and wearing away of rocks on the earth's surface by the action of water, waves, glaciers, wind and underground water. ▶

Fault: a fracture in the earth's crust along which there has been displacement of the rock on either side, relative to one another.

Geothermal energy: energy that can be extracted from the earth's internal heat, usually in the form of emissions of hot water, steam, and gas.

Glacier: a large ice mass formed on land by recrystallisation of compacted snow.

Ice Field: An extensive area of interconnected glaciers. An ice field is known as pack ice when floating on the sea.

Igneous Rock: Rock formed when a mass of molten magma cools and solidifies on or below earth's surface. One of three main classes of rock.

Magma: Molten rocky material (mostly silica) beneath the earth's surface. Reaching the surface red hot through volcanic activity, it cools and becomes lava.

Metamorphic Rock: Rock formed when preexisting rocks are altered by marked changes in temperature, pressure, or shearing stress. One of three major rock groups.

Sedimentary rock: Rock formed from the accumulation of loose material deposited by water, wind and ice, and solidified by compaction.

Seismograph: a device that records the seismic vibrations of an earthquake. The wave disturbances caused by earthquakes have different speeds and require different lengths of time to reach the surface.

Tectonic plates: Rigid outer layer of the earth's crust consists of about ten large plates, which "float" horizontally across the denser inner crust. The boundaries of these plates are zones of intense activity, and give rise to mountain building, volcanoes, changes in the ocean floor, and earthquakes.

Tsunami: Particular form of ocean wave produced by an earthquake in the ocean floor, noted for its destructive force.

Volcano: A vent in the earth's crust through which magma, rock fragments, dust, gases, and ash are ejected from below earth's surface.

Composition of the Earth

Core: The earth's core lies about 2,900 km below the surface, and consists of two layers: a solid inner core and an outer liquid layer. The inner core is a solid mass, 3,200 km in diameter, probably composed of compressed iron with small amounts of other metals such as nickel. The outer core (the only liquid layer) is about 3,470 km in radius and gives rise to earth's magnetic fields.

Mantle: Accounting for about 82 percent of earth's volume, the mantle is denser than the crust, and probably increases in density close to the core. The mantle extends from the core to about 90 km below the higher mountains, and to about 5 km beneath parts of the ocean crust.

Crust: The outside crust of planet earth ranges in thickness from 5 to 50 km. The relatively light, granite-like rock forming the continents overlies a thinner magnesium-iron layer that makes up the ocean floor. The continental blocks "float" on the denser layer forming the ocean bed.

Hydrosphere: A layer of water covering over 70% of the earth's crust, including all water on or near the surface of the planet.

Atmosphere: The lightest part of earth is the atmosphere, a gaseous envelope surrounding the planet. The atmosphere consists of nitrogen, oxygen, water vapour and argon. Less than 0.1% is composed of other gases. Gases have weight, so the atmosphere is densest near earth's surface, and thins towards the vacuum of space.

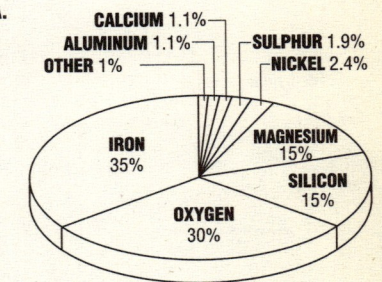

A.
CALCIUM 1.1%
ALUMINUM 1.1%
OTHER 1%
SULPHUR 1.9%
NICKEL 2.4%
MAGNESIUM 15%
SILICON 15%
OXYGEN 30%
IRON 35%

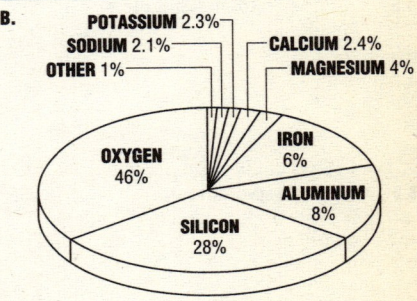

B.
POTASSIUM 2.3%
SODIUM 2.1%
OTHER 1%
CALCIUM 2.4%
MAGNESIUM 4%
IRON 6%
ALUMINUM 8%
SILICON 28%
OXYGEN 46%

▲
Relative abundance of elements by weight of elements in the whole earth (A) and in the earth's crust (B).

Earthquakes

Although the earth's surface seems completely stable, it is constantly moving and changing. Layers of rock in the earth's crust, called plates, push and pull each other until they bend or stretch.

Vibrations or "seismic waves" emanate from the source of the breakage out through the earth, causing the planet to quiver or ring like a tuning fork. The waves can be so minor that the quake will not be felt by humans, or so severe it will change the physical landscape of the area.

Earthquakes can happen all over the world, but they tend to reoccur along weaknesses in the crust, called faults. By studying the patterns of earthquakes, scientists determine the areas at greatest risk and compile the information in seismic zoning maps. In this way, building regulations can be applied to earthquake zones to minimize possible damage.

The most common method of measuring an earthquake's magnitude is the Richter Scale. It estimates the force from recordings of seismic waves taken by an instrument called a seismometer. the scale is logarithmic, so that each numeric reading is ten times greater in recorded amplitude.

The intensity of an earthquake can also be measured through the Modified Mercalli Scale. In addition to mechanical recordings, it uses witness accounts to describe the effects of an earthquake.

Measuring Earthquakes

Richter		Modified Mercali	
2.5	Generally felt, but not recorded.	I	Not felt except by a very few
		II	Felt only by a few persons at rest, especially on upper floors of buildings
3.5	Felt by many people.	III	Felt noticeably indoors. Standing cars may rock slightly. Most people do not recognize.
		IV	During daytime felt by many indoors, outdoors by a few. Dishes, windows and doors disturbed; walls creak. At night, some awaken. Sensation like a heavy truck passing.
		V	Felt by nearly everyone; many awakened. Some dishes and windows broken; some objects over-turned. Trees, poles and other tall objects disturbed.
4.5	Some local damage may occur.	VI	Felt by all, many run outdoors. Heavy furniture moves; occasionally plaster falls and chimneys damaged. Overall damage slight.
		VII	Everyone runs outdoors. Well-built structures suffer negligible damage; slight to moderate damage in well-built homes; poorly constructed buildings suffer considerable damage. Noticed by people in moving cars.
6.0	A destructive earthquake	VIII	Damage slight in specially designed structures; considerable in ordinary substantial buildings, with partial collapse; great in poorly-built structures. Chimneys fall. Heavy furniture overturned. Disturbs people driving cars. Sand and mud ejected in small amounts.
		IX	Damage to specially designed structures considerable. Buildings shifted off foundations. Conspicuous ground cracks. Underground pipes broken.

Earth Sciences

Richter		Modified Mercali	
7.0	A major earthquake, about 10 occur each year	X	Some well-built wooden structures destroyed; most masonry and frame structures destroyed. Ground badly cracked. Rails bent. Landslides considerable.
8.0	Great earthquake, occurs once every five to 10 years	XI	Few masonry structures remain standing. Bridges destroyed. Broad fissures in ground. Underground pipelines out of service. Earth slumps, and land slips in soft ground.
		XII	Damage total. Waves seen on ground surface. Lines of sight and levels distorted. Objects thrown upward into air.

World's Major Earthquakes

Date	Location	Deaths	Magnitude
1902 Dec. 16	Turkestan	4 500	—
1905 Apr. 4	India, Kangra	19 000	8.6
1905 Sep. 8	Italy, Calabria	2 500	7.9
1906 Aug. 17	Chile, Santiago	20 000	8.6
1907 Oct. 21	Central Asia	12 000	8.1
1908 Dec. 28	Italy, Messina	83 000	7.5
1915 Jan. 13	Italy, Avezzano	29 980	7.5
1920 Dec. 16	China, Gansu	200 000	8.6
1923 Sep. 1	Japan, Kwanto-Tokyo-Yokohama	143 000	8.3
1925 Mar. 16	China, Yunnan	5 000	7.1
1927 Mar. 7	Japan, Tango	3 020	7.9
1927 May 22	China, near Xining	200 000	8.3
1929 May 1	Iran	3 300	7.4
1932 Dec. 25	China, Gansu	70 000	7.6
1933 Mar. 2	Japan, Sanriku	2 990	8.9
1934 Jan. 15	India, Behar-Nepal	10 700	8.4
1935 Apr. 20	Formosa	3 280	7.1
1935 May 30	Pakistan, Quetta	30 000	7.6
1939 Jan. 25	Chile, Chillan	28 000	8.3
1939 Dec. 26	Turkey, Erzincan	30 000	7.6
1948 June 28	Japan, Fukui	5 390	7.3
1949 Aug. 5	Ecuador, Ambato	6 000	6.8
1960 Feb. 29	Morocco, Agadir	15 000	5.9
1960 May 22	Chile	5 000	7.3
1966 Aug. 19	Turkey, Varto	2 520	7.1
1968 Aug. 31	Iran	20 000	7.3
1969 July 25	Eastern China	3 000	5.9
1970 May 31	Peru	66 000	7.8
1972 Apr. 10	Southern Iran	5 054	7.1
1972 Dec. 23	Nicaragua, Managua	5 000	6.2
1974 Dec. 28	Pakistan	5 300	6.2
1976 Feb. 4	Guatemala	23 000	7.5
1976 June 30	Westirian, Indonesia	5 000	7.1
1976 July 27	China, Tangshan	255 000	8.0
1976 Aug. 16	Philippines, Mindanao	8 000	7.9
1976 Nov. 24	Turkey	4 000	7.3
1978 Sep. 16	Iran	25 000	7.8
1980 Oct. 10	Algeria	4 500	7.7
1980 Nov. 23	Southern Italy	4 800	7.2
1981 June 11	Southern Iran	3 000	6.9
1985 Sep. 19	Mexico, Michoacan	15 000	8.1
1988 Dec. 7	Turkey-USSR	25 000	7.0
1990 June 20	Western Iran	50 000	7.7
1993 Sept. 30	India	9 500	6.4
1995 Jan. 17	Kobe, Japan	6 000	7.2
1998 Feb. 1	Afghanistan	5,000	6.9
1999 Aug. 17	Turkey	12,000	7.4

Source: *Energy, Mines and Resources Canada; Swiss Re, sigma no 2/1996*

Earthquakes in Canada

Scientists estimate that more than 1,000 earthquakes are recorded in Canada each year. Most measure less than 3 on the Richter scale. The southwest corner of British Columbia is the most active earthquake region (more than 200 every year). Other active regions include coastal BC, the southern Yukon, the Mackenzie Valley in the Northwest Territories, the Arctic Islands, and parts of Ontario and Québec (especially the Ottawa and St Lawrence valleys).

Date		Location	Magnitude
1918	Dec. 6	Vancouver Island	7.0
1925	March 1	Charlevoix-Kamouraska region, Québec	6.7
1929	May 6	Off Queen Charlotte Islands	7.0
1929	Nov. 18	Atlantic Ocean. South of Newfoundland	7.2
1933	Nov. 20	Baffin Bay	7.3
1935	Nov. 1	Québec-Ontario border	6.2
1946	June 23	Vancouver Island	7.3
1949	August 22	Off Queen Charlotte Islands	8.1
1958	July 10	Alaska-BC border	7.9
1970	June 24	South of Queen Charlotte Islands	7.4
1976	Dec. 20	West of Vancouver Island	6.8
1979	Feb. 28	Yukon-Alaska border	7.5
1980	Dec. 17	West of Vancouver Island	6.8
1985	Dec. 23	Mackenzie region, NWT	6.9
1988	Nov. 25	Saguenay region, Quebec	6.0
1989	Dec. 25	Northern Quebec	6.1
1992	April 6	West of Vancouver Island	6.8

Source: *Geological Survey of Canada*

For more information on earthquakes, contact the following divisions of the Geological Survey of Canada:

Geophysics Division
1 Observatory Crescent
Ottawa, Ont.
K1A 0Y3
Tel (24 hrs): (613) 995-5558

Pacific Geoscience Centre
P.O. Box 6000
9860 West Saanich
Sidney, BC V8L 4B2
Tel (24 hrs): (604) 363-6500

Geological Time Periods

The story of planet earth is one of continuous change. Fossils, rock records and radioactive dating show three marked changes in the patterns of plant and animal life. These times of change in the most recent 570 million years of the earth's history are divided by geologists into three eras: Paleozoic (ancient life); Mesozoic (age of reptiles); and Cenozoic (age of mammals). The more than 4 billion years before the start of the Paleozoic era are referred to as Precambrian time. Each geological unit is divided further: the eras into periods, the periods into epochs.

The names of the time periods are taken either from the geographic locality where the fossil information was best displayed or first studied, or from some characteristic of the geological formations. For example, the Jurassic period is named from the Jura Mountains of France and Switzerland, and the Carboniferous is named from the coal-bearing sedimentary rocks.

▶

Earth Sciences

Era	Period	Epoch	Years Ago	Changes and Characteristics
▶ Precambrian Time			4.5 bil.?	Cooling and melting of the earth's crust. Evidence of bacteria, the first known living things, about 3.5 billion years ago.
Paleozoic	Cambrian		575 mil.	Seas spread across North America. First fishes appear. Greatest development of invertebrates.
	Ordovician		480 mil.	Floods sometimes cover two-thirds of North America. Jawless fish appear. Algae become plentiful.
	Silurian		435 mil.	Coral reefs are formed. First amphibians and forests of fernlike trees appear.
	Devonian		405 mil.	Gas and oil are formed. Many kinds of fish in seas and fresh water. First insects appear.
	Carboniferous —Mississippian		350 mil.	Warm, moist climate produces great forests that later become coal beds. Fish and amphibians plentiful.
	—Pennsylvanian		310 mil.	Appalachian Mountains are formed. Large amounts of coal are formed. First reptiles appear.
	Permian		270 mil.	Ural Mountains are formed. Glaciers in southern hemisphere melt. Gas, oil and salt are formed. Reptiles developing.
Mezozoic	Triassic		225 mil.	Reptiles dominate the earth. First mammals appear.
	Jurassic		180 mil.	Shallow seas invade continents. Dinosaurs reach their largest size. First birds appear.
	Cretaceous		130 mil.	Seas spread over the land. Flowering plants appear. Dinosaurs die out. Most chalk deposits are made.
Cenozoic	Tertiary	Paleocene	65 mil.	Mountains become higher. Climates less uniform. Mammals, flowering plants become common.
		Eocene	50 mil.	Climate mild. Seas flood shores of continents. Primitive apes, early horses and elephants appear.
		Oligocene	38 mil.	Climate mild. Alps and Himalayas begin to rise. Many volcanoes. Oil and natural gas are formed.
		Miocene	27 mil.	Climate mild. Rocky Mountains and Sierra Nevadas forming. Flowering plants and trees resemble modern kinds.
		Pliocene	10 mil.	Climate cooling. Mountains rising in western Canada. Many volcanoes. Birds and mammals spread around the world. Humans appear near end of epoch.
	Quaternary	Pleistocene	1.5 mil.	Great ice sheets cover northern hemisphere. Climate cool. Mountains continue to rise in North America. Early humans reach Europe and North America.
		Recent, or Holocene	10 000	Glaciers melt and Great Lakes are formed. Climate warm. Humans live in most parts of the earth, develop agriculture, use metals, domesticate animals.

Source: *Gage Canadian Dictionary* by Walter S. Avis, et al. Copyright © 1983 Gage Publishing Limited. Reproduced by permission.

Lithoprobe

(by Horst Heise, Communications Adviser)

When European explorers called North America the "New World" they reversed geological time. In reality, our ancestral continent, Laurentia, formed long before the forces of plate tectonics shaped their building blocks into Eurasia, South America and Africa.

Tracing our continent's dramatic assembly is the purpose of Canada's national Lithoprobe project (a probe or study of the lithosphere—the Earth's crust), our biggest earth-science undertaking ever and the first of its kind. More than 750 specialists (including over 400 post-graduate and post-doctoral students) from the various branches of the earth sciences have joined the project. Since 1984, Lithoprobe scientists have been constructing a "moving" image of what North America has gone through during the last four billion years, and published about 1,000 technical papers on the subject.

From its beginning, Lithoprobe has included experts from all earth science specialties, including geologists, geophysicists and geochemists, as well as the whole geoscience community. The project has been funded by the Natural Sciences and Engineering Research Council of Canada and the Geological Survey of Canada, and supported by provincial agencies, and mining and oil companies when operating in their spheres of interest.

In hard-rock mining areas Lithoprobe showed that seismic reflection surveys could provide good lithological and structural leads. Given Canada's reliance on mineral resources, this technique is of fundamental importance to existing as well as future mining communities.

The project intends to trace the growth of our continent from its beginning until today. Canada's four-billion-year-old rocks belong to a piece of old continental crust which then became part of the Slave Province.

The Slave Province (a geological designation) is one of six "original" microcontinents or **cratons** of the Archean age which eventually drifted into each other to form the heart of the Canadian Shield. The other cratons have been named Rae, Hearne, Wyoming, Superior and Nain. Whatever land had been in the oceans between the craton, even the ocean floor itself, was squeezed into a series of mountain belts (**orogens**) in the biggest, most widely spread round of continental collision the world has ever known, accompanied by an enormous outpouring of magma, which formed a brand new crust.

This giant welding process occurred in the **Early Proterozoic** period and the new mountain belts created included ranges that exist today as only eroded remains that look like welds uniting the Archean pieces.

Rifting turned into continent splitting in the west where a wide continental slope received the sediments on which the prairies now produce grain, and oil and gas reserves are found. The same happened in the east a while later, when a massive supercontinent resulted from an earlier orogen split (roughly where the St. Lawrence River is today) and a wide ocean developed. It in turn was pushed out of existence in a series of tectonic squeezes which ended with the creation of the Appalachians. Comparatively recently, the Atlantic opened, and is still widening today. Out west, the Rockies formed during the Early Tertiary, while tectonic processes have kept BC growing westward since Jurassic times.

■ Tracking the Canadian Mosaic

Many bits and pieces have become part of the "Canadian mosaic" during the continent's long geologic past, including portions of old and new continents, islands or ocean floor which have drifted in from many parts of the world. Depending on where in Canada we live, its underground once may be been in tropical seas (parts of Saskatchewan, for instance) or shivered at Himalayan heights (large portions of Ontario and Quebec) or, in geological terms, not existed until fairly recently. Piecing the geological story of our continent together is like having to choose from a pile of not one but several jigsaw puzzles of various ages in which individual pieces likely were reshaped before they occupied their present positions. They may have come from various depths in the crust, or been newly formed during tectonic activity; developed long ago or more recently, either here or far away.

Earth's geologic history began with our planet's cooling 4.6 billion years ago, leading to the formation of the planet's outer crust, which became a patchwork of individual, moving pieces or "plates." Our own continent, North America, currently is moving westward at a fairly good pace, about 4 or 5 cm per year, about as fast as one's fingernails grow. That translates into 4,000 to 5,000 km in 100 million years—a small portion of Earth's lifetime (comparable to just 31 minutes of a 24-hour day).

The North American continent grew through a progressive sticking together, or **accretion**, of smaller into bigger pieces of land. But there were also continental breakups that involved huge supercontinents. As well, the flowing magma created new lithosphere that was added to the continents and the ocean floors.

As crustal plates meet, one may slip below the other, for instance the heavier oceanic plates slide under lighter continental crust. This tectonic action is called **subduction**. Portions of a subducted plate may become attached to the underside of the overlying crustal pate, but most of the subduction plate will be recycled into the mantle, where it melts, perhaps to enter into another cycle of melting, outpouring and cooling.

Such a subduction zone was discovered under Vancouver Island in 1984, when a first geophysical test section proved the feasibility of the Lithoprobe project. This survey across Vancouver Island sounded the underground with seismic reflection signals. It showed conclusively how a portion of the Pacific Ocean seafloor was vanishing under Vancouver Island and on into the depths of Earth, causing a trail of earthquakes and tremors and, farther inland, volcanoes to line up parallel to the west coast. This investigation, and Lithoprobe's subsequent work there, was the first major earth-science investigation to cross an ocean-continent-subduction zone.

■ A Growing Continent

All of the Canadian Cordillera (with the exception of the volcanoes along the west coast), from the foothills in the east to the offshore in the west, is not where it used to be. All of it has been pushed, crunched or extended. The eastern portions are thrusted packages of sediments which previously had been laid down on the continental slope of the older North American continent. Part of this package still lies mostly undisturbed east of the Rockies in Alberta and in northeastern BC, and in the Western Canada Sedimentary Basin, which harbours western Canada's huge reserves of oil and gas.

Lithoprobe's west coast experiment was followed by an 1100-km long transect study and cross section all the way from the Juan de Fuca Ridge west of Vancouver Island to southwestern Alberta. This Southern Cordillera transect provided earth scientists with a rich record of how plate tectonics have worked in the recent past, and what the results of these processes look like.

Farther east, Lithoprobe looked at the Superior Province, in the heart of the Canadian Shield. Its age is Archean, the eon which comprises almost half of Earth's history, and the major period of its crustal formation. Archean rocks of the world, although a relatively small fraction of the exposed continental crust, contain a disproportionate amount of the world's mineral wealth, including more than half of the world's gold and significant base metal reserves. Also, the vast majority of useful diamond deposits come from deep lithospheric roots beneath Archean cratons and in some parts beneath the Superior craton.

The oldest rocks known on Earth, just over 4 billion years old, are in the Slave geological province, in the western Northwest Territories. The Slave contains rocks formed between 4 and 2.5 billion years ago; it is a relatively small member of the Archean family of microcontinents.

The Slave craton is significantly different from the much larger Superior Province. It has different rock compositions; the type, setting and timing of gold and base metal mineralization is different. More of the Slave's volcanic rocks are somewhat lighter, and a greater precentage of sedimentary rocks is present. Oldest rocks in the Slave craton are much older than in the Superior Province; still, the Slave Province appears to be a fragment of a yet earlier and bigger craton. Structures also differ, intensifying the quest for tectonic evidence from our oldest geological past.

Other revelations from Lithoprobe include evidence that the area from South Dakota, through the exposed shield in Saskatchewan-Manitoba and across Hudson Bay to northern Quebec was once part of a vast ocean—more than 5,000 kms wide—and scattered tropical islands and archipelagoes like those in the southwest Pacific. (Try to picture yourself on Bali while digging out from the next Saskatchewan blizzard.) The clues are geological markers such as the origin of the rocks and the time markers imprinted by various, mostly tectonic, processes. Saskatchewan's and Manitoba's South Sea remnants began to form after a previous continent split, which created an initial rift, comparable to the present Red Sea-Gulf of Aden area. This water body, comparable to the Pacific Ocean, was in the area where wheat fields now sway in the breeze.

Lithoprobe is scheduled to continue until 2003. Visit the project's Web site at http://www.geop.ubc.ca/Lithoprobe/public.html for an overview, an explanation of Lithoprobe techniques, and details of current research and educational resources. The program has a set of slides and other materials available for educational use; for more information you can also contact the Lithoprobe Secretariat at the University of British Columbia, Vancouver, BC V6T 1Z4.

Minerals

Minerals are all around us—everything from ice on the sidewalk in winter to the salt you sprinkle on French fries. Each mineral species has a definite chemical composition and a crystal structure. Therefore, ice is mineral because it is solid, but water is not because it is liquid. Sea shells are not minerals because, although they are solid, they are organic—formed by living creatures.

The physical properties of minerals—their form and hardness—are easy to recognize. Specimens may be composed of large showy crystals or millions of tiny crystals fused together. The external shape (or habit) is determined by the internal arrangement of atoms. The atoms are joined together in a framework to form minute building blocks. Called the crystal structure, the arrangement of atoms is unique for each mineral. The habit is also partly the result of the environment in which a mineral grows. If there is enough space during growth, the mineral develops smooth external crystals. However, conditions are seldom ideal and more often than not, minerals grow together as masses of fibres, grains, plates or spheres. The hardness of a mineral—its resistance to scratching—is measured by the Mohs scale.

The optical properties of minerals—lustre, colour and transparency—are easily observed by the unaided eye; other optical properties are determined with microscopes. Lustre is the quality of light reflected from the surface of a mineral. For instance, the highly reflective surfaces of pyrite produce the metallic lustre characteristics of most sulphide minerals. Many silicates, carbonates and other minerals have a softer, but still bright, glassy or vitreous lustre. Minerals with surfaces that reflect light more diffusely, such as serpentine asbestos or cyanotrichite, are said to have silky or earthly lustres. Lustre is reliable means of distinguishing minerals.

Colour can also be very distinctive, but is not always reliable in identifying most minerals because even minerals of the same species can occur in many colours. Quartz, which is quite common, can be as clear as water or the deepest purple because of flaws in the mineral's crystal structure. Colour can also be affected by the presence of major elements in the mineral: copper in azurite produces an intense azure blue; arsenic makes realgar appear red; and curite is coloured orange by uranium. Colour can also be produced by physical structure. When light strikes very thin layers within the structure of labradorite, the mineral glows with iridescent colours, an effect much like that of sunlight striking a film of gasoline on a puddle, causing a rainbow of colour.

Determining the chemical composition and crystal structure of minerals requires laboratory techniques and tools such as the electron microbe, a reliable tool for analysing chemical composition. Crystal structure is determined using an X-ray diffractometer. Other mineral properties such as magnetism, fluorescence and radioactivity are more easily detected: magnetite and pyrrhotite are noticeably magnetic; some minerals, such as scheelite, fluoresce strongly in ultra-violet light; and all uranium and thorium-bearing minerals are radioactive. The radiation can easily be detected with a Geiger counter or scintillometer.

Mohs Scale of Hardness

Mohs scale indicates the relative hardness of minerals. Each mineral listed is hard enough to scratch a smooth surface of those below it. On this scale, a polymer-like polyethylene would have a hardness of about 1, a finger nail 2.5, a penny 5, window glass 5.5, and the blade of a pocket knife 6.5. Tool steel has a hardness of about 7, and easily cuts glass.

10	Diamond
9	Corundum
8	Topaz
7	Quartz
6	Orthoclase
5	Apatite
4	Fluorite
3	Calcite
2	Gypsum
1	Talc

Source: *Geological Survey of Canada*

Earth Sciences Museums

Maritime Region:

☐ **St. Lawrence Miner's Museum**
P.O. Box 1992, St. Lawrence, Nfld A0E 2V0.
Tel: (709) 873-2222. No charge. Open in summer.

☐ **Fundy Geological Museum**
4028 Eastern Avenue, Parrsboro, NS B0M 1S0.
Tel: (902) 254-3814. Entrance fee. Open June to Oct. from 9:30 am to 5:30 pm, Nov. to May from Tues. to Sat. to 5:00 pm. Web site: http://www.ednet.ns.ca/educ/museum/fundy.html.

☐ **Inverness Miner's Museum**
Lower Railway Street, Inverness, NS B0E 1N0. Tel: (902) 258-2097. Entrance fee. Open all year.

☐ **Springhill Miner's Museum**
P.O. Box 610, Black River Road, Springhill, NS B0M 1X0. Tel: (902) 597-3449.
Entrance fee. Open spring, summer and fall.

Central Canada:

☐ **Alcan Museum and Archives**
1188 Sherbrooke Street West, Montreal, Que. H3A 3G2. Tel: (514) 848-8187. No charge. Open all year.

☐ **Canadian Museum of Nature,**
Viola Macmillan Mineral Gallery
240 McLeod St. at Metcalfe, Ottawa, Ont. K1P 6P4. Tel: (613) 566-4730. Entrance fee. Closed Monday (Oct.–Apr.), Christmas Day and New Year's Day.

☐ **Logan Hall**
Geological Survey of Canada, 601 Booth Street, Ottawa, Ont. K1A 0E8. Tel: (613)995-4261. No charge. Open all year. Closed on weekends and holidays.

☐ **Musée de Géologie**
Laval University, Pavillon Pouliot, 4th floor, Sainte Foy, Que. G1K 7P4. Tel: (418) 656-2131. No charge. Open all year.

☐ **Musée mineralogique et minier de Thetford Mines**   711 Smith Blvd. South, Thetford Mines, Que. G6G 5T3. Entrance fee. Open all year.
Tel: (418) 335-2123.

☐ **Musée régional mines de Malartic**
650 rue de la paix, Abitibi East, Malartic, Que. J0Y 1Z0. Tel: (819) 757-4677. Entrance fee. Open all year.

☐ **Earth Sciences Museum**
University of Waterloo, Waterloo, Ont. N2L 3G1. Tel: (519) 885-1211, ext. 2469. No charge.
Open weekdays from 8:30 am to 4:30 pm.
Web site: http://www.science.uwaterloo.ca/earth/museum/museum.html.

☐ **Miller Museum of Geology**
Queen's University, Miller Hall, Kingston, Ont. K7L 3N6. Tel: (613) 545-2597. No charge. Open all year.

☐ **Oil Museum of Canada**
2423 Kelly Road, Oil Springs, (35 km southeast of Sarnia), Ont. N0N 1P0. Tel: (519) 834-2840. Entrance fee. Open in summer and fall. Tours all year.

☐ **The Petrolia Discovery Foundation**
4381 Discovery Line, Petrolia, Ont. N0N 1R0.
Tel: (519) 882-0897. Entrance fee. Open in summer and fall.

☐ **Royal Ontario Museum,**
INCO Gallery of Earth Sciences
100 Queen's Park, Toronto, Ont. M5S 2C6.
Tel: (416) 586-5549. Entrance fee. Closed Christmas, New Year's Day.

☐ **Timmins Museum**
70 Legion Drive, South Porcupine, Ont. P4N 1B3. Tel: (705) 235-5066. No charge. Open all year.

Western Canada:

☐ **Stonewall Quarry Park**
200 North Main Street, Stonewall, Man. R0C 2Z0.
Tel: (204) 467-5354. Entrance fee. Open all year.

☐ **Geological Museum**
University of Saskatchewan, Geological Sciences Building, Saskatoon, Sask. S7N 0W0.
Tel: (306) 966-5683. No charge. Open all year.

☐ **Frank Slide Interpretive Centre**
1 km north of Frank, Alta T0K 0E0.
Tel: (403) 562-7388. No charge. Open all year.

☐ **Museum of Geology**
University of Alberta, basement of Earth Sciences Building, Edmonton, Alta T6G 2E3.
Tel: (403) 492-3265. No charge. Open all year.

☐ **Royal Tyrrell Museum of Palaeontology**
Hwy. 838, Midland Provincial Park, Drumheller, Alta T0J 0Y0. Tel: (403) 823-7707. Entrance fee.
Open all year. Web site: http://www.tyrrell.com/.

☐ **Dinosaur Provincial Park**
Patricia, Alta T0J 2K0. Tel: (403) 378-4342.
No charge. Open all year.

☐ **British Columbia Museum of Mining**
PO Box 188, Britannia Beach, BC V0N 1J0.
Tel: (604) 896-2233. Entrance fee. Open in summer and fall. All year for groups.

☐ **M.Y. Williams Geological Museum**
University of British Columbia, 6339 Stores Road, Vancouver, BC V6T 2B4. Tel: (604) 228-5586.
No charge. Open all year.

☐ **Princeton and District Museums**
167 Vermilion Street, Princeton, BC V0X 1W0.
Tel: (250) 295-7588. No charge. Summer (June 30–August 31.)

☐ **Keno City Mining Museum**
Centre Street, Keno City, Yukon Y0B 1M0.
Tel: (867) 995-2792. No charge. Open in summer.

PHYSICAL SCIENCES

Physics and chemistry constitute the physical sciences. **Chemistry** concerns itself with the composition, properties, and reactions of substances. Organic chemistry, one of the two main branches of chemistry, specializes in the composition, properties, and reactions of hydrocarbon compounds. The other branch, inorganic chemistry, deals primarily with the elements and compounds that do not include hydrocarbons. **Physics** concerns itself with universal aspects of nature—forces, energy, structure of matter, and their interactions. Some of its particular fields are: plasma physics, optics and quantum optics, particle physics, geophysics, biophysics, and acoustics. As basic sciences, physics and chemistry permeate all sciences and technologies.

Common Chemistry Terms

Acid: a substance that in liquid form will turn blue litmus paper red, react with alkalis (bases) to form salts, and dissolve metals to form salts.

Alkali: Any compound that has chemical qualities of a base, such as reacting with acid to form salts.

Atomic Weight (Mass): The relative mass of an atom, based on a scale in which a specific carbon atom is assigned a mass value of 12.

Base: an alkaline substance, either molecular or ionic in form, that will accept or receive a proton from another chemical unit.

Catalyst: a substance that accelerates a chemical reaction without becoming a part of the end product of the reaction.

Compound: A substance formed by the combination of two or more chemical elements that cannot be separated from the combination by physical means. The constituent atoms, however, can usually be separated by means of chemical reactions.

Electron: A negatively-charged particle that moves in orbit about the nucleus of an atom.

Element: A substance composed of atoms with the same atomic number or the same number of protons in their nuclei.

Isotope: One of two or more atoms having the same atomic number, but a different mass number.

Mass Number: the atomic weight of an isotope, calculated from the number of protons and neutrons in the nucleus.

Matter: Anything that has weight or fills space, such as a solid, liquid, or gas.

Polymer: a huge molecule composed of repeating units of the same molecule.

Valence: a number that represents the combining power of an element, ion, or radical.

Common Physics Terms

Acceleration: the rate of change of velocity with respect to time.

Anode: The positive terminal of an electric current flow. In a vacuum tube, electrons flow from the cathode to the anode.

Cathode: The negative terminal of an electric current system. In vacuum tube, the filament serves as the source electrons.

Conduction: the transfer of heat by molecular motion from a source of high temperature to a region of lower temperature, tending towards a result of equalized temperatures.

Convection: The mechanical transfer of heated molecules of a gas or liquid from a source to another area, as when a room is warmed by the movement of air molecules heated by a radiator.

Electromotive Force: The force that causes the movement of electrons through an electrical circuit.

Energy: the ability to perform work. Energy may be changed from one form to another, as from heat to light, but normally it cannot be created or destroyed.

Force: the influence on a body that causes it to accelerate.

Heat: A form of energy that results from the disordered motion of molecules. As the motion becomes more rapid and disordered, the amount of heat is increased.

Mass: a measure of the amount of matter. Near the surface of earth, it is roughly equivalent to weight.

Momentum: the mathematical product of the mass of a moving object and its velocity.

Velocity: The speed with which an object travels over a specified distance during a measured amount of time.

Weight: The force on a body produced by the downward pull of gravity on it.

Basic Laws of Physics

■ Newton's Laws of Motion

Newton's laws apply to objects in a vacuum, and are difficult to observe in the "real" world where forces such as friction affect all objects.

First Law: Any object at rest tends to stay at rest, and a body in motion will continue that motion with a constant velocity unless acted upon by some external unbalanced force.

Second Law: The acceleration of an object is directly proportional to the force acting upon it, and is inversely proportional to the mass of the object.

Third Law: Every action generates an equal and opposite reaction.

■ Gravity

When an object is dropped near the surface of the earth, it increases in speed as it falls. By rolling balls down inclined planes Galileo discovered that acceleration due to gravity is the same for all objects, independent of their weight (mass). For example, if you drop this book and a brick simultaneously, they will reach to floor at the same time. You can try the same experiment with a heavy book and a single sheet of paper. The paper is affected by the resistance of the air. Then crumple the paper, and try again.

Gravity is the force that tends to attract objects to the centre of a celestial body, such as the earth, the moon or Mars. The weight of an object at the earth's surface is mainly due to the force of gravity between the earth and the object. The force exerted by the earth varies with the object's distance from the centre of the earth. Therefore the weight of an object is not the same at the earth's surface as it is on the moon or in space.

■ Laws of Thermodynamics

Sadi Carnot (1796-1832) stated in his work *Reflections on the Motive Power of Fire* that mechanical energy could be produced by the simple transfer of heat.

First Law: In a closed system, energy appears to be conserved in all but nuclear reactions and other extreme conditions.

Second Law: In a closed system, heat never travels from a low to a higher temperature in a self sustaining process. In a closed system, entropy (disorder) always increases.

■ Two Basic Laws of Quantum Physics

Heisenberg's Uncertainty Principle: It is impossible to specify completely the position and momentum of a particle, such as an electron.

Pauli's Exclusion Principle: No two electrons of the same atom can have identical values for all four quantum numbers: at least one quantum number must be different.

Loudness of Sounds

Sound is measured in decibels. A decibel is a unit for measuring the relative intensity of a sound, equal to one-tenth of a bel. A bel indicates the amount of energy in the form of sound transmitted to one sq cm of the ear. The bel was named after Alexander Graham Bell.

The decibel scale advances geometrically instead of arithmetically. Twenty decibels represents not twice as much noise as ten, but 10 times as much. The 80-decibel level of a pneumatic drill is 100 times as noisy as the 60-decibel level of a quiet motor.

Source: *Dictionary of Science*, Barnhardt, American Heritage Series

Intensity (decibels)	Loudness
0	Threshold of hearing
10 (1 bel)	Virtual silence
20	Quiet room
30	Watch ticking at 1 m
40	Quiet street
50	Quiet conversation
60	Quiet motor at 1 m
70	Loud conversation
80	Door slamming
90	Busy typing room
100	Near loud motor horn
110	Pneumatic drill
120	Near airplane engine
130	Threshold of pain

The Elements

(name, symbol and atomic number)

An element is a substance composed of atoms that are chemically alike—each atom has an identical number of protons in its nucleus. Furthermore, there is no known process to break these elements down into more fundamental substances.

Name	Symbol	Number	Name	Symbol	Number	Name	Symbol	Number
actinium	Ac	89	gold	Au	79	potassium	K	19
aluminum	Al	13	hafnium	Hf	72	praseodymium	Pr	59
americium	Am	95	hassium	Hs	108	promethium	Pm	61
antimony	Sb	51	helium	He	2	protactinium	Pa	91
argon	Ar	18	holmium	Ho	67	radium	Ra	88
arsenic	As	33	hydrogen	H	1	radon	Rn	86
astatine	At	85	indium	In	49	rhenium	Re	75
barium	Ba	56	iodine	I	53	rhodium	Rh	45
berkelium	Bk	97	iridium	Ir	77	rubidium	Rb	37
beryllium	Be	4	iron	Fe	26	ruthenium	Ru	44
bismuth	Bi	83	krypton	Kr	36	rutherfordium	Rf	104
bohrium	Bh	107	lanthanum	La	57	samarium	Sm	62
boron	B	5	lawrencium	Lr	103	scandium	Sc	21
bromine	Br	35	lead	Pb	82	seaborgium	Sg	106
cadmium	Cd	48	lithium	Li	3	selenium	Se	34
calcium	Ca	20	lutetium	Lu	71	silicon	Si	14
californium	Cf	98	magnesium	Mg	12	silver	Ag	47
carbon	C	6	manganese	Mn	25	sodium	Na	11
cerium	Ce	58	meitnerium	Mt	109	strontium	Sr	38
cesium	Cs	55	mendelevium	Md	101	sulfur	S	16
chlorine	Cl	17	mercury	Hg	80	tantalum	Ta	73
chromium	Cr	24	molybdenum	Mo	42	technetium	Tc	43
cobalt	Co	27	neodymium	Nd	60	tellurium	Te	52
copper	Cu	29	neon	Ne	10	terbium	Tb	65
curium	Cm	96	neptunium	Np	93	thallium	Tl	81
dubnium	Db	105	nickel	Ni	28	thorium	Th	90
dysprosium	Dy	66	niobium	Nb	41	thulium	Tm	69
einsteinium	Es	99	nitrogen	N	7	tin	Sn	50
erbium	Er	68	nobelium	No	102	titanium	Ti	22
europium	Eu	63	osmium	Os	76	tungsten	W	74
fermium	Fm	100	oxygen	O	8	uranium	U	92
fluorine	F	9	palladium	Pd	46	vanadium	V	23
francium	Fr	87	phosphorus	P	15	xenon	Xe	54
gadolinium	Gd	64	platinum	Pt	78	ytterbium	Yb	70
gallium	Ga	31	plutonium	Pu	94	yttrium	Y	39
germanium	Ge	32	polonium	Po	84	zinc	Zn	30
						zirconium	Zr	40

What is the Periodic Table?

*T*he Periodic Table of Elements (shown opposite) has its roots in the 19th century when chemists calculated how much one atom of an element weighed in comparison to another. The resulting weight was known as the atomic mass and measured in atomic mass units (amu). (An amu is a mass equal to 1/12 of the mass of the most common form of carbon atom.) As the list of elements was compiled and ranked in order of mass, chemists noted that every seven or eight elements had similar properties.

By 1869 Dimitri Mendeleyev was confident enough to rearrange the list of elements to group those with similar properties and leave blanks for the missing ones that would make up the eight. Mendeleyev only had 63 elements but the periodic table now has 109 elements and still conforms to his 1869 rearrangement.

Early in the 20th century, the table was further refined when atoms were found to be made up of protons and electrons. The number of protons and electrons are equal in one atom and this number was designated the element's atomic number. The table now shows the elements in order according to their atomic number and their atomic mass.

Physical Sciences

Periodic Table of Elements

																	gases
1 H 1.00																	2 He 4.00
3 Li 6.94	4 Be 9.01											5 B 10.81	6 C 12.01	7 N 14.01	8 O 15.99	9 F 18.99	10 Ne 20.17
11 Na 22.98	12 Mg 24.30											13 Al 26.98	14 Si 28.08	15 P 30.97	16 S 32.06	17 Cl 35.45	18 Ar 39.94
19 K 39.09	20 Ca 40.08	21 Sc 44.95	22 Ti 47.88	23 V 50.94	24 Cr 51.99	25 Mn 54.93	26 Fe 55.84	27 Co 58.93	28 Ni 58.69	29 Cu 63.54	30 Zn 65.39	31 Ga 69.72	32 Ge 72.59	33 As 74.92	34 Se 78.96	35 Br 79.90	36 Kr 83.80
37 Rb 85.46	38 Sr 87.62	39 Y 88.90	40 Zr 91.22	41 Nb 92.90	42 Mo 95.94	43 Tc (98)	44 Ru 101.07	45 Rh 102.90	46 Pd 106.42	47 Ag 107.87	48 Cd 112.41	49 In 114.82	50 Sn 118.71	51 Sb 121.75	52 Te 127.60	53 I 126.90	54 Xe 131.29
55 Cs 132.90	56 Ba 137.33	57 La 138.90	72 Hf 178.49	73 Ta 180.94	74 W 183.85	75 Re 186.20	76 Os 190.2	77 Ir 192.22	78 Pt 195.08	79 Au 196.96	80 Hg 200.59	81 Tl 204.38	82 Pb 207.2	83 Bi 208.98	84 Po (209)	85 At (210)	86 Rn (222)
87 Fr (223)	88 Ra 226.02	89 Ac 227.02	104 Rf 261	105 Db 262	106 Sg 263	107 Bh 264	108 Hs 265	109 Mt 266	110 (271)	111 (272)	112 (277)	113 (282)					

transition metals — *other metals* — *non-metals*

— *rare earth elements* —

58 Ce 140.12	59 Pr 140.90	60 Nd 144.24	61 Pm (145)	62 Sm 150.36	63 Eu 151.96	64 Gd 157.25	65 Tb 158.93	66 Dy 162.50	67 Ho 164.93	68 Er 167.26	69 Tm 168.93	70 Yb 173.04	71 Lu 174.96
90 Th 232.03	91 Pa 231.03	92 U 238.02	93 Np 237.04	94 Pu (244)	95 Am (243)	96 Cm (247)	97 Bk (247)	98 Cf (251)	99 Es (252)	100 Fm (257)	101 Md (258)	102 No (259)	103 Lr (260)

This is a table which shows the properties of the elements, in the order of their atomic mass or number, and arranged in horizontal rows (periods) and vertical columns (groups) to illustrate the occurrence of similarities in the structure of their atoms. When the elements are arranged in this order, their chemical and physical properties show repeatable trends. This pattern in properties occurs periodically; that is, the pattern is repeated in an orderly manner over time.

The order of the elements is that of their atomic numbers, the integers which are equal to the positive electrical charges of the atomic nuclei expressed in electronic units.

The International System of Units (SI)

The Systeme Internationale (SI) or metric system was developed in France in 1799. By 1880 many European countries and much of South America had adopted the system as a common language of measurements.

The pressures of global trade have persuaded many of the English-speaking countries to adopt a uniform international standard of measure. Canada adopted the metric system in 1970.

Name	Symbol	Quantity
■ SI Base Units		
metre	m	length
kilogram	kg	mass
second	s	time
ampere	A	electric current
kelvin	K	thermodynamic temperature
mole	mol	amount of substance
candela	cd	luminous intensity
■ SI Supplementary Units		
radian	rad	plane angle
steradian	sr	solid angle
■ Common SI Derived Units With Special Names		
hertz	Hz	frequency
pascal	Pa	pressure, stress
watt	W	power, radiant flux
volt	V	electric potential, electromotive force
newton	N	force
joule	J	energy, work
coulomb	C	electric charge
ohm	Ω	electric resistance
farad	F	electric capacitance
■ Common Units Used With the SI		
litre	L	volume or capacity (= 1 dm^3)
degree Celsius	°C	temperature (= 1 K; 0°C = 273.2 K)
hectare	ha	area (= 10 000 m^2)
tonne	t	mass (= 1000 kg)
electronvolt	eV	energy (= 0.160 aJ)
nautical mile	M	distance (navigation) (= 1852 m)
knot	kn	speed (navigation) (= 1 M/h)
standard atmosphere	atm	atmospheric pressure (= 101.3 kPa)

■ SI Prefixes

Name	Symbol	Multiplying Factor*
exa-	E	10^{18}
peta-	P	10^{15}
tera-	T	10^{12}
giga-	G	10^{9}
mega-	M	10^{6}
kilo-	k	10^{3}
hecto-	h	10^{2}
deca-	da	10
deci-	d	10^{-1}
centi-	c	10^{-2}
milli-	m	10^{-3}
micro-	µ	10^{-6}
nano-	n	10^{-9}
pico-	p	10^{-12}
femto-	f	10^{-15}
atto-	a	10^{-18}

*10^2 = 100; 10^3 = 1 000; 10^{-1} = 0.1; 10^{-2} = 0.01; Thus, 2 km = 2 x 1 000 = 2 000 m ; 3 cm = 3 x 0.01 = 0.03 m

Source: *Gage Canadian Dictionary*

Large Numbers

1 thousand	1 000
1 million	1 000 000 or 10^6
1 milliard: used in Europe, USSR, former French possessions	1 000 000 000 or 10^9
1 billion:	1 000 000 000 000 or 10^{12}
—Canada, the United States and France	1 000 000 000 or 10^9
1 trillion:	1 000 000 000 000 000 000 or 10^{18}
—Canada and the United States	1 000 000 000 000 or 10^{12}

Source: *World Weights and Measures*

Science Centres and Museums

Maritime Region:

☐ **Discovery Centre**
1593 Barrington Street, Halifax, NS. Entrance fee.
Open daily. Tel: (902) 492-4422, Fax: (902) 492-3170
Web site: http://www.discoverycentre.ns.ca

☐ **Electrical Engineering Museum**
University of New Brunswick, Dept. of Electrical Engineering, Head Hall, Fredericton, NB No charge.
Open winter, spring and fall.

☐ **Nova Scotia Museum of Industry**
147 Foord Street, Stellarton, NS B0K 1S0.
Entrance fee. Open daily. Tel: (902) 755-5425.
Web site: http://www.museum.gov.ns.ca/moi/index.htm.

Central Canada:

☐ **Museum of Visual Science and Optometry**
University of Waterloo, Optometry Building, Columbia Street, Waterloo, Ont. N2L 3G1.
Tel: (519) 885-1211, ext. 3405. No charge.
Open all year. Web site:
http://www.optometry.uwaterloo.ca/~museum.

☐ **Hamilton Museum of Steam and Technology**
900 Woodward Avenue, Hamilton, Ont. L8H 7N2.
Tel: (416) 549-5225. Entrance fee. Open all year.

☐ **National Museum of Science and Technology**
1867 St. Laurent Blvd., Ottawa, Ont. K1G 5A3.
Tel: (613) 991-3044. Entrance fee. Open all year.
Web site: http://science-tech.nmstc.com/.

☐ **Ontario Science Centre**
770 Don Mills Road, Toronto, Ont. M3C 1T3.
Tel : (416) 696-1000. Open daily (except Christmas Day).
Web site: http://www.osc.on.ca/.

☐ **Science North**
100 Ramsay Lake Road, Sudbury, Ont. P3E 5S9.
Tel: (705) 522-3700 Entrance fee. Open all year.
Web site: http://www.sciencenorth.on.ca.

Western Canada:

☐ **Calgary Science Centre**
701-11 Street SW, Calgary, Alta T2P 2M5.
Tel: (403) 221-3700, Fax: (403) 237-0186
No charge. Open all year, closed Mondays.
Web site: http://www.calgaryscience.ca.

☐ **Edmonton Space and Science Centre**
11211-142 Street, Edmonton, Alta T5M 4A1.
Tel: (403) 452-9100, Fax: (403) 455-5882.
Entrance fee. Open all year.
Web site: http://www.planet.con.net/~essc/start.html.

☐ **Energeum**
640-5th Avenue S.W., Main Floor, Energy Resources Building, Calgary, Alta T2P 3G4. Tel: (403) 297-4293, Fax: (403) 297-3757. No charge. Open all year.

☐ **The Interior Space and Science Centre**
2704 Highway 6, Vernon, BC V1T 5G5. Tel: & Fax: (250) 545-3644. No charge. Open all year, Monday to Friday.

☐ **Saskatchewan Science Centre**
Winipeg Street and Wascana Drive, Regina, Sask. S4P 3M3. Entrance fee. Open all year.
Tel: 1 800 667-6300 or (306) 791-7900.
Web site: http://www.sciencecentre.sk.ca.

☐ **Science World**
1455 Quebec Street, Vancouver, BC V6A 3Z7.
Tel: (604) 443-7440, Fax: (604) 443-7430.
Entrance fee. Open daily, except Christmas Day.
Web site: www.scienceworld.bc.ca.

Sudbury Neutrino Observatory (SNO)

*T*he SNO's neutrino detector, situated over 2,000 m below ground in a Sudbury mine shaft, was turned on in spring, 1999 and collisions between neutrinos and heavy water molecules were recorded soon after. This event validated nearly two decades of study and conjecture by the Canada-US-UK team of physicists that designed and constructed the device.

The detector collects data that aid in the study of neutrinos and the core of the stars (including the sun) where they originate. The SNO suspends 1,000 tonnes of heavy water (on loan from Canada's AECL) in a 12-m acrylic sphere. Neutrinos, which pass through all matter, react with the heavy water to produce flashes of light. An array of photomultiplier tubes surrounding the heavy water detects those flashes. What do the flashes tell us? They will answer the question of whether or not neutrinos have mass. If they do, that will account for the missing mass in the universe and help scientists understand the fate of the universe. The 100 scientists from over 11 universities and labs in Canada and abroad expect to have that information within two years.

Visit http://www.physics.uoguelph.ca/sno/ for more information on the SNO.

SCIENCE AT WORK

This section takes a selective look at science as it is applied in industry and everyday life. Individual Canadians have been awarded recognition in the ranks of the world's preeminent scientists and researchers, as our lists of Nobel Prize winners and the Canadian Engineering and Science Hall of Fame both show.

Canadian Nobel Laureates in Science and Medicine

Year	Name	Field	Citation
1923	Drs. Banting, Macleod and Collip	Medicine and Physiology	For the discovery of insulin
1971	Dr. Gerhard Herzberg	Chemistry	For his contributions to the knowledge of electronic structure and geometry of molecules, particularly free radicals
1986	Dr. John Polyani	Chemistry	For contributions concerning the dynamics of elementary chemical reactions
1993	Dr. Michael Smith	Chemistry	Co-winner for work on genetic codes
1994	Bertram Brockhouse	Physics	Co-winner for study on atoms

Canadian Science and Engineering Hall of Fame

The inductees into the Canadian Science and Engineering Hall of Fame are outstanding researchers, inventors, and innovators who have won worldwide recognition for their accomplishments. The Hall of Fame portrait gallery is located at the NRC laboratories on Sussex Drive in Ottawa. Inductees are announced each October. The Hall of Fame web site can be accessed at http://www.nrc.ca.

The Inductees

- **Maude Abbott** (1869–1940) . . . . Pathologist and specialist in congenital heart disease
- **Sir Frederick Banting** (1891–1941) . . . . Co-discoverer of insulin; Nobel laureate
- **Alexander Graham Bell** (1847–1922) . . . . Inventor of the telephone
- **J. Armand Bombardier** (1907–1964) . . . . Inventor of the snowmobile
- **Bertram Brockhouse** (1918–) . . . . Physicist who pioneered use of neutron scattering in study of atoms
- **Reginald Fessenden** (1866–1932) . . . . Pioneer in the development of the radio
- **Sir Sanford Fleming** (1827–1915) . . . . Architect of the transcontinental railway; inventor of time zones
- **Gerald Heffernan** (1919–) . . . . Innovation in steel production, developer of the environment-friendly "mini-mill"
- **Gerhard Herzberg** (1904–99) . . . . Astrophysicist and Nobel laureate
- **George J. Klein** (1904–92) . . . . Design engineer, the most productive inventor in 20th century Canada
- **Hugh LeCaine** (1914–77) . . . . Physicist; designed the first musical synthesizer
- **Sir William Logan** (1798–1875) . . . . First director of the Geological Survey of Canada
- **Elizabeth "Elsie" MacGill** (1905–80) . . . . . . Aeronautical engineer, oversaw WWII production of Hawker Hurricane fighter aircraft
- **Frances G. McGill** (1877–1959) . . . . Pioneer in forensic pathology
- **Frère Marie-Victorin** (1885–1944) . . . . Botanist, author and teacher
- **Andrew G.L. MacNaughton** (1887–1966) . . . Inventor of cathode-ray detection finder and military leader
- **Margaret Newton** (1887–1971) . . . . Plant pathologist, who developed techniques to combat wheat rust
- **Joseph-Alphonse Ouimet** (1908–88) . . . . Inventor, engineer and CBC president
- **Wilder Penfield** (1891–1976) . . . . Neurosurgeon who developed surgical treatments for epilepsy
- **John Polanyi** (1929–) . . . . Nobel laureate; contributed to the development of laser chemistry
- **Charles E. Saunders** (1867–1937) . . . . Developed fast-ripening Marquis wheat
- **Michael Smith** (1932–) . . . . Chemistry researcher, genetic codes and DNA
- **Edgar William Richard Steacie** (1900–62) . . Researcher (free radical chemistry), educator; former president of the National Research Council
- **Wallace Turnbull** (1870–1954) . . . . Inventor of the variable pitch propeller

Source: *National Research Council*

1999 Nobel Prize Winners

Each October the Swedish academies for physics, chemistry and medicine announce the winners of the Nobel Prizes in science. The awards are named after Alfred Nobel, the Swedish-born chemist and businessman who invented dynamite and smokeless gunpowder. The science prizes, as well as a prize for literature and one for peace, are financed by an endowment from Nobel's estate. The prize for economics is financed by the Swedish national bank. Germany's Gunther Grass won the Nobel Prize for Literature; Doctors Without Borders won the Peace Prize for their efforts to bring medical aid to victims of war and disease. Robert Mundell won the economics prize for his demonstration of how international flows of capital affect economic planning.

The 1999 **Chemistry** prize was awarded to Ahmed Zwail of the California Institute of Technology for "his studies of the transition states of chemical reactions using femtosecond spectroscopy"—he uses laser technology to record chemical reactions at one quadrillion frames per second.

The 1999 prize for **Physiology and Medicine** was awarded to Guenter Blobel of Rockefeller University for solving the mystery of how the various proteins know which cells (plant or animal) to go to in living organisms.

The 1999 **Physics** prize was awarded jointly to Gerardu 't Hooft of the University of Utrecht and Martinus Veltman for developing new ways to predict the behaviour of subatomic particles.

> The offical Web site of the Nobel Foundation can be found at http://www.nobel.se. The site offers information on The Nobel Foundation, the various institutions that award the prizes and an Electronic Nobel Museum Project that allows browsers to look into a searchable database of all the prizes and winners; take a virtual tour of some Nobel facilities and access a library of related books and papers.
>
> There is also a Nobel Internet Archive (not affiliated with The Nobel Foundation) that can be searched by category, year or name. Winners biographies can also be accessed at this site. It can be found at http://www.nobelprizes.com.

1999 Manning Award Winners

The Manning Awards recognize and encourage innovation in Canada by honouring individuals who have created and promoted a new concept, process or product which is beneficial to society. Administered by the Calgary-based Ernest C. Manning Foundation, the awards are presented annually. For the 2000 winners, visit http://www.manningawards.ca.

PRINCIPAL AWARD: Roman Baldur of Waterloo, Ont. for development of IBIS (Integrated Ballistics Identification System), a computer-enhanced bullet and cartridge identification system used by law enforcement agencies around the world. The IBIS data bank compares information in a fraction of the time of manual process for linking crimes and sharing evidence.

AWARD OF DISTINCTION: Drs. Norman Dovichi and Jianzhong Zhang of Edmonton, Alta for developing the successful High-Speed DNA Sequencer. The High-Speed DNA Sequencer is poised to revolutionize genomics and DNA analysis. Fully automated, it is able to produce DNA sequences approximately ten times faster than earlier technology.

INNOVATION AWARDS: Stanley Isbister of Saskatoon, Sask. for the Gearless Angle Drive for socket wrench sets. The adapter replaces the hard-to-use universal joint. Available in several angles, the invention has been described by journeyman mechanics as a much-heralded addition to a toolbox.

Tom Van der Weide of Edmonton, Alta for the successful development of the Comfort Plus Anti Fatigue Mat. Designed to alleviate strain from standing on hard-surfaced floors for extended periods of time, the Comfort Mat is both durable and effective, reducing stress and fatigue of the worker.

YOUNG CANADIAN INNOVATION AWARDS: Xing Zeng, Montreal, Que. (The HEXAdb database); Kyle Doerksen, Calgary, Alta (3-D GPR Visualization and Interpretation); Alberto Da Rocha and Joe Barfett, London, Ont. (Hog Farms: A New Pollution Control Process); Robert Quick and Elena Andreeva, Toronto, Ont. (Computer Integrated Battery Manipulator).

Source: *The Manning Awards*

Canadian Inventors

The need to improve **transportation** has driven a number of inhabitants of Canadian soil to invent everything from toboggans, kayaks, birch bark canoes and snowshoes (all courtesy of *First Nations* people) to screw propellers (*John Patch*, 1833), compound steam engines (*Benjamin Franklin Tibbetts*, 1842), electric streetcars (*John Joseph Wright*, 1883) and snowmobiles (*Joseph-Armand Bombardier*, 1922). Other transportation innovations include *Thomas Turnbull*'s three-wheeled, crank-driven vehicle (he called it an Andromonon) of 1851; *John Gordie* and *Samuel Cunard*'s first steamship to cross the Atlantic in 1833; and *Alexander Graham Bell* and *Casey Baldwin*'s hydrofoil boats of 1908. *W.W. Gibson* brought us the first plane to be powered by an air-cooled engine in 1910; and *Walter Rupert Turnbull* developed the variable pitch propeller, patented in 1922 and tested by Canada's air force at Camp Borden in 1927. Oil-electric locomotives came to us in 1929 courtesy of *Samuel Hungerford*, while *Robert Noorduyn* designed and built the first bush plane in 1935. (These planes became the workhorses of the north, able to perform in the most rugged terrain.) In 1937, *John Gower* patented Canada's first all-terrain vehicle. In 1949, *James Floyd* showed the world the jetliner. *Bruce Kirby*, *Hans Fogh* and *Ian Bruce* contributed Laser sailboats to the recreation scene in 1970.

Navigation and **communication** are also a concern in a country this size. A Position Homing Indicator (*Parsons, Dunlop and Curran*, 1952) allowed aircraft personnel to calculate their course and position, while *Harry T. Stevinson* and *David Makow*'s Crash Position Indicator (1959) deployed just before a crash and aided in rescue efforts. *Fredrick N. Gisborne* patented the undersea telegraph cable in 1852. He had developed a method of insulating wire to make it resistant to saltwater and laid the first undersea telegraph cable in North America, linking New Brunswick and PEI. By 1866, the Atlantic Cable, connecting Ireland and Newfoundland, was in operation. Telephones (*Alexander Graham Bell*, 1876) and telephone handsets (*Cyril Duquet*, 1878) began the first personal communication revolution. *Sanford Fleming*'s Standard Time (1878) made the world of transportation and communication less chaotic. The new national railroad of the 1870s made the haphazard methods of timekeeping from town to town unworkable and Fleming set out to fix the problem by dividing the world into 24 time zones. In 1884, his system of Standard Time was adopted by the International Prime Meridian Conference in Washington, DC and we still use it today.

One of Canada's most prolific inventors (over 500 patents) was *Reginald Fessenden* and the products of his experiments have changed lives around the world. He was particularly active in the field of communications. Fessenden was convinced that sound could be transmitted without wires—he wanted to send them via radio waves. He had a wireless radio working by 1900; by 1904 he had transmitted voice via radio waves. The first trans-Atlantic voice transmission came in 1905 and Fessenden did the first radio broadcast from his transmitter at Brant Rock, Massachusetts in 1906. (He played Christmas carols on his violin; the program was heard by sailors aboard ships in the Caribbean.) When the Titanic sank in 1912, Fessenden set out to find a way for ships to detect icebergs in the fog; he developed sonar to help locate distant objects in front of ships and the depth sounder to keep them from running aground. During the First World War, Fessenden contributed tracer bullets (1914) to the Allied effort. He invented the electric gyroscope and built the first power generating station at Niagara Falls. He also took Thomas Edison's very expensive light bulb, which used platinum wiring, and reworked it with cheaper materials and a design that made it last longer. It was Fessenden's light bulb that lit up the nation. By 1927, he had mastered the basics of television. (Although Fessenden endured ridicule from all quarters over his idea that sound could be transmitted without wires and lived in poverty for most of his life, he was a wealthy man and had the satisfaction of watching many of his detractors turn on his radios before he died in 1932.)

Ted Rogers refined the radio even more when he developed the first AC radio tube in 1925. Before then, programs were prone to fading away at crucial moments as the batteries died. After Rogers' invention, a radio could be plugged in for a continuous supply of energy (and sound). Rogers went on to found the world's first all-electric broadcast station: CFRB.

In order to help us enjoy winter **sports**, *John Forbes* came up with a one-piece ice skate in 1868, while *J.A. Whepley* patented long-bladed speed skates in 1888. Around 1855, the game of ice hockey (presumably with strap-on blades) made its way from New Brunswick to points west, most notably in Montreal.

More practical inventors came up with the rotary railroad snowplow (*J.E. Elliott*, 1869), the snowblower (*Arthur Sicard*, 1925), propeller de-icer (*T.R. Griffith* and *John Orr*, 1941) and electric car heaters (*Thomas Ahearn*, 1890).

On the **home** front, *James Brown* invented the first washing machine in 1835, *Thomas Ahearn* patented an electric cooking range in 1882 (before tackling the problem of cold cars). *Dr. Archibald Hunstman* had frozen food for us by 1929, while consumers had to wait until 1962 for instant mashed potatoes (*Edward A. Asselbergs*). In 1930, *Drs. Alan Brown, Fredrick Tisdale* and *Theodore Drake* patented pablum to help nourish babies.

Outdoors enthusiasts remain grateful to *Charles Coll* for bringing them Muskol insect repellant by 1959. *Arthur Ganong* and his brother made outdoor life even more pleasant when they invented the chocolate bar in 1910 so they could take some along when they went fishing.

Canada's most prolific inventor to date is *Dr. George Klein* (1904–92). His work ranged from innovations for **medicine** (the microsurgical staple gun and the electric wheelchair for quadraplegics) to the design of Canada's first nuclear reactor. His early work helped put aircraft on skis; later he tackled problems in **space technology**. He invented the STEM antenna (our contribution to the Gemini and Apollo space programs) and came out of retirement to be the chief consultant on gear design for the CANADARM project.

This is a selective list of Canadians who have contributed innovations in all areas of life. For more information, do a search for the Canadian Science and Engineering Hall of Fame at www.nrc.ca or check out "Canadian Inventions, Innovations and Inventors" at www.stc.carleton.ca.

■ **What's the latest?**

Perhaps not the latest, but certainly something destined to have an impact on the way we live, the Ballard® Fuel Cell continues to be refined. Different from internal combustion engines and batteries, the fuel cell converts fuel (natural gas, methanol, gasoline or hydrogen) into electricity without burning it and creating pollutants the way a conventional engine does. And unlike batteries, it can operate continuously without needing to be recharged. It can use fuel from a tank, just like an internal combustion engine. The cells are quiet, efficient (because they convert fuel directly into electricity) and clean (because the byproducts of the process are heat and pure water vapour).

Although the theories on hydrogen power have been around for about 150 years, it took Geoffrey Ballard of BC to make a workable fuel cell a reality. Since the 1990s, research dollars from public funding and private enterprise have been poured into the project. The cell began a series of successful tests on buses in Germany (1997), Chicago (1998) and Vancouver (1998), with transit systems in Palm Springs and Oakland, California set to do more testing. Daimler-Benz (now DaimlerChrysler) unveiled the first fuel-cell-powered car in Germany in 1996. Ford Motor Company has also bought a share of the company and committed resources to making a fuel-cell-powered vehicle available to the public by 2004. The main challenge for the developer of this fuel cell (and its competitors) is to bring down the cost to make it comparable to the price of a conventional engine.

Patents

If you have an idea for a new gizmo, what is required to have it patented? The Patent Office judges the idea based the following criteria:
1) the gizmo must be the first of its kind in the world;
2) the gizmo must be useful, and most importantly, it must work;
3) the gizmo must be obviously ingenious to others familiar with the field.

A patent gives you the right to exclude others from making, using or selling an invention from the day the patent is granted until 20 years after filing. Patents also provide useful technical information to the public. Although individual inventors still apply for patents, the majority of applications now come from large corporations. Patents are granted by individual countries; so the protection of a Canadian patent extends throughout Canada alone. Patent rights in the United States or elsewhere must be applied for separately in the individual countries.

A Canadian patent application can be filed from any Canada Post outlet across the country. Detailed information on the application procedure for Patents, Trademarks, Copyrights and Industrial and Integrated Circuits Designs can be obtained from the Canadian Intellectual Property Office in Hull, Québec. (819) 953-7620.

There are now a number of World Wide Web sites that are of interest to inventors. These include:

The Canadian Intellectual Property Office (CIPO)
http://cipo.gc.ca
CIPO's web site has information on Canadian Patents, Trademarks, Copyrights, Industrial Designs and Integrated Circuit Topographies. Trademarks can now be filed on line.

The Canadian Innovation Centre
http://www.innovationcentre.ca
The Canadian Innovation Centre is a not-for-profit corporation dedicated to helping Canadians commercialize their technological innovations. (The Centre issues a publication, *Eureka!*, quarterly.)

Canadian Technology Network
http://www.nrc.ca/ctn
Part of the National Reseearch Council site, CTN gives small and medium-sized technology businesses access to a cross-country network of expert advisors.

US Patent and Trademark Office
http://www.uspto.gov/
General information about US Patents and Trademarks is available, and the site has direct links to other national patent offices.

The Centre for Networked Information Discovery and Retrieval (CNIDR-US Patent Project)
http://patents.cnidr.org
You can access the US Patent Classifications Database at this site. You can also access the patent database and do a search for existing patents.

Contact the Women Inventors Project

The Women Inventors Project is a non-profit organization founded in 1986 to provide education, advice and encouragement to innovators. A variety of activities and programs have been developed particularly to encourage girls and women to pursue careers in science, engineering and mathematics. Programs include resource materials, workshops, seminars, videos and presentations for entrepreneurs, teachers and members of service delivery ogranizations. Fledgling inventors have received assistance in everything from design to marketing.

Contact the organization at 107 Holm Crescent, Thornhill, Ont. L3T 5J4 or visit their Web site at http://www.interlog.com/~womenip/contact.html.

ATMOSPHERIC SCIENCE

A Glossary of Weather Terms

Air mass: an extensive body of air with a fairly uniform distribution of moisture and temperature throughout.

Alberta clipper: named after the clipper sailing ships, which at one time were the fastest vessels on the seas. These storms zip along at 64 km/h, preceded by about 5 cm of light, powdery snow and followed by violent winds capable of reaching 100 km/h. This often results in severe blowing and drifting with blizzard conditions that can leave many roads impassable.

Atmosphere: the envelope of air surrounding the earth. Most weather events are confined to the lower 10 km of the atmosphere.

Atmospheric pressure: the force exerted on the earth by the weight of the atmosphere.

Blizzard: severe winter weather condition characterized by low temperatures, strong winds above 40 km/h, and visibility of less than 1 km due to blowing snow; condition lasts three hours or more.

Blowing snow: snow lifted from the earth's surface by the wind to a height of two metres or more. Blowing snow is higher than drifting snow.

Bright sunshine: sunshine intense enough to burn a mark on recording paper mounted in the Campbell-Stokes sunshine recorder. The daily period of bright sunshine is less than that of visible sunshine because the sun's rays are not intense enough to burn the paper just after sunrise, near sunset and under cloudy conditions.

Chinook (also snow-eater): a dry, warm, strong wind that blows down the eastern slopes of the Rocky Mountains in North America. The warmth and dryness are due principally to heating by compression as the air descends the mountain slope.

Cold wave: an occurrence of dangerous cold conditions, when temperatures often dip below -18°C, that usually lasts longer than a few days.

Crepuscular rays: clouds to excite any sky photographer. Crepuscular rays are caused by streaks or beams of sunlight shining through openings in large cumulonimbus clouds on the horizon. The beams reach down and outward from behind the clouds. If they focus upward, toward a point in the sky opposite the sun, they are called anticrepuscular rays. Sometimes they are called sun beams crossing the sky or Jacob's ladder. Sailors refer to them as "the sun drawing water." The dark bands you see crossing the sky are the shadows from clouds.

Cyclone: a generic term that describes all classes of storms from local thunderstorms and tiny dust devils to monstrous hurricanes and typhoons. It comes from the Greek word, *kyklon*, meaning cycle, circle or coil of a snake and refers to all circular wind systems.

Deep low: used to describe the central barometric pressure of a low [usually when it is about 975 millibars (97.50 kPa or less)]. Often has winds of gale to storm force around the low.

Developing low: a low in which the central pressure is decreasing with time. Winds would normally increase as the low deepens.

Dew point temperature: the temperature at which air becomes saturated, allowing condensation of water vapour as frost, fog, dew, mist or precipitation.

Drizzle: precipitation consisting of numerous minute water droplets which appear to float; the droplets are much smaller than in rain.

El Niño: Near the end of most years, the normally cold Peru Current that sweeps northward along the South American coast from southern Chile to the equator is replaced by a warm southward flowing coastal current. Centuries ago the local fishermen named this the "Christ child current," because it appeared around the Christmas season. Every few years it was unusually intense and over time the term El Niño became more closely associated with occasional intense warmings.

Filling low: a low in which the central pressure is increasing with time., i.e. the low is gradually weakening.

Flash floods: a very rapid rise of water with little or no advance warning, most often when an intense thunderstorm drops a huge rainfall on a fairly small area in a very short space of time.

Fog: a cloud based at the earth's surface consisting of tiny water droplets or, under very cold conditions, ice crystals or ice fog; generally found in calm or low wind conditions. Under foggy conditions, visibility is reduced to less than one km. ▶

Frazil ice: [French Canadian] during the freeze-up period ice forms on the river surface and ice crystals or frazil develop within the river, especially in open turbulent water slightly below 0°C. Frazil ice is very common in rapids.

Freezing precipitation: supercooled water drops of drizzle, or rain which freeze on impact to form a coating of ice upon the ground or any objects they strike.

Front: the boundary between two different air masses which have originated from widely separated regions. A cold front is the leading edge of an advancing cold air mass, while a warm front is the trailing edge of a retreating cold air mass.

Frost: the deposit of ice crystals that occurs when the air temperature is at or below the freezing point of water. The term frost is also used to describe the icy deposits of water vapor that may form on the ground or on other surfaces like car windshields, which are colder than the surrounding air and which have a temperature below freezing.

Gale: a strong wind. A gale warning is issued for expected winds of 65 to 100 km/h (34 to 47 knots).

Gust: a sudden, brief increase in wind speed, for generally less than 20 seconds.

Heat wave: a period with more than three consecutive days of maximum temperatures at or above 32°C.

High pressure: a term for an area of high (maximum) pressure with a closed, clockwise (in the Northern Hemisphere) circulation of air.

Humidex: a measure of what hot weather "feels like." Air of a given temperature and moisture content is equated in comfort to air with a higher temperature and that of negligible moisture content. At a humidex of 30°C some people begin to experience discomfort. [*see* chart on p. 591.]

Hurricanes: tropical systems are classed into several categories depending on maximum strength, usually measured by maximum sustained wind speed. A *tropical disturbance* is simply a moving area of thunderstorms in the tropics that maintains its identity for 24 hours or more. A *tropical depression* is a cyclonic system originating over the tropics with a highest sustained wind speed of up to 61 km/h. A *tropical storm* has a highest sustained wind speed of between 62 and 117 km/h. A *hurricane* has wind speeds of 118 km/h or more.

Ice pellets: precipitation consisting of fragments of ice, 5 mm or less in diameter, that bounce when hitting a hard surface, making a sound upon impact.

Inversion: the term refers to a temperature increase with height, where the usual pattern is a decrease in temperature within increasing height.

Isobar: a line on a weather map or chart connecting points of equal pressure. The large concentric lines on television or newspaper weather maps are isobars.

Killing frost: a frost severe enough to end the growing season, usually when the air temperature falls below -2°C.

Land breeze: a small-scale wind set off when the air temperature over water is warmer than that over adjacent land. The land breeze develops at night and blows from the land out to the sea or onto the lake. Its counterpart is the sea or lake breeze.

Low pressure: an area of low (minimum) atmospheric pressure that has a closed counter-clockwise circulation in the Northern Hemisphere.

Peak wind (gust): the highest instantaneous wind speed recorded for a specific time period.

Plough winds: these belong to a family of strong, straight-line downburst winds found in thunderstorms. These winds rush to the ground with great force, maybe 100 to 150 km/h and occasionally even higher. Damage usually covers an area less than 3 km across. Plough winds are capable of toppling trees, lifting roofs, and ripping apart houses and other structures.

Precipitation: any and all forms of water, whether liquid or solid, that fall from the atmosphere and reach the earth's surface. A day with measurable precipitation is a day when the water equivalent of the precipitation is equal to or greater than 0.2 mm.

Probability of precipitation (POP): subjective numerical estimates of your chances of encountering measurable precipitation at some time during the forecast period. For example, a 40% probability of rain means there are four chances in 10 of getting wet. They cannot be used to predict when, where or how much precipitation will occur.

Relative humidity: the ratio of water vapour in the air at a given temperature to the maximum which could exist at that temperature. It is usually expressed as a percentage.

Ridge: an elongated area of high pressure extending from the centre of a high pressure region; the opposite of a trough.

Sea breeze: a small-scale wind set off when the air temperature over land is greater than that over the adjacent sea. The sea breeze develops during the day and blows from the sea to the land. Its counterpart is the land breeze.

Sleet: is not what you think. In the United States, sleet is frozen raindrops that bounce when they hit the surface. It is not as treacherous to drive on as is freezing rain. What Americans call sleet a Canadian would call ice pellets or frozen raindrops. They are spherical or irregular shapes with a diameter of 5 mm or less. Pellets do not stick to trees or wires. On the other hand, sleet to a British weather watcher is a mix of rain and partly melted snowflakes.

Small craft warning: issued when winds over the coastal marine areas are expected to reach and maintain speeds of 20 to 33 knots.

Snow: precipitation consisting of white or translucent ice crystals and often agglomerated into snowflakes. A day with measurable snow is a day when the total snowfall is at least 0.2 cm.

Squall: a strong, sudden wind which generally lasts a few minutes then quickly decreases in speed. Squalls are generally associated with severe thunderstorms.

Storm track: the path taken by a low-pressure centre.

Storm warning: the wind warning that is issued to mariners when winds are expected to be 48 to 63 knots.

Thunderstorm: a local storm, usually produced by a cumulonimbus cloud, and always accompanied by thunder and lightning. A thunderstorm day is a day when thunder is heard or when lightning is seen (rain and snow need not have fallen).

Tornado (also twister): a violently rotating column of air that is usually visible as a funnel cloud hanging from dark thunderstorm clouds. It is one of the least extensive of all storms, but in violence, it is the most destructive.

Trough: an elongated area of low pressure extending from the centre of a low pressure region; the opposite of a ridge.

Tsunami: also known (incorrectly) as a tidal wave. "Tsunami" comes from Japanese and means "harbour wave." It is a wave set in motion by an undersea movement such as an earthquake or a landslide. These waves can travel up to 1,000 km/h over long distances, hitting the shore with tremendous force.

Typhoon: a severe tropical cyclone in the Western Pacific Ocean, counterpart of the Atlantic hurricane.

Virga: streaks of falling rain that evaporate before reaching the ground.

Watches and warnings: Environment Canada alerts Canadians to severe storms by issuing weather watches and warnings. Usually the first message is the severe thunderstorm watch. If a watch is issued in your area, maintain your routine, but keep an eye skyward for threatening weather, and listen to radio and television for further weather information. When severe local storms are building, or have actually been sighted or detected by radar, then warnings are issued and updated. These may be either severe thunderstorm warnings or tornado warnings. Warnings mean you should be on the alert.

Waterspout: A waterspout is not really a waterspout. Often called a tornado over water, the actual water spray involved does not extend from the surface to the cloud, but 3 to 10 metres above the water surface. Like the tornado, the waterspout is very brief. Sailors believed one way of breaking up a waterspout was to fire a cannon through it.

Weatheradio: this is the name of Environment Canada's weather information broadcast network. The network has transmitters in every region and listeners need a receiver, which can be purchased from electronic equipment dealers, to pick up the broadcasts. Weatheradio signals warnings of severe weather automatically to receivers equipped with special alarm devices for that purpose.

Westerlies (west-wind belt): the pronounced west-to-east motion of the atmosphere centred over middle latitudes from about 35 to 65° latitude.

Willy-willies: refers to small, circular winds such as dust devils or whirlwinds in Australia, not very hazardous. Before 1950, willy-willies referred to much larger, more destructive typhoons or hurricanes.

Wind chill: a simple measure of the chilling effect experienced by the human body when strong winds are combined with freezing temperatures. The larger the wind chill, the faster the rate of cooling. The wind chill factor is expressed in watts per square metre or in °C (an equivalent temperature). [see chart on page 595, formula on page 597.]

Wind direction: the direction from which the wind is blowing.

Source: *Environment Canada*

Weather Records

	Canada	United States	World
Highest maximum air temperature	45.0° Midale and Yellowgrass, Sask. July 5, 1937	56.7° Death Valley, CA July 10, 1913	58.0° Al'azizyah, Libya Sept. 13, 1922
Lowest minimum air temperature	-63.0° Snag, YT Feb. 3, 1947	-62.1° Prospect Creek Camp, AK Jan. 23, 1971	-89.6° Vostok, Antarctica July 21, 1983
Coldest month	-47.9° Eureka, NWT Feb. 1979		
Highest sea-level pressure	107.95 kPa Dawson, YT Feb. 2, 1989	107.86 kPa Northway, AK Jan. 31, 1989	108.38 kPa Agata, Siberia USSR Dec. 31, 1968
Lowest sea-level pressure	94.02 kPa St. Anthony, Nfld Jan. 20, 1977	89.23 kPa Matecumbe Key, FL Sept. 2, 1935	87 kPa in eye of Typhoon Tip (Pacific Ocean) Oct. 12, 1979
Greatest precipitation in 24hrs	489.2 mm Ucluelet Brynnor Mines, BC Oct. 6, 1967	1 090 mm Alvin, TX	1 869.9 mm Cilaos, La Réunion Is. March 15, 1952
Greatest precipitation in one month	2 235.5 mm Swanson Bay, BC Nov. 1917	2 717.8 mm Kukui, HI March 1942	9 300 mm Cherrapunji, India July 1861
Greatest precipitation in one year	9 341.1 mm Henderson Lake, BC 1998	17 902.7 mm Kukui, HI 1982	26 461.2 mm Cherrapunji, India Aug. 1860-July 1861
Greatest average annual precipitation	7 m Henderson Lake, BC	11 684 mm Mt. Waialeaie, Kauai, HI	11 684 mm Mt. Waialeaie, Kauai, HI
Least annual precipitation	13.6 mm Arctic Bay, NWT 1949	0.0 Bagdad, CA Oct. 3, 1912 to Nov. 8, 1914	0.0 Arica, Chile—no rain for 14 years
Greatest average annual snowfall	1 518 cm Glacier Mt. Fidelity, BC	1 461 cm Rainer Paradise Ranger Station, WA	
Greatest snowfall in one season	2 446.9 cm Revelstoke/Mt. Copeland, BC 1971–72	2 850 cm Rainer Paradise Ranger Station, WA 1971–72	
Greatest snowfall in one month	535.8 cm Haines Apps. No 2, BC Dec. 1959	990.6 cm Tamarack, CA Jan. 1911	
Greatest snowfall in one day	145 cm Tahtsa Lake West, BC Feb. 11, 1999	196.6 cm Montague, N.Y. Jan. 11-12, 1997	
Highest average annual number of thunderstorm days	36 days London, Ont.	96 days Fort Meyers, FL	322 days Bogor, Indonesia
Heaviest hailstone	290 g Cedoux, Sask. Aug. 27, 1973	758 g Coffeyville, KS Sept. 3, 1970	15 000 g Guangdong province of China April 19, 1995
Highest average annual wind speed	36 km/h Cape Warwick, Resolution Island, NWT	56.3 km/h Mt. Washington, NH	
Highest wind speed for 1 hr	201.1 km/h Cape Hopes Advance (Quaqtaq), Que. Nov. 18, 1931	362.0 km/h Mt. Washington, NH April 12, 1934	
Highest average hours of fog	1 890 hrs Argentia, Nfld	2 552 hrs Cape Disappointment, WA	

Source: *Environment Canada*

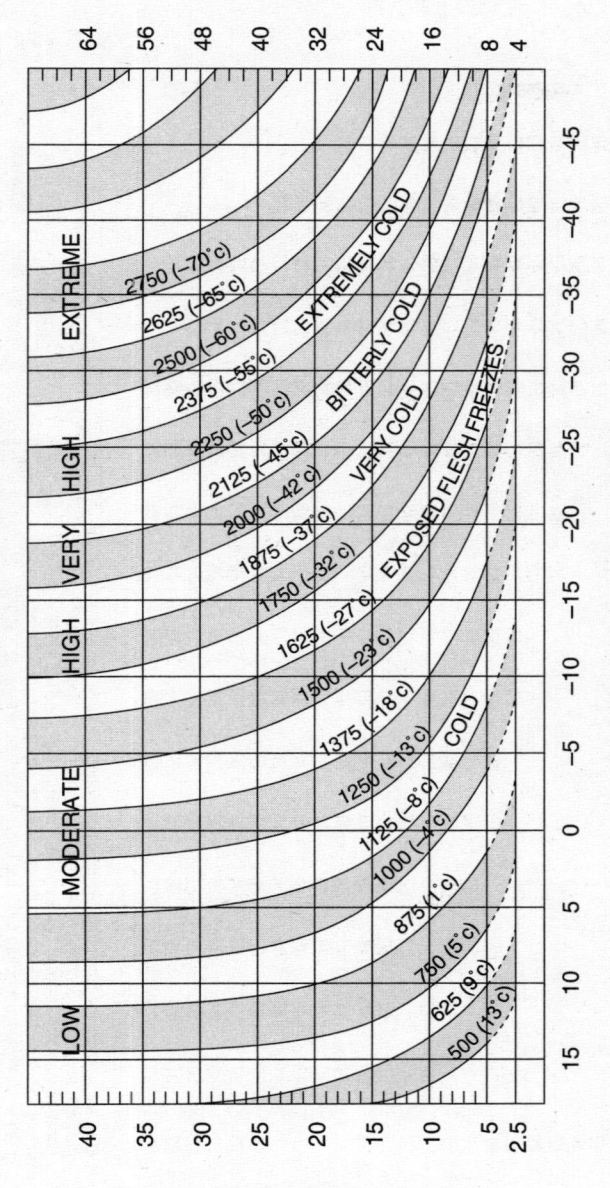

Humidex

RELATIVE HUMIDITY (%)

DBT (°C)	100	95	90	85	80	75	70	65	60	55	50	45	40	35	30	25	20
43												56	56	54	51	49	47
42											56	54	54	52	50	48	46
41										57	54	52	52	50	48	46	44
40									56	54	53	51	51	50	48	46	43
39								56	54	52	51	49	49	49	47	44	41
38							57	53	51	50	49	47	47	47	45	43	40
37						57	55	51	50	48	47	45	45	46	43	42	
36					58	54	53	49	48	47	45	43	43	43	42	40	
35			58	57	56	52	51	48	47	45	43	42	42	42	40	38	
34	58	58	57	56	54	51	49	46	44	43	42	40	41	41	38	37	
33	55	57	55	53	52	48	47	43	42	41	39	38	38	39	37	36	
32	52	54	52	51	50	46	45	41	40	39	38	36	37	37	36	34	
31	50	51	50	49	47	44	43	40	38	37	36	35	35	36	34	33	
30	48	49	48	46	45	42	41	38	37	36	34	33	34	34	33	31	
29	46	47	46	44	43	41	39	36	35	34	33	32	32	33	31	31	
28	43	45	44	43	42	38	37	35	33	32	31	31	31	31	30		
27	41	42	41	41	39	36	35	33	31	31	29	30	29	29	28		
26	39	40	39	38	37	34	33	32	30	29	28	28	28	28	28		
25	37	38	37	36	35	33	32	31	28	28	27	27	27	27			
24	35	36	35	34	33	31	30	29	27	26	25	26	26	25			
23	33	34	33	33	32	29	28	27	24	24	23	24	23				
22	31	32	32	31	30	27	26	26	24	23	23	23					
21	29	29	28	28	27	26	26	24				22					

Degree of Comfort

Humidex (°C)	Degree of Comfort
20 – 29	Comfortable
30 – 39	Varying degrees of discomfort
40 – 45	Almost everyone uncomfortable
46 and over	Many types of labour must be restricted

DRY BULB TEMPERATURE (DEGREES CELSIUS)

■ In hot weather, our bodies regulate core temperature by using our sweat glands to shed water. Sweating doesn't cool the body, but the evaporation of sweat on your skin removes heat because it takes energy (heat) to change the liquid on your skin to vapour in the air. However, when it's humid, the air itself is already full of moisture and it can't absorb the moisture we are trying to shed, making us sticky and uncomfortable.

Ultra-Violet Index

Ultra-violet radiation is short-wavelength radiation that is part of the spectrum, just beyond visible violet light. These waves can harm both plant and animal life—the shorter of the UV wavelengths, known as UV-B, can cause sunburn, skin cancer and cataracts in humans and animals, and can also reduce agricultural productivity.

These rays are usually blocked by the protective ozone layer in the stratosphere, found between 10 and 50 km above the Earth. Ozone is a form of oxygen that has thee atoms instead of two and is created when ordinary oxygen interacts with ultraviolet radiation from the sun. Ozone can be destroyed by chemicals released into the air—most notably by the breakdown of chlorofluorocarbons (CFCs). CFCs have been used in air-conditioning, refrigeration and in some plastics manufacturing and CFC molecules are stable enough to last 100 years in the atmosphere—long enough to drift into the stratosphere where UV-B rays can break them down to produce free chlorine atoms. It is the chlorine atoms that destroy ozone.

In the 1970s, scientists had a theory that the chemicals drifting in the atmosphere could destroy the ozone layer. In the winter of 1985 NASA discovered a hole in the ozone layer over Antarctica. In recent years the continuing depletion of the ozone layer has resulted its general thinning, and in holes of varying sizes at the poles from time to time. Various attempts have been made to phase out the use of ozone-depleting chemicals all over the world, particularly at the Earth Summit in Rio de Janeiro in June 1992. While progress has been made, it is important to realize that more UV-B rays are getting through the atmosphere and there is a higher risk of UV-B generated health problems.

In May 1992, Canada's weather service launched a daily ultraviolet index as part of the forecast, the first country in the world to do so. The purpose of the index is to warn people about the dangers of over-exposure to the sun. Several other countries, including Australia, New Zealand, the Netherlands, Germany, Great Britain and the United States, have now started their own programs closely modelled on the Canadian UV index.

The amount of UV-B is measured on a scale of 0 to 10, with 10 being a typical amount you would receive on a summer day in the tropics. The higher the number, the faster you'll sunburn. (Sunburn times are for light untanned skin; times would be somewhat longer for those with darker skin.)

UV Index	Category	Sunburn Time
over 9	extreme	less than 15 minutes
7-9	high	about 20 minutes
4-7	moderate	about 30 minutes
0-4	low	more than one hour

Source: *Environment Canada*

Calculating Wind Chill

You can calculate the wind chill equivalent temperature in degrees Celsius (°C) or the wind chill factor in watts per square metre for your own values of air temperature (°C) and wind speed in kilometres per hour, by using the following equations:

Wind Chill Equivalent Temperature [WET] in °C:

$$WET = 33 - ((12.1 + 6.12\sqrt{W} - 0.32 \times W) (33 - T)/27.8)$$

Wind Chill Factor [WCF] in watts per square metre:

$$WCF = (12.1 + 6.12\sqrt{W} - 0.32 \times W) (33 - T)$$

T = ambient air temperature in °C   W = wind speed in kilometres per hour

This calculation gives meaningful values of WET and WCF for any air temperature lower than 5°C, and for any wind speed between 8 and 80 kilometres per hour.

The Beaufort Wind Scale

Beaufort forces range from 0 in calm conditions, to 12 in a hurricane. Rear-Admiral Sir Francis Beaufort of the British Royal Navy devised the scale in 1805. It originally referred to the amount of sail a full-rigged ship could carry in specific wind conditions. In light air, just one sail would be taken in; in a moderate gale, seven would come down; and in a heavy storm the number would be eleven, therefore Beaufort force 11. The Beaufort scale has been modified and modernized several times. Basically though, the idea is to estimate wind speed by watching the effects of wind on such things as flags, trees, smoke, water surface and even people. The scale is still widely used today.

Beaufort Wind Force	Wind Speed (km/h)	Wind Type	Descriptive Effects
0	0–1	calm	smoke rises vertically
1	2–5	light air	smoke drifts slowly
2	6–11	light breeze	leaves rustle; wind vanes move
3	12–19	gentle breeze	leaves and twigs in constant motion
4	20–29	moderate breeze	small branches move; raises dust and loose paper moves along
5	30–38	fresh breeze	small trees sway
6	39–50	strong breeze	large branches in continuous motion; telephone wires whistle
7	51–61	near gale	whole trees in motion; wind affects walking
8	62–74	gale	twigs and small branches break off trees
9	75–87	strong gale	branches break; shingles blow from roofs
10	88–101	storm	trees snap and uproot; some damage to buildings
11	102–117	violent storm	property damage widespread
12	118–	hurricane	severe and extensive damage

Source: *Environment Canada*

Tornado Intensity Scale

Tornadoes are classified by the destruction they leave behind. They are rated from F0 to F5, F standing for Fujita, one of the world's leading experts on tornadoes.

F-Scale	Winds (km/h)	Length (km)	Width	Damage
0 (very weak)	under 116	< 1.5	under 15m	Light damage; minor roof, tree, chimney, antenna and sign damage
1 (weak)	117-180	1.6-5	50m	Moderate damage; barns torn apart; mobile homes pushed off foundations; trees snapped; cars pushed off roads; sheet metal buildings destroyed
2 (strong)	181-252	5.1-15.9	160m	Considerable damage; roofs torn off schools, homes and businesses; debris from barns scattered; trailers disintegrated; large trees uprooted; concrete block buildings destroyed
3 (severe)	253-332	16-50	161-500m	Severe damage; roofs and walls of schools, homes and buildings blown away; large trees uprooted; weaker homes completely disappear
4 (devastating)	333-419	51-159	0.5-1.4km	Interior and exterior walls of all homes blown apart; cars thrown more than 300m in the air
5 (incredible)	420-512	160-507	1.5-16km	Strongly built homes completely blown away; bizarre phenomena such as straw driven through fence posts

Source: *Environment Canada*

The Saffir-Simpson Hurricane Intensity Scale

Category	Maximum Sustained Wind Speed (km/h)	Minimum Surface Pressure (kPa)	Storm Surge (m)	Remarks
1 (minimal)	119-153	>=98.0	1.0-1.7	Damage to trees and signs. Low-lying flooding. Small craft torn from mooring.
2 (moderate)	154-177	97.9 - 96.5	1.8-2.6	Trees blown down; damage to mobile homes and roofs. Marinas flooded; evacuation of shores.
3 (extensive)	178-209	96.4 - 94.5	2.7-3.8	Some structural damage to small buildings; serious coastal flooding; mobile homes destroyed.
4 (extreme)	210-249	94.4 - 92.0	3.9-5.6	Extensive damage: doors, roofs, windows; major damage to lower floors of buildings near shore. Major beach erosion. Massive evacuation from shore possible.
5 (catastrophic)	>250	<92.0	>5.6	Small buildings blown away; complete destruction of mobile homes; massive evacuation within 10 to 20 km of shore possible.

Source: H.S. Saffir, P.E. and Dr. R. Simpson

Hurricane Names in 2001

*T*he names chosen for Atlantic Ocean, Gulf of Mexico and Caribbean Sea tropical storms are: Allison, Barry, Chantal, Dean, Erin, Felix, Gabrielle, Humberto, Iris, Jerry, Karen, Lorenzo, Michelle, Noel, Olga, Pablo, Rebekah, Sebastien, Tanya, Van and Wendy.

The names for Eastern Pacific tropical storms (east of 140°W) are: Adolph, Barbara, Cosme, Dalila, Erick, Flossie, Gil, Henriette, Israel, Juliette, Kiko, Lorena, Manuel, Narda, Octave, Priscilla, Raymond, Sonia, Tico, Velma, Wallis, Xina, York and Zelda. (A number of other areas have their own hurricane naming systems, including the NW Pacific; SW Indian Ocean; Western, Northern and Eastern Australian regions; Fiji area; and Papua New Guinea.)

Retired Atlantic Hurricane Names

Names are not used again when a particular storm causes a great deal of damage or death, in order to prevent confusion when referring to historically significant storms. Names of great Atlantic hurricanes dropped from the rotating list of names are: Agnes (1972), Alicia (1983), Allen (1980), Andrew (1992), Anita (1977), Audrey (1957), Betsy (1965), Beulah (1967), Bob (1991), Camille (1969), Carla (1961), Carmen (1974), Carol (1965), Celia (1970), Cesar (1996), Cleo (1964), Connie (1955), David (1979), Diana (1990), Diane (1955), Donna (1960), Dora (1964), Edna (1968), Elena (1985), Eloise (1975), Fifi (1974), Flora (1963), Fran (1996), Frederic (1979), Floyd (1999), Gilbert (1988), Gloria (1985), Georges (1998), Gracie (1959), Hattie (1961), Hazel (1954), Hilda (1964), Hortense (1996), Hugo (1989), Inez (1966), Ione (1955), Janet (1955), Joan (1988), Klaus (1990), Luis (1995), Lenny (1999), Marilyn (1995), Mitch (1998), Opal (1995) and Roxanne (1995).

Most Severe Weather Events of the Twentieth Century

Rogers Pass Avalanche, March 5, 1910: Sixty-two train men and labourers perished 2 km west of Rogers Pass, BC, when their engine was hit by an avalanche and hurtled 500 metres into Bear Creek. Over 600 volunteers used pick axes and shovels to dig through 10 m of snow in the search for survivors.

Deadliest Canadian Tornado, June 30, 1912: A late afternoon tornado slashed through six city blocks in Regina, killing up to 40 people, injuring 300 others, destroying 500 buildings and leaving a quarter of the population homeless.

Black Sunday Storm, November 7–13, 1913: One of the most severe Great Lakes storms on record swept winds of 140 km/h over lakes Erie and Ontario, taking down 34 ships and 270 sailors.

Storm Claims Sealers, April 1, 1914: Seventy-seven sealers froze to death on the ice during a violent storm off the southeast coast of Labrador. At the height of the storm, from March 31 to April 2, the temperature was -23°C with winds from the northwest at 64 km/h.

Killer Lightning, July 29, 1916: Lightning ignited a forest fire that burned down the towns of Cochrane and Matheson, Ontario, killing 233 people.

August Gale Kills 56 in Newfoundland, August 24–25, 1927: A hurricane swept through Atlantic Canada washing out roads, filling basements, and swamping boats. In Newfoundland, 56 people died at sea.

Dustbowl Era, 1930s: Between 1933 and 1937, the Prairies experienced only 60 percent of its normal rainfall. Thousands of livestock were lost to starvation and suffocation, crops withered and 250,000 people across the region abandoned their land to seek better lives elsewhere.

Cold Wave Grips Eastern North America, February 1934: A cold wave engulfed the continent from Manitoba to the Atlantic seaboard and down the east coast to Palm Beach, Florida. Ice trapped fishing vessels off Nova Scotia, hospitals were jammed with frostbite victims and, for only the second time in recorded history, Lake Ontario froze completely over.

The Deadliest Heat Wave in History, July 5–17, 1936: Temperatures exceeding 44°C in Manitoba and Ontario claimed 1,180 Canadians (mostly the elderly and infants) during the longest, deadliest heat wave on record. Four hundred of these deaths occurred when people drowned seeking refuge from the heat. In fact, the heat was so intense that steel rail lines and bridge girders twisted, sidewalks buckled, crops wilted and fruit baked on trees.

Hottest Day on Record, July 5, 1937: The highest temperature ever recorded in Canada was reached at Midale and Yellowgrass, Saskatchewan when the mercury soared to 45°C.

Worst Blizzard in Canadian Railway History, January 30 to February 8, 1947: A ten-day blizzard buried towns and trains from Winnipeg to Calgary, causing some Saskatchewan roads and rail lines to remain plugged with snow until spring. Children stepped over power lines to get to school and built tunnels to get to the outhouse. A Moose Jaw farmer had to cut a hole in the roof of his barn to get in to feed his cows.

Coldest Temperature in North America, February 3, 1947: The temperature in Snag, Yukon dipped to -63°C, establishing Canada's reputation for extreme cold.

BC's Worst Flood of the Century, May–June 1948: BC's Fraser River overflowed, drowning 10, inundating 22,200 hectares, destroying 2,300 homes and forcing 16,000 to flee. Row boats were the only means of transportation in much of the Fraser Valley, and for three weeks Vancouver had no rail connection with the rest of Canada.

Hurricane Hazel, October 15, 1954: Leaving a nightmare of destruction, Hazel dumped an estimated 300 million tonnes of rain on Toronto, causing lost streets, washed out bridges and untold personal tragedy. In all, 83 people died—some bodies washing up on the shores of Lake Ontario in New York State days later.

Fishing Fleet Disaster off Esuminac, NB, June 20, 1959: More than 30 fishermen drowned in the worst storm disaster ever to hit the Gulf of St. Lawrence fishing fleet. Twenty-two salmon boats sank by a sudden, smashing north-easterly gale.

Winnipeg's Snowstorm of the Century, March 4, 1966: This winter blizzard dropped 35 cm of snow with winds blowing at 120 km/h, paralyzing the city for four days. Winnipeg's mayor issued a warning for everyone to stay at home. The drifting snow blocked all highways in southern Manitoba and forced the cancellation of all air travel in and out of the Winnipeg airport.

Atmospheric Science

Blizzards in Southern Alberta, April 17–20 and 27–29, 1967: A series of intense winter storms dropped a record 175 cm of snow on southern Alberta. Thousands of cattle, unable to forage for food in the deep snow, perished on the open range.

Greatest Rainfall in One Day, October 6, 1967: A one-day rainfall of 489.2 mm occurred at Ucluelet Brynnor Mines, BC—a Canadian weather record that still stands.

Hurricane Beth Soaks Nova Scotia, August 15, 1971: Hurricane Beth brought punishing winds and up to 300 mm of rain, causing considerable crop damage and swamping highways and bridges, temporarily isolating communities on the eastern mainland of Nova Scotia.

Blizzard Isolates Iqaluit, February 8, 1979: Weather with -40°C temperatures, 100 km/h winds and zero visibility in snow kept residents of Iqaluit indoors for 10 days.

Blizzard Maroons PEI, February 22–26, 1982: A huge snowstorm with up to 60 cm of snow, 100 km/h winds, zero visibility and wind chills of -35°C paralyzed the Island for a week. The storm buried vehicles, snowplows and trains in 5- to 7-metre drifts and cut off all ties with the mainland.

Ocean Ranger Disaster, February 15, 1982: Bad weather caused the sinking of the largest semi-submersible drilling rig in the world, 300 km east of Newfoundland. In total, 84 people died in the world's second worst disaster involving an offshore drill ship. Winds of 145 km/h, waves of 21 metres and high seas hampered rescue efforts.

$4 Billion Drought, September 1987–August 1988: Across the southern Prairies, the hottest summer on record, combined with half the normal growing season rainfall and a virtually snow-free previous winter, produced a drought that rivaled the 1930s in terms of intensity and duration of the dry spell. About 10 percent of farmers and farm workers left agriculture in 1988. Effects of the drought were felt across the country as lower agricultural yields led to higher food and beverage prices for consumers.

Record Wind Chill, January 28, 1989: It was bad enough when the temperature dropped to -51°C in Pelly Bay, NWT but the wind made the air feel even colder when the wind chill equivalent reached -91°C.

Hailstorm Strikes Calgary, September 7, 1991: A supper-hour storm lasting 30 minutes dropped 10-cm diameter hail in Calgary subdivisions, splitting trees, breaking windows and siding, and crushing birds. Homeowners filed a record 116,000 insurance claims, with property damage losses exceeding $300 million—the most destructive hailstorm ever and the second costliest storm in Canada.

Saguenay Flood, July 18–21, 1996: Canada's first billion dollar disaster, this deluge triggered a surge of water, rocks, trees and mud that killed 10 people and forced 12,000 residents to flee their homes. Many roads and bridges in the region disappeared.

Red River Flood Levels Highest of Century, April–May, 1997: About 2,000 square km of valley lands were flooded as the Red River rose 12 m above winter levels. Thousands of volunteers and soldiers fought rising waters for days. Damage estimates reached a half a billion dollars.

Okanagan's $100 million Hailstorm, July 21, 1997: A destructive hail and wind storm ripped through the orchards of the Okanagan. It was the worst storm in memory with nearly 40 percent of the crop deemed unsuitable for fresh market. The rain and hail was accompanied by winds gusting to 100 km/h that capsized boats in the interior lakes, and caused power outages and traffic accidents.

Ice Storm of the Century, January 4–9, 1998: One of the most destructive and disruptive storms in Canadian history hit Eastern Canada causing hardship for 4 million people and costing $3 billion. Losses included millions of trees, 130 transmission towers and 120,000 km of power and telephone lines. Power outages lasted from several hours to four weeks.

Costliest Forest Fire Season on Record, 1998: Flames from forest fires destroyed 4.6 million hectares of forests, about 50 percent more than the normal amount. The 10,560 fires were the greatest number in 10 years and occurred after the country's second warmest winter and spring.

Greatest Single-Day Snowfall Record, February 11, 1999: Tahtsa Lake, BC, received 145 cm of snow, a new Canadian single-day snowfall record, but well below the world's record of 192 cm at Silver Lake, Colorado on April 15, 1921.

For a complete listing of the Top Weather Events of the Twentieth Century, visit http://www.ec.gc.ca/ weather_e.html and choose Top Weather Events.

Source: *Environment Canada.*

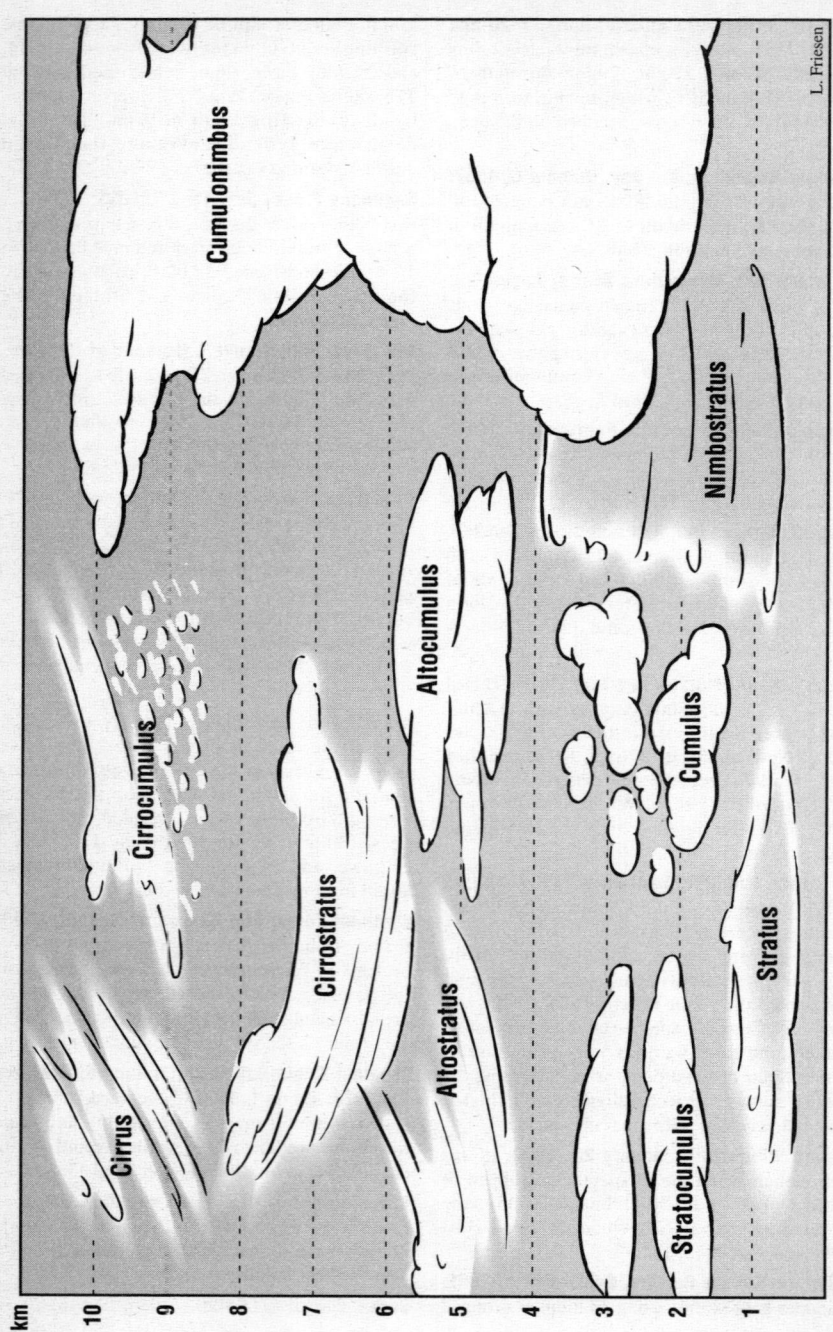

Ten Basic Cloud Types

1. Cirrus
Thin wispy small white clouds that often occur as feathery filaments or long streamers stretching across the sky. Often their ends are swept by strong winds giving it the look of a mare's tail.

2. Cirrostratus
White uniform veil of thin transparent cloud. Sky still appears bright with a halo around the sun. Cloud sheets are small or extensive.

3. Cirrocumulus
Thin bands of either continuous or patchy small clouds, white or pale grey in colour. Cloud base occurs above 6,000 m.; ripple or rib pattern gives it a look of fish-scales, referred to as a "mackerel sky."

4. Altocumulus
Either patchy or continuous middle cumulus cloud with a dappled or rippled appearance. Thicker and lower version of cirrocumulus that is associated with changeable weather and perhaps rain.

5. Alto stratus
Grey pale uniform layer of cloud in which the sun may appear weakly. Too thick and low for halos to be seen, however, through the overcast, the sun can be seen weakly. A sign of precipitation within a few hours.

6. Stratocumulus
Low layers of grey or whitish clouds with occasional dark patches that have a well-defined rounded or undulating appearance. May have a few breaks, but usually total cloud cover extends for hundreds of kilometres.

7. Stratus
A grey uniform low blanket of cloud that may be continuous or patchy, often producing light drizzle. The base is between the surface and 300 m, often obscuring hill tops and tall buildings. Looks like high drifting fog or making for a dull, grey day.

8. Nimbostratus
A thick low level (600 m) deck of cloud providing continuous rain or snow. Usually covers the entire sky and completely hides the sun.

9. Cumulus
White puffy clouds that often form by day and disappear by night. Well-defined base begins at 600 to 1,200 m; upper parts are cauliflower-like. Associated with fair weather, blue sky and no precipitation.

10. Cumulonimbus
Giant impressive cumulus clouds with dark base and a smooth anvil-shaped top. Called the kings of the sky, they are the biggest of all clouds, often towering in excess of 10 km. Often associated with severe thunderstorms and sometimes hail or tornadoes. In heavy rain, cumulonimbus clouds have a dark ominous base and a curtain of rain.

Source: *Environment Canada*

Weather Symbols

Meteorologists in Canada, China and Croatia—in fact, all around the world—use a standard set of symbols in constructing detailed weather maps. Here are some samples of these universal weather symbols:

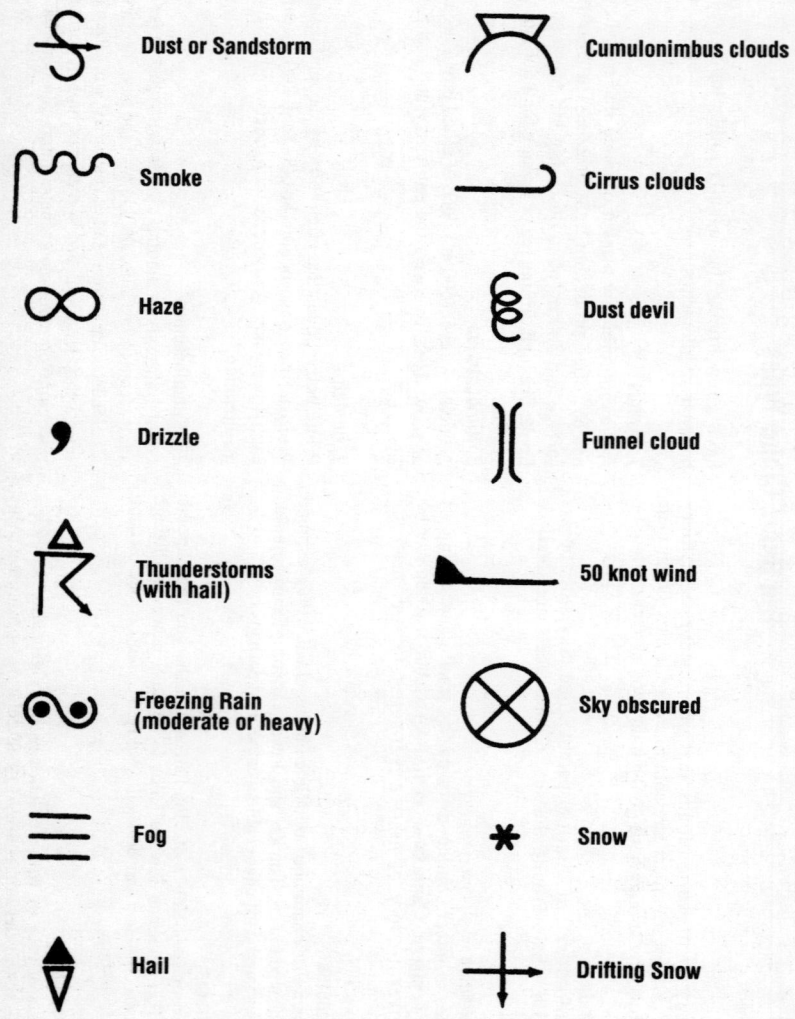

Source: *Environment Canada*

Climate Change and Canada

"Climate change" has always meant global warming, and for many Canadians, this doesn't sound like a bad idea—especially in January. Is it really getting warmer? Environment Canada has been keeping nationwide records since 1948 and reports general warming trends over the past two decades. In particular, we've experienced six of the warmest ten springs during the last 20 years. Most particularly, as of spring 2000, the country had experienced three years—twelve seasons in a row—of temperatures above normal. For most of the country the difference was 1° to 2°C above normal; for southern Manitoba and northern Ontario it was closer to 3°C above normal.

What about the rest of the world? In March 2000, scientists at the US National Oceanic and Atmospheric Administration reported that the world's oceans have grown warmer since the 1950s. The increase is from one-tenth to one-half a degree and was based on an analysis of over five million readings at various depths in the Indian, Pacific and Atlantic oceans. The most significant warming took place not just at the surface but to nearly 275 m below, with changes of up to 0.3°C. Elsewhere, signs such as an accelerated shrinking of Peru's Quelccaya ice cap documented in late 1999 and the appearance of water where ice was expected at the North Pole in the summer of 2000 have raised alarm in some quarters. Others insist it's all just part of the normal ebb and flow of climate over centuries.

What kind of impact could this degree of change have? Scientists suggest that it could mean anything from an increase in the severity of droughts, floods, winter storms and tornadoes to accelerated erosion and increased flooding in coastal regions. While the increase in temperature doesn't sound significant to us, it could change the environment enough to weaken plants (including trees and crops) and animals. Plants that get too much (or not enough) water and sunlight become more sensitive to disease and pests and less able to resist fire. A decrease in plant life would adversely affect the wildlife that feeds on it. For example, significant changes to water and wetland habitats could either weaken their current inhabitants or kill them if they can't adapt to the changed environment quickly.

■ Regional Impacts

In the **mountains** in the west, the seemingly small jump in temperature could mean decreased snowpack and a retreat of the glaciers; as well, the upper limit of continuous forest (the timberline) would slowly move northward. In the short term, this could mean flooding and flows of glacial debris; in the longer term, the interior plains and southern interior of BC could become drier because snowmelt and glacial melt are the main sources of water for the areas. From an economic perspective, the ability to produce crops could be adversely affected, as could recreational skiing and tourism.

Elsewhere, 50 percent of Canada's land surface has **permafrost** underneath it. While permafrost exists anywhere that ground temperatures are below freezing through the year, much of this territory has an average temperature only 2°C below freezing. The temperature change forecasted under the global warming model means that much of this could thaw, destabilizing the surface and affecting everything from cemeteries, building foundations, roads, railways, pipelines and dams to hillsides. In addition, thawing shorelines will be much more vulnerable to damage done by wave erosion. Another 14 percent of Canada's landmass is covered by **peatlands**—these are the areas with a layer of decaying plant material that could be over 40 cm deep. The peatlands are natural sources of carbon and a major warming trend would release it into the air, further contributing to global warming as well as accelerating the thawing of the permafrost in areas of frozen peatland.

Discussions of global warming have always included a warning about a **rise in sea level**. Canada's coastline is over 240,000 km long, making this a significant issue. A small rise in sea level would threaten low-lying areas that include the Bay of Fundy, Tuktoyaktut on the Beaufort Sea, the Fraser Delta near Vancouver and sites on the Queen Charlotte Islands. **Rivers** would be subject to an increase in flash floods if a warmer earth with more intense storms becomes the norm. While there would be a decrease in the amount of meltwater coming off glaciers and snowpacks, an increase in the intensity of storms would mean that rivers would have to change in order to accommodate the sudden influxes of water (or overflow). Still on the subject of water, **fish** populations need a limited range of water temperatures in order to survive; the kind of sudden temperature shift that could accompany global warming would mean that fish habitats would change overnight (relative to species adaptation). Scientists at Environment Canada predict that should the projected change take place, the habitat for the sockeye salmon, for example, would be eliminated from the Pacific Ocean.

Areas in northwest Ontario, Manitoba, Saskatchewan and the Northwest Territories have traditionally been the most prone to **forest fires**. While most of the attention in summer 2000 was on the beleaguered US state of Montana, forest fire activity is expected to be on the rise in areas formerly irrigated by meltwater. A warming climate is expected to bring a sizable increase in the size of the area subject to forest fires and longer fire seasons. An increased frequency of forest fires will mean shorter growth periods between fires and more young stands of trees. Forests in general are expected to be affected as the weather changes: pine forests will move north as the weather warms, replaced by the less commercially useful birch trees in traditional logging areas.

■ **Human Impact**

How will all this affect us? Changes in growing seasons and the capacity of the land to support crops and animals could affect our food supply, as could changes in the fisheries. The decrease in meltwater could diminish the country's vast water supplies. These changes would have an impact on our health as well as our economic well-being. Elsewhere in the world, changes in temperature and levels of precipitation are already affecting the levels of insect-borne diseases: malaria had moved into new areas in Kenya and Indonesia (the highlands) by 1997; Colombia also reported disease-carrying mosquitoes in communities previously thought to be safe from them.

Closer to home, some Canadians in Nunavut experienced sunburn for the first time in 1999. Those who speak Inuktitut as their first language did not have a word for the condition—this was the first time they had experienced the phenomenon. Generally, it is believed that the thinning of the ozone layer, which is part of the warming phenomenon, will lead to an increase in incidences of skin cancer, impaired vision and other conditions related to exposure to more intense ultraviolet rays.

Sea ice is thinner in Alaska, Siberia and northern Canada, making it more difficult for both humans and wildlife to find food. On the other hand, the Northwest Passage, formerly so choked with thick ice that ships could rarely get through is now navigable and northern residents are hopeful that a drier land will cut down on the clouds of mosquitoes in their area. Such is the growing evidence that the Earth's poles are warming. While no one can predict the outcomes of this warming, scientists are acutely aware of how the Earth's systems function as a whole. Long established deep ocean currents and wind patterns can change drastically if the relationship between the tropics and the poles change. Major changes in prevailing winds, rainfall patterns and ocean currents have meant the fall of civilizations (and the rise of new ones) in history and this era is unlikely to be an exception.

# LIFE SCIENCES

The life sciences consist of diverse disciplines that share a knowledge base centered around the same fundamental question, "What is life?" Beginning with biology (the study of living organisms), the life sciences soon included: zoology (the study of animals), botany (the study of plants), and taxonomy (the study of the classification of living things).

Over the last century, an ever increasing variety of subdisciplines and approaches to studying life have arisen: microbiology (the study of microorganisms), genetics (the study of heredity), biochemistry (the study of chemical compounds and reactions in living organisms), ecology (the study of the relationships between living things and their environment), and ethology (the study of animal behaviour). Most recently these disciplines have been joined by biotechnology (the study and use of organisms or their components for the manufacture or production of commercial substances, aided by techniques of genetic manipulation).

Common Life Sciences Terms

Aerobic: Life processes that depend on the presence of oxygen.

Algae: Simple rootless plants that grow in bodies of water in relative proportion to the amount of nutrients available.

Allergen: Any of various sorts of material that, as a result of coming into contact with appropriate tissues, induce a state of sensitivity and/or resistance to infection or toxic substances.

Anaerobic: Life processes that occur in the absence of oxygen.

Animal: A vertebrate (having a bony skeleton or one made of cartilage) or invertebrate (lacking a spine or skeleton) species including, but not limited to, humans and other mammals, birds, fish, and shellfish.

Bacteria: Single cell microorganisms that possess cell walls. Some cause disease and some are beneficial.

Baleen: Horny plates with fringed inner edges attached to the upper jaw of Mysticeti type whales, such as right and blue whales. The baleen are used to filter plankton and other food from water.

Biodiversity: The total diversity within an ecosystem, including genetic variation among species, diversity of life forms, and ecosystem diversity.

Biomass: The amount of living matter in a given unit of the environment.

Biosphere: The portion of Earth (upwards at least to a height of 10,000 m and downward to the ocean floor and a 100 km below the planet's surface) and the atmosphere surrounding it that supports life.

Bloom: A seasonal, dense growth of small marine plants, i.e., phytoplankton.

Coniferous: Refers to a softwood, cone bearing tree.

Deciduous: Refers to a hardwood, leaf dropping tree.

Effluent Waste: Material discharged into the environment, treated or untreated.

Flood Tide: Interim period of tide between low and high water; a rising tide.

Lagoon: Shallow pond where sunlight, bacterial action and oxygen work to purify waste water.

Marsh: Wet, soft, low-lying land that provides a natural habitat for many plants and animals.

Molt: The periodic casting off or shedding of the outer body covering (feathers, hair, skin, or cuticle) by birds, mammals, and reptiles.

Nutrients: Elements or compounds essential to growth and development of living things: carbon, oxygen, nitrogen, potassium, and phosphorus.

Osmosis: Tendency of a fluid to pass through a permeable membrane, such as the wall of a living cell, into a less concentrated solution, so as to equalize concentrations on both sides of the membrane.

Photosynthesis: A process of biochemical change in which plant cells, using light as an energy source, manufacture simple sugars from oxygen and carbon dioxide.

Regeneration (forests): The renewal of a forest by natural processes (self-sown seed or root suckers), as well as by sowing or planting new tree stock.

Synthesis: Production of a substance by the union of elements or simpler chemical compounds.

Tailings: Residue of raw materials or waste separated out during the processing of wood or minerals products.

Tidal Marsh: Low, flat marshlands crossed by interlaced channels and tidal sloughs, and subject to tidal inundation from the ocean, normally, the only vegetation present is salt-tolerant rushes and grasses.

Tide: Alternate rising and falling of water levels twice each lunar day, due to gravitational attraction of the moon and the sun in conjunction with the Earth's rotational force.

Major Groups of Living Organisms

All life forms are classified in a hierarchical series of groups. Taxonomy, the science of such classification, was introduced by Swedish scientist, Carolus Linneaus (1707–78).

The purpose of classification is to provide each plant or animal on the planet with a unique name by which it is known; to describe it so it may be recognized by anyone; and to place it within a system that shows its relationship to other plants and animals.

The system is flexible, allowing updating as more is learned about individual species and their history.

Naming

The scientific naming of species involves two Latin names. The first word in the species name denotes the Genus the species belongs to. For example, the first word in the scientific name of the Monarch butterfly is *Danaus*. The Monarch belongs to the Genus Danaus.

The second word in the scientific name is particular to a species and can be quite arbitrary. Sometimes species names refer to a person, a country, a particular feature of the animal or plant, or a food source. The second word in the scientific name for the Monarch is plexippus. Thus, the scientific name of the Monarch is *Danaus plexippus*.

A species usually also has a common or more familiar name. For example, people seldom refer to the Monarch butterfly as Danaus plexippus.

Species

The basic level in the system is species. The interpretation of differences and similarities between species is often subjective; so the number and name of a species may change. Also new species are still being found and identified.

Genus

Species with a number of common features are grouped together in Genera. The number of different species in a genus can vary from one to several hundred. Again identification is subjective and the number of genera is not fixed.

Family

Genera are further grouped into Families. Butterfly genera are broadly divided into four major families: 1) Papilionidae (swallowtails); 2) Pierodae (whites and sulphurs); 3) Nymphalidae (brush-footed); and 4) Lycaenidae (hairstreaks, coppers, and blues).

Order

Families that share major characteristics are grouped into Orders. For example, butterflies, along with moths, belong to the Order Lepidoptera or insects with scales. The word comes from the Greek words *lepis* (scale) and *pteron* (wing). Classification at this level can be a very complex structure of orders, sub-orders, and sub-sub-orders.

Class

Further up the hierarchy, all Orders belong to a Class. Members of each class show characteristics indicating a common evolutionary descent.

Phylum

At the next level, butterflies, for example, are members of the Phylum Arthropoda, along with millipedes, spiders, and crustaceans, among others. The word Phylum comes from the Greek *phulon* or race.

Kingdom

At the highest level of the hierarchy, butterflies along with other living creatures, including humans, are members of the Animal Kingdom.

Extinct and Endangered Species in Canada, 2000

The following list has been prepared by the Committee on the Status of Endangered Wildlife in Canada.

The "Extinct" category refers to any species that was indigenous to Canada that no longer exists anywhere in the world. The "Extirpated" category refers to any species that no longer exists in the wild but does occur elsewhere. The "Endangered" category refers to any species threatened with imminent extinction or extirpation throughout all or most of its Canadian range.

For more information, visit the Web site http://www.speciesatrisk.gc.ca.

Species	Habitat	Year Documented
EXTINCT CATEGORY		
Mammals		
Caribou, Woodland	(Queen Charlotte Islands population) BC	1920s, 1984
Mink, Sea	Atlantic coastal waters	1894
Birds		
Auk, Great	QC, NB, NS, NF	1844
Duck, Labrador	QC, NB, NS, NF	1875
Pigeon, Passenger	SK, MB, ON, QC, NB, NS, PE	1914
Fish		
Cisco, Deepwater	ON	1952
Cisco, Longjaw	ON	1975
Dace, Banff Longnose	AB	1986
Stickleback, Benthic (Hadley Lake)	BC	1999
Stickleback, Limnetic (Hadley Lake)	BC	1999
Walleye, Blue	ON	1965
Molluscs		
Limpet, Eelgrass	QC, NS, NF	1929
EXTIRPATED CATEGORY		
Mammals		
Bear, Grizzly	(Prairie population) AB, SK, MB	1880s
Ferret, Black-footed	AB, SK, MB	1974
Walrus, Atlantic	Atlantic coastal waters	1850
Whale, Grey	Atlantic population	prior 1800
Birds		
Grouse, Sage	(British Columbia population) BC	not observed since 1960's
Prairie-Chicken, Greater	AB, SK, MB, ON	last reported 1987 (SK)
Reptiles		
Lizard, Pygmy Short-Horned	(British Columbia population) BC	last reported 1898, near Osoyoos, BC
Fish		
Chub, Gravel	ON	last reported 1958, Thames River drainage
Paddlefish	ON	1917
Molluscs		
Wedgemussel, Dwarf	NB	1968
Lepidopterans[1]		
Blue, Karner	ON	1991
Elfin, Frosted	ON	1988
Marble, Island	BC	prior 1910
Plants		
Blue-eyed Mary	ON	not observed since 1954
Tick-trefoil, Illinois	ON	not observed since 1888

ENDANGERED CATEGORY

Mammals

Badger, American	BC, ON	2000
Caribou, Peary	(Banks Island population)	
	(High Arctic population) NT, NU	1991
Caribou, Woodland	(Atlantic - Gaspésie population) QC	2000
Fox, Swift	AB, SK	1998
Marmot, Vancouver Island	BC	1997
Marten, American	(Newfoundland population) NF	1996
Whale, Beluga	St. Lawrence River population	1997
	Ungava Bay population	1988
	Southeast Baffin Island–Cumberland Sound population	1990
Whale, Bowhead	Eastern Arctic population	1980
	Western Arctic population	1986
Whale, Right	Atlantic and Pacific Oceans	1990
Wolverine	(Eastern population) QC, NF	1989

Birds

Bobwhite, Northern	ON	1994
Crane, Whooping	NT, NU	1978
Curlew, Eskimo	All provinces and territories except BC	2000
Duck, Harlequin	(Eastern population) QC, NB, NS, NF	1990
Flycatcher, Acadian	ON	1994
Grouse, Sage	(Prairie population) AB, SK	1998
Owl, Barn	(Eastern population) ON, QC	1999
Owl, Burrowing	BC, AB, MB, SK	1995
Owl, Northern Spotted	BC	1999
Plover, Mountain	AB, SK	1987
Plover, Piping	AB, SK, MB, ON, QC, NB, NS, PE, NF	1985
Rail, King	ON	1994
Shrike, Loggerhead	(Eastern population) MB, ON, QC	1991
Sparrow, Henslow's	ON	1993
Tern, Roseate	QC, NB, NS	1999
Thrasher, Sage	BC, AB, SK	1992
Warbler, Kirtland's	ON	1999
Warbler, Prothonotary	ON	1996

Amphibians

Frog, Northern Cricket	ON	1990
Frog, Northern Leopard	(Southern Mountain population) BC	1998
Frog, Oregon Spotted	BC	1999
Frog, Tailed	(Southern Mountain population) BC	2000

Reptiles

Racer, Blue	ON	1991
Snake, Lake Erie Water	ON	1991
Snake, Sharp-tailed	BC	1999
Turtle, Leatherback	Atlantic & Pacific Oceans	1981

Fsih

Dace, Nooksack	BC	1996
Lamprey, Morrison Creek	BC	1999
Stickleback, Benthic Paxton Lake (Texada Island)	BC	1999
Stickleback, Benthic Vananda Creek	BC	1999
Stickleback, Limnetic Paxton Lake (Texada Island)	BC	1999
Stickleback, Limnetic Vananda Creek	BC	1999
Sucker, Salish	BC	1986
Trout, Aurora	ON	2000
Whitefish, Atlantic (Acadian)	NS	1984

Molluscs

Bean, Rayed	ON	1999
Lampmussel, Wavy-rayed	ON	1999

Physa, Hotwater	BC	1998
Riffleshell, Northern	ON	1999
Snail, Banff Springs	AB	1997

Lepidopterans[1]

Ringlet, Maritime	QC, NB	1997

Plants

Agalinis, Gattinger's	ON	1999
Agalinis, Skinner's	ON	1999
Ammannia, Scarlet	BC, ON	1999
Avens, Eastern Mountain	NS	1999
Balsamroot, Deltoid	BC	1996
Bulrush, Bashful (Few-flowered Club-rush)	ON	2000
Bluehearts	ON	1998
Braya, Long's	NF	1997
Buttercup, Water-plantain	BC	1996
Bush-clover, Slender	ON	1999
Cactus, Eastern Prickly Pear	ON	1998
Coreopsis, Pink	NS	1999
Cryptanthe, Tiny	AB, SK	1998
Fern, Southern Maidenhair	BC	1998
Gentian, White Prairie	ON	1991
Ginseng, American	ON, QC	1999
Goat's-rue, Virginia	ON	1996
Goldenrod, Showy	ON	1999
Lady's-slipper, Small White	MB, ON	1999
Lotus, Seaside Birds-foot	BC	1996
Lousewort, Furbish's	NB	1998
Lupine, Prairie	BC	1996
Milkwort, Pink	ON	1998
Mountain-mint, Hoary	ON	1998
Mulberry, Red	ON	1999
Orchid, Western Prairie Fringed	MB	2000
Owl-clover, Bearded	BC	1998
Paintbrush, Golden	BC	1995
Plantain, Heart-leaved	ON	1998
Pogonia, Large Whorled	ON	1998
Pogonia, Nodding	ON	1999
Pogonia, Small Whorled	ON	1998
Quillwort, Engelmann's	ON	1992
Sedge, False Hop	ON, QC	1997
Sedge, Juniper	ON	1999
Sundew, Thread-leaved	NS	1991
Thistle, Pitcher's	ON	1999
Toothcup	BC, ON	1999
Tree, Cucumber	ON	1999
Trillium, Drooping	ON	1996
Twayblade, Purple	ON	1999
Wintergreen, Spotted	YT, NT, BC, AB	2000
Wood-poppy	ON	1993
Woodsia, Blunt-lobed	ON, QC	1994

Lichens

Seaside Centipede	BC	1996

Mosses

Moss, Apple	BC	1997

Source: *Committee on Status of Endangered Wildlife in Canada*
(1) Lepidopteran: Order of insects with four wings covered by fine scales; butterflies and moths.

Geographical Locations

AB Alberta
BC British Columbia
MB Manitoba
NB New Brunswick
NF Newfoundland
NS Nova Scotia
NT Northwest Territories
NU Nunavut
ON Ontario
PE Prince Edward Island
QC Quebec
SK Saskatchewan
YT Yukon Territory

The Human Genome Project

On June 26, 2000, US scientists announced that they had finished "sequencing the genome." In some quarters the achievement was hailed as the greatest advance since Charles Darwin's *Origin of Species* was published. What's it all about? It's about the "mapping" or sequencing of all the DNA in an organism. In the case of the Human Genome Project, it's about mapping all the DNA in us. Why does it matter? (And what language are they speaking?)

■ It Starts with DNA

Deoxyribonucleic acid, better known as DNA, has four chemical components or bases. The bases are adenine, cytosine, guanine and thymine or A, C, G and T. It is the pattern of organization of A, C, G and T that determines how a particular gene (portion of DNA) directs the production of proteins and holds genetic information that gets passed (copied) to new cells.

What the participants in the Genome project did was take purified DNA and use computerized sequencing devices to read the order of the four chemicals in every chromosome and in each of the tens of thousands of genes that make up the human organism. While the sequencing is done, much work remains to find out what all of the information means. (Some have suggested that while we've got the "book of life" in our hands, it's written in a foreign language.)

■ What could it mean?

Figuring out the biochemical code for all our genes is likely the first (vital) step in figuring out what each protein does, how it works with the rest of the proteins and how the process all relates to making up and maintaining a healthy human being. (Or, conversely, what happens when things go wrong.) Some raise the spectre of designer babies or discrimination based on an analysis of an individual's genes (for instance, an insurance company could refuse coverage for those found to have a genetic predisposition to cancer—and these are genuine concerns. Others are hoping to go beyond the keys to hundreds of diseases—all the way to cures. Drugs could be designed to work with a particular person's genetic make-up, for maximum effectiveness with few side effects. Scientists can already see which of the thousands of genes are active in a particular tissue sample and are starting to probe the mysteries of diseases such as diabetes or Alzheimer's.

■ Who did the work?

Commercial enterprises raced an international consortium of scientists funded by the US and Great Britain to do the initial sequencing. A number of other countries have human genome research programs as well, including Australia, Brazil, Canada, China, Denmark, France, Germany, Israel, Italy, Japan, Korea, Mexico, the Netherlands, Russia and Sweden. A major issue has been "who owns the work"? The government-funded project has steadily posted its findings on a public database for all to use. In other quarters, the debate over the right to patent certain sequences has led to concerns that key information will be held for the benefit of only a few.

■ What's happening in Canada?

In February 2000, the federal budget set aside a $160 million grant for Genome Canada, a non-profit corporation set up to support national research initiatives into genomics on behalf of Canadians. The goal is to create five Genome Centres: in BC, the prairie region, Ontario, Quebec and the Atlantic region. These centres are to be partnerships among research hospitals, universities, industry, government and the public; the goal is to represent a broad range of participants and interests. Each centre will have at least one large-scale genomics project to concentrate on. Each will also devote resources to research into the issues surrounding the investigation and use of the genome information, specifically the legal, ethical, environmental and social issues. They will also be responsible for public education.

The province of Quebec, home to 40 percent of the country's biotechnology work, is in a strong position to take an international role in genome research. Dr. Thomas Hudson is director of the Montreal Genome Centre at Montreal General Hospital, a professor of Human Genetics at McGill University and also assistant director for the Centre for Genome Research at MIT in the US. Researchers at Toronto's Sick Children Hospital have established a Bioinformatics Supercomputing Centre to help take advantage of the Genome Database. They are working with Johns Hopkins University in Baltimore and Oak Ridge National Laboratory.

For more information, visit http://www.GenomeCanada.ca.

FOCUS ON...

Water Use in Canada

It is widely estimated that 20 percent of the Earth's population (the Earth's wealthiest citizens—including Canadians) use 80 percent of the resources available for annual consumption. This is possible in part because of an uneven distribution of those resources. Canada, a land rich in natural resources, is a case in point when it comes to water consumption.

■ Residential Use

The average Canadian household uses 340 L of water every day for household tasks and gardening; in the US, the figure is 425 L. In Israel, where there's less fresh water available, households get by on 135 L. This is water we use to cook, clean, wash clothes, shower, flush the toilet, wash cars and water lawns. (All of that water is treated in expensive filtration plants; less than 1 percent of it is actually for drinking.)

While some citizens in drier parts of the world simply do without—they don't worry about having a long, daily shower because there are no facilities, and they don't have a car, in the more affluent drier countries they have developed water efficient ways. For example, Canadian toilets generally use 20 L to do the job; elsewhere the facilities use just 6 L. (Low flow toilets have been criticized for being too low flow, but they are improving as consumers, particularly in the US, who must use them in all new installations, are demanding something more efficient.)

Dripping faucets, washing things under running water (including yourself—you can get wet, soap up without the water running and then rinse off), having a sparkling car at all times: everyone can think of some ways they waste water.

■ Industrial Use

An analysis of industrial use of water in Canada reveals which uses withdraw the most from our water resources: electric power generation; which are more efficient: manufacturing, on average, reuses its water twice while the mining industry reuses the water it withdraws four times; and which uses consume most of the water that is withdrawn, returning very little of the intake to its source: agriculture.

Environment Canada did a study water intake and use in 1991:

Water Use by Region:	Water Consumption by Use:
Ontario .... 63%[1]	Thermal Power 63%
Prairies 14%	Manufacturing 16%
Quebec 10%	Municipal .... 11%[2]
Atlantic Canada 7%	Agriculture 9%
BC and the Territories: 6%	Mining 1%

(1) Ontario's water use is largely for thermal power (as opposed to hydroelectric power, which is an "instream use")
(2) Includes residential water use.

■ Does it matter?

Canada has such an abundance of water—why does it matter how much we use? First, a portion of our fresh water is in the lakes in less accessible parts of the country. Having to transport water over long distances will send the price up considerably. (As well, reducing the amount of water available in those areas will hurt the local ecosystems—models predicting the effect of global warming have shown this.)

The Great Lakes watershed region, which supplies over 33 million people in two provinces and eight US states, is a more immediate concern. In 1999, the water level in several of the lakes had dropped nearly 56 cm in a year. It's expected that varying water levels will become the norm in the future.

Canada put a federal water policy in place in the 1970s and revised it in the 1990s to take a more direct approach to managing our water supplies, but it will take more than federal regulations to maintain abundant fresh water.

For more information, visit Environment Canada (http://www.ec.gc.ca) for a number of sites devoted to our water supply and how you can help.

Science and Nature

Zoos and Aquariums*

Maritime Region:

☐ **Aquarium and Marine Centre**
C.P. 1010, 2nd Avenue, Shippigan, NB E0B 2P0.
Tel: (506) 336-3013 Fax: (506) 336-3057.
Entrance fee. Open May to September.
http://inter.gov.nb.ca/dfa/aecm.htm

☐ **Cherry Brook Zoo**
901 Foster Thurston Drive, Saint John, NB E2K 5H9.
Tel: (506) 634-1440. Fax: (506) 634-0717.
Entrance fee. Open all year. E-mail: noah@nbnet.nb.ca

☐ **Magnetic Hill Zoo**
100 Worthington Avenue, Moncton, NB E1C 9Z3.
Tel: (506) 384-0303 Fax (506) 853-3569.
Open May to October, with limited openings on winter weekends. Entrance fee.
www.greatermoncton.com/mhzoo/index.html

Central Canada:

☐ **Aquarium du Québec**
1675, avenue des Hotels, Sainte-Foy, Que. G1W 4S3.
Tel: (418) 659-5266. Fax: (418) 646-9238.
Entrance fee. Open all year.
www.aquarium.qc.ca/aquarium.html

☐ **The Biodôme de Montréal**
An environmental museum. 4777, avenue Pierre-de Coubenin, Montréal, Que. H1V 1B3. Tel: (514) 868-3000. Fax: (514) 868-3065. Entrance fee. Open all year. www.ville.montreal.qc.ca/biodome/bdm.htm

☐ **Parc safari Africain**
850 Route 202, Hemmingford, Que. J0L 1H0.
Tel: (514) 247-2727 Fax: (514) 247-3563.
Entrance fee. Open mid-May to Labour Day.
www.parcsafari.com

☐ **Saint-Félicien Zoo**
2230 Boulevarde du Jardin, Saint-Félicien, Que. G8K 2P8. Tel: (418) 679-0543 Fax: (418) 679-3647.
Entrance fee. Open mid-May to mid-October.
www.zoosauvage@destination.ca

☐ **Société Zoologique de Granby**
525, rue Saint-Hubert, Granby, Que. J2G 5P3.
Tel: (450) 372-9113. Fax: (450) 372-5531.
Entrance fee. Open May to September.
www.zoogranby.qc.ca

☐ **African Lion Safari and Game Farm**
R.R#1, Cambridge, Ont. N1R 5S2.
Tel: (519) 623-2620. Fax: (519) 623-9542.
Entrance fee. Open summer. www.lionsafari.com

☐ **Bowmanville Zoological Park**
340 King Street East, Bowmanville, Ont. L1C 3K5.
Tel: (905) 623-5655 Fax: (905) 623-9675.

☐ **Jungle Cat World**
3667 Concession 6, Orono, Ont. L0B 1M0.
Tel: (905) 983-5016. Fax: (905) 983 9858.
Entrance fee. Open March to November.
www.junglecatworld.com

☐ **Toronto Zoo**
361A Old Finch Avenue, Scarborough, Ont. M1B 5K7.
Tel: (416) 392-5900. Fax: (416) 392-5934. Entrance fee. Open all year. www.torontozoo.com

Western Canada:

☐ **Assiniboine Park Zoo**
2355 Corydon Avenue, Winnipeg, Man. R3P 0R5.
Tel: (204) 986-6921 Fax: (204) 832-5420. Entrance fee. Open all year.

☐ **Saskatoon Zoo**
1903 Forest Drive, Saskatoon, Sask. S7S 1G9.
Tel: (306) 975-3382 Fax: (306) 975-3326.
Entrance fee. Open all year.

☐ **Alberta Birds of Prey**
P.O. Box 1150, Coaldale, Alta T1M 1M9.
Tel: (403) 345-4262.

☐ **Calgary Zoo, Botanical Garden and Prehistoric Park**
P.O. Box 3036, Station "B," 1300 Zoo Road NE, Calgary, Alta T2M 4R8. Tel: (403) 232-9300 Fax: (403) 237-7582. Entrance fee. Open all year.
www.calgaryzoo.ab.ca

☐ **Marine Life Department/Dolphin Lagoon**
West Edmonton Mall, #2472, 8770-170 Street, Edmonton, Alta T5T 4M2. Tel: (403) 444-5346 Fax: (403) 444-5266.
www.westedmall.com/parks/dolphin.htm

☐ **Valley Zoo and John Janzen Nature Centre**
P.O. Box 2359, 13315 Buena Vista Road, Edmonton, Alta T5J 2R7. Tel: (403) 496-6911 Fax: (403) 944-7529. Entrance fee. Open all year.
ww.ualberta.ca/EDMONTON/CONTRIB/jjanzen/

☐ **Barrett Aviaries**
3745 Melrose Road, Qualicum Beach, BC V9K 1V3.
Tel: (250) 752-2912 Fax: (250) 752-1600.

☐ **Crystal Garden**
713 Douglas Street, Victoria, BC V8W 1N8.
Tel: (250) 381-1277 Fax: (250) 383-1218.
Entrance fee. Open all year.
www.bcpcc.com/crystal

☐ **Greater Vancouver Zoological Centre**
5048-264 Street, Aldergrove, BC V4W 1N7.
Tel: (604) 856-6825 Fax: (604) 857-9008.
www.greatervancouverzoo.com

☐ **Kamloops Wildlife Park**
P.O. Box 698, East Trans Canada Highway, Kamloops, BC V2C 5L7. Tel: (250) 573-3242 Fax: (250) 573-2406.
Entrance fee. Open all year.
www.kamloopswildlife.com

☐ **Mountain View Farms Breeding and Conservation Centre** 8011-240th St., Langley, BC V3A 4P9. Tel: (604) 688-0553 Fax: (604) 688-7330.
www.mtnviewfarms.com

☐ **Vancouver Aquarium Marine Science Centre**
P.O. Box 3232, Stanley Park, Vancouver, BC V6B 3X8.
Tel: (604) 659-3474 Fax: (604) 659-3515. Entrance fee. Open all year. www.vanaqua.org

*Accredited by the Canadian Association of Zoos and Aquariums.

ARTS AND ENTERTAINMENT

Canada may well have been one of the best kept secrets on the world's arts and entertainment scene, but the secret is getting harder and harder to keep as artists like David Cronenberg, Alanis Morissette, Robert LePage, and Carol Shields make their mark. Historically, the small size and scattered nature of the Canadian market made dissemination of Canadian works of art and entertainment products difficult. But the years following World War II saw an explosion of activity in every sector, fuelled by public institutions such as the CBC, the Canada Council for the Arts, and the National Film Board and similar provincial and local agencies. Canadian content requirements for broadcasters and tax and investment measures favouring Canadian publishers have also helped foster successful, if fragile, publishing and recording industries. In 1996 all levels of government devoted $5.8 billion to culture (this includes federal support for the CBC and provincial and local support for public libraries). Restraints on public spending over the past two decades have caused emphasis to be placed on private investment and on production for foreign markets. During the 1990s, film and TV production saw a 200 percent increase in foreign investment and a 33 percent increase in private sector Canadian investment. At the same time Canadian authors, agents and publishers found the sale of foreign rights to be a lucrative stream of revenue in a world hungry to read the work of writers such as Shields, Michael Ondaatje, Anne Michaels and Anne-Marie MacDonald.

MAJOR ARTS COUNCILS

The Canada Council: 350 Albert St, Box 1047, Ottawa, Ont., K1P 5V8; tel: (613) 566-4414 (toll-free:1-800-263-5588); fax: (613) 566-4390; e-mail: [employee name]@canadacouncil.ca (see personnel directory at website);website: www.canadacouncil.ca.

Alberta Foundation for the Arts: Alberta Community Development, 901 Standard Life Centre, 10405 Jasper Ave, Edmonton, Alta, T5J 4R7; tel: (780) 427-9968; fax: (780)422-9132; e-mail: afa@mcd.gov.ab.ca; Website: http://www.affta.ab.ca

British Columbia Arts Council: Box 9819, Stn. Prov. Govt., Victoria, BC, V8W 9W3; tel: (250) 356-1718; fax: (250) 387-4099; e-mail: csbinfo@tbc.gov.bc.ca; Website: www.bcartscouncil.gov.bc.ca

Manitoba Arts Council: 525-93 Lombard Avenue, Winnipeg, Man., R3B 3B1; tel: (204) 945-2237; fax: 945-5925; website: www.gov.mb.ca/cgi-bin/print_hit_bold.pl/chc/archives/MAC/mac.html?Manitoba+Arts+Council#first_hit

New Brunswick Arts Board: P.O. Box 6000, Fredericton, NB, E3B-5H1; tel: (506) 453-4307; fax: (506) 453-6043; e-mail: artsboard@gov.nb.ca

Newfoundland and Labrador Arts Council: Box 98, St. John's, Nfld, A1C 5H5; tel: (709) 726-2212; fax: (709)726-0619; e-mail: nlacmail@newcomm.net; website: www.nlac.nf.ca

Northwest Territories Arts Council: Department of Education, Culture and Employment, Government of the Northwest Territories, Box 1320, Yellowknife, NWT, X1A 2L9; phone: (867) 920-3103; fax: (867) 873-0205

Nova Scotia Arts Council: P.O. Box 1559, CRO, Halifax, NS, B3J-2Y3; phone: (902) 422-1123; fax (902) 422-1445; e-mail: nsartscouncil@ns.sympatico.ca

Ontario Arts Council: 151 Bloor St. W., Toronto, ON M5S 1T6; phone: (416) 961-1660; fax: (416) 961-7796 (Toll-free: 1-800-387-0058); e-mail: info@arts.on.ca; website: www.arts.on.ca

P.E.I. Council of the Arts: tel:(902) 368-4410

Conseil des arts et des lettres du Quebec: Quebec bureau: 79, boulevard René-Lévesque Est, bureau 320, Quebec, G1R 5N5; tel: (418) 643-1707, (Toll-free) 1-800-897-1707; fax: (418) 643-4558; Montreal bureau: 500, Place d'Armes, 15e étage, Montréal, QC, H2Y 2W2; tel: (514) 864-3350, (Toll-free)1-800-608-3350; fax: (514) 864-4160; e-mail. affaires.publiques@calq.gouv.qc.ca; website: www.calq.gouv.qc.ca/fr/index.htm

Saskatchewan Arts Board: 3rd Floor, 3475 Albert Street Regina, Saskatchewan S4S 6X6; tel: (306) 787-4056, (Toll-free, Saskatchewan only)1-800-667-7526; fax: (306) 787-4199; e-mail: sab@artsboard.sk.ca

Yukon Tourism, Arts Branch: Box 2703, Whitehorse, Yukon, Y1A 2C6; tel: (867) 667-8589, (Toll-free within Yukon) 1-800-661-0408; fax: (867) 393-6456. e-mail: arts@gov.yk.ca; website: www.artsykon.com

TELEVISION

Television first reached Canada in the 1940s from border stations in the United States. The Canadian Broadcasting Corporation's TV services were launched in 1952. The launch in English Canada was less than auspicious; the first image to appear on the screen was the CBC logo presented upside down. The CBC recovered its poise and the network grew rapidly, opening stations across the country and broadcasting its programs on affiliated private stations.

CBC TV was joined by the private Canadian Television Network in 1961. The CanWest/Global system began in the 1970s and has become Canada's third major television network. Through the 1980s and 1990s the CRTC has licensed dozens of specialty cable services to ensure that Canadian services offer viewers a full range of choices.

While the most-watched television programs in Canada continue to be American dramas and situation comedies, Canadian broadcasters have scored considerable success with programs such as *Wojek*, *The King of Kensington*, *Street Legal*, and *Due South*. Canadian producers have been particularly successful with children's programs such as *Mr. Dressup* and with sketch comedy programs including *The Wayne and Shuster Comedy Hour*, *This Hour Has 22 Minutes*, and *SCTV*.

Today the television market accounts for 70 percent of the 14,000 film projects undertaken in Canada each year. Much of that production is destined for air in the United States and other countries as international coproduction becomes an increasingly popular way of funding television programs around the world.

Canada's Television Classification System

In the fall of 1997, a television classification system was formally launched on Canadian airwaves to help Canadians identify programming suitable to various age groups. There are seven classification levels. Although violence is the most important content consideration, each classification also includes information on coarse language, nudity and sex. The classifications are designed for use with V-chip technology which enables parents to block reception of undesirable programs. A Canadian V-chip system using the following classifications is expected to be operational in 2001.

 Children: Might contain occasional comedic, unrealistic depictions of violence. No offensive language. No sex or nudity.

 Children Over 8 Years: Might include mild physical violence, comedic violence, comic horror, special effects; fantasy, supernatural, or animated violence. No profanity. No sex or nudity.

 General: Violence is minimal and infrequent. Contains no frightening special effects not required by the storyline. May contain inoffensive slang. No profanity. No sex or nudity.

 Parental Guidance: Moderate violence which must be justified within the context of the storyline. Might contain mild profanity, suggestive language, some nudity.

 Over 14 Years: Might contain intense scenes of violence. Could include frequent profanity. Mght include scenes of nudity and/or sexual activity.

 Adults: Depictions of violence are intended for adult viewing, and thus are not suitable for audiences under 18 years of age. Might contain graphic language and explicit portrayals of sex and/or nudity.

Exempt: News, sports, documentaries, and other information programming, talk shows, music videos, and variety programming.

Source: Media Awareness Network, www.media-awareness.ca

The CRTC: Canada's Communications Watchdog

The Canadian Radio-television and Telecommunications Commission (CRTC) regulates all aspects of the Canadian broadcasting system. It grants licences to radio and television broadcasters, enforces the conditions of those licences and reviews broadcaster performance at regularly scheduled hearings. Created under the Broadcasting Act of 1968, the Commission inherited a long tradition of government supervision of broadcasting in Canada. Radio broadcasting was regulated in its early days under the Radiotelegraph Act. In the 1930s responsibility for radio was shifted to the newly-created Canadian Broadcasting Corporation. Private broadcasters were unhappy with a system that gave their public sector competitor the right to supervise their businesses and so an independent regulator, the Board of Broadcast Governors (BBG) was formed in 1958. The Broadcasting Act of 1968 replaced the BBG with the CRTC. The commission scored a success with the establishment of Canadian content regulations in 1971 for radio. Through the 1980s and 1990s it insisted on higher levels of quality Canadian programming from private television broadcasters and oversaw the introduction of dozens of new specialty services on cable and satellite television. While the CRTC also supervises telecommunications it announced in 1999 that it would not attempt to regulate the Internet.

Website: www.crtc.gc.ca

The Gemini Awards, 1999

The Gemini Awards were established in 1986 to honor outstanding contributions to the Canadian television industry. Given out annually by the Academy of Canadian Cinema and Television, the Geminis grew out of the former ACTRA Awards, last presented in 1985. These awards were presented Oct. 2, 1998. The 14th Geminis were given out Oct. 28-30, 2000.

Dramatic series	*Da Vinci's Inquest*
Comedy series	*Made in Canada*
TV movie	*Milgaard*
Actor (dramatic series)	Michael Riley, *Power Play*, "Seventh Game"
Actor (dramatic program)	Ian Tracey, *Milgaard*
Supporting actor (dramatic program or mini-series)	Hrothgar Matthews, *Milgaard*
Supporting actor (dramatic series)	Gordon Pinsent, *Power Play*, "Perambulate Me Back To My Habitual Abode"
Actress (dramatic series)	Arsinée Khanjian, *Foolish Heart*, "Lena"
Actress (dramatic program)	Wendy Crewson, *At the End of the Day: The Sue Rodriguez Story*
Supporting actress (dramatic program or mini-series)	Sabrina Grdevich, *Milgaard*
Supporting actress (dramatic series)	Marion Gilsenan, *Riverdale*, "Episode 33"
Guest performance in a series by an actress	Martha Henry, *Emily of New Moon*, "The Book Of Hours"
Guest performance in a series by actor	Sean McCann, *Power Play*, "Perambulate Me Back To My Habitual Abode"
Performance (performing arts program or series)	Joni Mitchell, *Joni Mitchell: Painting With Words and Music*
Performance (comedy program or series)	Cathy Jones, Rick Mercer, Greg Thomey, Mary Walsh, *This Hour Has 22 Minutes*, "Warrior Princess – Mike Harris/Talking To Americans"
Performance (variety program or series)	Jesse Cook, Natalie McMaster, *Juno Awards 1999*
Animated program or series	*Rolie Polie Olie*
Children's or Youth program or series	*The Inventors' Specials*, "Edison: The Wizard of Light"
Documentary series	*The View From Here*
Lifestyle information series	*Weird Homes*
Sports program	*The New Ice Age: A Year in the Life of the NHL*
Information series	*the fifth estate*
Performing arts program	*The Genius of Lenny Breau*
Short dramatic program	*The Dane*
Science, technology, nature and environment documentary program	*My Healing Journey: Seven Years with Cancer*

Source: *Academy of Canadian Cinema and Television*

The Most-Watched Television Programs in Canada[1]

Top 10 Programs

1. Academy Awards (CTV)
2. Academy Awards Pre-show (CTV)
3. Grammy Awards (CTV)
4. Golden Globe Awards (CTV)
5. Who Wants to be a Millionaire? [Mondays] (CTV)
6. Grey Cup Game '99 (CBC)
7. Who Wants to be a Millionaire? [Fridays] (CTV)
8. Anne of Green Gables 3 (CBC)
9. Emmy Awards (CTV)
10. American Music Awards (CTV)

Top 10 Regularly Scheduled Programs

1. Who Wants to be a Millionaire? (CTV)
2. E.R. (CTV)
3. Stanley Cup Finals (CBC)
4. Law and Order (CTV)
5. World Skating Championships (CTV)
6. Barbara Walters (CTV)
7. Whose Line Is It Anyway? (CTV)
8. NHL Playoffs Round 1 (CBC)
9. Wheel of Fortune (CTV)
10. Jeopardy (CTV)

Source: Nielsen Media Research (1) Persons 2+ for the period Aug. 30, 1999–Aug. 27, 2000

The Prime-Time Emmy Awards, 1999–2000

OUTSTANDING DRAMA SERIES	*The West Wing*, NBC
Actor (drama series)	James Gandolfini, *The Sopranos*, HBO
Actress (drama series)	Sela Ward, *Once And Again*, ABC
Supporting actor (drama series)	Richard Schiff, *The West Wing*, NBC
Supporting actress (drama series)	Allison Janney, *The West Wing*, NBC
Directing (drama series)	Thomas Schlamme, *The West Wing*, Pilot, NBC
Writing (drama series)	Aaron Sorkin, Rick Cleveland, *The West Wing*, "In Excelsis Deo," NBC
OUTSTANDING COMEDY SERIES	*Will & Grace*, NBC
Actor (comedy series)	Michael J. Fox, *Spin City*, ABC
Actress (comedy series)	Patricia Heaton, *Everybody Loves Raymond*, CBS
Supporting actor (comedy series)	Sean Hayes, *Will & Grace*, NBC
Supporting actress (comedy series)	Megan Mullally, *Will & Grace*, NBC
Writing (comedy series)	Linwood Boomer, *Malcolm In The Middle*, Pilot, FOX
OUTSTANDING MINISERIES	*The Corner*, HBO
Actor (miniseries or movie)	Jack Lemmon, *Tuesdays With Morrie*, ABC
Actress (miniseries or movie)	Halle Berry, *Introducing Dorothy Dandridge*, HBO
Supporting actor (miniseries or movie)	Hank Azaria, *Tuesdays With Morrie*, ABC
Supporting actress (miniseries or movie)	Vanessa Redgrave, *If These Walls Could Talk 2*, HBO
Directing (miniseries or movie)	Charles S. Dutton, *The Corner*, HBO
Writing (miniseries or movie)	David Simon, David Mills, *The Corner*, HBO
OUTSTANDING VARIETY, MUSIC OR COMEDY SERIES	*The Chris Rock Show*, HBO
OUTSTANDING VARIETY, MUSIC OR COMEDY SPECIAL	*Saturday Night Live: The 25th Anniversary Special*, NBC
Directing (variety or music)	Paul Miller, *1998 Tony Awards*, CBS
Writing (variety or music)	Eddie Izzard, *Eddie Izzard: Dress To Kill* • HBO
Performance (variety or music)	Eddie Izzard, *Eddie Izzard: Dress To Kill* • HBO
OUTSTANDING TV MOVIE	*Tuesdays With Morrie*, ABC

Television Networks and Cable Services

Arts & Entertainment Network (A&E): 235 E 45th St, New York, NY 10017. (212) 210-1328

Atlantic Television System & Atlantic Satellite Network: Box 1653, 2885 Robie St, Halifax, N.S. B3K 4P5. (902) 453-4000.

Bravo!: 299 Queen St W, Toronto, Ont. M5V 2Z5 (416) 591-5757

C-SPAN (Cable Satellite Public Affairs Network): 400 N. Capitol St. NW, Suite 650, Washington, DC 20001. (202) 737-3220

Cable News Network (CNN): 1 CNN Centre, Box 105366, Atlanta, GA 30348-5366. (404) 827-1700

Canadian Broadcasting Corporation (CBC): Box 500 Stn. A, Toronto, Ont. M5W 1E6. (416) 205-3311

Canal Famille: 2100 Sainte-Catherine ouest, Bureau 800, Montreal, Que. H3H 2T3. (514) 939-3150

CanWest/Global Communications Corp.: 201 Portage Ave, 31st Flr, TD Centre, Winnipeg, Man. R3B 3L7. (204) 956-2025

Capital Cities/ABC, Inc.: 77 W 66th St, New York, NY 10023-6298. (212) 456-7777

CHUM Limited: 1331 Yonge St, Toronto, Ont. M4T 1Y1. (416) 925-6666.

Columbia Broadcasting System (CBS): 51 W 52nd St, New York, NY 10019. (212) 975-4321

Country Music Television: 2806 Opreyland Dr., Nashville, TN 37214. (615) 871-5830

CTV Television Network Ltd.: Box Stn. O, 9 Channel Ct., Toronto, Ont. M4A 2M9. (416) 595-4100

Discovery Channel: 2225 Sheppard Ave E, Suite 100, Toronto, Ont. M2J 5C2

The Family Channel Inc.: BCE Place, 181 Bay St., Box 787, Toronto, Ont. M5J 2T3. (416) 956-2030

Fox Broadcasting Co.: P.O. Box 900, Beverly Hills, CA 90213-0900. (310) 369-1000

Global Television Network: 81 Barber Greene Rd, Don Mills, Ont. M3C 2A2 (416) 446-5311

Inuit Broadcasting Corporation: 217 Laurier Ave W, Ste 703, Ottawa, Ont. K1P 5J6. (613) 235-1892

Life Network: 1155 Leslie St, Toronto, Ont. M3C 2J6. (416) 444-9274

Maclean Hunter Limited: 777 Bay St, Toronto, Ont. M5W 1A7. (416) 596-5103

The Movie Network/First Choice: BCE Place, 181 Bay St., Box 787, Toronto, Ont. M5J 2T3. (416) 956-2010

MuchMusic Network: 299 Queen St W, Toronto, Ont. M5V 2Z5. (416) 591-5757

MusiquePlus: 1355 Sainte-Catherine est, Montreal, Que. H3B 1A5. (514) 284-7587

National Broadcasting Company (NBC): 30 Rockefeller Plaza, New York, NY 10112. (212) 664-4444

Premier Choix TVEC Inc.: 2100 Sainte-Catherine ouest, #800 Montreal, Que. H3H 2T3. (514) 939-3150

Public Broadcasting Service (PBS): 1320 Braddock Place, Alexandria, VA 22314-1698. (703) 739-5000

Le Reseau des Sports: 1755 Boul. René-Lévesque est, Bur. 300, Montreal, Que. H2K 4P6. (514) 599-2244

Rogers Broadcasting Ltd.: 36 Victoria St, Toronto, Ont. M5C 1H3. (416) 864-2000

Showcase Television Inc.: 121 Bloor St E, #200, Toronto, Ont. M4W 1B9 (416) 967-2473

Société de radio-télévision du Quebec (Radio-Quebec): 800, rue Fullum, Montreal, Que. H2K 3L7. (514) 521-2424

The Sports Network (TSN): 2225 Sheppard Ave E, Suite 100, Willowdale, Ont. M2J 5C2. (416) 494-1212

Telelatino Network Inc.: 5125 Steeles Ave W, Weston, Ont. M9L 1R5. (416) 744-8200

TVOntario (TVO): Box 200, Stn Q, Toronto, Ont. M4T 2T1. (416) 484-2600

Vision TV: 80 Bond St, Toronto, Ont. M5B 1X2. (416) 368-3194

The Weather Channel: 1 Robert Speck Parkway, Ste 1600, Mississauga, Ont. L4Z 4B3. (905) 566-9511

Women's Television Network: 300-1661 Portage Ave, Winnipeg, Man. R3J 3T7. (204) 783-5816

YTV Canada Inc.: 64 Jefferson Ave, Unit 18, Toronto, Ont. M6K 3H3. (416) 534-1191

RADIO

Radio Broadcasting has played an integral part in Canada's cultural development. The first radio licence was issued in 1919 to an experimental station based in Montreal. Radio stations proliferated in the 1920s. Railway companies were among Canada's first radio broadcasters, presenting programs for the enjoyment of passengers aboard their trains. However, most stations devoted themselves almost entirely to music and other programming imported from the United States. In 1936 the Canadian Broadcasting Corporation was formed to help remedy the situation. By the end of WWII, the corporation was operating two networks in English-the Trans-Canada and Dominion networks-and one network in French. CBC's news service was born out of the need to keep Canadians informed of overseas action during the war. Andrew Allan's *Stage* and other dramatic programs were the backbone of the "Golden Age" of Canadian radio from 1945 to 1955. Private radio continued to rely heavily on American music programming, a situation that remained unchanged until 1971, when they were compelled to accept quotas by the federal regulator (see **Music** p. 611, **CRTC** p.609). CBC Radio languished after the introduction of television until a 1971 revamp of its programming lead to the creation of *Morningside*, *As It Happens* and *Sunday Morning* and added popular morning and "drive-home" local information shows to the schedule. Private radio continues to embrace the trend towards specialized program "niches" (country, classical, "oldies," and "all-news" etc.). That trend is expected to intensify in the next few years as digital radio provides virtually unlimited signal capacity.

Weekly Reach and Share of Total Hours Tuned by Demographics[1]

Canada		Reach		Share	
		AM (%)	FM (%)	AM (%)	FM (%)
12+		44	78	31	69
Women 18+		45	77	32	68
Men 18+		47	78	31	69
Teens 12-17		21	84	9	91

Quebec		Reach		Share	
	Lang.	AM (%)	FM (%)	AM (%)	FM (%)
12+	Fr	29	86	20	80
	En	48	82	32	68
Women 18+	Fr	30	86	21	79
	En	49	80	35	65
Men 18+	Fr	33	86	20	80
	En	51	83	31	69
Teens 12-17	Fr	7	87	3	97
	En	20	89	8	92

Source: *Media Digest/BBM Fall '98*
(1) "Reach" is defined as the percentage of the population tuning to AM or FM radio at least once a week. "Share" is the percentage of the population's total listening time accounted for by each demographic group.

POPULAR MUSIC

The watershed year in the Canadian music industry was 1971, when the federal government imposed Canadian content regulations on the country's radio stations. These regulations helped build a domestic recording industry that has produced several generations of world-class pop stars including Bryan Adams, Céline Dion, Sarah MacLauchlan and Shania Twain.

Montreal, Toronto, and Vancouver have consistently served as centres for the Canadian popular music industry. But other cities have served as hotbeds at various periods. Winnipeg in the 1960s was dubbed the Liverpool of Canada for a scene that launched the careers of Neil Young and the Guess Who. The Ottawa Valley has long been a place of musical ferment owing to the interaction of the its Irish, Scottish, and French settlers. Bruce Cockburn and Alannis Morrissette are two of the National Capital Region's best known alumni.

Nova Scotia and Newfoundland have historically been home to vibrant Celtic folk traditions and the 1990s saw the rise of Atlantic Canada as a major centre for music production in Canada. Those traditions have been parlayed into commercial success for artists such as The Rankins, singer Rita MacNeil, and folk/rock fiddlers Ashley MacIsaac and Natalie McMaster.

The Juno Awards, 1990–2000

The Juno Awards were established in 1975 to honor achievement in the Canadian recording industry. The name was chosen to honor Pierre Juneau, former head of the Canadian Radio-television and Telecommunications Commission (CRTC) which instituted "Canadian content" requirements in the nation's broadcast industry.

Nominations for most major Juno categories are determined by record sales, although the actual winners are selected by a vote of members of the Canadian Academy of Recording Arts & Sciences.

Nominees must be Canadian citizens or landed immigrants and must have resided in Canada during the year prior to their nomination. Eligible recordings don't require national distribution, but must be available for retail sale in Canada.

The latest awards were announced March 12, 2000.

Canadian Entertainer of the Year
1990 . . . . The Jeff Healey Band
1991 . . . . The Tragically Hip
1992 . . . . Bryan Adams
1993 . . . . The Tragically Hip
1994 . . . . The Rankin Family
1995 . . . . The Tragically Hip
1996 . . . . Shania Twain

Best Selling Album (Foreign or Domestic)
2000 . . . . *Millennium*, Backstreet Boys

Album of the Year
1990 . . . . *Alannah Myles*, Alannah Myles
1991 . . . . *Unison*, Celine Dion
1992 . . . . *Mad Mad World*, Tom Cochrane
1993 . . . . *Ingenue*, k.d. lang
1994 . . . . *Harvest Moon*, Neil Young
1995 . . . . *Colour of My Love*, Celine Dion
1996 . . . . *Jagged Little Pill*, Alanis Morissette
1997 . . . . *Trouble at the Henhouse*, The Tragically Hip
1998 . . . . *Clumsy*, Our Lady Peace
1999 . . . . *Let's Talk About Love*, Celine Dion
2000 *Supposed Former Infatuation Junkie*, Alanis Morissette

Single of the Year
1990 . . . . "Black Velvet," Alannah Myles
1991 . . . . "Just Came Back," Colin James
1992 . . . . "Life Is a Highway," Tom Cochrane
1993 . . . "Beauty and the Beast," Celine Dion/Peabo Bryson
1994 . . . . "Fare Thee Well Love," The Rankin Family
1995 . . . . "Could I Be Your Girl," Jann Arden
1996 . . . . "You Oughta Know," Alanis Morissette
1997 . . . . "Ironic," Alanis Morissette
1998 . . . . "Building a Mystery," Sarah McLachlan
1999 . . . . "One Week," Barenaked Ladies
2000 . . . . "Bobcaygeon," The Tragically Hip

Female Vocalist of the Year
1990 . . . . Rita MacNeil
1991 . . . . Celine Dion
1992 . . . . Celine Dion
1993 . . . . Celine Dion
1994 . . . . Celine Dion
1995 . . . . Jann Arden
1996 . . . . Alanis Morissette
1997 . . . . Celine Dion
1998 . . . . Sarah McLachlan
1999 . . . . Celine Dion
2000 . . . . Chantal Kreviazuk

Male Vocalist of the Year
1990 . . . . Kim Mitchell
1991 . . . . Colin James
1992 . . . . Tom Cochrane
1993 . . . . Leonard Cohen
1994 . . . . Roch Voisine
1995 . . . . Neil Young
1996 . . . . Colin James
1997 . . . . Bryan Adams
1998 . . . . Paul Brandt
1999 . . . . Jim Cuddy
2000 . . . . Bryan Adams

Group of the Year
1990 . . . . Blue Rodeo
1991 . . . . Blue Rodeo
1992 . . . . Crash Test Dummies ▶

Arts and Entertainment

▶ 1993 .... Barenaked Ladies
1994 .... The Rankin Family
1995 .... The Tragically Hip
1996 .... Blue Rodeo
1997 .... The Tragically Hip
1998 .... Our Lady Peace
1999 .... Barenaked Ladies
2000 .... Matthew Good Band

Songwriter of the Year
1990 .... Greg Keelor and Jim Cuddy
1991 .... David Tyson
1992 .... Tom Cochrane
1993 .... k.d. lang
1994 .... Leonard Cohen
1995 .... Jann Arden
1996 .... Alanis Morissette (with Glen Ballard)
1997 .... Alanis Morissette (with Glen Ballard)
1998 .... Sarah McLachlan/Pierre Marchand
1999 .... Bryan Adams,(w' co-songwriter)
Phil Thornalley "On A Day Like Today;"
(w' co-songwriter) Eliott Kennedy,"When You're Gone"
2000 ...... Shania Twain, "Man! I Feel Like A Woman,"
(co-Songwriter Robert John "Mutt" Lange);
"You've Got A Way," (co-Songwriter Robert John "Mutt"
Lange); "That Don't Impress Me Much,"
(co-Songwriter Robert John "Mutt" Lange)

Best New Solo Artist
1994 .... Jann Arden
1995 .... Susan Aglukark
1996 .... Ashley MacIsaac
1997 .... Terri Clark
1998 .... Holly McNarland
1999 .... Melanie Doane
2000 .... Tal Bachman

Best New Group
1994 .... The Waltons
1995 .... Moist
1996 .... The Philosopher Kings
1997 .... The Killjoys
1998 .... Leahy
1999 .... Johnny Favourite Swing Orchestra
2000 .... Sky

Best Selling Francophone Album
1994 .... Album de Peuple: Tome 2
1995 .... Coup de tête
1996 .... D'eux
1997 .... Live À Paris
1998 .... Marie Michèle Desrosiers
Chante Les Classiques de Noël
1999 .... S'il Suffisait D'Aimer, Celine Dion
2000 .... En Catimini, La Chicane

Country Female Vocalist of the Year
1990 .... k.d. lang
1991 .... Rita MacNeil
1992 .... Cassandra Vasik
1993 .... Michelle Wright
1994 .... Cassandra Vasik
1995 .... Michelle Wright
1996 .... Shania Twain
1997 .... Shania Twain
1998 .... Shania Twain
1999 .... Shania Twain
2000 .... Shania Twain

Country Male Vocalist of the Year
1990 .... George Fox
1991 .... George Fox
1992 .... George Fox
1993 .... Gary Fjellgaard
1994 .... Charlie Major
1995 .... Charlie Major
1996 .... Charlie Major
1997 .... Paul Brandt
1998 .... Paul Brandt
1999 .... Paul Brandt
2000 .... Paul Brandt

Country Group or Duo of the Year
1990 .... The Family Brown
1991 .... Prairie Oyster
1992 .... Prairie Oyster
1993 .... Tracey Prescott & Lonesome Daddy
1994 .... The Rankin Family
1995 .... Prairie Oyster
1996 .... Prairie Oyster
1997 .... The Rankin Family
1998 .... Farmer's Daughter
1999 .... Leahy
2000 .... The Rankins

Best Pop/Adult Album
2000 ...... Colour Moving And Still, Chantal Kreviazuk

Best Rock Album
1991 .... Presto, Rush
1992 .... Roll the Bones, Rush
1993 .... Doin' the Nasty, Slik Toxik
1994 .... Dig, I. Mother Earth
1995 .... Suffersystem, Monster Voodoo Machine
1996 .... Jagged Little Pill, Alanis Morissette
2000 .... Beautiful Midnight, Matthew Good Band

Best Alternative Album
1991 .... One Chord to Another, Sloan
1998 .... Glee, Bran Van 3000
1999 .... Rufus Wainwright, Rufus Wainwright
2000 .... Julie Doiron and the Wooden Stars,
Julie Doiron and the Wooden Stars

Best Rap Recording
1991 .... "Symphony in Effect," Maestro Fresh-Wes
1992 .... "My Definition of a Boombastic Jazz Style,"
Dream Warriors
1993 .... Keep It Slammin', Devon
1994 .... One Track Mind, TBTBT
1995 .... Certified, Ghetto Concept
1996 .... E-Z On Tha Motion, Ghetto Concept
1997 .... What It Takes, Choclair
1998 .... Cash Crop, Rascalz
1999 .... Northern Touch, Rascalz featuring
Choclair, Kardinal Offishall, Thrust and Checkmate
2000 .... Ice Cold, Choclair ▶

Popular Music

Best Dance Recording
1990 .... "I Beg Your Pardon (I Never Promised You a Rose Garden)," Kon Kan
1991 .... "Don't Wanna Fall in Love," Jane Child
1992 .... "Everyone's a Winner (Chocolate Movement Mix)," Bootsauce
1993 . "Love Can Move Mountains (Club Mix)," Celine Dion
1994 .... "Thankful (Raw Club Mix)," Red Light
1995 .... "Higher Love (Club Mix)," Capital Sound
1996 .. "A Deeper Shade of Love (Extended Mix)," Camille
1997 .... "Astroplane" (City of Love Mix), BKS
1998 ..... "Euphoria" (Rabbit in the Moon Mix), Delerium
1999 .... Broken Bones, Love Inc.
2000 .... Silence, Delerium

Best Contemporary Jazz Album
1990 .. Skydance, Jon Ballantyne Trio featuring Joe Henderson
1991 .... Two Sides, Mike Murley
1992 .... For the Moment, Renee Rosnes; In Transition, Brian Dickinson; The Brass Is Back, Rob McConnell and The Boss Brass
1993 .... My Ideal, P.J. Perry
1994 .... Don't Smoke in Bed, Holly Cole Trio
1995 .. The Merlin Factor, Jim Hillman & The Merlin Factor
1996 .... NOJO, Neufeld-Occhipinti Jazz Orchestra
1997 .... Africville Suite, Joe Sealy
1998 .... Metalwood, Metalwood
1999 .... Metalwood 2, Metalwood
2000 ....so far, D.D. Jackson

Best Vocal Jazz Album
2000 .... When I Look In Your Eyes, Diana Krall

Best Mainstream Jazz Album
1994 . Fables and Dreams, Dave Young/Phil Dwyer Quartet
1995 .... Free Trade, Free Trade
1996 .... Vernal Fields, Ingrid Jensen
1997 .... Ancestors, Renee Rosnes
1998 .... In the Mean Time, The Hugh Fraser Quintet
1999 .... The Atlantic Sessions, Kirk MacDonald
2000 .... Deep In A Dream, Pat LaBarbera

Best R&B/Soul Recording
1990 .... "Spellbound," Billy Newton-Davis
1991 .... "Dance to the Music (Work Your Body)," Simply Majestic Featuring B. Kool
1992 .... "Call My Name," Love & Sas
1993 .... "Once in a Lifetime," Love & Sas
1994 .... "The Time is Right,"Rupert Gayle
1995 .... "First Impressions for the Bottom Jigglers," Bass is Base
1996 .... "Deborah Cox," Deborah Cox
1997 .... "Feelin' Alright," Carlos Morgan
1998 .... Things Just Ain't the Same, Deborah Cox
1999 .... One Wish, Deborah Cox
2000 .... Thinkin' About You, 2Rude featuring Latoya & Miranda

Best Blues/Gospel Album
1994 .... South at Eight/North at Nine, Colin Linden
1995 .... Joy to the World Jubilation V, Montreal Jubilation Gospel Choir
1996 .... That River, Jim Byrnes
1997 .... Right To Sing The Blues, Long John Baldry

Best Blues Album
1998 .... National Steel, Colin James
1999 .... Blues Weather, Fathead
2000 .... Gust Of Wind, Ray Bonneville

Best Gospel Album
1998 .... Romantics and Mystics, Steve Bell
1999 .... Life Is, Sharon Riley & Faith Chorale
2000 .... Legacy Of Hope, Deborah Klassen

Best Reggae/Calypso Recording
1990 .... Too Late To Turn Back Now, Sattalites
1991 .... Soldiers We Are All, Jayson & Friends
1994 .... Informer, Snow
1995 .... Class and Credential, Carla Marshall
1996 .... Now and Forever, Sattalites
1997 .... Nana Maclean, Nana Maclean
1998 .... Catch de Vibe, Messenjah
1999 .... Vision, Frankie Wilmot
2000 .... Heart & Soul, Lazo

Best Global Album
1992 .... The Gathering, Various Artists
1993 .... Spirits of Havana, Jane Bunnett
1994 .... El Camino Real, Ancient Cultures
1995 .... Africa+, Eval Manigat
1996 .... Music From Africa, Takadja
1997 .... Africa Do Brasil, Paulo Ramos Group
1998 .... La Llorona, Lhasa
1999 .... La Llorona, Lhasa
2000 .... Omnisource, Madagascar Slim

Best Roots and Traditional Album
1990 ... Je Voudrais Changer D'Chapeau, La Bottine Souriante
1991 .... Dance & Celebrate, Bourne & MacLeod
1992 ..... Saturday Night Blues, Various Artists; The Visit, Loreena McKennitt
1993 ..... Jusqu'aux P'tites Heures, La Bouttine Souriante
1994 .... My Skies, James Keelaghan
1995 ..... The Mask and Mirror, Loreena McKennitt
1996 .. Hi: How Are You Today?, Ashley MacIsaac (solo); Gypsies & Lovers, The Irish Descendants (group)
1997 .... drive-in movie, Fred Eaglesmith (solo); Matapedia, Kate & Anna McGarrigle (group)
1998 .... Other Songs, Ron Sexsmith (solo) Molinos, The Paperboys (group)
1999 .... Heartstrings, Willie P. Bennett (solo) The McGarrigle Hour, Kate & Anna McGarrigle (group)
2000 ..... Breakfast In New Orleans Dinner In Timbuktu, Bruce Cockburn (solo) Kings Of Love, Blackie & The Rodeo Kings (group)

Instrumental Artist(s) of the Year
1990 .... Manteca
1991 .... Ofra Harnoy
1992 .... Shadowy Men on a Shadowy Planet
1993 .... Ofra Harnoy
1994 .... Ofra Harnoy
1995 .... André Gagnon
1996 .... Liona Boyd
1997 .... Ashley MacIsaac
1998 .... Leahy

Best Instrumental Album
1999 ...... My Roots Are Showing, Natalie MacMaster
2000 .... In My Hands, Natalie MacMaster

Arts and Entertainment

Best Classical Album (solo or chamber ensemble)
1990 .... *20th Century Original Piano Transcriptions*, Louis Lortie
1991 .. *Schafer: Five String Quartets*, Orford String Quartet
1992 ..... *Franz Liszt: Années de Pelerinage*, Louis Lortie
1993 .... *Beethoven: Piano Sonatas*, Louis Lortie
1994 .... *Beethoven: Piano Sonatas, Op. 10, No. 1-3*, Louis Lortie
1995 .... *Erica Goodman Plays Canadian Harp Music*, Erica Goodman
1996. *Aikan: Grande Sonate/Sonatine*, Marc-André Hamelin
1997 .... *Scriabin: The Complete Piano Sonatas*, Marc-Andre Hamelin
1998 .... *Marc-André Hamelin plays Franz Liszt*, Marc-André Hamelin
1999 .... *Bach: Well-Tempered Clavier – Book 1*, Angela Hewitt
2000 .... *Schumann: String Quartets*, St. Lawrence String Quartet

Best Classical Album (large ensemble)
1990   *Boccherini: Cello Concertos and Symphonies*, Tafelmusik Baroque Orchestra
1991 .... *Debussy: Images, Nocturnes*, Orchestre .... Symphonique de Montréal, Charles Dutoit
1992 .... *Debussy: Pelleas et Melisande*, Orchestre Symphonique de Montréal, Charles Dutoit
1993 .... *Handel: Excerpts from Floridante*, Tafelmusik
1994 .. *Handel: Concerti Grossi, Op. 3, No. 1-6*, Tafelmusik
1995 .. *Bach: Brandenburg Concertos Nos. 1-6*, Tafelmusik
1996 .... *Shostakovich: Symphonies 5 & 9*, Orchestra Symphonique de Montréal
1997 .... *Ginastera/Villa-Lobos/Evangelista*, I Musici de Montreal
1998 .... *Mozart Horn Concertos*, James Sommerville, CBC Vancouver Orchestra, Mario Bernardi
1999 .... *Handel: Music For The Royal Fireworks*, Tafelmusik, Jeanne Lamon (Musical Director)
2000 ..... *Respighi: La Boutique Fantasque*, Orchestre Symphonique de Montréal

Best Classical Album (vocal or choral performance)
1995 .... *Berlioz: Les Troyens*, Vocal Soloists, Choeur et Orchestre symphonique de Montréal
1995 .. *Ben Heppner Sings Richard Strauss*, Ben Heppner, Toronto Symphony Orchestra, Andrew Davis, conductor
1997 .. *Berlioz: La Damnation de Faust*, Choeur et Orcheste symphonique de Montreal, Charles Dutoit, Conductor
1998 ..... *Soirée Francaise*, Michel Schade, Russel Braun, Canadian Opera Company Orchestra, Richard Bradshaw
1999 .... *Songs Of Travel*, Gerald Finley (baritone), Stephen Ralls (piano)
2000 .... *German Romantic Opera*, Ben Heppner

Best Classical Composition
1990 .... *Concerto For Harp and Chamber Orchestra/Morawetz Harp Concertos*, Oskar Morawetz
1991 .... *String Quartet No. 5 'Rosalind'*, R. Murray Schafer
1992 .... *Concerto For Piano & Chamber Orchestra*, Michael Conway Baker
1993 .... *Concerto for Flute and Orchestra*, R. Murray Schafer
1994 .... *Among Friends*, Chan Ka Nin
1995 .... *Sketches From Natal*, Malcolm Forsyth
1996 .... *Concerto For Violin and Orchestra*, Andrew P. MacDonald
1997 .... *Picasso Suite*, Harry Somers
1998 .... *Electra Rising*, Malcolm Forsyth
1999 ..... *Concerto For Wind Orchestra*, Colin McPhee
2000 ...... *Shattered Night, Shivering Stars*, Alexina Louie

Best Children's Album
1990 ...... *Beethoven Lives Upstairs*, Susan Hammond & Barbara Nichol
1991 .... *Mozart's Magic Fantasy*, Susan Hammond/Classical Kids
1992 .... *Vivaldi's Ring of Mystery*, Susan Hammond/Classical Kids
1993 .... *Waves of Wonder*, Jack Grunsky
1994 .... *Tchaikovsky Discovers America*, SusanHammond/Classical Kids
1995 .... *Bananaphone*, Raffi
1996 .... *Celery Stalks at Midnight*, Al Simmons
1997 .... *Songs From the Treehouse*, Martha Johnson
1998 .... *Livin' in a Shoe*, Judy & David
1999 . *Mozart's Magnificent Voyage*, Susan Hammond's Classical Kids
2000 .... *Skinnamarink TV*, Sharon, Lois and Bram

Producer of the Year
1990 .... Bruce Fairbairn
1991 .... David Tyson
1992 .... Bryan Adams
1993 ...... k.d. lang/Ben Mink (Greg Penny, co-producer)
1994 .... Steve MacKinnon/Marc Jordan (Greg Penny, co-producer)
1995 .... Robbie Robertson
1996 .... Michael-Phillip Wojewoda
1997 .... Garth Richardson
1998 .... Pierre Marchand
1999 .... Colin James (co-producer, Joe Hardy)
2000 .... Tal Bachman and Bob Rock

Best Video of the Year
1990 .... *Boomtown* (Andrew Cash), Cosimo Cavallaro
1991 .. *Drop the Needle* (Maestro Fresh-Wes), Joel Goldberg
1992 .... *Into the Fire* (Sarah McLachlan), Phil Kates
1993 ..... *Closing Time* (Leonard Cohen), Curtis Wehrfritz
1994 .... *I Would Die For You* (Jann Arden), Jeth Weinrich
1995 .... *Tunnel of Trees* (Gogh Van Go), Lyne Charlebois
1996 .... *Good Mother* (Jann Arden), Jeth Weinrich
1997 .... *Burned Out Car* (Junkhouse), Jeth Weinrich
1998 .... *Gasoline* (Moist), Javier Aguilera
1999 .... *Forestfire*, Javier Aguilera (David Usher)
2000 .... *So Pure*, Alanis Morissette

Best Music of Aboriginal Canada Recording
1995 .... Susan Aglukark
1996 .... Jerry Alfred & The Medicine Beat
1997 .... Buffy Ste. Marie
2000 .... *Falling Down*, Chester Knight & The Wind

Source: *Canadian Academy of Recording Arts & Sciences*

The East Coast Music Awards, 2000

The East Coast Music Awards were established in 1989 to honor outstanding contributions to the Canadian music industry by artists performing, recording, or rooted in Atlantic Canada, and to celebrate that region's distinct musical heritage in English and in French. The 12th annual ECMAs were presented Feb. 3-6, 2000 in Sydney, N.S.

Male Artist Of The Year	John Gracie
Female Artist Of The Year	Natalie MacMaster
Group Of The Year	Great Big Sea
Songwriter Of The Year	Gordie Sampson
Single Of The Year	"Sorry," Gordie Sampson
Video Of The Year	"Sorry," Gordie Sampson
Album Of The Year	Turn Great Big Sea
New Artist Of The Year	John Curtis Sampson
Entertainer Of The Year	Great Big Sea
Country Artist/Group Of The Year	John Curtis Sampson
Pop/Rock Artist/Group Of The Year	Kim Stockwood
Instrumental Artist/Group Of The Year	JP Cormier
Alternative Artist/Group Of The Year	An Acoustic Sin
Jazz Artist/Group Of The Year	Jive Kings
Blues Artist/Group Of The Year	Glamour Puss
Gospel Artist/Group Of The Year	The Nova Scotia Mass Choir
Children's Artist/Group Of The Year	Rik Barron
Urban Recording Of The Year	The Time, Jamie Sparks
Classical Recording Of The Year	Newfoundland Symphony Youth Choir
Roots/Traditional Solo Artist Of The Year	Natalie McMaster
Roots/Traditional Group Of The Year	Barachois
Francophone Recording Of The Year	Barachois
Aboriginial Artist/Group Of The Year	Morningstar

The Grammy Awards, 1989-99

Grammy winners are selected annually by the 6,000 voting members of The Recording Academy, based on artistic and/or technical excellence. The titles for song of the year are followed by the names of the songwriters. The 1999 Grammy winners were announced Feb. 23, 2000.

Best Record
- 1989 "Wind Beneath My Wings," Bette Midler
- 1990 "Another Day In Paradise," Phil Collins
- 1991 "Unforgettable," Natalie Cole (with Nat King Cole)
- 1992 "Tears in Heaven," Eric Clapton
- 1993 "I Will Always Love You," Whitney Houston
- 1994 "All I Wanna Do,' Sheryl Crow
- 1995 "Kiss From A Rose," Seal
- 1996 "Change the World," Eric Clapton
- 1997 "Sunny Came Home," Shawn Colvin
- **1998 "My Heart Will Go On," Celine Dion**
- 1999 "Smooth," Santana featuring Rob Thomas

Best Album
- 1989 *Nick of Time*, Bonnie Raitt
- 1990 *Back On The Block*, Quincy Jones
- 1991 *Unforgettable*, Natalie Cole
- 1992 *Unplugged*, Eric Clapton
- 1993 *The Bodyguard–Original Soundtrack Album*, Whitney Houston
- 1994 *MTV Unplugged*, Tony Bennett
- **1995 *Jagged Little Pill*, Alanis Morissette**
- **1996 *Falling Into You*, Celine Dion**
- 1997 *Time Out Of Mind*, Bob Dylan
- 1998 *The Miseducation of Lauryn Hill*, Lauryn Hill
- 1999 *Supernatural*, Santana

Best Song
- 1989 "Wind Beneath My Wings," Larry Henley, Jeff Silbar
- 1990 "From A Distance," Julie Gold
- 1991 "Unforgettable," Irving Gordon
- 1992 "Tears in Heaven," Eric Clapton, Will Jennings
- 1993 "A Whole New World (Aladdin's Theme)," Alan Menken, Tim Rice
- 1994 "Streets of Philadelphia," Bruce Springsteen
- 1995 "Kiss From A Rose," Seal
- 1996 "Change the World," Eric Clapton, Wynonna
- 1997 "Sunny Came Home," Shawn Colvin
- 1998 "My Heart Will Go On," James Harper, Will Jennings
- 1999 "Smooth," Itaal Shur & Rob Thomas, songwriters

Best Male Pop Vocal
- 1989 "How Am I Supposed to Live Without You," Michael Bolton
- 1990 "Oh, Pretty Woman," Roy Orbison
- 1991 "When a Man Loves a Woman," Michael Bolton
- 1992 "Tears in Heaven," Eric Clapton
- 1993 "If I Ever Lose My Faith in You," Sting
- 1994 "Can You Feel the Love Tonight," Elton John
- 1995 "Kiss From A Rose," Seal
- 1996 "Change the World," Eric Clapton
- 1997 "Candle in the Wind 1997," Elton John
- 1998 "My Father's Eyes," Eric Clapton
- 1999 "Brand New Day," Sting

Best Female Vocal
- 1989 "Nick of Time," Bonnie Raitt
- 1990 "Vision Of Love," Mariah Carey
- 1991 "Something to Talk About," Bonnie Raitt
- **1992 "Constant Craving," k.d. lang**

Arts and Entertainment

▶ 1993 "I Will Always Love You," Whitney Houston
1994 "All I Wanna Do," Sheryl Crow
1995 "No More 'I Love You's'," Annie Lennox
1996 "Un-Break My Heart," Toni Braxton
1997 "Building A Mystery," Sarah McLachlan
1998 "My Heart Will Go On," Celine Dion
1999 "I Will Remember You," Sarah McLachlan

Best Female Country Vocal Performance
1989 "Absolute Torch And Twang," k.d. lang
1990 "Where've You Been," Kathy Mattea
1991 "Down At The Twist And Shout," Mary-Chapin Carpenter
1992 "I Feel Lucky," Mary-Chapin Carpenter
1993 "Passionate Kisses," Mary-Chapin Carpenter
1994 "Shut Up And Kiss Me," Mary-Chapin Carpenter
1995 "Baby, Now That I've Found You," Alison Krauss
1996 "Blue," LeAnn Rimes
1997 "How Do I Live," Trisha Yearwood
1998 "You're Still The One," Shania Twain
1999 "Man! I Feel Like A Woman!" Shania Twain

Best Jazz Vocal Performance
1989 (Female) "Blues On Broadway," Ruth Brown; (Male) "When Harry Met Sally," Harry Connick Jr.
1990 (Female) "All That Jazz," Ella Fitzgerald; (Male) "We Are In Love," Harry Connick Jr.
1991 "He Is Christmas," Take 6 (Mark Kibble, Joey Kibble, Claude V. McKnight III, Cedric Dent, David Thomas & Alvin Chea)
1992 "'Round Midnight," Bobby McFerrin
1993 "Take A Look," Natalie Cole
1994 "Mystery Lady (Songs Of Billie Holiday)," Etta James
1995 "An Evening With Lena Horne," Lena Horne
1996 "New Moon Daughter," Cassandra Wilson
1997 "Dear Ella," DeeDee Bridgewater
1998 "I Remember Miles," Shirley Horn
1999 "When I Look In Your Eyes," Diana Krall

Best Instrumental Soloist(s) Performance (with Orchestra)
1989 Yo-Yo Ma, Barber: Cello Concerto, Op. 22; Britten: Symphony For Cello & Orch., Op. 68.
1990 Itzhak Perlman, Shostakovich: Violin Con. No. 1 In A Min.; Glazunov: Violin Con. In A Min
1991 John Browning, Barber: Piano Concerto
1992 Yo-Yo Ma, Prokofiev: Sinfonia Concertante; Tchaikovsky: Variations On A Rococo Theme
1993 Anne-Sophie Mutter, Berg: Violin Concerto; Rihm: Time Chant
1994 Yo-Yo-Ma, The New York Album (Works Of Albert, Bartok & Bloch)
1995 Itzhak Perlman, The American Album (Works Of Bernstein, Barber, Foss)
1996 Yefim Bronfman, Bartok: The Three Piano Concertos
1997 Yo-Yo Ma & David Zinman, Premieres – Cello Concertos (Works Of Danielpour, Kirchner, Rouse)
1998 Anne-Sophie Mutter & Krzysztof Penderecki, Penderecki: Violin Con. No. 2 Metamorphosen
1999 Prokofiev: Piano Concertos. Nos. 1 & 3; Bartók: Piano Con. No. 3, Martha Argerich & the Montreal Symphony Orchestra

Best New Artist
1989[1] Withdrawn
1990 Mariah Carey
1991 Mark Cohn
1992 Arrested Development
1993 Toni Braxton
1994 Sheryl Crow
1995 Hootie & The Blowfish
1996 LeAnn Rimes
1997 Paula Cole
1998 Lauryn Hill
1999 Christina Aguilera

Source: National Academy of Recording Arts & Sciences
Note: Canadian artist set in bold type.
(1) Initially awarded to Milli Vanilli who later admitted they had not performed on any of their recordings.

Canada at the Grammys

An inspection of our Grammy winners' list for the past decade shows that Canadians, particularly Canadian female vocalists, are no strangers to America's top music honours.

The 1999 Grammys saw the success of the country's divas reach new heights as Sarah McLachlan, Diana Krall, and Shania Twain brought home four high-profile awards. McLachlan took the prize for best female vocal for her song "I Will Remember You." Krall commandeered the best jazz vocal performance award for her album *When I Look In Your Eyes*, while Twain came home a double winner for best country vocalist and best country song ("Man! I Feel Like a Woman," and "Come on Over" respectively). In addition, U.S. singer Lenny Kravitz won best rock vocal honours for his rendition of "American Woman," a 1970s hit written by Randy Bachman and Burton Cummings for Winnipeg's The Guess Who. In the classical realm, the Montreal Symphony Orchestra won best instrumental soloist with orchestra for its recordings of piano concertos by Prokofiev and Bartók.

Canadian Music Hall of Fame

The Canadian Academy of Recording Arts and Sciences instituted a Hall of Fame Award in 1978 to honour Canadians who have contributed to the greater international recognition of Canadian artists and music.

■ Winners

1978	Guy Lombardo	1986	Gordon Lightfoot		Domenic Troiano
	Oscar Peterson	1987	The Guess Who		John Kay
1979	Hank Snow	1989	The Band		Zal Yanovsky
1980	Paul Anka	1990	Maureen Forrester	1997	Lenny Breau
1981	Joni Mitchell	1991	Leonard Cohen		Gil Evans
1982	Neil Young	1992	Ian & Sylvia		Maynard Ferguson
1983	Glenn Gould	1993	Anne Murray		Moe Kauffman
1984	The Crewcuts	1994	Rush		Rob McConnell
	The Diamonds	1995	Buffy Sainte-Marie	1998	David Foster
	The Four Lads	1996	David Clayton-Thomas	1999	Luc Plamondon
1985	Wilf Carter		Denny Doherty		

2000 INDUCTEE

■ Bruce Fairbairn

With blockbuster albums by Aerosmith, Bon Jovi, Cranberries, INXS, Loverboy, Van Halen and AC/DC to his credit, Vancouver's Bruce Fairbairn ranked in the top echelons of the world's record producers. In a business where healthy egos abound, Fairbairn was known for his unobtrusive, soft-spoken approach to studio work and his uncanny knack for getting musicians to work together in service of his vision.

Fairbarn held a bachelor's degree in biology and a master's in environmental planning. But he was also a classically trained trumpet player who formed his first band while still in high school. After university, Fairbairn worked as an environmental consultant for BC Hydro. His professional music career began with the rock band Prism. That work won him a Producer of the Year Juno Award in 1980. He shared the same award with Paul Dean in 1982 for his work with Loverboy. International success came with his production of Bon Jovi's 1986 album *Slippery When Wet* which sold 20 million copies world wide. His LPs for Aerosmith (*Permanent Vacation*, *Pump*, *Get a Grip*, *Big Ones*) sold 30 million copies. Fairbairn died in his sleep at his Vancouver home on May 17, 1999 at the age of 49.

Source: *Canadian Academy of Recording Arts and Sciences* http://www.juno-awards.ca/caras/

The Canadian Academy of Recording Arts and Sciences (CARAS)

This organization was originally created to administer and promote the Juno Awards. It has since expanded its mandate to link members of the Canadian music community and members of the public interested in the Canadian music and recording industry. The Junos themselves remain the centrepiece, to recognize (and reward) outstanding achievement in recorded music. The broadcast of the Junos brings singers, musicians, songwriters, producers and other creative talent together and to the attention of both a national audience and foreign markets.

CARAS uses a website to achieve its goals beyond the awards: a home page for the Canadian Music Hall of Fame has biographies, photos and sound clips from the inductees. In addition, CARAS is building a database containing information about Canadian music, and all of its artists and creators. Known as JAMA (Juno Awards Music Archive), the site boasted almost 2,000 entries in March of 1998 and is still growing. Browsers can access biographies, images, discographies and audio clips of Canadian artists. Check it out at http://www.juno-awards.ca

Canadian Country Music Awards, 1999

Awards and citations from the CCMA were presented September 2000, during Country Music Week. These were the nineteenth annual awards, the seventh to be broadcast in the US and Europe.

Fans' Choice Award:	The Wilkinsons
Female Artist of the Year	Michelle Wright
Male Artist of the Year	Paul Brandt
Single of the Year	"Jimmy's Got A Girlfriend," The Wilkinsons
Album of the Year	*Here and Now*, The Wilkinsons
Vocal Duo or Group of the Year	The Wilkinsons
Music Video of the Year	"That's The Truth," Paul Brandt
Song of the Year	"Daddy Won't Sell The Farm," Steve Fox and Robin Branda
Vocal/Instrumental Collaboration	"Get Me Through December," Natalie MacMaster and Alison Krauss
Rising Star	Tara Lyn Hart

Source: *Canadian Country Music Awards*

Top 50 CDs in Canada, 1999

1. *Millenium*, Backstreet Boys
2. *Baby, One More Time*, Britney Spears
3. ***Come On Over*, Shania Twain**
4. *Ricky Martin*, Ricky Martin
5. *Americana*, Offspring
6. *Believe*, Cher
7. *Significant Other*, Limp Bizkit
8. *Californications*, Red Hot Chili Peppers
9. *Fan Mail*, TLC
10. ***Mirrorball*, Sarah McLachlan**
11. *Now 4*, Various Artists
12. *Piece of Paradise*, Sky
13. *Sogna*, Andrea Bocelli
14. *Big Shiny Tunes 3*, Various Artists
15. *Miseducation*, Lauryn Hill
16. *Supernatural*, Santana
17. *On the 6*, Jennifer Lopez
18. *Austin Powers: The Spy Who Shagged Me*, Various Artists
19. *A Little Bit of Mambo*, Lou Bega
20. *1999 Grammy Nominees*, Various Artists
21. *Muchdance 1999*, Various Artists
22. *Women & Songs 2*, Various Artists
23. ***Tuesday's Child*, Amanda Marshall**
24. *Whitey Ford Sings The Blues*, Everlast
25. *Pure Dance 4*, Various Artists
26. *Christina Aguilera*, Christina Aguilera
27. ***Turn*, Great Big Sea 'X'**
28. *Notting Hill Original Sound Track*, Various Artists
29. *Human Clay*, Creed
30. ***When I Look In Your Eyes*, Diana Krall**
31. *Planet Pop 2000*, Various Artists
32. *Best of '80-'90*, U2
33. *The Matrix Original Sound Track*, Various Artists
34. *Vuelve*, Ricky Martin
35. *All Stars 2000*, Various Artists
36. ***Happiness…Is Not a Fish*, Our Lady Peace**
37. *The Party Album*, Vengaboys
38. *1999 Grammy Rap Nominees*, Various Artists
39. *Bury The Hatchet*, The Cranberries
40. *Astro Lounge*, Smash Mouth
41. ***TRIPtych*, Tea Party**
42. *Pure Energy 6*, Various Artists
43. ***Beautiful Midnight*, Matthew Good Band**
44. *The Fragile*, Nine Inch Nails
45. *Distance to Here*, Live
46. *Hits*, Phil Collins
47. *WWF The Music Vol. 3*, Various Artists
48. *Dasage*, Collective Soul
49. *Wild Wild West Original Sound Track*, Various Artists
50. *Sabrina the Teenage Witch Original Sound Track*, Various Artists

Source: *RPM Weekly*

Note: Canadian artists set in bold type.

Top 50 Hit Tracks, 1999

1. "Livin' La Vida Loca," Ricky Martin
2. "Every Morning," Sugar Ray
3. "I Want It That Way," Backstreet Boys
4. "All Star," Smash Mouth
5. "No Scrubs," TLC
6. "Love Song," Sky
7. "Mambo #5," Lou Bega
8. **"She's So High," Tal Bachman**
9. "Smooth," Santana
10. "If You Had My Love," Jennifer Lopez
11. "Kiss Me," Sixpence None the Richer
12. "Genie In A Bottle," Christina Aguilera
13. "Believe," Cher
14. "Beautiful Stranger," Madonna
15. "Steal My Sunshine," LEN
16. "Someday," Sugar Ray
17. "Bailamos," Enrique Iglesias
18. "Slide," Goo Goo Dolls
19. "Baby, One More Time," Britney Spears
20. "Wild Wild West," Will Smith
21. "Black Balloon," Goo Goo Dolls
22. "Unpretty," TLC
23. "Last Kiss," Pearl Jam
24. **"That Don't Impress Me Much," Shania Twain**
25. "The Animal Song," Savage Garden
26. **"It's All Been Done," Barenaked Ladies**
27. **"Keep A Lid On Things," Crash Test Dummies**
28. "You Get What You Give," New Radicals
29. "What It's Like," Everlast
30. "Praise You," Fatboy Slim
31. "Hands," Jewel
32. "Sometimes," Britney Spears
33. "12 Years Old," Kim Stockwood
34. "Heartreaker," Mariah Carey
35. "Millenium," Robbie Williams
36. **"When You're Gone," Bryan Adams**
37. "She's All I Ever Had," Ricky Martin
38. "Lullaby," Shawn Mullins
39. "Larger Than Life," Backstreet Boys
40. "Scar Tissue," Red Hot Chili Peppers
41. **"Cloud #9," Bryan Adams**
42. **"Unsent," Alanis Morissette**
43. "Angels Would Fall," Melissa Etheridge
44. "(You Drive Me) Crazy," Britney Spears
45. "Waiting For Tonight," Jennifer Lopez
46. "Angels of Mine," Monica
47. "Hey Leonardo," Blessed Union of Souls
48. **"Angel," Sarah McLachlan**
49. "Save Tonight," Eagle Eye Cherry
50. "Run," Collective Soul

Source: *RPM Weekly*
Note: Canadian artists set in bold type.

MTV Video Music Awards, 2000

Best Video of the Year	"The Real Slim Shady," Eminem
Best Rock Video	"Break Stuff," Limp Bizkit
Best R&B Video	"Say My Name," Destiny's Child
Best Hip Hop Video	"Thong Song," Sisqo
Viewer's Choice	"Bye Bye Bye," N Sync
Best Rap Video	"Can I Get A...," Jay-Z (featuring Ja Rule and Amil-Lion)
Best Direction	"Californication," Red Hot Chili Peppers
Best Female Video	"Try Again," Aaliyah
Best Pop Video	"Bye Bye Bye," N Sync
Best Video From a Fil	"Try Again," Aaliyah
Best New Artist	"I Try," Macy Gray
Best Group Video	"All The Small Things," Blink 182
Best Male Video	"The Real Slim Shady," Eminem
Best Dance Video	"Waiting For Tonight," Jennifer Lopez
Best Breakthrough Video	"All Is Full Of Love," Björk
Best Art Direction	"Californication," Colin Scrause
Special Effects	"All Is Full of Love," Chris Cunningham
Best Editing	"Bye Bye Bye," Dylan Tichneor
Best Choreography	"Bye Bye Bye," Darrin Henson
Best Cinematography	"Do Something," Jeff Cronenwett

Source: *MTV: Music Television*

The MuchMusic Video Awards, 2000

Best Rock Video	"Load Me Up," Matthew Good Band
Best Pop Video	"Misery," The Moffatts
Best Post-Production	"Rubbin'," Choclair
Best Cinematography	"Breathe Or Die," Dream Warriors
Best Video	"Load Me Up," Matthew Good Band
Best Director	The Tragically Hip, "My Music At Work"
Best Rap Video	"Let's Ride," Choclair
Best Soul/R and B Video	"Dissin' Us," 2 Rude featuring Jully Black and Grimmi Grimmi
Best Independent Video	"Money or Love," Saukrates
Best Dance Video	"Here Comes The Sunshine," Love Inc.
Best International Video	"Californication," Red Hot Chili Peppers
MuchMoreMusic Award	"Man, I Feel Like A Woman," Shania Twain
Best French Video	"Je Combats Le Spleen," Stefie Shock
VideoFACT Award	"DEEP," Serial Joe
Lifetime achievement award	The Guess Who
People's choice, favourite Canadian artist	"Alive," Edwin
People's choice, favourite Canadian group	"Is Anybody Home?," Our Lady Peace
People's choice, favourite Canadian video	"Is Anybody Home?," Our Lady Peace
People's choice, favourite international artist	"The Real Slim Shady," Eminem
People's choice, favourite international group	"Bye Bye Bye," N SYNC

Source: MuchMusic Network

Recording Industry Sales, 1999–2000[1]

These two charts examine the amount–and dollar value–of music purchased in a variety of forms in 2000, and compares those figures to the prior sales year. Sales information is supplied by members of the Canadian Recording Industry Association. Units and dollar amounts are expressed in the thousands.

Units Shipped	2000	1999	% change
VHS	407	879	-54%
DVDs	76	0	
Tl.Music Video	483279		-45%
Cassette Single	0	0	
Other Singles	193	375	-49%
Total Singles	193375		-49%
Cassette	1131	2231	-49%
CD	21884	22173	-1%
Total Albums	2301524404		-1%
Grand Total	23,691	25,658	-8%

Net Value of Sales ($000s)	2000	1999	% change
VHS	4039	7630	-47%
DVD	1537	0	
Tl. Music Videos	5576	7630	-27%
Cassette Single	0	0	
Other Singles	928	2057	-55%
Total Singles	9282057		-55%
Cassette	6805	13516	-50%
CD	259 749	263 316	-1%
Total Albums	266 554276 832		-4%
Grand Total	$273,058	$286,519	-5%

Source: Canadian Recording Industry Association

(1) For the period ending June 30th.

The Rock and Roll Hall of Fame

The Rock and Roll Hall of Fame was established in 1984. The Rock and Roll Hall of Fame and Museum opened in September 1995 in Cleveland, Ohio.

■ ARTISTS (Year Elected)

- The Allman Brothers Band (1995)
- The Animals (1994)
- LaVern Baker (1991)
- Hank Ballard (1990)
- The Band (1994)
- The Beach Boys (1988)
- The Beatles (1988)
- The Bee Gees (1997)
- Chuck Berry (1986)
- Bobby "Blue" Bland (1992)
- Booker T. & The MG's (1992)
- Buffalo Springfield (1997)
- David Bowie (1996)
- James Brown (1986)
- Ruth Brown (1993)
- The Byrds (1991)
- Johnny Cash (1992)
- Ray Charles (1986)
- Eric Clapton (2000)
- The Coasters (1987)
- Eddie Cochran (1987)
- Sam Cooke (1986)
- Cream (1993)
- Creedence Clearwater Revival (1993)
- Crosby, Stills and Nash (1997)
- Bobby Darin (1990)
- Bo Diddley (1987)
- Dion (1989)
- Fats Domino (1986)

▶

Popular Music

The Doors (1993)
The Drifters (1988)
Bob Dylan (1988)
The Eagles (1998)
Earth, Wind and Fire (2000)
Duane Eddy (1994)
The Everly Brothers (1986)
Fleetwood Mac (1998)
The Four Seasons (1990)
The Four Tops (1990)
Aretha Franklin (1987)
Marvin Gaye (1987)
Grateful Dead (1994)
Al Green (1995)
Bill Haley (1987)
Buddy Holly (1986)
The Jimi Hendrix Experience (1992)
John Lee Hooker (1991)
The Impressions (1991)
The Isley Brothers (1992)
Etta James (1993)
Jefferson Airplane (1996)
Billy Joel (1999)
Elton John (1994)
Janis Joplin (1995)
B.B. King (1987)
The Jackson Five (1997)
The Kinks (1990)
Gladys Knight and the Pips (1996)
Led Zeppelin (1995)
Lloyd Price (1998)
John Lennon (1994)
Jerry Lee Lewis (1986)
Little Richard (1986)
Little Willie John (1996)
The Lovin' Spoonful (2000)
Frankie Lyman and the Teenagers (1993)
The Mamas and the Papas (1998)
Bob Marley (1994)
Martha and the Vandellas (1995)
Curtis Mayfield (1999)
Paul McCartney (1999)
Joni Mitchell (1997)
Clyde McPhatter (1987)
The Moonglows (2000)
Van Morrison (1993)
Ricky Nelson (1987)
Roy Orbison (1987)
Parliament Funkadelic (1997)

Carl Perkins (1987)
Wilson Pickett (1991)
Pink Floyd (1996)
The Platters (1990)
Elvis Presley (1986)
Bonnie Raitt (2000)
Otis Redding (1989)
Jimmy Reed (1991)
Smokey Robinson (1987)
The Rolling Stones (1989)
Sam & Dave (1992)
Santana (1998)
Del Shannon (1999)
The Shirelles (1996)
Simon and Garfunkel (1990)
Sly and the Family Stone (1993)
Dusty Springfield (1999)
Bruce Springsteen (1999)
Rod Stewart (1994)
The Supremes (1988)
The Staple Singers (1999)
James Taylor (2000)
The Temptations (1989)
Ike and Tina Turner (1991)
Big Joe Turner (1987)
Gene Vincent (1998)
The Velvet Underground (1996)
Muddy Waters (1987)
The Who (1990)
Jackie Wilson (1987)
Stevie Wonder (1989)
The Yardbirds (1992)
The Young Rascals (1997)
Neil Young (1995)
Frank Zappa (1995)

■ NON-PERFORMERS

Paul Ackerman (1995)
Dave Bartholomew (1991)
Ralph Bass (1991)
Leonard Chess (1987)
Dick Clark (1993)
Clive Davis (2000)
Tom Donahue (1996)
Lamont Dozier, Brian Holland & Eddie Holland (1990)
Ahmet Ertegun (1987)
Leo Fender (1992)
Alan Freed (1986)
Milt Gabler (1993)

Gerry Goffin & Carole King (1990)
Berry Gordy, Jr. (1988)
Bill Graham (1992)
Jerry Leiber & Mike Stoller (1987)
George Martin (1999)
Syd Nathan (1997)
Johnny Otis (1994)
Sam Phillips (1986)
Doc Pomus (1992)
Phil Spector (1989)
Allen Toussaint (1998)
Jerry Wexler (1987)

■ LIFETIME ACHIEVEMENT AWARDS

Willie Dixon (1994)
Nesuhi Ertegun (1991)
John Hammond (1986)

■ EARLY INFLUENCES

Louis Armstrong (1990)
Charles Brown (1999)
Charlie Christian (1990)
Nat "King" Cole (2000)
Willie Dixon (1994)
Woody Guthrie (1988)
Billie Holiday (2000)
Howlin' Wolf (1991)
The Ink Spots (1989)
Mahalia Jackson (1997)
Elmore James (1992)
Robert Johnson (1986)
Louis Jordan (1987)
Lead Belly (1988)
Bill Monroe (1997)
Jelly Roll Morton (1998)
The Orioles (1995)
Les Paul (1988)
Professor Longhair (1992)
Ma Rainey (1990)
Jimmie Rodgers (1986)
Pete Seeger (1996)
Bessie Smith (1989)
The Soul Stirrers (1989)
T-Bone Walker (1987)
Dinah Washington (1993)
Hank Williams (1987)
Bob Wills & His Texas Playboys (1999)
Jimmy Yancey (1986)

Source: *Rock and Roll Hall of Fame Foundation*

MOVIES

Canada has been a world leader in documentary filmmaking, producing renowned artists such as Donald Brittain and Harry Rasky primarily through the National Film Board of Canada. The film board has also helped bring Canada to prominence as a producer of animation, and short subjects. Canadians have made an enormous contribution to the Hollywood feature film industry, from film mogul Louis B. Mayer to acclaimed director Norman Jewison to stars including Mary Pickford, Dan Ackroyd, Michael J. Fox, John Candy and Keanu Reeves. The Department of Canadian Heritage estimates that 20 percent of those employed in the Hollywood film industry are Canadian and that about 60 percent of the software used in U.S. film productions was developed by Canadians. Made-in-Canada features by filmmakers such as Denys Arcand, David Cronenburg, Atom Egoyan, and Patricia Rozema have enjoyed considerable critical and "art house" success around the world. In the 1990s, Canadian features twice won the Special Grand Jury Prize at the Cannes Film Festival. However, with U.S. distribution houses controlling 85 percent of the theatrical market, only one in twenty features gaining commercial release in Canada is produced in Canada.

■ Cameras Roll in Nova Scotia

During the past decade, Nova Scotia has secured its reputation as a major production centre in Canadian and international film production. Production activity brought a record $130 million into the Nova Scotia economy in 1999. American and other foreign producers accounted for $60 million of the total, a 200 percent increase over the previous year. Visiting productions to the province have included *Titanic*, *A Rumour of Angels* and *Catch a Falling Star*. Domestic film and television has enjoyed exponential growth in Nova Scotia, rising from $11.5 million in 1994 to $70 million in 1999.

Ten years ago, CBC Television identified Halifax as its third major production centre-after Toronto and Vancouver. The CBC gave local production companies such as Cochran Entertainment, Salter Street Films and Topsail Entertainment the opportunity to produce series including *Pit Pony*, *This Hour has 22 Minutes* and *Black Harbour* plus numerous movies of the week. Successful domestic feature films shot in Nova Scotia include *Margaret's Museum* and *New Waterford Girl*. The local industry is based in Halifax where three fully equipped sound stages are now in operation. The city ranks fourth in total film production after Toronto, Vancouver and Montreal, with approximately 2,500 people working in the industry. More than 50 percent of shooting takes place in locations outside the city, in picturesque locations such as Lunenberg, Cape Breton, Yarmouth and Chester.

Source: *Nova Scotia Film Development Corporation*

The National Film Board: Origins

On May 2, 1999, the National Film Board of Canada celebrated its 60th anniversary. It was established to improve Canadian Government Motion Picture Bureau productions and to increase their distribution in England. Canadian public servants working in London suggested that British documentary filmmaker John Grierson be invited to Canada to assess the film industry. Grierson submitted his report in June 1938, recommending that a coordinating body be established for Canadian film production.

A law was passed in May 1939, creating a National Film Commission (soon to be known as the National Film Board) to work alongside the Government Motion Picture Bureau. Its initial mandate was to make and distribute films designed to help Canadians in all parts of Canada understand each other's lives and problems. It was also responsible for coordinating the film activities of government departments.

Canada entered the war in September 1939, leading to a shift in film production towards patriotic propaganda. In October 1939, John Grierson became the first Government Film Commissioner. The NFB signed an agreement with The March of Time to distribute its films in the U.S., while Famous Players of Canada agreed to show NFB films in its 800 theatres.

Source: *The National Film Board of Canada*

Genie Awards, 1989–99

The Genie Awards have been presented since 1980 by the Academy of Canadian Cinema and Television to honor achievement in the Canadian film industry. Awards apply to films released in the previous year. Voting is conducted in a two-step process whereby the winners are chosen by all academy members from among the five nominees selected in each category by their respective craft branches. The 1999 awards were presented Jan. 30, 2000.

1989
Picture . . . . *Dead Ringers*
Actor . . . . Jeremy Irons, *Dead Ringers*
Actress . . . . Jackie Burroughs, *A Winter Tan*
Sup. Actor . . . . Remy Girard, *Les Portes tournantes*
Sup. Actress . . . . Colleen Dewhurst, *Obsessed*
Director . . . . David Cronenberg, *Dead Ringers*

1990
Picture . . . . *Jesus de Montréal*
Actor . . . . Lothaire Bluteau, *Jesus de Montréal*
Actress . . . . Rebecca Jenkins, *Bye Bye Blues*
Sup. Actor . . . . Remy Girard, *Jesus de Montréal*
Sup. Actress . . . . Robyn Stevan, *Bye Bye Blues*
Director . . . . Denys Arcand, *Jesus de Montréal*

1991
Picture . . . . *Black Robe*
Actor . . . . Remy Girard, *Amoureux fou*
Actress . . . . Pascale Montpetit, *H*
Sup. Actor . . . . August Schellenberg, *Black Robe*
Sup. Actress . . . . Danielle Proulx, *Amoureux fou*
Director . . . . Bruce Beresford, *Black Robe*

1992
Picture . . . . *Naked Lunch*
Actor . . . . Tony Nardi, *La Sarrasine*
Actress . . . . Janet Wright, *Bordertown Café*
Sup. Actor . . . . Michael Hogan, *Solitaire*
Sup. Actress . . . . Monique Mercure, *Naked Lunch*
Director . . . . David Cronenberg, *Naked Lunch*

1993
Picture . . . . *Thirty-Two Short Films about Glenn Gould*
Actor . . . . Tom McCamus, *I Love A Man in Uniform*
Actress . . . . Sheila McCarthy, *The Lotus Eaters*
Sup. Actor . . . . Kevin Tighe, *I Love A Man in Uniform*
Sup. Actress . . . . Nicola Cavendish, *The Grocer's Wife*
Director . . . . François Girard, *Thirty-Two Short Films about Glenn Gould*

1994
Picture . . . . *Exotica*
Actor . . . . Maury Chaykin, *Whale Music*
Actress . . . . Sandra Oh, *Double Happiness*
Sup. Actor . . . . Don McKellar, *Exotica*
Sup. Actress . . . . Martha Henry, *Mustard Bath*
Director . . . . Atom Egoyan, *Exotica*

1995
Picture . . . . *Le Confessionnal*
Actor . . . . David La Haye, *L'Enfant D'Eau*
Actress . . . . Helena Bonham Carter, *Margaret's Museum*
Sup. Actor . . . . Kenneth Welsh, *Margaret's Museum*
Sup. Actress . . . . Kate Nelligan, *Margaret's Museum*
Director . . . . Robert Lepage, *Le Confessionnal*

1996
Picture . . . . *Lilies*
Actor . . . . . . William Hutt, *Long Day's Journey Into Night*
Actress . . . Martha Henry, *Long Day's Journey Into Night*
Sup. Actor . . . Peter Donaldson, *Long Day's Journey Into Night*
Sup. Actress . . . . Martha Burns, *Long Day's Journey Into Night*
Director . . . . David Cronenburg, *Crash*

1997
Picture . . . . *The Sweet Hereafter*
Actor . . . . Ian Holm, *The Sweet Hereafter*
Actress . . . . Molly Parker, *Kissed*
Sup. Actor . . . . Peter MacNeill, *The Hanging Garden*
Sup. Actress . . . . . Seana McKenna, *The Hanging Garden*
Director . . . . Atom Egoyan, *The Sweet Hereafter*

1998
Picture . . . . *The Red Violin*
Actor . . . . Roshan Seth, *Such a Long Journey*
Actress . . . . Sandra Oh, *Last Night*
Sup. Actor . . . . Callum Keith Rennie, *Last Night*
Sup. Actress . . . . Monique Mercure, *Conquest*
Director . . . . François Girard, *The Red Violin*

1999
Picture . . . . *Sunshine*
Actor . . . . Bob Hoskins, *Felicia's Journey*
Actress . . . . Sylvie Moreau, *Post Mortem*
Sup. Actor . . . . Mark McKinney, *Dog Park*
Sup. Actress . . . . . Catherine O'Hara, *The Life Before This*
Director . . . . Jeremy Podeswa, *The Five Senses*
Original Screenplay . . . . Louis Bélanger, *Post Mortem*
Cinematography . . . . Paul Sarossy, *Felicia's Journey*
Film Editing . . . . Ronald Sanders, *eXistenZ*
Art Direction . . . . . . François Séguin, *Souvenirs intimes*
Costume Design . . . . Renée April, *Grey Owl*
Overall Sound . . . . Daniel Pellerin, Keith Elliott, Glen Gauthier, Peter Kelly, *Sunshine*
Sound Editing . . . . Jane Tattersall, Fred Brennan, Dina Eaton, Andy Malcolm, David McCallum, *Sunshine*
Music Score . . . . Mychael Danna, *Felicia's Journey*
Best Feature Length Documentary . . . . Gerry Flahive, Catherine Annau, Yves Bisaillon, *Just Watch Me: Trudeau and the '70s Generation*
Best Short Documentary . . . Bernard Lajoie, Erik Canuel, Tatsuo Shimamura, *Hemingway: A Portrait*
Best Live Action Short Drama . . . . Tina Goldlist, Chris Deacon, *Moving Day*

Motion Picture Academy Awards (Oscars™), 1989–99

1989
- Picture . . . . *Driving Miss Daisy*, Warner Bros.
- Actor . . . . Daniel Day Lewis, *My Left Foot*
- Actress . . . . Jessica Tandy, *Driving Miss Daisy*
- Sup. Actor . . . . Denzel Washington, *Glory*
- Sup. Actress . . . . Brenda Fricker, *My Left Foot*
- Director . . . . Oliver Stone, *Born on the Fourth of July*

1990
- Picture . . . . *Dances With Wolves*, Orion
- Actor . . . . Jeremy Irons, *Reversal of Fortune*
- Actress . . . . Kathy Bates, *Misery*
- Sup. Actor . . . . Joe Pesci, *Good Fellas*
- Sup. Actress . . . . Whoopi Goldberg, *Ghost*
- Director . . . . Kevin Costner, *Dances With Wolves*

1991
- Picture . . . . *The Silence of the Lambs*, Orion
- Actor . . . . Anthony Hopkins, *The Silence of the Lambs*
- Actress . . . . Jodie Foster, *The Silence of the Lambs*
- Sup. Actor . . . . Jack Palance, *City Slickers*
- Sup. Actress . . . . Mercedes Ruehl, *The Fisher King*
- Director . . . . Jonathan Demme, *The Silence of the Lambs*

1992
- Picture . . . . *Unforgiven*, Clint Eastwood, producer
- Actor . . . . Al Pacino, *Scent of A Woman*
- Actress . . . . Emma Thompson, *Howards End*
- Sup. Actor . . . . Gene Hackman, *Unforgiven*
- Sup. Actress . . . . Marisa Tomei, *My Cousin Vinny*
- Director . . . . Clint Eastwood, *Unforgiven*

1993
- Picture . . . . *Schindler's List*, Steven Spielberg, Gerald R. Molen, Branko Lustig, producers
- Actor . . . . Tom Hanks, *Philadelphia*
- Actress . . . . Holly Hunter, *The Piano*
- Sup. Actor . . . . Tommy Lee Jones, *The Fugitive*
- Sup. Actress . . . . Anna Paquin, *The Piano*
- Director . . . . Steven Spielberg, *Schindler's List*

1994
- Picture . . . . *Forrest Gump*, SteveTisch, Wendy Finerman, Steve Sharkey, producers
- Actor . . . . Tom Hanks, *Forrest Gump*
- Actress . . . . Jessica Lange, *Blue Sky*
- Sup. Actor . . . . Martin Landau, *Ed Wood*
- Sup. Actress . . . . Dianne Wiest, *Bullets Over Broadway*
- Director . . . . Robert Zemeckis, *Forrest Gump*

1995
- Picture . . . . *Braveheart*, Mel Gibson, Alan Ladd, Jr., and Bruce Davey, producers
- Actor . . . . Nicolas Cage, *Leaving Las Vegas*
- Actress . . . . Susan Sarandon, *Dead Man Walking*
- Sup. Actor . . . . Kevin Spacey, *The Usual Suspects*
- Sup. Actress . . . . Mira Sorvino, *Mighty Aphrodite*
- Director . . . . Mel Gibson, *Braveheart*

1996
- Picture . . . . . *The English Patient*, Saul Zaentz, producer
- Actor . . . . Geoffrey Rush, *Shine*
- Actress . . . . Frances McDormand, *Fargo*
- Sup. Actor . . . . Cuba Gooding, Jr., *Jerry Maguire*
- Sup. Actress . . . . . Juliette Binoche, *The English Patient*
- Director . . . . Anthony Minghella, *The English Patient*

1997
- Picture . . . . *Titanic*, James Cameron, Jon Landau, producers
- Actor . . . . Jack Nicholson, *As Good as It Gets*
- Actress . . . . Helen Hunt, *As Good as It Gets*
- Sup. Actor . . . . Robin Williams, *Good Will Hunting*
- Sup. Actress . . . . Kim Basinger, *L.A. Confidential*
- **Director** . . . . **James Cameron**, ***Titanic***

1998
- Picture . . . . *Shakespeare in Love*, Donna Gigliotti, Marc Norman, David Parfitt, Harvey Weinstein, Edward Zwick, producers
- Actor . . . . Roberto Benigni, *Life is Beautiful*
- Actress . . . . Gwyneth Paltrow, *Shakespeare in Love*
- Sup. Actor . . . . James Coburn, *Affliction*
- Sup. Actress . . . . . . Judi Dench, *Shakespeare in Love*
- Director . . . . Steven Spielberg, *Saving Private Ryan*

1999
- Picture . . . . *American Beauty*, Bruce Cohen and Dan Jinks, producers
- Actor . . . . Kevin Spacey, *American Beauty*
- Actress . . . . Hilary Swank, *Boys Don't Cry*
- Sup. Actor . . . . . . Michael Caine, *The Cider House Rules*
- Sup. Actress . . . . Angelina Jolie, *Girl Interrupted*
- Director . . . . Sam Mendes, *American Beauty*
- Foreign-Language Film . . . . *All About My Mother*, Spain
- Original Screenplay . . . . Alan Ball, *American Beauty*
- Screenplay Adaptation . . . . John Irving, *The Cider House Rules*
- Cinematography . . . . . . Conrad L. Hall, *American Beauty*
- Editing . . . . Zach Staenberg, *The Matrix*
- Original Score (Dramatic) . . . . Thomas Newman, *American Beauty*
- Original Song . . . . . Phil Collins, "You'll Be In My Heart"
- Art Direction . . . . Rick Heinrichs, *Sleepy Hollow*
- Costume Design . . . . Lindy Hemming, *Topsy-Turvy*
- Sound . . . . John Reitz, Gregg Rudloff, David Campbell and David Lee, *The Matrix*
- Sound Effects Editing . . . . Dane A. Davis, *The Matrix*
- Makeup . . . . Christine Blundell and Trefor Proud, *Topsy-Turvy*
- Visual Effects . . . . John Gaeta, Janek Sirrs, Steve Courtley and Jon Thum, *The Matrix*
- Documentary Feature . . . . Arthur Cohn and Kevin Macdonald, *One Day In September*
- Documentary Short Subject . . . . . Susan Hannah Hadary and William A. Whiteford, *King Gimp*

Source: © Academy of Motion Picture Arts and Sciences

1999 Oscar™ Nominations

Picture: *American Beauty*, *The Cider House Rules*, *The Green Mile*, *The Insider*, *The Sixth Sense*

Actor: Russell Crowe, *The Insider*; Richard Farnsworth, *The Straight Story*; Sean Penn, in *Sweet and Lowdown*; Kevin Spacey, *American Beauty*; Denzel Washington, *The Hurricane*.

Actress: Annette Benin, *American Beauty*; Janet McTeer, *Tumbleweeds*; Julianne Moore, in *The Ends of the Affair*; Meryl Streep, *Music of the Heart*; Hilary Swank, *Boys Don't Cry*.

Supporting Actor: Michael Caine, *The Cider House Rules*; Tom Cruise, *Magnolia*; Michael Clarke Duncan, *The Green Mile*; Jude Law, *The Talented Mr. Ripley*; Haley Joel Osment, *The Sixth Sense*.

Supporting Actress: Toni Collette, *The Sixth Sense*; Angelina Jolie, *Girl Interrupted*; Catherine Keener, *Being John Malkovich*; Samantha Morto, *Sweet and Lowdown*; Chloë Sevigny, *Boys Don't Cry*.

Director: Lasse Hallström, *The Cider House Rules*; Spike Jonze, *Being John Malkovich*; Michael Mann, *The Insider*; Sam Mendes, *American Beauty*; M. Night Shyamalan, *The Sixth Sense*.

Foreign-Language Film: *All About My Mother*, Spain; *Caravan*, Nepal; *East-West*, France; *Solomon and Gaenor*, UK; *Under the Sun*, Sweden.

Original Screenplay: Alan Ball, *American Beauty*; Charlie Kaufman, *Being John Malkovich*; Paul Thomas Anderson, *Magnolia*; M. Night Shyamalan, *The Sixth Sense*; Mike Leigh, *Topsy-Turvy*.

Screenplay Adaptation: John Irving, *The Cider House Rules*; Alexander Payne & Jim Taylor, *Election*; Frank Darabont, *The Green Mile*; Eric Roth & Michael Mann, *The Insider*; Anthony Minghella, *The Talented Mr. Ripley*.

Cinematography: Conrad L. Hall, *American Beauty*; Roger Pratt, *The End of the Affair*; Dante Spinotti, *The Insider*; Emmanuel Lubezki, *Sleepy Hollow*; Robert Richardson, *Snow Falling on Cedars*.

Original Song: Trey Parker and Marc Shaiman, "Blame Canada;" Diane Warren, "Music of My Heart;" Aimee Mann, "Save Me;" Randy Newman, "When She Loved Me;" Phil Collins, "You'll Be In My Heart."

Source: © *Academy of Motion Picture Arts and Sciences*

The Cannes Film Festival Awards, 1989–99

1989
Best Film . . . . *sex, lies and videotape* (USA)
Special Grand Jury Prize . . . . . *Trop Belle Pour Toi* (France); *Cinema Paradiso* (Italy)
Best Director . . . . Emir Kusturica, *Time of the Gypsies*
Best Actor . . . . James Spader, *sex, lies and videotape*
Best Actress . . . . Meryl Streep, *A Cry In The Dark*

1990
Best Film . . . . *Wild at Heart* (USA)
Special Grand Jury Prize . . . *Tilaï* (Burkina Faso); *The Sting of Death* (Japan)
Best Director . . . . Pavel Loungine, *Taxi Blues*
Best Actor . . . . Gerard Depardieu, *Cyrano de Bergerac*
Best Actress . . . . Krystyna Janda, *Interrogation*

1991
Best Film . . . . *Barton Fink* (USA)
Special Grand Jury Prize . . . . *La belle noiseuse* (France)
Best Director . . . . Joel Coen & Ethan Coen, *Barton Fink*
Best Actor . . . . John Turturro, *Barton Fink*
Best Actress . . . . . Irène Jacob, *The Double Life of Veronica*

1992
Best Film . . . . *The Best Intentions* (Switzerland)
Special Grand Jury Prize . . . . *Il Ladro di Bambini* (Italy)
Best Director . . . . Robert Altman, *The Player*
Best Actor . . . . Tim Robbins, *The Player*
Best Actress . . . . Pernilla August, *The Best Intentions*

1993
Best Film . . (tie) *The Piano*, (New Zealand), *Farewell To My Concubine* (China)
Special Grand Jury Prize . . . *Faraway, So Close!* (Germany)
Best Director . . . . Mike Leigh, *Naked*
Best Actor . . . . David Thewlis, *Naked*
Best Actress . . . . Holly Hunter, *The Piano*

1994
Best Film . . . . *Pulp Fiction*, (USA)
Special Grand Jury Prize . . . *Burnt by the Sun* (Russia) and *To Live!* (China)
Best Director . . . . Nanni Moretti, *Journal intime*
Best Actor . . . . Ge You, *To Live!*
Best Actress . . . . Virna Lisi, *la Reine Margot*

1995
Special Grand Jury Prize . . . . *Crash* (Canada)
Best Director . . . . Joel Coen, *Fargo* (U.S.)
Best Actor . . . . (tie) Daniel Autueil & Pascal Duquenne, *The Eighth Day* (France)
Best Actress . . . . Brenda Blethyn, *Secrets and Lies* (UK)
Palme d'Or . . . . *Secrets and Lies* (UK)

1996
Special Grand Jury Prize . . . . *The Sweet Hereafter* (Canada)
Best Director. . . . Wong Kar-Wai, *Happy Together* (Hong Kong)
Best Actor . . . . Sean Penn, *She's So Lovely* (U.S)
Best Actress . . . . Kathy Burke, *Nilby Mouth* (U.K)
Palme d'Or . . . . (tie) *Unagi* (The Eel) (Japan)
The Taste of Cherry (Iran)

1997

Grand Jury Prize .... *La Vita e Bella* (Italy)
Special Jury Prize .... *La Classe de Neige* (France);
Festen (Denmark)
Best Director ... John Boorman, *The General* (Great Britain)
Best Actor .... Peter Mullan, *My Name is Joe* (Great Britain)
Best Actress ...... Elodie Bouchez and Natacha Regnier, *La Vie Revee des Anges* (France)
Palme d'Or ...... *Eternity and a Day*, Theo Angelopoulos (Greece)

1998

Grand Jury Prize .... *L'humanité* (France)
Jury Prize .... *A Carta* (Portugal)
Best Director .... Pedro Almodovar, *Todo Sobre Mi Madre* (Spain)
Best Actor ..... Emmanuel Schotté, *L'humanité* (France)
Best Actress ..... Séverine Cancele, *L'humanité* (France) and Emilie Dequenne, *Rosetta* (Belgium)
Palme d'Or .... *Rosetta*, Luc and Jean-Pierre Dardenne (Belgium)

1999

Grand Prize .... *Guizi Lai Le*, Jiang Wen (China)
Jury Prize .... *Sånger Från Andra Våningen* (Sweden); *Takhté Siah* (Iran)
Best Director .... Edward Yang, *Yi Yi* (Taiwan)
Best Actor .... Tony Leung Chiu-Wai, *In the Mood for Love* (China)
Best Actress .... Björk, *Dancer in the Dark* (Denmark)
Palme d'Or *Dancer in the Dark*, Lars von Trier (Denmark)

Source: *The Cannes Film Festival*

(1) The Cannes Festival Jury is not obliged to select a winner in any category except that of Best Film.

Toronto International Film Festival, 2000

The 25th annual festival was held Sept. 7 to 16 in 2000, showing 328 films from over 56 countries. This is widely regarded as North America's major film festival.

People's Choice Award .... *Crouching Tiger, Hidden Dragon* (Taiwan), Ang Lee
Discovery Award (tie) .... *George Washington* (USA), David Gordon Green; *101 Reykjavík* (Iceland/Norway/Denmark/France), Baltasar Kormákur
Fipresci Award .... *Bangkok Dangerous* (Thailand), Oxide and Danny Pang
Best Canadian First Feature .... *La Moitié gauche du frigo*, **Philippe Falardeau**
Best Canadian Feature Film .... *Waydowntown*, **Gary Burns**
Best Canadian Short Film .... *Le Chapeau*, **Michèle Cournoyer**

Source: *Toronto International Film Festival*

Montreal World Film Festival, 2000

The 24th annual Festival des Films du Monde was held from Aug. 25th to Sept. 4th, 2000.

Grand Prix of the Americas (tie) .... *The Taste of Others (Le Goût des autres)* (France); *Innocence* (Australia)
Special Grand Prix of the Jury .... *Smell of Camphor, Fragrance of Jasmine* (Iran)
Best Director .... Silvio Caiozzi (Chile), *Coronación*
Best Actress ...... Gong Li (China), *Breaking the Silence*; Isabelle Huppert (USA), *Nightcap (Merci pour le chocolat)*
Best Actor .... Mark Ruffalo (USA), *You Can Count on Me*
Best Screenplay .... Pupi Avati and Antonio Avati (Italy), *La Via degli angeli*
Best Short Film .... *Unguent for Sore Hands* (Venezuela)
People's Choice Award .... *Innocence* (Australia)

Source: *Montreal World Film Festival*

GOVERNOR GENERAL'S PERFORMING ARTS AWARDS

The Governor General's Performing Arts Awards were inaugurated in 1992 to pay tribute to the lifetime achievements of outstanding artists in a variety of creative fields. The motto of the awards, "The Arts Engage and Inspire Us," reflects the cultural contribution made by recipients chosen from theatre, dance, classical music/opera, popular music, film and broadcasting. The awards are presented annually in November by the Governor General and are administered by the Governor General's Performing Arts Awards Foundation.

■ Winners 1994–1999

1994
Frédéric Back, animator/designer/artist
Robert Charlebois, popular singer
Celia Franca, dancer/artistic director of National Ballet
Frances Hyland, actor/director
Jean Papineau-Couture, composer/educator/musical administrator
Neil Young, musician/singer/songwriter

1995
Denys Arcand, writer/director
Maureen Forrester, opera singer
Peter Gzowski, writer/broadcaster
Paul Hébert, actor/director
Anne Murray, singer
Jeanne Renaud, dancer/choreographer

1996
Francois Barbeau, artist/designer/teacher
Michel Brault, cameraman/director
Martha Henry, actor/director
Joni Mitchell, singer/songwriter

Luc Plamondon, songwriter
Grant Strate, dancer/choreographer/teacher
Martha Lou Henley, arts volunteer/benefactor
Jon Kimura Parker, pianist

1998
Paul Buissoneau, theatre director/actor/writer
Bruce Cockburn, singer-songwriter
Rock Demers, film producer
The Royal Canadian Air Farce, comedians
Arnold Spohr, dancer/choreographer
Jon Vickers, opera singer
Joseph H. Shoctor, arts volunteer/benefactor
Denis Marleau, theatre director

1999
Mario Bernardi, conductor
David Cronenberg, film maker
Denise Filiatrault, actor/writer/director
Mavor Moore, actor/writer/director
Louis Quilico, opera singer
Ginette Reno, singer
Sam Sniderman, entrepreneur
Michel Tremblay, playwright

2000 WINNERS

■ Janette Bertrand

Journalist, radio and television scriptwriter, interviewer and host, actress and playwright, Janette Bertrand's exceptional career spans nearly 50 years. Born in 1925 in Montreal, she studied at the Université de Montréal. As a reporter for the *Petit Journal* she wrote the humorous column "Opinions de femmes" and then the advice column "Courrier du cœur" for 17 years. The latter column inspired the Robert Charlebois song *Madame Bertrand*. She began working in radio in the 1950s, hosting *Déjeuner en musique* for Radio-Canada and *Mon mari et nous* for CKAC. For television, she was a soap opera pioneer, writing scripts under her husband's name (actor Jean Lajeunesse) in an era when women writers were still regarded with suspicion. *Janette veut savoir* was the first of several series, including *SOS J'écoute*, *Parler pour parler*, *Janette...tout court*, and *Avec un grand A*, that demonstrated her understanding of human relations. Janette Bertrand has written three stage plays. She is currently working on her first feature film screenplay, *Le party de famille*, scheduled to begin production in 2001. She is above all a great communicator, interested in and passionate about life and humanity — a communicator whose contributions are underscored by the numerous awards and distinctions she has received.

■ Walter Carsen

Walter Carsen is recognized for more than a quarter-century of loyal and dedicated patronage of the performing and visual arts in Canada. He has been directly involved with and given generous financial support to many of Canada's leading cultural institutions, especially the National Ballet of Canada, the Shaw Festival, and several visual art institutions. He has personally underwritten several of the National Ballet's productions, including: *The Taming of the Shrew* in 1992 (the first time in the history of the arts in

Photo Credit: David Cooper

Canada that a complete production had been funded by a single individual or corporation), *Romeo and Juliet* in 1995 and *Inspired by Gould* in 1999. For the 2000–2001 season Mr. Carsen has underwritten the new production of *The Firebird*. In 1995 he sponsored The National Ballet School's Artist-in-Residence Program. A few years ago he paid for the renovation of the Shaw Festival's Royal George Theatre at a cost of some $600,000. In May of 1994, Mr. Carsen launched a campaign to build a loft in the Festival Theatre in honour of Artistic Director Christopher Newton's 15th anniversary season, and personally matched dollar for dollar every donation made to this project. Walter Carsen is one of the most beloved patrons on the Canadian arts scene today-indeed, his philanthropic efforts have earned him the nickname "Care Bear."

■ Tom C. ("Stompin' Tom") Connors

One of Canada's most beloved artists, "Stompin' Tom" Connors is known for his unwavering loyalty to Canada and his passionate commitment to Canadian music. In his 30-year performing career he has crisscrossed the country countless times,

singing about things Canadian to Canadians from coast to coast in his unique folk-country style and enriching the lives of all he has met. Born in Saint John, New Brunswick, in 1936, he was placed in the care of the Children's Aid Society and later adopted into a family from Prince Edward Island, where he lived until he began his hitchhiking career at the age of 15. Over the next 13 years he traveled to every corner of Canada. With his guitar, his Western boots and black cowboy hat, and his trademark plywood "stompin' board," Stompin' Tom Connors has become a beloved Canadian icon. From politics to potatoes, he has tackled just about everything that Canadians are passionate about (or should be). Over the last 30 years he has released 20 albums, all of which are unique bodies of work containing lyrics—sometimes poignant, often humorous—filled with his true sense of Canada's landscape and culture, set to a folk-country melody. Among his best-known compositions are *The Hockey Song, Bud the Spud*, and *Sudbury Saturday Night*.

■ Fernand Nault

In a career that spans over 50 years, Fernand Nault has inspired and enriched the lives of hundreds of dancers, and achieved national and international renown as one of Canada's most distinguished choreographers. He is known for the unwavering commitment to Canadian and international dance he has shown throughout his life. Born Fernand-Noël Boissonneault in Montreal in 1921, his love affair with dance started when he was 12 years old. He dared to become a dancer during a repressive time-dance was condemned from the pulpit in Quebec. But he found a way for his deep religious faith and his love of dance to co-exist. Nault studied in New York, London and Paris. From 1944 to 1965 he was a dancer, then Ballet Master at The American Ballet Theatre in New York. From 1960 to 1964 he was also director of the company's school.

Photo Credit: Michael Slobodian

He joined Les Grands Ballets Canadiens in 1965 as co-artistic director and resident choreographer. In his nearly 40 years with the company he has choreographed over thirty astonishingly diverse works. His creation of the rock ballet *Tommy* in the late 1970s put Les Grands Ballets Canadiens on the international map.

Nault has also created works for Alberta Ballet, the Opéra de Montréal, The American Ballet Theater, The Joffrey Ballet, The Atlanta Ballet, The Washington Ballet and The Colorado Ballet.

■ Christopher Newton

One of Canada's most distinguished and versatile stage directors, Christopher Newton has touched the lives and advanced the careers of some of Canada's most celebrated theatre artists. He has made a profound contribution to Canadian theatre, particularly during his twenty seasons as artistic director of the Shaw Festival in Niagara-on-the-Lake. Born in England, educated in England and the United States, he moved to Canada in 1961. Before taking over as Artistic Director of The Shaw, Mr. Newton founded Theatre Calgary (1968) and served as Artistic

Photo Credit: David Cooper

Director until 1971. He then took over as Artistic Director of The Vancouver Playhouse Theatre Company. At Shaw he has brought a new vitality to the festival and has been instrumental in the re-examination of many lesser-known playwrights. He has also established a permanent acting ensemble, recognized as one of North America's premiere acting companies. In 1985 he created The Academy, a forum for skills exchange among members of the Shaw Festival Acting Ensemble. The Academy has since grown into an exacting professional development programme featuring voice and movement classes, scene study, and specialized workshops. The Academy also sponsors workshop productions and the annual Directors' Project, as well as public outreach programmes.

■ Teresa Stratas

Teresa Stratas is nominated for an outstanding musical career spanning over 40 years. Her smooth, rich lyric soprano, her intuitive dramatic sense and her ability to convey genuine emotion have won her accolades from audiences and critics around the world. Born Anastasia Stratakis in Toronto, Ontario, in 1938, Teresa Stratas began her musical career at 13, singing Greek pop songs on the radio. After studying at Toronto's Royal Conservatory of Music and winning the prestigious Eaton Graduating Scholarship, she made her operatic debut in 1958 as Mimi in *La Bohème* at the Toronto Opera Festival. She won the 1959 Metropolitan Opera Auditions and made her debut with the company that year as Poussette in *Manon*. She moved quickly into major roles, and has sung more than 25 of them at the Met. Among her many international appearances, Ms. Stratas has sung at La Scala, the Bolshoi Opera, the Vienna State Opera, Covent Garden, the Deutsche Oper Berlin, the Bavarian State Opera, the San Francisco Opera and the Salzburg Festival. In 1981 she travelled to India where she joined Mother Teresa in nursing the terminally ill, and later the same year she turned her attention to nursing Lotte Lenya in her last days.

■ Donald Sutherland

Donald Sutherland, is one of Canada's most prolific and talented actors. His career has spanned 35 years and over 90 roles. With his offbeat elegance and often enigmatic screen presence, Sutherland has created a remarkable gallery of screen personae and garnered international acclaim for his amazing range and versatility. Born in Saint John, New Brunswick, in 1934, Donald Sutherland first trod the boards in 1952 at Hart House while studying engineering at the University of Toronto. His versatility as an actor was evident early in his film career. He appeared in the western *The Dirty Dozen* in 1967 and as a chorus leader in *Œdipus the King* in 1968. In 1970 he starred as the infamous Capt. Benjamin Franklin "Hawkeye" Pierce in Robert Altman's hit comedy *M*A*S*H*, and won rave reviews for his performance. His numerous and eclectic North American film credits include *The Dirty Dozen* (1967), *Klute* (1971, with Jane Fonda), *Invasion of the Body Snatchers* (1978), *Ordinary People* (1980, with Mary Tyler Moore), *JFK* (1991), and the title role in the controversial epic *Bethune: The Making of a Hero* (1990). He has also

Photo Credit: Myles Aronowitz

achieved enviable artistic success in Europe, actively seeking out such renowned directors as Nicolas Roeg (*Don't Look Now*, 1973), Federico Fellini (*Casanova*, title role, 1976), Bernardo Bertolucci (*1900*, 1976), and Werner Herzog (*Scream of Stone*, 1991).

THEATRE

Toronto is now considered the third largest production centre of live theatre in the English speaking world (following New York, and London, England). The English Canadian theatre scene has undergone exponential growth since the birth of the Stratford Shakespearean Festival at Stratford, Ont. in 1954. The alternative theatre movement that swept English Canada in the 1970s established producers of Canadian drama in every large centre. Diminishing government support in the 1980s and 1990s led to more emphasis on commercial Canadian productions of British, French and American "megamusicals" while development of new and experimental work has passed increasingly to independent artists often appearing at a cross-Canada network of "fringe" festivals.

Theatrical activity in French Canada burgeoned in the 1950s and 1960s as playwrights such as Marcel Dubé (*Un Simple Soldat*) and Gratien Gélinas (*'Tit Coq*) explored the social and moral issues confronting Québecers in their own dialect. This movement reached its apex in the work of Michel Tremblay in the early 1970s. More recently, Quebec theatre has also excelled in less verbal forms of theatre such as the spectacles produced by Cirque du Soleil, while the "total theatre" productions of Quebec City writer/performer/director Robert LePage have garnered critical acclaim around the world.

Dora Awards, 2000

The Doras, honoring excellence in Toronto theatrical productons, were first handed out in 1981. Named for Dora Mavor Moore, a teacher and director who helped establish professional theatre in Canada in the 1930s and 1940s, the awards are chosen annually from over 200 productions.

Outstanding New Play	*Alien Creature* by Linda Griffiths, *For the Pleasure of Seeing Her Again*, by Michel Tremblay, translated by Linda Gaboriau
Outstanding New Musical	*Anything That Moves*, by Ann-Marie MacDonald, Allen Cole, Alisa Palmer
Outstanding Production of a Play	*Endgame*, Soulpepper Theatre Company in assoc. with Harbourfront Centre
Outstanding Production of a Musical	*Cabaret*, Mirvish Productions and PACE Theatrical Group / SFX Entertainment
Outstanding Direction of a Play	László Marton, *Platonov*
Outstanding Direction of a Musical	Sam Mendes, *Cabaret*
Outstanding Performance by a Male in a Principle Role-Play	Diego Matamoros, *Endgame*
Outstanding Performance by a Female in a Principal Role-Play	Nora McLellan, *Music For Contortionist*
Performance by a Male in a Principal Role-Musical	Norbert Leo Butz, *Cabaret*
Outstanding Performance by a Female in a Principal Role-Musical	Paul Wolfson, *Shaking The Foundations*
Outstanding Performance in a Featured Role-Play or Musical	Jonathan Wilson, *The Lion King*
Outstanding Production for Young Audiences	*The General*, Theatre Direct Canada
Outstanding Set Design	Ken MacDonald, *The Overcoat*
Outrastanding Costume Design	Julie Taymor, Michael Curry, *The Lion King*

Independent Theatre

Outstanding New Play or Musical	*Building Jerusalem*, by Michael Redhill
Outstanding Production	*Building Jerusalem*, Volcano in association with Factory Theatre, *Chekhov's Shorts*, Theatre Smith-Gilmour
Outstanding Direction	Dean Gilmour & Michelle Smith, *Chekhov's Shorts*
Outstanding Performance by a Female	Barbara Gordon, *The Dogpatch*
Outstanding Performance by a Male	Dean Gilmour, *Chekhov's Shorts*
Outstanding Set Design	Michael Spence, Brenda Guldenstein, *The Epoch Project-Vision*
Outstanding Costume Design	Jacques LaMarre, *The Vile Governess & Other Psychodramas*

Source: *Toronto Theatre Alliance*

Jessie Awards, 2000

Named for professional theatre pioneer Jessie Richardson, these awards honour excellence in and raise awareness of professional theatre in Vancouver. Winners of the 17th annual awards were announced June 18, 2000.

Small Theatre

Outstanding Original Play or Musical	*The Score,* Electric Companyl
Outstanding Production	*The Score,* Electric Company
Outstanding Performance by an Actress in a Lead Role	Wendy VanRiessen, *War of the Worlds*
Outstanding Performance by an Actor in a Lead Role	Jeremy Tow, *Master Harold and the Boys*
Outstanding Performance by an Actress in a Supporting Role	Lois Anderson, *The Score*
Outstanding Performance by an Actor in a Supporting Role	Tom Pickett, *Master Harold and the Boys*
Outstanding Costume Design	Barbara Clayden, *War of the Worlds*
Outstanding Set Design of a Play	Robert Gardiner, *The Score*
Outstanding Lighting Design	Eduardo Meneses, *Reading Hebron*
Outstanding Sound Design or Original Composition	Peter Hannan, *War of the Worlds*

Large Theatre

Outstanding Production	*Sweeny Todd,* Arts Club Theatre
Larry Lillo Award for Outstanding Direction	Morris Panych, *Sweeny Todd*
Outstanding Performance by an Actress in a Lead Role	Corrine Koslo, *Sweeny Todd*
Outstanding Performance by an Actor in a Lead Role	Tom Macbeth, *Of Mice and Men*
Outstanding Performance by an Actress in a Supporting Role	Karin Konoval, *Sweeny Todd*
Outstanding Performance by an Actor in a Supporting Role	Alvin Sanders, *Of Mice and Men*
Outstanding Set Design of a Play or Musical	Helen Jarvis, *Of Mice and Men*
Outstanding Lighting Design of a Play or Musical	Gerald King, *Of Mice and Men*
Outstanding Sound Design or Original Composition	John Mann, *Of Mice and Men*
Outstanding Costume Design of a Play or Musical	Nancy Bryant, *Sweeny Todd*

Source: *Jessies Richardson Society*

Theatre Highlights for 2001

Belfry Theatre, Victoria

The Belfry's Theatre Festival 2001 kicks off with *In On It*, a two-man mystery cabaret in which we meet two men who might be angels or devils or anyone we know, written and directed by Daniel MacIvor. Feb 20–25. *Cirque Poule* follows Feb. 27–Mar 11, a collective creation that brings together clowns, acrobats, trapeze artists, flamenco dancers and accordionists for an evening of death-defying feats and endless play. *Cirque Poule* is good clean fun for anyone 10 and up. Running simultaneously is *Be Still*, a new play by Janet Munsil inspired by Victoria photographer Hannah Maynard and the macabre multiple exposure self-portraits she created in her Pandora Street studio.

Vancouver Playhouse

Wit is the Pulitzer Prize-winning drama by Margaret Edson which tells the story of of Dr. Vivian Bearing, a renowned English professor who is battling cancer. Directed by Glynis Leyshon Jan. 8–Feb. 3. Bernard Shaw's *Candida* follows Feb. 19–Mar. 17. Martin McDonagh's Tony Award-winning black comedy *The Beauty Queen of Leenane* runs April 23–May 19.

Alberta Theatre Projects, Calgary

PanCanadian PlayRites 2001: The Festival of New Canadian Plays runs Jan.26–Mar.4. Featured are: *Red Lips*, a magical, mystical comedy of personal discovery by Connie Gault; *Respectable*, a satiric black comedy about contemporary values and society's varied opinions of what is "respectable" by Ron Chambers; *24 Exposures*, a play about the everyday heartbreak and joy of family life by Serge Boucher, translated by Shelley Tepperman; *The Shape of a Girl* by Joan MacLeod tells the story of Braidie, a woman who must confront her capability for violence as she puts her own actions under scrutiny.

Globe Theatre, Regina

Wingfield Unbound by Dan Needles tells of stockbroker-turned farmer Walt Wingfield's comedic matrimonial and museological experiments. Runs Jan.10–24. *Wit* is the Pulitzer Prize-winning drama by Margaret Edson which tells the story of of Dr. Vivian Bearing, a renowned English professor who is battling cancer. Runs Feb. 7–21. Michael Healey's award-winning comedy *The Drawer Boy* runs Mar. 7–21. Peter Schaffer's drama about the life and death of Wofgang Amadeus Mozart, *Amadeus*, runs April 25–May 9.

Manitoba Theatre Centre

Lerner and Loewe's *Camelot* runs Jan. 4–27. Conor McPherson's rendition of Irish ghost stories, *The Weir*, runs Feb. 8–Mar. 3. Michael Healey's award-winning comedy *The Drawer Boy* runs Mar. 15–Apr. 7 followed by a musical adaptation of Carol Shields' *Larry's Party* with book and lyrics by Richard Ouzounian and music by Marek Norman, April 19–May 12, 2001.

Stratford Festival, Stratford, Ont.

The 2001 Stratford Festival runs Apr. 25–Nov. 4. This year's festival is the largest in 10 years featuring five Shakespearean productions and four Canadian premieres. The productions include: *The Merchant of Venice*, *Twelfth Night*, *Henry IV, Parts 1 & 2* and *Henry V* by William Shakespeare; *The Sound of Music* by Rodgers and Hammerstein, *Inherit the Wind* by Jerome Lawrence and Robert E. Lee and *Private Lives* by Noel Coward; *Who's Afraid of Virginia Woolf?* by Edward Albee, *The Seagull* by Anton Chekhov, *The New Wingfield* by Dan Needles, *The Trials of Ezra Pound* by Timothy Findley; *Tempest-Tost* by Richard Rose (adapted from the novel by Robertson Davies) and *A Robertson Davies Celebration*, a series of readings and performances paying homage to the great Canadian author and playwright.

Tarragon Theatre, Toronto

Midnight Sun by Maja Ardal opens Jan. 23: A small town in northern Iceland is overrun by U.S. troops in 1941 and the community's young people struggle with the seductiveness of the occupiers. With songs and music by John Roby. Opening March 13 is *An Acre of Time* by Jason Sherman. Based on the book by Phil Jenkins, which explored the history of a site near the Ottawa River, the play chronicles the story of a surveyor named Julia. In her study of the area, she finds a passageway not only to the history of the place, but to her personal history as well. *Earshot* by Morris Panych opens Feb 13, the story of a twitchy, paranoid recluse with extraordinary powers of hearing. *I, Claudia*, a multi-character, solo mask-play created and performed by Kristen Thomson opens April 3: A bright adolescent schoolgirl is caught out in the unfamiliar landscape of her parents' separation—a world in which relationships with her mother, her father, and her father's new girlfriend all need re-defining. *Anything That Moves* by Ann-Marie McDonald with music by Allen Cole opens May 1: Joel, hapless flower-shop owner, falls for Jinny, a microbiologist by day and party girl by night.

National Arts Centre, Ottawa

Clout by David Young examines the relationship between democracy and the press. Lionel K. Biggar, a powerful newspaper magnate, is thrown into an unlikely relationship with Trent, a dying journalist who is writing Biggar's biography. Runs Jan. 30–Feb. 10; *Larry's Party*, a musical adaptation of Carol Shields' by Richard Ouzounian and Marek Norman. Feb. 14–Mar. 3; *Midnight Sun* by Maja Ardal describes what happens when a small town in northern Iceland is overrun by U.S. troops in 1941 as the community's young people struggle with the seductiveness of the occupiers. With songs and music by John Roby. Mar. 6–17; Martin McDonagh's Tony Award-winning black comedy *The Beauty Queen of Leenane* runs Mar. 28–Apr. 14; William Shakespeare's *All's Well That Ends Well* runs May 9–26.

Theatre New Brunswick, Fredericton
The Attic, the Pearls & Three Fine Girls, a heartfelt comedy about family by Jennifer Brewin, Leah Cherniak, Ann-Marie MacDonald, Alisa Palmer, and Martha Ross runs Jan. 14–Feb. 3. Michael Healey's award-winning comedy *The Drawer Boy* runs Mar. 12–Apr. 1. *Wingfield Unbound* by Dan Needles tells of stockbroker-turned farmer Walt Wingfield's comedic matrimonial and museological experiments. Runs Apr. 22–May 12.

Neptune Theatre, Halifax
Art by Yasmina Rena, which runs Jan. 26–Feb. 18 was winner of the 1997 Olivier Award for Best Comedy. It describes how three men's relationship changes when one of them buys a work of modern art. *Homeward Bound* by Elliot Hayes runs Mar. 9–Apr. 11. This funny and moving play Margaret Atwood calls a "comedy of manners" is about one family's struggles to accept each other's imperfections. The Mainstage Series' grand finale is *Jesus Christ Superstar*, running Apr. 20–May 20.

Summer Theatre in Canada

Blyth Festival
P.O. Box 10, Blyth, Ont. N0M 1H0

Charlottetown Festival
Confederation Centre of Arts
145 Richmond St.
Charlottetown, PEI
C1A 1J1

Huron Country Playhouse
R.R. #1, Grand Bend, Ont. N0M 1T0

Kawartha Summer Theatre
P.O. Box 161, 2 Lindsay St. S.
Lindsay, Ont. K9V 4S1

Lighthouse Festival Theatre
P.O. Box 1208, Port Dover, Ont. N0A 1N0

Nanaimo Festival
P.O. Box 626, Nanaimo, B.C.
V9R 5L9 (Michael McLaughlin)

Port Credit Summer Theatre
161 Lakeshore Road W.
Mississauga, Ont. L5H 1G3

Red Barn Theatre
P.O. Box 291, Jackson's Point, Ont.
L0E 1L0

Shaw Festival Theatre
P.O. Box 774
Niagara-on-the-Lake, Ont. L0S 1J0

Stephenville Festival
149 Montana Dr.
Stephenville, Nfld. A2N 2T4

Stratford Shakespearean Festival
P.O. Box 520, Stratford, Ont. N5A 6V2

Theatre Orangeville
87 Broadway, Orangeville Opera House
Orangeville, Ont. L9W 1K1

Thousand Islands Playhouse
P.O. Box 241, Gananoque, Ont. K7G 2T8

Upper Canada Playhouse
P.O. Box 852, Morrisburg, Ont. K0C 1X0

Sources Include: *The Professional Association of Canadian Theatres*

Major Theatre Companies in Canada

MARITIMES

Mermaid Theatre of Nova Scotia: Box 2697, Windsor, N.S. B0N 2T0

Mulgrave Road Co-op Theatre: Box 219, Guysborough, N.S. B0H 1N0

Neptune Theatre Foundation: #B24, 1903 Barrington St., Halifax, N.S. B3J 3L7

Ship's Company Theatre: P.O. Box 275, Parrsboro, N.S. B0M 1S0

Theatre New Brunswick: Box 566, Fredericton, N.B. E3B 5A6

CENTRAL CANADA

Buddies in Bad Times: 12 Alexander St, Toronto, Ont. M5R 1E8

Canadian Stage Company: 26 Berkeley St, Toronto, Ont. M5A 2W3

Centaur Theatre Company: 453, rue Saint-François-Xavier, Montreal, Que. H2Y 2T1

La Compagnie Jean Duceppe: 1400 rue Saint-Urbain, Montreal, Que. H2X 2M5

Company of Sirens: 736 Bathurst St, Toronto, Ont. M5S 2R4

Factory Theatre: 125 Bathurst St, Toronto, Ont. M5V 2R2

Grand Theatre Company (Theatre London): 471 Richmond St, London, Ont. N6A 3E4

Great Canadian Theatre Company: 910 Gladstone Ave, Ottawa, Ont. K1R 6Y4

Gryphon Theatre: Box 454, Barrie, Ont. L4M 4T7

Magnus Theatre Company: The Central School Bldg., 10 South Algoma St, Thunder Bay, Ont. P7B 3A7

National Arts Centre: Box 1534, Stn. B, Ottawa, Ont. K1P 5W1

Native Earth Performing Arts: 503-720 Bathurst St, Toronto, Ont. M5S 2R4

Nightwood Theatre: 6000-317 Adelaide St W, Toronto, Ont. M5V 1T2

The Piggery: Box 390, North Hatley, Que. J0B 2C0

Princess of Wales Theatre: 300 King St W, Toronto, Ont. M5V 1J2

Royal Alexandra Theatre: 260 King St W, Toronto, Ont. M5V 1H9

Saidye Bronfman Centre for the Arts: 5170 Chemin de la Côte, Ste.-Catherine, Montreal, Que. H3Y 1M7

Soulpepper Theatre Company: P.O Box 199, 260 Adelaide St. E., Toronto, Ont. M5A 1N1

Sudbury Theatre Centre: Box 641, Stn. B, Sudbury, Ont. P3E 4P8

Tarragon Theatre: 30 Bridgman Ave, Toronto, Ont. M5R 1X3

Theatre Aquarius: 190 King William St., Hamilton, Ont. L8R 1A8

Théâtre de la Bordée: 1105, rue Saint-Jean, #201, Quebec, Que. G1R 1S3

Théâtre du Nouveau Monde: 137, Saint-Ferdinand, #201, Montreal, Que. H4C 2S7

Théâtre du Rideau Vert: 269 Rene Levesque G, Que., Que. G1R 2B3

Le Théâtre du Trident: 580, ave Grande-Allée est, #20, Quebec, Que. G1R 2K2

Theatre Passe Muraille: 16 Ryerson Ave, Toronto, Ont. M5T 2P3

Young People's Theatre: 165 Front St E, Toronto, Ont. M5A 3Z4

WESTERN CANADA

Alberta Theatre Projects: 220-9th Ave SE, Calgary, Alta. T2G 5C4

Arts Club Theatre: 1585 Johnson St, Vancouver, B.C. V6H 3R9

Belfry Theatre: 1291 Gladstone Ave, Victoria, B.C. V8T 1G5

Citadel Theatre: 9828-101A Ave, Edmonton, Alta. T5J 3C6

Globe Theatre: 1801 Scarth St, Regina, Sask. S4P 2G9

Manitoba Theatre Centre: 174 Market Ave, Winnipeg, Man. R3B 0P8

Manitoba Theatre for Young People: 89 Princess St, Winnipeg, Man. R3B 2X5

New Bastion Theatre Company: 625 Superior Ave, Victoria, BC V8V 1V1

Nightcap Productions: Box 1646, Saskatoon, Sask. S7K 3R8

Persephone Theatre: 2802 Rusholme Rd, Saskatoon, Sask. S7L 0H2

Popular Theatre Alliance of Manitoba: 2-413 Selkirk Ave, Winnipeg, Man. R2W 2M4

Prairie Theatre Exchange: 389 Portage Ave, Portage Place, Unit Y300, Winnipeg, Man. R3B 3H6

Tamahnous Theatre Workshop Society: 222-275 Woodland Dr, Vancouver, B.C. V5L 3S7

Theatre Calgary: 220-9th Ave. SE, Calgary, Alta. T2G 5C4

Theatre Network Society: 10708-124th St, Edmonton, Alta. T5M 0H1

25th Street Theatre: 420 Duchess St, Saskatoon, Sask. S7K 0R1

Vancouver Playhouse: 160 West 1st Ave, Vancouver, B.C. V5Y 1A4

Western Canada Theatre Company: Box 329, Kamloops, BC V2C 5K9

Sources Include: *The Professional Association of Canadian Theatres*

DANCE

Canada is home to strong traditions in both classical and contemporary dance. Founded in 1938, The Royal Winnipeg Ballet is the second oldest company in North America and was the first in the Commonwealth to receive a Royal charter. Since 1951, the Toronto-based National Ballet of Canada has provided a home to major talents including prima ballerinas Karen Kain and Veronica Tennant. It has also been a favoured stopping place for international greats such as the late Rudolph Nureyev. The National Ballet was instrumental in facilitating the 1979 defection of Russia's Mikhail Barishnykov in Toronto. Barishnykov danced his first performances as a free man with the National Ballet, an event whose anniversary was marked in 1999 with the presentation of an honorary doctorate to Baryshnikov at the University of Toronto.

Major Ballet Companies

Alberta Ballet: 141-18th Avenue SW, Calgary, AB, T2S 0B8

Ballet British Columbia: #102, 1101 West Broadway, Vancouver, B.C. V6H 1G2

Ballet Jorgen: 213B Glebeholme Blvd., Toronto, Ont., M4J 1S8

Ballet North: 12245-131 St., Edmonton, Alta. T5L 1M8

Les Grands Ballets Canadiens: 4816 rue Rivard, Montreal, Que. H2J 2N6

Royal Winnipeg Ballet: 380 Graham Ave., Winnipeg, Man. R3C 4K2

The National Ballet of Canada: The Walter Carson Centre, 470 Queen's Quay W, Toronto, Ont. M5V 3K4

Major Contemporary and Jazz Dance Companies

Les Ballets Jazz de Montréal: 3450 rue St-Urbain, Montreal, Que. H2X 2N5

Contemporary Dancers Canada: 109 Pulford St., Winnipeg, Man. R3L 1X8

Dancemakers: 927 Dupont St., Toronto, Ont. M6H 1Z1

Decidedly Jazz Danceworks: 1514 - 4 St. SW, Calgary, Alta. T2R 0Y4

Desrosiers Dance Theatre: 103-219 Broadview Ave., Toronto, Ont. M4M 2G3

Fortier Danse Création: Box 605, Stn. C., Montreal, Que. H2L 4L5

Margie Gillis Dance Foundation: 502-3575 boul. St. Laurent, #502, Montreal, Que. H2X 2T7

Danny Grossman Dance Company: 511 Bloor St. W., Toronto, Ont. M5S 1Y4

LaLaLa Human Steps: #206, 5655 av. du Parc, Montreal, Que. H2V 4H2

Le Groupe de la Place Royale: 2 Daly Ave., Ste. 2, Ottawa, Ont. K1N 6E2

Karen Jamieson Dance Company: 221 E. 16th Ave., Vancouver, B.C. V5T 2T5

Kompany!: #810, 10136-100th St., Edmonton, Alta. T5J 0P1

Mascall Dance: 1130 Jervis St., Vancouver, B.C. V6E 2C5

O Vertigo Danse: 4455 rue de Rouen, Montreal, Que. H1V 1H1

La Fondation Jean-Pierre Perreault: 2022 Rue Sherbrooke Est, Montreal, Que. H2K 1B9

Gina Lori Riley Dance Enterprises: 3277 Sandwich St., Windsor, Ont. N9C 1A9

Toronto Dance Theatre: 80 Winchester St., Toronto, Ont. M4X 1B2

Canadian Children's Dance Theatre: 509 Parliament St. Toronto, Ont. M4X 1P3

Compagnie Marie Chouinard: #615-3981 boul. St.-Laurent, Montreal, Wue. H2W 1Y5

Dance Arts Vancouver: #402-873 Beatty St. Vancouver, BC V6B 2M6

Source: *Dance Umbrella of Ontario*

BOOKS, MAGAZINES, NEWSPAPERS

The 326 Canadian-owned publishers account for half of all book sales in Canada, but they publish between 80 and 90 percent of new Canadian books. Canadian Heritage's most recent study puts total revenues for Canadian publishers at $1.8 billion plus annually. Magazine publishing in Canada is an $866 million business in which domestic magazines take a 30 percent share of the market. The magazine industry was dealt a serious blow in 2000 as the federal government was forced by the World Trade Organization to abandon tax measures aimed at protecting the advertising market from nominally Canadian "split run" editions of U.S. magazines. Canadian newspapers continue to enjoy increased profitability after advertising revenues slumped in the early 1990s. Recent years have seen major shifts in newspaper ownership as Montreal-based Québecor Inc. took control of the Sun newspaper chain. Canada's oldest newspaper dynasty, that of the Thomson family, divested itself of most of its newspaper holdings as it expanded its new media activities. The newspaper empire of Conrad Black's Hollinger Inc. expanded dramatically in the late 1990s, incorporating Southam Newspapers which launched the *National Post* in 1999 offering national competition to Thomson's *Globe and Mail*. In 2000, the newspaper industry saw yet another major shift in ownership as Black sold his interests in Southam to Winnipeg television magnate Izzy Asper's Canwest Global Corporation.

The Governor General's Literary Awards, 1989–99

The Governor General's Literary Awards, Canada's foremost literary prizes, are presented annually to recognize and reward Canadian writers. The awards were initiated in 1937 by the Canadian Authors' Association with the agreement of Governor General Baron Tweedsmuir (novelist John Buchan), and were administered by the Association until 1958.

The Awards are now administered by the Canada Council which appoints juries composed of literary specialists who select the best English and French-language works in each of 6 best categories: drama, fiction, poetry, non-fiction, and beginning in 1987, children's literature (text and illustration) and translation. The juries review all books by Canadian authors, illustrators and translators published in Canada or abroad during the previous year (Oct. 1–Sept. 30). In the case of translation, the original work must also be a Canadian-authored title. Winners receive a medal from the Governor General, $10,000 and a specially-bound copy of their award-winning book. The 1999 winners were announced Nov. 16, 1999.

English

—1989—

Fiction .... *Whale Music*, Paul Quarrington
Non-fiction .... *Willie: The Life of W. Somerset Maugham*, Robert Calder
Poetry .... *The Word for Sand*, Heather Spears
Drama .... *The Other Side of the Dark*, Judith Thompson

—1990—

Fiction .... *Lives of the Saints*, Nino Ricci
Non-fiction .... *Trudeau and Our Times*, Stephen Clarkson
Poetry .... *No Time*, Margaret Avison
Drama .... *Goodnight Desdemona (Good Morning Juliet)*, Ann-Marie MacDonald

—1991—

Fiction	*Such a Long Journey*, Rohinton Mistry
Non-fiction	*Occupied Canada*, Robert Hunter and Robert Calihoo
Poetry	*Night Field*, Don McKay
Drama	*Amigo's Blue Guitar*, Joan MacLeod

—1992—

Fiction	*The English Patient*, Michael Ondaatje
Non-fiction	*Revenge of the Land: A century of greed, tragedy and murder on a Saskatchewan Farm*, Maggie Siggins
Poetry	*Inventing the Hawk*, Lorna Crozier
Drama	*Possible Worlds, A Short History of Night*, John Mighton

—1993—

Fiction	*The Stone Diaries*, Carol Shields
Non-fiction	*Touch the Dragon*, Karen Connelly
Poetry	*Forest of the Medieval World*, Don Coles
Drama	*Fronteras Americanas*, Guillermo Verdecchia

—1994—

Fiction	*A Discovery of Strangers*, Rudy Wiebe
Non-fiction	*Rogue Primate: An Exploration of Human Domestication*, John A. Livingston
Poetry	*Cantos from a Small Room*, Robert Hilles
Drama	*The Ends of the Earth*, Morris Panych

—1995—

Fiction	*The Roaring Girl*, Greg Hollingshead
Non-fiction	*Shadow Maker: The Life of Gwendolyn MacEwen*, Rosemary Sullivan
Poetry	Voice, Anne Szumigalski
Drama	*Three in the Back, Two in the Head*, Jason Sherman

—1996—

Fiction	*The Englishman's Boy*, Guy Vanderhaeghe
Non-fiction	*The Unconscious Civilization*, John Raulston Saul
Poetry	*Apostrophes: Woman at a Piano*, E.D. Blodgett
Drama	*The Monument*, Colleen Wagner

—1997—

Fiction	*The Underpainter*, Jane Urquhart
Non-fiction	*Drumblair-Memories of an American Childhood*, Rachel Manley
Poetry	*Land to Light On*, Dionne Brand
Drama	*fareWel*, Ian Ross

—1998—

Fiction	*Forms of Devotion*, Diane Schoemperlen
Non-fiction	*Lines on the Water—A Fisherman's Life on the Miramichi*, David Adams Richards
Poetry	*White Stone: The Alice Poems*, Stephanie Bolster
Drama	*Harlem Duet*, Djanet Sears

—1999—

Fiction	*Elizabeth and After*, Matt Cohen
Non-fiction	*Water*, Marq de Villiers
Poetry	*Songs for Relinquishing the Earth*, Jan Zwicky
Drama	*The Drawer Boy*, Michael Healey
Translation	*Gabrielle Roy: A Life*, Patricia Claxton
Children's Literature (Illustration)	*The Great Poochini*, Gary Clement
Children's Literature (Text)	*A Screaming Kind of Day*, Rachna Gilmore

French

—1989—

Fiction	*La Rage*, Louis Hamelin
Non-fiction	*L'Intolérance : une problématique générale*, Lise Noël
Poetry	*Monème*, Pierre Desruisseaux
Drama	*Mademoiselle Rouge*, Michel Garneau

—1990—

Fiction	*La Mauvaise Foi*, Gérald Tougas
Non-fiction	*Dans l'oeil de l'aigle*, Jean François Lisée
Poetry	*Les Cendres bleues*, Jean-Paul Daoust
Drama	*Le Voyage magnifique d'Emily Carr*, Jovette Marchessault

—1991—

Fiction	*La Croix du Nord*, André Brochu
Non-fiction	*Le Jaguar et le Tamanoir*, Bernard Arcand
Poetry	*Chant pour un Québec Iointain*, Madeleine Gagnon
Drama	*Mon oncle Marcel qui vague vague près du métro Berri*, Gilbert Dupuis

—1992—

Fiction	*L'enfant chargé de songes*, Anne Hébert
Non-fiction	*La Radissonie. Le pays de la baie James*, Pierre Turgeon
Poetry	*Andromède attendra*, Gilles Cyr
Translation	*La mémoire postmoderne. Essai sur l'artcanadien contemporain*, Jean Papineau
Children's Literature (Illustration)	*Simon et la ville de carton*, Gille Tibo
Children's Literature (Text)	*Victor*, Christiane Duchesne

—1993—

Fiction	*Cartique des Plaines*, Nancy Huston
Non-fiction	*Le littérature de l'exiguité*, François Paré
Poetry	*Le Saut de L'ange*, Denise Desautels
Drama	*Celle-la*, Daniel Danis

—1994—

Fiction	*Le Petit Aigle à tête blanche*, Robert Lalonde
Non-fiction	*Du sida*, Chantal Saint-Jarre
Poetry	*Aknos*, Fulvio Caccia
Drama	*French Town*, Michel Ouellette

—1995—

Fiction	*Les Oiseaux de Saint-John Perse*, Nicole Houde
Non-fiction	*Louis-Antoine Dessaulles*, Yvan Lamonde
Poetry	*Pour orchestre et poète seul*, Émile Martel
Drama	*Les Quatre Morts de Marie*, Carole Fréchette

—1996—

Fiction	*Soifs*, Marie-Claire Blais
Non-fiction	*Le Naufrage de l'universite-Et autres essais d'epistemologie politique*
Poetry	*Le Quator de l' errance, La traversee du desert*
Drama	*Le Passage de L'Indiana*, Normand Charette

—1997—

Fiction	*Cet imperceptible mouvement*, Aude
Non-fiction	*Enfants du néant et mangeurs d'âmes-Guerre, culture et société en Iroquoisie ancienne*, Roland Viau
Poetry	*Romans-fleuves*, Pierre Nepveu
Drama	*Dits et Inédits*, Yvan Bienvenue

—1998—

Fiction	*La Terre ferme*, Christiane Frenette
Non-fiction	*Intérieurs du nouveau monde: essais dur les littératures du Québec et des Amériques*, Pierre Nepveu
Poetry	*Le Part de feu/Le Deuil de la rancune*, Suzanne Jacob
Drama	*15 secondes*, François Archambault

—1999—

Fiction	*La Danse juive*, Lise Tremblay
Non-fiction	*Le Mal du Nord*, Pierre Perrault
Poetry	*Conversations*, Herménégilde Chiasson
Drama	*Il n'y a que l'amour*, Jean Marc Dalpé
Translation	Jacques Brault, *Transfiguration*
Children's Literature (Illustration)	*Charlotte et l'île du destin*, Stéphane Jorisch
Children's Literature (Text)	*La Liberté? Connais pas...*, Charlotte Gingras

Source: *The Canada Council*

The Giller Prize, 1994-99

The Giller Prize awards $25,000 annually to the author of the best Canadian novel or short story collection published in English. The award was founded in 1994 by Toronto businessman Jack Rabinovitch in honour of his late wife, literary journalist Doris Giller.

The 1999 Giller Prize was presented November 3, 1999.

Year	Author	Title
1994	M.G. Vassanji	The Book of Secrets
1995	Rohinton Mistry	A Fine Balance
1996	Margaret Atwood	Alias Grace
1997	Mordecai Richler	Barney's Version
1998	Alice Munro	The Love of a Good Woman
1999	Bonnie Burnard	A Good House

The Booker Prize, 1989-99

The Booker Prize recognizes the best work of English fiction published in the Commonwealth, South Africa and Ireland. It is sponsored by Booker McConnell Ltd., an international food and agriculture business, and administered by the Booker Prize Book Trust, a British educational charity. Since 1984, the value of the Booker Prize has been £15,000.

Year	Author	Title
1989	Kazuo Ishiguro	The Remains of the Day
1990	A.S. Byatt	Possession
1991	Ben Okri	The Famished Road
1992 (joint winners)	Michael Ondaatje	The English Patient
	Barry Unsworth	Sacred Hunger
1993	Roddy Doyle	Paddy Clarke Ha Ha Ha
1994	James Kelman	How Late it Was, How Late
1995	Pat Barker	The Ghost Road
1996	Graham Swift	Last Orders
1997	Arundhati Roy	God of Small Things
1998	Ian McEwan	Amsterdam
1999	J.M. Coetzee	Disgrace

Pulitzer Prizes, 1999

The winners of these annual American literary awards were announced on April 10, 2000.

Fiction .... Jhumpa Lahiri, *Interpreter of Maladies*

Non-fiction .... John W. Dower, *Embracing Defeat: Japan in the Wake of World War II*

Poetry .... C.K. Williams, *Repair*

Drama .... Donald Margulies, *Dinner With Friends*

Biography .... Stacy Schiff, *Vera (Mrs. Vladimir Nabokov)*

History .... David M. Kennedy, *From Fear: The American People in Depression and War, 1929-1945*

News Reporting .... Staff, *Denver Post*, (Columbine H.S. shooting)

Investigative Reporting .... Sang-Hun Choe, Charles J. Hanley and, Martha Mendoza, Associated Press

(Massacre at No Gun Ri)

Bestselling Books in Canada, 1999

(Canadian books in bold type)

Fiction

1. *Tara Road*, by Maeve Binchy
2. *Hannibal*, by Thomas Harris
3. *The Testament*, by John Grisham
4. *The Girl Who Loved Tom Gordon*, by Stephen King
5. **Pilgrim, by Timothy Findley**
6. **A Good House, by Bonnie Burnard**
7. *Hearts In Atlantis*, by Stephen King
8. **The Love Of A Good Woman, by Alice Munro**
9. *Bag Of Bones*, by Stephen King
10. *White Oleander*, by Janet Fitch

Non-fiction

1. *'Tis*, by Frank McCourt
2. *The Ice Storm*, by Mark Abley
3. **The Canadian Oxford Dictionary, edited by Katherine Barber**
4. **Canada: Our Century, by Mark Kingwell and Christopher Moore**
5. *Tuesdays With Morrie*, by Mitch Albom
6. *Conversations With God, Book I*, by Neale Donald Walsch
7. *Angela's Ashes*, by Frank McCourt
8. **Becoming Human, by Jean Vanier**
9. **Titans, by Peter C. Newman**
10. **My Life In Pictures, by Wayne Gretzky with John Davidson**

Source: *The Globe and Mail*

Canadian books set in bold type.

National Magazine Awards, 1999

These annual awards were given May 26, 2000 by the National Magazine Awards Foundation. In 1999 there were gold and silver awards in 33 categories, including writing, design and photography.

One-of-a-Kind Articles	Chris Turner, "Flip flops, a desktop & one billion reasons never to leave," *Shift*
Humour	Miriam Toews, "Gunthered," *Saturday Night*
Business	Peter Foster, "The Money Pit," *Toronto Life*
Science & Technology	Curtis Gillespie, "Ground Zero" *Saturday Night*
Health and Medicine	Mary Rogan, "Acts of Faith," *Saturday Night*
Still-Life Photography	Colin Faulkner, Technical Expertise, *Toronto Life Fashion*
Fashion	Marc Stewart, Chris Nicholls and Jimmy Moorhouse, "Zen and Now," *Wedding Bells*
Politics	Naomi Klein, "The Real APEC Scandal," *Saturday Night*
Investigative Reporting	Paul Kaihla, "Mayhem Man," *Canadian Business*
Fiction	Bill Richardson, "It's in the Cards," the *Georgia Straight*
Arts and Entertainment	Jack Batten, "For Doris," *Toronto Life*
Environments	Deborah Samuel, Breaking the Waves, *enRoute*
Sports and Recreation	Bruce Grierson, "Court Jester," *Saturday Night*
Photojournalism	Robert Bourdeau, "The Station Point," *Border Crossings*; Larry Towell, "The Road to Bountiful," *Canadian Geographic*
Personal Journalism	Timothy Wilson, "Boo," *Saturday Night*
Portrait Photography	Bryce Duffy, "The Cutting Edge," *Shift*
Columns	Mireille Silcott, "The New Satanism/Not-so-cool Britannia/Rhyme Pays," *Shift*
Service	Leanne Delap and Jacob Richler, Sin City, *Toronto Life*
Travel	Jake MacDonald, "Fishing Papa's Paradise," *Outdoor Canada*
Spot Illustration	Gerard DuBois, "Canadian Letters – November," *Saturday Night*
How-To	Ken Bailey, "The Book on Whitetails," *Outdoor Canada*
Essays	Michel Legault, "Le médecin et la mort," *L'actualité médicale*
Profiles	Gerald Hannon, "A Monumental Man," *Toronto Life*
Poetry	Julie Bruck, "Six Poems," *The Malahat Review*
Art Direction for a Single Article	Carmen Dunjko, Malcolm Brown, "The Cutting Edge," *Shift*
Editorial Package	Diane Bérard, Jacinthe Tremblay, René Vézina, Laurent Fontaine, Daniel Germain and Sandrine L'Herminier, "Power!," *Revue Commerce*
Words and Pictures	Laas Turnbull, Matthew McKinnon, Carmen Dunjko, Malcolm Brown and Floria Sigismondi, "Work Wear," *Shift*
Social Affairs	Mark Bourrie, "The System That Killed Santa," *Ottawa City Magazine*
Magazine Covers	Stephen Hanks, "Through the Lens," *Canadian Geographic*
President's Medal	Mary Rogan, *Fashion*
Magazine of the Year	*Chatelaine*
Best New Magazine	*Montage*
Alexander Ross Award for Best New Magazine Writer	Yan Muckle
Foundation Award for Outstanding Achievement	Peter C. Newman

Source: National Magazine Awards Foundation

Bill C-55: "Split Run" Magazines in Canada

*C*anada-U.S. relations were strained through the first half of 1999 by the threatened passage into law of Bill C-55 by the federal government. The bill would have made it illegal for Canadian advertisers to purchase space in American "split run" magazines (magazines produced in the United States with small additions of Canadian content and beamed via satellite into Canada for printing). In 1998, the World Trade Organization overturned the tax measures that Canada had used to protect the domestic advertising market after a complaint from the American government. Bill C-55 was intended as a replacement for the disallowed tariffs. It was passed by the federal parliament in March, causing American Trade Officials to threaten retaliation in key trade sectors including steel, wood products and textiles. Before the bill was given royal assent, an agreement was reached, allowing certain split runs to sell up to 18 percent of their advertising space to Canadian advertisers provided they meet yet-to-be agreed on quotas for Canadian content. Some Canadian industry spokespersons saw the agreement as a major blow to the financial viability of Canadian magazines. Others spoke of a future in which Canadian magazines might either adopt a more intensely local focus, or seek U.S. production partners to keep competitive.

Top Canadian Paid-Circulation Magazines, 2000

Magazine	Circulation[1]
Reader's Digest (Canadian English edition)	1 083 413
Chatelaine (English language edition)	763 778
TV Guide	630 739
Canadian Living	551 884
Maclean's	503 369
Time (Canadian edition)	319 041
Sélection du Reader's Digest (Canadian French edition)	226 533
Canadian Geographic	205 488
TV Hebdo	200 672
Châtelaine (French language edition)	187 913
L'Actualité	180 364
Flare	172 362
Coupe de Pouce	161 696
7 Jours	145 008

Source: *CARD: Media Information Network*
(1) Average total paid circulation for most recently reported 6 month period as of August 2000.

The Stephen Leacock Award for Humour

*S*tephen Butler Leacock was born in England in 1869. His education included Upper Canada College, a B.A. at U of T, and a Ph.D from the University of Chicago. He taught at UCC, and later lectured in political science at McGill. His literary output included works in history, economics and political science, although by far the most popular were his humour books. By the time of his death in 1944, he was the best-known humourist in the English-speaking world.

Canada's highest award for humour is named in Leacock's honour and is given annually at a ceremony in his hometown of Orillia, Ontario. The 2000 winner was Arthur Block for **Black Tie and Tales.**

Top Canadian Daily Newspapers, 2000

Newspaper	Daily[2]	Circulation[1] Saturday	Sunday
Toronto Star	467 638	701 805	485 373
Globe and Mail	322 834	39 638	
National Post	268 747	314 385	
Journal de Montreal	267 374	334 726	277 830
Toronto Sun	239 288	188 474	400 717
La Presse	187 400	286 293	195 911
Vancouver Sun	183 075 (M–Th.) 220 391 (F.)	247 085	
Vancouver Province	160 597		196 731
Ottawa Citizen	140 909	185 384	136 733
Montreal Gazette	140 592	188 144	133 374
Edmonton Journal	137 326(M–Th./Sat.); 163 373 (Fri.)		134 205
Winnipeg Free Press	131 385	181 486	144 324
Calgary Herald	112 642 (M–Th.) 152 542 (Fri.)	130 488	116 563
Halifax Chronicle Herald	112 139		54 773
Hamilton Spectator	108 437	127 539	
London Free Press	99 366	125 623	
Le Journal de Quebec	97 999	126 611	101 391
Le Soleil	80 640	126 771	89 134
Victoria-Times Columnist	76 431 (Mon.–Sat.)		76 165
Windsor Star	75 271	87 333	
Edmonton Sun	73 576 (Mon.–Sat.)		110 017

Sources: CARD Media Information Network
(1) Average total paid circulation for most recently reported 6 month period as of August 2000. Ranked by weekday circulation.
(2) Monday to Friday unless otherwise indicated.

National Newspaper Awards, 1999

These annual awards were announced in Montreal on May 12, 2000.

Editorial Writing	Alain Dubuc, *La Presse*
Spot News Photography	Leonard LePage, *St. Catharines Standard*
Feature Photography	Chris Schwarz, *Edmonton Journal*
Spot News Reporting	Canadian Press, Montreal Bureau
International Reporting	John Stackhouse, *Globe and Mail*
Sports Writing	Jack Todd, *Montreal Gazette*
Feature Writing	John Stackhouse, *Globe and Mail*
Columns	Christie Blatchford, *National Post*
Sports Photography	Fred Chartrand, Canadian Press
Enterprise Reporting	William Marsden, *Montreal Gazette*
Critical Writing	Doug Saunders, *Globe and Mail*
Layout and Design	Marc Duplain, *Le Soleil*
Editorial Cartooning	Serge Chapleau, *La Presse*
Business Reporting	David Bains, Richard Blackwell, Susanne Craig, Karen Howlett, Dawn Walton and Mark MacKinnon, *Globe and Mail*
Special Projects	*Montreal Gazette*
Local Reporting	Elaine Smith, *Simcoe Reformer*

Source: Canadian Newspaper Association

GALLERIES AND MUSEUMS

Canadian art is a time-honoured tradition with the oldest surviving work of prehistoric First Nations carving dating back to 5,000 B.C. European traditions were slow to take hold in the colonnial regime. Bishop Laval established the country's first school of art near Quebec in 1675 and religious art dominated the Canadian scene until the 19th century when Paul Kane and Cornelius Krieghoff became the country's first genre painters, rendering scenes of native and settler life respectively. After the establishment of major art instituions such as the Royal Canadian Academy of Art (1880) and the Ontario College of Art (1875), landscape became the dominant form of Canadian painting, a trend that peaked with the formation of the Group of Seven in 1920 (see article below). Abstract art reached Canada in the 1940s and gained its first domestic expression in the work of Montreal's automatiste painters, lead by Jean Paul Riopelle and Paul-Emile Borduas, working under the influence of cubism and the French surreallists. Art in English Canada remained under the sway of the Group of Seven and that of British representational trends in portraiture and urban landscape until the formation in 1954 and subsequent international success of Painters Eleven in Toronto. This group which featured Jack Bush, Kazuo Nakamura, Jock MacDonald, William Ronald, and Harold Town drew heavily on the abstract expressionist movement in the United States for inspiration and its members scored success in New York critical circles of the period. Leadership reverted to Montreal in the 1960s with the emergence of painters devoted to the op art school focussing on experiments in visual effects and surface dynamics. While magic realist painters such as Nova Scotia's Alex Colville, and Newfoundland's Christopher Pratt and Manitoba-born naïve painter William Kurelek kept representational painting popular through the 1970s, a new generation of artists such as Michael Snow, Greg Curnoe, General Idea, and Iain Baxter followed the international trend away from painting into conceptual art exploring new media such as film, photography, performance and installation art. The 1980s saw a rebirth in interest in representational painting with the emergence of neo-expressionist influenced work from groups such as Vancouver's New Romantics and Toronto's ChromaZone Collective. Today the Canadian art scene features artists working in every conceivable medium and genre. Their work is shown in artist run collectives, commercial galleries and larger public galleries in every major centre.

Group of Seven

The Group of Seven held its first exhibition at the Art Gallery of Toronto in May 1920. The original members included J.E.H. MacDonald, Lawren Harris, A.Y. Jackson, Arthur Lismer, F.H. Varley, Frank Johnston and Franklin Carmichael.

In 1924, Johnston resigned from the Group and, in 1926, A.J. Casson was invited to join. In the later years of the Group, two new members, Edwin Holgate and Lionel Lemoine FitzGerald, were added. The Group held its final exhibition in Dec. 1931 and disbanded in 1932.

Tom Thomson, who drowned in 1917, was never a member of the Group of Seven, though his boldly-colored works depicting the rugged landscape of northern Ontario became associated with its style of painting.

By breaking with the traditional, European, painting style popular in Canada in the 1920s, The Group of Seven made a huge impact on Canadian art. Although originally reviled by critics, the Group had gained wide acceptance and popularity by the 1930s. Today, the Group's paintings are exhibited in every major gallery in Canada.

J.E.H. **MacDonald** (1873–1932)
Lawren **Harris** (1885–1970)
Alexander Young (A.Y.) **Jackson** (1882–1974)
Arthur **Lismer** (1885–1969)
Frederick Horsman **Varley** (1881–1969)
Frank Hans **Johnston** (1888–1949)
Frank **Carmichael** (1890–1945)
Alfred Joseph (A.J.) **Casson** (1898–1992)
Edwin **Holgate** (1892–1977)
Lionel Lemoine **FitzGerald** (1890–1956)
Tom **Thomson** (1877–1917)

Source: *Looking at Landscape*, Dwight Siegner, The McMichael Canadian Art Collection

Gallery and Museum Highlights, 2000

Vancouver Art Gallery
Global Conceptualism: Points of Origin 1950–1980s is the first major exhibition to explore in depth the history of conceptual art as it developed around the world. Continues through April, 2001. *Krieghoff: Images of Canada*, the first large-scale retrospective of the work of Canada's foremost 19th century painter Cornelius Krieghoff (1812–1872), Feb.–May 2001. *Colouring the West: A Century of B.C. Painting* examines the trends within painting in British Columbia throughout the 20th century and continues to May 2001.

Glenbow Museum, Calgary
Mysteries of Egypt, organized by the Canadian Museum of Civilization, features over 350 artifacts and reproductions from the world's oldest civilization, ranging from real mummies and objects used in everyday life to reproductions of wall murals and a copy of the Rosetta Stone. To March 11, 2001. *Treasures From Glenbow*, A rare opportunity to see some of the highlights from Glenbow's collections of over one million artifacts. July–November, 2001. *Nitawah-Sinnanii: Our Land, The Story of the Blackfoot People* shares the history and culture of the Blackfoot people as told in their own voices. This new permanent gallery has been created through a unique partnership with the Blackfoot Confederacy and features artifacts from Glenbow's outstanding Blackfoot collection. Opening September 2001.

Art Gallery of Ontario, Toronto
Matisse: From The Baltimore Museum of Art includes more than 60 of the drawings and sculptures by Henri Matisses collected by Baltimore sisters Dr. Claribel Cone (1864–1929) and Miss Etta Cone (1870–1949). The collection provides a unique perspective on one of the most revolutionary and recognizable artis of the 20th century. Continues to Jan. 14, 2001. *Greg Curnoe: Retrospective* (working title) will be the first major retrospective of Curnoe's work since his death in 1992 and will consist of works from the AGO's permanent collection—now the largest public collection of Curnoe's work in the world. Multi-media constructions (part painting, part sculpture, part installation), text works, found objects (often in the form of collages), watercolours and prints on plexiglass will form the nucleus of the exhibition. March 9–June 17, 2001. *Rubens and His Times: From the State Hermitage Museum* features works by the three most accomplished and influential Flemish painters of the 17th century: Peter Paul Rubens, Anthony van Dyck, and Jacob Jordaens. Also included are works by Jan Brueghel, Frans Synders, Adriaen Brouwer and David Teniers the Younger. A selection of some 93 pictures—religious scenes, landscapes, portraits, still lifes, and more—traces the development of a unique school of painting. The exhibition is further enhanced by the inclusion of Flemish drawings and a splendid selection of decorative works of art. May 5–Aug. 12, 2001.

Royal Ontario Museum, Toronto
Passionate Vision: Intimate Portraits of Canada's National Parks presents photographs of all 41 Canadian national parks taken by Dr. Roberta Bondar, Canada's premier astronaut. Nov. 4, 2000–Feb. 25, 2001. *Treasures of Japanese Art* from the ROM's Collection showcases Japanese paintings and woodblock prints from the 17th to 19th centuries, drawn exclusively from the ROM's Asian collections. Nov. 30, 2000–Apr. 2001. *Legacy in Gold: Scythian Treasures from Ancient Ukraine* is the largest and most complete assemblage of Scythian art, exclusively from Ukrainian collections.

More than 170 rare works of art from the 7th to 2nd centuries B.C., mostly crafted in gold, exemplify the extraordinary design qualities and spectacular visual impact of the art produced by the fierce nomadic warriors of the steppes. Feb. 18–May 6, 2001. *Dionysus to Bacchus: Wine and Revelry* is the fascinating story of the god of wine and revelry from ancient Greece and Rome until the present. Examining the ways in which wine has influenced society and art throughout the ages, the exhibition traces the fascinating history of wine production and consumption through unique works of art and artifacts. June 13–October 21, 2001.

National Gallery of Canada, Ottawa

Elusive Paradise: The Millennium Prize is an invitational exhibition. A group of 10 artists, of whom half will be Canadian, will be invited to submit new works, some of which will be created on site, reflecting a significant direction in contemporary art at the beginning of the new millennium. Feb. 9–May 13, 2001. *Gustav Klimt (1862–1918): Modernism in the Making* brings together some 40 paintings, and between 60 and 70 works on paper to present, for the first time to a North American public, the various components of this great Symbolist's art. The exhibition will feature a selection of both early and later works, and a fair and even representation of portraits, history paintings, and landscapes. June 15–Sept. 16, 2001. *Louis-Philippe Hébert* is considered the greatest Canadian sculptor of his time (1850–1917) and one of the major figures in the history of Canadian art. This exhibition will include approximately 150 works which illustrate the artist's wide range of themes, materials, and techniques, and represent all the periods of his career and production. Oct. 12, 2001–Jan. 6, 2002.

Montreal Museum of Fine Art

Alfred Hitchcock is the first exhibition of its kind to be devoted to a filmmaker. Through film clips, production stills, posters, annotated scripts, set models and so on, visitors will follow the chronological and thematic development of Hitchcock's works from his initial English period under the aesthetic influence of German cinema to the masterpieces of his maturity in Hollywood. The museum will also presentpaintings, sculptures, prints and other art works that have facilitated an aesthetic understanding of his films. Nov. 16, 2000–Mar. 18, 2001. *Erotic Picasso* presents 50 paintings and sculptures, 100 gouaches, collages, drawings and sketchbooks, as well as 100 prints. The works examine the subjects of love and sex that enriched Picasso's art throughout his life. June 14–Sept. 16, 2001. *Pierre Ayot*, was a key player on the Montreal arts scene from the early 1960s to his accidental death in 1995. Inspired by Pop images, he was at the centre of the extraordinary growth in Quebec printmaking in the early 1980s, as both a leader and an artist. Apr. 26–July 15, 2001.

Art Gallery of Nova Scotia

Relative Marks, Relative Surfaces—Bryan Maycock: since 1996, Bryan Maycock has been working on a series of two- and three-dimensional works that investigate and reflect upon personal genealogical research. This has led to work that is about exploring aspects of several individuals' work and lives through a connection between materials used and occupations practised by various forebearers and Maycock's own art practice. Dec. 2, 2000–Feb. 4, 2001. *Joe Norris: Painted Visions of Nova Scotia*: Joe Norris (1924–1996) was one of Nova Scotia's and Canada's finest folk artists. His rural scenes depict a disappearing culture while evoking joy and optimism in a most delightful manner. He painted prolifically until his death, leaving a legacy of artworks, painted furniture, and panels that are alive with his remarkable sense of colour and symmetry. Nov. 25, 2000–Jan. 28, 2001.

GOVERNOR GENERAL'S AWARDS IN VISUAL AND MEDIA ARTS

These annual awards, funded and administered by the Canada Council for the Arts, were created in June 1999. Six prizes are awarded for distinguished career achievement in the visual and media arts, and one prize for distinguished contributions to the visual and media arts through voluntarism, philanthropy, board governance or community outreach activities. The first annual Governor General's awards were announced March 23, 2000.

2000 Winners

■ **Jocelyne Alloucherie,** Sculpture
Over the last 30 years Jocelyne Alloucherie's work has played an increasingly significant role in Canadian sculpture and installation art. Her work is rooted in intellectual rigor and clarity and defined by a very personal visual vocabulary and definition of space. Her exceptional body of work, often integrating drawing and photography into installations, has established Alloucherie as a seminal artist and has attracted important critical attention across Canada and abroad.

■ **Ghitta Caiserman-Roth,** Painting
Ghitta Caiserman-Roth has distinguished herself for over 60 years as a figurative artist. Her paintings, etchings, lithographs and drawings, represented in over 100 public collections, reflect an ongoing concern with the human condition. In addition to her untiring activity as a practicing artist, Caiserman-Roth has played, and continues to play, a significant role as teacher, lecturer and mentor to numerous artists in Montreal and across Canada.

■ **John Chalke,** Fine Crafts
John Chalke has been at the forefront of Canadian ceramics for over 30 years. He is recognized world-wide for his important and innovative discoveries in the technology of ceramics as well as for the aesthetic quality of his work. In addition to being an influential teacher and author, he is considered one of the most important and influential ceramists of the last 50 years.

■ **Jacques Giraldeau,** Film
For 30 years the work of Jacques Giraldeau has established him as a pre-eminent documentary filmmaker. His longstanding career at the National Film Board, his unique visual exuberance and extraordinary approach to the film medium as well as his numerous productions mark him as a pioneer of documentary cinema.

■ **John Scott,** Painting
For over 20 years John Scott has used his apocalyptic vision and the unique visual idiom of his drawings, sculptures and installation work as a catalyst for social and political change. His work speaks directly and forcefully about the social, political and cultural condition of our times, in particular the plight of the ordinary person. Through the format of painted drawings, John Scott expresses both apprehension and hope for the human collectivity.

■ **Michael Snow,** Film
Michael Snow's work, which includes photography, film, holography, painting, sculpture, installation and experimental jazz, has touched on just about everything that allowed him to discover new ground. It is his pioneering work as an independent filmmaker, however, that is celebrated by this award. His films have been shown throughout North America, Europe and the Far East and are included in the curricula of film schools around the globe.

■ **Doris Shadbolt,** Voluntarism
The development of Vancouver as an important centre for the visual arts would not have been possible without Doris Shadbolt's wisdom, generosity and aesthetic sensitivity. She has participated on countless committees, juries and boards. With her husband, Jack Shadbolt, she provided an enduring legacy by establishing the Vancouver Institute for the Visual Arts (VIVA).

Major Public Art Galleries in Canada

Art Gallery of Greater Victoria: 1040 Moss St., Victoria, B.C. V8V 4P1 (604) 384-4101

Art Gallery of Nova Scotia: P.O. Box 2262, Halifax, N.S. B3J 3C8 (902) 424-7542

Art Gallery of Ontario: 317 Dundas St. W., Toronto, Ont. M5T 1G4 (416) 979-6648

Art Gallery of Windsor: 3100 Howard Ave., Windsor, Ont. N8X 3Y8 (519) 258-7111

Beaverbrook Art Gallery: P.O. Box 605, Fredericton, N.B. E3B 5A6 (506) 458-8545

Confederation Centre Art Gallery and Museum: 145 Richmond St., Charlottetown, P.E. C1A 1J1 (902) 628-6111

Dunlop Art Gallery: P.O. Box 2311, Regina, Sask. S4P 3Z5 (306) 777-6040

Edmonton Art Gallery: 2 Sir Winston Churchill Sq., Edmonton, Alta. T5J 2C1 (403) 422-6223

McMichael Canadian Art Collection: 10365 Islington Ave., Kleinburg, Ont. L0J 1C0 (905) 893-1121

Montreal Museum of Fine Arts: 1379-1380 Sherbrooke St. W., P.O. Box 3000, Stn. H, Montreal, Que. H3G 2T9 (514) 285-1600

Musee d'Art Contemporain de Montreal: 185 St. Catherine St. W, Montreal, Que. H2X 1Z8 (514) 847-6212

Musée du Québec: Parc des Champs de Bataille, 1, rue Wolfe/Montcalm, Quebec, Que. G1R 5H3 (418) 643-2150

National Gallery of Canada: 380 Sussex Dr., Ottawa, Ont. K1N 9N4 (613) 990-1985

Thunder Bay Art Gallery: P.O. Box 1193, Station F, Thunder Bay, Ont. P7C 4X9 (807) 577-6427

Vancouver Art Gallery: 750 Hornby St., Vancouver, B.C. V6Z 2H7 (604) 662-4700

Winnipeg Art Gallery: 300 Memorial Blvd., Winnipeg, Man. R3C 1V1 (204) 786-6641

Major Public Museums in Canada

Canadian Centre for Architecture: 1920 rue Baile, Montreal, Que. H3A 1E9 (514) 939-7000

Canadian Museum of Civilization: 100 Laurier St., Box 3100, Stn B, Hull, Que. J8X 4H2 (819) 776-7000

Canadian Museum of Contemporary Photography: 1 Rideau Canal, P.O. Box 465, Station A, Ottawa, Ont. K1N 9N6 (613) 990-8257

Canadian Museum of Nature: P.O. Box 3443, Station D, Ottawa, Ont. K1P 6P4 (613) 566-4700

Canadian War Museum: 330 Sussex Dr., Ottawa, Ont. K1A 0M8 (613) 996-1420

Glenbow-Alberta Institute: 130-9th Ave. SE, Calgary, Alta. T2G 0P3 (403) 268-4100

Manitoba Museum of Man and Nature: 190 Rupert Ave., Winnipeg, Man. R3B 0N2 (204) 956-2830

Maritime Museum of the Atlantic: 1675 Lower Water St., Halifax, N.S. B3J 1S3 (902) 429-7490

McCord Museum of Canadian History: 690, rue Sherbrooke ouest, Montreal, Que. H3A 1E9 (514) 398-7100

Musée de la Civilisation: 85, rue Dalhousie, C.P. 155, Succursale B, Quebec, Que. G1K 7A6 (418) 643-2158

New Brunswick Museum: 277 Douglas Ave., Saint John, N.B. E2K 1E5 (506) 643-2300

Newfoundland Museum: 285 Duckworth St., P.O. Box 8700, St. John's, Nfld. A1B 4J6 (709) 729-2329

Nova Scotia Museum: 1747 Summer St., Halifax, N.S. B3H 3A6 (902) 424-6471

Prince of Wales Northern Heritage Centre: P.O. Box 1320, Yellowknife, N.W.T. X1A 2L9 (867) 873-7551

Provincial Museum of Alberta: 12845-102nd Ave., Edmonton, Alta. T5N 0M6 (403) 453-9100

Royal British Columbia Museum: P.O. Box 9815, Stn. Prov. Govt., Victoria, B.C. V8W 9W2 (250) 387-3701

Royal Ontario Museum: 100 Queen's Park, Toronto, Ont. M5S 2C6 (416) 586-8000

Royal Saskatchewan Museum: Wascana Park, College and Albert, Regina, Sask. S4P 3V7 (306) 787-2815

Vancouver Museum: 1100 Chestnut St., Vancouver, B.C. V6J 3J9 (604) 736-4431

Prince Edward Island Museum and Heritage Foundation: 2 Kent St., Charlottetown, PEI C1A 1M6 (902) 368-6600

CANADIAN HALL OF FAME

The following list is not meant to be exhaustive, but rather a listing of prominent Canadians, and those whose reputations are inextricably linked with Canada, from all fields.

A

ABBOTT, John Joseph Caldwell (Sir), politics. St Andrews, Lower Canada, 1821–93. Canada's third prime minister.

ABBOTT, Maude Elizabeth Seymour, medicine. St Andrews, Que., 1869–1940. Specialist in congenital heart disease. *History of Medicine in the Province of Quebec.*

ABBOTT, Roger, performing arts. Eng., 1946. Actor and co-producer of CBC's *Royal Canadian Air Farce*, noted for impersonation of Jean Chrétien.

ABEL, Sidney Gerald (Sid), sports. Melville, Sask., 1918-2000. Hockey player; 1949–52 considered best offensive unit when centred with Gordie Howe and Ted Lindsay (Detroit Red Wings); four-time all-star.

ABERDEEN, Ishbel Maria Marjoribanks Gordon (Lady), reformer. Eng., 1857–1939. Helped create National Council of Women, Victorian Order of Nurses.

ABERHART, William "Bible Bill", politics. Hibbard Twp, Ont., 1878–1943. Founded Social Credit party; Alberta premier 1935–43.

ACORN, Milton, literary arts. Charlottetown, PEI, 1923–86. Radical poet. "The Island Means Minago."

ADAMS, Bryan, performing arts. Kingston, Ont., 1959. Singer/songwriter; rock star. *Reckless.*

ADAMS, Ian, literary arts. Tanzania, 1937. Novelist, nonfiction writer. *S, Portrait of a Spy; The Trudeau Papers.*

ADAMS, Thomas, city planner. Scot., 1871–1940. Father of the Canadian Planning Movement.

AFFLECK, Raymond Tait, visual arts. Penticton, BC, 1922–89. Architect; designed Place Ville Marie, Place Bonaventure.

AGLUKARK, Susan, performing arts. Arviat, NWT, 1966. Singer/songwriter; first Inuit recording artist.

AIRD, John Black, politics. Toronto, Ont., 1923–95. Liberal senator; Ontario lieutenant-governor 1980–85.

AISLIN (b. Christopher Terry Mosher), visual arts. Ottawa, Ont., 1942. *Montreal Gazette* cartoonist; sports caricaturist.

AITKEN, William Maxwell (Lord Beaverbrook), literary arts. Maple, Ont., 1879–1964. Publisher; newspaper magnate; British Conservative cabinet minister.

AKEEAKTASHUK, visual arts. Hudson Bay, Ont., 1898–1954. Sculptor; first important Inuit carver.

ALBANI, Emma (b. Louise Cecile Emma Lajeunesse), performing arts. Chambly, Que., 1847–1930. Opera singer; grand diva excelled in Wagnerian opera, popular in Britain and US.

ALEXANDER, Lincoln MacCauley, politics. Toronto, Ont., 1922. First Black in Parliament; Ont. lieutenant-governor 1985–91.

ALLAN, Hugh (Sir), business. Scot., 1810–82. Railway promoter; suspected of electoral bribery for soliciting favours in Pacific Scandal (1873).

ALLAN, Ted (b. Allan Herman), performing arts. Montreal, Que., 1916–95. Author; screenwriter. *Lies My Father Told Me; Bethune: The Making of a Hero.*

ALLEN, Charlotte Vale, literary arts. Toronto, Ont., 1941. Writer, lecturer on child abuse. *Daddy's Girl.*

ALLEN, John F. (Jack), science. Winnipeg, Man., 1908. Co-discoverer of superfluidity in liquid helium.

ALLEN, Montagu (Sir), sports. Montreal, Que., 1860–1951. Financier and sportsman who donated Allen Cup in 1908 for senior amateur competition in Canada.

ALLEN, Ralph, literary arts. Winnipeg, Man., 1913–66. Influential *Maclean's* editor (1946–60).

ALMOND, Paul, performing arts. Montreal, Que., 1931. Film director. *Act of the Heart.*

ALTMAN, Sidney, science. Montreal, Que., 1939. Microbiologist; 1989 Nobel Prize in chemistry for role in research into chemical cell reactions.

AMIEL, Barbara, media. Eng., 1940s. Journalist; conservative political and social columnist.

AMOS, Beth (b. Bessie Rymer), performing arts. St Catharines, Ont., 1915–95. Actor. *Jake and the Kid; Miracle at Indian Creek; Canadian Bacon.*

ANDERSON, Doris Hilda, literary arts. Toronto, Ont., 1921. Writer; feminist; editor, *Chatelaine* 1958–77.

ANDERSON, Pamela Denise, performing arts. Ladysmith, BC, 1967. Voluptuous actress who has starred in *Baywatch, Barb Wire.*

ANDRE, Brother (b. Alfred Bissette), religion. St Gregoire d'Iberville, Lower Canada, 1845–1937. Mystic; built Montreal's St Joseph's Oratory.

ANGILIK, Paul Apak, performing arts. Hall Beach, NWT, 1954–98. Documentary filmmaker of Inuit life; adventurer; contributor to Inuit Broadcasting Corporation.

ANKA, Paul Albert, performing arts. Ottawa, Ont., 1941. Singer/songwriter; composed more than 400 songs. "My Way."

APPLEBAUM, Louis, performing arts. Toronto, Ont., 1918-2000. Composer; writer of opera, concerts, film scores.

APPLEYARD, Peter, performing arts. Eng., 1928. Jazz musician; vibraphonist; TV personality. "Swing Fever."

APPS, Charles Joseph Sylvanus (Syl), sports. Paris, Ont., 1915–98. Hockey player; Toronto Maple Leafs (1936–48); 3-time all-star; pole vault contender in 1936 Olympics; 1937 Canadian Athlete of the Year.

AQUIN, Hubert, literary arts. Montreal, Que., 1929–77. Novelist; modernist writer. *Neige Noire.*

ARCAND, Denys, performing arts. Deschambault, Que., 1941. Film director. *Decline of the American Empire.*

ARCHAMBAULT, Louis, visual arts. Montreal, Que., 1915. Sculptor; his work is in many museum collections.

ARCHER, Violet, performing arts. Montreal, Que., 1913-2000. Internationally recognized classical music composer, inspired by Canadian folk music. *Prairie Profiles.*

ARDEN, Elizabeth (b. Florence Nightingale Graham), business. Woodbridge, Ont., 1884-1966. Founder of the Elizabeth Arden cosmetics empire, Arden was a pioneer in mass advertising and built the business from a small shop in New York City in 1914 to today's vast chain of spas and beauty salons.

ARDEN, Jann (b. Jann Arden Richards), performing arts. Calgary, Alta, 1962. Juno-award winning pop singer, songwriter. *Happy?; Time for Mercy.*

ARTHUR, Eric Ross, visual arts. New Zealand, 1898-1982. Architectural conservancy advocate; writer. *Toronto: No Mean City; The Barn: A Vanishing Landmark in North America.*

ASPER, Israel Harold, business. Minnedosa, Man., 1932. Financier; founder Global-TV; columnist; author.

ATHANS, George S. Jr., sports. Kelowna, BC, 1952. Three-time world water ski champion.

ATKINSON, Joseph, media. Newcastle, Ont., 1865-1948. Journalist; built *Toronto Star* into nation's largest newspaper.

ATWOOD, Margaret Eleanor, literary arts. Ottawa, Ont., 1939. Prolific novelist with international following. *The Handmaid's Tale, Alias Grace.*

AUBERT de GASPE, Philippe-Ignace François, literary arts. Quebec City, Que., 1814-41. Novelist; wrote first French-Cdn novel. *L'influence d'un livre* (1837).

AUF DER MAUR, Nick, journalism. Montreal, Que., 1942-98. Long-time columnist for *Montreal Gazette;* co-wrote biography of Brian Mulroney: *The Boy from Baie Comeau.*

AUGUSTYN, Frank Joseph, performing arts. Hamilton, Ont., 1953. Former principal dancer, National Ballet of Canada; director, Ottawa Ballet.

AVERY, Oswald, science. Halifax, NS, 1877-1955. First person to show agent responsible for transferring genetic information was DNA, not a protein as previously thought.

AXWORTHY, Norman Lloyd, politics. North Battleford, Sask., 1939. Liberal Minister of External Affairs.

AYKROYD, Daniel Edward (Dan), performing arts. Ottawa, Ont., 1952. Actor/comedian. *Saturday Night Live, Ghostbusters.*

B

BACHMAN, Randy, performing arts. Winnipeg, Man., 1946. Rock musician; guitarist for Guess Who, Bachman-Turner Overdrive. *American Woman.*

BAETZ, Reuben, politics. Chelsey, Ont., 1923-96. Executive director of Canadian Council on Social Development; proponent of national unemployment insurance program.

BAFFIN, William, exploration and discovery. Eng., 1584-1622. Made two Arctic voyages in search of the Northwest Passage; first to conclude Hudson Bay did not lead westward; explored Baffin Island.

BAILEY, Donovan, sports. Jamaica, 1967. Track star who won 100 m race at world record time, 9.84, at 1996 Olympics in Atlanta.

BAKER, Carroll, performing arts. Bridgewater, NS, 1949. Singer; country music star.

BALDWIN, Robert, politics. York, Ont., 1804-58. Proponent of responsible government; co-premier (with LaFontaine) of Upper Canada.

BALLARD, Harold Edwin, sports. Toronto, Ont., 1903-90. Sports capitalist; irascible owner of Toronto Maple Leafs, Hamilton Tiger Cats.

BANTING, Frederick Grant, (Sir) medicine. Alliston, Ont., 1891-1941. Medical researcher; co-discoverer of insulin; Nobel Prize for medicine, 1923.

BARBEAU, Charles Marius, ethnologist. St-Marie-de-Beauce, Que., 1883-1969. Eminent folklorist.

BARFOOT, Joan Louise, literary arts. Owen Sound, Ont., 1947. Novelist. *Dancing in the Dark; Family News; Charlotte and Claudia Keeping in Touch.*

BARKER, William George (Billy), military. Dauphin, Man., 1894-1930. Fighter pilot awarded Victoria Cross for 60 solo combat missions against German aircraft during WWI.

BARLOW, Maude Victoria, politics. Toronto, Ont., 1947. Political/human rights activist, author. Chair, Council of Canadians.

BARR, Murray Llewellyn, medicine. Belmont, Ont., 1908. Anatomist; developed chromosome analysis to diagnose genetic disorders.

BARRY, James (b. Miranda Stewart), medicine. Eng., 1795-1865. In 1857 appointed inspector general of military hospitals in Province of Canada; as a woman disguised as a man, was the first woman doctor to work in Canada.

BASINSKI, Zbigniew Stanislaw, science. Poland, 1928. Outstanding metal physics researcher.

BASSETT, John White Hughes, media. Ottawa, Ont., 1915-98. Media executive.

BASSETT-SEGUSO, Carling Kathrin, sports. Toronto, Ont., 1967. Top-ranked Canadian tennis player.

BATA, Sonja Ingrid, public service. Switzerland, 1926. Founder of the Bata Shoe Museum in Toronto; wife of shoe retailing entrepreneur Thomas Bata.

BATA, Thomas John, business. Czech., 1914. Industrialist; chairman, Bata Shoes; in over 70 countries.

BATEMAN, Robert McLellan, visual arts. Toronto, Ont., 1930. Painter; major international wildlife artist.

BAUER, David William (Father), sports. Kitchener, Ont., 1925-88. Hockey coach; father of Cdn Olympic hockey.

BAUMANN, Alexander (Sasha), sports. Czech., 1964. Swimmer; gold medals in 200 m, 400 m individual medley, 1984 Olympics; 1984 top male athlete.

BEARDY, Quentin Pickering Jackson, visual arts. Island Lake, Man., 1944-84. Graphic stylist using Cree legends.

BEATTY, Henry Perrin, politics. Toronto, Ont., 1950. President of CBC, 1995-98; former PC cabinet minister.

BECK, Adam (Sir), business. Baden, Canada W, 1857-1925. Hydro commissioner; built Ontario Hydro.

BECKER, Abigail, military. Frontenac Cty, UC, 1831-1905. Heroine; saved men shipwrecked on Lake Erie.

BECKWITH, John, literary arts/performing arts. Victoria, BC, 1927. Composer; writer; critic. *The Shivaree.*

BEDARD, Myriam, sports. Lorretteville, Que., 1969. Biathlete; two gold medals, biathlon, '94 Olympics.

BEDDOES, Dick, media. Daysland, Alta, 1926-91. Colourful sportswriter, broadcaster, hockey commentator with the Vancouver *Sun, Globe & Mail,* Edmonton *Bulletin;* broadcaster on CFRB radio in Toronto. *Pal Hal,* a profile of Harold Ballard.

BEECROFT, Norma Marian, performing arts. Oshawa, Ont., 1934. Composer; avant-garde musician. *"From Dreams of Brass."*

BEERS, William George, medicine/sports. Montreal, Que., 1843–1900. Popularized lacrosse; Dean, Canada's first dental college.

BEGIN, Monique, politics. Italy, 1936. First Quebec woman in Commons; health minister.

BELANGER, Michel, business. Lévis, Que., 1929–97. President of Quebec's National Bank; 1991–92 was co-chairman of Belanger-Campeau Commission which examined constitutional concerns in Quebec.

BELIVEAU, Jean Arthur, sports. Trois-Rivières, Que., 1931. Hockey player; stylish Montreal Canadiens centre, 1953–71; 507 goals.

BELL, Alexander Graham, invention. Scot., 1847–1922. Invented telephone; worked on iron lung, phonograph, sea-water desalination.

BELL, George Maxwell (Max), business. Regina, Sask., 1912–72. Industrialist; principal, FP Publications and sportsman.

BELL, Marilyn, sports. Toronto, Ont., 1937. First person to swim Lake Ontario (1954).

BELL, Robert Edward, science. Ladner, BC, 1918–92. Nuclear physicist; discovered proton radioactivity.

BELLOW, Saul, literary arts. Lachine, Que., 1915. Nobel Prize for Literature. *Herzog.*

BELZBERG, Samuel, business. Calgary, Alta, 1928. Financier; developed real estate financing in W Canada; founder, First City Trust.

BENNETT, Richard Bedford, first Viscount, politics. Hopewell Hill, NB, 1870–1947. Prime minister of Canada 1930–35.

BENNETT, William Andrew Cecil (W.A.C.), politics. Hastings, NB, 1900–79. Social Credit premier of BC, 1952–72.

BENNETT, William Richards, politics. Kelowna, BC, 1932. Social Credit premier of BC, 1975–86.

BENOIT, Jehane, media. Montreal, Que., 1904–87. Food expert; cookbook writer; featured on TV; authority on Cdn/Québécois cooking.

BENY, Roloff (b. Wilfred Roy), visual arts. Medicine Hat, Alta, 1924–84. Photographer; lavish travel books. *India.*

BERBICK, Trevor, sports. Jamaica, 1952. Boxer; Canadian heavyweight champion (1978–85); WBC world heavyweight champion (1986).

BERCZY, William (b. Johann Albrecht Ulrich Moll), visual arts. Germany, 1744-1813. Painter, architect; most famous for his portraits of the native leader Joseph Brant. Also designed church decorations for Christ Church Montreal, in 1903.

BERESFORD-HOWE, Constance Elizabeth, literary arts. Montreal, Que., 1922. Novelist. *Night Studies.*

BERGER, Thomas Rodney, politics. Victoria, BC, 1933. Jurist; proponent of aboriginal rights; commissioner, Mackenzie Valley Pipeline Inquiry.

BERNARDI, Mario, performing arts. Kirkland Lake, Ont., 1930. Conductor, Calgary Philharmonic.

BERNIER, Sylvie, sports. Quebec City, Que., 1964. Diver; gold medal, 3 m springboard,1984 Olympics.

BERTON, Pierre, literary arts. Whitehorse, YT, 1920. Popular historian; author and media personality. *The Last Spike.*

BESSETTE, Gerard, literary arts. Ste-Anne-de-Sabrevois, Que., 1920. Novelist, poet, literary critic. *Mes romans et moi.*

BEST, Charles Herbert, medicine. USA, 1899–1978. Physiologist; co-discoverer of insulin.

BETHUNE, Henry Norman, medicine. Gravenhurst, Ont., 1890–1939. Surgeon; hero in China, where he died helping revolutionary army.

BEY, Salome, performing arts. USA, 1938?. Singer, songwriter, actress. Noted for jazz, blues, spirituals. Wrote and starred in *Indigo,* a history of blues. *Shimmytime.*

BIG BEAR, politics. Ft. Carlton, Sask., 1825–88. Cree leader; opposed treaties on grounds they would destroy Cree way of life.

BIGELOW, Dr. Wilfred Gordon, medicine. Brandon, Man., 1913. Surgeon; developed first cardiac pacemaker.

BILLES, Alfred Jackson, business. Toronto, Ont., 1902–95. Co-founder in 1922 of Canada-wide chain Canadian Tire Corporation.

BILLES, John William, business. Toronto, Ont., 1896–1956. Original founder of Canadian Tire chain of hardware stores.

BINNS, Patrick George, politics. Weyburn, Sask., 1948. PC premier of PEI, elected 1996.

BIRDSELL, Sandra, literary arts. Hamiota, Man., 1942. Novelist who weaves domestic and feminist themes into her work. *The Missing Child; The Chrome Suite.*

BIRKS, Henry, business. Montreal, Que., 1840-1928. Silversmith who founded national jewelry chain Henry Birks and Sons, opening his first store in 1879 in Montreal.

BIRNEY, Alfred Earle, literary arts. Calgary, Alta, 1904–1995. Narrative poet and professor. *David and Other Poems.*

BISHOP, William Avery (Billy), military. Owen Sound, Ont., 1894–1956. WWI flying ace; downed 72 enemy planes.

BISSELL, Keith, performing arts. Meaford, Ont., 1912–92. Composer of choral, vocal, organ, orchestral and chamber music; folksong arrangements for piano and voice; commissioned by Lois Marshall, Charles Peaker and others.

BISSOONDATH, Neil Devindra, literary arts. Trinidad, 1955. Novelist, short story writer. *A Casual Brutality.*

BLACK, Conrad Moffat, business. Montreal, Que., 1944. Press baron; owner of Hollinger Inc. newspaper empire.

BLAIS, Marie-Claire, literary arts. Quebec City, Que., 1939. Influential novelist. *Une Saison dans la vie d'Emmanuel.*

BLAISE, Clark Lee, literary arts. USA, 1940. Writer; explorer of the displaced person. *Resident Alien.*

BLAKE, Hector "Toe", sports. Victoria Mines, Ont., 1912–95. Hockey player; coached Montreal Canadiens to eight Stanley Cups, 1955–68.

BLAKENEY, Allan Emrys, politics. Bridgewater, NS, 1925. NDP premier of Saskatchewan 1971–82.

BLISS, John William Michael, politics. Leamington, Ont., 1941. Author, history commentator. *Right Honorable Men: The Descent of Canadian Politics from Macdonald to Mulroney.*

BLOHM, Hans Ludwig, visual arts. Germany, 1927. Photographer; author of many photography books. *The Beauty of the Maritimes.*

BLONDIN-ANDREWS, Ethel, politics. Fort Norman, NWT, 1951. In 1988, first native woman elected to Parliament; for Western Arctic (Lib).

BLUMENFELD, Hans, city planner. Germany, 1892–1988. Urban planner; author. *The Modern Metropolis.*

BLYTHE, Dominic, performing arts. Eng., 1947. Actor with Stratford Festival, Ont.

BOCHNER, Lloyd, performing arts. Toronto, Ont., 1924. Character actor who has appeared in TV series *Dynasty* and *Santa Barbara* and in movies. *Naked Gun 2½.*

BODOGH, Marilyn, sports. Toronto, Ont., 1955. Curling. Two-time world champion (skip) in women's curling; member of Team Canada.

BOGGS, Jean Sutherland, visual arts. Peru, 1922. Art curator; National Gallery curator, 1966–76.

BOLDT, Arnie, sports. Osler, Sask., 1957. One-legged high jumper holds disabled world record (2.08 m).

BOLT, Carol, literary arts. Winnipeg, Man., 1941. Playwright; socially conscious writer. *One Night Stand.*

BOMBARDIER, Joseph Armand, invention. Valcourt, Que., 1908–64. Inventor; developer of snowmobiles.

BONDAR, Roberta Lynn, science. Sault Ste Marie, Ont., 1945. Astronaut; first Canadian woman in space.

BONISTEEL, Roy, media. Ameliasburg, Ont., 1930. Host of CBC television's *Man Alive* series 1967–89; early career as a radio producer for church organizations. *In Search of Man Alive.*

BORDEN, Robert Laird (Sir), politics. Grand Pré, NS, 1854–1937. Canada's prime minister throughout WWI (1911–20).

BORDUAS, Paul-Emile, visual arts. St-Hilaire, Que., 1905–60. Painter; founded Automatistes. *L'etoile noire.*

BORSOS, Phillip, performing arts. Tasmania, 1954–95. Filmmaker. *The Grey Fox* (winner of Best Picture and Best Director, 1982 Genie Awards); *Bethune.*

BOSSY, Michael, sports. Montreal, Que., 1957. Hockey player; NY Islanders winger; nine 50-goal seasons.

BOTSFORD, Sara, performing arts. Dobie, Ont., 1952. Stage, film and TV actress. *Bay Boy; E.N.G.*

BOTTERELL, Edmund Henry, science. Vancouver, BC, 1906–97. Neurosurgeon who initiated program into spinal chord injury research; during WWII devoted to rehabilitation of veterans.

BOUCHARD, Lucien, politics. St-Coeur-de-Marie, Que., 1938. Founder and leader of Bloc Québécois; leader of Parti Québécois; premier of Quebec, 1996–.

BOUCHER, Gaetan, sports. Charlesbourg, Que., 1958. Speedskater; two gold medals (1000 m,1500 m) and a bronze medal (500 m) 1984 Winter Olympics.

BOUEY, Gerald Keith, business. Axford, Sask., 1920. Banker; governor.

BOURASSA, Henri, politics. Montreal, Que., 1868–1952. Federalist; founded *Le Devoir* newspaper.

BOURASSA, Jocelyne, sports. Shawinigan-Sud, Que., 1947. Golf champion, winner of many awards, including La Canadienne 1973 LPGA event; Golf Personality of the Year, Golf Canada, 1972.

BOURASSA, Robert, politics. Montreal, Que., 1933–96. Quebec premier 1970–76, 1985–93.

BOURGEOYS, Marguerite, religion. France, 1620–1700. Religious educator; canonized, 1982.

BOURGET, Ignace, religion. Lauzon, Que., 1799–1885. Catholic bishop of Montreal; avid ultra-Montanist opposed secular Quebec.

BOURNE, Shae-Lynn, sports. Chatham, Ont., 1976. Ice dancing; with Victor Kraatz won Canadian title, 1993–96; third in World Championships, 1996.

BOURQUE, James, politics. Wandering River, Alta, 1935–96. Aboriginal activist appointed to Privy Council, 1992. Co-director of policy for Royal Commission on Aboriginal Peoples, 1994.

BOURQUE, Raymond, sports. Montreal, Que., 1960. Hockey player; Boston Bruins defenceman; four-time Norris Trophy winner.

BOWELL, Mackenzie (Sir), politics. Eng., 1823–1917. Canada's fifth prime minister (1894–96).

BOWER, John William (Johnny), sports. Prince Albert, Sask., 1924. Hockey player. Long-time goalkeeper for New York Rangers, Toronto Maple Leafs; led Leafs to four Stanley Cup wins.

BOWERING, George Harry, literary arts. Penticton, BC, 1935. Prolific poet and prose writer. "Burning Water."

BOWMAN, Scotty, sports. Montreal, Que., 1933. Hockey coach; won six Stanley Cups; five with Montreal.

BOYD, Liona, performing arts. Eng., 1950. Acclaimed classical guitarist. *The Guitar–Liona Boyd.*

BOYLE, Joseph Whiteside, exploration and discovery. Toronto, Ont., 1867–1923. Adventurer "Klondike Joe"; mining entrepreneur; national hero in Romania.

BOYLE, Willard S., invention. Amherst, NS, 1924. Physicist who co-invented the charge-coupled device for camcorders and telescopes.

BRACKEN, John, politics. Ellisville, Ont., 1883–1969. Cons. Manitoba premier 1922–42.

BRAITHWAITE, Max, literary arts. Nokomis, Sask., 1911–95. Prairie novelist noted for autobiographical novel *Why Shoot the Teacher?*

BRAND, Oscar, performing arts. Winnipeg, Man., 1920. Folksinger; recorded 80 albums; author folk song collections. *Squid Jiggin' Ground.*

BRANT, Joseph (b. Thayendanegea), politics/religion. USA, 1742–1807. Mohawk leader; British loyalist during American Revolution; translated Bible into Mohawk.

BRASSARD, Jean-Luc, sports. Valleyfield, Que., 1972. Skier; gold medal moguls 1994 Olympics.

BRASSEUR, Isabelle, sports. Kingsbury, Que., 1970. Skater; with Lloyd Eisler won 1993 pairs world title, two Olympic bronze medals (1992).

BRAULT, Jacques, literary arts. Montreal, Que., 1933. Poet; playwright; novelist. *Agonie.*

BREAU, Lenny, performing arts. USA, 1941–84. Guitarist, singer, composer of jazz, country, folk and pop; aired on CBC radio in 1940s and 1950s.

BREBEUF, Jean de, religion. France, 1593–1649. Jesuit martyr; missionary at Sainte Marie among the Hurons.

BRILL, Debbie, sports. Mission, BC, 1953. High jumper; originated "Brill bend" jumping style.

BRITTAIN, Donald, visual arts. Ottawa, Ont., 1928–89. Documentary filmmaker. *On Guard for Thee.*

BROADBENT, John Edward (Ed), politics. Oshawa, Ont., 1936. National leader, NDP 1975–89.

BROADFOOT, Dave, performing arts. Toronto, Ont., 1925. Comedian; Sergeant Renfrew character on *Royal Canadian Air Farce.*

BROCK, Isaac (Sir), military. Eng., 1769–1812. Soldier; War of 1812 hero; died at Queenston Heights.

BROCKHOUSE, Bertram Neville, science. Lethbridge, Alta, 1918. Pioneer of use of thermal neutrons to study aspects of behaviour of condensed matter systems at atomic level. Won 1994 Nobel Prize for physics.

BRONFMAN, Charles Rosner, business. Montreal, Que., 1931. Industrialist; chairman, Cemp Investments Ltd; former owner, Montreal Expos.

BRONFMAN, Edgar M., business. Montreal, Que., 1929. Industrialist; CEO, Seagram's Ltd; president, World Jewish Congress.

BRONFMAN, Samuel, business. Brandon, Man., 1891–1971. Capitalist; distiller (Seagram Co. Ltd) and philanthropist.

BROSSARD, Nicole, literary arts. Montreal, Que., 1943. Formalist poet. "Mecanique jongleuse suivi de masculin grammaticale."

BROWN, Arthur Royal "Roy", military. Carleton Place, Ont., 1893–1944. On April 21, 1918, shot down Germany's Red Baron, Manfred von Richthofen.

BROWN, George, media/politics. Scot., 1818–80. Journalist; founded *Toronto Globe* (1844); as Reformer, played major role in Confederation.

BROWN, John George "Kootenai", exploration and discovery. Ire., 1839–1916. Adventurer; army official; prospector; whisky trader; established Waterton Lakes Natl Park.

BROWN, Rosemary, politics. Jamaica, 1930. Activist; head, Ontario Human Rights Assn; former NDP leadership candidate.

BROWNING, Kurt, sports. Rocky Mountain House, Alta, 1966. World figure skating champion, 1989–91, 1993.

BRUHN, Erik Belton Evers, performing arts. Denmark, 1928–86. Dancer; choreographer; guiding figure for National Ballet.

BRULE, Etienne, exploration and discovery. France, 1592–1633. Explorer; first known European to reach Lake Superior.

BRZOZOWICZ, Czelaw Peter, engineering. Poland, 1911–97. Structural engineer consulted on Toronto's original subway line, Niagara Falls Skylon Tower and CN Tower in Toronto.

BUCHAN, John, first Baron Tweedsmuir, literary arts. Scot., 1875–1940. Thriller novelist, wrote *The 39 Steps*; governor general, 1935–40.

BUCHANAN, John MacLennan, politics. Sydney, NS, 1931. Conservative premier of NS.

BUCK, Tim, politics. Eng., 1891–1973. Radical politician; led Canadian Commmunist Party, 1929–61.

BUCKE, Richard Maurice, medicine. Eng., 1837–1902. Physician; writer; advocate for the mentally ill; spiritual writer. *Cosmic Consciousness.*

BUCZYNSKI, Walter, performing arts. Toronto, Ont., 1933. Pianist and composer of orchestral, chamber, vocal and piano music; soloist internationally in 1960s and 1970s. *Songs of War, Ressurrection II.*

BUJOLD, Geneviève, performing arts. Montreal, Que., 1942. Actress; international star. *Dead Ringers.*

BULL, Gerald Vincent, invention. North Bay, Ont., 1928–90. Inventor; weapons designer; murdered mysteriously.

BURKA, Petra, sports. Holland, 1946. Figure skater; women's world champion, 1965.

BURNARD, Bonnie, literary arts. Petrolia, Ont., 1945. Novelist; her *A Good House* won the 1999 Giller Prize. *Women of Influence,* short stories.

BURNS, Tommy (b. Noah Brusso), sports. Hanover, Ont., 1881–1955. Boxer; world heavyweight champion, 1906–08.

BURR, Raymond William Stacy, performing arts. New Westminster, BC, 1917–93. Actor; TV's Perry Mason, 1957–66, 1985–93.

BURROUGHS, Jackie, performing arts. Eng., 1942. Actress; versatile performer; Hetty in *Road to Avonlea.*

BUSH, John Hamilton (Jack), visual arts. Toronto, Ont., 1909–77. Abstract artist. "Bridge Passage."

BUTALA, Sharon Annette, literary arts. Nipawin, Sask., 1940. Novelist, short story writer, playwright. *Coming Attractions; The Fourth Archangel.*

BUTCHART, Robert Pim, business. Owen Sound, Ont., 1856-1943. In 1888 founded Owen Sound Portalnd Cement Co.; later turned quarries in Victoria, BC, into famed Butchart Gardens.

BY, John, military. Eng., 1779–1836. Engineer; built Rideau Canal, Quebec fortifications.

BYNG, Julian Hedworth George, first Viscount, military. Eng., 1862–1935. Soldier; governor general, 1921–26.

C

CABOT, John (b. Giovanni Caboto), exploration and discovery. Italy, c. 1450–99. First N American landing since the Vikings.

CABOT, Sebastian, performing arts. Eng., 1918–76. Portly, bearded character actor in film and television. *The Captain's Paradise, The Beachcombers, Family Affair.*

CAIN, Larry, sports. Toronto, Ont., 1963. Canoeist; gold (500 m) and silver (1000 m) medals, 1984 Olympics.

CALDER, Frank Arthur, politics. Nass Harbour, BC, 1915. Native politician; Nishga leader; BC MLA.

CALDWELL, Zoe, performing arts. Australia, 1933. Actor, director. *The Prime of Miss Jean Brodie.*

CALLAGHAN, Barry, literary arts. Toronto, Ont., 1937. Founder of *Exile: A Literary Quarterly*; novelist, journalist; son of Morley Callaghan.

CALLAGHAN, Morley Edward, literary arts. Toronto, Ont., 1903–90. Novelist; memoirist. *The Loved and the Lost.*

CALLBECK, Catherine, politics. Central Bedeque, PEI, 1939. First woman to be elected premier. Liberal premier of PEI 1993–96.

CALLUM, Keith Rennie, performing arts. England, 1960. Actor noted for role as Stanley Raymond Kowalski in CBC Mountie comedy/drama *Due South;* also appeared in movies *My Life as a Dog; Hard Core Logo;* and in TV series *The X-Files.*

CALLWOOD, June, public service. Chatham, Ont., 1924. Journalist; civil libertarian, AIDS activist.

CAMERON, Elspeth MacGregor, literary arts. Toronto, Ont., 1943. Biographer. *Robertson Davies: An Appreciation; Hugh MacLennan: A Writer's Life; Irving Layton: A Portrait.*

CAMERON, James, literary arts. Eng., 1910. Philosopher; essayist; poet. "Images of Authority."

CAMERON, James, performing arts. Kapuskasing, Ont., 1954. Hollywood-based director of action movies including *Terminator* series, *Aliens, True Lies, Titanic.*

CAMERON, Michelle, sports. Calgary, Alta, 1962. Gold medalist in sychronized swimming with Carolyn Waldo, 1988 Olympics.

CAMERON, Silver Donald, literary arts. Toronto, Ont., 1937. Novelist, critic, editor, playwright. *Dragon Lady; Wind, Whales and Whisky: A Cape Breton Voyage.*

CAMERON, Thomas Wright Moir, medicine. Scot., 1894–1947. Parasitologist; pioneered study of parasitic worms.

CAMP, Dalton Kingsley, politics. Woodstock, NB, 1920. PC consultant; newspaper columnist.

CAMPBELL, Alexander (Sir), politics. Eng., 1822–92. Tory leader; Father of Confederation.

CAMPBELL, Avril Phaedra "Kim", politics. Port Alberni, BC, 1947. First woman prime minister of Canada, June 1993–December 1993.

CAMPBELL, Clarence, sports. Fleming, Sask., 1905–84. Sports administrator; headed NHL, 1946–77.

CAMPBELL, Douglas, performing arts. Scot., 1922. Actor at Stratford Festival, Ont. Co-founder of Canadian Players.

CAMPBELL, Neve, performing arts. Guelph, Ont., 1973. Actress/dancer noted for role in Canadian TV series *Catwalk;* appeared in the US TV series *Party of 5;* also films *The Craft;* and the cult hit *Scream.*

CAMPBELL, Nicholas, performing arts. Toronto, Ont., 1952. Versatile actor, screenwriter, director; star of CBC's *DaVinci's Inquest;* also film *The Omen;* and TV production of *Come Back Little Sheba.*

CAMPBELL, Norman Kenneth, performing arts. USA, 1924. Music producer; innovative developer of ballet and musicals.

CAMPEAU, Robert, business. Sudbury, Ont., 1923. Financier; exemplar of 1980s expansionist business mania; developer; retail store magnate.

CANDY, John Franklin, performing arts. Toronto, Ont., 1950–94. Actor; comedian; bearish *SCTV* regular (Johnny LaRue, William B.); film star. *Uncle Buck.*

CARDINAL, Douglas Joseph, visual arts. Red Deer, Alta, 1934. Métis architect; Canadian Museum of Civilization.

CARDINAL, Tantoo, performing arts. Fort McMurray, Alta, 1951. Native actress who has appeared in films, *Big Bear, Smoke Signals, Black Robe* and CBC's *North of 60.*

CARIOU, Len, performing arts. St Boniface Man., 1939. Theatre director and actor; associated with Manitoba Theatre Centre; Stratford Festival, Ont.; and in England and US. Tony Award for Stephen Sondheim's *Sweeney Todd* in New York, 1979.

CARLE, Gilles, visual arts. Maniwaki, Que., 1929. Film director. *La Vrai Nature de Bernadette.*

CARLETON, Guy (Sir), first Baron Dorchester, politics. Ire., 1724–1808. Quebec governor, 1768–78, 1785–95; supporter of French traditions.

CARMAN, William Bliss, literary arts. Fredericton, NB, 1861–1929. Poet; journalist. "The Pipes of Pan."

CARMICHAEL, Franklin, visual arts. Orillia, Ont., 1890–1945. Group of Seven founding member.

CARR, Emily, visual arts. Victoria, BC, 1871–1945. Painter of NW coastal Indians and nature.

CARR, Shirley, politics. Niagara Falls, Ont., First Woman to lead CUPE, Canada's largest union. President Emeritus, Canadian Labour Congress.

CARREY, James (Jim), performing arts. Jackson's Point, Ont., 1962. Comedic actor. *Ace Ventura; The Mask; Batman Forever.*

CARRIER, Roch, literary arts. Beauce, Que., 1937. Novelist; playwright. *La Guerre, Yes Sir!*

CARSON, John Elmer (Jack), performing arts. Carman, Man., 1910–63. Square-jawed film actor. *Mildred Pierce.*

CARTER, Emmett (Cardinal), religion. Montreal, Que., 1912. As Toronto Cardinal, helped get full funding for Catholic schools.

CARTER, Wilf, performing arts. Port Hilford, NS, 1904–96. Singer; father of Canadian country music.

CARTIER, Georges-Etienne (Sir), politics. St Antoine, UC, 1814–73. Father of Confederation; joint premier of United Canada, 1857–62.

CARTIER, Jacques, exploration and discovery. France, 1491–1557. Credited with European discovery of Canada; first explorer of St. Lawrence River.

CARVER, Humphrey Stephen Mumford, politics. Eng., 1902–95. Key figure in Central Mortgage and Housing Corporation 1950s–60s; formed Co-operative Commonwealth Federation, forerunner of NDP.

CASGRAIN, Thérèse, politics. Montreal, Que., 1896–1981. Won Quebec women the right to vote (1940) and hold provincial office; leader of Quebec's CCF party in 1951.

CASSON, Alfred Joseph (A.J.), visual arts. Toronto, Ont., 1898–1992. Member, Group of Seven. "Country Store."

CATHERWOOD, Ethel, sports. Haldimand Cty, Ont., 1909. High jumper; gold in high jump, 1928 Olympics.

CAVOUKIAN, Artin and Lucie, visual arts. Egypt, Armenia, 1915–95, 1923–95. Clientele of photographer Artin with wife Lucie included world leaders.

CHALMERS, Floyd Sherman, public service. USA, 1898–1993. Instituted Floyd S. Chalmers Foundation funding for arts in Canada.

CHAMPLAIN, Samuel de, exploration and discovery. France, 1567–1635. Explorer; important cartographer/geographer; "Father of New France."

CHANG, Simon, business. China, 1950. Fashion designer; also branched into fragrances, accessories, uniforms for restaurants and salon design.

CHANG, Thomas Ming Sui, medicine/science. China, 1933. Physiologist; expert on artificial cells and organs.

CHAPMAN, John Herbert, science. London, Ont., 1921–79. Physicist; lead role in Canada's satellite program.

CHAPUT-ROLLAND, Solange, media. Montreal, Que., 1919. Writer; broadcaster; Québécoise federalist.

CHAREST, Jean J., politics. Sherbrooke, Que., 1958. Led PC rump after '93 federal electoral debacle.

CHARLEBOIS, Robert, performing arts. Montreal, Que., 1945. Singer/songwriter. "Solidaritude."

CHARLEVOIX, Pierre François Xavier de, literary arts. France, 1682–1761. Historian; first complete history of New France.

CHAYKIN, Maury, performing arts. USA, 1949. Prolific actor has appeared in *Jacob Two-Two Meets the Hooded Fang; Dances With Wolves.*

CHEE CHEE, Benjamin (b. Kenneth Thomas Benjamin), visual arts. Temagami, Ont., 1944-77. Ojibwa artist; block-stamped abstract and animal, bird images; noted for use of movement and humour.

CHERRY, Don, sports. Kingston, Ont., 1934. Hockey coach; commentator; feisty nationalist.

CHERRY, Zena, media. Prince Albert, Sask., 1915-2000. Longtime social columnist for Toronto's *Globe and Mail.* "After a Fashion."

CHEVALIER, Leo, business. Montreal, Que., 1934-2000. Fashion designer of international lines.

CHIPMAN, Ward, law. St John, NB, 1787–1851. Jurist; chief justice of NB; noted abolitionist.

CHIRAEFF, Ludmilla, performing arts. Latvia, 1924. Choreographer; founder, Les Grands Ballets Canadiennes.

CHISHOLM, George Brock, medicine. Oakville, Ont., 1896–1971. Psychiatrist; early opponent of pollution, nuclear arms; first head of World Health Org.

CHONG, Rae Dawn, performing arts. Vancouver, BC, 1962. Film actress. *Quest for Fire.*

CHONG, Thomas (Tommy), performing arts. Edmonton, Alta, 1938. Actor; half of Cheech and Chong comedy team. *Cheech and Chong's Nice Dreams.*

CHOUART DES GROSEILLIERS, Medard, exploration and discovery. France, 1618–90. Explorer; fur trader; with Radisson opened western fur trade.

CHOUINARD, Josée, sports. Rosemont, Que., 1969. Three-time Canadian figure skating champion.

CHRETIEN, Joseph Jacques Jean, politics. Shawinigan, Que., 1934. Became prime minister of Canada, general election 1993.

CHRISTENSEN, Hayden, performing arts. Vancouver, BC, 1981. Actor; has gained new role in *Star Wars* series as the young Anakin Skywalker. *Higher Ground.*

CHRISTIE, Robert Wallace, performing arts. Toronto, Ont., 1920–96. Played at Ontario's Stratford Festival; Old Vic in London, Eng.; famous for portrayal of John A. MacDonald.

CHRISTIE, William Mellis, business. Scot., 1829–1900. Biscuit manufacturer; Christie Biscuits founder.

CHUVALO, George, sports. Toronto, Ont., 1937. Boxer; fought three world champions; never knocked down. Anti-drug crusader.

CLAIR, Frank, sports. USA, 1917. Football coach; 174 wins (Ottawa Rough Riders) tops CFL coaches.

CLANCY, Francis Michael "King", sports. Ottawa, Ont., 1903–86. Hockey player; defenceman, Ottawa Senators, Toronto Maple Leafs; lively raconteur.

CLARK, Charles Joseph (Joe), politics. High River, Alta, 1939. Prime minister of Canada 1979–80. Leader of Federal Progressive Conservative Party, 1998—.

CLARK, Greg, literary arts. Toronto, Ont., 1892–1977. Journalist and humorist, winner of Leacock Award for Humour.

CLARK, Susan, performing arts. Sarnia, Ont., 1940. Actress who has appeared in Hollywood movies, television. *Murder by Decree; Coogan's Bluff; Webster.*

CLARK, Wayne, business. Drumheller, Alta, 1949. Canadian fashion designer noted for his dramataic evening wear and high-quality sportswear.

CLARKE, Austin Chesterfield, literary arts. Barbados, 1934. Novelist, short story writer. *Proud Empires; Nine Men Who Laughed.*

CLARKSON, Adrienne Louise, media/politics. Hong Kong, 1939. Broadcaster; long-time CBC host. *Take Thirty.* Appointed governor-general of Canada, 1999.

CLAYTON-THOMAS, David, performing arts. Eng., 1941. Singer; member, Blood, Sweat and Tears. *Spinning Wheel.*

COCHRANE, Tom, performing arts. Lynn Lake, Man., 1953. Singer, songwriter, guitarist. Led Toronto-based quintet, Tom Cochrane and Red Rider, formed in 1976. *Breaking Curfew.* Went solo in 1991 with *Mad, Mad World.* "Life is a Highway."

COCKBURN, Bruce, performing arts. Ottawa, Ont., 1945. Singer/songwriter; politically conscious performer. *Dancing in the Dragon's Jaws.*

COE-JONES, Dawn, sports. Lake Cowichan, BC, 1961. Golfer; leading pro; 1993 LPGA title.

COHEN, Leonard, literary arts/performing arts. Montreal, Que., 1934. Poet; singer. *Flowers for Hitler, I'm Your Man.*

COHEN, Matt, literary arts. Kingston, Ont., 1942-2000. Short story writer, novelist, translator. *The Colour of War; Living on Water; Freud: The Paris Notebooks.*

COHEN, Morris (Moishe) Abraham "Two-Gun", military. Eng., 1889–1970. China hand; confidant of Sun Yat-sen; general in Chinese army.

COHEN, Samuel Nathan, literary arts. Sydney, NS, 1923–71. Critic; Canada's first serious drama critic.

COHON, George, business. USA, 1937. CEO, Cdn McDonald's restaurants; philanthropist.

COLDWELL, James William (Major), politics. Eng., 1888–1974. CCF founder; leader, 1942–60.

COLE, Holly, performing arts. Halifax, NS, 1963. Jazz/pop singer with distinctive contralto voice; founder of the Holly Cole Trio. *Don't Smoke in Bed; Christmas Blues; Dear Dark Heart.*

COLE, Jack, business. Toronto, Ont., 1920–97. With brother Carl started Coles chain of bookstores in Toronto, which later became national; created Coles Notes, study booklets for students, in 1947.

COLEMAN, Kathleen Blake (Kit), media. Toronto, Ont., 1864–1915. First woman war correspondent.

COLICOS, John, performing arts. Toronto, Ont., 1928-2000. Stage actor; Stratford Festival regular.

COLLIP, James Bertram, medicine. Belleville, Ont., 1892–1965. Biochemist; co-discoverer of insulin.

COLOMBO, John Robert, literary arts. Kitchener, Ont., 1936. Anthologist; prolific compiler of reference books. *Colombo's Canadian Quotations.*

Canadian Hall of Fame 667

COLVILLE, Alexander, visual arts. Toronto, Ont., 1920. Realistic painter; designed centennial coins.

COMFORT, Charles Fraser, visual arts. Scot., 1900–94. Artist, graphic designer, created murals for Toronto Stock Exchange; director of National Gallery of Canada 1960–65.

CONACHER, Lionel Pretoria, sports. Toronto, Ont., 1901–54. Canada's Athlete of the Half-Century (1900–1950).

CONNOR, Ralph (b. Charles William Gordon), literary arts. West Indian Lands, Glengarry County, Canada West 1860–1937. Popular novelist, preacher of "red-blooded" Christianity. *The Sky Pilot.*

CONNORS, Charles Thomas "Stompin' Tom", performing arts. Saint John, NB, 1936. Country singer; nationalist performer. *Across This Land with Stompin' Tom.*

COOK, George Ramsay, literary arts. Alameda, Sask., 1931. Prolific historian. *Canada: A Modern Study; The Maple Leaf Forever.*

COOK, James, exploration and discovery. Eng., 1728–79. Navigator; explored Newfoundland and Northwest coasts.

COOKE, Jack Kent, business. Hamilton, Ont., 1912–97. Capitalist; flamboyant owner of newspapers, radio stations, sports teams (Washington Redskins).

COOMBS, Ernest Arthur (Ernie), performing arts. USA, 1927. Children's entertainer; CBC's "Mr. Dressup."

COPP, Harold, science. Toronto, Ont., 1915. Physiologist; discovered calcitonon, hormone that regulates calcium in blood.

COPPS, Sheila Maureen, politics. Hamilton, Ont., 1952. Liberal deputy prime minister.

CORMIER, Ernest, visual arts. Montreal, Que., 1885–1980. Architect; designed University of Montreal.

CORRIGAL, Jim, sports. Barrie, Ont., 1946. Football player. Lineman with Toronto Argonauts 1970–81; four-time CFL all-star.

COSENTINO, Frank, sports. Hamilton, Ont., 1937. Football player; CFL quarterback, 1960–69; sports history writer; prof., physical education.

COSTAIN, Thomas Bertram, literary arts. Brantford, Ont., 1885–1965. Historical novelist. *High Towers.*

COUGHTRY, Graham, visual arts. St Lambert, Que., 1931–99. Abstract figurative painter; exhibited in New York's Guggenheim Museum, Museum of Modern Art, as well as across Canada.

COULTHARD, Jean, performing arts. Vancouver, BC, 1908. Composer. "The Pines of Emily Carr."

COUPLAND, Douglas Campbell, literary arts. Germany, 1961. Novelist; humorist. *Generation X.*

COURNOYEA, Nellie J., politics. Aklavik, NWT, 1940. First woman aboriginal leader of Northwest Territories.

COWAN, Garry, sports. Kitchener, Ont., 1938. Golfer; twice US amateur champion (1966, 1971).

CRANSTON, Toller, sports. Hamilton, Ont., 1949. Skater; brought innovation and artistry to men's figure skating.

CRAWLEY, Frank Radford "Budge", visual arts. Ottawa, Ont., 1911–87. Film producer. *The Rowdyman.*

CREIGHTON, Donald Grant, literary arts. Toronto, Ont., 1902–79. Historian; developed literary side of history.

CREMAZIE, Claude Joseph Olivier "Octave", literary arts. Quebec City, Que., 1827–79. Father of French Canadian poetry. "Le Drapeau de Carillon."

CREMO, Lee, performing arts. Cape Breton, NS, 1939–99. Six-time winner of Maritime Old-Time Fiddling Contest; mix of Irish, Scottish, Mi'kmaq Indian music; winner of Canadian title at Alberta Tar Sands Competition.

CROLL, David Arnold, politics. Russia, 1900–91. Liberal MLA in 1934; first Jewish cabinet minister (1955).

CROMBIE, David Edward, politics. Toronto, Ont., 1936. Civic reformer; Toronto mayor 1973–78.

CRONENBERG, David, visual arts. Toronto, Ont., 1943. Film director; inventive horror; science fiction filmmaker. *Videodrome, Crash.*

CRONYN, Hume (b. Hume Blake), performing arts. London, Ont., 1911. Stage actor; film character player. *Cocoon.*

CROSBIE, John Carnell, politics. St John's, Nfld. 1931. PC minister of fisheries and oceans; international trade; justice.

CROTHERS, William, sports. Markham, Ont., 1940. Runner; silver medal (800 m), 1964 Olympics.

CROW, John William, business. Eng., 1937. Economist; governor of Bank of Canada, 1987–94.

CROWFOOT, military. Belly R, Alta, 1830–90. Blackfoot chief, diplomat.

CUDDY, James Gordon (Jim), performing arts. Toronto, Ont., 1955. Lead singer for rock group Blue Rodeo.

CUMMINGS, Burton, performing arts. Winnipeg, Man., 1947. Rock singer; lead singer, The Guess Who; later solo artist. *My Own Way to Rock.*

CUNARD, Samuel (Sir), business. Halifax, NS, 1787–1865. Shipowner; founded Cunard Line forerunner.

CURNOE, Gregory Richard, visual arts. London, Ont., 1936–92. Fine artist whose paintings often incorporated written words; also created collages, drawings, prints.

CURRIE, Arthur William (Sir), military. Strathroy, Ont., 1875–1933. Commander, Canadian corps, WWI.

CURRIE, Philip, science. Toronto, Ont., 1948. Curator of dinosaurs for Alberta's Royal Tyrrel Museum in Drumheller and world leader in paleontology; recently discovered a feathered dinosaur that proved birds were dinosaurs.

CURTOLA, Robert Allen (Bobby), performing arts. Thunder Bay, Ont., 1944. Singer; early teen idol. "Fortune Teller."

CYR, Louis, sports. Napierville, Que., 1863–1912. World's strongest man, 1880–1990.

DAFOE, Allan Roy, medicine. Madoc, Ont., 1883–1943. Small-town physician who delivered the Dionne quintuplets, 28 May 1934; later faced accusations of exploiting the sisters.

DAFOE, John Wesley, media. Combermere, Ont., 1866–1944. Journalist; influential editor, *Winnipeg Free Press.*

DAIR, Carl, visual arts. Welland, Ont., 1912–67. Internationally recognized designer, topographer; created Cartier, first modern Canadian typeface. *Design with Type.*

DALE, Cynthia, performing arts. Toronto, Ont., 1961. Actress known for roles in TV series *Street Legal; Taking the Falls.* Also movie *Moonstruck.*

DANBY, Kenneth Edison (Ken), visual arts. Sault Ste Marie, Ont., 1940. Painter of realistic sports figures.

DANKO, Rick, performing arts. Simcoe, Ont., 1943-99. Founder and vocal/bass member of folk, blues, rock group The Band, subject of director Martin Scorcese's film *The Last Waltz*.

DAUDELIN, Robert, performing arts. West Shefford, Que., 1939. Film administrator; writer; producer; director. Founder of movie critic magazine *Objectif*; International Film Festival in Montreal; director of Cinémathèque québécoise.

DAVEY, Keith, politics. Toronto, Ont., 1926. Long-time Liberal Party strategist.

DAVIES, Robertson William, literary arts. Thamesville, Ont., 1913-95. Novelist, playwright. *Fifth Business*.

DAVIS, Andrew, performing arts. Eng., 1944. Conductor of Toronto Symphony Orchestra 1975-88; participated in 1978 TSO visit to People's Republic of China.

DAVIS, Donald, performing arts. Newmarket, Ont., 1928-98. Distinguished Shakespearean actor, played Ontario's Stratford Festival; also appeared in TV roles: *Mission Impossible*. Co-founder of Toronto's Crest Theatre.

DAVIS, Fred, media. Toronto, Ont., 1921-96. Broadcaster and host of long-running CBC panel show "Front Page Challenge" (1957-95).

DAVIS, Victor, sports. Guelph, Ont., 1964-89. Swimmer; three medals 1984 Olympics; gold in 200 m breaststroke.

DAVIS, Warren, performing arts. Peterborough, Ont., 1926-95. CBC newsman. *The National; This Hour Has Seven Days*.

DAVIS, William Grenville, politics. Brampton, Ont., 1929. PC premier of Ontario, 1971-85.

DAWSON, George Mercer, science. Pictou, NS, 1849-1901. Geologist; surveyed much of northern and western Canada.

DAWSON, John William (Sir), science. Pictou, NS, 1820-99. Geologist; made McGill a leading university; founded Royal Society of Canada.

DAY, James, sports. Thornhill, Ont., 1946. Equestrian; team gold medal, 1968 Olympics.

DAY, Stockwell, politics. Barrie, Ont., 1950. Former provincial treasurer for Alberta; Canadian Alliance Reform Party leadership contender.

DE CARLO, Yvonne (b. Peggy Yvonne Middleton), performing arts. Vancouver, BC, 1924. Actress; film/TV star. *The Munsters*.

DE LA ROCHE, Mazo (b. Maisie Roche), literary arts. Newmarket, Ont., 1879-1961. Prolific popular novelist. *Jalna*.

de VILLIERS, Priscilla, politics. Pretoria, S. Africa, 1942. Activist and founder of CAVEAT, Canadians Against Violence Everywhere Advocating Its Termination.

DEL GRANDE, Louis, performing arts. USA, 1942. Actor, producer, writer. Starred in CBC TV series *Seeing Things*.

DENNYS, Louise, literary arts. Egypt, 1948. Vice-president and publisher at Knopf Canada.

DEPOE, Norman Reade, media. USA, 1917-80. CBC's Ottawa correspondent in the 1960s, Depoe was respected for his high standards in both national and international reporting during his career; also helped build CBC network in the 1950s.

DESCHENES, Jules, law. Montreal, Que., 1923-2000. Jurist; Que. chief justice; chairman, Inquiry of War Criminals in Canada.

DESJARDINS, Alphonse, business. Lévis, Que., 1854-1920. Banker; established first Caisse populaire (credit union) in 1900.

DESMARAIS, Paul, business. Sudbury, Ont., 1927. Industrialist; chairman of Power Corp., controlling trust, insurance and paper companies.

DESMOND, Trudy, performing arts. USA, 1946-99. Ballad and jazz singer, appeared in 1970 revue Spring Thaw. *My One and Only Love,* a tribute to Gershwin.

DEWAR, Marion, politics. Montreal, Que., 1928. Mayor, Ottawa, 1978-85; NDP MP.

DEWDNEY, Christopher, literary arts. London, Ont., 1951. Eclectic poet. *The Immaculate Perception: The Recent Artifacts from the Institute of Applied Fiction*.

DEWHURST, Colleen, performing arts. Montreal, Que., 1926-91. Actress who cultivated an earth-mother persona; noted for TV and film roles and performances in Albee and O'Neill plays. *Annie Hall; Murphy Brown*.

DIAMOND, Abel Joseph (Jack), visual arts. South Africa, 1932. Leading architect; designed Toronto's central YMCA; York University (Toronto) Student Centre; Jerusalem City Hall; Burns Building, Calgary.

DICKENS, Francis Jeffrey, military. Eng., 1844-86. Policeman; novelist's son; inspector in NWMP.

DICKINS, Clennell Haggerston "Punch", exploration and discovery. Portage la Prairie, Man., 1899-1995. Adventurer. First to fly length of MacKenzie River and above Arctic Circle.

DICKINSON, Peter Allgood Rastall, visual arts. England, 1925-61. International style architect responsible for postwar development: Benvenuto Apartments, Prudential Building (Toronto); CIBC, Windsor Plaza (Montreal).

DICKSON, Robert George Brian, law. Yorkton, Sask., 1916-98. Chief justice of Canada, 1984-90.

DIEFENBAKER, John George, politics. Neustadt, Ont., 1895-1979. Prime minister of Canada 1957-63. (PC)

DION, Celine, performing arts. Montreal, Que., 1968. Popular Quebec chanteuse. "Unison."

DION, Stéphane, politics. Quebec City, Que., 1955. Political scientist; Liberal Minister of Intergovernmental Affairs 1996–.

DIONNE, Marcel, sports. Drummondville, Que., 1951. Hockey player; centre; 731 goals, third all-time.

DIONNE sisters, medicine. Corbeil, Ont., 1934. Annette, Emilie (d. 1954), Yvonne, Cecile and Marie (d. 1970), identical quintuplets born to poor rural family, became tourist attraction through government exploitation.

DMYTRYK, Edward, visual arts. Grand Forks, BC, 1908-99. Film director; film noir specialist. One of Hollywood Ten during McCarthy era. *Detour*.

DOBBS, Kildare Robert Eric, literary arts. India, 1923. Short story writer, essayist. *Coastal Canada; Historic Canada*.

DOER, Gary, politics. Winnipeg, Man., 1948. NDP premier of Manitoba, elected in 1999.

DOHERTY, Denny, performing arts. Halifax, NS, 1941. Pop singer; founding member, The Mamas and the Papas.

DONKIN, Eric Albert, performing arts. Eng., 1930-98. Classical actor who played 26 seasons at Ontario's Stratford Festival.

DOOHAN, James Montgomery, performing arts. Vancouver, BC, 1920. Actor; played Scotty (Lt. Commander Montgomery "Scotty" Scott) in *Star Trek* series.

DOSANJH, Ujjal, politics. India, 1947. NDP premier of BC, elected 2000.

DOUGHTY, Arthur George (Sir), archivist. Eng., 1860–1936. Established Public Archives of Canada.

DOUGLAS, James (Sir), politics. British Guiana, 1803–77. Administrator; governor of BC, 1858–64.

DOUGLAS, Robert John Wilson, science. Southampton, Ont., 1920. Geologist; famous for geographical survey of structure of Rockies and foothills of southern Alberta.

DOUGLAS, Thomas Clement (Tommy), politics. Scot., 1904–86. Eloquent socialist; Sask. premier, 1944–61; NDP federal leader, 1961–71.

DRABINSKY, Garth Howard, performing arts. Toronto, Ont., 1948. Impresario; Cineplex founder, theatrical producer. *Show Boat.*

DRAPEAU, Jean, politics. Montreal, Que., 1916–99. Montreal mayor for 29 years; brought city Expo 67, 1976 Olympics, Montreal Expos.

DRESSLER, Marie (b. Leila von Koerber), performing arts. Cobourg, Ont., 1869–1934. Actress; oversize film star. *Min and Bill.*

DRYDEN, Kenneth Wayne, sports. Hamilton, Ont., 1947. Hockey goaltender; six-time all-star for Montreal; also lawyer and writer. *The Game.*

DUCKWORTH, Henry Edmison, science. Brandon, Man., 1915. With associates constructed highy accurate mass spectrometers for determination of atomic masses.

DUDEK, Louis, literary arts. Montreal, Que., 1918. Socially aware poet; critic. "East of the City."

DUGUID, Don, sports. Winnipeg, Man., 1935. Curler; Canadian and world champion, 1970, 1971.

DUMONT, Fernand, politics. Montmorency, Que., 1927–97. Quebec sovereigntist named deputy minister of cultural development for PQ in 1976; drafter of Bill 101, French Language Charter.

DUMONT, Gabriel, military. Red River, Sask., 1837–1906. Métis leader; guerrilla leader in NW Rebellion.

DUNNING, George, performing arts. Toronto, Ont., 1920. Animator and director; creator of Beatles *Yellow Submarine* film animation.

DUPLESSIS, Maurice Le Noblet, politics. Trois-Rivières, Que., 1890–1959. Powerful premier of Quebec, 1936–39, 1944–59.

DURBIN, Deanna (b. Edna Mae Durbin), performing arts. Winnipeg, Man., 1921. Actress; singer; teenage movie star. *3 Smart Girls.*

DURELLE, Yvon, sports. Baie Ste Anne, Que., 1929. Canadian middleweight boxing title 1953; light heavyweight 1953–54; British empire light heavyweight champion 1957.

DURHAM, John George Lambton, first Earl of, politics. Eng., 1792–1840. Statesman; "Radical Jack" urged union of English and French Canada.

DURNAN, William Arnold (Bill), sports. Toronto, Ont., 1915–72. Hockey goaltender; six-time Vezina Trophy winner for Montreal Canadiens.

DUTOIT, Charles Edouard, performing arts. Switz., 1936. Conductor of Montreal Symphony Orchestra.

DWAN, Allan, visual arts. Toronto, Ont., 1885–1981. Film director from silent era, made over 200 Hollywood films. *Sands of Iwo Jima.*

EATON, Cyrus Stephen, business. Pugwash, NS, 1883–1979. Financier; promoter of international peace.

EATON, Fredrik Stefan, business. Toronto, Ont., 1938. Retailer; former chairman, T. Eaton Co.

EATON, Timothy, business. Ire., 1834–1907. Retailer; innovative founder of T. Eaton Co. in 1867.

EDWARDS, Robert Chambers (Bob), media. Scot., 1864–1922. Journalist; published satirical *Calgary Eye Opener.*

EGOYAN, Atom, visual arts. Egypt, 1960. Film director; guitarist; playwright. *The Sweet Hereafter.*

EISLER, Lloyd, sports. Seaforth, Ont., 1963. Figure skater; with Isabelle Brasseur won world pairs title, 1993; Olympic bronze medals.

ELDER, Jim, sports. Toronto, Ont., 1934. Equestrian; team gold medal, 1968 Olympics.

ELGAARD, Ray, sports. Edmonton, Alta, 1959. Football player; Sask. Roughriders star wide receiver.

ELGIN, James Bruce, eighth Earl of, politics. Eng., 1811–63. Governor general, 1847–54.

EMERY, Victor, sports. Montreal, Que., 1933. Bobsledder; piloted 1964 Olympic gold medal team.

EMSLIE, Robert Daniel, sports. Guelph, Ont., 1859–1943. Major league baseball pitcher; won 32 games for Baltimore Orioles in 1884; umpire in National League, strove to improve working conditions and umpires' image.

ENGEL, Howard, literary arts. Toronto, Ont., 1931. Mystery writer. *Murder Sees the Light.*

ENGEL, Marian, literary arts. Toronto, Ont., 1933–85. Novelist. *Bear.*

ERASMUS, Georges Henry, politics. Ft Rae, NWT, 1948. Dene leader; former head, Assembly of First Nations.

ERICKSON, Arthur Charles, visual arts. Vancouver, BC, 1924. Architect; Simon Fraser University (Burnaby, BC).

ESPOSITO, Phillip Anthony (Phil), sports. Sault Ste Marie, Ont., 1942. Hockey player; Boston centre; 717 goals, fourth all-time.

ESTEY, Willard Zebedee "Bud", law. Saskatoon, Sask., 1919. Supreme Court justice, 1977–88; headed several royal commissions.

ETROG, Sorel, visual arts. Romania, 1933. Monumental sculptor; designer. "Ritual Head."

EVANGELISTA, Linda, media. St Catharines, Ont., 1965. International top model.

EVANS, Gil, performing arts. Toronto, Ont., 1912–88. Composer, arranger, pianist. Played free jazz, rock and funk. Gil Evans Orchestra.

EVANS, James, education. Eng., 1801–46. English Methodist missionary, invented Cree syllabic writing system. *Cree Syllabic Hymn Book.*

EVANSHEN, Terrance Anthony (Terry), sports. Montreal, Que., 1944. Football player; outstanding CFL receiver.

EYTON, Trevor, business. Quebec City, Que., 1934. Executive; president, Brascan Ltd; many corporate boards.

F

FACKENHEIM, Emil Ludwig, literary arts. Germany, 1916. Philosopher; works on religion and the Holocaust. *Quest for Past and Future.*

FAIRCLOUGH, Ellen Louks, politics. Hamilton, Ont., 1905. First woman Cabinet minister (1957).

FAIRFIELD, Robert, visual arts. St Catharines, Ont., 1918–95. Designed Stratford Festival Theatre, Ont.; Ontario pavilion at Expo 67.

FAIRLEY, Barker, visual arts. Eng., 1887–1986. Critic; essential Goethe scholar; portrait painter.

FAITH, Percy, performing arts. Toronto, Ont., 1908–76. Bandleader; top music arranger. "Canadian Sunset."

FALK, Gathie, visual arts. Alexander, Man., 1928. Multimedia artist, specializes in performance art, watercolour, drawings. Work shown at National Gallery of Canada.

FALONEY, Bernie, sports. USA, 1932. Football player; long-time star QB for Edmonton, Hamilton.

FAVREAU, Marc, performing arts. Montreal, Que., 1929. Actor; author, noted for role as the hapless, naïve clown Sol, performed on TV and in theatre. *Sol et Gobelet.*

FAVRO, Murray, visual arts. Huntsville, Ont., 1940. Artist noted for his "projected reconstruction"; he has projected slide images on life-size objects, also introduced invention themes into his work. *Windmill Electric Generator; Perpetual Motion Machine.*

FEINBERG, Abraham (Rabbi) (b. Abraham Nisselevicz, aka Anthony Frome), politics. USA, 1899–1986. Peace activist; champion of radical causes.

FERGUSON, Don, performing arts. Montreal, Que., 1946. Actor, writer, director of CHC documentaries; on team of CBC's *Royal Canadian Air Farce.* Impersonates Lucien Bouchard, Preston Manning.

FERGUSON, Ivan Graeme, invention. Toronto, Ont., 1929. Inventor; developed IMAX and OMNIMAX film systems.

FERGUSON, James Francis, performing arts. Ire., 1940–97. Founder, with George Millar, of the Irish Rovers, a singing group that popularized Irish pub music from the sixties on; appeared on CBC television.

FERGUSON, Max "Rawhide", media. Eng., 1924. Broadcaster; popular host of CBC Radio's *Rawhide.*

FERGUSON, Maynard, performing arts. Verdun, Que., 1928. Jazz trumpeter; versatile stylist made 50 albums.

FERRON, Jacques, literary arts/politics. Louiseville, Que., 1921–85. Playwright, *Contes du pays incertain,* Rhinoceros Party founder.

FESSENDEN, Reginald Aubrey, invention. Milton-Est, Canada E, 1866–1932. Inventor; transmitted world's first radio broadcast (1906).

FIELDING, Joy, literary arts. Toronto, Ont., 1945. Novelist, journalist, scriptwriter. *Tell Me No Stories.*

FILION, Herve, sports. Angers, Que., 1940. Harness driver; all-time leader in victories; 12,000+.

FILMON, Gary Albert, politics. Winnipeg, Man., 1942. PC Manitoba premier since 1988.

FINDLEY, Timothy, literary arts. Toronto, Ont., 1930. Novelist; versatile writer. *The Wars.*

FITZ-JONES, Philip Chester, science. Vancouver, BC, 1920. Researched structure and chemical nature of bacterial spores.

FITZGERALD, Lionel LeMoine, visual arts. Winnipeg, Man., 1890–1956. Impressionist turned to abstracts. "Doc Snider's House."

FLAVELLE, Joseph Wesley (Sir), business. Peterborough, Ont., 1858–1939. Financier; executive for Canada Packers, Bank of Commerce, National Trust.

FLEMING, Sandford (Sir), invention. Scot., 1827–1915. Engineer; developed standard time; designed Canada's first postage stamp; built railways.

FOLEY, Dave, performing arts. Toronto, Ont., 1963. Actor, role of Dave Nelson in TV series *News Radio;* member of comedy troupe Kids in the Hall.

FOLLOWS, Megan, performing arts. Toronto, Ont., 1969. Actor who portrayed Anne of Green Gables in CBC TV series. *Silver Bullet.*

FONYO, Stephen Charles (Steve), sports. Montreal, Que., 1965. Handicapped runner; "Journey for Lives" raised funds for cancer research, 1985.

FORD, Glenn (b. Gwyllyn Samuel Newton Ford), performing arts. Quebec City, Que., 1916. Noted American actor of the 1940s and 1950s. *Gilda, Teahouse of the August Moon.*

FORRESTER, Helen, literary arts. Eng., 1919. Novelist. Wrote semiautobiographical Liverpool series: *Twopence to Cross the Mersey; Liverpool Miss; By the Waters of Liverpool; Lime Street at Two.*

FORRESTER, Maureen, performing arts. Monteal, Que., 1930. Operatic contralto; Canada's prima diva.

FORSEY, Eugene Alfred, politics. Grand Bank, Nfld. 1904–91. Intellectual; commentator on public affairs; social radical; strong federalist.

FORTIER, L. Yves, politics. Quebec City, Que., 1935. Former Canadian ambassador to the United Nations.

FOSTER, David Walter, performing arts. Victoria, BC, 1949. Musician; produced many major acts (Chicago, Barbra Streisand); 12 Grammy awards.

FOSTER, George Eulas (Sir), politics. Carleton, NB, 1847–1931. Statesman; central in Cdn political life; acting PM during Borden's illness (1920).

FOTHERINGHAM, Allan, media. Hearne, Sask., 1932. Journalist; popular political columnist.

FOWKE, Edith Margaret, literary arts. Lumsden, Sask., 1913–96. Music ethnologist, published traditional Canadian folksongs. *Penguin Book of Canadian Folksongs; Sally Go Round the Sun.*

FOX, Michael James (J.), performing arts. Edmonton Alta, 1961. Actor; diminutive leading man. *Back to the Future.*

FOX, Terrance Stanley (Terry), sports. Winnipeg, Man., 1958–81. Began "Marathon of Hope" cross-Canada run to raise funds for cancer research; Lou Marsh Trophy as Canada's top athlete, 1980.

FRANCA, Celia (b. Celia Franks), performing arts. Eng., 1921. Choreographer; founder of National Ballet of Canada.

FRANCK, Albert Jacques, visual arts. Holland, 1899–1973. Painter especially noted for his depiction of old houses and back lanes in the old city of Toronto.

FRANCKS, Don Harvey, performing arts. Burnaby, BC, 1932. Veteran actor, jazz musician, appeared in revue *Spring Thaw.* Also TV and film roles. *The Man From U.N.C.L.E.; Finian's Rainbow.*

FRANKLIN, John (Sir), exploration and discovery. Eng., 1786–1847. Bold, doomed Arctic explorer.

FRANKS, Wilbur Rounding, invention. Weston, Ont., 1901–86. Inventor; devised pressure suit for airplane pilots.

FRAPPIER, Armand, science. Valleyfield, Que., 1904–91. Influential microbiologist.

FRASER, Anna, sports. Ottawa, Ont., 1963. Free-style skier; World Cup Aerial Champion (1986).

FRASER, Brendan, performing arts. USA, 1968. Comedic actor who has appeared in films *George of the Jungle; Airheads;* and *Dudley Do-Right.*

FRASER, John Anderson, literary arts. Montreal, Que., 1944. Author; former editor of *Saturday Night* magazine; master of Massey College, Toronto. *The Chinese: A Portrait of a People.*

FRASER, Simon, exploration and discovery. USA, 1776–1862. First white man to explore Fraser River.

FRASER, Sylvia Lois, literary arts. Hamilton, Ont., 1935. Novelist. *Pandora; Berlin Solstice; My Father's House; The Emperor's Virgin.*

FRECHETTE, Sylvie, sports. Laval, Que., 1967. Received post-event gold medal in synchronized swimming, 1992 Olympics.

FRENCH, David, literary arts. Coley's Point, Nfld, 1939. Playwright. *Salt-Water Moon; Jitters; Leaving Home.*

FREUND, Kurt, medicine. Czech., 1914–96. Psychiatrist; noted researcher into human sexuality.

FROBISHER, Martin (Sir), exploration and discovery. Eng., 1539–94. Mariner; discovered Frobisher Bay.

FRONTENAC ET PALLUAU, (Louis de Buade) Comte de, politics. France, 1622–98. Gov. gen, New France, 1672–82, 1689–98.

FROST, Leslie Miscampbell, politics. Orillia, Ont., 1895–1973. PC premier of Ontario, 1949–61.

FRUM, Barbara Ruth, media. USA, 1937–92. Broadcaster; interviewer. *As It Happens; The Journal.*

FRUM, David, literary arts. Toronto, Ont., 1960. Journalist of "new right."

FRYE, Herman Northrop, literary arts. Sherbrooke, Que., 1912–91. Canada's most influential literary critic. *Anatomy of Criticism.*

FULFORD, Robert Marshall Blount, media. Ottawa, Ont., 1932. Journalist; former editor, *Saturday Night*; columnist.

FULTON, E. Davie, politics. Kamloops, BC, 1916-2000. Justice minister in John Diefenbaker's government, beginning 1957; became BC Supreme Court judge 1973-81.

FUNG, Donna Lori, sports. Vancouver, BC, 1963. Rhythmic gymnast; gold medal, 1984 Olympics.

FURST, Judith, performing arts. New Westminster, BC, 1943. Opera singer; internationally renowned diva.

GABEREAU, Vicki Frances, media. Vancouver, BC, 1946. Broadcaster, author. Host of CBC Radio's *Gabereau,* 1988–97. Host of TV talk show on Baton Broadcasting.

GABRIEL, Tony, sports. Hamilton, Ont., 1948. Football player; CFL tight end; held record 138 straight games with receptions until 1995.

GAGNON, André, performing arts. Saint-Pacôme-de-Kamouraska, Que., 1942. Pianist; composer. "Le Saint-Laurent."

GAGNON, André Phillipe, performing arts. Loretteville, Que., 1961. Comedian, impressionist, noted for one-man shows.

GALBRAITH, John Kenneth, business/literary arts. Iona Station, Ont., 1908. Economist; author; influential intellectual. *The Affluent Society.*

GALLANT, Mavis Leslie, literary arts. Montreal, Que., 1922. Author of more than 100 short stories. "A Fairly Good Time."

GALLEY, Harry A., invention. Montreal, Que., 1903–95. Inco employee; designer of first mass-produced stainless steel sink.

GALLIVAN, Danny, sports. Montreal, Que., 1917–93. Hockey announcer; voice of the Montreal Canadiens.

GALT, Alexander Tilloch, politics. Eng., 1817–93. Railway promoter; proposed union of all British colonies.

GARBER, Victor, performing arts. London, Ont., 1949. Character actor in Hollywood, formerly led folk band The Sugar Shoppe. Roles include Jesus in *Godspell;* also appeared in films *Titanic* and *First Wives Club.*

GARNEAU, François Xavier, literary arts. Quebec City, Que., 1809–66. Writer; early historian. *Histoire du Canada.*

GARNEAU, Hector de Saint Denys, literary arts. Montreal, Que., 1912–43. Poet. "Regards et jeux dans l'espace."

GARNEAU, Marc, science. Quebec City, Que., 1949. First Canadian astronaut (1984) to achieve liftoff.

GARNER, Hugh, literary arts. Eng., 1913–79. Working class novelist. *Cabbagetown.*

GASCON, Jean, performing arts. Montreal, Que., 1921–88. Actor; director; influential man of the theatre; headed Stratford Festival, Natl Arts Centre.

GAYFORD, Thomas Franklin, sports. Toronto, Ont., 1928. Equestrian; won gold medal Prix des Nations in 1968 Olympics.

GEDGE, Pauline, literary arts. New Zealand, 1945. Novelist. *Scroll of Saqqara; The Twelfth Transforming; The Covenant.*

GEHRY, Frank, visual arts. Toronto, Ont., 1929. Internationally recognized architect. Guggenheim Museum in Bilbao, Spain; Art and Teaching Museum, University of Minnesota.

GELBER, Arthur Ellis, public service. Toronto, Ont., 1915–98. Philanthropist who was prominent on arts boards, including National Arts Centre, National Ballet of Canada and the Ontario Arts Council.

GELINAS, Gratien, performing arts. St Tite, Que., 1909–99. Actor; director; playwright; crucial to modern Quebec theatre.

GEOFFRION, Joseph André Bernard "Boom Boom", sports. Montreal, Que., 1931. Hockey player; right-winger, Montreal Canadiens (1950–64), noted for strength and speed.

GEORGE, Dan (Teswahno), performing arts. Burrard Reserve, BC, 1899–1981. Actor; helped redefine image of Aboriginal peoples in media. *Little Big Man.*

GERUSSI, Bruno, performing arts. Medicine Hat, Alta, 1928–95. Actor; regular on *The Beachcombers.*

GESNER, Abraham, invention. Cornwallis, NS, 1797–1864. Inventor of kerosene oil.

GETTY, Donald Ross, politics/sports. Montreal, Que., 1933. Edmonton Eskimos quarterback; PC premier of Alberta, 1985–92.

GHIZ, Joseph Atallah, politics. Charlettetown, PEI, 1945–97. Liberal premier of PEI 1986–93. Avid supporter of Meech Lake Accord and Charlettetown Accord.

GIAUQUE, William Francis, science. Niagara Falls, Ont., 1895–1982. Chemist who won 1949 Nobel Prize in chemistry for studies of properties of substances at temperatures near absolute zero.

GIBSON, George "Mooney", sports. London, Ont., 1880–1967. Baseball player; pro catcher, 1905–18.

GIBSON, Graeme C., literary arts. London, Ont., 1934. Novelist. *Five Legs; Perpetual Motion.*

GIBSON, William, literary arts. USA, 1948. Science fiction writer, pioneered "Cyberpunk" paradigm; novel *Neuromancer* won Hugo and Nebula awards; wrote screenplay for *Johnny Mnemonic.*

GILLIS, Margie, performing arts. Montreal, Que., 1953. Dancer, choreographer; depicts social and political themes; an internationally acclaimed soloist, she has toured with Les Grands Ballet Canadiens, and introduced modern dance to China after the revolution. *Mercy.*

GILMOUR, Clyde, media. Calgary, Alta, 1912–97. Journalist; arts radio broadcaster. *Gilmour's Albums.*

GIMBY, Bobbie (b. Robert Stead), performing arts. Cabri, Sask., 1918–98. Trumpeter, songwriter. Appeared in CBC radio series *The Happy Gang.* Composed "CA-NA-DA" in 1967 for centennial celebrations.

GISBORNE, Frederick Newton, invention. Eng., 1824–92. Inventor; developed undersea telegraph cable (1852).

GIVENS, Philip, politics. Toronto, Ont., 1922–95. Mayor of Toronto 1964–66; responsible for acquisition of Henry Moore's *The Archer* sculpture at Toronto's New City Hall.

GOLDSMITH, Robert, literary arts. St Andrews, NB, 1794–1861. First Canadian-born poet to write in English: *The Rising Village* described Acadian experience.

GOMEZ, Avelino, sports. Cuba, 1928–80. Jockey; over 4,000 career wins, including four Queen's Plates.

GOODERHAM, William, business. England, 1790–1881. With nephew James built Canada West's largest distillery, in 1859; Gooderham and Worts eventually had interests in distilleries, railways, transportation and retailing.

GOODMAN, Henry George, business. USA, 1907–97. Philanthropist, volunteer and lawyer who helped initiate and served as president of the Jewish Children's Aid Society in Toronto.

GOODYEAR, Scott, sports. Toronto, Ont., 1959. Indy car driver; winner of Canadian Racing Drivers Association Driver of the Year award; first Canadian to win oval race.

GORDON, Charles William, literary arts. Glengarry Cty, Canada W, 1860–1937. Presbyterian minister who wrote western-style novels, *The Sky Pilot, The Prospector,* as well as *Glengarry School Days.*

GORDON, Donald, business. Scot., 1901–69. Executive; controversial head of CNR, 1950–66.

GORDON, Walter Lockhart, politics. Toronto, Ont., 1906–87. Economic nationalist; inspired creation of Committee for an Independent Canada.

GORMAN, Charles, sports. Saint John, NB, 1897–1940. Speed skater; held seven world records.

GOTLIEB, Allan Ezra, politics. Winnipeg, Man., 1928. Career public servant; Canadian ambassador to US 1981–89.

GOTLIEB, Phyllis Fay, literary arts. Toronto, Ont., 1926. Poet, science fiction writer. *Heart of Red Iron; The Kingdom of the Cats.*

GOTLIEB, Sondra, literary arts. Winnipeg, Man., 1936. Newspaper columnist with *Washington Post, Globe and Mail.* Writer: *"Wife Of": An Irreverent Account of Life in Washington; True Confections.*

GOUGEON, Hélène Carroll, media. Ottawa, Ont., 1924–2000. Veteran journalist on radio, TV and in print; culinary expertise led to her *The Original Canadian Cookbook.* Also wrote for *Weekend; Toronto Star; Ottawa Journal.*

GOUIN, Jean-Lomer (Sir), politics. Canada E, 1861–1929. Liberal premier of Quebec, 1905–20.

GOULD, Glenn Herbert, performing arts. Toronto, Ont., 1932–82. Classical pianist; *Goldberg Variations* stand out in brilliant, eccentric career.

GOULET, Robert Gerard, performing arts. USA, 1933. Singer/actor, noted for romantic male leads. *South Pacific; Camelot.*

GOUZENKO, Igor Sergeievich, military. USSR, 1919–82. Spy; defector exposed Soviet espionage network.

GOVIER, Katherine Mary, literary arts. Edmonton, Alta, 1948. Novelist, short story writer. *Random Descent; Angel Walk.*

GOWAN, Elsie Park, literary arts. Scot., 1905–99. Internationally recognized playwright for radio and stage. *Beeches from Bond Street; The Building of Canada.*

GOWDY, Barbara, literary arts. Windsor, Ont., 1950. Editor, writer. *Through the Green Valley; We So Seldom Look on Love.*

GOY, Luba, performing arts. Germany, 1946. Comedian on *Royal Canadian Air Farce*; impersonations include Sheila Copps, Pamela Wallin.

GRANT, Charles, law. Toronto, Ont., 1902–80. Activist; fought anti-Semitism, racism, bigotry.

GRANT, George Parkin, literary arts. Toronto, Ont., 1918–88. Philosopher; influential pessimistic thinker and nationalist. *Lament for a Nation.*

GRAY, George R., sports. Canada W, 1865–1933. Shot putter; world record holder during 1880s.

GRAY, James Henry, literary arts. Whitemouth, Man., 1906–98. Social historian whose works reflected Western Canadian society. *The Winter Years,* a story about the Depression; *The Boy From Winnipeg.*

GREENE, Graham, performing arts. Six Nations Reserve, Ont., 1952. Film/TV actor. *Dances with Wolves.*

GREENE, Lorne Hyman, performing arts. Ottawa, Ont., 1915–87. Actor; Ben Cartwright on TV's *Bonanza* for 14 years.

GREENE, Nancy Catherine, sports. Ottawa, Ont., 1943. Skier; World Cup winner, 1967, 1968; gold and silver slalom medals.

GREENOUGH, Gail, sports. Edmonton, Alta, 1960. Equestrian; 1986 world champion, individual show jumping.

GREENSPAN, Edward Leonard, law. Niagara Falls, Ont., 1944. Distinguished criminal lawyer.

GRENFELL, Wilfred Thomason (Sir), medicine. Eng., 1865–1940. Medical missionary; builder of hospitals in Nfld.

GRETZKY, Wayne, sports. Brantford, Ont., 1961. Hockey player; all-time leading NHL scorer.

GREY OWL (b. Archibald Stansfield Belaney), literary arts. Eng., 1888–1938. Writer; conservationist who identified with Aboriginal peoples. *Pilgrims of the Wild.*

GRIERSON, John, visual arts. Scot., 1898–1972. Documentarist; creator of National Film Board.

GRIFFITH, Linda, performing arts. Toronto, Ont., 1953. Film, TV and stage actress. *Maggie and Pierre.*

GROSS, Paul, performing arts. Calgary, Alta, 1959. Actor, playwright; starred in TV series *Due South.*

GROSSMAN, Daniel Williams, performing arts. USA, 1942. Founder of the Danny Groosman Dance Co.; specializes in contemporary dance, set to jazz, rock music. *Higher; Nobody's Business.*

GROSSMAN, Lawrence S. (Larry), politics. Toronto, Ont., 1943–97. High-profile minister in Bill Davis's Ontario PC government, ran unsuccessfully as Tory leader against David Peterson in 1985.

GROULX, Lionel Adolphe, religion. Vaudreuil, Que., 1878–1967. Historian; Quebec religious nationalist.

GROVE, Frederick Philip, literary arts. Prussia, 1879–1948. Writer. *In Search of Myself.*

GUERIN, Gertrude Ettershank (Klaw Law We Leth), politics. Mission Reserve, N. Vancouver, BC. A Musqueam chief, considered to be the first native woman to hold such a high-ranking position.

GUILLET, James Edwin Dr., invention. Toronto, Ont., 1927. Inventor of biodegradable plastics.

GUSTAFSON, Ralph Barker, literary arts. Lime Ridge, Que., 1909–95. Founder of League of Canadian Poets. Governor General's Award, 1974. *Fire and Stone.*

GWYN, Sandra (Alexandra) Jean Fraser, literary arts. St John's, Nfld, 1935-2000. Governor General's Award, 1984. *The Private Capital; Tapestry of War.*

GWYNNE, Horace "Lefty", sports. Toronto, Ont., 1912. Boxer; bantamweight gold medal, 1932 Olympics.

GZOWSKI, Casimir Stanislaus (Sir), exploration and discovery. Russia, 1813–98. Engineer; built roads, bridges, and railroads.

GZOWSKI, Peter, media. Toronto, Ont., 1934. Broadcaster; author; long-time radio host. *Morningside.*

H

HACKNER, Allan, sports. Nipigon, Ont., 1954. Curler; Canadian and world champion, 1982, 1985.

HADFIELD, Chris Austin, science. Sarnia, Ont., 1959. Astronaut, first Canadian mission specialist on space shuttle, 1996.

HAILEY, Arthur, literary arts. Eng., 1920. Writer; produced string of best-sellers. *Airport.*

HAIM, Corey, performing arts. Toronto, Ont., 1972. Actor, producer. *Demolition High; Life 101.*

HALDER, Walter (Wally), sports. Toronto, Ont., 1925–94. Leading goal scorer on Canada's gold medallist team at 1948 Olympic Winter Games.

HALIBURTON, Thomas Chandler, literary arts. Windsor, NS, 1796–1865. Writer; social satirist. *The Clockmaker.*

HALL, Emmett Matthew, public service. Saint-Columban, Que., 1898–1995. Chief Justice of Saskatchewan; co-author of Ontario's 1966 Hall-Dennis education report.

HALL, Glenn Henry, sports. Humboldt, Sask., 1931. Hockey goaltender; 11-time all-star; record 502 consecutive games.

HALL, Monty, performing arts. Winnipeg, Man., 1925. Long-time TV host of *Let's Make a Deal* show.

HAMEL, Theophile, visual arts. Ste-Foy, LC, 1817–70. Painted life-like official portraits.

HAMILTON, Barbara, performing arts. Toronto, Ont., 1926–96. Veteran screen and stage actor. *Anne of Green Gables; Crazy for You.*

HAMM, John F., politics. New Glasgow, NS, 1938. PC premier of Nova Scotia, elected in 1999.

HAMPSON, Sharon, performing arts. Toronto, Ont., 1943. Member of children's musical entertainment group Sharon, Lois and Bram; live and on TV. *The Elephant Show.*

HANLAN, Edward (Ned), sports. Toronto, Ont., 1855–1908. World champion oarsman, 1880–84.

HANSEN, Rick, sports. Port Alberni, BC, 1957. Wheelchair athlete; "Man in Motion" tour raised $20M for medical research.

HANSON, Melvin "Fritzie", sports. USA, 1912. Football player; led Winnipeg to first western Grey Cup (1935).

HARCOURT, Michael Franklin, politics. Edmonton, Alta, 1943. NDP Premier of BC 1991–96.

HARDY, Hagood, performing arts. USA, 1937–97. Pop/jazz pianist and composer; Juno award-winner. "The Homecoming"; scores for *Anne of Green Gables, Road to Avonlea.*

HARE, Frederick Kenneth, science. Eng., 1919. Environmentalist; expert on climate change, greenhouse effect.

HARNOY, Ofra, performing arts. Israel, 1965. International virtuoso cellist.

HARPER, Elijah, politics. Red Sucker L, Man. MLA in Manitoba legislature who blocked passage of Meech Lake Accord.

HARPER, J. Russell, visual arts. Caledonia, Ont., 1914–83. Art historian; pioneered study of art history.

HARRINGTON, Michael Francis, performing arts. St John's, Nfld, 1916–99. Supporter of an independent Newfoundland prior to 1949 confederation, Harrington hosted popular 1940s Newfoundland radio program *The Barrelman;* co-edited complete National Convention debates.

HARRIS, Lawren Stewart, visual arts. Brantford, Ont., 1885–1970. Founder of Group of Seven; noted for stark landscapes. *Above Lake Superior.*

HARRIS, Micheal Deane, politics. Toronto, Ont., 1945. PC premier of Ontario 1995–.

HARRIS, Mike, sports. Georgetown, Ont., 1967. Skip of the silver-medal-winning curling team during the 1998 winter Olympics in Nagano, Japan.

HARRIS, Wayne, sports. USA, 1938. Football player; outstanding Calgary Stampeders linebacker.

HARRON, Donald (Don), performing arts. Toronto, Ont., 1924. Actor; comedian; host of *Morningside* 1977–82; also noted for portraying farmer Charlie Farquharson.

HART, Corey Mitchell, performing arts. Montreal, Que., 1962. Pop singer; teen heartthrob. *Boy in the Box*.

HART, Evelyn Anne, performing arts. Toronto, Ont., 1956. Prima ballerina, Royal Winnipeg Ballet.

HARTMAN, Grace, business. Toronto, Ont., 1918. Labour leader; first woman to head Canadian Union of Public Employees (1975–83).

HARVEY, Douglas N. (Doug), sports. Montreal, Que., 1924–90. Hockey player; Montreal Canadiens defenceman; won seven Norris Trophies.

HARWOOD, Vanessa Clare, performing arts. Eng., 1947. National Ballet soloist.

HATFIELD, Richard Bennett, politics. Woodstock, NB, 1931–91. PC premier of NB, 1970–87.

HAWKINS, Ronald "Rompin' Ronnie", performing arts. USA, 1935. Pop/country singer; pioneer of Canadian rock. "Mary Lou."

HAWLEY, Sanford Desmond (Sandy), sports. Oshawa, Ont., 1949. Jockey; winner of more than 6,000 races.

HAYDEN, Melissa (b. Mildred Herman), performing arts. Toronto, Ont., 1923. Virtuoso with New York City Ballet.

HEALEY, Jeff, performing arts. Toronto, Ont., 1966. Pop singer; blind blues guitarist. "See the Light."

HEARNE, Samuel, exploration and discovery. Eng., 1745–92. Explorer; *A Journey from Prince of Wales's Fort in Hudson's Bay to the Northern Ocean* is one of the great travel narratives.

HEATH, John Geoffrey "Jeff", sports. Ft William, Ont., 1915–75. Baseball player; hit .293 in 14-year career.

HEBB, Donald Olding, science. Chester, NS, 1904–85. Psychologist; developmental work showed importance of environmental stimulation.

HEBERT, Anne, literary arts. Ste-Catherine-de-Fossambault, Que., 1916–2000. Novelist. *Kamouraska*.

HEBERT, Louis-Philippe, visual arts. Megantic, Que., 1850–1917. Commemorative sculptor of many public monuments. *Queen Victoria*.

HEDDLE, Kathleen, sports. Vancouver, BC, 1965. With Marnie McBean won women's double sculls rowing medals: two golds in 1992 at Barcelona Olympics; one gold, one bronze in 1996 Olympics in Atlanta.

HEES, George Harris, politics. Toronto, Ont., 1910–96. PC cabinet minister for John Diefenbaker and Brian Mulroney.

HEGGTVEIT, Anne, sports. Ottawa, Ont., 1939. Skier; Canada's first Olympic gold medal in skiing; women's slalom, 1960.

HELLSTROM, Sheila Anne (Brig-Gen.), military. Bridgewater, NS, 1935. Soldier; first Cdn woman general.

HELWIG, David Gordon, literary arts. Toronto, Ont., 1938. Poet; novelist. "Figures in a Landscape."

HENLEY, Garney, sports. USA, 1935. Football player; Hamilton star CFL's most versatile player.

HENNING, Douglas, performing arts. Ft Garry, Man., 1947–2000. Magician; co-founder, Natural Law Party.

HENRY, Martha, performing arts. USA, 1938. TV/film actress; Stratford regular. *The Wars*.

HENSON, Josiah, politics. USA, 1789–1883. Black leader; escaped slave; model for *Uncle Tom's Cabin*.

HENSTRIDGE, Natasha, performing arts. Springdale, Nfld, 1974. Model turned actress; appeared in *Species* movie series; also films *Dog Park* and *The Whole Nine Yards*.

HEPBURN, Doug, sports. Vancouver, BC, 1926. Weight lifter; world heavyweight title, 1953.

HEPBURN, Mitchell Frederick, politics. St Thomas, Ont., 1896–1953. Liberal Ontario premier, 1934–42.

HEPPNER, Ben, performing arts. Murrayville, BC, 1956. Tenor opera singer, Metropolitan debut in 1991.

HERBERT, Paul, performing arts. Thetford Mines, Que., 1924. Actor; screenwriter; director.

HERIOT, George, visual arts. Scot., 1759–1839. Watercolourist. *Lake St Charles Near Quebec*.

HEROUX, Denis, visual arts. Montreal, Que., 1940. Film producer. *Atlantic City*.

HERZBERG, Gerhard, medicine. Germany, 1904–99. Physicist; molecular analyst; Nobel Prize, chemistry, 1971.

HEWITT, Foster William, sports. Toronto, Ont., 1903–85. Hockey announcer; voice of Toronto Maple Leafs.

HIGHWAY, Tomson, literary arts. Brovchet, Man., 1951. Playwright. *Dry Lips Oughta Move to Kapuskasing*.

HILL, Arthur, performing arts. Melfort, Sask., 1922. Stage and film performer. *The Ugly American*.

HILL, Dan Jr, performing arts. Toronto, Ont., 1954. Ballad singer and composer. "Sometimes When We Touch."

HILL, Daniel Grafton Sr, politics. USA, 1923. Reformer; human rights; black history activist and writer.

HILL, James Jerome, business. Rockwood, Ont., 1838–1916. In 1890 consolidated vast railway holdings into the Great Northern Railway Co., also was integral in the building of the Canadian Pacific Railway.

HILLER, Arthur Garfin, visual arts. Edmonton, Alta, 1923. Filmmaker/director. *Love Story*.

HILLIARD, Anna Marion, medicine. Morrisburg, Ont., 1902-58. In 1947 helped develop the Pap test to detect cervical cancer; facilitated its initiation at Women's College Hospital in Toronto in 1948. Wrote *A Woman Doctor Looks at Love and Life*.

HILLIER, James, invention. Brantford, Ont., 1915. Inventor; pioneered electron microscopes.

HIRSCH, John Stephen, performing arts. Hungary, 1930–89. Stage director; founded Manitoba Theatre Centre; headed Stratford Festival, CBC TV drama.

HITSCHMANOVA, Lotta, politics. Czech., 1909–80. Activist; founding director, Unitarian Service Committee of Canada development agency.

Canadian Hall of Fame

HNATYSHYN, Ramon John, politics. Saskatoon, Sask., 1934. Governor general of Canada 1990–95.

HODGINS, Jack Stanley, literary arts. Comox, BC, 1938. Novelist. *The Resurrection of Joseph Bourne.*

HODGSON, George Ritchie, sports. Montreal, Que., 1893–1983. Swimmer; first Canadian Olympic gold medals in swimming; 400 m, 1500 m freestyle in 1912.

HOFFMAN, Abigail (Abbie), sports. Toronto, Ont., 1947. Sports feminist; director of Sport Canada.

HOFFMEISTER, Bertram Meryl, military. Vancouver, BC, 1907-99. Canadian general in WWII, considered brilliant battle strategist, later chairman of lumber conglomerate MacMillan Bloedel.

HOGG-PRIESTLY, Helen Battles, science. USA, 1905–93. Astronomer; star clusters expert; asteroid named for her.

HOHL, Elmer, sports. Wellesley, Ont., 1919–87. Horseshoe pitcher; world champion, 1965–87.

HOLGATE, Edwin, visual arts. Allandale, Ont., 1892–1977. Group of Seven artist, noted for portraiture; member of Royal Canadian Academy of Arts.

HOLLINGSHEAD, Gregory Albert Frank, literary arts. Toronto, Ont., 1947. Governor General's Award for fiction, 1995, *The Roaring Girl.*

HOMME, Robert, performing arts. USA, 1919–2000. Portrayed the Friendly Giant on long-running CBC children's program of same name.

HOOD, Hugh John Blagdon, literary arts. Toronto, Ont., 1928. Novelist; essayist. *The Swing in the Garden.*

HORTON, Miles Gilbert "Tim", sports. Cochrane, Ont., 1930–74. Toronto Maple Leaf hockey player, five Stanley Cup wins; founder of national doughnut chain.

HOSPITAL, Janette Turner, literary arts. Australia, 1942. Winner of the Seal first Novel Award, 1982, *The Ivory Swing. Isobars.*

HOUSSER, Yvonne McKague, visual arts. Toronto, Ont., 1898–1996. Group of Seven-influenced paintings: National Art Gallery; Art Gallery of Ontario; McMichael Gallery.

HOUSTON, Heather, sports. Thunder Bay, Ont., 1959. Curler; skip of 1989 world championship team; Canadian championships 1988, 1989.

HOUSTON, James Archibald, literary/visual arts. Toronto, Ont., 1921. In the 1950s became a major buyer and supporter of Inuit art. *White Dawn; Confessions of an Igloo Dweller.*

HOWARD, Russ, sports. Penetanguishene, Ont., 1955. Curler; Canadian and world champion, 1987, 1993.

HOWE, Clarence Decatur (C.D.), business/politics. USA, 1886–1960. Foremost grain elevator builder of his day, Howe was a Liberal minister of transport; helped create Trans-Canada Airlines, forerunner of Air Canada.

HOWE, Gordon (Gordie), sports. Floral, Sask., 1928. Hockey player; Detroit Red Wings great; 801 NHL goals.

HOWE, Joseph, politics. Halifax, NS, 1804–73. Led fight against Nova Scotia entry into Confederation; later joined cabinet.

HUBEL, David Hunter, science. Windsor, Ont., 1926. Winner of 1981 Nobel Prize in medicine and physiology for research in processing the visual system.

HUGGINS, Charles Brenton, science. Halifax, NS, 1901. Won Nobel Prize for medicine in 1966 for discoveries concerning hormonal treatment of prostate cancer.

HULL, Robert Marvin, sports. Pte Anne, Ont., 1939. Hockey player; "Golden Jet," left winger for Chicago and Winnipeg; 610 NHL goals.

HUMPHREY, John Peters, public service. Hampton, NB, 1905–95. Principal author of the Universal Declaration of Human Rights; founder of the Canadian Human Rights Foundation and Amnesty International (Can.).

HUNGERFORD, George William, sports. Vancouver, BC, 1944. Rower; gold medal, coxless pairs, 1964 Olympics.

HUNTER, Thomas James (Tommy), performing arts. London, Ont., 1937. Country singer; *Tommy Hunter Show* on CBC, 1965–92.

HUNTSMAN, Archibald Gowanlock, science. Tintern, Ont., 1883–1973. Biologist; pioneered fisheries science.

HURTIG, Melvyn (Mel), literary arts. Edmonton, Alta, 1932. Publisher; Canadian nationalist. *The Canadian Encyclopedia.*

HUSTON, Walter (b. Walter Houghston), performing arts. Toronto, Ont., 1884–1960. Actor. *Treasure of the Sierra Madre.*

HUTCHISON, William Bruce, literary arts. Prescott, Ont., 1901–92. Political historian; biographer of W. L. Mackenzie King, *The Incredible Canadian.*

HUTT, William Ian deWitt, performing arts. Toronto, Ont., 1920. Stage actor; distinguished Stratford leading player.

HYLAND, Francis, performing arts. Regina, Sask., c. 1932. Actor with Stratford Festival, Ont.

I

IBERVILLE, Pierre Le Moyne, Sieur d', military. Montreal, Que., 1661–1706. soldier; daring, often cruel, adventurer.

IDE, Thomas Ranald (Ran), media. Ottawa, Ont., 1919–96. Appointed in 1966 to set up TVOntario, an innovative education network.

IGNATIEFF, George, politics. Russia, 1913–89. Diplomat; expert in East-West relations; UN ambassador.

IGNATIEFF, Michael, literary arts/media. Toronto, Ont., 1947. Writer; broadcaster. *The Russian Album.*

IMLACH, George "Punch", sports. Toronto, Ont., 1918–87. Hockey coach and manager; during 11 seasons with Toronto Maple Leafs won four Stanley Cups.

INNIS, Harold Adams, politics. Otterville, Ont., 1894–1952. Political economist; communications theorist. *Empire and Communications.*

IRELAND, John, performing arts. Vancouver, BC, 1914. Actor; often played a heavy. *Red River.*

IRONSIDE, Michael, performing arts. Toronto, Ont., 1950. Character actor, specializes in heavies and thugs; has appeared in films *Top Gun; Highlander II.* Also on TV's *ER* series.

IRVIN, Dick Sr, sports. Limestone Ridge, Ont., 1892–1957. Hockey executive; innovative coach/mgr of Montreal Canadiens, Toronto Maple Leafs.

IRVING, Kenneth Colin (K.C.), business. Buctouche, NB, 1899–1992. Industrialist; founder of NB business empire, from oil to broadcasting.

IRWIN, Mary (b. May Campbell), performing arts. Whitby, Ont., 1862–1938. Broadway, vaudeville star; famous for first screen kiss in film *The Kiss,* in 1896. Sang "After the Ball."

ISELER, Elmer Walter, performing arts. Port Colbourne, Ont., 1927–98. Choral conductor who founded Festival Singers of Canada; from 1964 to 1997 conductor of the Toronto Mendelssohn Choir; also founded the Elmer Iseler Singers.

ISRAEL, Werner, science. Germany, 1931. Physicist; pioneered study of black holes, gravitation.

ISSAJENKO, Angella (Taylor), sports. Jamaica, 1958. Sprinter; many medals in 100 m races.

JACKS, Terry, performing arts. Winnipeg, Man., 1944. Singer; founding member, the Poppy Family.

JACKSON, Alexander Young (A.Y.), visual arts. Montreal, Que., 1882–1974. Painter; landscape artist; member, Group of Seven. *Barns.*

JACKSON, Donald, sports. Oshawa, Ont., 1940. Figure skater; men's world champion, 1962.

JACKSON, Roger, sports. Toronto, Ont., 1942. Rower; gold medal, coxless pairs, 1964 Olympics.

JACKSON, Russell Stanley (Russ), sports. Hamilton, Ont., 1936. Football player; Ottawa quarterback; 3-time Schenley Award winner as CFL top player.

JACKSON, Tom, performing arts. Winnipeg, Man. Native actor and singer, has appeared on CBC's *North of 60; Medicine River; The Diviners.*

JACOBS, "Indian" Jack, sports. USA, 1920–74. Football player; fiery quarterback for Winnipeg Blue Bombers; helped popularize CFL.

JACOBS, Jane, literary arts. USA, 1916. Urban critic; major urban thinker. *Systems of Survival.*

JAMES, Colin, performing arts. Regina, Sask., 1964. Songwriter, guitarist; plays blues, pop, swing. *Hook, Line & Single; Colin James.*

JAMES, Gerry, sports. Regina, Sask., 1934. Football/hockey player; rare pro double; Winnipeg Blue Bombers, Toronto Maple Leafs.

JANES, Percy Maxwell, literary arts. St John's, Nfld, 1922–99. Newfoundland writer whose gritty works depicted the reality of life on the island. *House of Hate.*

JARVIS, Judy, performing arts. Ottawa, Ont., 1946-86. Dancer, founder of the Judy Jarvis Dance and Theatre Co.; innovative teacher and choreographer and instrumental in development of Canadian contemporary dance. *Bird; Three Women.*

JELINEK, Otto John, sports/politics. Czech., 1940. PC minister; with sister Maria won world pairs figure skating title (1972).

JENKINS, Ferguson Arthur, sports. Chatham, Ont., 1943. Baseball pitcher; only Canadian in Hall of Fame, 284 career wins.

JENNESS, Diamond, literary arts. New Zealand, 1886–1969. Anthropologist; author; expert on native Canadians. *The People of the Twilight.*

JENNINGS, Peter Charles, media. Toronto, Ont., 1938. Broadcaster; anchorman, *ABC Evening News.*

JEROME, Harry Winston, sports. Prince Albert, Sask., 1940–82. Sprinter; one-time world record holder in 100 m.

JEWISON, Norman Frederick, visual arts. Toronto, Ont., 1926. Film director; founded Canadian Film Centre in Toronto. *In the Heat of the Night.*

JOHANSSON, Herman Smith "Chief Jackrabbit", sports. Norway, 1875–1986. Skier; popularizer of cross-country skiing.

JOHNS, Harold Elford (Dr), medicine. China, 1915. Physician; developed cobalt bomb for treating cancer.

JOHNSON, Ben, sports. Jamaica, 1961. Sprinter; stripped of 100 m world record time gold medal in 1988 Olympics for using banned drug.

JOHNSON, Daniel, politics. Montreal, Que., 1944. Liberal opposition leader in Quebec 1994–98.

JOHNSON, Edward, performing arts. Guelph, Ont., 1878–1959. Opera singer, performed at Metropolitan Opera in New York; later chairman of board of Royal Conservatory of Music in Toronto.

JOHNSON, Emily Pauline "Tekahionwake", literary arts. Six Nations Reserve, UC, 1861–1913. Her poetry celebrated Canada and her native heritage. "Flint and Feather."

JOHNSTON, Francis Hans (Franz), visual arts. Toronto, Ont., 1888–1949. Early Group of Seven member. *Batchawana Falls.*

JOHNSTON, Lynn, visual arts. Collingwood, Ont., 1947. Cartoonist; creator, "For Better or For Worse."

JOHNSTON, Rita Margaret, politics. Melville, Sask., 1935. First woman premier in Canada (BC) in 1991, succeeded Bill Vander Zalm.

JOLIAT, Aurele, sports. Ottawa, Ont., 1908–86. Hockey player; left winger for Montreal Canadiens.

JOLLIET, Louis, exploration and discovery. Quebec City, Que., 1645–1700. Co-discoverer of the Mississippi R.

JONAS, George, literary arts. Hungary, 1935. Poet, writer, scriptwriter. Script for CBC's *The Scales of Justice; Vengeance; By Persons Unknown: The Strange Death of Christine Demeter.*

JONES KONIHOWSKI, Diane, sports. Vancouver, BC, 1951. Canadian pentathlon record holder.

JORY, Victor, performing arts. Yukon, 1902–82. Actor; Hollywood villain. *Huckleberry Finn.*

JUCKES, Gordon, sports. Watrous, Sask., 1914–95. Hockey and Sports Hall of Fame member, established national team program.

JULIEN, Pauline, performing arts. Trois-Rivières, Que., 1928–98. Quebec singer, political activist, separatist and feminist, Julien embodied the spirit of Quebec through songs of her own composition as well as Kurt Weill, Bertolt Brecht and Gilles Vigneault.

JULIETTE (b. Juliette Augustina Sysak), performing arts. Winnipeg, Man., 1927. Singer; early TV star; own show, 1954–66.

JUNEAU, Pierre, business. Verdun, Que., 1922. Broadcast executive; headed CRTC, 1968–75.

JUTRA, Claude, visual arts. Montreal, Que., 1930–87. Film director. *Mon Oncle Antoine.*

K

KAIN, Karen, performing arts. Hamilton, Ont., 1951. Prima ballerina, National Ballet of Canada.

KALVAK, Helen, visual arts. Victoria I., NWT, 1901-84. Inuit artist; over 300 prints portray the life of the Copper Inuit, frequent spiritual themes. *Kidnapper.*

KANE, Lori, sports. Charlottetown, PEI, 1964. Golfer: member of Canadian Inernational Team 1989–92; member of Commonwealth Team in 1991; 1992 Canadian World Amateur Team; 1997, Canadian Athlete of the Year.

KANE, Paul, visual arts. Ire., 1810–71. Painter of the Canadian West and native peoples.

KARPIS, Alvin (b. Albin Karpowicz). Montreal, Que., 1908–79. Barker Gang member; US Public Enemy No. 1.

KARSH, Yousuf, visual arts. Armenia, 1908. Photographer; portraitist of the famous, e.g., Churchill.

KEDROVA, Lila Howard, performing arts. Russia, 1920-2000. Actress noted for role as Madame Hortense in film *Zorba the Greek,* also appeared in *High Wind in Jamaica.*

KEELER, Ruby (b. Ethel Keeler), performing arts. Halifax, NS, 1909–93. Actress; dancer. *42nd Street.*

KEITH, Vicki, sports. Winnipeg, Man., 1961. Swam all five Great Lakes in 1988.

KELESI, Helen Mersi, sports. Victoria, BC, 1969. Tennis player; Canadian women's championship 1987–90.

KELLY, Leonard "Red", sports. Simcoe, Ont., 1927. Hockey player; star defenceman with Detroit and Toronto; two-time Liberal MP.

KELLY, Milton Terrence (M.T.), literary arts. Toronto, Ont., 1947. Poet, playwright, novelist. *A Dream Like Mine.*

KELSO, John Joseph, politics. Ire., 1864–1935. Reformer; founded Toronto Humane Society, Children's Aid.

KENOJUAK Ashevak, visual arts. Baffin Island, NWT, 1927. Artist noted for bird graphics.

KEON, David Michael, sports. Noranda, Que., 1940. Hockey player with Toronto Maple Leafs 1960–75. Team Canada member 1977. Winner of Conn Smythe trophy, 1967.

KHANJIAN, Arsinée, performing arts. Lebanon, 1958. Film and theatre actress, wife of film director Atom Egoyan. *Next of Kin; Exotica.*

KHORANA, Har Gobind, science. India, 1922. Chemist; Nobel Prize in medicine (1968) for DNA research.

KIDD, Bruce, sports. Ottawa, Ont., 1943. Runner; many wins at various distances; outstanding athlete in Canada, 1961 and 1962.

KIDDER, Margot, performing arts. Yellowknife, NWT, 1948. Actress; Hollywood star. *Superman.*

KIERANS, Eric William, politics. Montreal, Que., 1914. Economist; outspoken nationalist.

KILBOURN, William, literary arts. Toronto, Ont., 1926–95. Writer; historian; biographer of C.D. Howe.

KILLAM, Isaac Walton, business. Yarmouth, NS, 1885–1955. Industrialist; built business empire; known for philanthropy.

KING, Allan Winton, visual arts. Vancouver, BC, 1930. Filmmaker; documentarist. *Warrendale.*

KING, Thomas, literary arts. USA, 1943. Aboriginal writer, novelist. Creator of "Dead Dog Café" on CBC radio programs *Morningside* and *This Morning. Medicine River.*

KING, William Lyon Mackenzie, politics. Kitchener, Ont., 1874–1950. Prime minister of Canada during WWII.

KINSELLA, William Patrick (W. P.), literary arts. Edmonton, Alta, 1935. Writer; known for poetic baseball fiction. *Shoeless Joe.*

KIRKE, David (Sir), exploration and discovery. France, 1597–1654. First governor of Nfld, 1637.

KLEIN, Abraham Moses, literary arts. Ukraine, 1909–72. Poet of Jewish themes. "The Rocking Chair."

KLEIN, George John, invention. Hamilton, Ont., 1904–92. Productive inventor: wind tunnels, gearing systems, Canadarm gear design.

KLEIN, Ralph Philip, politics. Calgary, Alta, 1942. PC premier of Alberta, 1992–.

KNOTT, Elsie Marie, politics. Curve Lake, Ont., 1922–95. First native woman in Canada to be elected chief, at Ojibwa reserve near Peterborough, Ont.

KNOWLES, Stanley Howard, politics. USA, 1908–97. A founder of the New Democratic Party; represented Winnipeg North Centre riding 1942–81. Admired for his support of old-age pensions; president of Canadian Labour Congress 1958–62.

KNUDSON, George, sports. Winnipeg, Man., 1937–89. Golfer; Canada's top pro; 12 PGA tour victories.

KOFFLER, Murray Bernard, business. Toronto, Ont., 1924. Entrepreneur; made Shopper's Drug Mart Canada's largest pharmacy chain.

KOFFMAN, Morris (Moe), performing arts. Toronto, Ont., 1928. Jazz flautist. "Swinging Shepherd Blues."

KOGAWA, Joy Nozomi, literary arts. Vancouver, BC, 1935. Writer. *Obasan; Itsuka.*

KOTCHEFF, William Theodore (Ted), visual arts. Toronto, Ont., 1931. Film director. The Apprenticeship of Duddy Kravitz.

KRAATZ, Victor, sports. Germany, 1971. Ice dancing; with Shae-Lynn Bourne won Canadian title, 1993–96; third in World Championships, 1996.

KRALL, Diana, performing arts. Nanaimo, BC, 1964. Sultry jazz vocalist. *When I Look Into Your Eyes.*

KREINER, Kathy, sports. Timmins, Ont., 1957. Skier; gold medal, giant slalom, 1976 Olympics.

KREVER, Horace, law. Montreal, Que., 1929. Judge who led Royal Commission of Inquiry on the Blood System in Canada, 1997–97.

KRIEGHOFF, Cornelius David, visual arts. Holland, 1815–72. Known for paintings of Quebec life. *The Habitant Farm.*

KROL, Joseph "Joe King", sports. Hamilton, Ont., 1919. Football player; Toronto Argos star; top athlete, 1946.

KUDELKA, James, performing arts. Newmarket, Ont., 1955. Artistic director for the National Ballet of Canada; also choreographer, dancer. Critically acclaimed work with classical and modern influences. *Spring Awakening.*

KUERTI, Anton Emil, performing arts. Austria, 1938. Leading pianist; composer; Beethoven specialist.

KURELEK, William (Wasyl), visual arts. Whitfield, Alta, 1927–77. Symbolist religious painter.

KUWABARA, Bruce, visual arts. Hamilton, Ont., 1949. Partner with Toronto-based architecture firm Kuwabara Payne McKenna Blumberg; award-winning designer of Kitchener, Ont., City Hall; City Hall in Richmond, BC.

LA SALLE, Rene Robert Cavelier, Sieur de, exploration and discovery. France, 1643–87. Became commandant of Fort Frontenac in present-day Kingston, Ont., 1673.
LA VERENDRYE, Pierre Gaultier de Varennes, Sieur de, exploration and discovery. Trois-Rivières, Que., 1685–1749. Explorer of W Canada.
LABATT, John Kinder, business. Ireland, 1803-66. In 1855 became owner of a small brewery in London, Ont., the origin of the giant brewery empire.
LAFLEUR, Guy Damien, sports. Thurso, Que., 1951. Hockey player; Canadiens star right winger; 560 goals.
LAFONTAINE, Louis Hippolyte (Sir), politics. Boucherville, LC, 1807–64. In effect, Canada's first PM, 1848–51.
LALONDE, Donny, sports. Kitchener, Ont., 1960. Boxer; WBC light heavyweight champion (1987–88).
LALONDE, Edouard Charles, sports. Cornwall, Ont., 1887–1970. In 1950 named as one of Canada's outstanding lacrosse players of the half-century; played NHL Montreal Canadiens, scoring 124 goals in 98 games 1913–18.
LAMBERT, Natalie, sports. Montreal, Que., 1963. Speed skater; short track title, 500 m, 1993.
LAMBERTS, Heath, performing arts. Toronto, Ont., 1941. Actor at Stratford Festival, Ont. *Glengarry Glen Ross; Cyrano de Bergerac.*
LAMER, Antonio, law. Montreal, Que., 1933. Chief justice of the Supreme Court 1990-99.
LAMPMAN, Archibald, literary arts. Morpeth, Canada W, 1861–99. Nature poet. "Lyrics of Earth."
LANCASTER, Ron, sports. USA, 1938. Football player; coach; quarterback set 30 CFL records.
LANCTOT, Françoise, performing arts. Montreal, Que., 1947. Actress, film director; winner of Etrog for *La vrai nature du Bernadette. The Apprenticeship of Duddy Kravitz.*
LANDRY, G. Yves, business. Thetford Mines, Que., 1938–98. Died while chairman, president and CEO of Chrysler Canada; co-chairman of Automotive Advisory Committee to the Minister of Industry Canada.
LANG, Katherine Dawn (k.d.), performing arts. Consort, Alta, 1961. Country-torch singer; vegetarian activist. *Shadowlands.*
LANGFORD, Sam, sports. Weymouth Falls, NS, 1886–1956. Boxer; great fighter; denied title shot.
LANOIS, Daniel, performing arts. Hamilton, Ont., 1953. Singer; producer of Peter Gabriel's "Sledgehammer" and with Brian Eno U2's *Joshua Tree.*
LANTOS, Robert, visual arts. Hungary, 1949. Film producer; CEO, Alliance Communications. *Black Robe.*
LAPIERRE, Laurier L., media. Megantic, Que., 1929. TV personality, author; co-host, *This Hour Has Seven Days.*
LASKIN, Bora, law. Ft William, Ont., 1912–84. Chief justice of Canada, 1973–84.

LASTMAN, Melvin Douglas (Mel), politics. Toronto, Ont., 1933. Elected mayor of the amalgamated City of Toronto in 1997; formerly long-time mayor of North York, a satellite "city" of the former Metropolitan Toronto.
LAU, Evelyn, literary arts. Vancouver, BC, 1971. Poet, novelist, short story writer, used own experiences to portray the lives of street kids. *Runaway: Diary of a Street Kid; You Are Not Who You Claim; Oedipal Dreams.*
LAUMANN, Silken, sports. Toronto, Ont., 1964. Rower; braved broken leg for bronze medal in 1992 Olympics; Athlete of the Year 1991, 1992.
LAURE, Carole (b. Carol Champagne), performing arts. Montreal, Que., 1949. Actress; screen star. *Maria Chapdelaine.*
LAURENCE, Jean Margaret, literary arts. Neepawa, Man., 1926–87. Writer; created fictional setting of Manawaka. *The Diviners.*
LAURENDEAU, Joseph-Edmond-André, politics. Montreal, Que., 1912–68. Co-chairman of Royal Commission on Bilingualism and Biculturalism 1963–68; editor of Montreal's *Le Devoir* 1958–68.
LAURIER, Wilfrid (Sir), politics. St-Lin, Canada E, 1841–1919. Canada's first French-speaking prime minister.
LAURIN, Camille, politics. Charlemagne, Que., 1922–99. Drafted Bill 101, Quebec's French Language Charter; joined Quebec National Assembly in 1970, member of Parti Québécois.
LAVAL, François de, religion. France, 1623–1708. First bishop of Quebec (1674–88).
LAVALLEE, Calixa, performing arts. Verchères, Canada E, 1842–1891. Composer of "O Canada."
LAW, Andrew Bonar, politics. Rexton, NB, 1858–1923. Prime Minister of Britain 1922–23; signed Treaty of Versailles on behalf of Great Britain in 1919.
LAWRENCE, Florence, performing arts. Hamilton, Ont., 1890-1938. Film and vaudeville actress; first to use publicity stunt to launch career. *Daniel Boone; Resurrection.*
LAYTON, Irving Peter, literary arts. Romania, 1912. Prolific, flamboyant poet. "A Red Carpet for the Sun."
LE CAINE, Hugh, performing arts/science. Port Arthur, Ont., 1914–77. Physicist; composer; designed the sackbut, the first musical synthesizer.
LEACOCK, Stephen Butler, literary arts. Eng., 1869–1944. Humorist. *Sunshine Sketches of a Little Town.*
LEBLANC, Romeo, politics. Memramcook, NB, 1927. Governor-General of Canada 1994–99; former Liberal MP.
LEBLOND, Charles Philippe, science. France, 1910. Anatomist; pioneer in cell biology.
LECLERC, Felix, performing arts. La Tuque, Que., 1914–88. Singer/songwriter; influential chansonnier and Quebec nationalist.
LEE, Dennis Beynon, literary arts. Toronto, Ont., 1939. Poet, children's writer. *Alligator Pie; Garbage Delight.*
LEE, Geddy, performing arts. Toronto, Ont., 1953. Singer/songwriter; lead singer for Rush. *Moving Pictures.*
LEE-GARTNER, Kerrin, sports. Trail, BC, 1966. Skier; gold medal, women's downhill, 1992 Olympics.

LEGER, Gabrielle Carmel, politics. Montreal, Que., 1916–98. Wife of the late governor general Jules Leger; acted for her husband when he suffered a stroke shortly after taking office.

LEGER, Jules, politics. St-Anicet, Que., 1913–80. Canada's governor general, 1974–79.

LEGER, Paul-Emile, religion. Valleyfield, Que., 1904–91. Cardinal; eloquent, compassionate religious leader; became missionary in Africa.

LEMELIN, Roger, literary arts. Quebec City, Que., 1919–92. Writer; creator of the popular Plouffe family.

LEMIEUX, Jean-Paul, visual arts. Quebec City, Que., 1904–90. Landscape painter. *Le Visiteur du Soir; Lazare.*

LEMIEUX, Mario, sports. Montreal, Que., 1965. Hockey player; Pittsburgh Penguins centre, one of two players to average two points per game.

LENNOX, Edward James, visual arts. Toronto, Ont., 1854-1933. Architect of "Richardson Romanesque" style. Toronto's Old City Hall, Casa Loma; powerhouse at Niagara Falls, Ont.

LEONARD, Stanley, sports. Vancouver, BC, 1915. Golfer; won many Canadian titles; three US tour wins.

LESAGE, Jean, politics. Montreal, Que., 1912–80. Liberal premier of Quebec, 1960–66.

LETHEREN, Carol Anne, sports. Toronto, Ont., 1942. Chief executive of Canadian Olympic Association.

LEVESQUE, Georges-Henri, politics. Roberval, Que., 1902-2000. Dominican priest, founded Faculty of Social Sciences at Laval University; major figure in Quebec's Quiet Revolution.

LEVESQUE, Jean-Louis, business. Nouvelle, Que., 1911. Financier; co-founder of Levesque Beaubien Inc., Quebec's largest brokerage house.

LEVESQUE, René, politics. New Carlisle, Que., 1922–87. Led Parti Québécois; Quebec premier 1976–85.

LEVY, Eugene, performing arts. Hamilton, Ont., 1946. Actor; comedian; *SCTV* regular (Earl Camembert, Bobby Bitman).

LEWIS, David, politics. Russia, 1909–81. Federal NDP leader, 1971–75; eloquent speaker.

LEWIS, Lennox, sports. Eng., 1965. Boxer; super heavyweight gold medal, 1988 Olympics.

LEWIS, Stephen Henry, politics. Ottawa, Ont., 1937. Ont. NDP leader; Cdn UN ambassador.

LEWIS, Wilfrid Bennett, science. Eng., 1908–87. Physicist; prime role in developing CANDU reactor.

LEYRAC, Monique, performing arts. Montreal, Que., 1928. Actress; popular Quebec chanteuse.

LIGHTFOOT, Gordon Meredith, performing arts. Orillia, Ont., 1938. Singer/songwriter; popular vocalist with many hits. "Canadian Railroad Trilogy."

LILIENSTEIN, Lois, performing arts. USA, 1936. Member of children's musical entertainment group Sharon, Lois and Bram; live and on TV. *The Elephant Show.*

LILLIE, Beatrice Gladys, performing arts. Toronto, Ont., 1894–1989. Stage comedienne. *Auntie Mame.*

LINDER, Cec, performing arts. Poland, 1921–92. Television, stage and film character actor. *Goldfinger; A Touch of Class; The Edge of Night.*

LINDROS, Eric, sports. London, Ont., 1973. Hockey player; centre for Philadelphia Flyers; winner of Hart Trophy, 1995.

LINDSAY, Robert Blake Theodore (Ted), sports. Renfrew, Ont., 1925. Hockey player; left winger 17 seasons with Detroit and Chicago.

LINKLETTER, Art (b. Arthur Brown), performing arts. Moose Jaw, Sask., 1912. Radio/TV host. *People Are Funny.*

LISMER, Arthur, visual arts. Eng., 1885–1969. Painter; Group of Seven founding member. *September Gale.*

LITTLE, Jean, literary arts. Taiwan, 1932. Popular writer of children's literature, poetry; blends themes of alienation and troubled relationships. *From Anna; Mama's Going to Buy You a Mockingbird; His Banner Over Me.*

LITTLE, Richard Carruthers (Rich), performing arts. Ottawa, Ont., 1938. Impersonator; night club and television performer.

LIVESAY, Dorothy, literary arts. Winnipeg, Man., 1909–96. Poet; sensitive feminist writer. *Poems for People.*

LOATES, Glen Martin, visual arts. Toronto, Ont., 1945. Wildlife artist; painter and naturalist.

LOCKHART, Gene, performing arts. London, Ont., 1891–1957. Character actor appeared in *Miracle on 34th Street, Carousel,* and on Broadway. Father of actress June Lockhart.

LOGAN, William Edmond (Sir), science. Montreal, Que., 1798–1875. Geologist; first head of Geological Survey of Canada; first to map Laurentian Shield.

LOMBARDO, Gaetano Alberto "Guy", performing arts. London, Ont., 1902–77. Bandleader; his Royal Canadians most popular band in N America; 300 million records sold. Also won International World Cup in speed boating in 1946; US champion 1946-49; Canadian title in 1955, 1956.

LONGBOAT, Thomas Charles, sports. Brantford, Ont., 1887–1949. Runner; set record in 1907 Boston Marathon.

LONGDEN, John (Johnny), sports. Eng., 1910. Jockey; first N American with 4,000 winners (career: 6,032).

LORD, Bernard, politics. Moncton, NB, 1965. PC premier of NB, elected in 1999.

LORTIE, Louis, performing arts. Montreal, Que., 1959. Pianist; five-time winner of Canadian Music Competition, 1968–72, 1990 Juno for Best Classical Album.

LOUGHEED, Edgar Peter, politics. Calgary, Alta, 1928. PC premier of Alberta, 1971–85; played strong role in federal politics.

LOVELL, Jocelyn, sports. Eng., 1950. Canada's leading cyclist 1970–83; winner of 1000 m silver medal in 1978 world championships; paralysed in training accident 1983.

LOWRY, (Clarence) Malcolm, literary arts. Eng., 1909–57. British novelist whose powerful novels reflected his turbulent life; lived in BC 1937–54. *Under the Volcano.*

LUBA (b. Luba Kowalchyk), performing arts. Montreal, Que., 1958. Pop singer-songwriter. "Between the Earth and Sky"; "All or Nothing."

LUND, Alan, performing arts. Toronto, Ont., 1927–92. Dancer/choreographer. With wife Blanche Harris performed as an Astaire/Rogers-style dancing team; Stratford Festival, Charlottetown Festival.

LUNDSTROM, Linda, business. Red Lake, Ont., 1951. Founder of fashion business with boutiques across North America; her signature LaParka has long been her Canadian culture statement, as are her all-Canadian made clothes.

M

MacDONALD, Flora Isabel, politics. Sydney, NS, 1926. First woman to hold senior cabinet post; external affairs in Clark govt (1979).

MacDONALD, James Edward Hervey (J.E.H.), visual arts. Eng., 1874–1932. Landscape painter; Group of Seven founder. *Mist Fantasy.*

MacDONALD, James Williamson Galloway (Jock), visual arts. Scot., 1897–1960. Early abstract painter; member, Painters Eleven.

MACDONALD, John Alexander (Sir), politics. Scot., 1815–91. Canada's first official prime minister.

MacDOUGALL, Fraser, media. Stratford, Ont., 1907-2000. Longtime journalism figure; Ottawa bureau chief for Canadian Press; active on Ontario Press Council; chairman of Michener journalism awards.

MacEWEN, Gwendolyn, literary arts. Toronto, Ont., 1941–87. Poet. *The Shadow-Maker.*

MacGILL, Elizabeth "Elsie" Muriel Gregory, science. Vancouver, BC, 1905–80. Designer of Maple Leaf Trainer aircraft during WWII; designed winterized version of Hawker Hurricane fighter plane.

MacGREGOR, Roy, literary arts. Whitney, Ont., 1948. Novelist, columnist. *Home Game: Hockey and Life in Canada; The Last Season.*

MacGUIGAN, Mark Rudolph, politics. Charlottetown, PEI, 1931–98. Liberal politician who served with Pierre Trudeau, ran unsuccessfully for leader in 1984, later appointed judge of the Federal Court of Appeal. Founding member of the Canadian Civil Liberties Association.

MacISAAC, Ashley, performing arts. Antigonish, NS, 1975. Eclectic musician who blends pop music with traditional Celtic sound. *How Are You Today?; Fine Thank You Very Much.*

MACKENZIE, Alexander, politics. Scot., 1822–1892. Canada's second prime minister.

MacKENZIE, Alexander (Sir), exploration and discovery. Scot., 1764–1820. Charted MacKenzie R. (1789); crossed from L. Athabasca to Pacific Ocean (1793).

MacKENZIE, Maj.-Gen. Lewis W., military. Truro, NS, 1940. Soldier; led UN soldiers from 33 nations (incl. Canada) in opening Sarajevo airport for delivery of humanitarian aid during Bosnian civil war.

MacKENZIE, William Lyon, politics. Scot., 1795–1861. Led 1837 rebellion for reform in Upper Canada; Toronto's first mayor.

MacLEAN, John Angus, politics. Lewes, PEI, 1914-2000. Premier PEI 1979-81; instigator of equalization payments for troubled Atlantic fisheries.

MACLEAN, John Bayne, media. Crieff, Ont., 1862–1950. Founder of *Maclean's* magazine in 1905; also of *Financial Post, Chatelaine.*

MacLEAN, Steven Glenwood, science. Ottawa, Ont., 1954. Laser physicist who trained with NASA's astronaut program, specializes with NASA's robotics branch.

MacLENNAN, John Hugh, literary arts. Glace Bay, NS, 1907–90. Respected Canadian novelist. *The Watch That Ends the Night.*

MacLEOD, John James Rickard, medicine. Scot., 1876–1935. Medical researcher, co-winner with Drs. Banting and Best of Nobel Prize in 1923 for discovery of insulin.

MacMILLAN, Ernest Campbell (Sir), performing arts. Mimico, Ont., 1893–1973. Renowned conductor, composer, arranger; championed Canadian works.

MacMILLAN, Harvey Reginald (H.R.), business. Newmarket, Ont., 1885–1976. Industrialist; established forerunner of logging giant MacMillan Bloedel.

MacNAUGHTON, Andrew George Latta, military. Moosomin, NWT, 1887–1966. Soldier; led Cdn army in WWII; endorsed Dieppe raid; diplomat; UN Atomic Energy Assn.

MacNEIL, Rita, performing arts. Big Pond, NS, 1944. Cape Breton country singer; star of CBC's *Rita MacNeil Show.*

MacNEIL, Robert Breckenridge Ware, media. Toronto, Ont., 1932. TV host, newscaster, reporter, co-hosted public television series in USA, *MacNeil-Lehrer Newshour.*

MacNUTT, Walter, performing arts. Charlottetown, PEI, 1910–96. Composer of orchestral, chamber, choral, vocal, and keyboard music; noted for compositions for Anglo-Catholic service.

MACPHAIL, Agnes Campbell, politics. Proton Twp, Ont., 1890–1954. Only woman MP in 1921 (first women's vote); founded Elizabeth Fry Society.

MacPHERSON, Cluny, invention. St John's, Nfld, 1879–1966. Invented the gas helmet.

MacPHERSON, Duncan, visual arts. Toronto, Ont., 1925–93. Long-time *Toronto Star* cartoonist.

MAGEE, Helen Gagan, journalism. Toronto, Ont., 1908–98. Author and food writer for the Toronto *Globe and Mail* and former *Telegram.*

MAGNUSSEN, Karen Diane, sports. North Vancouver, BC, 1952. Figure skater; world champion, 1973.

MAHOVLICH, Francis William, sports. Timmins, Ont., 1938. Toronto Maple Leaf hockey player, 1957–68; winner of Calder Trophy, 1958.

MAILLET, Antonine, literary arts. Buctouche, NB, 1929. Novelist of Acadian life. Winner of France's *La Prix Goncourt. La Sagouine.*

MAISONNEUVE, Paul de Chomedey, Sieur de, politics. France, 1612–76. Founder of Montreal, 1642.

MAITLAND, (Herbert) Alan, performing arts. Lilburn, Ont., 1920–99. Long-running CBC radio host noted for his rich, resonant voice; appeared on *Maitland Manor, Read to Me* and most notably, *As It Happens,* with co-hosts Barbara Frum and Michael Enright, among others, from 1974–93.

MAK, Tak Wah, medicine. China, 1946. Research led him to discover the T-cell receptor, crucial to understanding the human immune system.

MANDEL, Howie, performing arts. Toronto, Ont., 1955. Manic comic and TV actor. *St Elsewhere.*

MANGUEL, Alberto Adrian, literary arts. Argentina, 1948. Critic, anthologist, novelist. *News from a Foreign Country; The Oxford Book of Canadian Ghost Stories.*

MANLEY, Elizabeth, sports. Belleville, Ont., 1965. Figure skater; silver medal, 1988 Olympics.

MANNING, Ernest Charles, politics. Carnduff, Sask., 1908–96. Alberta's Social Credit premier 1943–68; father of Reform Party leader Preston Manning.

MANNING, Ernest Preston, politics. Edmonton, Alta, 1942. Led Reform Party to breakthrough in 1993 federal election.

MANNING, Thomas Henry, exploration and discovery. Eng., 1911–98. Mapmaker who charted vast territories of the Arctic; also biologist and naturalist focusing on Arctic environment.

MANSBRIDGE, Peter, media. Eng., 1948. Broadcaster; anchorman, CBC national news.

MANSOURI, Lotfallah (Lotfi), performing arts. Iran, 1929. Former general director of Canadian Opera Company; creator of "surtitles", English translations of opera house librettos screened above stage.

MARCHAND, Leonard Stephen, politics. Vernon, BC, 1933. Native politician; first native federal cabinet minister.

MARCHILDON, Philip Edward, sports. Penetanguishene, Ont., 1913. Began career with Philadelphia Athletics in 1940; won 68 major league games before retirement in 1950.

MARCUS, Egerton, sports. Guyana, 1919–65. Boxer; silver medalist, middleweight category in 1988 Olympics.

MARCUS, Rudolph A., science. Montreal, Que., 1923. Winner of 1992 Nobel Prize in chemistry for work on electron transfer reactions in chemical systems.

MARGISON, Richard, performing arts. Victoria, BC, 1953. Tenor opera singer whose repertoire includes Verdi, Puccini and Bizet; international reputation.

MARIE-VICTORIN, Frère, science. Kingsley Falls, Que., 1885–1944. Distinguished botanist, author of *Croquis laurentiens; Les filicinée de Québec.*

MARK, J. Carson, science. Lindsay, Ont., 1913–97. Head of theoretical division of Los Alamos Scientific Library, influence in creation of hydrogen bomb.

MARQUETTE, Jacques, exploration and discovery. France, 1637–75. Jesuit priest explored North America with Louis Jolliet; served at Sault Ste Marie, 1666.

MARSHALL, Amanda, performing arts. Toronto, Ont., 1964. Singer, songwriter with powerful voice. "Birmingham."

MARSHALL, Donald, law. Sydney, NS, 1953. Acquitted of murder after serving 11 years in prison.

MARSHALL, Lois Catherine, performing arts. Toronto, Ont., 1924–97. Soprano, career began with Sir Ernest MacMillan's Bach's *St Matthew's Passion* with Mendelssohn Choir and Toronto Symphony; Toronto Arts Award for Music, 1989.

MARSHALL, Phyllis, performing arts. Barrie, Ont., 1921–96. Jazz singer; pioneer among black Canadian performers; performed with Cab Calloway, Percy Faith; 1949–52 on CBC radio's *Blues for Friday.*

MARTIN, Andrea, performing arts. USA, 1947. Stage, television and film actor particularly well known for comic roles in *SCTV* series.

MARTIN, Clara Brett, law. Toronto, Ont., 1874–1923. First woman lawyer in British Empire.

MARTIN, Paul Edgar Philippe, politics. Windsor, Ont., 1938. Liberal minister of finance.

MARTIN, Paul Joseph James, politics. Ottawa, Ont., 1903–92. Long-time Liberal cabinet minister.

MARTINI, Paul, sports. Weston, Ont., 1960. Figure skater; world pairs champion (with Barbara Underhill), 1984.

MASON, Roger Burford, literary arts. Eng., 1943–98. Editor and writer, short stories: *The Beaver Picture & Other Stories;* biography of John Evans, who devised a Cree alphabet (*Travels in the Shining Island*); and a biography of artist Franz Johnson.

MASSEY, Charles Vincent, politics. Toronto, Ont., 1887–1967. First Canadian-born governor general, 1952–59.

MASSEY, Hart Almerrin, business. Haldemand Twp, Ont., 1823–96. Capitalist; developed Massey-Ferguson Ltd.

MASSEY, Raymond Hart, performing arts. Toronto, Ont., 1896–1983. Craggy-faced actor often played Lincoln. *Dr. Kildare.*

MASSON, Henri Leopold, visual arts. Belgium, 1907–96. Paintings of city and landscapes in the 1940s; National Gallery.

MAXWELL, Lois (b. Lois Ruth Hooker), performing arts. Kitchener, Ont., 1927. Actress, columnist. Played character Moneypenny in James Bond movie series from 1963–83. Former columnist for Toronto *Sun.*

MAYER, Louis B. (Burt) (b. Eliezer Mayer), performing arts. Russia, 1885–1957. Grew up in Saint John, NB; with Samuel Goldwyn formed MGM movie studio in 1924; co-founded the Academy of Motion Picture Arts and Sciences in 1927.

McBEAN, Marnie, sports. Toronto, Ont., 1968. With Kathleen Heddle won women's double sculls rowing medals: two gold in 1992 Barcelona Olympics; one gold, one bronze in 1996 Olympics in Atlanta.

McBRIDE, Robert Bruce (Bob), performing arts. Toronto, Ont., 1946–98. Juno–award-winning lead singer of the 1970s rock band Lighthouse.

McCAIN, H. Harrison, business. Florenceville, NB, 1927. Industrialist; turned potato-processing plant into international firm.

McCARTHY, Doris, visual arts. Calgary, Alta, 1910. Artist, calligrapher, more than 90 solo exhibitions.

McCLELLAND, John Gordon (Jack), literary arts. Toronto, Ont., 1922. Publisher; his McClelland & Stewart nurtured Canadian writing; over 5,000 Canadian titles.

McCLUNG, Nellie Letitia, law. Chatsworth, Ont., 1873–1951. Reformer; fought for women's suffrage.

McCONNELL, Robert Murray Gordon, performing arts. London, Ont., 1935. Jazz musician; founded Boss Brass, major big band.

McCRAE, John, literary arts. Guelph, Ont., 1872–1918. Poet; physician who wrote "In Flanders Field."

McCULLOCH, Bruce Ian, performing arts. Edmonton, Alta, 1961. Versatile comedic actor, director, writer.

McCURDY, Edward Potts, performing arts. USA, 1919-2000. Folk singer, played in Ontario's Mariposa Folk Festival; noted for his huge repertoire of folk music that reflected the cultural history of Canada, specializing in Maritimes music.

McCURDY, Howard Douglas, politics. London, Ont., 1932. Black activist; also biologist.

McCURDY, John Alexander Douglas, exploration and discovery. Baddeck, NS, 1886–1961. Pilot; first airplane flight in British Empire in Silver Dart (1909).

McDERMOTT, Dennis, business. Eng., 1922. Labour leader; former president, Canadian Labour Congress.

McDONALD, Bruce, performing arts. Kingston, Ont., 1959. Film director. *Poadkill; Highway 61; Dance Me Outside.*

McDOUGALL, Barbara Jean, politics. Toronto, Ont., 1937. PC External Affairs minister 1991–93; political commentator and journalist.

McELCHERAN, William, visual arts. Hamilton, Ont., 1927–99. Internationally renowned sculptor; designer of ACTRA's Nellie award; famous for bronze "Everyman" sculptures depicting burly businessmen in striking poses.

McEWEN, Jean Albert, visual arts. Montreal, Que., 1923–99. "Nonfigurative" artist inspired by Riopelle, French Impressionists and American abstract artists.

McFARLANE, Leslie (F. W. Dixon), literary arts. Ottawa, Ont., 1903–77 Author of *Hardy Boys* adventure series.

McFARLENE, Todd, literary arts. Calgary, Alta, 1961. Creator of cult comic book *Spawn;* the first issue in 1992 was best-selling independent comic at 1.7 million copies sold.

McGARRIGLE, Anna and Kate, performing arts. Montreal, Que., 1944, 1946. Songwriters/ singers. Unique duo sings folk, own compositions. "Love Over and Over."

McGEE, Thomas D'Arcy, politics. Ire., 1825–68. Eloquent proponent of Confederation; assassinated 1868.

McGIBBON, Pauline Emily, politics. Sarnia, Ont., 1910. Cda's first woman lieutenant-governor (Ont., 1974).

McINTOSH, John, invention. USA, 1777–1845. Inventor; breeder of McIntosh apple.

McKENNA, Frank Joseph, politics. Apolaqui, NB, 1948. Liberal premier of NB since 1987.

McKENNA, Patrick Ivan Peter, performing arts. Hamilton, Ont., 1960. Comic actor plays Harold on *Red Green Show.* Also appears on drama series *Traders.*

McKENNITT, Loreena, performing arts. Morden, Man., 1957. Singer; harpist; Celtic music repertoire.

McKENZIE, Robert Tait, visual arts. Almonte, Ont., 1867–1938. Sculptor, orthopedic surgeon; designer of war memorials, sculptures.

McKINNON, Catherine, performing arts. Saint John, NB, 1944. Singer, actress. Appeared in CBC's *Don Messer's Jubilee; Spring Thaw* revue; *The Catherine McKinnon Show;* Charlottetown Festival. Married to actor/humorist Don Harron.

McKOY, Mark, sports. Guyana, 1961. Hurdler; gold medal, 110 m hurdles, 1992 Olympics.

McLACHLAN, Beverly, public service. Pincher Creek, Alta, 1943. Former BC Chief Justice of Supreme Court; in January 2000 became Chief Justice of Supreme Court of Canada.

McLACHLAN, Sara, performing arts. Halifax, NS, 1968. Singer-songwriter of pop music. *Surfacing.*

McLAREN, Norman, visual arts. Scot., 1914–87. Filmmaker; innovative NFB animator; *Pas de deux.*

McLARNIN, Jimmy, sports. Ire., 1907. Boxer; world welterweight champion, 1933–35.

McLAUCHLAN, Murray Edward, performing arts. Scot., 1948. Country performer; *Swingin' on a Star,* CBC Radio (1990); seven-time Juno award winner.

McLAUGHLIN, Audrey, politics. Dutton, Ont., 1936. NDP national leader 1989–95. First woman to lead a national party.

McLAUGHLIN, Robert Samuel (Col.), business. Enniskillen, Ont., 1871–1972. Industrialist; founded firm that became General Motors of Canada.

McLEAN, Stuart, media. Montreal, Que., 1948. Broadcaster on CBC's *Morningside; Vinyl Café;* author of *Welcome Home: Travels in Small Town Canada.*

McLUHAN, Herbert Marshall, media. Edmonton, Alta, 1911–80. Media theorist; developed theory about "hot" and "cool" media. *The Gutenburg Galaxy.*

McMURTRY, Roland Roy, politics. Toronto, Ont., 1932. Chief Justice of Ontario Court of Justice.

McNAUGHTON, Andrew George Latta, military. Moosomin, NWT, 1887–1966. Army officer, scientist, as chief of general staff of Armed Forces 1929–35 began modernization of nonpermanent militia; 1935–39 president of National Research Council of Canada.

McNAUGHTON, Duncan Anderson, sports. Cornwall, Ont., 1910. High jumper; 1932 Olympic high jump gold medal.

McPHERSON, Aimee Semple, religion. Ingersoll, Ont., 1890–1944. Controversial evangelist.

McPHERSON, Donald, sports. Windsor, Ont., 1945. World professional champion figure skater, 1965.

MEAGHER, Blanche Margaret, public service. Halifax, NS, 1911–99. Canada's first woman ambassador beginning in 1942, Meagher was posted in various locations: Mexico, Israel, Sweden, Uganda and London.

MEIGHEN, Arthur, politics. Anderson, Ont., 1874–1960. Succeeded Sir Robert Borden as prime minister of Canada.

MEILLEUR, Marie Louise Febronie Chasse, Kamouraska, Que., 1880–1998. Recognized in 1997 as the world's oldest person, lived in rural Ontario for most of her life.

MERCER, Ruby, performing arts. USA, 1906–99. Former opera singer who debuted at New York's Metropolitan Opera in 1936, Mercer was instrumental in the development of Canadian opera; founder of *Opera Canada* magazine, Canadian Children's Opera Chorus and host of CBC radio's *Opera Time* and *Opera in Stereo.*

MERCREDI, Ovide William, politics. Grand Rapids, Man., 1946. National chief of the Assembly of First Nations 1991.

MERRIL, Judith, literary arts. USA, 1923–97. Science fiction writer, novelist, editor, short story writer, critic. *Survival Ship and Other Stories; Daughters of the Earth and Other Stories.*

MESSER, Donald Charles Frederick (Don), performing arts. Tweedside, NB, 1909–73. Bandleader; popular maker of traditional fiddle and dance music. *Don Messer's Jubilee.*

METCALF, John Wesley, literary arts. Eng., 1938. Essayist; short story writer. *Going Down Slow; Private Parts: A Memoir; Adult Entertainment.*

MICHAELS, Lorne (b. Lorne Lipowitz), media. Toronto, Ont., 1945. TV producer; founding producer, *Saturday Night Live.*

MICHENER, Daniel Roland, politics. Lacombe, Alta, 1900–91. Governor general of Canada, 1967–74.

MIKITA, Stan (b. Stanislaus Gvoth, sports. Czech., 1940. Hockey player; centre with Chicago Blackhawks (1959–80); first Czech to play in NHL.

MILLAR, Ian D., sports. Halifax, NS, 1947. Eight-time Canadian show-jumping champion, Cdn Athlete of the Year, 1987, 1989.

MILLAR, Margaret, literary arts. Kitchener, Ont., 1915. Thriller writer. *Beast in View*.

MILLS, Frank, performing arts. Montreal, Que., 1942. Pianist, composer; early career was member of pop group The Bells; solo career on TV and the concert stage. "Love Me Love Me Love"; "Music Box Dancer".

MILNE, David Brown, visual arts. Paisley, Ont., 1882–1953. Versatile painter. *Raspberry Jam*.

MILNER, Brenda, science. Eng., 1915. Neuropsychologist; ground-breaking brain researcher.

MINER, John Thomas (Jack), science. USA, 1865–1944. Conservationist; pioneered bird sanctuaries, migratory banding.

MIRVISH, Edwin (Ed) (b. Yehudi Mirvish), business. USA, 1914. Entrepreneur; retailer (Honest Ed's) and theatre owner.

MISTRY, Rohinton, literary arts. India, 1952. Novelist, short story writer. *Such a Long Journey; A Fine Balance*.

MITCHELL, Joni (b. Roberta Joan Anderson), performing arts. Ft Macleod, Alta, 1943. Singer/songwriter; influential lyricist. *Court and Spark*.

MITCHELL, Ray, sports. Peace River, Alta, 1931. Bowler; winner of 1972 Canadian and world 10-pin championship.

MITCHELL, William Ormond (W.O.), literary arts. Weyburn, Sask., 1914–98. Prairie novelist. *Who Has Seen the Wind?*

MOLSON, John, business. Eng., 1764–1836. Founded Molson brewery; built railroads.

MONTCALM DE SAINT VERAN, Louis Joseph de Montcalm Grozon, military. France, 1712–59. Soldier; French commander in Seven Years War; died on Plains of Abraham.

MONTGOMERY, Lucy Maud, literary arts. Clifton, PEI, 1874–1942. Writer; creator of *Anne of Green Gables*.

MONTGOMERY, Robert Douglas, performing arts. Bradford, Ont., 1908–66. Movie actor, played Laurie in 1933 version of *Little Women* opposite Katharine Hepburn.

MOODIE, Susanna, literary arts. Eng., 1803–85. Writer; pioneer author of *Roughing It in the Bush*.

MOORE, Brian, literary arts. N Ire., 1921–99 Prolific novelist; winner of two Governor General's Awards. *The Luck of Ginger Coffey; Black Robe*.

MOORE, Dora Mavor, performing arts. Scotland, 1888–1979. Actress appeared in Canada and US; founded Village Players in 1938 in Toronto, Ont.; toured schools. *Spring Thaw*.

MOORE, Gregory William, sports. Vancouver, BC, 1975–99. Four time winner of Championship Auto Racing Teams (CART) circuit; died in Marlboro 500 race in California.

MOORE, James Mavor, literary arts. Toronto, Ont., 1919. TV producer; librettist; columnist; critic.

MOORES, Frank Duff, politics. Carbonear, Nfld, 1933. PC premier of Newfoundland, 1972–79.

MORANIS, Rick, performing arts. Toronto, Ont., 1953. Comedian; actor; *SCTV* regular. *Ghostbusters*.

MORAWETZ, Oskar, performing arts. Czech., 1917. Composer. From the Diary of Anne Frank.

MORENZ, Howarth Williams (Howie), sports. Mitchell, Ont., 1902–37. Hockey player; centre; Canada's player of half century (CP), 1950; died of on-ice injuries.

MORGAN, Henry, business. Scotland, 1819–93. In 1852 Morgan founded a dry goods store in Montreal, which by 1950 became the national chain Henry Morgan & Co.; merged with Hudson's Bay Company in 1960.

MORGAN, John, performing arts. Wales. Comedian who appears on CBC's *Royal Canadian Air Farce*, roles include Jock McBile and Mike from Canmore.

MORGENTALER, Henry, medicine. Poland, 1923. Physician; challenge of abortion laws led to Supreme Court ruling them unconstitutional.

MORISSETTE, Alanis Nadine, performing arts. Ottawa, Ont., 1974. Singer-songwriter. Juno award winner 1996 for *Jagged Little Pill* (Best Album) and Female Vocalist of the Year; Grammy Award winner, 1996.

MORIYAMA, Raymond, visual arts. Vancouver, BC, 1929. Architect; Ontario Science Centre.

MORRICE, James Wilson (J.W.), visual arts. Montreal, Que., 1864–1924. Artist; early modernist. *The Ice Bridge*.

MORRIS, Alwyn, sports. Montreal, Que., 1957. With Hugh Fisher won gold medal in 1000 m and bronze in 500 m kayak doubles at 1984 Olympics.

MORRIS, Joseph (Joe), politics. Eng., 1913–96. Former president of Canadian Labour Congress; chairman of International Labour Organization.

MORRISON, Bram, performing arts. Toronto, Ont., 1940. Member of children's musical entertainment group Sharon, Lois and Bram; live and on TV. *The Elephant Show*.

MORRISSEAU, Norval, visual arts. Sand Point Reserve, Ont., 1932. Ojibway artist originated pictographic style.

MORSE, Barry, performing arts. Eng., 1918. Stage/film/TV actor; regular on *The Fugitive*.

MORTON, William Lewis (W.L.), literary arts. Gladstone, Man., 1908–80. Historian. *Manitoba: A History*.

MOSS, Carrie-Anne, performing arts. Vancouver, BC, 1967. Model turned actress who has appeared in *Dark Justice* TV series, as well as *Matrix; Models Inc.,* and *F/X The Series*.

MOWAT, Claire Angel, literary arts. Toronto, Ont., 1933. Graphic artist, fiction writer, wife of writer Farley Mowat. *The Girl From Away; The Outport People; The French Isles*.

MOWAT, Farley McGill, literary arts. Belleville, Ont., 1921. Controversial, popular naturalist writer. *A Whale for the Killing*.

MOWAT, Oliver (Sir), politics. Kingston, UC, 1820–1903. Ontario premier, 1872–96; lieutenant-governor, 1897–1903.

MUKHERJEE, Bharati, literary arts. India, 1940. Novelist, *The Middleman and Other Stories; Jasmine*.

MULRONEY, Brian Martin, politics. Baie Comeau, Que., 1939. Prime minister of Canada 1984–93.

MUNDELL, Robert, business. Kingston, Ont., 1932. Winner of 1999 Nobel Prize for economics for 1960s study of exchange rates and their relationship to monetary policy.

MUNK, Peter, business. Hungary, 1927. Capitalist; CEO, American Barrick Resources gold mining company.

MUNRO, Alice, literary arts. Wingham, Ont., 1931. Short story writer. Winner of 1998 Giller prize. *Lives of Girls and Women.*

MUNSCH, Robert, literary arts. USA, 1945. Children's writer. *The Paper Bag Princess; Love You Forever.*

MURPHY, Emily Cowan, law. Cookstown, Ont., 1868–1933. Legal reformer; first woman magistrate in British Empire; fought for women's rights.

MURPHY, Rex, media. Carbonear, Nfld, 1947. CBC news journalist with acerbic style. *Cross Country Checkup.*

MURRAY, Anne, performing arts. Springhill, NS, 1945. Singer; Canada's most successful performer; many Junos and Grammys. "Snowbird."

MURRAY, George Henry, politics. Grand Narrows, NS, 1861–1929. Lib. premier of NS, 1896–1923.

MURRAY, John Wilson, law. Scot., 1840–1906. Detective; pioneered scientific crime detection.

MURRAY, Margaret Teresa "Ma", media. USA, 1888–1982. Journalist; pungent editorialist in own magazines.

MURRAY, Robert George Everitt, science. Eng., 1919. With Philip Fitz-Jones, researched structure and chemical nature of bacterial spores.

MUSGRAVE, Susan, literary arts. USA, 1951. Poet, novelist, children's writer. *The Embalmer's Art: Poems; The Charcoal Burners.*

MUSTARD, James Fraser, medicine. Toronto, Ont., 1927. Physician; medical humanitarian; found connection between aspirin and blood clotting.

MUSTARD, William, medicine. Clinton, Ont., 1914–87. Physician; beloved children's surgeon developed operations for blue babies, polio cripples.

MYERS, Barton, visual arts. USA, 1934. Architect. Seagram Museum in Waterloo, Ont.; U of Toronto's Woodsworth College; UCLA Northwest Commons and Housing; Housing Union Building, U of Alta.

MYERS, Mike, performing arts. Toronto, Ont., 1963. Comic actor has appeared in movies *Austin Powers; It's a Dog's Life; Wayne's World,* also appeared on *Saturday Night Live.*

MYLES, Alannah, performing arts. Toronto, Ont., 1958. Pop singer/composer of hard rock, ballads. "Lover of Mine"; *Black Velvet; Al-Lan-Nah.*

N

NAISMITH, James A., sports. Almonte, Ont., 1861–1939. Physician; invented basketball in 1891.

NAKAMURA, Kazio, visual arts. Vancouver, BC, 1926. Japanese-Canadian artist who was interned during World War II; a member of Painters Eleven group, he represents the chaos of the universe through abstracts, landscapes and surreal images.

NAMARO, James (Jimmy), performing arts. USA, 1913–98. A member of the CBC's *Happy Gang,* the longest-running program on the radio network; also led his own jazz band.

NANOGAK, Agnes, visual arts. Baillie I., NWT, 1925. Inuit artist whose prints depict Inuit myths and legends, operating out of Holman I. Artist co-op. Illustrated *Tales from the Igloo.*

NASH, Cyril Knowlton, media. Toronto, Ont., 1927. Broadcaster; former anchorman, CBC national news.

NATTRASS, Susan Marie, sports. Medicine Hat, Alta, 1950. Shooter; six women's world trapshooting titles.

NAULT, Fernand (b. Fernand-Noel Boissonneault), performing arts. Montreal, Que., 1921. Dancer; choreographer, Les Grands Ballets Canadiens.

NELLIGAN, Emile, literary arts. Montreal, Que., 1879–1941. Romantic poet. "Romance du Vin."

NELLIGAN, Kate, performing arts. London, Ont., 1951. Actor; appears on both stage and film. *Eleni.*

NEMETZ, Nathaniel "Sonny", law. Winnipeg, Man., 1913–97. Chief Justice of British Columbia 1979–88, leading judicial administrator in BC.

NEVILLE, John, performing arts. Eng., 1925. Actor, director. Stratford Festival, Ont.; director of Stratford's The Young Company.

NEWMAN, Peter Charles, media. Austria, 1929. Journalist; popular historian. *The Canadian Establishment; Maclean's* editor, 1971–82.

NEWTON, Margaret, science. Montreal, Que., 1887–1971. Plant pathologist; first scientist to research rust in wheat.

NICHOL, Barrie Phillip (bp), literary arts. Vancouver, BC, 1944–88. Concrete and sound poet, novelist. *Journeying and Returns; Love: A Book of Remembrance.*

NICHOL, Dave, business. Chatham, Ont., 1940. Made Loblaws stores market leader with President's Choice label.

NICHOLAS, Cynthia (Cindy), sports. Toronto, Ont., 1957. Marathon swimmer; first woman to swim English Channel both ways.

NICOL, Eric, media. Kingston, Ont., 1919. Humour columnist. "Girdle Me a Globe."

NIELSEN, Erik Hersholt, politics. Regina, Sask., 1924. PC MP elected in Yukon 1957, served as deputy prime minister in Mulroney government.

NIELSEN, Leslie, performing arts. Regina, Sask., 1926. Deadpan film/TV comedian. *Naked Gun.*

NORQUAY, John, politics. St Andrews, Man., 1841–89. Manitoba premier of mixed European and native ancestry, 1878–87.

NORTHCOTT, Ronald Charles, sports. Innisfail, Alta, 1935. Curler; skipped three Brier and world champion rinks.

NOWLAN, Alden, literary arts. Windsor, NS, 1933–83. Poet. "Bread, Wine and Salt."

O

O'BRIEN, Mary, public service. Scot., 1926–98. Midwife, philosopher; founding member of the Feminist Party of Canada, wrote *The Politics of Reproduction; Reproducing the World.*

O'HARA, Catherine, performing arts. Toronto, Ont., 1954. Actor; comedian; *SCTV* regular (Lola Heatherton).

O'NEILL, James Edward "Tip", sports. Canada W, 1859–1918. Baseball player; batted .326 in 10-year career.

OAKS, Sir Harry, business. USA, 1874-1943. Oaks made his fortune through hold mine near Swastika, Ont., became North America's second largest gold mine; retired to the Bahamas, victim of unsolved murder.

ODJIG, Daphne, visual arts. Manitoulin Island, Ont., 1919. Blends western and native styles. *The Indian in Transition.*

OKALIK, Paul, politics. Pangnirtung, NWT, 1964. First premier of 19-member Legislative Assembly for Nunavit in the Eastern Arctic, created in 1999.

OLCOTT, Sidney, performing arts. Toronto, Ont., 1873–1949. Director of Hollywood silent films, pioneered locations shots, westerns. *Ben Hur.*

OLIPHANT, Betty, performing arts. Eng., 1918. Founded National Ballet School.

ONDAATJE, Christopher, business/literary arts. Sri Lanka, 1933. Financier; author. *Leopard in the Afternoon.*

ONDAATJE, Michael, literary arts. Sri Lanka, 1943. Poet; editor; novelist. *The English Patient* (Booker Prize).

OONARK, Jessie, visual arts. Back River, NWT, 1906-85. Inuit artist who employed brilliant colours to depict both traditional images and Christian themes in her drawings and wall hangings.

ORBINSKI, James, medicine. England, 1960. President, International Council, for Doctors Without Borders; accepted 1999 Nobel Peace Prize on behalf of the international organization.

ORR, Robert Gordon (Bobby), sports. Parry Sound, Ont., 1948. Hockey player; spectacular offensive defenceman; won eight consecutive Norris trophies.

ORSER, Brian Ernest, sports. Belleville, Ont., 1961. Figure skater; 1987 world champion, twice Olympic silver medallist (1984, 1988).

ORTON, George W., sports. Strathroy, Ont., 1873–1958. Runner; Canada's first Olympic gold medallist, winning for USA in 1900 (2500 m steeplechase).

OSLER, William (Sir), medicine. Bond Head, UC, 1849–1919. Physician; renowned medical educator; author of authoritative textbooks.

OTTENBRITE, Anne, sports. Whitby, Ont., 1966. Swimmer; gold medal, 200 m, 1984 Olympics.

OUIMET, Joseph Alphonse, media. Montreal, Que., 1908–88. TV executive; designed first Canadian TV receiver; CBC president, 1958–67.

P

PACE, Kate, sports. North Bay, Ont., 1969. Skier; World Cup downhill champion, 1993.

PACHTER, Charles, visual arts. Toronto, Ont., 1942. Painter famous for flag series; 1973 acrylic sketch titled *Queen on Moose.*

PAGE, Patricia Kathleen, (P.K.), literary arts. Eng., 1916. Poet; novelist; artist. "The Metal and the Flower."

PANNETON, Philippe (Ringuet), literary arts. Trois-Rivières, Que., 1895–1960. Man of letters; acclaimed Quebec writer. *Trente Arpents.*

PAPINEAU, Louis Joseph, politics. Montreal, Que., 1786–1871. Led political reform movement in Lower Canada.

PARIS, Erna, literary arts. Toronto, Ont., 1938. Writer. *The Garden and the Gun; End of Days.*

PARIZEAU, Jacques, politics. Montreal, Que., 1930. Leader, Parti Québécois 1987–95.

PARKER, Jackie, sports. USA, 1932. Football player; coach; Edmonton Eskimos star quarterback; named CFL outstanding player three times.

PARKER, Jon Kimura, performing arts. Vancouver, BC, 1959. Concert pianist, performed for Queen, prime ministers, and at Carnegie Hall.

PARKIN, John Burnett, visual arts. Toronto, Ont., 1911-75. Partnered with John Cresswell Parkin (no relation) to build major public buildings, including hospitals, schools, airports. Largest firm in Canada in the 1950s and '60s. Union Station (Ottawa), IBM head office (Toronto).

PARROT, Jean-Claude, business. Montreal, Que., 1936. Labour leader; leader of militant postal union.

PARTRIDGE, Edward Alexander, business. Canada W, 1862–1931. Farm reformer; visionary in grain industry fought monopolies, started growers' cooperative.

PASSAGLIA, Lui, sports. Vancouver, BC, 1954. Football player; kicker with BC Lions; CFL's all-time scoring leader.

PATRICK, Lester, sports. Drummondville, Que., 1883–1960. Hockey executive; NHL builder.

PATTISON, James Allen, business. Saskatoon, Sask., 1928. Industrialist; developed car dealership into business empire; chairman, Expo 86.

PAUL, Robert, sports. Toronto, Ont., 1937. Figure skater; with Barbara Wagner, won four pairs titles, 1960 Olympic gold.

PAYETTE, Julie, science. Montreal, Que., 1963. Astronaut and mission specialist on crew of STS-96 Atlantis, a 10-day logistics and resupply mission that launched in May 1999.

PAYETTE, Lise, media/politics. Montreal, Que., 1931. Broadcaster, writer, politician; her radio show with Radio-Canada, *Place Aux Femmes,* aired in the 1960s; Parti Québécois MNA1976-80.

PEAKER, Charles, performing arts. Eng., 1899–1978. Organist, choirmaster, writer. Foremost concert organist in Canada. Edited *Organ Music of Canada.*

PEARSON, Lester Bowles, politics. Newtonbrook, Ont., 1897–1972. Prime minister of Canada 1963–1968; awarded Nobel Peace Prize in 1957.

PECKFORD, Alfred Brian, politics. Whitbourne, Nfld. 1942. PC premier of Nfld, 1979–89.

PEEL, Paul, visual arts. London, Ont., 1860–92. Painter famous for *After the Bath,* which depicts two children warming themselves before a fireplace. *The Tired Model; Good News, Toronto.*

PELADEAU, Pierre, media. Outremont, Que., 1925–97. Publisher; head of newspaper giant Quebecor.

PELLAN, Alfred, visual arts. Quebec City, Que., 1906–88. Painter; cubist and surrealist artist.

PELLATT, Henry Mill (Sir), military. Kingston, Canada W, 1860–1939. Soldier; builder of eccentric Toronto mansion, Casa Loma.

PELLETIER, Gerard, politics. Victoriaville, Que., 1919–97. Chief editor for *La Presse* (1961–65); federal deputy minister for Montreal riding of Hochelaga 1965–75. Later ambassador for Canada in Paris and for United Nations.

PENFIELD, Wilder Groves Dr, medicine. USA, 1891–1976. Neurologist; writer; pioneered mapping of brain functions; founded Montreal Neurological Inst.

PENNELL, Nicholas, performing arts. Eng., 1938–95. Former actor at Stratford Festival; starred in British TV series *The Forsyte Saga.*
PENTLAND, Barbara Lally, performing arts. Winnipeg, Man., 1912-2000. Celebrated avant-garde composer; noted for anti-tonal style. *Concerto for Piano and String Orchestra.*
PEPIN, Jean-Luc, politics. Drummondville, Que., 1924–95. Longtime Liberal cabinet minister; served on Anti-Inflation Board, co-chairman of 1977 unity task force.
PEPIN, Marcel, politics. Montreal, Que., 1926-2000. Became president of Confederation of National Trade unions in 1965; responsible for uniting public service unions in Quebec and instigator of illegal Common Front Strike of 1972; later head of World Confederation of Labour.
PERCY, Karen, sports. Edmonton, Alta, 1966. Skier; won two bronze medals, 1988 Olympics.
PERRAULT, Pierre, visual arts. Montreal, Que., 1927. Filmmaker; realist director. *L'Acadie, L'Acadie.*
PETERSON, Eric, performing arts. Indian Head, Sask., 1946. Actor. *Billy Bishop Goes to War;* CBC's *Street Legal* series.
PETERSON, Oscar Emmanuel, performing arts. Montreal, Que., 1925. Jazz pianist; "Canadiana Suite"; over 90 albums.
PETRIE, Daniel, performing arts. Glace Bay, NS, 1920. Film director, won Genie award for *Bay Boy; A Raisin in the Sun.*
PEZER, Vera, sports. Melfort, Sask., 1939. Curler; Canadian women's champion, 1971–73.
PFLUG, Christiane, visual arts. Germany, 1936–72. Painter of melancholy landscapes and domestic scenes. *Cottingham School After the Rain; Kitchen Door with Esther.*
PHILLIPS, Robin, performing arts. Eng., 1942. Director, Stratford Festival, 1975–80, 1986–87.
PICKFORD, Mary (b. Gladys Smith), performing arts. Toronto, Ont., 1893–1979. Actress; "America's Sweetheart" was early movie star. *Sparrows.*
PIDGEON, Walter, performing arts. E Saint John, NB, 1897–1984. Leading man. *Mrs. Miniver.*
PINSENT, Gordon Edward, performing arts. Grand Falls, Nfld, 1930. Versatile actor. *The Rowdyman; Due South.*
PITSEOLAK Ashoona, visual arts. NWT, 1904–83. Artist of Inuit myth and legend.
PITSEOLAK, Peter, visual arts. NWT, 1902–73. Photographer; recorded passing of traditional Inuit life.
PLAMONDON, Antoine, visual arts. Lorette, Que., 1804–95. Portraitist and religious painter.
PLAMONDON, Luc, performing arts. St Raymond-de-Portneuf, Que., 1945. Lyricist; wrote rock opera *Starmania;* collaborated with Britain's Tim Rice; has written songs for Celine Dion.
PLANTE, Jacques, sports. Mt Carmel, Que., 1929–86. Hockey goaltender; seven-time Vezina winner; originated face mask.
PLAUT, Gunther, religion. Germany, 1912. Rabbi (Toronto's Holy Blossom Temple); author; advocate of modern secular Judaism. Wrote *The Torah: A Modern Commentary; The Man Who Would Be Messiah,* a novel.
PLUMMER, Arthur Christopher Orme, performing arts. Toronto, Ont., 1929. Stage and film star. *Murder By Decree.*

POCKINGTON, Peter H., business. Regina, Sask., 1941. Entrepreneur; owner of Edmonton Oilers.
POCOCK, Nancy Meek, philanthropy. USA, 1911–98. Quaker and pacifist, an antiwar and refugee advocate; won the Medal of Friendship from Socialist Republic of Vietnam.
PODBORSKI, Steve, sports. Toronto, Ont., 1957. Skier; world downhill champion, 1982.
POLANYI, John Charles, science. Germany, 1929. Chemist; Nobel Prize (1986) for work on infrared chemiluminescence.
POLLEY, Sarah, performing arts. Toronto, Ont., 1979. Actress; *The Road to Avonlea; The Sweet Hereafter.*
POLLOCK, Sam, sports. Montreal, Que., 1925. Hockey executive; built Montreal Canadiens dynasty.
POLLOCK, Sharon, literary arts. Fredericton, NB, 1936. Playwright; writer of conscience. *Blood Relations.*
PONTIAC, military. USA, 1720?–69. Ottawa Indian chief who formed alliance with various Indian federations to attack English, including a fort at Point Pelee, Ont.; in 1765 key signer of peace treaties with the English.
PORTER, Anna Maria, literary arts. Hungary. Publisher, author. CEO and director of Key Porter Books; mystery writer. *The Bookfair Murders; Mortal Sins.*
POST, Sandra, sports. Oakville, Ont., 1943. Golfer; Canada's first woman touring professional.
POTTS, Jerry (b. Ky-yo-Kosi), military. USA, 1840–96. Native scout; Blackfoot became NWMP special constable.
POTVIN, Dennis, sports. Ottawa, Ont., 1953. Hockey player; as defenceman with New York Islanders (1973–88) all-time leader in goals and assists.
POWELL, Marion, medicine. Toronto, Ont., 1923–97. Former president of Planned Parenthood in Toronto; a pioneer in introducing birth control information in the 1960s.
PRATLEY, Gerald Arthur, performing arts. England, 1923. Film critic; founder of Ontario Film Institute in 1968; CBC's first film critic 1948-75. *Pratley at the Movies.*
PRATT, Edwin James (E.J.), literary arts. Western Bay, Nfld, 1883–1964. Leading pre-WWII poet. "Newfoundland Verse."
PRATT, John Christopher, visual arts. St John's, Nfld, 1935. Artist; developed style of "conceptual realism."
PRATT, Mary, visual arts. Fredericton, NB, 1935. Artist; her paintings portray kitchen imagery and domestic themes. Illustrated Cynthia Wine's *Across the Table: An Indulgent Look at Food in Canada.*
PRIESTLEY, Jason Bradford, performing arts. Vancouver, BC, 1969. Popular actor noted for his brooding looks. *Beverly Hills, 90210.*
PURDY, Alfred Wellington, literary arts. Wooler, Ont., 1918-2000. Working-class poet. "The Cariboo Horses."

Q

QUARRINGTON, Paul Lewis, literary arts. Toronto, Ont., 1953. Governor General's Award for Fiction, 1990. *Home Game; Whale Music.*
QUILICO, Louis, performing arts. Montreal, Que., 1925-2000. Operatic baritone; appeared with most major companies.

R

RADDAL, Thomas Head, literary arts. Eng., 1903–94. Governor General's Award winning historical novelist. *The Pied Piper of Dipper Creek and Other Tales; His Majesty's Yankees.*

RADISSON, Pierre Esprit, exploration and discovery. France, 1636–1710. Explorer; fur trader; important in early history of Hudson's Bay Co as guide and advisor.

RAE, Robert Keith (Bob), politics. Ottawa, Ont., 1948. NDP premier of Ontario 1990–95.

RAFFI (b. Raffi Cavoukian), performing arts. Egypt, 1948. Singer. *Baby Beluga.*

RANKIN, John Morris, performing arts. Mabou, NS, 1959-2000. Head of musical group The Rankin Family, later The Rankins, Cape Breton musicians instrumental in popular revival of East Coast Celtic tradition.

RASKY, Harry, performing arts. Toronto, Ont., 1928. Filmmaker; noted documentarist. *The Dispossessed: The War Against the Indians.*

RASMINSKY, Louis, business. Montreal, Que., 1908–98. Governor, Bank of Canada, 1961–72.

RAYNER, Gordon, visual arts. Toronto, Ont., 1935. Realist, abstract painter, landscapes and cityscapes; northern Ontario landscapes. *Magnetawan No. 2.*

READ, Ken, sports. 1955. Skier; winner of five World Cup downhill victories (1975–80).

REANEY, James Crerar, literary arts. Easthope, Ont., 1926. Playwright; poet; critic. "A Suit of Nettles."

REBICK, Judy, politics. USA, 1945. Former head, Natl Action Committee on Status of Women.

REED, George Robert, sports. USA, 1939. Football player; running back with Sask. Roughriders; 44 CFL records.

REEVES, Keanu, performing arts. Lebanon, 1965. Actor. *Bill and Ted's Excellent Adventure; My Own Private Idaho.*

REGAN, Gerald Augustine, politics. Windsor, NS, 1928. Liberal premier of NS, 1970–78.

REICHMANN, Paul, business. Austria, 1930. Developer; philanthropist; with brothers Albert and Ralph, built Olympia & York into world's largest real estate developers in 1980s.

REID, Daphne Kate, performing arts. Eng., 1930–93. Primarily stage actress; Stratford mainstay.

REID, Fiona, politics. Eng., 1951. Dramatic and comedic actor. CBC's *King of Kensington* series; Stratford Festival, Ont.

REID, William Ronald (Bill), visual arts. Victoria, BC, 1920–98. Noted artist who promoted Northwest Coast native carving; also a sculptor whose works appear in major galleries and buildings.

REITMAN, Ivan, visual arts. Czech., 1946. Film director; producer; went from exploitation movies to blockbusters. *Ghostbusters.*

RENO, Ginette, performing arts. Montreal, Que., 1946. Popular chanteuse of sentimental ballads. "Tu vivras toujours dans mon Coeur"; "A ma manière."

REYNOLDS, John McCombe "Mac", visual arts. Toronto, Ont., 1916-99. Internationally renowned sculptor, painter and social historian for CBC.

RICCI, Nino Pio, literary arts. Leamington, Ont., 1959. Novelist, recipient of Governor General's Award for Fiction, 1990, for Lives of the Saints.

RICHARD, Joseph Henry Maurice "Rocket", sports. Montreal, Que., 1921-2000. Hockey player; legendary right winger; hockey's first 50-goal, 500-goal scorer.

RICHARDSON, Ernie, sports. Stoughton, Sask., 1931. Curler; skipped four Brier and world title rinks.

RICHARDSON, James Armstrong, business. Kingston, Ont., 1885–1939. Financier; founded family grain business and investment house.

RICHLER, Mordecai, literary arts. Montreal, Que., 1931. Novelist; essayist; acerbic comic writer. *St Urbain's Horseman.*

RIDOUT, Godfrey, performing arts. Toronto, Ont., 1918–94. Composer of chamber, symphonic and religious choral works.

RIEL, Louis, politics. St Boniface, Man., 1844–85. Métis leader; led North West Rebellion, 1870 and 1885; hanged for treason; rehabilitated and recognized as a founder of Manitoba in 1992.

RIOPELLE, Jean-Paul, visual arts. Montreal, Que., 1923. Acclaimed painter, sculptor. *Autrich.*

RITCHIE, Charles Stewart Almon, politics. Halifax, NS, 1906–95. Diplomat post–WWII; author of a number of books. *The Siren Years.*

RITTER, Erika, literary arts. Regina, Sask., 1948. Playwright, essayist, broadcaster. Her plays are a lighthearted look at serious women's issues. *The Visitor From Charleston; Automatic Pilot; Urban Scrawl.*

ROBARTS, John Parmenter, politics. Banff, Alta, 1917–82. PC premier of Ontario, 1961–71.

ROBERTS, Charles George Douglas (Sir), literary arts. Douglas, NB, 1860–1943. Poet; animal story writer. *Eyes of the Wilderness.*

ROBERTSON, Heather Margaret, literary arts. Winnipeg, Man., 1942. Novelist, critic. *More Than a Rose: Prime Ministers, Wives and Other Women.*

ROBERTSON, Jaime Robbie, performing arts. Toronto, Ont., 1944. Singer/songwriter; founding member of The Band; later soloist. *Music from Big Pink.*

ROBERTSON, John Ross, business. Toronto, Ont., 1841–1918. Financier; publisher and philanthropist.

ROBERTSON, Lloyd, media. Stratford, Ont., 1934. Broadcaster; chief anchor, CTV news.

ROBICHAUD, Louis Joseph, politics. St-Antoine, NB, 1925. Liberal premier of NB, 1960–70.

ROBINETTE, John Josiah (J.J.), law. Toronto, Ont., 1906–96. Lawyer; prominent in criminal and constitutional law.

ROBINSON, Svend J., politics. USA, 1952. NDP MP, British Columbia; social activist, gay rights.

ROBLIN, Dufferin (Duff), politics. Winnipeg, Man., 1917. PC premier of Manitoba, 1958–67.

ROBLIN, Rodmond Palen (Sir), politics. Sophiasburg, Canada W, 1853–1937. PC premier of Manitoba, 1900–15.

ROCK, Allan Michael, politics. Ottawa, Ont., 1947. Liberal MP made minister of justice and attorney general in 1993, introduced major changes in Young Offender's Act and gun control legislation, minister of health in Chrétien government.

RODRIGUEZ, Sue, public service. Winnipeg, Man., 1959–94. Lou Gehrig's disease victim who championed right to die.

ROGERS, Edward S. (Ted), business. Toronto, Ont., 1933. Cable TV executive; runs Canada's largest cable system; 1994 take-over of Maclean Hunter.

ROGERS, Edward Samuel, invention. Toronto, Ont., 1900–39. Radio inventor; perfected alternating current radio tube, revolutionizing the industry.

ROGERS, Shelagh, media. Ottawa, Ont., 1956. CBC radio personality. Co-host of CBC's *Morningside; Take Five with Shelagh Rogers.*

ROGERS, Stan, performing arts. Hamilton, Ont., 1949–83. Folk singer/songwriter. "Between the Breaks."

ROHMER, Richard, literary arts. Hamilton, Ont., 1924. Writer. *Triad, Red Arctic, Death by Deficit.*

ROLPH, John, medicine. Eng., 1793–1870. Physician; ran medical school; constitutional reformer.

ROMAN, Stephen Boleslav, business. Slovakia, 1921–88. Industrialist; founded Denison Mines Ltd.

ROMANOW, Roy John, politics. Saskatoon, Sask., 1939. NDP premier of Sask. since 1991.

RONALD, William (b. William Smith), visual arts. Stratford, Ont., 1926–98. Abstract artist; host, *As It Happens.*

ROOKE, Leon, literary arts. USA, 1934. Short story writer, novelist, playwright. *Krokodile; Shakespeare's Dog; How I Saved the Province; A Bit of White Cloth.*

ROSE, Fred (b. Fred Rosenburg), politics. Poland, 1907–83. Only Canadian Communist MP (1945); jailed as spy.

ROSENFELD, Fanny "Bobbie", sports. Russia, 1905–69. Track star; Canada's female athlete of half century.

ROSS, Anne Glass, medicine. Ukraine, 1911–98. Executive director of Winnipeg's Mount Carmel community health clinic, the first of its kind in Canada; birth control advocate. *Pregnant and Alone; Clinic with a Heart.*

ROSS, James Sinclair, literary arts. Shellbrook, Sask., 1908–96. Novelist. *As for Me and My House.*

ROTHSTEIN, Aser, science. Vancouver, BC, 1918. Physiologist; introduced radioisotopes in biology.

ROULEAU, Joseph, performing arts. Matane, Que., 1929. Operatic bass; internationally famous singer.

ROUX, Jean-Louis, performing arts/politics. Montreal, Que., 1923. Actor, playwright with successful career was rejected as proposed lieutenant governor of Quebec in 1997 due to youthful support of Nazi regime during WWII; appointed head of Canada Council in 1998.

ROY, Gabrielle, literary arts. St Boniface, Man., 1909–83. Popular novelist. *The Tin Flute.*

ROY, Patrick, sports. Quebec City, Que., 1965. Hockey player with Montreal Canadiens, youngest ever to win Conn Smythe trophy; in 1989–92 considered to be one of best goalies in the world.

ROZEMA, Patricia, politics. Kingston, Ont., 1958. Filmmaker; *I've Heard the Mermaids Singing, White Room.*

RUBENSTEIN, Louis, sports. Montreal, Que., 1861-1931. Canadian figure skating champion 1883-89; in 1890 won unofficial world title in Russia; also cyclist, bowler.

RUBES, Jan, performing arts. Czech., 1920. Singer; actor; operatic bass; TV host; film actor.

RUBINEK, Saul, performing arts. Toronto, Ont., 1948. Versatile character player. *The Quarrel.*

RUBINSKY, Yuri, business. Lebanon, 1952–96. Founder of Banff Publishing Workshop; co-director of SoftQuad Inc.; software designer.

RULE, Jane Vance, literary arts. USA, 1931. Novelist, short story writer. *Desert of the Heart; After the Fire; Contract With the World.*

RUSSELL, Loris Shano, science. USA, 1904. Paleontologist; suggested dinosaurs might be warm-blooded.

RUTHERFORD, Ann, performing arts. Toronto, Ont., 1917. Actress who appeared as Andy Hardy's girlfriend, Polly Benedict, in 12 Hardy films. *Secret Life of Walter Mitty.*

RUTHERFORD, Ernest (Rutherford of Nelson), science. NZ, 1871–1937. Physicist; much of his seminal work done at McGill University.

RYAN, Pat, sports. Winnipeg, Man., 1955. Curler; skip of world championship team in 1989; Canadian championship 1988, 1989.

RYAN, Thomas F. (Tommy), business. Guelph, Ont., 1872–1961. Entrepreneur; invented five-pin bowling (1909).

RYBCZYNSKI, Witold, literary arts/visual arts. Scot., 1943. Architect; critic; writer. *Paper Heroes.*

RYERSON, Adolphus Egerton, politics. Norfolk County, UC, 1803–82. Leading figure in 19th century politics and education.

RYGA, George, literary arts. Deep Creek, Alta, 1932–87. Playwright, novelist. *Ecstasy of Rita Joe; Night Desk.*

SABIA, Laura Louise, public service. Pembroke, Ont., 1916–96. Headed Royal Commission on the Status of Women in 1960s; became president of National Action Committee on the Status of Women 1973.

SAFDIE, Moshe, visual arts. Israel, 1938. Architect; Habitat, National Gallery of Canada.

SAFER, Morley, media. Toronto, Ont., 1931. Broadcaster; co-host, *60 Minutes* since 1971.

SAHL, Mort, performing arts. Montreal, Que., 1926. Comedian; delivered political satire in monologues.

SAINTE-MARIE, Buffy, performing arts. Craven, Sask., 1941. Native singer. "Soldier Blue."

SALABERRY, Charles Michel D'Irumberry de, military. Beauport, Que., 1778–1829. Soldier; repelled American force in Battle of Chateaugay (1813).

SALTZMAN, Harry, performing arts. Saint John, NB, 1915–94. Co-producer of James Bond films. *The Man With the Golden Gun; The Ipcress File.*

SALUTIN, Rick, literary arts. Toronto, Ont., 1942. Playwright, columnist; leftist commentator. *Marginal Notes; Challenges to the Mainstream; Globe and Mail* columnist.

SARLOS, Andrew, business. Hungary, 1931–97. Financial trader with Toronto Stock Exchange. Realized $22 million profit from Hiram-Walker-Consumer's Gas merger.

SARRAZIN, Michael, performing arts. Quebec City, Que., 1940. Leading man. *They Shoot Horses, Don't They?*

SAUL, John Ralston, literary arts. Ottawa, Ont., 1947. Novelist, essayist. *The Paradise Eater; Voltaire's Bastards: The Dictatorship of Reason in the West.*

SAUNDERS, Charles Edward (Sir), science. London, Ont., 1867–1937. Agriculturalist; introduced Marquis wheat to W Canada.

SAUVE, Jeanne Mathilde, politics. Prud'homme, Sask., 1922–93. Governor general, 1984–89.

SAWCHUK, Terrence Gordon, sports. Winnipeg, Man., 1929–70. Hockey goaltender; all-time shutouts leader (103).

SAWYER, Robert, literary arts. Ottawa, Ont., 1960. Science fiction writer, winner of US Nebula award, awards in Japan, France, Spain. *Flashforward; Factoring Humanity.*

SCHAEFER, Carl Fellman, visual arts. Hanover, Ont., 1903–95. Painter of rural Ontario landscapes, director of Ontario College of Art.

SCHAFER, Raymond Murray, performing arts. Sarnia, Ont., 1933. Composer of contemporary music, first recipient of Glenn Gould Award in 1987.

SCHALLY, Andrew Victor, science. Poland, 1926. Winner of 1977 Nobel Prize in medicine and physiology, for research into understanding peptide hormones in the brain.

SCHAWLOW, Arthur, science. USA, 1921–99. Canadian educated scientist, winner of 1964 Nobel Prize with Charles Hand Townes, co-patented the laser.

SCHLESINGER, Joe, media. Austria, 1928. Journalist; long-time CBC foreign correspondent.

SCHMIRLER, Sandra Marie, sports. Biggar, Sask., 1963-2000. Skip of the gold-medal-winning curling team at the 1998 Winter Olympics in Nagano, Japan.

SCHNARRE, Monika, performing arts. Toronto, Ont., 1971. Won 1986 Face of the 1980s modeling award; acting career includes role on *The Bold and the Beautiful.*

SCHOLES, Myron, economics. Timmins, Ont., 1941. Stanford University-based co-winner (with Harvard academic Robert Merton) of Nobel Prize for economics, for developing a mathematical formula for estimating values in the worldwide market of derivatives, known as the Black-Scholes formula.

SCHREYER, Edward Richard, politics. Beausejour, Man., 1935. NDP premier of Man., 1969–77; governor general of Canada, 1979–84.

SCOTT, Barbara Ann, sports. Ottawa, Ont., 1928. Figure skater; women's world champion, 1947–48; Olympic gold medal, 1948.

SCOTT, Duncan Campbell, literary arts. Ottawa, Ont., 1862–1947. Poet. "New World Lyrics and Ballads."

SCOTT, Francis (Frank) Reginald, literary arts. Quebec City, Que., 1899–1985. Poet. "Collected Poems."

SCOTT, Jack, performing arts. Windsor, Ont., 1936. Singer; 1950s rockabilly star. "My True Love."

SCRIVEN, Joseph Medlicott, religion. Ire., 1819–86. Hymn writer; wrote "What a Friend We Have in Jesus."

SEAGRAM, Joseph Emm, business. Fishers Mills, Ont., 1841-1919. Founder of world's largest distillery for spirits and wine-making; active as race horse owner; PC MP in Waterloo, Ont.

SECORD, Laura, military. USA, 1775–1868. Heroine; warned British of American attack (1813).

SEGAL, Hugh, politics. Montreal, Que., 1950. Back-room PC advisor to Robert Stanfield, William Davis and Brian Mulroney.

SELKIRK, George, sports. Huntsville, Ont., 1899–1987. Baseball player; outfielder on several NY Yankee champions; replaced Babe Ruth in 1934.

SELKIRK, Thomas Douglas, fifth Earl of, exploration and discovery. Scot., 1771–1820. Colonizer; established Red River settlement in Manitoba.

SELYE, Hans, medicine. Austria, 1907–82. Endocrinologist; author; pioneer in stress research. *The Stress of Life.*

SENNETT, Mack (b. Mikail Sinnott), visual arts. Danville, Que., 1880–1960. Producer; silent comedy pioneer; Keystone Kops.

SERVICE, Robert William, literary arts. Eng., 1874–1958. Poet of the Yukon, "Songs of a Sourdough."

SETON, Ernest Thompson, literary arts. Eng., 1860–1946. Naturalist; writer. *Wild Animals I Have Known.*

SHADBOLT, John Leonard (Jack), visual arts. Eng., 1909–98. BC artist noted for nature and native Canadian influenced work.

SHANNON, Kathleen, performing arts. Vancouver, BC, 1935-98. Founder of National Film Board's Studio D in 1974, which provided female filmmakers an opportunity to create documentaries with a feminist perspective. *If You Love This Planet; Not a Love Story.*

SHARPE, Isadore Nataniel, business. Toronto, Ont., 1931. Opened first Four Seasons Hotel in Toronto in 1961 on Jarvis Street, now a worldwide chain of luxury hotels.

SHATNER, William, performing arts. Montreal, Que., 1931. Actor; Capt. Kirk on TV/movies *Star Trek.*

SHAVER, Helen, performing arts. St Thomas, Ont., 1951. Actress appeared in *The Amityville Horror; Bethune: the Making of a Hero.*

SHEARER, Douglas, performing arts. Westmount, Que., 1899–1971. Sound recording technician, 40 years with MGM; won 12 Academy Awards; brother of actress Norma Shearer. *The Great Caruso; The Big House.*

SHEARER, Norma, performing arts. Edmonton, Alta, 1900–83. Actress; Hollywood star. *Romeo and Juliet.*

SHEBIB, Donald, visual arts. Toronto, Ont., 1939. Acclaimed filmmaker: *Goin' Down the Road; Heartaches.*

SHIELDS, Carol, literary arts. USA, 1935. Writer; won 1993 Booker and Pulitzer prizes for *The Stone Diaries.*

SHORE, Eddie, sports. Ft Qu'Appelle, Sask., 1902–85. Hockey player; Boston defenceman; four-time Hart Trophy winner.

SHORT, Martin, performing arts. Toronto, Ont., 1951. Comedian; TV/film star; *SCTV's* Ed Grimley. *3 Amigos.*

SHULMAN, Morton (Dr), business/medicine. Toronto, Ont., 1925-2000. Investor; physician; author; stock promoter; introduced anti-Parkinson's disease drug into Canada.

SHUSTER, Frank, performing arts. Toronto, Ont., 1918. Comedian; straighter half of Wayne & Shuster team.

SHUSTER, Joe, visual arts. Toronto, Ont., 1914–92. Cartoonist; co-creator of Superman.

SIBERRY, Jane, performing arts. Ottawa, Ont., 1955. Singer, songwriter, guitarist. Contemporary folk style. *Jane Siberry; No Borders Here.*

SIFTON, Clifford (Sir), politics. Arva, Canada W, 1861–1929. Promoted immigration to settle western Canada.

SILVERHEELS, Harold Jay Smith, performing arts. Six Nations Reserve, Ont., 1919–80. Actor; played Tonto in *Lone Ranger*.

SIMARD, Réné, performing arts. Chicoutimi, Que., 1961. Quebec pop singer began as boy soprano turned international pop star. *The Rene Simard Show* on CBC.

SIMCOE, John Graves, politics. Eng., 1752–1806. Upper Canada's first lieutenant-governor, 1792–96.

SIMPSON, Allan John, public service. Ottawa, Ont., 1939–98. Co-founder of Canadians with Disabilities and the Canadian Association of Independent Living Centres; created first Pan-Am Wheelchair Games and Canadian Wheelchair Sports Association. Lobbied to have disabled included in Charter of Rights and Freedoms.

SIMPSON, Sir George, business. Scot., 1787–1860. Financier; governor, Hudson's Bay Co., 1820–60.

SINCLAIR, Gordon Allan, media. Toronto, Ont., 1900–84. Journalist; feisty commentator; long-time *Front Page Challenge* panelist.

SITTLER, Darryl Glen, sports. St Jacob's, Ont., 1950. Hockey player; with Toronto Maple Leafs set NHL record 10 points in one game.

SKVORECKY, Josef, literary arts. Czech., 1924. Intellectual writer; novelist; critic. *The Engineer of Human Souls*.

SLADE, Bernard (b. Bernard Slade Newbound), performing arts. St Catharines, Ont., 1930. Sitcom pilot writer for *The Flying Nun; The Partridge Family; Bridget loves Bernie*. Wrote screenplay for *Same Time Next Year*.

SLOCUM, Joshua, literary arts. Wilmot Twp, NS, 1844–1909. Sailor; wrote classic *Sailing Alone Around the World*.

SMALLWOOD, Joseph Roberts (Joey), politics. Gambo, Nfld, 1900–92. Led Newfoundland into Confederation, 1949; premier 1949–72.

SMART, Elizabeth, literary arts. Ottawa, Ont., 1913–86. Novelist. *By Grand Central Station I Sat Down and Wept*.

SMELLIE, Elizabeth Lawrie, medicine. Port Arthur, Ont., 1884–1968. Nurse; builder, Victorian Order of Nurses.

SMITH, Alexis, performing arts. Penticton, BC, 1921–93. Film and television actress appeared in *Marcus Welby; Rhapsody in Blue; Of Human Bondage*.

SMITH, Byron, exploration and discovery. Winnipeg, Manitoba, 1960. Leader of AGF Everest 2000 expedition, reached summit May 21, 2000, with team members Tim Rippel and Brad Wrobleski.

SMITH, Donald Graham, sports. Edmonton, Alta, 1958. Swimmer; six gold medals, 1978 Commonwealth Games.

SMITH, Lois Irene, performing arts. Vancouver, BC, 1929. National Ballet's first prima ballerina.

SMITH, Michael, science. Eng., 1932. Biochemist; 1993 Nobel Prize winner in chemistry.

SMITH, Michael, sports. Kenora, Ont., 1967. Decathlete; silver medal, 1991 world championships.

SMITH, Stephen Richard (Steve), performing arts. Toronto, Ont., 1945. Comedian who stars in *Red Green Show*, also plays stand-up comedy.

SMITH, Wilfred Cantwell, literary arts. Toronto, Ont., 1916–2000. Founder of McGill University's Islamic Institute; co-founder of Harvard's Center for Study of World Religions. *Islam in Modern History*.

SMITS, Sonja, performing arts. Sudbury, Ont., 1958. Star of CBC series *Street Legal*; CBC's *The Diviners*. Appeared in stage production of *Nothing Sacred*.

SMYTH, Constantine Falkland Cary (Conn), sports. Toronto, Ont., 1895–1980. Hockey executive; owner of Toronto Maple Leafs, 1930–61.

SNIDERMAN, Sam, business. Toronto, Ont., 1920. Retailer; established Sam the Record Man; 130 stores.

SNOW, Clarence Eugene "Hank", performing arts. Liverpool, NS, 1914–2000. Country music singer. "I'm Movin' On."

SNOW, Michael James Aleck, visual arts. Toronto, Ont., 1929. Painter; sculptor; filmmaker; photographer.

SOBEY, Frank, business. Lyons Brook, NS, 1902–85. Industrialist; turned family grocery business into a major industry.

SOMERS, Harry Stewart, performing arts. Toronto, Ont., 1925–99. Composer of opera, orchestral, vocal and ballet music, acclaimed for operas *Louis Riel* and *The Fool*; commissioned by Yehudi Menuhin to write *Music for Solo Violin*.

SOPINKA, John, law/sports. Broderick, Sask., 1933–97. Supreme Court justice; former CFL player.

SOUSTER, Raymond Holmes, literary arts. Toronto, Ont., 1921. Poet; editor. "The Colour of the Times."

SOUTHAM, William, media. Montreal, Que., 1843–1932. Publisher; founded Southam newspaper dynasty.

SPICER, Keith, media. Toronto, Ont., 1934. Civil servant; chairman, Canadian Radio-Television and Telecommunications Commission.

SPOHR, Arnold, performing arts. Rhein, Sask., 1927. Ballet teacher; led Royal Winnipeg Ballet to world fame.

ST LAURENT, Louis Stephen, politics. Compton, Que., 1882–1973. Prime minister of Canada 1948–57; one of the architects of NATO.

STAEBLER, Edna, media. Kitchener, Ont., 1906. Journalist, cookbook writer, specializing in Mennonite cuisine. *Food That Really Schmecks; Whatever Happened to Maggie?*

STANFIELD, Robert Lorne, politics. Truro, NS, 1914. PC premier of NS, 1956–67; as federal PC leader, lost three elections to Trudeau.

STANLEY, George Frances Gillman, literary arts. Westmount, Que., 1907. Historian; proposed basic design of Maple Leaf flag in 1965.

STARYK, Steven, performing arts. Toronto, Ont., 1932. Violinist; virtuoso performer and teacher.

STEACIE, Edgar William Richard, science. Montreal, Que., 1900–62. Chemist; authority on free radical kinetics.

STEELE, Samuel Benfield (Sir), military. Purbrook, Canada W, 1849–1919. NWMP and WWI officer.

STEFANSSON, Vilhjalmur, exploration and discovery. Arnes, Man., 1879–1962. Controversial Arctic explorer. Wrote *My Life with the Eskimo; The Friendly Arctic*.

STEINBERG, David (b. Duddy Steinberg), performing arts. St Boniface, Man., 1942. Stand-up comic; talk show host.

STEINBERG, Samuel, business. Hungary, 1905–78. Retailer; turned family grocery into supermarket empire.

STEPHENSON, William Samuel (Sir), military. Winnipeg, Man., 1896–1989. Spy; "Intrepid," head of British counter-espionage during WWII; invented wirephotos.

STEWART, Walter Douglas, literary arts. Toronto, Ont., 1931. Journalist, editor, social commentator; noted for acerbic wit. Author of *Shrug: Trudeau in Power; Towers of Gold, Feet of Clay;* and *True Blue,* a history of United Empire Loyalists.

STOJKO, Elvis, sports. Newmarket, Ont., 1972. Figure skater; silver medal, 1994 Olympics; world champion, 1995.

STOWE, Emily Howard, medicine. Norwich, UC, 1831–1903. Physician; first Canadian woman to practice medicine; had to obtain degree in US.

STRACHAN, John, religion. Scot., 1778–1867. Anglican bishop; strove to keep Upper Canada British.

STRATAS, Teresa (b. Anastasia Stratakis), performing arts. Toronto, Ont., 1938. Opera soprano; diva with strong stage presence.

STRATHCONA, Donald Alexander Smith (Sir), first Baron, politics. Scot., 1820–1914. Politician, businessman, diplomat; drove the Last Spike.

STRATTON, Dorothy (b. Dorothy Ruth Hoogstratten), performing arts. Vancouver, BC, 1960–80. *Playboy* model; murdered by estranged husband. Her story was told in film *Star 80,* starring Mariel Hemingway.

STREIT, Marlene Stewart, sports. Cereal, Alta, 1934. Golfer; won many international titles. Canadian Athlete of the Year, 1951, 1956.

STRONACH, Frank, business. Austria, 1954. Industrialist; chairman, Magna Intl; built machine company into global enterprise.

STRONG, Lori, sports. Toronto, Ont., 1972. Gymnast; winner of four gold medals at 1990 Commonwealth Games.

STRONG, Maurice Frederick, business. Oak Lake, Man., 1929. Headed Canadian International Development Agency; secretary-general of UN Conference in the Human Environment; head of Petro-Canada and Ontario Hydro; Canadian Ambassador to the UN.

SULLIVAN, Kevin Roderick, performing arts. Toronto, Ont., 1955. Producer; made *Anne of Green Gables;* launched popular *Road to Avonlea* TV series.

SUNG, Alfred (b. Sung Wang Moon), business. Toronto, Ont., 1948. Fashion designer; top designer of the 1980s.

SURIN, Bruny, sports. Haiti, 1967. Sprinter; world 100 m outdoor champion, 1993.

SUTHERLAND, Donald, performing arts. Saint John, NB, 1934. Versatile actor of Hollywood and Canadian films. *Murder by Decree; Don't Look Now.*

SUTHERLAND, Kiefer, performing arts. Eng., 1964. Actor. *Bay Boy, Flatliners, Stand By Me.*

SUZUKI, David Takayoshi, media/science. Vancouver, BC, 1936. Geneticist; promoter of environmental causes; columnist; host of CBC's *The Nature of Things.*

SWAN, Anna Haining, performing arts. Mill Brook, NS, 1846–88. Giantess, at 7 ft. 6 in., 352 lbs; was P.T. Barnum star.

SWAN, Susan, literary arts. Midland, Ont., 1945. Novelist. *Women of the World; The Last of the Golden Girls.*

SYDOR, Alison, sports. Vancouver, BC, 1966. Champion mountain biker; won 1996 Olympics silver award, three-time World MTB champion, 1994, 1995, 1996.

SZNAJDER, Andrew, sports. Toronto, Ont., 1968. Four-time Canadian singles tennis champ.

TALON, Jean-Baptiste, politics. France, 1625–94. Governor; as intendant, sought to diversify economy of New France with minerals, timber, farming.

TANNER, Elaine, sports. Vancouver, BC, 1951. Canada's best woman swimmer by age 15; world records in individual medley and butterfly; won silver and bronze medals in 1968 Olympics.

TASCHEREAU, Louis-Alexandre, politics. Quebec City, Que., 1867–1952. Liberal premier of Quebec, 1920–36; anti-nationalist leader.

TAUBE, Henry, science. Neudorf, Sask., 1915. Nobel Prize winner in 1983 in chemistry for research into electron transfer reactions, especially in metal complexes.

TAYLOR, Edward Plunket (E.P.), business. Ottawa, Ont., 1901–89. Industrialist; founded Argus Corp; notable horseman.

TAYLOR, Fred "Cyclone", sports. Tara, Ont., 1883–1979. Hockey's first great star.

TAYLOR, Kenneth Douglas, politics. Calgary, Alta, 1934. Diplomat; engineering freedom for six US hostages in Iran made him an instant celebrity in 1980.

TAYLOR, Richard Edward, science. Medicine Hat, Alta, 1929. Physicist; nuclear accelerator pioneer; 1990 Nobel Prize in physics.

TAYLOR, Ronald, medicine/sports. Toronto, Ont., 1937. Major league relief pitcher (1962–72) and sports medicine pioneer.

TECUMSEH, military. USA, 1768?–1813. Chief of Shawnee Indians, ally of Britain and Canada during the War of 1812.

TEMPLETON, Charles Bradley, media. Toronto, Ont., 1915. Author, broadcaster, playwright, evangelist, journalist; wrote controversial *Act of God.*

TENNANT, Veronica, performing arts. Eng., 1947. Prima ballerina, National Ballet of Canada.

TEWKSBURY, Mark, sports. Calgary, Alta, 1968. Swimmer; gold medal, 100 m backstroke, 1992 Olympics.

THERIAULT, Yves, literary arts. Quebec City, Que., 1915–83. Novelist, dramatist. *Contes pour un homme seul; Agaguk.*

THICKE, Alan (b. Alan Jeffery), performing arts. Kirkland Lake, Ont., 1948. Actor and talk show host, host of TV game show *Pictionary,* formerly host of talk show *Thicke of the Night.*

THIRSK, Robert Brent (Bob), science. New Westminster, BC, 1953. In 1996 flew a 17-day journey on space shuttle Columbia, conducting experiments on space sickness and researching other areas.

THOM, Linda, sports. Hamilton, Ont., 1943. Shooter; gold medal, women's sports pistol, 1984 Olympics.

THOM, Ronald James, visual arts. Penticton, BC, 1923. Architect; Shaw Festival Theatre, Toronto Zoo.

THOMAS, Dave, performing arts. Toronto, Ont., 1953. Comedic actor noted for roles on *SCTV*, portrayed with Rick Moranis one of the McKenzie Brothers in *Strange Brew*.

THOMPSON, David, exploration and discovery. Eng., 1770–1857. Charted Columbia River.

THOMPSON, John Sparrow David (Sir), politics. Halifax, NS, 1845–94. Canada's fourth prime minister, 1892–94; largely responsible for establishment of the Criminal Code.

THOMSON, David Kenneth Roy, business. Toronto, Ont., 1923. Businessman; art collector; chairman, Thomson Newspapers Ltd.

THOMSON, Roy Herbert (R. H.), performing arts. Toronto, Ont., 1947. Stage and television actor. *Charlie Grant's War; Cry from the Heart; Ticket to Heaven.*

THOMSON, Roy (Lord Thomson of Fleet), media. Toronto, Ont., 1894–1976. Publisher; owned major newspapers in English-speaking world.

THOMSON, Thomas John (Tom), visual arts. Claremont, Ont., 1877–1917. Influential painter. *Autumn Foliage*.

THORBURN, Clifford Charles Devlin, sports. Victoria, BC, 1948. Snooker player; world champion, 1980.

TILLY, Jennifer, performing arts. USA, 1959. Actress, appeared in Woody Allen's *Bullets Over Broadway*.

TILLY, Margaret (Meg), performing arts. Texada Is., BC, 1960. Actress whose winsome face appeared in *The Body Snatchers; The Big Chill.*

TIMMINS, Noah Anthony, business. Mattawa, Ont., 1867–1936. Mining operator; developed N America's largest gold mine; town named for him.

TINTNER, George, performing arts. Vienna, 1917–99. Conductor of Nova Scotia Symphony Orchestra 1987–94; noted for recordings of Anton Bruckner.

TOBIN, Brian Vincent, politics. Stephenville, Nfld, 1954. Began "cod war" with Spain while serving as Liberal Minister of Fisheries and Oceans, 1995; premier of Nfld, 1996–.

TORGOV, Morley Edward, literary arts. Sault Ste Marie, Ont., 1927. Story writer. *The Abramsky Variations; The Outside Chance of Maximilian Glick.*

TORY, Henry Marshall, educator. Pt Shoreham, NS, 1864–1947. University founder: UBC, Carleton.

TOTH, Jerry (Jaroslav), performing arts. Windsor, Ont., 1929–99. Saxophonist, clarinetist, arranger, conductor and producer, Toth was responsible for the *Hockey Night in Canada* theme on CBC, as well as many other network productions: *Wayne and Shuster; Parade*. Member of Boss Brass ensemble for 20 years.

TOWN, Harold Barling, visual arts. Toronto, Ont., 1924–90. Influential painter, sculptor, writer.

TOWNSEND, Eleanor, performing arts. Goderich, Ont., 1944–98. Fiddling champion who was first woman to win North American Fiddle Championship at Shelburne, Ont.; member of both Canada's and US Fiddling Halls of Fame.

TRACY, Paul, sports. Scarborough, Ont., 1968. Auto racer; winner of three Indy titles in 1993.

TRAILL, Catharine Parr, literary arts. Eng., 1802–99. Writer. The Backwoods of Canada.

TREBEK, Alex, performing arts. Sudbury, Ont., 1940. TV host of *Jeopardy* quiz show.

TREMBLAY, Jean-Claude, sports. Bagotville, Ont., 1939–94. Star defenceman for Montreal Canadiens in 1960s.

TREMBLAY, Michel, literary arts. Montreal, Que., 1942. Playwright; novelist. *Le Vrai Monde*.

TROIANO, Dominic, performing arts. Italy, 1946. Rock guitarist collaborated with the Mandalas, The Guess Who; wrote for CBC TV. *Night Heat; Diamonds.*

TRUDEAU, Pierre Elliott, politics. Montreal, Que., 1919–2000. Prime minister of Canada 1968–79, 1980–84.

TRYGGVASON, Bjarni V., science. Iceland, 1945. Astronaut who flew aboard the Discovery in 1997 for 11 days to test Canadian-made equipment at zero gravity.

TSUI, Dr Lap-Chee, science. China, 1950. Geneticist; identified gene carrying cystic fibrosis.

TUPPER, Charles (Sir), politics. Amherst, NS, 1821–1915. Appointed as Canada's sixth prime minister, 1896.

TURCOTTE, Ron, sports. Drummond, NB, 1941. Jockey; long-time leading jockey rode Secretariat to Triple Crown (1973).

TURNBULL, Wallace, invention. Saint John, NB, 1870–1954. Inventor of variable pitch propeller in 1927, contributed to improved flying safety.

TURNER, John Napier, politics. Eng., 1929. Prime minister of Canada June 1984–July 1984.

TUROFSKY, Riki, performing arts. Toronto, Ont., 1944. Debuted in 1972 at New York City Opera in *Carmen*; host of CBC's *Summer Festival* in 1978; *Festival Today* in 1984.

TWAIN, Shania (b. Eileen Regina Edwards), performing arts. Windsor, Ont., 1965. Winner of Country Music of the Year Award (US) 1995. *The Woman in Me.*

TYRRELL, Joseph Burr, science. Weston, Canada W, 1858–1957. Geologist; discovered S Alberta dinosaur beds.

TYSON, Ian Dawson, performing arts. Victoria, BC, 1933. Singer/songwriter; half of Ian and Sylvia. "Four Strong Winds."

TYSON, Sylvia Fricker, performing arts. Chatham, Ont., 1940. Singer; half of Ian and Sylvia. "You Were on My Mind."

UNDERHILL, Barbara Ann, sports. Pembroke, Ont., 1963. Figure skater; world pairs champion (with Paul Martini), 1984.

UNGER, James, visual arts. Eng., 1937. Cartoonist; creator of popular "Herman" cartoon strip.

VAILLANCOURT, Armand J. R., visual arts. Black L., Que., 1932. Sculpts in aid of social activism.

VALDY, (b. Vladimir Horsdal), performing arts. Ottawa, Ont., 1946. Country-folk singer-songwriter, guitarist. "Rock and Roll Song"; *Valdy; Notes from Places*.

VALLIERES, Pierre, politics. Montreal, Que., 1938–98. Journalist and former leader of Front de Libération de Québec (FLQ); author of *White Niggers of America*, which compared Québécois with American Blacks; fell out with FLQ after murder of labour minister Pierre Laporte.

VAN HERK, Aritha, literary arts. Wetaskiwin, Alta, 1954. Novelist. *Judith; No Fixed Address; Places Far from Ellesmere.*

VAN HORNE, William Cornelius (Sir), business. USA, 1843–1915. Driving force behind Canadian Pacific Railroad.

VAN VOGT, Alfred Elton (A.E.), literary arts. Winnipeg, Man., 1912. Writer; science fiction standout. *Slan.*

VANCOUVER, George, exploration and discovery. Eng., 1757–98. Navigator; surveyor of BC coastline.

VANDER ZALM, William Nick, politics. Holland, 1934. Social Credit premier of BC 1986–91, proponent of free trade.

VANDERBURG, Helen, sports. Calgary, Alta, 1959. Synchronized swimmer; dominated sport in 1979.

VANDERHAEGHE, Guy Clarence, literary arts. Esterhazy, Sask., 1951. Novelist, won 1982 Governor General's Award for *Man Descending. My Present Age; Homesick.*

VANIER, Georges Phileas, politics. Montreal, Que., 1888–1967. Governor general, 1959–67.

VANIER, Jean, public service. Switz., 1928. Spiritual leader; man of great moral conviction established homes for handicapped around the world.

VANNELLI, Gino, performing arts. Montreal, Que., 1954. Pop singer. *Brother to Brother; Nightwalker.*

VARLEY, Frederick Horsman, visual arts. Eng., 1881–1969. Member, Group of Seven. *Vera.*

VEREGIN, Peter Vasilevich, religion. Russia, 1859–1924. Charismatic Doukhobor leader.

VERNON, John, performing arts. Montreal, Que., 1931. TV and film actor. *Wojeck.*

VEZINA, Georges, sports. Chicoutimi, Que., 1887–1926. Hockey goalie; NHL trophy named for him.

VICKERS, Jonathan Stewart (Jon), performing arts. Prince Albert, Sask., 1926. Tenor; operatic star; Wagner specialist.

VICKREY, William, economics. Victoria, BC, 1914–96. Winner of Nobel Prize in economics in 1996. Worked with United Nations on tax issues in African countries.

VIGNEAULT, Gilles, performing arts. Natashquan, Que., 1928. Beloved poet and cultural icon of Québécois. "Mon Pays."

VILLENEUVE, Gilles, sports. St-Jean, Que., 1950–82. Auto racer; won six Grand Prix titles.

VILLENEUVE, Jacques, sports. St-Jean, Que., 1971. Winner of Indianapolis 500 in 1995; Lou Marsh trophy for Canadian Athlete of the Year, 1995.

VINCENT, Anthony Gustave, public service. Eng., 1939. Canadian ambassador to Peru when, in December 1996, Tupac Amaru guerrillas stormed Japanese ambassador's residence in Lima, taking 575 hostages. Vincent attempted negotiations with leader Nestor Cerpa; the remaining hostages were freed when troops stormed residence in April 1997.

WAGNER, Barbara Aileen, sports. Toronto, Ont., 1938. Figure skater; with Robert Paul, won four pairs titles and 1960 Olympic gold.

WALDO, Carolyn, sports. Montreal, Que., 1964. Synchronized swimmer; two gold medals, 1988 Olympics.

WALKER, Larry, sports. Maple Ridge, BC, 1966. Baseball player; star outfielder for Montreal Expos, Colorado Rockies. NL MVP, 1997. NL batting champion, 1998.

WALLIN, Pamela, media. Wadena, Sask., 1953. Longtime CBC journalist and independent news magazine host. *Pamela Wallin.*

WALLS, Earl, sports. Puce, Ont., 1928–96. Canadian heavyweight boxing champion, 1952.

WALSH, Richard "Hock", performing arts. Toronto, Ont., 1948-2000. Co-founder in 1969 with brother Donnie of Downchild Blues Band; inspiration for Dan Aykroyd and John Belushi in movie *The Blues Brothers.*

WALTERS, Angus, exploration and discovery. Lunenburg, NS, 1882–1968. *Bluenose* captain; skipper of celebrated schooner.

WARD, Maxwell William, business. Edmonton, Alta, 1921. Capitalist; charter flights pioneer; founded Wardair.

WARNER, Jack L., performing arts. London, Ont., 1892–1978. Head of production at Warner Brothers in 1927; launched talkies with *The Jazz Singer,* starring Al Jolson.

WATKINS, Melville Henry, business. Toronto, Ont., 1932. Economist; founded left-wing Waffle Movement.

WATSON, Hilda Pauline, politics. Kuest, Sask., 1922–96. Leader of the Yukon Territorial Progressive Conservatives 1978. First woman to lead a political party in Canada.

WATSON, Homer Ransford, visual arts. Doon, Canada W, 1855–1936. Landscape painter. *The Pioneer Mill.*

WATSON, John, literary arts. Scot., 1847–1939. Philosopher; metaphysician. "Kant and His English Critics."

WATSON, Ken, sports. Minnedosa, Man., 1904–86. Curler; three-time Brier winner; curling teacher.

WATSON, Patrick, media. Toronto, Ont., 1929. TV host; actor; writer; producer.

WATSON, Sheila Doherty, literary arts. New Westminster, BC, 1909–98. Author of *Double Hook,* considered to be the first modern Canadian novel; also *Deep Hollow Creek.* Described experiences as schoolteacher in central BC in the 1930s.

WATSON, William "Whipper Billy", sports. Toronto, Ont., 1917–1990. Wrestler; twice world pro champion.

WAXMAN, Albert Samuel (Al), performing arts. Toronto, Ont., 1935. Movie and TV performer. *King of Kensington.*

WAYNE, John Louis (Johnny), performing arts. Toronto, Ont., 1918–90. Comedian; wilder half of Wayne and Shuster comedy team.

WEBSTER, Donald Colin "Ben", invention. Montreal, Que., 1928–97. Founder of high-tech Helix Investments (Canada), credited with introduction of the fastening material Velcro.

WEBSTER, John Edgar (Jack), media. Scot., 1918–99. Broadcaster; journalist on Vancouver *Sun.* Noted for outspoken opinions.

WEINZWEIG, John Jacob, performing arts. Toronto, Ont., 1913. Influential composer using 12-tone technique. "Red Ear of Corn."

WEIR, Mike, sports. Sarnia, Ont., 1970. First Canadian in seven years to win PGA (golf) Tour event, in 1999; close second to Tiger Woods at Motorola event.

WEIR, Robert Stanley, literary arts. Hamilton, Ont., 1856–1926. Jurist; author; wrote English lyrics of National Anthem, "O Canada."

WELLS, Clyde Kirby, politics. Buchans Junction, Nfld, 1937. Newfoundland premier 1989–96.

WELSH, Kenneth, politics. Edmonton, Alta, 1942. Versatile actor noted for roles in *Empire Inc.; And Then You Die; The Tar Sands.*

WESTON, Hilary M., politics. Ire., 1942. Appointed lieutenant governor of Ontario in 1997, wife of grocery magnate Galen Weston.

WESTON, W. Galen Gordon, business. Eng., 1940. Industrialist; Canadian head for George Weston Ltd.

WESTON, Willard Garfield, business. Toronto, Ont., 1893–1978. Industrialist; pioneer in food retailing.

WHEELER, Anne, visual arts. Edmonton, Alta, 1946. Filmmaker. *A Change of Heart; Bye Bye Blues.*

WHEELER, Lucille, sports. Montreal, Que., 1935. Skier; first N American to win world title, downhill and slalom (1958).

WHITE, Bob, business. Ire., 1935. Labour leader; first head of Canadian Auto Workers' Union.

WHITTON, Charlotte Elizabeth, politics. Renfrew, Ont., 1896–1975. Reformer; outspoken Ottawa mayor.

WIEBE, Rudy Henry, literary arts. Speedwell, Sask., 1934. Mennonite novelist. *Temptations of Big Bear.*

WILLAN, James Healey, performing arts. Eng., 1880–1968. Classical composer and musician. "O Lord, Our Governour" sung at Queen Elizabeth II's coronation in Westminster Abbey.

WILLIAMS, Daffyd (Dave) Rhys, science. Saskatoon, Sask., 1954. Astronaut, flew on 16-day Spacelab flight aboard Space Shuttle Columbia in 1998; coordinator of Canadian Astronaut Program Space Unit Life Simulation (CAPSULS) project.

WILLIAMS, Percy Alfred, sports. Vancouver, BC, 1908–82. Sprinter; Olympic gold in 100 m and 200 m, 1928.

WILSON, Bertha, law. Scot., 1923. First woman named to Supreme Court of Canada (1982).

WILSON, Cairine Reay, politics. Montreal, Que., 1885–1962. Canada's first woman senator, 1930 (Lib.).

WILSON, Daniel (Sir), educator. Scot., 1816–92. Darwinian opposed idea of natural selection; energetic administrator, author, scholar.

WILSON, Ethel Davis, literary arts. S Africa, 1888–1980. BC novelist. *Swamp Angel.*

WILSON, John Tuzo, science. Ottawa, Ont., 1908–93. Geophysicist; pioneered plate tectonics theory.

WILSON, Lois Miriam, religion. Winnipeg, Man., 1927. First woman president of Canadian Council of Churches, in 1976; first woman Moderator of United Church of Canada in 1980. Peace advocate and active in antipoverty initiatives.

WILSON, Michael Holcombe, politics. Toronto, Ont., 1937. PC minister of industry, science and technology; international trade; finance minister (1984–91).

WISEMAN, Adele, literary arts. Winnipeg, Man., 1928–92. Novelist, poet. *The Sacrifice; Crackpot.*

WISEMAN, Joseph, performing arts. Montreal, Que., 1918. Actor; title role in James Bond movie, *Dr. No.*

WOLFE, James, military. Eng., 1727–59. Soldier; took Quebec for British; died on Plains of Abraham.

WONG, Celia Jan, media. Montreal, Que., 1952. *Globe and Mail* correspondent in China, 1988–94. *Red China Blues.*

WOOD, Elizabeth Wyn, visual arts. Orillia, Ont., 1903–66. Sculptor; fountains and panels for Rainbow Bridge Gardens, monument to King George VI, Niagara Falls.

WOODCOCK, George, literary arts. Winnipeg, Man., 1912–95. Historian; journalist; activist. *Anarchism.*

WOODSWORTH, James Shaver, politics. Etobicoke, Ont., 1874–1942. Founder Cooperative Commonwealth Federation (later NDP).

WRAY, Fay, performing arts. Medicine Hat, Alta, 1910. Famous as screaming heroine in *King Kong.*

WRIGHT, Eric Stanley, literary arts. Eng., 1929. Mystery writer. *A Sensitve Case; Final Cut.*

WRIGHT, Michelle, performing arts. Merlin, Ont., 1960. Sultry country songstress. "Now and Then."

YANOFSKY, Abe (b. Daniel Abraham), sports. Poland, 1925-2000. First chess grandmaster in Commonwealth; child prodigy in 1939 Chess Olympics in Buenos Aires; active in Winnipeg city council.

YANOVSKY, Zal, performing arts. Toronto, Ont., 1944. Singer; member of folk-rock group, Lovin' Spoonful.

YOST, Elwy, performing arts. Toronto, Ont., 1925. Affable and knowledgeable host of TVOntario's popular *Saturday Night at the Movies.*

YOUNG, Neil Percival, performing arts. Toronto, Ont., 1945. Singer/songwriter; seminal rocker. *After the Gold Rush.*

YOUNG, Scott Alexander, literary arts. Glenboro, Man., 1918. Novelist, short story writer, children's writer, biographer. *The Boys of Saturday Night; Power Play.*

YOUVILLE, Marie Marguerite d', religion. Varennes, Que., 1701–71. First Canadian to be beatified by Pope; founded Grey Nuns.

ZEIDLER, Eberhard Heinrich, visual arts. Germany, 1936. Award-winning architect of Toronto Eaton Centre, Toronto's Queen's Quay Terminal, Ontario Place.

ZNAIMER, Moses, business. Toronto, Ont., 1942. TV executive; founder of CITY-TV, Much Music.

ZOLF, Larry, media. Winnipeg, Man., 1934. Broadcaster; journalist; writer. CBC's *Fifth Estate.*

ZUCKERMAN, Mortimer, business. Montreal, Que., 1937. Financier; developer, magazine publisher.

SPORTS

BASEBALL

American League Final Standings, 2000

Eastern Division

CLUB	W	L	%	GB
x-New York	87	74	.540	—
Boston	85	77	.525	2½
Toronto	83	79	.512	4½
Baltimore	74	88	.457	13½
Tampa Bay	69	92	.429	18

Central Division

CLUB	W	L	%	GB
x-Chicago	95	67	.586	—
Cleveland	90	72	.556	5
Detroit	79	83	.488	16
Kansas City	77	85	.475	18
Minnesota	69	93	.426	26

Western Division

CLUB	W	L	%	GB
x-Oakland	91	70	.565	—
y-Seattle	91	71	.562	½
Anaheim	82	80	.506	9½
Texas	71	91	.438	20½

Source: *Canadian Press*   x=Clinched division title; y=Clinched wild card.

American League Leaders, 2000

Batting

Batting Average
- Garciaparra, Bos ... .372
- Erstad, Ana ... .355
- M. Ramirez, Clev ... .351
- Delgado, Tor ... .344
- Jeter, NY ... .339
- Segui, Clev ... .334
- Ja. Giambi, Oak ... .333
- Sweeney, KC ... .333
- Thomas, Chi ... .328
- Damon, KC ... .327

On-Base Percentage
- Ja. Giambi, Oak ... .476
- Delgado, Tor ... .470
- M. Ramirez, Clev ... .457
- Thomas, Chi ... .436
- Garciaparra, Bos ... .434
- Martinez, Sea ... .423
- A. Rodriguez, Sea. ... .420
- Posada, NY ... .417
- Jeter, NY ... .416
- Erstad, Ana ... .409

Runs
- Damon, KC ... 136
- A. Rodriguez, Sea. ... 134
- Durham, Chi ... 121
- Erstad, Ana. ... 121
- Glaus, Ana. ... 120
- Jeter, NY ... 119
- Delgado, Tor ... 115
- Thomas, Chi. ... 115
- R. Alomar, Clev ... 111
- 3 tied ... 108

Hits
- Erstad, Ana. ... 240
- Damon, KC ... 214
- Sweeney, KC ... 206
- Jeter, NY ... 201
- Garciaparra, Bos ... 197
- Delgado, Tor ... 196
- Dye, KC ... 193
- Segui, Clev ... 192
- Thomas, Chi ... 191
- R. Alomar, Clev ... 189

Runs Batted In
- Martinez, Sea ... 145
- Sweeney, KC ... 144
- Thomas, Chi. ... 143
- Delgado, Tor ... 137
- Ja. Giambi, Oak ... 137
- A. Rodriguez, Sea. ... 132
- Ordonez, Chi ... 126
- M. Ramirez, Clev ... 122
- Williams, NY ... 121
- Palmeiro, Tex. ... 120

Doubles
- Delgado, Tor ... 57
- Garciaparra, Bos ... 51
- D. Cruz, Det ... 46
- Olerud, Sea ... 45
- Higginson, Det ... 44
- Lawton, Minn. ... 44
- Thomas, Chi. ... 44
- DeShields, Balt. ... 43
- Stewart, Tor ... 43
- 2 tied ... 42

Triples
- Guzman, Minn ... 20
- Kennedy, Ana. ... 11
- Damon, KC. ... 10
- Durham, Chi. ... 9
- Alicea, Tex ... 8
- Nixon, Bos ... 8
- Hunter, Minn ... 7
- 4 tied ... 6

Home Runs
- Glaus, Ana. ... 47
- Ja. Giambi, Oak ... 43
- Thomas, Chi. ... 43
- Batista, Tor. ... 41
- Delgado, Tor ... 41
- Justice, NY. ... 41
- A. Rodriguez, Sea. ... 41
- Palmeiro, Tex. ... 39
- M. Ramirez, Clev ... 38
- 2 tied ... 37

Slugging Average
- M. Ramirez, Clev ... .697
- Delgado, Tor ... .664
- Ja. Giambi, Oak ... .647
- Thomas, Chi ... .625
- A. Rodriguez, Sea. ... .606
- Glaus, Ana. ... .604
- Garciaparra, Bos ... .599
- Everett, Bos ... .587
- Justice, NY ... .584
- Martinez, Sea ... .579

Stolen Bases
- Damon, KC. ... 46
- R. Alomar, Clev ... 39
- DeShields, Balt. ... 37
- Henderson, Sea ... 31
- Lofton, Clev ... 30
- McLemore, Sea ... 30
- Cairo, T.B. ... 28
- Erstad, Ana. ... 28
- Guzman, Minn ... 28
- Durham, Chi. ... 25

Walks
- Ja. Giambi, Oak ... 137
- Delgado, Tor ... 123
- Thome, Clev ... 118
- Glaus, Ana ... 112
- Thomas, Chi. ... 112
- Posada, NY ... 107
- Salmon, Ana ... 104
- Palmeiro, Tex. ... 103
- Olerud, Sea ... 102
- A. Rodriguez, Sea. ... 100

Total Bases
- Delgado, Tor ... 378
- Erstad, Ana. ... 366
- Thomas, Chi. ... 364
- Glaus, Ana ... 340
- Dye, KC ... 337
- Anderson, Ana ... 336
- A. Rodriguez, Sea. ... 336
- Ja. Giambi, Oak ... 330
- Damon, KC. ... 324
- Sweeney, KC ... 323

Pitching

Wins – Losses		Earned Run Average	
Hudson, Oak	20–6	P. Martinez, Bos	1.74
D. Wells, Tor	20–8	Clemens, NY	3.70
Pettitte, NY	19–9	Mussina, Balt	3.79
P. Martinez, Bos	18–6	Sirotka, Chi	3.79
Sele, Sea	17–10	Colon, Clev	3.88
Burba, Clev	16–6	D. Wells, Tor	4.11
Finley, Clev	16–11	Heredia, Oak	4.12
Helling, Tex	16–13	Lopez, T.B.	4.13
4 tied	15	Hudson, Oak	4.14
		Finley, Clev	4.17

Strikeouts		Saves		Shutouts	
P. Martinez, Bos	284	Jones, Det	42	P. Martinez, Bos	4
Colon, Clev	212	Lowe, Bos	42	Hudson, Oak	2
Mussina, Balt	210	Sasaki, Sea	37	Sele, Sea	2
Finley, Clev	189	Rivera, NY	36	26 tied	1
Clemens, NY	188	Foulke, Chi	34		
Nomo, Det	181	Wetteland, Tex	34		
Burba, Clev	180	Isringhausen, Oak	33		
Hudson, Oak	169	Koch, Tor	33		
D. Wells, Tor	166	Hernandez, T.B.	32		
Milton, Minn	160	Percival, Ana	32		

Innings Pitched		Games		Complete Games	
Mussina, Balt	237.2	Wunsch, Chi	83	D. Wells, Tor	9
D. Wells, Tor	229.2	Venafro, Tex	77	P. Martinez, Bos	7
Rogers, Tex	227.1	Wells, Minn	76	Mussina, Balt	6
Radke, Minn	226.2	Trombley, Balt	75	Ponson, Balt	6
Ponson, Balt	222.0	Lowe, Bos	74	Lopez, T.B.	4
Finley, Clev	218.0	Nelson, NY	73	Radke, Minn	4
Helling, Tex	217.0	Foulke, Chi	72	6 tied	3
P. Martinez, Bos	217.0	Karsay, Clev	72		
Suppan, KC	217.0	Rhodes, Sea	72		
Sele, Sea	211.2	Tam, Oak	72		

Source: *Canadian Press*

National League Final Standings, 2000

Eastern Division					Central Division					Western Division				
CLUB	W	L	%	GB	CLUB	W	L	%	GB	CLUB	W	L	%	GB
x-Atlanta	95	67	.586		x-St. Louis	95	67	.586		x-San Francisco	97	65	.599	
y-New York	94	68	.580	1	Cincinnati	85	77	.525	10	Los Angeles	86	76	.531	11
Florida	79	82	.491	15½	Milwaukee	73	89	.451	22	Arizona	85	77	.525	12
Montreal	67	95	.414	28	Houston	72	90	.444	23	Colorado	82	80	.506	15
Philadelphia	65	97	.401	30	Pittsburgh	69	93	.426	26	San Diego	76	86	.469	21
					Chicago	65	97	.401	30					

Source: *Canadian Press*   x=Clinched division title; y=Clinched wild card.

National League Leaders, 2000

Batting

Batting Average		On-Base Percentage		Runs	
Helton, Col	.372	Helton, Col	.463	Bagwell, Hou	152
Alou, Hou	.355	Bonds, SF	.440	Helton, Col	138
V. Guerrero, Mtl	.345	Sheffield, LA	.438	Bonds, SF	129
Hammonds, Col	.335	Giles, Pitt	.432	Edmonds, StL	129
Castillo, Fla	.334	Alfonzo, NY	.425	A. Jones, Atl	122
Kent, SF	.334	Kent, SF	.424	Hidalgo, Hou	118
Vidro, Mtl	.330	Bagwell, Hou	.424	C. Jones, Atl	118
Cirillo, Col	.326	Castillo, Fla	.418	Kent, SF	114
Sheffield, LA	.325	Abreu, Phil	.416	Kendall, Pitt	112
Piazza, NY	.324	Alou, Hou	.416	2 tied	111

Hits

Helton, Col	216
Vidro, Mtl	200
A. Jones, Atl	199
V. Guerrero, Mtl	197
Kent, SF	196
Cirillo, Col	195
Sosa, Chi	193
Gonzalez, Ari	192
Perez, Col	187
Kendall, Pitt	185

Runs Batted In

Helton, Col	147
Sosa, Chi	138
Bagwell, Hou	132
Kent, SF	125
Giles, Pitt	123
V. Guerrero, Mtl	123
Hidalgo, Hou	122
Wilson, Fla	121
Griffey, Cin	118
Cirillo, Col	115

Doubles

Helton, Col	59
Cirillo, Col	53
Vidro, Mtl	51
Gonzalez, Ari	47
Green, LA	44
Abreu, Phil	42
Hidalgo, Hou	42
Grace, Chi	41
Kent, SF	41
2 tied	40

Triples

Womack, Ari	14
V. Guerrero, Mtl	11
Perez, Col	11
Abreu, Phil	10
Belliard, Mil	9
Goodwin, LA	9
7 tied	7

Home Runs

Sosa, Chi	50
Bonds, SF	49
Bagwell, Hou	47
V. Guerrero, Mtl	44
Hidalgo, Hou	44
Sheffield, LA	43
Edmonds, StL	42
Helton, Col	42
Griffey, Cin	40
Piazza, NY	38

Slugging Average

Helton, Col	.698
Bonds, SF	.688
V. Guerrero, Mtl	.664
Sheffield, LA	.643
Hidalgo, Hou	.636
Sosa, Chi	.634
Alou, Hou	.623
Bagwell, Hou	.615
Piazza, NY	.614
Kent, SF	.596

Stolen Bases

Castillo, Fla	62
Goodwin, LA	55
E. Young, Chi	54
Womack, Ari	45
Furcal, Atl	40
Wilson, Fla	36
Glanville, Phil	31
Owens, SD	29
Reese, Cin	29
2 tied	28

Walks

Bonds, SF	117
Giles, Pitt	114
Bagwell, Hou	107
Edmonds, StL	103
Helton, Col	103
Sheffield, LA	101
Abreu, Phil	100
Burnitz, Mil	99
3 tied	95

Total Bases

Helton, Col	405
Sosa, Chi	383
V. Guerrero, Mtl	379
Bagwell, Hou	363
Hidalgo, Hou	355
A. Jones, Atl	355
Kent, SF	350
Gonzalez, Ari	336
Giles, Pitt	332
Bonds, SF	330

Pitching

Wins – Losses

Glavine, Atl	21–9
Kile, StL	20–9
Johnson, Ari	19–7
Maddux, Atl	19–9
Park, LA	18–10
Elarton, Hou	17–7
Hernandez, SF	17–11
Leiter, NY	16–8
Stephenson, StL	16–9
3 tied	15

Earned Run Average

Brown, LA	2.58
Johnson, Ari	2.64
Maddux, Atl	3.00
Hampton, NY	3.14
Leiter, NY	3.20
Park, LA	3.27
Glavine, Atl	3.40
Ankiel, StL	3.50
Person, Phil	3.63
Dempster, Fla	3.66

Strikeouts

Johnson, Ari	347
Park, LA	217
Brown, LA	216
Dempster, Fla	209
Leiter, NY	200
Vazquez, Mtl	196
Ankiel, StL	194
Astacio, Col	193
Kile, StL	192
Lieber, Chi	192

Saves

Alfonseca, Fla	45
Hoffman, SD	43
Benitez, NY	41
Nen, SF	41
Graves, Cin	30
Aguilera, Chi	29
Veres, StL	29
Shaw, LA	27
3 tied	24

Shutouts

Johnson, Ari	3
Maddux, Atl	3
Estes, SF	2
Glavine, Atl	2
Hernandez, SF	2
Sanchez, Fla	2
Schilling, Ari	2
Stephenson, StL	2
20 tied	1

Innings Pitched

Lieber, Chi	251.0
Maddux, Atl	249.1
Johnson, Ari	248.2
Glavine, Atl	241.0
Hernandez, SF	240.0
Kile, StL	232.1
Brown, LA	230.0
Dempster, Fla	226.1
Park, LA	226.0
3 tied	217.2

Games

Kline, Mtl	83
Sullivan, Cin	79
Myers, Col	78
Wendell, NY	77
Benitez, NY	76
Rodriguez, SF	76
Sauerbeck, Pitt	75
Heredia, Chi	74
Leskanic, Mil	73
Looper, Fla	73

Complete Games

Johnson, Ari	8
Schilling, Ari	8
Lieber, Chi	6
Maddux, Atl	6
Brown, LA	5
Hernandez, SF	5
Kile, StL	5
Estes, SF	4
Glavine, Atl	4
W. Williams, SD	4

Source: *Canadian Press*

Major League Pennant Winners, 1960–1999

	National League					American League			
	Winner	Won	Lost	%		Winner	Won	Lost	%
1960	Pittsburgh	95	59	.617	1960	New York	97	57	.630
1961	Cincinnati	93	61	.604	1961	New York	109	53	.673
1962	San Francisco	103	62	.624	1962	New York	96	66	.593
1963	Los Angeles	99	63	.611	1963	New York	104	57	.646
1964	St. Louis	93	69	.574	1964	New York	99	63	.611
1965	Los Angeles	97	65	.599	1965	Minnesota	102	60	.630
1966	Los Angeles	95	67	.586	1966	Baltimore	97	63	.606
1967	St. Louis	101	60	.627	1967	Boston	92	70	.568
1968	St. Louis	97	65	.599	1968	Detroit	103	59	.636
1969	New York	100	62	.617	1969	Baltimore	109	53	.673
1970	Cincinnati	102	60	.630	1970	Baltimore	108	54	.667
1971	Pittsburgh	97	65	.599	1971	Baltimore	101	57	.639
1972	Cincinnati	95	59	.617	1972	Oakland	93	62	.600
1973	New York	82	79	.509	1973	Oakland	94	68	.580
1974	Los Angeles	102	60	.630	1974	Oakland	90	72	.556
1975	Cincinnati	108	54	.667	1975	Boston	95	65	.594
1976	Cincinnati	102	60	.630	1976	New York	97	62	.610
1977	Los Angeles	98	64	.605	1977	New York	100	62	.617
1978	Los Angeles	95	67	.586	1978	New York	100	63	.613
1979	Pittsburgh	98	64	.605	1979	Baltimore	102	57	.642
1980	Philadelphia	91	71	.562	1980	Kansas City	97	65	.599
1981	Los Angeles	63	47	.573	1981	New York	59	48	.551
1982	St. Louis	92	70	.568	1982	Milwaukee	95	67	.586
1983	Philadelphia	90	72	.556	1983	Baltimore	98	64	.605
1984	San Diego	92	70	.568	1984	Detroit	104	58	.642
1985	St. Louis	101	61	.623	1985	Kansas City	91	71	.562
1986	New York	108	54	.667	1986	Boston	95	66	.590
1987	St. Louis	95	67	.586	1987	Minnesota	85	77	.525
1988	Los Angeles	94	67	.584	1988	Oakland	104	58	.642
1989	San Francisco	92	70	.568	1989	Oakland	99	63	.611
1990	Cincinnati	91	71	.562	1990	Oakland	103	59	.636
1991	Atlanta	94	68	.580	1991	Minnesota	95	67	.586
1992	Atlanta	98	64	.605	1992	**Toronto**	**96**	**66**	**.593**
1993	Philadelphia	97	65	.599	1993	**Toronto**	**95**	**67**	**.586**
1994[1]	no winner				1994[1]	no winner			
1995	Atlanta	90	54	.625	1995	Cleveland	100	44	.694
1996	Atlanta	96	66	.593	1996	New York	92	70	.569
1997	Florida	92	70	.568	1997	Cleveland	86	75	.534
1998	San Diego	98	64	.605	1998	New York	114	48	.704
1999	Atlanta	103	59	.639	1999	New York	98	64	.605

Source: *Canadian Press*

(1) Players strike Aug. 12, 1994; owners suspended season, Sept. 14, 1994.

World Series Results, 1960–1999

Year	Champion	Final Opponent	Series Result
1960	Pittsburgh Pirates, NL	New York Yankees, AL	4–3
1961	New York Yankees, AL	Cincinnati Reds, NL	4–1
1962	New York Yankees, AL	San Francisco Giants, NL	4–3
1963	Los Angeles Dodgers, NL	New York Yankees, AL	4–0
1964	St. Louis Cardinals, NL	New York Yankees, AL	4–3
1965	Los Angeles Dodgers, NL	Minnesota Twins, AL	4–3
1966	Baltimore Orioles, AL	Los Angeles Dodgers, NL	4–0
1967	St. Louis Cardinals, NL	Boston Red Sox, AL	4–3
1968	Detroit Tigers, AL	St. Louis Cardinals, NL	4–3
1969	New York Mets, NL	Baltimore Orioles, AL	4–1
1970	Baltimore Orioles, AL	Cincinnati Reds, NL	4–1
1971	Pittsburgh Pirates, NL	Baltimore Orioles, AL	4–3
1972	Oakland Athletics, AL	Cincinnati Reds, NL	4–3
1973	Oakland Athletics, AL	New York Mets, NL	4–3
1974	Oakland Athletics, AL	Los Angeles Dodgers, NL	4–1
1975	Cincinnati Reds, NL	Boston Red Sox, AL	4–3
1976	Cincinnati Reds, NL	New York Yankees, AL	4–0
1977	New York Yankees, AL	Los Angeles Dodgers, NL	4–2
1978	New York Yankees, AL	Los Angeles Dodgers, NL	4–2
1979	Pittsburgh Pirates, NL	Baltimore Orioles, AL	4–3
1980	Philadelphia Phillies, NL	Kansas City Royals, AL	4–2
1981	Los Angeles Dodgers, NL	New York Yankees, AL	4–2
1982	St. Louis Cardinals, NL	Milwaukee Brewers, AL	4–3
1983	Baltimore Orioles, AL	Philadelphia Phillies, NL	4–1
1984	Detroit Tigers, AL	San Diego Padres, NL	4–1
1985	Kansas City Royals, AL	St. Louis Cardinals, NL	4–3
1986	New York Mets, NL	Boston Red Sox, AL	4–3
1987	Minnesota Twins, AL	St. Louis Cardinals, NL	4–3
1988	Los Angeles Dodgers, NL	Oakland Athletics, AL	4–1
1989	Oakland Athletics, AL	San Francisco Giants, NL	4–0
1990	Cincinnati Reds, NL	Oakland Athletics, AL	4–0
1991	Minnesota Twins, AL	Atlanta Braves, NL	4–3
1992	**Toronto Blue Jays, AL**	Atlanta Braves, NL	4–2
1993	**Toronto Blue Jays, AL**	Philadelphia Phillies, NL	4–2
1994	No World Series: season suspended Sept. 15, 1994		
1995	Atlanta Braves, NL	Cleveland Indians, AL	4–2
1996	New York, AL	Atlanta, NL	4–2
1997	Florida, NL	Cleveland, AL	4–3
1998	New York Yankees, AL	San Diego, NL	4–0
1999	New York Yankees, AL	Atlanta Braves, NL	4–0

Source: *Canadian Press*

World Series MVPs, 1960–1999

1960	Bobby Richardson, NY (AL)
1961	Whitey Ford, NY (AL)
1962	Ralph Terry, NY (AL)
1963	Sandy Koufax, LA
1964	Bob Gibson, StL
1965	Sandy Koufax, LA
1966	Frank Robinson, Bal
1967	Bob Gibson, StL
1968	Mickey Lolich, Det
1969	Donn Clendenon, NY (NL)
1970	Brooks Robinson, Bal
1971	Roberto Clemente, Pgh
1972	Gene Tenace, Oak
1973	Reggie Jackson, Oak
1974	Rollie Fingers, Oak
1975	Pete Rose, Cin
1976	Johnny Bench, Cin
1977	Reggie Jackson, NY (AL)
1978	Bucky Dent, NY (AL)
1979	Willie Stargell, Pgh
1980	Mike Schmidt, Pha
1981	Ron Cey, LA[1]
1981	Pedro Guerrero, LA[1]
1981	Steve Yeager, LA[1]
1982	Darrell Porter, StL
1983	Rick Dempsey, Bal
1984	Alan Trammell, Det
1985	Bret Saberhagen, KC
1986	Ray Knight, NY (NL)
1987	Frank Viola, Min
1988	Orel Hershiser, LA
1989	Dave Stewart, Oak
1990	Jose Rijo, Cin
1991	Jack Morris, Min
1992	**Pat Borders, Tor**
1993	**Paul Molitor, Tor**
1994	No award
1995	Tom Glavine, Atl
1996	John Wetteland, NY
1997	Livan Hernandez, Fla
1998	Scott Brosius, NY
1999	Mariano Rivera, NY

Source: *Canadian Press*   (1) Joint winners.

Cy Young Award Winners, 1960–1999

Year	League	Player, Club
1960[1]		Vernon Law, Pittsburgh Pirates
1961[1]		Whitey Ford, New York Yankees
1962[1]		Don Drysdale, Los Angeles Dodgers
1963[1]		Sandy Koufax, Los Angeles Dodgers
1964[1]		Dean Chance, California Angels
1965[1]		Sandy Koufax, Los Angeles Dodgers
1966[1]		Sandy Koufax, Los Angeles Dodgers
1967	(NL)	Mike McCormick, San Francisco Giants
	(AL)	Jim Lonborg, Boston Red Sox
1968	(NL)	Bob Gibson, St. Louis Cardinals
	(AL)	Dennis McLain, Detroit Tigers
1969	(NL)	Tom Seaver, New York Mets
	(AL)	Dennis McLain, Detroit Tigers
	(AL)	Mike Cuellar, Baltimore Orioles
1970	(NL)	Bob Gibson, St. Louis Cardinals
	(AL)	Jim Perry, Minnesota Twins
1971	(NL)	Ferguson Jenkins, Chicago Cubs
	(AL)	Vida Blue, Oakland A's
1972	(NL)	Steve Carlton, Philadelphia Phillies
	(AL)	Gaylord Perry, Cleveland Indians
1973	(NL)	Tom Seaver, New York Mets
	(AL)	Jim Palmer, Baltimore Orioles
1974	(NL)	Mike Marshall, Los Angeles Dodgers
	(AL)	Jim (Catfish) Hunter, Oakland A's
1975	(NL)	Tom Seaver, New York Mets
	(AL)	Jim Palmer, Baltimore Orioles
1976	(NL)	Randy Jones, San Diego Padres
	(AL)	Jim Palmer, Baltimore Orioles
1977	(NL)	Steve Carlton, Philadelphia Phillies
	(AL)	Sparky Lyle, New York Yankees
1978	(NL)	Gaylord Perry, San Diego Padres
	(AL)	Ron Guidry, New York Yankees
1979	(NL)	Bruce Sutter, Chicago Cubs
	(AL)	Mike Flanagan, Baltimore Orioles
1980	(NL)	Steve Carlton, Philadelphia Phillies
	(AL)	Steve Stone, Baltimore Orioles
1981	(NL)	Fernando Valenzuela, Los Angeles Dodgers
	(AL)	Rollie Fingers, Milwaukee Brewers
1982	(NL)	Steve Carlton, Philadelphia Phillies
	(AL)	Pete Vuckovich, Milwaukee Brewers
1983	(NL)	John Denny, Philadelphia Phillies
	(AL)	LaMarr Hoyt, Chicago White Sox
1984	(NL)	Rick Sutcliffe, Chicago Cubs
	(AL)	Willie Hernandez, Detroit Tigers
1985	(NL)	Dwight Gooden, New York Mets
	(AL)	Bret Saberhagen, Kansas City Royals
1986	(NL)	Mike Scott, Houston Astros
	(AL)	Roger Clemens, Boston Red Sox
1987	(NL)	Steve Bedrosian, Philadelphia Phillies
	(AL)	Roger Clemens, Boston Red Sox
1988	(NL)	Orel Hershiser, Los Angeles Dodgers
	(AL)	Frank Viola, Minnesota Twins
1989	(NL)	Mark Davis, San Diego Padres
	(AL)	Bret Saberhagen, Kansas City Royals
1990	(NL)	Doug Drabek, Pittsburgh Pirates
	(AL)	Bob Welch, Oakland A's
1991	(NL)	Tom Glavine, Atlanta Braves
	(AL)	Roger Clemens, Boston Red Sox
1992	(NL)	Greg Maddux, Chicago Cubs
	(AL)	Dennis Eckersley, Oakland A's
1993	(NL)	Greg Maddux, Atlanta Braves
	(AL)	Jack McDowell, Chicago White Sox
1994	(NL)	Greg Maddux, Atlanta Braves
	(AL)	David Cone, Kansas City Royals
1995	(NL)	Greg Maddux, Atlanta Braves
	(AL)	Randy Johnson, Seattle Mariner
1996	(NL)	John Smoltz, Atlanta Braves
	(AL)	**Pat Hentgen, Toronto Blue Jays**
1997	**(NL)**	**Pedro Martinez, Montreal Expos**
	(AL)	**Roger Clemens, Toronto Blue Jays**
1998	(NL)	Tom Glavine, Atlanta Braves
	(AL)	**Roger Clemens, Toronto Blue Jays**
1999	(NL)	Randy Johnson, Arizona
	(AL)	**Pedro Martinez, Boston**

Source: *Canadian Press*

(1) One award, 1960–66.

Most Valuable Player, 1960–99

	National League	American League
1960	Dick Groat, Pittsburgh Pirates	Roger Maris, New York Yankees
1961	Frank Robinson, Cincinnati Reds	Roger Maris, New York Yankees
1962	Maury Wills, Los Angeles Dodgers	Mickey Mantle, New York Yankees
1963	Sandy Koufax, Los Angeles Dodgers	Elston Howard, New York Yankees
1964	Ken Boyer, St. Louis Cardinals	Brooks Robinson, Baltimore Orioles
1965	Willie Mays, San Francisco Giants	Zoilo Versalles, Minnesota Twins
1966	Roberto Clemente, Pittsburgh Pirates	Frank Robinson, Baltimore Orioles
1967	Orlando Cepeda, St. Louis Cardinals	Carl Yastrzemski, Boston Red Sox
1968	Bob Gibson, St. Louis Cardinals	Denny McLain, Detroit Tigers
1969	Willie McCovey, San Francisco Giants	Harmon Killebrew, Minnesota Twins
1971	Joe Torre, St. Louis Cardinals	Vida Blue, Oakland Athletics
1972	Johnny Bench, Cincinnati Reds	Dick Allen, Chicago White Sox
1975	Joe Morgan, Cincinnati Reds	Fred Lynn, Boston Red Sox
1976	Joe Morgan, Cincinnati Reds	Thurman Munson, New York Yankees
1979	Keith Hernandez, St. Louis Cardinals; Willie Stargell, Pittsburgh Pirates	Don Baylor, California Angels
1980	Mike Schmidt, Philadelphia Phillies	George Brett, Kansas City Royals
1981	Mike Schmidt, Philadelphia Phillies	Rollie Fingers, Milwaukee Brewers
1982	Dale Murphy, Atlanta Braves	Robin Yount, Milwaukee Brewers
1983	Dale Murphy, Atlanta Braves	Cal Ripken, Jr., Baltimore Orioles
1984	Ryne Sandberg, Chicago Cubs	Willie Hernandez, Detroit Tigers
1985	Willie McGee, St. Louis Cardinals	Don Mattingly, New York Yankees
1986	Mike Schmidt, Philadelphia Phillies	Roger Clemens, Boston Red Sox
1987	André Dawson, Chicago Cubs	**George Bell, Toronto Blue Jays**
1988	Kirk Gibson, Los Angeles Dodgers	Jose Canseco, Oakland Athletics
1989	Kevin Mitchell, San Francisco Giants	Robin Yount, Milwaukee Brewers
1990	Barry Bonds, Pittsburgh Pirates	Rickey Henderson, Oakland Athletics
1991	Terry Pendleton, Atlanta Braves	Cal Ripken, Jr., Baltimore Orioles
1992	Barry Bonds, Pittsburgh Pirates	Dennis Eckersley, Oakland A's
1993	Barry Bonds, San Francisco Giants	Frank Thomas, Chicago White Sox
1994	Jeff Bagwell, Houston Astras	Frank Thomas, Chicago White Sox
1995	Barry Larkin, Cincinnati Reds	Mo Vaughn, Boston Red Sox
1996	Ken Caminiti, San Diego Padres	Juan Gonzalez, Texas Rangers
1997	Larry Walker, Colorado Rockies	Ken Griffey Jr., Seattle Mariners
1998	Sammy Sosa, Chicago Cubs	Juan Gonzalez, Texas Rangers
1999	Chipper Jones, Atlanta Braves	Ivan Rodriguez, Texas Rangers

Source: *Canadian Press*

Larry Walker's Season Ended

Colorado Rockies outfielder Larry Walker, on the disabled list since Aug. 21, 2000, underwent surgery on his right elbow on Sept. 8. Walker, from Maple Ridge, BC, had a long piece of cartilage and a bone spur removed from the back of his elbow joint.

Walker, the NL's MVP in 1997 and the league's batting champion in 1998 and 1999, played in pain for most of the 2000 season. In 87 games, he hit .309 with nine homers and 51 RBIs, a far cry from 1997 when he hit .366 with 49 homers and 130 RBIs. Walker was in the first year of a US$75 million, six-year contract.

Source: *The Canadian Press*

Batting Champions, 1960–1999

National League

Year	Player, Club	%
1960	Dick Groat, Pittsburgh	.325
1961	Roberto Clemente, Pittsburgh	.351
1962	Tommy Davis, Los Angeles	.346
1963	Tommy Davis, Los Angeles	.326
1964	Roberto Clemente, Pittsburgh	.339
1965	Roberto Clemente, Pittsburgh	.329
1966	Matty Alou, Pittsburgh	.342
1967	Roberto Clemente, Pittsburgh	.357
1968	Pete Rose, Cincinnati	.335
1969	Pete Rose, Cincinnati	.348
1970	Rico Carty, Atlanta	.366
1971	Joe Torre, St. Louis	.363
1972	Billy Williams, Chicago	.333
1973	Pete Rose, Cincinnati	.338
1974	Ralph Garr, Atlanta	.353
1975	Bill Madlock, Chicago	.354
1976	Bill Madlock, Chicago	.339
1977	Dave Parker, Pittsburgh	.338
1978	Dave Parker, Pittsburgh	.334
1979	Keith Hernandez, St. Louis	.344
1980	Bill Buckner, Chicago	.324
1981	Bill Madlock, Pittsburgh[1]	.341
1982	**Al Oliver, Montreal**	**.331**
1983	Bill Madlock, Pittsburgh	.323
1984	Tony Gwynn, San Diego	.351
1985	Willie McGee, St. Louis	.353
1986	**Tim Raines, Montreal**	**.334**
1987	Tony Gwynn, San Diego	.370
1988	Tony Gwynn, San Diego	.313
1989	Tony Gwynn, San Diego	.336
1990	Willie McGee, St. Louis	.335
1991	Terry Pendleton, Atlanta	.319
1992	Gary Sheffield, San Diego	.330
1993	Andres Galarraga, Colorado	.370
1994	Tony Gwynn, San Diego[1]	.394
1995	Tony Gwynn, San Diego	.368
1996	Tony Gwynn, San Diego	.353
1997	Tony Gwynn, San Diego	.372
1998	Larry Walker, Colorado	.363
1999	Larry Walker, Colorado	.379

American League

Year	Player, Club	%
1960	Pete Runnels, Boston	.320
1961	Norm Cash, Detroit	.361
1962	Pete Runnels, Boston	.326
1963	Carl Yastrzemski, Boston	.321
1964	Tony Oliva, Minnesota	.323
1965	Tony Oliva, Minnesota	.321
1966	Frank Robinson, Baltimore	.316
1967	Carl Yastrzemski, Boston	.326
1968	Carl Yastrzemski, Boston	.301
1969	Rod Carew, Minnesota	.332
1970	Alex Johnson, California	.329
1971	Tony Oliva, Minnesota	.337
1972	Rod Carew, Minnesota	.318
1973	Rod Carew, Minnesota	.350
1974	Rod Carew, Minnesota	.364
1975	Rod Carew, Minnesota	.359
1976	George Brett, Kansas City	.333
1977	Rod Carew, Minnesota	.388
1978	Rod Carew, Minnesota	.333
1979	Fred Lynn, Boston	.333
1980	George Brett, Kansas City	.390
1981	Carney Lansford, Boston	.336
1982	Willie Wilson, Kansas City	.332
1983	Wade Boggs, Boston	.361
1984	Don Mattingly, New York	.343
1985	Wade Boggs, Boston	.368
1986	Wade Boggs, Boston	.357
1987	Wade Boggs, Boston	.363
1988	Wade Boggs, Boston	.366
1989	Kirby Puckett, Minnesota	.339
1990	George Brett, Kansas City	.329
1991	Julio Franco, Texas	.341
1992	Edgar Martinez, Seattle	.343
1993	**John Olerud, Toronto**	**.363**
1994	Paul O'Neill, New York[1]	.359
1995	Edgar Martinez, Seattle	.356
1996	Alex Rodriguez, Seattle	.358
1997	Frank Thomas, Chicago	.347
1998	Bernie Williams, New York	.339
1999	Nomar Garciaparra, Boston	**.357**

Source: *Canadian Press*

(1) Strike abbreviated season.

Greatest Home Run Seasons

HR	Player, Team	Year
70	Mark McGwire, StL	1998
66	Sammy Sosa, Chi Cubs	1998
65	Mark McGwire, StL	1999
63	Sammy Sosa, Chi Cubs	1999
61	Roger Maris, NYY	1961
60	Babe Ruth, NYY	1927
59	Babe Ruth, NYY	1921
58	Jimmie Foxx, Phi Athletics	1932
58	Hank Greenberg, Det	1938
58	Mark McGwire, Oak/ StL	1997
56	Hack Wilson, Chi Cubs	1930
56	Ken Griffey Jr., Sea	1998
56	Ken Griffey Jr., Sea	1997
54	Babe Ruth, NYY	1920
54	Babe Ruth, NYY	1928
54	Ralph Kiner, Pit	1949
54	Mickey Mantle, NYY	1961
54	Mickey Mantle, NYY	1956
52	Willie Mays, SF	1965
52	George Foster, Cin	1977
52	Mark McGwire, Oak	1996
51	Ralph Kiner, Pit	1947
51	Johnny Mize, NY Giants	1947
51	Willie Mays, NY Giants	1955
51	Cecil Fielder, Det	1990
50	Jimmie Foxx, Bos	1938
50	Albert Belle, Cle	1995
50	Brady Anderson, Bal	1996
50	Greg Vaughn, SD	1998

Source: *Canadian Press*

Individual Earned Run Average Leaders, 1960–2000

National League

Year	Player, Team	ERA
1960	Mike McCormick, SF	2.70
1961	Warren Spahn, Mil	3.02
1962	Sandy Koufax, LA	2.54
1963	Sandy Koufax, LA	1.88
1964	Sandy Koufax, LA	1.74
1965	Sandy Koufax, LA	2.04
1966	Sandy Koufax, LA	1.73
1967	Phil Niekro, Atl	1.87
1968	Bob Gibson, StL	1.12
1969	Juan Marichal, SF	2.10
1970	Tom Seaver, NY	2.81
1971	Tom Seaver, NY	1.76
1972	Steve Carlton, Pha	1.97
1973	Tom Seaver, NY	2.08
1974	Buzz Capra, Atl	2.28
1975	Randy Jones, SD	2.24
1976	John Denny, StL	2.52
1977	John Candelaria, Pgh	2.34
1978	Craig Swan, NY	2.43
1979	J.R. Richard, Hou	2.71
1980	Don Sutton, LA	2.21
1981	Nolan Ryan, Hou	1.69[1]
1982	**Steve Rogers, Mtl**	**2.40**
1983	Atlee Hammaker, SF	2.25
1984	Alejandro Pena, LA	2.48
1985	Dwight Gooden, NY	1.53
1986	Mike Scott, Hou	2.22
1987	Nolan Ryan, Hou	2.76
1988	Joe Magrane, StL	2.18
1989	Scott Garrelts, SF	2.28
1990	Danny Darwin, Hou	2.21
1991	**Dennis Martinez, Mtl**	**2.39**
1992	Bill Swift, S	2.08
1993	Greg Maddux, Atl	2.36
1994	Greg Maddux, Atl	1.56[1]
1995	Greg Maddux, Atl	1.63
1996	Kevin Brown, Fla	1.89
1997	Pedro Martinez, Mtl	1.90
1998	Greg Maddux, Atl	2.22
1999	Randy Johnson, Ari	2.48
2000	Kevin Brown, LA	2.58

American League

Year	Player, Team	ERA
1960	Frank Baumann, Chi	2.67
1961	Dick Donovan, Wash	2.40
1962	Hank Aguirre, Det	2.21
1963	Gary Peters, Chi	2.33
1964	Dean Chance, LA	1.65
1965	Sam McDowell, Cle	2.18
1966	Gary Peters, Chi	1.98
1967	Joel Horlen, Chi	2.06
1968	Luis Tiant, Cle	1.60
1969	Dick Bosman, Wash	2.19
1970	Diego Segui, Oak	2.56
1971	Vida Blue, Oak	1.82
1972	Luis Tiant, Bos	1.91
1973	Jim Palmer, Bal	2.40
1974	Catfish Hunter, Oak	2.49
1975	Jim Palmer, Bal	2.09
1976	Mark Fidrych, Det	2.34
1977	Frank Tanana, Cal	2.54
1978	Ron Guidry, NY	1.74
1979	Ron Guidry, NY	2.78
1980	Rudy May, NY	2.47
1981	Steve McCatty, Oak	2.32[1]
1982	Rick Sutcliffe, Cle	2.96
1983	Rick Honeycutt, Tex	2.42
1984	Mike Boddicker, Bal	2.79
1985	**Dave Stieb, Tor**	**2.48**
1986	Roger Clemens, Bos	2.48
1987	**Jimmy Key, Tor**	**2.76**
1988	Allan Anderson, Min	2.45
1989	Bret Saberhagen, KC	2.16
1990	Roger Clemens, Bos	1.93
1991	Roger Clemens, Bos	2.62
1992	Roger Clemens, Bos	2.41
1993	Kevin Appier, KC	2.56
1994	Steve Ontiveras, Oak	2.65[1]
1995	Randy Johnson, Sea	2.48
1996	Juan Guzman, Tor	2.93
1997	Roger Clemens, Tor	2.05
1998	Roger Clemens, Tor	2.65
1999	Pedro Martinez, Bos	2.07
2000	Pedro Martinez, Bos	1.74

Source: *The Baseball Encyclopedia*

(1) Strike abbreviated season.

Directory of Selected Baseball Organizations in Canada

Canadian Federation of Amateur Baseball
1600 James Naismith Dr.
Gloucester, Ont.
K1B 5N4
Tel: (613) 748-5606
Fax: (613) 748-5706

Major League Baseball
350 Park Ave.
New York, NY 10022
Tel: (212) 339-7800
www.majorleague
baseball.com

Montreal Expos Baseball Club
P.O. Box 500, Station M
Montreal, Que
H1V 3P2
Tel: (514) 253-3434
Fax: (514) 253-8282
www.montrealexpos.com

Toronto Blue Jays
The Skydome
300 The Esplanade West,
Suite 3200
Toronto, Ont.
M5V 3B3
Tel: (416) 341-1000
www.bluejays.ca

Canadian Players in Major League Baseball, 2000

Batter	AVG	OBA	AB	R	H	2B	3B	HR	RBI	BB	SO	SB	CS	E
Larry Walker, Colorado	.309	.409	314	64	97	21	7	9	51	46	40	5	5	1
Corey Koskie, Minnesota	.300	.400	474	79	142	32	4	9	65	77	104	5	4	12
Danny Klassen, Arizona	.237	.318	76	13	18	3	0	2	8	8	24	1	1	2
Matt Stairs, Oakland	.227	.333	476	74	108	26	0	21	81	78	122	5	2	4
Kevin Nicolson, San Diego	.216	.255	97	7	21	6	1	1	8	4	31	1	0	4
Rob Ducey, Philadelphia	.197	.322	152	24	30	4	1	6	25	29	47	1	0	3

Pitchers	W	L	ERA	G	GS	SV	IP	H	R	ER	HR	BB	SO
Ryan Dempster, Florida	14	10	3.66	33	33	0	226.1	210	102	92	30	97	209
Eric Gagne, Los Angeles	4	6	5.15	20	19	0	101.1	106	62	58	20	60	79
Mike Johnson, Montreal	5	6	6.39	41	13	0	101.1	107	73	72	18	53	70
Jeff Zimmerman, Texas	4	5	5.30	65	0	1	69.2	80	45	41	10	34	74
Rheal Cormier, Boston	3	3	4.61	64	0	0	68.1	74	40	35	7	17	43
Paul Quantrill, Toronto	2	5	4.57	67	0	1	80.2	97	44	41	6	25	44
Jason Dickson, Anaheim	2	2	6.11	6	6	0	28.0	39	20	19	5	7	18
Dave Wainhouse, St. Louis	0	1	9.35	9	0	0	8.2	13	10	9	2	4	5
Paul Spoljaric, Kansas City	0	0	6.52	13	0	0	9.2	9	7	7	4	5	6

Source: *Canadian Press*

Career Records of Some Canadian Major League Players of the Past

Player	G	AB	R	H	2B	3B	HR	RBI	BA	OBA	SA
Jeff Heath, 1936–49	1 383	4 937	777	1 447	279	102	194	887	.293	.370	.509
Terry Puhl, 1977–90	1 531	4 855	676	1 361	226	56	62	435	.280	.350	.388
George Gibson, 1905–18	1 213	3 776	295	893	142	49	15	335	.236	.294	.312
Tip O'Neill, 1883–92	1 054	4 255	880	1 386	222	92	52	435	.326	.392	.458
Pete Ward, 1962–70	973	3 060	345	776	136	17	98	427	.254	.342	.405
George Selkirk 1934–42	846	2 790	503	810	131	41	108	576	.290	.400	.483
Jack Graney 1908–22	1 402	4 705	706	1 178	219	79	18	420	.250	.354	.342
Frank O'Rourke 1917–31	1 131	4 069	547	1 032	196	42	15	430	.254	.315	.333

Pitcher	W	L	%	G	SHO	SV	IP	H	BB	SO	ERA
Ferguson Jenkins, 1965–83	284	226	.557	664	49	7	4 498	4 142	997	3 192	3.34
Reggie Cleveland, 1969–81	105	106	.498	203	12	25	1 809	1 813	543	930	4.01
Russ Ford, 1909–15	99	71	.582	199	15	9	1 487	1 318	376	710	2.59
Phil Marchildon, 1942–50[1]	68	75	.476	185	6	2	1 214	1 084	684	481	3.93
Oscar Judd, 1941–48	40	51	.440	161	4	7	770	744	397	304	3.90
John Hiller 1965–80	87	76	.534	545	6	125	1 242	1 040	535	1 036	2.83
Dick Fowler 1941–52	66	79	.455	221	11	4	1 303	1 367	578	382	4.11
Ron Taylor 1962–72	45	43	.511	491	0	72	800	794	209	464	3.93

G = Games played. AB = At bats. R = Runs. H = Hits. 2B = Doubles. 3B = Triples. HR = Home runs. RBI = Runs batted in. BA = Batting average. OBA = On-base percentage. SA = Slugging average.

W = Wins. L = Losses. % = Percentage. G = Games pitched. SHO = Shutouts. SV = Saves. IP = Innings pitched. H = Hits allowed. BB = Walks. SO = Strikeouts. ERA = Earned run average.

(1) Marchildon was in the Canadian Armed Forces in 1943–44.

Montreal Expos Year-By-Year Record, 1969–2000

Year	Won	Lost	%	Pos.	Home Attendance	Manager
1969	52	110	.321	6th	1 212 608	Gene Mauch
1970	73	89	.451	6th	1 424 683	Gene Mauch
1971	71	90	.441	5th	1 290 963	Gene Mauch
1972	70	86	.449	5th	1 142 145	Gene Mauch
1973	79	83	.488	4th	1 246 863	Gene Mauch
1974	79	82	.491	4th	1 019 134	Gene Mauch
1975	75	87	.463	5th	908 292	Gene Mauch
1976	55	107	.340	6th	646 704	K. Kuehl/C. Fox
1977	75	87	.463	5th	1 433 757	Dick Williams
1978	76	86	.469	4th	1 427 007	Dick Williams
1979	95	65	.594	2nd	2 102 173	Dick Williams
1980	90	72	.556	2nd	2 208 175	Dick Williams
1981	60	48	.556	—	1 534 564	Dick Williams/ Jim Fanning
1982	86	76	.531	3rd	2 318 292	Jim Fanning
1983	82	80	.506	3rd	2 320 651	Bill Virdon
1984	78	83	.484	5th	1 606 531	Bill Virdon/ Jim Fanning
1985	84	77	.522	3rd	1 502 494	Buck Rodgers
1986	78	83	.484	4th	1 128 981	Buck Rodgers
1987	91	71	.562	3rd	1 850 324	Buck Rodgers
1988	81	81	.500	3rd	1 478 659	Buck Rodgers
1989	81	81	.500	4th	1 783 533	Buck Rodgers
1990	85	77	.525	3rd	1 421 388	Buck Rodgers
1991	70	91	.441	6th	978 045	Buck Rodgers/ Tom Runnells
1992	87	75	.537	2nd	1 731 566	Tom Runnells/ Felipe Alou
1993	94	68	.580	2nd	1 641 437	Felipe Alou
1994	74	40	.649	1st(a)	1 276 250	Felipe Alou
1995	66	78	.458	5th	1 309 618	Felipe Alou
1996	88	74	.543	2nd	1 618 573	Felipe Alou
1997	78	84	.481	4th	1 175 000	Felipe Alou
1998	65	97	.401	4th	914 909	Felipe Alou
1999	68	94	.420	4th	773 277	Felipe Alou
2000	67	95	.414	4th	926 427	Felipe Alou

Source: *Canadian Press*

(a) Eastern Division: first year with three divisions.

Montreal Expos Individual Statistics, 2000

Batters

	Avg	OBA	AB	R	H	2B	3B	HR	RBI	BB	SO	SB	CS	E
V. Guerrero	.345	.410	571	101	197	28	11	44	123	58	74	9	10	10
Vidro	.330	.379	606	101	200	51	2	24	97	49	69	5	4	10
White	.307	.370	290	52	89	24	0	11	54	28	67	5	1	1
De La Rosa	.288	.365	66	7	19	3	1	2	9	7	11	2	1	2
Mordecai	.284	.335	169	20	48	16	0	4	16	12	34	2	2	8
Blum	.283	.335	343	40	97	20	2	11	45	26	60	1	4	9
Seguignol	.278	.326	162	22	45	8	0	10	22	9	46	0	1	5
W. Guerrero	.267	.312	288	30	77	7	2	2	23	19	41	8	1	4
Stevens	.265	.337	449	60	119	27	2	22	75	48	105	0	0	11
Tracy	.260	.339	192	29	50	8	1	11	32	22	61	1	0	6
Jones	.250	.292	168	30	42	8	2	0	13	10	32	7	2	3
Bergeron	.245	.320	518	80	127	25	7	5	31	58	100	11	13	5
Widger	.238	.311	281	31	67	17	2	12	34	29	61	1	2	8
Cabrera	.237	.279	422	47	100	25	1	13	55	25	28	4	4	10
Schneider	.235	.276	115	6	27	6	0	0	11	7	24	0	1	6
Bradley	.221	.288	154	20	34	8	1	2	15	14	32	2	1	2
Barrett	.214	.277	271	28	58	15	1	1	22	23	35	0	1	15
O'Brien	.211	.286	19	4	1	0	1	2	2	7	0	0	0	
Webster	.210	.264	81	6	17	3	0	0	5	6	14	0	0	0
Coquillette	.203	.284	59	6	12	4	0	1	8	7	19	0	0	1
Nunnari	.200	.583	5	2	1	0	0	0	1	6	2	0	0	0
Valera	.000	.167	10	1	0	0	0	0	1	1	5	0	0	0
Team Totals	.266	.326	5 535	738	1 475	310	35	178	705	476	1 048	58	48	132

Source: *Canadian Press*

AVG = Batting average; OBA = On base average; AB = Times at bat; R = Runs; H = Hits; 2B = Doubles; 3B = Triples; HR = Home runs; RBI = Runs batted in; BB = Walks; SO = strikeouts; SB = Stolen bases; CS = Caught stealing; E = Errors.

Pitchers

	W	L	ERA	G	GS	SV	IP	H	R	ER	HR	BB	SO
Strickland	4	3	3.00	49	0	9	48.0	38	18	16	3	16	48
Pavano	8	4	3.06	15	15	0	97.0	89	40	33	8	34	64
Kline	1	5	3.50	83	0	14	82.1	88	36	32	8	27	64
Telford	5	4	3.79	64	0	3	78.1	76	38	33	10	23	68
Urbina	0	1	4.05	13	0	8	13.1	11	6	6	1	5	22
Vazquez	11	9	4.05	33	33	0	217.2	247	104	98	24	61	196
Armas	7	9	4.36	17	17	0	95.0	74	49	46	10	50	59
Hermanson	12	14	4.77	38	30	4	198.0	226	128	105	26	75	94
Rigby	0	0	5.06	6	0	1	5.1	8	5	3	0	3	2
Blank	0	1	5.14	13	0	0	14.0	12	8	8	1	5	4
Downs(LG)	4	3	5.29	19	19	0	97.0	122	62	57	13	40	63
Downs	0	0	9.00	1	1	0	3.0	5	3	3	0	3	0
Lira	5	8	5.40	53	7	0	101.2	129	71	61	11	36	51
Spencer	0	0	5.40	8	0	0	6.2	7	4	4	2	3	6
Santana	1	5	5.67	36	4	0	66.2	69	45	42	11	33	58
Mota	1	1	6.00	29	0	0	30.0	27	21	20	3	12	24
Lara	0	0	6.35	6	0	0	5.2	5	4	4	0	8	3
Johnson	5	6	6.39	41	13	0	101.1	107	73	72	18	53	70
Thurman	4	9	6.42	17	17	0	88.1	112	69	63	9	46	52
Moore	1	5	6.62	8	8	0	35.1	55	31	26	7	21	24
Irabu	2	5	7.24	11	11	0	54.2	77	45	44	9	14	42
Forster	0	1	7.88	42	0	0	32.0	28	31	28	5	25	23
Powell	0	3	7.96	11	4	0	26.0	35	27	23	6	9	19
Team Totals	67	95	5.13	162	162	39	1 424.2	1 475	902	132	178	579	1 011

Source: *Canadian Press*

W = Games won; L = Games lost; ERA = Earned run average; G = Games played in; GS = Games started; SV = Saves; IP = Innings pitched; H = Hits allowed; R = Runs allowed; ER = Earned runs; HR = Home runs allowed; BB = Walks allowed; SO = Strikeouts.

Montreal Expos Team Records up to 2000 Season

Batting

Single Season

Batting Average: Tim Raines, 1986, .334; Moises Alou, 1994, .339 (106g)
At Bats: Warren Cromartie, 1979, 659
Games: Rusty Staub, 1971, 162; Ken Singleton, 1973, 162; Warren Cromartie, 1980, 162
Hits: Al Oliver, 1982, 204
Runs: Tim Raines, 1983, 133
Singles: Tim Raines, 1986, 140
Doubles: Mark Grudzielanek, 1997, 54
Triples: Rodney Scott, 1980, 13; Tim Raines, 1985, 13; Mitch Webster, 1986, 13
Home Runs: Vladimir Guerrero, 2000, 44
Runs Batted In: Vladimir Guerrero, 1999, 131
Total Bases: Andre Dawson, 1983, 341
Slugging Average: Moises Alou, 1994, .592 (106g); Andre Dawson, 1981, .553
On-Base Average: Tim Raines, 1987, .431
Stolen Bases: Ron LeFlore, 1980, 97
Strikeouts: Andres Galarraga, 1990, 169
Walks: Ken Singleton, 1973, 123
Hit By Pitch: Ron Hunt, 1971, 50
Hitting Streak: Vladimir Guerrero, 1999, 31
Pinch Hits: Jose Morales, 1976, 25

Career Leaders

Batting Average: Al Oliver, .315
At Bats: Tim Wallach, 6 529
Games: Tim Wallach, 1 767
Hits: Tim Wallach, 1 694
Runs: Tim Raines, 934
Singles: Tim Raines, 1,148
Doubles: Tim Wallach, 360
Triples: Tim Raines, 81
Home Runs: Andre Dawson, 225
Runs Batted In: Tim Wallach, 905
Total Bases: Tim Wallach, 2,728

Stolen Bases: Tim Raines, 634
Strikeouts: Tim Wallach, 1,008
Walks: Tim Raines, 775

Pitching

Single Season

Games: Mike Marshall, 1973, 92
Games Started: Steve Rogers, 1977, 40
Complete Games: Bill Stoneman, 1971, 20
Innings Pitched: Steve Rogers, 1977, 302
Wins: Ross Grimsley, 1978, 20
Losses: Steve Rogers, 1974, 22
Saves: John Wetteland, 1993, 43
Earned Run Average: Ugueth Urbina, 1998, 1.30
Strikeouts: Pedro Martinez, 1991, 305

Career Leaders

Games: Tim Burke, 425
Games Started: Steve Rogers, 393
Complete Games: Steve Rogers, 129
Innings Pitched: Steve Rogers, 2 839
Wins: Steve Rogers, 158
Losses: Steve Rogers, 152
Saves: Jeff Reardon, 152
Earned Run Average: Dennis Martinez, 2.93

Source: *Canadian Press*

Montreal Expos Player of the Year, 1969–1999

Year	Player	Year	Player	Year	Player	Year	Player
1969	Rusty Staub	1977	Gary Carter	1984	Gary Carter	1992	Larry Walker
1970	Carl Morton	1978	Ross Grimsley	1985	Tim Raines	1993	Marquis Grissom
1971	Ron Hunt	1979	Larry Parrish	1986	Tim Raines	1994	Moises Alou
1972	Mike Marshall	1980	Gary Carter	1987	Tim Wallach	1995	David Segui
1973	Mike Marshall	1981	Andre Dawson	1988	Andres Galarraga	1996	Hank Rodriguez
1974	Willie Davis	1982	Al Oliver	1989	Tim Wallach	1997	Pedro Martinez
1975	Gary Carter	1983	Andre Dawson;	1990	Tim Wallach	1998	Vladimir Guerrero
1976	Woodie Fryman		Tim Raines (tie)	1991	Dennis Martinez	1999	Vladimir Guerrero

Directory of Sports Organizations

A number of Canadian amateur sports organizations can be reached at 1600 James Naismith Drive, Gloucester, Ont. K1B 5N4. These include:

Basketball Canada
Tel: (613) 748-5607
www.cdnsport.cu/basketball

Canadian Amateur Boxing Assn
Tel: (613) 748-5611
Fax: (613) 748-5740
www.boxing.ca/cuba.html

Canadian Amateur Diving Assn
Tel: (613) 748-5631

Canadian Amateur Hockey Association
Tel: (613) 748-5613
Fax: (613) 748-5709

Canadian Curling Association
Tel: (613) 748-5628
Fax: (613) 748-5713
www.curling.ca

Canadian Cycling Assn
Tel: (613) 748-5629
Fax: (613) 748-5692
www.canadian-cycling.com

Canadian Federation of Amateur Baseball
Tel: (613) 748-5606
Fax: (613) 748-5706

Canadian Figure Skating Association
Tel: (613) 748-5635
Fax: (613) 748-5718
www.cfsa.ca

Canadian Interuniversity Athletic Union
Tel: (613) 748-5619
Fax: (613) 748-5764
www.ciau.ca

Canadian Soccer Association
Tel: (613) 748-5667
Fax: (613) 745-1938

Canadian Track and Field Assn
Tel: (613) 748-5678
Fax: (613) 748-5645

Canadian Volleyball Assn
Tel: (613) 748-5681

Football Canada
Tel: (613) 748-5636
Fax: (613) 748-5702

Rowing Canada
Tel: (613) 748-5656
Fax: (613) 748-5712

Softball Canada
Tel: (613) 748-5668

Swimming Canada
Tel: (613) 748-5673
Fax: (613) 748-5715
www.swimming.ca

Canadian Automobile Sports Clubs
Tel: (905) 667-9500
Fax: (905) 667-9555
www3.sympatico.ca/case.or

Other sports organizations include:

Canadian Trotting Assn
2150 Meadowvale Blvd.
Mississauga, Ont.
L5N 6R6
Tel: (905) 858-3060
Fax: (905) 858-3111

Royal Canadian Golf Association
1333 Dorval Dr.
Oakville, Ont.
L6J 4Z3
Tel: (416) 849-9700
Fax: (416) 845-7040
www.rcga.org

Toronto Blue Jays Year-By-Year Record, 1977–2000

	Won	Lost	%	Pos.	Home Attendance	Manager		Won	Lost	%	Pos.	Home Attendance	Manager
1977 ..	54	107	.335	7th	1 701 052	Roy Hartsfield	1989 ..	89	73	.549	1st	3 375 573	Williams/
1978 ..	59	102	.366	7th	1 562 585	Roy Hartsfield							Cito Gaston
1979 ..	53	109	.327	7th	1 431 651	Roy Hartsfield	1990 ..	86	76	.531	2nd	3 885 284	Cito Gaston
1980 ..	67	95	.414	7th	1 400 327	Bob Mattick	1991 ..	91	71	.562	1st	4 001 526	Cito Gaston
1981 ..	37	69	.349	—	755 083	Bob Mattick	1992 ..	96	66	.593	1st	4 028 318	Cito Gaston
1st half	16	42	.276	7th	—		1993 ..	95	67	.586	1st	4 057 947	Cito Gaston
2nd half	21	27	.438	7th	—								
1982 ..	78	84	.481	6th[1]	1 275 978	Bobby Cox	1994 ..	55	60	.476	3rd[2]	2 907 933	Cito Gaston
1983 ..	89	73	.549	4th	1 930 415	Bobby Cox	1995 ..	56	88	.389	5th	2 826 483	Cito Gaston
1984 ..	89	73	.549	2nd	2 110 009	Bobby Cox	1996 ..	74	88	.457	4th	2 559 563	Cito Gaston
1985 ..	99	62	.615	1st	2 468 925	Bobby Cox	1997 ..	76	86	.469	5th	2 589 297	Cito Gaston[3]
1986 ..	86	76	.531	4th	2 455 477	Jimy Williams	1998 ..	88	74	.543	3rd	2 454 303	Tim Johnson
1987 ..	96	66	.593	2nd	2 778 459	Jimy Williams	1999 ..	84	78	.518	3rd	2 163 473	Jim Fregosi
1988 ..	87	75	.537	3rd	2 595 175	Jimy Williams	2000 ..	83	78	.516	3rd	1 819 886	Jim Fregosi

Source: *Canadian Press*
(1) Tied. (2) Eastern Division: first year with three divisions (3) Gaston was fired with five games remaining in the 1997 season.

Toronto Blue Jays Individual Statistics, 2000

Batters

	AVG	OBA	AB	R	H	2B	3B	HR	RBI	BB	SO	SB	CS	E
Delgado	.344	.470	569	115	196	57	1	41	137	123	104	0	1	13
Fletcher	.320	.355	416	43	133	19	1	20	58	20	45	1	0	4
Stewart	.319	.363	583	107	186	43	5	21	69	37	79	20	5	2
Fullmer	.295	.340	482	76	142	29	1	32	104	30	68	3	1	0
Grebeck	.295	.364	241	38	71	19	0	3	23	25	33	0	0	9
Martinez	.311	.393	180	29	56	10	1	2	22	24	28	4	2	2
Martinez(LG)	.285	.362	403	55	115	18	4	5	46	48	65	7	7	2
Morandini	.271	.316	107	10	29	2	1	0	7	7	23	1	0	1
Mondesi	.271	.329	388	78	105	22	2	24	67	32	73	22	6	7
Batista	.263	.307	620	96	163	32	2	41	114	35	121	5	4	17
Gonzalez	.252	.313	527	68	133	31	2	15	69	43	113	4	4	16
Cordova	.245	.317	200	23	49	7	0	4	18	18	35	3	2	1
Cruz	.242	.323	603	91	146	32	5	31	76	71	129	15	5	3
Greene, T.	.235	.278	85	11	20	2	0	5	10	5	18	0	0	0
Mottola	.222	.300	9	1	2	0	0	0	2	0	4	0	0	0
Bush	.215	.271	297	38	64	8	0	1	18	18	60	9	4	6
A. Castillo	.211	.287	185	14	39	7	0	1	16	21	36	0	0	3
Woodward	.183	.254	104	16	19	7	0	3	14	10	28	1	0	5
Thompson	.167	.444	6	2	1	0	0	0	1	3	2	0	0	0
Ducey	.154	.267	13	2	2	1	0	0	1	2	2	0	0	1
Wise	.136	.208	22	3	3	0	0	0	0	1	5	1	0	0
Greene, C.	.111	.111	9	0	1	0	0	0	0	0	5	0	0	0
Phelps	.000	.000	1	0	0	0	0	0	0	0	1	0	0	0
Wells, V.	.000	.000	2	0	0	0	0	0	0	0	0	0	0	0
Team Totals	.275	.341	5 677	861	1 562	328	21	244	826	526	1 026	89	34	100

Source: *Canadian Press*
AVG = batting average; OBA = on base average; AB = times at bat; R = runs; H = hits; 2B = doubles; 3B = triples; HR = home runs; RBI = runs batted in; BB = walks; SO = strikeouts; SB = stolen bases; CS = caught stealing; E = errors.

Pitchers

	W	L	ERA	G	GS	SV	IP	H	R	ER	HR	BB	SO
▶ Andrews	1	2	10.02	8	2	0	20.2	34	23	23	6	9	12
Bale	0	0	14.73	2	0	0	3.2	5	7	6	1	3	6
Borbon	1	1	6.48	59	0	1	41.2	45	37	30	5	38	29
Carpenter	10	12	6.26	34	27	0	175.1	203	130	121	29	83	113
Castillo	10	5	3.59	25	24	0	138.0	112	58	55	18	56	104
Coco	0	0	9.00	1	0	0	4.0	5	4	4	1	5	2
DeWitt	1	0	8.56	8	0	0	13.2	20	13	13	4	9	6
Escobar	10	15	5.35	43	24	2	180.0	183	118	105	24	85	142
Estrella	0	0	5.79	2	0	0	4.2	9	3	3	1	0	3
Frascatore	2	4	5.42	60	0	0	73.0	85	51	43	13	33	30
Gunderson	0	1	7.11	6	0	0	6.1	15	6	5	0	2	2
Guthrie	3	6	4.67	76	0	0	71.1	17	41	7	1	37	63
Halladay	4	7	10.64	19	13	0	67.2	107	87	80	14	42	44
Koch	9	3	2.63	68	0	33	78.2	77	28	23	6	18	60
Loaiza	10	13	4.56	34	31	1	199.1	88	112	35	8	57	137
Munro	1	1	5.96	9	3	0	25.2	38	22	17	1	16	16
Painter	2	0	4.73	42	2	0	66.2	69	37	35	9	22	53
Quantril	2	5	4.52	68	0	1	83.2	97	45	41	6	25	47
Trachsel	8	15	4.80	34	34	0	200.2	67	116	32	9	74	110
D. Wells	20	8	4.11	35	35	0	229.2	259	115	100	22	31	166
Totals	83	79	5.14	162	162	37	1 437.1	1 583	908	805	186	560	978

Source: *Canadian Press*

W = Games won; L = Games lost; ERA = Earned run average; G = Games played in; GS = Games started; SV = Saves; IP = Innings pitched; H = Hits allowed; R = Runs allowed; ER = Earned runs; HR = Home runs allowed; BB = Walks allowed; SO = Strikeouts.

Toronto Blue Jays Team Records up to 2000 Season

Batting

Single Season

Batting Average: John Olerud, 1993, .363
At Bats: Tony Fernandez, 1986, 687
Games: Tony Fernandez, 1986, 163
Hits: Tony Fernandez, 1986, 213
Runs: Paul Molitor, 1993, 121
Singles: Tony Fernandez, 1986, 161
Doubles: Carlos Delgado, 2000, 57
Triples: Tony Fernandez, 1990, 17
Home Runs: George Bell, 1987, 47
Runs Batted In: Carlos Delgado, 2000, 137
Total Bases: Carlos Delgado, 2000, 378
Slugging Average: George Bell, 1987, .605
On-Base Average: John Olerud, 1993, .473
Stolen Bases: Dave Collins, 1984, 60
Strikeouts: José Canseco, 1998, 154
Walks: Carlos Delgado, 2000, 123
Hit By Pitch: Ed Sprague, 1996, 18
Hitting Streak: Shawn Green, 1999, 27

Career Leaders

Batting Average: Roberto Alomar, .310
At Bats: Lloyd Moseby, 5,124
Games: Lloyd Moseby, 1,392
Hits: Tony Fernandez, 1,406
Runs: Lloyd Moseby, 768
Singles: Tony Fernandez, 1,035
Doubles: Tony Fernandez, 246
Triples: Tony Fernandez, 72
Home Runs: Joe Carter, 203
Runs Batted In: George Bell, 740
Total Bases: George Bell, 2,201
Slugging Average: Fred McGriff, .530
On-Base Average: Fred McGriff, .391
Stolen Bases: Lloyd Moseby, 255
Strikeouts: Lloyd Moseby, 1,015
Walks: Lloyd Moseby, 547
Hit By Pitch: Lloyd Moseby, 50

Pitching

Single Season

Games: Mark Eichhorn, 1987, 89
Games Started: Jim Clancy, 1982, 40
Complete Games: Dave Stieb, 1982, 19
Innings Pitched: Dave Stieb, 1982, 288.1
Wins: Jack Morris, 1992, 21
Roger Clemens, 1997, 21
Losses: Jerry Garvin, 1977, 18; Phil Huffman, 1979, 18
Saves: Duane Ward, 1993, 45
Earned Run Average: Roger Clemens, 1997, 2.05
Shutouts: Dave Stieb, 1982, 5
Strikeouts: Roger Clemens, 1997, 292
Walks: Jim Clancy, 1980, 128
Home Runs Allowed: Woody Williams, 1998, 36
Hit Batsmen: Dave Stieb, 1986, 15

Career Leaders

Games: Tom Henke, 446
Games Started: Dave Stieb, 408
Complete Games: Dave Stieb, 103
Innings Pitched: Dave Stieb, 2 872.1

Wins: Dave Stieb, 175
Losses: Jim Clancy, 140
Saves: Tom Henke, 217
Earned Run Average: Tom Henke, 2.48
Shutouts: Dave Stieb, 30
Strikeouts: Dave Stieb, 1 658
Walks: Dave Stieb, 1 020
Home Runs Allowed: Jim Clancy, 219
Hit Batsmen: Dave Stieb, 129

Source: *Canadian Press*

Toronto Blue Jays Player of the Year, 1977–1999

Year	Player	Year	Player	Year	Player
1977	Bob Bailor	1985	Jesse Barfield	1993	Paul Molitor
1978	Bob Bailor	1986	Jesse Barfield	1994	Joe Carter
1979	Alfredo Griffin	1987	George Bell	1995	Roberto Alomar
1980	John Mayberry	1988	Fred McGriff	1996	Ed Sprague
1981	Dave Stieb	1989	George Bell	1997	Carlos Delgado
1982	Damaso Garcia	1990	Kelly Gruber	1998	Carlos Delgado
1983	Lloyd Moseby	1991	Roberto Alomar	1999	Shaun Green
1984	Dave Collins	1992	Roberto Alomar		

Want to Surf for Sports Info?

Football

Canadian Football League
www.cfl.ca
All you need to know about the CFL

National Football League
www.nfl.com
All the information you want on the NFL

Canadian Junior Football League
www.cjfl.ca
Scores, standings and stats

Hockey
Canadian Hockey League
www.canoe.ca/CHL/
Info on Canadian junior hockey with links to various leagues

Ontario Hockey League
www.ontariohockeyleague.com
Scores, standings, game recaps and news

American Hockey League
www.theahl.com
Stats, rosters and team info

The Hockey News
www.thn.com
News and stats

Hockey Future: The Hockey Propects Resource
www.hockeysfuture.com
Learn about the stars of tomorrow today

BASKETBALL

National Basketball Association, 1999–2000
Final Regular Season Standings

Eastern Conference

■ Atlantic Division

	W	L	%	GB
a-Miami (2)	52	30	.634	0.0
x-New York (3)	50	32	.610	2.0
x-Philadelphia (5)	49	33	.598	3.0
Orlando	41	41	.500	11.0
Boston	35	47	.427	17.0
New Jersey	31	51	.378	21.0
Washington	29	53	.354	23.0

■ Central Division

	W	L	%	GB
c-Indiana (1)	56	26	.683	0.0
x-Charlotte (4)	49	33	.598	7.0
x-Toronto (6)	**45**	**37**	**.549**	**11.0**
x-Detroit (7)	42	40	.512	14.0
x-Milwaukee (8)	42	40	.512	14.0
Cleveland	32	50	.390	24.0
Atlanta	28	54	.341	28.0
Chicago	17	65	.207	39.0

a-Clinched Atlantic Division Title
c-Clinched Central Division Title
m-Clinched Midwest Division Title

Western Conference

■ Midwest Division

	W	L	%	GB
m-Utah (2)	55	27	.671	0.0
x-San Antonio (4)	53	29	.646	2.0
x-Minnesota (6)	50	32	.610	5.0
Dallas	40	42	.488	15.0
Denver	35	47	.427	20.0
Houston	34	48	.415	21.0
Vancouver	**22**	**60**	**.268**	**33.0**

■ Pacific Division

	W	L	%	GB
p-L.A. Lakers (1)	67	15	.817	0.0
x-Portland (3)	59	23	.720	8.0
x-Phoenix (5)	53	29	.646	14.0
x-Seattle (7)	45	37	.549	22.0
x-Sacramento (8)	44	38	.537	23.0
Golden State	19	63	.232	48.0
L.A. Clippers	15	67	.183	52.0

p-Clinched Pacific Division Title
x-Clinched Playoff Berth

NBA Playoff Results, 1999–2000

QUARTERFINAL
New York defeated Toronto 3-0
Knicks 92   Raptors 88
Knicks 84   Raptors 83
Knicks 87   Raptors 80
Indiana defeated Milwaukee 3-2
Miami defeated Detroit 3-0
Philadelphia defeated Charlotte 3-1

SEMIFINAL
New York defeated Miami 4-3
Indiana defeated Philadelphia 4-2

**EASTERN CONFERENCE
FINAL**
Indiana defeated New York 4-2

QUARTERFINAL
Utah Jazz defeated Seattle 3-2
Los Angeles Lakers defeated Sacramento 3-2
Portland defeated Minnesota 3-1
Phoenix defeated San Antonio 3-1

SEMIFINAL
Los Angeles Lakers defeated Phoenix 4-1
Portland defeated Utah 4-1

**WESTERN CONFERENCE
FINAL**
Los Angeles Lakers defeated Portland 4-3

FINAL
Los Angeles Lakers defeated Indiana 4-2

Source: *Canadian Press*

1999–2000 NBA Season Review

The Los Angles Lakers did as expected and captured the NBA Championship. With a roster blessed with NBA MVP Shaquille O'Neal, young flash forward Kobe Bryant, and controlled by Zen-master coach Phil Jackson, the Lakers defeated the Indiana Pacers 4-2 in the championship final after barnstorming their way through a 67-15 regular season.

The Lakers were pushed in the playoffs by Portland and Sacramento, but on the strength of Shaquille O'Neal's 41-point, 12-rebound performance in the series-clinching 116-111 victory over the Indiana Pacers, the team won its first league title in 12 seasons. Shaq was a unanimous playoff MVP selection after earning NBA MVP honours during the regular season.

The Toronto Raptors regular season was its best-ever as the team posted a franchise-high 45-37 regular season record, good for sixth in the Eastern Conference and the team's first playoff berth. Toronto lost the best-of-five Eastern Conference quarter-final to the New York Knicks 3-0, but did not lose by more than seven points. Raptors Vince Carter enjoyed a breakout second season. Among his accomplishments were a career-high 51-point scoring performance in a 103-102 win over Phoenix on February 27, a 12-point scoring effort as a starter in the 2000 NBA all-star game, and a victory in the NBA.com slam dunk competition.

The Vancouver Grizzlies followed their fifth consecutive losing season (22-60) without a berth in the playoffs with an end-of-season ownership change and front office house cleaning.

Details on the Grizzlies and Raptors off-seasons follow on pages 714–16.

Individual Statistical Leaders, 1999-2000

(Final Regular Season)

■ Scoring

	FG	PTS	AVG
O'Neal, LAL	956	2 344	29.7
Iverson, Pha	729	1 989	28.4
Hill, Det	696	1 906	25.8
Carter, Tor	788	2 107	25.7
Malone, Utah	752	2 095	25.5
Webber, Sac	748	1 834	24.5
Payton, Sea	747	1 982	24.2
Stackhouse, Det	619	1 939	23.6
Duncan, S.A.	628	1 716	23.2
Garnett, Minn	759	1 857	22.9

■ Rebounds Per Game

	DEG	TOT	AVG
Mutombo, Atl	853	1 157	14.1
O'Neal, LAL	742	1 078	13.6
Duncan, S.A.	656	918	12.4
Garnett, Min	733	956	11.8
Webber, Sac	598	787	10.5
Abdur-Rahim, Vcr	607	825	10.1
Brand, Chi	462	810	10.0
Davis, Ind	473	729	9.9
Robinson, S.A.	577	770	9.6
Williams, Det	512	789	9.6

■ Field Goal Percentage

	FG	FGA	%
O'Neal, LAL	956	1 665	.574
Mutombo, Atl	322	573	.562
Mourning, Mia	652	1 184	.551
Patterson, Sea	354	661	.536
Wallace, Por	542	1 045	.519
Robinson, S.A.	528	1 031	.512
Szczerbiak, Min	342	669	.511
Malone, Utah	752	1 476	.509
McDyess, Den	614	1 211	.507
Harrington, Vcr	420	830	.506

■ Free Throw Percentage

	FT	FTA	%
Hornacek, Utah	171	180	.950
Miller, Ind	373	406	.919
Armstrong, Orl	225	247	.911
Brandon, Min	187	208	.899
Allen, Mil	353	398	.887
Stojakovic, Sac	135	153	.882
Jackson, Atl	186	212	.877
Anderson, LAC	271	309	.877
Richmond, Wash	298	340	.876
Cassell, Mil	390	445	.876 ▶

Basketball

■ Assists Per Game

	G	AST	AVG
Kidd, Phx.	67	678	10.1
Van Exel, Den.	79	714	9.0
Cassell, Mil.	81	729	9.0
Payton, Sea.	82	732	8.9
Brandon, Min.	71	629	8.9
Stockton, Utah	82	703	8.6
Marbury, N.J.	74	622	8.4
Bibby, Vcr.	82	665	8.1
Jackson, Ind.	81	650	8.0
Snow, Pha.	82	624	7.6

■ 3-Point Field Goal Percentage

	FG	3FGA	%
Davis, Dal.	82	167	.491
Hornacek, Utah	66	138	.478
Bullard, Hou.	79	177	.446
Rogers, Phx.	115	262	.439
Houston, NY	106	243	.436
Porter, SA	90	207	.435
Hunter, Det.	168	389	.432
Murray, Wash.	113	263	.430
Barry, Sac.	66	154	.429
Person, Cle.	106	250	.424

Source: *Canadian Press*

■ Steals Per Game

	G	STL	AVG
Jones, Cha.	72	192	2.67
Pierce, Bos.	73	152	2.08
Armstrong, Orl.	82	169	2.06
Iverson, Pha.	70	144	2.06
Blaylock, G.S.	73	146	2.00
Kidd, Phx.	67	134	2.00
Brandon, Min.	71	134	1.89
Payton, Sea.	82	153	1.87
Gill, N.J.	76	139	1.83
Stockton, Utah	82	143	1.74

■ Blocked Shots Per Game

	G	BLK	AVG
Mourning, Mia.	79	294	3.72
Mutombo, Atl.	82	269	3.28
O'Neal, LAL	79	239	3.03
Ratliff, Pha.	67	171	3.00
Bradley, Dal.	77	190	2.47
Robinson, SA	80	183	2.29
Duncan, SA	74	165	2.23
LaFrentz, Den.	81	180	2.22
Ostertag, Utah	81	172	2.12
Camby, NY	59	116	1.97

All-Time NBA Statistical Leaders

(as of the end of the 1999–2000 season)

All-Time Points
1. Kareem Abdul-Jabbar ... 38 387
2. Wilt Chamberlain ... 31 419
3. Karl Malone[a] ... 31 041
4. Michael Jordan ... 29 277
5. Moses Malone ... 27 409
6. Elvin Hayes ... 27 313
7. Oscar Robertson ... 26 710
8. Dominique Wilkins ... 26 676
9. John Havlicek ... 26 395
10. Hakeem Olajuwon[a] ... 25 822

All-Time Assists
1. John Stockton[a] ... 13 798
2. Magic Johnson ... 10 141
3. Oscar Robertson ... 9 887
4. Isiah Thomas ... 9 061
5. Mark Jackson[a] ... 8 572
6. Maurice Cheeks ... 7 392
7. Len Wilkens ... 7 215
8. Bob Cousy ... 6 955
9. Guy Rodgers ... 6 917
10. Rod Strickland[a] ... 6 723

All-Time Rebounds
1. Wilt Chamberlain ... 23 924
2. Bill Russell ... 21 620
3. Kareem Abdul-Jabbar ... 17 440
4. Elvin Hayes ... 16 279
5. Moses Malone ... 16 212
6. Robert Parish ... 14 715
7. Nate Thurmond ... 14 464
8. Walt Bellamy ... 14 241
9. Wes Unseld ... 13 769
10. Buck Williams ... 13 023

All-Time Blocks
1. Hakeem Olajuwon[a] ... 3 648
2. Kareem Abdul-Jabbar ... 3 189
3. Mark Eaton ... 3 064
4. Patrick Ewing[a] ... 2 757
5. Tree Rollins ... 2 543
6. David Robinson[a] ... 2 485
7. Robert Parish ... 2 361
8. Manute Bol ... 2 086
9. George Johnson ... 2 082
10. Larry Nance ... 2 027

Source: *Canadian Press*

(a) Active player.

Toronto Raptors Individual Statistics 1999–2000

Player Averages

	G	MPG	FG%	3P%	FT%	OFF	DEF	TOT	TO	PF	PPG
V. Carter	82	38.1	.465	.403	.791	1.8	4.0	5.8	2.2	3.2	25.7
McGrady	79	31.2	.451	.277	.707	2.4	4.0	6.3	2.0	2.5	15.4
Christie	73	31.0	.407	.360	.843	0.9	3.0	3.9	2.0	2.3	12.4
A. Davis	79	31.4	.440	—	.765	3.0	5.8	8.8	1.5	3.4	11.5
Willis	79	21.3	.415	.333	.799	2.5	3.6	6.1	1.2	3.2	7.6
D. Curry	67	16.3	.427	.393	.750	0.2	1.3	1.5	0.6	1.0	7.6
D. Brown	38	17.7	.360	.358	.688	0.2	1.2	1.4	1.0	1.6	6.9
Oakley	80	30.4	.418	.341	.776	1.5	5.3	6.8	1.9	3.7	6.9
Al. Williams	55	14.2	.397	.291	.738	0.5	1.1	1.5	0.9	1.4	5.3
Bogues	80	21.6	.439	.333	.908	0.3	1.4	1.7	0.7	1.5	5.1
Workman	36	9.7	.344	.326	.667	0.0	0.7	0.7	0.5	1.0	2.4
Padojevic	3	8.0	.286	—	.500	0.7	2.0	2.7	1.7	1.7	2.3
Jo. Thomas	55	8.7	.458	.000	.390	0.7	0.7	1.4	0.3	1.9	2.1
Marks	5	2.4	.333	.000	1.000	0.0	0.4	0.4	0.6	0.6	1.6
Stewart	42	9.3	.377	—	.563	0.8	1.5	2.2	0.4	1.9	1.4
Team	82	240.9	.433	.363	.765	13.4	29.9	43.3	13.2	24.3	97.2
Opponents	82	240.9	.454	.339	.764	11.7	31.1	42.8	15.2	22.9	97.3

Player Totals

	G	MIN	FGM-A	3PM-A	FTM-A	OFF	DEF	TOT	AST	STL	BLK	TO	PF	PTS
V. Carter	82	3126	788-1696	95-236	436-551	150	326	476	322	110	92	178	263	2107
McGrady	79	2462	459-1018	18-65	277-392	188	313	501	263	90	151	160	201	1213
Christie	73	2264	311-764	99-275	182-216	63	222	285	321	102	43	144	167	903
A. Davis	79	2479	313-712	0-0	284-371	235	461	696	105	38	100	121	267	910
Willis	79	1679	236-569	1-3	131-164	201	281	482	49	36	48	98	256	604
D. Curry	67	1095	194-454	95-242	24-32	11	89	100	89	32	9	40	66	507
D. Brown	38	673	93-258	67-187	11-16	9	45	54	86	24	5	39	62	264
Oakley	80	2431	234-560	14-41	66-85	117	423	540	253	102	45	154	294	548
Al. Williams	55	779	114-287	16-55	48-65	27	58	85	126	34	11	47	78	292
Bogues	80	1731	157-358	17-51	79-87	25	110	135	299	65	4	59	119	410
Workman	36	350	31-90	14-43	10-15	1	25	26	61	20	0	18	37	86
Radojevic	3	24	2-7	0-0	3-6	2	6	8	1	2	1	5	5	7
Jo. Thomas	55	477	49-107	0-1	16-41	37	38	75	9	12	14	14	106	114
Marks	5	12	2-6	0-1	4-4	0	2	2	0	1	1	3	3	8
Stewart	42	389	20-53	0-0	18-32	33	61	94	6	5	19	17	81	58
Team Totals	82	19755	2980-6882	425-1171	1583-2068	1098	2449	3547	1947	666	544	1085	1989	7968
Opponents	82	19755	3002-6615	346-1021	1631-2436	961	2552	3513	1790	557	434	1250	1874	7981

Source: *Canadian Press*

3P = three-point field goal; 3PM-A = three-point field goal-attempts; AST = assists; BLK = block; DEF = defensive rebounds; FG = field goal; FGM-A = field goals made-attempts; FT = free throw; FTM-A = free throw made-attempts; G = games played; MIN = minutes; MPG = minutes per game; OFF = offensive rebounds; PF = personal fouls; PPG = points per game; PTS = points; STL = steals; TO = turnovers; TOT = total.

Vancouver Grizzlies 1999–2000 Statistics

Player Averages

TEAM	G	MPG	FG%	3P%	FT%	OFF	DFF	TOT	TO	PF	PPG
Abdur-Rahim	82	39.3	.465	.302	.809	2.7	7.4	10.1	3.0	3.0	20.3
Dickerson	82	37.8	.436	.409	.830	1.0	2.5	3.4	2.0	2.8	18.2
Bibby	82	38.5	.445	.363	.780	0.9	2.8	3.7	3.0	2.1	14.5
O. Harrington	82	32.6	.506	.000	.792	2.4	4.5	6.9	2.6	3.5	13.1
Reeves	69	25.7	.448	.000	.648	1.8	3.8	5.7	1.7	3.6	8.9
Scott	66	19.1	.375	.376	.842	0.2	1.4	1.6	0.5	1.6	5.6
Long	42	21.9	.443	000	.775	2.0	3.5	5.6	1.2	2.6	4.8
Lopez	65	12.0	.425	.167	.615	0.9	1.0	1.9	0.8	1.4	4.5
D. West	38	15.3	.407	.000	.850	0.5	1.4	1.9	0.5	2.1	4.0
Price	41	10.3	.345	.368	872	0.2	0.7	0.9	1.1	1.5	3.4
Pkezie	39	9.0	.466	—	.672	0.9	1.5	2.4	0.7	1.6	3.2
A. Carr	21	10.5	.438	—	.786	0.4	1.1	1.5	0.4	2.0	3.2
Parks	56	14.4	.497	.000	.649	1.0	2.3	3.3	0.5	2.1	3.0
Palacio	33	7.4	.439	.000	.595	0.3	0.6	1.0	0.8	0.6	2.0
Team Totals	82	242.1	.449	.361	.774	12.3	28.3	40.6	16.0	22.9	93.9
Opponents	82	242.1	.474	.333	.769	11.8	28.5	40.3	15.0	23.3	99.5

Player Totals

TEAM	G	MIN	FGM-A	3PM-A	FTM-A	OFF	DEF	TOT	AST	STL	BLK	TO	PF	PTS
Abdur-Rahim	82	3223	594-1277	29-96	446-551	218	607	825	271	89	87	249	244	1663
Dickerson	82	3103	554-1270	119-291	269-324	78	201	279	208	116	45	165	226	1496
Bibby	82	3155	459-1031	77-212	195-250	73	233	306	665	132	15	247	171	1190
O. Harrington	82	2677	420-830	0-2	236-298	196	367	563	97	36	58	217	287	1076
Reeves	69	1773	252-562	0-4	107-165	126	264	390	82	33	38	119	245	611
Scott	66	1263	125-333	71-189	48-57	16	90	106	69	28	9	30	104	369
Long	42	920	74-167	0-4	55-71	86	148	234	43	45	10	49	108	203
Lopez	65	781	111-261	3-18	67-109	59	65	124	44	32	17	53	94	292
D. West	38	381	59-145	0-3	34-40	18	53	71	43	12	8	19	80	152
Price	41	424	41-119	25-68	34-39	8	29	37	69	17	1	47	63	141
Ekezie	39	351	41-88	0-0	43-64	34	58	92	8	9	4	26	61	125
A. Carr	21	221	28-64	0-0	11-14	8	24	32	7	3	6	9	42	67
Parks	56	808	72-145	0-1	24-37	55	128	183	35	29	45	28	115	168
Palacio	53	394	43-98	0-2	22-37	17	34	51	48	20	0	44	32	108
Team Totals	82	19855	x892-6441	324-898	1594-2060	1005	2324	3329	1700	608	346	1308	1881	7702
Opponents	82	19855	3136-6613	361-1083	1530-1989	970	2336	3306	1932	725	519	1234	1912	8163

Source: *Canadian Press*

3P = three-point field goal; 3PM-A = three-point field goal-attempts; AST = assists; BLK = block; DEF = defensive rebounds; FG = field goal; FGM-A = field goals made-attempts; FT = free throw; FTM-A = free throw made-attempts; G = games played; MIN = minutes; MPG = minutes per game; OFF = offensive rebounds; PF = personal fouls; PPG = points per game; PTS = points; STL = steals; TO = turnovers; TOT = total.

Changes in Canadian Front Offices for the 2000-2001 Season

The Raptors

The Toronto Raptors fired coach Butch Carter on June 13, 2000. Despite helping the Raptors improve from 16 wins three years ago to 45 in 1999–2000, Carter seemed to find embarrassment off the court. In a book written with his brother Cris and released while the Raptors were trying to secure a playoff berth, coach Carter attacked Indiana coach Bobby Knight for his behaviour while Carter played there. Then, with the Raptors about to begin a playoff series with the New York Knicks, he sued former Raptor Marcus Camby for calling him a liar. He dropped the lawsuit after it was widely criticized. Carter also came under fire from veterans Antonio Davis and Charles Oakley after he said there was a lack of leadership in the Raptors' dressing room. Soon after the season he sought the GM's title—though not its power—in a meeting with team management.

Carter took the unusual step of meeting the media the day he was fired—in the offices of the team that had fired him.

"This was the way for all of us to be as healthy as possible," Carter said. Carter was bought out of the three years and $6 million US he had remaining on a contract extension signed halfway through the 1999 season—before the controversies started snowballing.

On June 21, the Raptors named the NBA's all-time winningest coach to lead its bench. Lenny Wilkens, 62, reportedly signed a four-year, $20-million US deal with Toronto. He has a life-time record of 1,179–981, the most wins in NBA history. He also has a reputation of being a player's coach. Wilkens had spoken to both the Vancouver Grizzlies and New Jersey Nets about their vacant coaching positions but found Toronto the most attractive.

Wilkens was a first-round draft pick out of Providence College and spent 15 years as a player with St. Louis, Seattle and Cleveland. He played in 1,077 games, averaging 16.5 points, 6.7 assists and 4.7 rebounds.

The Grizzlies

Canada's other NBA team, the Vancouver Grizzlies, enjoyed a similar off-season soap opera.

On May 10, new Grizzlies owner Michael Heisley, a Chicago millionaire, served notice that he was in charge. Heisley replaced much of the senior management staff with his own people, including former NBA coaches Dick Versace and Chuck Daly, plus former Pacers senior vice-president Billy Knight as the Grizzlies GM.

In the week prior to Heisley's sweeping West Coast entrance, Stu Jackson, Vancouver's president and GM, announced his resignation, after interim coach Lionel Hollins was fired the day before. Hollins, an original Grizzlie along with Jackson, was told of his dismissal by telephone at his Phoenix home. (On July 1, Jackson became the NBA's senior vice-president for basketball operations. Jackson will chair the league's competition and rules committee, oversee officiating and impose discipline for misconduct by players and coaches.)

Vancouver's challenge for the post-season is usually finished by Christmas, and the 1999–2000 was no different. The franchise's lifetime record is 78-300. The Grizzlies went 22-60 in 1999–2000 and lost an estimated $20 million in the process.

The Grizzlies selected Sidney Lowe to coach the team. Lowe spent seven seasons as an assistant coach in Cleveland and Minnesota. (He was the Wolves' head coach from January 1993 until the end of the 1993–94 season.) Last season the team had a 50-32 record. Lowe is the Grizzlies' fifth head coach as they enter their sixth NBA season.

One positive note came July 17 when Grizzlie Shareef Abdur-Rahim was added to the U.S. Olympic basketball team for the Games in Sydney. Abdur-Rahim replaced Grant Hill, who withdrew after breaking his ankle in April during the NBA playoffs. In his fourth NBA season, Abdur-Rahim, 23, led Vancouver in scoring (20.3 points per game) and rebounding (10.1). He joins 11 other NBA players on the team, including Vince Carter of the Toronto Raptors, to be coached by the Houston Rockets' Rudy Tomjanovich.

Source: *Canadian Press*

New Canadian in the NBA

Toronto native Jamaal Magloire was the only Canadian taken in the 2000 NBA draft, after a stellar season at Kentucky.

Magloire, a six-foot-10 centre, averaged 13.2 points and 9.1 rebounds in 33 games as a senior, and is Kentucky's career leader in blocked shots with 268. The 19th pick in the first round, Magloire signed a three-year contract with the Charlotte Hornets worth about $2.6 million. He was the highest Canadian picked in the NBA Draft since Steve Nash of Victoria went 15th overall to the Phoenix Suns in 1996. The highest ever is Bob Houbregs of Vancouver, who went third overall to Milwaukee in 1953.

Source: *Canadian Press*

FOOTBALL

Canadian Football League

(1999 Regular Season Standings)

Team	W	L	T	F	A	PTS
East Division						
Montreal	12	6	0	495	395	24
Hamilton	11	7	0	603	378	22
Toronto	9	9	0	386	373	18
Winnipeg	6	12	0	362	601	12

Team	W	L	T	F	A	PTS
West Division						
British Columbia	13	5	0	429	373	26
Calgary	12	6	0	503	393	24
Edmonton	6	12	0	459	502	12
Saskatchewan	3	15	0	370	592	6

Divisional Semi-finals:
Edmonton 17, Calgary 30
Toronto 6, Hamilton 27

Divisional Finals:
Hamilton 27, Montreal 26
Calgary 26, BC 24

Grey Cup:
Hamilton 32, Calgary 21

Source: *Canadian Football League*

Canadian Football League All-Stars, 1999

(voted by Football Reporters of Canada)

Offence

Quarterback: Danny McManus, Hamilton
Running Back: Kelvin Anderson, Calgary
Running Back: Mike Pringle, Montreal
Slotback: Allen Pitts, Calgary
Slotback: Darren Flutie, Hamilton
Wide Receiver: Travis Moore, Calgary
Wide Receiver: Ben Cahoon, Montreal
Centre: Jamie Taras, BC
Guard: Leo Groenewegen, Edmonton
Guard: Pierre Vercheval, Montreal
Tackle: Uzooma Okeke, Montreal
Tackle: Rocco Romano, Calgary
Punter: Noel Prefontaine, Toronto
Kicker: Mark McLoughlin, Calgary
Special Teams: Jimmy Cunningham, BC

Defence

Defensive Tackle: Demetrious Maxie, Toronto
Defensive Tackle: Johnny Scott, BC
Defensive End: Daved Benefield, BC
Defensive End: Joe Montford, Hamilton[1]
Linebacker: Mike O'Shea, Toronto
Linebacker: Calvin Tiggle, Hamilton[1]
Linebacker: Maurice Kelly, Winnipeg
Cornerback: William Hampton, Calgary
Cornerback: Adrion Smith, Toronto
Halfback: Gerald Vaughn, Hamilton
Halfback: Barron Miles, Montreal[1]
Safety: Rob Hitchcock, Hamilton

Source: *Canadian Football League*

(1) unanimous selection

The Grey Cup, 1909–1999

The Grey Cup was donated in 1909 by Governor General Earl Grey for the "Rugby Football Championship of Canada." Since 1954, only teams in the Canadian Football League have challenged for the trophy, with the winners of the East and West divisions meeting in the championship game.

1909	U. of Toronto 26, Parkdale 6
1910	U. of Toronto 16, Ham. Tigers 7
1911	U. of Toronto 14, Toronto 7
1912	Ham. Alerts 11, Toronto 4
1913	Ham. Tigers 44, Parkdale 2
1914	Toronto 14, U. of Toronto 2
1915	Ham. Tigers 13, Tor. R.A.A. 7
1916–19	No games held.
1920	U. of Toronto 16, Toronto 3
1921	Toronto 23, Edmonton 0
1922	Queen's U. 13, Edmonton 1
1923	Queen's U. 54, Regina 0
1924	Queen's U. 11, Balmy Beach 3
1925	Ott. Senators 24, Winnipeg 1
1926	Ott. Senators 10, U. of Toronto 7
1927	Balmy Beach 9, Ham. Tigers 6
1928	Ham. Tigers 30, Regina 0
1929	Ham. Tigers 14, Regina 3
1930	Balmy Beach 11, Regina 6
1931	Mtl. A.A.A. 22, Regina 0
1932	Ham. Tigers 25, Regina 6
1933	Toronto 4, Sarnia 3
1934	Sarnia 20, Regina 12
1935	Winnipeg 18, Ham. Tigers 12
1936	Sarnia 26, Ott. R.R. 20
1937	Toronto 4, Winnipeg 3
1938	Toronto 30, Winnipeg 7
1939	Winnipeg 8, Ottawa 7
1940[1]	Ottawa 12, Balmy Beach 5
	Ottawa 8, Balmy Beach 2
1941	Winnipeg 18, Ottawa 16
1942	Tor. R.C.A.F. 8, Win. R.C.A.F. 5
1943	Ham. F. Wild 23, Win. R.C.A.F. 14
1944	Mtl. St. H.D. Navy 7, Ham. F. Wild 6
1945	Toronto 35, Winnipeg 0
1946	Toronto 28, Winnipeg 6
1947	Toronto 10, Winnipeg 9
1948	Calgary 12, Ottawa 7
1949	Mtl. Als. 28, Calgary 15
1950	Toronto 13, Winnipeg 0
1951	Ottawa 21, Saskatchewan 14
1952	Toronto 21, Edmonton 11
1953	Hamilton 12, Winnipeg 6
1954	Edmonton 26, Montreal 25
1955	Edmonton 34, Montreal 19
1956	Edmonton 50, Montreal 27
1957	Hamilton 32, Winnipeg 7
1958	Winnipeg 35, Hamilton 28
1959	Winnipeg 21, Hamilton 7
1960	Ottawa 16, Edmonton 6
1961	Winnipeg 21, Hamilton 14
1962	Winnipeg 28, Hamilton 27
1963	Hamilton 21, BC 10
1964	BC 34, Hamilton 24
1965	Hamilton 22, Winnipeg 16
1966	Saskatchewan 29, Ottawa 14
1967	Hamilton 24, Saskatchewan 1
1968	Ottawa 24, Calgary 21
1969	Ottawa 29, Saskatchewan 11
1970	Montreal 23, Calgary 10
1971	Calgary 14, Toronto 11
1972	Hamilton 13, Saskatchewan 10
1973	Ottawa 22, Edmonton 18
1974	Montreal 20, Edmonton 7
1975	Edmonton 9, Montreal 8
1976	Ottawa 23, Saskatchewan 20
1977	Montreal 41, Edmonton 6
1978	Edmonton 20, Montreal 13
1979	Edmonton 17, Montreal 9
1980	Edmonton 48, Hamilton 10
1981	Edmonton 26, Ottawa 23
1982	Edmonton 32, Toronto 16
1983	Toronto 18, BC 17
1984	Winnipeg 47, Hamilton 17
1985	BC 37, Hamilton 24
1986	Hamilton 39, Edmonton 15
1987	Edmonton 38, Toronto 36
1988	Winnipeg 22, BC 21
1989	Saskatchewan 43, Hamilton 40
1990	Winnipeg 50, Edmonton 11
1991	Toronto 36, Calgary 21
1992	Calgary 24, Winnipeg 10
1993	Edmonton 33, Winnipeg 23
1994	BC 26, Baltimore 23
1995	Baltimore 37, Calgary 20
1996	Toronto 43, Edmonton 37
1997	Toronto 47, Saskatchewan 23
1998	Calgary 26, Hamilton 24
1999	Hamilton 32, Calgary 21

Source: *Canadian Press*

(1) A 2-game total point series.

All-Time Leading CFL Players

(up to the end of the 1999 season)

Touchdowns

	TD	SEASONS		TD	SEASONS
George Reed, Sask.	137	13 (1963-75)	Matt Dunigan, Edm./BC/Tor./Wpg./Bhm./Ham.	77	14 (1983-96)
Allen Pitts, Cal.	111	10 (1990-99)	Mike Pringle, Edm./Sac./Balt./Mtl.		8 (1992-99)
Brian Kelly, Edm.	97	9 (1979-87)	Hal Patterson, Mtl./Ham.	75	14 (1954-67)
Dick Shatto, Tor.	91	12 (1954-65)	Leo Lewis, Wpg.		12 (1955-66)
Tom Scott, Wpg./Edm./Cal.		11 (1974-84)	Donald Narcisse, Sask.		13 (1987-99)
Jackie Parker, Edm./Tor./BC	88	13 (1954-68)	Mike Saunders, S.A./Mtl./Ham./Tor./Sask.		8 (1992-99)
Craig Ellis, Wpg./Cal./Sask./Tor./Edm.		10 (1982-93)	Damon Allen, Edm./Ott./Ham./Mps./BC	74	15 (1985-99)
Earl Winfield, Ham.	87	11 (1987-97)	Tony Gabriel, Ham./Ott.	72	11 (1971-81)
Willie Fleming, BC	86	8 (1959-68)	Johnny Bright, Cal./Edm.	71	13 (1952-64)
Norm Kwong, Cal., Edm.	83	13 (1948-60)	Jim Germany, Edm.		7 (1977-83)
Michael Clemons, Tor.		11 (1989-99)	Bob Simpson, Ott.	70	13 (1950-62)
Terry Evanshen, Mtl./Cal./Ham./Tor.	80	14 (1965-78)	Jeff Boyd, Wpg./Tor.		9 (1983-91)
Virgil Wagner, Mtl.	79	9 (1946-54)	Jim Sandusky, BC/Edm.		12 (1984-96, 98)
David Williams, BC/Ott./Edm./Tor./Wpg.	78	8 (1988-95)	Jim Young, BC	68	13 (1967-79)
Ray Elgaard, Sask.		14 (1983-96)	Ron Stewart, Ott.	67	12 (1959-70)

Points

Scoring	SEAS	TD	CONS	FGS	SINGLES	PTS
Lui Passaglia, BC	24	1	995	835	305	3 811
Dave Ridgway, Sask.	13	0	541	574	111	2 374
Paul Osbaldiston, BC, Wpg., Ham.	14	0	549	520	223	2 332
Mark McLoughlin, Cal.	12	0	647	517	120	2 318
Dave Cutler, Edm.	16	0	627	464	218	2 237
Trevor Kennerd, Wpg.	12	0	509	394	149	1 840
Bernie Ruoff, Wpg., Ham., BC	14	0	401	384	219	1 772
Terry Baker, Sask., Ott., Tor., Mtl.	13	0	393	330	157	1 540
Lance Chomyc, Tor.	9	9	412	337	75	1 498
Gerry Organ, Ott.	12	2	391	318	105	1 462
Troy Westwood, Wpg.	9	1	375	332	76	1 453
J.T. Hay, Cal.	11	0	363	308	124	1 411
Don Sweet, Mtl., Ham.	14	0	327	314	73	1 342
Sean Fleming, Edm.	8	0	345	276	95	1 268
Larry Robinson, Cal.	14	9	362	171	101	1 030
Zenon Andrusyshyn, Tor., Ham. Edm. Mtl.	12	0	222	215	143	1 010
Tommy Joe Coffey, Edm., Ham., Tor.	14	65	204	108	53	971
Dean Dorsey, Tor., Ott., Edm.	8	0	244	219	50	951
Jack Abendschan, Sask.	11	0	312	159	74	863
George Reed, Sask.	13	137	0	0	1	823
Jackie Parker, Edm., Tor., BC	13	88	103	40	19	750
Don Sutherin, Ham., Ott., Tor.	12	4	270	114	78	714
Allen Pitts, Cal.	10	111	x4	0	0	674
Gerry James, Wpg., Sask.	11	63	143	40	21	645
Ian Sunter, Ham., Tor.	6	0	155	135	66	626
Paul McCallum, BC, Ott., Sask.	7	0	150	137	43	604
Brian Kelly, Edm.	9	97	x2	0	0	586

Rushing

	YRS	C	YDS	AVG	TD
George Reed, Sask.	13	3 243	16 116	5.0	134
Johnny Bright, Cal, Edm.	13	1 969	10 909	5.5	69
Mike Pringle, Edm., Sac., Bal., Mtl.	8	1 803	10 579	5.9	69

▶ Damon Allen, Edm., Ham., Ott., Mps., BC	15	1 322	9 179	6.9	74
Normie Kwong, Cal., Edm.	13	1 745	9 022	5.2	78
Leo Lewis, Wpg.	11	1 351	8 861	6.6	48
Dave Thelen, Ott., Tor.	9	1 530	8 463	5.5	47
Tracy Ham, Edm., Tor., Bal., Mtl.	13	1 059	8 043	7.6	62
Jim Evenson, BC, Ott.	7	1 460	7 060	4.8	37
Earl Lunsford, Cal.	6	1 199	6 994	5.8	55
Dick Shatto, Tor.	12	1 322	6 958	5.3	39
Lovell Coleman, Cal., Ott., BC	10	1 135	6 556	5.8	42
Willie Burden, Cal.	8	1 242	6 234	5.0	32

Passing Yards

	YRS	ATT	CMP	YARDS	%	TD	INT
Ron Lancaster, Ott., Sask.	19	6 233	3 384	50 535	54.3	333	396
Damon Allen, Edm., Ott., Ham., Mps., BC	15	5 955	3 264	45 949	54.8	253	203
Matt Dunigan, Edm., BC, Tor., Wpg., Bhm., Ham	14	5 476	3 057	43 857	55.8	306	211
Doug Flutie, BC, Cal., Tor.	8	4 854	2 975	41 355	61.3	270	155
Tracy Ham, Edm., Tor., Bal., Mtl.	12	4 945	2 670	40 534	53.9	284	164
Tom Clements, Ot., Sask., Ham., Wpg.	12	4 657	2 807	39 041	60.3	252	214
Kent Austin, Sask., BC, Tor., Wpg.	10	4 700	2 709	36 030	57.6	198	191
Dieter Brock, Wpg., Ham.	11	4 535	2 602	34 830	57.4	210	158
Tom Burgess, Ott., Sask., Wpg.	10	4 034	2 118	30 308	52.5	190	191
Danny McManus, Wpg., BC, Ed., Ham.	10	3 599	1 953	29 316	54.3	146	147
Sam Etcheverry, Mtl.	7	2 829	1 630	25 582	53.6	185	125
Conredge Holloway, Ott., Tor., BC.	13	3 013	1 710	25 193	56.8	155	94
Russ Jackson, Ott.	12	2 530	1 356	24 592	53.6	185	125
Bernie Faloney, Ham., Ham., Mtl., BC.	12	2 876	1 493	24 264	51.9	151	201
Roy Dewalt, BC, Wpg., Ott.	9	3 130	1 803	24 147	57.6	132	96
Danny Barrett, Cal., Tor., BC, Ott.	14	3 078	1 656	23 419	53.8	133	93
Joe Kapp, Cal., BC	8	2 709	1 476	22 725	54.5	136	130
Tom Wilkinson, Tor., BC, Edm.	15	2 662	1 613	22 579	60.6	154	126
Joe Paopao, BC, Sask., Ott.	11	3 008	1 721	22 474	57.2	117	157
Mike Kerrigan, Ham., Tor.	11	2 870	1 534	21 714	53.4	126	163
John Hufnagel, Cal., Sask., Wpg.	12	2 694	1 495	21 594	55.5	127	131
Peter Liske, Tor., Cal., BC.	7	2 571	1 449	21 266	56.4	130	133
Warren Moon, Edm.	6	2 382	1 369	21 228	57.5	144	77
David Archer, Sac., S.A., Ott., Edm.	5	2 434	1 388	20 671	57.0	120	71
Joe Barnes, Mtl., Sask., Tor., Cal.	11	2 454	1 350	18 491	55.0	94	117

(1) Yards per pass completed. (2) Did not play in 1988 or 1989.

Pass Receiving

	YRS	C	YDS	AVG	TD
Allen Pitts, Cal.	10	889	13 846	15.6	111
Ray Elgaard, Sask.	14	830	13 198	16.0	78
Don Narcisse, Sask.	13	919	12 366	13.5	75
Brian Kelly, Edm.	9	575	11 169	19.4	97
Darren Flutie, BC, Edm., Ham.	9	749	11 104	14.8	52
Tony Gabriel, Ham., Ott.	11	614	9 832	16.0	69
Rocky DiPietro, Ham.	14	706	9 762	13.8	45
Jim Sandusky, BC, Edm.	12	586	9 737	16.6	69
Terry Evanshen, Mtl., Cal., Ham., Tor.	14	600	9 697	16.2	80
Hal Patterson, Mtl., Ham.	14	460	9 473	20.6	64
Jim Young, BC	13	522	9 248	17.7	65
James Murphy, Wpg.	8	573	9 036	15.8	61
Ray Alexander, Cal, BC, Ott.	8	556	8 842	15.9	40
Paul Massoti, Tor.	12	556	8 772	15.8	44
Joe Poplawski, Wpg.	9	549	8 341	15.2	48

Source: *Canadian Press*

CFL Outstanding Player Awards[1]

Outstanding Player

1980 Deiter Brock, Wpg	1987 Tom Clements, Wpg	1994 Doug Flutie, Cal
1981 Deiter Brock, Wpg	1988 David Williams, BC	1995 Mike Pringle, Bal
1982 Condredge Holloway, Tor	1989 Tracy Ham, Edm	1996 Doug Flutie, Tor
1983 Warren Moon, Edm	1990 Mike Clemons, Tor	1997 Doug Flutie, Tor
1984 Willard Reaves, Wpg	1991 Doug Flutie, BC	1998 Mike Pringle, Mtl
1985 Mervyn Fernandez, BC	1992 Doug Flutie, Cal	1999 Danny McManus, Ham
1986 James Murphy, Wpg	1993 Doug Flutie, Cal	

Outstanding Canadian

1980 Gerry Dattilio, Mtl	1987 Scott Flagel, Wpg	1994 Gerald Wilcox, Wpg
1981 Joe Poplawski, Wpg	1988 Ray Elgaard, Sask	1995 Dave Sapunjis, Cal
1982 Rocky DiPietro, Ham	1989 Rocky DiPietro, Ham	1996 Leroy Blugh, Edm
1983 Paul Bennett, Wpg	1990 Ray Elgaard, Sask	1997 Sean Millington, BC
1984 Nick Arakgi, Mtl	1991 Blake Marshall, Edm	1998 Mike Morreale, Ham
1985 Paul Bennett, Ham	1992 Ray Elgaard, Sask	1999 Mike O'Shea, Tor
1986 Joe Poplawski, Wpg	1993 Dave Sapunjis, Cal	

Outstanding Defensive Player

1980 Dan Kepley, Edm	1987 Gregg Stumon, BC	1994 Willie Pless, Edm
1981 Dan Kepley, Edm	1988 Grover Covington, Ham	1995 Willie Pless, Edm
1982 James Parker, Edm	1989 Danny Bass, Edm	1996 Willie Pless, Edm
1983 Greg Marshall, Ott	1990 Greg Battle, Wpg	1997 Willie Pless, Edm
1984 James Parker, BC	1991 Greg Battle, Wpg	1998 Joe Montford, Ham
1985 Tyrone Jones, Wpg	1992 Willie Pless, Edm	1999 Calvin Tiggle, Ham
1986 James Parker, BC	1993 Jearld Baylis, Sask	

Outstanding Offensive Lineman

1980 Mike Wilson, Edm	1987 Chris Walby, Wpg	1994 Shar Pourdanesh, Bal
1981 Larry Butler, Wpg	1988 Roger Aldag, Sask	1995 Mike Withycombe, Bal
1982 Rudy Phillips, Ott	1989 Rod Connop, Edm	1996 Mike Kiselak, Tor
1983 Rudy Phillips, Ott	1990 Jim Mills, BC	1997 Mike Kiselak, Tor
1984 John Bonk, Wpg	1991 Jim Mills, BC	1998 Fred Childress, Cal
1985 Nick Bastaja, Wpg	1992 Rob Smith, Ott	1999 Uzooma Okeke, Mtl
1986 Roger Aldag, Sask	1993 Chris Walby, Wpg	

Outstanding Rookie

1980 William Miller, Wpg	1987 Gill Fenerty, Tor	1994 Matt Goodwin, Bal
1981 Vince Goldsmith, Sask	1988 Orville Lee, Ott	1995 Shalon Baker, Edm
1982 Chris Isaac, Ott	1989 Stephen Jordan, Ham	1996 Kelvin Anderson, Cal
1983 Johnny Shepherd, Ham	1990 Reggie Barnes, Ott	1997 Derrell Mitchell, Tor
1984 Dwaine Wilson, Mtl	1991 Jon Volpe, BC	1998 Steve Muhammad, BC
1985 Michael Gray, BC	1992 Mike Richardson, Wpg	1999 Pat LaCoste, BC
1986 Harold Hallman, Cal	1993 Michael O'Shea, Ham	

Source: *Canadian Football League*

(1) Winners are chosen by a vote of the Football Reporters of Canada; prior to 1989 they were known as the Schenley Awards.

Canadian Football Hall of Fame

(only players listed (year of election))

Player, Year Elected, Team(s)

Ah You, Junior (1997) Mtl
Atchison, Ron, (1978) Sask
Bailey, Byron (1975) BC
Baker, Bitt (1994) Sask/BC
Barrow, John (1976) Ham
Bass, Danny (2000) Tor/Cgy/Edm
Batstone, Harry (1963) Tor/Queen's
Beach, Ormond (1963) Sarnia
Benecick, Al (1996) Sask
Box, Ab (1965) Balmy Beach/Tor
Breen, Joseph (1963) U of Toronto/Tor
Bright, Johnny (1970) Edm/Cal
Brock, Ralph Dieter (1995) Wpg/Ham
Brown, Tom (1984) BC
Campbell, Jerry "Soupy" (1996) Cal/Ott
Casey, Tom (1964) Wpg
Charlton, Ken (1992) Ott/Sask
Clements, Tom (1994) Ott/Sask/Ham/Wpg
Clark, Bill (1996) Sask
Coffey, Tommy Joe (1977) Edm/Cal
Conacher, Lionel (1963) Tor
Copeland, Royal (1988) Tor
Corrigal, Jim (1990) Tor
Covington, Grover (2000) Ham
Cox, Ernest (1963) Ham
Craig, Ross (1964) Ham
Cronin, Carl (1967) Wpg
Cutler, Dave (1998) Edm
Cutler, Wes (1968) Tor
Dalla Riva, Peter (1993) Mtl
Dipietro, Rocky (1997) Ham
Dixon, George (1974) Mtl
Eliowitz, Abe (1969) Ott/Mtl
Emerson, Eddie (1963) Ott
Etcheverry, Sam (1969) Mtl
Evanshen, Terry (1984) Mtl/Cal/Ham/Tor
Faloney, Bernie (1974) Edm/Ham
Fear, Cap (1967) Tor/Mtl/Ham
Fennell, Dave (1990) Edm
Ferraro, John (196)6 Ham/Mtl
Fieldgate, Norm (1979) BC
Fleming, Willie (1982) BC
Gabriel, Tony (1984) Ham/Ott
Gaines, Geve (1994) Mtl/Ott
Gall, Hugh (1963) U of Toronto

Player, Year Elected, Team(s)

Golab, Tony (1964) Ott
Grant, Tom (1995) Ham/Wpg
Gray, Herb (1983) Wpg
Griffing, Dean (1965) Sask/Cal
Hanson, Fritz (1963) Wpg
Harris, Dickie (1998) Mtl
Harris, Wayne (1976) Cal
Harrison, Herman (1993) Cal
Helton, John (1985) Cal/Wpg
Henley, Garney (1979) Ham
Hinton, Tom (1991) BC
Holloway, Condredge (1998) O /Tor/BC
Huffman, Dick (1987) Wpg/Cal
Isbister, Bob (1965) Ham
Jackson, Russ (1973) Ott
Jacobs, Jack (1963) Wpg
James, Eddie (1963) Wpg/Reg
James, Gerry (1981) Wpg
Kabat, Greg (1966) Wpg
Kapp, Joe (1984) Cal/BC
Keeling, Jerry (1989) Cal/Ott/Ham
Kelly, Brian (1991) Edm
Kelly, Ellison (1992) Edm/Ham
Kepley, Dan (1996) Edm
Krol, Joe (1963) Tor/Ham
Kwong, Normie (1969) Cal/Edm
Lawson, Smirle (1963) U. of Toronto
Leadlay, Frank (1963) Queen's/Ham
Lear, Les (1974) Wpg/Cal
Lewis, Leo (1973) Wpg
Lunsford, Earl (1983) Cal
Luster, Marv (1990) Mtl/Tor
Luzzi, Don (1985) Cal
McCance, Chester (1976) Wpg/Mtl
McGill, Frank (1965) Mtl
McQuarters, Ed (1988) Sask
Miles, Rollie (1980) Edm
Morris, Frank (1983) Tor/Edm
Morris, Ted (1964) Tor
Mosca, Angelo (1987) Ham
Murphy, James (2000) Wpg
Nelson, Roger (1985) Edm
Neumann, Peter (1979) Ham
O'Quinn, Red (1981) Mtl
Pajaczkowski, Tony (1988) Cal/Mtl

▶

Parker, Jackie (1971) Edm/Tor/BC
Patterson, Hal (1971) Mtl/Ham
Perry, Gordon (1970) Mtl
Perry, Norman (1963) Sarnia
Ploen, Ken (1975) Wpg
[1]Poplawski, Joe (1998) Wpg
Quilty, Silver (1966) U. of Ottawa
Raimy, Dave (2000) Wpg/Tor
Rebholz, Russ (1963) Wpg
Reed, George (1979) Sask
Reeve, Ted (1963) Tor
Rigney, Frank (1984) Wpg
[1]Robinson, Larry (1998) Cal
Rodden, Michael (1964) Queen's/Tor
Rowe, Paul (1964) Cal
Ruby, Martin (1974) Sask
Russel, Jeff (1963) Ott
[1]Scott, Tom (1998) Wpg/Edm
Scott, Vince (1982) Ham
Shatto, Dick (1975) Tor
Simpson, Benjamin (1963) Ham
Simpson, Bob (1976) Ott

Sprague, David (1963) Ham/Ott
Stevenson, Art (1969) Wpg
Stewart, Ron (1977) Ott
Stirling, Bummer (1966) Sarnia
Sutherin, Don (1992) Ham/Ott
Symons, Bill (1997) BC/Tor
Thelen, Dave (1989) Ott/Tor
Timmis, Brian (1963) Ham/Ott
Tinsley, Buddy (1982) Wpg
Tommy, Andrew (1989) Ott/Tor
Trawick, Herb (1975) Mtl
Tubman, Joe (1968) Ott
Tucker, Whit (1993) Ott
Urness, Ted (1989) Sask
Vaughn, Kaye (1978) Ott
Wagner, Virgil (1980) Mtl
Welch, Huck (1964) Ham/Mtl
Wilkinson, Tom (1987) Edm
Wilson, Al (1997) BC
Wylie, Harvey (1980) Cal
Young, Jim (1991) BC
Zock, William (1984) Tor/Edm

Source: *Canadian Football League* (1) new inductee

2000 CFL HALL OF FAME INDUCTEES

■ **Danny Bass (Player):**
Danny Bass began his CFL playing career in 1980 with the Toronto Argonauts. After playing with Calgary for two seasons, he went on to play with the Edmonton Eskimos from 1984 to 1991. He retired in 1991 after twelve years in the CFL. Bass was named CFL all-star six times, a western all-star eight times, Schenley Most Outstanding Defensive Player and played in three Grey Cup games, winning with Edmonton in 1987.

■ **Hugh Campbell (Builder):**
Hugh Campbell has been in the CFL for 26 seasons, as a player, coach, general manager and president & CEO. Campbell became the head coach of the Edmonton Eskimos in 1977. He coached the Eskimos to a Canadian Football League record of six Grey Cup appearances in a row, winning five from 1978 to 1982. His regular season coaching record of 70 wins, 21 losses and five ties is the best percentage in league history.

■ **Grover Covington (Player):**
Grover Covington began his CFL career in 1981 with Hamilton. For eleven years he played defensive end position and was the CFL sack leader in 1988 with 25. Covington still holds the CFL's all-time quarterback sack record with 157. Covington was named CFL all-star four times, Eastern all-star seven times, and won the Schenley for Most Outstanding Defensive Player. He played in four Grey Cup games, winning in 1986.

■ **James Murphy (Player):**
James Murphy joined the Winnipeg Blue Bombers in 1982 where he played eight seasons and established himself as the Bomber's all time leading receiver. James Murphy was named CFL all- star two times, an Eastern all-star four times, he won a Schenley for Most Outstanding Player, played in three Grey Cup games winning all three in 1984, 1988 and 1990.

■ **Dave Raimey (Player):**
Dave Raimey came to the Winnipeg Blue Bombers in 1965 and was a running back for four years before being traded to the Toronto Argonauts, where he played defensive halfback. Raimey was named a CFL all-star in 1969, and a Blue Bomber all-star on four occasions.

The five individuals were formally inducted into the Canadian Football Hall of Fame during the Induction Weekend festivities in Hamilton, Ontario from September 28 to September 30, 2000.

NFL Final Standings, 1999

American Football Conference

■ Eastern Division

	W	L	T	PF	PA
Indianapolis	13	3	0	423	333
Buffalo	11	5	0	320	229
Miami	9	7	0	326	336
NY Jets	8	8	0	308	309
New England	8	8	0	299	284

■ Central Division

	W	L	T	PF	PA
Jacksonville	14	2	0	396	217
Tennessee	13	3	0	392	324
Baltimore	8	8	0	324	277
Pittsburgh	6	10	0	317	320
Cincinnati	4	12	0	283	460
Cleveland	2	14	0	217	437

■ Western Division

	W	L	T	PF	PA
Seattle	9	7	0	338	298
Kansas City	9	7	0	390	322
Oakland	8	8	0	390	329
San Diego	8	8	0	269	316
Denver	6	10	0	314	318

National Football Conference

■ Eastern Division

	W	L	T	PF	PA
Washington	10	6	0	443	377
Dallas	8	8	0	352	276
NY Giants	7	9	0	299	358
Arizona	6	10	0	245	382
Philadelphia	5	11	0	272	357

■ Central Division

	W	L	T	PF	PA
Tampa Bay	11	5	0	270	235
Minnesota	10	6	0	399	335
Detroit	8	8	0	322	323
Green Bay	8	8	0	357	341
Chicago	6	10	0	272	341

■ Western Division

	W	L	T	PF	PA
St Louis	13	3	0	526	242
Carolina	8	8	0	421	381
Atlanta	5	11	0	285	380
San Francisco	4	12	0	295	453
New Orleans	3	13	0	260	434

Playoffs

■ Wild Cards
Tennessee Titans 22, Buffalo Bills 16
Washington Redskins 27, Detroit Lions 13
Minnesota Vikings 27, Dallas Cowboys 10
Miami Dolphins 20, Seattle Seahawks 17

■ Conference Championship
Tennessee Titans 33, Jacksonville Jaguars 14
St. Louis Rams 11, Tampa Bay Buccaneers 6

■ Divisional Playoffs
Jacksonville Jaguars 62, Miami Dolphins 7
Tampa Bay Buccaneers 14, Washington Redskins 13
St. Louis Rams 49, Minnesota Vikings 37
Tennessee Titans 19, Indianapolis Colts 16

■ SUPER BOWL XXXIV at Georgia Dome
Sunday, Jan. 30, 2000
St. Louis Rams 23, Tennessee Titans 16

Source: National Football League

New League on the Block

*I*n February 2001, a new professional league is scheduled to begin play in the United States. The XFL—or Extra Fun League—will have the broadcast backing of NBC, which will televise the games on Saturday nights and is also a league co-owner. (UPN will broadcast games on Sunday nights and TNN on cable will do the Sunday afternoon games.) The XFL is the brainchild of the World Wrestling Federation's president and marquee marketer, president Vince McMahon.

The 8-team league will feature the New York-New Jersey Hitmen, the Chicago Enforcers and the San Jose Demons and the Memphis Maniax. Also, the Orlando Rage, the Birmingham Thunderbolts, the Los Angeles X-treme and the Las Vegas Outlaws. The league bills itself as the "anti-NFL" and plans a 10-game season in the non-NFL months of February, March and April. Players will get a flat US$45,000 for the season, plus an equal share of US$100,000 for each game won. There will be no domed-stadiums in the league and the game will go on no matter what the weather. Other innovations include helmet-cams, announcers sitting in the stands with the fans and more than a few storylines—like Greg Mohns of the BC Lions, who resigned as coach August 20—midway through the CFL season—for a management job in the XFL; — and yes, there will be cheerleaders.

Source: The Canadian Press

National Football League Individual Statistics by Top Ten, 1999

PASSING

	ATT.	COMP.	COMP%	YDS	YDS/ATT.	TD	TD%	LONG	INT.	RATING
K. Warner, StL	499	325	65.1	4 353	8.7	41	8.2	75t	13	109.2
S. Beuerlein, Car	571	343	60.1	4 436	7.8	36	6.3	88t	15	94.6
J. George, Min	329	191	58.1	2 816	8.6	23	7.0	80t	12	94.2
P. Manning, Ind	533	331	62.1	4 135	7.8	26	4.9	80t	15	90.7
B. Johnson, Was	519	316	60.9	4 005	7.7	24	4.6	65t	13	90.0
R. Gannon, Oak	515	304	59.0	3 840	7.5	24	4.7	50	14	86.5
R. Lucas, NYJ	272	161	59.2	1 678	6.2	14	5.1	56t	6	85.1
C. Batch, Det	270	151	55.9	1 957	7.3	13	4.8	74t	7	84.1
G. Frerotte, Det	288	175	60.8	2 117	7.4	9	3.1	77t	7	83.6
C. Chandler, Atl	307	174	56.7	2 339	7.6	16	5.2	60t	11	83.5

RECEIVING

	YDS	REC.	YDS/REC.	LONG	TD
M. Harrison, Ind	1 663	115	14.5	57t	12
J. Smith, Jac	1 636	116	14.1	62	6
R. Moss, Min	1 413	80	17.7	67t	11
M. Robinson, Chi	1 400	84	16.7	80t	9
T. Brown, Oak	1 344	90	14.9	47	6
G. Crowell, Det	1 338	81	16.5	77t	7
M. Muhammad, Car	1 253	96	13.1	60t	8
C. Carter, Min	1 241	90	13.8	68	13
M. Westbrook, Was	1 191	65	18.3	65	9
A. Toomer, NYG	1 183	79	15.0	80	6

RUSHING

	ATT.	YDS	YDS/ATT.	LONG	TD
E. James, Ind	369	1 553	4.2	72	13
C. Martin, NYJ	367	1 464	4.0	50	5
S. Davis, Was	290	1 405	4.8	76t	17
E. Smith, Dal	329	1 397	4.2	63t	11
M. Faulk, StL	253	1 381	5.5	58	7
E. George, Ten	320	1 304	4.1	40	9
D. Staley, Phi	325	1 273	3.9	29	4
C. Garner, SFO	241	1 229	5.1	53	4
R. Watters, Sea	325	1 210	3.7	45	5
C. Dillon, Cin	263	1 200	4.6	50	5

Source: *Canadian Press*

More NFL Individual All-Time Records

Most Passes Attempted in a Game: 70: Drew Bledsoe, New England vs. Minnesota, Nov. 13, 1994 (OT)
Most Passes Completed in a Game: 45, Drew Bledsoe, New England vs. Minnesota, Nov. 13, 1994 (OT)
Most Passes Completed in a Season: 404, Warren Moon, Houston, 1991
Longest Pass Completion: 99 yards:
  Frank Filchock (to Farkas) Washington vs. Pittsburgh, Oct. 15, 1939
  George Izo (to Mitchell), Washington vs. Cleveland, Sept. 15, 1963
  Karl Sweetan (to Studstill), Detroit vs. Baltimore, Oct. 16, 1966
  Sonny Jurgensen (to Allen), Washington vs. Chicago, Sept. 15, 1968
  Jim Plunkett (to Branch), L.A. Raiders vs. Washington, Oct. 2, 1983
  Ron Jaworski (to Quick) Philadelphia vs. Atlanta, Nov. 10, 1985
  Stan Humphries (to Martin), San Diego vs. Seattle, Sept. 18, 1994
  Brett Favre (to Brooks), Green Bay vs. Chicago, Sept. 11, 1995
Source: *Canadian Press*

Super Bowl Results, 1980–2000

Date	Results	MVP
Jan. 20, 1980	Pittsburgh 31, L.A. Rams 19	Terry Bradshaw, Pittsburgh
Jan. 25, 1981	Oakland 27, Philadelphia 10	Jim Plunkett, Oakland
Jan. 24, 1982	San Francisco 26, Cincinnati 21	Joe Montana, San Francisco
Jan. 30, 1983	Washington 27, Miami 17	John Riggins, Washington
Jan. 22, 1984	L.A. Raiders 38, Washington 9	Marcus Allen, L.A. Raiders
Jan. 20, 1985	San Francisco 38, Miami 16	Joe Montana, San Francisco
Jan. 26, 1986	Chicago 46, New England 10	Richard Dent, Chicago
Jan. 25, 1987	N.Y. Giants 39, Denver 20	Phil Simms, N.Y. Giants
Jan. 31, 1988	Washington 42, Denver 10	Doug Williams, Washington
Jan. 22, 1989	San Francisco 20, Cincinnati 16	Jerry Rice, San Francisco
Jan. 28, 1990	San Francisco 55, Denver 10	Joe Montana, San Francisco
Jan. 27, 1991	N.Y. Giants 20, Buffalo 19	Ottis Anderson, N.Y. Giants
Jan. 26, 1992	Washington 37, Buffalo 24	Mark Rypien, Washington
Jan. 31, 1993	Dallas 52, Buffalo 17	Troy Aikman, Dallas
Jan. 30, 1994	Dallas 30, Buffalo 13	Emmitt Smith, Dallas
Jan. 29, 1995	San Francisco 49, San Diego 26	Steve Young, San Francisco
Jan. 28, 1996	Dallas 27, Pittsburgh 17	Larry Brown, Dallas
Jan. 26, 1997	Green Bay 35, New England 21	Desmond Howard, Green Bay
Jan. 25, 1998	Denver 31, Green Bay 24	Terrell Davis, Denver
Jan. 31, 1999	Denver 34, Atlanta 19	John Elway, Denver
Jan. 30, 2000	St. Louis 23, Tennessee 16	Kurt Warren, St. Louis

Who Was the Greatest? (NFL-style)

John Unitas was selected as quarterback of the NFL's All-time Team on August 1, 2000 in Canton, Ohio.

The All-time Team is an eclectic group. In addition to Unitas—a former Colts' star—are Jim Brown, who played for Cleveland and Walter Payton, the former Bear, both of whom are in the backfield. Jerry Rice, who has played for San Francisco since 1985 is paired at wide receiver with Don Hutson, who starred for Green Bay in the 1930s.

The team includes four members of the 1970s edition of the Pittsburgh Steelers that won four Super Bowls: centre Mike Webster; defensive tackle Joe Greene; linebacker Jack Ham and cornerback Mel Blount, however, there are no players from Vince Lombardi's Packers of the '50s and '60s. Those teams won five NFL titles, including the first two Super Bowls.

The team also features three active players—Rice, Reggie White and Deion Sanders—and is heavily weighted with players from the last four decades. All were chosen by the 36 Pro Football Hall of Fame voters.

The offensive tackles are Anthony Munoz, who played for the Bengals in the '80s and '90s and Roosevelt Brown, a star for the Giants in the '50s and '60s. The guards are John Hannah of the Patriots of the '70s and '80s and Jim Parker, who played with Unitas on the Colts during the '50s and '60s.

Joining Reggie White (who signed with Carolina in 2000 after retiring after the 1998 season) and Joe Greene is Deacon Jones of the '70s Rams and Bob Lilly of the '70s Cowboys.

In addition to Jack Ham, linebackers include Dick Butkus of the Bears of the '60s and '70s and Lawrence Taylor, who starred for the Giants in the '80s and early '90s.

And along with Mel Blount, the defensive backs are Dick "Night Train" Lane of the Lions of the '50s; Ronnie Lott, the former 49er inducted into the Hall of Fame in September 2000 and Larry Wilson, who starred for the Cardinals from 1960-72.

Jan Stenerud, the former Chief, is the kicker; former Bear Gale Sayers is the kick returner; former Raider Ray Guy is the punter; Sanders is the punt returner and Steve Tasker of the Bills is the special teams player.

Source: *Canadian Press*

HOCKEY

NHL Season Review, 1999–2000

October 1999

1 The NHL opened its 1999–2000 regular season with the Dallas Stars defeating the Pittsburgh Penguins, 6-4, and the New York Rangers tying the Edmonton Oilers, 1-1. In Dallas, the Stars raised their first Stanley Cup championship banner and in Edmonton, the Oilers honored Wayne Gretzky in a special pre-game ceremony televised throughout North America.

2 The NHL's newest team and 28th franchise, the Atlanta Thrashers, played its first regular season game, a 4-1 loss to the New Jersey Devils at Philips Arena in Atlanta.

Boston's Ray Bourque moved past Paul Coffey as the NHL's all-time leading goal-scorer among defensemen by scoring his 386th career goal versus Carolina.

14 The Atlanta Thrashers won their first NHL game with a 2-0 victory over the New York Islanders.

November 1999

18 Geoff Courtnall, who played 17 seasons in the NHL with Boston, Edmonton, Washington, St. Louis and Vancouver, announced his retirement. Courtnall recorded 367 goals and 432 assists for 1,465 points in 1,048 NHL games.

January 2000

4 Los Angeles King's left wing Luc Robitaille played in the 1,000th game of his 14-year NHL career at Kiel Center in St. Louis.

February 2000

6 The World all-stars defeated the North America All-Stars, 9-4, in the 50th NHL All-Star Game at Air Canada Centre in Toronto. The Florida Panthers' Pavel Bure became the 11th player in all-star history, and the second European player, to net a hat trick. Bure added an assist, capturing MVP honours. Prior to the game the NHL retired Wayne Gretzky's #99 throughout the League in a special ceremony.

11 Colorado's Ray Bourque became only the second defencemen in NHL history to reach 1,500 career points with a first-period goal versus the New York Rangers. Bourque became the ninth player in NHL history to reach the 1,500-point plateau and the fourth this season, joining Detroit's Steve Yzerman and Carolina's Ron Francis and Paul Coffey.

26 Toronto Maple Leafs right wing Steve Thomas played in the 1,000th game of his 16-year NHL career.

March 2000

4 Colorado Avalanche goaltender Patrick Roy climbed into second place on the NHL's all-time wins list with his 435th career victory, passing Hall of Famer Jacques Plante in a 4-1 win over the Tampa Bay Lightning.

19 Detroit Red Wings defenceman Larry Murphy appeared in his 1,550th NHL game, surpassing former Red Wing Alex Delvecchio to rank second on the all-time games played list. Murphy's 1,558 games played trails Gordie Howe (1,767).

April 2000

1 Calgary Flames goaltender Fred Brathwaite tied a 25 year-old Flames franchise record with his fifth shutout of the season.

9 The Colorado Avalanche and Detroit Red Wings played the first penalty-free game in 20 years when the Avalanche defeated the Red Wings, 4-3, The last penalty-free game in the NHL prior to the Detroit-Colorado game was on Feb. 17, 1980, Montreal at Buffalo (a 2-2 tie).

25 The San Jose Sharks became the fifth No. 8 seed to upset a No. 1 seed in the Conference quarter-finals since the inception of the current conference playoff format in 1994. San Jose's 4-3 series upset of the St. Louis Blues marked the second time the Sharks defeated the top seed, having ousted the Detroit Red Wings, 4-3, in 1994.

May 2000

4 Philadelphia Flyers centre Keith Primeau ended the third-longest game in NHL history by scoring at 12:01 of the fifth overtime to give the Flyers a 2-1 victory over Pittsburgh in Game 4 of their Eastern Conference semifinal series. The win tied the series at 2-2.

4 The Columbus Blue Jackets and Minnesota Wild signed their first players. Columbus signed Niagara University goaltender Greg Gardner and Minnesota signed forward Johnathon Gagnon.

8 The New Jersey Devils allowed only six shots on goal, the fewest in the playoffs or regular season since the league's expansion in 1967, when they defeated Toronto, 3-0, to advance to the Eastern Conference final.

12 Scott Gomez, Brian Rafalski, Brian Boucher, Simon Gagne, Brad Stuart and Mike York were voted to the 1999–2000 all-rookie team.

27 NHL legend Maurice "Rocket" Richard passed away. Recognized as both an icon and an ▶

ambassador of the game, his legacy will carry forth for generations to come.

June 2000

11 Jason Arnott scored in double overtime to give the New Jersey Devils their second Stanley Cup victory in six seasons. It marked the second consecutive Stanley Cup winning goal scored in overtime; last year being scored by Brett Hull of the Dallas Stars. New Jersey defenceman Scott Stevens was selected the winner of the Conn Smythe Trophy, awarded to the MVP of the playoffs.

15 Steve Yzerman, Jaromir Jagr, Brendan Shanahan, Chris Pronger, Nicklas Lidstrom and Olaf Kolzig were voted to the 1999-2000 first all-star team. It was Jagr's fifth first-team selection in the last six years.

23 The Columbus Blue Jackets and the Minnesota Wild made their selections in the NHL Expansion Draft 2000. Each team was allowed to take 26 players from teams around the league with the exception of the most recent Atlanta and Nashville squads. The Columbus selections were highlighted by Rick Tabaracci, Lyle Odelein and Mathieu Schneider. Amongst the Wild's picks were veterans Mike Vernon, Chris Terreri and Joe Juneau.

24 Calgary was the host of the NHL Entry Draft 2000. The New York Islanders had the number one pick, and selected goaltender Rick DiPietro from Boston University. This marked the first time a goaltender was selected number one overall since Montreal chose Michel Pleasse in 1968. The Atlanta Thrashers held the second draft slot and selected University of Wisconsin standout Dany Heatley. Rounding out the top three was Minnesota's selection of Marian Gaborik, an offensive star from Slovakia.

With draft day at hand, several trades took place. The Islanders were the most active team, trading goaltenders Kevin Weekes and Roberto Luongo to make room for their top draft choice in Rick DiPietro. Colorado traded all-star defenceman Sandis Ozolinsh and a second round pick to Carolina for defenceman Nolan Pratt and a first round pick. Vancouver traded veteran winger Brad May to Phoenix for a conditional pick in the 2001 Entry Draft.

National Hockey League, 1999–2000

Final Standings

Eastern Conference

■ Atlantic Division

	W	L	T	GF	GA	PTS
Philadelphia	45	25	123	237	179	105
New Jersey	45	29	8	251	203	103
Pittsburgh	37	37	8	241	236	88
NY Rangers	29	41	12	218	246	73
NY Islanders	14	49	9	194	275	58

■ Northeast Division

	W	L	T	GF	GA	PTS
Toronto	45	30	7	246	222	100
Ottawa	41	30	11	244	210	95
Buffalo	35	36	11	213	204	85
Montreal	35	38	9	196	194	83
Boston	24	39	19	210	248	73

■ Southeast Division

	W	L	T	GF	GA	PTS
Washington	44	26	12	227	194	102
Florida	43	33	6	244	209	98
Carolina	37	35	10	217	216	84
Tampa Bay	19	54	9	204	309	54
Tampa Bay	19	54	9	179	292	47
Atlanta	14	61	7	170	313	39

Western Conference

■ Central Division

	W	L	T	GF	GA	PTS
St. Louis	51	20	11	248	165	114
Detroit	48	24	10	278	210	108
Chicago	33	39	10	241	245	78
Nashville	28	47	7	199	240	70

■ Northwest Division

	W	L	T	GF	GA	PTS
Colorado	42	29	11	233	201	96
Edmonton	32	34	16	226	212	88
Vancouver	30	37	15	227	237	83
Calgary	31	41	10	211	256	77

■ Pacific Division

	W	L	T	GF	GA	PTS
Dallas	43	29	10	211	184	102
L.A.	39	31	12	246	228	94
Phoenix	39	35	8	232	228	90
San Jose	35	37	10	225	214	87
Anaheim	34	36	12	217	227	83

Source: *Canadian Press*

Note: A team scoring a goal in overtime is credited with two points and a victory in the W column; the team giving up a goal in overtime gets one point and the game is counted in the RT (Regulation Tie) and the loss column.

Hockey **729**

NHL Playoff Results, 1998-2000

■ CONFERENCE QUARTER-FINALS

Eastern Conference – 1

Date	Matchup	Result
Thu., April 13	Buf at Pha	PHA, 3-2
Fri., April 14	Buf at Pha	PHA, 2-1
Sun., April 16	Pha at Buf	PHA, 2-0
Tue., April 18	Pha at Buf	BUF, 3-2 (OT)
Thu., April 20	Buf at Pha	PHA, 5-2

Philadelphia Wins Series, 4-1

Eastern Conference – 2

Date	Matchup	Result
Thu., April 13	Pgh at Wash	PGH, 7-0
Sat., April 15	Wash at Pgh	PGH, 2-1 (OT)
Mon., April 17	Wash at Pgh	PGH, 4-3
Wed., April 19	Pgh at Wash	WASH, 3-2
Fri., April 21	Pgh at Wash	PGH, 2-1

Pittsburgh Wins Series, 4-1

Eastern Conference – 3

Date	Matchup	Result
Wed., April 12	Ott at Tor	TOR, 2-0
Sat., April 15	Ott at Tor	TOR, 5-1
Mon., April 17	Tor at Ott	OTT, 4-3
Wed., April 19	Tor at Ott	OTT, 2-1
Sat., April 22	Ott at Tor	TOR, 2-1 (OT)
Mon., April 24	Tor at Ott	TOR, 4-2

Toronto Wins Series, 4-2

Eastern Conference – 4

Date	Matchup	Result
Thu., April 13	Fla at N.J.	NJ, 4-3
Sun., April 16	Fla at N.J.	NJ, 2-1
Tue., April 18	N.J. at Fla	NJ, 2-1
Thu., April 20	N.J. at Fla	NJ, 4-1

New Jersey Wins Series, 4-0

Western Conference – 1

Date	Matchup	Result
Wed., April 12	S.J. at St.L.	StL, 5-3
Sat., April 15	S.J. at St.L.	S.J., 4-2
Mon., April 17	St.L. at S.J.	S.J., 2-1
Wed., April 19	St.L. at S.J.	S.J., 3-2
Fri., April 21	S.J. at St.L.	StL, 5-3
Sun., April 23	St.L. at S.J.	StL, 6-2
Tue., April 25	S.J. at St.L.	S.J., 3-1

San Jose Wins Series, 4-3

Western Conference – 2

Date	Matchup	Result
Wed., April 12	Edm at Dal	DAL, 2-1
Thu., April 13	Edm at Dal	DAL, 3-0
Sun., April 16	Dal at Edm	EDM, 5-2
Tue., April 18	Dal at Edm	DAL, 4-3
Fri., April 21	Edm at Dal	DAL, 3-2

Dallas Wins Series, 4-1

Western Conference – 3

Date	Matchup	Result
Thu., April 13	Phx at Col	COL, 6-3
Sat., April 15	Phx at Col	COL, 3-1
Mon., April 17	Col at Phx	COL, 4-2
Wed., April 19	Col at Phx	PHO, 3-2
Fri., April 21	Phx at Col	COL, 2-1

Colorado Wins Series, 4-1

Western Conference – 4

Date	Matchup	Result
Thu., April 13	L.A. at Det	DET, 2-0
Sat., April 15	L.A. at Det	DET, 8-5
Mon., April 17	Det at L.A.	DET, 2-1
Wed., April 19	Det at L.A.	DET, 3-0

Detroit Wins Series, 4-0

■ CONFERENCE SEMI-FINALS

Eastern Conference – 1

Date	Matchup	Result
Thu., April 27	Pgh at Pha	PGH, 2-0
Sat., April 29	Pgh at Pha	PGH, 4-1
Tue., May 2	Pha at Pgh	PHA, 4-3 (OT)
Thu., May 4	Pha at Pgh	PHA, 2-1 (5OT)
Sun., May 7	Pgh at Pha	PHA, 6-3
Tue., May 9	Pha at Pgh	PHA, 2-1

Philadelphia Wins Series, 4-2

Eastern Conference – 2

Date	Matchup	Result
Thu., April 27	N.J. at Tor	TOR, 2-1
Sat., April 29	N.J. at Tor	NJ, 1-0
Mon., May 1	Tor at N.J.	NJ, 5-1
Wed., May 3	Tor at N.J.	TOR, 3-2
Sat., May 6	N.J. at Tor	NJ, 4-3
Mon., May 8	Tor at N.J.	NJ, 3-0

New Jersey Wins Series, 4-2

Western Conference – 1

Date	Matchup	Result
Fri., April 28	S.J. at Dal	DAL, 4-0
Sun., April 30	S.J. at Dal	DAL, 1-0
Tue., May 2	Dal at S.J.	SJ, 2-1
Fri., May 5	Dal at S.J.	DAL, 5-4
Sun., May 7	S.J. at Dal	DAL, 4-1

Dallas Wins Series, 4-1

Western Conference – 2

Date	Matchup	Result
Thu., April 27	Det at Col	COL, 2-0
Sat., April 29	Det at Col	COL, 3-1
Mon., May 1	Col at Det	DET, 3-1
Wed., May 3	Col at Det	COL, 3-2 (OT)
Fri., May 5	Det at Col	COL, 4-2

Colorado Wins Series, 4-1

▶

▶ ■ **CONFERENCE FINALS**

Eastern Conference
Philadelphia (No. 1) vs. New Jersey (No. 4)

Date	Matchup	Result
Sun., May 14	N.J. at Pha	NJ, 4-1
Tue., May 16	N.J. at Pha	PHA, 4-3
Thu., May 18	Pha at N.J.	PHA, 4-2
Sat., May 20	Pha at N.J.	PHA, 3-1
Mon., May 22	N.J. at Pha.	NJ, 4-1
Wed., May 24	Pha at N.J.	NJ, 2-1
Fri., May 26	N.J. at Pha	NJ, 2-1

New Jersey wins series, 4-3

Western Conference

Date	Matchup	Result
Sat., May 13	Col. at Dal.	COL, 2-0
Mon., May 15	Col. at Dal.	DAL, 3-2
Fri., May 19	Dal. at Col.	COL, 2-0
Sun., May 21	Dal. at Col.	DAL, 4-1
Tue., May 23	Col. at Dal.	DAL, 3-2
Thu., May 25	Dal. at Col.	COL, 2-1
Sat., May 27	Col. at Dal.	DAL, 3-2

Dallas wins series, 4-3

STANLEY CUP FINAL

Date	Matchup	Result
Tue., May 30	Dal at N.J.	NJ, 7-3
Thu., June 1	Dal at N. J.	DAL, 2-1
Sat., June 3	N.J. at Dal	NJ, 2-1
Mon., June 5	N.J. at Dal	NJ, 3-1
Thu., June 8	Dal at N.J.	DAL, 1-0 (3OT)
Sat., June 10	N.J. at Dal	NJ, 2-1 (2OT)

New Jersey wins series, 4-2

Source: *Canadian Press*

The Latest Expansion

The NHL, criticized for watered-down play and a shrinking talent-pool in recent seasons, will welcome two more teams to the league in the fall of 2000 to bring the league total to an unprecedented 30.

Owner Robert Naegele Jr. led a group that paid $80 million for the franchise rights to the Minnesota Wild, the team that will debut in the 2000–2001 season alongside the Columbus Blue Jackets.

"We've reached the pinnacle now with the team," said principal Columbus owner John H. McConnell on July 23, 2000 after the club selected 26 players in the expansion draft. "We've got flesh-and-blood guys. That's more than the numbers and talk that we had before."

Columbus general manager Doug MacLean, a former coach of the Florida Panthers, built a roster consisting of enforcer Krzysztof Oliwa, goalie Dwayne Roloson and left-winger Geoff Sanderson. Sanderson had 26 points in 67 games last year for Buffalo.

"I'm obviously very excited about going to Columbus," Sanderson said. "I've heard a lot of good things about the organization. It looks like we've got some good players."

The Blue Jackets will be coached by Dave King, who once coached the Calgary Flames and most recently was an assistant coach in Montreal.

Jacques Lemaire will coach the Wild, while Doug Riseborough is the general manager. Risebrough and Lemaire spent eight seasons together in Montreal, winning four Stanley Cups.

Minnesota's roster consists of tough guy Jeff Odgers, taken from Colorado, Scott Pellerin and goalies Jamie McLennan, a back-up in St. Louis last year, and Manny Fernandez, acquired earlier from Dallas.

The Florida Panthers had the best expansion season among teams that entered the NHL since 1991. In 1993–94, the Panthers were 33-34-17. The worst of the seven new entries came in 1992–93, when the Ottawa Senators were 10-74-4.

Stanley Cup Champions, 1926–2000

The Stanley Cup, the oldest trophy competed for by professional athletes in North America, was donated by Frederick Arthur, Lord Stanley of Preston, in 1893. Originally presented to the amateur hockey champions of Canada, it has been awarded to the top professional team since 1910 and, since 1926, has been competed for only by NHL teams.

Year	Champion	Final Opponent	Series Result	Winning Coach	Winning Manager
1926	Montreal Maroons	Victoria	3-1	Eddie Gerard	Eddie Gerard
1927	Ottawa Senators	Boston	2-0	Dave Gill	Dave Gill
1928	New York Rangers	Montreal	3-2	Lester Patrick	Lester Patrick
1929	Boston Bruins	New York	2-0	Cy Denneny	Art Ross
1930	Montreal Canadiens	Boston	2-0	Cecil Hart	Cecil Hart
1931	Montreal Canadiens	Chicago	3-2	Cecil Hart	Cecil Hart
1932	Toronto Maple Leafs	New York	3-0	Dick Irvin	Conn Smythe
1933	New York Rangers	Toronto	3-1	Lester Patrick	Lester Patrick
1934	Chicago Black Hawks	Detroit	3-1	Tommy Gorman	Tommy Gorman
1935	Montreal Maroons	Toronto	3-0	Tommy Gorman	Tommy Gorman
1936	Detroit Red Wings	Toronto	4-0	Jack Adams	Jack Adams
1937	Detroit Red Wings	New York	3-2	Jack Adams	Jack Adams
1938	Chicago Black Hawks	Toronto	4-1	Bill Stewart	Bill Stewart
1939	Boston Bruins	Toronto	4-1	Art Ross	Art Ross
1940	New York Rangers	Toronto	4-2	Frank Boucher	Lester Patrick
1941	Boston Bruins	Detroit	4-0	Cooney Weiland	Art Ross
1942	Toronto Maple Leafs	Detroit	4-3	Hap Day	Conn Smythe
1943	Detroit Red Wings	Boston	4-0	Jack Adams	Jack Adams
1944	Montreal Canadiens	Chicago	4-0	Dick Irvin	Tommy Gorman
1945	Toronto Maple Leafs	Detroit	4-3	Hap Day	Conn Smythe
1946	Montreal Canadiens	Boston	4-1	Dick Irvin	Tommy Gorman
1947	Toronto Maple Leafs	Montreal	4-2	Hap Day	Conn Smythe
1948	Toronto Maple Leafs	Detroit	4-0	Hap Day	Conn Smythe
1949	Toronto Maple Leafs	Detroit	4-0	Hap Day	Conn Smythe
1950	Detroit Red Wings	New York	4-3	Tommy Ivan	Jack Adams
1951	Toronto Maple Leafs	Montreal	4-1	Joe Primeau	Conn Smythe
1952	Detroit Red Wings	Montreal	4-0	Tommy Ivan	Jack Adams
1953	Montreal Canadiens	Boston	4-1	Dick Irvin	Frank Selke
1954	Detroit Red Wings	Montreal	4-3	Tommy Ivan	Jack Adams
1955	Detroit Red Wings	Montreal	4-3	Jimmy Skinner	Jack Adams
1956	Montreal Canadiens	Detroit	4-1	Toe Blake	Frank Selke
1957	Montreal Canadiens	Boston	4-1	Toe Blake	Frank Selke
1958	Montreal Canadiens	Boston	4-2	Toe Blake	Frank Selke
1959	Montreal Canadiens	Toronto	4-1	Toe Blake	Frank Selke
1960	Montreal Canadiens	Toronto	4-0	Toe Blake	Frank Selke
1961	Chicago Black Hawks	Detroit	4-2	Rudy Pilous	Tommy Ivan
1962	Toronto Maple Leafs	Chicago	4-2	Punch Imlach	Punch Imlach
1963	Toronto Maple Leafs	Detroit	4-1	Punch Imlach	Punch Imlach
1964	Toronto Maple Leafs	Detroit	4-3	Punch Imlach	Punch Imlach
1965	Montreal Canadiens	Chicago	4-3	Toe Blake	Sam Pollock

Year	Champion	Final Opponent	Series Result	Winning Coach	Winning Manager
▶ 1966	Montreal Canadiens	Detroit	4-2	Toe Blake	Sam Pollock
1967	Toronto Maple Leafs	Montreal	4-2	Punch Imlach	Punch Imlach
1968	Montreal Canadiens	St. Louis	4-0	Toe Blake	Sam Pollock
1969	Montreal Canadiens	St. Louis	4-0	Claude Ruel	Sam Pollock
1970	Boston Bruins	St. Louis	4-0	Harry Sinden	Milt Schmidt
1971	Montreal Canadiens	Chicago	4-3	Al MacNeil	Sam Pollock
1972	Boston Bruins	New York	4-2	Tom Johnson	Milt Schmidt
1973	Montreal Canadiens	Chicago	4-2	Scotty Bowman	Sam Pollock
1974	Philadelphia Flyers	Boston	4-2	Fred Shero	Keith Allen
1975	Philadelphia Flyers	Buffalo	4-2	Fred Shero	Keith Allen
1976	Montreal Canadiens	Philadelphia	4-0	Scotty Bowman	Sam Pollock
1977	Montreal Canadiens	Boston	4-0	Scotty Bowman	Sam Pollock
1978	Montreal Canadiens	Boston	4-2	Scotty Bowman	Sam Pollock
1979	Montreal Canadiens	New York	4-1	Scotty Bowman	Irving Grundman
1980	N.Y. Islanders	Philadelphia	4-2	Al Arbour	Bill Torrey
1981	N.Y. Islanders	Minnesota	4-1	Al Arbour	Bill Torrey
1982	N.Y. Islanders	Vancouver	4-0	Al Arbour	Bill Torrey
1983	N.Y. Islanders	Edmonton	4-0	Al Arbour	Bill Torrey
1984	Edmonton Oilers	New York	4-1	Glen Sather	Glen Sather
1985	Edmonton Oilers	Philadelphia	4-1	Glen Sather	Glen Sather
1986	Montreal Canadiens	Calgary	4-1	Jean Perron	Serge Savard
1987	Edmonton Oilers	Philadelphia	4-3	Glen Sather	Glen Sather
1988	Edmonton Oilers	Boston	4-0	Glen Sather	Glen Sather
1989	Calgary Flames	Montreal	4-2	Terry Crisp	Cliff Fletcher
1990	Edmonton Oilers	Boston	4-1	John Muckler	Glen Sather
1991	Pittsburgh Penguins	Minnesota	4-2	Bob Johnson	Craig Patrick
1992	Pittsburgh Penguins	Chicago	4-0	Scotty Bowman	Craig Patrick
1993	Montreal Canadiens	Los Angeles	4-1	Jacques Demers	Serge Savard
1994	New York Rangers	Vancouver	4-3	Mike Keenan	Neil Smith
1995	New Jersey Devils	Detroit	4-0	Jacques Lemaire	Lou Lamoriello
1996	Colorado Avalanche	Florida	4-0	Marc Crawford	Pierre Lacroix
1997	Detroit Red Wings	Philadelphia	4-0	Scotty Bowman	Scotty Bowman
1998	Detroit Red Wings	Washington	4-0	Scotty Bowman	Ken Holland
1999	Dallas Stars	Buffalo	4-2	Ken Hitchcock	Bob Gainey
2000	New Jersey Devils	Dallas	4-2	Larry Robinson	Lou Lamoriello

Source: *National Hockey League*

NHL Scoring Leaders, 1999–2000

(Regular Season)

Player	GP	G	A	PTS	+/-	PIM	SHFT	S
Jaromir Jagr, Pitt	63	42	54	96	25	50	21.52	290
Pavel Bure, Fla	74	58	36	94	25	16	24.93	360
Mark Recchi, Pha	82	28	63	91	20	50	23.22	223
Paul Kariya, Ana	74	42	44	86	22	24	26.36	324
Teemu Selanne, Ana	79	33	52	85	6	12	24.05	236
Owen Nolan - S.J.	78	44	40	84	-1	110	22.33	261
Tony Amonte, Chi	82	43	41	84	10	48	25.18	260
Mike Modano, Dal	77	38	43	81	0	48	27.73	188
Joe Sakic, Col	60	28	53	81	30	28	28.42	242
Steve Yzerman, Det	78	35	44	79	28	34	22.95	234
Jeremy Roenick, Phx	75	34	44	78	11	102	22.95	192
Brendan Shanahan, Det	78	41	37	78	24	105	20.95	283
John Leclair, Pha	82	40	37	77	8	36	21.67	249
Valeri Bure, Cal	82	35	40	75	-7	50	21.84	308
Pavol Demitra, Stl	71	28	47	75	34	8	21.65	241
Luc Robitaille, L.A	71	36	38	74	11	68	20.58	221
Ron Francis, Car	78	23	50	73	10	18	24.40	150
Mats Sundin, Tor	73	32	41	73	16	46	21.16	184
Nicklas Lidstrom, Det	81	20	53	73	19	18	27.25	218
Doug Weight, Edm	77	21	51	72	6	54	21.70	167

Playoffs

Player	GP	G	A	PTS	+/-	PIM	SHFT	S
Brett Hull, Dal	23	11	13	24	3	4	25.65	79
Mike Modano, Dal	23	10	13	23	3	10	32.78	67
Jason Arnott, N.J	23	8	12	20	7	18	21.00	56
Patrik Elias, N.J	23	7	13	20	9	9	23.04	60
Mark Recchi, Pha	18	6	12	18	3	6	26.50	53
Petr Sykora, N.J	23	9	8	17	8	10	19.87	45
Jaromir Jagr, Pitt	11	8	8	16	5	6	24.36	42
Peter Forsberg, Col	16	7	8	15	9	12	29.62	54
Adam Deadmarsh, Col	17	4	11	15	7	21	28.47	41
Chris Drury, Col	17	4	10	14	7	4	30.47	44
John Leclair, Pha	18	6	7	13	3	6	24.78	64
Keith Primeau, Pha	18	2	11	13	-4	13	25.67	37
Eric Desjardins, Pha	18	2	10	12	1	2	33.00	31
Martin Straka, Pitt	11	3	9	12	5	10	28.63	23
Jan Hrdina, Pitt	9	4	8	12	9	2	28.55	9
Scott Stevens, N.J	23	3	8	11	9	6	28.17	29
Rick Tocchet, Pha	18	5	6	11	-2	49	21.61	46
Bobby Holik, N.J	23	3	7	10	-1	14	22.09	73
Claude Lemieux, N.J	23	4	6	10	7	28	23.48	78
Joe Nieuwendyk, Dal	23	7	3	10	-2	18	23.87	45

Source: *Canadian Press*
GP = Games played; G = Goals; A = Assists; Pts = Points; +/- = Plus/minus statistic, which shows the number of even-strength and shorthanded goals scored by a player's team, minus those scored against, while he is on the ice; PIM = Penalties in minutes; S = Shots on goal;

NHL All Time Individual Scoring Leaders

(at the end of the 1999–2000 season)

	Seasons	Goals	Assists	PTS
1. Wayne Gretzky, Edm/LA/StL/NYR	20	894	1 963	2 857
2. Gordie Howe, Det/Hfd	26	801	1 049	1 850
3. Marcel Dionne, Det/LA/NYR	18	731	1 040	1 771
4. **Mark Messier, Edm/NYR/Vcr**	21	627	1 087	1 714
5. Phil Esposito, Chi/Bos/NYR	18	717	873	1 590
6. **Steve Yzerman, Det**	16	621	929	1 550
7. **Ron Francis, Hfd/Pitt/Car**	19	472	1 075	1 547
8. **Paul Coffey, Edm/Pitt/La/Det/Hfd/Pha/Chi/Car**	20	392	1 128	1 520
9. **Ray Bourque, Bos/Col**	21	397	1 113	1 510
10. Mario Lemieux, Pitt	12	613	881	1 494
11. Stan Mikita, Chi	22	541	926	1 467
12. Bryan Trottier, NYI/Pitt	18	524	901	1 425

Source: *Canadian Press* Active players are in bold.

Directory of Selected Hockey Organizations

Hockey Hall of Fame
30 Yonge St.
Toronto, Ont.
M5E 1X8
Tel: (416) 360-7735
Fax: (416) 360-1501
http://www.hhof.com

National Hockey League
1155 Metcalfe St.
Suite 960
Montreal, Que.
H3B 2W2
Tel: (514) 871-9220
http://www.nhl.com

National Hockey League Players' Association
777 Bay St., Suite 2400
Toronto, Ont. M5G 2C8
Tel: (416) 408-4040
Fax: (416) 408-3685
http://nhlpa.medius.com

Alexei Yashin—booed coast-to-coast

With Alexi Yashin, the jury ruled, and the jury is still out. Canadian hockey fans haven't been shy in letting the Ottawa Senators' star centre know what they think of his return from a season-long holdout over a demand to renegotiate the last year of a contract scheduled to pay him CDN$3.6 million.

The sentiments of Ottawa fans were more complex when they got to see the team's talented former captain on home ice at the Corel Centre for the first time in 17 months, during an exhibition game against Calgary on September 18. The boos they delivered every time Yashin touched the puck reflexively turned into cheers when he scored the first goal of his reluctant return, then quickly switched back to boos when the goal was announced. Yashin rejoined the Senators only, he said, because he had nowhere else to play. He lost an arbitrator's decision on restricted free agency. The 26-year-old Russian was the NHL's top goal-scoring centre in 1998–99 with 44 goals and 94 points.

Source: *The Canadian Press*

Regular Season NHL Scoring Champions, 1959–99

Season	Player, Team	GP	G	A	PTS	Season	Player, Team	GP	G	A	PTS
1959–60	Bobby Hull, Chi	70	39	42	81	1980–81	Wayne Gretzky, Edm	80	55	109	164
1960–61	Bernie Geoffrion, Mtl	64	50	45	95	1981–82	Wayne Gretzky, Edm	80	92	120	212
1961–62	Bobby Hull, Chi	70	50	34	84	1982–83	Wayne Gretzky, Edm	80	71	125	196
1962–63	Gordie Howe, Det	70	38	48	86	1983–84	Wayne Gretzky, Edm	74	87	118	205
1963–64	Stan Mikita, Chi	70	39	50	89	1984–85	Wayne Gretzky, Edm	80	73	135	208
1964–65	Stan Mikita, Chi	70	28	59	87	1985–86	Wayne Gretzky, Edm	80	52	163	215
1965–66	Bobby Hull, Chi	65	54	43	97	1986–87	Wayne Gretzky, Edm	79	62	121	183
1966–67	Stan Mikita, Chi	70	35	62	97	1987–88	Mario Lemieux, Pitt	77	70	98	168
1967–68	Stan Mikita, Chi	72	40	47	87	1988–89	Mario Lemieux, Pitt	76	85	114	199
1968–69	Phil Esposito, Bos	74	49	77	126	1989–90	Wayne Gretzky, LA	73	40	102	142
1969–70	Bobby Orr, Bos	76	33	87	120	1990–91	Wayne Gretzky, LA	78	41	122	163
1970–71	Phil Esposito, Bos	78	76	76	152	1991–92	Mario Lemieux, Pitt	64	44	87	131
1971–72	Phil Esposito, Bos	76	66	67	133	1992–93	Mario Lemieux, Pitt	60	69	91	160
1972–73	Phil Esposito, Bos	78	55	75	130	1993–94	Wayne Gretzky, LA	81	38	92	130
1973–74	Phil Esposito, Bos	78	68	77	145	1994–95	Jaromir Jagr[2], Pitt	48[3]	32	38	70
1974–75	Bobby Orr, Bos	80	46	89	135	1995–96	Mario Lemieux, Pitt	70	69	92	161
1975–76	Guy Lafleur, Mtl	80	56	69	125	1996–97	Mario Lemieux, Pitt	76	50	72	122
1976–77	Guy Lafleur, Mtl	80	56	80	136	1997–98	Jaromir Jagr, Pitt	77	35	67	102
1977–78	Guy Lafleur, Mtl	78	60	72	132	1998–99	Jaromir Jagr, Pitt	81	44	83	127
1978–79	Bryan Trottier, NYI	76	47	87	134	1999–00	Jaromir Jagr, Pitt	63	42	54	96
1979–80	Marcel Dionne, LA	80	53	84	137						

Source: National Hockey League
(1) Number of assists not recorded. (2) Jagr tied with Lindros (Phi); awarded title based on most goals scored. (3) Season shortened to 48 games due to owner/player dispute.

The NHL $4-Million Dollar Club for the 1999–2000 Season

(as of Sept. 1, 1999. All figures in U.S. dollars)

Player	Club	Salary	Player	Club	Salary
Peter Forsberg	COL	$10 000 000	Niklas Lidstrom	DET	$7 250 000
Paul Kariya	ANA	10 000 000	Brett Hull	DAL	7 000 000
Jaromir Jagr	PGH	9 482 708	Mike Modano	DAL	7 000 000
Pavel Bure	FLA	9 000 000	Brendan Shanahan	DET	6 500 000
Eric Lindros	PHA	8 500 000	Curtis Joseph	TOR	6 150 000
Keith Tkachuk	PHX	8 300 000	Theo Fleury	NYR	6 000 000
Teemu Selanne	ANA	8 000 000	Doug Gilmour	BUF	6 000 000
Steve Yzerman	DET	8 000 000	Mike Richter	NYR	5 600 000
Brian Leetch	NYR	7 680 000	Ed Belfour	DAL	5 500 000
Dominik Hasek	BUF	7 500 000	Ray Bourque	COL	5 500 000
Patrick Roy	COL	7 500 000	Chris Chelios	DET	5 500 000
Mats Sundin	TOR	7 500 000	Rob Blake	LA	5 267 500
			Alex Mogilny	NJ	5 200 000

Source: National Hockey League Player's Association

2000 NHL Draft—First Round Selections

Pick, Team, Player, Position, Last Team (league)

1. **NY Islanders:** Rick DiPietro, G, Boston University (HE)
2. **Atlanta:** Dany Heatley, LW, Univ. of Wisconsin (WCHA)
3. **Minnesota:** Marian Gaborik, LW, Dukla Trencin (Slovakia)
4. **Columbus:** Rostislav Klesla, D, Bramptom (OHL)
5. **NY Islanders** (from TB): Raffi Torres, LW, Brampton (OHL)
6. **Nashville:** Scott Hartnell, RW, Prince Albert (WHL)
7. **Boston:** Lars Jonsson, D, Leksand (Sweden)
8. **Tampa Bay** (from NYR): Nikita Alexeev, RW, Erie (OHL)
9. **Calgary:** Brent Krahn, G, Calgary (OHL)
10. **Chicago:** Mikhail Yakubov, C, Lada Togliatti (Russia)
11. **Chicago** (from Van): Pavel Vorobiev, RW, Yaroslavl (Russia)
12. **Anaheim:** Alexei Smirnov, LW, Dynamo (Russia)
13. **Montreal:** Ron Hainsey, D, Mass.-Lowell (HE)
14. **Colorado** (from Car): Vaclav Nedorost, C, Budejovice (Czech Republic)
15. **Buffalo:** Artem Kriukov, C, Yaroslavl (Russia)
16. **Montreal** (from S.J.): Marcel Hossa, C, Portland (WHL)
17. **Edmonton:** Alexei Mikhnov, W, Yaroslavl (Russia)
18. **Pittsburgh:** Brooks Orpik, D, Boston College (HE)
19. **Phoenix:** Krystofer Kolanos, C, Boston College (HE)
20. **Los Angeles:** Alexander Frolov, LW, Yaroslavl (Russia)
21. **Ottawa:** Anton Volchenkov, D, CSKA (Russia)
22. **New Jersey** (from Col): David Hale, D, Sioux City (USHL)
23. **Vancouver** (from Fla): Nathan Smith, C, Swift Current (WHL)
24. **Toronto:** Brad Boyes, C, Erie (OHL)
25. **Dallas:** Steve Ott, C, Windsor (OHL)
26. **Washington:** Brian Sutherby, C, Moose Jaw (WHL)
27. **Boston** (from Col, NJ)[1]: Martin Samuelsson, W, MoDo (Sweden)
28. **Philadelphia:** Justin Williams, RW, Plymouth (OHL)
29. **Detroit:** Niklas Kronvall, D, Djurgarden (Sweden)
30. **St. Louis:** Jeff Taffe, C, Univ. of Minnesota (WCHA)

Source: *Canadian Press*

NHL All-Star Teams, 1995–2000[1]

First Team	Second Team	First Team	Second Team
1995		**1998**	
Dominik Hasek, Buf, g	Jim Carey, Wash, g	Dominik Hasek, Buf, g	Martin Brodeur, NJ, g
Chris Chelios, Chi, d	Raymond Bourque, Bos, d	Rob Blake, LA, d	Raymond Bourque, Bos, d
Paul Coffey, Det, d	Larry Murphy, Pitt, d	Nicklas Lidstrom, Det, d	Chris Pronger, StL, d
Eric Lindros, Phi, c	Alexei Zhamnov, Wpg, c	Peter Forsberg, Col, c	Wayne Gretzky, NYR, c
Jaromir Jagr, Pitt, rw	Theoren Fleury, Cal, rw	Jaromir Jagr, Pitt, rw	Teemu Selanne, Ana, rw
John Leclair, Phi, lw	Keith Tkachuk, Wpg, lw	John LeClair, Phi, lw	Keith Tkachuk, Pho, lw
1996		**1999**	
Jim Carey, Wash, g	Chris Osgood, Det, g	Dominik Hasek, Buf, g	Byron Dafoe, Bos, g
Chris Chelios, Chi, d	Brian Leetch, NYR, d	Al MacInnis, StL, d	Raymond Bourque, Bos, d
Raymond Bourque, Bos, d	Vladimir Konstantinov, Det, d	Nicklas Lidstrom, Det, d	Eric Desjardins, Pha, d
Mario Lemieux, Pitt, c	Eric Lindros, Phi, c	Peter Forsberg, Col, c	Alexei Yashin, Ott, c
Jaromir Jagr, Pitt, rw	Alexander Mogilny, Van, rw	Jaromir Jagr, Pit, rw	Teemu Selanne, Ana, rw
Paul Kariya, Ana, lw	John Leclair, Phi, lw	Paul Kariya, Ana, lw	John LeClair, Phi, lw
1997		**2000**	
Dominik Hasek, Buf, g	Martin Brodeur, NJ, g	**First team**	**Second Team**
Sandis Ozolinsh, Col, d	Chris Chelios, Chi, d	Olaf Kolzig, Was, g	Roman Turek, St.L, g
Brian Leetch, NYR, d	Scott Stevens, NJ, d	Chris Pronger, St.L, d	Rob Blake, LA, d
Mario Lemieux, Pitt, c	Wayne Gretzky, NYR, c	Nicklas Lidstrom, Det, d	Eric Desjardins, Phil, d
Teemu Selanne, Ana, rw	Jaromir Jagr, Pitt, rw	Steve Yzerman, Det., c	Mike Modano, Dal. c
Paul Kariya, Ana, lw	John LeClair, Phi, lw	Jaromir Jagr, Pitt, rw	Pavel Bure, Fla, rw
		Brendan Shanahan, Det, lw	Paul Kariya, Ana, lw

Source: *Canadian Press*

(1) As selected by members of the Professional Hockey Writers' Association.

NHL Individual Award Winners, 1980–2000

Hart Trophy (Most Valuable Player)[1]

1980 Wayne Gretzky, Edm	1987 Wayne Gretzky, Edm	1994 Sergei Fedorov, Det
1981 Wayne Gretzky, Edm	1988 Mario Lemieux, Pitt	1995 Eric Lindros, Phi
1982 Wayne Gretzky, Edm	1989 Wayne Gretzky, LA	1996 Mario Lemieux, Pitt
1983 Wayne Gretzky, Edm	1990 Mark Messier, Edm	1997 Dominik Hasek, Buf
1984 Wayne Gretzky, Edm	1991 Brett Hull, StL	1998 Dominik Hasek, Buf
1985 Wayne Gretzky, Edm	1992 Mark Messier, NYR	1999 Jaromir Jagr, Pitt
1986 Wayne Gretzky, Edm	1993 Mario Lemieux, Pitt	2000 Chris Pranger, StL

Calder Trophy (Best Rookie)[1]

1980 Raymond Bourque, Bos	1987 Luc Robitaille, LA	1994 Martin Brodeur, NJ
1981 Peter Stastny, Que	1988 Joe Nieuwendyk, Cal	1995 Peter Forsberg, Que
1982 Dale Hawerchuk, Wpg	1989 Brian Leetch, NYR	1996 Daniel Alfredsson, Ott
1983 Steve Larmer, Chi	1990 Sergei Makarov, Cal	1997 Bryan Berard, NYI
1984 Tom Barrasso, Buf	1991 Ed Belfour, Chi	1998 Sergei Samsonov, Bos
1985 Mario Lemieux, Pit	1992 Pavel Bure, Vcr	1999 Chris Drury, Col
1986 Gary Suter, Cal	1993 Teemu Selanne, Wpg	2000 Scott Gomez, NJ

James Norris Trophy (Best Defenceman)[1]

1980 Larry Robinson, Mtl	1987 Raymond Bourque, Bos	1994 Raymond Bourque, Bos
1981 Randy Carlyle, Pitt	1988 Raymond Bourque, Bos	1995 Paul Coffey, Det
1982 Doug Wilson, Chi	1989 Chris Chelios, Mtl	1996 Chris Chelios, Chi
1983 Rod Langway, Wash	1990 Raymond Bourque, Bos	1997 Brian Leetch, NYR
1984 Rod Langway, Wash	1991 Raymond Bourque, Bos	1998 Rob Blake, LA
1985 Paul Coffey, Edm	1992 Brian Leetch, NYR	1999 Al MacInnis, StL
1986 Paul Coffey, Edm	1993 Chris Chelios, Chi	2000 Chris Pranger, StL

Vezina Trophy (Best Goalkeeper)[2]

1980 Bob Suavé, Buf	1985 Pelle Lindbergh, Phi	1993 Ed Belfour, Chi
Don Edwards, Buf	1986 John Vanbiesbrouck, NYR	1994 Dominik Hasek, Buf
1981 Richard Sevigny, Mtl	1987 Ron Hextall, Phi	1995 Dominik Hasek, Buf
Denis Herron, Mtl	1988 Grant Fuhr, Edm	1996 Jim Carey, Wash
Michel Larocque, Mtl	1989 Patrick Roy, Mtl	1997 Dominik Hasek, Buf
1982 Bill Smith, NYI	1990 Patrick Roy, Mtl	1998 Dominik Hasek, Buf
1983 Pete Peeters, Bos	1991 Ed Belfour, Chi	1999 Dominik Hasek, Buf
1984 Tom Barrasso, Buf	1992 Patrick Roy, Mtl	2000 Olaf Kolzig, Wash

Lady Byng Trophy (Most Sportsmanlike)[1]

1980 Wayne Gretzky, Edm	1987 Joe Mullen, Cal	1994 Wayne Gretzky, LA
1981 Rick Kehoe, Pitt	1988 Mats Naslund, Mtl	1995 Ron Francis, Pitt
1982 Rick Middleton, Bos	1989 Joe Mullen, Cal	1996 Paul Kariya, Ana
1983 Mike Bossy, NYI	1990 Brett Hull, StL	1997 Paul Kariya, Ana
1984 Mike Bossy, NYI	1991 Wayne Gretzky, LA	1998 Ron Francis, Pitt
1985 Jari Kurri, Edm	1992 Wayne Gretzky, LA	1999 Wayne Gretzky, NYR
1986 Mike Bossy, NYI	1993 Pierre Turgeon, NYI	2000 Paul Demitro, StL

Conn Smythe Trophy (Most Valuable in Playoffs) [3]

1980 Bryan Trottier, NYI	1987 Ron Hextall, Phi	1994 Brian Leetch, NYR
1981 Butch Goring, NYI	1988 Wayne Gretzky, Edm	1995 Claude Lemieux, NJ
1982 Mike Bossy, NYI	1989 Al MacInnis, Cal	1996 Joe Sakic, Col
1983 Bill Smith, NYI	1990 Bill Ranford, Edm	1997 Mike Vernon, Det
1984 Mark Messier, Edm	1991 Mario Lemieux, Pitt	1998 Steve Yzerman, Det
1985 Wayne Gretzky, Edm	1992 Mario Lemieux, Pitt	1999 Joe Nieuwendyk, Dal
1986 Patrick Roy, Mtl	1993 Patrick Roy, Mtl	2000 Scott Stevens, NJ

Frank J. Selke Trophy (Best Defensive Forward) [1]

1980 Bob Gainey, Mtl	1987 Dave Poulin, Phi	1994 Sergei Fedorov, Det
1981 Bob Gainey, Mtl	1988 Guy Carbonneau, Mtl	1995 Ron Francis, Pitt
1982 Steve Kasper, Bos	1989 Guy Carbonneau, Mtl	1996 Sergei Fedorov, Det
1983 Bobby Clarke, Phi	1990 Rick Meagher, StL	1997 Mike Peca, Buf
1984 Doug Jarvis, Wash	1991 Dirk Graham, Chi	1998 Jere Lehtinen, Dal
1985 Craig Ramsay, Buf	1992 Guy Carbonneau, Mtl	1999 Jere Lehtinen, Dal
1986 Troy Murray, Chi	1993 Doug Gilmour, Tor	2000 Steve Yzerman, Det

Jack Adams Trophy (Coach of the Year)

1980 Pat Quinn, Phi	1987 Jacques Demers, Det	1994 Jacques Lemaire, NJ
1981 Red Berenson, StL	1988 Jacques Demers, Det	1995 Marc Crawford, Que
1982 Tom Watt, Wpg	1989 Pat Burns, Mtl	1996 Scotty Bowman, Det
1983 Orval Tessier, Chi	1990 Bob Murdoch, Wpg	1997 Ted Nolan, Buf
1984 Bryan Murray, Wash	1991 Brian Sutter, StL	1998 Pat Burns, Bos
1985 Mike Keenan, Phi	1992 Pat Quinn, Van	1999 Jacques Martin, Ott
1986 Glen Sather, Edm	1993 Pat Burns, Tor	2000 Joel Quenneville, StL

Source: *Canadian Press*

(1) As selected at the end of the regular season by members of the Professional Hockey Writers' Association in the NHL cities. (2) Since the 1981–82 season, Vezina Trophy winners have been selected by general managers of the NHL clubs. In earlier seasons the trophy was awarded to the goalkeeper(s) of the team allowing the fewest goals during the regular season. (3) As selected by members of the Professional Hockey Writers' Association at the end of the last game of the Stanley Cup finals.

Top NHL Draft Picks Since 1980

Player, Team Selected by, Position, Junior Team

1980 Doug Wickenheiser, Montreal, C, Regina (WHL)	1991 Eric Lindros, Quebec, C, Oshawa (OHL)
1981 Dale Hawerchuk, Winnipeg, C, Cornwall (QMJHL)	1992 Roman Hamrlik, Tampa Bay, D, ZPS Zin (Czech)
1982 Gord Kluzak, Boston, D, Billings (WHL)	1993 Alexandre Daigle, Ottawa, C, Victoriaville (QMJHL)
1983 Brian Lawton, Minnesota, C, Mount St. Charles HS	1994 Ed Jovanovski, Florida, D, Windsor (OHL)
1984 Mario Lemieux, Pittsburgh, C, Laval (QMJHL)	1995 Bryan Berard, Ottawa, D, Detroit (OHL)
1985 Wendel Clark, Toronto, LW-D, Saskatoon (WHL)	1996 Chris Phillips, Ottawa, D, Prince Albert (WHL)
1986 Joe Murphy, Detroit, C, Michigan State	1997 Joe Thornton, Boston, C, Sault Ste. Marie (OHL)
1987 Pierre Turgeon, Buffalo, C, Granby (QMJHL)	1998 Vincent Lecavalier, Tampa Bay, C, Rimouski (QMJHL)
1988 Mike Modano, Minnesota, C, Prince Albert (WHL)	
1989 Mats Sundin, Quebec, RW, Nacka (Sweden)	1999 Patrik Stefan, Atlanta, C, Long Beach (IHL)
1990 Owen Nolan, Quebec, RW, Cornwall (OHL)	2000 Rick DiPietro, N.Y. Islanders, G, Boston University

Source: *Canadian Press*

The New York-Edmonton Connection

The saga started May 19 when Glen Sather—orchestrator of some of the most potent offensives in the history of the league during the 1980s—resigned as president and general manager of the Edmonton Oilers after 21 years as GM, and five Stanley Cups.

On June 1, Sather went east and uptown as new general manager and president of the New York Rangers. The Rangers hope Sather, 56, will change the fortunes of the struggling team. New York won the Stanley Cup six years ago, but has missed the playoffs for the last three seasons. The Rangers were 29-41-12 last season despite a league-high payroll of US$61 million.

On June 9, the Oilers named Kevin Lowe as general manager of the team to cap his two-year ride through the upper echelons of hockey management. His appointment came less than two years after he retired from the NHL as a player and less than one year after he became the Oilers' head coach. He guided the team to a 32-34-16 record, followed by a first-round playoff loss to the Dallas Stars.

On June 12, the Rangers announced former Oilers' coach Ron Low as head coach and Ted Green and Walt Kyle as assistant coaches. Green, 60, had been part of the Oilers' coaching staff since 1981. Kyle, 44, had been hired by Sather to coach Edmonton's AHL farm team in Hamilton two years ago.

On June 22, the Oilers promoted former team captain Craig MacTavish from assistant to headcoach. MacTavish, 41, from London, Ont. became the eighth coach in the Oilers' history. A two-way centre, MacTavish starred on three Stanley Cup winners during the Oiler dynasty of the 1980s. He was team captain for two seasons in the early 1990s before being traded to the New York Rangers, where he won one more Cup.

On July 13, The Moose returned to Manhattan. Mark Messier, 39, agreed to a two-year deal reportedly worth US$11 million and was given the captain's C. The Rangers team to which Messier returns to has only four players remaining from the 1997 team he left: Brian Leetch, Adam Graves, Mike Richter and Darren Langdon.

Messier first joined the Rangers in 1991 in a trade Glen Sather made from Edmonton, and in his third season, led the team to its first championship in 54 years. Messier, a 21-year veteran, has appeared in 1,479 career NHL games with the Rangers, Canucks and Oilers, registering 627 goals and 1,087 assists for 1,714 points. He is the leading career scorer among active NHL players and fourth on the NHL's all-time list with 1,714 points. Messier also ranks fourth in assists (1,087), sixth in goals (627), and seventh in games played (1,479).

Source: Canadian Press

It was a very bad year

*A*fter a season of disappointments, including losing his captain's C, Philadelphia Flyers' Eric Lindros came off a ten-week absence to play his second playoff game—his first at home. His game lasted seven minutes 50 seconds. On May 26, Lindros, 27 suffered his fourth concussion of the 1999–2000 season and sixth in the last two years. (His younger brother, Brett, retired from the NHL after a series of concussions.) The burly centre was limp as he was helped off the ice after a legal, open-ice check by New Jersey's Scott Stevens in the first period of Game 7 of the Eastern Conference final.

Lindros arrived in Philadelphia in 1992 following a trade with Quebec that included six players, two first-round draft choices and US$15 million. He has made six all-star teams and won an MVP award in 1995, but the Flyers lost in their only Stanley Cup final with him.

On August 1, 2000 Lindros rejected the US$8.5-million qualifying offer from Philadelphia to become a restricted free agent. Lindros has a personal US$20-million insurance policy that covers him in 2000–2001. If he doesn't play 20 games, the 27-year-old centre will receive the full premium tax-free.

Source: Canadian Press

Men's World Hockey Championship, 2000

(St. Petersburg, Russia)

(Top four in each group advance to quarter-finals)

STANDINGS

Group E	W	L	T	GF	GA	PTS	Group F	W	L	T	GF	GA	PTS
Team							Team						
U.S.	3	0	2	13	7	8	Czech Republic	4	1	0	25	11	8
Switzerland	2	1	2	14	12	6	Finland	3	1	1	22	15	7
Sweden	2	2	1	16	11	5	**Canada**	**3**	**2**	**0**	**19**	**10**	**6**
Latvia	2	2	1	12	13	5	Slovakia	2	2	1	22	15	5
Belarus	2	3	0	9	17	4	Norway	1	3	1	10	24	3
Russia	1	4	0	8	12	2	Italy	0	4	1	5	28	1

Semifinals Czech Republic 2, Canada 1
Slovakia 3, Finland 1
Third Place Finland 2, **Canada** 1
Championship Czech Republic 5, Slovakia 3

Source: *Canadian Press*

IIHF Women's World Hockey Championship, 1999

(Mississauga, Ont.)

STANDINGS

Pool A	GP	W	L	T	GF	GA	PTS	Pool B	GP	W	L	T	GF	GA	PTS
Canada	**3**	**3**	**0**	**0**	**21**	**1**	**6**	U.S.	3	3	0	0	35	4	6
Sweden	3	1	1	1	11	5	3	Finland	3	2	1	0	14	6	4
Japan	3	1	2	0	3	19	2	Russia	3	1	2	0	8	24	2
China	3	0	2	1	2	12	1	Germany	3	0	3	0	4	27	0

5th/6th place – Russia 4, China 0
7th/8th place – Germany 3, Japan 2
Semifinals – **Canada 3**, Finland 2
U.S. 7, Sweden 1
Bronze Medal – Finland 7, Sweden 1
Gold Medal – **Canada 3**, U.S. 2 (OT)

Source: *Canadian Press*

2000 World Junior Hockey Championship

(Final Round Robin)

STANDINGS

Group A	GP	W	L	T	GF	GA	PTS	Group B	GP	W	L	T	GF	GA	PTS
Czech Republic	4	2	0	2	12	7	6	Russia	4	4	0	0	30	4	8
Canada	4	2	0	2	9	5	6	Sweden	4	3	1	0	27	8	6
USA	4	1	1	2	5	6	4	Switzerland	4	2	2	0	13	16	4
Finland	4	1	2	1	8	9	3	Kazakhstan	4	1	3	0	7	34	2
Slovakia	4	0	3	1	4	11	1	Ukraine	4	0	4	0	6	21	0

7th place Finland 9 – Kazakhstan 1
5th place Sweden 5 – Switzerland 2
Bronze **Canada 4** – USA 3 (OT/shootout)
Gold Czech Rep 1 – Russia 0 (OT/shootout)

Source: *Canadian Press*

World Hockey Championships, 1981–2000
Team Canada's Leading Scorers

		GP	G	A	PTS			GP	G	A	PTS
1981	Dennis Maruk	8	5	3	8	1992	Steve Thomas	6	2	2	4
1982	Wayne Gretzky	10	6	8	14	1993	Eric Lindros	8	11	6	17
1983	Michel Goulet	10	1	8	9	1994	Paul Kariya	8	5	7	12
1984	Marcel Dionne	10	6	3	9	1995	Andrew McKim	8	6	7	13
1985	Mario Lemieux	9	4	6	10	1996	Yanic Perrault	8	6	3	9
1986	Brent Sutter	8	4	7	11	1997	Travis Green	11	3	5	8
1987	Tony Tanti	10	6	2	8	1998	Ray Whitney	6	4	2	6
1989[1]	Brian Bellows	10	8	7	15	1999	Corey Stillman	10	4	4	8
1990	Steve Yzerman	10	9	10	19	2000	Todd Bertuzzi	9	5	4	9
1991	Joe Sakic	10	6	5	11						

Source: *Canadian Press*   (1) No championship in 1988.

World Hockey Championships
First All-Star Teams since 1990

(forwards, defence, goalie)

1990 Steve Yzerman (Cda), Robert Reichel (Tch), Andrei Khomutov (Urs), Viacheslav Fetisov (Urs), Dominik Hasek (Tch), Mikhail Tatarinov (Urs)

1991 Valeri Kamensky (Urs), Thomas Rundquist (Swe), Jari Kurri (Fin), Alexei Kasatonov (Urs), Sean Burke (Cda), Viacheslav Fetisov (Urs)

1992 Mats Sundin (Swe), Petr Hrbek (Tch), Jarkko Varvio (Fin), Frantisek Musil (Tch), Markus Ketterer (Fin); Timo Jutila (Fin)

1993 Ulf Dahlen (Swe), Eric Lindros (Cda), Mikael Renberg (Swe), Ilya Byakin (Rus), Petr Briza (Cze), Dave Manson (Cda)

1994 Paul Kariya (Cda), Saku Koivu (Fin), Jari Kurri (Fin), Magnus Svensson (Swe), Timo Jutila (Fin), Bill Ranford (Cda)

1995 Ville Peltonen (Fin), Saku Koivu (Fin), Jere Lehtinen (Fin), Tommy Sjodin (Swe), Timo Jutila (Fin), Roman Turek (Cze)

1996 Robert Reichel (Cze), Otakar Vejvoda (Cze), Paul Kariya (Cda), Michal Sykora (Cze), Alexei Zhitnik (Rus), Roman Turek (Cze)

1997 Vladimir Vujtek (Cze), Michael Nylander (Swe), Martin Prochazka (Cze), Rob Blake (Cda), Teppo Numminen (Fin), Tommy Salo (Swe)

1998 Peter Forsberg (Swe), Mats Sundin (Swe), Ville Peltonen (Fin), Frantisek Kucera (Cze), Jere Karalahti (Fin), Tommmy Salo (Swe)

1999 Martin Rucinsky, (Cze), Saku Koivu (Fin), Teemu Selanne (Fin), Jere Karalahti (Fin), Pavel Kubina (Cze), Tommy Salo (Swe)

2000 Jiri Dopita (Cze), Miroslav Satan (Slv), Tomas Vlasak (Cze), Michal Sykora (Cze), Petteri Nummelin (Fin), Roman Cechmanek (Cze).

Source: *Canadian Press*

World Junior Hockey Medal Winners, 1980–1999

Year	Medalists
1980	Soviet Union, Finland, Sweden
1981	Sweden, Finland, Soviet Union
1982	Canada, Czechoslovakia, Finland
1983	Soviet Union, Czechoslovakia, Canada
1984	Soviet Union, Finland, Czechoslovakia
1985	Canada, Czechoslovakia, Soviet Union
1986	Soviet Union, Canada, United States
1987	Finland, Czechoslovakia, Sweden
1988	Canada, Soviet Union, Finland
1989	Soviet Union, Sweden, Czechoslovakia
1990	Canada, Soviet Union, Czechoslovakia
1991	Canada, Soviet Union, Czechoslovakia
1992	C.I.S., Sweden, United States
1993	Canada, Sweden, Czech-Slovak
1994	Canada, Sweden, Russia
1995	Canada, Russia, Sweden
1996	Canada, Sweden, Russia
1997	Canada, United States, Russia
1998	Finland, Russia, Switzerland
1999	Russia, Canada, Slovakia

Source: *Canadian Press*

Memorial Cup Winners, 1960–2000

(Canadian Junior Hockey Champions)

1960	St. Catharines Tee Pees
1961	St. Michael's Majors
1962	Hamilton Red Wings
1963	Edmonton Oil Kings
1964	Toronto Marlboros
1965	Niagara Falls Flyers
1966	Edmonton Oil Kings
1967	Toronto Marlboros
1968	Niagara Falls Flyers
1969	Montreal Jr. Canadiens
1970	Montreal Jr. Canadiens
1971	Quebec Ramparts
1972	Cornwall Royals
1973	Toronto Marlboros
1974	Regina Pats
1975	Toronto Marlboros
1976	Hamilton Fincups
1977	New Westminster Bruins
1978	New Westminster Bruins
1979	Peterborough Petes
1980	Cornwall Royals
1981	Cornwall Royals
1982	Kitchener Rangers
1983	Portland Winter Hawks
1984	Ottawa 67's
1985	Prince Albert Raiders
1986	Guelph Platers
1987	Medicine Hat Tigers
1988	Medicine Hat Tigers
1989	Swift Current Broncos
1990	Oshawa Generals
1991	Spokane Chiefs
1992	Kamloops Blazers
1993	Sault Ste. Marie Greyhounds
1994	Kamloops Blazers
1995	Kamloops Blazers
1996	Granby Predateurs
1997	Hull Olympiques
1998	Portland Winterhawks
1999	Ottawa 67s
2000	Rimouski Oceanic

Source: *Canadian Amateur Hockey Association*

Memorial Cup, 2000

STANDINGS

Team	W	L	T	GF	GA	PTS
Halifax	2	0	0	12	3	4
Rimouski	2	0	0	10	3	4
Barrie	0	2	0	4	12	0
Kootenay	0	2	0	2	10	0

Semifinal, May 27   Barrie 6, Halifax 3
Final, May 28   Rimouski 6, Barrie 2

Source: *Canadian Press*

Memorial Cup Awards

HAP EMMS MEMORIAL TROPHY
Outstanding Goaltender
1990	Mike Torchia, Kitchener
1991	Felix Potvin, Chicoutimi
1992	Corey Hirsch, Kamloops
1993	Kevin Hodson, Sault Ste. Marie
1994	Eric Fichaud, Chicoutimi
1995	Jason Saal, Detroit
1996	Frederic Deschenes, Granby
1997	Christian Bronsard, Hull
1998	Chris Madden, Guelph
1999	Cory Campbell, Belleville
2000	Sebastien Caron, Rimouski

ED CHYNOWETH TROPHY
Memorial Cup Top Scorer
1996	Philippe Audet, Granby
1997	Christian Dube, Hull
1998	Andrej Podkonicky, Portland
1999	Justin Davis, Ottawa
2000	Ramzi Abid, Halifax

Stafford Smythe Memorial Trophy
Memorial Cup MVP
1990	Iain Fraser, Ottawa
1991	Pat Falloon, Spokane
1992	Scott Niedermayer, Kamloops
1993	Ralph Intranuovo, S.S. Marie
1994	Darcy Tucker, Kamloops
1995	Shane Doan, Kamloops
1996	Cameron Mann, Peterborough
1997	Christian Dube, Hull
1998	Chris Madden, Guelph
1999	Nick Boynton, Ottawa
2000	Brad Richards, Rimouski

Source: *Canadian Press*

Memorial Cup All-Stars, 1990-2000

1990 *Goal:* Mike Torchia, Kitchener. *Defence:* Cory Keenan, Kitchener; Paul O'Hagan, Oshawa. *Forwards:* Eric Lindros, Oshawa; Iain Fraser, Oshawa; Steven Rice, Kitchener.

1991 *Goal:* Félix Potvin, Chicoutimi. *Defence:* Patrice Brisebois, Drummondville; Brad Tiley, Sault Ste. Marie. *Forwards:* Pat Falloon, Spokane; Ray Whitney, Spokane; Brent Thurston, Spokane.

1992 *Goal:* Corey Hirsch, Kamloops. *Defence:* Scott Niedermayer, Kamloops; Drew Bannister, S.S. Marie. *Forwards:* Colin Miller, Sault Ste. Marie; Mike Mathers, Kamloops; Turner Stevenson, Seattle.

1993 *Goal:* Kevin Hodson, Sault Ste. Marie. *Defence:* Michael Gaul, Laval; Drew Bannister, S.S. Marie. *Forwards:* Ralph Intranuovo, S.S. Marie; Chad Penney, Sault Ste. Marie; Martin Lapointe, Laval.

1994 *Goal:* Eric Fichaud, Chicoutimi. *Defence:* Aaron Keller, Kamloops; Nolan Baumgartner, Kamloops. *Forwards:* Darcy Tucker, Kamloops; Alain Côté, Laval; Rod Stevens, Kamloops.

1995 *Goal:* Jason Saal, Detroit. *Defence:* Nolan Baumgartner, Kamloops; Bryan McCabe, Brandon. *Forwards:* Darcy Tucker, Kamloops; Sean Haggerty, Detroit; Shane Doan, Kamloops.

1996 *Goal:* Frédéric Deschenes, Granby. *Defence:* Wade Redden, Brandon; Jason Doig, Granby. *Forwards:* Xavier Delisle, Granby; Philippe Audet, Granby; Cameron Mann, Peterborough.

1997 *Goal:* Christian Bronsard, Hull. *Defence:* Chris Phillips, Lethbridge; Jan Snopek, Oshawa. *Forwards:* Christian Dube, Hull; Byron Ritchie, Lethbridge; Martin Menard, Hull.

1998 *Goal:* Chris Madden, Guelph. *Defence:* Brad Ference, Spokane; Francis Lessard, Val d'Or. *Forwards:* Andrej Podkonicky, Portland; Manny Malhotra, Guelph; Marian Hossa, Portland.

1999 *Goal:* Cory Campbell, Belleville. *Defence:* Matt Kinch, Calgary; Nick Boynton, Ottawa. *Forwards:* Pavel Brendl, Calgary; Glenn Crawford, Belleville; Joe Talbot, Ottawa.

2000 *Goal:* Sebastien Caron, Rimouski. *Defence:* Eric Reitz, Barrie; Michel Periard, Rimouski. *Forwards:* Brad Richards, Rimouski; Juraj Kolnik, Rimouski; Sheldon Keefe, Barrie.

Source: *Canadian Press*

OLYMPICS

Summer Olympics

Location	Date of Competition	Competitors Men	Women	Nations Represented	Unofficial Winners
1896 Athens, Greece	Apr. 6–15	311	0	13	United States
1900 Paris, France	May 20–Oct. 28	1 319	11	22	United States
1904 St. Louis, United States	July 1–Nov. 23	681	6	12	United States
1906[1] Athens, Greece	Apr. 22–May 2	877	7	20	United States
1908 London, England	Apr. 27–Oct. 31	1 999	36	23	United States
1912 Stockholm, Sweden	May 5–July 22	2 490	57	28	United States
1916 Cancelled because of World War I					
1920 Antwerp, Belgium	Apr. 20–Sept. 12	2 543	64	29	United States
1924 Paris, France	May 4–July 27	2 956	136	44	United States
1928 Amsterdam, Netherlands	May 17–Aug. 12	2 724	290	46	United States
1932 Los Angeles, United States	July 30–Aug. 14	1 281	127	37	United States
1936 Berlin, Germany	Aug. 1–16	3 738	328	49	Germany
1940 Cancelled because of World War II					
1944 Cancelled because of World War II					
1948 London, England	July 29–Aug. 14	3 714	385	59	United States
1952 Helsinki, Finland	July 19–Aug.3	4 407	518	69	United States
1956 Melbourne, Australia[2]	Nov. 22–Dec. 8	2 958	384	67	USSR
1960 Rome, Italy	Aug. 25–Sept. 11	4 738	610	83	USSR
1964 Tokyo, Japan	Oct. 10–24	4 457	683	93	United States
1968 Mexico City, Mexico	Oct. 12–27	4 750	781	112	United States
1972 Munich, West Germany	Aug. 26–Sept. 10	5 848	1 299	122	USSR
1976 Montreal, Canada	July 17–Aug. 1	4 834	1 251	92[3]	USSR
1980 Moscow, USSR	July 19–Aug. 3	4 265	1 088	81	USSR
1984 Los Angeles, United States	July 28–Aug. 12	5 458	1 620	141	United States
1988 Seoul, South Korea	Sept. 17–Oct. 2	7 105	2 476	160	USSR
1992 Barcelona, Spain	July 25–Aug. 9	7 555	3 008	172	Unified Team
1996 Atlanta, United States	July 19–Aug. 4	7 000	3 800	197	United States
2000 Sydney, Australia	Sept. 16-Oct. 1				United States
2004 Athens, Greece					

Source: *Canadian Olympic Association*

(n.a.) not available.
(1) 1906 Games were not recognized by the International Olympic Committee.
(2) The equestrian events were held in Stockholm, Sweden, June 10–17, 1956.
(3) Most sources list this figure as 88. Cameroon, Egypt, Morocco and Tunisia all boycotted the 1976 Olympics; however, their athletes had already competed before the boycott was officially announced.

Canada's Olympic Gold Medalists, 1920–2000

■ Winter Olympic Games

1920 Winnipeg Falcons, Ice Hockey (Although the Olympic Winter Games did not begin until 1924, ice hockey was an official event at the 1920 Olympic Games.)

1924 Toronto Granites, Ice Hockey

1928 University of Toronto Graduates, Ice Hockey

1932 Winnipeg Hockey Team, Ice Hockey

1948 Barbara Ann **Scott,** Women's Figure Skating; **RCAF Flyers,** Ice Hockey

1952 Edmonton Mercurys, Ice Hockey

1960 Anne **Heggtveit,** Alpine Skiing, Women's Slalom; Barbara **Wagner** & Robert **Paul,** Pairs Figure Skating

1964 Vic **Emery,** John **Emery,** Douglas **Anakin** & Peter **Kirby,** Four-Man Bobsled

1968 Nancy **Greene,** Alpine Skiing, Women's Giant Slalom

1976 Kathy **Kreiner,** Alpine Skiing, Women's Giant Slalom

1984 Gaetan **Boucher,** Speed Skating, Men's 1 000 m; Gaetan **Boucher,** Speed Skating, Men's 1 500 m

1992 Kerrin **Lee-Gartner,** Alpine Skiing, Women's Downhill; Sylvie **Daigle,** Nathalie **Lambert,** Annie **Perreault,** Angela **Cutrone,** Speed Skating, Women's Short Track Relay; Philippe **Laroche,** Freestyle Skiing, Men's Aerials (demonstration)

1994 Jean-Luc **Brassard,** Freestyle Skiing, Men's Alpine; Myriam **Bedard,** Biathlon, Women's 7.5 km Sprint; Myriam **Bedard,** Biathlon, Women's 15 km

1998 Pierre **Lueders** and Dave **MacEachern,** Bobsled (Two-man); Sandra **Schmirler,** Jan **Betker,** Joan **McCusker,** Marcia **Gudereit** and Atina **Ford,** Curling (Women); Ross **Rebagliati,** Snowboarding (Giant Slalom); Catriona **Le May Doan,** Speed Skating, Long Track (500 metres); Annie **Perreault,** Speed Skating, Short Track (500 metres); Eric **Bedard,** Derrick **Campbell,** Francois **Drolet,** and Marc **Gagnon,** Speed Skating, Short Track (5,000-metre relay).

■ Summer Olympic Games

1900 George **Orton,** 2 500 Steeplechase (Although a Canadian citizen, he represented the University of Pennsylvania; Canada did not officially appear at the Olympics until 1904.)

1904 Étienne **Desmarteau,** 56-pound Weight Throw; George **Lyon,** Golf; **The Galt Association Football Club,** Football (Soccer); **The Winnipeg Shamrocks Lacrosse Club,** Lacrosse 190; William **Sherring,** Marathon (The 1906 Games are not officially recognized by the I.O.C.)

1908 Walter **Ewing,** Trapshooting; Robert **Kerr,** Men's 200 m Run; **The All Canadas,** Lacrosse

1912 George **Goulding,** 10 000 m Walk; George **Hodgson,** Swimming, Men's 400 m Freestyle; George **Hodgson,** Swimming, Men's 1 500 m Freestyle

1920 Albert **Schneider,** Boxing, Welterweight; Earl **Thomson,** Men's 110 m Hurdles

1928 Ethel **Catherwood,** Women's High Jump; Percy **Williams,** Men's 100 m Run; Percy **Williams,** Men's 200 m Run; Women's Relay Team (Fanny **Rosenfeld,** Ethel **Smith,** Florence **Bell** & Myrtle **Cook**), Women's 4 x 100 m Relay

1932 Horace **Gwynne,** Boxing, Bantamweight; Duncan ▶

McNaughton, Men's High Jump

1936 Francis **Amyot**, Canoeing, Canadian Singles 1 000 m

1952 George **Genereux**, Trapshooting

1956 Gerald **Ouellette**, Small-Bore Rifle (Prone); University of British Columbia Team (Archibald **McKinnon**, Lorne **Loomer**, Walter **D'Hondt** & Donald **Arnold**, Rowing, Four-Oared Shell without Coxswain

1964 George **Hungerford** & Roger **Jackson**, Rowing, Pair-Oared Shell without Coxswain

1968 Equestrian Team (James **Elder**, James **Day** & Thomas **Gayford**), Grand Prix (Jumping)

1984 Alex **Baumann**, Swimming, Men's 200 m Individual Medley; Alex **Baumann**, Swimming, Men's 400 m Individual Medley; Sylvie **Bernier**, Women's Spring-board Diving; Larry **Cain**, Canoeing, Canadian Singles 500 m; Victor **Davis**, Swimming, 200 m Breaststroke; Hugh **Fisher** & Alwyn **Morris**, Canoeing, Kayak Pairs 1 000 m; Lori **Fung**, Rhythmic Gymnastics, All-Around; Anne **Otten-brite**, Swimming, Women's 200 m Breast-stroke; Linda **Thom**, Women's Sport Pistol; National Team (Patrick **Turner**, Kevin **Neufeld**, Mark **Evans**, Grant **Main**, Paul **Steele**, J. Michael **Evans**, Dean **Crawford**, Blair **Horn** & Brian **McMahon**), Eight-Oared Shell with Coxswain

1988 Lennox **Lewis**, Boxing, Super heavyweight; Carolyn **Waldo**, Synchronized Swimming, Solo; Carolyn **Waldo** & Michelle **Cameron**, Synchronized Swimming, Duet

1992 Marnie **McBean** and Kathleen **Heddle**, Rowing, Women's Pairs; Mark **McKoy**, Track, Men's 110 m Hurdles; Mark **Tewksbury**, Swimming, Men's 100 m Backstroke; Women's Fours, Rowing (Kirsten **Barnes**, Brenda **Taylor**, Jessica **Monroe**, Kay **Worthington**); Men's Eights, Rowing (John **Wallace**, Bruce **Robertson**, Michael **Forgeron**, Darren **Barber**, Robert **Marland**, Michael **Rascher**, Andy **Crosby**, Derek **Porter**, Terry **Paul**); Women's Eights, Rowing (Kirsten **Barnes**, Brenda **Taylor**, Megan **Delehanty**, Shannon **Crawford**, Marnie **McBean**, Kay **Worthington**, Jessica **Monroe**, Kathleen **Heddle**, Lesley **Thompson**); Sylvie **Frechette**, synchronized swimming

1996 Donovan **Bailey**, Track, Men's 100m; Donovan **Bailey**, Bruny **Surin**, Glenroy **Gilbert**, Robert **Esmie**, Carlton **Chambers**, Men's 4x100 Relay; Marnie **McBean** and Kathleen **Heddle**, Rowing, Women's Double Sculls.

2000 GOLD: Daniel **Igali**, Freestyle Wrestling, 69-kg; Sebastien **Lareau** and Daniel **Nestor**, Tennis, Men's Doubles; Simon **Whitfield**, Men's Triathlon.

SILVER: Caroline **Brunet**, Kayak, Singles 500m; Nicolas **Gill**, Judo, 100-kg; Emilie **Heymans** and Anne **Montminy**, Diving, 10m Synchronized Platform.

BRONZE: Dominique **Bosshart**, Taekwondo, +67-kg; Karen **Cockburn**, Trampoline, Women's; Steve **Giles**, Canoeing, Singles 1 000 m; Anne **Montminy**, Diving, 10 m Platform; Rowing, Women's Eight (Buffy **Alexander**, Laryssa **Biesenthal**, Heather **Davis**, Alison **Korn**, Theresa **Luke**, Heather **McDermid**, Emma **Robinson**, Lesley **Thompson**, Dorota **Urbaniak**); Synchronized Swimming, Women's Team (Lyne **Beaumont**, Claire **Carver-Dias**, Erin **Chan**, Jessica **Chase**, Catherine **Garceau**, Fanny **Letourneau**, Kirstin **Normand**, Jacinthe **Taillon**, Reidun **Tatham**); Curtis **Myden**, Swimming, Men's 400m Individual Medley; Mathieu **Turgeon**, Trampoline, Men's.

Source: *Canadian Press*

Olympic Wrap-Up

As the Sydney Games wound down after two intense weeks of competition, Canada's Olympians bid Australia farewell by unfurling a gigantic Maple Leaf flag and bouncing to the beat of a party watched worldwide.

Flag-bearer for the closing ceremonies, Simon Whitfield, the gold medallist in the triathlon, was the first Canadian athlete to make his way into the packed Stadium Australia. Whitfield sported a huge grin as he proudly waved the Maple Leaf. Other medal-winning marchers included Daniel Igali, who wrestled his way into Canadian Olympic history by winning Canada's first ever Olympic wrestling gold and Caroline Brunet, the flag-bearer in the opening ceremonies, who won silver in the K-1 500 on the final day of competition.

Igali's gold and Brunet's silver boosted Canada's final medal total to 14: three gold, three silver and eight bronze. Igali, from Surrey, B.C., arrived in Canada just six years ago. He defeated Arsen Gitinov of Russia 7–4 to finish the Olympics with a perfect record of 5–0. The 26-year-old grew up in a family of 21 children in Nigeria, a country where wrestling is as much a passion as hockey is in Canada.

Canada's medal total was eight less than the total from the 1996 Games in Atlanta, but the fourth-highest total at any Summer Olympics. The United States topped the medal standings with 97, including 39 gold. Russia was next with 88 (32 gold) and China third at 59 (28 gold). Host Australia was fourth with 58 medals—16 of them gold.

The Canadian team won 22 medals four years ago at Atlanta, including 3 gold—the most for Canada at a non-boycotted Games. This meant the bar of expectation had been raised. Before Atlanta, Canada's best Olympic showing had been 18 medals at Barcelona in 1992. Canada has won 15 medals at a Summer Games three times: in 1932 in Los Angeles; 1928 in Amsterdam and 1908 in London.

Canada ended the Games with 54 top-eight finishes. This compares to 54 in Atlanta, and 53 in Barcelona in 1992 but is less than the 65 at Montreal in 1976. However the medals did not come from the sports Canadians are accustomed to triumphing in: five were won in sports like trampoline (two bronze), taekwondo (a bronze), triathlon (a gold) and synchronized diving (a silver). And our third gold came from the tennis doubles team of Sebastien Lareau and Daniel Nestor, who won Canada's first Olympic gold medal in tennis.

At the track, Canada was shut out for the first time since 1972 in Munich. In boxing, Canadian fighters failed to win a medal for the first time since 1976. In the pool, Curtis Myden won our sole swimming medal—a bronze. The last time Canada emerged with just one swimming medal was 1972. The frustration continued for 53-year-old equestrian Ian Millar of Perth, Ont., who has now competed in seven Olympics but has yet to win a medal. There also were personal disappointments. Carol Montgomery was a favourite to win the women's triathlon but was knocked out of the race after a crash. A respiratory virus prevented Donovan Bailey from defending his Olympic 100-metre title, while Bruny Surin was knocked out of the race with a hamstring injury. Rower Marnie McBean was forced to withdraw due to injury before the Games started. Cyclist Clara Hughes competed despite a nasty virus and track star Katie Anderson was also sidelined. Richard Clarke came into sailing ranked No. 1 in the world in the Finn class, but finished 17th.

Bright spots included diver Alexandre Despatie who finished fourth, despite being only 15 and competing in his first Olympics, while the Canadian men's basketball team finished seventh.

For the rest of the world, it was the Olympics of the Thorpedo, 17-year-old Australian swimmer Ian Thorpe, who earned three gold medals and two silvers. Of Cathy Freeman, the Aboriginal sprinter who shouldered a country's racial burden. Of Eric Moussambani, the swimmer from Equatorial Guinea who barely finished and captured the imagination of an underdog-friendly world. It was an Olympics of whooshes—Thorpe, Susie O'Neill, Jenny Thompson and Inge de Bruijn whooshing through the water. Marion Jones and Freeman and Maurice Greene whooshing along the track. Stacy Dragila and Tatiana Grigorieva whooshing over the bar and claiming their spots in pole-vaulting history. It was an Olympics of firsts, especially for women. Trampoline and taekwondo and synchronized diving made their debuts, as did women's pole vault, women's water polo and women's weightlifting.

Source: *The Canadian Press*

Sydney 2000 Multiple Medal Winners

Six: Alexei Nemov, Russia, artistic gymnastics, 2 gold, 1 silver, 3 bronze.

Five: Marion Jones, US, athletics, 3 gold, 2 bronze.
Ian Thorpe, Australia, swimming, 3 gold, 2 silver.
Dara Torres, US, swimming, 2 gold, 3 bronze.

Four: Inge de Bruijn, Netherlands, swimming, 3 gold, 1 silver.
Gary Hall Jr., US, swimming, 2 gold, 1 silver, 1 bronze.
Michael Klim, Australia, swimming, 2 gold, 2 silver.
Susie O'Neill, Australia, swimming, 1 gold, 3 silver.
Jenny Thompson, US, swimming, 3 gold, 1 bronze.
Pieter van den Hoogenband, Netherlands, swimming, 2 gold, 2 bronze.
Leontien Zijlaard, Netherlands, cycling, 3 gold, 1 silver.

Three: Therese Alshamer, Sweden, swimming, 2 silver, 1 bronze.
Simona Amanar, Romania, artistic gymnastics, 2 gold, 1 bronze.
Svetlana Khorkina, Russia, artistic gymnastics, 1 gold, 2 silver.
Yana Klochkova, Ukraine, swimming, 2 gold, 1 silver.
Lenny Krayzelburg, US, swimming, 3 gold.
Adam Pine, Australia, swimming, 2 gold, 1 silver.
Massimiliano Rosolino, Italy, swimming, 1 gold, 1 silver, 1 bronze.
Florian Rousseau, France, cycling, 2 gold, 1 silver.
Dmitri Saoutine, Russia, diving, 1 gold, 1 silver, 1 bronze.
Petria Thomas, Australia, swimming, 2 silver, 1 bronze.
Matthew Welsh, Australia, swimming, 2 silver, 1 bronze.
Liu Xuan, China, artistic gymnastics, 1 gold, 2 bronze.
Elena Zamolodtchikova, Russia, artistic gymnastics, 2 gold, 1 silver.

Two: 96 athletes, including Anne Montminy of Montreal won two medals

Source: *Canadian Press*

Final Medal Standings of the Summer Olympics, 2000

(Sydney, Australia; September 16 to October 1, 2000)

Country	Gold	Silver	Bronze	Total	Country	Gold	Silver	Bronze	Total
United States	39	25	33	97	Uzbekistan	1	1	2	4
Russia	32	28	28	88	Yugoslavia	1	1	1	3
China	28	16	15	59	Latvia	1	1	1	3
Australia	16	25	17	58	The Bahamas	1	1	0	2
Germany	14	17	26	57	New Zealand	1	0	3	4
France	13	14	11	38	Thailand	1	0	2	3
Italy	13	8	13	34	Estonia	1	0	2	3
Netherlands	12	9	4	25	Croatia	1	0	1	2
Cuba	11	11	7	29	Mozambique	1	0	0	1
Great Britain	11	10	7	28	Colombia	1	0	0	1
Romania	11	6	9	26	Cameroon	1	0	0	1
Korea	8	9	11	28	Brazil	0	6	6	12
Hungary	8	6	3	17	Jamaica	0	4	3	7
Poland	6	5	3	14	Nigeria	0	3	0	3
Japan	5	8	5	18	South Africa	0	2	3	5
Bulgaria	5	6	2	13	Belgium	0	2	3	5
Greece	4	6	3	13	Argentina	0	2	2	4
Sweden	4	5	3	12	Chinese Tapei	0	1	4	5
Norway	4	3	3	10	Morocco	0	1	4	5
Ethiopia	4	1	3	8	North Korea	0	1	3	4
Ukraine	3	10	10	23	Trinidad & Tobago	0	1	1	2
Kazakhstan	3	4	0	7	Saudi Arabia	0	1	1	2
Belarus	3	3	11	17	Moldova	0	1	1	2
Canada	**3**	**3**	**8**	**14**	Vietnam	0	1	0	1
Spain	3	3	5	11	Uruguay	0	1	0	1
Turkey	3	0	1	4	Ireland	0	1	0	1
Iran	3	0	1	4	Georgia	0	0	6	6
Czechoslovakia	2	3	3	8	Portugal	0	0	2	2
Kenya	2	3	2	7	Costa Rica	0	0	2	2
Denmark	2	3	1	6	Qatar	0	0	1	1
Finland	2	1	1	4	Macedonia	0	0	1	1
Austria	2	1	0	3	Sri Lanka	0	0	1	1
Lithuania	2	0	3	5	Kuwait	0	0	1	1
Azerbaijan	2	0	1	3	Kirgistan	0	0	1	1
Slovenia	2	0	0	2	Israel	0	0	1	1
Switzerland	1	6	2	9	Iceland	0	0	1	1
Indonesia	1	3	2	6	India	0	0	1	1
Slovakia	1	3	1	5	Chile	0	0	1	1
Mexico	1	2	3	6	Barbados	0	0	1	1
Algeria	1	1	3	5	Armenia	0	0	1	1

Source: *Canadian Olympic Association*

2000 Olympic Games Results

Held in Sydney, Australia; Sept. 16 to Oct. 1, 2000
(*Olympic record; **Olympic and World record)

	Event	Date	2000 Results
Archery	Men's Individual	Sept. 16, 18, 20	1. Simon Fairweather, Australia 2. Victor Wunderle, United States 3. Wietse van Alten, Netherlands
	Men's Team	Sept. 16, 22	1. Korea 2. Italy 3. United States
	Women's Individual	Sept. 17, 19	1. Mi-Jin Yun, Korea 2. Nam-Soon Kim, Korea 3. Soo-Nyung Kim, Korea
	Women's Team	Sept. 21	1. Korea 2. Ukraine 3. Germany
Athletics (Track and Field)	Men's 100-Metre	Sept. 22, 23	1. Maurice Greene, United States 2. Ato Boldon, Trinidad & Tobago 3. Obadele Thomoson, Barbados 5. (prelim. heat) Nicolas Macrozonaris, Laval, Que. 8. (prelim. heat) Donovan Bailey, Oakville, Ont. 8. (prelim. heat) Bruny Surin, Montreal, Que.
	Men's 200-metre	Sept. 27, 28	1. Konstantinos Kenteris, Greece 2. Darren Campbell, Britain 3. Ato Bolden, Trinidad & Tobago 6. (prelim. heat) Pierre Browne, Toronto, Ont.
	Men's 400-metre	Sept. 22, 23, 24, 25	1. Michael Johnson, United States 2. Alvin Harrison, United States 3. Gregory Haughton, Jamaica
	Men's 800-metre	Sept. 23, 25, 27	1. Nils Schumann, Germany 2. Wilson Kipketer, Denmark 3. Aissa Said Guerni, Algeria 4. (prelim. heat) Zach Whitmarsh, Victoria, BC
	Men's 1 500-metre	Sept. 25, 27, 29	1. Noah Ngeny, Kenya 2. Hicham El Guerrouj, Morocco 3. Bernard Lagat, Kenya 5. (final) Kevin Sullivan, Brantford, Ont.

Olympics

Event	Date	2000 Results
Men's 5 000-metre	Sept. 27, 28, 30	1. Millon Wolde, Ethiopia 2. Ali Saidi-Sief, Algeria 3. Brahim Lahlafi, Morocco
Men's 10 000-metre	Sept. 22, 25	1. Haile Gebrselassie, Ethiopia 2. Paul Tergat, Kenya 3. Assefa Mezgebu, Ethiopia **12. (prelim. heat) Sean Kaley, Ottawa, Ont.** **15. (prelim. heat) Jeff Schiebler, Vancouver, BC**
Men's 110-metre Hurdles	Sept. 24, 25	1. Anier Garcia, Cuba 2. Terrence Trammell, United States 3. Mark Crear, United States
Men's 400-metre Hurdles	Sept. 24, 25, 27	1. Angelo Taylor, United States 2. Hadi Souan Somayli, Saudi Arabia 3. Llewellyn Herbert, South Africa
Men's 3 000-metre Steeplechase	Sept. 27, 29	1. Reuben Kosgei, Kenya 2. Wilson Bolt Kipketer, Kenya 3. Ali Ezzine, Morocco
Men's 20K Walk	Sept. 22	1. Robert Korzeniowski, Poland 2. Noe Hernandez, Mexico 3. Vladimir Andreyev, Russia **24. (final) Arturo Huerta, Toronto, Ont.** **26. (final) Tim Berrett, Edmonton, alta.**
Men's 50-Kilometre Walk	Sept. 29	1. Robert Korzeniowski, Poland 2. Aigars Fadejevs, Latvia 3. Joel Sanchez, Mexico **Tim Berrett, Edmonton, Alta and Arturo Huerta, Toronto, Ont. (both disqualified in final)**
Men's 4x100 Relay	Sept. 29, 30	1. United States 2. Brazil 3. Cuba **6. (prelim. heat) Canada**
Men's 4x400 Relay	Sept. 29, 30	1. United States 2. Nigeria 3. Jamaica
Men's Decathalon	Sept. 27, 28	1. Erki Nool, Estonia 2. Roman Sebrle, Czech Republic 3. Chris Huffins, United States
Men's High Jump	Sept. 22, 24	1. Sergey Kliugin, Russia 2. Javier Sotomayor, Cuba 3. Abderrahmane Hammad, Algeria **6. (final) Mark Boswell, Brampton, Ont.** **12. (final) Kwaku Boateng, Montreal, Que.**

Event	Date	2000 Results
Men's Long Jump	Sept. 25, 28	1. Ivan Pedroso, Cuba 2. Jai Taurima, Australia 3. Roman Schurenko, Ukraine 16. (prelim. heat) Richard Duncan, St. Catherines, Ont. 20. (prelim. heat) Ian Lowe, Montreal, Que.
Men's Triple Jump	Sept. 23, 25	1. Jonathan Edwards, Britain 2. Yoel Garcia, Cuba 3. Denis Kapustin, Russia
Men's Discus	Sept. 24, 25	1. Virgilijus Alekna, Lithuania 2. Lars Riedel, Germany 3. Frantz Kruger, South Africa 6. (final) Jason Tunks, London, Ont.
Men's Hammer	Sept. 23, 24	1. Szymon Ziolkowski, Poland 2. Nicola Vizzoni, Italy 3. Igor Astapkovich, Belarus
Men's Javelin	Sept. 22, 23	1. Jan Zelezny, Czech Republic 2. Steve Backley, Britain 3. Sergey Makarov, Russia
Men's Pole Vault	Sept. 23, 27, 29	1. Nick Hysong, United States 2. Lawrence Johnson, United States 3. Maksim Tarasov, Russia
Men's Shot Put	Sept. 22, 29	1. Arsi Harju, Finland 2. Adam Nelson, United States 3. John Godina, United States 13. (prelim. heat) Brad Snyder, Windsor, Ont.
Men's Marathon	Oct. 1	1. Gezahgne Abera, Ethiopia 2. Eric Wainaina, Kenya 3. Tesfaye Tola, Ethiopia 44. (final) Bruce Deacon, Victoria, BC
Women's 100-Metre	Sept. 22, 23	1. Marion Jones, United States 2. Ekaterini Thanou, Greece 3. Tanya Lwarence, Jamaica 4. (prelim. heat) Esi Benyarku, Toronto, Ont. 6. (prelim. heat) Martha Adussi, Toronto, Ont.
Women's 200-metre	Sept. 27, 28	1. Marion Jones, United States 2. Pauline Davis-Thompson, Bahamas 3. Susanthika Jayasinghe, Sri Lanka

Event	Date	2000 Results
Women's 400-metre	Sept. 22, 23, 25	1. Cathy Freeman, Australia 2. Lorraine Graham, Jamaica 3. Katharine Merry, Britain **5. (prelim. heat) Ladonna Antoine, Regina, Sask.** **8. (prelim. heat) Foy Williams, Toronto, Ont.**
Women's 800-metre	Sept. 22, 23, 25	1. Maria Mutola, Mozambique 2. Stephanie Graf, Austria 3. Kelly Holmes, Britain
Women's 1 500-metre	Sept. 27, 28, 30	1. Nouria Merah-Benida, Algeria 2. Violeta Szekely, Romania 3. Gabriela Szabo, Romania **Leah Pells, Langley, BC (did not finish)**
Women's 5 000-metre	Sept. 22, 25	1. Gabriela Szabo, Romania 2. Sonia O'Sullivan, Ireland 3. Gete Wami, Ethiopia
Women's 10 000-metre	Sept. 27, 30	1. Derartu Tulu, Ethiopia 2. Gete Wami, Ethiopia 3. Fernanda Ribeiro, Portugal **19. (heat—eliminated) Tina Connelly, Port Coquitlam, BC** **Carol Montgomery, North Vancouver, BC (did not start)**
Women's 100-metre Hurdles	Sept. 25, 27	1. Olga Shishigina, Kazakhstan 2. Glory Alozie, Nigeria 3. Melissa Morrison, United States **Perdita Felicien, Pickering, Ont. (eliminated, first-round)** **Katie Anderson, Toronto, Ont. (injured)**
Women's 400-metre Hurdles	Sept. 24, 26, 27	1. Irina Privalova, Russia 2. Deon Hemmings, Jamaica 3. Nouzha Bidouane, Morocco **(did not start) Karlene Haughton, Calgary, Alta**
Women's 20K Walk	Sept. 28	1. Liping Wang, China 2. Kjersti Plaetzer, Norway 3. Maria Vasco, Spain **Janice McCaffrey, Calgary, Alta (disqualified)**
Women's 4x100 Relay	Sept. 29, 30	1. Bahamas 2. Jamaica 3. United States **5. (prelim. heat) Canada** **15. (prelim. heat) Canada**

	Event	Date	2000 Results
	Women's 4x400 Relay	Sept. 29, 30	1. United States 2. Jamaica 3. Russia
	Women's Heptathlon	Sept. 23, 24	1. Denise Lewis, Britain 2. Yelena Prokhorova, Russia 3. Natalya Sazanovich, Belarus
	Women's High Jump	Sept. 28, 30	1. Yelena Yelesina, Russia 2. Hestrie Cloete, South Africa 3. Kajsa Bergqvist, Sweden 3. Oana Pantelimon, Romania
	Women's Long Jump	Sept. 27, 29	1. Heike Drechsler, Germany 2. Fiona May, Italy 3. Marion Jones, United States
	Women's Triple Jump	Sept. 22, 24	1. Tereza Marinova, Bulgaria 2. Tatyana Lebedeva, Russia 3. Olena Hovorova, Ukraine
	Women's Discus	Sept. 25, 27	1. Ellina Zvereva, Belarus 2. Anastasia Kelesidou, Greece 3. Irina Yatchenko, Belarus
	Women's Hammer	Sept. 27, 29	1. Kamila Skolimowska, Poland 2. Olga Kuzenkova, Russia 3. Kirsten Muenchow, Germany **13. (prelim. round) Michelle Fournier, Pierrefonds, Que.**
	Women's Javelin	Sept. 29, 30	1. Trine Hattestad, Norway 2. Mirella Maniani-Tzelli, Greece 3. Osleidys Menendez, Cuba
	Women's Pole Vault	Sept. 23, 25	1. Stacy Dragila, United States 2. Tatiana Grigorieva, Australia 3. Vala Flosadottir, Iceland
	Women's Shot Put	Sept. 27, 28	1. Yanina Korolchik, Belarus 2. Larisa Peleshenko, Russia 3. Astrid Kumbernuss, Germany
	Women's Marathon	Sept. 24	1. Naoko Takahashi, Japan 2. Lidia Simon, Romania 3. Joyce Chepchumba, Kenya
Badminton	Men's Singles	Sept. 17, 18, 19, 20	1. Xinpeng Ji, China 2. Henra Wan, Indonesia 3. Xuanze Xia, China

	Event	Date	2000 Results
	Men's Doubles	Sept. 16, 17, 18	1. Indonesia 2. Korea 3. Korea **Canada (eliminated second-round)**
	Women's Singles	Sept. 16, 17, 18, 19	1. Zhichao Gong, China 2. Camilla Martin, Denmark 3. Zhaoying Ye, China **Milaine Cloutier, Granby, Que. (eliminated second-round)**
	Women's Doubles	Sept. 18, 19, 20	1. China 2. China 3. China **Canada (eliminated)**
	Mixed Doubles	Sept. 16, 17, 18	1. China 2. Indonesia 3. Britain
Baseball		Sept. 17, 18, 19, 20	1. United States 2. Cuba 3. Korea
Basketball	**Men's**	Sept. 17, 19, 21, 23	1. United States 2. France 3. Lithuania **7. (final) Canada**
	Women's	Sept. 16, 18, 20, 22	1. United States 2. Australia 3. Brazil
Boxing	**Men's 48 kg**	Sept. 17, 22, 26, 28, 30	1. Brahim Asloum, France 2. Rafael Lozano Munoz, Spain 3. Un Chol Kim, North Korea 3. Maikro Romero Esquirol, Cuba
	Men's 51 kg	Sept. 19, 24, 27, 29, Oct. 1	1. Wijan Ponlid, Thailand 2. Bulat Jumadilov, Kazakhstan 3. Vladimir Sidorenko, Ukraine 3. Jerome Thomas, France
	Men's 54 kg	Sept. 16, 21, 26, 28, 30	1. Guillermo Ortiz, Cuba 2. Raimkoul Malakhbekov, Russia 3. Serguey Daniltchenko, Ukraine 3. Clarence Vinson, United States
	Men's 57 kg	18, 23, 27, 29, Oct. 1	1. Bekzat Sattarkhanov, Kazakhstan 2. Ricardo Juarez, United States 3. Kamil Dzamalutdinov, Russia 3. Tahar Tamsamani, Morocco

Event	Date	2000 Results
Men's 60 kg	Sept. 17, 22, 26, 28, 30	1. Mario Kindelan, Cuba 2. Andriy Kotelnyk, Ukraine 3. Cristian Benitez, Mexico 3. Alexandr Maletin, Russia
Men's 63.5 kg	Sept. 20, 24, 27, 29, Oct. 1	1. Mahamadkadyz Abdullaev, Uzbekistan 2. Ricardo Williams, United States 3. Mohamed Allalou, Algeria 3. Diogenes Luna Martinez, Cuba
Men's 67 kg	Sept. 16, 21, 26, 28, 30	1. Oleg Saitov, Russia 2. Sergey Dotsenko, Ukraine 3. Vitalii Grusac, Moldova 3. Dorel Simion, Romania
Men's 71 kg	Sept. 19, 23, 27, 29, Oct. 1	1. Yermakhan Ibraimov, Kazakhstan 2. Marin Simion, Romania 3. Jermaine Taylor, United States 3. Pornchai Thongburan, Thailand **Scotty MacIntosh, Sydney, NS (eliminated)**
Men's 75 kg	Sept. 18, 22, 26, 28, 30	1. Jorge Gutierrez, Cuba 2. Gaidarbek Gaidarbekov, Russia 3. Vugar Alekperov, Azerbaijan 3. Zsolt Erdei, Hungary
Men's 81 kg	Sept. 20, 24, 27, 29, Oct. 1	1. Alexander Lebziak, Russia 2. Rudolf Kraj, Czech Republic 3. Andri Fedtchouk, Ukraine 3. Sergei Mikhailov, Uzbekistan
Men's 91 kg	Sept. 21, 23, 26, 27, 28, 29, 30, Oct. 1	1. Felix Savon, Cuba 2. Sultanahmed Ibzagimov, Russia 3. Sebastian Kober, Germany 3. Vladimir Tchantouria, Georgia
Men's +91 kg	Sept. 23, 27, 29, Oct. 1	1. Audley Harrison, Britain 2. Mukhatarkhan Dildabekov, Kazakhstan 3. Rustam Saidov, Uzbekistan 3. Paulo Vidoz, Italy **Artur Biknowski, Kitchener, Ont.** **(outclassed, second-round)**

Canoe-Kayak

Event	Date	2000 Results
Men's Canoe Single 500	Sept. 27, 29, Oct. 1	1. Gyorgy Kolonics, Hungary 2. Maxim Opalev, Russia 3. Andreas Dittmer, Germany **4. Maxime Boilard, Lac-Beauport, Que.**
Men's Canoe Single 1000	Sept. 26, 28, 30	1. Andreas Dittmer, Germany 2. Ledys Frank Balceiro, Cuba **3. Steve Giles, Canada**

Event	Date	2000 Results
Men's Canoe Double 500	Sept. 27, 29, Oct.1	1. Hungary 2. Poland 3. Romania
Men's Canoe Double 1000	Sept. 26, 28, 30	1. Romania 2. Cuba 3. Germany **7. (prelim. heat) Canada**
Men's Kayak Single 500	Sept. 27, 29, Oct. 1	1. Knut Holman Norway 2. Petar Merkov Bulgaria 3. Michael Kolganov Israel **7. (prelim. heat) Mihai Apostol, Dartmouth, NS**
Men's Kayak Single 1000	Sept. 26, 28, 30	1. Knut Holmann, Norway 2. Petar Merkov, Bulgaria 3. Tim Brabants, Britain
Men's Kayak Double 500	Sept. 27, 29, Oct. 1	1. Hungary 2. Australia 3. Germany
Men's Kayak Double 1000	Sept. 26, 28, 30	1. Italy 2. Sweden 3. Hungary
Men's Kayak Fours 1000	Sept. 26, 28, 30	1. Hungary 2. Germany 3. Poland
Women's Kayak Single 500	Sept. 27, 29, Oct. 1	1. Josefa Idem Guerrini, Italy **2. Caroline Brunet, Canada** 3. Katrin Borchert, Australia **13. (final) Margaret Langford, Lions Bay, BC**
Women's Kayak Double 500	Sept. 27, 29, Oct. 1	1. Germany 2. Hungary 3. Poland **5. (final) Canada**
Women's Kayak Fours 500	Sept. 26, 28, 30	1. Germany 2. Hungary 3. Romania **9. (final) Canada**
Men's Slalom Canoe Singles	Sept. 17, 18	1. Tony Estanguet, France 2. Michal Martikan, Slovakia 3. Juraj Mincik, Slovakia

Event	Date	2000 Results
Men's Slalom Canoe Doubles	Sept. 19, 20	1. Slovakia 2. Poland 3. Czech Republic
Men's Slalom Kayak Singles	Sept. 19, 20	1. Thomas Schmidt, Germany 2. Paul Ratcliffe, Britain 3. Pierpaolo Ferrazzi, Italy
Women's Slalom Kayak Singles	Sept. 17, 18	1. Stepanka Hilgertova, Czech Republic 2. Brigitte Guibal, France 3. Anne-Lise Bardet, France

Cycling

Event	Date	2000 Results
Men's Sprint	Sept. 18, 19, 20	1. Marty Nothstein, United States 2. Florian Rousseau, France 3. Jens Fiedler, Germany
Men's Points Race	Sept. 20	1. Juan Llaneras, Spain 2. Milton Wynants, Uruguay 3. Alexey Markov, Russia **9. Mike Walton, Vancouver, BC**
Men's Individual Pursuit	Sept. 16, 17	1. Robert Bartko, Germany 2. Jens Lehmann, Germany 3. Brad McGee, Australia
Men's Road Race	Sept. 27	1. Jan Ullrich, Germany 2. Alexandre Vinokourov, Kazakhstan 3. Andreas Kloeden, Germany **16. (final) Gord Fraser, Nepean, Ont.** **72. (final) Brian Walton, Vancouver, BC** **Czeslaw Lukaszewicz, Quebec City, Que. (did not finish)**
Men's Individual Time Trial	Sept. 30	1. Viacheslav Ekimov, Russia 2. Jan Ullrich, Germany 3. Lance Armstrong, United States **20. (final) Eric Wohlberg, Levack Ont.**
Men's Mountain Bike	Sept. 24	1. Miguel Martinez, France 2. Filip Meirhaeghe, Belgium 3. Christoph Sauser, Switzerland **9. (final) Geoff Kabush, Victoria, BC** **14. (final) Roland Green, Victoria, BC**
Men's 1km Time Trial	Sept. 16	1. Jason Queally, Britain 2. Stefan Nimke, Germany 3. Shane Kelly, Australia
Men's Team Pursuit	Sept. 18, 19	1. Germany 2. Ukraine 3. Britain

	Event	Date	2000 Results
	Men's Olympic Sprint	Sept. 17	1. France 2. Britain 3. Australia
	Men's Keirin	Sept. 21	1. Florian Rousseau, France 2. Gary Neiwand, Australia 3. Jens Fiedler, Germany
	Men's Madison	Sept. 21	1. Australia 2. Belgium 3. Italy
	Women's Sprint	Sept. 18, 19, 20	1. Felicia Ballanger, France 2. Oxana Grichina, Russia 3. Iryna Yanovych, Ukraine **7. Tanya Dubincoff, Winnipeg, Man.**
	Women's Points Race	Sept. 21	1. Antonella Bellutti, Italy 2. Leontin Zijlaard, Netherlands 3. Olga Slioussareva, Russia
	Women's Individual Pursuit	Sept. 17, 18	1. Leontien Zijlaard, Netherlands 2. Marion Clignet, France 3. Yvonne McGregor, Britain
	Women's Road Race	Sept. 26	1. Leontien Zijlaard, Netherlands 2. Hanka Kupfernagel, Germany 3. Diana Ziliute, Lithuania
	Women's Individual Time Trial	Sept. 30	1. Felicia Ballanger, France 2. Michelle Ferris, Australia 3. Cuihua Jiang, China **6. (final) Clara Hughes, Winnipeg, Man.** **15. (final) Genevieve Jeanson, Lachine, Que.**
	Women's Mountain Bike	Sept. 24	1. Paola Pezzo, Italy 2. Barbara Blatter, Switzerland 3. Margarita Fullana, Spain **5. Alison Sydor, Vancouver, BC** **8. Chrissy Redden, Campbellville, Ont.** **19. Lesley Tomlinson, Victoria, BC**
Diving	**Men's Platform**	Sept. 29, 30	1. Liang Tian, China 2. Jia Hu, China 3. Dmitri Saoutine, Russia **4. (final) Alexander Despatie, Montreal, Que.** **17. (prelim. round) Christ Kalec, Laval, Que.**

	Event	Date	2000 Results
	Men's Springboard	Sept. 25, 26	1. Ni Xiong, China 2. Fernando Platas, Mexico 3. Dmitri Saoutine, Russia **19. (prelim. round) Jeff Liberty, Winnipeg, Man.**
	Men's Springboard Synchronized	Sept. 25, 26, 28	1. China 2. Russia 3. Australia
	Men's Platform Synchronized	Sept. 23	1. Russia 2. China 3. Germany
	Women's Platform	Sept. 22, 24	1. Laura Wilkinson, United States 2. Na Li, China **3. Anne Montminy, Canada** **5. (final) Emily Haymans, Greenfield Park, Que.**
	Women's Springboard	Sept. 27, 28	1. Mingxia Fu China 2. Jingjing Guo China 3. Doerte Lindner Germany **10. (final) Blythe Hartley, Vancouver, BC** **20. (prelim. round) Eryn Bulmer, Edmonton, Alta**
	Women's Platform Synchronized	Sept. 28	1. China **2. Canada** 3. Australia
	Women's Springboard Synchronized	Sept. 23	1. Russia 2. China 3. Ukraine **5. Canada**
Equestrian	Individual Dressage	Sept. 26, 27	1. Anky van Grunsven, Netherlands 2. Isabell Werth, Germany 3. Ulla Salzgeber, Germany
	Individual Jumping	Sept. 25, 28, Oct. 1	1. Jeroen Dubbeldam, Netherlands 2. Albert Voorn, Netherlands 3. Khaled Al Eid, Saudi Arabia **13. (final) Ian Miller, Perth, Ont.** **15. Jonathan Asselin, Calgary, Alta** **62. (prelim. round) John Pearce, Stouffville, Ont.** **63. (prelim. round) Jay Hayes, Cheltenham, Ont.**

	Event	Date	2000 Results
	Individual Three Day Event	Sept. 20, 21, 22	1. David O'Connor, United States 2. Andrew Hoy, Australia 3. Mark Todd, New Zealand **22. (final) Bruce Mandeville, New Westminster, BC** **Wyn St. John, Edmonton, Alta (withdrew)**
	Team Dressage	Sept. 26, 27	1. Germany 2. Netherlands 3. United States
	Team Jumping	Sept. 28	1. Germany 2. Switzerland 3. Brazil **9. (final) Canada**
	Team Three Day Event	Sept. 16, 17, 18, 19	1. Australia 2. Britain 3. United States
Fencing	**Men's Individual Epee**	Sept. 16	1. Pavel Kolobkov, Russia 2. Hugues Obry, France 3. Sang-Ki Lee, Korea
	Men's Individual Foil	Sept. 20	1. Young Ho Kim, Korea 2. Ralf Bissdorf, Germany 3. Dmitri Chevtchenko, Russia
	Men's Individual Sabre	Sept. 21	1. Mihai Claudiu Covaliu, Romania 2. Mathieu Gourdain, France 3. Wiradech Kothny, Germany
	Men's Team Epee	Sept. 18	1. Italy 2. France 3. Cuba
	Men's Team Foil	Sept. 22	1. France 2. China 3. Italy
	Men's Team Sabre	Sept. 24	1. Russia 2. France 3. Germany
	Women's Individual Epee	Sept. 17	1. Timea Nagy, Hungary 2. Gianna Buerki, Switzerland 3. Laura Flessel-Colovic, France **Sherraine Schalm, Brooks, Alta (eliminated)**

	Event	Date	2000 Results
	Women's Individual Foil	Sept. 21	1. Valentina Vezzali, Italy 2. Rita Koenig, Germany 3. Giovanna Trillini, Italy **Jujie Luan, Edmonton, Alta (eliminated)**
	Women's Team Epee	Sept. 19	1. Russia 2. Switzerland 3. China
	Women's Team Foil	Sept. 23	1. Italy 2. Poland 3. Germany **Canada (eliminated)**
Field Hockey	Men's	Sept. 16–21, 23–30	1. Netherlands 2. Korea 3. Australia **10. (final) Canada**
	Women's	Sept. 16–22, 24	1. Australia 2. Argentina 3. Netherlands
Gymnastics	Men's, Artistic All-around	Sept. 20	1. Alexei Nemov, Russia 2. Wei Yang, China 3. Oleksandr Beresh, Ukraine
	Men's Team Medal Event	Sept. 18	1. China 2. Ukraine 3. Russia
	Men's Floor	Sept. 24	1. Igors Vihrovs, Latvia 2. Alexei Nemov, Russia 3. Iordan Iovtchev, Bulgaria
	Men's Horizontal Bar	Sept. 25	1. Alexei Nemov, Russia 2. Benjamin Varonian, France 3. Joo Hyung Lee, Korea
	Men's Parallel Bar	Sept. 25	1. Xiaopeng Li, China 2. Joo Hyung Lee, Korea 3. Alexi Nemov, Russia
	Men's Pommel Horse	Sept. 24	1. Marius Urzica, Romania 2. Eric Poujade, France 3. Alexei Nemov, Russia
	Men's Rings	Sept. 24	1. Szilveszter Csollany, Hungary 2. Dimosthenis Tampakos, Greece 3. Iordan Iovtchev, Bulgaria

	Event	Date	2000 Results
	Men's Trampoline	Sept. 23	1. Alexandre Moskalenko, Russia 2. Ji Wallace, Australia **3. Mathieu Turgeon, Canada**
	Men's Vault	Sept. 25	1. Gervasio Deferr, Spain 2. Alexev Bondarenko, Russia 3. Leszek Blanik, Poland
	Women's Artistic All-around	Sept 21	1. Andreaa Raducan, Romania 2. Simona Amanar, Romania 3. Maria Olaru, Romania **16. (final) Kate Richardson, Coquitlam, BC** **34. (final) Yvonne Tousek, Cambridge, Ont.**
	Women's Team Medal Event	Sept. 19	1. Romania 2. Russia 3. China
	Women's Balance Beam	Sept. 25	1. Xuan Liu, China 2. Ekaterina Lobazniouk, Russia 3. Elena Prodounova, Russia
	Women's Floor	Sept. 25	1. Elena Zamolodtchikova, Russia 2. Svetlana Khorkina, Russia 3. Simona Amanar, Romania
	Women's Rhythmic, Group	Sept. 28, 30	1. Russia 2. Belarus 3. Greece
	Women's Rhythmic, Individual	Sept. 28, 29, 30	1. Yulia Barsukova, Russia 2. Yulia Raskina, Belarus 3. Alina Kabaeva, Russia **18. (prelim. round) Emilie Livingston, Toronto, Ont.**
	Women's Trampoline	Sept. 22	1. Irina Karavaeva, Russia 2. Oxana Tsyhuleva, Ukraine **3. Karen Cockburn, Canada**
	Women's Uneven Bars	Sept. 24	1. Svetlana Khorkina, Russia 2. Jie Ling, China 3. Yun Yang, China
	Women's Vault	Sept. 24	1. Elena Zamolodtchikova, Russia 2. Andreaa Raducan, Romania 3. Ekaterina Lobazniouk, Russia
Handball	Men's Team	Sept. 16, 18, 20 22, 24, 26, 29, 30	1. Russia 2. Sweden 3. Spain

	Event	Date	2000 Results
	Women's Team	Sept. 17, 19, 21, 23, 25, 28, 29, 30	1. Denmark 2. Hungary 3. Norway
Judo	Men's 60 kg	Sept. 16	1. Tadahiro Nomura, Japan 2. Bu-Kyung Jung, Korea 3. Manolo Poulot, Cuba 3. Aidyn Smagulov, Kyrgyzstan
	Men's 66 kg	Sept. 17	1. Kosei Inoue, Japan **2. Nicolas Gill, Canada** 3. Iouri Stepkine, Russia 3. Stephane Traineau, France
	Men's 73 kg	Sept. 18	1. Giuseppe Maddaloni, Italy 2. Tiago Camilo, Brazil 3. Anatoly Laryukov, Belarus 3. Vsevolods Zelonijs, Latvia
	Men's 81 kg	Sept. 19	1. Makoto Takimoto, Japan 2. In-Chul Cho, Korea 3. Aleksei Budolin, Estonia 3. Nuno Delgado, Portugal
	Men's 90 kg	Sept. 20	1. Mark Huizinga, Netherlands 2. Carlos Honorato, Brazil 3. Frederic Demontfaucon, France 3. Ruslan Mashurenko, Ukraine
	Men's 100 kg	Sept. 21, 22	1. Kosei Inoue, Japan **2. Nicolas Gill, Canada** 3. Iouri Stepkine, Russia 3. Stephane Traineau, France
	Men's +100 kg	Sept. 22	1. David Douillet, France 2. Shinichi Shinohara, Japan 3. Selim Tataroglu, Turkey 3. Tamerlan Tmenov, Russia
	Women's 48 kg	Sept. 16	1. Ryoko Tamura, Japan 2. Lioubov Brouletova, Russia 3. Anna-Maria Gradante, Germany 3. Ann Simons, Belgium
	Women's 52 kg	Sept. 17	1. Legna Verdecia, Cuba 2. Noriko Narazaki, Japan 3. Sun Hui Kye, North Korea 3. Yuxiang Liu, China

	Event	Date	2000 Results
	Women's 57 kg	Sept. 18	1. Isabel Fernandez, Spain 2. Driulys Gonzalez, Cuba 3. Kie Kusakabe, Japan 3. Maria Pekli, Australia **Michelle Buckingham, Ottawa, Ont. (eliminated)**
	Women's 63 kg	Sept. 19	1. Severine Vandenhende, France 2. Shufang Li, China 3. Sung-Sook Jung, Korea 3. Gella Vandecaveye, Belgium **Sophie Roberge, Beauport, Que. (eliminated)**
	Women's 70 kg	Sept. 20	1. Sibelis Veranes, Cuba 2. Kate Howey, Britain 3. Min-Sun Cho, Korea 3. Ylenia Scapin, Italy
	Women's 78 kg	Sept. 21, 22	1. Lin Tang, China 2. Celine Lebrun, France 3. Simona Marcela Richter, Romania 3. Emanuela Pierantozzi, Italy **Kimberly Ribble, Hamilton, Ont. (injured)**
	Women's +78 kg	Sept. 22	1. Hua Yuan, China 2. Daima Mayelis Beltran, Cuba 3. Seon-Young Kim, Korea 3. Mayumi Yamashita, Japan
Pentathlon	Men's	Sept. 30th.	1. Dmitry Svatkovsky, Russia 2. Gabor Balogh, Hungary 3. Pavel Dovgal, Belarus
	Women's	Oct. 1st	1. Stephanie Cook, Britain 2. Emily de Riel, United States 3. Kate Allenby, Britain
Rowing	Men's Single sculls	Sept. 17, 19, 21	1. Rob Waddell 2. Xeno Mueller 3. Marcel Hacker **4. Derek Porter, Victoria, BC**
	Men's Double sculls	Sept. 17, 19, 21	1. Slovenia 2. Norway 3. Italy **4. (prelim. heat) Canada**
	Men's Coxless pair	Sept. 17, 19, 21	1. France 2. United States 3. Australia

	Event	Date	2000 Results
	Men's Coxless fours	Sept. 17, 19, 21	1. Britain 2. Italy 3. Australia
	Men's Lightweight	Sept. 18, 20, 22	1. Poland 2. Italy 3. France
	Men's Lightweight four	Sept. 18, 20, 22	1. France 2. Australia 3. Denmark **4. (prelim. heat) Canada**
	Men's Quad sculls	Sept. 18, 20, 22	1. Italy 2. Netherlands 3. Germany
	Men's Eights	Sept. 18, 20, 23, 24	1. Britain 2. Australia 3. Croatia **3. (prelim. heat) Canada**
	Women's Single sculls	Sept. 17, 19, 21	1. Ekaterina Karsten, Belarus 2. Rumyana Neykova, Bulgaria 3. Katrin Rutschow, Germany
	Women's Double sculls	Sept. 17, 19, 22, 23	1. Germany 2. Netherlands 3. Lithuania
	Women's Coxless pair	Sept. 17, 19, 22, 23	1. Romania 2. Australia 3. United States **4. (final) Canada**
	Women's Lightweight Double sculls	Sept. 18, 20, 22, 23, 24	1. Romania 2. Germany 3. United States **5. (prelim. heat) Canada**
	Women's Quad sculls	Sept. 18, 20, 23, 24	1. Germany 2. Britain 3. Russia
	Women's Eights	Sept. 18, 20, 24	1. Romania 2. Netherlands **3. Canada**
Sailing	**Open, Laser**	Sept. 20, 21, 23, 26, 28, 29	1. Ben Ainslie, Britain 2. Robert Scheidt, Brazil 3. Michael Blackburn, Australia **24. (final) Marty Essig, Carlisle, Ont.**

	Event	Date	2000 Results
	Star	Sept. 23, 25, 26, 27, 28, 30	1. United States 2. Britain 3. Brazil **5. (final) Canada**
	Tornado	Sept. 17, 18, 19, 21, 22, 24	1. Austria 2. Australia 3. Germany
	3-Person Keelboat (Soling)	Sept. 17, 18, 19, 23, 24, 25, 26, 27, 29, 30	1. Austria 2. Australia 3. Germany **13. (prelim. round) Canada**
	High Performance Dinghy (49er)	Sept. 18, 19, 20, 22, 23, 25	1. Finland 2. Britain 3. United States
	Men's Finn	Sept. 23, 25, 26, 27, 28, 30	1. Ian Percy, Britain 2. Luca Devoti, Italy 3. Fredrik Loof, Sweden **17. (final) Richard Clarke, Toronto, Ont.**
	Men's Mistral	Sept. 17, 18, 19, 20, 21, 22, 24, 25, 27	1. Christoph Sieber, Austria 2. Carlos Espinola, Argentina 3. Aaron McIntosh, New Zealand
	Men's 470	Sept. 20, 21, 22, 24, 25, 27	1. Australia 2. United States 3. Argentina
	Women's Europe	Sept. 20, 21, 23, 26, 28, 29	1. Shirley Robertson, Britain 2. Margriet Matthysse, Netherlands 3. Serena Amato, Argentina **11. (final) Beth Calkin, West Vancouver, BC**
	Women's Mistral	Sept. 17, 18, 19, 21, 22, 24	1. Alessandra Sensini, Italy 2. Amelie Lux, Germany 3. Barbara Kendall, New Zealand **17. (final) Caroll-Ann Alie, Gracefield, Que.**
	Women's 470	Sept. 20, 21, 22, 24, 25, 27	1. Australia 2. United States 3. Ukraine
Shooting	Men's Air Pistol	Sept. 16	1. Franck Dumoulin, France 2. Yifu Wang, China 3. Igor Basinsky, Belarus
	Men's Free Pistol	Sept. 19	1. Tanyu Kiriakov, Bulgaria 2. Igor Basinsky, Belarus 3. Martin Tenk, Czech Republic

Event	Date	2000 Results
Men's Rapid Fire Pistol	Sept. 20, 21	1. Serguei Alifirenko, Russia 2. Michal Ansermet, Switzerland 3. Iulian Raicea, Romania
Men's Running Target	Sept. 21, 22	1. Ling Yang, China 2. Oleg Moldovan, Moldova 3. Zhiyuan Niu, China
Men's Air Rifle	Sept. 18	1. Yalin Cai, China 2. Artem Khadjibekov, Russia 3. Evgueni Aleinikov, Russia
Men's Small-Bore Rifle, Prone	Sept. 21	1. Jonas Edman, Sweden 2. Torben Grimmel, Denmark 3. Sergei Martynov, Belarus 10. (tie prelim. heat) **Wayne Sorensen, Calgary, Alta** 38. (tie prelim. heat) **Roger Caron, Baie-Comeau, Que.**
Men's Small-Bore Rifle, 3-Position	Sept. 23	1. Rajmond Debevec, Slovenia 2. Juha Hirvi, Finland 3. Harald Stenvaag, Norway
Men's Trap	Sept. 16, 17	1. Michael Diamond, Australia 2. Ian Peel, Britain 3. Giovani Pellielo, Italy 10. **George Leary, Newmarket, Ont.**
Men's Double Trap	Sept. 20	1. Richard Faulds, Britain 2. Russell Mark, Australia 3. Fehaid Al Deehani, Kuwait
Skeet	Sept. 22, 23	1. Mykola Milchev, Ukraine 2. Petr Malek, Czech Republic 3. James Grave, United States 12. (tie final) **Jason Caswell, Winnipeg, Man.**
Men's Free Rifle	Sept. 23	1. Jonas Edman, Sweden 2. Torben Grimmel, Denmark 3. Sergei Martynov, Belarus
Women's Air Pistol	Sept. 17	1. Luna Tao, China 2. Jasna Sekaric, Yugoslavia 3. Annemarie Forder, Australia 39. (prelims) **Kim Eagles, Maple Ridge, BC**
Women's Air Rifle	Sept. 16	1. Nancy Johnson, United States 2. Cho-Hyun Kang, Korea 3. Jing Gao, China

	Event	Date	2000 Results
	Women's Sport Pistol	Sept. 22	1. Maria Grozdeva, Bulgaria 2. Luna Tao, China 3. Lolita Evglevskaya, Belarus **35. (final) Kim Eagles, Maple Ridge, BC**
	Small-Bore Rifle, 3-Position	Sept. 20	1. Renata Mauer-Rozanska, Poland 2. Tatiana Goldobina, Russia 3. Maria Feklisova, Russia **26. (tie final) Sharon Bowes, Waterloo, Ont.** **40. (final) Carol Johnson, Campbell River, BC**
	Women's Double Trap	Sept. 19	1. Pia Hansen, Sweden 2. Deborah Gelisio, Italy 3. Kimberly Rhode, United States **5. (final) Cynthia Meyer, Bowen, BC** **15. (prelim. round) Sue Nattrass, Edmonton**
	Women's Trap	Sept. 18	1. Daina Gudzineviciute, Lithuania 2. Delphine Racinet, France 3. E Gao, China **9. (prelim. round) Sue Nattrass, Edmonton, Alta** **10. (tie) Cynthia Meyer, Bowen Island, BC**
	Women's Skeet	Sept. 21	1. Zemfira Meftakhetdinova, Azerbaijan 2. Svetlana Demina, Russia 3. Diana Igaly, Hungary
Softball	Women's	Sept. 17–26	1. United States 2. Japan 3. Australia
Swimming	Men's 50-metre free style	Sept. 21, 22	1. Anthony Ervin, United States 1. Gary Hall Jr., United States 3. Pieter Hoogenband, Netherlands **Craig Hutchinson, Pointe-Claire, Que. (disqualified)**
	Men's 100-metre free style	Sept. 19, 20	1. Pieter Hoogenband, Netherlands 2. Alexander Popov, Russia 3. Gary Hall, United States **5. (prelim. heat) Craig Hutchinson, Pointe-Claire, Que.** **7. (prelim. heat) Yannick Lupien, Ste-Foy, Que.**

Event	Date	2000 Results
Men's 200-metre free style	Sept. 17, 18	1. Pieter Hoogenband, Netherlands 2. Ian Thorpe, Australia 3. Massimiliano Rosolino, Italy 7. (final) **Rick Say, Salmon Arm, BC** 8. (prelim. Heat) **Mark Johnston, St. Catherines, Ont.**
Men's 400-metre free style	Sept. 16	1. Ian Thorpe, Australia 2. Massimiliano Rosolino, Italy 3. Klete Keller, United States
Men's 1,500-metre free style	Sept. 22, 23	1. Grant Hackett, Australia 2. Kieren Perkins, Australia 3. Chris Thompson, United States 7. (prelim. heat) **Andrew Hurd, Oakville, Ont.** 8. (prelim. heat) **Tim Peterson, Vancouver, BC**
Men's 100-metre back stroke	Sept. 17, 18	1. Lenny Krayzelburg, United States 2. Matthew Welsh, Australia 3. Stev Theloke, Germany 7. (prelim. Heat) **Mark Versfeld, Fort McMurray, Alta**
Men's 200-metre back stroke	Sept. 20, 21	1. Lenny Krayzelburg, United States 2. Aaron Peirsol, United States 3. Matthew Welsh, Australia 6. (prelim. heat) **Chris Renault, Calgary, Alta** 7. (prelim. heat) **Dustin Hersee, Vancouver, BC**
Men's 100-metre breast stroke	Sept. 16, 17	1. Domenico Fioravanti, Italy 2. Ed Moses, United States 3. Roman Sloudnov, Russia 6. (final) **Morgan Knabe, Edmonton, Alta**
Men's 200-metre breast stroke	Sept. 19, 20	1. Domenico Fioravanti, Italy 2. Terence Parkin, South Africa 3. Davide Rummolo, Italy 5. (prelim. heat) **Morgan Knabe, Calgary, Alta**
Men's 100-metre butterfly	Sept. 21, 22	1. Lars Froelander, Sweden 2. Michael Klim, Australia 3. Geoff Huegill, Australia 5. (tie final) **Michael Mintenko, Moose Jaw, Sask.** 8. (prelim. heat) **Shamek Pietucha, Edmonton, Alta**

Event	Date	2000 Results
Men's 200-metre butterfly	Sept. 18, 19	1. Tom Malchow, United States 2. Denys Sylant'yev, Ukraine 3. Justin Norris, Australia 8. (eliminated heat) **Shamek Pietucha, Edmonton, Alta**
Men's 200-metre individual medley	Sept. 20, 21	1. Massimiliano Rosolino, Italy 2. Tom Dolan, United States 3. Tom Wilkens, United States 6. (prelim. heat) **Curtis Myden, Calgary, Alta** 8. (prelim. heat) **Brian Johns Richmond, BC**
Men's 400-metre individual medley	Sept. 17	1. Tom Dolan, United States 2. Erik Vendt, United States 3. **Curtis Myden, Canada (Canadian record of 4:15:33)** 7. (prelim. heat) **Owen von Richter, Mississauga, Ont.**
Men's 400-metre free style relay	Sept. 16	1. Australia 2. United States 3. Brazil
Men's 4x200-metre free style relay	Sept. 19	1. Australia 2. United States 3. Netherlands 7. (final) **Canada**
Men's 400-medley relay	Sept. 22, 23	1. United States 2. Australia 3. Germany 6. (final) **Canada**
Women's 50-metre free style	Sept. 22, 23	1. Inge de Bruijn, Netherlands 2. Therese Alshammar, Sweden 3. Dara Torres, United States 7. (prelim. heat) **Nadine Rolland, Brossard, Que.** 8. (prelim. heat) **Jenna Gresdal, Huntsville, Ont.**
Women's 100-metre free style	Sept. 20, 21	1. Inge de Bruijn, Netherlands 2. Therese Alshammar, Sweden 3. Jenny Thompson, United States 3. Dana Torres, United States 7. (prelim. heat) **Laura Nicholls, Waterloo, Ont.**

Event	Date	2000 Results
Women's 200-metre free style	Sept. 18, 19	1. Susie O'Neill, Australia 2. Martina Moravcova, Slovakia 3. Claudia Poll, Costa Rica **6. (prelim. heat) Jessica Deglau, Vancouver, BC** **7. (prelim. heat) Laura Nicholls, Waterloo, Ont.**
Women's 400-metre free style	Sept. 17	1. Brooke Bennett, United States 2. Diana Munz, United States 3. Claudia Poll, Costa Rica **7. (prelim. heat) Karine Legault, St-Eustache, Que.**
Women's 800-metre free style	Sept. 21, 22	1. Brooke Bennett, United States 2. Yana Klochkova, Ukraine 3. Kaitlin Sandeno, United States **5. (prelim. heat) Karine Legault, St-Eustache, Que.** **Joanne Malar, Hamilton (did not start)**
Women's 100-metre back stroke	Sept. 17, 18	1. Diana Mocanu, Romania 2. Mai Nakamura, Japan 3. Nina Zhivanevskaya, Spain
Women's 200-metre back stroke	Sept. 21, 22	1. Diana Mocanu, Romania 2. Roxana Maracineanu, France 3. Miki Nakao, Japan **8. (final) Kelly Stefanyshyn, Winnipeg, Man.**
Women's 100-metre breast stroke	Sept. 17, 18	1. Megan Quann, United States 2. Leisel Jones, Australia 3. Penny Heyns, South Africa
Women's 200-metre breast stroke	Sept. 20, 21	1. Agnes Kovacs, Hungary 2. Kristy Kowal, United States 3. Amanda Beard, United States **6. (prelim. heat) Christin Petelski, Victoria, BC**
Women's 100-metre butterfly	Sept. 16, 17	1. Inge de Bruijn, Netherlands 2. Martina Moravcova, Slovakia 3. Dara Torres, United States
Women's 200-metre butterfly	Sept. 19, 20	1. Misty Hyman, United States 2. Susie O'Neill, Australia 3. Petria Thomas, Australia **6. (prelim. heat) Jen Button, Waterloo, Ont.** **7. (prelim. heat) Jessica Deglau, Vancouver, BC**

	Event	Date	2000 Results
	Women's 200-metre individual medley	Sept. 18, 19	1. Yana Klochkova, Ukraine 2. Beatrice Caslaru, Romania 3. Cristina Teuscher, United States **4. (final) Marianne Limpert, Fredericton, NB** **5. (final) Joanne Malar, Hamilton, Ont.**
	Women's 400-metre individual medley	Sept. 16	1. Yana Klochkova, Ukraine 2. Yasuko Tajima, Japan 3. Beatrice Caslaru, Romania
	Women's 400-metre free style relay	Sept. 16	1. United States 2. Netherlands 3. Sweden
	Women's 4x200-metre free style relay	Sept. 20	1. United States 2. Australia 3. Germany **5. (final) Canada**
	Women's 400-metre medley relay	Sept. 22, 23	1. United States 2. Australia 3. Japan
Synchronized Swimming	Team	Sept. 28, 29	1. Russia 2. Japan **3. Canada**
	Duet	Sept. 24, 25, 26	1. Russia 2. Japan 3. France
Table Tennis	Men's Singles	Sept. 17, 18, 19, 20, 21, 22, 23, 24, 25	1. Linghui Kong, China 2. Jan-Ove Waldner, Sweden 3. Guoliang Liu, China
	Men's Doubles	Sept. 16, 18, 20, 21, 22, 23	1. China 2. China 3. France
	Women's Singles	Sept. 17, 18, 19, 20, 21, 22, 23, 24	1. Nan Wang, China 2. Ju Li, China 3. Jing Chen, Chinese Taipai
	Women's Doubles	Sept. 16, 18, 20, 21, 22	1. China 2. China 3. Korea
Taekwondo	Men's, Under 58-kg	Sept. 27	1. Michail Mouroutsis, Greece 2. Gabriel Esparaza, Spain 3. Chih-Hsiung Huang, Chinese Taipei

Event	Date	2000 Results
Men's 58-68 kg	Sept. 28	1. Steven Lopez, United States 2. Joon-Sik Sin, Korea 3. Hadi Saeibonehkohal, Iran
Men's 68-80 kg	Sept. 29	1. Angel Matos Fuentes, Cuba 2. Faissal Ebnoutalib, Germany 3. Victor Estrada-Garibay, Mexico
Men's Over 80-kg	Sept. 30	1. Kyong-Hun Kim, Korea 2. Daniel Trenton, Australia 3. Pascal Gentil, France
Women's Under 49-kg	Sept. 27	1. Lauren Burns, Australia 2. Urbia Rodriguez, Cuba 3. Shu-Ji Chi, Chinese Taipei
Women's 49-57 kg	Sept. 28	1. Jae-Eun Jung, Korea 2. Hieu Ngan Tran, Vietnam 3. Hamide Bikcin, Turkey
Women's 57-67 kg	Sept. 29	1. Sun-Hee Lee, Korea 2. Trude Gundersen, Norway 3. Yoriko Okamoto, Japan
Women's Over 67-kg	Sept. 30	1. Zhong Chen, China 2. Natalia Ivanova, Russia **3. Dominique Bosshart, Canada**

Tennis

Event	Date	2000 Results
Men's Singles	Sept. 19–28	1. Yevgeny Kafelnikov, Russia 2. Tommy Haas, Germany 3. Arnaud Di Pasquale, France **Sebastien Lareau, Boucherville, Que.** **(eliminated prelim. match)** **Daniel Nestor, Toronto, Ont.** **(eliminated prelim. match)**
Men's Doubles	Sept. 20–27	**1. Canada** 2. Australia 3. Spain
Women's Singles	Sept. 19–27	1. Venus Williams, United States 2. Elena Dementieva, Russia 3. Monica Seles, United States
Women's Doubles	Sept. 21–28	1. United States 2. Netherlands 3. Belgium

Olympics

	Event	Date	2000 Results
Track and Field (See Athletics)			
Triathlon	Men's	Sept. 17	**1. Simon Whitfield, Canada** 2. Stefan Vuckovic, Germany 3. Jan Rehula, Czech Republic
	Women's	Sept. 16	1. Brigitte McMahon, Switzerland 2. Michellie Jones, Australia 3. Magali Messmer, Switzerland **31. Isabelle Turcotte-Baird, Quebec City, Que.** **38. Sharon Donnelly, Ottawa, Ont.** **Carol Montgomery, North Vancouver, BC (did not qualify)**
Volleyball, Beach	Men's	Sept. 17, 19, 22, 24, 26	1. United States 2. Brazil 3. Germany **Canada, John Child and Mark Heese, Toronto, Ont. (eliminated)** **Canada, Jody Holden, Shelburne, NS and Conrad Leinemann, Kelowna, BC (eliminated)**
	Women's	Sept. 16, 18, 21, 23, 25	1. Australia 2. Brazil 3. Brazil
Volleyball, Indoor	Men's	Sept. 17, 19, 21, 23, 25, 27, 28, 29, Oct. 1	1. Yugoslavia 2. Russia 3. Italy
	Women's	Sept. 16, 18, 20, 22, 24, 26, 27, 28, 30	1. Cuba 2. Russia 3. Brazil
Water Polo	Men's	Sept. 23, 24, 25, 26, 27, 29, 30, Oct. 1	1. Hungary 2. Russia 3. Yugoslavia
	Women's	Sept. 16, 17, 18, 19, 20, 22, 23	1. Australia 2. United States 3. Russia Broadcast **5. (final) Canada**
Weightlifting	Men's 56-kg	Sept. 16	1. Halil Mutlu, Turkey 2. Wenxiong Wu, China 3. Xiangxiang Zhang, China
	Men's 62-kg	Sept. 17	1. Nikolay Pechaliv, Croatia 2. Leonidas Sabanis, Greece 3. Gennady Oleschchuk, Belarus

Event	Date	2000 Results
Men's 69-kg	Sept. 20	1. Galabin Boevski, Bulgaria 2. Georgi Markov, Bulgaria 3. Sergei Lavrenov, Belarus
Men's 77-kg	Sept. 22	1. Xugang Zhan, China 2. Viktor Mitrou, Greece 3. Arsen Melikyan, Armenia
Men's 85-kg	Sept. 23	1. Pyrros Dimas, Greece 2. Marc Huster, Germany 3. George Asanidze, Georgia
Men's 94-kg	Sept. 24	1. Akakios Kakiasvilis, Greece 2. Szymon Kolecki, Poland 3. Alexei Petrov, Russia
Men's 105-kg	Sept. 25	1. Hossein Tavakoli, Iran 2. Alan Tsagaev, Bulgaria 3. Said S Asaad, Qatar
Men's 105-kg plus	Sept. 26	1. Hossein Rezazadeh, Iran 2. Ronny Weller, Germany 3. Andrei Chemerkin, Russia
Women's 48-kg	Sept. 17	1. Tara Nott, United States 2. Raema Lisa Rumbewas, Indonesia 3. Sri Indriyani, Indonesia
Women's 53-kg	Sept. 18	1. Xia Yang, China 2. Feng-Ying Li, Chinese Taipei 3. Winarni Binti Slamet, Indonesia
Women's 58-kg	Sept. 18	1. Soraya Mendivil, Mexico 2. Song Hui Ri, North Korea 3. Khassaraporn Suta, Thailand **4. Maryse Turcotte, Brossard, Que.**
Women's 63-kg	Sept. 19	1. Xiaomin Chen, China 2. Valentina Popova, Russia 3. Ioanna Chatziioannou, Greece
Women's 69-kg	Sept.19	1. Weining Lin, China 2. Erzsebet Markus, Hungary 3. Karnam Malleswari, India
Women's 75-kg	Sept. 20	1. Maria Isabel Urrutia, Colombia 2. Ruth Ogbeifo, Nigeria 3. Yi Hang Kuo, Chinese Taipei

	Event	Date	2000 Results
	Women's 75-kg plus	Sept. 22	1. Meiyuan Ding, China 2. Agata Wrobel, Poland 3. Cheryl Haworth, United States
Wrestling	**Freestyle, 54-kg**	Sept. 28, 29, 30	1. Namig Abdullayev, Azerbaijan 2. Samuel Henson, United States 3. Amiran Karntanov, Greece
	Freestyle, 58-kg	Sept. 29, 30, Oct. 1	1. Alireza Dabir, Iran 2. Yevgen Buslovych, Ukraine 3. Terry Brands, United States **Gia Sissaouri, Montreal, Que.** **(eliminated first-round)**
	Freestyle, 63-kg	Sept. 28, 29, 30	1. Mourad Oumakhanov, Russia 2. Serafim Barzakov, Bulgaria 3. Jae Sung Jang, Korea
	Freestyle, 69-kg	Sept. 29, 30, Oct. 1	**1. Daniel Igali, Canada** 2. Arsen Gitinov, Russia 3. Lincoln McIlravy, United States
	Freestyle, 76-kg	Sept. 28, 29, 30	1. Alexander Leipold, Germany 2. Brandon Slay, United States 3. Eui Jae Moon, Korea
	Freestyle, 85-kg	Sept. 29, 30, Oct. 1	1. Adam Saitiev, Russia 2. Yoel Romero, Cuba 3. Mogamed Ibragimov, Macedonia **Justin Abdou, Moose Jaw, Sask.** **(eliminated prelim. round)**
	Freestyle, 97-kg	Sept. 28, 29, 30	1. Saghid Mourtasaliyev, Russia 2. Islam Bairamukov, Kazakhstan 3. Eldar Kurtanidze, Georgia **Dean Schmeichel, Prince Albert, Sask.** **(eliminated)**
	Freestyle, 130-kg	Sept. 29, 30, Oct. 1	1. David Moussoulbes, Russia 2. Artur Taymazov, Uzbekistan 3. Alexis Rodriguez, Cuba
	Greco-Roman, 54-kg	Sept. 24, 25, 26	1. Kwon Ho Sim, Korea 2. Lazaro Rivas, Cuba 3. Young Gyun Kang, North Korea
	Greco-Roman, 58-kg	Sept. 25, 26, 27	1. Armen Nazarian, Bulgaria 2. In Sub Kim, Korea 3. Zetian Sheng, China

Event	Date	2000 Results
Greco-Roman, 63-kg	Sept. 24, 25, 26	1. Varteres Samourgachev, Russia 2. Juan Luis Maren, Cuba 3. Akaki Chachua, Georgia
Greco-Roman, 69-kg	Sept. 25, 26, 27	1. Filiberto Azcuy, Cuba 2. Katsuhiko Nagata, Japan 3. Alexei Glouchkov, Russia
Greco-Roman, 76-kg	Sept. 24, 25, 26	1. Mourat Kardanov, Russia 2. Matt James Lindland, United States 3. Marko Yli-Hannuksela, Finland
Greco-Roman, 85-kg	Sept. 25, 26, 27	1. Hamza Yerlikaya, Turkey 2. Sandor Istvan Bardosi, Hungary 3. Mukhran Vakhtangadze, Georgia
Greco-Roman, 97-kg	Sept. 24, 25, 26	1. Mikael Ljungberg, Sweden 2. Davyd Saldadze, Ukraine 3. Garrett Lowney, United States
Greco-Roman, 130-kg	Sept. 25, 26, 27	1. Rulon Gardner, United States 2. Alexandre Karelin, Russia 3. Dmitry Debelka, Belarus

Source: *Canadian Press*

Record-setting Olympics

*O*rganizers of Sydney 2000 announced that Day 8 was the record-setter as far as attendance at the Olympic Park was concerned: 400,345 attended events at that venue alone.

By September 30th, 4,472,495 people had travelled to the Olympic Park. And those visitors ate and drank while they were there. Daily consumption was estimated at: 10,000 cups of beer; 70,000 bottles of Coke; 3,000 bottles of water; 4,000 ice creams; 2,000 pizzas; 2,000 seafood baskets; 3,000 hot dogs and 3,000 cups of hot chips. Not to be outdone, the athletes also ate well: the one millionth meal was served in the Athlete's Dining Hall on September 28th. (Char grilled Tasmanian salmon kebabs were reported to be the most popular dish on the menu.) Organizers also reported that staff consumed one billion lollies—6 each per day.

Despite all the consumption, 80 percent of all waste and garbage collected at the Olympic sites was recycled or composted through special recycling bins at the park and other venues. For these, and other fascinating bits of information, visit http://www.olympics.com

OTHER SPORTS

Canadian Curling Champions

Men

Skip, Province	Skip, Province	Skip, Province
1927 Murray Macneill, NS	**1954** Matt Baldwin, Alta	**1978** Ed Lukowich, Alta
1928 Gordon Hudson, Man.	**1955** Garnet Campbell, Sask.	**1979** Barry Fry, Man.
1929 Gordon Hudson, Man.	**1956** Billy Walsh, Man.	**1980** Rick Folk, Sask.
1930 Howard Wood, Man.	**1957** Matt Baldwin, Alta	**1981** Kerry Burtnyk, Man.
1931 Bob Gourley, Man.	**1958** Matt Baldwin, Alta	**1982** Al Hackner, N. Ont.
1932 Jim Congalton, Man.	**1959** Ernie Richardson, Sask.	**1983** Ed Werenich, Ont.
1933 Cliff Manahan, Alta	**1960** Ernie Richardson, Sask.	**1984** Mike Riley, Man.
1934 Leo Johnson, Man.	**1961** Hec Gervais, Alta	**1985** Al Hackner, N. Ont.
1935 Gordon Campbell, Ont.	**1962** Ernie Richardson, Sask.	**1986** Ed Lukowich, Alta
1936 Ken Watson, Man.	**1963** Ernie Richardson, Sask.	**1987** Russ Howard, Ont.
1937 Cliff Manahan, Alta	**1964** Lyall Dagg, BC	**1988** Pat Ryan, Alta
1938 Ab Gowanlock, Man.	**1965** Terry Braunstein, Man.	**1989** Pat Ryan, Alta
1939 Bert Hall, Ont.	**1966** Ron Northcott, Alta	**1990** Ed Werenich, Ont.
1940 Howard Wood, Man.	**1967** Alf Phillips, Jr., Ont.	**1991** Kevin Martin, Alta
1941 Howard Palmer, Alta	**1968** Ron Northcott, Alta	**1992** Vic Peters, Man.
1942 Ken Watson, Man.	**1969** Ron Northcott, Alta	**1993** Russ Howard, Ont.
1946 Billy Rose, Alta	**1970** Don Duguid, Man.	**1994** Rick Folk, BC
1947 Jimmy Welsh, Man.	**1971** Don Duguid, Man.	**1995** Kerry Burtnyk, Man
1948 Frenchy D'Amour, BC	**1972** Orest Meleschuk, Man.	**1996** Jeff Stoughton, Man
1949 Ken Watson, Man.	**1973** Harvey Mazinke, Sask.	**1997** Kevin Martin, Alta
1950 Tom Ramsay, N. Ont.	**1974** Hector Gervais, Alta	**1998** Wayne Middaugh, Ont.
1951 Don Oyler, NS	**1975** Bill Tetley, N. Ont.	**1999** Jeff Stoughton, Man.
1952 Billy Walsh, Man.	**1976** Jack MacDuff, Nfld.	**2000** Greg McAuley, BC
1953 Ab Gowanlock, Man.	**1977** Jim Ursel, Que.	

Women

Skip, Province	Skip, Province	Skip, Province
1961 Joyce McKee, Sask.	**1975** Lee Tobin, Que.	**1989** Heather Houston, Ont.
1962 Ina Hansen, BC	**1976** Lindsay Davie, BC	**1990** Alison Goring, Ont.
1963 Mabel DeWare, NB	**1977** Myrna McQuarrie, Alta.	**1991** Julie Sutton, BC
1964 Ina Hansen, BC	**1978** Cathy Pidzarko, Man.	**1992** Connie Laliberte, Man.
1965 Peggy Casselman, Man.	**1979** Lindsay Sparkes, BC	**1993** Sandra Peterson, Sask.
1966 Gail Lee, Alta.	**1980** Marj Mitchell, Sask.	**1994** Sandra Peterson, Sask
1967 Betty Duguid, Man.	**1981** Susan Seitz, Alta.	**1995** Connie Laliberte, Man.
1968 Hazel Jamieson, Alta.	**1982** Colleen Jones, NS	**1996** Marilyn Bodogh, Ont.
1969 Joyce McKee, Sask.	**1983** Penny LaRocque, NS	**1997** Sandra Schmirler, Sask.
1970 Dorenda Schoenhais, Sask.	**1984** Connie Laliberte, Man.	**1998** Cathy Borst, Alta.
1971 Vera Pezer, Sask.	**1985** Linda Moore, BC	**1999** Colleen Jones, NS
1972 Vera Pezer, Sask.	**1986** Marilyn Darte, Ont.	**2000** Kelly Law, BC
1973 Vera Pezer, Sask.	**1987** Pat Sanders, BC	
1974 Emily Farnham, Sask.	**1988** Heather Houston, Ont.	

Source: *Canadian Press*

Canadian Interuniversity Athletic Union (CIAU) Champions, 1999–2000

	Men	Women
Field Hockey	—	UBC Thunderbirds
Rugby	—	Alberta Pandas
Soccer	Western Mustangs	Dalhousie Tigers
Cross Country	Guelph Gryphons	Victoria Vikes
Football	Laval Rouge et Or	—
Swimming	UBC Thunderbirds	UBC Thunderbirds
Wrestling	Brock Badgers	Calgary Dinos
Hockey	Alberta Golden Bears	Alberta Pandas
Volleyball	Manitoba Bisons	Alberta Pandas
Basketball	St FX X-Men	Victoria Vikes
Track & Field	Sherbrooke Vert et Or	Saskatchewan Huskies

Medal Count	Gold	Silver	Bronze	Total	Medal Count	Gold	Silver	Bronze	Total
Alberta Golden Bears / Pandas	4	2	3	9	StFX X-Men	1	—	—	1
Victoria Vikes	2	2	2	6	Brandon Bobcats	—1	—1		
Calgary Dinos	1	3	1	5	McGill Martlets	—1	—1		
UBC Thunderbirds	3	1	—	4	Saint Mary's Huskies	—1	—1		
Guelph Gryphons	1	1	2	4	Toronto Varsity Blues	—1	—1		
Saskatchewan Huskies	1	2	—	3	UNB Varsity Reds	—1	—1		
Sherbrooke Vert et Or	1	1	1	3	Concordia Stingers	—	1		1
Brock Badgers	1	1		—2	Lakehead Thunderwolves	—	1		1
Manitoba Bisons	1	1		—2	Regina Cougars	—	1		1
Western Mustangs	1	1		—2	Waterloo Warriors	—	1		1
Dalhousie Tigers	1	—		1	Windsor Lancers	—	1		1
Laval Rouge et Or	1	—		1	Winnipeg Wesmen	—	1		1

Source: *Canadian Press*

CIAU Championship Summaries, 1999–2000

WOMEN'S FIELD HOCKEY (November 4–7, 1999)
Champions: UBC; **Silver:** Victoria; **Bronze:** Alberta
The UBC Thunderbirds captured their second straight field hockey title with a 1–0 victory over their provincial rivals, the Victoria Vikes. Stephanie Hume scored the eventual winner in just the ninth minute of the game.

WOMEN'S RUGBY (November 10–11, 1999)
Champions: Alberta; **Silver:** Guelph; **Bronze:** Waterloo
The Alberta Pandas used their size advantage to overpower the defending CIAU Champion Guelph Gryphons 20–3 in a game dominated by heavy winds. Flanker Cara Denkhaus scored two tries, leading Alberta to the CIAU crown in their first trip to the national tournament.

MEN'S SOCCER (November 11–14, 1999)
Champions: Western; **Silver:** Alberta; **Bronze:** Victoria
The Western Mustangs repeated as champions with a 1–0 win over the Alberta Golden Bears. Xavier Paturel's goal in the 46th minute was the difference. Alberta, with a number of unsuccessful goal scoring opportunities, settled for the silver for the second straight season.

WOMEN'S SOCCER (November 11–14, 1999)
Champions: Dalhousie; **Silver:** Alberta; **Bronze:** Guelph
In the 23rd minute of the game, tournament MVP Stef Finateri scored her fourth goal of the championship, and the eventual game winner as the Dalhousie Tigers went on to claim their first CIAU crown since 1995 by the score of 2–0. ▶

CIAU Champions

▶ **MEN'S CROSS COUNTRY (November 13, 1999)**
Champions: Guelph; Silver: Toronto; Bronze: Sherbrooke
The Guelph Gryphons captured their first CIAU men's championship in thirty years on a day when running conditions were ideal.

WOMEN'S CROSS COUNTRY (November 13, 1999)
Champions: Victoria; Silver: Western; Bronze: Guelph
With five All-Canadians in the mix, the Victoria Vikes ran away with the 2000 CIAU Women's Cross Country title.

FOOTBALL
Vanier Cup Champions (November 27, 1999): Laval.
Atlantic Bowl Champions: Saint Mary's
Canada West Champions: Saskatchewan
OUA Champions: Waterloo
In just its fourth season as a program, the Laval Rouge et Or won the national title with a 14–10 victory over the Saint Mary's Huskies. The 35th Vanier Cup was the sixth-lowest scoring final in CIAU history.

SWIMMING (February 25–27, 2000)
Men: Champions: UBC; Silver: Calgary; Bronze: Victoria
Women: Champions: UBC; Silver: Victoria; Bronze: Calgary
Both of the UBC Thunderbirds' men's and women's teams repeated as national champions for the third straight time. The men edged the University of Calgary while the women dominated their nearest rival, Victoria, by 133.5 points.

WRESTLING (February 25–26, 2000)
Men: Champions: Brock; Silver: Calgary; Bronze: Lakehead
Women: Champions: Calgary; Silver: Brock; Bronze: Alberta
The Brock Badger men's team and the Calgary Dinosaurs women's team repeated as CIAU champions when they each captured their second consecutive national title in 2000.

WOMEN'S HOCKEY (February 24–27, 2000)
Champions: Alberta; Silver: McGill; Bronze: Concordia
The Alberta Pandas defeated the McGill Martlets 2–0, to win their first-ever CIAU women's hockey Championship.

MEN'S VOLLEYBALL (March 3–5, 2000)
Champions: Manitoba; Silver: Saskatchewan; Bronze: Winnipeg
The Bisons, who earned a wild-card spot to the tournament, defeated the third-seeded Saskatchewan Huskies 3–1 for the title. The fourth set, a marathon, was won by Manitoba 32–30.

WOMEN'S VOLLEYBALL (March 2–4, 2000)
Champions: Alberta; Silver: Manitoba; Bronze: UBC
The University of Alberta won it's sixth straight CIAU Women's Volleyball Championship, one shy of the national all-time record.

TRACK AND FIELD (March 10–11, 2000)
Men: Champions: Sherbrooke; Silver: Saskatchewan; Bronze: Alberta
Women: Champions: Saskatchewan; Silver: Sherbrooke; Bronze: Windsor
The University of Sherbrooke won the CIAU's men's championship for a fourth consecutive year. On the women's side, the University of Saskatchewan triumphed over 19 other teams.

WOMEN'S BASKETBALL (March 10–12, 2000)
Champions: Victoria; Silver: Calgary; Bronze: Regina
The University of Victoria Vikes won their eighth national title with a 57–41 victory over the Calgary Dinos.

MEN'S BASKETBALL (March 17–19, 2000)
Champions: StFX; Runner Up: Brandon
St FX earned its second title and first since 1993 as they defeated the Brandon Bobcats 61–60 in the national final.

MEN'S HOCKEY (March 23–26, 2000)
Champions: Alberta; Runner Up: UNB
CIAU player of the year Russ Hewson scored 8:18 into the second overtime period to lift the Alberta Golden Bears to 5–4 victory over the UNB Varsity Reds in the national final. The victory gave the Golden Bears back-to-back titles and ties them with the University of Toronto with a record 10 University Cup titles.

Source: *Canadian Press*

Canadian Interuniversity Athletic Union Champions, 1975–1999

Men

	Basketball	Football	Ice Hockey	Soccer	Swimming	Volleyball	Track & Field
1975–76	Manitoba	Ottawa	Toronto	Alberta	Toronto	BC	—
1976–77	Acadia	Western	Toronto	Concordia	Waterloo	Winnipeg	—
1977–78	St. Mary's	Western	Alberta	York	Waterloo	Manitoba	—
1978–79	St. Mary's	Queen's	Alberta	Manitoba	Waterloo	Saskatchewan	—
1979–80	Victoria	Acadia	Alberta	Alberta	Toronto	Manitoba	—
1980–81	Victoria	Alberta	Moncton	New Brunswick	Toronto	Alberta	Toronto
1981–82	Victoria	Acadia	Moncton	McGill	Calgary	Calgary	Toronto
1982–83	Victoria	BC	Saskatchewan	McGill	Calgary	BC	York
1983–84	Victoria	Calgary	Toronto	Laurentian	Calgary	Manitoba	York
1984–85	Victoria	Guelph	York	BC	Calgary	Manitoba	Toronto
1985–86	Victoria	Calgary	Alberta	BC	Toronto	Winnipeg	Toronto
1986–87	Brandon	BC	Trois-Rivières	BC	Calgary	Winnipeg	Saskatchewan
1987–88	Brandon	McGill	York	Victoria	Calgary	Manitoba	Manitoba
1988–89	Brandon	Calgary	York	Toronto	Calgary	Calgary	Manitoba
1989–90	Concordia	Western	Moncton	BC	Calgary	Laval	Manitoba–Toronto
1990–91	Western	Saskatchewan	Trois-Rivières	BC	Calgary	Manitoba	Windsor
1991–92	Brock	Wilfrid Laurier	Alberta	BC	Toronto	Laval	Manitoba
1992–93	St. Francis Xavier	Queen's	Acadia	BC	Toronto	Calgary	Windsor
1993–94	Alberta	Toronto	Lethbridge	Sherbrooke	Toronto	Laval	Manitoba
1994–95	Alberta	Western	Moncton	BC	Calgary	Manitoba	Manitoba
1995–96	Brandon	Calgary	Acadia	Dalhousie	Calgary	Manitoba	Manitoba
1996–97	Victoria	Saskatchewan	Guelph	Victoria	Calgary	Alberta	Sherbrooke
1997–98	Bishop's	BC	New Brunswick	McGill	BC	Winnipeg	Sherbrooke
1998–99	St Mary's	Saskatchewan	Alberta	Western	BC	Saskatchewan	Sherbrooke

Women

	Basketball	Field Hockey	Swimming	Track & Field	Volleyball	Soccer	Ice Hockey
1975–76	Laurentian	Toronto	—	—	Western		
1976–77	Laurentian	Dalhousie	Acadia	—	BC		
1977–78	Laurentian	Toronto	Acadia	—	BC		
1978–79	Laurentian	BC	Toronto	—	Saskatchewan		
1979–80	Victoria	Toronto	Toronto	—	Saskatchewan		
1980–81	Victoria	BC	Toronto	Western	Saskatchewan		
1981–82	Victoria	Toronto	Toronto	Western	Dalhousie		
1982–83	Bishop's	BC	Toronto	Western	Winnipeg		
1983–84	Bishop's	BC	Toronto	York	Winnipeg		
1984–85	Victoria	Victoria	BC	Alta & Sask.	Winnipeg		
1985–86	Toronto	Toronto	BC	Saskatchewan	Winnipeg		
1986–87	Victoria	Toronto	Toronto	Calgary	Winnipeg		
1987–88	Manitoba	Victoria	Toronto	York	Winnipeg	BC	
1988–89	Calgary	Toronto	Toronto	Toronto	Calgary	Queen's	
1989–90	Laurentian	Victoria	Toronto	York	Manitoba	Alberta	
1990–91	Laurentian	BC	Toronto	Calgary	Manitoba	Acadia	
1991–92	Victoria	Victoria	Toronto	Windsor	Manitoba	McMaster	
1992–93	Winnipeg	Victoria	Toronto	Windsor	Winnipeg	Laurier	
1993–94	Winnipeg	Toronto	BC	Windsor	Calgary	BC	
1994–95	Winnipeg	Victoria	BC	Windsor	Alberta	Dalhousie	
1995–96	Manitoba	Victoria	BC	Windsor	Alberta	Laurier	
1996–97	Manitoba	Toronto	Toronto	Toronto	Alberta	Ottawa	
1997–98	Victoria	Victoria	BC	Toronto	Alberta	Alberta	
1998–99	Alberta	BC	BC	Windsor	Alberta	Calgary	Concordia

Source: Canadian Interuniversity Athletic Union

Association of Tennis Professionals—2000 Grand Slam Events

Event	Date	Winner	Event	Date	Winner
Australian Open	Jan. 17-30	Andre Agassi	Wimbledon	June 26-July 9	Pete Sampras
French Open	May 29-June 11	Gustavo Kuerten	U.S. Open	Aug. 28-Sept. 10	Marat Safin

Source: *Canadian Press*

Men's ATP Rankings, 2000
(as of September 11, 2000, including top Canadians)

Rank		Country	Rank		Country
1.	Pete Sampras	United States	8.	Thomas Enqvist	Sweden
2.	Gustavo Kuerten	Brazil	9.	Yevgeny Kafelnikov	Russia
3.	Marat Safin	Russia	10.	Tim Henman	Great Britain
4.	Magnus Norman	Sweden	111.	Sebastian Lareau	Canada
5.	Lleyton Hewitt	Australia	141.	Daniel Nestor	Canada
6.	Alex Corretia	Spain	197.	Simon Larose	Canada
7.	Andre Agassi	United States	280.	Frederic Niemeyer	Canada

Source: *Canadian Press*

Women's Tennis Association—2000 Grand Slam Events

Event	Date	Winner	Event	Date	Winner
Australian Open	Jan. 17-30	Lindsay Davenport	Wimbledon	June 26-July 9	Venus Williams
French Open	May 29-June 11	Mary Pierce	U.S. Open	Aug. 28-Sept. 10	Venus Williams

Source: *Canadian Press*

Women's Final WTA Rankings, 2000
(as of September 11, 2000)

Rank		Country	Rank		Country
1.	Martina Hingis	Switzerland	126.	Maureen Drake	Canada
2.	Lindsay Davenport	United States	221.	Renata Kolbovic	Canada
3.	Venus Williams	United States	224.	Marie-Eve Pelletier	Canada
4.	Mary Pierce	France	495.	Alison Nash	Canada
5.	Monica Seles	United States	608.	Martina Nejedly	Canada
6.	Conchita Martinez	Spain	717.	Melanie Marois	Canada
7.	Nathalie Tauziat	France	745.	Nicole Havlicek	Canada
8.	Serena Williams	United States	767.	Kavitha Krishnamurthy	Canada
9.	Arantxa Sanchez-Vicario	Spain	778.	Debbie Larocque	Canada
10.	Anke Huber	Germany	828.	Aneta Soulup	Canada
58.	Sonya Jeyaseelen	Canada	832.	Anya Loncaric	Canada
67.	Jana Nejedly	Canada	914.	Lauren Colalillo	Canada
109.	Vanessa Webb	Canada	934.	Nancy Loeffler-Caro	Canada

Source: *Canadian Press*

The Quiet Gold

Canada's Daniel Nestor and Sebastien Lareau were downright subdued after winning an Olympic gold medal by beating Australia's Todd Woodbridge and Mark Woodforde, the best doubles team in modern tennis history, 5-7, 6-3, 6-4, 7-6 (2) in the finals.

Lareau, 27, and Nestor, 28, have known each other for 18 years, playing doubles as juniors and together in the odd satellite event. In 2000, they have reached the quarter-finals of three Grand Slams, won the Tennis Master Series Canada in Toronto in August and capped it with Olympic gold. Nestor and Lareau will perhaps play in the Australian Open in 2001. But they will play fewer events together in the future as both want to focus more on their singles games.

Source: *The Canadian Press*

Canadian Alpine Skiing Champions, 1980–2000

Men

	Downhill	Slalom	Giant Slalom	Super Giant Slalom
1980	Ken Read	Peter Monod	Peter Monod	—
1981	Robin McLeish	Peter Monod	Peter Monod	—
1982	Urs Raeber (SUI)	Peter Monod	Jim Read	—
1983	Steve Podborski	Francois Jodoin	Mike Tommy	—
1984	Steve Podborski	Mike Tommy	Jim Read	Jim Read
1985	Steven Lee (AUS)	Gordon Perry	Jim Read	Mike Brown (USA)
1986	Don Stevens	Jim Read	Jim Read	Derek Trussler
1987	Brian Stemmle	Alain Villiard	Alain Villiard	Jim Read
1988	Steven Lee (AUS)	Jack Miller (USA)	Tiger Shaw (USA)	Leonard Stock (AUT)
1989	Mike Carney	Alain Villiard	Alain Villiard	Felix Belczyk
1990	Felix Belczyk	Rob Crossan	Robbie Parisien	David Duchesne
1991	Edi Podivinsky	Eric Villiard	Eric Villiard	Rob Boyd
1992	Reggie Crist (USA)	Rob Crossan	Thomas Grandi	Reggie Crist (USA)
1993	John Mealey	Rob Crossan	Thomas Grandi	Eric Villiard
1994	Ralf Socher	Stanley Hayer	Christopher Pickett (US)	Ralf Socher
1995	Edi Podivinsky	Stanley Hayer	Thomas Grandi	Brian Stemmle
1996	Edi Podivinsky	Stanley Hayer	Thomas Grandi	(cancelled)
1997	Graydon Oldfield	Thomas Grandi	Thomas Grandi	Ryan Oughtred
1998	Daimion Applegath	Thomas Grandi	Thomas Grandi	Darin McBeath
1999	Kevin Wert	Munroe Hunsicker	Vincent Lavoie	Brian Stemmle
2000	Cancelled	Michael Tichy	Jean-Phillipe Roy	Cancelled

Women

	Downhill	Slalom	Giant Slalom	Super Giant Slalom
1980	Laurie Graham	Lynn Lacasse	Ann Blackburn	—
1981	Gerry Sorensen	Josée Lacasse	Diana Haight	—
1982	Dianne Lehodey	Lynn Lacasse	Lynn Lacasse	—
1983	Gerry Sorensen	Lynn Lacasse	Liisa Savijarvi	—
1984	Diana Haight	Andréa Bedard	Liisa Savijarvi	Laurie Graham
1985	Laurie Graham	Andréa Bedard	Liisa Savijarvi	Karen Percy
1986	Karen Percy	Josée Lacasse	Josée Lacasse	Karen Percy
1987	Liisa Savijarvi	Julie Klotz	Josée Lacasse	Karen Percy
1988	Laurie Graham	Josée Lacasse	Karen Percy	Karen Percy
1989	Lucie LaRoche	Sonja Rusch	Karen Percy	Kendra Kobelka
1990	Lucie LaRoche	Josée Lacasse	Josée Lacasse	Nancy Gee
1991	Kerrin Lee-Gartner	Sonja Rusch	Annie Laurendeau	Michelle McKendry
1992	Kerrin Lee-Gartner	Annie Laurendeau	Michelle McKendry	Michelle McKendry
1993	Kerrin Lee-Gartner	Nanci Gee	Melanie Turgeon	Michelle Ruthven[1]
1994	Kate Pace	Katarina Tichy (Czech)	Edith Rozsa	Michelle Ruthven[1]
1995	Lindsey Roberts	Edith Rozsa	Melanie Turgeon	Melanie Turgeon
1996	Kate Pace	Melanie Turgeon	Melanie Turgeon	(cancelled)
1997	Kate Pace Lindsay	Edith Rozsa	Allison Forsyth	Melanie Turgeon
1998	Jennifer Mickelson	Allison Forsyth	Allison Forsyth	Emily Brydon
1999	Emily Brydon	Amy Prohal	Allison Forsyth	Allison Forsyth
2000	Cancelled	Allison Forsyth	Allison Forsyth	Cancelled

Source: *Ski Canada*   (1) Michelle McKendry's married name is Ruthven.

Figure Skating Champions, 1953–2000

	Canadian Champions		World Champions	
	Men	**Women**	**Men**	**Women**
1953	Peter Firstbrook	Barbara Gratton	Hayes Jenkins, US	Tenley Albright, US
1954	Charles Snelling	Barbara Gratton	Hayes Jenkins, US	Gundi Busch, W. Germany
1955	Charles Snelling	Carole Jane Pachl	Hayes Jenkins, US	Tenley Albright, US
1956	Charles Snelling	Carole Jane Pachl	Hayes Jenkins, US	Carol Heiss, US
1957	Charles Snelling	Carole Jane Pachl	Dave Jenkins, US	Carol Heiss, US
1958	Charles Snelling	Margaret Crosland	Dave Jenkins, US	Carol Heiss, US
1959	Donald Jackson	Margaret Crosland	Dave Jenkins, US	Carol Heiss, US
1960	Donald Jackson	Wendy Griner	Alain Giletti, France	Carol Heiss, US
1961	Donald Jackson	Wendy Griner	—[1]	—[1]
1962	Donald Jackson	Wendy Griner	Don Jackson, Canada	Sjoukje Dijkstra, Neth.
1963	Donald McPherson	Wendy Griner	Don McPherson, Canada	Sjoukje Dijkstra, Neth.
1964	Charles Snelling	Petra Burka	Manfred Schnelldorfer, W. Germany	Sjoukje Dijkstra, Neth.
1965	Donald Knight	Petra Burka	Alain Calmat, France	Petra Burka, Canada
1966	Donald Knight	Petra Burka	Emmerich Danzer, Austria	Peggy Fleming, US
1967	Donald Knight	Valerie Jones	Emmerich Danzer, Austria	Peggy Fleming, US
1968	Jay Humphry	Karen Magnussen	Emmerich Danzer, Austria	Peggy Fleming, US
1969	Jay Humphry	Linda Carbonetto	Tim Wood, US	Gabriele Seyfert, E. Germany
1970	David McGillivray	Karen Magnussen	Tim Wood, US	Gabriele Seyfert, E. Germany
1971	Toller Cranston	Karen Magnussen	Ondrej Nepela, Czech.	Beatrix Schuba, Austria
1972	Toller Cranston	Karen Magnussen	Ondrej Nepela, Czech.	Beatrix Schuba, Austria
1973	Toller Cranston	Karen Magnussen	Ondrej Nepela, Czech.	Karen Magnussen, Canada
1974	Toller Cranston	Lynn Nightingale	Jan Hoffman, E. Germany	Christine Errath, E. Germany
1975	Toller Cranston	Lynn Nightingale	Sergei Volkov, USSR	Dianne de Leeuw, Neth.-US
1976	Toller Cranston	Lynn Nightingale	John Curry, Gr. Brit.	Dorothy Hamill, US
1977	Ron Shaver	Lynn Nightingale	Vladimir Kovalev, USSR	Linda Fratianne, US
1978	Brian Pockar	Heather Kemkaran	Charles Tickner, US	Anett Poetzsch, E. Germany
1979	Brian Pockar	Janet Morrisey	Vladimir Kovalev, USSR	Linda Fratianne, US
1980	Brian Pockar	Heather Kemkaran	Jan Hoffmann, E. Germany	Anett Poetzsch, E. Germany
1981	Brian Orser	Tracey Wainman	Scott Hamilton, US	Denise Biellmann, Switzerland
1982	Brian Orser	Kay Thomson	Scott Hamilton, US	Elaine Zayak, US
1983	Brian Orser	Kay Thomson	Scott Hamilton, US	Rosalyn Sumners, US
1984	Brian Orser	Kay Thomson	Scott Hamilton, US	Katarina Witt, E. Germany
1985	Brian Orser	Elizabeth Manley	Alexandre Fadeev, USSR	Katarina Witt, E. Germany
1986	Brian Orser	Tracey Wainman	Brian Boitano, US	Debi Thomas, US
1987	Brian Orser	Elizabeth Manley	Brian Orser, Canada	Katarina Witt, E. Germany
1988	Brian Orser	Elizabeth Manley	Brian Boitano, US	Katarina Witt, E. Germany
1989	Kurt Browning	Karen Preston	Kurt Browning, Canada	Midori Ito, Japan
1990	Kurt Browning	Lisa Sargeant	Kurt Browning, Canada	Jill Trenary, US
1991	Kurt Browning	Josée Chouinard	Kurt Browning, Canada	Kristi Yamaguchi, US
1992	Michael Slipchuk	Karen Preston	Victor Petrenko, Russia	Kristi Yameguchi, US
1993	Kurt Browning	Josée Chouinard	Kurt Browning, Canada	Oksana Baiul, Ukraine
1994	Elvis Stojko	Josée Chouinard	Elvis Stojko, Canada	Yuka Sato, Japan
1995	Sebastien Britten	Netty Kim	Elvis Stojko, Canada	Lu Chen, China
1996	Elvis Stojko	Jennifer Robinson	Todd Eldredge, US	Michelle Kwan, US
1997	Elvis Stojko	Susan Humphreys	Elvis Stojko, Canada	Tara Lipinski, US
1998	Elvis Stojko	Angela Derochie	Alexei Yagudin, Russia	Michelle Kwan, US
1999	Elvis Stojko	Jennifer Robinson	Alexei Yagudin, Russia	Maria Butyrskaya, Russia
2000	Elvis Stojko	Jennifer Robinson	Alexei Yagudin, Russia	Michelle Kwan, US

Source: *Canadian Figure Skating Association*

(1) The 1961 world championships were cancelled after an air crash killed the entire US team travelling to the competition.

Lacrosse—The Mann Cup, 1910–2000

The Mann Cup was presented by the late Sir Donald Mann, builder of the Canadian Northern Railway, for the Senior Amateur Championship of Canada and was originally a challenge cup.

1910	Young Torontos, Toronto, Ont.
1911	Vancouver Athletic Club, Vancouver, BC
1912	Vancouver Athletic Club, Vancouver, BC
1913	Vancouver Athletic Club, Vancouver, BC
1914	Vancouver Athletic Club, Vancouver, BC
1915	Salmonbellies, New Westminster, BC
1916	Salmonbellies, New Westminster, BC
1917	Salmonbellies, New Westminster, BC
1918	Coughlans, Vancouver, BC
1919	Foundation Club, Vancouver, BC
1920–1925	Salmonbellies, New Westminster, BC
1926	Westonmen, Weston, Ont.
1927	Salmonbellies, New Westminster, BC
1928	Emmets, Ottawa, Ont.
1929	Generals, Oshawa, Ont.
1930	Excelsiors, Brampton, Ont.
1931	Excelsiors, Brampton, Ont.
1932	Mountaineers, Mimico, Ont.
1933	Tigers, Hamilton, Ont.
1934	Terriers, Orillia, Ont.
1935	Terriers, Orillia, Ont.
1936	Terriers, Orillia, Ont.
1937	Salmonbellies, New Westminster, BC
1938	Athletics, St. Catharines, Ont.
1939	Adanacs, New Westminster, BC
1940	Athletics, St. Catharines, Ont.
1941	Athletics, St. Catharines, Ont.
1942	Combines, Mimico/Brampton, Ont.
1943	Salmonbellies, New Westminster, BC
1944	Athletics, St. Catharines, Ont.
1945	Burrards, Vancouver, BC
1946	Athletics, St. Catharines, Ont.
1947	Adanacs, New Westminster, BC
1948	Tigers, Hamilton, Ont.
1949	Burrards, Vancouver, BC
1950	Crescents, Owen Sound, Ont.
1951	Timbermen, Peterborough, Ont.
1952	Timbermen, Peterborough, Ont.
1953	Timbermen, Peterborough, Ont.
1954	Timbermen, Peterborough, Ont.
1955	Shamrocks, Victoria, BC
1956	Timbermen, Nanaimo, BC
1957	Shamrocks, Victoria, BC
1958	Salmonberries, New Westminster, BC
1959	O'Keefes, New Westminster, BC
1960	Sailors, Port Credit, Ont.
1961	Burrards, Vancouver, BC
1962	O'Keefes, New Westminster, BC
1963	Carlings, Vancouver, BC
1964	Carlings, Vancouver, BC
1965	Salmonbellies, New Westminster, BC
1966	Lakers, Peterborough, Ont.
1967	Carlings, Vancouver, BC
1968	Redmen, Brooklin, Ont.
1969	Redmen, Brooklin, Ont.
1970	Salmonbellies, New Westminster, BC
1971	Warriors, Brantford, Ont.
1972	Salmonbellies, New Westminster, BC
1973	Lakers, Peterborough, Ont.
1974	Salmonbellies, New Westminster, BC
1975	Burrards, Vancouver, BC
1976	Salmonbellies, New Westminster, BC
1977	Burrards, Vancouver, BC
1978	Red Oaks, Peterborough, Ont.
1979	Shamrocks, Victoria, BC
1980	Excelsiors, Brampton, Ont.
1981	Salmonbellies, New Westminster, BC
1982	Lakers, Peterborough, Ont.
1983	Payless, Victoria, BC
1984	Lakers, Peterborough, Ont.
1985	Redmen, Brooklin, Ont.
1986	Salmonbellies, New Westminster, BC
1987	Redmen, Brooklin, Ont.
1988	Redmen, Brooklin, Ont.
1989	Salmonbellies, New Westminster, BC
1990	Redmen, Brooklin, Ont.
1991	Salmonbellies, New Westminster, BC
1992	Excelsiors, Brampton, Ont.
1993	Excelsiors, Brampton, Ont.
1994	Chiefs, Six Nations, Ont.
1995	Chiefs, Six Nations, Ont.
1996	Chiefs, Six Nations, Ont.
1997	Shamrocks, Victoria, BC
1998	Excelsiors, Brampton, Ont.
1999	Shamrocks, Victoria, BC
2000	Redmen, Brooklin, Ont.

Source: *Canadian Lacrosse Association*

Auto Racing—1990–2000

Molson Indy

	Toronto				Vancouver		
1990	Al Unser Jr.	1996	Adrian Fernandez	1990	Al Unser Jr.	1996	Michael Andretti
1991	Michael Andretti	1997	Mark Blundell	1991	Michael Andretti	1997	Alex Zanardi
1992	Michael Andretti	1998	Alex Zanardi	1992	Michael Andretti	1998	Dario Franchitti
1993	Paul Tracy[1]	1999	Dario Franchitti	1993	Al Unser Jr.	1999	Juan Montoya
1994	Michael Andretti	2000	Michael Andretti	1994	Al Unser Jr.	2000	**Paul Tracy[1]**
1995	Michael Andretti			1995	Al Unser Jr.		

Source: *Canadian Press*   (1) Canadian.

Championship Auto Racing Teams (CART), 2000

	Date	Winner
Marlboro Grand Prix	March 26	Max Papis
Toyota Grand Prix	April 16	**Paul Tracy**
Rio 200	April 30	Adrian Fernandez
Firestone Firehawk 500	May 13	Michael Andretti
Bosch Spark Plug Grand Prix	May 27	Gil de Ferran
Miller Lite 225	June 4	Juan Montoya
Tenneco Automotive Grand Prix	June 18	Helio Castroneves
Freightliner/G.I. Joe's 200	June 25	Gil de Ferran
Marconi Grand Prix	July 2	Roberto Moreno
Molson Indy, Toronto	July 16	Michael Andretti
Michigan 500	July 23	Juan Montoya
Target Grand Prix	July 30	Cristiano da Matta
Miller Lite 200	Aug. 13	Helio Castroneves
Texaco Havoline 200	Aug. 20	**Paul Tracy**
Molson Indy, Vancouver	Sept. 3	**Paul Tracy**
Honda Grand Prix	Sept. 10	Helio Castroneves

Source: *Canadian Press*

Formula One, 2000

	Date	Winner
Grand Prix of Australia	March 12	Michael Schumacher
Brazilian Grand Prix	March 26	Michael Schumacher
San Marino Grand Prix	April 9	Michael Schumacher
British Grand Prix	April 22	David Coulthard
Spanish Grand Prix	May 7	Mika Hakkinen
European Grand Prix	May 21	Michael Schumacher
Grand Prix of Monaco	June 4	David Coulthard
Canadian Grand Prix	June 18	Michael Schumacher
French Grand Prix	July 2	David Coulthard
Grand Prix of Austria	July 16	Mika Hakkinen
German Grand Prix	July 30	Rubens Barrichello
Hungarian Grand Prix	Aug. 13	Mika Hakkinen
Belgium Grand Prix	Aug. 27	Mika Hakkinen
Italian Grand Prix	Sept. 10	Michael Schumacher

Source: *Canadian Press*

Canadian Open Golf Tournament, 1980–2000

	Winner	Score		Winner	Score
1980	Bob Gilder	274	1991	Nick Price	273
1981	Peter Oosterhuis	280	1992	Greg Norman	280
1982	Bruce Lietzke	277	1993	David Frost	279
1983	John Cook	277	1994	Nick Price	275
1984	Greg Norman	278	1995	Mark O'Meara	274
1985	Curtis Strange	279	1996	Dudley Hart	202[1]
1986	Bob Murphy	280	1997	Steve Jones	275
1987	Curtis Strange	276	1998	Billy Andrade	275
1988	Ken Green	275	1999	Hal Sutton	275
1989	Steve Jones	271	2000	Tiger Woods	266
1990	Wayne Levi	278			

Source: *Canadian Press* (1) Held to 54 holes by bad weather.

Du Maurier Ltd. Women's Golf Classic, 1980–2000

	Winner	Score		Winner	Score		Winner	Score
1980	Pat Bradley	277	1987	Jodi Rosenthal	272	1994	Martha Nause	279
1981	Jan Stephenson	278	1988	Sally Little	279	1995	Jenny Lidback	280
1982	Sandra Haynie	280	1989	Tammie Green	279	1996	Laura Davies	277
1983	Hollis Stacy	277	1990	Cathy Johnston	276	1997	Colleen Walker	278
1984	Juli Inkster	274	1991	Nancy Scranton	279	1998	Brandie Burton	270[2]
1985	Pat Bradley	278	1992	Sherri Steinhauer	277	1999	Karrie Webb	277
1986	Pat Bradley	276	1993	Brandie Burton[1]	277	2000	Meg Mallon	282

Source: *Canadian Press* (1) Won on first playoff hole vs. Betsy King. (2) Tournament Record.

Kane was Able

*A*fter firing a 6-under-par 66 and taking the lead after the second round, Charlottetown's Lorie Kane erased a career resume that had nine second-place finishes but no LPGA titles. This changed August 6, 2000 when Kane, 35, won the Michelob Light Classic at Fox Run Golf Club after a final-round 71 to win the tournament with an 11-under 205.

"I know all the members at my club back in (Charlottetown) were watching. I have a feeling that when the putt went everybody pretty much went crazy," Kane said. After Kane bogeyed the 18th, several LPGA players and caddies rushed the green and doused the champion with beer to celebrate her victory.

"I think I've waited my whole life for this," said an emotional Kane.

Then, on October, 1, 2000, Kane came from five shots back before birdying the first playoff hole to win the New Albany Golf Classic in Ohio. Kane shot her second straight 68, overcoming an opening-round 74. She and Mi Hyun Kim were tied after 72 holes. Kane rolled in a nine-foot birdie putt on the first sudden-death hole to record her second Tour victory of the season.

Kane was named The Canadian Press Female Athlete of the year in 1997 after four second-place finishes and $425,964 in earnings on her first full-time year on the tour. She played only nine LPGA events in 1996.

Source: *Canadian Press*

PGA Major Tournaments

Event	Date	Winner
The Masters	Apr. 3–9, 2000	Vijay Singh
US Open Championship	June 12–18, 2000	Tiger Woods
British Open Championship	July 17–23, 2000	Tiger Woods
PGA Championship	Aug. 14–20, 2000	Tiger Woods

Source: *Canadian Press*

2000 PGA Tour Money Leaders

(as of October 1, 2000)

	Events	Winnings (US$)		Events	Winnings (US$)
1. Tiger Woods	17	$8 286 821	9. Kirk Triplett	22	$1 865 882
2. Phil Mickelson	21	3 387 457	10. Jim Furyk	22	1 845 919
3. Ernie Els	18	3 207 739	33. Mike Weir	23	1 027 379
4. Hal Sutton	22	2 976 444	57. Stephen Ames	26	636 254
5. Jesper Parnevik	18	2 322 345	91. Glen Hnatiuk	25	424 342
6. Davis Love III	21	2 087 612	161. Richard Zokol	7	152 400
7. Vijay Singh	23	1 987 368	190. David Morland IV	23	76 930
8. Tom Lehman	19	1 948 739	246. Dave Barr	5	5 200

Source: *Canadian Press*

LPGA Major Tournaments

Event	Date	Winner
Nabisco Dinah Shore	Mar. 23–26, 2000	Karrie Webb
LPGA Championship	June 22–25, 2000	Juli Inkster
US Open Championship	July 20–23, 2000	Karrie Webb
Du Maurier Canadian Open	Aug 10–13, 2000	Meg Mallon

Source: *Canadian Press*

2000 LPGA Tour Money Leaders and Canadians

(as of October 1, 2000)

	Events	Winnings (US$)		Events	Winnings (US$)
1. Karrie Webb	18	$1 687 241	9. Laura Davies	19	$510 652
2. Annika Sorenstam	18	1 158 917	10. Michele Redman	24	502 071
3. Meg Mallon	22	1 063 598	32. A.J. Eathorne	26	239 437
4. Juli Inkster	16	790 256	47. Dawn Coe-Jones	18	165 360
5. Pat Hurst	22	749 407	74. Gail Graham	23	105 439
6. Rosie Jones	21	572 183	134. Nancy Harvey	19	21 201
7. Mi Hyun Kim	23	567 371	150. Liz Earley	15	21 201
8. Lorie Kane	24	555 365	191. Barb Bunkowsky Scherbak	8	2 704

Source: *Canadian Press*

The Queen's Plate, 1960–2000

The Queen's Plate, first run in 1860, is North America's oldest annual sports event. The race for 3-year-olds foaled in Canada, is run at Toronto's Woodbine Race Track in late June or July.

	Winner	Jockey	Time[1]		Winner	Jockey	Time[1]
1960	Victoria Park	Avelino Gomez	2:02	1980	Driving Home	Bill Parsons	2:04.1
1961	Blue Light	Hugo Dittfach	2:05	1981	Fiddle Dancer Boy	David Clark	2:04.4
1962	Flaming Page	Jim Fitzsimmons	2:04.3	1982	Son of Briartic	John-Paul Souter	2:04.3
1963	Canebora	Manuel Ycaza	2:04	1983	Bompago	Larry Attard	2:04.1
1964	Northern Dancer	Bill Hartack	2:02.1	1984	Key to the Moon	Robin Platts	2:03.4
1965	Whistling Sea	Tak Inouye	2:03.4	1985	La Lorgnette	David Clark	2:04.3
1966	Titled Hero	Avelino Gomez	2:03.3	1986	Golden Choice	Vince Bracciale	2:07.1
1967	Jammed Lovely	Jim Fitzsimmons	2:03	1987	Market Control	Ken Skinner	2:03.2
1968	Merger	Wayne Harris	2:05.2	1988	Regal Intention	Jack Lauzon	2:06.1
1969	Jumpin Joseph	Avelino Gomez	2:04.1	1989	With Approval	Don Seymour	2:03
1970	Almoner	Sandy Hawley	2:04.4	1990	Izvestia	Don Seymour	2:01.4
1971	Kennedy Road	Sandy Hawley	2:03	1991	Dance Smartly	Pal Day	2:03.2
1972	Victoria Song	Robin Platts	2:03.1	1992	Alydeed	Craig Perret	2:04.6
1973	Royal Chocolate	Ted Colangelo	2:08	1993	Peteski	Craig Perret	2:04.2
1974	Amber Herod	Robin Platts	2:09.1	1994	Basqueian	Jack Laron	2:03.4
1975	L'Enjoleur	Sandy Hawley	2:02.3	1995	Regal Discovery	Todd Kabel	2:03.4
1976	Norcliffe	Jeffrey Fell	2:05	1996	Victor Cooley	Emke Ramsammy	2:03.8
1977	Sound Reason	Robin Platts	2:06.3	1997	Awesome Again	A.E. Smith	2:04
1978	Regal Embrace	Sandy Hawley	2:02	1998[2]	Archer's Bay	Kent Desormeaux	2:02.1
1979	Steady Growth	Brian Swatuk	2:06.3	1999	Woodcarver	Mickey Walls	2:03
				2000	Scatter the Gold	Todd Kabel	1:56.0

Source: *Ontario Jockey Club*

(1) Fractions of a second are in fifths. (2) Held June 21, 1998.

Thoroughbred Racing

Triple Crown	Date	Winner
Kentucky Derby	May 6, 2000	Fusaichi Pegasus
Preakness Stakes	May 20, 2000	Red Bullet
Belmont Stakes	June 10, 2000	Commendable

Source: *Canadian Press*

Canadian Triple Crown Winners in Thoroughbred Racing

(since the three-race series—The Queen's Plate, Prince of Wales and Breeders' Stakes—began in 1959)

New Providence (1959)
Caneboro (1963)
With Approval (1989)

Izvestia (1990)
x-Dance Smartly (1991)
Peteski (1993)

Source: *Canadian Press*

x = Denotes filly.

Prince of Wales Stakes, 1960–2000

	Winner	Jockey	Time[1]		Winner	Jockey	Time[1]
1960	Bulpamiru	Hugo Dittfach	2:19.4	1980	Allan Blue	Joe Belowus	2:34.4
1961	Song of Even	Jim Fitzsimmons	2:29.0	1981	Cadet Corps	Robin Platts	2:34.4
1962	King Gorm	Hugo Dittfach	2:21.1	1982	Runaway Groom	Robin Platts	2:38.2
1963	Canebora	Hugo Dittfach	2:30.3	1983	Archdeacon	Vince Bracciale	2:32.0
1964	Canadillis	Avelino Gomez	2:35.0	1984	Val Dansant	John LeBlanc	2:48.3
1965	Good Old Mort	S. McComb	2:22.4	1985	Imperial Choice	Irwin Driedger	2:34.3
1966	He's A Smoothie	Hugo Dittfach	2:19.0	1986	Golden Choice	Vince Bracciale	2:44.2
1967	Battling	Hugo Dittfach	2:21.0	1987	Coryphee	Brian Swatuk	2:39.3
1968	Rouletabille	Richard Grubb	2:18.3	1988	Regal Classic	Sandy Hawley	2:00.1
1969	Sharp-Eyed Quillo	H. Gustines	2:16.3	1989	With Approval	Don Seymour	1:56.4
1970	Almoner	Sandy Hawley	2:19.4	1990	Izvestia	Don Seymour	1:56.2
1971	New Pro	Jim Kelly	2:15.1	1991	Dance Smartly	Pal Day	1:56.3
1972	Presidial	John LeBlanc	2:16.3	1992	Benburb	Larry Attard	1:57.2
1973	Tara Road	Sandy Hawley	2:16.4	1993	Peteski	Dave Penna	1:34.4
1974	Rushton's Corsair	Jim Kelly	2:23.2	1994	Bruce's Mill	Craig Perret	1:53.4
1975	L'Enjoleur	Sandy Hawley	2:32.2	1995	Kiridashi	Larry Attard	1:55.0
1976	Norcliffe	Jeff Fell	2:30.1	1996	Stephanotis	Mickey Walls	1:55.2
1977	Dance in Time	Gary Stahlbaum	2:31.4	1997	Cryptocloser	W. Martinez	1:56
1978	Overskate	Robin Platts	2:34.2	1998[2]	Archer's Bay	Robert Landry	1:55.1
1979	Mass Rally	George Ho Sang	2:33.2	1999	Gandria	Constant Montpellier	1:56.4
				2000	Scatter the Gold	Todd Kabel	1:56.0

Source: *Ontario Jockey Club* (1) Fractions of a second are in fifths. (2) Held July 25, 1999.

Breeders Stakes, 1960–2000

	Winner	Jockey	Time[1]		Winner	Jockey	Time[1]
1960	Hidden Treasure	Al Coy	2:34.2	1979	Bridle Path	Sandy Hawley	2:29.3
1961	Song of Even	Jim Fitzsimmons	2:31.3	1980	Ben Fab	Gary Stahlbaum	2:31.3
1962	Crafty Lace	Ron Turcotte	2:52	1981	Social Wizard	George Ho Sang	2:48.4
1963	Canebora	Manuel Ycaza	2:32.1	1982	Runaway Groom	Robin Platts	2:32.1
1964	Artic Hills	R. Armstrong	2:33.3	1983	Kingsbridge	Robin Platts	2:32.2
1965	Good Old Mort	P. Kallai	2:43	1984	Bounding Away	David Clark	2:32.3
1966	Titled Hero	Avelino Gomez	2:31.2	1985	Crowning Honors	Brian Swatuk	2:50
1967	Pine Point	Avelino Gomez	2:32.1	1986	Carotene	Richard Dos Ramos	2:32.3
1968	No Parando	John LeBlanc	2:30	1987	Hangin On a Star	Dave Penna	2:30
1969	Grey Whiz	John LeBlanc	2:29	1988	King's Deputy	Sandy Hawley	2:30.3
1970	Mary of Scotland	Richard Grubb	2:38.2	1989	With Approval	Don Seymour	2:29
1971	Belle Geste	Noel Turcotte	2:28	1990	Izvestia	Don Seymour	2:33.2
1972	Nice Dancer	Sandy Hawley	2:35.4	1991	Dance Smartly	Pal Day	2:31.2
1973	Come In Dad	Wayne Green	2:33.3	1992	Blitzer	Don Seymour	2:35.3
1974	Haymaker's Jig	Robin Platts	2:30.4	1993	Peteski	Craig Perret	2:30.4
1975	Momigi	Gary Melanson	2:38.1	1994	Basqueian	Jack Lauzon	2:47.4
1976	Tiny Tinker	Sandy Hawley	2:31.1	1995	Charlie's Dewan	Craig Perret	2:26.4
1977	Dance in Time	Gary Stahlbaum	3:01.3	1996	Chief Bearheart	Mickey Walls	2:28.3
1978	Overskate	Robin Platts	2:29.2	1997	John The Magician	Steven Bahen	2:35
				1998[2]	Pinafore Park	Robert Landry	2:30.1
				1999	Free Vacation	Laurie Gulas	2:28.4
				2000	Lodge Hill	Todd Pletcher	2:28

Source: *Ontario Jockey Club* (1) Fractions of a second are in fifths. (2) August 15, 1999.

Canadian Sports Hall of Fame

(living members as of October 1, 2000)[2]

Anakin, Douglas, bobsled
Arnold, Don, rowing
Athans, George, Jr., water skiing
Aubut, Marcel, hockey builder
Balding, Al, golf
Baldwin, Matt, curling
Baumann, Alex, swimming
Bédard, Myriam, biathlon
Bedard, Robert, tennis
Béliveau, Jean, hockey
Bell, Marilyn, marathon swimming
Bernier, Sylvie, diving
Betger, Jan, curling[1]
Boldt, Arnie, field high jump
Boucher, Gaetan, speed skating
Bowyer, Johnny, hockey
Box, Ab, football
Boys, Bev, diving
Brasseur, Isabelle, figure skating
Brooks, Lela, speed skating
Brouillard, Lou, boxing
Browning, Kurt, figure skating
Burka, Ellen, figure skating builder
Burka, Petra, figure skating
Burka, Sylvia, speed skating
Cain, Larry, canoeing
Cameron, Michelle, synchro swimming
Chuvalo, George, boxing
Cliff, Leslie, swimming
Clifford, Betsy, skiing
Coleman, Jim, sports journalism
Cowan, Gary, golf
Cranston, Toller, figure skating
Crothers, Bill, track mid-distance
D'hondt, Walter, rowing
Dafoe, Frances, figure skating
Day, James, equestrian
Dexter, Glen, yachting
Dionne, Marcel, hockey
Dojack, Paul, football builder
Drake, Clare, hockey builder
Drayton, Jerome, marathon running
Dryden, Ken, hockey
Duguid, Don, curling
Dunnell, Milt, sports broadcaster
Durrelle, Yvon, boxing
Eisler, Lloyd, figure skating
Elder, James, equestrian
Emery, Dr. John, bobsled
Emery, Victor, bobsled
Esaw, Johnny, all-around builder
Esposito, Phil, hockey
Filion, Hervé, harness racing
Fisher, Hugh, canoeing[1]
Fogh, Hans, yachting
Fortier, Sylvie, synchro swimming
Frechette, Sylvie, synchro swimming
Gabriel, Tony, football
Gainey, Bob, hockey
Galbraith, Sheldon, figure skating builder
Gate, George, swimming builder
Gaudaur, Jake, Jr., football builder
Gayford, Tom, equestrian
Geoffrion, Bernard "Boom Boom," hockey
Golab, Tony, football
Graham, Laurie, skiing
Greene, Nancy, skiing
Grenier, Jean, speed skating builder
Gretzky, Wayne, hockey[1]
Gudereit, Marcia, curling[1]
Gwynne, Horace, boxing
Hall, Glenn, hockey
Hartman, Barney, skeet shooting
Hawley, Sandy, horse racing
Heddle, Kathleen, rowing
Heggtveit, Anne, skiing
Henderson, Paul, hockey
Hepburn, Doug, weightlifting
Hildebrand, Ike, lacrosse
Hiller, John, baseball
Howe, Gordie, hockey
Hull, Bobby, hockey
Hungerford, George W., rowing
Huot, Jules, golf
Hutton, Ralph, swimming
Jackson, Donald, figure skating
Jackson, Dr. Roger, rowing
Jackson, Russ, football
Jelinek, Maria, figure skating
Jelinek, Otto, figure skating
Jenkins, Ferguson, baseball
Josenhans, Andreas, yachting

▶ **Kelly**, Leonard (Red), hockey
Kidd, Bruce, track mid-distance
Kirby, Peter, bobsled
Kreiner, Kathy, skiing
Krol, Joe, football
Kwong, Norm, football
Lafleur, Guy, hockey
Lancaster, Ron, football
Laumann, Silken, rowing
Lee-Gartner, Kerrin, skiing
Lemieux, Mario, hockey
Leonard, Stan, golf
Lessard, Lucille, archery
Lidstone, Dorothy, archery
Loney, Don, football builder
Longden, Johnny, horse racing
Loomer, Lorne, rowing
Lovell, Jocelyn, cycling
Luftspring, Sammy, boxing
MacDonald, Irene, diving
MacDonald, Noel, basketball
MacMillan, Sandy, yachting
Magnussen, Karen, figure skating
Mahovlich, Frank, hockey
Mara, George, multi-sport builder
Martini, Paul, figure skating
McBean, Marnie, rowing
McCusker, Joan, curling[1]
McLarnin, Jimmy, boxing
McPherson, Donald, figure skating
Miles, John C., marathon swimming
Millar, Ian, equestrian
Mitchell, Ray, bowling
Morris, Alwyn, canoeing[1]
Muir, Debbie, synchro swim builder
Nattrass, Susan, trap shooting
Nicholas, Cindy, marathon swimming
Northcott, Ron, curling
O'Donnell, Bill, harness racing
Orr, Robert (Bobby), hockey
Orser, Brian, figure skating
Ottenbrite, Anne, swimming
Parker, Jackie, football
Pashby, Dr. Tom, multi-sport builder[1]
Paul, Robert, figure skating
Peden, Doug, multi-sport
Percy, Karen, skiing

Perry, Gordon, football
Podborski, Steve, skiing
Pollock, Sam, hockey builder
Post, Sandra, golf
Presley, Gerald, bobsled
Primrose, John, trap shooting
Ramage, Pat, skiing builder
Read, Ken, skiing
Reed, George, football
Richard, Henri, hockey
Richardson, Arnold, curling
Richardson, Ernie, curling
Richardson, Garnet, curling
Richardson, Wes, curling
Robertson, Bruce, swimming
Rogers, Doug, judo
Saunders, Claude, rowing builder
Schmidt, Milt, hockey
Scott, Barbara Ann, figure skating
Shedd, Marjory, badminton
Smith, Graham, swimming
Sorensen, Gerry, skiing
Steen, Dave, decathlon
Stewart, Marlene, golf
Stewart, Ron, football
Storey, R.A. (Red), all-around
Stukus, Annis, football builder
Tanner, Elaine, swimming
Taylor, Ron, baseball
Tewksbury, Mark, swimming
Thom, Linda, pistol shooting
Thompson, James, speedboating builder
Townsend, Cathy, bowling
Turcotte, Ron, horse racing
Underhill, Barbara, figure skating
Van Vliet, Maury, builder
Vanderburg, Helen, synchro swimming
Wagner, Barbara, figure skating
Waldo, Carolyn, synchro swimming
Waples, Keith, harness racing
Weslock, Nick, golf
Wheeler, Lucille, skiing
Whitaker, Brig. Gen. Denis, equestrian builder
Wilson, Bruce, soccer[1]
Worrall, Jim, builder
Young, Michael, bobsled

Source: *Canadian Sports Hall of Fame*
(1) New members in 2000.
(2) For a complete listing of all members, visit http://home.inforamp.net/~cshof

Newest Hall of Famers

Wayne Gretzky added another sporting honour after induction into Canada's Sports Hall of Fame in November, 2000. There were nine new additions, including the late champion curler Sandra Schmirler, and teammates Jan Betker, Joan McCusker and Marcia Gudereit. Paddlers Alwyn Morris and Hugh Fisher and former soccer star Bruce Wilson were inducted, as was Dr. Tom Pashby, a developer of equipment to make sport safer for players, who goes in the builders' category.

In a Canadian Press poll last year, Gretzky was named the country's male athlete of the century. The NHL's all-time leading scorer, already a member of Hockey's Hall of Fame, retired last spring after winning the scoring championship 10 times and the league's MVP award eight times. Schmirler's Saskatchewan rink won three Canadian and world curling championships. They also won Olympic gold in Nagano, Japan. Cancer claimed Schmirler earlier this year. Morris and Fisher won kayak gold and bronze at the 1984 Olympics in Los Angeles. Wilson earned a Canadian-record 48 caps to play for Canada internationally during his soccer career. He was for many years captain of the national team. Pashby is a leading Canadian ophthalmologist. He has led the way in developing helmets, faceguards, visors and other protective equipment.

The addition of eight athletes and one builder brings the total number of honoured members in Canada's Sports Hall of Fame to 419.

Source: Canadian Press

Canadian Press Athlete of the Century[1]

Wayne Gretzky was the runaway winner as Canadian male athlete of the century in The Canadian Press/Broadcast News survey of newspaper sports editors and broadcasters. Gretzky finished with 1,315 points and 112 of 136 first-place votes cast. Gretzky's boyhood idol, Gordie Howe, was second (836 points, four first-place votes), a whisker ahead of Bobby Orr (833, seven first place-votes).

All-round athlete Lionel Conacher, voted Canada's athlete of the half century, was fourth with 516 points and eight first-place votes. Conacher was a big winner himself in 1950, collecting 33 votes to two for runner-up Percy Williams, the 1928 double Olympic gold medalist sprinter who was 13th in the century poll.

"It's obviously a very special honour," Gretzky said.

The late Maurice (Rocket) Richard was fifth in the voting (497 points, one first-place vote), followed by Donovan Bailey (455), Fergie Jenkins (391), Mario Lemieux (333), Larry Walker (321) and Gaetan Boucher (255, one first-place vote).

Gretzky's commanding century win capped a year—and career—to remember for the 38-year-old. He retired in April after a 20-year NHL career that produced 61 records and was inducted into the Hockey Hall of Fame without the usual waiting period.

The all-seeing centre left the NHL with 894 goals, 1,963 assists and 2,857 points in 1,487 regular-season games with Edmonton, Los Angeles, St. Louis and the New York Rangers. Gretzky was the NHL's scoring leader ten times, MVP nine times and played in 17 all-star games. He also won enough cars and trucks (21 in all) to start his own dealership. In typical Gretzky fashion, he gave all but one away.

For many around the world, Gretzky is the face of Canada. And while his hockey career is over, The Great One has not left the public domain. Companies still want the Gretzky seal of approval and he is a more popular pitchman than ever.

Gretzky was joined by skier Nancy Greene and the 1972 Team Canada as other century winners. Greene, who won Olympic gold and silver in 1968, was chosen female athlete of the century, while the Summit Series winners were named team of the century.

---

(1) The Canadian Press Athlete of the Year awards were replaced by Athlete of the Century awards in 1999.

QUICK REFERENCE

Temperature Equivalents
(Celsius and Fahrenheit)

°C	°F	°C	°F	°C	°F	°C	°F	°C	°F
-50	-58	-30	-22	-10	14	10	50	30	86
-49	-56.2	-29	-20.2	-9	15.8	11	51.8	31	87.8
-48	-54.4	-28	-18.4	-8	17.6	12	53.6	32	89.6
-47	-52.6	-27	-16.6	-7	19.4	13	55.4	33	91.4
-46	-50.8	-26	-14.8	-6	21.2	14	57.2	34	93.2
-45	-49	-25	-13	-5	23	15	59	35	95
-44	-47.2	-24	-11.2	-4	24.8	16	60.8	36	96.8
-43	-45.4	-23	-9.4	-3	26.6	17	62.6	37	98.6
-42	-43.6	-22	-7.6	-2	28.4	18	64.4	38	100.4
-41	-41.8	-21	-5.8	-1	30.2	19	66.2	39	102.2
-40	-40	-20	-4	0	32	20	68	40	104
-39	-38.2	-19	-2.2	1	33.8	21	69.8	41	105.8
-38	-36.4	-18	-0.4	2	35.6	22	71.6	42	107.6
-37	-34.6	-17	1.4	3	37.4	23	73.4	43	109.4
-36	-32.8	-16	3.2	4	39.2	24	75.2	44	111.2
-35	-31	-15	5	5	41	25	77	45	113
-34	-29.2	-14	6.8	6	42.8	26	78.8	50	122
-33	-27.4	-13	8.6	7	44.6	27	80.6	100	212
-32	-25.6	-12	10.4	8	46.4	28	82.4	150	302
-31	-23.8	-11	12.2	9	48.2	29	84.2	200	392

Household Measures, Metric Equivalents

Volume

Imperial	Metric	Imperial	Metric	Imperial	Metric
1/4 tsp	1 mL	1/3 cup	50 mL	4 cups	1 L
1/2 tsp	2 mL	1/3 cup	75 mL	5 cups	1.25 L
3/4 tsp	4 mL	1/2 cup	125 mL	6 cups	1.5 L
1 tsp	5 mL	2/3 cup	150 mL	7 cups	1.75 L
2 tsp	10 mL	3/4 cup	175 mL	8 cups	2 L
1 tbsp (3 tsp)	15 mL	1 cup	250 mL		

Weight

Imperial	Metric	Imperial	Metric	Imperial	Metric
1 oz	25 g	1/2 lb	250 g	1 3/4 lb	875 g
2 oz	50 g	2/3 lb	350 g	2.2 lb	1 kg
3 oz	75 g	3/4 lb	375 g	3 lb	1.5 kg
1/4 lb	125 g	1 lb	500 g	5 lb	2.2 kg
1/3 lb	175 g	1 1/2 lb	750 g	10 lb	4.5 kg

Oven Temperatures

Imperial (°F)	Metric (°C)	Imperial (°F)	Metric (°C)	Imperial (°F)	Metric (°C)
250	120	350	180	450	230
275	135	375	190	475	245
300	150	400	200	500	260
325	160	425	220		

Canadian Imperial and Metric Measures

Name	Abbrev.	Equivalent in Related Units	Metric Equivalent
■ Length			
inch	in.	—	2.54 cm
foot	ft.	12 in.	30.48 cm
yard	yd.	3 ft.; 36 in.	0.91 m
mile	mi.	1 760 yd.; 5 280 ft.	1.609 km
■ Mass (Weight)			
grain	gr.	—	0.06 g
dram	dr.	27.343 gr.	1.77 g
ounce	oz.	16 dr.	28.35 g
pound	lb.	16 oz.	0.453 kg
hundredweight			
(short)	cwt.	100 lb.	45.36 kg
(long)	cwt.	112 lb.	50.80 kg
ton (short)	—	2 000 lb.	0.907 t
ton (long)	—	2 240 lb.	1.016 t
■ Volume and Capacity			
fluid dram	fl. dr.	0.22 cu. in.	3.55 cm^3
fluid ounce	fl. oz.	8 fl. dr.; 1.7 cu. in.	28.41 cm^3
pint	pt.	20 fl. oz.; 34.7 cu. in.	568.3 cm^3
quart	qt.	2 pt.; 69.4 cu. in.	1.14 dm^3
gallon	gal.	4 qt.; 277 cu. in.	4.55 dm^3
peck	pk.	2 gal.; 555 cu. in.	9.09 dm^3
bushel	bu.	4 pk.; 2 219 cu. in.	36.37 dm^3
barrel (oil)	bbl	35 gal.	0.159 m^3
cubic foot	ft.^{3}	1 728 in.^{3}	0.028 m^3
cubic yard	yd.^{3}	27 ft.^{3}	0.765 m^3
■ Area			
square foot	ft.^{2}	144 sq. in.	0.09 m^2
square yard	yd.^{2}	9 sq. ft.	0.836 m^2
acre	—	4 840 sq. yd.	4 047 m^2
square mile	sq. mi.	640 acres	2.590 km^2

Source: *Gage Canadian Dictionary*

Roman Numerals

I	1	VII	7	XX	20	C	100	$\overline{\text{V}}$	5 000
II	2	VIII	8	XXX	30	CC	200	$\overline{\text{X}}$	10 000
III	3	IX	9	XL	40	CD	400	$\overline{\text{L}}$	50 000
IV	4	X	10	L	50	D	500	$\overline{\text{C}}$	100 000
V	5	XI	11	LX	60	CM	900	$\overline{\text{D}}$	500 000
VI	6	XIX	19	XC	90	M	1 000	$\overline{\text{M}}$	1 000 000

Canada's Food Guide To Healthy Eating[1]

Canada's Food Guide, revised in November of 1992, recognizes that the amount of food each Canadian needs every day from the four food groups and other foods depends on age, body size, activity level, whether the individual is male or female, and if the individual is pregnant or breast-feeding. That's why the Food Guide gives a range of possible servings for each food group—young children can choose the lower number of recommended servings from a particular group, while male teenagers can go to the higher number. Most other people can choose servings somewhere in between.

Canada's Food Guide recommends, every day:

- 5 to 12 servings from the grain products group. An example of one serving would be one slice of bread; 30 g of cold cereal or 175 mL of hot cereal. Two servings would be a bagel, pita or bun; or 250 mL of rice or pasta.

- 5 to 10 servings of vegetables and fruit. One serving would be one medium size vegetable or fruit; 125 mL of fresh, frozen or canned vegetables or fruit; 250 mL of salad; or 125 mL of juice.

- 2 to 3 servings of meat or alternatives. One serving would be 50-100 g of meat, poultry or fish; 1-2 eggs; 125-250 mL of beans; 100 g of tofu; or 30 mL of peanut butter.

- Recommended servings of milk products vary according to age: 2-3 servings for children aged 4-9; 3-4 servings for young people aged 10-16; 2-4 servings for adults; and 3-4 servings for pregnant or breast-feeding women. Examples of one serving would be 250 mL of milk, 50 g of cheese or 175 g of yogurt.

Taste and enjoyment can also come from other foods and beverages that are not part of the four food groups. Some of these foods are higher in fat or calories, so it is recommended that these foods be used in moderation. The important things to remember are: enjoy a variety of foods from each group every day and choose lower-fat foods more often.

Source: Health and Welfare Canada

(1) For people four years and over.

Functions of Nutrients

Calcium aids in the formation and maintenance of strong bones and teeth; promotes healthy nerve function and normal blood clotting.
Carbohydrate supplies energy; assists in the utilization of fats.
Fat supplies energy; aids in the absorption of fat-soluble vitamins.
Fibre provides undigestible bulk, which encourages the normal elimination of body wastes.
Folacin (folic acid) aids red blood cell formation.
Iodine aids in function of the thyroid gland.
Iron combines with protein to form hemoglobin, the red blood cell constituent that transports oxygen and carbon dioxide.
Magnesium aids in formation and maintenance of strong bones and teeth; aids in energy metabolism and tissue formation.
Phosphorus aids in formation and maintenance of strong bones and teeth.

Protein builds and repairs body tissues; builds antibodies, the blood components that fight infection.
Riboflavin (vitamin B_2) maintains healthy skin and eyes; maintains a normal nervous system; releases energy to body cells during metabolism.
Thiamin (vitamin B_1) releases energy from carbohydrate; aids normal growth and appetite.
Vitamin A aids normal bone and tooth development; promotes good night vision; maintains the health of skin and membranes.
Vitamin B_{12} (cobalamin) aids in red blood cell formation; maintains healthy nerve and gastrointestinal tissues.
Vitamin C (ascorbic acid) maintains healthy teeth and gums; maintains strong vessel walls.
Vitamin E (tocopherol) protects the fat in body tissues from oxidation.
Zinc aids in energy and metabolism and tissue formation.

Source: Canada's Food Guide Handbook

Quick Reference

CANADA'S Food Guide TO HEALTHY EATING
FOR PEOPLE FOUR YEARS AND OVER

Different People Need Different Amounts of Food

The amount of food you need every day from the 4 food groups and other foods depends on your age, body size, activity level, whether you are male or female and if you are pregnant or breast-feeding. That's why the Food Guide gives a lower and higher number of servings for each food group. For example, young children can choose the lower number of servings while male teenagers can go to the higher number. Most other people can choose servings somewhere in between.

Grain Products
5-12 SERVINGS PER DAY

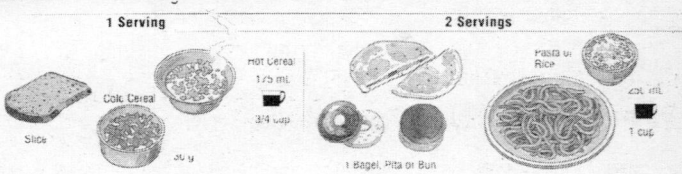

1 Serving: Slice, Cold Cereal, Hot Cereal 175 mL 3/4 cup
2 Servings: 1 Bagel, Pita or Bun, Pasta or Rice 250 mL 1 cup

Vegetables & Fruit
5-10 SERVINGS PER DAY

1 Medium Size Vegetable or Fruit

Fresh, Frozen or Canned Vegetables or Fruit 125 mL 1/2 cup

Salad 250 mL 1 cup

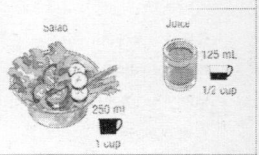
Juice 125 mL 1/2 cup

Milk Products
SERVINGS PER DAY
Children 4-9 years: 2-3
Youth 10-16 years: 3-4
Adults: 2-4
Pregnant & Breast-feeding Women: 3-4

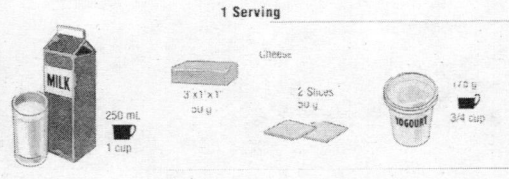

1 Serving: Milk 250 mL 1 cup • Cheese 3"x1"x1" 50 g • 2 Slices 50 g • Yogourt 175 g 3/4 cup

Other Foods

Taste and enjoyment can also come from other foods and beverages that are not part of the 4 food groups. Some of these foods are higher in fat or Calories, so use these foods in moderation.

Meat & Alternatives
2-3 SERVINGS PER DAY

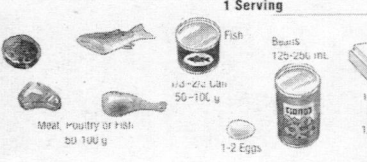

1 Serving: Meat, Poultry or Fish 50-100 g • Fish 1/3-2/3 can 50-100 g • 1-2 Eggs • Beans 125-250 mL

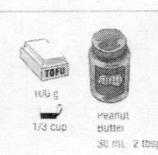

TOFU 100 g • 1/3 cup • Peanut Butter 30 mL 2 tbsp

Enjoy eating well, being active and feeling good about yourself. That's VITALITY

© Minister of Supply and Services Canada 1992. Cat. No. H39-252/1902E. No changes permitted. Reprint permission not required.
ISBN 0-662-19648-1

In 1997, Federal, Provincial and Territorial Ministers responsible for fitness, active living, recreation and sport recognized physical inactivity as a serious health issue and set a target to reduce inactivity by 10 percent by 2003. In response, Health Canada and partners launched "Canada's Physical Activity Guide to Healthy Active Living" in 1998, our first-ever set of national guidelines designed to help Canadians improve their health through regular physical activity. In 1999, "Canada's Physical Activity Guide for Older Adults" was launched. To order free copies of both Guides, call toll free 1-888-334-9769, or visit the Guide's Web site (http://www.paguide.com).

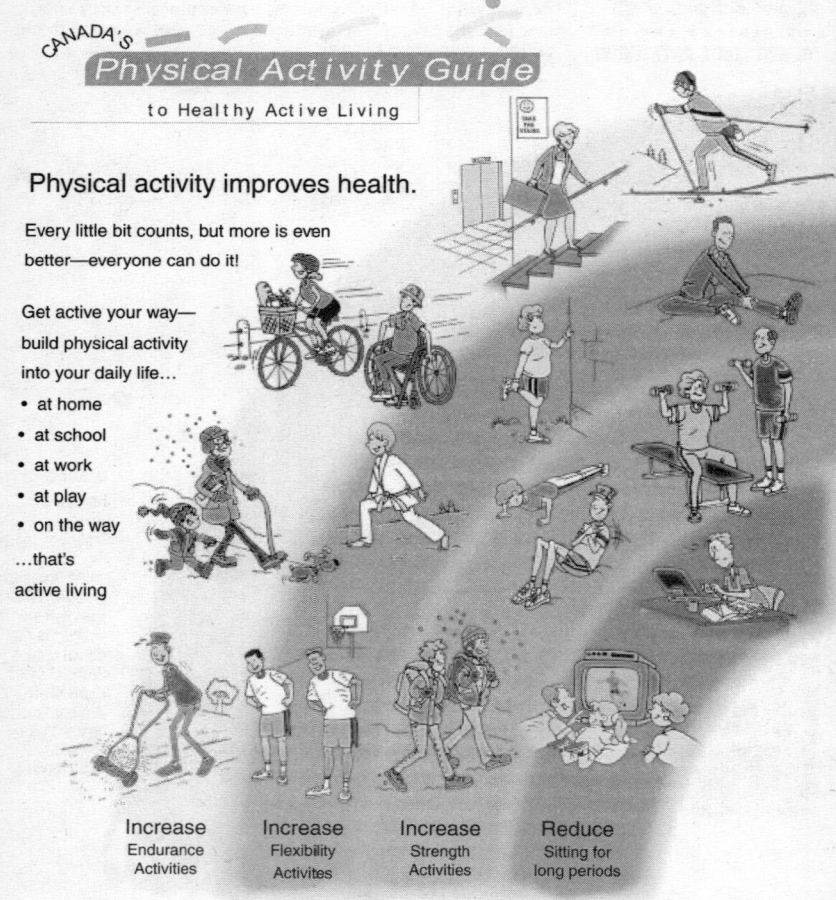

Quick Reference 801

Choose a variety of activities from these three groups:

Endurance
4–7 days a week
Continuous activities for your heart, lungs and circulatory system.

Flexibility
4–7 days a week
Gentle reaching, bending and stretching activities to keep your muscles relaxed and joints mobile.

Strength
2–4 days a week
Activities against resistance to strength muscles and bones and improve posture.

Starting slowly is very safe for most people. Not sure? Consult your health professional.

For a copy of the Guide Handbook and more information:
1-888-334-9769, or
www.paguide.com

Eating well is also important. Follow Canada's Food Guide to Healthy Eating to make wise food choices.

Get Active Your Way, Every Day—For Life!

Scientists say accumulate 60 minutes of physical activity every day to stay healthy or improve your health. As you progress to moderate activities you can cut down to 30 minutes, 4 days a week. Add-up your activities in periods of at least 10 minutes each. Start slowly... and build up.

Time needed depends on effort

Very Light Effort	Light Effort 60 minutes	Moderate Effort 30–60 minutes	Vigorous Effort 20-30 minutes	Maximum Effort
• Strolling • Dusting	• Light walking • Volleyball • Easy gardening • Stretching	• Brisk walking • Biking • Raking leaves • Swimming • Dancing • Water aerobics	• Aerobics • Jogging • Hockey • Basketball • Fast swimming • Fast dancing	• Sprinting • Racing

Range needed to stay healthy

You Can Do It – Getting started is easier than you think

Physical activity doesn't have to be very hard. Build physical activities into your daily routine.

- Walk whenever you can – get off the bus early, use the stairs instead of the elevator.
- Reduce inactivity for long periods, like watching TV.
- Get up from the couch and stretch and bend for a few minutes every hour.
- Play actively with your kids.
- Choose to walk, wheel or cycle for short trips.

- Start with a 10 minute walk – gradually increase the time.
- Find out about walking and cycling paths nearby and use them.
- Observe a physical activity class to see if you want to try it.
- Try one class to start – you don't have to make a long-term commitment.
- Do the activities you are doing now, more often.

Benefits of regular activity:
- better health
- improved fitness
- better posture and balance
- better self-esteem
- weight control
- stronger muscles and bones
- feeling more energetic
- relaxation and reduced stress
- continued independent living in later life

Health risks of inactivity:
- premature death
- heart disease
- obesity
- high blood pressure
- adult-onset diabetes
- osteoporosis
- stroke
- depression
- colon cancer

No changes permitted. Permission to photocopy this document in its entirety not required.
Cat. No. H39-429/1998-1E ISBN 0-662-86627-7

Laundry Care Symbols

The Canadian Care Labelling Program is a voluntary one that provides consumer information on the care of textiles, usually clothing. It uses five basic symbols, illustrated in the conventional "traffic light" colours. The program takes into consideration the fabric's colourfastness (i.e. whether the dye will bleed into the water and other clothing); whether it will shrink or stretch; how bleach will affect the garment; and how it may be ironed safely.

This labelling program does not apply to upholstered furniture, mattresses, carpets, leather, fur, or yarn.

The basic symbols represent washing, bleaching, drying, ironing and drycleaning, and the colours represent stop/do not (red), be careful (yellow), and go ahead (green). The red/crossed out symbol is only used when the procedure would damage the article.

Symbol	Red — Stop	Yellow — Be careful	Green — Go ahead
Washing	Do not wash	Hand wash in cool water; Machine wash in cool water at a gentle setting—reduced agitation (30°C); Machine wash in lukewarm water at a gentle setting—reduced agitation (40°C); Machine wash in warm water at a gentle setting—reduced agitation (50°C)	Machine wash in warm water at a normal setting (50°C); Machine wash in hot water at a normal setting (70°C)
Bleaching	Do not use chlorine bleach	Use chlorine bleach with care	
Drying		Dry flat; Tumble dry at low temperature	Tumble dry at medium to high temperature; Hang to dry; Drip dry
Ironing	Do not iron	Iron at low setting (110°C); Iron at medium setting (150°C)	Iron at high setting (200°C)
Dry Cleaning	Do not dry clean	Dry clean—with caution	Dry clean

Source: Industry Canada

Product Safety Symbols

Health Canada has devised a set of safety symbols for containers of household chemicals and other materials. These symbols indicate possible hazards associated with various products such as cleaning liquids and powders, paint thinners, drain cleaners, windshield washer fluids and polishes, as well as some glues and treatments for household surfaces such as brick and metal, and garden chemicals.

The symbols indicate the type of danger and are contained in a frame that indicates the degree of danger—the more sides the frame has, the more dangerous the product is. In addition to the symbols, the labels on most of these containers include a safety warning. Learn the symbols opposite and handle the materials with care, especially if children live in the home or visit often.

Follow these steps to Safety:

- Teach children that the symbols mean Danger! Do Not Touch!
- Chemical product containers, even if sealed or empty, are not toys. Never let children play with them.
- If there is anything in the label instructions that you don't understand, ask for help. Make sure the symbols and labels on containers are not removed or covered up.
- Keep household chemicals in their original containers. Never mix them together. Some mixtures can produce harmful gases.
- Close the cap on the container tightly, even if you set it down for just a moment. Make sure that child-resistant containers are working.
- Keep all chemical products out of sight and out of reach of children.

Corrosive: the product can burn skin or eyes, and if swallowed, will damage the throat and stomach.

Explosive: the container can explode if heated or punctured. Flying pieces of metal or plastic from the container can cause serious injury, especially to the eyes.

Flammable: the product or its vapous will catch fire easily if it is near heat, flames or sparks

Poison: if the product is swallowed, licked or even, in some cases inhaled, it can cause sickness or death

If someone is injured:

- Call your doctor or the Poison Control Centre immediately.
- Give the information from the label to the person answering.
- Take the container with you when you go for help.

CANADIAN IDENTITY

Sooner or later all Canadians acquire a number of pieces of identification. These can include birth certificates, Social Insurance Numbers and health cards at a minimum, plus passports. All of these documents are necessary at some time or another to prove identity (including citizenship) or to establish eligibility for social benefits in various situations.

■ What if you've lost your birth certificate?

A birth certificate is the document that initially establishes your legal identity. Individuals should be registered at birth; the Canadian certificate that is issued is necessary to obtain health cards, passports and SINs. Foreign birth certificates are also the starting point for establishing identity or eligibility in Canada.

If you need to replace a lost Canadian birth certificate, information on how to do so can be obtained from the following:

Newfoundland
Vital Statistics
Government Service Centre
Department of Government Services & Lands
5 Mews Place, P.O. Box 8700
St. John's, Nfld. A1B 4J6
Tel: (709) 729-3308
Fax: (709) 729-0946
http://www.gov.nf.ca/gsl/

Prince Edward Island
Division of Vital Statistics
Department of Health & Community Services
35 Douses Road, P.O. Box 3000,
Montague, PEI C0A 1R0
Tel: (902) 838-0880 or (902) 838-0881
Fax: (902) 838-0883
http://www.gov.pe.ca/vitalstatistics

Nova Scotia
Deputy Registrar General
1723 Hollis Street, P.O. Box 157
Halifax, NS B3J 2M9
Tel: (902) 424-4381
(902) 424-4380 (recording)
http://www.gov.ns.ca/bacs/vstat

New Brunswick
Registrar General
Division of Vital Statistics
Department of Gov't Services and Lands
Centennial Building, P.O. Box 6000
Fredericton, NB E3B 5H1
Tel: (506) 453-2385
(506) 444-5525 (recording)
http://www.gov.nb.ca/0379/en/index.htm

Quebec
Direction de l'etat civil
Ministere des Relations avec les citoyens et de l'Immigration
205, rue Montmagny
Quebec, Que. G1N 2Z9
Tel: (418) 643-3900
http://www.etatcivil.gouv.qc.ca/english/default.htm

Ontario
Office of the Registrar General
P.O. Box 4600, 189 Red River Road
Thunder Bay, Ont. P7B 6L8
Tel: (416) 325-8305
In Ontario call: 1-800-461-2156
http://www.ccr.gov.on.ca/mccr/orgindex.htm

Manitoba
Division of Vital Statistics
Community Services
254 Portage Avenue
Winnipeg, Man. R3C 0B6
Tel: (204) 945-8177
(204) 945-3701 (recording)
http://www.gov.mb.ca

Saskatchewan
Division of Vital Statistics
Department of Health
1942 Hamilton Street
Regina, Sask. S4P 3V7
Tel: (306) 787-3092

Alberta
Government Services, Alberta Registries
Vital Statistics, P.O. Box 2023
Edmonton, Alta T5J 4W7
Tel: (780) 427-7013 (recording)

British Columbia
Division of Vital Statistics Ministry of Health
818 Fort Street
Victoria, BC V8W 1H8
Tel: 1-800-663-8328
Fax: (250) 952-1829
http://www.hlth.gov.bc.ca/vs

Yukon Territories
Registrar of Vital Statistics
P.O. Box 2703
Whitehorse, YT Y1A 2C6
Tel: (403) 667-5207

Northwest Territories
Registrar General
Vital Statistics
Department of Health and Social Services
Government of NWT, P.O. Bag 9

Inuvik, NT X0E 0T0
Tel: (867) 777-7420
Fax: (867) 777-3197

Nunavut
Registrar General of Vital Statistics
Nunavut Health and Social Services, P.O. Bag 3
Rankin Inlet, NT X0C 0G0
Tel: (867) 645-5002
Toll-free: 1-800-661-0833
Fax: (867) 645-2997

■ Social Insurance Number (SIN)

Social Insurance Numbers are issued by Human Resources Development Canada. The nine-digit number is how the federal government identifies you for taxation, premiums (and payments) for pensions and employment insurance premiums. The SIN is also used as a form of identification when applying for jobs or trying to gain admittance to an academic program.

How do you get a SIN? You can apply for one in person at a Human Resources Centre (check the blue pages in your local telephone book for the office nearest you) or you can apply by mail. You can obtain the form from an HRDC office or you can download it from HRDC's web site (http://www.hrdc-drhc.gc.ca).

In both cases, you must fully complete the application, which asks for your name, date of birth, place of birth, and your mother's and father's birth names. You must also provide the original (or a certified copy) of the document(s) that prove your identity and your status in Canada. If you are a Canadian citizen born in Canada, you may use your birth certificate or passport; in the cases of Quebec and Newfoundland, a baptismal certificate is also acceptable. If you are a Canadian citizen born outside the country, a Certificate of Canadian Citizenship or a passport is required. A Permanent Resident can use a Canadian Immigration Record and Visa or Record of Landing, a Confirmation of Landing Document, a Canada Travel Document, a Canadian Certificate of Identity, a foreign passport stamped "Permanent Resident" by Canada Immigration or a Returning Resident Permit.

If the name you are currently using (the name that will appear on your Social Insurance Number card) is different from the name on the original documents, you must also supply evidence that your name was legally changed either by marriage/divorce or by law.

If the card is lost or stolen, notify the local HRDC office immediately. The staff there will advise you of what steps need to be taken to protect yourself from SIN fraud. (This usually takes the form of someone else applying for government benefits under your name.)

SIN fraud is also defined as: knowingly applying for more than one SIN; using someone else's number to obtain financial benefits or establish an identity; loaning or selling a SIN or card to another party; or manufacturing a SIN card.

■ Just in Case: How to get on the voters' list

Canadian citizens over the age of 18 on polling day are entitled to vote in federal elections and referendums. (Check your provincial/territorial electoral authority for the voting age in your province or territory.) Canadian citizens who have lived away from Canada for less than five years in a row are eligible to vote under the Special Voting Rules. Canadian citizens who are serving time of less than two years in a Canadian correctional institution also have the right to vote.

Elections Canada now maintains a permanent register of eligible voters, based on the list from the previous elections, by-elections and referendums. (Federal elections must be held every five years by law.) They use sources such as motor vehicle registers, Canada Customs and Revenue Agency, Citizenship Canada and permanent provincial lists of electors to keep information up-to-date.

If you have moved since the last election, you may still be registered to vote in the area of your previous address. It is also possible, however, that Elections Canada's sources have kept your address information current. (Ticking "Yes" on your tax form is a quick and easy way to keep your voter registration current. Ticking "No" doesn't mean you can't vote. It simply means that your registration information may be out-of-date.) To find out if your registration is correct, you can write to the National Registrar of Electors asking for confirmation. Send your query along with a photocopy of a piece (or pieces) of identification that include your address and your signature (a driver's licence will do, or a phone bill plus a library or health card, for example).

If you have recently turned 18, Elections Canada should send you a letter asking you to confirm your citizenship, consent to being added to the Register and provide your signature. If you are a new citizen, ticking off the consent box on the application for citizenship is enough to get your name on the voters' list.

When an election is called, you should receive a notification of your polling station in the mail. If you have not received the notice in the few weeks prior to the election, contact Elections Canada to get yourself on the voters' list. You can also get on the list by presenting proof of citizenship and sufficient identification at the polling station on the day of the election. For more information, visit http://www.elections.ca.

Note: See page 64 for information on how to become a Canadian citizen

Canadian Passports

The best of proof of citizenship when you are outside Canada is a valid passport. It is the only proof that is accepted in all countries. While passports are not officially required for entry into the US, many Canadians have been stopped for failure to have photo identification and proof of citizenship with them. In addition, passports can be useful when cashing travellers' cheques or completing legal transactions in the US, and a passport is essential if the US is only one stop in a multi-destination tour. A passport can be replaced if it is stolen or lost during a trip—unlike a birth certificate or a driver's licence.

Any Canadian citizen may obtain a passport. The passport is good for five years; it cannot be renewed or extended. Make sure that you will be back home before the expiry date. (Some countries will not allow you in unless you have a passport that is valid long after you plan to return home.) Many countries require a visa in addition to a valid passport. Always check with your travel agent or that country's representative (listed in "Nations of the World") before you leave home, to ensure you have all of the required documentation.

■ How to get a passport

Application forms are available at post offices and passport offices (there are 28 of them across the country). The form requires basic information about birth, citizenship, marital status and residence, in addition to two copies of a passport photo, which must conform to specific requirements relating to size and type of shot. (Passport photos can be obtained at many photo supply stores as well as other outlets. They can be in black and white or colour. Family snapshots are not suitable.)

The completed form must be witnessed by a "guarantor," someone who has known you for at least two years and can attest to the truth of the information submitted. A guarantor must come from a recognized profession such as engineering, medicine or clergy or be in a senior administrative position in an academic or financial institution.

When you present your fully completed and witnessed application form at a passport office, you must also present the photos (one of which has been signed by your guarantor), the original of your proof of citizenship (birth certificate or citizenship certificate) and the fee ($60 for a 24-page passport). You must also present any expired passports. These will be voided and returned to you.

If you choose to send the application in rather than presenting it in person, it can be mailed to Passport Office, Department of Foreign Affairs and International Trade, Ottawa, ON K1A 0G3 or couriered to The Passport Office, Commercial Level 2, Place du Centre, 200 Promenade du Portage, Hull, QC J8X 4B7.

Children under 16 can either be listed on one of their parent's passports or have their own. Those listed on a parent's passport can only travel outside the country with that parent. Those who are travelling alone must have their own passport. The application form for a child under 16 is Form B; be sure to specify if you require an application form for a child's passport.

When is the best time to apply? If you go in person, the offices tend to be less busy between opening time and 11 a.m. Wednesday and Thursdays are usually slower days. June to November is considered "off season."

It generally takes eight working days to get your passport ready for pick up (or delivery by Priority Courier). If there are problems with your application, it will take longer. An average of 650 passports are issued every working hour of the day.

What if your passport expires while you are abroad?

If you are residing abroad and need to renew your passport during that time you must obtain the standard passport application form from any Canadian diplomatic or consular mission and complete it as required. The completed application form, new photos and proof of citizenship must be submitted to the closest office issuing Canadian passports in the country where you reside. (If you are living in the US, you can mail the form to the Ottawa address noted above, or courier it to the processing office in Hull, Que.) Processing time varies from country to country and you should allow two to three months from the time you get the application form to the time you need the passport to make sure it will be available in time.

What if you lose your passport?

To ensure your passport is safe, consider locking it in your hotel room or accommodation—many hotels offer safe places for valuables. Carry a photocopy with you as a back up document. If you carry your passport with you, check for it and other valuables at least once a day, even if you are not using them. That way, a lost passport or credit card will have been missing for no more than 24 hours and you have a better chance of retracing your steps to find it. Remember that as proof of citizenship, your passport is an important document to both yourself and someone who may want to use it illegally.

While it is your responsibility to protect your passport and other valuables during your trip, the nearest Canadian diplomatic or consular mission can help you if your passport is lost or stolen. The loss must also be reported to the local police. (The same applies if your passport is lost or stolen at home. The police must be notified as well as the nearest passport office.)

Consular Services

Canada's Department of Foreign Affairs and International Trade maintains a network of 250 offices, embassies, high commissions, consulates, honorary consuls and development offices in over 180 countries. (Australian diplomatic officers provide services to Canadians where Canada does not have a presence.) For a list of Canadian representation abroad, consult the country-by-country listings in "Nations of the World." The offices are also listed in a government booklet entitled *Bon Voyage, But....*

Should you lose your passport, become ill or incapacitated, become a victim of crime (or be arrested), the staff are there to provide assistance. In addition, emergency services can be obtained by calling (613) 996-8885 at any time. (Collect calls will be accepted.)

Pre-trip Planning

Before you go on a trip—be it a brief or extended one—make sure that you have **proper identification** before you go, and any **visas** you require. In addition, always take out-of-country **medical insurance** and enough medication or other medical appliances you may require in case it is difficult to replace them at your destination—even eyeglasses can be hard to come by in some places.

If you have any doubt about the political stability of the country you are about to visit (or even if you don't), you can check to see if any **Travel Advisories** have been issued for travellers abroad before you go by calling 1-800-575-2500 or visiting the department's Web site at http://voyage.dfaitmaeci.gc.ca/destinations/menu_e.htm. Travel advisories can cover anything from the local political situation to an outbreak of Yellow Fever. While Canada's representatives abroad can assist you if you get into trouble, it's best to plan from the beginning to avoid difficulties.

Source: *Department of Foreign Affairs and International Trade*

Canadian Postal Rates

(as of October 1, 2000)

Within Canada		
Lettermail and postcards (letter size max. 245 mm x 150 mm x 5 mm)	0-30 g	$0.46
	31-50 g	$0.73
Non-standard and oversize items (max. 380 mm x 270 mm x 20 mm)	0-100 g	$0.92
	101-200 g	$1.50
	201-500 g	$2.00
Registered mail		$4.00 plus applicable postage

To the USA		
Lettermail and postcards (airmail) (letter size max. 245 mm x 150 mm x 5 mm)	0-30 g	$0.55
	31-50 g	$0.80
Non-standard and oversize items (max. 38 mm x 270 mm x 20 mm)	0-100 g	$1.25
	101-200 g	$2.35
	201-500 g	$4.05
Registered mail		$4.00 plus applicable postage

Note: GST is applicable to all postal charges. Other services for parcels, bulk mailings or expedited delivery are also available.

■ What's the best way to address an envelope?

A wide variety of packages and styles of address make it through Canada Post's system, however there are ways to ensure that your mail is handled most efficiently. While the computerized systems can read a range of addresses—including handwriting—the system's preferred style is as follows:

Line 1: name of the recipient
Line 2: title, floor number, attention line
Line 3: If business, company name
Line 4: unit number (if applicable) –
street number and name
If post office box, information should appear above municipality name
Line 5: municipality, province   postal code

While the system can read upper and lower case, upper case is preferred, with an aligned left margin. Address lines should be less than 40 characters long. The first three elements of the postal code should be separated from the final three by a space, never a hyphen.

The return address should be formatted the same way, in the upper left corner (or on the back at the top). If on the front, it should be clearly separated from the destination address and preferably be smaller than the destination address.

Characters should be larger than 2 mm and smaller than 5 mm (10 to 12 point).

When addressing mail to the United States, the US Postal Service prefers the use of the two-character state symbol rather than having the name of the state spelled out. The ZIP code should come two spaces after the state code and appear on the same line. The final line should be USA. When addressing international mail, the name of the country should be spelled out in full (GREAT BRITAIN) and should appear on the last line of the address, below any other municipality, city name or code information.

■ Province and Territory Symbols

The two-character symbols have been designated by Canada Post in order to make mailing more efficient. The codes for Canada's ten provinces and three territories are:

Newfoundland	NF
Prince Edward Island	PE
Nova Scotia	NS
New Brunswick	NB
Quebec	QC
Ontario	ON
Manitoba	MB
Saskatchewan	SK
Alberta	AB
British Columbia	BC
Yukon Territory	YT
Northwest Territories	NT
Nunavut	NT

Source: *Canada Post*

OBITUARIES 2001

October 1, 1999–September 30, 2000

ABEL, Sidney Gerald, 81. Centre for Detroit Red Wings and captain of the team 1942-3 and 1946-52, playing with Gordie Howe and Ted Lindsay; a Hart Trophy winner, he also served as the Red Wings general manager and coach. February 8, 2000.

APPLEBAUM, Louis, 82. A composer and arts administrator, Applebaum wrote scores for film, theatre and television. Integral to the creation of the National Arts Centre Orchestra in Ottawa and active on the National Film Board and Ontario Arts Council, he wrote the score for CBC TV's *The National Dream* and won an Oscar nomination for the score of the movie *The Story of G.I. Joe* (1945); his last work was the opera *Ereewhon*. April 20, 2000.

ARAB, John Joseph, 69. Leading tenor with the Canadian Opera Company between 1958 and 1977. Noted for roles in operas including *The Barber of Seville, Otello, La Bohème* and *La Traviata,* as well as Harry Somers's *Louis Riel*. June 11, 2000.

ARCHER, Violet (b. Violetta Balistreri), 86. Internationally recognized classical music composer who taught at the University of Alberta, Archer studied under Béla Bartók and Paul Hindemith. Many of her choral and orchestral works were inspired by folk music of French Canada, the Maritimes and Inuit culture. *Ten Folk Songs for Four Hands; Prairie Profiles*. February 21, 2000.

ARKAN (Zeljko Raznatovic), 47. Serbian warlord, head of paramilitary Tigers; accused of war crimes in Bosnian and Croatian wars between 1991 and 1995; was on Interpol's most-wanted list for crimes including bank robbery and extortion. Assassinated in Belgrade hotel. January 15, 2000.

BATES, Daisy, 84. American civil-rights activist who was instrumental in the fight against segregation when she enabled nine black students to enter Little Rock Central High School in 1957; barred by the National Guard, the students were finally escorted in by troops on the orders of Dwight Eisenhower. *The Long Shadow of Little Rock*. November 4, 1999.

BIONDA, Jack, 66. Lacrosse champion whose teams (Victoria Shamrocks and New Westminster Salmonbellies) won five Mann cups; also played for NHL in the 1950s. November 3, 1999.

BISSELL, Claude Thomas, 83. Former president of University of Toronto and Carleton University in Ottawa, and chairman of the Canada Council; biographer of Vincent Massey. *The Imperial Canadian*. June 21, 2000.

BLACK, Sir Robert "Robin" Brown, 93. As British governor of Hong Kong, 1958-64, Black encouraged the growth and financial stability of the city, and was instrumental in the vast construction of housing when Chinese mainlanders flooded Hong Kong in the 1960s. October 29, 1999.

BOURGUIBA, Habib, 96. President of Tunisia from 1956, when the country gained independence from France, to 1987, when he was deposed. Bourguiba was instrumental in bringing about the westernisation of the Muslim country, discouraging Muslim traditions that hindered progress, and supporting equal rights for women. April 6, 2000.

BOWLES, Paul, 88. American author whose first book, *The Sheltering Sky,* set in North Africa, was named by the Modern Library as one of the century's best books; he also was a Broadway composer and translator of Moroccan writers. *Let It Come Down; Up Above the World*. November 18, 1999.

BRESSON, Robert, 98. French film director who inspired Francois Trufffaut and Jean-Luc Godard; a forerunner of New Wave cinema. Bresson employed a realistic style in films including *A Man Escaped, Pickpocket,* and *Diary of a Country Priest,* based on the Georges Bernanos novel. December 18, 1999.

BUDGE, Donald, 84. The first tennis player to win international Grand Slam tennis tournaments, in 1938, in France, USA, Australia and at Wimbleton. January 26, 2000.

CADMUS, Paul, 94. American artist both celebrated and denounced for his Italian Renaissance-inspired figurative works depicting dramatic subjects and gay cultural themes. *The Fleet's In; Sailors and Floozies.* December 12, 1999.

CARTLAND, Dame Barbara, 98. Flamboyant, pink-clad author of bodice-ripping romances that eschewed blatant sex, Cartland was the hugely prolific writer of 723 romance novels; her books, with individual print runs exceeding one million copies, were internationally popular. Cartland also made headlines as the step-grandmother of the late Princess Diana. May 21, 2000.

CASHIN, Bonnie, 84. American fashion designer of the 1940s and '50s; started out as a designer for Twentieth Century Fox in L.A., designing costumes for *Anna and the King of Siam* among other films, later based in New York where her ponchos, canvas raincoats and big zippers became stylistic trademarks. February 3, 2000.

CAUDWELL, Sarah, 60. British best-selling writer whose career as a London barrister led to her popular novels with legal themes. Her mother was said to be the model for Sally Bowles in Christopher Isherwood's stories of Berlin, later adapted to the musical *Cabaret. The Shortest Way to Hades; The Sirens Sang of Murder.* January 28, 2000.

CHAMBERLAIN, Wilt, 63. Celebrated basketball player who set eight NBA records during his 14-year career, once scoring 100 points in one game, the seven-foot-one Chamberlain was lambasted for boasting that he had had sex with 20,000 women, a fact he later retracted as having been made in jest. October 12, 1999.

CHERRY, Zena Mary MacMillan, 84. Longtime Toronto *Globe and Mail* society columnist; her "After a Fashion" column was often parodied for its extensive lists of Toronto's social elite (and their wives), but a mention by Cherry was regarded by many as a social asset. January 21, 2000.

CHRISTMAS, Eric, 84. British-born character actor who played extensively in British, Canadian and American television and films; he appeared at the Stratford Festival in Ontario, on television with Wayne and Shuster, and in many American films.*The Andromeda Strain; Bugsy.* July 22, 2000.

CHEVALIER, Leo, 65. Montreal-based fashion designer whose elegant couture collections won him international fame; fashion columnist for the Montreal *Gazette.* June 16, 2000.

CLAIBORNE, Craig, 79. For 29 years, Claiborne served as the *New York Times* food editor; his prolific career as a cookbook writer brought fine cuisine to North Americans. *The New York Times Cookbook; French Cooking;* and the autobiographical *A Feast Made for Laughter.* January 23, 2000.

COHEN, Alexander, 79. Highly successful producer for popular Broadway and London's West End theatre, Cohen's hits included *Hellzapoppin',* Jules Feiffer's *Little Murders, Hamlet* (starring Richard Burton), and Harold Pinter's *Homecoming.* April 22, 2000.

COHEN, Matt, 56. Novelist, short story writer, winner of 1999 Governor General's Literary Award for fiction with *Elizabeth and After;* also wrote semi-autobiographical *Last Seen* and *Spanish Doctor,* and *Emotional Arithmetic.* Noted for his versatility in both the literary and academic disciplines, writing short stories, poetry and children's stories. December 2, 1999.

COLICOS, John, 71. Veteran character actor who appeared in film (*Anne of the Thousand Days; Star Trek; Scorpio),* CBC productions (*The National Dream; Love and Hate)* and on the soap opera *General Hospital,* Colicos also played many roles, such as King Lear and Cyrano, in Ontario's Stratford Theatre, at London, Eng.'s Old Vic, and on Broadway. March 6, 2000.

COMFORT, Alexander, 80. Author of the highly successful sex manual *The Joy of Sex: A Gourmet Guide to Lovemaking,* published in 1972. Sold internationally, the manual, with its explicit drawings and sometimes humorous tone, has sold 12 million copies. Comfort was also a novelist, medical biologist and gerontologist. March 26, 2000.

CORNELL, Ward MacLaurin, 75. Long-time host of the CBC's *Hockey Night in Canada,* Cornell became the NHL's "voice of hockey"; later served under Bill Davis's Ontario PC party as a deputy minister and agent-general based in

London, Eng., a controversial appointment that critics denounced as patronage. February 5, 2000.

COULTHARD, Jean, 92. Classical composer of symphonies, operas, concertos, choral works, Coulthard, with Violet Archer and Barbara Pentland, was internationally celebrated for her innovative style. *Return of the Native* (opera); *Cradle Song*. March 9, 2000.

CREMO, Lee, 60. Cape Breton-born fiddler whose Celtic-style music made him a six-time winner of the Maritime Old-Time Fiddling Contest and of the Alberta Tar Sands Competition; performed for the Queen during Expo '67. October 10, 1999.

CRISP, Quentin (b. Dennis Pratt), 90. Flamboyant British writer and actor whose 1968 autobiographical novel, *The Naked Civil Servant*, launched his career. The book, later made into a 1976 movie starring John Hurt, profiled the life of a gay man in the unenlightened days of 1930s Britain. *How to Have a Life-Style; Manners from Heaven*. November 21, 1999.

DANKO, Rick, 56. Founder of the rock, folk, blues group, the Band, Danko was a singer and bass guitar player. The Band played Woodstock in 1969, toured with Bob Dylan, and was the subject of director Martin Scorcese's film *The Last Waltz*. December 10, 1999.

DESCHENES, Jules, 76. Chief Justice of the Quebec Superior Court; in the 1980s headed royal commission on war criminals in Canada; also commission on Quebec language laws as they pertained to education. May 10, 2000.

DEUTSCH, André, 82. Hungarian-born British publisher whose career began when he published controversial German texts; later became internationally renowned, publishing American classics such as Norman Mailer's *The Naked and the Dead*. April 13, 2000.

DIESTELMEYER, Wally, 74. With partner Suzie Morrow Francis won the Olympic bronze medal for pairs skating in 1948; they invented the "death spiral" skating manoeuvre still used by skaters today. December 23, 1999.

DUNN, Gerald Patrick, 97. Owner of Dunn's Pavilion in Bala, Ontario, in the Muskoka vacation area, which, in its heyday, hosted such luminaries as Louis Armstrong, the Dorsey Brothers and Duke Ellington. December 5, 1999.

DURY, Ian, 57. Lead singer of Ian Dury and the Blockheads, a British New Wave rock group that was founded in 1977. Later appeared in films such as Peter Greenaway's *The Book, the Thief, His Wife and Her Lover*. "Sex, Drugs and Rock and Roll." March 27, 2000.

FAIRBANKS, Douglas Jr., 90. Hollywood actor and son of movie legend Douglas Fairbanks, he appeared on stage and on film; although never achieving his swashbuckling father's reputation, he appeared in several Hollywood movies, including *Sinbad the Sailor, A Woman of Affairs* and *Little Caesar*, as well as on television. May 7, 2000.

FITCH, James Marston, 90. American architect who rebelled against the trend of the 1950s and '60s to demolish historic buildings, leading the movement to restore and preserve vernacular architecture. Instrumental in South Street Seaport development in New York City. April 10, 2000.

FORTIN, André "Dédé", 38. Quebec pop star, head of group Les Colocs, whose combination of rock, reggae, rap and blues led him to winning Quebec's coveted Félix award in 1998. "La Rue Principale"; *Dehors Novembre*. May 10, 2000.

FOTI, Joseph, 80. Italian-born civil servant whose fund-raising barbecues for the Liberal Party brought friendship and respect from the country's high-fliers, including Jean Chrétien, former Ontario Liberal leader David Peterson and Toronto mayor Mel Lastman. May 10, 1999.

FUCHS, Dr. Vivian, 91. British explorer who led the Trans-Antarctic Expedition, the first to cross the surface of Antarctica, in 1957-58; his adaptation of the vehicle used to cross the rough land led to the development of the Sno-Cat, a caterpillar-wheeled vehicle. November 11, 1999.

FULTON, E. Davie, 84. Seven times elected as a PC MP for Kamloops, BC, Fulton, a Rhodes scholar and confrontational politician, served as Justice minister in John Diefenbaker's government, also held attorney-general, citizenship and immigration, and public works portfolios. Fulton became a BC Supreme Court judge in 1973. May 22, 2000.

GANONG, Randol Whidden, 93. Head of family-owned Ganong Bros. Ltd., a leading confectionery company based in St. Stephen, NB. March 18, 2000.

GHERMEZIAN, Jacob, 97. Businessman who moved his company, Triple Five Corp., from Iran to Canada; built the West Edmonton Mall. Also a stakeholder in Minnesota's vast Mall of America. June 3, 2000.

GIELGUD, Sir John (b. Gelgaudas), 96. A highly regarded British stage and film actor, Gielgud, noted for his sonorous voice, performed a vast Shakespearean repertoire, and also appeared in contemporary works, including the Dudley Moore film *Arthur* and the British television production of *Brideshead Revisited.* He directed Richard Burton in *Hamlet* in Toronto and starred in Stratford, Ont., in his one-man show *The Ages of Man.* Also appeared in *Shine, Summer's Lease* and Peter Greenaway's *Prospero's Books,* an adaptation of *The Tempest.* May 21, 2000.

GOREY, Edward St. John, 75. American artist and author, Gorey was well known for his sometimes macabre pen and ink sketches; he created the drawings for the opening credits of the PBS *Mystery!* series, also illustrated books by Samuel Beckett and Edward Lear. April 15, 2000.

GUINNESS, Sir Alec, 86. Beloved British actor whose rather bland appearance belied his ability to take on a diversity of roles in film, on stage and television, in both dramatic and comedic roles. His almost 70-year career included parts in *The Bridge on the River Kwai, Kind Hearts and Coronets, The Captain's Paradise* and *Star Wars.* Wrote an autobiography titled *Blessings in Disguise.* August 5, 2000.

GWYN, Sandra (Alexandra), 65. Social historian and journalist whose first love was the celebration of her native Newfoundland, Gwyn was a major contributor to Canada's leading magazines and author of the noteworthy books *Tapestry of War: A Private View of Canadians in the Great War* and *The Private Capital: Ambition and Love in the Age of Macdonald and Laurier.* May 26, 2000.

HAMILTON, Willie, 82. Scottish Labour MP (1951-87) who made a career of criticizing the British royal family in vitriolic attacks. Wrote *My Queen and I; Blood on the Wall: The Memoirs of an Anti-Royalist.* January 27, 2000.

HENNING, Doug, 52. A magician and entertainer, Henning became famous with *Spellbound,* a combination rock opera and magic show, also appeared on television and Broadway; he joined the Natural Law Party of Canada in the late 1980s. February 7, 2000.

HEBERT, Anne, 83. Quebec-born poet and novelist and winner of international literary awards, including three Governor General's awards and a recent nomination for the Giller Prize for her last book, *Am I Disturbing You?* Hébert was celebrated for her passionate, romantic novels based on Quebec rural life. Her novel *Kamouraska* was made into a film of the same name, starring Genevieve Bujold. Hébert was based in Paris for much of her life. January 22, 2000.

HELLER, Joseph, 76. American author whose book *Catch-22* spawned the popular catchphrase, and whose theme was a harbinger of the upcoming Vietnam War. Other works include *No Laughing Matter, Closing Time,* and the posthumous *Portrait of an Artist as an Old Man.* December 12, 1999.

HOFFMEISTER, Bertram Meryl, 92. Highly regarded Canadian general during World War II, noted as a successful battlefield strategist, he fought throughout Europe; later became chairman of lumber conglomerate MacMillan Bloedel in 1956. December 4, 1999.

HOMME, Robert, 81. The Friendly Giant on CBC television's third-longest-running program, Homme was beloved by children for his gentle approach. To the strains of "Early One Morning," Homme, the kindly giant, invited his young audience into his castle with its miniature furniture, where he read stories and chatted with his sidekick puppets, Rusty and Jerome. May 2, 2000.

HUNDERTWASSER, Friedensreich, 71. Controversial Austrian architect and artist who designed Vienna's Hundertwasser-Haus, a distinctive asymmetrical apartment building whose bright colours and wavy designs exemplified his artistic vision. February 19, 2000.

JONES, Robert Trent, 93. American golf course architect whose difficult courses, with multiple hazards, challenged professional golfers; designed more than 450 courses. June 14, 2000.

KAHN, Madeline, 57. American comedic actress who starred in several Mel Brooks comedies, including *Blazing Saddles, Young Frankenstein* and *High Anxiety;* her baby voice and ditzy persona were her signatures. December 3, 1999.

KEDROVA (HOWARD), Lila, 80(?). Russian-born actress who won an Oscar for her role as Madame Hortense in the film *Zorba the Greek,* starring Anthony Quinn and Irene Pappas, and later appeared in the Broadway version; other films included *High Wind in Jamaica* and *Torn Curtain;* also noted for role in Chekhov's *The Cherry Orchard.* February 16, 2000.

KEELEY, Glen, 30. Ranked the ninth top bull rider in the world, Keeley died in competition in Albuquerque, New Mexico, trampled by a one tonne bull. March 24, 2000.

KENNER-JACKSON, Doris 58. A member of the 1950s all-women quartet, The Shirelles, whose "uptown rhythm and blues" hits immortalized the angst of teenage girls. "Will You Love Me Tomorrow"; "Tonight's the Night." February 4, 2000.

KIRBY, Durward, 88. American comedian, broadcaster and television personality, Kirby was best known as the co-star of the *Gary Moore Show* and co-host with Allen Funt, during the 1960s, of *Candid Camera.* March 15, 2000.

KITCHENER, Lord (b. Aldwyn Roberts), 77. Trinidadian calypso/jazz musician whose island culture themes and political messages made him an international celebrity. "Shops Too Early"; "Green Fig." February 11, 2000.

LAMARR, Hedy (b. Hedwig Kiesler), 86. Austrian-born actress debuted in a 1933 Czech film, *Ecstasy,* in which she appeared nude. Her Hollywood career as a beautiful temptress peaked in the 1930s and '40s with *Algiers, Samson and Delilah* and *My Favorite Spy.* In 1942 received a patent, with composer George Antheil, for a radio-signalling device, a forerunner of today's "spread spectrum." January 19, 2000.

LAMPORT, Allan Austin, 96. Elected mayor of Toronto in 1952, Lamport also held positions as the Toronto Transit Commission's chairman and served on the Ontario Legislature. He championed cocktail bars in Toronto, Sunday sporting events, the Metro system of government, and promoted the building of Toronto's Bloor Street subway line. November 18, 1999.

LANG, Serge, 79. French journalist who co-instigated the World Cup skiing championships in the 1966-67 season; was president of the International Ski Federation's World Cup committee from 1973 to 1986. November 21, 1999

LEVESQUE, Georges-Henri, 96. Dominican priest who founded, in 1938, the Faculty of Social Sciences at Laval University. Lévesque was instrumental in the inception of Quebec's Quiet Revolution, opposing the authoritarianism of premier Maurice Duplessis. January 15, 2000.

LIBERMAN, Alexander, 87. For 30 years, Ukrainian-born Liberman was the editorial director of the magazine conglomerate Conde Nast; credited with setting the stage for the company's phenomenal growth. Also author of art and photography books. *Prayers in Stone; Them.* November 19, 1999.

LITTLE, Stanley, 89. A founding member of the Canadian Union of Public Employees (CUPE), Little was a leading figure in Canada's public labour sector. He was instrumental in building the fledgling organization, an amalgamation of the National Union of Public Service Employees and the National Union of Public Employees, to become Canada's largest union. May 16, 2000.

LLEWELYN, Desmond, 85. Veteran British actor who portrayed the eccentric, gadget-loving Q in seventeen James Bond movies; memorable for his exploding pens, auto-ejector seats and deadly umbrellas. Died in an auto accident shortly after filming his last Bond movie, *The World Is Not Enough.* December 19, 1999.

LYNCH, Jack, 82. Irish prime minister during 1966-73 and 1977-78 for the Fianna Fail party, Lynch supported the Catholic minority in Northern Ireland during the 1969 violence in Londonderry. While he advocated the withdrawal of British Protestant forces in Northern

Ireland, he hoped the two sides could achieve peace. October 20, 1999.

MacDOUGALL, Fraser, 92. Formerly, until 1972, Ottawa bureau chief of Canadian Press; joined Ontario Press Council after retirement; chairman of board of judges for Michener Awards for journalism. January 24, 2000.

MacEWAN, John Grant Walter, 97. A champion of western Canadian culture, MacEwan served as Alberta's lieutenant governor for 10 years, beginning 1965; he also served as mayor of Calgary and as a Liberal member of Legislature. His prodigious output of books on Albertan history gained him notoriety and respect. *Eye-opener Bob; Poking into Politics.* June 15, 2000.

MacLEAN, J. Angus, 95. Premier of Prince Edward Island 1979-81; minister of fisheries under John Diefenbaker 1958-63. MacLean was credited with bringing national attention to the economic plight of the Atlantic fisheries, leading to equalization payments. February 15, 2000.

MacNELLY, Jeffrey Kenneth, 52. American cartoonist whose editorial cartoons won him three Pulitzer Prizes; from 1977 till his death authored cartoon strip *Shoe.* June 8, 2000.

MARCHAND, Nancy, 71. American actress well known for her role as newspaper publisher Mrs. Pynchon on the television series *Lou Grant;* she appeared extensively on Broadway, in classical theatre, and on television and in film roles. Her last role was as a Mafia mother in the TV series *The Sopranos.* June 18, 2000.

MARTIN, Donald Edward, 68. *Mad Magazine* cartoonist whose irreverent style and black humour entertained readers for more than 30 years. January 6, 2000.

MASSON, Claude, 58. Well-respected deputy publisher and editorial writer of Montreal's *La Presse* newspaper, Masson died with his wife, Jeannine Bourdages, in the crash of EgyptAir Flight 990. October 31, 1999.

MATHIAS, Joe, 56. Chief of Vancouver's Squamish Indians, Mathias was a co-founder of the Union of British Columbia chiefs, and an integral force behind the native land claims disputes in the province. March 10, 2000.

MATTHAU, Walter, 79. American actor famous for playing gruff, curmudgeonly characters; his role as the lovable slob in Neil Simon's *The Odd Couple,* opposite the fastidious Jack Lemmon, launched his career. *The Fortune Cookie; Grumpy Old Men.* July 1, 2000.

MAYNARD, Owen, 75. Aeronautical engineer who was instrumental in the development of NASA's Apollo space program, employed mainly in the systems engineering department; previously involved in the development of the Avro Arrow's weapons pack and landing gear. July 15, 2000.

McCURDY, Ed, 81. American-born folk singer who hosted a CBC Radio folk music program in 1946 and appeared frequently at Ontario's Mariposa Folk Festival; noted for his vast repertoire and extensive folk collection. March 23, 2000.

MERRICK, David, 88. Award-winning Broadway producer of hit musicals such as *Gypsy, 42nd Street, Oliver! Becker* and *Hello, Dolly!* Merrick was famous for outlandish publicity stunts; his career blossomed in the 1950s and '60s. April 25, 2000.

MILLER, Frank Stuart, 73. PC premier of Ontario in 1985 for five months, succeeding Bill Davis; a strong advocate for small business and the rights of "ordinary Canadians." His premiership ended 42 years of Conservative supremacy. July 21, 2000.

MILLS, Donald, 84. The last surviving member of the harmonizing singing group the Mills Brothers, which started in 1922 and became a groundbreaker for black musical artists; their recording "Tiger Rag" sold one million copies in 1931; also recorded "Glow Worm" and "Yellow Bird." November 13, 1999.

MOORE, Clayton, 85. Star of the television western *The Lone Ranger,* Moore played the masked hero whose horse, Silver, and companion, Tonto (played by the late Canadian-born actor Jay Silverheels), helped him conquer the bad guys. Rossini's *William Tell Overture* introduced each program. December 28, 1999.

MOORE, Gregory William, 24. Four-time winner of the Championship Auto Racing Teams (CART) circuit, Moore, from Vancouver, died while driving 600 kilometres per hour in the Marlboro 500 race in Fontana, California. October 31, 1999.

MORITA, Akio, 78. Japanese businessman and co-founder of Sony Corp., Morita is credited with developing Sony into a world leader in the electronics and entertainment business and becoming the first Japanese company to sell stock on the New York Stock Exchange. Also developed the Walkman portable stereo. October 3, 1999.

NEBIOLO, Primo, 76. President of the International Amateur Athletic Federation (IAAF) and a member of the International Olympic committee; credited for allowing amateur athletes to obtain lucrative contracts, for encouraging more women to compete, for tightening drug offence testing and for enabling more nations to join the IAAF; criticized for his lavish life-style and sometimes unpopular decisions. November 7, 1999.

NYERERE, Julius Kambarage, 77. Formerly president of Tanganyika, Nyerere became president of the United Republic of Tanzania after it joined with Zanzibar in 1964. Although his political career was tumultuous, he was respected for his modest leadership style and strong support of education. October 14, 1999.

OBUCHI, Keizo, 62. Liberal Democrat prime minister of Japan since July 1998, Obuchi died from complications following a stroke, suffered while he was in office. Credited with pulling Japanese economy out of a recession with massive public spending programs in his short period of office and bringing a measure of stability to the ailing economy. Succeeded by Yoshiro Mori. May 14, 2000.

PATTON, Frances Gray, 94. American short-story writer whose work appeared for several decades in magazines including the *New Yorker, Colliers* and *Harpers;* also wrote the novel *Good Morning, Miss Dove.* March 28, 2000.

PENTLAND, Barbara, 88. Noted composer of avant-garde music, Pentland adapted the antitonal style of Schoenberg and other twentieth-century composers whose compositions rejected traditional harmonic music; her *Sonata Fantasy for Piano* was performed by Harry Somers in 1948; later works included *Concerto for Piano and String Orchestra* and *Symphony in Ten Parts.* February 5, 2000.

PEPIN, Marcel, 74. A Quebec union organizer, Pépin became president of the Confederation of National Trade Unions in 1965. Responsible for uniting and organizing public service unions in Quebec while the Quiet Revolution was evolving, he was a chief instigator in the massive illegal Common Front strike in 1972 and was briefly jailed for contempt of court. Later became head of the World Confederation of Labour. March 5, 2000.

PETRIE, Doris Lloyd Sharford, 82. Actress who initiated her career in her late 40s; she appeared on stage, television and on film. Noted for roles in the movie *Wedding in White,* stage versions of *Driving Miss Daisy* and Michel Tremblay's *Albertine in Five Times.* August 22, 2000.

POWELL, Anthony Dymoke, 94. British novelist whose satirical work portrayed the life of the English upper classes. Wrote twelve-volume *A Dance to the Music of Time.* March 28, 2000.

PURDY, Alfred Wellington, 81. Distinguished poet and writer whose working-class origins and experiences travelling across Canada strongly affected his work; also wrote prolifically for television and radio, and magazines. Winner of two Governor General's Awards for poetry. *The Enchanted Echo; Beyond Remembering;* and his memoir, *Reaching for the Beaufort Sea.* April 21, 2000.

QUILICO, Louis, 75. Leading baritone who, during his 45-year career, sang at London's Covent Garden and the Paris Opera House, and enjoyed a 25-year tenure at New York's Metropolitan Opera. Nicknamed "Mr. Rigoletto" for his success in the role of the same name. Co-recorded *Two of a Kind* with wife, Christina Petrowski, a concert pianist. July 15, 2000.

RAMPAL, Jean-Pierre, 78. French flutist and conductor whose 50-year career brought him international fame, Rampal revived interest in the flute as a solo instrument. His musical range was wide, but he specialized in the music of Baroque composers. May 20, 2000.

RANKIN, John Morris, 40. As head of the Rankin Family (later The Rankins), Morris was instrumental in introducing Cape Breton's Celtic music tradition to a worldwide audience. Originally a fiddler, Rankin played piano for the group during their 10-year career (they retired in September 1999). Collaborated with the Chieftains on the album *Fire in the Kitchen.*

Rankin died when his car plunged into the frigid Gulf of St. Lawrence near his home in Mabou, Cape Breton; his son and two friends escaped unharmed. January 16, 2000.

RICHARD, Joseph Henri Maurice "Rocket", 78. Montreal Canadiens hockey great, Richard was a hugely popular, record-setting player; he was the first NHL player to score 50 goals in one season in 1944-45 (unbroken until Wayne Gretzky's 1980-81 season) and the first player to score 500 goals (1957). He was a five-time leading scorer in the NHL, and played in eight Stanley Cup championship teams. In 1955 his suspension for fighting led to rioting in the streets of Montreal. May 27, 2000.

RUNCIE, Robert, 78. Archbishop of Canterbury between 1979 and 1991, Runcie became involved in controversial issues, including the ordination of women into the Anglican ministry, the new liturgy, and his role in the release of hostages in Lebanon in 1987, when he sent Terry Waite as an envoy, who then became a hostage himself. July 11, 2000.

SCHMIRLER, Sandra, 36. Skip of the first gold-medal-winning women's curling team in the 1998 Nagano Olympics; also three-time Canadian and world champions in 1993, '94 and '97. March 2, 2000.

SCHULZ, Charles Monroe, 77. Creator of the *Peanuts* comic strip, since 1950, which portrayed a community of children whose foibles were both poignant and familiar: Charlie Brown, the perpetual loser; the vain and nasty Lucy; blanket-toting Linus; and Snoopy, the beagle who aspired to be the Red Baron. His Christian themes were celebrated in *The Gospel According to the Peanuts*. Schulz died on the eve of his last strip. February 12, 2000.

SCOTT, George C., 71. Crusty American actor best known for his film portrayal of General George Patton in the 1970 film *Patton*, he also starred on Broadway and in films *Dr. Strangelove* and *The Hustler*. Although he disdained the award, he won Best Actor for his portrayal of Patton. September 23, 1999.

SHULMAN, Dr. Morton, 75. A man with many careers, Shulman was a family doctor who became Toronto's chief coroner; he served as an NDP member of the Ontario Legislature; became an investment counsellor and writer of how-to books in the investment field; and due to his battle with Parkinson's disease, introduced North Americans to the drug Deprenyl, which alleviated Parkinson's symptoms. A multimillionaire, he was noted for his philanthropy. August 17, 2000.

SLONIM, Rabbi Reuben, 85. A self-described maverick rabbi, Slonim raised dissension in religious circles when he denounced Israel's stand against Palestinians; also a severe critic of wealthy Jewish synagogues and overpaid rabbis. Worked in both the U.S. and in Toronto congregations, author of several books. *To Kill a Rabbi; The United Church and the Jews*. January 20, 2000.

SMITH, Wilfred Cantwell, 83. Founder of Montreal's McGill University's Islamic Institute and co-developer of Harvard's Center for Study of World Religions, Smith was an internationally regarded expert in Islamic studies. Wrote *Islam in Modern History; The Meaning and End of Religion*. February 7, 2000.

SNOW, Hank, 85. A country music legend, Nova Scotia-born Snow recorded more than 40 Top Ten songs in a career that spanned 50 years; appearing in trademark flashy glittering suits, he was a regular on Nashville's Grand Ole Opry. "I'm Movin' On."; "I Don't Hurt Anymore." December 20, 1999.

STEWART, Payne, 42. Champion golfer whose doomed plane carried him and six others halfway across the United States before crashing. Payne, who sported traditional knickers and Tam o' Shanter, enjoyed nine PGA Tour victories that included two major championships. October 25, 1999.

TAKESHITA, Noboru, 76. Prime minister of Japan 1987-89, Takeshita, a member of the Liberal Democratic Party, was forced to resign after a stock scandal; he was instrumental in the grooming of subsequent Japanese leaders and led Japan through a period of growth and prosperity. June 19, 2000.

THOMS, Leslie Russell, 61. Former Liberal member of Newfoundland's House of Assembly; in 1988 was appointed the High Sheriff of Newfoundland and Labrador. December 5, 1999.

TINTNER, Georg, 82. Conductor of the Nova Scotia Symphony Orchestra from 1987-94, Tintner was world-renowned for his skill, especially for his recordings of composer Anton Bruckner, and a member of the Order of Canada; he died in an apparent suicide from a fall from an eleventh-storey balcony after suffering from ill health. October 2, 1999.

TRUDEAU, Pierre Elliott, 80. Prime minister of Canada, 1968-79; 1980-84. During his tenure as head of the Liberal Party he supported multiculturalism and official bilingualism; repatriated the Constitution; and initiated the Charter of Rights and Freedoms. Noted for his intellectual prowess and emphatic personal style. September 28, 2000. For an extended biography see pages 132-33.

TREVOR, Claire (b. Claire Wemlinger), 90(?). Sultry, tough American character actress remembered for roles in major films such as *Key Largo, Stagecoach* and a television production of Sinclair Lewis's *Dodsworth*. April 8, 2000.

TUDJMAN, Franjo, 77. President of Croatia, Tudjman was a driving force behind Croatia's split from Yugoslavia in 1990, favouring a nationalist state in his mainly Roman Catholic country, and behind the war in Bosnia, again backing the Croatian cause against the Serbian forces in the war-torn state. December 11, 1999.

TURCOTTE, Sheldon, 64. Long-time CBC anchorman, producer, writer, reporter and foreign correspondent, Turcotte anchored the CBC's *Midday News* from 1985-95; also producer of *The National*. February 18, 2000.

VADIM, Roger (b. Roger Vladimir Plemiannikov), 72. French film director whose celebrated movies starred actresses including Brigitte Bardot, Catherine Deneuve and Jane Fonda, all of whom he was romantically linked with. His films included *And God Created Women, Barbarella,* and *Vice and Virtue*. February 11, 1999.

VAUGHAN, Colin, 68. Acerbic political analyst for Toronto's CITY-TV, Vaughan was a respected critic and commentator of urban affairs. A two-term Toronto alderman 1972-76, Vaughan, trained as an architect, was instrumental in the city's nonprofit housing movement; he designed the Canadian pavilion for Expo '67 in Montreal, as well as the interior of Toronto's O'Keefe Centre (now Hummingbird). January 1, 2000.

WALSH, Richard "Hock", 51. Co-founded in 1969 the Downchild Blues Band with brother Donnie; their band was the inspiration for Dan Aykroyd and John Belushi's *Blues Brothers* movie. January 2, 2000.

WASHINGTON, Grover, 56. American jazz saxophonist whose ability to mix rock and jazz led to a successful career. Winner of five gold albums. *Inner City Blues; Come Morning; Time Out of Mind.* December 17, 1999.

WEBB, Todd, 94. American photographer whose images recorded the diversity of American life and architecture; his photographic career was especially active during the 1930s to '50s. April 15, 2000.

WEST, Morris, 83. Australian best-selling novelist whose blockbusters *The Shoes of the Fisherman, The Devil's Advocate* and *Children of the Son* were translated and popular throughout the world. Also wrote for radio, TV and stage. October 9, 1999.

WICKS, Ben (b. Alfred Wicks), 73. Cockney cartoonist, illustrator and author, Wicks was the leading syndicated newspaper cartoonist in Canada during the 1970s; his whimsical satirical political cartoon, *The Outcasts,* appeared in major newspapers across Canada. Also a fervent advocate for children's literacy. *Ben Wick's Canada; Born to Read and Count.* September 11, 2000.

YANOFSKY, Daniel Abraham (Abe), 74. First chess grandmaster in the Commonwealth, and Grand Champion eight times, Yanofsky was hailed as a child prodigy in the Chess Olympics in Buenos Aires in 1939 at the age of 14. He was also active in Winnipeg city council, and a practicing lawyer. March 5, 2000.

YOUNG, Loretta (b. Gretchen Michaela), 87. American actress whose movie career spanned the decades between the 1920s and the '40s; she later became a pioneer in television, appearing in and producing *The Loretta Young Show,* a dramatic anthology series. *The Farmer's Daughter; The Stranger; The Bishop's Wife.* August 12, 2000.

NEWS EVENTS OF 1999–2000

October 1, 1999 to September 30, 2000

(See also Obituaries pages 809–17.)

October

INTERNATIONAL

Antarctica: Jerri Nielsen, an American doctor suffering from breast cancer, was evacuated from the South Pole Oct. 16 after a five-month wait caused by bad weather. She treated herself until a US military plane could make the rescue. **Argentina:** Fernando de la Rua won the presidential election on Oct. 24, ending a decade of Peronist rule. **Armenia:** Nationalist gunmen surrendered on Oct. 28 after storming the Armenian parliament and killing the prime minister and seven others on the 27th. The five gunmen released 40 hostages after holding them overnight. **Austria:** The far right Freedom Party, led by the controversial Jorg Haider, won 27% of the votes for parliament on an anti-immigrant platform. **Bosnia-Herzegovina:** The UN declared the Oct. 12 birth of a baby boy in Sarajevo as the symbolic 6 billionth resident on the planet to highlight concerns about population growth. **Britain:** On Oct. 10 an express commuter train from Cheltenham collided with a local train in Britain's worst train accident since 1915; the crash in London killed 127 and injured 160. **Central America:** Honduras, Nicaragua, Costa Rica, El Salvador and Mexico were battered by weeks of torrential rains and flash floods which killed nearly 50, severely damaged roads and buildings and drove thousands from their homes. **East Timor:** The last of the Indonesian troops left as the UN cemented its earl control of the battered region; guerrillas and refugees began to return to their razed villages. **India:** A supercyclone, the worst in the Bay of Bengal in three decades, hit eastern India on Oct. 29, killing 10,000 and leaving 15 million homeless. On Oct. 17 an earlier cyclone had hit the same area, causing 56 deaths. Parliamentary elections were held during five weekends in Sept. and Oct. (Sept. 5, 12, 18, 25 and Oct. 3) in an effort to forestall violence. Despite these measures, almost 100 died during election-related confrontations. The ruling BJP took the most seats in the 545-seat parliament, however none of the 38 parties winning seats came close to a clear majority. **Indonesia:** Parliament elected Abdurrahman Wahid, an ailing but revered Muslim moderate, as Indonesia's new leader on Oct. 20, hours after President B. J. Habibie withdrew from the race. **Japan:** The Japanese government concluded that shoddy work practices at a uranium-processing plant set off the country's worst nuclear accident on Sept. 30. The three workers mixing uranium in containers had skipped safety steps. **Korea:** At fire in a bar on the second floor of a four-storey building in Inchon, near Seoul, killed 55, mostly teenagers. The fire started in a basement karaoke bar and spread up through the building. **Mexico:** Severe rains early in the month caused flooding and mudslides that killed 450 and left 315,000 homeless in several southern states. Later in the month, an earthquake measuring 7.5 on the Richter scale struck the southern state of Oaxaca, killing 20. **Nigeria:** Heavy seasonal rains flooded the Niger and Kaduna Rivers; officials opened three dams and flooded the central states, submerging hundreds of villages and leaving over 300,000 homeless. **Norway:** The Paris-based group Medicins sans frontier (Doctors Without Borders) won the Nobel Peace Prize on Oct. 15 for their work risking personal injury to help victims of war and natural disaster. **Pakistan:** Gen Pervez Musharraf seized power Oct. 12 in a bloodless coup, just hours after the army chief of staff had been fired by Prime Minister Nawaz Sharif. The cabinet was sacked and the constitution was suspended as martial law was imposed. **United States:** On Oct. 4 an Illinois jury ordered State Farm Insurance company to pay $456 million to 4.7 million customers in a lawsuit accusing that nation's largest car insurer of using inferior parts for auto body repairs. MCI Worldcom announced and planned takeover of Sprint that would create the world's biggest telecom company. A veteran parachutist plunged to her death on Oct. 22 when her chute failed to open while jumping off the top of 3,200-foot *El Capitan* in Yosemite National Park in California to protest park rules banning such jumps because they are not safe. A Learjet carrying champion golfer Payne Stewart and four other people flew a ghostly journey halfway across the US from Florida to South Dakota on Oct. 25; US military planes sent to make contact reported the plane's windows were iced over and its occupants apparently incapacitated. The plane crashed when it ran out of fuel. An EgyptAir jetliner, Flight 990, bound for Cairo with 217 people on board, plunged 33,000 feet in two minutes, crashing into the ocean off Nantucket Island on Oct. 31. Experts later speculated that the plane was deliberately crashed by the co-pilot.

CANADA

On Oct. 3 non-natives, angry that Aboriginals had been allowed to fish in the off-season, took matters into their own hands, destroying native lobster traps in Miramichi Bay off the coast of northeastern New Brunswick. (The Supreme Court of Canada judgement on Sept. 17, 1999 ruled that terms of a 1760 Mi'kmaq treaty allow East Coast natives to earn a moderate livelihood from hunting, fishing and gathering was still valid.) On Oct. 10 Fisheries Minister Herb Dhaliwal announced there would be limits on native fishing. Adrienne Clarkson, a former broadcaster, was sworn in as Governor General on Oct. 7. On Oct. 11 Quebec provincial police cracked down on a week-long highway blockade by truckers protesting high fuel prices. On Oct. 12 the Liberal government's Throne Speech promised financial breaks for families and broader tax relief. The World Trade Organization ruled Oct. 13 that the 1965 Canada-US auto pact was unfair because it violated rules that call for freer global trade. Robert Rabinovitch, who has worked in the broadcasting field both as a public servant and a high-powered executive, was named CBC president on Oct. 18. A Quebec judge struck down language law provisions requiring French predominance on commercial signs. The judge ruled Oct. 20 that a sign outside an antiques store in Knowlton, Que., did not violate the law even though its French and English lettering were of equal size. On Oct. 29 Ottawa agreed to pay $3.6 billion in back pay to thousands of mostly female workers to compensate for wage gaps between men and women. The Federal Court had upheld a Human Rights Tribunal ordering the payment.

November

INTERNATIONAL

Afghanistan: On Nov. 14 the United Nations imposed sanctions on Afghanistan for refusing to hand over suspected terrorist Osama bin Laden, the man accused of masterminding the 1998 bombings of US embassies in Kenya and Tanzania. **Australia:** On Nov. 5, Australians rejected a referendum to make their nation the world's 147th republic and drop Queen Elizabeth as head of state. By mid-month, authorities had detained four new boatloads of illegal immigrants from Asia. **Chechny**a: On Nov. 1 Russia reopened several border crossings with Chechnya, allowing terrified refugees to flee Russian air and rocket attacks. **China:** On Nov. 25, a ferry being pummelled by towering waves caught fire and cracked open off the coast of eastern China; more than 280 people were killed. **India:** On Nov. 4 officials set fire to hundreds of bodies stacked on the beach in Paradadwip to stave off disease in eastern India, a week after a devastating storm that killed 10,000. On Nov. 6 in New Dehli, Pope John Paul declared the Roman Catholic church an ally of Asia's poor. **New Zealand:** On Nov. 27, New Zealand's Labour Party, led by Helen Clark, defeated the 9-year National Party regime led by Jenny Shipley. **Northern Ireland:** Peace talks brokered by US senator George Mitchell reach agreement that allows for the creation of a government made up of Sinn Fein and Ulster Unionists, despite the IRA's refusal to decommission its arsenal. On Nov. 29, Protestant and Catholic adversaries joined forces to form the Ulster Assembly. **Israel:** On Nov. 5, Israel and Palestinians began negotiations on final peace treaty with a 100-day deadline to craft the broad outlines of a peace that has eluded them for a half century. By Nov. 28 the talks were at an impasse over the fate of the Golan Heights, with Israel refusing to give up the territory and Syria demanding it back. **Italy:** On Nov. 11, a five-storey apartment building in the southern city of Foggia collapsed, killing 67. Tenants had complained for years that they felt the building was unsafe. **Mexico:** On Nov. 30, Mexican police found the bodies of more than 100 victims of a drug gang in Mexico, in a mass grave near the US border with Texas. **Nigeria:** Zafara, the country's northern state, introduced Islamic Shari'a law. The Muslim majority of the population supported the move; while promises to safeguard the rights of non-Muslims did little to calm concerns. **Pakistan:** On Nov. 18 ousted Pakistani prime minister Nawaz Sharif was handed over to police as the military government widened its crackdown on corruption. Sharif was accused of conspiracy, hijacking, kidnapping and attempted murder. **South Africa:** On Nov. 2 South African President Thabo Mbeki's claim that a widely used AIDS drug is dangerous set off an uproar, shocking physicians who say AZT is safe. **Turkey:** On Nov. 12, a strong earthquake, measuring 7.2 on the Richter scale, rocked western Turkey, killing 550 and injuring 3,000 around the town of Duzce, 185 km east of Instanbul. **United States:** On Nov. 2 in Honolulu a Xerox copier repairman shot and killed seven co-workers in his office building. He was arrested after a five-hour standoff with police. The following day in Seattle, a man in camouflage clothing calmly walked in and shot four employees at a boat repair company, killing two of them. On Nov. 3 13-year-old Christopher Beamon's scary Halloween essay earned him extra credit—and five days in jail. The seventh-grader from Ponder, Tex. was arrested for writing a story about shooting two classmates and a teacher. On Nov. 5, a federal judge declared Microsoft Corp. a monopoly, ruling that aggressive actions by Bill Gates's software empire to protect its technology dominance were "stifling innovation" and hurting consumers. On Nov. 7, the space shuttle *Discovery* returned from a ten-day mission that including a return to space by 1962 astronaut (and 77-year-old) John Glenn. (NASA scientists later said that the former US senator had withstood the rigors of space as well as astronauts half his age.) On Nov. 16, in Pontiac Mich., a boy was convicted of second-degree murder for shooting a stranger outside a convenience store with a rifle when he was 11. On Nov. 18, a huge stack of logs being prepared for a bonfire at Texas A&M university collapsed, killing 12. On Nov. 25, 6-year old Elian Gonzalez was rescued at sea off the coast of Florida. He was the sole survivor of a boat that sank while attempting to reach the United States from Cuba. Twelve Cubans died, including his mother. He was released into temporary custody of relatives in Miami. On Nov. 30, protesters disrupted a World Trade Organization meeting in Seattle. Thousands of protesters faced pepper spray-equipped anti-riot officers, backed by armoured cars and mounted police.

CANADA

On Nov. 2, Finance Minister Paul Martin said Canadians must decide what to do with a budget surplus of $95.5 billion over the next five years. On Nov. 3, Beverley

McLachlin was appointed chief justice of the Supreme Court of Canada, the first female to hold the key post. On Nov. 3, federal Environment Minister David Anderson gave the go-ahead to develop Canada's second diamond mine in the Northwest Territories. The $1.3-billion Diavik project is "not likely to cause significant environmental effects," Anderson said. On Nov. 5, Onex Corp. scrapped its $2.1-billion bid to restructure Canada's airline industry after a Quebec court ruled that its hostile attempt to buy Air Canada was illegal. Air Canada eventually acquired competitor Canadian Airlines. On Nov. 5, cigarette taxes in parts of Central and Eastern Canada were hiked in a bid to cut smoking. (Taxes had been slashed to fight smuggling.) On Nov. 7, a labour dispute shut West Coast ports for everything but bulk grain shipments for a week costing, the Port of Vancouver alone $90 million a day. About 2,000 dockworkers were locked out in a dispute over work done by a non-union company. On Nov. 16, a judge in Surrey, BC said five skinheads who beat an elderly Sikh man to death outside a temple were "social misfits" motivated by racism. He sentenced them to 12- to 15-years for killing Nirmal Singh Gill. On Nov. 17, the Supreme Court of Canada said native people who claimed broad treaty rights under its Sept. 17 ruling read too much into that decision, giving the government power to regulate resource use. On Nov. 19, federal Health Minister Allan Rock said about half of the $115 million pledged by Ottawa to fight diabetes will go to aboriginal communities, where the disease has been a particular scourge. On Nov. 23, Wayne Gretzky was inducted into the Hockey Hall of Fame. On Nov. 23, the federal government vowed to step up efforts to counter tobacco research and marketing. Health Canada released 1,200 pages of industry documents showing Canadian-based Imperial Tobacco Ltd. assessed smokers as young as nine and 'fortified' products to increase their addictive qualities. On Nov. 23, a jury in Yorkton, Sask. convicted Larry Fisher of the killing of Gail Miller in 1969, the sex slaying for which David Milgaard was wrongly convicted. Milgaard spent 23 years in prison before being exonerated by DNA evidence. On Nov. 24, Reform MP Jack Ramsay, 62, was convicted of attempting to rape a 14-year-old girl on a Saskatchewan reserve when he was an RCMP corporal in 1969. On Nov. 27, McCain Foods of Florenceville, N.B. said it would refuse to accept genetically engineered potatoes for processing into french fries.

December

INTERNATIONAL

Australia: An Australian commuter train slammed into the back of another passenger train outside Sydney on Dec. 2, killing seven people and injuring 50. **Chechnya:** Russian military gave the residents of the capital Grozny until Dec. 11 to evacuate the area; they launched an all-out assault on the city to capture it the next day. **Croatia:** Hardline (and founding) president Franjo Tudjman died on Dec. 11, throwing the country into political turmoil. **Cuba:** The father of 6-year-old Elian Gonzalez demanded the return of his son, with the backing of the Castro government. **Finland:** European Union leaders wrapped up a successful summit on Dec. 11 endowing the EU with new military powers, preparing a move eastward that will almost double its membership and healing relations with Turkey by acknowledging it could one day join the bloc. **France:** France bore the brunt of two storms that hit Western Europe in late December. On Dec. 26 winds up to 220 km/h killed 60 people. On the 27th another storm caused 120 deaths across Europe, including 70 in France, and left millions without electricity. The army was called out to clear debris and deliver drinking water. For many, power was not restored until mid-January. **Germany:** US and German negotiators agreed Dec. 14 to a US$5.2 billion fund to compensate former Nazi slave and forced laborers. **Guatemala:**

The first presidential elections since the end of the 36-year civil war in 1996 resulted in victory for Alfonso Portillo Cabrera. **Ivory Coast:** President Henri Konan Bedie was replaced in a bloodless military coup on Dec. 24. He fled to France two days later. **Korea, North:** A Japanese delegation brokered the start to talks between North and South Korea on establishing diplomatic ties. Japan later announced an end to its freeze on food aid for the struggling nation. **Kuwait:** The all-male parliament rejected a bill that would allow women to vote and stand for election by a vote of 32 to 30. **Macau:** Portugal handed over Macau to China, ending 442 years of colonial rule. **Macedonia:** A Nov. 14 election was marred by ballot stuffing and proxy voting; a repeat vote was held in much of the Albanian sector. Boris Trajkovski, a pro-Western coalition candidate was eventually declared the winner. **Netherlands:** A Scottish judge ruled Dec. 8 that two Libyans suspected of blowing up Pan Am Flight 103 over Lockerbie, Scotland, will stand trial on conspiracy charges—despite a defence motion to have them dropped. **Panama:** Control of the Panama Canal was transferred from the US to Panama on Dec. 31. **Romania:** In an effort to solve the country's economic woes, Pres. E. Constantinescu fired the prime minister and appointed the head of the central bank as prime minister, giving him until Dec. 20 to submit an economic plan and form a cabinet. **Russia:** Pres. Boris Yeltsin surprised the nation by announcing that he was stepping down immediately on Dec. 31 and handing presidential powers over to Prime Min. Valdimir Putin. **Sri Lanka:** President Chandrika Kumaratunga was injured Dec 18 in one of two bomb blasts that killed at least 18 people and injured 150 others at opposite election rallies. **Switzerland:** On Dec. 12, the International Olympic Committee banned member visits to bid cities, a practice that led to the organization's worst corruption scandal. Despite complaints that a ban implies they cannot be trusted, delegates fell into line behind a sweeping reform package designed to boost the committee's credibility. **Turkey:** An oil tanker broke up in the sea of Marmara, threatening the link between the Bosporus and the Dardenelles with massive pollution and coating a 10-km stretch of coastline with fuel oil. **United Nations:** On Dec. 16 an inquiry panel into the massacre of some 800,000 Rwandans in 1994 blamed the then-UN secretary general, the Security Council, UN staff and the UN mission in Rwanda, which was under the command of Canadian Gen. Romeo Dallaire. **United States:** The Mars Polar Lander slammed into Mars on Dec. 3 and NASA was unable to make contact with the deep space probe. Dec. 4, the streets of Seattle erupted in protest and rioting as the closed-door WTO meetings were scheduled to begin. The meetings were disrupted by those concerned with the effect of globalization; Seattle's police chief resigned Dec. 7, accepting part of the blame for violent protests. Six farmers opposed to genetically engineered crops filed a suit Dec. 12 alleging that Monsanto Co. and other firms had conspired to take over the seed trade and push biotech crops to market without adequate environmental and health testing. On Dec. 18, Julia 'Butterfly' Hill, who had been sitting for two years on a tree 50 m in the air to protest logging, reached a deal to come down. On Dec. 22 Canadian porn star Kathryn Gannon, known as Marylin Star, was accused of illegally profiting from inside information gained from an intimate relationship with an influential Wall Street executive. Two astronauts ventured out on a Christmas Eve walk in space and finished fixing the Hubble Space Telescope by installing a new radio transmitter, digital recorder and large sun shades. **Venezuela:** Deadly rain hit mid-month causing flooding and mudslides that reached a crisis on Dec. 15 when an estimated 30,000 were killed, 35,000 homes were destroyed and 400,000 left homeless. Despite the devastation, over 54% of voters turned out to cast ballots on the proposed changes to their constitution. 71% of those who voted supported the measures, which eliminated the Senate, gave the state more power for economic intervention and extended the presidential term. **Viet Nam:** Severe flooding along the central coast prompted the government to organize an airlift of food by military helicopters. Heavy rains killed 115 and left 750,000 homeless just a month after the country's worst flooding in a century killed 600

CANADA

On Dec. 3 the jobless rate was reported at 6.9 per cent, the lowest in 18 years. Air Canada gained control of Canadian Airlines on Dec. 8 and reached a release agreement with AMR Corp., Canadian's largest shareholder. Reform MPs protesting a Nisga'a land claims agreement moved 471 amendments that took 43 consecutive hours of voting to defeat on Dec. 9. Ontario introduced a bill on Dec. 9 to create a province-wide registry to track pedophiles and other sex offenders who move from one community to another. On Dec. 12, about 30 workers ended a three-week occupation of a Molson Breweries plant in Barrie, Ont. that had been set up to protest plans to close the brewery. Merchant mariners and the federal government reached a deal Dec. 15 on compensation for civilian seamen who served aboard cargo ships during the Second World War, paying from $5,000 to $24,000. Canadian National Railway announced Dec. 20 that it is combining with American railway giant Burlington Northern Santa Fe to create the largest freight carrier in North America, with 67,000 employees. On Dec. 20 a Vancouver police officer became a millionaire when a provincial court judge awarded him a bag full of money he had found in a city park. But Constable Mel Millas was warned not to spend the cash for six years in case the true owner came forward. On Dec. 21 Ottawa announced a US$1 billion lawsuit accusing world giant RJ Reynolds Tobacco of running a huge cigarette smuggling scheme that it says undermined efforts to stop young Canadians from smoking. Quebec Justice Louis LeBel was named to the Supreme Court of Canada on Dec. 21 to fill the last vacancy on the bench.

January

INTERNATIONAL

The New Year arrived with little impact by the much-feared Y2K computer bug around the world. No major problems were reported, after hundreds of billions of dollars had been spent preparing computer networks for the transition. Meanwhile, celebrations swept the globe as most people marked a new millennium. **Afghanistan:** On Jan. 1, Shirley Macklin of Winnipeg and 154 other hostages were freed after an eight-day kidnapping ordeal that had begun on Christmas Eve. An Indian Airlines flight from Katmandu, Nepal to New Delhi, India was hijacked by militants linked to the separatist movement in Kashmir. Macklin said the hijackers were well organized and cruel. The hostages were freed after India agreed to release two Kashmiri militants and a Pakistani fundamentalist cleric. **Algeria:** A six-month amnesty period came to an end and the government claimed that 6,000 Islamic guerrillas had surrendered; the government vowed to fight on against the estimated 1,500 who remained at large. **Britain:** On Jan. 11 doctors in London ruled that Gen. Augusto Pinochet was unfit to stand trial, opening the possibility that the former Chilean dictator could win his battle against extradition to Spain. **Chile:** Presidential elections on Jan. 16 saw victory for the first Socialist president since the 1973 overthrow of Salvador Allende. **Croatia:** Parliamentary elections were held Jan. 3 and the ruling nationalist party was swept from office by the opposition. On Jan. 24, presidential elections were held and Stjepan Mesiæ was the eventual winner after a run-off vote on Feb. 7. **Cuba:** On Jan. 15 about 150,000 Cubans rallied to protest the US refusal to return 6-year-old Elian Gonzalez. His grandmothers visited him in Miami on Jan. 26. **Ecuador:** On Jan. 21, thousands of protesters stormed

Ecuador's national palace hours after a rebellion led by Indians and backed by the military forced Ecuador's unpopular president to flee. A three-man junta claimed power and hours later turned it over to the Vice Pres. Gustavo Noboa to resume civilian rule. **Ivory Coast:** On Jan. 30 a Kenya Airways jet carrying 169 passengers and 10 crew members crashed into the sea, shortly after taking off from Abidjan. **Spain:** One million people gathered in Madrid on Jan. 22; the crowd was protesting a car-bomb attack blamed on Basque separatists. **Sri Lanka:** Two attempts were made on the prime minister's life during the month. Both attempts by suicide bombers were unsuccessful although 40 others died in the two attacks, 123 were injured, including the prime minister. **Thailand:** On Jan. 24, Thai security forces stormed a hospital and killed ten heavily armed insurgents from a Myanmar rebel group who had taken 700 of patients, visitors and staff hostage. **United States:** On Jan. 4 US Federal Reserve chairman Alan Greenspan was nominated for a fourth term as head of the agency that controls that country's interest rates. On Jan. 10, the Internet giant America OnLine (AOL) bought Time Warner for US$162 billion, creating a media and entertainment giant that merges new and old media. On Jan. 14 the US government returned 840 hectares to the Northern Ute tribe in Utah as part of a deal to clean up millions of tonnes of uranium waste along the Colorado River. Democrat candidate Al Gore and Republican candidate George W. Bush won the Iowa caucuses on Jan. 24, validating their front-runner status in the opening contest of the 2000 presidential election season. An Alaska Airlines jet carrying 88 people from Mexico to San Francisco crashed Jan 31 in the Pacific Ocean after reporting mechanical difficulties.

CANADA

On Jan. 2, 25 Chinese men were discovered aboard a cargo ship in Vancouver; the illegal migrants were locked inside two canvas-covered containers buried beneath thousands of tonnes of other cargo. The men, who were en route to Seattle when they were discovered, had been on the boat for two weeks. Larry Fisher was sentenced Jan. 4 to life in prison for the brutal 1969 sex-slaying of Gail Miller. On Jan. 6, a mother and son were charged with trying to smuggle 10 teenage Chinese girls into the United States. Their van was stopped in Wallaceburg, Ont., on its way to Detroit. Inco Ltd. announced Jan. 11 that it was shelving plans to construct a nickel processing facility in Newfoundland to handle the oree from the Voisey's Bay deposit. On Jan. 12, Beverley McLachlin was officially sworn in as chief justice of the Supreme Court of Canada. Ottawa announced Jan. 13 it would pay C$1 billion over the next two years to help cash-crunched farmers through the latest crisis in agricultural prices, but critics complained the promised aid wasn't enough. On Jan. 14, a shipment of weapons-grade plutonium from the US arrived at a Chalk River, Ont., lab by helicopter, thwarting protesters plans to block highways along its route. On Jan. 18 Ottawa offered tax breaks to keep National Hockey League teams in Canada, but three days later, amid a storm of protest from across the country, it rescinded the offer. On Jan. 24, James Kopp, a US anti-abortion activist, was named in Canada-wide warrant charging him with the attempted murder of a Hamilton-area doctor. Kopp, who is a fugitive, already faced charges in the murder of a Buffalo doctor. On Jan. 25 Shannon Murrin was found not guilty in Vancouver of murdering eight-year-old Mindy Tran of Kelowna, BC in 1994. Murrin had spent five years in prison awaiting the trial. On Jan. 27 the Reform Party opened the convention destined to change its course and lead to the creation of the Canadian Alliance party. Human Resources Minister Jane Stewart spent much of the month on the defensive trying to play down reports that her department had misspent C$1 billion on dubious projects. The Supreme Court of Canada ruled Jan. 31 that criminals who commit violent crimes should be eligible for conditional sentences, rejecting calls from Ottawa and the provinces to increase prison sentences. Also on Jan. 31, Ottawa approved the C$8 billion takeover of Canada Trust by Toronto Dominion Bank.

February

INTERNATIONAL

Afghanistan: An Afghan passenger airline was hijacked Feb. 6. After nine passengers were freed in Moscow the plant flew to Britain and landed at Stansted airport with 142 passengers. The stand off ended peacefully after four days, with 105 of the hostages seeking asylum in Britain. **Austria**: Right-wing Austrian leader Joerg Haider was forced to resign after weeks of protests at home and around the world when his party became part of a coalition government on Feb. 3. Haider had campaigned on an anti-immigrant platform and once applauded aspects of the Nazi regime. **Chechnya**: On Feb. 6 acting Russian President Vladimir Putin announced that Russian troops had captured the last rebel stronghold in Grozny, the Chechen capital. The city itself was little more than rubble after a six-month bombardment that left no home intact and much of the city booby-trapped or littered with unexploded Russian shells. **Finland**: On Feb. 6, Tarja Halonen became the first woman elected president of that country after 80.2% turnout gave her 51.6% of the popular vote. **Iran**: First round voting on Feb. 18 saw a strong turnout and strong support for the president's reform policies among the electorate of 38.7 million, half of which is under 25. **Kosovo**: Ethnic Albanians and Serbs exchanged sniper fire and then turned their guns on French peacekeepers, injuring two in Mitrovica. A security sweep resulted in the arrest of 57 and confiscation of a small arsenal hidden in an ambulance. **Mexico**: Police raided a university in Mexico City on Feb. 6 and arrested 632 striking students, ending a 9 _ month occupation. **Mozambique**: The worst flooding in 50 years hit much of southern Africa during the first two weeks of the month, killing thousands and leaving several hundred thousand homeless. On Feb. 22 a cyclone struck, causing more deaths and flooding. **Northern Ireland**: On Feb. 11 Britain resumed direct control over Northern Ireland, stripping power from the province's new Protestant-Catholic administration in an effort to save the coalition. It was clear that the IRA would not meet any conditions set for the Feb. 12 decommissioning of weapons and the British government wished to avert the resignation of First Minister David Trimble. **Romania:** A cyanide spill from a gold mine contaminated the Tisza and Danube rivers killing tonnes of fish and birds downstream in Yugoslavia and as far as Bulgaria. **United States:** On Feb. 6 Hillary Clinton officially announced she was seeking a US Senate seat in New York in the November, 2000 elections. On Feb. 7 President Bill Clinton introduced a US$1.84 trillion budget aiming to expand health care and shrink the country's national debt. Major Internet sites including CNN, Yahoo and eBay were hit by computer disruption Feb. 7 and 8 when powerful computers overwhelmed their systems with thousands of messages (SPAM). (In April, a Montreal teen known as Mafiaboy was charged with the attacks and in August he pleaded not guilty to 64 charges.) After spending more than $66 million of his own money in a relentless six-year bid for political viability, Republican publisher Steve Forbes abandoned his second presidential campaign on Feb. 9. *Peanuts* creator Charles Schulz died Feb. 13 on the day his last original cartoon was published in newspapers worldwide. In New York a former executive with the Bank of New York and her husband pleaded guilty to charges of laundering US$1.8 million on behalf of members of the Russian mob. On Feb. 25 a jury acquitted four white New York City police officers on all charges in the killing of unarmed African immigrant Amadou Diallo, whose death in a barrage of 41 bullets touched off weeks of civil disobedience over police treatment of minorities.

On Feb. 14, tornadoes hit rural Georgia, killing 22 and injuring 100 as they slept. On Feb. 24, Texas Gov. George W. Bush rejected Betty Lou Beets's claim that she killed her fifth husband in self-defence and an appeal for clemency; the 62-year-old woman was executed. A 6-year-old Michigan boy pulled a gun from his pants on Feb. 29 and shot a little girl to death in front of her first-grade teacher and classmates. **Zimbabwe:** 55% of voters rejected Pres. Mugabe's constitutional changes, which would have allowed for expropriation of white-owned commercial farms and extended the president's power.

CANADA

More than 1,500 students demonstrated on Parliament Hill on Feb. 2 to protest the lack of money for university students and the high debt load they face. On Feb. 3 the Toronto police union called off a controversial fundraising campaign aimed at financing bids to defeat politicians the union leadership didn't like. Quebec Premier Lucien Bouchard said on Feb. 6 that Quebec must solve its health care crisis before calling another sovereignty referendum. Many bars, restaurants and pubs in British Columbia continued to let customers smoke, despite a tough non-smoking policy that became law on Jan. 1. About 150 angry farmers occupied Saskatchewan's legislature on Feb. 7 demanding more financial help. The Crown announced Feb. 9 that no charges would be laid against Nadia Hama, whose 18-month-old daughter fell from her arms on the Capilano Suspension bridge near Vancouver on Sept. 22, 1999. Half the social service workers in Newfoundland paramedics walked off the job on Feb. 9 to protest low wages and a crushing workload. The illegal strike came less than a week after the province's private ambulance operators parked their backup vehicles for a day to push for a better budget proposal from the government. Soaring gasoline and diesel prices led to several protests across the country, including truck blockades in Quebec, Nova Scotia and Ontario. On Feb. 16 Austrian far-right leader Joerg Haider made a surprise visit to Montreal. New consumer laws to protect consumers from price gouging by Air Canada were introduced Feb. 17. BC Attorney General Ujjal Dosanjh's first ballot win Feb. 20 at the NDP convention set the stage for him to become Canada's first Indo-Canadian premier four days later. Police in Saskatoon were investigated in mid-February after allegations concerning their treatment of natives. Critics charged that natives were dropped off at the edge of the city in the winter and forced to walk to their reserves, possibly causing four deaths. NHL tough guy Marty McSorley was charged with assault and suspended for the rest of the season following a Feb. 21 stick-swinging attack in Vancouver on Canucks forward Donald Brashear. On Feb. 25 BCE Inc. announced an offer to buy broadcaster CTV for $2.3 billion.

March

INTERNATIONAL

Britain: On March 2, former Chilean dictator Gen. Augusto Pinochet departed Britain a free man, ending a 16-month legal saga. He received a hero's welcome from thousands of cheering supporters when he returned to Chile the next day. **Indonesia:** Forest fires in West Kalimantan and Riau created serious pollution problems in neighbouring Malaysia and Singapore as charges of illegal clearing by fire were levelled at plantation companies. **Israel:** Pope John Paul began his Jubilee pilgrimage in Bethlehem after the first visit by a Roman Catholic pontiff to Egypt. **Kosovo:** The city of Mitrovica was again the site of violence as grenade blasts and gunfire injured 40, including 16 peacekeepers. The difficulty of keeping the Serbs and Albanians from killing each other led the peacekeepers to establish a "confidence" zone around a disputed bridge that links the two communities. **Mongolia:** The government called for international aid for 500,000 affected by a summer drought and an unusually severe winter that lead to the death of 1.4 million of the population's animals. **Mozambique:** On March 1 a woman gave birth to a baby girl in a treetop where she had lived for four days above raging flood waters that had forced about 1 million people from their homes. **Russia:** On March 26 Vladimir Putin was elected president, promising to bring stability to the country. He had been acting president since Boris Yeltsin stepped aside. **Rwanda:** Pres. Bizimungu, a Hutu, resigned after the tensions between himself and the Tutsi dominated parliament made it impossible to continue. **Syria:** Syrian Pres. Assad appoint the first prime minister in 13 years as he tried to revive the economy and strengthen ties with the west. **Taiwan:** Voters in the March 18 presidential election ignored Beijing's tough rhetoric and elected pro-independence Chen Shui-bian. **Uganda:** More than 900 members of a religious cult were found dead on March 17 and the following days in one of the world's largest mass murders. Dozens of charred bodies were found on the floor of a church and hundreds were found strangled and dismembered. **Ukraine:** On March 11, a methane gas explosion in a coal mine in eastern Ukraine killed 80 workers. **United States**: On March 7, George W. Bush won Republican primaries in Ohio and Georgia, while John McCain won in Vermont. Al Gore defeated Bill Bradley in the Democratic races on Super Tuesday. Two days later, McCain and Bradley withdrew from the presidential race. On March 14, a Florida judge threw out the first statewide school voucher system, ruling that Florida's constitution bars public money from being spent on private education. On March 17, Canadian National Railway's ambitious plan to merge with US giant Burlington Northern Santa Fe received a setback when the US government ordered a moratorium on all railway mergers for at least 15 months. Also on that day, the giant gun manufacturer Smith & Wesson agreed to install locks on its weapons to make them more childproof. In exchange, governments dropped lawsuits seeking damages for gun violence. Six juvenile offenders were killed March 20 as they collected trash alongside a highway near Las Vegas. The teens, who were wearing bright orange vests, were struck by a car driven by a woman who had been drinking. On March 20, two men who worked for the trucking company hired to deliver Academy Awards statues were charged with stealing the 55 Oscars, all but three of which were found over the weekend beside a trash bin by a man scavenging for valuables. Former hostage Terry Anderson was awarded US$341 million from Iran by a federal judge who said his treatment during his nearly seven years of captivity in Beirut was "savage and cruel by any civilized standards." **Vatican City:** On March 12, Pope John Paul II asked God's forgiveness for the sins of Roman Catholics through the ages, including wrongs inflicted on Jews, women and minorities. The apology was a personal landmark for a frail, ailing pope who vowed to cleanse and reinvigorate Catholicism for its third millennium.

CANADA

Alberta tabled a bill March 2 to allow for-profit clinics to compete with public hospitals, setting off a storm of protest by people who felt the new law would undermine universal health care. A Cuban envoy who had been holed up in his country's embassy in Ottawa for four days left on March 2. Jose Imperatori maintained he had been wrongly accused of spying in the United States and came to Ottawa from Washington. On March 7 a Quebec Court judge ruled that two Montreal police officers convicted of assault causing bodily harm in the fatal 1993 beating of taxi driver Richard Barnabe could keep their jobs. Quebec announced a day later that it would change the law so it can fire officers convicted of criminal offences. On March 9, the already controversial Human Resources and Development department, under fire for bungling job grants, took over the high-risk $1.5 billion a year Canada Student Loans program. On March 14 Quebec announced it would cut personal income taxes by $4.5 billion over three years. On March 15, the House of Commons voted overwhelmingly in favour of legislation to clarify the rules if Quebec, or any other province, holds a referendum on secession. After months of acrimonious debate and political manoeuvring aimed at scuttling the bill, the Bloc Quebecois failed to neutralize Ottawa's clarity and it passed 208-55. Also on March 15, an Ontario court struck down media baron Conrad Black's lawsuit against Prime Minister Jean Chretien, saying his decision to block Black's appointment to the British House of Lords is beyond judicial review. Eight toddlers were killed in St-Jean-Baptiste-de-Nicolet, Que. on March 16 when the minivan they were in crashed, tossing many of the kids into a nearby field. On March 20 a BC farmer arrived in Ottawa after a journey across the country on a combine to raise awareness of the need for farm aid. Nick Parsons met the Prime Minister before heading home. On March 22 a BC judge struck down part of the toughest anti-smoking policy in the country, saying restaurants and bars didn't get enough notice of the change. On March 31, a BC court found Kelly Ellard guilty of second-degree murder in the killing of 14-year-old Reena Virk in Victoria in November 1997.

April

INTERNATIONAL

Austria: Nine of the 11-member OPEC, including Iran, voted to increase crude oil production in an effort to bring the price down. **Britain:** On April 11, a judge branded historian David Irving an anti-Semite racist and an apologist for Hitler. He ruled that an American scholar was justified in calling him a Holocaust denier. **Colombia:** 21 police and at least 9 others were killed in a leftist guerrilla attack in two towns on the Atrato River, in an attempt to seize control of the waterway. Earlier in the month, leftists had shut down the power supply to large parts of the country as the government announced plans to privatize the state-run utilities. **Congo:** On April 14 a blast in the Kinshasa airport killed 40 people. **Ecuador:** Local cash machines began dispensing American dollars instead of sucres as the government moved forward its plan to abandon the devalued currency and switch to a more stable one. A country-wide education program was put in place to ease the transition. **Ethiopia:** A drought in Ethiopia left more than eight million people short of food and seeking international assistance. **Iran:** President Mohammad Khatami took an assertive stand against hard-liners who have launched a crackdown against the pro-democracy movement, insisting that political and social reform cannot be stopped. **Japan:** Yoshiro Mori was sworn in as prime minister on April 5, three days after incumbent Keizo Obuchi suffered a massive stroke. (Obuchi died on May 14.) 16,000 were evacuated from villages on Hakkaido as Mount Usu sent smoke, ash and rocks into the air and mudslides down its slopes after a series of earth tremors. **Korea, North and South:** The two countries, divided since 1945, announced a planned bi-lateral summit for mid-June. Topics will include food aid for the North and family reunification. **Netherlands:** On April 22 Bosnian Serb Dragan Nikolic, commander of a detention camp for more than five years, was arrested after the Yugoslave war crimes tribunal accused him of raping, torturing and killing Muslims. His indictment included the highest number of counts contained in a public indictment issued by the Tribunal to that date. **Peru:** President Alberto Fujimori, the iron-fisted leader who crushed Maoist rebels and tamed runaway inflation, won a third term on April 9 after his opponent withdrew from a planned runoff vote on May 28 to protest election irregularities. **Philippines:** On April 18 an Air Philippines passenger plane carrying about 120 people crashed in the southern Philippines. **Portugal:** On April 16, seven people were killed when gas canisters were hurled inside a nightclub in Lisbon. **Russia:** The lower house of parliament ratified the

START II treaty between the US and Russia; the agreement calls for cutting the number of nuclear warheads on ballistic missiles to 3,500 each by 2007. (The US approved the treaty in 1996.) **United States:** On April 3 a judge ruled that Microsoft Corp. violated US antitrust laws by keeping "an oppressive thumb" on competitors during the race to link Americans to the Internet. On April 28, the U.S government moved to split the software giant in half. By April 5, technology stocks on the New York stock markets had suffered record drops sending the NASDAQ from a US$6.71 trillion high on Mar. 10 to US$5.61 trillion on April 4; by April 6, the index had begun to climb back up again. On April 6, Celera Genomics, a private company mapping the human genetic blueprint, said it had decoded all of the DNA pieces that make up the genetic pattern of a single human being. On April 9 a Marine Corps aircraft attempting to land during a nighttime training mission in Marana, Ariz., crashed and burst into flames, killing all 19 aboard. On April 12 a Cleveland, Ohio jury unanimously rejected the claim of Dr. Sam Sheppard's son that his father was wrongfully imprisoned for his mother's 1954 slaying, ending another chapter in the sensational case that inspired "The Fugitive" television series. In the early morning hours of April 22, US agents from the Immigration and Naturalization Service broke down the door of Elian Gonzalez's Miami relatives and seized the boy in a 3-minute raid. The child was flown to Andrews Air Force base in Maryland where he was reunited with his father, but not allowed to leave the US. Protesters failed to disrupt world leaders meeting in Washington for the World Bank and International Monetary Fund. On April 28 a white man opened fire in several suburban Pittsburgh communities, killing five people and critically wounding a sixth in a racially motivated shooting spree. **Zimbabwe:** President Robert Mugabe sought to shore up his flagging popularity among Zimbabwe's landless poor by backing squatters as they took over commercial farm property; the government passed legislation on April 6 that allowed the government to seize white-owned farms without compensation. On April 13, Zimbabwe's highest court ordered the government to remove squatters from nearly 1,000 of the country's mostly white-owned commercial farms. Police refused to enforce the order, citing lack of resources. The international community responded to the impasse by freezing millions of dollars of aid for land reform.

CANADA

On April 2, the BC government passed emergency legislation to end a week-long school strike and reopened the schools for 350,000 students. On April 6 Ottawa introduced a tough new immigration act to crack down on human smuggling and refugees who are criminals while welcoming the "best and brightest." In response to the announcement concerning the mapping of the human genome and the looming battles over the patenting of portions of the DNA, internationally known futurist Frank Ogden formally filed an application to have his own DNA trademarked in an effort to protect himself and his identity. On April 11, the federal government's same-sex bill ended its turbulent passage through the Commons as MPs voted overwhelmingly for the proposed legislation. The bill gives same-sex pairs the same social and tax benefits as heterosexual couples. On April 13, Nisga'a leaders smiled, clapped and fought tears as a land-claim treaty started 113 years ago by their ancestors cleared its last Parliamentary hurdle. The British Columbia First Nation received self-government powers and C$253 million in cash and economic funding. Ottawa will kick in C$255 million toward the deal that will cost a total of C$487 million. On April 17, voters in Prince Edward Island gave Premier Pat Binns a second mandate. The ruling Tories received over 50 per cent of the popular vote to win their second majority. On April 19, Wiebo Ludwig was convicted on five charges of vandalism in the northern Alberta oilpatch. He was sentenced to 28 months in jail and co-accused

Richard Boonstra received 21 days. A man was killed in Winkler, Man. on April 19 when a massive straw fire created a 50-metre wide tornado that sucked up his pick-up truck and tossed it like a toy. Irvin Harder, 63, died after he was plucked from the truck he was driving by a fire funnel, created by the intense heat of a blaze. On April 20, five students in an Ottawa-area high school were wounded in a knife attack by a 15-year-old boy. The federal government denounced Vietnamese government's April 24 execution in of a Canadian citizen accused of smuggling heroin. Foreign Affairs Minister Lloyd Axworthy said Nguyen Thi Hiep, who was born in Vietnam but became a Canadian citizen after moving to Canada and settling in Montreal in 1982, may have been duped into transporting drugs.

May

INTERNATIONAL

Chile: The court of appeals voted in favour of stripping Gen. Augusto Pinochet of political immunity, setting the stage for a trial for human rights violations during his 17-year reign as dictator. **Fiji:** Rebels holding Fiji's elected government released 10 hostages on May 19 after they signed documents backing nationalist rebel leader George Speight. (The remaining 18 hostages were released on July 13.) Speight took Fiji's first ethnic Indian Prime Minister Mahendra Chaudhry and most of his government captive in a bid to reassert native Fijian control over the country's politics. Speight was granted amnesty in return for freeing the hostages. **Indonesia:** On May 12, a cease-fire was declared in 25-year guerrilla war in the oil province of Aceh. **Iran:** Despite the reform policies of the government, a crackdown on free speech was initiated by the conservative judiciary, which ordered 16 pro-reform journals and newspapers shut down and the imprisonment of two editors. **Lebanon:** South Lebanon was in chaos May 22 after units of an Israeli-allied militia abandoned their positions and Shiite Muslim guerrillas and their supporters rushed in to reclaim villages held by Israeli forces for two decades. **Malaysia:** On May 24 armed assailants stormed one of the world's top diving resorts and sped off with 20 hostages. Philippine Muslim rebels who are seeking the release of militants jailed in the United States claimed responsibility for the kidnapping. **Netherlands:** A blaze inside a fireworks warehouse on May 13 triggered multiple explosions that killed at least 20 people, and injured 540. Over 400 homes were destroyed in the residential area. **Northern Ireland:** The IRA agreed to international monitoring of arms dumps as a way around the impasse over weapons decommissioning which has derailed the Ulster Assembly. **Peru:** Protestors attacked the National Election Board to back demands for postponement of a May 28 presidential run-off vote which they claimed was rigged in favour of incumbent Fujimori. **Philippines:** A man was arrested May 8 man suspected of being linked to the ILOVEYOU computer virus that hit machines around the world after raiding his apartment and finding computer equipment. The student was released because of insufficient evidence. Days later another student said he may have inadvertently set the virus free. The cost of the attack was estimated at US$10 billion worldwide. Supporters of a Muslim separatist group kidnapped 21 people, including ten tourists, from a remote holiday island, days after the government launched an assault on the group's base, where 27 teachers and children had been held hostage for over a month. **Portugal:** Ending an enduring mystery that some had feared hid an apocalyptic prediction, the Vatican on May 13 disclosed the so-called third secret of Fatima and said it was related to the 1981 assassination attempt against Pope John Paul II. The announcement came after the pope beatified two shepherd children who are said to have viewed an apparition of the mother of Christ above an olive tree in Fatima in

1917 and were told three secrets. **Serbia and Montenegro:** Pres. Milosevic shut down the country's largest opposition TV station and raided the offices of independent media outlets in an effort to slow the growing opposition forces. **Sierra Leone**: More than 300 United Nations peacekeepers were seized by rebels in four cities on May 5. 800 British paratroopers arrived to assist in restoring order. Rebwel leader Foday Sankoh was captured and airlifted to custody of the Sierra Leone government. Ten days later the rebels freed 139, after UN officials secured the release of 18 others. On May 28 the last of the hostages were released. **Sri Lanka:** Tamil Tigers made considerable gains during the month, advancing on their former capital of Jaffna and warning residents to flee the coming firefight. Early in the months they captured the strategically important Elephant Pass which holds the key to Jaffna. **Uganda:** Another 55 bodies were found in a mass grave linked to the Movement for the Restoration of the Ten Commandments of God, the sixth mass grave brought the death toll to over 970. **United States:** Driven by swirling wind of up to 80 kilometres an hour, fire rolled from block to block in abandoned Los Alamos on May 13 burning scores of homes down to their foundations in the town where the atomic bomb was built. The National Park Service had ordered a brush-clearing fire in a bid to avoid a major blaze. Mothers Day was marked by a Million Mom March for gun control in Washington. A 13-year-old student sent home from school in Lake Worth, Fla. for throwing water balloons returned and fatally shot a teacher in the face on May 26. **Venezuela**: The country's Supreme Court suspended the national elections slated for May 28, citing problems with the voting machine software and calling for rescheduled elections in late June. **Zimbabwe:** Pres. Mugabe continued to defy opinion at home and abroad, supporting the squatters on commercial farms and using the situation to bolster his faltering political fortunes.

CANADA

Three Barrie, Ont. children died May 5 when they hid inside a trunk and suffocated. On May 10, 90 Chinese migrants were put aboard a plane under armed guard to return to their homeland. They were among the almost 600 migrants who arrived illegally off the West Coast in 1999. Alberta MP Jack Ramsay walked out of a Melfort, Sask. court on May 10 cleared of an allegation that he once ordered a teenage girl to take down her underwear and threatened to shoot her in the back. A week earlier Ramsay, a former RCMP officer, was sentenced to nine months in jail for the attempted rape of a 14-year-old girl in the same isolated community in northern Saskatchewan. Federal Privacy Commissioner Bruce Phillips warned May 16 that Ottawa's Human Resources and Development department has a massive database containing data relating to the lives of ordinary Canadians. After weeks of protest, the government announced it would dismantle the database. An unknown Canadian soldier who was killed during the First World War was exhumed from a cemetery near Vimy Ridge in France to be brought home. After lying in state in Ottawa the body was buried at the foot of the National War Memorial. In late May six deaths in Walkerton, Ont. were blamed on the worst E. coli outbreak in Canadian history. The contamination by the potentially deadly bacteria was traced to the town's water supply; local officials were accused of failing to alert townspeople to the danger. As the controversy grew, the Ontario Ministry of Environment and government cutbacks were also drawn into the debate over responsibility for the outbreak. Hundreds of elective surgeries were cancelled in Alberta on May 23 and patients were sent home early from stressed hospitals as 10,000 health-care workers staged an illegal strike for higher wages. The Alberta Union of Provincial Employees was fined $400,000 for the two-day illegal strike. A 30-year-old high school teacher in Sechelt,

BC who was convicted of sexual exploitation was ordered to spend 10 months under house arrest in the home she shares with her victim.

June

INTERNATIONAL

Australia: A fire set by an arsonist in a youth hostel in Childers on June 23 killed 16 and injured at least 10 visitors from around the world. **Brazil:** As part of its campaign against crime, the government banned the sale of firearms. The Justice department hopes to make it illegal for anyone not a member of the police, military or a private security company to own a gun. **Britain:** Fifty-eight Chinese immigrants were found dead in the unrefrigerated, sealed compartment of a tomato truck when it was examined in Dover on June 19. **Chechnya:** The day after a suicide bomb attack killed up to 27 at a military command post in Alkhan-Yurt, Russian Pres. Putin established direct presidential rule over the region. **Cuba:** Elian Gonzalez returned to Havana with his father on June 28, seven months after he was cast adrift in the Florida straits, rescued and taken to the United States. The lengthy legal battle polarized the anti-Castro Cuban community in Miami and the rest of the US population. **Ethiopia:** The government announced the end of the two-year war with Eritrea, however the Eritreans vowed to fight on until all disputed territory was returned to them. **Greece:** A British defence attache was assassinated and police found evidence pointing to the terrorist group November 17, whose members have eluded capture despite a 25-year legacy of bloodshed. **India:** Thirty-four low-caste villagers were killed in Miapur on June 17 by an upper-caste militia amid ongoing violence over India's ancient system of social hierarchy. **Indonesia:** A powerful earthquake and several strong aftershocks rocked the Indonesian island of Sumatra, killing at least 25 people. On June 20, 160 Christians were killed in eastern Indonesia, victims of religious violence. On June 29, hundreds of refugees fleeing the religious fighting drowned when their overloaded ship sank in stormy waters. **Korea:** The leaders of North and South Korea met June 13 in a historic summit aimed at the eventual reunification of the divided Korean Peninsula; an agreement to ease tensions was signed and a plan put in place to begin the reunification of families. The US responded by easing sanctions against the North. **Luxembourg:** Police posing as journalists shot and critically wounded a hostage-taker holding a child and a grenade on June 1, freeing 25 children and three teachers held captive during a 30-hour standoff. **New Zealand:** On June 5 the prime minister of the Solomon Islands was taken hostage and armed rebels put up road blocks in the capital, Honiara. **Nigeria:** A government announcement that the price of fuel would rise by 50% sparked riots in many cities and a nationwide strike. **Poland:** Five cabinet ministers resigned from the coalition government, leaving the president determined to lead a minority government rather than calling elections. **Rumania:** The collapse of a high-risk investment fund left 300,000 investors demanding restitution; they blocked traffic and converged on the presidential palace in an effort to recover the money they lost. **Solomon Islands:** Rebels took the prime minister hostage and seized the capital city of Honiara in a wave of ethnic violence; the prime minister resigned in an effort to find a solution to the state's problems. **Sri Lanka**: A suicide bomber shattered Sri Lanka's first-ever War Heroes Day on June 7, killing a cabinet minister and 20 other people during a fund-raiser for the families of slain soldiers. **Syria:** President Hafez Assad died on June 10; his son Bashar took over his post and vowed to continue his father's policies. **United States:** On June 7 a federal judge ordered the breakup of Microsoft Corp., declaring the software giant should be split into two because it "proved untrustworthy in the past." **Zimbabwe:** Zimbabweans voted peacefully and in strong numbers on June 25 in the final day of parliamentary elections, but international observers declared the polls tainted by a dirty campaign plagued by violence and intimidation.

CANADA

On June 4 in Windsor, Ont. anti-globalization protesters were blasted with pepper spray and arrested as police riot squads braced for the opening of the annual general assembly of the Organization of American States. Dozens of Chinese migrants smashed windows and set fires on June 12 at the BC detention facility where they had been held since arriving illegally in Canada a year earlier. Paul Bernardo's former lawyer Ken Murray was acquitted of obstructing justice on June 13; Ontario Superior Court Justice Patrick Gravely said there was a reasonable doubt that Murray intended to impede the course of justice by forever keeping Bernardo's gruesome sex-and-torture videotapes from those trying convict him. Human Resources Development Minister Jane Stewart announced that the "Big Brother" database, a set of e-files cross-referencing up to 2,000 bits of information about each Canadian, would be dismantled, citing the potential for invasion of privacy. The Supreme Court of Canada reserved decision on June 14 after a day of hearings into Robert Latimer's 1993 killing of his disabled daughter, Tracy. The next day, the Supreme Court upheld the five-year-old Firearms Act that requires every gun owner to get a licence and register every firearm by the end of 2000. Baton-wielding riot police dodged bricks, paint bombs and Molotov cocktails on June 15 as more than 1,000 protesters attempted to storm the Ontario legislature in a show of civil disobedience over the policies of the Harris government concerning the poor. A glass-bottomed tugboat sank June 16 near Tobermory, Ont. plunging 17 Grade 7 students and their teachers into the cold, choppy waters of Georgian Bay. Two children—a boy and a girl—were drowned. Nearly 10 years after the Oka crisis, Kanesatake Mohawks signed a tentative agreement with Ottawa on June 21 to give them control over hundreds of hectares of land. Preston Manning placed second to Stockwell Day on June 24 as the Canadian Alliance party voted for its first leader. He was defeated two weeks later in a second ballot.

July

INTERNATIONAL

Denmark: Eight Pearl Jam fans were killed and 25 injured July 1 when some of the 50,000 fans at a rock festival in Roskilde pushed forward, trampling those at the front. **Fiji:** On July 13 coup leader George Speight ended a two-month-long hostage standoff by freeing the ousted prime minister and 26 others after the military refused to continue negotiations. On July 26 Speight was arrested by the military. **France:** An Air France Concorde crashed shortly after taking off from Paris on July 25, killing 113 people, most of them German tourists on their way to New York for a Caribbean cruise. **Greece:** A heat wave sent temperatures in southeastern Europe to over 40°C on July 6, killing 25 and melting roads in Turkey. Over 184 wildfires raged for over two weeks; killing two firefighters and injuring nine others. **India:** A Boeing 737-200 jet that crashed and burst into flames on July 23, killing 55 people on board and on the ground was scheduled to be taken out of service by the end of the year. **Israel:** Prime Minister Ehud Barak survived an attempt to bring down his government and bought himself time to push the peace process on July 31, but he lost another battle when his party's candidate for president was defeated. Peace talks held in the US collapsed over rival claims to East Jerusalem. **Ivory Coast:** A constitutional amendment requiring that any presidential candidate to have both parents of Ivorian descent was approved by 90% of voters. **Japan:** Over 13,000 people came down with food poisoning in the worst crisis in 30 years. Contaminated milk products were cited as the cause. **Mexico:** Vicente Fox was elected president on July 2, promising to be a pro-business leader when he takes power on Dec. 1. His election ended 71 years of rule by the Institutional Revolutionary Party (PRI). **Nigeria**: More than 200 charred bodies were found July 11 after a damaged gasoline pipeline exploded in southern Nigeria, killing villagers scavenging fuel with buckets and chamber pots. **Northern Ireland:** The traditional marching season saw the usual barricades and riots over parade bans in Catholic areas. The violence brought British troops back into the streets in Belfast amid growing signs that support was waning for the hardline Protestant Orange Order. **Peru:** Growing protests against Pres. Fujimori turned violent as fires were set and six were killed in the demonstrations. **Philippines:** Both scavengers and residents were killed July 9 when a mountain of garbage, loosened by rain, collapsed and burst into flames at Manila's biggest dump; squatters' shanties were flattened and 136 people were reported killed with another 150 unaccounted for. **Saudi Arabia:** The government announced another increase in production in the continuing effort to bring the price of crude oil down to US$25/barrel. **Sierra Leone:** A United Nations military operation on July 15 rescued 222 peacekeepers and 11 military observers who had been trapped by rebels inside a UN base since May. **United States:** The US and Vietnamese governments signed an agreement to lower trade barriers and increase US investment in the country. In a decision handed down in a class action suit by 500,000 Florida residents against five big tobacco firms, the Miami judge awarded US$145 billion in damages. On July 28 two federal appeals judges granted Napster Inc. a stay in the injunction aimed at shutting the online music site down, allowing the popular music trading service to remain online while it continues its legal battle with the music industry. The US Representatives voted to end restrictions on travel to Cuba as well as limits on the sale of food and medicine but the measure was expected to encounter trouble getting through the Senate. **Venezuela:** Voters in the July 30 presidential election re-elected Hugo Rafael Chàvez Fríaz to a new six-year term.

CANADA

Canadian athlete Mary-Beth Miller of Yellowknife, NWT, was killed by a bear on July 3 while training for the biathlon, a sport combining shooting and cross-country skiing at CFB Valcartier, Que. An Ontario judge ruled July 5 that parents and teachers are allowed to spank kids, but said it's time for clearer rules governing the use of corporal punishment. Canada's agriculture ministers signed a $5.5 billion-dollar agreement designed to take at least some of the uncertainty out of the risky business of farming, Federal Agriculture Minister Lyle Vanclief said July 5. A Vancouver gynecologist who survived a 1994 murder attempt was stabbed July 11 in his office building, prompting police to urge abortion providers to go on high alert. The assailant escaped. Matthew Coon Come, a tough-talking Cree leader from northern Quebec, unseated Phil Fontaine as national chief of the Assembly of First Nations on July 12. A tornado hit a Pine Lake, Alta. campsite on July 15, killing 10 people and injuring more than 130. On July 20 Canadian National Railway Co. and Burlington Northern Santa Fe Corp. called off their planned merger, which would have created North America's largest railway after a US appeals court upheld a 15-month moratorium on mergers by the US rail industry regulator. Ninety Chinese migrants who arrived in British Columbia by boat in 1999 were returned to China on July 27 to face jail and fines upon arrival in their homeland. A groundbreaking Alberta law that allowed authorities to temporarily detain suspected child prostitutes in safe houses was ruled unconstitutional by a judge on July 28. A new multimedia colossus was created July 31 as CanWest Global Communications Corp. announced a C$3.5 billion takeover of all the major Canadian newspapers held by Conrad Black's Hollinger Inc. On July 31 Ontario's highest court declared the law prohibiting the possession of marijuana unconstitutional and gave Ottawa one year to amend it. The Ontario Court of Appeal ruled that Canada's marijuana law fails to recognize that people who suffer from chronic illnesses can use pot as medicine.

August

INTERNATIONAL

Bahrain: A Gulf Air Airbus A320 crashed into shallow Persian Gulf waters on Aug. 23 after circling and trying to land in Bahrain, killing 143 people. **Chile:** The Supreme Court rejected Pinochet's appeal of the lifting of his political immunity, leaving the way clear for over 150 charges of human rights abuses during his regime. **India:** Suspected Islamic guerrillas mowed down Hindu Pilgrims on Aug. 2, sparking a 24-hour wave of violence that left 101 people dead and the prospect of peace shattered in the Himalayan province of Kashmir. **Indonesia:** Pres. Wahid handed the daily affairs of business over to his vice president, Magawati Sukarnoputri after severe criticism of his handling of the government. **Korea, North and South:** 100 families were reunited in Seoul and Pyongyang 50 years after Korea was split in two during the run-up to the Korean War. **Lebanon:** Local security forces moved into territory formerly occupied by Israel; UN peacekeepers are stationed along the border. **Malaysia:** The long-running show trial of former deputy prime minister Anwar Ibrahim finally came to an end with an expected conviction on charges of sodomy and a nine-year sentence. **Philippines:** On Aug. 29, six hostages released after months in captivity in the Philippines went to Libya to meet the man who helped buy their freedom: Moammar Gadhafi. **Russia:** On Aug. 9 an explosion in Moscow killed seven people and reawakened memories of a 1999 bombing campaign that left hundreds dead. On Aug. 14, the Russian nuclear sub Kursk with 118 sailors onboard went to the bottom of the Barents Sea, apparently after an explosion blew a hole in its starboard side. The Russian navy refused offers of international help to rescue the crew until there was very little hope that they would be found alive. A fire in Moscow's television tower on Aug. 27 knocked out most TV channels in the Russian capital. **Somalia:** On Aug. 13, after almost a decade of chaos, more than 2,000 Somali clan elders, religious leaders, businesspeople and peace activists formed a central government, but the country is so unstable that they met in neighboring Djibouti. **United States:** George W. Bush won the Republican party's presidential nomination on Aug. 3 setting up a race with Democrat Al Gore, who officially received his party's nomination on Aug. 16. On Aug. 9 Bridgestone/Firestone Inc. recalled 6.5 million tires used on light trucks and sport utility vehicles that were involved in over 100 deaths, primarily on Ford vehicles. Shares of Emulex, a computer network equipment maker, plummeted by more than 60 per cent on Aug. 25 after financial news agencies picked up a false Internet news release claiming the CEO had quit and the company was under investigation by the Securities and Exchange Commission. A man was later charged with stock fraud. North Texas endured its longest dry spell, going more than 60 days without rain, breaking a record of 59 days set during the Dust Bowl of the Depression. By the end of August, 72,000 wild fires had destroyed more than 60,000 hectares across the US west, burning in Montana, California, Nevada, Washington, Idaho, Colorado and Wyoming. **Zimbabwe:** On Aug. 1 Zimbabwe's government confirmed plans to take more than half of all the white-owned farming land in the country without paying for it and redistribute it to 500,000 poor black families. Trade unions called for a general strike to protest. By month end authorities had moved to evict some of the squatters.

CANADA

On Aug. 1 Ottawa appointed former NHL referee Bruce Hood to monitor airline restructuring and handle complaints from angry Air Canada customers. Oil from a ruptured pipeline caused an oil slick on the Pine River in northeastern British Columbia that endangered the water supply of Chetwynd, a town with 4,000 residents. Toronto council decided Aug. 2 to send the city's garbage by train to an abandoned mine near Kirkland Lake, Ont., setting off a storm of protest in that community. On Aug. 3 armed Canadian soldiers dropped from helicopters to take charge of the American cargo ship GTS Katie, loaded with Canadian military equipment, which was refusing to complete its delivery because of a dispute over payment. The ship was escorted from an area off the coast of Newfoundland to port in Quebec by two warships. A 16-year-old, known as Mafiaboy, accused of paralysing major Web sites, including CNN.com and Yahoo, in attacks that halted online business for several hours pleaded not guilty in Montreal on Aug. 3 to more than 60 new charges. Nine South Korean sailors sobbed with relief in a Victoria, BC court on Aug. 3 after they were acquitted of smuggling a boatload of Chinese migrants into Canada. Prime Minister Jean Chretien was hit in the face with a cream pie on Aug. 15 while visiting a summer festival in Charlottetown, prompting a review of security arrangements. The photo of a 4-year-old boy abandoned in a Calgary supermarket was released Aug. 16 in a bid to identify him and find his mother. The woman was located in Washington State. British Columbia announced Aug. 24 that its booming economy let the province have a surplus in 1999-2000, the first in a decade. BC announced Aug. 29 that it would raise its minimum wage to $7.60 per hour on Nov. 1, the highest in Canada. The long-running dispute over native lobster fishing near Burnt Church, N.B., took a dangerous turn Aug. 29 when federal fisheries officers sank removed illegal lobster traps from the water. Victims of Canada's tainted blood tragedy agreed to a $79-million compensation plan on Aug. 30. The people infected by hepatitis C and HIV were infected before 1986 or after 1990, making them ineligible for the $1.5 billion federal-provincial compensation package announced two years earlier.

September

INTERNATIONAL

Australia: The 2000 Summer Olympics opened in Sydney on Sept. 15. **Austria:** Meeting in Vienna, the Organization of Petroleum Exporting Countries said Sept. 9 they would raise their official output by at least half a million barrels a day in a bid to stem surging fuel prices. **Britain:** From the remote Scottish highlands to the shadow of Big Ben, gasoline pumps ran dry all over Britain on Sept. 12 as protesters, furious over high prices and high taxes, blockaded fuel depots, and the shortages set off panic buying. On Sept. 21 police found part of a grenade launcher near the scene of an attack on the headquarters of Britain's MI6 intelligence service, in what they believed was the work of Irish Republican Army dissidents. No one was injured in the attack. A judge ruled Sept. 24 that conjoined twins should be separated in order to save life of one twin. The parents, from Malta, wanted the twins left together, trusting in God's will to determine whether they would live. Doctors said both would die unless they were separated. **Burundi:** Hutu rebels killed 11 civilians in an attack on the outskirts of Burundi's capital, the latest violence in the country's seven-year civil war. **China:** On Sept. 12 China executed a legislator who made nearly US$5 million in bribes in hopes of marrying his mistress—the most senior official put to death for corruption since the communist takeover a half-century ago. **Denmark:** A

Sept. 28 referendum on joining the European common currency (€) was rejected by 53% of those voting. **France:** Protests against high fuel prices continued to block French ports, access to the Channel Tunnel and main roadways as the fishermen ended their siege and truckers and taxi drivers took up the cause. **India:** More than 400 people were killed in flooding in eastern Indian late in the month when several rivers, including the Ganges, overflowed. **Indonesia:** A car bomb ripped through an underground garage in the Jakarta Stock Exchange building on Sept. 13, killing 13 people, injuring 27 and shaking confidence in Indonesia's attempts to reform after decades of corrupt dictatorship. **Israel:** Eight people died in Israel by September from the West Nile virus and dozens of others were hospitalized. The government dusted towns with insecticide to fight the mosquito-borne disease. **Lebanon:** Two years after Rafik Hariri was ousted as prime minister because of economic problems, voters overwhelmingly re-elected the billionaire real estate developer. **Netherlands:** The Dutch Parliament voted Sept. 12 to give same-sex couples the right to marriage and all the trappings, including adoption and divorce—approving legislation by a margin of more than three to one that gives gays rights beyond those offered in any other country. **Peru**: Opposition to Pres. Fujimori mounted as evidence of a bribery scandal was released to the public. Fujimori responded by vowing to step down by July 2001. **Philippines:** On Sept. 9 Muslim rebels released four European hostages, ending 140 days of captivity. Government negotiators called in helicopters following a bloody ambush of two go-betweens en route to remote Jolo Island. **Serbia and Montenegro:** The presidential election on Sept. 24 was marred by charges of corruption and ballot irregularities. Despite official attempts to downplay the results, it was clear that President Slobodan Milosevic's opposition had won the vote. Milosevic responded by calling for a run-off vote on October 8, while the opposition called for him to step down. **United States:** On Sept. 5 UN Secretary-General Kofi Annan urged 150 international leaders to use the Millennium Summit to forge peace and end poverty in the 21st century. On Sept. 6 A federal judge ordered MP3.com to pay as much as $250 million to Universal Music Group for violating the record company's copyrights by making thousands of CDs available for listening over the Internet. MP3.com was fined $25,000 per CD to send a warning to Internet companies, the judge said. On Sept. 7 the UN Security council voted unanimously to overhaul United Nations peacekeeping operations—to create a more potent, better financed force that could respond more quickly to threats to international peace. The US government reached a deal Sept. 11 to release Wen Ho Lee, who had been held for nine months on charges of stealing nuclear secrets. Lee agreed to plead guilty to one of the 59 charges. The judge apologized for the government's actions, which he said "embarrassed our entire nation." Chase Manhattan Corp. reached a deal Sept. 13 to buy J.P. Morgan & Co. for about US$36 billion, combining two distinguished Wall Street institutions. Federal prosecutors concluded Sept. 20 there is "insufficient" evidence that President Bill Clinton or his wife Hillary committed a crime in Whitewater. The conclusion brought the six-year investigation to an end four months before the president left office. **Vatican**: On Sept. 3, Pope John Paul II beatified controversial 19th century Pope Pius IX and the 20th century's popular Pope John XXIII. Some Jews said the recognition of Pius—known for allegedly referring to followers of their faith as "dogs"—threatened the historic progress John Paul had made in Christian-Jewish relations.

CANADA

A judge's decision Sept. 1 to uphold a law banning private visits between federal inmates upset prisoners-rights groups who say such meetings are crucial. Justice Francois Lemieux ruled the gay couple in question couldn't be granted the privilege —not because of their homosexual relationship but because current legislation says two inmates cannot share a conjugal visit. The law has been in effect for more than 20 years. Alberta hammer-thrower Robin Lyons was dropped from Canada's Olympic team Sept. 5 after she tested positive for anabolic steroids. Lyons, 23, tested positive for the anabolic steroid norandrosterone, a metabolite of nandrolone, at the Canadian Olympic trials in August. Two days later, equestrian Eric Lamaze was kicked off the team after it was revealed that traces of cocaine had shown up in an earlier drug test, a violation of his agreement with the Canadian athletic authorities. RCMP officers netted 156 kilograms of heroin and disrupted an international Asian-based crime gang in two separate, massive busts in Vancouver and Toronto on Sept. 5. About 200 commercial fishermen and politicians gathered on the Yarmouth, N.S. waterfront on Sept. 5 to urge Ottawa to end the native lobster fishery. Natives from the land-locked Indian Brook reserve near Shubenacadie, N.S., had been fishing in St. Mary's Bay near Yarmouth for months. Premiers struck a health care deal on Sept. 11 with Prime Minister Jean Chretien that will raise federal transfers to C$18.3 billion next year. The provinces wanted federal transfer payments restored to 1994 levels of $18.7 billion, which they said would cost $4.2 billion annually. Several British Columbia doctors withdrew their services on Sept. 11, adding to a lengthy list of physicians who have been waging a battle with the province's Health Ministry over funding. Former Ontario premier Bob Rae tried to mediate an agreement between Mi'kmaq fishermen from the Burnt Church First Nation and the federal Fisheries and Oceans Department over control of the lobster fishery in Miramichi Bay, but gave up when he concluded the two sides were too far apart. On Sept. 23 three non-natives were arrested after shots were fired at fishing boats. On Sept. 11 Canadian Alliance leader Stockwell Day (Okanagan-Coquihalla) and Progressive Conservative party leader Joe Clark (King's/Hants) won federal by-elections. Michel Auger, Quebec's leading crime reporter, was shot five times in the back on Sept. 13, the day after publication of his latest expose on organized crime. Auger, 55, survived the hail of bullets and summoned the strength to ring the emergency 911 number with his cell phone as he lay bleeding in the parking lot of his employer, *Le Journal de Montreal*. On Sept. 13 Groupe Videotron Ltee. Agreed to be taken over by Quebecor Inc. for C$5.4 billion. Two luxury cruise ships were seized in Halifax for unpaid bills on Sept. 14 and about 1,700 passengers were put ashore. Finance Minister Paul Martin announced Sept. 20 that the surplus for 1999-2000 was C$12.3 billion, with a C$11.4 billion surplus in the first four months of the latest fiscal year. Second Cup cafes in Quebec can continue selling coffee and biscotti under the chain's English-language banner a provincial advisory group said Sept. 21. The English signs advertising Home Depot, Future Shop and Burger King, among others, also can stay. A provincial advisory body has decided chains with trademark names don't have to adopt French monikers to comply with Quebec's language laws. Sept. 25, Long-serving Saskatchewan premier Roy Romanow announced that he would be stepping down as soon as a new leader could be chosen. On Sept. 28, former Prime Minister Pierre Trudeau died at the age of 80; his body was brought to Ottawa to lie in state on Sept. 30.

Index

A

Abbot, Sir John 125, 152
Aboriginal
  languages 143
  population 48
  records 624
Abortion 60
Academic
  attainment 80, 81
  awards 151
  degrees 81
Academic Medal 151
Academy Awards 634–35
Accommodation industry
  e-commerce 225
  labour force 228–29
  operating profits 227
Action démocratique 188
Active living guide 800–1
Addressing envelopes 808
Afghanistan 317–18
Africa
  area 248
  highest, lowest points 248
  immigration to Canada 66
  map M12–M13
  mountains 250
  population 248, 253
African unity, intl. org 263
Agriculture
  Canada 217
    growing season 22–23
    hardiness zones 23
    labour force 228–29
    income 231
      by prov./terr. 217
      by region 7–8
    value of products 217
  world
    by country 318–556
Aid, humanitarian 193
Air force
  bases 193
  humanitarian missions 193
  ranks 191
  strength 190
Air masses/circulation 12–13
Airlines, revenues 220
Airports
  by country 318–556
  intl 25–31
  weather at 10
Air traffic, by country 318–556
Albania 319–20
Alberta
  agriculture 8, 217
  bankruptcies 199
  cabinet 176

climate 29
crime 85
economy 29
education 29, 80
election results
  fed 180–82
  prov 187
enters Confed 29
families
  income 76
  lone-parent 73
  size 74
fertility rate 72
frost dates 22
fuel production 218
geography 29
highest point 4
Internet usage 75
labour force 29, 228–30
lieut-gov 29
manufacturing 222
marriages/divorces 71
merchandising 223
migration
  emigration 68
  immigration 67
  interprov 29, 69
mining 216
motto/symbols 29
MPs 162–63
official langs 29
parks 29
party leaders 189
political profile 29
population 29, 42
  cities/towns 53–54
  native 48
  urban/rural 49
premiers (historical) 172–73
RRSP contribs 246
Senate seats 138
taxation 236–39
transfer payments 105
unemployment 29, 200
vital stats 29, 58, 62
wages 235
water use 613
web site 30
Alcohol, spending 196
Algeria 320–21
Altitudes
  highest, lowest points
    Canada 1, 4
    world 248
  mountains 250–51
Ambassadors (Cdn.) to U.N. 261
American Samoa 321, 543
Amphibians, endangered 610
Ancient history 270–73

Andorra 321–22
Angola 322–23
Anguilla 323–24, 542
Animals
  classifying 608
  endangered/extinct 609–11
Antarctica
  area 248
  highest, lowest points 248
  mountains 250
Anthems
  Canada
    ntl 1, 87
    prov./terr. 25–30
    royal 1
Antigua & Barbuda 324–25
APEC 266
Appellate courts 141
Aquariums 614
Arab League 262
Archery (2000 Olympics) 750
Arctic Council 262
Argentina 325–26
Armenia 326–27
Army
  bases 193
  ranks 191
  strength 191
Art galleries 655–57
  directory 659
  highlights (2000) 656–57
Arts & entertainment 615–59
  arts councils 615
  awards (See Awards)
  dance 646
  galleries/museums 655-57, 659
  e-commerce 225
  movies 632–36
  music 621–31
  radio 620
  television 616-19
  theatre 641–45
  writing 647–54
Arts councils 615
Aruba 327–28, 468
ASEAN 262
Ashmore & Cartier Islands 328
Asia
  area 248
  highest, lowest points 248
  immigration to Canada 66
  mountains 250
  population 248, 253
Asia-Pacific Economic Coop. (APEC) . 266
Assault 83–86
Assoc. Southeast Asian Nations 262
Asteroids 563
Asthma, incidence of 61
Astronauts 560, 567

840 Index

Astronomy
  constellations... 568
  eclipses (2001)... 565
  events (2001)... 564
  observatories/planetariums... 568–69
  orgs... 563
  solar system... 557–58
  terms... 561
  web sites... 565
Athlete of the century... 794
Athletics
  CIAU champs... 780, 781, 782
  org... 707
  2000 Olympics... 750–54
Atmospheric science... 591–606
Auditor General... 164
Australia... 328–29
  highest, lowest points... 248
  map... M14
  population... 248
Australian Antarctic Territory... 328
Austria... 329–30
Automobiles
  merchandising... 223
  ownership, by country... 318–556
  prices... 226
  sales... 226
  theft... 83–85
Automotive industry
  operating profits... 223
  retail... 223, 233
Auto sports
  org... 707
  racing... 787
Aviation, intl. org... 262
Awards/prizes
  academic... 151
  baseball... 700
  bravery... 150–51
  broadcasting... 617, 618
  drama... 641–42
  film... 633–35, 658
  humanitarian... 151
  humour... 653
  illustration... 649, 650
  innovation... 587
  literary... 647–51
  journalism... 652, 654
  medicine... 586
  military... 149–51
  music... 621–26, 628
    video... 629–30
  performing arts (Gov.–Gen)... 637–40
  science... 586, 587
  sports (See Sports, awards)
  television... 617, 618
  theatre... 641–42
  translation... 649, 650
  visual/media arts... 658
  voluntarism... 658
Azerbaijan... 330–31

B

Badminton (2000 Olympics)... 754–55
Bahamas... 331–32
Bahrain... 332–33
Baker Island... 543
Balance of payments, Cdn... 210, 211
Ballet, Cdn. companies... 646
Bangladesh... 333–34
Bankruptcies... 199
Banks
  interest rates... 197
  intl... 265
  labour force... 231
  operating profits... 227
  prime rate... 197
Barbados... 335–36
Barbuda (See Antigua & Barbuda)
Barley, Cdn. production... 217
Baseball
  American League
    batting champs... 702
    final standings... 695
    leaders... 695–96
    runs... 703
    MVPs... 701
    pennant winners... 698
    awards... 700
    Cdn. players... 704
    records... 704
    greatest home run seasons... 702
  National League
    battting champs... 702
    final standings... 696
    leaders... 696–97
    runs... 703
    pennant winners... 698
  orgs... 697, 707
  2000 Olympics... 755
  World Series... 699
    MVPs... 699
  (See also Montreal Expos; Toronto Blue Jays)
Basketball... 711–16
  CIAU champs... 780, 781, 782
  org... 707
  2000 Olympics... 755
  (See also National Basketball Association)
Beach volleyball... 769
Beaufort Wind Scale... 598
Beef production... 7, 8, 217
Belarus... 336–37
Belgium... 337–38
Belize... 338–39
Benin... 339–40
Bennett, Richard,... 129–30, 152
Bermuda... 340, 542
Bestsellers... 652
Beverages
  labour force... 232

value of products... 221–22
Bhutan... 340–42
Bill C–55... 653
Bills, stages to passage of... 139, 143
Biomass... 218
Birds
  classifying... 608
  endangered/extinct... 609, 610
  prov./terr... 25–30
Birth certificates... 804–5
Birth rates
  Canada... 25–31, 58
  world... 318–555
Bloc Québécois,... 178, 185
Bolivia... 342–43
Bonds, govt.
  average yields... 246
  interest rates on... 197
Booker Prize... 651
Books
  awards... 647–51
  bestsellers... 652
Borden, Sir Robert... 127–28, 152
Bosnia & Herzegovina... 343–44
Botanical gardens... 614
Botswana... 344–45
Bouchard, Lucien... 185
Bouvet Island... 477
Bowell, Sir Mackenzie... 126, 152
Boxing
  org... 707
  2000 Olympics... 755–56
Bravery awards... 150–51
Brazil... 345–46
Break & enters... 83–86
Breeders Stakes... 791
Bridges... 247
Britain (See United Kingdom)
British Antarctic Territory... 542
British Columbia
  agriculture... 8, 217
  bankruptcies... 199
  cabinet... 177
  climate... 29
  crime... 85
  economy... 29
  education... 29, 80
  election results
    fed... 179–83
    prov... 187
  enters Confed... 29
  families
    income... 76
    lone-parent... 73
    size... 74
  fertility rate... 72
  frost dates... 22
  fuel production... 218
  geography... 29
  highest point... 4
  Internet usage... 75
  labour force... 29, 228–30
  lieut.-gov... 29
  manufacturing... 222
  marriages/divorces... 71
  merchandising... 223
  migration
    emigration... 68
    immigration... 67

Index

interprov. 29, 69
mining 216
motto/symbols. 29
MPs 163
official langs. 29
parks 29
party leaders 189
political profile 29
population 29, 42
  cities/towns 54
  native 48
  urban/rural. 49
premier (historical) 173
RRSP contribs. 246
Senate seats. 138
taxation 236–39
transfer payments 205
unemployment. 29, 200
vital statistics. 29, 58, 62
wages. 235
water use 613
web site 30
British Indian Ocean Territory .. 342–542
British Virgin Islands 346–47, 542
Broadcasting
  awards 617, 618
  revenues/expenses. 219
  TV networks/servs. 619
  (See also Radio broadcasting)
Brunei Darussalam. 347–48
Building
  materials 216
  permits. 198
  tallest 247
Bulgaria 348–49
Burkina Faso 349–50
Burundi 350–51
Burma (See Myanmar)
Business, Canada
  bankruptcies 199
  credit summary 234
  e-commerce 224–25
  immigration 65
  investment
    abroad 215
    foreign 214
  productivity 233
Business services
  labour force 228–29
  income. 231
  operating profits 227

C

Cabinet (Cdn.) 139–40
  members 153–55
    role. 136
    salary 166
    ministries 174–77
Cable TV servs
  directory 619
  revenues/expenses. 219
Caicos Island (See Turks & Caicos Island)
Calcium 797

Calder Trophy. 736
Calendars. 857–58
Calgary (AB). 31
  crime rate. 86
  Intenet use. 75
  population 53, 55
Cambodia. 351–53
Cameroon 353–54
Campbell, Kim 135, 152
Canada. 354–55
  agriculture 7–8, 22-23, 217
  anthems. 1, 87
  area 1
  bankruptcies 199
  borders/boundaries 1
  Charter of Rights 146–49
  cities 31–37
  citizenship 64, 67, 806–7
  climate. 9–23, 605–6
  coat of arms. 88
  Constitution 143–44
  Consumer Price Index 196
  currency. 198, 234
  debt 203
  defence 190–93
  economy 194–246
  education 80–82
  election results. 179–83
  embassies 318–556, 807
  emigration 68
  energy 256
  flag. 87
  foreign investment 214, 215
  foreign trade 210–15
  frost dates 22–23
  geography 1, 3–6, 354
  geological regions 3–6
  govt. of. 137–67
    (See also Fed. govt.)
  health care 209
  history 89–135
  identification, documents 804–5
  inflation rate 197, 354
  judiciary 141–44, 168
  labour force 228–33
  manufacturing 221–22
  map 2
  marriages/divorces 71
  merchandising 223
  migration 64–70
  mining 216
  monarchy. 137
  motto 1
  ntl. game 1
  North 8
  official langs. 1, 147–48
    prov./terr. 25–31
  orders & decorations 149–51
  parks 37–41
  passports. 806–7
  pension policy 207
  population 42–57, 354
  postal rates 808
  prime ministers 124–35, 152

  provinces (See Provinces & territories)
  rights & freedoms 146–49
  SIN numbers 805
  social security 206–8
  superlative facts. 1, 4, 5
  symbols. 1, 87, 88
  taxation 236–39
  territories (See Provinces & territories)
  time zones 2, 563
  trade. 210–13
  unemployment 200
  vegetation 7–8
  vital statistics 58–63
  water use 613
Canada Astronaut Program 567
Canada Elections Act 184
Canada Football Hall of Fame 722–23
Canada-France-Hawaii Telescope.... 559
Canada Pension Plan 207
Canada Post. 808
Canada Site 145
Canadarm. 566, 567
Canada's Food Guide to Healthy Eating
  797–99
Cdn. Acad. Rec. Arts & Sciences 627
Cdn. Action Party 178
Cdn. Astronaut Program 567
Cdn. Broadcasting Corp. (See CBC)
Cdn. Country Music Awards. 628
Cdn. Football League
  all-stars 717
  all-time leading players 719–20
  awards 721
  hall of fame 723
  standings. 717
  web site 710
  (See also National Football League)
Cdn. Forces
  bases 192–93
  medal. 149–51
  missions
    humanitarian 193
    peacekeeping 191–92
  ranks 191
  senior personnel 190
  strength 190
Cdn. Hall of Fame 660–94
Cdn. Heritage Party of Canada .. 178
Cdn. Heritage Rivers System 6
Cdn. identity, documents 804–7
Cdn. Innovation Centre 590
Cdn. Intellectual Property Office. 590
Cdn. Interuniv. Athletic Union (CIAU), 780
Cdn. Open Golf tournament 788
Cdn. Reform Conservative Alliance
  .... 178, 185
Cdn. Space Agency 566
Cdn. Space Program, quiz 559
Cdn. Sports Hall of Fame 792–93
Cdn. Technology Network 590
Cancer (cause of death) 60
Cannes Film Festival. 635–36
Canoe-Kayak (2000 Olympics)... 756–58
Canola production 217

Index

Cape Verde 355–56
Carbohydrates 797
Cardiovascular disease (cause of death) 60
Caribbean
  immigration to Canada 66
  population 254
Caring Canadian Award 151
Cartooning (editorial) award 654
Cassini Mission to Saturn 565
Cayman Islands 356, 542
CBC 620
CDs, top 50 628
Celsius scale 795
Census families 73
Census metro areas 31–37, 55
  crime in 86
Census 2001 56–57
Central African Republic 356–58
Central America
  area 248
  population 254
Chad 358–59
Championship Auto Racing Teams .. 787
Channel Islands 359, 542
Charlottetown (PEI) 25
  population 50
Charter of Rights & Freedoms ... 146–49
Chemical products
  labour force 232
  value of product 221–2
  safety symbols 803
Chemistry
  awards 586
  elements 582
    periodic table 583
  terms 580
Chicoutimi-Jonquière (Que.) 31–32
  population 50, 55
Children('s)
  lit. awards 649, 650
  music awards 624
Chile 359–60
China 360–62
  population 247, 252
Chrétien, Jean 135, 152
Christian Heritage Party of Canada ... 178
Christmas Island 328, 362
Churches, world council 263
CIAU champs 780–82
Cities
  Canada 31–37
    area 50–55
    capitals 1, 25–31
    crime 86
    incorporation dates 31–37
    Internet use in 75
    latitude, longitude, elevations. 24
    municipal govt. 142
    official langs. 31–37
    population 31–37, 50–55
    superlative stats. 1
    wages 235
    weather 10, 20

(See also Towns)
world
  capitals 317–555
  elevations 248
  population, largest 247
  superlative stats. 247
  weather records 594
Citizenship
  passports 806–7
  persons granted 67
  qualifying/applying 64
  Welcome Home Campaign 45
Clark, Joe 133, 152
Classical music awards 624
Classification, living organisms 608
Classification system, TV 616
Cleaning symbols 802
Climate
  Canada
    change 605–6
    cities 31–37
    prov./terr. 25–31
    factors affecting 9, 11
    maps 11, 12–13
  world
    by country 317–555
Clothing
  care of (symbols) 802
  industry
    labour force 232
    value of products 221, 223
    price index 196
    stores 223, 233
Clouds 602–3
CNIDR-US Patent Project 590
Coal
  consumption 256
  labour force 232
  supply 218
  value of products 218, 221–22
Coastlines
  Canada 1
  prov./terr. 25–31
  world 317–555
Coats of arms
  ntl. 88
  prov./terr. 25–31
Cocos (Keeling) Island 328, 362
Colleges, enrolment 80, 81
Colombia 363–64
Commissioners (terr.) 30, 31, 142
Committee of the Regions 265
Commonwealth 262
Communications industry
  Canada
    labour force 228–29
    income 231
    operating profits 227
    telephones 219
  world
    by country 318–556
Communications satellites
  (See satellites/space probes)
Communist Party of Canada 178

Comoros 364–65
Confederation
  dates 1
  fathers of 118
Congo 365–66
Conn Smythe Trophy 738
Constellations 568
Constitution of Canada 143–44
Construction
  building permits 198
  labour force 228–29
  income 231
  operating profits 227
Consumer
  bankruptcies 199
  credit 234
Consumer goods & services
  operating profits 227
  prices 196
  purchasing power 234
  time base 197
  value of products 221–22
Consumer Price Index 196
  purchasing power, dollar 234
  time base 197
Continents
  area 248
  highest, lowest points 248
  maps M1–M16
  mountains 250–51
  population 248
  superlatives 247
Cook Islands 366, 477
Coral Sea Island Territory 328
Corn production 217
Costa Rica 366–67
Côte d'Ivoire 367–69
Council of the European Union 265
Countries of the world
  events of '99–00 818–38
  energy consumption 256
  humanitarian missions to. 193
  immigration from 44–45
  maps M1–M16
  peacekeeping missions 191–92
  population projections 252–54
  superlative stats. 247
  trade 211–13
Country music, awards 628
County courts 141
Courage, awards for 150–51
Courts
  Canada 141–42
  world 257, 265
Credit summary 234
Crime
  incidents 83
  by age, gender 83
  by prov. 84–85
  rate of
    change in 86
    youth 86
Crimes (Cdn.) 122–23
Critical writing, awards 654

Index

Croatia 369–70
Cross of Valour 151
Crown corporations 140
CRTC 617
Cuba......................... 370–71
Cultural industries (See Information & cultural industries)
Curling
  Cdn. medals.................... 745
  champs 779
  org. 707
Currency
  by country 318–556
  dollar, purchasing power 234
  foreign rates.................. 198
Current events 818–38
Currents....................... 9, 11
Cycling
  org. 707
  2000 Olympics.............. 755–59
Cyprus 371–72
Cy Young Award................ 700
Czech Republic 372–73

D

Dairy production
  Canada
    by region 7, 8
    value of product............... 217
Dairy products, food guide 797–99
Dance
  awards........................ 637
  companies
    ballet 646
    jazz dance 646
Dark Ages 273–77
Daylight Saving Time............ 563
Death(s)
  disease (cause of) 60, 63
  earthquakes (cause of)........... 573
  rates
    Canada................... 25–31, 62
    by country 318–550
  (See also Obituaries)
Debt
  bankruptcies 199
  national
    Canada....................... 203
    by country 318–556
  public
    interest on 204
Decorations (military) 149–51
Defence
  Canada (See Cdn. Forces)
  expenditures, by country 318–556
Deficit, govt..................... 203
Degrees, academic............... 81
Dem. Republic of the Congo .. 373–75
Denmark 375–76
Dental servs., expenditures 209
Deputy leader, govt., salary........ 166
Deputy leader, opposition, salary.... 166
Deputy prime ministers
  role........................... 136

terms 155
Deputy speaker, salary 166
Deserts, world 247
Diabetes........................ 61
Diefenbaker, John 131, 152
Diet & health 797–99
Dinosaurs
  geological time period 575
  museum....................... 579
Diplomacy
  embassies 318–556, 807
  UN ambassadors 261
Directories
  aquariums 614
  arts councils 615
  art galleries 659
  astronomy orgs................. 563
  baseball orgs............. 697, 707
  Cdn. documentation......... 804–5
  dance comps................... 646
  govt........................... 145
  hockey orgs. 707, 734
  museums......... 579, 585, 659
  observatories............... 568–69
  planetariums 569
  political parties................ 178
  science centres 585
  sports orgs.............. 697, 707
  television/cable servs............ 619
  theatre comps.................. 644
  vital stats. offices........... 804–5
  zoos........................... 614
Disabilities pensions 207
Disasters 119–21
Diseases
  cause of death 63
  chronic conditions 61
  and health indicators 60
District courts 141
Diving
  org........................... 707
  2000 Olympics.............. 759–60
  (See also Synchronized diving)
Divorce rates 71
Djibouti 376–77
DNA, mapping (See Human Genome Project)
Doctors, expenditures 209
Documents, Cdn. identification ... 804–5
Dollar, Cdn.
  exchange rates................. 198
  price index.................... 196
  purchasing power 234
Dominica 377–78
Dominican Republic........... 378–79
Dora Awards 641
Drama awards 637–42
Drug offences 83
Drug stores 233
Drugs, expenditure............... 209
Drunk driving 83
Drycleaning, symbols 802
Du Maurier Ltd. Women's Golf Classic
  788
Dutch Guiana (See Suriname)

E

Earth
  composition of................. 571
  Lithoprobe 576–77
Earthquakes
  in Canada..................... 574
  measuring 572–73
  world 573
Earth sciences 570–79
  museums...................... 579
  terms 570–71
  web site 570
East Coast Music Awards......... 625
East Timor 379–80
Eating, food guide 797–99
Eclipses (2001) 565
E-commerce................. 224–25
Economic immigrants 65
Economics
  Canada.................... 194–246
  CPI 196
  exchange rates................. 198
  GDP 195
  inflation rate................... 197
  interest rates.................. 197
  productivity 233
  by prov./terr. 25–31
  terms 194–95
  world 255–56
  by country 318–556
Ecuador 380–81
Editorial cartooning award 654
Editorial writing awards 652, 654
Edmonton 29, 32
  crime rate..................... 86
  Internet use 75
  population 54, 55
Education
  Canada
    attainment 80
    enrolment................... 80–81
    expenditure 82
    price index................... 196
    prov./terr. 25–31, 80
    university grads................. 81
  by country 318–556
Educational servs.
  e-commerce................... 225
  labour force 228–29
  operating profits 227
Egg production, value of product.... 217
Egypt 381–82
Elections, Canada
  results
    fed....................... 179–83
    prov...................... 186–89
  voters
    lists 805
    turnout 183
Electoral districts, fed............. 182
Electrical/electronic production
  labour force 232
  operating profits 227

844 Index

value of product........... 221–22
Electricity
  labour force............... 228–29
  income...................... 231
  supply....................... 218
Elementary schools.............. 80
Elements (chemical)............ 582
  periodic table........... 582, 583
El Niño........................ 591
El Salvador................. 382–83
Embassies............ 318–556, 807
Emigration, by prov./terr......... 68
Emmy Awards.................. 618
Employment
  distribution
    by city (selected).......... 31–37
    by prov./terr......... 25–31, 230
    by country............. 318–556
    by industry............ 228, 233
  insurance..................... 206
Endangered species.......... 609–11
Energy
  Canada
    labour force............. 228–29
    income.................... 231
    operating profits........... 227
    supply.................... 218
  museums..................... 585
  world consumption........... 256
Engineering
  hall of fame.................. 586
  museums..................... 585
England (See United Kingdom)
English language (See Official langs.)
Entertainment (See Arts & entertainment)
Equatorial Guines........... 383–84
Equestrian sports
  org......................... 707
  2000 Olympics........... 760–61
  (See also Horse racing)
Eritrea..................... 384–85
Equivalencies
  metric/imperial........... 795–96
  temperature.................. 795
Estonia.................... 385–86
Ethiopia................... 386–88
Ethnicity
  in Canada..................... 46
  world, by country........ 318–555
Europe
  area......................... 248
  highest, lowest points........ 248
  immigration................... 66
  map....................... M8–M9
  mountains.................... 250
  population........... 248, 253–54
European Central Bank........... 265
European Commission........... 265
European Community (EC)...... 264
European Council............... 265
European Parliament............ 265
European Council (EU)...... 264–65
  Cdn. investment in............ 215
  and foreign investment........ 214

institutions of................. 265
members of................... 265
European Space Agency......... 558
Exchange rates................ 198
Expenditures
  consumer................ 79, 196
  govt.
    education................... 82
    health care................. 209
    social programs......... 206–8
Exercise guide............. 800–1
Explosives, symbols............ 803
Exports
  Canada...................... 213
  trade balance................ 211
  by country.............. 318–556
Extinct species................ 609
Extirpated species............. 609

F

Fahrenheit scale............... 795
Fairbairn, Bruce............... 627
Falkland Islands........... 388, 542
Families
  cities (selected)............ 31–37
  composition of................ 74
  income
    average..................... 76
    min. level................ 78–79
  lone-parent................... 73
  size of....................... 74
Farms (See Agriculture)
Faroe Islands.................. 388
Fathers of Confederation....... 118
Fats (in foods)................ 797
Federal Court of Canada........ 141
Fed. govt., Canada
  cabinet depts................ 140
  debt........................ 203
  executive............... 139–40
  expenditure(annual).......... 204
  financial statement ('99).. 200–1
  judiciary................ 141–44
  labour force.............. 228–29
  income..................... 231
  leg. authority............... 142
  leg. costs............... 166–67
  Parliament.............. 138–39
  party leaders................ 185
  political
    figures, salaries of...... 166–67
    parties..................... 178
  spending................ 200–9
  surplus/deficit.............. 203
  system.................. 137–44
  transfer payments............ 205
  watchdogs............... 164–65
Federated States of Micronesia
  .... 254, 457, 543
Fencing (2000 Olympics)..... 761–62
Fertility rates
  Canada....................... 72
  world................... 318–556

Festival
  film..................... 635–36
  theatre...................... 644
Fibre (in foods)............... 797
Fiction awards.......... 647–50, 651
Field hockey
  CIAU champs............ 780, 782
  2000 Olympics............... 759
Figure skating
  Cdn. champs................. 785
  org......................... 707
Fiji....................... 389–90
Film
  awards............... 633–35, 658
  festivals................ 635–36
Finance industry
  e-commerce.................. 225
  labour force............. 228–29
  income...................... 231
Finance, personal........... 234–43
  bankruptcies................. 199
Finland.................... 390–91
Fish, endangered/extinct...... 609, 610
Fishing industry
  labour force............. 228–29
  income...................... 231
Flag, ntl...................... 87
Flammable products, symbols..... 803
Flowers
  endangered/extinct....... 609, 611
  hardiness zones............... 23
  prov./terr................ 25–30
Fog...................... 10, 594
Folacin....................... 797
Food(s)
  healthy eating guide...... 797–99
  nutrients in................. 797
  price index.................. 196
Food industry
  Canada
    e-commerce................ 225
    labour force............... 232
    income.................... 231
    operating profits........... 227
    value of products....... 221–22
Food stores................... 223
Football................... 717–726
  bowl games.................. 726
  CIAU champs....... 780, 781, 782
  Grey Cup.................... 718
  hall of fame............. 722–23
  org......................... 707
  2000 Olympics............... 759
  web site.................... 710
  XFL (Extra Fun League)....... 724
  (See also Cdn. Football League;
    National Football League)
Foreign currency exchange rates.... 198
Foreign investment
  abroad, by industry.......... 214
  in Canada................... 214
Foreign trade............. 210–15
Forestry
  e-commerce.................. 225

Index

forested land, by prov. 25–30
  labour force 228–29
  income 231
  operating profits 227
  value of product 221–22
Formula One 787
France 391–92
  La Francophonie 263
Frank J. Selke Trophy 738
Fraud 83
Fredericton (NB) 26
  population 26, 50
French Guiana 391, 392–93
French language
  awards 649–50
  rights 147–48
French Polynesia 391, 393
Frost 10
Frost dates 22–23
Fruit, food guide 797–99
Fruit production
  by region 7, 8
  value of product 217
Fuel production 218
  (See also Petroleum production)
Furniture mfg.
  labour force 232
  value of product 221–2
Furniture stores 223, 233
Futuna. See Wallis & Futuna

G

Gabon 393–94
Galleries 655
  highlights (2000) 656–57
Gambia 394–95
Game farms 614
Gas stations 223, 233
Gaza Strip 395–96
Gemini Awards 617
Genie Awards 633
Genome Project 612
Geography
  Canada 1
    landforms 3–6
    by prov./terr. 25–31
  world 248–51
    by country 317–558
    maps M1–M16
Geological Survey of Canada . . . 570, 574
Geology
  Lithoprobe 576–77
  museums 579
  terms 570–71
  time periods 3, 4, 574–75
  web sites 570
  (See also Earth sciences)
Georgia 396–97
Germany 397–98
Ghana 398–99
Gibraltar 399–400, 542
Giller Prize 651
Glenbow Museum (Calgary) 656

Global
  information 247–556
  superlatives 247
  warming 9, 605-6
Glossaries
  astronomy 561
  chemistry 580
  economy 194–95
  geology 570–71
  investment 244–45
  life sciences 607–8
  meteorology 591–93
  physics 580
  space 561
  U.N. acronyms 258
  weather 591–93
Gold reserves, by country 318–556
Golf
  org. 707
  tournaments 788–89
Gorges 247
Govt.
  Canada
    defeat of 143
    organization of 137–44
    spending 200–9
    web sites 145
    (See also Fed. govt.)
  world 318–556
Govt. bonds
  average yields 246
  interest rates on 197
Govt. holidays 858
Govt. house leader 136
Govt. leaders
  by country 318–556
  salaries 166
  Yukon/NWT/Nunavut 142
Govs.-gen. 137–38
  salary 166, 167
  as symbol 138
  terms 152
Govs.-gen.'s awards
  academic 151
  humanitarian 151
  literary 647–650
  performing arts 637–40
  visual/media arts 658
Grains
  food guide 797–99
  production, Canada 217
Grammy Awards 625–26
Gravity 581
Great Lakes 5
Greece 400–1
Greenland 401
Green Party 178
Grenada 401–2
Grenadines (See Saint Vincent &
  the Grenadines)
Gretzky, Wayne 794
Grey Cup 718
Grizzlies (Vancouver) 715, 716
Groceries

price index 196
stores 223
Gross domestic product (GDP)
  Canada 195
  by prov./terr. 25–31
  by country 318–556
Groundwater, quality of 8
Group of Seven 655
Growing season, Canada 22–23
Guadeloupe 391, 402–3
Guam 403, 543
Guaranteed Income Supplement 208
Guatemala 403–4
Guernsey 542
Guiana (French) 391
Guinea 404–6
Guinea-Bissau 406–7
Guyana 407–8
Gymnastics (2000 Olympics) 762–63

H

Hail 594
Haiti 408–9
Halifax (NS) 26, 32
  Internet use 75
  population 50, 55
Halls of fame
  Cdn. 660–94
  Cdn. football 722–23
  Cdn. sports 792–93
  hockey 734
  music
    Cdn. 627
    rock & roll 630–1
  science/eng. 586
Hamilton (ON) 32
  crime rate 86
  Internet use 75
  population 52, 55
Handball (2000 Olympics) 763–64
Hardiness zones 23
Hardness (mineral), measuring 578
Hart Trophy 737
Haze 10
Health
  nutrition/food 797–99
    exercise 800–1
    health indicators 60
    smoking 60
  price index 196
Health cards 804–5
Health care
  e-commerce 225
  labour force 228–29
  income 231
  operating profits 227
  spending 209
Healthy eating guide 797–98
Heard & McDonald Islands 328
Heart disease (cause of death) 60
Heavy equipment mfg. 214, 221
Heinbecker, Paul 261

Index **845**

846 Index

Herzogovena (*See* Bosnia & Herzogovena)
History
  Canada.................89–135
  world................270–316
Hockey......................727–43
  awards/trophies......737–38, 742–43
  hall of fame..................734
  junior champs.........740, 742–43
  orgs...................707, 734
  Stanley Cup champs........731–32
  web sites.....................710
  world champs.............740–41
  (*See also* National Hockey League)
Holidays
  govt. & bank..................858
  ntl., by country............318–556
Holland (*See* Netherlands)
Homicide....................83–86
Honduras....................409–10
Honey production..............217
Hong Kong....................410
Horse racing................790–91
Hospitals, expenditures.........209
House of Commons..............139
  expenses......................166
  members...................174–77
    pensions....................167
    salaries.....................166
Household
  chemicals, safety..............803
  credit........................234
  goods, value of................223
  Internet use....................75
  measures, metric equiv........795
  spending..................79, 196
  water use....................613
Housing
  affordability..................242
  building permits..............198
  price index..................196
  resale value..................240
Howland Island.................543
Human Genome Project..........612
Humanitarian
  award........................151
  missions.....................193
Humidex..................592, 596
Humour award..................653
Hungary....................410–12
Hurricanes
  intensity scale................599
  names........................599
Hydroelectricity
  Canada, supply................218
  world consumption.............256

I

Identification, documents.......804–7
Illustration, Gov.-gen.'s award..649, 650
Immigration
  changes in.....................70
  interprov. migration..........25–31

by origin.......................66
program........................66
by prov.destination..............67
refugees.......................66
totals..........................65
Immigration & Refugee Protection Act 70
Imperial measures..............795
Imports
  Canada........................212
    trade balance................211
  by country................318–556
Income(s)
  by amount.....................77
  avg., by type...................77
  avg. weekly...................231
  cities, selected..............31–37
  family........................76
  by industry...................231
  low.........................78–79
  median........................235
  of political figures........166, 167
  and savings...................243
  taxable
    by age/gender................239
    by prov./terr.................236
Income taxes (*See* Taxes)
Incorporation dates, cities....31–37
Independence dates, by country 317–555
Identification (documents)....804–5
India.......................413–14
Indonesia...................414–15
Industrial Revolution.......281–84
Industries
  e-commerce..................225
  foreign investment by........214
  labour force..............228–29
    income.....................231
  operating profits..............227
  principal
    by country...............318–556
    by prov./terr...............25–31
  water use by..................613
Infant mortality rates
  Canada........................60
  by country................318–556
Inflation rates
  by country................318–556
  by year......................197
Information Commissioner....164–65
Information & cultural industries
  e-commerce..................225
  operating profits..............227
Innovation award..............587
Insurance industry
  e-commerce..................225
  labour force..............228–29
    income.....................231
  operating profits..............227
Intellectual property..........590
Interest rates
  on mortgage payments....240, 241
  on public debt................204
Intl. Civil Av. Org. (ICAO).......262
Intl. Court of Justice...........257

Intl. Fed. Red Cross & Red Cres. Soc. 262
Intl. Monetary Fund (IMF).......262
Intl. news..................818–38
Intl. Olympic Com. (IOC).......262
Intl. Org. of Francophones......263
Intl. Org. for Standardization...263
Intl. orgs..................257–69
Intl. payments.................210
Intl. reserves, by country....318–556
Intl. Space Station.............560
Intl. system of units (SI).......584
Intl. Trade Org................268
Internet
  sales......................224–25
  usage, by prov.................75
Inter-Parliamentary Union......263
Interpol........................262
Interprov. migration.....25–31, 69
Inuit, population................48
Inventions
  awards......................587
  Cdn.......................588–89
  patents......................590
  web sites....................590
  women's project..............590
Investigative reporting awards..651, 652
Investment
  abroad......................215
  balance of payments.........210
  bonds........................246
  foreign, in Canada...........214
  RRSP holdings...............246
  stock exchange..............246
  terms....................244–45
Iodine (nutrient)...............797
Iqaluit.........................31
Iran.......................415–16
Iraq.......................416–18
Ireland....................418–19
Iron (nutrient).................797
Ironing symbols................802
Islands..............1, 247, 249
Isle of Man...............419, 542
Israel.....................419–20
Italy......................420–22
Ivory Coast................367–69

J

Jack Adams Trophy.............738
Jamaica....................422–23
James Norris Trophy...........737
Jan Mayen.....................477
Japan......................423–24
Jarvis Island..................543
Jersey.........................542
Jessie Awards..................642
Jockeys..................790, 791
Johnston Atoll.................543
Jordan.....................424–25
Journalism awards.......651, 652, 654
Judges & justices........141–42, 168
Judo (2000 Olympics).......764–65
Junior hockey championships...742–43

Index

Juno Awards 621–24
Justice system
  Canada
    courts. 141–42
    judges/justices. 168
  intl. 257

K

Kane, Lori. 788
Kazakhstan. 425–26
Keeling Islands. 328, 362
Kenya. 426–27
Kermadec Islands 470
King, William Lyon Mackenzie. . . 129, 152
Kingman Reef 543
Kiribati 427–28
Kitchener (ON). 32–33
  Internet use 75
  population 52, 55
Korea (See North Korea; South Korea)
Kuwait 430–32
Kyrgyzstan 432–33

L

Labelling (symbols)
  laundry care. 802
  product safety 803
Labour force
  by age 230
  cities (selected) 31–37
  by country 318–556
  income 231
    by industry. 228, 232, 233
  productivity 233
  by prov. 230
Lady Byng Trophy 737
Lacrosse 786
La Francophonie 263
Lakes
  Canada. 1, 5
  world 249
Land force bases 193
Landforms
  Canada. 3–6, 9
  prov./terr. 25–31
  world 317–555
Languages
  Canada
    aboriginal. 143
    Charter of Rights & Freedoms . 147–48
    minority (lang.) rights 148
    mother tongues . . . . , 47
    prov./terr. stats. 25–31
    (See also Official languages)
  by country 318–555
  most common 247
Laos. 433–34
Large numbers. 584
Latin America. 248
  population projection 254
Latvia 434–35
Laundry care symbols 802

Laurier, Sir Wilfrid 127, 152
Leacock award 653
League of Arab States 262
Leather industry
  labour force 232
  value of products 221–22
Lebanon 435–36
Legal identify, documents 804–5
Legislation, passage of 139, 143
Legislature (See Parliament)
Lepidopterans, extirpated/endangered
. . . . 609, 611
Lesotho 436–47
Letters, postal info. 808
Liberal International 263
Liberal Party of Canada 178
  leaders
    fed. 185
    prov. 188–89
Liberia 437–38
Libya 438–49
Lichens, endangered 611
Liechtenstein 439–40
Lieut.-govs.
  by prov. 25–30, 169
  salary 166
Life expectancy
  Canada
    prov./terr.stats 25–31
    years remaining, by age. 59
  by country 318–556
Life sciences 607–14
  taxonomy. 608
  terms 607–8
Lindros, Eric. 739
Literacy, by country 318–556
Literature
  awards/prizes. 647–51
  bestsellers 652
Lithoprobe 576–77
Lithuania 440–42
Livestock production
  by region 7, 8
  value of product 217
London (ON) 33
  Internet use 75
  population 52, 55
Longitude/latitude 1, 24
Loudness, measuring. 581
LPGA tournament 789
Lunar eclipses 565
Luxembourg. 442–43

M

Macau 443
Macdonald, John A. 124, 152
Mackenzie, Alexander. 124–25, 152
Macedonia 443–44
Machinery (mfg.)
  labour force 232
  operating profits 227
  value of product 221–22
Madagascar 444–45

Magazines
  awards. 652
  Bill C-55 653
  top circulation 653
Magloire, Jamaal 716
Magnesium (nutrient) 797
Mail, rates 808
Major League Baseball. 697
Malawi. 446–47
Malaysia. 447–48
Maldives. 448–49
Mali 449–50
Malta 450–51
Mammals
  classifying 608
  endangered/extinct. 609, 610
Management services
  e-commerce. 225
  operating profits 227
Manitoba
  agriculture 8, 217
  bankruptcies 199
  cabinet 176
  climate 28
  crime 85
  economy 28
  education 28, 80
  election results
    fed. 179–83
    prov. 187
  enters Confederation 28
  families
    income 76
    lone-parent. 73
    size of 74
  fertility rate. 72
  frost dates 22
  fuel production. 218
  geography 28
  highest point 4
  Internet usage 75
  labour force 28, 228–30
  lieut.-gov. 28
  manufacturing 222
  marriages/divorces 71
  merchandising 223
  migration
    emigration 68
    immigration 67
    interprov. 28, 69
  mining 216
  motto/symbols. 28
  MPs. 162
  official langs. 28
  parks 28
  party leaders 189
  political profile 28
  population 28, 42
    cities/towns 53
    native 48
    urban/rural. 49
  premiers (historical) 172
  RRSP contribs. 246
  Senate seats. 138

Index

taxation 236–39
transfer payments to 205
unemployment. 28, 200
vital stats. 28, 58, 62
wages. 235
water use. 613
web site 30
Mann Cup 786
Manning Award 587
Manufacturing
  e-commerce. 225
  labour force 228, 229, 232
  income. 231
  value of products 221
  by prov. 222
Maps
  air masses/circulation 12–13
  ocean currents. 11
  prov./terr. 2
  solar system 558
  weather symbols 604
  world M1–M16
Marriages
  marital status, by age. 72
  rates
    by prov/terr. 71
    by year 71
Mars, missions to 558
Marshall Islands. 451–52, 543
Martinique 391, 452–53
Marxist-Leninist Party of Canada. . . . 178
Mauritania 453–54
Mauritius 454–55
Mayotte 391, 455
Meat, food guide 797–99
  (See also Beef production; Livestock
  production)
Medal of Bravery 151
Medal of Military Valour. 150
Medals
  military. 149–51
  Olympic 744–46
Media arts awards 658
Medicine, Nobel Prize 586, 587
Meighen, Arthur 128, 152
Members of Parliament (See MPs)
Memorial Cup 742–43
Merchandising
  labour force 228–29
  income. 231
  value of products 223
Meritorious Service Cross 151
Meritorious Service Medal 151
Metal production
  labour force 232
  operating profits 227
  value of product 216, 221–22
Métis 48
Metric system
  conversion 795, 796
  SI 584
Mexico 455–56
Micronesia 457, 543
Middle Ages 273–77

Middle & Near East, map M16
Midway Islands 543
Migraine headaches. 61
Migration
  Canada
    interprov. 25–31, 69
    by country 318–556
Military
  awards 149–51
  bases 192–93
  personnel 190
  ranks 191
Military Valour Decorations 150
Milk products, food guide 797–99
Minerals
  hardness of 578
  museums. 579
Minerals (nutrients) 797
Minimum wage 235
Mining
  e-commerce. 225
  labour force 228–29
  income. 231
  museums. 579
  value of product 216
Modern era 284–316
Modified Mercali Scale. 572–73
Mohs scale. 578
Moldova. 458–59
Molluscs, extinct/endangered . . 609, 610
Molson Indy. 787
Monaco 459
Monarchy. 137
Mongolia 459–61
Montenegro (See Serbia & Montenegro)
Montreal. 33
  crime rate. 86
  Internet use 75
  population 51, 55
Montreal Expos. 697, 705-7
Montreal Museum of Fine Art. 656
Montreal Stock Exchange. 246
Montreal World Film Festival 636
Montserrat 461, 542
Moon, phases of 563
MOPITT 559
Morocco. 461–62
Mortality rates
  Canada 62
  prov./terr. 62
  by country 318–555
Mortgages
  credit summary 234
  interest rates 240, 241
Mosses, endangered 611
Motion Picture Academy Awards . 634–35
Motion, laws of 581
Mottoes 1, 25–31
Mountains 4, 250–51
Movies
  awards 633–36
  Cdn. 633
  festivals 635–36
Mozambique 462–63

MPs 158–63
  office budget 166–67
  pension plan 167
  salary 166
  writing to 167
MTV Video Music Awards 629
MuchMusic Video Awards 630
Mulroney, Brian 134, 152
Municipal govt. 142
  interest on debt 204
Museums
  highlights (2000) 656–657
  major public. 659
  rock & roll 630–31
  science. 579, 585, 659
Music. 621–31
  awards 621–26, 628
  videos 629–30
  halls of fame
    Cdn. 627
    rock & roll 630–31
  industry sales. 630
  top 50 CDs 628
  top 50 tracks 629
Myanmar 463–65

N

Names
  constellations. 568
  hurricanes 599
  living organisms 608
Namibia 465–66
NASA
  missions 558, 560
  web site 565
National Basketball Association (NBA)
  all-time leaders 713
  management changes 716
  playoff results 711
  reg. season standings 711
  season review 712
  statistical leaders 712–13
  2000 draft, ... 716
  (See also Toronto Raptors;
  Vancouver Grizzlies)
National Film Board 632
National Football League
  all-time scoring records 725
  all-time team 726
  final standings 724
  individual stats. 725
  (See also Cdn. Football League)
National Hockey League (NHL)
  all-star teams 736
  draft
    first round selections 736
    top picks 738
  final standings 728
  indiv. award winners 737–38
  management changes 739
  players assn. 734
  playoff results 729–30

Index

scoring
 champs 735
 leaders 733–34
 season highlights........... 727–28
 Stanley Cup champs 731–32
National Magazine Awards......... 652
National Newspaper Awards 654
Nationalities, by country 317–555
Nations of the world......... 317–555
 maps M1–M16
 population 252–54
 superlative facts.............. 247
 world history 270–316
Native people of Canada
 languages.................... 143
 largest bands.................. 48
 population 48
 Status Indians 48
NATO 269
Natural gas
 Canada
  production 218
  operating profits 227
 world, consumption............ 256
Natural Law Party of Canada 178
Natural resources
 Canada.................... 216–18
 world 318–556
Nature (See Science & Nature)
Nauru 466–67
Navy
 bases 193
 ranks 191
 strength 190
Near-Earth Objects............... 563
Near East, map................. M16
Nepal 467–68
Netherlands 468–69
Netherlands Antilles 468, 469–70
Neutrino observatory 585
Nevis. See Saint Kitts & Nevis
New Brunswick
 agriculture 217
 bankruptcies 199
 cabinet 174
 climate 26
 crime 84
 economy 26, 84
 education 26, 80
 election results
  fed......................... 179–83
  prov........................ 186
 enters Confederation 26
 families
  income....................... 76
  lone-parent................... 73
  size......................... 74
 fertility rate................... 72
 frost dates 22
 fuel production................. 218
 geography 26
 highest point 4
 Internet usage 75
 labour force 228–30
 lieut.-gov..................... 26
 manufacturing 222
 marriages/divorces 71
 merchandising 223
 migration
  emigration 68
  immigration 67
  interprov................... 26, 69
 mining 216
 motto/symbols................. 26
 MPs 158
 official langs................... 26
 parks 26
 party leaders 188
 political profile 26
 population 26, 42
  cities/towns 50
  native 48
  urban/rural................... 49
 premiers (historical) 170–71
 RRSP contribs. 246
 Senate seats................... 138
 taxation 236–39
 transfer payments to 205
 unemployment................. 200
 vital stats................. 26, 58, 62
 wages....................... 235
 water use 613
 web site 30
New Caledonia 391, 469–70
New Democratic Party 178
 leaders
  fed......................... 185
  prov...................... 188–89
Newfoundland
 agriculture 7, 217
 bankruptcies 199
 cabinet 174
 crime 84
 economy 25
 education 25, 80
 election results
  fed......................... 180–83
  prov........................ 186
 enters Confederation 25
 families
  income....................... 76
  lone-parent................... 73
  size......................... 74
 fertility rate................... 72
 frost dates 22
 fuel production................. 218
 geography 25
 highest point 4
 Internet usage 75
 labour force 25, 228–30
 lieut.-gov..................... 25
 manufacturing 222
 marriages/divorces 71
 merchandising 223
 migration
  emigration 68
  immigration 67
  interprov................... 25, 69
 mining 216
 motto/symbols................. 25
 MPs 158
 official langs................... 25
 parks 25
 party leaders 188
 political profile 25
 population 25, 42
  cities/towns 50
  native 48
  urban/rural................... 49
 premiers (historical) 169
 RRSP contribs. 246
 Senate seats................... 138
 taxation 236–39
 transfer payments to 205
 unemployment............. 25, 200
 vital stats................. 25, 58, 62
 wages....................... 235
 water use 613
 web site 30
New Guinea (See Papua New Guinea)
News events ('99–'00)......... 818–38
News reporting awards 651, 654
Newspaper
 awards 654
 number of, by country 318–556
 top dailies (Cdn.) 654
Newton's Laws of Motion.......... 581
New Zealand 470–72
 map (See Oceania)
Nicaragua................... 471–72
Niger 472–73
Nigeria 473–74
Niue 470, 475
Nobel Prize................. 586, 587
Nonfiction
 awards 651
 bestsellers 652
Non-metals production
 labour force 232
 value of product............... 216
Non-prescription drugs, expenditure . 209
Norfolk Island 328, 475
North America
 area 248
 highest, lowest points 248
 map M1
 mountains 251
 population 248, 254
North Korea 428–29
Northern Marianas 475–76, 543
Northwest Territories
 bankruptcies 199
 cabinet 177
 census divisions 49
 climate 30
 commissioner 30
 crime 85
 economy 30
 education 30, 80
 election results............. 179–83
 enters Confederation 30
 families 74

fertility rate. 72
frost dates 23
fuel production. 218
geography 30
government 142–43
highest point 4
marriages/divorces 71
merchandising 223
migration
  emigration 68
  immigration 67
  interprov. 30, 69
mining 216
MPs 163
official langs. 30
parks 30
political profile 30
population 30, 42
  cities/towns 54
  native 48
  urban/rural 49
premiers (historical) 173
RRSP contribs. 246
Senate seats. 138
taxation 236–39
transfer payments to 205
vital stats. 30, 58, 62
wages. 235
water use 613
web site 30
Norway 476–77
Nova Scotia
  agriculture 217
  bankruptcies 199
  cabinet. 174
  climate. 26
  crime 84
  economy 26
  education 26, 80
  election results
    fed. 179–83
    prov. 186
  enters Confederation 26
  families
    income 76
    lone-parent. 73
    size of 74
  fertility rate. 72
  film production in. 632
  frost dates 22
  fuel production. 218
  geography 26
  highest point 4
  Internet usage 75
  labour force 26, 228–30
  lieut.-gov. 26
  manufacturing 222
  marriages/divorces 71
  merchandising 223
  migration
    emigration 68
    immigration 67
    interprov. 26, 69
  mining 216

motto/symbols. 26
MPs 158
official langs. 26
parks 26
party leaders 188
political profile 26
population 26, 42
  cities/towns 50
  native 48
  urban/rural 49
premiers (historical) 170
RRSP contribs. 246
Senate seats. 138
taxation 236–39
transfer payments to 205
unemployment. 26, 200
vital stats. 26, 58, 62
wages. 235
water use 613
web site 30
Nuclear energy
  consumption 256
  supply 218
Numbers
  large. 584
  Roman numerals 796
Nunavut
  bankruptcies 199
  cabinet. 177
  census divisions 49
  commissioner 31
  economy 31
  education 31
  fertility rate. 72
  frost dates 23
  geography 31
  govt. 142–43
  highest point 4
  labour force 31
  marriages/divorces 71
  migration
    emigration 68
    interprov. 69
  MPs 163
  parks 31
  political profile 31
  population 31, 42
  native 48
  urban/rural 49
  premier 173
  RRSP contribs. 246
  Senate seats. 138
  taxation 236
  transfer payments to 205
  unemployment. 31
  vital stats. 31, 58, 62
  wages. 235
  water use 613
  weather 14–15
  water use 613
  web site 30
Nursery products. 217
Nutrients, functions of 797
Nutrition. 797–99

O

Obituaries. 809–17
Observatories. 568–69
O Canada 1, 87
Oceania
  area 248
  immigration to Canada. 66
  map. M14–15
  mountains 251
  population 248, 254
Oceans & seas
  areas, depths 248, 249
  currents 11
  superlative stats. 247
Official languages, Canada
  aboriginal. 143
  Charter of Rights & Freedoms . . 147–48
  cities (selected) 31–37
  prov./terr. 25–31
Oil production
  Canada
    labour force 228-29, 232
    income. 231
    operating profits 227
    supply 218
    value of products 218, 221–22
  intl. org. 263
  museum. 579
  world consumption 256
Old Age Security 208
Olympic Games
  Cdn. gold medalists 745-46
  summer, by year 744
  2000
    medal standings. 746, 749
    multiple medal winners 748
    results 750–78
    summary of events 747–48
  winter. 745
Oman 477–78
Ombudsman 165
Ontario
  agriculture 7, 8, 217
  bankruptcies 199
  cabinet. 175
  climate. 27
  crime 84
  economy 27
  education 27, 80
  election results
    fed. 179–83
    prov. 186
  enters Confederation 27
  families
    income 76
    lone-parent. 73
    size of 74
  fertility rate. 72
  frost dates 22
  fuel production. 218
  geography 27
  highest point 4

Index 851

Internet usage 75
labour force 27, 228–30
lieut.-gov. 27
manufacturing 222
marriages/divorces 71
merchandising 223
migration
  emigration 68
  immigration 67
  interprov. 27, 69
mining 216
motto/symbols 27
MPs 160–61
official langs. 27
parks 27
party leaders 188
political profile 27
population 27, 42
  cities/towns 52–53
  native 48
  urban/rural 49
premiers (historical) 171–72
RRSP contribs. 246
Senate seats 138
taxation 236–39
transfer payments to 205
unemployment 27, 200
vital stats 27, 58, 62
wages 235
water use 613
web site 30
OPEC 263
Opposition, salaries 166
Opera awards 637
Opposition party leaders
  by prov./terr. 25–31
  salaries 166
Order of Canada 149
Order of Military Merit 149–50
Orders & decorations 149–51
Organisms (classifying) 608
Org. of African Unity 263
Org. of American States 263
Org. for Economic Co-op. & Dev. . 267
Org. of Petroleum Exp. Countries. ... 263
Orgs., intl. 261–72
Oscars 634–65
Oshawa (ON) 33
  population 53, 55
Ottawa-Hull (ON) 1, 33
  crime rate 86
  Internet use 35
  population 53, 55
Ozone, measurement 559

P

Pakistan 478–79
Palaeontology, museum 579
Palau 480, 543
Palymyra Atoll 543
Panama 481–82
Paper & allied products
  labour force 232

value of product 221–22
Papua New Guinea 482–83
Paraguay 483–84
Parks, ntl. 25–31, 37–41
Parliament of Canada 138–39
  members of 158–63
  salaries 166
  pension plan 167
Parliament, European 265
Parliament, intl. org. 263
Parti Libéral (Que.) 188
Parti Québécois 188
Party leaders
  fed 185
  prov. 188–89
  salaries 166
Passports 806–7
Patents 590
Pay TV (directory) 619
Peacekeeping missions 191–92
Pearson, Lester 131–32, 152
Pension plans 207
  parliamentary 167
Pentathlon (2000 Olympics) 765
Performing arts awards 637–40
Periodic Table of Elements 583
  defined 582
Personal
  bankruptcies 199
  finance 234–43
  care, consumer index 196
  health, labour force 228–29
  services, labour force 228–29
  income 231
Peru 484–85
Peter I Island 477
Petroleum production
  Canada
    labour force 228–29, 232
    income 231
    operating profits 227
    supply 218
    value of product 218, 221–2
    intl. org. 263
    museum 579
    world consumption 256
PGA tournaments 789
Pharmaceuticals, expenditures ... 209
Philippines 485–86
Phosphorus (nutrient) 797
Photography
  awards 652, 654
  museum 659
Physical Activity Guide 800–1
Physical sciences
  awards/prizes 586, 587
  hall of fame 586
  museums 585
  terms 580
Physicians, expenditures 209
Physics
  laws of 581
  Neutrino Observatory 585
  Nobel Prize winners 586, 587

  terms 580
Pitcairn Islands 486–87, 542
Planetariums 569
Planets 557–58
  astronomical events 564
  Terrestrial Planet Finder 562
Plant(s)
  classifying 608
  extirpated/endangered 609, 611
  hardiness zones 23
plastics industry
  labour force 232
  value of products 221–22
Playwriting awards 647–50
Poetry awards 647–50, 651
Poisons, symbols 803
Poland 487–88
Police, intl. org. 262
Political parties
  fed. 178
  leaders
    fed. 185
    prov. 188–89
Polynesia 254
Population
Canada
  age structure of 42
  births/deaths 25–31
  census 56–57
  cities 31–37, 50–55
  by country, birth 44–45
  ethnicity of 46
  by gender 43
  growth of 69
  marital status 72
  by mother tongue 47
  native people 48
  projections 43, 254
  by prov./terr. 25–31, 42
  urban/rural 49
  visible minorities 46
world
  continents 248
  by country 252, 317–555
  least populous nation 247
  most populous nation 247
  projections 252–54
Portugal 488–89
Postal rates 808
Potato production 217
Poverty line 79
Precipitation
  at airports 10
  cities 31–37
  factors affecting 9, 11
  prov. averages 14
  records 14, 247, 594
  seasonal 20–21
  terms 21
  and water supply 9
Premiers
  historical 169–73
  prov. 25–31
Prescription drugs, expenditures 209

852 Index

Prices, consumer index 196
Prime ministers 139
  biographies 124–35
  birth/death dates 152
  role of 136
  salary 166
  terms 152
Prime rate 197
Prince Edward Island
  agriculture 217
  bankruptcies 199
  cabinet 174–75
  climate 25
  crime 84
  economy 25
  education 25, 80
  election results
    fed 179–83
    prov 186
  enters Confederation 25
  families
    income 76
    lone-parent 73
    size of 74
  fertility rate 72
  frost dates 22
  fuel production 218
  geography 25
  highest point 4
  Internet usage 75
  labour force 25, 228–30
  lieut.-gov. 25
  manufacturing 222
  marriages/divorces 71
  merchandising 223
  migration
    emigration 68
    immigration 66
    interprov 25, 69
  mining 216
  motto/symbols 25
  MPs 158
  official langs 25
  parks 25
  party leaders 188
  political profile 25
  population 25, 42
    cities/towns 50
    native 48
    urban/rural 49
  premiers (historical) 169–70
  RRSP contribs. 246
  Senate seats 138
  taxation 236–39
  transfer payments to 205
  unemployment 25, 200
  vital stats. 25, 58, 62
  wages 235
  water use 613
  web site 30
Prince of Wales Stakes 791
Príncipe (See São Tomé & Príncipe)
Printing industry
  labour force 232

value of product 221–22
Privacy Commissioner 165
Privy Council Office 140
Product safety symbols 803
Productivity 233
Professional servs.
  e-commerce 225
  operating profits 227
Profits, by industry 227
Progressive Conservative Party
  of Canada 178
  leaders
    fed 185
    prov 188–89
Property crime 83–86
Prostitution 83
Protein 797
Provinces & territories
  agriculture 217
  area 24, 25–31
  arts councils 615
  bankruptcies 199
  births/deaths 58, 62
  cabinets of 174–77
  capital cities 25–31
  coats of arms 25–31
  courts 141–42
  crime stats 84–85
  documents, offices 804–5
  economy 25–31
  education 80
  election results 186–87
  employment distrib 25–31, 228–30
  enter Confederation 25–30
  families
    income 76
    lone-parent 73
    size of 74
  fertility rates 72
  frost dates 22–23
  fuel production 218
  geography 25–31
  govt 25–31, 142–43
    cabinets 174–77
  income 236
  Internet usage 75
  labour force 25–31, 228–29
  leg. authority 142
  lieut.-govs 25–30, 169
  manufacturing 222
  map 2
  marriages/divorces 71
  merchandising 223
  migration
    emigration 68
    immigration 67
    interprov 25–31, 69
  mining 216
  MPs 158–63
  official langs 25–31
  party leaders 188–89
  population 25–31, 42
    cities/towns 50–54
    native 48

urban/rural 49
postal symbols 808
premiers (historical) 169–73
refugees 68
ridings 158–63
RRSP contribs. 246
superlative facts 1, 4
symbols 25–30
taxes 236–39
transfer payments to 205
unemployment 25–31
vital stats. 25–31, 58–63
  offices 804
  wages 235
  water use 613
  weather 14–15
  web sites 30
Provincial courts 141–42
Provincial govt. 142–43
  cabinets 174–77
  interest on debt 204
Public administration
  ecommerce 225
  labour force 228–29
  income 231
Public debt, interest on 204
Public health, expenditure 209
Publishing industry
  labour force 232
  value of product 221–22
Puerto Rico 489–90, 543
Pulitzer Prize 651
Pulp & paper industry
  labour force 228–29
  income 231
  operating profits 227
  value of products 221–22

Q

Qatar 490–91
Quantum physics, laws 581
Quebec
  agriculture 7, 8, 217
  bankruptcies 199
  cabinet 175
  climate 27
  crime 84
  economy 27
  education 27, 80
  election results
    fed 179–83
    prov 186
  enters Confederation 27
  families
    income 76
    lone-parent 73
    size of 74
  fertility rate 72
  frost dates 22
  fuel production 218
  geography 27
  highest point 4
  Internet usage 75

Index

labour force 27, 228–30
lieut.-gov. 27
manufacturing 222
marriages/divorces 71
merchandising 223
migration
  emigration 68
  immigration 67
  interprov. 27, 69
mining 216
motto/symbols. 27
MPs 159–60
official langs. 27
parks 27
party leaders 188
political profile 27
population 27, 42
  cities/towns 50–52
  native 49
  urban/rural 49
premiers (historical) 171
RRSP contribs. 246
Senate seats. 138
taxation 236–39
transfer payments to 205
unemployment 27, 200
vital stats.. .... 27, 58, 62
wages. 235
water use 613
web site 30
Quebec City 27, 34
  crime rate. 86
  Internet use 75
  population 51, 55
Quebec Pension Plan 207
Queen Elizabeth II 137
Queen Maud Land 477
Queen's Plate 790
Question Period 139
Quick reference 795–808

R

RadarSat 566
Radio broadcasting 620
Radios, ratio to pop. 318–556
Railways
  Canada, revenues. 220
  by country 318–556
Real estate industry
  e-commerce. 225
  labour force 228–29
    income. 231
  operating profits 227
  (See also Housing)
Recording industry
  org. 627
  sales. 630
Recreational services
  e-commerce. 225
  labour force 228–29
  operating profits 227
  price index. 196
Red Cross. See Intl. Fed. Red Cross &

Red Crescent Soc.
Reefs 247
Reform Party of British Columbia ... 189
Refugees 68, 70
Regina (SK) 28
  population 53, 55
Relief
  agencies (intl.) 258
  missions 193
Religion
  by country 318–555
  most common 247
Renaissance. 277–81
Reptiles, extirpated/endangered. 609, 610
Respiratory diseases (cause of death) . 63
Rest of Canada (ROC) Party 178
Retail trade
  e-commerce. 225
  labour force 228–29
    income. 231
  value of products 223
  (See also Merchandising)
Retirement
  benefit plans 207–8
  RRSPs 246
  savings. 243
Réunion 391, 491
Rhythmic gymnastics (2000 Olympics)
  763
Riboflavin. 797
Richter scale 572–73
Ridings (prov.) 158–63
Rivers
  Canada. 1, 5–6
  world 247, 251
Roads, by country 318–556
Robbery 83–86
Rock & roll hall of fame 630–31
Roman numerals 796
Romania. 491–92
Ross Dependency 470
Rowing
  org. 707
  2000 Olympics. 765–66
Royal
  anthem. 1
  family. 138
  RRSPs 246
Rubber products
  labour force 232
  value of products 221–22
Rugby, CIAU champs. 780
Running (See Athletics)
Russia 492–93
Rwanda 494–95

S

Safety symbols 803
Saffer-Simpson Hurricane Intensity
  Scale 599
Sailing (2000 Olympics). 766–67
St. Catharines–Niagara (ON) 34
  Internet use 75

population 53, 55
Saint Helena. 495, 542
Saint John (NB) 34
  population 50, 55
St. John's (NF) 34–35
  population 50, 55
Saint Kitts & Nevis 495–96
St. Laurent, Louis. 130–31, 152
Saint Lucia. 496–97
Saint Pierre & Miquelon. ... 391, 497–98
Saint Vincent & the Grenadines .. 498–99
Salaries
  hockey players 735
  political figures 166, 167
  prov. 235
Samoa 499–500
San Marino 500–1
São Tomé & Príncipe 501–2
Saskatchewan
  agriculture 8, 217
  bankruptcies 199
  cabinet. 176
  climate. 28
  crime. 85
  economy. 28
  education. 28, 80
  election results
    fed. 179–83
    prov. 187
  enters Confederation 28
  families
    income. 76
    lone-parent. 73
    size of 74
  fertility rate. 72
  frost dates 22
  fuel production. 218
  geography 28
  highest point 4
  Internet usage 75
  labour force 28, 228–30
  lieut.-gov. 28
  manufacturing 222
  marriages/divorces 71
  merchandising 223
  migration
    emigration 68
    immigration 67
    interprov. 28, 69
  mining 216
  motto/symbols. 28
  MPs 162
  official langs. 28
  parks 28
  party leaders 189
  political profile 28
  population 28, 42
    cities/towns 53
    natives 49
    urban/rural. 49
  premiers (historical) 172
  RRPS contribs. 246
  Senate seats. 138
  taxation 236–39

854 Index

transfer payments to 205
unemployment................. 200
vital stats................ 28, 58, 62
wages........................ 235
water use..................... 613
web site 30
Saskatoon (SK) 35
population 53, 55
Satellites/space probes 558, 559, 566, 567
Saturn, mission to, web site....... 565
Saudi Arabia................. 502–3
Savings (income)............... 243
interest rates on............. 197
Schools
enrolment................... 80
prov./terr. stats............ 25–31
Science centres 585
Science & nature
astronomy & space......... 557–69
atmospheric science 591–606
awards/prizes............. 586–87
earth sciences............ 570–79
hall of fame................ 586
inventions 588–89
life sciences............. 607–14
museums........... 579, 585, 659
physical sciences.......... 580–85
SCISAT-1 559
Seas (See Oceans & seas)
Secretaries-general (U.N.)......... 261
Secretaries of state 155
salaries..................... 166
Senate of Canada............ 138–39
members............... 156–57
salaries.................. 166
web site 145
Senegal 503–4
Serbia & Montenegro........... 504–5
Service industries
e-commerce................. 225
labour force............. 228–29
income................... 231
operating profits 227
Sexual assaults............... 83–86
Sexually transmitted diseases 60
Seychelles 505–6
Sherbrooke (Que.)................ 35
population 52, 55
Shooting (2000 Olympics)...... 767–69
Shrubs, hardiness zones 23
SI units 584
Sierra Leone................. 506–8
Singapore................... 508–9
Skating
(See Figure Skating)
Sky, astronomical events (2001) 564
Slovakia.................... 509–10
Slovenia.................... 510–11
Smoke/haze 10
Smoking....................... 60
Snowfall
average annual............ 10, 15
cities (selected) 31–37
records............... 247, 594

Soccer
CIAU champs........... 780, 782
org. 707
Social assistance
Internet usage 225
operating profits 227
Social insurance numbers 804, 805
Social security
disability pensions 207
employment insurance......... 206
Guaranteed Income Supplement ... 208
Old Age Security 208
Socialist Intl................... 263
Softball
org. 707
2000 Olympics.............. 769
Solar eclipses.................. 565
Solar storms 563
Solar system 557–58
at a glance 558
eclipses (2001) 565
terms 561
Solomon Islands 511–12
Somalia................... 512–13
Sound, loudness 581
South Africa 513–14
South America
area 248
highest, lowest points 248
immigration to Canada.......... 66
map..................... M6–M7
mountains 251
population 248, 254
South Georgia (UK) 542
South Korea................ 429–30
South Sandwich Islands.......... 542
Southern & Antarctic Territories..... 391
Space
agency, Cdn................. 566
debris...................... 563
exploration............. 558, 560
intl. station................. 560
quiz 559
terms 561
web sites 565, 566
Space Telescope Science Instit....... 565
Spain 515–16
Speaker of the House, salary 166
Speaker of the Senate, salary....... 166
Species
classifying 608
endangered/extinct......... 609–11
Split-run magazines............. 653
Sports
awards................. 695–794
athlete of the century........... 794
baseball................... 700
football.................... 718
hockey 731–32, 737–38, 742–43
lacrosse 786
CIAU champs........... 780–82
halls of fame 722–23
networks, addresses 619
Olympics................ 744–78

orgs. 697, 707
web sites 710
Sports writing awards 654
Spouses' Allowance............. 208
Sri Lanka................... 516–17
Standard Time Zones............ 563
Standards, intl. org............. 263
Stanley Cup................ 731–32
Star of Courage 151
Star of Military Valour 150
Stars 568
Status Indians 48
Steam & biomass energy......... 218
Stephen Leacock Award for Humour . 653
Stock exchange 246
Storage industry 220
Stores
employment................. 233
revenues 223
Storms
average annual............... 10
records.................... 594
solar....................... 563
terms 591–93
worst 600–1
Street, longest 247
Stroke 60
Structural materials prod.......... 216
Sudan..................... 517–18
Sudbury (ON).................... 35
population 53, 55
Sudbury Neutrino Observatory 585
Suicide........................ 60
Summer Olympics......... 744, 745–46
(See also 2000 Olympics)
Summer theatre................ 644
Sun 562
solar storms................. 563
Sunburn times................. 597
Sunshine
hours of 10, 14, 31–37
UV index 597
Super Bowl 726
Superior Court of Original Jurisdic. ... 141
Supermarkets.................. 229
Supreme Court of Canada 136, 141
contacting 168
justices.................... 168
Suriname.................. 518–19
Svalbard.............. 477, 519–20
Swaziland.................. 520–21
Sweden.................... 521–22
Swimming
CIAU champs........... 780, 781
2000 Olympics............ 769–73
(See also Synchronized Swimming)
Switzerland................ 522–23
Sydney 2000 (See 2000 Olympics
Symbols
laundry care................ 802
ntl..................... 1, 87, 88
postal..................... 808
product safety 803
prov./terr.................. 25–31

Index

SI units 584
  television classification 616
  weather 604
Synchronized diving (2000 Olympics) 760
Synchronized swimming
  (2000 Olympics) 773
Syria 523–24

T

Table tennis (2000 Olympics) 773
Taekwondo (2000 Olympics) 773–74
Taiwan 524–26
Tajikistan 526–27
Tanzania 527–28
Taxes
  by age/gender 239
  credits 238
  filing returns 236
  individuals 237
  prov. rates 236
  by prov./terr. 236
  reductions 243
  revenues 239
  2000 tables 238
Taxonomy 608
Team Canada 741
Telephones
  revenues/lines in serv. 219
  ratio to pop. 318–556
Telesat Canada 559
Television 616–20
  awards 617, 618
  classification system 616
  CRTC 617
  most-watched programs 618
  networks/cable servs. 619
Temperature
  at airports 10
  in cities 31–37
  equivalents 795
  factors affecting 9, 11
  frost dates 22–23
  global warming 9, 605–6
  humidex 592, 596
  plant hardiness zones 23
  records 14, 247, 594
  seasonal 20–21
  terms 591–93
Tennis
  tournaments 783
  2000 Olympics 774
Terrestrial Planet Finder 562
Territories (See Provinces & Territories)
Textile mfg.
  labour force 232
  value of product 221–22
Textiles, care of 802
Thailand 528–29
Theatre
  awards 641–42
  companies 645
  highlights (2001) 642–44
  summer 644

Theft 83–86
Thermodynamics, laws of 581
Thiamin 797
Thompson, Sir John 125–26, 152
Thoroughbred racing 790
Thunder Bay (ON) 35–36
  population 53, 55
Thunderstorms (See Storms)
Tides, greatest 247
Time periods (geological) 574–75
Time zones 2, 563
Tobacco
  price index 196
  smoking 60
Tobacco production
  labour force 232
  value of products 217, 221–22
Tobago (See Trinidad & Tobago)
Togo 529–30
Tokelau 470, 530–31
Tonga 531–32
Tornadoes 598
Toronto (ON) 27, 36
  crime rate 86
  Internet use 75
  population 53, 55
Toronto Blue Jays 697, 708–10
Toronto Intl. Film Festival 636
Toronto Raptors 714, 716
Toronto Stock Exchange 246
Towns, Canada 50–55
Track & field (See Athletics)
Trade
  balance of 211
  by country 318–556
  intl. org. 268
  operating profits 227
  payments 210
  (See also Exports; Imports)
Trademarks 590
Traffic deaths 60
Trampoline gymn. (2000 Olympics) . 763
Transfer payments 205
Translation awards 649, 650
Transportation
  airlines, revenues 220
  consumer index 196
  by country 318–556
  labour force 228–29
    income 231
  operating profits 227
  railways, revenues 220
Transportation
  labour force 228–29, 232
    income 231
  value of product 221–22
Transportation & storage 220
  e-commerce 225
  labour force 228–29
    income 231
Trapping
  labour force 228–29
    income 231
Treasury Board 140

Trees, hardiness zones 23
Triathlon (2000 Olympics) 775
Trinidad & Tobago 532–33
Triple Crown 790
Trois-Rivières (Que.) 36
  population 52, 55
Trudeau, Pierre Elliott 132–33, 152
Tunisia 533–34
Tupper, Sir Charles 126–27, 152
Turkey 534–35
Turkmenistan 535–36
Turks & Caicos 536–37, 542
Turner, John 130–31, 152
Tuvalu 537–38
2000 Olympics (Sydney)
  medals standings 746, 749
  multiple medal winners 748
  results 750–78
  summary of events 747–48

U

Uganda 538–39
Ukraine 539–40
Ultra-violet index 597
Unemployment
  Canada 200
  by city 31–37
  by prov./terr. 25–31, 230
  by country 318–556
United Arab Emirates 540–41
United Kingdom 541–43
United Nations
  acronyms 258
  Cdn. ambassadors to 261
  members of 260–61
  peacekeeping missions 191–92
  related orgs. 262–63
  Sec.-gens. 261
  structure of 257, 259
United States 543–44
  immigration to Canada 66
  map M4–M5
  population 252, 254
  weather records 594
Universities
  academic attainment 81
  enrolment 80
  sports champs 780–82
Uruguay 544–45
U.S. Patent & Trademark Office ... 590
U.S. Virgin Islands 538, 543
Utilities
  e-commerce 225
  labour force 228–29
    income 231
  operating profits 227
UV index 597
Uzbekistan 545–46

V

Vancouver (BC) 36
  crime rate 86

856 Index

Internet use	75	
population	54, 55	
Vancouver Grizzlies	715, 716	
Vanuatu	546–47	
Vatican City	548	
Vegetables, food guide	797–99	
Vegetable prod., Canada	7–8, 217	
Vegetation, Canada	7–8	
Venezuela	548–50	
Vezina Trophy	737	
Video Music Awards	624, 629–30	
Victoria (BC)	29, 36–37	
Internet use	75	
population	54, 55	
Victoria Cross	150	
Vietnam	550–51	
Virgin Islands (British)	346–47, 542	
Virgin Islands (U.S.)	538, 543	
Visible minorities	46	
Vision-care servs., expenditures	209	
Visual arts awards	658	
Vital statistics		
Canada	58–63	
offices	804–5	
by prov./terr.	25–31	
by country	317–555	
Vitamins	797	
Volcanoes	3, 4, 247	
Volleyball, beach (2000 Olympics)	775	
Volleyball, indoor	769	
CIAU champs	780, 781, 782	
org.	707	
2000 Olympics	775	
Voluntarism award	658	
Voters		
lists	805	
turnout	183	

W

Wages		
min. hourly	235	
prov.	235	
(See also Income; Salaries)		
Wake Island	543	
Wales *(See* United Kingdom)		
Walker, Larry	701	
Wallis & Futuna	391, 551	
Warehousing	220	
e-commerce	225	
labour force	228–29	
income	231	
Watchdogs, fed.	164–65	
Water		
quality	8	
use	613	
Waterfalls	247, 249	
Water polo (2000 Olympics)	775	
Weather		
Canada		
at airports	10	
by city	31–37	
events, most severe	600–1	
frost dates	22–23	
highlights	16–19	
maps	11, 12–13	
by prov.	14–15	
records	14–15, 594	
symbols	604	
terms	20, 21, 591–93	
world		
records	247, 594	
Weather Channel	619	
Weatheradio	593	
Weightlifting (2000 Olympics)	775–77	
Weights & measures		
imperial measures	796	
intl. system (SI)	584	
metric conversion	796	
temperature equivalents	782	
Welcome Home Campaign	45	
West Bank	551	
Western Sahara	552	
Wheat production		
Canada		
by region	7, 8	
value of product	217	
Whips	136, 166	
Whitehorse (Yukon)	30	
population	54	
Wholesale trade		
e-commerce	225	
labour force	228–29	
income	231	
Wildlife		
endangered/extinct	609–11	
intl. org.	263	
Wind		
at airports	10	
direction	9, 10	
prov. stats.	15	
records	15	
speed, estimating	598	
terms	591–93	
Wind chill		
calculating	597	
defined	21, 593	
factor	595	
prov. stats.	15	
Windsor (ON)	37	
Internet use	75	
population	53, 55	
Winnipeg (MB)	28, 37	
crime rate	86	
Internet use	75	
population	53, 55	
Winter Olympics, gold medalists	745	
Women Inventors Project	590	
Women's golf	788, 789	
Women's tennis	783	
Women's hockey	740	
World Council of Churches	263	
World Court	257	
World history	270–316	
World news	818–38	
World Series	699	
World Trade Org.	268	
World Wide Fund for Nature	263	
Wrestling		
CIAU champs	780, 781	
2000 Olympics	777–78	
Writing awards	647–51, 652, 654	

X

XFL (Extra Fun League)	724

Y

Yashin, Alexei	734
Yellowknife (NWT)	30
population	54
Yemen	552–54
Youth crime	86
Yukon Party	189
Yukon Territory	
agriculture	8
bankruptcies	199
cabinet	177
climate	30
commissioner	30
crime	85
economy	30
education	30, 80
election results	
fed.	179–83
prov.	187
enters Confederation	30
families	74
fertility rate	72
frost dates	23
fuel production	218
geography	30
govt.	142–43
leaders	30, 173
highest point	4
marriages/divorces	71
merchandising	223
migration	
emigration	68
immigration	67
interprov.	30, 69
mining	216
MPs	163
official langs.	30
parks	30
party leaders	189
political profile	30
population	30, 42
cities/towns	54
native	49
urban/rural	49
RRSP contribs.	246
Senate seats	138
symbols	30
taxation	236–39
transfer payments to	205
vital stats.	30, 58, 62
wages	235
water use	613
web site	31

Z

Zambia	554–55
Zimbabwe	555–56
Zinc (nutrient)	797
Zoos	614